8 ACT Practice Tests

RELATED TITLES FOR COLLEGE-BOUND STUDENTS

8 ACT Practice Tests

KAPLAN PUBLISHING

New York

© 2016 by Kaplan, Inc.
Published by Kaplan Publishing, a division of Kaplan, Inc.
750 Third Avenue
New York, NY 10017

10   9   8   7   6   5   4   3   2   1

ISBN-13: 978-1-5062-0903-6

Kaplan Publishing print books are available at special quantity discounts to use for sales promotions, employee premiums, or educational purposes. For more information or to purchase books, please call the Simon & Schuster special sales department at 866-506-1949.

Table of Contents

Practice Makes Perfect

Don't be scared of the ACT. Why? Because we know what's on the exam, and we know exactly how you should prepare for it. Kaplan has been teaching kids how to succeed on standardized tests for more than 75 years—longer than anyone else, period.

This book contains 8 practice exams that mirror the ACT you will face on Test Day—more ACT practice than can be found between the covers of any other book. Practice is one of the keys to mastery, and these 8 exams give you plenty of practice to assess your strengths and weaknesses before you take the real thing.

Just as important as taking practice tests is understanding why you got a question right or wrong when you're done. The detailed answers and explanations that follow each practice test provide you with a thorough explanation of the correct answer as well as strategic advice, so you will start to learn some ways you can approach similar questions on Test Day. In addition, every answer explanation lets you know the difficulty level of each question. If you're missing a lot of "Low" difficulty questions, you might need to do some extra review. If you are acing many of the "High" difficulty questions, you're on the right track.

Every practice question and answer explanation in this book is geared toward one thing—getting you more points on the actual ACT. So don't stress out—Kaplan's got you covered.

HOW TO USE THIS BOOK

This book is filled with over 1,700 practice questions to help you master the ACT. Follow these steps to get the most out of these 8 practice tests:

1. Read about the ACT structure in the next section. This way, you'll know what to expect—not only as you work through the book but, more importantly, on Test Day.

2. Begin your practice! Buying this book has given you an advantage—after you've worked your way through the exams, the format and timing of the ACT will be second nature to you. All you will have to concentrate on is improving your skills in the areas that need work.

3. Keep track. Turn to the Score Tracker on page xi, where you can track your score as you take each exam. Keep a record of your scores and watch how much you improve from test to test.

4. Assess your strengths and weaknesses. After you finish each test, carefully read the detailed explanations—pay attention to the questions you got wrong, but don't forget to read about the ones you got right. It's important to note your areas of strength as well as weakness. Take your own personal inventory of the skills you've mastered and the skills you need to work on.

5. Watch your scores improve! After you've made your way halfway through the book, compare your scores on Test 1 and Test 4. You've made progress, haven't you? See if your strengths and weaknesses have changed. Then work your way through the remaining tests, building skills and ACT competency along the way.

After making your way through these steps, we guarantee that you will have the test expertise and improved skills to tackle the ACT with confidence.

ACT TEST DATES

As a general rule, students take the ACT at least once in their junior year, often taking it for the first time in the early spring. The ACT is administered on select Saturdays during the school year. Sunday testing is also available for students who cannot take the Saturday test because of religious observances. Check the official ACT website at actstudent.org/regist/dates.html for the most up-to-date test dates.

ACT REGISTRATION

To register for the ACT by mail, you'll need to get an ACT Paper Registration Guide from your high school guidance counselor.

You can register online at actstudent.org/regist/. Note: Not all students are eligible to register online, so read the instructions and requirements carefully.

Register early to secure the time you want at the test center of your choice and to avoid late registration fees.

Students with disabilities can go to actstudent.org/regist/disab/ to learn how to apply for accommodations.

In the United States, the fee for the ACT is $56.50 with the essay, and $39.50 without the essay. This price includes reports for you, your high school, and up to four colleges and scholarship programs. To get the most up-to-date information on test fees, please check actstudent.org/regist/actfees.html.

You will receive an admission ticket at least a week before the test. The ticket confirms your registration on a specified date, at a specified test center. Make sure to bring this, along with proper identification, to the test center. Some acceptable forms of identification include photo IDs such as a driver's license, a school identification card, or a valid passport. (Unacceptable forms of identification include a Social Security card, credit card, or birth certificate.)

Your ACT scores will be available online approximately three weeks after the test.

Remember to check actstudent.org for all the latest information on the ACT. Every effort has been made to keep the information in this book as up-to-date as possible, but changes may occur after the book is published.

Finally, bookmark the ACT's website: actstudent.org.

HOW THE ACT IS STRUCTURED

The ACT is about three hours long (three and a half with the Writing Test). The test consists of four subject tests, with a total of 215 scored multiple-choice questions, and one optional essay.

Below is the breakdown of the test:

Test	Questions	Timing	Content
English	75 questions	45 minutes	Measures standard written English and rhetorical skills.
Mathematics	60 questions	60 minutes	Measures mathematical skills students have typically acquired in courses taken up to the beginning of grade 12.
Reading	40 questions	35 minutes	Measures reading comprehension.
Science	40 questions	35 minutes	Measures the interpretation, analysis, evaluation, reasoning, and problem-solving skills required in the natural sciences.
Optional Writing Test	1 prompt	40 minutes	Measures writing skills emphasized in high school English classes and in entry-level college composition courses.

* There will be a short break between the Math and Reading subject tests.

HOW THE ACT IS SCORED

The ACT is scored differently from most tests that you take at school. Your ACT score on a test section is not reported as the total number of questions you answered correctly, nor does it directly represent the percentage of questions you answered correctly. Instead, the test makers add up all of your correct answers in a section to get what's called your raw score. They then use a conversion chart, or scale, that matches up a particular raw score with what's called a scaled score. The scaled score is the number that gets reported as your score for that ACT subject test.

You gain one point for every question you answer correctly. You lose no points for answering a question wrong OR for leaving a question blank. This means you should ALWAYS answer EVERY question on the ACT—even if you have to guess.

SCORE TRACKER

1. **Figure out your score for each subject test.** Refer to the answer keys to determine the correct number for each test. Enter the results in the chart:

RAW SCORES

	TEST 1	TEST 2	TEST 3	TEST 4	TEST 5	TEST 6	TEST 7	TEST 8
English:	72	70	71					
Math:	43	58	54					
Reading:	37	35	32					
Science:	30	24	35					

2. **Find your Practice Test scores.** Find your raw score for each subject test in the following table. The score in the far left column indicates your estimated scaled score if this were an actual ACT.

SCALED SCORE	RAW SCORES			
	English	**Mathematics**	**Reading**	**Science**
36	75	60	40	40
35	74	60	40	40
34	73	59	39	39
33	72	58	39	39
32	71	57	38	38
31	70	55–56	37	37
30	69	53–54	36	36
29	68	50–52	35	35
28	67	48–49	34	34
27	65–66	45–47	33	33
26	63–64	43–44	32	32
25	61–62	40–42	31	30–31
24	58–60	38–39	30	28–29
23	56–57	35–37	29	26–27
22	53–55	33–34	28	24–25
21	49–52	31–32	27	21–23
20	46–48	28–30	25–26	19–20
19	44–45	26–27	23–24	17–18
18	41–43	23–25	21–22	16
17	39–40	20–22	19–20	15
16	36–38	17–19	17–18	14
15	34–35	15–16	15–16	13
14	30–33	13–14	13–14	12
13	28–29	11–12	12–13	11
12	25–27	9–10	10–11	10
11	23–24	8	9	9
10	20–22	7	8	8
9	17–19	6	7	7
8	14–16	5	6	6
7	12–13	4	5	5
6	9–11	3	4	4
5	7–8	2	3	3
4	4–6	1	2	2
3	3	1	1	1
2	2	0	0	0
1	1	0	0	0

SCALED SCORES

	TEST 1	TEST 2	TEST 3	TEST 4	TEST 5	TEST 6	TEST 7	TEST 8
English:	33	31	32					
Math:	26	33	30					
Reading:	31	29	26					
Science:	26	22	29					

3. **Find your estimated Composite score.** To calculate your estimated Composite score, simply add together your scaled scores for each subject test and divide by four.

COMPOSITE SCORES

TEST 1	TEST 2	TEST 3	TEST 4	TEST 5	TEST 6	TEST 7	TEST 8
28	28	29					

ACT ESSAY SCORING RUBRIC

There are four separate scoring domains for the ACT Essay: Ideas and Analysis, Development and Support, Organization, and Language Use. Each domain is scored on a scale of 1 to 6. Two readers assign a score for each domain, and the scores are added together to generate a raw score that is between 8 and 48. The raw score is then converted to a scaled score that will be between 1 and 36. The graders will use a rubric similar to the following to determine each domain score.

6	5	4
Ideas and Analysis		
• Skillfully explores multiple perspectives on the given issue • Includes a comprehensive, detailed, and insightful thesis • Establishes thorough context for analysis of the issue and its perspectives • Evaluates implications, intricacies, and/or assumptions	• Effectively explores multiple perspectives on the given issue • Includes a detailed, insightful thesis • Establishes effective context for analysis of the issue and its perspectives • Discusses implications, intricacies, and/or assumptions	• Adequately explores multiple perspectives on the given issue • Includes a detailed thesis • Establishes adequate context for analysis of the issue and its perspectives • Identifies implications, intricacies, and/or assumptions
Development and Support		
• Provides additional insight and context • Skillfully provides relevant reasoning • Explores the significance of the argument	• Provides additional understanding • Effectively provides relevant reasoning • Discusses the significance of the argument	• Provides additional clarity • Adequately provides relevant reasoning • Identifies the significance of the argument
Organization		
• Demonstrates a skillful structure • Focuses on a well-defined main idea • Includes transitions that skillfully connect ideas	• Demonstrates an effective structure • Focuses on a main idea • Includes transitions that effectively connect ideas	• Demonstrates an adequate structure • Reflects a main idea • Includes transitions that adequately connect ideas
Language Use		
• Features skillful, precise, appropriate word choice • Consistently includes varied sentence structure • May include a few minor errors in grammar that do not distract from clarity or readability	• Features precise, appropriate word choice • Often includes varied sentence structure • May include minor errors in grammar that do not distract from clarity or readability	• Features appropriate word choice • Sometimes includes varied sentence structure • Includes minor errors in grammar that rarely distract from clarity or readability

3	2	1
Ideas and Analysis		
• Somewhat explores multiple perspectives on the given issue • Includes a thesis • Establishes some context for analysis of the issue and its perspectives • May mention implications, intricacies, and/or assumptions	• Somewhat responds to multiple perspectives on the given issue • Does not include a clear thesis • Does not provide context for analysis of the issue and its perspectives • Does not discuss implications, intricacies, and/or assumptions	• Fails to explore multiple perspectives on the given issue • Does not include a thesis • Does not provide context for analysis of the issue and its perspectives • Does not identify implications, intricacies, and/or assumptions
Development and Support		
• Provides general information • Provides relevant reasoning in a redundant or inexact way	• Weakly provides information • Inadequately provides relevant reasoning	• Lacks development • Does not provide relevant reasoning
Organization		
• Demonstrates a basic structure • Contains a main idea • Includes transitions that sometimes connect ideas	• Demonstrates a simplistic structure • May not reflect a main idea • Does not use transitions that adequately connect ideas	• Demonstrates a confusing structure • Does not reflect a main idea • Does not use transitions that adequately connect ideas
Language Use		
• Features basic word choice • Rarely includes varied sentence structure • Includes errors in grammar that somewhat distract from clarity and readability	• Features unclear word choice • Often includes unclear sentence structure • Includes numerous errors in grammar that distract from clarity and readability	• Features confusing word choice • Often includes unclear, confusing sentence structure • Includes numerous errors in grammar that distract from clarity and readability

ACT Practice Test One
ANSWER SHEET

ENGLISH TEST

1. Ⓐ Ⓑ Ⓒ Ⓓ   11. Ⓐ Ⓑ Ⓒ Ⓓ   21. Ⓐ Ⓑ Ⓒ Ⓓ   31. Ⓐ Ⓑ Ⓒ Ⓓ   41. Ⓐ Ⓑ Ⓒ Ⓓ   51. Ⓐ Ⓑ Ⓒ Ⓓ   61. Ⓐ Ⓑ Ⓒ Ⓓ   71. Ⓐ Ⓑ Ⓒ Ⓓ
2. Ⓕ Ⓖ Ⓗ Ⓙ   12. Ⓕ Ⓖ Ⓗ Ⓙ   22. Ⓕ Ⓖ Ⓗ Ⓙ   32. Ⓕ Ⓖ Ⓗ Ⓙ   42. Ⓕ Ⓖ Ⓗ Ⓙ   52. Ⓕ Ⓖ Ⓗ Ⓙ   62. Ⓕ Ⓖ Ⓗ Ⓙ   72. Ⓕ Ⓖ Ⓗ Ⓙ
3. Ⓐ Ⓑ Ⓒ Ⓓ   13. Ⓐ Ⓑ Ⓒ Ⓓ   23. Ⓐ Ⓑ Ⓒ Ⓓ   33. Ⓐ Ⓑ Ⓒ Ⓓ   43. Ⓐ Ⓑ Ⓒ Ⓓ   53. Ⓐ Ⓑ Ⓒ Ⓓ   63. Ⓐ Ⓑ Ⓒ Ⓓ   73. Ⓐ Ⓑ Ⓒ Ⓓ
4. Ⓕ Ⓖ Ⓗ Ⓙ   14. Ⓕ Ⓖ Ⓗ Ⓙ   24. Ⓕ Ⓖ Ⓗ Ⓙ   34. Ⓕ Ⓖ Ⓗ Ⓙ   44. Ⓕ Ⓖ Ⓗ Ⓙ   54. Ⓕ Ⓖ Ⓗ Ⓙ   64. Ⓕ Ⓖ Ⓗ Ⓙ   74. Ⓕ Ⓖ Ⓗ Ⓙ
5. Ⓐ Ⓑ Ⓒ Ⓓ   15. Ⓐ Ⓑ Ⓒ Ⓓ   25. Ⓐ Ⓑ Ⓒ Ⓓ   35. Ⓐ Ⓑ Ⓒ Ⓓ   45. Ⓐ Ⓑ Ⓒ Ⓓ   55. Ⓐ Ⓑ Ⓒ Ⓓ   65. Ⓐ Ⓑ Ⓒ Ⓓ   75. Ⓐ Ⓑ Ⓒ Ⓓ
6. Ⓕ Ⓖ Ⓗ Ⓙ   16. Ⓕ Ⓖ Ⓗ Ⓙ   26. Ⓕ Ⓖ Ⓗ Ⓙ   36. Ⓕ Ⓖ Ⓗ Ⓙ   46. Ⓕ Ⓖ Ⓗ Ⓙ   56. Ⓕ Ⓖ Ⓗ Ⓙ   66. Ⓕ Ⓖ Ⓗ Ⓙ
7. Ⓐ Ⓑ Ⓒ Ⓓ   17. Ⓐ Ⓑ Ⓒ Ⓓ   27. Ⓐ Ⓑ Ⓒ Ⓓ   37. Ⓐ Ⓑ Ⓒ Ⓓ   47. Ⓐ Ⓑ Ⓒ Ⓓ   57. Ⓐ Ⓑ Ⓒ Ⓓ   67. Ⓐ Ⓑ Ⓒ Ⓓ
8. Ⓕ Ⓖ Ⓗ Ⓙ   18. Ⓕ Ⓖ Ⓗ Ⓙ   28. Ⓕ Ⓖ Ⓗ Ⓙ   38. Ⓕ Ⓖ Ⓗ Ⓙ   48. Ⓕ Ⓖ Ⓗ Ⓙ   58. Ⓕ Ⓖ Ⓗ Ⓙ   68. Ⓕ Ⓖ Ⓗ Ⓙ
9. Ⓐ Ⓑ Ⓒ Ⓓ   19. Ⓐ Ⓑ Ⓒ Ⓓ   29. Ⓐ Ⓑ Ⓒ Ⓓ   39. Ⓐ Ⓑ Ⓒ Ⓓ   49. Ⓐ Ⓑ Ⓒ Ⓓ   59. Ⓐ Ⓑ Ⓒ Ⓓ   69. Ⓐ Ⓑ Ⓒ Ⓓ
10. Ⓕ Ⓖ Ⓗ Ⓙ   20. Ⓕ Ⓖ Ⓗ Ⓙ   30. Ⓕ Ⓖ Ⓗ Ⓙ   40. Ⓕ Ⓖ Ⓗ Ⓙ   50. Ⓕ Ⓖ Ⓗ Ⓙ   60. Ⓕ Ⓖ Ⓗ Ⓙ   70. Ⓕ Ⓖ Ⓗ Ⓙ

MATHEMATICS TEST

1. Ⓐ Ⓑ Ⓒ Ⓓ Ⓔ   11. Ⓐ Ⓑ Ⓒ Ⓓ Ⓔ   21. Ⓐ Ⓑ Ⓒ Ⓓ Ⓔ   31. Ⓐ Ⓑ Ⓒ Ⓓ Ⓔ   41. Ⓐ Ⓑ Ⓒ Ⓓ Ⓔ   51. Ⓐ Ⓑ Ⓒ Ⓓ Ⓔ
2. Ⓕ Ⓖ Ⓗ Ⓙ Ⓚ   12. Ⓕ Ⓖ Ⓗ Ⓙ Ⓚ   22. Ⓕ Ⓖ Ⓗ Ⓙ Ⓚ   32. Ⓕ Ⓖ Ⓗ Ⓙ Ⓚ   42. Ⓕ Ⓖ Ⓗ Ⓙ Ⓚ   52. Ⓕ Ⓖ Ⓗ Ⓙ Ⓚ
3. Ⓐ Ⓑ Ⓒ Ⓓ Ⓔ   13. Ⓐ Ⓑ Ⓒ Ⓓ Ⓔ   23. Ⓐ Ⓑ Ⓒ Ⓓ Ⓔ   33. Ⓐ Ⓑ Ⓒ Ⓓ Ⓔ   43. Ⓐ Ⓑ Ⓒ Ⓓ Ⓔ   53. Ⓐ Ⓑ Ⓒ Ⓓ Ⓔ
4. Ⓕ Ⓖ Ⓗ Ⓙ Ⓚ   14. Ⓕ Ⓖ Ⓗ Ⓙ Ⓚ   24. Ⓕ Ⓖ Ⓗ Ⓙ Ⓚ   34. Ⓕ Ⓖ Ⓗ Ⓙ Ⓚ   44. Ⓕ Ⓖ Ⓗ Ⓙ Ⓚ   54. Ⓕ Ⓖ Ⓗ Ⓙ Ⓚ
5. Ⓐ Ⓑ Ⓒ Ⓓ Ⓔ   15. Ⓐ Ⓑ Ⓒ Ⓓ Ⓔ   25. Ⓐ Ⓑ Ⓒ Ⓓ Ⓔ   35. Ⓐ Ⓑ Ⓒ Ⓓ Ⓔ   45. Ⓐ Ⓑ Ⓒ Ⓓ Ⓔ   55. Ⓐ Ⓑ Ⓒ Ⓓ Ⓔ
6. Ⓕ Ⓖ Ⓗ Ⓙ Ⓚ   16. Ⓕ Ⓖ Ⓗ Ⓙ Ⓚ   26. Ⓕ Ⓖ Ⓗ Ⓙ Ⓚ   36. Ⓕ Ⓖ Ⓗ Ⓙ Ⓚ   46. Ⓕ Ⓖ Ⓗ Ⓙ Ⓚ   56. Ⓕ Ⓖ Ⓗ Ⓙ Ⓚ
7. Ⓐ Ⓑ Ⓒ Ⓓ Ⓔ   17. Ⓐ Ⓑ Ⓒ Ⓓ Ⓔ   27. Ⓐ Ⓑ Ⓒ Ⓓ Ⓔ   37. Ⓐ Ⓑ Ⓒ Ⓓ Ⓔ   47. Ⓐ Ⓑ Ⓒ Ⓓ Ⓔ   57. Ⓐ Ⓑ Ⓒ Ⓓ Ⓔ
8. Ⓕ Ⓖ Ⓗ Ⓙ Ⓚ   18. Ⓕ Ⓖ Ⓗ Ⓙ Ⓚ   28. Ⓕ Ⓖ Ⓗ Ⓙ Ⓚ   38. Ⓕ Ⓖ Ⓗ Ⓙ Ⓚ   48. Ⓕ Ⓖ Ⓗ Ⓙ Ⓚ   58. Ⓕ Ⓖ Ⓗ Ⓙ Ⓚ
9. Ⓐ Ⓑ Ⓒ Ⓓ Ⓔ   19. Ⓐ Ⓑ Ⓒ Ⓓ Ⓔ   29. Ⓐ Ⓑ Ⓒ Ⓓ Ⓔ   39. Ⓐ Ⓑ Ⓒ Ⓓ Ⓔ   49. Ⓐ Ⓑ Ⓒ Ⓓ Ⓔ   59. Ⓐ Ⓑ Ⓒ Ⓓ Ⓔ
10. Ⓕ Ⓖ Ⓗ Ⓙ Ⓚ   20. Ⓕ Ⓖ Ⓗ Ⓙ Ⓚ   30. Ⓕ Ⓖ Ⓗ Ⓙ Ⓚ   40. Ⓕ Ⓖ Ⓗ Ⓙ Ⓚ   50. Ⓕ Ⓖ Ⓗ Ⓙ Ⓚ   60. Ⓕ Ⓖ Ⓗ Ⓙ Ⓚ

READING TEST

1. Ⓐ Ⓑ Ⓒ Ⓓ   6. Ⓕ Ⓖ Ⓗ Ⓙ   11. Ⓐ Ⓑ Ⓒ Ⓓ   16. Ⓕ Ⓖ Ⓗ Ⓙ   21. Ⓐ Ⓑ Ⓒ Ⓓ   26. Ⓕ Ⓖ Ⓗ Ⓙ   31. Ⓐ Ⓑ Ⓒ Ⓓ   36. Ⓕ Ⓖ Ⓗ Ⓙ
2. Ⓕ Ⓖ Ⓗ Ⓙ   7. Ⓐ Ⓑ Ⓒ Ⓓ   12. Ⓕ Ⓖ Ⓗ Ⓙ   17. Ⓐ Ⓑ Ⓒ Ⓓ   22. Ⓕ Ⓖ Ⓗ Ⓙ   27. Ⓐ Ⓑ Ⓒ Ⓓ   32. Ⓕ Ⓖ Ⓗ Ⓙ   37. Ⓐ Ⓑ Ⓒ Ⓓ
3. Ⓐ Ⓑ Ⓒ Ⓓ   8. Ⓕ Ⓖ Ⓗ Ⓙ   13. Ⓐ Ⓑ Ⓒ Ⓓ   18. Ⓕ Ⓖ Ⓗ Ⓙ   23. Ⓐ Ⓑ Ⓒ Ⓓ   28. Ⓕ Ⓖ Ⓗ Ⓙ   33. Ⓐ Ⓑ Ⓒ Ⓓ   38. Ⓕ Ⓖ Ⓗ Ⓙ
4. Ⓕ Ⓖ Ⓗ Ⓙ   9. Ⓐ Ⓑ Ⓒ Ⓓ   14. Ⓕ Ⓖ Ⓗ Ⓙ   19. Ⓐ Ⓑ Ⓒ Ⓓ   24. Ⓕ Ⓖ Ⓗ Ⓙ   29. Ⓐ Ⓑ Ⓒ Ⓓ   34. Ⓕ Ⓖ Ⓗ Ⓙ   39. Ⓐ Ⓑ Ⓒ Ⓓ
5. Ⓐ Ⓑ Ⓒ Ⓓ   10. Ⓕ Ⓖ Ⓗ Ⓙ   15. Ⓐ Ⓑ Ⓒ Ⓓ   20. Ⓕ Ⓖ Ⓗ Ⓙ   25. Ⓐ Ⓑ Ⓒ Ⓓ   30. Ⓕ Ⓖ Ⓗ Ⓙ   35. Ⓐ Ⓑ Ⓒ Ⓓ   40. Ⓕ Ⓖ Ⓗ Ⓙ

SCIENCE TEST

1. Ⓐ Ⓑ Ⓒ Ⓓ   6. Ⓕ Ⓖ Ⓗ Ⓙ   11. Ⓐ Ⓑ Ⓒ Ⓓ   16. Ⓕ Ⓖ Ⓗ Ⓙ   21. Ⓐ Ⓑ Ⓒ Ⓓ   26. Ⓕ Ⓖ Ⓗ Ⓙ   31. Ⓐ Ⓑ Ⓒ Ⓓ   36. Ⓕ Ⓖ Ⓗ Ⓙ
2. Ⓕ Ⓖ Ⓗ Ⓙ   7. Ⓐ Ⓑ Ⓒ Ⓓ   12. Ⓕ Ⓖ Ⓗ Ⓙ   17. Ⓐ Ⓑ Ⓒ Ⓓ   22. Ⓕ Ⓖ Ⓗ Ⓙ   27. Ⓐ Ⓑ Ⓒ Ⓓ   32. Ⓕ Ⓖ Ⓗ Ⓙ   37. Ⓐ Ⓑ Ⓒ Ⓓ
3. Ⓐ Ⓑ Ⓒ Ⓓ   8. Ⓕ Ⓖ Ⓗ Ⓙ   13. Ⓐ Ⓑ Ⓒ Ⓓ   18. Ⓕ Ⓖ Ⓗ Ⓙ   23. Ⓐ Ⓑ Ⓒ Ⓓ   28. Ⓕ Ⓖ Ⓗ Ⓙ   33. Ⓐ Ⓑ Ⓒ Ⓓ   38. Ⓕ Ⓖ Ⓗ Ⓙ
4. Ⓕ Ⓖ Ⓗ Ⓙ   9. Ⓐ Ⓑ Ⓒ Ⓓ   14. Ⓕ Ⓖ Ⓗ Ⓙ   19. Ⓐ Ⓑ Ⓒ Ⓓ   24. Ⓕ Ⓖ Ⓗ Ⓙ   29. Ⓐ Ⓑ Ⓒ Ⓓ   34. Ⓕ Ⓖ Ⓗ Ⓙ   39. Ⓐ Ⓑ Ⓒ Ⓓ
5. Ⓐ Ⓑ Ⓒ Ⓓ   10. Ⓕ Ⓖ Ⓗ Ⓙ   15. Ⓐ Ⓑ Ⓒ Ⓓ   20. Ⓕ Ⓖ Ⓗ Ⓙ   25. Ⓐ Ⓑ Ⓒ Ⓓ   30. Ⓕ Ⓖ Ⓗ Ⓙ   35. Ⓐ Ⓑ Ⓒ Ⓓ   40. Ⓕ Ⓖ Ⓗ Ⓙ

ENGLISH TEST

45 Minutes—75 Questions

Directions: In the following five passages, certain words and phrases are underlined and numbered. In the right-hand column are alternatives for each underlined portion. Select the one that best conveys the idea, creates the most grammatically correct sentence, or is the most consistent with the style and tone of the passage. If you decide that the original version is best, select NO CHANGE. You may also find questions that ask about the entire passage or a section of the passage. These questions will correspond to small numbered boxes in the text. For these questions, decide which choice best accomplishes the purpose set out in the question stem. After you've selected the best choice, fill in the corresponding oval in your Answer Grid. For some questions, you'll need to read the context in order to answer correctly. Be sure to read until you have enough information to determine the correct answer choice.

PASSAGE I

ORIGINS OF URBAN LEGENDS

[1]

Since primitive times, societies have <u>created, and told</u> legends. Even before the development of written language, cultures would orally pass down these popular stories.

[2]

[2] These stories served the dual purpose of entertaining audiences and of transmitting values and beliefs from generation to generation.

1. A. NO CHANGE
    B. created then subsequently told
    C. created and told
    D. created, and told original

2. Suppose that the author wants to insert a sentence here to describe the different kinds of oral stories told by these societies. Which of the following sentences would best serve that purpose?

    F. These myths and tales varied in substance, from the humorous to the heroic.
    G. These myths and tales were often recited by paid storytellers.
    H. Unfortunately, no recording of the original myths and tales exists.
    J. Sometimes it took several evenings for the full story to be recited.

GO ON TO THE NEXT PAGE ▷

<u>Indeed</u> today we have many more permanent ways
    3
of handing down our beliefs to future generations, we

continue to create and tell legends. In our technological

society, a new form of folktale has emerged:

<u>the</u> urban legend.
 4

3. **A.** NO CHANGE
    B. However,
    C. Indeed,
    D. Although

4. **F.** NO CHANGE
    G. it is called the
    H. it being the
    J. known as the

[3]

Urban legends are stories we all have heard; they

are supposed to have really happened, but are never

<u>verifiable however.</u> It seems that the people involved can
        5
never be found. Researchers of the urban legend call the

elusive participant in such supposed "real-life" events a

FOAF—a Friend of a Friend.

5. **A.** NO CHANGE
    B. verifiable, however.
    C. verifiable, furthermore.
    D. verifiable.

[4]

Urban legends have some characteristic features.

They are often humorous in nature with a surprise

<u>ending and a conclusion.</u> One such legend is the tale of
          6
the hunter who was returning home from an unsuccess-

ful hunting trip. On his way home, he accidentally hit

and killed a deer on a deserted highway. Even though he

knew it was illegal, he decided to keep the deer, and he

<u>loads it in</u> the back of his station wagon. As the hunter
    7
continued driving, the deer,

<u>he was</u> only temporarily knocked unconscious by the
    8
car, woke up and began thrashing around. The hunter

panicked, stopped the car, ran to hide in the roadside

ditch, and watched the enraged deer destroy his car.

6. **F.** NO CHANGE
    G. ending.
    H. ending, which is a conclusion.
    J. ending or conclusion.

7. **A.** NO CHANGE
    B. loaded it in
    C. is loading it in
    D. had loaded it in

8. **F.** NO CHANGE
    G. which being
    H. that is
    J. which was

GO ON TO THE NEXT PAGE ⟩

[5]

One legend involves alligators in the sewer systems of major metropolitan areas. According to the story, before alligators were a protected <u>species, people</u> vacationing in Florida purchased baby alligators to take home as souvenirs.

<u>Between 1930 and 1940, nearly a million alligators in Florida were killed for the value of their skin, used to make expensive leather products such as boots and wallets.</u>
After the novelty of having a pet alligator wore off, many people flushed their baby souvenirs down toilets. Legend has it that the baby alligators found a perfect growing and breeding environment in city sewer systems, where they thrive to this day on the ample supply of rats.

[6]

In addition to urban legends that are told from friend to friend, a growing number of urban legends are passed along through the Internet and email. One of the more popular stories <u>are about</u> a woman who was unwittingly charged $100 for a cookie recipe she requested at an upscale restaurant. To get her money's worth, this

<u>woman supposed</u> copied the recipe for the delicious cookies and forwarded it via email to everyone she knew.

9. **A.** NO CHANGE
   B. species; people
   C. species. People
   D. species people

10. **F.** NO CHANGE
   G. Because their skin is used to make expensive leather products such as boots and wallets, nearly a million alligators in Florida were killed between 1930 and 1940.
   H. Killed between 1930 and 1940, the skin of nearly a million alligators from Florida was used to make expensive leather products such as boots and wallets.
   J. OMIT the underlined portion.

11. **A.** NO CHANGE
   B. would be about
   C. is about
   D. is dealing with

12. **F.** NO CHANGE
   G. woman supposedly
   H. women supposedly
   J. women supposed to

GO ON TO THE NEXT PAGE

[7]

Although today's technology enhances our ability to tell and retell urban legends, the Internet can also serve as a monitor of urban legends. <u>Dedicated to commonly told urban legends, research is done by many websites.</u>
13

According to those websites, most legends, including the ones told here, have no basis in reality.

13. **A.** NO CHANGE
    B. Many websites are dedicated to researching the validity of commonly told urban legends.
    C. Researching the validity of commonly told urban legends, many websites are dedicated.
    D. OMIT the underlined portion.

> Questions 14–15 ask about the preceding passage as a whole.

14. The author wants to insert the following sentence:

> Other urban legends seem to be designed to instill fear.

What would be the most logical placement for this sentence?

F. After the last sentence of paragraph 3
G. After the second sentence of paragraph 4
H. Before the first sentence of paragraph 5
J. After the last sentence of paragraph 6

15. Suppose that the author had been assigned to write an essay comparing the purposes and topics of myths and legends in primitive societies and in our modern society. Would this essay fulfill that assignment?

A. Yes, because the essay describes myths and legends from primitive societies and modern society.
B. Yes, because the essay provides explanations of possible purposes and topics of myths and legends from primitive societies and modern society.
C. No, because the essay does not provide enough information about the topics of the myths and legends of primitive societies to make a valid comparison.
D. No, because the essay does not provide any information on the myths and legends of primitive societies.

PASSAGE II

HENRY DAVID THOREAU: A SUCCESSFUL LIFE

What does it mean to be successful? <u>Do one</u> meas-
                                        16
ure success by money? If I told you about a

man: working as a teacher, a land surveyor, and a
     17
factory worker (never holding any of these jobs for more

than a few years), would that man sound like a success

to you? If I told you that he spent

16. F. NO CHANGE
G. Does we
H. Does one
J. Did you

17. A. NO CHANGE
B. man who worked
C. man and worked
D. man, which working

GO ON TO THE NEXT PAGE ⟹

<u>two solitary years living alone</u> in a small cabin that he
                18
built for himself and that he spent those years looking at

plants and writing in a diary—would you think of him

as a celebrity or an important figure? What if I told you

that

<u>he rarely ventured</u> far from the town where he was
         19
born, that he was thrown in jail for refusing to pay his

taxes, and that he died at the age of forty-five? Do any of

these facts seem to point to a man whose life should be

studied and emulated?

    You may already know about this man. You may

even have read some of his writings. His name <u>was:</u>
                                               20
<u>Henry David Thoreau, and he</u> was, in addition to the
                20
jobs listed above, a poet, an essayist, a naturalist, and

a social critic. Although the facts listed about him

may not seem to add up to much, he <u>was, in fact a</u>
                                         21
tremendously influential person. Along with writers

such as Ralph Waldo Emerson, Mark Twain, and Walt

Whitman, Thoreau helped to create the first literature

and philosophy that most people identify as <u>unique</u>
                                              22
American.

    In 1845, Thoreau built a <u>cabin. Near</u> Walden Pond
                                  23
and remained there for more than two years, living

alone, fending for himself, and observing the nature

around him. He kept scrupulous notes in his diary,

notes that he later distilled into his most famous work

titled *Walden.*

18. **F.** NO CHANGE
   G. two years living alone
   H. two solitary years all by himself
   J. a couple of lonely years living in solitude

19. **A.** NO CHANGE
   B. he is rarely venturing
   C. he has rare ventures
   D. this person was to venture rarely

20. **F.** NO CHANGE
   G. was Henry David Thoreau and he
   H. was: Henry David Thoreau; and he
   J. was Henry David Thoreau, and he

21. **A.** NO CHANGE
   B. was, in fact, a
   C. was in fact a
   D. was in fact, a

22. **F.** NO CHANGE
   G. uniquely
   H. uniqueness
   J. the most unique

23. **A.** NO CHANGE
   B. cabin. On
   C. cabin, by
   D. cabin near

GO ON TO THE NEXT PAGE ⇒

Walden is read by many literature students today.
24

[1] To protest slavery, Thoreau refused to pay his taxes in 1846. [2] Thoreau was a firm believer in the abolition of slavery, and he objected to the practice's extension into the new territories of the West. [3] For this act of rebellion, he was thrown in the Concord jail. 25

Thoreau used his writing to spread his message of resistance and activism; he published an essay entitled
26
Civil Disobedience (also known as Resistance to Civil Government). In it, Thoreau laid out his argument for refusing to obey unjust laws.

Although Thoreau's life was very brief, his works
27
and his ideas continue to touch and influence people. Students all over the country—all over the world—continue to read his essays and hear his unique voice, urging them to lead lives of principle, individuality, and freedom. 28 To be able to live out the ideas that burn in

the heart of a person—surely that is the meaning of
29
success.

24. **F.** NO CHANGE
    G. This book is read by many literature students today.
    H. Today, many literature students read *Walden*.
    J. OMIT the underlined portion.

25. What is the most logical order of sentences in this paragraph?
    A. NO CHANGE
    B. 3, 2, 1
    C. 2, 1, 3
    D. 3, 1, 2

26. **F.** NO CHANGE
    G. activism, he published:
    H. activism, he published
    J. activism, he published,

27. **A.** NO CHANGE
    B. he's
    C. their
    D. those

28. The purpose of this paragraph is to:
    F. explain why Thoreau was put in jail.
    G. prove a point about people's conception of success.
    H. suggest that Thoreau may be misunderstood.
    J. discuss Thoreau's importance in today's world.

29. **A.** NO CHANGE
    B. one's heart
    C. the heart and soul of a person
    D. through the heart of a person

GO ON TO THE NEXT PAGE

Question 30 asks about the preceding passage as a whole.

30. By including questions throughout the entire first paragraph, the author encourages the reader to:

    F. answer each question as the passage proceeds.

    G. think about the meaning of success.

    H. assess the quality of Thoreau's work.

    J. form an opinion about greed in modern society.

PASSAGE III

THE SLOTH: SLOW BUT NOT SLOTHFUL

[1]

More than half of the world's <u>currently living plant</u> and
                                        31
animal species live in tropical rain forests. Four square

miles of a Central American rain forest can be home

to up to 1,500 different species of flowering plants, 700

species of trees, 400 species of birds, and 125 species of

mammals. Of these mammals, the sloth is one of the

most unusual.

[2]

Unlike most mammals, the sloth is usually upside

down. A sloth does just about everything upside down,

including sleeping, eating, mating, and giving birth.

<u>Its' unique</u> anatomy allows the sloth to spend most of
      32
the time hanging from one tree branch or another, high

in the canopy of a rain forest tree. About the size of a

large domestic <u>cat, the</u> sloth hangs from its unusually
                  33
long limbs and long, hooklike claws.

31. A. NO CHANGE
    B. currently existing plant
    C. living plant
    D. plant

32. F. NO CHANGE
    G. It's unique
    H. Its unique
    J. Its uniquely

33. A. NO CHANGE
    B. cat; the
    C. cat. The
    D. cat, but the

GO ON TO THE NEXT PAGE ⟹

Specially designed for limbs, the sloth's muscles seem to
                              34
cling to things.
  34

34. F. NO CHANGE
   G. The sloth's muscles seem to cling to things for specially designed limbs.
   H. The muscles in a sloth's limbs seem to be specially designed for clinging to things.
   J. OMIT the underlined portion.

[3]

In fact, a sloth's limbs are so specific adapted to
                              35
upside-down life that a sloth is essentially incapable

35. A. NO CHANGE
   B. so specific and
   C. so specified
   D. so specifically

of walking on the ground. Instead, they must crawl or
                              36
drag itself with its massive claws. This makes it easy to

see why the sloth rarely leaves its home in the trees.

36. F. NO CHANGE
   G. Instead, it
   H. However, they
   J. In addition, it

Because it can not move swiftly on the ground, the sloth
    37
is an excellent swimmer.

37. A. NO CHANGE
   B. Despite
   C. Similarly,
   D. Though

[4]

38 A sloth can hang upside down and, without

38. The author wants to insert a sentence here to help connect paragraph 3 and paragraph 4. Which of the following sentences would best serve that purpose?

   F. Of course, many other animals are also excellent swimmers.
   G. Another unique characteristic of the sloth is its flexibility.
   H. In addition to swimming, the sloth is an incredible climber.
   J. Flexibility is a trait that helps the sloth survive.

GO ON TO THE NEXT PAGE ▷

moving the rest of its <u>body turn</u> its face 180 degrees so
                        39

that it <u>was looking</u> at the ground. A sloth can rotate
              40
its forelimbs in all directions, so it can easily reach the

leaves that make up its diet. The sloth can also roll itself

up into a ball in order to <u>protect and defend itself from</u>
                           41

predators. <u>The howler monkey, another inhabitant of</u>
                                42
<u>the rain forest, is not as flexible as the sloth.</u>
            42

[5]

The best defense a sloth has from predators such as

jaguars and large snakes, though, is its camouflage. Dur-

ing the rainy season, a sloth's thick brown or gray fur is

usually covered with a coat of blue-green <u>algae. Which</u>
                                               43
helps it blend in with its forest surroundings. Another

type of camouflage is the sloth's incredibly slow move-

ment: it often moves less than 100 feet during a 24-hour

period.

[6]

It is this slow movement that earned the sloth its

name. *Sloth* is also a word for laziness or an aversion to

work. But even though it sleeps an average of 15 hours a

day, the sloth isn't necessarily lazy. It just moves, upside

39. A. NO CHANGE
    B. body turns
    C. body, it has the capability of turning
    D. body, turn

40. F. NO CHANGE
    G. had been looking
    H. will have the ability to be looking
    J. can look

41. A. NO CHANGE
    B. protect itself and defend itself from
    C. protect itself so it won't be harmed by
    D. protect itself from

42. F. NO CHANGE
    G. Another inhabitant of the rain forest, the howler monkey, is not as flexible as the sloth.
    H. Not as flexible as the sloth is the howler monkey, another inhabitant of the rain forest.
    J. OMIT the underlined portion.

43. A. NO CHANGE
    B. algae, which
    C. algae, being that it
    D. algae

GO ON TO THE NEXT PAGE ⟩

down, at its own slow pace through its world of rain

forest trees. 44

44. The author is considering deleting the last sentence of paragraph 6. This change would:

F. diminish the amount of information provided about the habits of the sloth.

G. make the ending of the passage more abrupt.

H. emphasize the slothful nature of the sloth.

J. make the tone of the essay more consistent.

Question 45 asks about the preceding passage as a whole.

45. The author wants to insert the following description:

An observer could easily be tricked into thinking that a sloth was just a pile of decaying leaves.

What would be the most appropriate placement for this sentence?

A. After the last sentence of paragraph 1

B. After the third sentence of paragraph 2

C. Before the last sentence of paragraph 5

D. Before the first sentence of paragraph 6

GO ON TO THE NEXT PAGE

PASSAGE IV

FIRES IN YELLOWSTONE

During the summer of 1988, I watched Yellowstone

National Park go up in flames. In June, <u>fires ignited</u>
                                              46
<u>by lightning</u> had been allowed to burn unsuppressed
   46
because park officials expected that the usual summer

rains would douse the flames. However, the rains never

<u>will have come</u>. A plentiful fuel supply of fallen logs and
   47
pine needles was available, and winds of up to 100 miles

per hour whipped the spreading fires along and carried

red-hot embers to other areas, creating new fires. By the

time park officials succumbed to the pressure of public

opinion and <u>decide</u> to try to extinguish the
              48

flames. <u>It's</u> too late. The situation remained out of con-
         49
trol in spite of the efforts of 9,000 firefighters who were

using state-of-the-art equipment. By September, more

than 720,000 acres of Yellowstone had been affected by

fire. <u>Nature was only able to curb the destruction</u>; the
                        50
smoke did not begin to clear until the first snow arrived

on September 11.

   <u>Being that I was</u> an ecologist who has studied
       51
forests for 20 years, I know that this was not nearly

the tragedy it seemed to be. Large fires are, after

46. **F.** NO CHANGE
    G. fires having been ignited by lightning
    H. fires, the kind ignited by lightning,
    J. fires ignited and started by lightning

47. **A.** NO CHANGE
    B. came
    C. were coming
    D. have come

48. **F.** NO CHANGE
    G. are deciding
    H. decided
    J. OMIT the underlined portion.

49. **A.** NO CHANGE
    B. flames, it's
    C. flames, it was
    D. flames; it was

50. **F.** NO CHANGE
    G. Only curbing the destruction by able nature
    H. Only nature was able to curb the destruction
    J. Nature was able to curb only the destruction

51. **A.** NO CHANGE
    B. Being that I am
    C. I'm
    D. As

GO ON TO THE NEXT PAGE

all, necessary <u>in order that the continued health in</u>
<u>the forest ecosystem be maintained.</u> Fires thin out
overcrowded areas and allow the sun to reach species of
plants stunted by shade. Ash fertilizes the soil, and fire
smoke kills forest bacteria. In the case of the lodgepole

pine, fire is essential to reproduction: the <u>pines' cone</u>
open only when exposed to temperatures greater than
112 degrees.

The fires in Yellowstone did result in some loss of
wildlife, but overall, the region's animals proved to be
fire-tolerant and fire-adaptive. <u>However,</u> large animals

such as bison were often seen <u>grazing, and</u> bedding
down in meadows near burning forests. Also, the fire
posed little threat to the members of any endangered
animal species in the park.

My confidence in the natural resilience of the forest
has been borne out in the years since the fires ravaged
Yellowstone. <u>Judged from recent pictures of the park</u>

the forest was not destroyed; <u>it</u> was rejuvenated.

---

52. **F.** NO CHANGE
G. for the continued health of the forest ecosystem to be maintained.
H. in order to continue the maintenance of the health of the forest ecosystem.
J. for the continued health of the forest ecosystem.

53. **A.** NO CHANGE
B. pines cones'
C. pine's cones
D. pine's cone

54. **F.** NO CHANGE
G. Clearly,
H. In fact,
J. Instead,

55. **A.** NO CHANGE
B. grazing; and bedding
C. grazing: and bedding
D. grazing and bedding

56. **F.** NO CHANGE
G. Recent pictures of the park show that
H. Judging by the recent pictures of the park,
J. As judged according to pictures taken of the park recently,

57. **A.** NO CHANGE
B. they
C. the fires
D. I

GO ON TO THE NEXT PAGE ⇨

Questions 58–59 ask about the preceding passage as a whole.

58. The writer is considering inserting the following true statement after the first sentence of the second paragraph:

> Many more acres of forest burned in Alaska in 1988 than in Yellowstone Park.

Would this addition be appropriate for the essay?

F. Yes, the statement would add important information about the effects of large-scale forest fires.

G. Yes, the statement would provide an informative contrast to the Yellowstone fire.

H. No, the statement would not provide any additional information about the effect of the 1988 fire in Yellowstone.

J. No, the statement would undermine the author's position as an authority on the subject of forest fires.

59. Suppose that the writer wishes to provide additional support for the claim that the fire posed little threat to the members of any endangered animal species in the park. Which of the following additions would be most effective?

A. A list of the endangered animals known to inhabit the park

B. A discussion of the particular vulnerability of endangered species of birds to forest fires

C. An explanation of the relative infrequency of such an extensive series of forest fires

D. A summary of reports of biologists who monitored the activity of endangered species in the park during the fire

PASSAGE V

MY FIRST WHITE-WATER RAFTING TRIP

[1]

White-water rafting being a favorite pastime of mine
60
for several years. I have drifted down many challenging

North American rivers, including the Snake, the Green,

and the Salmon, and there are many other rivers in
61
America as well. I have spent some of my best moments
61
in dangerous rapids, yet nothing has matched the thrill

60. F. NO CHANGE
G. have been
H. has been
J. was

61. A. NO CHANGE
B. Salmon, just three of many rivers existing in North America.
C. Salmon; many other rivers exist in North America.
D. Salmon.

GO ON TO THE NEXT PAGE ▷

I experienced facing my <u>first, rapids, on the Deschutes</u>
                                    62
<u>River.</u>
  62

[2]

My father and I spent the morning floating down a calm and peaceful stretch of the Deschutes in his wooden MacKenzie river boat. This trip <u>it being</u> the
                                                    63
wooden boat's first time down rapids, as well as mine.

<u>Rapids are rated according to a uniform scale of relative</u>
                                    64
<u>difficulty.</u>
  64

[3]

<u>Roaring, I was in the boat approaching Whitehorse</u>
                          65
<u>Rapids.</u> I felt much like a novice skier peering down her
  65
first steep slope: I was scared, but even more excited.

The water <u>churned and covering me</u> with a refreshing
                          66
spray. My father, toward the stern, controlled the oars. The carefree expression he usually wore on the river had

been replaced<u>, and instead he adopted</u> a look of intense
                          67
concentration as he maneuvered around boulders dotting our path. To release tension, we began to holler

62. **F.** NO CHANGE
    G. first: rapids on the Deschutes River.
    H. first rapids; on the Deschutes River.
    J. first rapids on the Deschutes River.

63. **A.** NO CHANGE
    B. it happened that it was
    C. was
    D. being

64. **F.** NO CHANGE
    G. Rated according to a uniform scale, rapids are relatively difficult.
    H. (Rapids are rated according to a uniform scale of relative difficulty.)
    J. OMIT the underlined portion.

65. **A.** NO CHANGE
    B. It roared, and the boat and I approached Whitehorse Rapids.
    C. While the roaring boat was approaching Whitehorse Rapids, I could hear the water.
    D. I could hear the water roar as we approached Whitehorse Rapids.

66. **F.** NO CHANGE
    G. churned, and covering me
    H. churning and covering me
    J. churned, covering me

67. **A.** NO CHANGE
    B. with
    C. by another countenance altogether:
    D. instead with another expression;

GO ON TO THE NEXT PAGE ▷

like kids on a roller-coaster, our voices echoing <u>across</u> [68] the water as we lurched violently about.

[4]

Suddenly we came to a jarring halt <u>and we stopped</u>; [69] the left side of the bow was wedged on a large rock. A whirlpool swirled around us; if we capsized, we would be sucked into the undertow. Instinctively, I threw all of my weight toward the right side of the tilting boat. Luckily, <u>it was</u> just enough force to dislodge us, and [70] we continued on downstream to enjoy about 10 more minutes of spectacular rapids.

[5]

Later that day, we went through Buckskin Mary Rapids and Boxcar Rapids. When we pulled up on the bank that evening, we saw that the boat had received its first scar: <u>that scar was a</u> small hole on the upper bow [71] from the boulder we had wrestled with. In the years to come, we went down many rapids and the boat

<u>receiving many</u> bruises, but Whitehorse remains the [72] most

68. F. NO CHANGE
     G. throughout
     H. around
     J. from

69. A. NO CHANGE
     B. which stopped us
     C. and stopped
     D. OMIT the underlined portion.

70. F. NO CHANGE
     G. it's
     H. it is
     J. its

71. A. NO CHANGE
     B. that was a
     C. which was a
     D. a

72. F. NO CHANGE
     G. received many
     H. received much
     J. receives many

memorable rapids of all. 73

73. Which of the following concluding sentences would most effectively emphasize the final point made in this paragraph while retaining the style and tone of the narrative as a whole?

   A. The brutal calamities that it presented the unwary rafter were more than offset by its beguiling excitement.

   B. Perhaps it is true that your first close encounter with white water is your most intense.

   C. Or, if not the most memorable, then at least a very memorable one!

   D. Call me crazy or weird if you want, but white-water rafting is the sport for me.

Questions 74–75 ask about the preceding passage as a whole.

---

74. The writer has been assigned to write an essay that focuses on the techniques of white-water rafting. Would this essay meet the requirements of that assignment?

   F. No, because the essay's main focus is on a particular experience, not on techniques.

   G. No, because the essay mostly deals with the relationship between father and daughter.

   H. Yes, because specific rafting techniques are the essay's main focus.

   J. Yes, because it presents a dramatic story of a day of white-water rafting.

75. Suppose that the writer wants to add the following sentence to the essay:

> It was such a mild summer day that it was hard to believe dangerous rapids awaited us downstream.

What would be the most logical placement of this sentence?

   A. After the last sentence of paragraph 1

   B. After the last sentence of paragraph 2

   C. Before the first sentence of paragraph 4

   D. After the last sentence of paragraph 4

IF YOU FINISH BEFORE TIME IS CALLED, YOU MAY CHECK YOUR WORK ON THIS SECTION ONLY. DO NOT TURN TO ANY OTHER SECTION IN THE TEST.   **STOP**

MATHEMATICS TEST

60 Minutes—60 Questions

Directions: Solve each of the following problems, select the correct answer, and then fill in the corresponding space on your answer sheet.

Don't linger over problems that are too time-consuming. Do as many as you can, then come back to the others in the time you have remaining.

The use of a calculator is permitted on this test. Though you are allowed to use your calculator to solve any questions you choose, some of the questions may be most easily answered without the use of a calculator.

Note: Unless otherwise noted, all of the following should be assumed.

1. Illustrative figures are *not* necessarily drawn to scale.
2. All geometric figures lie in a plane.
3. The term *line* indicates a straight line.
4. The term *average* indicates arithmetic mean.

1. In a recent survey, 14 people found their mayor to be "very competent." This number is exactly 20% of the people surveyed. How many people were surveyed?

    A. 28
    B. 35
    C. 56
    D. 70
    E. 84

2. A train traveled at a rate of 90 miles per hour for x hours, and then at a rate of 60 miles per hour for y hours. Which expression represents the train's average rate in miles per hour for the entire distance traveled?

    F. $\dfrac{540}{xy}$

    G. $\dfrac{90}{x} \times \dfrac{60}{y}$

    H. $\dfrac{90}{x} + \dfrac{60}{y}$

    J. $\dfrac{90x + 60y}{x + y}$

    K. $\dfrac{150}{x + y}$

3. In a certain string ensemble, the ratio of men to women is 5:3. If there are a total of 24 people in the ensemble, how many women are there?

    A. 8
    B. 9
    C. 10
    D. 11
    E. 12

4. If $x \neq 0$, and $x^2 - 3x = 6x$, then $x = ?$

    F. -9
    G. -3
    H. $\sqrt{3}$
    J. 3
    K. 9

GO ON TO THE NEXT PAGE

5. Two overlapping circles below form three regions, as shown:

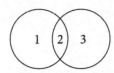

What is the maximum number of regions that can be formed by three overlapping circles?

A. 5
B. 6
C. 7
D. 8
E. 9

6. If $x^2 + 6x + 8 = 4 + 10x$, then x equals which of the following?

F. −2
G. −1
H. 0
J. 1
K. 2

7. Nine less than the number c is the same as the number d, and d less than twice c is 20. Which two equations could be used to determine the value of c and d?

A. $d - 9 = c$
   $d - 2c = 20$
B. $c - 9 = d$
   $2c - d = 20$
C. $c - 9 = d$
   $d - 2c = 20$
D. $9 - c = d$
   $2c - d = 20$
E. $9 - c = d$
   $2cd = 20$

8. An ice cream parlor offers five flavors of ice cream and four different toppings (sprinkles, hot fudge, whipped cream, and butterscotch). There is a special offer that includes one flavor of ice cream and one topping, served in a cup, sugar cone, or waffle cone. How many ways are there to order ice cream with the special offer?

F. 4
G. 5
H. 12
J. 23
K. 60

9. At a recent audition for a school play, 1 out of 3 students who auditioned were asked to come to a second audition. After the second audition, 75% of those asked to the second audition were offered parts. If 18 students were offered parts, how many students went to the first audition?

A. 18
B. 24
C. 48
D. 56
E. 72

10. One number is 5 times another number, and their sum is −60. What is the lesser of the two numbers?

F. −5
G. −10
H. −12
J. −48
K. −50

GO ON TO THE NEXT PAGE ▷

11. In the following figure, which is composed of equilateral triangles, what is the greatest number of parallelograms that can be found?

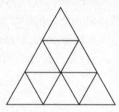

A. 6

B. 9

C. 12

D. 15

E. 18

12. The circle in the following figure is inscribed in a square with a perimeter of 16 inches. What is the area of the shaded region?

F. 4π

G. $16 - 2\pi$

H. $16 - 4\pi$

J. $8 - 2\pi$

K. $8 - 4\pi$

13. How many positive integers less than 50 are multiples of 4 but *not* multiples of 6 ?

A. 4

B. 6

C. 8

D. 10

E. 12

14. Given that $f(x) = (8 - 3x)(x^2 - 2x - 15)$, what is the value of $f(3)$?

F. -30

G. -18

H. 12

J. 24

K. 30

15. A class contains five juniors and five seniors. If one member of the class is assigned at random to present a paper on a certain subject, and another member of the class is randomly assigned to assist him, what is the probability that both will be juniors?

A. $\dfrac{1}{10}$

B. $\dfrac{1}{5}$

C. $\dfrac{2}{9}$

D. $\dfrac{2}{5}$

E. $\dfrac{1}{2}$

16. In triangle XYZ shown, $\overline{XS}$ and $\overline{SZ}$ are 3 and 12 units, respectively. If the area of triangle XYZ is 45 square units, how many units long is altitude $\overline{YS}$?

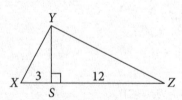

F. 3

G. 6

H. 9

J. 12

K. 15

GO ON TO THE NEXT PAGE

17. At which y-coordinate does the line described by the equation $6y - 3x = 18$ intersect the y-axis?

    A. 2
    B. 3
    C. 6
    D. 9
    E. 18

18. If $x^2 - y^2 = 12$ and $x - y = 4$, what is the value of $x^2 + 2xy + y^2$?

    F. 3
    G. 8
    H. 9
    J. 12
    K. 16

19. What is the area in square units of the following figure?

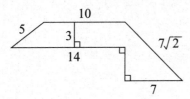

    A. $39 + 7\sqrt{2}$
    B. 60.5
    C. 91
    D. 108.5
    E. 147

20. A carpenter is cutting wood to make a new bookcase with a board that is 12 feet long. If the carpenter cuts off three pieces, each of which is 17 inches long, how many inches long is the remaining fourth and final board? (A foot contains 12 inches.)

    F. 36
    G. 51
    H. 93
    J. 108
    K. 144

21. If $x^2 - 4x - 6 = 6$, what are the possible values for x ?

    A. 4, 12
    B. −6, 2
    C. −6, −2
    D. 6, 2
    E. 6, −2

22. If −3 is a solution for the equation $x^2 + kx - 15 = 0$, what is the value of k ?

    F. 5
    G. 2
    H. −2
    J. −5
    K. Cannot be determined from the information given.

23. If the lengths of all three sides of a triangle are integers, and one side is 7 inches long, what is the smallest possible perimeter of the triangle, in inches?

    A. 9
    B. 10
    C. 12
    D. 15
    E. 18

GO ON TO THE NEXT PAGE

24. If $0° < \theta < 90°$ and $\sin \theta = \dfrac{\sqrt{11}}{2\sqrt{3}}$, then $\cos \theta = ?$

   F. $\dfrac{1}{2\sqrt{3}}$

   G. $\dfrac{1}{\sqrt{11}}$

   H. $\dfrac{2}{\sqrt{3}}$

   J. $\dfrac{2\sqrt{3}}{\sqrt{11}}$

   K. $\dfrac{11}{2\sqrt{3}}$

25. Which of the following expressions is equivalent to $\dfrac{\sqrt{3+x}}{\sqrt{3-x}}$ for all x such that $-3 < x < 3$?

   A. $\dfrac{3-x}{3+x}$

   B. $\dfrac{3+x}{3-x}$

   C. $\dfrac{-3\sqrt{3}+x}{\sqrt{3-x}}$

   D. $\dfrac{\sqrt{9-x^2}}{3-x}$

   E. $\dfrac{x^2-9}{3+x}$

26. In a certain cookie jar containing only macaroons and gingersnaps, the ratio of macaroons to gingersnaps is 2 to 5. Which of the following could be the total number of cookies in the cookie jar?

   F.   24

   G.   35

   H.   39

   J.   48

   K.   52

27. What is the sum of $\dfrac{3}{16}$ and 0.175 ?

   A.   0.3165

   B.   0.3500

   C.   0.3625

   D.   0.3750

   E.   0.3875

28. What is the maximum possible area, in square inches, of a rectangle with a perimeter of 20 inches?

   F.   15

   G.   20

   H.   25

   J.   30

   K.   40

29. $\dfrac{\dfrac{3}{2} + \dfrac{7}{4}}{\left(\dfrac{15}{8} - \dfrac{3}{4}\right) - \left(\dfrac{4+3}{-4+3}\right)} = ?$

   A. $\dfrac{3}{8}$

   B. $\dfrac{2}{5}$

   C. $\dfrac{9}{13}$

   D. $\dfrac{5}{2}$

   E. $\dfrac{8}{3}$

30. If $x - 15 = 7 - 5(x - 4)$, then $x = ?$

   F.   0

   G.   2

   H.   4

   J.   5

   K.   7

GO ON TO THE NEXT PAGE

31. The following sketch shows the dimensions of a flower garden. What is the area of this garden in square meters?

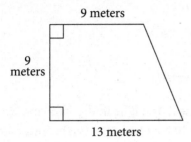

9 meters

9 meters

13 meters

A. 31
B. 85
C. 99
D. 101
E. 117

32. What is the slope of the line described by the equation $6y - 3x = 18$?

F. -2
G. $-\dfrac{1}{2}$
H. $\dfrac{1}{2}$
J. 2
K. 3

33. Line m passes through the point (4,3) in the standard (x,y) coordinate plane and is perpendicular to the line described by the equation $y = -\dfrac{4}{5}x + 6$. Which of the following equations describes line m ?

A. $y = \dfrac{5}{4}x - 2$

B. $y = -\dfrac{5}{4}x + 6$

C. $y = -\dfrac{4}{5}x - 2$

D. $y = -\dfrac{4}{5}x + 2$

E. $y = -\dfrac{5}{4}x - 2$

34. Line t in the standard (x,y) coordinate plane has a y-intercept of -3 and is parallel to the line having the equation $3x - 5y = 4$. Which of the following is an equation for line t ?

F. $y = -\dfrac{3}{5}x + 3$

G. $y = -\dfrac{5}{3}x - 3$

H. $y = \dfrac{3}{5}x + 3$

J. $y = \dfrac{5}{3}x + 3$

K. $y = \dfrac{3}{5}x - 3$

35. If $y = mx + b$, which of the following equations expresses x in terms of y, m, and b ?

A. $x = \dfrac{y - b}{m}$

B. $x = \dfrac{b - y}{m}$

C. $x = \dfrac{y + b}{m}$

D. $x = \dfrac{y}{m} - bx$

E. $x = \dfrac{y}{m} + b$

GO ON TO THE NEXT PAGE ▷

36. In the following figure, $\overline{AB} = 20$, $\overline{BC} = 15$, and $\angle ADB$ and $\angle ABC$ are right angles. What is the length of $\overline{AD}$?

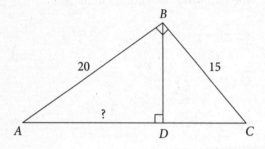

F. 9

G. 12

H. 15

J. 16

K. 25

37. In the standard (x,y) coordinate plane shown in the figure, points A and B lie on line m, and point C lies below it. The coordinates of points A, B, and C are $(0,5)$, $(5,5)$, and $(3,3)$, respectively. What is the shortest possible distance from point C to a point on line m?

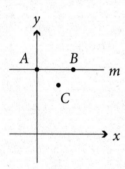

A. 2

B. $2\sqrt{2}$

C. 3

D. $\sqrt{13}$

E. 5

38. For all $x \neq 8$, $\dfrac{x^2 - 11x + 24}{8 - x} = ?$

F. $8 - x$

G. $3 - x$

H. $x - 3$

J. $x - 8$

K. $x - 11$

39. Points A and B lie in the standard (x,y) coordinate plane. The (x,y) coordinates of A are $(2,1)$, and the (x,y) coordinates of B are $(-2,-2)$. What is the distance from A to B?

A. $3\sqrt{2}$

B. $3\sqrt{3}$

C. 5

D. 6

E. 7

40. In the following figure, $\overline{AB}$ and $\overline{CD}$ are both tangent to the circle as shown, and $ABCD$ is a rectangle with side lengths $2x$ and $5x$ as shown. What is the area of the shaded region?

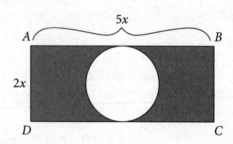

F. $10\pi x^2$

G. $10x^2 - \pi x^2$

H. $10x^2 - 2\pi x$

J. $9\pi x^2$

K. $6\pi x^2$

GO ON TO THE NEXT PAGE ▷

41. If $0° < \theta < 90°$ and $\cos\theta = \dfrac{5\sqrt{2}}{8}$, then $\tan\theta = ?$

    A. $\dfrac{5}{\sqrt{7}}$

    B. $\dfrac{\sqrt{7}}{5}$

    C. $\dfrac{\sqrt{14}}{8}$

    D. $\dfrac{8}{\sqrt{14}}$

    E. $\dfrac{8}{5\sqrt{2}}$

42. Consider fractions of the form $\dfrac{7}{n}$, where n is an integer. How many integer values of n make this fraction greater than 0.5 and less than 0.8 ?

    F. 3
    G. 4
    H. 5
    J. 6
    K. 7

43. The figure below shows two tangent circles. The circumference of circle X is 12π, and the circumference of circle Y is 8π. What is the greatest possible distance between two points, one of which lies on the circumference of circle X and one of which lies on the circumference of circle Y ?

    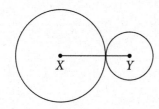

    A. 6
    B. 10
    C. 20
    D. 10π
    E. 20π

44. $\sqrt{(x^2+4)^2} - (x+2)(x-2) = ?$

    F. $2x^2$
    G. $x^2 - 8$
    H. $2(x-2)$
    J. 0
    K. 8

45. If $s = -3$, then $s^3 + 2s^2 + 2s = ?$

    A. -15
    B. -10
    C. -5
    D. 5
    E. 33

46. How many different numbers are solutions for the equation $2x + 6 = (x+5)(x+3)$?

    F. 0
    G. 1
    H. 2
    J. 3
    K. Infinitely many

47. In square $ABCD$ shown, $\overline{AC} = 8$. What is the perimeter of $ABCD$?

    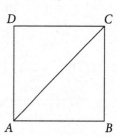

    A. $4\sqrt{2}$
    B. 8
    C. $8\sqrt{2}$
    D. 16
    E. $16\sqrt{2}$

GO ON TO THE NEXT PAGE

48. The front surface of a fence panel is shown here with the lengths labeled representing inches. The panel is symmetrical along its center vertical axis. What is the surface area of the front surface of the panel in square inches?

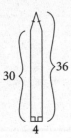

F.   144

G.   132

H.   120

J.   80

K. $64 + 6\sqrt{5}$

49. In the following figure, O is the center of the circle, and C, D, and E are points on the circumference of the circle. If $\angle OCD$ measures 70° and $\angle OED$ measures 45°, what is the measure of $\angle CDE$?

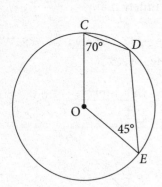

A.   25°

B.   45°

C.   70°

D.   90°

E.   115°

50. Which of the following systems of equations does NOT have a solution?

F. $x + 3y = 19$
     $3x + y = 6$

G. $x + 3y = 19$
     $x - 3y = 13$

H. $x - 3y = 19$
     $3x - y = 7$

J. $x - 3y = 19$
     $3x + y = 6$

K. $x + 3y = 6$
     $3x + 9y = 7$

51. What is the 46th digit to the right of the decimal point in the decimal equivalent of $\frac{1}{7}$?

A.   1

B.   2

C.   4

D.   7

E.   8

52. Which of the following inequalities is equivalent to $-2 - 4x \le -6x$?

F. $x \ge -2$

G. $x \ge 1$

H. $x \ge 2$

J. $x \le -1$

K. $x \le 1$

GO ON TO THE NEXT PAGE

53. If $x > 0$ and $y > 0$, $\dfrac{\sqrt{x}}{x} + \dfrac{\sqrt{y}}{y}$ is equivalent to which of the following?

A. $\dfrac{2}{xy}$

B. $\dfrac{\sqrt{x} + \sqrt{y}}{\sqrt{xy}}$

C. $\dfrac{x + y}{xy}$

D. $\dfrac{\sqrt{x} + \sqrt{y}}{\sqrt{x + y}}$

E. $\dfrac{x + y}{\sqrt{xy}}$

54. In the following diagram, $\overline{CD}$, $\overline{BE}$, and $\overline{AF}$ are all parallel and are intersected by two transversals as shown. What is the length of $\overline{EF}$?

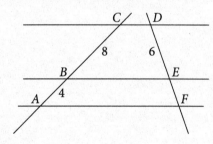

F. 2

G. 3

H. 4

J. 6

K. 9

55. What is the area, in square units, of the square whose vertices are located at the (x,y) coordinate points indicated in the following figure?

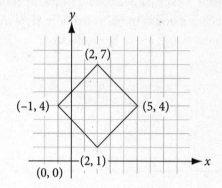

A. 9

B. 12

C. 16

D. 18

E. 24

56. Compared to the graph of $y = \cos\theta$, the graph of $y = 2\cos\theta$ has:

F. twice the period and the same amplitude.

G. half the period and the same amplitude.

H. twice the period and half the amplitude.

J. half the amplitude and the same period.

K. twice the amplitude and the same period.

GO ON TO THE NEXT PAGE

57. Brandy has a collection of comic books. If she adds 15 to the number of comic books in her collection and multiplies the sum by 3, the result will be 65 less than 4 times the number of comic books in her collection. How many comic books are in her collection?

  A.   50
  B.   85
  C.   110
  D.   145
  E.   175

58. One empty cylinder has three times the height and twice the diameter of another empty cylinder. How many fillings of the smaller cylinder would be equivalent to one filling of the larger cylinder?

  (Note: The volume of a cylinder of radius r and height h is $\pi r^2 h$.)

  F.   6
  G. $6\sqrt{2}$
  H.   12
  J.   18
  K.   24

59. What is the perimeter of a 30°-60°-90° triangle with a long leg of 12 inches?

  A. $5\sqrt{3} + 12$
  B. $4\sqrt{3} + 18$
  C. $8\sqrt{3} + 18$
  D. $12\sqrt{3} + 12$
  E. $12\sqrt{3} + 18$

60. A baseball team scores an average of x points in its first n games and then scores y points in its next and final game of the season. Which of the following represents the team's average score for the entire season?

  F. $x + \dfrac{y}{n}$

  G. $x + \dfrac{y}{n+1}$

  H. $\dfrac{x + ny}{n+1}$

  J. $\dfrac{nx + y}{n+1}$

  K. $\dfrac{n(x + y)}{n+1}$

READING TEST

35 Minutes—40 Questions

Directions: There are four passages in this test. Each passage is followed by several questions. After reading a passage, choose the best answer to each question and fill in the corresponding oval on your Answer Grid. You may refer to the passages as often as necessary.

PASSAGE I

PROSE FICTION

This passage is adapted from the novel Emma *by Jane Austen. It was originally published in 1815.*

Emma Woodhouse, handsome, clever, and rich, with a comfortable home and happy disposition, seemed to unite some of the best blessings of existence. She had lived
(5) nearly twenty-one years in the world with very little to distress or vex her. She was the youngest of the two daughters of a most affectionate, indulgent father, and had, in consequence of her sister's marriage, been
(10) mistress of his house from a very early period. Her mother had died too long ago for her to have more than an indistinct remembrance of her caresses, and her place had been taken by an excellent governess
(15) who had fallen little short of a mother in affection.

Sixteen years had Miss Taylor been in Mr. Woodhouse's family, less as a governess than a friend, very fond of both daughters,
(20) but particularly of Emma. Between them it was more the intimacy of sisters. Even before Miss Taylor had ceased to hold the nominal office of governess, the mildness of her temper had hardly allowed her
(25) to impose any restraint. The shadow of authority being now long passed away, they had been living together as friend and friend very mutually attached, and Emma doing just what she liked, highly esteeming Miss
(30) Taylor's judgment, but directed chiefly by her own. The real evils, indeed, of Emma's situation were the power of having rather too much her own way, and a disposition to think a little too well of herself; these were
(35) the disadvantages which threatened alloy to her many enjoyments. The danger, however, was at present so unperceived, that they did not by any means rank as misfortunes with her.

(40) Sorrow came—a gentle sorrow—but not at all in the shape of any disagreeable consciousness. Miss Taylor married. It was Miss Taylor's loss which first brought grief. It was on the wedding-day of this beloved
(45) friend that Emma first sat in mournful thought of any continuance. The wedding over, and the bride-people gone, she and her father were left to dine together, with no prospect of a third to cheer a long evening.
(50) Her father composed himself to sleep after dinner, as usual, and she had then only to sit and think of what she had lost.

The marriage had every promise of happiness for her friend. Mr. Weston was
(55) a man of unexceptionable character, easy fortune, suitable age, and pleasant manners. There was some satisfaction in considering with what self-denying, generous friendship she had always wished and promoted the
(60) match, but it was a black morning's work for her. The want of Miss Taylor would be felt every hour of every day. She recalled her past kindness—the kindness, the affection of sixteen years—how she had taught her
(65) and how she had played with her from five years old—how she had devoted all her

GO ON TO THE NEXT PAGE ➔

powers to attach and amuse her in health—
and how she had nursed her through the
various illnesses of childhood. A large

(70) debt of gratitude was owing here, but the
intercourse of he last seven years, the equal
footing and perfect unreserve which had
soon followed Isabella's marriage, on their
being left to each other, was yet a dearer,

(75) tenderer recollection. She had been a friend
and companion such as few possessed:
intelligent, well-informed, useful, gentle,
knowing all the ways of the family, interested
in all its concerns, and peculiarly

(80) interested in her, in every pleasure, every
scheme of hers—one to whom she could
speak every thought as it arose, and who
had such an affection for her as could never
find fault.

(85)   How was she to bear the change? It was
true that her friend was going only half a
mile from them, but Emma was aware that
great must be the difference between a Mrs.
Weston, only half a mile from them, and

(90) a Miss Taylor in the house. With all her
advantages, natural and domestic, she was
now in great danger of suffering from intellectual
solitude.

1. According to the passage, what are the great-
    est disadvantages facing Emma?

    A. Her father is not a stimulating conversa-
        tionalist, and she is bored.

    B. She is lonely and afraid that Mrs.
        Weston will not have a happy marriage.

    C. She is used to having her way too much,
        and she thinks too highly of herself.

    D. She misses the companionship of her
        mother, her sister, and Miss Taylor.

2. The name of Emma's sister is:

    F. Mrs. Weston.

    G. Isabella.

    H. Miss Taylor.

    J. Mrs. Woodhouse.

3. As described in the passage, Emma's relation-
    ship with Miss Taylor can be characterized as:

    A. similar to a mother-daughter relation-
        ship.

    B. similar to the relationship of sisters or
        best friends.

    C. weaker than Emma's relationship with
        her sister.

    D. stronger than Miss Taylor's relationship
        with her new husband.

4. As used in line 33, *disposition* can most closely
    be defined as:

    F. a tendency.

    G. control.

    H. placement.

    J. transfer.

5. Which of the following are included in
    Emma's memories of her relationship with
    Miss Taylor?

         I. Miss Taylor taking care of Emma
             during childhood illnesses

        II. Miss Taylor entertaining Emma

       III. Miss Taylor teaching her mathemat-
             ics

        IV. Miss Taylor scolding her for being
             selfish

    A. I, III, and IV only

    B. I and III only

    C. II, III, and IV only

    D. I and II only

GO ON TO THE NEXT PAGE ⇨

6. It is most reasonable to infer from Emma's realization that "great must be the difference between a Mrs. Weston, only half a mile from them, and a Miss Taylor in the house" (lines 88–90) that:

   F. Miss Taylor will no longer be a part of Emma's life.

   G. Emma is happy about the marriage because now she will have more freedom.

   H. Emma regrets that her relationship with Miss Taylor will change.

   J. Emma believes that her relationship with Miss Taylor will become stronger.

7. Based on the passage, Emma could best be described as:

   A. sweet and naïve.

   B. self-centered and naïve.

   C. self-centered and headstrong.

   D. unappreciative and bitter.

8. The passage suggests that the quality Emma values most in a friend is:

   F. charisma.

   G. devotion.

   H. honesty.

   J. intelligence.

9. How does Emma view Mr. Weston?

   A. She thinks that he is an excellent match, and it required considerable self-sacrifice not to pursue him herself.

   B. She considers him to be a respectable if somewhat average match for her friend.

   C. She sees him as an intruder who has carried away her best friend in "a black morning's work" (line 60).

   D. She believes he is an indulgent, easily swayed man, reminiscent of her father.

10. From the passage, it can be inferred that Emma is accustomed to:

    F. behaving according to the wishes of her affectionate father.

    G. taking the advice of Miss Taylor when faced with deciding upon a course of action.

    H. doing as she pleases without permission from her father or governess.

    J. abiding by strict rules governing her behavior.

PASSAGE II

SOCIAL SCIENCE

The period of active experimentation to develop the airplane began in the 1890s. Many scientists and engineers attempted to solve the problem in the decade following, but with limited progress until Orville and Wilbur Wright made the first successful powered, heavier-than-air flight in 1903. Both of the passages below discuss aspects of the Wright brothers' invention.

PASSAGE A

What about the method used by the Wright brothers allowed them to succeed where so many scientists, engineers, and crackpots had
Line failed to make progress for a dozen years? In
(5) the decade leading up to their success, there had been so many unsuccessful attempts that newspaper reporters became jaded, tired of investigating each yokel who claimed to have made an airplane. In fact, the reporter present
(10) at that historical first flight didn't even bother to take his camera out of its bag, deciding that two unassuming brothers from Ohio without college educations would be two more in a long line. Instead, the Wrights, quite systematically
(15) and without much fuss or outside assistance, changed the world dramatically in 1903. What made Orville and Wilbur so different from the rest of the pack?

GO ON TO THE NEXT PAGE →

Most inventors of the time were working
(20) on their planes with a fairly simple and logical
approach: They would design an airplane, build
it, test it in the field, and then use the results of
that test to tinker with their designs in an attempt to improve the next model. The problem
(25) with this method, though, was that the field
test of a new airplane only provided information about whether it flew or not, for how
long, and how high. There was no way of knowing whether the wings were good but the
(30) engine was bad, or the shape was right but
the materials were too heavy. With no way of
discerning which parts worked and which
parts didn't, inventors' second attempts often
flew worse than their initial ones, because
(35) their creators had inadvertently removed
design features that were effective and exag-
gerated features that were not.

The Wright brothers proved to be adept
scientists. With their keen analytical insight
(40) and love of engineering and all things mechanical, they were able to escape that endless loop
of misguided "improvements." They worked
on their machine one aspect at a time. After
familiarizing themselves with all the published
(45) literature on flight, they began working on a
method of control. They theorized that twisting the wings one way or another would steer
a craft. Instead of building an entire airplane
to test their theory, they built a five-foot bi-
(50) plane kite. Sure enough, twisting the wings
controlled the craft laterally. Having settled
that aspect of the craft's design, they turned
to wing shape.

After building two failed gliders based
(55) on their original design, the brothers realized
that it was too expensive and time consuming
to continue designing and making whole
machines. As an alternative, they invented
the first wind tunnel with instruments capable
(60) of quantifying the lift and drag of wing segments. In this wind tunnel, they could test
wings alone for their efficiency and aerodynamics. In the process of testing 80 to 200
wing shapes in this way, they disproved a com-

(65) monly accepted theory of lift (called "Smeaton's
coefficient") and settled on a new and highly
efficient wing shape for their craft.

The Wrights returned to the wind tunnel
to perfect designs for their propeller and
(70) then designed an effective four-cylinder
engine to power the craft. When the time
came to marry all of these carefully designed
components into a complete craft, there was
no guesswork involved. The Wright brothers
(75) knew they had built an airplane, and they
knew that each piece was beautifully designed and perfectly functioning. That first historic flight was merely proof of their scientific
genius.

PASSAGE B

(80) Few people recognize that the Wright
brothers are tragic figures in American
history. Today, they are hailed as great inventors, but during their lives they were scorned
and discredited publicly, even though the
(85) entire world copied their successful designs.
The prevailing opinion among those who
made airplanes was that two rustic, uneducated fellows from Ohio could never have
accomplished such a historic feat, let alone
(90) deliberately marry the disparate components
of air travel that are required for successful
flight. They hadn't paid their dues to the
scientific community. The French aviation
community especially mocked the brothers,
(95) and the secrecy of Orville and Wilbur during
the years in which they prepared their patents
only fueled derision of and doubts about
their accomplishments.

The Wright brothers finally received a
(100) U.S. patent for their system of lateral control,
perhaps their most important contribution to
aviation, in May of 1906. Manufacturers
unwilling to pay the modest fee the brothers
asked for use of their system launched a vast
(105) and sadly successful smear campaign against
the brothers, impugning the importance of
their contribution to flight. Some European
countries simply refused to issue the brothers

GO ON TO THE NEXT PAGE →

a patent, and as a result airplane manufacturers (110) in those countries could legally copy the Wrights' technology unchecked.

In the midst of the legal battle over rights and license fees against several airplane manufacturers, Wilbur sadly succumbed to typhoid (115) fever. He was thus deprived of seeing his claims vindicated in court, and, though Orville was accorded a tidy sum, this small victory was hardly commensurate with the enormous contribution the two brothers had made. The (120) court case also did nothing to compensate the brothers for the taxing and unfair period of ridicule and doubt and the obstinate refusal by much of the world to acknowledge their achievements. Perhaps most tellingly, the Smithsonian Museum (125) didn't display the brothers' historic craft until 1948, when it finally bestowed on them the title of the first men to fly in a heavier-than-air craft. Sadly, this was too little, too late, as the brothers had both passed away.

Questions 11–13 ask about Passage A.

---

11. The main purpose of Passage A is to:

    A. describe how the Wright brothers were regarded.

    B. emphasize the process of designing the airplane.

    C. criticize the attitude of other inventors.

    D. explore the practical application of science.

12. What does Passage A suggest about the method used by most inventors at the time of the Wright brothers?

    F. They did not take Smeaton's coefficient into account.

    G. They scorned the methods used by the Wright brothers.

    H. They weren't able to learn effectively from previous failures.

    J. They didn't believe it was possible to build an airplane.

13. Passage A suggests that the wind tunnel played what role in the Wright brothers' research?

    A. It provided more reliable data than their experiments with kites.

    B. It allowed them to isolate single aspects of design from other considerations.

    C. It helped them develop a method of twisting the wings to control the plane laterally.

    D. It confirmed the accuracy of Smeaton's coefficient.

Questions 14–16 ask about Passage B.

---

14. In Passage B, the author mentions a "legal battle" (line 112) in order to:

    F. emphasize the poor way in which the Wright brothers were treated.

    G. illustrate the dangers of publicizing new knowledge.

    H. help explain why the Wright brothers' discovery was of little importance.

    J. suggest a reason for Wilbur's fatal illness.

15. What does Passage B suggest about the Smithsonian Museum's choice to display the brothers' historic craft in 1948?

    A. It was a small victory for Orville, who lost his brother Wilbur to typhoid fever.

    B. It was a direct result of the obstinate refusal by much of the world to acknowledge their achievements.

    C. While it was a great honor, it did not fully atone for the poor treatment of the brothers.

    D. The historic craft would have been displayed sooner if European countries had issued the brothers a patent.

GO ON TO THE NEXT PAGE

16. In Passage B, the statement "They hadn't paid their dues to the scientific community" (lines 92–93) is presented as the opinion of:

F. the French aviation community.

G. the Wright brothers.

H. the author.

J. those who made airplanes.

Questions 17–20 ask about both passages.

17. The author of Passage B would likely agree that the "inventors of the time" (line 19) mentioned in Passage A:

A. thought that the Wright brothers didn't actually make the first airplane.

B. didn't believe that the Wright brothers deserved credit for the magnitude of their achievement.

C. were grateful for the breakthrough that the Wrights had engineered.

D. felt the Wright brothers had likely copied the design from a more accomplished inventor.

18. In lines 72 and 90, "marry" most nearly means:

F. prove.

G. test rigorously.

H. bring together.

J. satisfy.

19. According to Passage A, while the brothers "hadn't paid their dues to the scientific community" (lines 92–93), as mentioned in Passage B, they were indeed skilled inventors because:

A. they designed an airplane, built it, tested it in the field, and then used the results of that test to adjust their designs.

B. they used analytical insight to work on machines one aspect at a time to perfect their design.

C. they invented the first wind tunnel, which was a greater accomplishment than inventing the first successful aircraft.

D. their claims were eventually vindicated in court, and Orville received monetary reimbursement.

20. Both passages provide support for the idea that the Wright brothers:

F. used a method of scientific inquiry that was different from everyone else's.

G. were poorly treated following their discovery.

H. were exceptional scientists.

J. should have protected the rights to their discovery more carefully.

PASSAGE III

HUMANITIES

This passage is excerpted from A History of Women Artists, *© 1975 by Hugo Munsterberg; Clarkson N. Potter (a division of Random House, Inc.), publisher. Reprinted by permission of the author's family.*

There can be little doubt that women artists have been most prominent in photography and that they have made their greatest
Line contribution in this field. One reason for
(5) this is not difficult to ascertain. As several

GO ON TO THE NEXT PAGE ▷

historians of photography have pointed out, photography, being a new medium outside the traditional academic framework, was wide open to women and offered them

(10) opportunities that the older fields did not....

All these observations apply to the first woman to have achieved eminence in photography, and that is Julia Margaret Cameron....Born in 1815 in Calcutta into an

(15) upper-middle-class family and married to Charles Hay Cameron, a distinguished jurist and member of the Supreme Court of India, Julia Cameron was well-known as a brilliant conversationalist and a woman of personality

(20) and intellect who was unconventional to the point of eccentricity. Although the mother of six children, she adopted several more and still found time to be active in social causes and literary activities. After

(25) the Camerons settled in England in 1848 at Freshwater Bay on the Isle of Wight, she became the center of an artistic and literary circle that included such notable figures as the poet Alfred Lord Tennyson and the

(30) painter George Frederick Watts. Pursuing numerous activities and taking care of her large family, Mrs. Cameron might have been remembered as still another rather remarkable and colorful Victorian lady had it not

(35) been for the fact that, in 1863, her daughter presented her with photographic equipment, thinking her mother might enjoy taking pictures of her family and friends. Although forty-eight years old, Mrs. Cameron took

(40) up this new hobby with enormous enthusiasm and dedication. She was a complete beginner, but within a very few years she developed into one of the greatest photographers of her period and a giant in the

(45) history of photography. She worked ceaselessly as long as daylight lasted and mastered the technical processes of photography, at that time far more cumbersome than today, turning her coal house into a darkroom

(50) and her chicken house into a studio. To her, photography was a "divine art," and in it she found her vocation. In 1864, she wrote

triumphantly under one of her photographs, "My First Success," and from then until her

(55) death in Ceylon in 1874, she devoted herself wholly to this art.

Working in a large format (her portrait studies are usually about 11 inches by 14 inches) and requiring a long exposure

(60) (on the average five minutes), she produced a large body of work that stands up as one of the notable artistic achievements of the Victorian period. The English art critic Roger Fry believed that her portraits were

(65) likely to outlive the works of artists who were her contemporaries. Her friend Watts, then a very celebrated portrait painter, inscribed on one of her photographs, "I wish I could paint such a picture as this."...Her

(70) work was widely exhibited, and she received gold, silver, and bronze medals in England, America, Germany, and Austria. No other female artist of the nineteenth century achieved such acclaim, and no other woman

(75) photographer has ever enjoyed such success.

Her work falls into two main categories on which her contemporaries and people today differ sharply. Victorian critics were particularly impressed by her allegorical

(80) pictures, many of them based on the poems of her friend and neighbor Tennyson.... Contemporary taste much prefers her portraits and finds her narrative scenes sentimental and sometimes in bad taste. Yet,

(85) not only Julia Cameron, but also the painters of that time loved to depict subjects such as *The Five Foolish Virgins* or *Pray God, Bring Father Safely Home*. Still, today her fame rests upon her portraits for, as she herself

(90) said, she was intent upon representing not only the outer likeness but also the inner greatness of the people she portrayed. Working with the utmost dedication, she produced photographs of such eminent

(95) Victorians as Tennyson, Browning, Carlyle, Trollope, Longfellow, Watts, Darwin, Ellen Terry, Sir John Herschel, who was a close friend of hers, and Mrs. Duckworth, the mother of Virginia Woolf.

GO ON TO THE NEXT PAGE ▷

21. Which of the following conclusions can be reasonably drawn from the passage's discussion of Julia Margaret Cameron?

    A. She was a traditional homemaker until she discovered photography.

    B. Her work holds a significant place in the history of photography.

    C. She was unable to achieve in her lifetime the artistic recognition she deserved.

    D. Her eccentricity has kept her from being taken seriously by modern critics of photography.

22. According to the passage, Cameron is most respected by modern critics for her:

    F. portraits.

    G. allegorical pictures.

    H. use of a large format.

    J. service in recording the faces of so many twentieth century figures.

23. The author uses which of the following methods to develop the second paragraph (lines 11–56)?

    A. A series of anecdotes depicting Cameron's energy and unconventionality

    B. A presentation of factual data demonstrating Cameron's importance in the history of photography

    C. A description of the author's personal acquaintance with Cameron

    D. A chronological account of Cameron's background and artistic growth

24. As it is used in the passage, *cumbersome* (line 48) most closely means:

    F. difficult to manage.

    G. expensive.

    H. intense.

    J. enjoyable.

25. When the author says that Cameron had found "her vocation" (line 52), his main point is that photography:

    A. offered Cameron an escape from the confines of conventional social life.

    B. became the main interest of her life.

    C. became her primary source of income.

    D. provided her with a way to express her religious beliefs.

26. The main point of the third paragraph is that Cameron:

    F. achieved great artistic success during her lifetime.

    G. is the greatest photographer who ever lived.

    H. was considered a more important artist during her lifetime than she is now.

    J. revolutionized photographic methods in the Victorian era.

27. According to the passage, the art of photography offered women artists more opportunities than did other art forms because it:

    A. did not require expensive materials.

    B. allowed the artist to use family and friends for subject matter.

    C. was nontraditional.

    D. required little artistic skill.

28. *The Five Foolish Virgins* and *Pray God, Bring Father Safely Home* are examples of:

    F. portraits of celebrated Victorians.

    G. allegorical subjects of the sort that were popular during the Victorian era.

    H. photographs in which Cameron sought to show a subject's outer likeness and inner greatness.

    J. photographs by Cameron that were scoffed at by her contemporaries.

29. According to the passage, which of the following opinions of Cameron's work was held by Victorian critics but is NOT held by modern critics?

    A. Photographs should be based on poems.

    B. Her portraits are too sentimental.

    C. Narrative scenes are often in bad taste.

    D. Her allegorical pictures are her best work.

30. The author's treatment of Cameron's development as a photographer can best be described as:

    F. admiring.

    G. condescending.

    H. neutral.

    J. defensive.

PASSAGE IV

NATURAL SCIENCE

This passage discusses aspects of the harbor seal's sensory systems.

The harbor seal, *Phoca vitulina*, lives amphibiously along the northern Atlantic and Pacific coasts. This extraordinary
Line mammal, which does most of its fishing at
(5) night when visibility is low and in places where noise levels are high, has developed several unique adaptations that have sharpened its acoustic and visual acuity. The need for such adaptations has been
(10) compounded by the varying behavior of sound and light in each of the two habitats of the harbor seal—land and water.

While the seal is on land, its ear operates much like the human ear, with sound waves
(15) traveling through air and entering the inner ear through the auditory canal. The directions from which sounds originate are distinguishable because the sound waves

arrive at each inner ear at different times.
(20) In water, however, where sound waves travel faster than they do in air, the ability of the brain to differentiate arrival times between each ear is severely reduced. Yet it is crucial for the seal to be able to pinpoint the exact
(25) origins of sound in order to locate both its offspring and its prey. Therefore, the seal has developed an extremely sensitive quadraphonic hearing system, composed of a specialized band of tissue that extends
(30) down from the ear to the inner ear. In water, sound is conducted to the seal's inner ear by this special band of tissue, making it possible for the seal to identify the exact origins of sounds.

(35) The eye of the seal is also uniquely adapted to operate in both air and water. The human eye, adapted to function primarily in air, is equipped with a cornea, which aids in the refraction and focusing
(40) of light onto the retina. As a result, when a human eye is submerged in water, light rays are further refracted and the image is blurry. The seal's cornea, however, refracts light as water does. Therefore, in water, light
(45) rays are transmitted by the cornea without distortion and are clearly focused on the retina. In air, however, the cornea is astigmatic, resulting in a distortion of incoming light rays. The seal compensates for this by
(50) having a stenopaic pupil, which constricts into a vertical slit. Since the astigmatism is most pronounced in the horizontal plane of the eye, the vertical pupil serves to minimize its effect on the seal's vision.

(55) Since the harbor seal hunts for food under conditions of low visibility, some scientists believe it has echolocation systems akin to those of bats, porpoises, and dolphins. This kind of natural radar involves
(60) the emission of high-frequency sound pulses that reflect off obstacles such as predators, prey, or natural barriers. The reflections are received as sensory signals by the brain, which processes them into an image. The

GO ON TO THE NEXT PAGE ▷

(65) animal, blinded by unfavorable lighting
conditions, is thus able to perceive its
surroundings. Such echolocation by harbor
seals is suggested by the fact that they emit
"clicks," high-frequency sounds produced in
(70) short, fast bursts that occur mostly at night,
when visibility is low.

Finally, there is speculation that the
seal's whiskers, or vibrissae, which are
unusually well developed and highly
(75) sensitive to vibrations, act as additional
sensory receptors. Scientists speculate that
the vibrissae may sense wave disturbances
produced by nearby moving fish, allowing
the seal to home in on and capture prey.

31. The harbor seal's eye compensates for the distortion of light rays on land by means of its:

   A. vibrissae.

   B. cornea.

   C. stenopaic pupil.

   D. echolocation.

32. The passage implies that a harbor seal's vision
is:

   F. inferior to a human's vision in the
      water, but superior to it on land.

   G. superior to a human's vision in the
      water, but inferior to it on land.

   H. inferior to a human's vision both in the
      water and on land.

   J. equivalent to a human's vision both in
      the water and on land.

33. According to the passage, scientists think
vibrissae help harbor seals to catch prey by:

   A. improving underwater vision.

   B. sensing vibrations in the air.

   C. camouflaging predator seals.

   D. detecting underwater movement.

34. According to the passage, the speed of sound
in water is:

   F. faster than the speed of sound in air.

   G. slower than the speed of sound in air.

   H. the same as the speed of sound in air.

   J. unable to be determined exactly.

35. According to the passage, which of the following have contributed to the harbor seal's need
to adapt its visual and acoustic senses?

   I. Night hunting

   II. The need to operate in two habitats

   III. A noisy environment

   A. I and II only

   B. II and III only

   C. I and III only

   D. I, II, and III

36. Which of the following claims expresses the
writer's opinion and not a fact?

   F. The human eye is adapted to function
      primarily in air.

   G. When the seal is on land, its ear
      operates like a human ear.

   H. The "clicks" emitted by the harbor seal
      mean it uses echolocation.

   J. The need for adaptation is increased if
      an animal lives in two habitats.

37. The passage suggests that the harbor seal lives
in:

   A. cold ocean waters with accessible coasts.

   B. all areas with abundant fish popula-
      tions.

   C. most island and coastal regions.

   D. warm coastlines with exceptionally clear
      waters.

GO ON TO THE NEXT PAGE ⇨

38. According to the passage, a special band of tissue extending from the ear to the inner ear enables the harbor seal to:

    F. make its distinctive "clicking" sounds.

    G. find prey by echolocation.

    H. breathe underwater.

    J. determine where a sound originated.

39. The author compares harbor seal sensory organs to human sensory organs primarily in order to:

    A. point out similarities among mammals.

    B. explain how the seal's sensory organs function.

    C. prove that seals are more adaptively successful than humans.

    D. prove that humans are better adapted to their environment than seals.

40. According to the passage, one way in which seals differ from humans is:

    F. that sound waves enter a seal's inner ear through the auditory canal.

    G. the degree to which their corneas refract light.

    H. that seal's eyes focus light rays on the retina.

    J. that seals have adapted to live in a certain environment.

SCIENCE TEST

45 Minutes—40 Questions

Directions: There are several passages in this test. Each passage is followed by several questions. After reading a passage, choose the best answer to each question and fill in the corresponding oval on your Answer Grid. You may refer to the passages as often as necessary. You are NOT permitted to use a calculator on this test.

PASSAGE I

The following table contains some physical properties of common optical materials. The refractive index of a material is a measure of the amount by which light is bent upon entering the material. The transmittance range is the range of wavelengths over which the material is transparent.

Table 1

Physical Properties of Optical Materials				
Material	Refractive index for light of 0.589 μm	Transmittance range (μm)	Useful range for prisms (μm)	Chemical resistance
Lithium fluoride	1.39	0.12–6	2.7–5.5	Poor
Calcium fluoride	1.43	0.12–12	5–9.4	Good
Sodium chloride	1.54	0.3–17	8–16	Poor
Quartz	1.54	0.20–3.3	0.20–2.7	Excellent
Potassium bromide	1.56	0.3–29	15–28	Poor
Flint glass*	1.66	0.35–2.2	0.35–2	Excellent
Cesium iodide	1.79	0.3–70	15–55	Poor

*Flint glass is lead oxide–doped quartz.

1. According to the table, which material(s) will transmit light at 25 μm?

   A. Potassium bromide only
   B. Potassium bromide and cesium iodide
   C. Lithium fluoride and cesium iodide
   D. Lithium fluoride and flint glass

2. A scientist hypothesizes that any material with poor chemical resistance would have a transmittance range wider than 10 μm. The properties of which of the following materials contradicts this hypothesis?

   F. Lithium fluoride
   G. Flint glass
   H. Cesium iodide
   J. Quartz

GO ON TO THE NEXT PAGE ⟹

3. When light travels from one medium to another, total internal reflection can occur if the first medium has a higher refractive index than the second. Total internal reflection could occur if light were traveling from:

   A. lithium fluoride to flint glass.

   B. potassium bromide to cesium iodide.

   C. quartz to potassium bromide.

   D. flint glass to calcium fluoride.

4. Based on the information in the table, how is the transmittance range related to the useful prism range?

   F. The transmittance range is always narrower than the useful prism range.

   G. The transmittance range is narrower than or equal to the useful prism range.

   H. The transmittance range increases as the useful prism range decreases.

   J. The transmittance range is wider than and includes within it the useful prism range.

5. The addition of lead oxide to pure quartz has the effect of:

   A. decreasing the transmittance range and the refractive index.

   B. decreasing the transmittance range and increasing the refractive index.

   C. increasing the transmittance range and the useful prism range.

   D. increasing the transmittance range and decreasing the useful prism range.

6. Which of the following materials would provide the greatest range of transmittance as well as the greatest useful range for prisms?

   F. Lithium fluoride

   G. Sodium chloride

   H. Quartz

   J. Flint glass

PASSAGE II

Osmosis is the diffusion of a solvent (often water) across a semipermeable membrane from the side of the membrane with a lower concentration of dissolved material to the side with a higher concentration of dissolved material. The result of osmosis is an equilibrium—an even distribution—on both sides of the membrane. In order to prevent osmosis, external pressure must be applied to the side with the higher concentration of dissolved material. *Osmotic pressure* is the external pressure required to prevent osmosis. The apparatus shown was used to measure osmotic pressure in the following experiments.

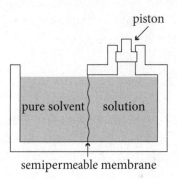

EXPERIMENT 1

Aqueous (water-based) solutions containing different concentrations of sucrose were placed in the closed side of the apparatus. The open side was filled with water. The sucrose solutions also contained a blue dye that binds to sucrose. The osmotic pressure created by the piston was measured for each solution at various temperatures. The results are given in Table 1.

GO ON TO THE NEXT PAGE

Table 1

Concentration of sucrose solution (mol/L)	Temperature (K)	Osmotic pressure (atm)
1.00	298.0	24.47
0.50	298.0	12.23
0.10	298.0	2.45
0.05	298.0	1.22
1.00	348.0	28.57
0.50	348.0	14.29
0.10	348.0	2.86
0.05	348.0	1.43

EXPERIMENT 2

Sucrose solutions of four different organic solvents were investigated in the same manner as in Experiment 1 with all trials at 298 K. The results are shown in Table 2.

Table 2

Solvent	Concentration of sucrose solution (mol/L)	Osmotic pressure (atm)
Ethanol	0.50	12.23
Ethanol	0.10	2.45
Acetone	0.50	12.23
Acetone	0.10	2.45
Diethyl ether	0.50	12.23
Diethyl ether	0.10	2.45
Methanol	0.50	12.23
Methanol	0.10	2.45

7. Osmotic pressure can be calculated using the formula $\Pi = MRT$, where Π represents the calculated osmotic pressure, M = mol/L, R is a constant equal to 0.0821 and T is temperature in Kelvins. Which of the following can be inferred from the data in Table 1?

  I. In order to maintain osmotic pressure, temperature must stay constant.

  II. Temperature and volume must have an inverse relationship in order to maintain a constant osmotic pressure.

  III. Osmotic pressure will increase as volume and temperature increase.

  A. I only

  B. II only

  C. III only

  D. II and III only

8. According to the experimental results, osmotic pressure is dependent upon the:

  F. solvent and temperature only.

  G. solvent and concentration only.

  H. temperature and concentration only.

  J. solvent, temperature, and concentration.

9. According to Experiment 2, if methanol was used as a solvent, what pressure must be applied to a 0.5 mol/L solution of sucrose at 298 K to prevent osmosis?

  A. 1.23 atm

  B. 2.45 atm

  C. 12.23 atm

  D. 24.46 atm

GO ON TO THE NEXT PAGE ⇒

10. A 0.10 mol/L aqueous sucrose solution is separated from an equal volume of pure water by a semipermeable membrane. If the solution is at a pressure of 1 atm and a temperature of 298 K:

F. water will diffuse across the semipermeable membrane from the sucrose solution side to the pure water side.

G. water will diffuse across the semipermeable membrane from the pure water side to the sucrose solution side.

H. water will not diffuse across the semipermeable membrane.

J. water will diffuse across the semipermeable membrane, but the direction of diffusion cannot be determined.

11. In Experiment 1, the scientists investigated the effect of:

A. solvent and concentration on osmotic pressure.

B. volume and temperature on osmotic pressure.

C. concentration and temperature on osmotic pressure.

D. temperature on atmospheric pressure.

12. Which of the following conclusions can be drawn from the experimental results?

I. Osmotic pressure is independent of the solvent used.

II. Osmotic pressure is only dependent upon the temperature of the system.

III. Osmosis occurs only when the osmotic pressure is exceeded.

F. I only

G. III only

H. I and II only

J. I and III only

13. What was the most likely purpose of the dye placed in the sucrose solutions in Experiments 1 and 2?

A. The dye showed when osmosis was completed.

B. The dye showed the presence of ions in the solutions.

C. The dye was used to make the experiment more colorful.

D. The dye was used to make the onset of osmosis visible.

PASSAGE III

A series of experiments was performed to study the environmental factors affecting the size and number of leaves on the *Cycas* plant.

EXPERIMENT 1

Five groups of 25 *Cycas* seedlings, all 2–3 cm tall, were allowed to grow for 3 months, each group at a different humidity level. All of the groups were kept at 75°F and received 9 hours of sunlight a day. The average leaf lengths, widths, and densities are given in Table 1.

Table 1

% Humidity	Average length (cm)	Average width (cm)	Average density* (leaves/cm)
15	5.6	1.6	0.13
35	7.1	1.8	0.25
55	9.8	2.0	0.56
75	14.6	2.6	0.61
95	7.5	1.7	0.52

*Number of leaves per 1 cm of plant stalk

EXPERIMENT 2

Five new groups of 25 seedlings, all 2–3 cm tall, were allowed to grow for three months, each group receiving different amounts of sunlight at a constant humidity of 55%. All other conditions were the same as in Experiment 1. The results are listed in Table 2.

Table 2

Sunlight (hrs/day)	Average length (cm)	Average width (cm)	Average density* (leaves/cm)
0	5.3	1.5	0.32
3	12.4	2.4	0.59
6	11.2	2.0	0.56
9	8.4	1.8	0.26
12	7.7	1.7	0.19

*Number of leaves per 1 cm of plant stalk

EXPERIMENT 3

Five new groups of 25 seedlings, all 2–3 cm tall, were allowed to grow at a constant humidity of 55% for three months at different daytime and night-time temperatures. All other conditions were the same as in Experiment 1. The results are shown in Table 3.

Table 3

Day/night temperature (°F)	Average length (cm)	Average width (cm)	Average density* (leaves/cm)
85/85	6.8	1.5	0.28
85/65	12.3	2.1	0.53
65/85	8.1	1.7	0.33
75/75	7.1	1.9	0.45
65/65	8.3	1.7	0.39

*Number of leaves per 1 cm of plant stalk

14. Based on the data in Experiment 3, which day/night temperatures produced the smallest leaves?

F. 85/85

G. 85/65

H. 75/75

J. 65/85

15. Which of the following conclusions can be made based on the results of Experiment 2 alone?

A. The seedlings do not require long daily periods of sunlight to grow.

B. The average leaf density is independent of the humidity the seedlings receive.

C. The seedlings need more water at night than during the day.

D. The average length of the leaves increases as the amount of sunlight increases.

GO ON TO THE NEXT PAGE ⟹

16. Seedlings grown at a 40% humidity level under the same conditions as in Experiment 1 would have average leaf widths closest to:

    F. 1.6 cm.

    G. 1.9 cm.

    H. 2.2 cm.

    J. 2.5 cm.

17. According to the experimental results, under which set of conditions would a *Cycas* seedling be most likely to produce the largest leaves?

    A. 95% humidity and 3 hours of sunlight

    B. 75% humidity and 3 hours of sunlight

    C. 95% humidity and 6 hours of sunlight

    D. 75% humidity and 6 hours of sunlight

18. Which variable remained constant throughout all of the experiments?

    F. The number of seedling groups

    G. The percent of humidity

    H. The daytime temperature

    J. The nighttime temperature

19. It was assumed in the design of the three experiments that all of the *Cycas* seedlings were:

    A. more than 5 cm tall.

    B. equally capable of germinating.

    C. equally capable of producing flowers.

    D. equally capable of further growth.

20. As a continuation of the three experiments listed, it would be most appropriate to next investigate:

    F. how many leaves over 6.0 cm long there are on each plant.

    G. which animals consume *Cycas* seedlings.

    H. how the mineral content of the soil affects the leaf size and density.

    J. what time of year the seedlings have the darkest coloring.

PASSAGE IV

The resistance (R) of a conductor is the extent to which it opposes the flow of electricity. Resistance depends not only on the conductor's resistivity (ρ) but also on the conductor's length (L) and cross-sectional area (A). The resistivity of a conductor is a physical property of the material that varies with temperature.

A research team designing a new appliance was researching the best type of wire to use in a particular circuit. The most important consideration was the wire's resistance. The team studied the resistance of wires made from four metals—gold (Au), aluminum (Al), tungsten (W), and iron (Fe). Two lengths and two gauges (diameters) of each type of wire were tested at 20°C. The results are recorded in the following table.

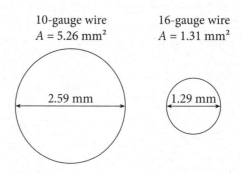

10-gauge wire
$A = 5.26 \text{ mm}^2$

2.59 mm

16-gauge wire
$A = 1.31 \text{ mm}^2$

1.29 mm

Note: area of circle = πr^2

GO ON TO THE NEXT PAGE

Table 1

Material	Resistivity (mV–cm)	Length (cm)	Cross-sectional area (mm²)	Resistance (mV)
Au	2.44	1.0	5.26	46.4
Au	2.44	1.0	1.31	186.0
Au	2.44	2.0	5.26	92.8
Au	2.44	2.0	1.31	372.0
Al	2.83	1.0	5.26	53.8
Al	2.83	1.0	1.31	216.0
Al	2.83	2.0	5.26	107.6
Al	2.83	2.0	1.31	432.0
W	5.51	1.0	5.26	105.0
W	5.51	1.0	1.31	421.0
W	5.51	2.0	5.26	210.0
W	5.51	2.0	1.31	842.0
Fe	10.00	1.0	5.26	190.0
Fe	10.00	1.0	1.31	764.0
Fe	10.00	2.0	5.26	380.0
Fe	10.00	2.0	1.31	1,528.0

21. Of the wires tested, resistance increases for any given material as which parameter is decreased?

   A. Length

   B. Cross-sectional area

   C. Resistivity

   D. Gauge

22. Given the data in the table, which of the following best expresses resistance in terms of resistivity (ρ), cross-sectional area (A), and length (L)?

   F. $\dfrac{\rho^A}{L}$

   G. $\dfrac{\rho^L}{A}$

   H. ρAL

   J. $\dfrac{AL}{\rho}$

23. Which of the following wires would have the highest resistance?

   A. A 1-cm aluminum wire with a cross-sectional area of 0.33 mm²

   B. A 2-cm aluminum wire with a cross-sectional area of 0.33 mm²

   C. A 1-cm tungsten wire with a cross-sectional area of 0.33 mm²

   D. A 2-cm tungsten wire with a cross-sectional area of 0.33 mm²

24. According to the information given, which of the following statements is (are) correct?

   I. 10-gauge wire has a larger diameter than 16-gauge wire.

   II. Gold has a higher resistivity than tungsten.

   III. Aluminum conducts electricity better than iron.

   F. I only

   G. II only

   H. III only

   J. I and III only

GO ON TO THE NEXT PAGE

25. Which of the following graphs best represents the relationship between the resistivity of a tungsten wire and its length?

A.

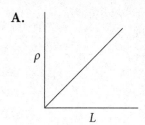

B.

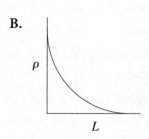

C.

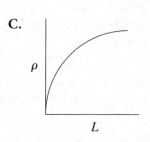

D.

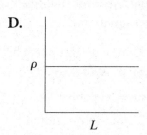

26. If the length of the wires were increased to 4 cm, what could be expected in terms of resistance?

- **F.** Resistance would increase, but only with a 10 gauge wire.
- **G.** Resistance would decrease, but only with a 16 gauge wire.
- **H.** Resistance would not change because 2 cm is the maximum length that affects resistance.
- **J.** Resistance would increase on both the 10 and 16 gauge wires.

PASSAGE V

How does evolution occur? Two views are presented here.

SCIENTIST 1

Evolution occurs by natural selection. Random mutations are continually occurring in a species as it propagates. A number of these mutations result in traits that help the species adapt to environmental changes. Because these mutant traits are advantageous, the members of the species who possess them tend to survive and pass on their genes more often than those who do not have these traits. Therefore, the percentage of the population with an advantageous trait increases over time. Long necks evolved in giraffes by natural selection. The ancestors of giraffes had necks of various sizes; however, their average neck length was much shorter than the average neck length of modern-day giraffes. Since the food supply was limited, the individuals with necks on the long range of the spectrum had access to more food (the leaves of trees) and therefore were more likely to survive and pass on their traits than individuals with shorter necks. Therefore, the proportion of the individuals with long necks was slightly greater in each subsequent generation.

SCIENTIST 2

Evolution occurs by the inheritance of acquired characteristics. Characteristics that are acquired by an individual member of a species during its lifetime are passed on to its offspring. Therefore, each generation's traits are partially accounted for by all the changes that occurred in the individuals of the previous generation. This includes changes that occurred as a result of accidents, changes in the environment, overuse of muscles, etc. The evolution of long necks of giraffes is an example. Ancestors of giraffes had short necks and consequently had to stretch their necks to reach the leaves of trees that were their main source of food. This repeated stretching of their necks caused them to elongate

GO ON TO THE NEXT PAGE

slightly. This trait was passed on, so that the individuals of the next generation had slightly longer necks. Each subsequent generation also stretched their necks to feed; therefore, each generation had slightly longer necks than the previous generation.

27. Both scientists agree that:

    A. the environment affects evolution.

    B. the individuals of a generation have identical traits.

    C. acquired characteristics are inherited.

    D. random mutations occur.

28. How would the two hypotheses be affected if it were found that all of the offspring of an individual with a missing leg due to an accident were born with a missing leg?

    F. It would support Scientist 1's hypothesis, because it is an example of random mutations occurring within a species.

    G. It would refute Scientist 1's hypothesis, because it is an example of random mutations occurring within a species.

    H. It would support Scientist 2's hypothesis, because it is an example of an acquired characteristic being passed on to the next generation.

    J. It would support Scientist 2's hypothesis, because it is an example of random mutations occurring within a species.

29. Which of the following characteristics can be inherited according to Scientist 2?

    I. Fur color

    II. Bodily scars resulting from a fight with another animal

    III. Poor vision

    A. I only

    B. II only

    C. I and III only

    D. I, II, and III

30. Scientist 1 believes that the evolution of the long neck of the giraffe:

    F. is an advantageous trait that resulted from overuse of neck muscles over many generations.

    G. is an advantageous trait that resulted from a random mutation.

    H. is an advantageous trait that resulted from a mutation that occurred in response to a change in the environment.

    J. is a disadvantageous trait that resulted from a random mutation.

31. The fundamental point of disagreement between the two scientists is whether:

    A. giraffes' ancestors had short necks.

    B. evolved traits come from random mutations or from the previous generation.

    C. the environment affects the evolution of a species.

    D. the extinction of a species could be the result of random mutations.

GO ON TO THE NEXT PAGE

32. Suppose evidence was found that suggested that before the discovery of fire, human skin lacked the nerve endings necessary to detect extreme heat. Which of the following pieces of information, if true, would most seriously weaken the hypothesis of Scientist 2?

F. Human skin is capable of generating nerve endings with new functions during life.

G. The total number of nerve endings in the skin of a human is determined at birth and remains constant until death.

H. An excess of nerve endings that are sensitive to extreme heat is a relatively common human mutation.

J. No evidence exists to suggest that an excess of nerve endings that are sensitive to heat could be acquired through mutation.

33. The average height of a full-grown person today is significantly greater than was the average height of a full-grown person 1,000 years ago. If it was proven that the increase in average height was due only to evolutionary changes, how would Scientist 1 most likely explain this increase?

A. People genetically prone to growing taller have been more likely to produce offspring over the last 1,000 years.

B. Over the last 1,000 years, improvements in nutrition and medicine have led to greater average growth over a person's lifetime, and this growth has been passed from one generation to the next.

C. Increased height is not a trait that can be acquired through mutation.

D. Measurements of average height were less accurate 1,000 years ago than they are today.

PASSAGE VI

Bovine spongiform encephalopathy (BSE) is caused by the spread of a misfolded protein that eventually kills infected cattle. BSE is diagnosed postmortem from the diseased cavities that appear in brain tissue and is associated with the use in cattle feed of ground-up meat from scrapie-infected sheep. A series of experiments was performed to determine the mode of transmission of BSE. The results of both experiments are provided in Table 1.

EXPERIMENT 1

Sixty healthy cows were divided into two equal groups. Group A's feed included meat from scrapie-free sheep; and Group B's feed included meat from scrapie-infected sheep. Eighteen months later, the two groups were slaughtered and their brains examined for BSE cavities.

EXPERIMENT 2

Researchers injected ground-up sheep brains directly into the brains of two groups of 30 healthy cows. The cows in Group C received brains from scrapie-free sheep. The cows in Group D received brains from scrapie-infected sheep. Eighteen months later, both groups were slaughtered and their brains examined for diseased cavities.

Table 1

Group	Mode of transmission	Scrapie present	Number of cows infected with BSE*
A	feed	no	1
B	feed	yes	12
C	injection	no	0
D	injection	yes	3

*As determined visually by presence/absence of spongiform encephalopathy

GO ON TO THE NEXT PAGE

34. Based on the information provided in Table 1, a cow is at greatest risk for contracting BSE if the cow:

   F. consumes meat from scrapie-free sheep.

   G. consumes meat from scrapie-infected sheep.

   H. is injected with ground-up sheep brains from scrapie-free sheep.

   J. is injected with ground-up sheep brains from scrapie-infected sheep.

35. Which of the following hypotheses was investigated in Experiment 1?

   A. The injection of scrapie-infected sheep brains into cows' brains causes BSE.

   B. The ingestion of wild grasses causes BSE.

   C. The ingestion of scrapie-infected sheep meat causes scrapie.

   D. The ingestion of scrapie-infected sheep meat causes BSE.

36. What is the purpose of Experiment 2?

   F. To determine whether BSE can be transmitted by injection

   G. To determine whether BSE can be transmitted by ingestion

   H. To determine whether ingestion or injection is the primary mode of BSE transmission

   J. To determine the healthiest diet for cows

37. Which of the following assumptions is made by the researchers in Experiments 1 and 2?

   A. Cows do not suffer from scrapie.

   B. A year and a half is a sufficient amount of time for BSE to develop in a cow.

   C. Cows and sheep suffer from the same diseases.

   D. Cows that eat scrapie-free sheep meat will not develop BSE.

38. A researcher wishes to determine whether BSE can be transmitted through scrapie-infected goats. Which of the following experiments would best test this?

   F. Repeating Experiment 1, using a mixture of sheep and goat meat in Group C's feed

   G. Repeating Experiments 1 and 2, replacing sheep with healthy goats

   H. Repeating Experiments 1 and 2, replacing healthy sheep with healthy goats and scrapie-infected sheep with scrapie-infected goats

   J. Repeating Experiment 2, replacing healthy cows with healthy goats

39. What is the control group in Experiment 1?

   A. Group A

   B. Group B

   C. Group C

   D. Group D

GO ON TO THE NEXT PAGE ⟩

40. Which of the following conclusions can be drawn based on the results of the experiments?

    I. Cows that are exposed to scrapie-infected sheep are more likely to develop BSE than cows that are not.

    II. BSE is only transmitted by eating scrapie-infected sheep meat.

    III. A cow that eats scrapie-infected sheep meat is more likely to develop BSE than a cow that is injected with scrapie-infected sheep brains.

F. II only

G. III only

H. I and III only

J. II and III only

IF YOU FINISH BEFORE TIME IS CALLED, YOU MAY CHECK YOUR WORK ON THIS SECTION ONLY. DO NOT TURN TO ANY OTHER SECTION IN THE TEST.   STOP

WRITING TEST

40 Minutes—1 Question

Directions: This is a test of your writing skills. You will have forty (40) minutes to write an essay in English. Before you begin planning and writing your essay, read the writing prompt carefully to understand exactly what you are being asked to do. Your essay will be evaluated on the evidence it provides of your ability to do the following:

- Express judgments by evaluating the three perspectives given in the prompt, taking a position on an issue, and explaining the relationship among all four ideas
- Develop a position by using logical reasoning and by supporting your ideas
- Maintain a focus on the topic throughout the essay
- Organize ideas in a logical way
- Use language clearly and effectively according to the conventions of standard written English

You may use a separate piece of paper to plan your essay. *You must write your essay in pencil on the lined pages provided after the prompt.* Your writing on those lined pages will be scored. You may not need all the lined pages, but to ensure you have enough room to finish, do NOT skip lines. You may write corrections or additions neatly between the lines of your essay, but do NOT write in the margins of the lined pages. *Illegible essays cannot be scored, so you must write (or print) clearly.*

DO NOT OPEN THIS BOOKLET UNTIL TOLD TO DO SO.

GO ON TO THE NEXT PAGE

CAREER READINESS PROGRAMS

High school curricula are designed to ready students for future career paths, many of which include higher education. Whether or not students choose to attend college, a comprehensive high school education provides an essential foundation. Some educators argue that high schools have an obligation to provide career readiness training for students who do not intend to pursue a college degree. Should high schools invest time and money to develop programs for students who do not wish to continue their education beyond 12th grade? Given the many factors that students weigh when considering if, where, and when to attend college, it is prudent for educators to explore programs that contribute to a better-skilled workforce.

Read and carefully consider these perspectives. Each offers suggestions regarding high school–based career readiness programs.

Perspective One	Perspective Two	Perspective Three
Rather than concentrating solely on students who may not pursue higher education, high schools should help all students develop valuable skills for the workforce. Requiring students to complete classes that focus on key cognitive strategies, content knowledge, and relevant skills and techniques will help them enter the workforce, either immediately after high school or later in their lives.	Career-readiness training should be provided for students who do not wish to pursue college, and it should be particularly targeted at students who are at risk for dropping out. When their high school experience is reframed as training for successful careers rather than government-mandated learning, students can succeed where they may previously have failed.	Students who do not want to pursue higher education should not be given additional accommodations in high school, because they should not be provided any incentives to not attend college. College is the best way to learn how to be productive in the workforce, and students should be encouraged to attend since it is in their best interest.

ESSAY TASK

Write a unified, coherent essay in which you evaluate multiple perspectives on high school–based career readiness programs. In your essay, be sure to:

- analyze and evaluate the perspectives given
- state and develop your own perspective on the issue
- explain the relationship between your perspective and those given

Your perspective may be in full agreement with any of the others, in partial agreement, or wholly different. Whatever the case, support your ideas with logical reasoning and detailed, persuasive examples.

GO ON TO THE NEXT PAGE

PLANNING YOUR ESSAY

You may wish to consider the following as you think critically about the task:

Strengths and weaknesses of the three given perspectives
- What insights do they offer, and what do they fail to consider?
- Why might they be persuasive to others, or why might they fail to persuade?

Your own knowledge, experience, and values
- What is your perspective on this issue, and what are its strengths and weaknesses?
- How will you support your perspective in your essay?

_____

_____

_____

_____

_____

_____

_____

_____

_____

_____

_____

_____

_____

_____

_____

GO ON TO THE NEXT PAGE ⟶

_____

_____

_____

_____

_____

_____

_____

_____

_____

_____

_____

_____

_____

_____

_____

_____

_____

_____

_____

_____

_____

_____

_____

Practice Test One
ANSWER KEY

ENGLISH TEST

1. C	11. C	21. B	31. D	41. D	51. D	61. D	71. D
2. F	12. G	22. G	32. H	42. J	52. J	62. J	72. G
3. D	13. B	23. D	33. A	43. B	53. C	63. C	73. B
4. F	14. H	24. J	34. H	44. G	54. H	64. J	74. F
5. D	15. C	25. C	35. D	45. C	55. D	65. D	75. B
6. G	16. H	26. F	36. G	46. F	56. G	66. J	
7. B	17. B	27. A	37. D	47. B	57. A	67. B	
8. J	18. G	28. J	38. G	48. H	58. H	68. F	
9. A	19. A	29. B	39. D	49. C	59. D	69. D	
10. J	20. J	30. G	40. J	50. H	60. H	70. F	

MATHEMATICS TEST

1. D	9. E	17. B	25. D	33. A	41. B	49. E	57. C
2. J	10. K	18. H	26. G	34. K	42. H	50. K	58. H
3. B	11. D	19. B	27. C	35. A	43. C	51. E	59. D
4. K	12. H	20. H	28. H	36. J	44. K	52. K	60. J
5. C	13. C	21. E	29. B	37. A	45. A	53. B	
6. K	14. H	22. H	30. K	38. G	46. G	54. G	
7. B	15. C	23. D	31. C	39. C	47. E	55. D	
8. K	16. G	24. F	32. H	40. G	48. G	56. K	

READING TEST

1. C	6. H	11. B	16. J	21. B	26. F	31. C	36. H
2. G	7. C	12. H	17. B	22. F	27. C	32. G	37. A
3. B	8. G	13. B	18. H	23. D	28. G	33. D	38. J
4. F	9. B	14. F	19. B	24. F	29. D	34. F	39. B
5. D	10. H	15. C	20. H	25. B	30. F	35. D	40. G

SCIENCE TEST

1. B	6. G	11. C	16. G	21. B	26. J	31. B	36. F
2. F	7. D	12. F	17. B	22. G	27. A	32. G	37. B
3. D	8. H	13. D	18. F	23. D	28. H	33. A	38. H
4. J	9. C	14. F	19. D	24. J	29. D	34. G	39. A
5. B	10. G	15. A	20. H	25. D	30. G	35. D	40. G

ANSWERS AND EXPLANATIONS

ENGLISH TEST

PASSAGE I

1. C
Category: Punctuation
Difficulty: Medium
Getting to the Answer: Choice (C) is the correct and most concise answer choice. Choice A uses an unnecessary comma. Choice B is unnecessarily wordy. Choice D is redundant—if the societies created the legends, there is no need to describe the legends as "original."

2. F
Category: Writing Strategy
Difficulty: High
Getting to the Answer: The question stem gives an important clue to the best answer: The purpose of the inserted sentence is "to describe the different kinds" of stories. Choice (F) is the only choice that does this. Choice G explains how the stories were told. Choice H explains why more is not known about the stories. Choice J describes the length of some stories.

3. D
Category: Connections
Difficulty: Medium
Getting to the Answer: Choices A, B, and C create run-on sentences. Choice (D) describes a relationship that makes sense between our "many more permanent ways of handing down our beliefs" and the fact that "we continue to create and tell legends." It also creates a complete sentence.

4. F
Category: Verb Tenses
Difficulty: Low
Getting to the Answer: Choices H and J are ungrammatical after a colon. Choice G is unnecessarily wordy.

5. D
Category: Wordiness
Difficulty: Medium
Getting to the Answer: Choices A, B, and C are redundant or unnecessarily wordy. Because the contrasting word *but* is already used, *however* is repetitive and should be eliminated.

6. G
Category: Wordiness
Difficulty: Low
Getting to the Answer: Choices F, H, and J are all redundant. The word *conclusion* is unnecessary because the word *ending* has already been used.

7. B
Category: Verb Tenses
Difficulty: Medium
Getting to the Answer: Choice (B) is the only choice that is consistent with the verb tense established by *knew* and *decided*.

8. J
Category: Verb Tenses
Difficulty: Medium
Getting to the Answer: Choice F creates a run-on sentence and also makes it seem that the hunter, not the deer, "was only temporarily knocked unconscious by the car." Choices G and H use incorrect verb tenses.

9. A
Category: Punctuation
Difficulty: High
Getting to the Answer: Choice B is incorrect because the words preceding the semicolon could not be a complete sentence on their own. Choice C would create a sentence fragment. Choice D would create a run-on sentence.

10. J
Category: Wordiness
Difficulty: Medium
Getting to the Answer: Regardless of the sequence of the words, the information provided in F, G, and H is irrelevant to the passage's topic of urban legends.

11. C
Category: Verb Tenses
Difficulty: Medium
Getting to the Answer: The subject of the sentence is *One*, so the verb must be singular. Choices B and D use incorrect verb tenses.

12. G
Category: Word Choice
Difficulty: Low
Getting to the Answer: Choice F creates a sentence that does not make sense. Choices H and J use the plural *women* instead of the singular *woman*.

13. B
Category: Sentence Sense
Difficulty: Medium
Getting to the Answer: Choice (B) most clearly expresses the idea that several websites research "the validity of commonly told urban legends." Because this information is relevant to the topic of urban legends, "OMIT the underlined portion" is not the best answer.

14. H
Category: Writing Strategy
Difficulty: High
Getting to the Answer: Paragraph 4 describes an urban legend that is "humorous in nature." Paragraph 5 describes a rather frightening legend: alligators living underneath the city in the sewer system. The sentence "Other urban legends seem to be designed to instill fear" is an appropriate topic sentence for paragraph 5, and it also serves as a needed transition between paragraph 4 and paragraph 5.

15. C
Category: Writing Strategy
Difficulty: Medium
Getting to the Answer: Although paragraph 1 provides *some* general information about the purpose and topics of the myths and legends of primitive societies, no specifics are given. This makes (C) the best answer.

PASSAGE II

16. H
Category: Verb Tenses
Difficulty: Medium
Getting to the Answer: Correct choices here could be *do you* or *does one*. The latter appears in (H).

17. B
Category: Punctuation
Difficulty: Medium
Getting to the Answer: Choice A incorrectly uses a colon. Choices C and D are grammatically incorrect.

18. G
Category: Wordiness
Difficulty: Medium
Getting to the Answer: *Solitary* and *alone* are redundant in the same sentence. Choices H and J also have redundancy.

19. A
Category: Word Choice
Difficulty: Low
Getting to the Answer: The underlined portion is clearest the way it is written.

20. J
Category: Punctuation
Difficulty: Medium
Getting to the Answer: The colon is incorrect, so eliminate F and H. Because this sentence is a compound sentence, a comma is needed before *and*.

21. B
Category: Sentence Sense
Difficulty: Medium
Getting to the Answer: *In fact* is nonessential—it should be set off by commas.

22. G
Category: Word Choice
Difficulty: Medium
Getting to the Answer: *American* (an adjective) is the word being modified. Therefore, the adverb form of *unique*—*uniquely*— is needed.

23. D
Category: Sentence Sense
Difficulty: Low
Getting to the Answer: "Near Walden Pond…" is a long sentence fragment. The best way to fix the error is to simply combine the sentences by eliminating the period.

24. J
Category: Sentence Sense
Difficulty: Medium
Getting to the Answer: This paragraph and the ones that immediately follow outline Thoreau's life. His influence on the people of today is not discussed until the end of the essay. Therefore, the underlined sentence does not belong here.

25. C
Category: Organization
Difficulty: High
Getting to the Answer: Sentence 3 logically follows sentence 1. Choice (C) is the only choice that lists this correct order.

26. F
Category: Punctuation
Difficulty: Medium
Getting to the Answer: There is one independent clause on each side of the semicolon, so the sentence is punctuated correctly. Choice G would need *and* after the comma to be correct. Choices H and J create run-on sentences.

27. A
Category: Word Choice
Difficulty: Low
Getting to the Answer: A possessive pronoun is needed because the works belong to Thoreau. Eliminate B and D. Choice C relates to more than one person, so it is incorrect as well.

28. J
Category: Writing Strategy
Difficulty: Medium
Getting to the Answer: This paragraph discusses Thoreau's impact on modern society; only (J) expresses the correct topic.

29. B
Category: Wordiness
Difficulty: Medium
Getting to the Answer: Choices A, C, and D are excessively wordy.

30. G
Category: Writing Strategy
Difficulty: High
Getting to the Answer: The use of questions prompts a reader to think about the answers to those questions. Choice F is too literal, and J is too broad for the topic of the essay. Choice H is incorrect because the author establishes the quality of Thoreau's work.

PASSAGE III

31. D
Category: Wordiness
Difficulty: Medium
Getting to the Answer: Because the word *live* is used later in the sentence, A, B, and C contain redundant information.

32. H
Category: Word Choice
Difficulty: Low
Getting to the Answer: In this sentence, the *its* must be possessive because the "unique anatomy" belongs to the sloth. The word describing *anatomy* must be an adjective, not an adverb.

33. A
Category: Punctuation
Difficulty: Medium
Getting to the Answer: The comma is correctly used in (A) to separate the nonessential descriptive phrase "about the size of a large domestic cat" from the rest of the sentence.

34. H
Category: Sentence Sense
Difficulty: Medium
Getting to the Answer: The information about the sloth's limbs is relevant to the topic, so it should not be omitted. Choice (H) clearly and directly expresses how the sloth's muscles are designed to allow this animal to cling to things.

35. D
Category: Word Choice
Difficulty: Medium
Getting to the Answer: *Adapted* needs to be modified by an adverb, so (D) is the best choice.

36. G
Category: Connections
Difficulty: Medium
Getting to the Answer: *Instead* describes the right relationship between the two sentences. The

pronouns must be consistent, and because *its* is already used in the sentence, (G) is the best choice.

37. D
Category: Connections
Difficulty: Low
Getting to the Answer: Choice (D) is the only choice that correctly establishes the relationship between the sloth's inability to "move swiftly on the ground" and its ability to swim.

38. G
Category: Writing Strategy
Difficulty: High
Getting to the Answer: Choice (G) connects the sloth's unique characteristics discussed in paragraph 3 with the description of its flexibility in paragraph 4.

39. D
Category: Punctuation
Difficulty: Medium
Getting to the Answer: Choice (D) correctly uses the second comma necessary to separate the phrase "without moving the rest of its body" from the rest of the sentence. Choice C can be eliminated because it is unnecessarily wordy.

40. J
Category: Verb Tenses
Difficulty: Medium
Getting to the Answer: Choice (J) is the only choice that contains a verb tense consistent with the sentence.

41. D
Category: Wordiness
Difficulty: Low
Getting to the Answer: Choices A, B, and C contain redundant information.

42. J
Category: Wordiness
Difficulty: Medium
Getting to the Answer: This information about the howler monkey is irrelevant to the topic of the passage.

43. B

Category: Sentence Sense

Difficulty: Medium

Getting to the Answer: Choice A creates a sentence fragment. Choice C is unnecessarily wordy and awkward. Choice D creates a run-on sentence.

44. G

Category: Writing Strategy

Difficulty: Medium

Getting to the Answer: The last sentence aptly concludes the entire passage, and removing it would make the ending more abrupt.

45. C

Category: Organization

Difficulty: High

Getting to the Answer: The description of the sloth's "camouflage" is in paragraph 5.

PASSAGE IV

46. F

Category: Verb Tenses

Difficulty: Medium

Getting to the Answer: The underlined portion is best left as is. The other answer choices make the sentence unnecessarily wordy.

47. B

Category: Verb Tenses

Difficulty: Low

Getting to the Answer: The verb tense must agree with the tense that has been established up to this point. The passage is in the past tense, so (B) is correct.

48. H

Category: Verb Tenses

Difficulty: Medium

Getting to the Answer: As with the answer to the previous question, the simple past tense is correct.

49. C

Difficulty: Medium

Category: Verb Tenses

Getting to the Answer: Choice A creates a sentence fragment and uses an incorrect verb tense. Choice B also uses the wrong verb tense. Choice D incorrectly uses a semicolon, as the words preceding the semicolon do not constitute an independent clause.

50. H

Category: Sentence Sense

Difficulty: High

Getting to the Answer: In the context of the rest of the passage, only (H) makes sense. The firefighters' attempts to extinguish the flames failed; *only* nature could stop the fire with the first snowfall.

51. D

Category: Wordiness

Difficulty: Medium

Getting to the Answer: Choices A and B are unnecessarily wordy and awkward. Choice C creates a run-on sentence.

52. J

Category: Wordiness

Difficulty: Medium

Getting to the Answer: All of the other answer choices are unnecessarily wordy and/or repetitive.

53. C

Category: Verb Tenses

Difficulty: High

Getting to the Answer: From the plural verb *open*, you can determine that the best answer will contain *cones*. This makes (C) the only possible answer, as the apostrophe is incorrectly used in B.

54. H

Category: Connections

Difficulty: Medium

Getting to the Answer: This is the only choice that makes sense in the context of the passage. The sighting of the large animals near burning forests is used as evidence that the animals of the region were "fire-tolerant and fire-adaptive."

55. D
Category: Punctuation
Difficulty: Medium
Getting to the Answer: The comma in A is unnecessary because the sentence has a list of only two examples, not three. The semicolon in B is incorrectly used because "and bedding down" does not begin an independent clause. The colon in C is incorrectly used because it is not being used to introduce or emphasize information.

56. G
Category: Sentence Sense
Difficulty: High
Getting to the Answer: The problem with "judging from recent pictures of the park" is that the phrase is modifying *forest*, and a forest obviously can't judge anything. The phrase would have been correct if the sentence had read "judging from the recent pictures of the park, I think that the forest was not destroyed." In this case, the phrase would modify *I*, the author, who is capable of judging. Choice (G) takes care of the problem by rewriting the sentence to eliminate the modifying phrase.

57. A
Category: Word Choice
Difficulty: Low
Getting to the Answer: The pronoun refers to *forest*.

58. H
Category: Writing Strategy
Difficulty: Medium
Getting to the Answer: The introduction of information about fires in Alaska is unwarranted, so F and G can be eliminated. Choice J is incorrect because the additional information would actually uphold the author's position as an authority.

59. D
Category: Writing Strategy
Difficulty: High
Getting to the Answer: The reports mentioned in (D) directly substantiate the author's claims much more than do any of the other answer choices.

PASSAGE V

60. H
Category: Verb Tenses
Difficulty: Medium
Getting to the Answer: Choice F creates a sentence fragment, and G incorrectly uses a plural verb with a singular subject. The verb tense of the paragraph makes (H) a better choice than J.

61. D
Category: Wordiness
Difficulty: Medium
Getting to the Answer: The final part of the sentence "…and there are many other rivers in America as well" is completely irrelevant to the rest of the sentence and the paragraph, in which the author discusses white-water rafting and the rivers she's rafted.

62. J
Category: Punctuation
Difficulty: Medium
Getting to the Answer: Choice F is wrong because *rapids* is essential information and should not be set off by commas. Choice G is wrong because what follows the colon is not an explanation. Choice H is incorrect because what follows the semicolon cannot stand alone as a sentence.

63. C
Category: Wordiness
Difficulty: Low
Getting to the Answer: Choices A and D create sentence fragments, and B is extremely awkward.

64. J
Category: Wordiness
Difficulty: Medium
Getting to the Answer: This sentence is irrelevant to the topic of the passage.

65. D
Category: Word Choice
Difficulty: Medium
Getting to the Answer: This sentence makes it sound as though the author were roaring, not the rapids; *roaring* is a misplaced modifier. Choice B doesn't fix the problem because the reader has no idea what *it* refers to. Choice C has *the boat* roaring. Choice (D) is the clearest choice.

66. J
Category: Sentence Sense
Difficulty: Medium
Getting to the Answer: Either the word *cover* must be in past tense, or the structure of the sentence must change. Choice (J) does the latter.

67. B
Category: Wordiness
Difficulty: Medium
Getting to the Answer: Choice (B) is the simplest, most concise way of expressing the idea. Replacing "and instead he adopted" with "with" and removing the comma make the sentence much less awkward.

68. F
Category: Word Choice
Difficulty: Low
Getting to the Answer: Choices G and J make it sound as though the author were in the water. Choice (F) expresses the idea more accurately than H does.

69. D
Category: Wordiness
Difficulty: High
Getting to the Answer: The phrase "and we stopped" is redundant because "we came to a jarring halt" says the same thing much more expressively. Omit the underlined portion.

70. F
Category: Word Choice
Difficulty: Low
Getting to the Answer: "It was" is fine here because the author is telling her story in the past tense. Choices G and H are in the present tense, and J incorrectly introduces the possessive form.

71. D
Category: Wordiness
Difficulty: Medium
Getting to the Answer: The other answer choices are unnecessarily wordy; the simplest choice, (D), is the best.

72. G
Category: Verb Tenses
Difficulty: Medium
Getting to the Answer: The participle *receiving* has to be changed into a verb in the past tense, *received*, in order to be consistent with *went*. Choice (G) is correct as opposed to H, because the number of bruises something has can be counted, necessitating *many* bruises, not *much* bruises.

73. B
Category: Writing Strategy
Difficulty: Medium
Getting to the Answer: Choice A wouldn't work as a concluding sentence because its style and tone are off; nowhere in the passage does the writer use language such as "brutal calamities" and "beguiling excitement." Also, the writer and her father were not "unwary rafters." Choice C contradicts the writer's main theme that nothing was as memorable as her first ride through the rapids. This is also a sentence fragment. The tone in D, "call me crazy or weird…," is much different from the writer's. Choice (B) closely matches the author's style and tone while restating the main theme of the passage.

74. F

Category: Writing Strategy

Difficulty: Medium

Getting to the Answer: This essay relates a personal experience of the writer: her first time rafting down a rapids. There is very little mention of the techniques of white-water rafting, so the essay would not meet the requirements of the assignment. Choice G is incorrect because the essay does not focus on the relationship between father and daughter but on their first rafting experience together.

75. B

Category: Organization

Difficulty: High

Getting to the Answer: The sentence foreshadows things to come, so it must appear toward the beginning of the essay. That eliminates C and D. The second paragraph is about the peaceful setting, so (B) is the most sensible answer.

MATHEMATICS TEST

1. D

Category: Proportions and Probability

Difficulty: Medium

Getting to the Answer: You know that 14 people are 20% of the total, and you need to find 100% of the total. You could set up an equation, or you could multiply 14 by 5, because 100% is 5 times as much as 20%. The number of people surveyed is 14×5, or 70.

2. J

Category: Proportions and Probability

Difficulty: Medium

Getting to the Answer: One safe way to answer this question is by Picking Numbers. For instance, if you let $x = 2$ and $y = 3$, the train would have traveled $90 \times 2 + 60 \times 3 = 360$ miles in 5 hours, or $\frac{360}{5} = 72$ miles per hour. If you then plug $x = 2$ and

$y = 3$ into the answer choices, it's clear that the correct answer is (J). No other answer choice equals 72 when $x = 2$ and $y = 3$.

3. B

Category: Proportions and Probability

Difficulty: High

Getting to the Answer: If the ratio of men to women is 5:3, then the ratio of women to the total is $3:(3 + 5) = 3:8$. Because you know the total number of string players is 24, you can set up the equation $\frac{3}{8} = \frac{x}{24}$ to find that $x = 9$. Also, without setting up the proportion, you could note that the total number of players is 3 times the ratio total, so the number of women will be 3 times the part of the ratio that represents women.

4. K

Category: Variable Manipulation

Difficulty: Medium

Getting to the Answer: In a pinch, you could Backsolve on this question, but this one is fairly easy to solve algebraically:

$$x^2 - 3x = 6x$$

$$x^2 = 9x$$

Now you can divide both sides by x because $x \neq 0$:

$$\frac{x^2}{x} = \frac{9x}{x}$$

$$x = 9$$

5. C

Category: Patterns, Logic, and Data

Difficulty: Medium

Getting to the Answer: With visual perception problems such as this one, the key is to play around with possibilities as you try to draw a solution. Eventually, you should be able to come up with a picture like this:

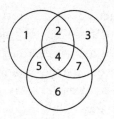

6. K

Category: Variable Manipulation

Difficulty: High

Getting to the Answer: This problem could be solved algebraically, but look at the answer choices. They are all simple numbers, making this a great opportunity for Backsolving. Begin with H.

Plugging in 0, you get:

$$(0)^2 + 6(0) + 8 = 4 + 10(0)$$

$$8 = 4$$

Because 8 does not equal 4, you know this isn't the correct answer. But it is difficult to know which answer to try next. Should you aim higher or lower? If you're unsure of which direction to go, just try whatever looks easiest. Choice J, 1, looks like a good candidate:

$$(1)^2 + 6(1) + 8 = 4 + 10(1)$$

$$1 + 6 + 8 = 4 + 10$$

$$15 = 14$$

So J doesn't work either, but it looks like the numbers are getting closer, so you're going in the right direction. Try (K) just to be sure.

$$(2)^2 + 6(2) + 8 = 4 + 10(2)$$

$$4 + 12 + 8 = 4 + 20$$

$$24 = 24$$

Choice (K) is the correct answer.

7. B

Category: Variable Manipulation

Difficulty: Medium

Getting to the Answer: Translate piece by piece:

"Nine less than c" indicates subtraction: $c - 9$.

"Nine less than c is the same as the number d": $c - 9 = d$. There's one equation. The answer is either (B) or C.

"d less than" also indicates subtraction: $- d$.

"d less than twice c is 20": $2c - d = 20$. There's the second equation.

Choice (B) matches what you found.

8. K

Category: Proportions and Probability

Difficulty: Medium

Getting to the Answer: To determine the total number of possible arrangements on a question like this one, simply determine the number of possibilities for each component and then multiply them together. There are three ways of serving the ice cream, five flavors, and four toppings. Therefore, there are $3 \times 5 \times 4 = 60$ ways to order ice cream, and (K) is correct.

9. E

Category: Proportions and Probability

Difficulty: High

Getting to the Answer: Backsolving is a great technique to use for this problem. Start with C. The director asked 1 out of 3 students to come to the second audition and $\frac{1}{3}$ of 48 is 16, so 16 students were invited to a second audition. Then 75% of 16, which is $\frac{3}{4}(16) = 12$ students, were offered parts. The question states that 18 students were offered parts, so you already know that C is too small.

(You can also, thus, eliminate A and B.) Because

the director invited $\frac{1}{3}$ of the students to a second audition, the number of students at the first audition must be divisible by 3. (You can't have a fraction of a student.) That eliminates D, leaving only (E).

10. K

Category: Variable Manipulation

Difficulty: Medium

Getting to the Answer: Begin by translating the English into math: $x + 5x = -60$, $6x = -60$, so $x = -10$, and the two numbers are -10 and -50. Thus, the lesser number is -50.

By the way, this is where most people mess up. They forget that the lesser of two negative numbers is the negative number with the larger absolute value (because *less* means *to the left of* on the number line):

11. D

Category: Patterns, Logic, and Data

Difficulty: High

Getting to the Answer: You're looking for the total number of parallelograms that can be found among the triangles, and parallelograms could be formed two ways from these triangles, either from two adjacent triangles or from four adjacent triangles, like so:

Begin by looking for the smaller parallelograms. If you look for parallelograms leaning in the same direction as the one we drew, you'll find 3. But there are two other possible orientations for the smaller parallelogram; it could be flipped horizontally, or it could be rotated 90 degrees so that one triangle sits atop the other in the form of a diamond; both of these orientations also have 3 parallelograms, for a total of 9 smaller parallelograms.

Now look for larger parallelograms. Perhaps the easiest way to count these is to look along the sides of the larger composite triangle. You should be able to spot 2 of the larger parallelograms along each side, one originating at each vertex, for a total of 6 larger parallelograms.

Thus, there are a total of $9 + 6 = 15$ parallelograms in all.

12. H

Category: Plane Geometry

Difficulty: Medium

Getting to the Answer: The square has a perimeter of 16 inches, so each side of the square is 4 inches; the area of the square is, therefore, 16 square inches. If the side of the square is 4 inches, then the diameter of the circle is also 4 inches. The radius of the circle is then 2 inches, making the area of the circle 4π square inches. The area of the shaded region is then $16 - 4\pi$ square inches.

13. C

Category: Number Properties

Difficulty: Medium

Getting to the Answer: The safest strategy is simply to list out the possibilities. It's also helpful to realize that multiples of both 4 and 6 are multiples of 12 (the least common multiple between the two), so skip over all multiples of 12:

4, 8, ~~12~~, 16, 20, ~~24~~, 28, 32, ~~36~~, 40, 44, ~~48~~

So there are 8 in all.

14. H

Category: Variable Manipulation

Difficulty: Medium

Getting to the Answer: Don't be intimidated by the expression $f(x)$. In this case, you should just plug in the number that appears in the parentheses for the x in the expression the question has given you. So, if $f(x) = (8 - 3x)(x^2 - 2x - 15)$, $f(3) = [8 - 3(3)][(3)^2 - 2(3) - 15]$.

Once you get to this point, just remember PEMDAS.

$[8 - 3(3)][(3)^2 - 2(3) - 15] = (8 - 9)(9 - 6 - 15) = (-1)(-12) = 12$, (H).

15. C
Category: Proportions and Probability
Difficulty: Medium
Getting to the Answer: A class contains five juniors and five seniors. If one member of the class is assigned at random to present a paper on a certain subject, and another member of the class is randomly assigned to assist him, then:

The probability that the first student picked will be a

$$\text{junior} = \frac{\text{\# of juniors}}{\text{Total \# of students}} = \frac{5}{10} = \frac{1}{2}.$$

Given that the first student picked was a junior, the probability that the second student picked will be a

$$\text{junior} = \frac{\text{\# of juniors remaining}}{\text{Total \# of students remaining}}.$$

So the probability that both students will be

$$\text{juniors} = \frac{1}{2} \times \frac{4}{9} = \frac{2}{9}.$$

16. G
Category: Plane Geometry
Difficulty: Medium

Getting to the Answer: Because the formula to find the area of a triangle is $\frac{1}{2}$(base)(height), you can plug in the base and area to find the height. You know that the area of this triangle is 45 units and that the base is $3 + 12 = 15$. Let x be the length of altitude $\overline{YS}$. Plug these into the area formula to get

$45 = \frac{15x}{2}$. Solve for x to get $x = 6$.

17. B
Category: Coordinate Geometry
Difficulty: Medium
Getting to the Answer: The y-coordinate is the point at which the x value is zero, so plug $x = 0$ into the equation:

$$6y - 3(0) = 18$$
$$6y = 18$$
$$y = 3$$

18. H
Category: Variable Manipulation
Difficulty: High
Getting to the Answer: This question involves common quadratics, so the key is to write these quadratic expressions in their other forms. For instance, $x^2 - y^2 = 12$, so $(x + y)(x - y) = 12$. Because $x - y = 4$, $(x + y)(4) = 12$, so $x + y = 3$. Finally, $x^2 + 2xy + y^2 = (x + y)^2 = (3)^2 = 9$.

19. B
Category: Plane Geometry
Difficulty: High
Getting to the Answer: This shape must be divided into three simple shapes. By drawing two perpendicular line segments down from the endpoints of the side that is 10 units long, you are left with a 3×10 rectangle, a triangle with a base of 4 and a height of 3, and a triangle with a base of 7 and a hypotenuse of $7\sqrt{2}$. The rectangle has an area of $3 \times 10 = 30$ square units. The smaller triangle has an area of $\frac{4 \times 3}{2} = 6$ square units. The larger triangle is a 45°-45°-90° triangle, so the height must be 7. Therefore, it has an area of $\frac{7 \times 7}{2} = 24.5$ square units. The entire shape has an area of $6 + 30 + 24.5 = 60.5$ square units.

20. H

Category: Operations

Difficulty: High

Getting to the Answer: Although Backsolving is certainly possible with this problem, it's probably quicker to solve with arithmetic. The board is 12 feet long, which means it is $12 \times 12 = 144$ inches. The carpenter cuts off $3 \times 17 = 51$ inches. That leaves $144 - 51 = 93$ inches.

21. E

Category: Variable Manipulation

Difficulty: Low

Getting to the Answer: To answer this question, begin by setting the right side of the equation equal to zero:

$$x^2 - 4x - 6 = 6$$

$$x^2 - 4x - 12 = 0$$

Now use reverse-FOIL to factor the left side of the equation:

$$(x - 6)(x + 2) = 0$$

Thus, either $x - 6 = 0$ or $x + 2 = 0$, so $x = 6$ or -2.

22. H

Category: Variable Manipulation

Difficulty: Medium

Getting to the Answer: Here's another question that tests your understanding of FOIL, but you have to be careful. The question states that -3 is a possible solution for the equation $x^2 + kx - 15 = 0$, so in its factored form, one set of parentheses with a factor inside must be $(x + 3)$. Because the last term in the equation in its expanded form is -15, that means that the entire factored equation must read $(x + 3)(x - 5) = 0$, which in its expanded form is $x^2 - 2x - 15 = 0$. Thus, $k = -2$.

23. D

Category: Plane Geometry

Difficulty: Medium

Getting to the Answer: To solve this problem, you need to understand the triangle inequality theorem, which states: The sum of the lengths of any two sides of a triangle is always greater than the length of the third side. Therefore, the other sides of this triangle must add up to more than 7. You know from the problem that every side must be an integer. That means that the sides must add up to at least 8 inches (4 inches and 4 inches, or 7 inches and 1 inch, for example). The smallest possible perimeter is $7 + 8 = 15$.

24. F

Category: Trigonometry

Difficulty: Medium

Getting to the Answer: It's time to use SOHCAH-TOA, and drawing a triangle might help as well. If the sine of θ (opposite side over hypotenuse) is $\dfrac{\sqrt{11}}{2\sqrt{3}}$, then one of the legs of the right triangle is $\sqrt{11}$, and the hypotenuse is $2\sqrt{3}$. Now apply the Pythagorean theorem to come up with the other (adjacent) leg: $\left(\sqrt{11}\right)^2 + \left(n\right)^2 = \left(2\sqrt{3}\right)^2$, so $11 + n^2 = 12$, which means that $n^2 = 1$, and $n = 1$. Thus, cosine (adjacent side over hypotenuse) θ is $\dfrac{1}{2\sqrt{3}}$.

25. D

Category: Operations

Difficulty: Medium

Getting to the Answer: Take a quick look at the answer choices before simplifying an expression like this one. Notice that only one of these choices contains a radical sign in its denominator. So when you simplify the expression, try to eliminate that radical sign. Your calculations should look something like this:

$$\frac{\sqrt{3+x}}{\sqrt{3-x}} \times \frac{\sqrt{3-x}}{\sqrt{3-x}} = \frac{\sqrt{(3+x)(3-x)}}{\sqrt{(3-x)^2}} =$$

$$\frac{\sqrt{9-3x+3x-x^2}}{3-x} = \frac{\sqrt{9-x^2}}{3-x}$$

So (D) is correct.

26. G
Category: Proportions and Probability

Difficulty: Low

Getting to the Answer: If the ratio of the parts is 2:5, then the ratio total is $2+5=7$. Thus, the actual total number of cookies must be a multiple of 7. The only choice that's a multiple of 7 is (G), 35.

27. C
Category: Number Properties

Difficulty: Medium

Getting to the Answer: This question is a great opportunity to use your calculator. Notice that all your choices are decimals. In order to solve, convert $\frac{3}{16}$ into a decimal and add that to 0.175: $\frac{3}{16} = 0.1875$, so the sum equals $0.1875 + 0.175 = 0.3625$. Thus, (C) is correct.

28. H
Category: Plane Geometry

Difficulty: Low

Getting to the Answer: Remember that if you are given a perimeter for a rectangle, the rectangle with the greatest area for that perimeter will be a square. So you are looking for the area of a square with a perimeter of 20. The perimeter of a square equals $4s$, where s is the length of one side of the square. If $4s = 20$, then $s = 5$. The area of the square equals $s^2 = 5^2 = 25$, (H).

29. B
Category: Operations

Difficulty: High

Getting to the Answer: Be careful on this one. You can't start plugging numbers into your calculator without paying attention to the order of operations. This one is best solved on your own.

$$\frac{\frac{3}{2}+\frac{7}{4}}{\frac{15}{8}-\frac{3}{4}-\frac{4+3}{-4+3}} =$$

$$\frac{\frac{3}{2}+\frac{7}{4}}{\frac{9}{8}-\frac{7}{-1}} = \frac{\frac{13}{4}}{\frac{65}{8}} = \frac{13}{4} \times \frac{8}{65} = \frac{2}{5}$$

30. K
Category: Variable Manipulation

Difficulty: Medium

Getting to the Answer: You could solve this algebraically for x as follows:

$$x - 15 = 7 - 5(x-4)$$
$$x - 15 = 7 - 5x + 20$$
$$x - 15 = -5x + 27$$
$$6x = 42$$
$$x = 7$$

Remember also that if you are ever stuck, you can Backsolve using the answer choices. Here, if you try them all out, only 7 works:

$$7 - 15 = 7 - 5(7-4)$$
$$-8 = 7 - 5(3)$$
$$-8 = 7 - 15$$
$$-8 = -8$$

31. C

Category: Plane Geometry

Difficulty: Medium

Getting to the Answer: Break strange figures like this one up into shapes that are more familiar and easier to handle. In this case, the quadrilateral can be split into a square and a right triangle. The square is 9 × 9, so the area of that part of the figure is 81 square meters. The right triangle has a height of 9 and a base of 4, so the area of the triangle would be

$$\frac{1}{2}bh = \frac{1}{2}(4 \times 9) = \frac{1}{2}(36) = 18$$

square meters. Therefore, the total area of the figure is (81 + 18) square meters = 99 square meters, (C).

32. H

Category: Coordinate Geometry

Difficulty: Medium

Getting to the Answer: The easiest way to solve this question is to put it in the form $y = mx + b$, where m equals the slope. In other words, you want to isolate y:

$$6y - 3x = 18$$
$$6y = 3x + 18$$
$$y = \frac{3x + 18}{6}$$
$$y = \frac{1}{2}x + 3$$

So the slope equals $\frac{1}{2}$.

33. A

Category: Coordinate Geometry

Difficulty: Low

Getting to the Answer: To answer this question, you have to know that perpendicular lines on the standard (x, y) coordinate plane have slopes that are negative reciprocals of each other. In other words, the line described by the equation $y = -\frac{4}{5}x + 6$ has a slope of $-\frac{4}{5}$, so a line perpendicular to it

has a slope of $\frac{5}{4}$. This eliminates all choices but (A). However, if you want to double-check, you can plug the coordinates you're given (4, 3) into the equation found in (A).

$$3 = \frac{5}{4}(4) - 2$$
$$3 = 5 - 2$$
$$3 = 3$$

34. K

Category: Coordinate Geometry

Difficulty: Medium

Getting to the Answer: Because the problem gives you the y-intercept, it is easy to look at the answer choices and rule out F, H, and J. Put the equation from the question in slope-intercept form to find its slope:

$$3x - 5y = 4$$
$$-5y = -3x + 4$$
$$y = \frac{-3x + 4}{-5}$$
$$y = \frac{3}{5}x - \frac{4}{5}$$

Because line t is parallel, it has the same slope. This matches (K).

35. A

Category: Variable Manipulation

Difficulty: Low

Getting to the Answer: To solve for x in the equation $y = mx + b$, isolate x on one side of the equation. Begin by subtracting b from both sides. You will be left with $y - b = mx$. Then divide both sides by m, and you will be left with $x = \frac{y - b}{m}$, (A).

36. J

Category: Plane Geometry

Difficulty: Medium

Getting to the Answer: In this figure, there are many right triangles and many similar triangles. If you know to be on the lookout for 3-4-5 triangles, it should be easy to spot that triangle *ABC* has sides of 15-20-25, so $\overline{AC}$ is 25. Now turn your attention to triangle *ABD*. Because it's a right triangle that shares ∠*BAC* with triangle *ABC*, it too must be a 3-4-5 triangle. So if the hypotenuse is 20, the shorter leg ($\overline{BD}$) must have a length of 12, and the longer leg ($\overline{AD}$) must have a length of 16.

37. A

Category: Coordinate Geometry

Difficulty: High

Getting to the Answer: The shortest distance to line *m* will be a line perpendicular to *m*. So the distance will be the difference between the *y*-coordinates of point *C* and the nearest point on line *m*. Because every point on *m* has a *y*-coordinate of 5, and point *C* has a *y*-coordinate of 3, the difference is 2.

38. G

Category: Variable Manipulation

Difficulty: Medium

Getting to the Answer: While you could try factoring the numerator, you'll find that you can't easily cancel out the denominator by doing so. Perhaps the easiest approach here is to Pick Numbers. Pick a simple number such as *x* = 2. Thus,

$$\frac{x^2 - 11x + 24}{8 - x} = \frac{(2)^2 - 11(2) + 24}{6} =$$
$$\frac{4 - 22 + 24}{6} = \frac{6}{6} = 1.$$

So 1 is your target number. When you plug *x* = 2 into the choices, the only choice that gives you 1 is (G).

39. C

Category: Coordinate Geometry

Difficulty: Medium

Getting to the Answer:

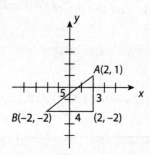

The textbook method for this problem would be to use the distance formula, but that's time-consuming. Instead, it may help to draw a picture. Draw a right triangle on the coordinate plane as shown above. Note that the distance between the two points represents the hypotenuse of the triangle. The legs of the triangle have lengths of 3 and 4, so the distance between the two points must be 5, (C).

40. G

Category: Plane Geometry

Difficulty: Medium

Getting to the Answer: To find the area of the shaded region, you must subtract the area of the circle from the area of the rectangle. Because the sides of the rectangle are 2*x* and 5*x*, it has an area of $2x \times 5x = 10x^2$. By examining the diagram, you can see that the circle has a diameter of 2*x*, so it has a radius of *x*. Its area is, therefore, πx^2. Thus, the shaded region has an area of $10x^2 - \pi x^2$.

41. B

Category: Trigonometry

Difficulty: High

Getting to the Answer: Because you are not given a diagram for this problem, it's best to draw a quick sketch of a right triangle to help keep the sides separate in your mind. Mark one of the acute angles θ. Because $\cos \theta = \frac{5\sqrt{2}}{8}$, mark the adjacent side $5\sqrt{2}$ and the hypotenuse as 8. (Remember SOHCAHTOA.) Use the Pythagorean theorem to find that the side opposite θ is $\sqrt{14}$. The problem asks you to find tan θ. Tangent = $\frac{\text{opposite}}{\text{adjacent}}$, so tan θ = $\frac{\sqrt{14}}{5\sqrt{2}}$, which can be simplified to $\frac{\sqrt{7}}{5}$.

42. H

Category: Proportions and Probability

Difficulty: Medium

Getting to the Answer: This question is one where your calculator can come in handy. Divide 7 by integer values for n, and look for values between 0.5 and 0.8. Begin by looking for the integer values of n where $\frac{7}{n}$ is greater than 0.5. If $n = 14$, then $\frac{7}{n} = 0.5$, so n must be less than 14. Work through values of n until you get to the point where $\frac{7}{n} + 0.8$. When $n = 9$, $\frac{7}{n} = 0.778$, but when $n = 8$, $\frac{7}{n} = 0.875$. So the integer values that work in this case are $n = 9$, 10, 11, 12, and 13. Five integer values work, making (H) correct.

43. C

Difficulty: Medium

Category: Plane Geometry

Getting to the Answer: The points are as far apart as possible when separated by a diameter of X and a diameter of Y.

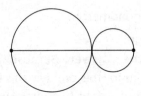

The circumference of a circle is π × (diameter), so the diameter of circle X is 12, and the diameter of circle Y is 8. The greatest possible distance between points then is 12 + 8 = 20.

44. K

Category: Variable Manipulation

Difficulty: Medium

Getting to the Answer: Begin by getting rid of the square root sign. If $y \geq 0$, then $\sqrt{y^2} = y$, so $\sqrt{(x^2 + 4)^2} = x^2 + 4$. Then $(x + 2)(x - 2) = x^2 - 4$, so you now have $(x^2 + 4) - (x^2 - 4) = ?$ Get rid of the parentheses, and you have $x^2 + 4 - x^2 + 4 = x^2 - x^2 + 4 + 4 = 8$.

45. A

Category: Variable Manipulation

Difficulty: Medium

Getting to the Answer: Here, you need to substitute −3 for s and solve. That gives you the expression $(-3)^3 + 2(-3)^2 + 2(-3)$, which equals −27 + 18 − 6, or −15. If you missed this problem, you probably made a mistake with the signs of the numbers.

46. G

Category: Variable Manipulation

Difficulty: High

Getting to the Answer: Be careful on this one. Begin by simplifying the equation by FOILing one side:

$$2x + 6 = (x + 5)(x + 3)$$

$$2x + 6 = x^2 + 8x + 15$$

Then get the right side of the equation to equal zero: $x^2 + 6x + 9 = 0$.

The left side of this equation is the perfect square $(x + 3)^2$, so $(x + 3)^2 = 0$, which has only one solution, $x = -3$. Choice (G) is correct.

47. E

Category: Pythagorean Theorem

Difficulty: Low

Getting to the Answer: The textbook method for this would be to use the Pythagorean theorem to find the length of a side and then multiply that by 4, but there's an easier way: eyeball it! The perimeter is greater than $\overline{AC}$, so you can get rid of A and B.

It appears to be quite a bit greater than $\overline{AC}$, more than twice as great, so C and D are out as well. That only leaves (E).

If you wanted to solve this the conventional way, because the perimeter is the sum of the lengths of all the sides of the square, you need to find the length of the square's sides. Let the length of each of the square's sides be x. $\overline{AC}$ divides the square into two right triangles, so you can apply the Pythagorean theorem: $\overline{AB}^2 + \overline{BC}^2 = \overline{AC}^2$. Because $\overline{AB}$ and $\overline{BC}$ are sides of the square, they have the same length. You can write that as $x^2 + x^2 = \overline{AC}^2$. $\overline{AC} = 8$, so $2x^2 = 8^2$, $2x^2 = 64$, $x^2 = 32$, $x = \sqrt{32} = \sqrt{16 \times 2} = 4\sqrt{2}$.

So each side of the square is $4\sqrt{2}$, and the perimeter of the square is $4 \times 4\sqrt{2} = 16\sqrt{2}$.

48. G
Category: Plane Geometry
Difficulty: Medium
Getting to the Answer: To find the area of this complex shape, you could divide it into two simple shapes by drawing a line 30 inches up, parallel to the horizontal base. This leaves you with a 4 × 30 rectangle and a triangle with height of 6 and a base of 4. The rectangle has an area of 4 × 30 = 120 square inches, and the triangle has an area of $\frac{4 \times 6}{2} = 12$ square inches. That makes a total of 120 + 12 = 132 square inches.

49. E
Category: Plane Geometry
Difficulty: Medium
Getting to the Answer: Triangles are the secret to solving this one. Drawing $\overline{OD}$ divides quadrilateral *OCDE* into two triangles, *OCD* and *ODE*. Both triangles are isosceles because $\overline{OC}$, $\overline{OD}$, and $\overline{OE}$ are all radii of circle *O*. Angles *ODC* and *OCD* have equal measures, because they're opposite equal sides, so $\angle ODC$ measures 70°. Similarly, $\angle ODE$ measures 45°.

Together, angles *ODC* and *ODE* make up $\angle CDE$, so its measure is 70° + 45° = 115°.

50. K
Category: Coordinate Geometry
Difficulty: High
Getting to the Answer: Remember that lines intersect at the point that is a solution to both equations. So equations with no common solution don't intersect—they have the same slope and are parallel. To solve this problem, search through the answer choices to find the pair of equations representing lines with the same slope. If you write the equations in (K) in slope-intercept form, you'll get

$$y = -\frac{1}{3}x + 2, y = -\frac{1}{3}x + \frac{7}{9},$$

so the slope is clearly the same for both equations.

51. E
Category: Number Properties
Difficulty: Medium
Getting to the Answer: To solve a repeating decimal question, begin by determining the pattern of the decimal on your calculator: $\frac{1}{7} = 0.142857142857\ldots$ so you know that this fraction repeats every six decimal places. Because you are looking for the 46th decimal place, you need to determine where in the six-term pattern you would be at the 46th place. Divide 46 by 6 and look for the remainder. The remainder in this case is 4, so you are looking for the 4th term in the sequence, which is 8, (E).

52. K
Category: Variable Manipulation
Difficulty: Medium
Getting to the Answer: Remember that you treat an inequality exactly like an equality, except that you need to flip the sign when you multiply or divide by a negative number. In this problem, you start with the inequality $-2 - 4x \le -6x$. Add $4x$ to

both sides to get $-2 \leq -2x$. Divide by -2 and flip the sign to get $1 \geq x$, which matches (K).

53. B
Category: Operations
Difficulty: High
Getting to the Answer: For this problem, it would probably be easiest to Pick Numbers. Because you will be taking the square root of the numbers, it's easiest to pick perfect squares, like 4 and 9:

$$\frac{\sqrt{4}}{4} + \frac{\sqrt{9}}{9} = \frac{2}{4} + \frac{3}{9} = \frac{1}{2} + \frac{1}{3} = \frac{5}{6}$$

When you plug 4 and 9 into the answer choices, only (B) gives you $\frac{5}{6}$.

54. G
Category: Plane Geometry
Difficulty: Medium

Getting to the Answer: When transversals intersect parallel lines, corresponding line segments on the transversals are proportional. In other words, $\frac{\overline{DE}}{\overline{CB}} = \frac{\overline{EF}}{\overline{BA}}$. Thus, $\frac{6}{8} = \frac{\overline{EF}}{4}$, so $EF = 3$.

55. D
Category: Coordinate Geometry
Difficulty: High
Getting to the Answer: Divide the square into two right triangles by drawing the diagonal from (2, 7) to (2, 1). Remember that the area of each triangle is half its base times its height. Treat the diagonal as the base of a triangle. Its length is the distance from (2, 7) to (2, 1). Because the x-coordinates are the same, that distance is simply the difference between the y-coordinates, $7 - 1$, or 6. The diagonal bisects the square, so the height of the triangle is half the distance from $(-1, 4)$ to $(5, 4)$. You already know that a diagonal of this square is 6, so half the distance is 3. Therefore, the base and height of either triangle are 6 and 3, making the area of each triangle $\frac{6 \times 3}{2}$, or 9 square units. The square is made up of

two such triangles and so has twice the area, or 18 square units.

Alternatively, you could use the Distance Formula to find the length of one side and square that side to find the area.

56. K
Category: Trigonometry
Difficulty: Medium
Getting to the Answer: Compared to the graph of $y = \cos \theta$, the graph of $y = 2 \cos \theta$ would have twice the amplitude and the same period, (K). Here you are doubling y, which represents the vertical coordinates, but the θ coordinates stay the same. The amplitude of a trigonometric equation refers to how high or low the curve moves from the horizontal axis. The period refers to the distance required to complete a single wave along the horizontal axis.

57. C
Category: Variable Manipulation
Difficulty: Medium
Getting to the Answer: To solve this problem with algebra, you need to translate each phrase into mathematics. Translated, the problem is $3(x + 15) = 4x - 65$. Solve for x to get 110. Alternatively, you could Backsolve starting with the middle value:

$$3(110 + 15) = 4(110) - 65$$

$$3(125) = 440 - 65$$

$$375 = 375$$

Because the two sides are equal, (C) is correct.

58. H
Category: Proportions and Probability
Difficulty: Medium
Getting to the Answer: You're given the formula for the volume of a cylinder in the equation so you can find the volume of both cylinders described. Then this becomes a ratio problem in which you're comparing the volumes of both cylinders. Pick Numbers to make this question more concrete and plug them into this volume formula.

Let's say the smaller cylinder has a height of 1 and a radius of 1 (diameter of 2), for a volume of $\pi(1)^2 \times 1 = \pi$. The larger cylinder would then have a height of 3 and a radius of 2 (diameter of 4), for a volume of $\pi(2)^2 \times 3 = 12\pi$. Thus, it would take 12 fillings of the smaller cylinder to fill the larger cylinder.

59. D

Category: Plane Geometry

Difficulty: High

Getting to the Answer: Draw a picture of the triangle and carefully apply your knowledge of the ratio of the lengths of the sides of a 30°-60°-90° triangle ($x : x\sqrt{3} : 2x$). If the longer leg has a length of 12, the shorter leg has a length of

$$\frac{12}{\sqrt{3}} = \frac{12\sqrt{3}}{\sqrt{3} \times \sqrt{3}} = \frac{12\sqrt{3}}{3} = 4\sqrt{3}.$$

Then, the hypotenuse is twice this, or $8\sqrt{3}$. Finally, the perimeter is the sum of the three sides, or

$$4\sqrt{3} + 12 + 8\sqrt{3} = 12\sqrt{3} + 12.$$

60. J

Category: Proportions and Probability

Difficulty: Medium

Getting to the Answer: Remember the average formula on this one. The average formula states,

$$\text{Average} = \frac{\text{Sum of the terms}}{\text{Number of the terms}}. \text{ So to find the}$$

total average, find the total sum and divide it by the total number of terms. If a team averages x points in n games, then it scored nx points in n games. In the final game of the season, it scored y points. So the total sum of points for the season is $nx + y$, and the total number of games is $n + 1$. So the team's average score for the entire season is $\frac{nx + y}{n + 1}$, (J).

READING TEST

PASSAGE I

1. C

Category: Detail

Difficulty: Medium

Getting to the Answer: The answer can be found in lines 31–36: "The real evils, indeed, of Emma's situation were the power of having rather too much her own way, and a disposition to think a little too well of herself; these were the disadvantages which threatened alloy to her many enjoyments."

2. G

Category: Detai

Difficulty: High

Getting to the Answer: Isabella's name is given in line 73.

3. B

Category: Detail

Difficulty: Medium

Getting to the Answer: The answer can be found in lines 20–21: "Between them it was more the intimacy of sisters."

4. F

Category: Vocab-in-Context

Difficulty: Low

Getting to the Answer: As it is used in the sentence, *disposition* means "tendency" or "inclination." It would not make sense for Emma to have G, control; H, placement; or J, transfer "to think a little too well of herself" (lines 33–34).

5. D

Category: Detail

Difficulty: High

Getting to the Answer: The answer can be found in lines 62–69: "She recalled her past kindness—the kindness, the affection of sixteen years—how she had taught her and…how she had devoted all her powers to attach and amuse her in health—and how she had nursed her through the various illnesses of childhood."

6. H

Category: Inference
Difficulty: Medium

Getting to the Answer: Miss Taylor will continue to be a part of Emma's life, but they will not be as close because Miss Taylor no longer lives with Emma and because Miss Taylor will be primarily concerned with her husband's, not Emma's, well-being.

7. C

Category: Inference
Difficulty: Medium

Getting to the Answer: Emma is self-centered, as evidenced by her description of her relationship with Miss Taylor. Among Miss Taylor's admirable qualities, Emma includes the fact that Miss Taylor was "interested in her, in every pleasure, every scheme of hers—one to whom she could speak every thought as it arose, and who had such an affection for her as could never find fault" (lines 80–84). Emma is also clearly headstrong. She is described as "having rather too much her own way" (lines 32–33).

8. G

Category: Generalization
Difficulty: Medium

Getting to the Answer: Emma's description of her friendship with Miss Taylor suggests that Emma most highly values devotion in her friends.

9. B

Category: Detail
Difficulty: Medium

Getting to the Answer: The description of Mr. Weston is in lines 53–56: "The marriage had every promise of happiness for her friend. Mr. Weston was

a man of unexceptionable character, easy fortune, suitable age, and pleasant manners." None of the other choices match this description.

10. H

Category: Inference
Difficulty: Low

Getting to the Answer: The answer to the question is in lines 28–31: "Emma doing just what she liked, highly esteeming Miss Taylor's judgment, but directed chiefly by her own."

PASSAGE II

11. B

Category: Generalization
Difficulty: Medium

Getting to the Answer: Passage A discusses the Wright brothers' process for designing a successful airplane; (B) is correct. Although the passage mentions how the Wright brothers were regarded, A, this information appears in the first paragraph only, and is not the main focus of the passage. The passage discusses the approaches used by other inventors, but the author does not criticize them, as represented in C. The practical application of science, D, is too broad to be correct.

12. H

Category: Inference
Difficulty: High

Getting to the Answer: According to paragraph 2, most inventors would design an airplane, build it, and test it, but not know specifically what caused a plane to succeed or fail, (H). Choice F is opposite because Smeaton's coefficient was commonly accepted during that time in history. There's no indication that they considered the methods and rejected them, G. Choice J is opposite; people who were trying to build an airplane likely believed it was possible.

13. B
Category: Inference
Difficulty: High
Getting to the Answer: The passage says that the Wright brothers invented the wind tunnel as an alternative to building and testing "whole machines." They tested only parts of their design in the tunnel, such as wing shape. You can infer that the wind tunnel made it possible for them to deal with their airplane design one piece at a time. The author never implies that the data from the kites, A, was inaccurate. To work on controlling the plane laterally, they used a five-foot biplane kite rather than the wind tunnel, which rules out C. Choice D is opposite; they disproved a commonly-accepted theory of lift (called Smeaton's coefficient).

14. F
Category: Function
Difficulty: High
Getting to the Answer: Passage B deals mainly with how the Wright brothers were treated publicly following their discovery. The "legal battle" is mentioned as another example of how the brothers didn't receive the money and respect they deserved for their important contribution, (F). The author does not imply that it is unwise to publicize knowledge, G. Choice H is opposite; the author feels that their discovery was quite important. Choice J isn't directly related to the court case.

15. C
Category: Inference
Difficulty: Medium
Getting to the Answer: In the last paragraph, the author states that "this was too little, too late," so the author would agree that the honor did not properly compensate for the poor treatment of the brothers, (C). It was not a victory for Orville, A, because both brothers had passed away by 1948. The Smithsonian's choice was not a result of a refusal to recognize the brothers' achievements, B, because it was a great honor. There is no evidence to suggest that the craft would have been displayed sooner if European countries had issued the brothers a patent, D.

16. J
Category: Detail
Difficulty: High
Getting to the Answer: This Detail question requires very careful reading. The previous sentence talks about how "those who made airplanes" thought little of the Wright brothers' accomplishments. The following sentence is a continuation of that thought, and so it is "those who made airplanes," (J), who are expressing this opinion. The discussion of "the French aviation community" begins a new thought, ruling out F. The Wright brothers, G, didn't have a poor view of themselves. The author, H, has a positive view of the Wright brothers.

17. B
Category: Inference
Difficulty: Medium
Getting to the Answer: The passage says "the prevailing opinion among those who made airplanes was that two rustic, uneducated fellows from Ohio could never have accomplished such an historic feat except by accident." From this, you can infer that those who made airplanes didn't think that the Wright brothers were exceptional; in their eyes, the brothers' discovery must have been sheer luck, not the result of scientific experimentation. Eliminate A because the passage never says that they thought the Wrights hadn't made a working airplane, only that they thought little of the accomplishment. Choice C is opposite; they had a negative opinion the Wrights' breakthrough. Choice D is a distortion; they felt the brothers were lucky, not dishonest.

18. H
Category: Vocab-in-Context
Difficulty: Low
Getting to the Answer: The authors state that the Wrights were able to "marry all of these carefully designed components into a complete craft" (lines 72–73) and "deliberately marry the disparate components of air travel that are required for successful flight" (line 90–93). So, the Wright brothers brought together all the separate pieces into a whole airplane. Predict that "marry" means "bring together,"

(H). The airplane did prove, F, that the components worked when together, but it doesn't make sense to say that the brothers were able to deliberately prove the components. The Wright brothers had already rigorously tested each component separately, so G is incorrect. Airplane components can't be satisfied, so J won't work.

19. B
Category: Detail
Difficulty: Medium
Getting to the Answer: At the beginning of paragraph 3, Passage A states, "The Wright brothers proved to be adept scientists. With their keen analytical insight and love of engineering and all things mechanical, they were able to escape that endless loop of misguided 'improvements.'" This matches perfectly with (B). Choice A describes the approach that other, unsuccessful inventors used. Passage A does not provide evidence that the invention of the wind tunnel was a greater accomplishment than the airplane, C. The court case cited in D is included in Passage B, not in Passage A.

20. H
Category: Detail
Difficulty: Low
Getting to the Answer: Wrong answer choices for this type of question are commonly those that are true for one passage but not the other. Both passages agree that the Wright brothers did something great that no one else was capable of at the time, which is reflected in (H). The brothers' method of inquiry, F, is discussed in Passage A only. Choices G and J are included in Passage B, but not in Passage A.

PASSAGE III

21. B
Category: Inference
Difficulty: Medium
Getting to the Answer: In lines 11–13, Julia Margaret Cameron is described as "the first woman to

have achieved eminence in photography." The other answer choices contradict information supplied in the passage.

22. F
Category: Detail
Difficulty: Low
Getting to the Answer: The answer to this question can be found in lines 82–83, "Contemporary taste much prefers her portraits...," and in lines 88–89, "today her fame rests upon her portraits...."

23. D
Category: Detail
Difficulty: High
Getting to the Answer: The dates used in the passage tell you that this is a chronological account; the author begins with Cameron's birth in 1815, tells of her marriage and then her move to England in 1848, points out that she received her first photographic equipment in 1863, describes one of her photographs from 1864, and then concludes the paragraph with her death in 1874.

24. F
Category: Vocab-in-Context
Difficulty: Medium
Getting to the Answer: The dictionary definition of *cumbersome* is "difficult to handle because of weight or bulk." Choice (F) most closely fits this definition, and it is the only answer choice that makes sense within the context of the sentence.

25. B
Category: Inference
Difficulty: Medium
Getting to the Answer: Lines 55–56 describe how Cameron "devoted herself wholly to this art," which matches (B). Choice A contradicts information from the passage, which suggests that Cameron led anything but a conventional life. Neither the money that Cameron earned as a photographer nor her religious beliefs are discussed in the passage, making C and D incorrect.

26. F

Category: Generalization

Difficulty: Medium

Getting to the Answer: Lines 60–63 say, "she produced a large body of work that stands up as one of the notable artistic achievements of the Victorian period." To say that she is "the greatest photographer who ever lived" goes beyond anything stated or implied in the passage. The third paragraph does not compare her importance as an artist during her lifetime to her importance today. The passage also does not state that she "revolutionized" any photographic methods.

27. C

Category: Detail

Difficulty: Medium

Getting to the Answer: The answer to this question can be found in lines 7–10: "photography, being a new medium outside the traditional academic framework, was wide open to women and offered them opportunities that the older fields did not…"

28. G

Category: Detail

Difficulty: Low

Getting to the Answer: These titles refer to allegorical pictures, as described in lines 78–81: "Victorian critics were particularly impressed by her allegorical pictures, many of them based on the poems of her friend and neighbor Tennyson…."

29. D

Category: Detail

Difficulty: Medium

Getting to the Answer: The answer to this question can be found in lines 82–84: "Contemporary taste much prefers her portraits and finds her narrative scenes sentimental and sometimes in bad taste."

30. F

Category: Inference

Difficulty: Low

Getting to the Answer: The author says that Cameron "achieved eminence" (line 12) in her field, that she "devoted herself wholly to this art" (lines 55–56), and that "no other woman photographer has ever enjoyed such success" (lines 74–75). Only (F) fits these descriptions.

PASSAGE IV

31. C

Category: Detail

Difficulty: Low

Getting to the Answer: For details about the eye, look at paragraph 3. Only the cornea and stenopaic pupil are relevant, eliminating A and D. But the cornea, B, is helpful underwater, not on land.

32. G

Category: Inference

Difficulty: Medium

Getting to the Answer: The eye is covered in paragraph 3. The seal's cornea improves vision in the water (note the comparison to human underwater vision), but it distorts light moving through the air. Another adaptation was then needed to *minimize* (line 53) distortion, but that doesn't mean distortion is completely eliminated, so the seal's vision in the air is distorted, (G).

33. D

Category: Detail

Difficulty: Low

Getting to the Answer: The vibrissae are discussed only in the last paragraph. They sense wave disturbances made by nearby moving fish, so (D) is correct. Choice B, by using the phrase "in the air," distorts information in the passage.

34. F

Category: Detail

Difficulty: Low

Getting to the Answer: This is stated in the second paragraph, where the seal's hearing is discussed.

35. D

Category: Detail

Difficulty: Medium

Getting to the Answer: This appears in the first paragraph, which introduces the influences on the seal's adaptations. They include that the seal "does most of its fishing at night," that "noise levels are high," and that these factors are compounded by the seal's "two habitats."

36. H

Category: Detail

Difficulty: Medium

Getting to the Answer: Locating each of these claims in the passage, you find that (H) is *suggested* (line 68) and the subject of speculation, rather than stated as fact. All of the other choices are given in support of claims.

37. A

Category: Inference

Difficulty: High

Getting to the Answer: You learn in the first paragraph that they live along the northern Atlantic and Pacific coasts. Because they live both on the land and in the water, the coastlines must be accessible. You can infer that the waters are cold rather than warm, eliminating D. Choices B and C are too broad.

38. J

Category: Detail

Difficulty: Medium

Getting to the Answer: This feature is mentioned at the end of paragraph 2. It shouldn't be confused with echolocation, which is discussed in paragraph 4 but not associated with any particular sensory organ.

39. B

Category: Function

Difficulty: Medium

Getting to the Answer: The entire passage is about how the seal's sensory organs have adapted to life on land and in the water, making (B) the best choice. Generally, you are told about differences, not similarities, between the sensory organs of humans and harbor seals, eliminating A. The relative success of human and seal adaptation to their environments isn't discussed, thus eliminating C and D.

40. G

Category: Detail

Difficulty: Medium

Getting to the Answer: In paragraph 3, we see that human corneas refract light badly in water, while the seal's corneas perform well.

SCIENCE TEST

PASSAGE I

1. B

Category: Figure Interpretation

Difficulty: Medium

Getting to the Answer: To answer this question, you have to examine the third column of the table, transmittance range. For a material to transmit light at a wavelength of 25 μm, its transmittance range—the range of wavelengths over which the material is transparent—must include 25 μm. Only potassium bromide (0.3–29 μm) and cesium iodide (0.3–70 μm) have transmittance ranges that include 25 μm, so (B) is correct.

2. F

Category: Figure Interpretation

Difficulty: Medium

Getting to the Answer: The material that contradicts this hypothesis is going to have poor chemical resistance but a transmittance range less than 10 μm. Lithium fluoride, (F), fits the bill: Its chemical resistance is poor, and its transmittance range is less than 6 μm wide. Choices G and J are wrong because both flint glass and quartz have excellent chemical resistance. Choice H is out because cesium iodide has a transmittance range nearly 70 μm wide.

3. D

Category: Scientific Reasoning

Difficulty: High

Getting to the Answer: The correct answer is a pair of materials in which the refractive index of the first material is greater than that of the second. In A, B, and C, the refractive index of the first material is less than that of the second. In (D), however, flint glass has a refractive index of 1.66 while calcium fluoride's refractive index is only 1.43. That makes (D) the correct answer.

4. J

Category: Scientific Reasoning

Difficulty: Medium

Getting to the Answer: The easiest way to answer this question is to use the first couple materials and test each hypothesis on them. Choices F and G are incorrect because the transmittance range of lithium fluoride is wider than its useful prism range. Comparing the data on lithium fluoride and calcium fluoride rules out H because transmittance range does NOT increase as useful prism range decreases. In fact, looking down the rest of the table, you see that transmittance range seems to decrease as useful prism range decreases. Choice (J) is the only one left, and the data on lithium fluoride and calcium fluoride as well as all the other materials confirm that the transmittance range is always wider than, and includes within it, the useful prism range.

5. B

Category: Figure Interpretation

Difficulty: Medium

Getting to the Answer: According to the footnote to the table, quartz infused with lead oxide is flint glass. Comparison of the properties of pure quartz

and flint glass shows that the transmittance range of flint glass is narrower than that of quartz but its refractive index is greater. This supports (B).

6. G

Category: Scientific Reasoning

Difficulty: Medium

Getting to the Answer: Begin this question by looking at the answer choices and finding the transmittance range and useful range for prisms for lithium fluoride, sodium chloride, quartz, and flint glass. A quick glance at the chart shows that the ranges for lithium flouride (for transmittance and prisms, respectively) are slightly below 6 and 2. Sodium chloride shows ranges of just under 17 and 8. Quartz has ranges of less than 3 and 2, while flint glass has ranges of less than 2 for both categories. Therefore, sodium chloride, (G), is the correct answer.

PASSAGE II

7. D

Category: Scientific Reasoning

Difficulty: High

Getting to the Answer: Begin by looking at the equation in the question. Given that osmotic pressure is already isolated on one side, using some basic rules of math will make this question go much faster. R is a constant and therefore does not factor into the answer choices. Because temperature and osmotic pressure increase together, you can eliminate roman numeral I as well as A. Statement II describes what happens to Π when M and T are inversely related. The statement says that as one goes up and the other goes down, Π remains constant. That is true: Because both M and T are on the same side of the equation, the only way to keep Π constant and still vary M and T is to have an inverse relationship between the latter two variables. Statement II is correct, so you can eliminate C. For statement III, you can look at the equation and recognize that because M, R, and T are all multiplied together,

Π must increase if even one of those increases. Because statement III is also true, (D) is correct.

8. H
Category: Scientific Reasoning
Difficulty: Medium
Getting to the Answer: Use the results of both experiments to answer this question. The answer choices all involve temperature, concentration, and solvent in different combinations. To determine whether osmotic pressure is dependent upon a variable, look for a pair of trials in which all conditions except for that variable are identical. In doing so, you see that temperature and concentration affect osmotic pressure, but solvent does not.

9. C
Category: Figure Interpretation
Difficulty: High
Getting to the Answer: Find methanol at 0.5 mol/L, which is in Table 2. The text above the table states that all the trials were conducted under the same temperature (298 K). Therefore, simply look across the row that you identified. The osmotic pressure is 12.23, (C).

10. G
Category: Scientific Reasoning
Difficulty: High
Getting to the Answer: To figure out whether or not the sucrose solution will diffuse across the membrane under the conditions described in the question, go back to the definition of osmotic pressure given in the introduction. Once the external pressure reaches the osmotic pressure, osmosis will not occur. In order for osmosis to occur, the external pressure must be less than the osmotic pressure of the solution. The solution in this question is a 0.1 mol/L aqueous sucrose solution at 298 K; those conditions correspond to an osmotic pressure of 2.45 atm. Because the external pressure is 1 atm, which is less than the osmotic pressure, osmosis will occur. From the definition of osmosis in the passage, it is

clear that the solution will diffuse from the side of the membrane with a lower concentration of dissolved material, in this case pure water, to the side with a higher concentration, in this case sucrose solution. Choice (G) is correct.

11. C
Category: Figure Interpretation
Difficulty: Medium
Getting to the Answer: To determine what the scientists investigated in Experiment 1, look at what they varied and what they measured. In Experiment 1, the scientists varied the concentration and the temperature of sucrose solutions, and they measured the osmotic pressure. Therefore, they were investigating the effect of concentration and temperature on osmotic pressure, (C). Watch out for A: It states what was investigated in Experiment 2, not Experiment 1.

12. F
Category: Patterns
Difficulty: Low
Getting to the Answer: The results in Table 2 indicate that osmotic pressure doesn't depend on the solvent, as discussed in the explanation to question 6. So Statement I is a valid conclusion, and G can be eliminated. Statement II is false. The results in Table 1 indicate that osmotic pressure is dependent on concentration as well as temperature. So H can be ruled out. Now consider Statement III. It is not a valid conclusion because osmotic pressure is the pressure required to prevent osmosis, so osmosis occurs only if the external pressure is less than the osmotic pressure.

13. D
Category: Scientific Reasoning
Difficulty: Medium
Getting to the Answer: To answer questions that ask about the design of an experiment, look at what the scientists are trying to measure. You're told that osmotic pressure is the pressure required to prevent osmosis. In order to measure the osmotic pressure

of a solution, scientists need to be able to tell when osmosis begins. If you have two clear solutions with sucrose dissolved in one of them, how can you tell when there's any movement of solvent between the two of them? If the sucrose is dyed, the blue solution will become paler when osmosis starts, i.e., when solvent moves across the membrane to create an equilibrium. Therefore, (D) is correct.

PASSAGE III

14. F
Category: Figure Interpretation
Difficulty: Low
Getting to the Answer: The question refers to Experiment 3, so look at Table 3. You see that when the temperature is 85 during the day and 85 at night, the leaves have the smallest measurements. Choice (F) is correct.

15. A
Category: Scientific Reasoning
Difficulty: Low
Getting to the Answer: The question refers to Experiment 2 only, so the correct answer will involve sunlight. Table 2 shows that the average length of the leaves increased from 5.3 cm to 12.4 cm as the amount of sunlight increased from 0 to 3 hours per day. But as the amount of sunlight increased further, leaf size decreased. Therefore, D is incorrect. Neither humidity, B, nor water, C, is relevant to Experiment 2.

16. G
Category: Figure Interpretation
Difficulty: Low
Getting to the Answer: Table 1 gives leaf widths at 35% and 55% humidity at 1.8 cm and 2.0 cm, respectively. The leaf width at 40% humidity would most likely be between those two figures. Choice (G) is the only choice within that range.

17. B
Category: Scientific Reasoning
Difficulty: Medium
Getting to the Answer: All the answer choices involve humidity and sunlight, which were investigated in Experiments 1 and 2, respectively. In Table 1, leaf length and width were greatest at 75% humidity. In Table 2, they were greatest at three hours per day of sunlight. Combining those two conditions, as in (B), would probably produce the largest leaves.

18. F
Category: Scientific Reasoning
Difficulty: Medium
Getting to the Answer: This question relates to the method of the study. Each experiment begins with a statement that five groups of seedlings were used. Therefore, (F) is correct. The other choices list variables that were manipulated.

19. D
Category: Scientific Reasoning
Difficulty: High
Getting to the Answer: Choice (D) is an assumption that underlies the design of all three experiments. If the seedlings were not equally capable of further growth, then changes in leaf size and density could not be reliably attributed to researcher-controlled changes in humidity, sunlight, and temperature. Choice A is incorrect because all the seedlings were 2–3 cm tall. The seedlings' abilities to germinate, B, or to produce flowers, C, were not mentioned in the passage.

20. H
Category: Scientific Reasoning
Difficulty: Medium
Getting to the Answer: Each of the three experiments investigated a different factor related to leaf growth. To produce the most useful new data, researchers would probably vary a fourth condition. Soil mineral content would be an appropriate factor to examine. None of the other choices relate directly

to the purpose of the experiments as expressed in paragraph 1 of the passage.

PASSAGE IV

21. B
Category: Figure Interpretation
Difficulty: Medium
Getting to the Answer: According to the table, decreasing the cross-sectional area of a given wire always increases resistance, so (B) is correct. Choice C is incorrect because resistivity, displayed in the second column, is constant for each material and thus cannot be responsible for variations in resistance for any given material. Gauge varies inversely with cross-sectional area, so D is incorrect.

22. G
Category: Patterns
Difficulty: High
Getting to the Answer: Because resistance varies inversely with cross-sectional area A, as discussed in the previous explanation, the correct answer to this question must place A in the denominator. The only choice that does so is (G).

23. D
Category: Patterns
Difficulty: Medium
Getting to the Answer: Compare the choices two at a time. The wires in A and B are made of the same material and have the same cross-sectional area; only their length is different. Doubling the length doubles the resistance, so B would have a higher resistance than A. By similar reasoning, (D) would have a higher resistance than C. The only difference between B and (D) is the material. Even though the research team didn't test wire with a 0.33 mm^2 cross-sectional area, Table 1 shows that tungsten wire has higher levels of resistance than aluminum wire across all factors.

24. J
Category: Scientific Reasoning
Difficulty: Medium
Getting to the Answer: The larger circle represents 10-gauge wire; its diameter is 2.59 mm. The smaller circle has a diameter of only 1.29 mm, but it represents 16-gauge wire, so Statement I is true, and you can eliminate G and H without even checking Statements II or III. To check Statement III, the table shows that the resistance of an iron (Fe) wire is much higher than that of an aluminum (Al) wire with the same length and cross-sectional area. The first sentence of paragraph 1 defined the resistance of a conductor as "the extent to which it opposes the flow of electricity." Because iron has a higher resistance than aluminum, iron must not conduct electricity as well. Therefore, Statement III is true, and (J) is correct.

25. D
Category: Patterns
Difficulty: Medium
Getting to the Answer: The data indicate that the resistivity of a material doesn't change when wire length changes. Therefore, the graph of resistivity versus length for tungsten (or any other) wire is a horizontal line.

26. J
Category: Patterns
Difficulty: Medium
Getting to the Answer: Refer to Table 1 to see the effect that wire length has on resistance. Regardless of wire gauge, resistance increases for each material when length is increased. Choice (J) is correct.

PASSAGE V

27. A
Category: Scientific Reasoning
Difficulty: Medium
Getting to the Answer: To answer this question, you have to refer to the examples presented by the scientists to find a point of agreement. Both use the

example of giraffes to show how scarcity of food and the need to reach higher and higher branches led to the evolution of long necks; thus, they both agree that environment affects evolution.

28. H
Category: Scientific Reasoning
Difficulty: Medium
Getting to the Answer: This Principle question requires that you figure out how new evidence affects the two hypotheses. To answer it, all you have to consider are the hypotheses of the two scientists. Scientist 2 believes that characteristics acquired by an individual over a lifetime are passed on to its offspring, a theory that would be supported by this finding.

29. D
Category: Scientific Reasoning
Difficulty: Low
Getting to the Answer: This question requires some reasoning. Scientist 2 states that all of the changes that occur in an individual's life can be passed on to offspring. Because he believes that any characteristic can undergo change, he must also believe that any characteristic can be inherited.

30. G
Category: Scientific Reasoning
Difficulty: Medium
Getting to the Answer: You don't need any information other than the hypothesis of Scientist 1 to answer this question. He believes that random mutations continually occur within a species as it propagates and that advantageous mutations, such as long necks on giraffes, help the species adapt to environmental changes and thus become more prevalent within the species. This is what (G) states.

31. B
Category: Scientific Reasoning
Difficulty: Low
Getting to the Answer: Here, you don't need any information other than the hypotheses of the two

scientists. The crux of their disagreement is over how evolution occurs—whether through random mutations or through the inheritance of acquired characteristics.

32. G
Category: Scientific Reasoning
Difficulty: High
Getting to the Answer: Recall that Scientist 2 states that evolution occurs through the inheritance of acquired characteristics. In order to account for humans possessing nerve endings now that were not present before the discovery of fire, Scientist 2 would have to believe that new nerve endings could be acquired during a single lifetime. Choice (G) directly contradicts this idea and would therefore refute the hypothesis.

33. A
Category: Scientific Reasoning
Difficulty: Medium
Getting to the Answer: Recall that Scientist 1 explains that evolution occurs as a result of random mutation, while Scientist 2 credits the inheritance of acquired characteristics. Choice B can then be eliminated, because it is related to the explanation of the wrong scientist. Choice C would actually refute Scientist 1's hypothesis, and D is irrelevant. Only (A) provides a valid explanation for the increase in average height based on the random mutations described by Scientist 1.

PASSAGE VII

34. G
Category: Figure Interpretation
Difficulty: Low
Getting to the Answer: According to Figure 1, Group B had the greatest number of cows infected with BSE. Group B was fed meat from scrapie-infected sheep, which matches (G).

35. D

Category: Figure Interpretation

Difficulty: Medium

Getting to the Answer: In Experiment 1, the researchers vary what is fed to the cows by giving them meat from scrapie-free sheep and from scrapie-infected sheep. The cows are later examined for signs of BSE. One common type of incorrect answer choice for Experiment questions are choices, such as B for this question, that include factors that are outside the parameters of the experiment.

36. F

Category: Figure Interpretation

Difficulty: Medium

Getting to the Answer: In Experiment 2, the researchers vary what is injected into cows' brains. Any answer choice that discusses ingestion as a focus of this experiment is incorrect. This eliminates G, H, and J. Often, incorrect answer choices for Experiment questions, such as G for this question, will include the appropriate information from the wrong experiment.

37. B

Category: Scientific Reasoning

Difficulty: Medium

Getting to the Answer: By examining the method used in a given experiment, one can determine the assumptions the researchers made in carrying out the experiment and the sources of error. Often, an error enters the experiment because of the assumptions researchers make. In Experiments 1 and 2, the researchers examined the brains of cows a year and a half after the cows were fed scrapie-infected sheep meat or were injected with scrapie-infected sheep brains. If a year and a half is not a sufficient amount of time for BSE to develop, some of the cows that were counted as not infected might have developed BSE if they had been given more time.

38. H

Category: Scientific Reasoning

Difficulty: Low

Getting to the Answer: To answer this question, you need to determine how to test whether BSE can be transmitted via scrapie-infected goats. To test this, one would compare the effects of feeding cows scrapie-free goat meat with the effects of feeding cows scrapie-infected goat meat and compare the effects of injecting cows with scrapie-free goat brains with the effects of injecting them with scrapie-infected goat brains.

39. A

Category: Scientific Reasoning

Difficulty: Medium

Getting to the Answer: Remember that control groups are used as standards of comparison. The control group used in Experiment 1 is the group that is fed scrapie-free sheep meat. If the same proportion of Group A developed BSE as that of Group B, then the researchers would not have any evidence to support the hypothesis that the ingestion of scrapie-infected sheep meat causes BSE.

40. G

Category: Scientific Reasoning

Difficulty: High

Getting to the Answer: Because the proportion of the group of cows that ate scrapie-infected sheep meat and developed BSE was greater than the proportion of the group that were injected with scrapie-infected sheep brains and developed BSE, one can conclude that a cow that eats scrapie-infected sheep meat is more likely to develop BSE than a cow that is injected with scrapie-infected sheep brains. Mere exposure to scrapie-infected sheep, as opposed to ingestion of it, is never studied in either experiment, so conclusion I can be eliminated.

WRITING TEST

MODEL ESSAY

Below is an example of what a high-scoring essay might look like. Notice that the author states her position clearly in the introductory paragraph and supports that position with evidence in the following paragraphs. This essay also uses transitions, some advanced vocabulary, and an effective "hook" to draw in the reader.

Children are often asked, "What do you want to be when you grow up?" Little do they know, whether or not they go to college has a huge impact on their career choices. The issue under discussion is whether or not schools should develop dual curricula to serve both those students who are college bound and those who intend to forego college, instead entering a career directly after high school graduation. The fundamental concern is how to best serve all students, which I believe should be through two curricula working together.

The first point of view supports having all students pursue the same curriculum, one primarily directed at college-bound students. It essentially states that an academic-only curriculum is valuable for all students, regardless of their future plans. It is true that the ability to think critically, have a wide range of content knowledge, and be adept at the skills and techniques required to live a full and productive life are important to all students. A well-rounded person is able to take advantage of many more opportunities than those with limited skills. Furthermore, should a career-bound student change his mind and decide to go to college, he will have the basic requirements for a successful college experience. However, if a student is determined to start his career directly after high school, the college curriculum could be a waste of his time, and he would be better served by taking courses that prepare him for his career. I am in partial agreement with option one, since a broad, basic education is important for all students. However, it is similarly important to prepare students for their future lives, which may begin immediately after high school.

The second option supports career-readiness education. As stated above, it is important to recognize that some students are set on a embarking on a career after high school rather than on going to college. High school is the place to prepare these students, since it can offer the courses that are most applicable to them. Furthermore, students in danger of dropping out of high school are generally those who are uninterested in or bored by the academic curriculum. Such students would be more engaged and successful if they were able to take classes that fit their goals and interests, and they would be more likely not only to stay in school but also to be well-prepared for their careers. This option purposes a dual curriculum, one for the college bound and one for career readiness, and thus provides the best education for both. On the assumption that non-college-bound students are also taking an adequate number of general education classes, and supplementing them with courses designed to provide them with the skills they need for their careers, these students will now have a solid academic foundation as well as career skills. College-bound students will still have the option to take more academic classes. Thus, I support this option because it provides the best solution for both groups.

Those who agree that students who are not planning on going to college should not be offered career-centered classes are denying the fact that not all students go to college, even if given incentives to do so.

This option does not take into consideration the numerous facts that can affect whether or not a student goes to college. Some students cannot afford college fees, even with scholarships; some have a low GPA that would prohibit their acceptance at college; and some do poorly on pre-college tests such as the ACT. Encouraging students to go to college is not enough to ensure that they will. Though it may be true that college teaches how to be productive in the workforce, it is also true that being a fully qualified mechanic or electrician after high school is extremely productive for those who choose these careers. This option is an elitist one that would disregard those for whom college is not a goal, and it is one with which I completely disagree.

It is vital to all students that high schools prepare them for their future, whatever that may be. Those who choose college are well-served by an intensive academic curriculum that gives them a solid foundation for college. On the other hand, for those who choose, or are forced by circumstances, to forego college in favor of immediate entry into the workforce, it is important that, along with a sufficient academic foundation, they also receive training in their intended careers. Thus the second perspective, that of providing both an academic and a career-oriented curriculum, serves the needs of both and is the most effective one for all students.

You can evaluate your essay and the model essay based on the following criteria, which is covered in the Practice Makes Perfect section of this book:

- Does the author discuss all three perspectives provided in the prompt?

- Is the author's own perspective clearly stated?

- Does the body of the essay assess and analyze each perspective?

- Is the relevance of each paragraph clear?

- Does the author start a new paragraph for each new idea?

- Is each sentence in a paragraph relevant to the point made in that paragraph?

- Are transitions clear?

- Is the essay easy to read? Is it engaging?

- Are sentences varied?

- Is vocabulary used effectively? Is college-level vocabulary used?

ACT Practice Test Two
ANSWER SHEET

ENGLISH TEST

1. Ⓐ Ⓑ Ⓒ Ⓓ   11. Ⓐ Ⓑ Ⓒ Ⓓ   21. Ⓐ Ⓑ Ⓒ Ⓓ   31. Ⓐ Ⓑ Ⓒ Ⓓ   41. Ⓐ Ⓑ Ⓒ Ⓓ   51. Ⓐ Ⓑ Ⓒ Ⓓ   61. Ⓐ Ⓑ Ⓒ Ⓓ   71. Ⓐ Ⓑ Ⓒ Ⓓ
2. Ⓕ Ⓖ Ⓗ Ⓙ   12. Ⓕ Ⓖ Ⓗ Ⓙ   22. Ⓕ Ⓖ Ⓗ Ⓙ   32. Ⓕ Ⓖ Ⓗ Ⓙ   42. Ⓕ Ⓖ Ⓗ Ⓙ   52. Ⓕ Ⓖ Ⓗ Ⓙ   62. Ⓕ Ⓖ Ⓗ Ⓙ   72. Ⓕ Ⓖ Ⓗ Ⓙ
3. Ⓐ Ⓑ Ⓒ Ⓓ   13. Ⓐ Ⓑ Ⓒ Ⓓ   23. Ⓐ Ⓑ Ⓒ Ⓓ   33. Ⓐ Ⓑ Ⓒ Ⓓ   43. Ⓐ Ⓑ Ⓒ Ⓓ   53. Ⓐ Ⓑ Ⓒ Ⓓ   63. Ⓐ Ⓑ Ⓒ Ⓓ   73. Ⓐ Ⓑ Ⓒ Ⓓ
4. Ⓕ Ⓖ Ⓗ Ⓙ   14. Ⓕ Ⓖ Ⓗ Ⓙ   24. Ⓕ Ⓖ Ⓗ Ⓙ   34. Ⓕ Ⓖ Ⓗ Ⓙ   44. Ⓕ Ⓖ Ⓗ Ⓙ   54. Ⓕ Ⓖ Ⓗ Ⓙ   64. Ⓕ Ⓖ Ⓗ Ⓙ   74. Ⓕ Ⓖ Ⓗ Ⓙ
5. Ⓐ Ⓑ Ⓒ Ⓓ   15. Ⓐ Ⓑ Ⓒ Ⓓ   25. Ⓐ Ⓑ Ⓒ Ⓓ   35. Ⓐ Ⓑ Ⓒ Ⓓ   45. Ⓐ Ⓑ Ⓒ Ⓓ   55. Ⓐ Ⓑ Ⓒ Ⓓ   65. Ⓐ Ⓑ Ⓒ Ⓓ   75. Ⓐ Ⓑ Ⓒ Ⓓ
6. Ⓕ Ⓖ Ⓗ Ⓙ   16. Ⓕ Ⓖ Ⓗ Ⓙ   26. Ⓕ Ⓖ Ⓗ Ⓙ   36. Ⓕ Ⓖ Ⓗ Ⓙ   46. Ⓕ Ⓖ Ⓗ Ⓙ   56. Ⓕ Ⓖ Ⓗ Ⓙ   66. Ⓕ Ⓖ Ⓗ Ⓙ
7. Ⓐ Ⓑ Ⓒ Ⓓ   17. Ⓐ Ⓑ Ⓒ Ⓓ   27. Ⓐ Ⓑ Ⓒ Ⓓ   37. Ⓐ Ⓑ Ⓒ Ⓓ   47. Ⓐ Ⓑ Ⓒ Ⓓ   57. Ⓐ Ⓑ Ⓒ Ⓓ   67. Ⓐ Ⓑ Ⓒ Ⓓ
8. Ⓕ Ⓖ Ⓗ Ⓙ   18. Ⓕ Ⓖ Ⓗ Ⓙ   28. Ⓕ Ⓖ Ⓗ Ⓙ   38. Ⓕ Ⓖ Ⓗ Ⓙ   48. Ⓕ Ⓖ Ⓗ Ⓙ   58. Ⓕ Ⓖ Ⓗ Ⓙ   68. Ⓕ Ⓖ Ⓗ Ⓙ
9. Ⓐ Ⓑ Ⓒ Ⓓ   19. Ⓐ Ⓑ Ⓒ Ⓓ   29. Ⓐ Ⓑ Ⓒ Ⓓ   39. Ⓐ Ⓑ Ⓒ Ⓓ   49. Ⓐ Ⓑ Ⓒ Ⓓ   59. Ⓐ Ⓑ Ⓒ Ⓓ   69. Ⓐ Ⓑ Ⓒ Ⓓ
10. Ⓕ Ⓖ Ⓗ Ⓙ   20. Ⓕ Ⓖ Ⓗ Ⓙ   30. Ⓕ Ⓖ Ⓗ Ⓙ   40. Ⓕ Ⓖ Ⓗ Ⓙ   50. Ⓕ Ⓖ Ⓗ Ⓙ   60. Ⓕ Ⓖ Ⓗ Ⓙ   70. Ⓕ Ⓖ Ⓗ Ⓙ

MATHEMATICS TEST

1. Ⓐ Ⓑ Ⓒ Ⓓ Ⓔ   11. Ⓐ Ⓑ Ⓒ Ⓓ Ⓔ   21. Ⓐ Ⓑ Ⓒ Ⓓ Ⓔ   31. Ⓐ Ⓑ Ⓒ Ⓓ Ⓔ   41. Ⓐ Ⓑ Ⓒ Ⓓ Ⓔ   51. Ⓐ Ⓑ Ⓒ Ⓓ Ⓔ
2. Ⓐ Ⓑ Ⓒ Ⓓ Ⓔ   12. Ⓕ Ⓖ Ⓗ Ⓙ Ⓚ   22. Ⓕ Ⓖ Ⓗ Ⓙ Ⓚ   32. Ⓕ Ⓖ Ⓗ Ⓙ Ⓚ   42. Ⓕ Ⓖ Ⓗ Ⓙ Ⓚ   52. Ⓕ Ⓖ Ⓗ Ⓙ Ⓚ
3. Ⓐ Ⓑ Ⓒ Ⓓ Ⓔ   13. Ⓐ Ⓑ Ⓒ Ⓓ Ⓔ   23. Ⓐ Ⓑ Ⓒ Ⓓ Ⓔ   33. Ⓐ Ⓑ Ⓒ Ⓓ Ⓔ   43. Ⓐ Ⓑ Ⓒ Ⓓ Ⓔ   53. Ⓐ Ⓑ Ⓒ Ⓓ Ⓔ
4. Ⓕ Ⓖ Ⓗ Ⓙ Ⓚ   14. Ⓕ Ⓖ Ⓗ Ⓙ Ⓚ   24. Ⓕ Ⓖ Ⓗ Ⓙ Ⓚ   34. Ⓕ Ⓖ Ⓗ Ⓙ Ⓚ   44. Ⓕ Ⓖ Ⓗ Ⓙ Ⓚ   54. Ⓕ Ⓖ Ⓗ Ⓙ Ⓚ
5. Ⓐ Ⓑ Ⓒ Ⓓ Ⓔ   15. Ⓐ Ⓑ Ⓒ Ⓓ Ⓔ   25. Ⓐ Ⓑ Ⓒ Ⓓ Ⓔ   35. Ⓐ Ⓑ Ⓒ Ⓓ Ⓔ   45. Ⓐ Ⓑ Ⓒ Ⓓ Ⓔ   55. Ⓐ Ⓑ Ⓒ Ⓓ Ⓔ
6. Ⓕ Ⓖ Ⓗ Ⓙ Ⓚ   16. Ⓕ Ⓖ Ⓗ Ⓙ Ⓚ   26. Ⓕ Ⓖ Ⓗ Ⓙ Ⓚ   36. Ⓕ Ⓖ Ⓗ Ⓙ Ⓚ   46. Ⓕ Ⓖ Ⓗ Ⓙ Ⓚ   56. Ⓕ Ⓖ Ⓗ Ⓙ Ⓚ
7. Ⓐ Ⓑ Ⓒ Ⓓ Ⓔ   17. Ⓐ Ⓑ Ⓒ Ⓓ Ⓔ   27. Ⓐ Ⓑ Ⓒ Ⓓ Ⓔ   37. Ⓐ Ⓑ Ⓒ Ⓓ Ⓔ   47. Ⓐ Ⓑ Ⓒ Ⓓ Ⓔ   57. Ⓐ Ⓑ Ⓒ Ⓓ Ⓔ
8. Ⓕ Ⓖ Ⓗ Ⓙ Ⓚ   18. Ⓕ Ⓖ Ⓗ Ⓙ Ⓚ   28. Ⓕ Ⓖ Ⓗ Ⓙ Ⓚ   38. Ⓕ Ⓖ Ⓗ Ⓙ Ⓚ   48. Ⓕ Ⓖ Ⓗ Ⓙ Ⓚ   58. Ⓕ Ⓖ Ⓗ Ⓙ Ⓚ
9. Ⓐ Ⓑ Ⓒ Ⓓ Ⓔ   19. Ⓐ Ⓑ Ⓒ Ⓓ Ⓔ   29. Ⓐ Ⓑ Ⓒ Ⓓ Ⓔ   39. Ⓐ Ⓑ Ⓒ Ⓓ Ⓔ   49. Ⓐ Ⓑ Ⓒ Ⓓ Ⓔ   59. Ⓐ Ⓑ Ⓒ Ⓓ Ⓔ
10. Ⓕ Ⓖ Ⓗ Ⓙ Ⓚ   20. Ⓕ Ⓖ Ⓗ Ⓙ Ⓚ   30. Ⓕ Ⓖ Ⓗ Ⓙ Ⓚ   40. Ⓕ Ⓖ Ⓗ Ⓙ Ⓚ   50. Ⓕ Ⓖ Ⓗ Ⓙ Ⓚ   60. Ⓕ Ⓖ Ⓗ Ⓙ Ⓚ

READING TEST

1. Ⓐ Ⓑ Ⓒ Ⓓ   6. Ⓕ Ⓖ Ⓗ Ⓙ   11. Ⓐ Ⓑ Ⓒ Ⓓ   16. Ⓕ Ⓖ Ⓗ Ⓙ   21. Ⓐ Ⓑ Ⓒ Ⓓ   26. Ⓕ Ⓖ Ⓗ Ⓙ   31. Ⓐ Ⓑ Ⓒ Ⓓ   36. Ⓕ Ⓖ Ⓗ Ⓙ
2. Ⓕ Ⓖ Ⓗ Ⓙ   7. Ⓐ Ⓑ Ⓒ Ⓓ   12. Ⓕ Ⓖ Ⓗ Ⓙ   17. Ⓐ Ⓑ Ⓒ Ⓓ   22. Ⓕ Ⓖ Ⓗ Ⓙ   27. Ⓐ Ⓑ Ⓒ Ⓓ   32. Ⓕ Ⓖ Ⓗ Ⓙ   37. Ⓐ Ⓑ Ⓒ Ⓓ
3. Ⓐ Ⓑ Ⓒ Ⓓ   8. Ⓕ Ⓖ Ⓗ Ⓙ   13. Ⓐ Ⓑ Ⓒ Ⓓ   18. Ⓕ Ⓖ Ⓗ Ⓙ   23. Ⓐ Ⓑ Ⓒ Ⓓ   28. Ⓕ Ⓖ Ⓗ Ⓙ   33. Ⓐ Ⓑ Ⓒ Ⓓ   38. Ⓕ Ⓖ Ⓗ Ⓙ
4. Ⓕ Ⓖ Ⓗ Ⓙ   9. Ⓐ Ⓑ Ⓒ Ⓓ   14. Ⓕ Ⓖ Ⓗ Ⓙ   19. Ⓐ Ⓑ Ⓒ Ⓓ   24. Ⓕ Ⓖ Ⓗ Ⓙ   29. Ⓐ Ⓑ Ⓒ Ⓓ   34. Ⓕ Ⓖ Ⓗ Ⓙ   39. Ⓐ Ⓑ Ⓒ Ⓓ
5. Ⓐ Ⓑ Ⓒ Ⓓ   10. Ⓕ Ⓖ Ⓗ Ⓙ   15. Ⓐ Ⓑ Ⓒ Ⓓ   20. Ⓕ Ⓖ Ⓗ Ⓙ   25. Ⓐ Ⓑ Ⓒ Ⓓ   30. Ⓕ Ⓖ Ⓗ Ⓙ   35. Ⓐ Ⓑ Ⓒ Ⓓ   40. Ⓕ Ⓖ Ⓗ Ⓙ

SCIENCE TEST

1. Ⓐ Ⓑ Ⓒ Ⓓ   6. Ⓕ Ⓖ Ⓗ Ⓙ   11. Ⓐ Ⓑ Ⓒ Ⓓ   16. Ⓕ Ⓖ Ⓗ Ⓙ   21. Ⓐ Ⓑ Ⓒ Ⓓ   26. Ⓕ Ⓖ Ⓗ Ⓙ   31. Ⓐ Ⓑ Ⓒ Ⓓ   36. Ⓕ Ⓖ Ⓗ Ⓙ
2. Ⓕ Ⓖ Ⓗ Ⓙ   7. Ⓐ Ⓑ Ⓒ Ⓓ   12. Ⓕ Ⓖ Ⓗ Ⓙ   17. Ⓐ Ⓑ Ⓒ Ⓓ   22. Ⓕ Ⓖ Ⓗ Ⓙ   27. Ⓐ Ⓑ Ⓒ Ⓓ   32. Ⓕ Ⓖ Ⓗ Ⓙ   37. Ⓐ Ⓑ Ⓒ Ⓓ
3. Ⓐ Ⓑ Ⓒ Ⓓ   8. Ⓕ Ⓖ Ⓗ Ⓙ   13. Ⓐ Ⓑ Ⓒ Ⓓ   18. Ⓕ Ⓖ Ⓗ Ⓙ   23. Ⓐ Ⓑ Ⓒ Ⓓ   28. Ⓕ Ⓖ Ⓗ Ⓙ   33. Ⓐ Ⓑ Ⓒ Ⓓ   38. Ⓕ Ⓖ Ⓗ Ⓙ
4. Ⓕ Ⓖ Ⓗ Ⓙ   9. Ⓐ Ⓑ Ⓒ Ⓓ   14. Ⓕ Ⓖ Ⓗ Ⓙ   19. Ⓐ Ⓑ Ⓒ Ⓓ   24. Ⓕ Ⓖ Ⓗ Ⓙ   29. Ⓐ Ⓑ Ⓒ Ⓓ   34. Ⓕ Ⓖ Ⓗ Ⓙ   39. Ⓐ Ⓑ Ⓒ Ⓓ
5. Ⓐ Ⓑ Ⓒ Ⓓ   10. Ⓕ Ⓖ Ⓗ Ⓙ   15. Ⓐ Ⓑ Ⓒ Ⓓ   20. Ⓕ Ⓖ Ⓗ Ⓙ   25. Ⓐ Ⓑ Ⓒ Ⓓ   30. Ⓕ Ⓖ Ⓗ Ⓙ   35. Ⓐ Ⓑ Ⓒ Ⓓ   40. Ⓕ Ⓖ Ⓗ Ⓙ

ENGLISH TEST

45 Minutes—75 Questions

Directions: In the following five passages, certain words and phrases are underlined and numbered. In the right-hand column are alternatives for each underlined portion. Select the one that best conveys the idea, creates the most grammatically correct sentence, or is the most consistent with the style and tone of the passage. If you decide that the original version is best, select NO CHANGE. You may also find questions that ask about the entire passage or a section of the passage. These questions will correspond to small numbered boxes in the text. For these questions, decide which choice best accomplishes the purpose set out in the question stem. After you've selected the best choice, fill in the corresponding oval in your Answer Grid. For some questions, you'll need to read the context in order to answer correctly. Be sure to read until you have enough information to determine the correct answer choice.

PASSAGE I

DUKE ELLINGTON, A JAZZ GREAT

[1]

By the time Duke Ellington published his autobiography, *Music is My Mistress,* in <u>1973 he had</u> traveled to
₁
dozens of countries and every continent. "I pay rent in New York City," he answered when asked of his residence.

1. **A.** NO CHANGE
   B. 1973. He had
   C. 1973, it had
   D. 1973, he had

[2]

  In the 1920s, though, Ellington <u>pays</u> more than rent
₂
in New York; he paid his dues on the bandstand. Having moved to Harlem from Washington, D.C., in 1923, Ellington

2. **F.** NO CHANGE
   G. paid
   H. has to pay
   J. pay

<u>established: his own</u> band and achieved critical
₃
recognition with a polished sound and appearance. The first New York review of the Ellingtonians in 1923 commented, "The boys look neat in dress suits and labor hard but not in vain at their music." As Ellington made

3. **A.** NO CHANGE
   B. established the following: his own
   C. established his own
   D. took the time and effort to establish his own

GO ON TO THE NEXT PAGE ⟶

a name for himself as a leader arranger and pianist,
4
his Harlem Renaissance compositions and recordings
highlighted two enduring characteristics of the man.
First, Ellington lived for jazz. Second, Harlem sustained
it, physically and spiritually.
5

[3]

Ellington himself admitted he was not a very

good pianist. As a teenager in Washington. He missed
6
more piano

lessons then he took with his teacher, Mrs. Clinkscales,
7
and spent more time going to dances than practicing the
the piano.

Mrs. Clinkscales was really the name of his piano
8
teacher! In the clubs,
8

therefore, Ellington and his friends eventually caught
9
word of New York and the opportunities

that awaited and were there for young musicians.
10
Ellington wrote, "Harlem, to our minds, did indeed have
the world's most glamorous atmosphere. We had to go
there."

4. **F.** NO CHANGE
   G. leader arranger, and pianist,
   H. leader, arranger, and pianist
   J. leader, arranger, and pianist,

5. **A.** NO CHANGE
   B. him,
   C. them,
   D. itself,

6. **F.** NO CHANGE
   G. good pianist as a teenager
   H. good pianist, a teenager
   J. good pianist, as a teenager

7. **A.** NO CHANGE
   B. lessons then he had taken
   C. lessons; he took
   D. lessons than he took

8. **F.** NO CHANGE
   G. That was really the name of his piano
      teacher: Mrs. Clinkscales!
   H. Mrs. Clinkscales was really the name of
      his piano teacher.
   J. OMIT the underlined portion.

9. **A.** NO CHANGE
   B. however
   C. despite
   D. then

10. **F.** NO CHANGE
    G. awaiting and being there for
    H. that awaited
    J. that were there for

GO ON TO THE NEXT PAGE ⟶

He left Washington with drummer Sonny Greer. Before
11
they could even unpack in Harlem, though, they found
themselves penniless. Not until Ellington was lucky
enough to find fifteen dollars on the street could he
return to Washington and recollect himself.

[4]

Ellington eventually did return to Harlem, and he
achieved great success as the bandleader at the Cotton
Club from 1927 to 1932. Located in the heart of Harlem at
142nd Street and Lenox Avenue, he played at the Cotton
                                        12
Club, which was frequented by top entertainers and rich
12
patrons. Harlem's nightlife, "cut out of a very luxurious,
royal-blue bolt of velvet," was an inspirational backdrop,
and Ellington composed, arranged, and recorded prolifi-
cally to the rave of excited critical acclaim. "Black and Tan
Fantasy," "Hot and Bothered," and "Rockin' in Rhythm"
were Ellington's early hits during this period.

[13] They exhibited his unique ability to compose music
that animated both dancers in search of a good time and
improvising musicians in search of good music.

11. **A.** NO CHANGE
    B. With drummer Sonny Greer, it was
       Washington that he left.
    C. Leaving Washington, he, Ellington, left
       with drummer Sonny Greer.
    D. OMIT the underlined portion.

12. **F.** NO CHANGE
    G. he played at the Cotton Club, a club
       that was frequented
    H. the Cotton Club, which was frequented
    J. the Cotton Club was frequented

13. The purpose of including the names of
    Ellington's songs is to:
    A. provide some details about Ellington's
       early music.
    B. contradict an earlier point that
       Ellington did not create his own music.
    C. illustrate the complexity of Ellington's
       music.
    D. discuss the atmosphere at the Cotton
       Club.

GO ON TO THE NEXT PAGE ⇨

Before long, the once fumbling pianist from Washington, D.C., became the undisputed leader of hot jazz in decadent Harlem. [14]

14. The purpose of paragraph 4, as it relates to the previous paragraphs, is primarily to:

F. demonstrate how accomplished Ellington had become.

G. suggest that Ellington did not like living in New York.

H. remind us how difficult it is to be a musician.

J. make us skeptical of Ellington's abilities.

Question 15 asks about the preceding passage as a whole.

15. The writer wishes to insert the following detail into the essay:

The combination of fun and seriousness in his music led to critical acclaim and wide mass appeal.

The sentence would most logically be inserted into paragraph:

A. 1, after the last sentence.

B. 3, before the first sentence.

C. 4, after the first sentence.

D. 4, before the last sentence.

GO ON TO THE NEXT PAGE

PASSAGE II

COLORING AS SELF-DEFENSE IN ANIMALS

The following paragraphs may or may not be in the most logical order. Each paragraph is numbered in brackets, and question 29 will ask you to choose the appropriate order.

[1]

Some animals change <u>its</u> coloring with the seasons. The
        16
ptarmigan sheds its brown plumage

<u>in winter, replacing</u> it with white feathers. The stoat,
        17
a member of the

<u>weasel family is known</u> as the *ermine* in winter because
        18
its brown fur changes to white. The chameleon is

perhaps the most versatile of all animals

<u>having changed</u> their protective coloration. The
        19
chameleon changes its color in just a few minutes to

whatever surface it happens to be sitting on.

[2]

    While animals like the chameleon <u>use their</u>
                                              20
<u>coloring</u> as a way of hiding from predators, the skunk
    20
uses its distinctive white stripe as a way of standing out

from its surroundings. Far from placing it in

16. **F.** NO CHANGE
    G. their
    H. it's
    J. there

17. **A.** NO CHANGE
    B. in winter and replacing
    C. in winter: replacing
    D. in winter replacing

18. **F.** NO CHANGE
    G. weasel family known
    H. weasel family, which is known
    J. weasel family, is known

19. **A.** NO CHANGE
    B. who changes
    C. that change
    D. that changed

20. **F.** NO CHANGE
    G. their use coloring
    H. use coloring their
    J. coloring their use

GO ON TO THE NEXT PAGE

danger; the skunk's visibility actually protects it. By
    21
distinguishing itself from other

animals. The skunk warns its predators to avoid its infa-
    22
mous stink. Think about it:

the question is would your appetite be whetted by the
                           23
skunk's odor?
  23

[3]

    Researchers have been investigating how animal
                        24
species have come to use coloring as a means of pro-

tecting themselves. One study has shown that certain

animals have glands that release special hormones,

resulting in the change of skin or fur color. Therefore,
                                25
not all the animals that camouflage themselves have

these glands.

The topic remains and endures as one of the many mys-
                    26
teries of the natural world.

21. **A.** NO CHANGE
    B. danger, the skunk's
    C. danger; the skunks'
    D. danger, it is the skunk's

22. **F.** NO CHANGE
    G. animals, therefore, the
    H. animals because
    J. animals, the

23. **A.** NO CHANGE
    B. would your appetite be whetted by the
skunk's odor?
    C. the question is as follows, would your
appetite be whetted by the skunk's
odor?
    D. the question is would your appetite be
whetted by the odor of the skunk?

24. **F.** NO CHANGE
    G. investigated
    H. were investigating
    J. investigate

25. **A.** NO CHANGE
    B. Nevertheless,
    C. However,
    D. Finally,

26. **F.** NO CHANGE
    G. remaining and enduring as
    H. remains and endures
    J. remains

GO ON TO THE NEXT PAGE ⟹

[4]

Animals have a variety of ways of protecting themselves from enemies. Some animals adapt in shape and color to their environment. The tree frog, for example, blends perfectly into its surroundings. When it sits motionless, <u>a background of leaves completely hides the tree frog.</u>
27

27

<u>This camouflage enables the tree frog to hide from other animals that would be interested in eating the tree frog.</u>
28

28

27. **A.** NO CHANGE
    B. the tree frog is completely hidden in a background of leaves.
    C. completely hidden is the tree frog in a background of leaves.
    D. a background of leaves and the tree frog are completely hidden.

28. **F.** NO CHANGE
    G. This camouflage enables the tree frog to hide from predators.
    H. This camouflage enables the tree frog to hide from other animals interested in eating the tree frog.
    J. OMIT the underlined portion.

Questions 29–30 ask about the preceding passage as a whole.

---

29. What would be the most logical order of paragraphs for this essay?
    A. 3, 1, 4, 2
    B. 1, 2, 4, 3
    C. 4, 1, 2, 3
    D. 2, 1, 3, 4

30. Suppose the author had been asked to write an essay on how animals use their coloring to protect themselves in the wild. Would this essay meet the requirement?
    F. Yes, because the author covers several aspects of how animals use their coloring to protect themselves.
    G. Yes, because the author thoroughly investigates how one animal protects itself with its coloring.
    H. No, because the author does not consider animals that exist in the wild.
    J. No, because the author does not include information from research studies.

GO ON TO THE NEXT PAGE ⟹

PASSAGE III

THE HISTORY OF CHOCOLATE

The word *chocolate* is used to describe a variety of

foods made from the beans of the cacao tree. The first
          31
people known to have made chocolate were the

Aztecs, a people who used cacao seeds to make a bit-
              32
ter but tasty drink. However, it was not until Hernan

Cortez's exploration of Mexico in

1519. That Europeans first learned of chocolate.
     33
     Cortez came to the New World in search of gold,

but his interest was also fired by the Aztecs' strange

drink. When Cortez returned to Spain, his ship's cargo

included and held three chests of cacao beans. It was
              34
from these beans that Europe experienced its first taste

of what

seemed to be a very unusual beverage. The drink soon
          35
became popular among those people wealthy enough to

afford it.

31. **A.** NO CHANGE
    B. foods, which are made
    C. foods and made
    D. foods and are

32. **F.** NO CHANGE
    G. Aztecs, and they used
    H. Aztecs a people that use
    J. Aztecs, who used

33. **A.** NO CHANGE
    B. 1519 that
    C. 1519, that
    D. 1519:

34. **F.** NO CHANGE
    G. included, held
    H. included
    J. including and holding

35. **A.** NO CHANGE
    B. seems to be
    C. seemingly is
    D. seemed being

GO ON TO THE NEXT PAGE

Over the next century cafes specializing in chocolate
                              36
drinks began to appear throughout Europe. 37

36. **F.** NO CHANGE
    G. Over the next century cafes specialize
    H. Over the next century, cafes specializing
    J. Over the next century, there were cafes specializing

37. The author is considering the addition of another sentence here that briefly describes one of the first European cafes to serve a chocolate drink. This addition would:
    A. weaken the author's argument.
    B. provide some interesting details.
    C. contradict the topic of the paragraph.
    D. highlight the author's opinion of chocolate.

Of course, chocolate is very popular today. People all over the world enjoy chocolate bars chocolate
                                                                  38
sprinkles and even chocolate soda.
          38

38. **F.** NO CHANGE
    G. chocolate, bars, chocolate, sprinkles, and even chocolate soda.
    H. chocolate bars chocolate sprinkles— even chocolate soda.
    J. chocolate bars, chocolate sprinkles, and even chocolate soda.

In fact, Asia has cultivated the delicacy of chocolate-
    39
covered ants! People enjoy this food as a snack at the movies or sporting events. The chocolate ant phenomenon has yet to take over America,

but enjoy their chocolate Americans do nonetheless.
          40

Many chocolate lovers around the world were ecstatic to hear that chocolate may actually be good for you. Researchers

39. **A.** NO CHANGE
    B. Unfortunately
    C. In spite of this
    D. The truth is

40. **F.** NO CHANGE
    G. but Americans enjoy their chocolate
    H. but enjoy their chocolate is what Americans do
    J. but Americans do enjoy their chocolate

GO ON TO THE NEXT PAGE ⟩

say: chocolate contains a chemical that could prevent
41
cancer and heart disease. New research measures the

amount of catechins, the chemical thought to be behind

the benefits, in different types of chocolate.

The substance is also found in tea. The studies show
42
that chocolate is very high in catechins. The research is

likely to be welcomed

by those with a sweet tooth, although dentists
43

may less be pleased.
44

41. **A.** NO CHANGE
    B. have said the following: chocolate contains
    C. say that chocolate contains
    D. say: chocolate contained

42. **F.** NO CHANGE
    G. Another place where the substance is found is tea.
    H. Also, tea contains the substance.
    J. OMIT the underlined portion.

43. **A.** NO CHANGE
    B. with them
    C. by us
    D. to those

44. **F.** NO CHANGE
    G. pleased less they will be.
    H. may be pleased less.
    J. may be less pleased.

Question 45 asks about the preceding passage as a whole.

---

45. Suppose the author had been given the assignment of writing about culinary trends in history. Would this essay satisfy the requirement?

    A. Yes, because the essay discusses many culinary trends in history.
    B. Yes, because the essay shows how chocolate has been used over time.
    C. No, because the essay focuses too much on chocolate in present times.
    D. No, because the essay only covers chocolate.

GO ON TO THE NEXT PAGE

PASSAGE IV

THE MILITARY UNIFORM OF THE FUTURE

[1]

Scientists, in programs <u>administers by</u> the United States
46
Army, are experimenting to develop the military uni-

form of the future. As imagined, it

<u>would be light as silk, bulletproof, and able to</u> rapidly
47
change at the molecular level to adapt to biological or

chemical threats. In response to a detected anthrax

threat, for example, it would become an impermeable

shield. The pant leg of a

<u>soldier who's</u> leg had been broken
48

<u>would have been</u> able to morph into a
49

<u>splint, or, even form</u> an artificial muscle. Nanosensors
50
would transmit vital signs back to a medical team or

monitor the breath for increased nitric oxide, a sign of

stress.

[2]

The especially promising Invisible Soldier program

aims to make the long-held dream of human invisibility

a reality by using

46. F. NO CHANGE
G. administering by
H. administered by
J. administers with

47. A. NO CHANGE
B. would: be light as silk, bulletproof, and able to
C. would be light as silk bulletproof and able to
D. light as silk, bulletproof, and was able to

48. F. NO CHANGE
G. soldier whose
H. soldier, who's
J. soldier that's

49. A. NO CHANGE
B. would be
C. will have been
D. is

50. F. NO CHANGE
G. splint or even form
H. splint, or even, form
J. splint or, even, form

GO ON TO THE NEXT PAGE

technology. To create a covering capable of
      51

concealing a soldier and making him invisible from
                        52
most wavelengths of visible light. 53 54

51. A. NO CHANGE
  B. technology to create
  C. technology, which were creating
  D. technology; create

52. F. NO CHANGE
  G. making a soldier invisible and concealing him
  H. concealing a soldier making that soldier invisible
  J. concealing a soldier

53. The writer's description of the U.S. Army's Invisible Soldier program seems to indicate that the army's opinion of the program is:
  A. skeptical.
  B. curious.
  C. enthusiastic.
  D. detailed.

54. What is the purpose of this paragraph, as it relates to the rest of the essay?
  F. To highlight one of the successes of the scientists' programs
  G. To predict the future of U.S. military uniforms
  H. To outline what will follow in the essay
  J. To introduce a specific example of the uniform of the future

[3]

A solution proposed in the early stages near the
                                            55
beginning of the program's development was to construct
      55
a suit or cape from fabric linked to sensors that could

detect the coloring and pattern of the background. The

sensors would then send varying intensities of electrical

current to the appropriate areas of the fabric,

55. A. NO CHANGE
  B. beginning and the early stages of
  C. early stages of
  D. OMIT the underlined portion.

GO ON TO THE NEXT PAGE ⇒

they would be impregnated with chemicals sensitive to
56

electricity. The coveralls would change colors continu-

ally as the soldier moved.

[4]

The problem with this solution from a military

standpoint, you know, is
57

power: the fact that the suit would require a continuous
58

flow of electricity means that a soldier would have to

carry a large number of batteries, which would hardly

contribute to ease of movement and camouflage.

[5]

[1] To address this problem, Army researchers have

developed a new kind of color-changing pixel, known as

the intererometric modulator or i-mod. [2] The research-

ers hope that a flexible suit made of i-mod pixels could

completely blend into any background. [3] In addition to

matching a background, the pixels could also be set to show

other colors, for example, a camouflage mode that would

render a soldier effectively invisible in the forest and a flash

mode that would enhance a soldier's visibility in a rescue

situation. [4] Changing the distance between the mirrors

changes the color of the light that they reflect. [5] Each i-

mod pixel is made up of a pair of tiny mirrors. 59

56. **F.** NO CHANGE
    G. that
    H. it
    J. which

57. **A.** NO CHANGE
    B. is, like,
    C. however, is
    D. therefore, is

58. **F.** NO CHANGE
    G. power; the fact that the suit
    H. power the fact that the suit
    J. power the fact that, the suit

59. Which of the following sequences would
    make paragraph 5 most logical?
    A. 2, 4, 5, 3, 1
    B. 2, 3, 1, 5, 4
    C. 1, 4, 5, 2, 3
    D. 1, 5, 4, 2, 3

GO ON TO THE NEXT PAGE

Question 60 asks about the preceding passage as a whole.

60. The writer wishes to insert the following material into the passage:

> When H.G. Wells wrote *The Invisible Man*, there was no interest in camouflaging soldiers; the British army was garbed in bright red uniforms. Since that time, governments have learned the value of making soldiers difficult to see, first by using camouflage fabrics, and today by envisioning something even more effective that would change color to match the terrain.

The new material would most logically be placed in paragraph:

F. 2.

G. 3.

H. 4.

J. 5.

GO ON TO THE NEXT PAGE ▷

PASSAGE V

CALIFORNIA: A STATE BUILT ON DREAMS

It lasted fewer than 10 years, but when it was over, the United States had been radically and forever changed. The population had exploded on the West Coast of the country, <u>fortunes had been made and those same fortunes were lost,</u> and a new state had entered the union—a state that would become a state of mind for all

61

61. **A.** NO CHANGE

    B. fortunes had been made and lost,

    C. fortunes, which had been made, were then lost,

    D. made and lost were fortunes,

<u>Americans: California.</u>

62

62. **F.** NO CHANGE

    G. Americans, and that place was called California.

    H. Americans, California.

    J. Americans. California.

The United States <u>acquiring</u> the territory that

63
would later become California during the Mexican War (1846–1848). One of the many settlers who traveled to the new territory was

63. **A.** NO CHANGE

    B. has acquired

    C. is acquiring

    D. acquired

<u>John Sutter who was a shopkeeper</u> from Switzerland

64
who had left behind his wife, his children, and his debts, in search of a new life.

64. **F.** NO CHANGE

    G. John Sutter, a shopkeeper

    H. John Sutter; a shopkeeper

    J. John Sutter, who was a shopkeeper

GO ON TO THE NEXT PAGE

<u>Hired he did</u> a carpenter named James Marshall to build
65
a sawmill for him on the American River in the foothills

of the Sierra Nevada mountains.

65. **A.** NO CHANGE
    B. He hired
    C. Hiring
    D. He did hire

    On January 24, 1848, <u>while inspecting the mill's</u>
66
<u>runoff into the river</u>, Marshall saw two shiny objects
66
below the surface of the water. He took the nuggets to

Sutter, who was annoyed by the discovery; Sutter didn't

want

66. **F.** NO CHANGE
    G. (he was inspecting the mill's runoff into the river)
    H. inspecting the mill's runoff into the river all the while
    J. OMIT the underlined portion.

<u>them</u> mill workers distracted by gold fever.
67

67. **A.** NO CHANGE
    B. this
    C. his
    D. there

<u>Keeping the discovery</u> quiet for a while, but then he
68
couldn't resist bragging about it. Word got out, and

workers began quitting their jobs and heading into the

hills to look for the source of the gold that had washed

down the river.

    69 Thousands of people poured into California in

search of fortune and glory.

68. **F.** NO CHANGE
    G. The discovery he was keeping
    H. He kept the discovery
    J. Keeps he the discovery

69. Which of the following would provide the best transition here, guiding the reader from the topic of the previous paragraph to the new topic of this paragraph?
    A. Sutter and Marshall did not make a profit.
    B. The gold rush had officially begun.
    C. Can you image how a small discovery led to such a large state?
    D. Most of the "gold" turned out to be a hoax.

GO ON TO THE NEXT PAGE ⟩

This is similar to recent stock market increases. Dur-
70
ing the two years after Marshall's discovery, more than

90,000 people made their way to California, looking for

gold. In fact, so many people moved West in just

singularly one of those years, 1849, that all the prospec-
71
tors, regardless of when they arrived, became known as

Forty-niners. By 1850, so many people had moved to

the California territory that the United States Congress

was forced to declare it a new state. In 1854, the popula-

tion had increased by another 300,000 people. In fact, 1
72
out of every 90 people then living in the United States

was living in California.

Even after all of the gold had been taken from the

ground, California remained a magical place in the

American imagination. The 31st state had become a

place that lives could change, fortunes could be made,
73
and dreams could come true. For many

people, and California is still such a place.
74

---

70. **F.** NO CHANGE

    G. The rush for gold was similar to recent stock market increases.

    H. This was similar to recent stock market increases.

    J. OMIT the underlined portion.

71. **A.** NO CHANGE

    B. one

    C. one and only one

    D. singular

72. **F.** NO CHANGE

    G. In spite of this,

    H. Believe it or not,

    J. Therefore,

73. **A.** NO CHANGE

    B. where

    C. through which

    D. in

74. **F.** NO CHANGE

    G. Forty-niners, California

    H. people and California

    J. people, California

GO ON TO THE NEXT PAGE ▷

Question 75 asks about the preceding passage as a whole.

75. Suppose the writer had been assigned to write a brief essay detailing the life of a Forty-niner during the California gold rush. Would this essay successfully fulfill the assignment?

   A. Yes, because the essay tells about the lives of John Sutter and James Marshall.

   B. No, because the essay covers a historical rather than biographical perspective of the gold rush.

   C. Yes, because one can imagine the life of a Forty-niner from the details provided in the essay.

   D. No, because the essay does not discuss Forty-niners.

MATHEMATICS TEST

60 Minutes—60 Questions

Directions: Solve each of the following problems, select the correct answer, and then fill in the corresponding space on your answer sheet.

Don't linger over problems that are too time-consuming. Do as many as you can, then come back to the others in the time you have remaining.

The use of a calculator is permitted on this test. Though you are allowed to use your calculator to solve any questions you choose, some of the questions may be most easily answered without the use of a calculator.

Note: Unless otherwise noted, all of the following should be assumed.

1. Illustrative figures are *not* necessarily drawn to scale.
2. All geometric figures lie in a plane.
3. The term *line* indicates a straight line.
4. The term *average* indicates arithmetic mean.

1. The regular price for a certain bicycle is $125.00. If that price is reduced by 20%, what is the new price?

   A. $100.00
   B. $105.00
   C. $112.50
   D. $120.00
   E. $122.50

2. If $x = -5$, then $2x^2 - 6x + 5 = ?$

   F. −15
   G. 15
   H. 25
   J. 85
   K. 135

3. How many distinct prime factors does the number 36 have?

   A. 2
   B. 3
   C. 4
   D. 5
   E. 6

4. In the following figure, what is the value of x ?

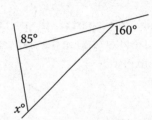

   F. 105°
   G. 115°
   H. 135°
   J. 245°
   K. 255°

5. What is the average of $\frac{1}{20}$ and $\frac{1}{30}$?

   A. $\frac{1}{25}$

   B. $\frac{1}{24}$

   C. $\frac{2}{25}$

   D. $\frac{1}{12}$

   E. $\frac{1}{6}$

GO ON TO THE NEXT PAGE

6. The toll for driving a segment of a certain freeway is $1.50 plus 25 cents for each mile traveled. Joy paid a $25 toll for driving a segment of the freeway. How many miles did she travel?

   F. 10
   G. 75
   H. 94
   J. 96
   K. 100

7. For all x, the product $3x^2 \times 5x^3 = ?$

   A. $8x^5$
   B. $8x^6$
   C. $15x^5$
   D. $15x^6$
   E. $15x^8$

8. How many units apart are the points $P\,(-1,-2)$ and $Q\,(2,2)$ in the standard (x,y) coordinate plane?

   F. 2
   G. 3
   H. 4
   J. 5
   K. 6

9. In a group of 25 students, 16 are female. What percentage of the group is female?

   A. 16%
   B. 40%
   C. 60%
   D. 64%
   E. 75%

10. For how many integer values of x will $\dfrac{7}{x}$ be greater than $\dfrac{1}{4}$ and less than $\dfrac{1}{3}$?

    F. 6
    G. 7
    H. 12
    J. 28
    K. Infinitely many

11. Which of the following is a polynomial factor of $6x^2 - 13x + 6$?

    A. $2x + 3$
    B. $3x - 2$
    C. $3x + 2$
    D. $6x - 2$
    E. $6x + 2$

12. What is the value of a if $\dfrac{1}{a} + \dfrac{2}{a} + \dfrac{3}{a} + \dfrac{4}{a} = 5$?

    F. $\dfrac{1}{2}$
    G. 2
    H. 4
    J. $12\dfrac{1}{2}$
    K. 50

GO ON TO THE NEXT PAGE

13. In the following figure, $\overline{AD}$, $\overline{BE}$, and $\overline{CF}$ all intersect at point G. If the measure of $\angle AGB$ is 40° and the measure of $\angle CGE$ is 105°, what is the measure of $\angle AGF$?

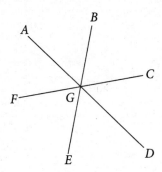

  A. 35°

  B. 45°

  C. 55°

  D. 65°

  E. 75°

14. Which of the following is the solution statement for the inequality $-3 < 4x - 5$?

  F. $x > -2$

  G. $x > \dfrac{1}{2}$

  H. $x < -2$

  J. $x < \dfrac{1}{2}$

  K. $x < 2$

15. In the following figure, $\overline{BD}$ bisects $\angle ABC$. The measure of $\angle ABC$ is 100°, and the measure of $\angle BAD$ is 60°. What is the measure of $\angle BDC$?

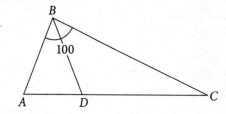

  A. 80°

  B. 90°

  C. 100°

  D. 110°

  E. 120°

16. If $x + 2y - 3 = xy$, where x and y are positive, then which of the following equations expresses y in terms of x?

  F. $y = \dfrac{3 - x}{2 - x}$

  G. $y = \dfrac{3 - x}{x - 2}$

  H. $y = \dfrac{x - 3}{2 - x}$

  J. $y = \dfrac{x - 2}{x - 3}$

  K. $y = \dfrac{6 - x}{x - 2}$

17. In a group of 50 students, 28 speak English and 37 speak Spanish. If everyone in the group speaks at least one of the two languages, how many speak both English and Spanish?

  A. 11

  B. 12

  C. 13

  D. 14

  E. 15

GO ON TO THE NEXT PAGE

18. A car travels 288 miles in 6 hours. At that rate, how many miles will it travel in 8 hours ?

    F. 216

    G. 360

    H. 368

    J. 376

    K. 384

19. When $\frac{4}{11}$ is written as a decimal, what is the 100th digit after the decimal point?

    A. 3

    B. 4

    C. 5

    D. 6

    E. 7

20. What is the solution for x in the following system of equations?

    $$3x + 4y = 31$$

    $$3x - 4y = -1$$

    F. 4

    G. 5

    H. 6

    J. 9

    K. 10

21. In the standard (x,y) coordinate plane, points P and Q have coordinates $(2,3)$ and $(12,-15)$, respectively. What are the coordinates of the midpoint of $\overline{PQ}$?

    A. (6,–12)

    B. (6,–9)

    C. (6,–6)

    D. (7,–9)

    E. (7,–6)

22. In the following figure, $\angle B$ is a right angle, and the measure of $\angle C$ is θ. What is the value of $\cos \theta$?

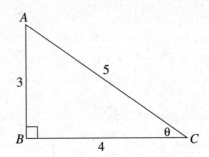

    F. $\dfrac{3}{4}$

    G. $\dfrac{3}{5}$

    H. $\dfrac{4}{5}$

    J. $\dfrac{5}{4}$

    K. $\dfrac{4}{3}$

23. In the following figure, the circle centered at P is tangent to the circle centered at Q. Point Q is on the circumference of circle P. If the circumference of circle P is 6 inches, what is the circumference, in inches, of circle Q ?

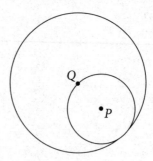

    A. 12

    B. 24

    C. 36

    D. 12π

    E. 36π

GO ON TO THE NEXT PAGE

24. If $f(x) = x^3 - x^2 - x$, what is the value of $f(-3)$?

   F. −39

   G. −33

   H. −21

   J. −15

   K. 0

25. If the lengths, in inches, of all three sides of a triangle are integers, and one side is 4 inches long, what is the least possible perimeter of the triangle, in inches?

   A. 6

   B. 8

   C. 9

   D. 12

   E. 16

26. What is the complete factorization of $2x + 3x^2 + x^3$?

   F. $x(x^2 + 2)$

   G. $x(x - 2)(x + 3)$

   H. $x(x - 1)(x + 2)$

   J. $x(x + 1)(x + 2)$

   K. $x(x + 2)(x + 3)$

27. If $xyz \neq 0$, which of the following is equivalent to $\dfrac{x^2 y^3 z^4}{\left(xyz^2\right)^2}$?

   A. $\dfrac{1}{y}$

   B. $\dfrac{1}{z}$

   C. y

   D. $\dfrac{x}{yz}$

   E. xyz

28. As a decimal, what is the sum of $\dfrac{2}{3}$ and $\dfrac{1}{12}$?

   F. 0.2

   G. 0.5

   H. 0.75

   J. 0.833

   K. 0.875

29. The formula for converting a Fahrenheit temperature reading to Celsius is $C = \dfrac{5}{9}(F - 32)$, where C is the reading in degrees Celsius and F is the reading in degrees Fahrenheit. Which of the following is the Fahrenheit equivalent to a reading of 95° Celsius?

   A. 35°F

   B. 53°F

   C. 63°F

   D. 203°F

   E. 207°F

30. A jar contains 4 green marbles, 5 red marbles, and 11 white marbles. If 1 marble is chosen at random, what is the probability that it will be green?

   F. $\dfrac{1}{3}$

   G. $\dfrac{1}{4}$

   H. $\dfrac{1}{5}$

   J. $\dfrac{1}{16}$

   K. $\dfrac{5}{15}$

GO ON TO THE NEXT PAGE

31. What is the average of the expressions $2x + 5$, $5x - 6$, and $-4x + 2$?

A. $x + \dfrac{1}{3}$

B. $x + 1$

C. $3x + \dfrac{1}{3}$

D. $3x + 3$

E. $3x + 3\dfrac{1}{3}$

32. The line that passes through the points $(1,1)$ and $(2,16)$ in the standard (x,y) coordinate plane is parallel to the line that passes through the points $(-10,-5)$ and $(a,25)$. What is the value of a ?

F. -8

G. 3

H. 5

J. 15

K. 20

33. In the following figure, $\overline{QS}$ and $\overline{PT}$ are parallel, and the lengths of $\overline{QR}$ and $\overline{PQ}$, in units, are as marked. If the perimeter of $\triangle QRS$ is 11 units, how many units long is the perimeter of $\triangle PRT$?

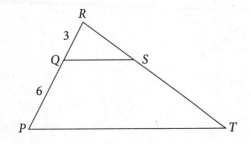

A. 22

B. 33

C. 66

D. 88

E. 99

34. The figure shown belongs in which of the following classifications?

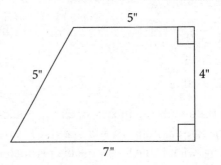

   I. Polygon
  II. Quadrilateral
 III. Rectangle
 IV. Trapezoid

F. I only

G. II only

H. IV only

J. I, II, and III only

K. I, II, and IV only

35. If one solution to the equation $2x^2 + (a - 4)x - 2a = 0$ is $x = -3$, what is the value of a ?

A. 0

B. 2

C. 4

D. 6

E. 12

36. A menu offers 4 choices for the first course, 5 choices for the second course, and 3 choices for dessert. How many different meals, consisting of a first course, a second course, and a dessert, can one choose from this menu?

F. 12

G. 24

H. 30

J. 36

K. 60

GO ON TO THE NEXT PAGE ⟩

37. If an integer is divisible by 6 and by 9, then the integer must be evenly divisible by which of the following?

      I. 12

     II. 18

    III. 36

  A. I only

  B. II only

  C. I and II only

  D. I, II, and III

  E. None

38. For all $x \neq 0$, $\dfrac{x^2 + x^2 + x^2}{x^2} = ?$

  F. 3

  G. $3x$

  H. x^2

  J. x^3

  K. x^4

39. Joan has q quarters, d dimes, n nickels, and no other coins in her pocket. Which of the following represents the total number of coins in Joan's pocket?

  A. $q + d + n$

  B. $5q + 2d + n$

  C. $0.25q + 0.10d + 0.05n$

  D. $(25 + 10 + 5)(q + d + n)$

  E. $25q + 10d + 5n$

40. Which of the following graphs represents the solutions for x of the inequality $5x - 2(1 - x) \geq 4(x + 1)$?

F.

G.

H.

J.

K.

41. In the standard (x,y) coordinate plane, line m is perpendicular to the line containing the points $(5,6)$ and $(6,10)$. What is the slope of line m ?

  A. -4

  B. $-\dfrac{1}{4}$

  C. $\dfrac{1}{4}$

  D. 4

  E. 8

GO ON TO THE NEXT PAGE

42. In the right triangle below, sin θ = ?

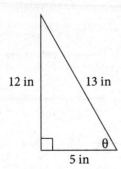

F. $\dfrac{5}{13}$

G. $\dfrac{5}{12}$

H. $\dfrac{12}{13}$

J. $\dfrac{13}{12}$

K. $\dfrac{13}{5}$

43. If $9^{2x-1} = 3^{3x+3}$, then $x = $?

A. -4

B. $-\dfrac{7}{4}$

C. $-\dfrac{10}{7}$

D. 2

E. 5

44. From 1970 through 1980, the population of City Q increased by 20%. From 1980 through 1990, the population increased by 30%. What was the combined percent increase for the period 1970–1990 ?

F. 25%

G. 26%

H. 36%

J. 50%

K. 56%

45. Martin's average score after four tests is 89. What score on the fifth test would bring Martin's average up to exactly 90 ?

A. 90

B. 91

C. 92

D. 93

E. 94

46. Which of the following is an equation for the circle in the standard (x,y) coordinate plane that has its center at $(-1,-1)$ and passes through the point $(7,5)$?

F. $(x - 1)^2 + (y - 1)^2 = 10$

G. $(x + 1)^2 + (y + 1)^2 = 10$

H. $(x - 1)^2 + (y - 1)^2 = 12$

J. $(x - 1)^2 + (y - 1)^2 = 100$

K. $(x + 1)^2 + (y + 1)^2 = 100$

47. Which of the following is an equation for the graph in the following standard (x,y) coordinate plane?

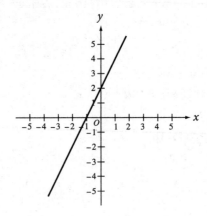

A. $y = -2x + 1$

B. $y = x + 1$

C. $y = x + 2$

D. $y = 2x + 1$

E. $y = 2x + 2$

GO ON TO THE NEXT PAGE

48. What is $\frac{1}{4}$% of 16 ?

    F. 0.004

    G. 0.04

    H. 0.4

    J. 4

    K. 64

49. For all s, $(s + 4)(s - 4) + (2s + 2)(s - 2) = ?$

    A. $s^2 - 2s - 20$

    B. $3s^2 - 12$

    C. $3s^2 - 2s - 20$

    D. $3s^2 + 2s - 20$

    E. $5s^2 - 2s - 20$

50. Which of the following is an equation of the parabola graphed in the following (x, y) coordinate plane?

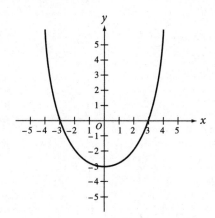

    F. $y = \dfrac{x^2}{3} - 3$

    G. $y = \dfrac{x^2 - 3}{3}$

    H. $y = \dfrac{x^2}{3} + 3$

    J. $y = \dfrac{x^2 + 3}{3}$

    K. $y = 3x^2 - 3$

51. In the following figure, $\sin a = \dfrac{4}{5}$. What is $\cos b$?

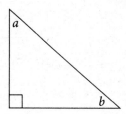

    A. $\dfrac{3}{4}$

    B. $\dfrac{3}{5}$

    C. $\dfrac{4}{5}$

    D. $\dfrac{5}{4}$

    E. $\dfrac{4}{3}$

52. For all $x \neq 0$, $\dfrac{x^2 + x^2 + x^2}{x} = ?$

    F. $3x$

    G. x^3

    H. x^5

    J. x^7

    K. $2x^2 + x$

53. One can determine a student's score S on a certain test by dividing the number of wrong answers (w) by 4 and subtracting the result from the number of right answers (r). This relation is expressed by which of the following formulas?

    A. $S = \dfrac{r - w}{4}$

    B. $S = r - \dfrac{w}{4}$

    C. $S = \dfrac{r}{4} - w$

    D. $S = 4r - w$

    E. $S = r - 4w$

GO ON TO THE NEXT PAGE ▷

54. What is the volume, in cubic inches, of the cylinder shown in the following figure?

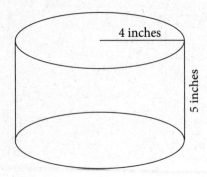

4 inches

5 inches

F. 20π

G. 40π

H. 60π

J. 80π

K. 100π

55. In the following figure, $\overline{AB}$ is perpendicular to $\overline{BC}$. The lengths of $\overline{AB}$ and $\overline{BC}$, in inches, are given in terms of x. Which of the following represents the area of $\triangle ABC$, in square inches, for all $x > 1$?

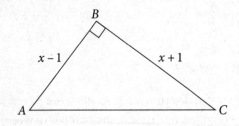

A. x

B. $2x$

C. x^2

D. $x^2 - 1$

E. $\dfrac{x^2 - 1}{2}$

56. In 1990, the population of Town A was 9,400 and the population of Town B was 7,600. Starting then, each year the population of Town A decreased by 100, and the population of Town B increased by 100. In what year were the two populations equal?

F. 1998

G. 1999

H. 2000

J. 2008

K. 2009

57. In a certain club, the average age of the male members is 35, and the average age of the female members is 25. If 20% of the members are male, what is the average age of all the club members?

A. 26

B. 27

C. 28

D. 29

E. 30

GO ON TO THE NEXT PAGE

58. To determine the height h of a tree, Roger stands b feet from the base of the tree and measures the angle of elevation to be θ, as shown in the following figure. Which of the following relates h and b ?

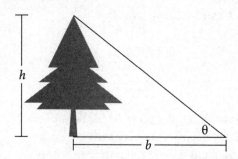

F. $\sin\theta = \dfrac{h}{b}$

G. $\sin\theta = \dfrac{b}{h}$

H. $\sin\theta = \dfrac{b}{\sqrt{b^2 + h^2}}$

J. $\sin\theta = \dfrac{h}{\sqrt{b^2 + h^2}}$

K. $\sin\theta = \dfrac{\sqrt{b^2 + h^2}}{b}$

59. The formula for the lateral surface area S of a right circular cone is $S = \pi r\sqrt{r^2 + h^2}$, where r is the radius of the base and h is the altitude. What is the lateral surface area, in square feet, of a right circular cone with base radius 3 feet and altitude 4 feet?

A. $3\pi\sqrt{5}$

B. $3\pi\sqrt{7}$

C. 15π

D. 21π

E. $\dfrac{75\pi}{2}$

60. In the following figure, line t crosses parallel lines m and n. Which of the following statements must be true?

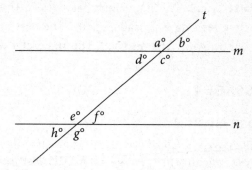

F. $a = b$

G. $a = d$

H. $b = e$

J. $c = g$

K. $d = g$

READING TEST

35 Minutes—40 Questions

Directions: There are four passages in this test. Each passage is followed by several questions. After reading a passage, choose the best answer to each question and fill in the corresponding oval on your Answer Grid. You may refer to the passages as often as necessary.

PASSAGE I

PROSE FICTION

This passage is adapted from Bleak House, *by Charles Dickens, which was first published in 1853. In this excerpt, Esther recounts some of her childhood experiences.*

I can remember, when I was a very little girl indeed, I used to say to my doll when we were alone together, "Now, Dolly, I am not
Line clever, you know very well, and you must be
(5) patient with me, like a dear!"

…My dear old doll! I was such a shy little thing that I seldom dared to open my lips, and never dared to open my heart, to anybody else. It almost makes me cry
(10) to think what a relief it used to be to me when I came home from school of a day to run upstairs to my room and say, "Oh, you dear faithful Dolly, I knew you would be expecting me!" and then to sit down on
(15) the floor, leaning on the elbow of her great chair, and tell her all I had noticed since we parted…

I was brought up, from my earliest remembrance—like some of the princesses
(20) in the fairy stories, only I was not charming—by my godmother. At least, I only knew her as such. She was a good, good woman! She went to church three times every Sunday, and to morning prayers on
(25) Wednesdays and Fridays, and to lectures whenever there were lectures, and never missed. She was handsome; and if she had ever smiled, would have been (I used to think) like an angel—but she never smiled.
(30) She was always grave and strict. She was so very good herself, I thought, that the

badness of other people made her frown all her life. It made me very sorry to consider how good she was and how unworthy of
(35) her I was, and I used ardently to hope that I might have a better heart; and I talked it over very often with the dear old doll, but I never loved my godmother as I ought to have loved her and as I felt I must have
(40) loved her if I had been a better girl.

I had never heard my mama spoken of. I had never been shown my mama's grave. I had never been told where it was.

Although there were seven girls at
(45) the neighboring school where I was a day boarder, and although they called me little Esther Summerson, I knew none of them at home. All of them were older than I, to be sure (I was the youngest there by a good
(50) deal), but there seemed to be some other separation between us besides that, and besides their being far more clever than I was and knowing much more than I did. One of them in the first week of my going to
(55) the school (I remember it very well) invited me home to a little party, to my great joy. But my godmother wrote a stiff letter declining for me, and I never went. I never went out at all.
(60) It was my birthday. There were holidays at school on other birthdays—none on mine. There were rejoicings at home on other birthdays, as I knew from what I heard the girls relate to one another—there were none
(65) on mine. My birthday was the most melancholy

GO ON TO THE NEXT PAGE ▷

day at home in the whole year…

Dinner was over, and my godmother and I were sitting at the table before the fire. The clock ticked, the fire clicked; not (70) another sound had been heard in the room or in the house for I don't know how long. I happened to look timidly up from my stitching, across the table at my godmother, and I saw in her face, looking gloomily at me, (75) "It would have been far better, little Esther, that you had had no birthday, that you had never been born!"

I broke out crying and sobbing, and I said, "Oh, dear godmother, tell me, pray do (80) tell me, did Mama die on my birthday?"

"No," she returned. "Ask me no more, child!"

…I put up my trembling little hand to clasp hers or to beg her pardon with what (85) earnestness I might, but withdrew it as she looked at me, and laid it on my fluttering heart. She…said slowly in a cold, low voice—I see her knitted brow and pointed finger—"The time will come—and soon (90) enough—when you will understand this better and will feel it too.…I have forgiven her"—but her face did not relent—"the wrong she did to me, and I say no more of it, though it was greater than you will ever (95) know…Forget your mother and leave all other people to forget her.…Now, go!"

.…I went up to my room, and crept to bed, and laid my doll's cheek against mine wet with tears, and holding that solitary (100) friend upon my bosom, cried myself to sleep. Imperfect as my understanding of my sorrow was, I knew that I had brought no joy at any time to anybody's heart and that I was to no one upon earth what Dolly was (105) to me.

Dear, dear, to think how much time we passed alone together afterwards, and how often I repeated to the doll the story of my birthday and confided to her that I would (110) try as hard as ever I could to repair the fault I had been born with.…I hope it is not self-indulgent to shed these tears as I think of it.

1. According to the passage, Esther only remembers:

   A. being brought up by her parents for a short time.
   B. being brought up by her mother for a short time.
   C. being brought up by her godmother for a short time.
   D. being brought up by her godmother.

2. It is most likely that Esther thought of her doll as:

   F. only an amusing plaything.
   G. her only friend and confidante.
   H. a princess in a fairy tale.
   J. a beautiful toy that was too fragile to touch.

3. As it is used in the passage, *stiff* (line 57) most closely means:

   A. difficult to bend.
   B. rigidly formal.
   C. unchanging.
   D. not moving easily or freely.

4. Which of the following most likely contributed to Esther's belief that she had been born with a fault (lines 110–111)?

   F. She is not very clever.
   G. Her birthday was never celebrated.
   H. She did not have any friends at school.
   J. Her mother died in childbirth.

GO ON TO THE NEXT PAGE ▷

5. Esther's godmother's words, actions, and facial expression as described in paragraph 10 (lines 83–96) suggest that she:

   A. had a change of heart about celebrating Esther's birthday.

   B. did not know what had happened to Esther's mother.

   C. continued to resent Esther's mother.

   D. had truly forgiven Esther's mother.

6. According to the passage, Esther's childhood could be most accurately characterized as:

   F. an adventure.

   G. a time of loneliness and confusion.

   H. a period of dedication to education and self-improvement.

   J. a period of attempting to become more like her godmother.

7. From Esther's statement, "I was to no one upon earth what Dolly was to me" (lines 104–105), it is reasonable to infer that Esther:

   A. believed that her godmother loved her.

   B. believed that she would be able to become friends with the girls at school.

   C. believed that no one loved her.

   D. believed that her mother was alive.

8. In the passage, it is implied that all of the following contributed to separating Esther from the other girls at her school EXCEPT:

   F. the other girls were older than Esther.

   G. Esther's godmother did not allow Esther to socialize with the other girls outside of school.

   H. Esther believed that the other girls were much smarter.

   J. Esther was self-indulgent.

9. According to the passage, one reason that Esther thinks of her godmother as a "good, good woman" (lines 22–23) is:

   A. that when she smiles, she looks like an angel.

   B. that she forgave Esther's mother.

   C. that she frequently attends church services.

   D. that she gave Esther a doll.

10. In the passage, Esther describes herself as a child as:

    F. self-indulgent and not very clever.

    G. shy and not very clever.

    H. shy and faithful.

    J. self-indulgent and faithful.

PASSAGE II

SOCIAL SCIENCE

This passage is excerpted from "The Return of the Big Cats," by Mac Margolis, Newsweek, December 11, 2000, © 2000 by Newsweek, Inc. All rights reserved. Reprinted by permission.

Marcos Nunes is not likely to forget his first holiday in Brazil's Pantanal wilderness. One afternoon last October he was coaxing his
Line horse through a lonely tuft of woods when
(5) he suddenly found himself staring down a fully grown spotted jaguar. He held his breath while the painted cat and her cub paraded silkily through the grove, not 10 meters away....."Thank you," he wrote later
(10) in a hotel visitor's log, "for the wonderful fright!"

As Nunes and other ecotourists are discovering, these big, beautiful animals, once at the brink of extinction, are now
(15) staging a comeback. Exactly how dramatic a comeback is difficult to say because jaguars—*Panthera onca*, the largest feline in the New World—are solitary, secretive,

GO ON TO THE NEXT PAGE ⇨

nocturnal predators. Each cat needs to
(20) prowl at least 35 square kilometers by itself.
Brazil's Pantanal, vast wetlands that spill
over a 140,000-square-kilometer swath of
South America the size of Germany, gives
them plenty of room to roam. Nevertheless,
(25) scientists who have been tagging jaguars
with radio transmitters for two decades
have in recent years been reporting a big
increase in sightings. Hotels, campgrounds,
and bed-and-breakfasts have sprung up to
(30) accommodate the half-million tourists a year
(twice the number of five years ago) bent on
sampling the Pantanal's wildlife, of which
the great cats must be the most magnificent
example.

(35)   Most sightings come from local cattle
herders—but their jaguar stories have a very
different ring. One day last September, ranch
hand Abel Monteiro was tending cattle near
the Rio Vermelho, in the southern Pantanal,
(40) when, he says, a snarling jaguar leaped from
the scrub and killed his two bloodhounds.
Monteiro barely had time to grab his .38
revolver and kill the angry cat. Leonelson
Ramos da Silva says last May he and a group
(45) of field hands had to throw flaming sticks
all night to keep a prowling jaguar from
invading their forest camp....The Brazilian
interior, famous for its generous spirit and
cowboy *bonhomie*, is now the scene of a
(50) political catfight between the scientists,
environmentalists, and ecotourists who want
to protect the jaguars and the embattled
ranchers who want to protect themselves
and their livelihood.

(55) The ranchers, to be sure, have enough
headaches coping with the harsh, sodden
landscape without jaguars attacking their
herds and threatening their livelihoods.
Hard data on cattle losses due to jaguars in
(60) the Pantanal are nonexistent, but there are
stories. In 1995, Joo Julio Dittmar bought a
6,200-hectare strip of ideal breeding ground,
only to lose 152 of his 600 calves to jaguars,
he claims. Ranchers chafe at laws that forbid

(65) them to kill the jaguars. "This is a question
of democracy," says Dittmar. "We ranchers
ought to be allowed to control our own
environment."

Man and jaguar have been sparring for
(70) territory ever since 18th-century settlers,
traders, and herdsmen began to move into
this sparsely populated *serto*, or back lands.
By the 1960s, the Pantanal was a vast, soggy
canvas, white with gleaming herds of Nelore
(75) cattle. Game hunters were bagging 15,000
jaguars a year in the nearby Amazon Basin
(no figures exist on the Pantanal) as the
worldwide trade in pelts reached $30 million
a year. As the jaguars grew scarce, their
(80) chief food staple, the capybaras—a meter-
long rodent, the world's largest—overran
farmers' fields and spread trichomoniasis,
a livestock disease that renders cows sterile.

Then in 1967, Brazil outlawed jaguar
(85) hunting, and a world ban on selling pelts
followed in 1973. Weather patterns also
shifted radically—due most likely to global
warming—and drove annual floods to
near-Biblical proportions. The waters are
(90) only now retreating from some inundated
pasturelands. As the Pantanal herds shrank
from 6 million to about 3.5 million head,
the jaguars advanced. Along the way they
developed a taste for the bovine intruders.

(95)   The ranchers' fear of the big cats is
partly cultural. The ancient Inca and Maya
believed that jaguars possessed supernatural
powers. In Brazil, the most treacherous
enemy is said to be *o amigo da onca*, a
(100) friend to the jaguar....

Some people believe there may be a way
for ranchers and jaguars to coexist. Sports
hunters on "green safaris" might shoot
jaguars with immobilizing drugs, allowing
(105) scientists to fit the cats with radio collars.
Fees would help sustain jaguar research and
compensate ranchers for livestock losses.
(Many environmentalists, though, fear
fraudulent claims.) Scientists are setting up
(110) workshops to teach ranchers how to protect

GO ON TO THE NEXT PAGE ⟩

their herds with modern husbandry, pasture management, and such gadgets as blinking lights and electric fences.

(115) Like many rural folk, however, the wetland ranchers tend to bristle at bureaucrats and foreigners telling them what to do. When the scholars go home and the greens log off, the *pantaneiros* will still be there— left on their own to deal with the jaguars as
(120) they see fit.

11. As it is used in the passage, *canvas* (line 74) most closely means:

   A. a survey of public opinion.
   B. a background.
   C. a coarse cotton fabric.
   D. a painting.

12. According to the passage, one result of the decline of the jaguar population during the 1960s was:

   F. an increase in the population of human settlers.
   G. an increase in Brazil's ecotourist business.
   H. an increase in the price of a jaguar pelt.
   J. an increase in the population of jaguars' most common source of food, the capybaras.

13. According to the passage, it is difficult to determine the extent of the jaguar's comeback because:

   A. the area they inhabit is so large.
   B. the stories that the local ranchers tell about jaguars contradict the conclusions reached by scientists.
   C. jaguars are solitary, nocturnal animals that can have a territory of 35 square kilometers.
   D. scientists have only used radio transmitters to track the movements of the jaguar population.

14. The information about ecotourism in the first and second paragraphs of the passage (lines 1–34) suggests that:

   F. the jaguars are seen as a threat to the safety of tourists.
   G. the jaguars are important to the success of Brazil's growing ecotourism industry.
   H. the growth of the ecotourism industry is threatening the habitat of the jaguars.
   J. it is common for ecotourists to spot one or more jaguars.

15. According to the passage, which of the following is NOT a method for protecting cattle herds that scientists are teaching ranchers?

   A. "Green safaris"
   B. Pasture management
   C. The use of blinking lights and electric fences
   D. Modern husbandry

GO ON TO THE NEXT PAGE ⟹

16. It is most likely that the author of the passage included the jaguar stories of three ranchers (lines 35–47, 61–68) in order to:

    F. express more sympathy toward the ranchers than toward the environmentalists and scientists.

    G. illustrate the dangers and economic losses that the jaguars currently pose to ranchers.

    H. show the violent nature of the ranchers.

    J. provide a complete picture of the Pantanal landscape.

17. From information in the passage, it is most reasonable to infer that the cattle herds "shrank from 6 million to about 3.5 million head" (lines 91–92) because:

    A. the jaguars had killed so many cattle.

    B. environmentalists and scientists worked to convert pastureland into refuges for the jaguars.

    C. many cows had become sterile from trichomoniasis, and annual floods submerged much of the pastureland used by ranchers.

    D. the cattle could not tolerate the increase in the average temperature caused by global warming.

18. The main conclusion reached about the future of the relationship between the people and the jaguars in the Pantanal is that:

    F. the increase in ecotourism will ensure the continued growth in the jaguar population.

    G. the ranchers themselves will ultimately determine how they will cope with the jaguars.

    H. the jaguar population will continue to fluctuate with the number of tourists coming into the Pantanal.

    J. the scientists' new ranching methods will make it easy for the ranchers and jaguars to coexist.

19. According to the passage, which of the following groups want to protect the jaguar?

    I. Ecotourists

    II. Environmentalists

    III. Scientists

    A. I and II only

    B. I and III only

    C. II and III only

    D. I, II, and III

20. According to the passage, there are no accurate data available on:

    F. the number of cattle killed by jaguars.

    G. the number of ranchers attacked by jaguars.

    H. the growth rate of ecotourism in Brazil.

    J. the percentage of the Pantanal wetlands inhabited by jaguars.

GO ON TO THE NEXT PAGE

PASSAGE III

HUMANITIES

This passage is excerpted from Music Through the Ages *Revised Edition,* © 1987 by Marion Bauer and Ethel R. Peyser, edited by Elizabeth E. Rogers, copyright © 1932 by Marion Bauer and Ethel R. Peyser, renewed copyright © 1960 by Ethel R. Peyser. Reprinted by permission of G. P. Putnam's Sons, a division of Penguin Group (USA), Inc.

Greek instruments can be classified into two general categories—string and pipe, or lyre and aulos. Our knowledge of them comes
Line from representations on monuments, vases,
(5) statues, and friezes and from the testimony of Greek authors. The lyre was the national instrument and included a wide variety of types. In its most antique form, the chelys, it is traced back to the age of fable and
(10) allegedly owed its invention to Hermes. Easy to carry, this small lyre became the favorite instrument of the home, amateurs, and women, a popular accompaniment for drinking songs and love songs as well as
(15) more noble kinds of poetry....Professional Homeric singers used a kithara, a larger, more powerful instrument, which probably came from Egypt. The kithara had a flat wooden sound box and an upper horizontal
(20) bar supported by two curving arms. Within this frame were stretched strings of equal length, at first but three or four in number. Fastened to the performer by means of a sling, the kithara was played with both
(25) hands. We are not sure in just what manner the instrument was used to accompany the epics. It may have been employed for a pitch-fixing prelude and for interludes, or it may have paralleled or decorated the vocal
(30) melody in more or less free fashion.

...Two types of tuning were used: the dynamic, or pitch method, naming the degrees "according to function"; and the thetic, or tablature, naming them "according
(35) to position" on the instrument.

As early as the eighth century B.C., lyres of five strings appeared. Terpander

(fl. c. 675 B.C.), one of the first innovators, is said to have increased the number
(40) of strings to seven. He is also supposed to have completed the octave and created the Mixolydian scale. Aristoxenos claimed that the poetess Sappho, in the seventh century B.C., in addition to introducing a mode in
(45) which Dorian and Lydian characteristics were blended, initiated use of the plectrum or pick. At the time of Sophocles (495–406 B.C.), the lyre had eleven strings.

Another harplike instrument was the
(50) magadis, whose tone was described as trumpetlike. Of foreign importation, it had twenty strings, which, by means of frets, played octaves. As some of the strings were tuned in quarter tones, it was an instrument
(55) associated with the enharmonic mode. Smaller versions, the pectis and the barbitos, were also tuned in quarter tones. Greek men and boys had a style of singing in octaves that was called magadizing, after the octave-
(60) playing instruments.

The kithara was identified with Apollo and the Apollonian cult, representing the intellectual and idealistic side of Greek art. The aulos or reed pipe was the instrument of
(65) Dionysians, who represented the unbridled, sensual, and passionate aspect of Greek culture.

Although translated as "flute," the aulos is more like our oboe. Usually found
(70) in double form, the pipes set at an angle, the aulos was imputed to have a far more exciting effect than that produced by the subdued lyre. About 600 B.C., the aulos was chosen as the official instrument of
(75) the Delphian and Pythian festivals. It was also used in performances of the Dionysian dithyramb as well as a supplement of the chorus in classic Greek tragedy and comedy.

There was a complete family of auloi
(80) covering the same range as human voices. One authority names three species of simple pipes and five varieties of double pipes. (The double pipe was the professional

GO ON TO THE NEXT PAGE ⟶

instrument.) An early specimen
(85) was supposed to have been tuned to the
chromatic tetrachord D, C sharp, B flat, A—
a fact that points to Oriental origin. Elegiac
songs called aulodia were composed in
this mode to be accompanied by an aulos.
(90) Although the first wooden pipes had only
three or four finger holes, the number later
increased so that the Dorian, Phrygian, and
Lydian modes might be performed on a
single pair. Pictures of auletes show them
(95) with a bandage or phorbeia over their faces;
this might have been necessary to hold the
two pipes in place, to modulate the tone or,
perhaps, to aid in storing air in the cheeks
for the purpose of sustained performance.

21. The passage suggests that the aulos was considered "the instrument of the Dionysians"
(lines 64–65) because:

    A. it expressed the excitement and passion
       of that aspect of Greek culture.
    B. it was chosen as the official instrument
       of the Delphian and Pythian festivals.
    C. it represented the intellectual and ideal-
       istic side of Greek art.
    D. it was invented around the time that the
       Dionysian cult originated.

22. The statement that the chelys can be "traced
back to the age of fable" (line 9) implies that
the chelys:

    F. was invented by storytellers.
    G. was used to accompany the epics.
    H. probably existed in legend only.
    J. was a particularly ancient instrument.

23. The main purpose of the passage is to describe
the:

    A. use of the lyre in different musical
       settings.
    B. connection between the ancient Greek
       arts of music and drama.
    C. references to music in ancient Greek
       literature.
    D. origin and development of various
       Greek instruments.

24. According to the passage, the kithara was:

    F. most likely of Greek origin.
    G. played with one hand.
    H. used by professional musicians.
    J. less powerful than a chelys.

25. Which of the following is NOT cited as a
change that occurred to the lyre between the
eighth and fifth centuries B.C.?

    A. Musicians began to use a plectrum.
    B. Lyres featured increasing numbers of
       strings.
    C. Musicians began to use different scales
       and modes.
    D. Lyres were used to accompany dramatic
       productions.

26. It can be inferred from the passage that the
chromatic tetrachord D, C sharp, B flat, A
(line 86) was:

    F. not appropriate for elegaic songs.
    G. only used by professional musicians.
    H. impossible on the first wooden pipes.
    J. present in ancient Oriental music.

GO ON TO THE NEXT PAGE

27. According to the passage, the most ancient form of the lyre was called a:

    A. magadis.

    B. kithara.

    C. chelys.

    D. barbitos.

28. According to the passage, one of Sappho's contributions to ancient Greek music was that she:

    F. completed the octave and created the Mixolydian scale.

    G. introduced a mode blending Dorian and Lydian characteristics.

    H. incorporated poetry into recitals of lyre music.

    J. helped increase the number of strings on the lyre.

29. According to the passage, which of the following is/are characteristic of the aulos?

    I. It was used in performances of the Dionysian dithyramb.

    II. It sounded more exciting than the lyre.

    III. It resembles the modern-day flute more than it does the oboe.

    A. I only

    B. I and II only

    C. II and III only

    D. I, II, and III

30. Which of the following does the passage suggest is true about our knowledge of ancient Greek instruments?

    F. Our knowledge is dependent on secondary sources.

    G. Little is known about how instruments were tuned.

    H. Very few pictures of ancient Greek instruments have survived.

    J. More is known about string instruments than about pipe instruments.

PASSAGE IV

NATURAL SCIENCE

The immune system can be divided into two major divisions: nonspecific and specific. The nonspecific immune system is composed of defenses that are used to fight off infection in general and are not targeted at specific pathogens. The specific immune system is able to attack very specific disease-causing organisms by means of protein-to-protein interaction and is responsible for our ability to become immune to future infections from pathogens we have fought off already.

PASSAGE A

Nonspecific defenses serve as the first line of defense for the body to fight off infection. The skin and mucous membranes form one part of these nonspecific defenses, which our body uses against (5) foreign cells or viruses. Intact skin cannot normally be penetrated by bacteria or viruses, and oil and sweat secretions give the skin a pH that ranges from 3 to 5, which is acidic enough to discourage most microbes from growing there. In addition, (10) saliva, tears, and mucous all contain the enzyme lysozyme, which can destroy bacterial cell walls (causing bacteria to rupture due to osmotic pressure) and some viral capsids. Mucous is able to trap foreign particles and microbes and transport them (15) to the stomach through swallowing or to the outside by coughing or blowing the nose. Also, movement in the stomach due to peristalsis and in the airways due to cilia helps remove harmful agents. The gut

GO ON TO THE NEXT PAGE ▷

flora, microorganisms that live in the stomach
(20) and intestines, secrete substances harmful to the
invader and compete with it for food. Inflamma-
tion is also a nonspecific defense as it attempts to
form a physical barrier, trapping the pathogen and
preventing it from spreading.

(25)   Certain white blood cells are another part of
the nonspecific defense systems. Macrophages are
large white blood cells that circulate, looking for
foreign material or cells to engulf, which
they do through phagocytosis. Macrophages circ-
(30) late through the blood and are able to transport
themselves through capillary walls and into tissues
that have been infected or wounded. Once in the
tissues, macrophages use their pseudopodia (like
amoebas) to pull in foreign particles and destroy
(35) them within lysosomes. Macrophages are called
antigen-presenting cells (APCs) because of their
ability to display on their own cell surface the
proteins that were on the surface of the cell or
viral particle they have just digested. Because
(40) macrophages and other APCs do not distinguish
between "self-proteins" destined for their cell
membrane and "non-self" proteins previously on
another organism's membrane, both types of proteins get shipped to the macrophage's cell surface.
(45) The advantage of this is that macrophages are able
to display to other more specific immune system
cells the antigens (foreign proteins) they have just
encountered. That, in turn, often results in a more
intensive immune response from these more speci-
(50) fic cells like B and T cells.

     Neutrophils are white blood cells that are
actively phagocytic like macrophages, but are not
APCs. Our bodies normally produce approximately
1 million neutrophils per second, and they can be
(55) found anywhere in the body. They usually destroy
themselves as they fight off pathogens.

     People who have decreased numbers of neutro-
phils circulating through their blood are extremely
susceptible to bacterial and fungal infections. Other
(60) white blood cells that secrete toxic substances without fine-tuned specificity include the eosinophils,
basophils, and mast cells.

PASSAGE B

     The major specific defense of the immune
system includes specialized white blood cells
(65) known as lymphocytes which come in two varieties, B cells and T cells. Both are produced by stem
cells in the bone marrow, and although T cells
mature in the thymus, B cells do not. The thymus
is essential for "educating" T cells; those that recog-
(70) nize "self" antigens (proteins found on one's own
cell surfaces) are killed off to prevent the body from
attacking itself. This negative selection results in
the development of T cell tolerance, a necessity of
the specific immune system. Yet a positive selection
(75) process also exists whereby T cells that do not react
to a specific set of glycoproteins, called MHC (major histocompatibility complex) proteins, are killed
off because T cells need to be able to bond to both
self-MHC and foreign antigens simultaneously.

(80)   There are three types of T cells: helper (TH),
cytotoxic (TC), and suppressor (TS). While TH
cells are mediators between macrophages and B
cells, TC cells are essential in defending against
viruses because they can kill virally infected cells
(85) directly. Since virally infected cells display some
viral proteins on their surfaces, TC cells can bind
to those proteins and secrete enzymes that tear the
cell membrane, thereby killing the cell. TS cells are
involved in controlling the immune response so
(90) that it does not run amok; they do this by suppress-
ing the production of antibodies by B cells.

     T cells cannot detect free antigens; they can
only respond to displayed antigens and MHC on
the surfaces of cells. When they do recognize a
(95) displayed antigen, it is always in combination with
a self-MHC protein displayed along with the antigen on the host cell surface. Interactions between
T cells and APCs are enhanced by certain proteins
that hold the T cell to the APC as it recognizes the
(100) antigen-MHC combination.

     Every B cell has surface receptors that can
recognize a specific set of foreign antigens (proteins
found on the surfaces of foreign cells and viruses).
B cells can be "activated" in one of two ways: either
(105) they can come into contact with a foreign antigen
that can bind to the B cell surface receptors, or they
can engulf a pathogen, displaying its antigens on

GO ON TO THE NEXT PAGE ⟩

the B cell surface much as a macrophage would. Then they can get activated to divide by chemicals
(110) released by a helper T cell that recognizes the foreign proteins sitting on the B cell surface.

B and T cells each have unique cell receptors. That means that almost every one of the several billion B and T cells in the body is capable of
(115) responding to a slightly different foreign antigen. When a particular B or T cell gets activated, it begins to divide rapidly to produce identical clones.

In the case of B cells, these clones will all produce antibodies of the same structure, capable
(120) of responding to the same invading antigens. B cell clones are known as plasma B cells and can produce thousands of antibody molecules per second as long as they live.

Questions 31–33 ask about Passage A.

31. According to first paragraph (lines 1–24), which of the following nonspecific defenses can kill bacteria?

   I. White blood cells that can engulf bacteria

   II. Skin secretions that have an acidic pH

   III. Mucous membranes that contain lysozyme

A. I only
B. III only
C. II and III only
D. I, II, and III

32. Which specific characteristic of macrophages often results in a more intensive immune response?

F. The specific immune system detects the pathogens that the macrophage is engulfing.
G. Macrophages are antigen-presenting cells.
H. Macrophages will pass "non-self" proteins to the specific immune system division.
J. Foreign particles are digested within macrophage lysosomes.

33. According to the passage, neutrophils:

A. may cause people to be more susceptible to disease.
B. are similar to macrophages because they engulf foreign material.
C. display non-self proteins on their cell walls as do macrophages.
D. will always destroy themselves in battling pathogens.

Questions 34–36 ask about Passage B.

34. As it is used in the passage, the word *mediators* (line 82) most nearly means:

F. regulators.
G. peacemakers.
H. instigators.
J. intermediaries.

35. According the passage, once a particular B cell gets activated, the cell:

A. divides quickly to create plasma B cells.
B. produces a foreign antigen.
C. uses pseudopodia to destroy foreign particles.
D. creates identical clones called neutrophils.

36. The passage describes a B cell as:

F. a type of macrophage that can display antigens on its surface.
G. using entirely different methods to capture foreign antigens than do macrophages.
H. being able to self-replicate as soon as it displays foreign proteins on its cells surface.
J. requiring other lymphocytes to act before it can replicate to produce antibodies.

GO ON TO THE NEXT PAGE

Questions 37–40 ask about both passages.

37. The specific immune system differs from the nonspecific immune system in that it:

   A. is more complicated.

   B. uses white blood cells.

   C. is responsible for the body's ability to become immune.

   D. does not target specific pathogens.

38. Which of the following statements provides the most accurate comparison of the passages?

   F. Passage A provides a generic overview, while Passage B provides specific detail.

   G. Passage A includes nonspecific information about a concept, while Passage B provides specific information.

   H. Passage A provides information about one aspect of a system, while Passage B provides additional information about that system.

   J. Passage A provides an explanation of a process, while Passage B provides a different explanation of that same process.

39. It can be most reasonably inferred from both passages that:

   A. certain nonspecific defenses are required to occur before certain specific defenses can commence.

   B. nonspecific and specific defenses of the immune system operate independently.

   C. nonspecific defenses serve to communicate information to specific defenses.

   D. specific defenses are more important than nonspecific passages.

40. According to both passages, which defense mechanisms are cited as being able to kill pathogens by rupturing the cell membranes?

   I. Secretions such as mucous and saliva
   II. TC cells
   III. Disease-causing organisms

   F. I only

   G. I and II only

   H. III only

   J. I, II, and III

IF YOU FINISH BEFORE TIME IS CALLED, YOU MAY CHECK YOUR WORK ON THIS SECTION ONLY. DO NOT TURN TO ANY OTHER SECTION IN THE TEST. STOP

SCIENCE TEST

35 Minutes—40 Questions

Directions: There are several passages in this test. Each passage is followed by several questions. After reading a passage, choose the best answer to each question and fill in the corresponding oval on your Answer Grid. You may refer to the passages as often as necessary. You are NOT permitted to use a calculator on this test.

PASSAGE I

Acid-base indicators are used to determine changes in pH. The pH is a quantitative measure of the hydrogen ion concentration of a solution. For any solution, the pH ranges from 0 to 14. An acid-base indicator is a weak acid or base that is sensitive to the hydrogen ion concentration and changes color at a known pH. At any other pH, the acid-base indicator is clear.

Table 1

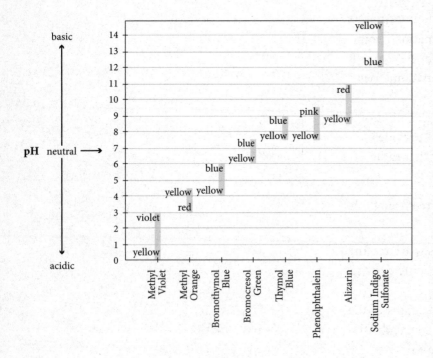

Figure 1

	ph of Common Items
14	Liquid drain cleaner
13	Bleach
12	Soapy water
11	Ammonia
10	Milk of magnesium
9	Toothpaste
8	Baking soda, seawater, eggs
7	Pure water
6	Milk
5	Black coffee
4	Tomato juice
3	Orange juice, soda
2	Lemon juice, vinegar
1	Gastric acid
0	Battery acid

GO ON TO THE NEXT PAGE

1. Which indicators undergo a color change in the region from pH 8 to pH 12?

   A. Bromocresol green, bromothymol blue, and thymol blue

   B. Thymol blue, phenolphthalein, and alizarin

   C. Phenolphthalein, alizarin, and sodium indigo sulfonate

   D. Phenolphthalein and bromothymol blue

2. Which of the following indicators undergoes a red-to-yellow or yellow-to-red color change?

   I. Alizarin

   II. Thymol blue

   III. Methyl orange

   F. I only

   G. II only

   H. I and III only

   J. I, II, and III

3. A chemist is running an experiment in a solution that becomes basic upon completion. According to the diagram, the reaction is complete when:

   A. the addition of bromocresol green results in a blue color.

   B. any indicator turns violet.

   C. a white solid appears.

   D. the addition of bromothymol blue results in a blue color.

4. Which of the following hypotheses is consistent with the information in the passage and the diagram?

   F. Color changes for any given acid-base indicator occur in a solution with a pH less than 7.

   G. Color changes for any given acid-base indicator occur in a solution with a pH greater than 7.

   H. Color changes for acid-base indicators always occur within the same pH range.

   J. Color changes for acid-base indicators vary within the pH range.

5. Compared to bromothymol blue, phenolphthalein undergoes a color change at:

   A. a higher pH.

   B. a lower pH.

   C. the same pH.

   D. Cannot be determined from the data provided.

6. Based on Figure 1 and Table 1, which of the following indicators would be most useful in determining the pH of black coffee?

   F. Methyl Orange

   G. Bromothymol Blue

   H. Bromocresol Green

   J. Alizarin

GO ON TO THE NEXT PAGE

PASSAGE II

The Brazilian tree frog (*Hyla faber*) exchanges gases through both its skin and lungs. The exchange rate depends on the temperature of the frog's environment. A series of experiments was performed to investigate this dependence.

EXPERIMENT 1

Fifty frogs were placed in a controlled atmosphere that, with the exception of temperature, was designed to simulate their native habitat. The temperature was varied from 5°C to 25°C, and equilibrium was attained before each successive temperature change. The amount of oxygen absorbed by the frogs' lungs and skin per hour was measured, and the results for all the frogs were averaged. The results are shown in Table 1.

Table 1

Temperature (°C)	Moles O_2 absorbed/hr	
	Skin	Lungs
5	15.4	8.3
10	22.7	35.1
15	43.6	64.9
20	42.1	73.5
25	40.4	78.7

EXPERIMENT 2

The same frogs were placed under the same conditions as in Experiment 1. For this experiment, the amount of carbon dioxide eliminated through the skin and lungs was measured. The results are averaged and given in Table 2.

Table 2

Temperature (°C)	Moles CO_2 eliminated/hr	
	Skin	Lungs
5	18.9	2.1
10	43.8	12.7
15	79.2	21.3
20	91.6	21.9
25	96.5	21.4

7. Scientists want to determine if other atmospheric conditions affect gas exchange in frogs. Which of the following variables should they test?

    I. Skin color
   II. Humidity level
  III. Altitude
  IV. Wind speed

A. I and II
B. I, II, and III
C. II and III
D. II, III, and IV

8. The results of Experiment 1 suggest that the total amount of O_2 absorbed per hour is:

F. affected by the temperature.
G. independent of the temperature.
H. an indication of how healthy a Brazilian tree frog is.
J. always less than the total amount of CO_2 eliminated per hour.

9. According to Experiment 2, the total amount of CO_2 eliminated per hour at 17°C is closest to:

A. 21 mol/hr.
B. 85 mol/hr.
C. 106 mol/hr.
D. 115 mol/hr.

GO ON TO THE NEXT PAGE

10. Ectotherms are animals whose bodily functions are affected by the temperature of their environment. Which of the following results supports the conclusion that *Hyla fabers* is an ectotherm?

    F. The oxygen absorbed at 25°C
    G. The carbon dioxide released by the lungs
    H. The oxygen absorbed over the entire temperature range
    J. The results do not support this conclusion.

11. According to the results of Experiment 2, which of the following plots best represents the amount of carbon dioxide eliminated through the skin and lungs as a function of temperature?

    A.

    B.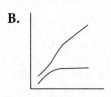

    C.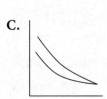

    D.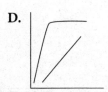

12. On the basis of the experimental results, one could conclude that as temperature increases:

    F. O_2 absorbed by the lungs increases, and CO_2 released by the skin decreases.
    G. O_2 absorbed by the lungs increases, and CO_2 released by the skin increases.
    H. O_2 absorbed by the lungs decreases, and CO_2 released by the lungs increases.
    J. O_2 absorbed by the lungs decreases, and CO_2 released by the lungs decreases.

13. According to the results of these experiments, as the temperature rises above 15°C, which of the following phenomena can be observed?

    A. The Brazilian tree frog's ability to absorb oxygen through the skin decreases, as does its ability to release carbon dioxide through the lungs.
    B. The Brazilian tree frog's ability to absorb oxygen through the skin decreases, while its ability to release carbon dioxide through the lungs remains about the same.
    C. The Brazilian tree frog's ability to absorb oxygen through the skin remains about the same, as does its ability to release carbon dioxide through the lungs.
    D. The Brazilian tree frog's ability to absorb oxygen through the skin increases, while its ability to release carbon dioxide through the lungs remains about the same.

GO ON TO THE NEXT PAGE

PASSAGE III

While the focus (point of origin) of most earthquakes lies less than 20 km below Earth's surface, certain unusual seismographic readings indicate that some activity originates at considerably greater depths. Below, two scientists discuss the possible causes of deep-focus earthquakes.

SCIENTIST 1

Surface earthquakes occur when rock in Earth's crust fractures to relieve stress. However, below 50 km, rock is under too much pressure to fracture normally. Deep-focus earthquakes are caused by the pressure of fluids trapped in Earth's tectonic plates. As a plate is forced down into the mantle by convection, increases in temperature and pressure cause changes in the crystalline structure of minerals such as serpentine. In adopting a denser configuration, the crystals dehydrate, releasing water. Other sources of fluid include water trapped in pockets of deep-sea trenches and carried down with the plates. Laboratory work has shown that fluids trapped in rock pores can cause rock to fail at lower shear stresses. In fact, at the Rocky Mountain Arsenal, the injection of fluid wastes into the ground accidentally induced a series of shallow-focus earthquakes.

SCIENTIST 2

Deep-focus earthquakes cannot result from normal fractures because rock becomes ductile at the temperatures and pressures that exist at depths greater than 50 km. Furthermore, mantle rock below 300 km is probably totally dehydrated because of the extreme pressure. Therefore, trapped fluids could not cause quakes below that depth. A better explanation is that deep-focus quakes result from the slippage that occurs when rock in a descending tectonic plate undergoes a phase change in its crystalline structure along a thin plane parallel to a stress. Just such a phase change and

resultant slippage can be produced in the laboratory by compressing a slab of calcium magnesium silicate. The pattern of deep-quake activity supports this theory. In most seismic zones, the recorded incidence of deep-focus earthquakes corresponds to the depths at which phase changes are predicted to occur in mantle rock. For example, little or no phase change is thought to occur at 400 km, and indeed, earthquake activity at this level is negligible. Between 400 and 680 km, activity once again increases. Although seismologists initially believed that earthquakes could be generated at depths as low as 1,080 or 1,200 km, no foci have been confirmed below 700 km. No phase changes are predicted for mantle rock below 680 km.

14. If deep-focus earthquakes were found to be the result of rising liquid magma in the asthenosphere, this information would support which of the following?

    I.   Scientist 1
    II. Scientist 2
    III. Neither scientist 1 nor scientist 2

    F. I only
    G. II only
    H. III only
    J. I and II

15. Scientists 1 and 2 agree on which point?

    A. Deep-earthquake activity does not occur below 400 km.
    B. Fluid allows tectonic plates to slip past one another.
    C. Water can penetrate mantle rock.
    D. Rock below 50 km will not fracture normally.

GO ON TO THE NEXT PAGE ⟶

16. Which of the following is evidence that would support Scientists 1's hypothesis?

    F. The discovery that water can be extracted from mantle-like rock at temperatures and pressures similar to those found below 300 km

    G. Seismographic indications that earthquakes occur 300 km below Earth's surface

    H. The discovery that phase changes occur in the mantle rock at depths of 1,080 km

    J. An earthquake underneath Los Angeles that was shown to have been caused by water trapped in sewer lines

17. Both scientists assume that:

    A. deep-focus earthquakes are more common than surface earthquakes.

    B. trapped fluids cause surface earth-quakes.

    C. earth's crust is composed of mobile tectonic plates.

    D. deep-focus earthquakes cannot be felt on Earth's crust without special recording devices.

18. To best refute Scientist 2's hypothesis, Scientist 1 might:

    F. find evidence of other sources of underground water.

    G. record a deep-focus earthquake below 680 km.

    H. find a substance that does not undergo phase changes even at depths equivalent to 680 km.

    J. show that rock becomes ductile at depths of less than 50 km.

19. According to Scientist 1, the earthquake at Rocky Mountain Arsenal occurred because:

    A. serpentine or other minerals dehydrated and released water.

    B. fluid wastes injected into the ground compressed a thin slab of calcium magnesium silicate.

    C. fluid wastes injected into the ground flooded pockets of a deep-sea trench.

    D. fluid wastes injected into the ground lowered the shear stress failure point of the rock.

20. Scientist 2's hypothesis would be strengthened by evidence showing that:

    F. water evaporates at high temperatures and pressures.

    G. deep-focus earthquakes can occur at 680 km.

    H. stress has the same effect on mantle rock that it has on calcium magnesium silicate.

    J. water pockets exist at depths below 300 km.

21. According to Scientist 2, phase changes in the crystalline structure of a descending tectonic plate:

    A. occur only at Earth's surface.

    B. are not possible.

    C. cause certain minerals to release water, which exerts pressure within the plate.

    D. cause slippage that directly results in an earthquake.

GO ON TO THE NEXT PAGE

PASSAGE IV

Astronomers want to know the effects of atmospheric conditions on the impact of an asteroid-to-Earth collision. The most common hypothesis is that the presence of moisture in Earth's atmosphere significantly reduces the hazardous effects of such a collision. One researcher has decided to create a laboratory model of Earth. The researcher has the ability to control the amount of moisture surrounding the model. The researcher has also created models of asteroids of various sizes. The researcher will use a collision indicator (see table below) based on the Torino Scale to measure the results of two experiments.

Collision Indicator	
Torino Scale Collision Rating	Impact Effect
0 to 0.9	A collision capable of little destruction
1 to 3.9	A collision capable of localized destruction
4 to 6.9	A collision capable of regional destruction
7 to 10	A collision capable of global catastrophe

EXPERIMENT 1

The researcher simulated collisions on the Earth model of asteroid models representing mass equivalent to 1,000 kg to 1,000,000 kg. The controlled moisture level of the model Earth's atmosphere was 86%. The effects of the collisions were recorded and rated according to the collision indicator.

EXPERIMENT 2

The researcher simulated collisions on the Earth model of asteroid models representing the same masses as in Experiment 1. The controlled moisture level of the model Earth's atmosphere in this experiment was 12%. The effects of the collisions were recorded and rated according to the collision indicator. The results of both experiments are shown in the graph.

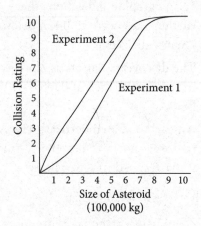

22. How was the experimental design of Experiment 1 different from that of Experiment 2?

 F. The impacts of more asteroids were measured.

 G. The impacts of larger asteroids were measured.

 H. There was more moisture in the atmosphere.

 J. There was a different collision indicator.

23. If the atmospheric moisture in Experiment 2 was increased to 50%, the collision rating for an asteroid with a mass of 400,000 kg would most likely be between:

 A. 2 and 3.

 B. 4.5 and 5.5.

 C. 6 and 7.

 D. 9 and 10.

GO ON TO THE NEXT PAGE ⟩

24. Based on the experimental results, one can generalize that an increase of moisture in the atmosphere would:

F. decrease the impact of an asteroid-to-Earth collision, regardless of the size of the asteroid.

G. decrease the impact of an asteroid-to-Earth collision involving an asteroid under 700,000 kg.

H. increase the impact of an asteroid-to-Earth collision, regardless of the size of the asteroid.

J. increase the impact of an asteroid-to-Earth collision involving an asteroid under 700,000 kg.

25. In a simulated asteroid-to-Earth collision, a 400,000 kg asteroid received a collision rating of 4. The amount of moisture in the atmosphere was most likely closest to:

A. 0%.

B. 12%.

C. 86%.

D. 100%.

26. According to the researcher's model, a 100,000 kg asteroid colliding in an atmosphere with a moisture level of 12% would be likely to have the same impact as an asteroid colliding in an atmosphere with a moisture level of 86% with a size closest to which of the following?

F. 50,000 kg

G. 120,000 kg

H. 270,000 kg

J. 490,000 kg

27. To be minimally capable of regional destruction, an asteroid entering an atmosphere with a moisture level of 86% would have to be roughly what percent larger than an asteroid capable of the same level of destruction entering an atmosphere with a moisture level of 12%?

A. 20%

B. 70%

C. 150%

D. 220%

28. If researchers were to find evidence of a 350,000 kg collision on Earth that resulted in a Torino Scale Collision Rating of 1.5, the moisture level would be:

F. less than 12%.

G. greater than 86%.

H. exactly 12%.

J. exactly 86%.

GO ON TO THE NEXT PAGE

PASSAGE V

The electrical conductivity of a material determines how it will react to various temperature conditions in a consumer product. Product researchers need to know how a material will react in order to determine its safety for consumer use. The electrical conductivity of two different samples of a platinum dithiolate compound was measured from 10 K to 275 K. The results and general conductivity versus temperature plots for conductors and semiconductors are shown here.

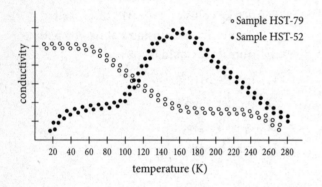

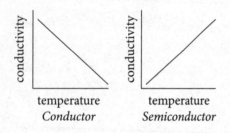

Conductor   Semiconductor

29. At what temperature do both samples demonstrate semiconductor-like behavior?

   A. 115 K
   B. 160 K
   C. 275 K
   D. They do not share a common temperature for semiconductor behavior.

30. For Sample HST-52, which of the following describes its behavior when the temperature is dropped from 200 K to 100 K?

   F. The sample remains a semiconductor.
   G. The sample remains a conductor.
   H. The sample undergoes a conductor to semiconductor transition.
   J. The sample undergoes a semiconductor to conductor transition.

31. In a material exhibiting conductor-like behavior, the conductivity:

   A. increases as the temperature increases.
   B. decreases as the temperature increases.
   C. decreases as the temperature decreases.
   D. remains the same at all temperatures.

GO ON TO THE NEXT PAGE

32. A newly developed material has a semiconductor to conductor transition at about 10 K
as the temperature increases. Its conductivity versus temperature plot would resemble
which of the following?

F.

G.

H.

J.

33. An industrial firm wishes to use HST-52
as a semiconductor in an assembly-line
component. The experimental results indicate
that:

A. HST-52 is not a semiconductor; a new
material will have to be chosen.

B. HST-52 is suitable for the planned application.

C. HST-52 is too brittle to be used in this
manner.

D. HST-52 will be usable only if the
assembly line is maintained at less than
150 K.

34. The temperature at which a compound's
conductivity-versus-temperature plot declines
most quickly is known as its "optimal conductor" temperature. Which of the following
could be the optimal conductor temperature
for Sample HST-52?

F. 20 K

G. 80 K

H. 160 K

J. 180 K

GO ON TO THE NEXT PAGE

PASSAGE VI

Siamese cats have a genotype for dark fur, but the enzymes that produce the dark coloring function best at temperatures below the cat's normal body temperature. A Siamese cat usually has darker fur on its ears, nose, paws, and tail, because these parts have a lower temperature than the rest of its body. If a Siamese cat spends more than one hour a day for six consecutive days outdoors (an "outdoor" cat) during very cold weather, darker fur grows in other places on its body. If a Siamese cat does not spend this amount of time outdoors, it is an "indoor" cat. The amount of dark fur on its body remains constant throughout the year.

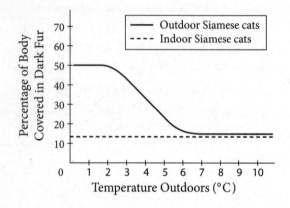

35. According to the graph, if the average temperature outdoors drops from 2°C to 0°C over the course of a month, what will most likely happen to the fur of an outdoor Siamese cat during the same time period? Over that time, the percentage of the cat's body covered in dark fur will:

    A. increase.
    B. decrease.
    C. remain the same.
    D. increase, then decrease.

36. A particular Siamese cat goes outdoors a total of three hours per week during the coldest part of the year. One could predict that the percentage of its body covered by dark fur would be closest to:

    F. 0%.
    G. 10%.
    H. 40%.
    J. 60%.

37. According to the graph, what is the most likely temperature outside if outdoor Siamese cats have 45% of their bodies covered in dark fur?

    A. 0°C
    B. 3°C
    C. 6°C
    D. 9°C

38. If a Siamese cat that lived indoors was lost and later found with dark fur over 30% of its body, which of the following could be inferred about the period during which it was missing:

    I. It was living in an area where temperatures fell below 5°C.
    II. It spent more time outdoors than indoors.
    III. It was missing for at least six days.

    F. I and II only
    G. I and III only
    H. II and III only
    J. I, II, and III

GO ON TO THE NEXT PAGE

39. If a Siamese cat has dark fur over 10% of its body, which of the following must be true about the cat?

A. It lives indoors.

B. It lives in an area where the temperature outdoors is usually 7°C or higher.

C. It either lives indoors or it lives in an area where the temperature outdoors is usually 7°C or higher.

D. None of the above

40. If a researcher wants to find out how fur color is affected by the amount of time a Siamese cat spends outside in cold weather, which experiment would be the most helpful?

F. The indoor cats in the original experiment should be used as the control group, and their fur color should be compared to a group of Siamese cats spending six hours or more a day outside in cold weather for six consecutive days.

G. A new group of Siamese cats should be formed and kept outside two or more hours a day at varying temperatures. Their fur color at different outdoor temperatures should be compared to that of the outdoor cats already charted.

H. Siamese cats should be split into two groups, one group spending only one hour per day outside for six consecutive days in cold weather and the other group spending at least two hours a day outside for six consecutive days in the same weather.

J. No new experiment is needed. The data already gathered show that the more time a Siamese cat spends outside in cold weather, the darker its fur will be.

WRITING TEST

40 Minutes—1 Question

Directions: This is a test of your writing skills. You will have forty (40) minutes to write an essay in English. Before you begin planning and writing your essay, read the writing prompt carefully to understand exactly what you are being asked to do. Your essay will be evaluated on the evidence it provides of your ability to do the following:

- Express judgments by evaluating the three perspectives given in the prompt, taking a position on an issue, and explaining the relationship among all four ideas
- Develop a position by using logical reasoning and by supporting your ideas
- Maintain a focus on the topic throughout the essay
- Organize ideas in a logical way
- Use language clearly and effectively according to the conventions of standard written English

You may use a separate piece of paper to plan your essay. *You must write your essay in pencil on the lined pages provided after the prompt.* Your writing on those lined pages will be scored. You may not need all the lined pages, but to ensure you have enough room to finish, do NOT skip lines. You may write corrections or additions neatly between the lines of your essay, but do NOT write in the margins of the lined pages. *Illegible essays cannot be scored, so you must write (or print) clearly.*

DO NOT OPEN THIS BOOKLET UNTIL TOLD TO DO SO.

GO ON TO THE NEXT PAGE

STUDENT ENGAGEMENT

Studies show that students not only retain more information but also enjoy learning more when they actively participate in the classroom. Teachers therefore strive to optimize engagement to foster a positive, effective instructional environment. In an effort to increase student interaction in the high school classroom, some educators argue that curriculum should take into account the interests and suggestions of students. Since teachers cannot allow students to choose every aspect of a lesson, is it worth the time and effort to actively seek relevant student feedback? As high schools aim to improve the quality of the education they offer to students, student opinion may prove to be valuable.

Read and carefully consider these perspectives. Each discusses the relevance of student feedback in lesson planning.

Perspective One	Perspective Two	Perspective Three
Many colleges require students to complete a course survey before they are eligible to receive their semester grades. Colleges use students' responses to evaluate course materials to ensure quality education. High schools would benefit from implementing a similar system of regular feedback on classroom lesson plans by students.	Students are not qualified to provide insight regarding lesson planning or curriculum design. Improving education quality is the responsibility of educators, and they are rightfully in charge of making effective changes.	Many school districts evaluate teachers using students' test scores and conducting in-classroom observations. Information gathered from student surveys could not only inform lesson design, but also provide another source of evaluation by which to measure teacher effectiveness.

ESSAY TASK

Write a unified, coherent essay in which you evaluate multiple perspectives on the relevance of student feedback in lesson planning. In your essay, be sure to:

- analyze and evaluate the perspectives given
- state and develop your own perspective on the issue
- explain the relationship between your perspective and those given

Your perspective may be in full agreement with any of the others, in partial agreement, or wholly different. Whatever the case, support your ideas with logical reasoning and detailed, persuasive examples.

GO ON TO THE NEXT PAGE

PLANNING YOUR ESSAY

You may wish to consider the following as you think critically about the task:

Strengths and weaknesses of the three given perspectives

- What insights do they offer, and what do they fail to consider?
- Why might they be persuasive to others, or why might they fail to persuade?

Your own knowledge, experience, and values

- What is your perspective on this issue, and what are its strengths and weaknesses?
- How will you support your perspective in your essay?

_____

_____

_____

_____

_____

_____

_____

_____

_____

_____

_____

_____

_____

_____

_____

_____

_____

GO ON TO THE NEXT PAGE

Practice Test Two
ANSWER KEY

ENGLISH TEST

1. D	11. A	21. B	31. A	41. C	51. B	61. B	71. B
2. G	12. J	22. J	32. J	42. J	52. J	62. F	72. F
3. C	13. A	23. B	33. B	43. A	53. C	63. D	73. B
4. J	14. F	24. F	34. H	44. J	54. J	64. G	74. J
5. B	15. D	25. C	35. A	45. D	55. C	65. B	75. B
6. G	16. G	26. J	36. H	46. H	56. J	66. F	
7. D	17. A	27. B	37. B	47. A	57. C	67. C	
8. J	18. J	28. G	38. J	48. G	58. F	68. H	
9. B	19. C	29. C	39. A	49. B	59. D	69. B	
10. H	20. F	30. F	40. G	50. G	60. F	70. J	

MATHEMATICS TEST

1. A	9. D	17. E	25. C	33. B	41. B	49. C	57. B
2. J	10. F	18. K	26. J	34. K	42. H	50. F	58. J
3. A	11. B	19. D	27. C	35. D	43. E	51. C	59. C
4. G	12. G	20. G	28. H	36. K	44. K	52. F	60. J
5. B	13. D	21. E	29. D	37. B	45. E	53. B	
6. H	14. G	22. H	30. H	38. F	46. K	54. J	
7. C	15. D	23. A	31. A	39. A	47. E	55. E	
8. J	16. F	24. G	32. F	40. K	48. G	56. G	

READING TEST

1. D	6. G	11. B	16. G	21. A	26. J	31. B	36. J
2. G	7. C	12. J	17. C	22. J	27. C	32. G	37. C
3. B	8. J	13. C	18. G	23. D	28. G	33. B	38. H
4. G	9. C	14. G	19. D	24. H	29. B	34. J	39. A
5. C	10. G	15. A	20. F	25. D	30. F	35. A	40. G

SCIENCE TEST

1. B	6. G	11. B	16. F	21. D	26. H	31. B	36. G
2. H	7. D	12. G	17. C	22. H	27. B	32. H	37. B
3. A	8. F	13. B	18. G	23. B	28. J	33. D	38. G
4. J	9. C	14. H	19. D	24. G	29. D	34. J	39. C
5. A	10. H	15. D	20. H	25. C	30. H	35. C	40. H

ANSWERS AND EXPLANATIONS

ENGLISH TEST

PASSAGE I

1. D
Category: Punctuation
Difficulty: Medium
Getting to the Answer: A comma is needed to set off the introductory phrase, so A cannot be correct. Choice B creates a sentence fragment, and the pronoun *it* in C does not match the subject of the sentence—Duke Ellington.

2. G
Category: Verb Tenses
Difficulty: Low
Getting to the Answer: The whole passage is in past tense, and there is no reason why this verb should not be in past tense as well. Also, the part of the sentence on the other side of the semicolon gives you a big clue by using *paid*.

3. C
Category: Punctuation
Difficulty: Medium
Getting to the Answer: The colon is used incorrectly in the original sentence, and B does not solve the problem. Choice D is unnecessarily wordy.

4. J
Category: Punctuation
Difficulty: High
Getting to the Answer: Commas are needed between items in a series, so eliminate F and G. A comma is also needed to set off the introductory phrase, so eliminate H.

5. B
Category: Word Choice
Difficulty: Medium
Getting to the Answer: In order to figure out the appropriate pronoun, identify the noun to which the pronoun refers. The only possible corresponding noun is *Ellington*; therefore, (B) is the correct answer.

6. G
Category: Sentence Sense
Difficulty: High
Getting to the Answer: "As a teenager in Washington" is not a complete sentence. Choice H does not make sense, and J is incorrect because the comma is unnecessary.

7. D
Category: Word Choice
Difficulty: Medium
Getting to the Answer: The word *then* should be *than*—(D) makes this correction.

8. J
Category: Wordiness
Difficulty: Low
Getting to the Answer: Even though the piano teacher's name is mentioned in the preceding sentence, more information about her name is unnecessary to make the sentence relevant to the passage.

9. B
Category: Connections
Difficulty: Medium
Getting to the Answer: There is a contrast between Ellington's not being a good pianist and his hearing about the opportunities for musicians in New York. The correct contrast is established by (B).

10. H
Category: Wordiness
Difficulty: Medium
Getting to the Answer: *Awaited* and *were there for* mean the same thing, so one part of the underlined portion should be deleted—that eliminates F and G. Choice J is also unnecessarily wordy.

11. A
Category: Sentence Sense
Difficulty: Medium
Getting to the Answer: The sentence is logical in the flow of the paragraph, so eliminate D. The paragraph discusses Ellington's move to Harlem, and the *they* in the next sentence indicates Ellington wasn't alone. Choice (A) is the simplest and most correct way to phrase the sentence.

12. J
Category: Word Choice
Difficulty: Medium
Getting to the Answer: The subject of the sentence is the Cotton Club, so choices with the pronoun *he*—F and G—should be eliminated. Choice H creates a sentence fragment.

13. A
Category: Writing Strategy
Difficulty: Low
Getting to the Answer: This list of songs follows a description of Ellington's early musical career, so (A) is correct. The songs do not contradict anything, so eliminate B. The names of the songs themselves do not illustrate complexity; therefore, C is incorrect. This part of the paragraph is no longer about the Cotton Club, so eliminate D.

14. F
Category: Writing Strategy
Difficulty: Medium
Getting to the Answer: The last paragraph of the essay lists the accomplishments of Ellington. Choice (F) is the only answer choice that makes sense.

15. D
Category: Organization
Difficulty: High
Getting to the Answer: Paragraph 4 is the only paragraph that covers elements of Ellington's music. The logical place for the insertion is before the last sentence of the essay where his musical ability is discussed.

PASSAGE II

16. G
Category: Word Choice
Difficulty: Medium
Getting to the Answer: The subject is *animals*, so a plural pronoun is needed. Choice F is a singular pronoun, H is a contraction, and J uses *there* instead of *their*.

17. A
Category: Punctuation
Difficulty: Medium
Getting to the Answer: The comma is needed to set off the second clause from the first, so eliminate B and D. Choice C incorrectly uses a colon.

18. J
Category: Punctuation
Difficulty: High
Getting to the Answer: The phrase "a member of the weasel family" is a nonessential clause and should be set off by commas. Eliminate G and H because they create sentence fragments.

19. C
Category: Verb Tenses
Difficulty: Medium
Getting to the Answer: "Having changed" is the incorrect verb tense. Ermines are nonhuman, so B is incorrect; choice (C) uses *that* correctly. The whole passage is in present tense, so eliminate D because it is in past tense.

20. F
Category: Sentence Sense
Difficulty: Low
Getting to the Answer: Choose the most logical order of the words. Choice (F) makes the most sense.

21. B
Category: Punctuation
Difficulty: Medium
Getting to the Answer: "Far from placing it in danger" is an introductory phrase and should be set off by a comma. Eliminate A and C. Choice D is unnecessarily wordy and doesn't make sense with the rest of the sentence.

22. J
Category: Wordiness
Difficulty: Medium
Getting to the Answer: "By distinguishing itself from other animals" is a sentence fragment. These words make sense as an introductory phrase and should therefore be set off by a comma. Choice (J) is the only choice that accomplishes this concisely.

23. B
Category: Wordiness
Difficulty: Low
Getting to the Answer: The unnecessary phrase "the question is" should be eliminated. Choice (B) is the simplest and most correct way to phrase the question.

24. F
Category: Verb Tenses
Difficulty: High
Getting to the Answer: The investigating has occurred in the past, and it is still occurring. The tense of the answer choice should be present perfect. Choices G and H only refer to the past, and J refers only to the present.

25. C
Category: Connections
Difficulty: Medium
Getting to the Answer: The previous sentence speaks of special glands, but this sentence says that some animals do not have these glands. This is a contrast, and *however* sets it up best.

26. J
Category: Wordiness
Difficulty: Low
Getting to the Answer: *Remains* and *endures as* are the same thing, so the correct choice will eliminate one of them. Choice (J) does just that.

27. B
Category: Word Choice
Difficulty: Low
Getting to the Answer: The pronoun *it* refers to the tree frog, not a background of leaves. Choice (B) fixes this modifier error by placing "the tree frog" after the modifying phrase.

28. G
Category: Wordiness
Difficulty: Medium
Getting to the Answer: The information pertains to the paragraph's topic, so eliminate J. Choice (G) is a simple and logical way of rephrasing all of the excess words.

29. C
Category: Organization
Difficulty: High
Getting to the Answer: Paragraph 4 begins with an introduction, and paragraph 3 ends with a conclusion. Choice (C) is the only choice that features this correct order.

30. F
Category: Writing Strategy
Difficulty: Medium
Getting to the Answer: The author covers a range of topics in the area and uses several animals as examples. All of the other answer choices are incorrect because they contradict things that the author does in the essay.

PASSAGE III

31. A
Category: Wordiness
Difficulty: Medium
Getting to the Answer: The other answer choices are unnecessarily wordy.

32. J
Category: Wordiness
Difficulty: Medium
Getting to the Answer: The other answer choices are unnecessarily wordy.

33. B
Category: Sentence Sense
Difficulty: High
Getting to the Answer: The sentences on both sides of the period are fragments. The best way to fix this mistake is to simply combine the sentences as (B) does.

34. H
Category: Wordiness
Difficulty: Low
Getting to the Answer: *Included* and *held* relay the same information. Choice (H) deletes one of the unnecessary words.

35. A
Category: Verb Tenses
Difficulty: Medium
Getting to the Answer: The drink was unusual to the people who had never experienced it before.

In other words, the verb form should be past tense. Eliminate B and C. Choice D does not make sense, so eliminate it.

36. H
Category: Sentence Sense
Difficulty: Medium
Getting to the Answer: "Over the next century" is an introductory phrase and should be set off by a comma. Choices (H) and J add the comma, but J also adds unnecessary words.

37. B
Category: Writing Strategy
Difficulty: Medium
Getting to the Answer: This description would add some "color" to the essay. It would not weaken or contradict anything, so eliminate A and C. It would not say anything about the author's opinion of chocolate either, so eliminate D.

38. J
Category: Punctuation
Difficulty: Low
Getting to the Answer: Commas are needed between items in a series. Choice G is incorrect because there are too many commas.

39. A
Category: Connections
Difficulty: Medium
Getting to the Answer: The sentence provides an example of the uses of chocolate worldwide. Choices B and C set up an unwarranted contrast. Choice D is not a good transition between the two sentences.

40. G
Category: Sentence Sense
Difficulty: Medium
Getting to the Answer: The word *do* is unnecessary in the sentence, especially with the presence of *nonetheless*. Choice (G) is the most concise statement of the information.

41. C
Category: Punctuation
Difficulty: Medium
Getting to the Answer: The colon is not used properly here, so eliminate A, B, and D.

42. J
Category: Wordiness
Difficulty: Low
Getting to the Answer: Tea has nothing to do with the topic, so the sentence should be eliminated.

43. A
Category: Word Choice
Difficulty: Low
Getting to the Answer: The research will be welcomed *by* people, not *to* or *with* them. Therefore, eliminate B and D. "Us with a sweet tooth" does not make sense, so (A) is the correct answer.

44. J
Category: Wordiness
Difficulty: Medium
Getting to the Answer: Choices F and G do not make any sense at all. Between H and (J), the latter is the best style.

45. D
Category: Writing Strategy
Difficulty: Medium
Getting to the Answer: This essay is about only chocolate, and it does not cover any other culinary trends in history. Therefore, it would not meet the requirement.

PASSAGE IV

46. H
Category: Word Choice
Difficulty: Medium
Getting to the Answer: Here, the verb is being used as part of a modifying phrase. Choice (H) is idiomatically correct.

47. A
Category: Punctuation
Difficulty: Medium
Getting to the Answer: Commas are needed in a series, so eliminate C. A colon is not appropriate; eliminate B. Choice D incorrectly switches to the past tense.

48. G
Category: Word Choice
Difficulty: Medium
Getting to the Answer: The form needed is the possessive of *who,* so (G) is correct.

49. B
Category: Verb Tenses
Difficulty: Medium
Getting to the Answer: This sentence is part of a list of proposed "uniform of the future" developments. The other sentences in that list use the verbs *would be, would become,* and *would transmit;* the correct form is (B).

50. G
Category: Punctuation
Difficulty: High
Getting to the Answer: No commas are needed in a list of only two items.

51. B
Category: Sentence Sense
Difficulty: Low
Getting to the Answer: Be wary of sentences that begin with *to;* they are often fragments like the one here. Choice (B) is the best and most concise way to combine the two parts of the sentence.

52. J
Category: Wordiness
Difficulty: Medium
Getting to the Answer: Two words in the underlined portion of the sentence have closely related meanings: *concealing* means "keeping from being

observed" or "hiding," and *invisible* means "hidden" or "impossible to see." Because these words convey the same idea, this is a redundancy that can be fixed by eliminating one of the two words. Therefore, eliminate F, G, and H and select (J) as the answer.

53. C
Category: Writing Strategy
Difficulty: Medium
Getting to the Answer: To determine the U.S. Army's opinion of the Invisible Soldier program, look at the words used to introduce and describe it: the army has dreamed of such a program and invested in it. So the army attitude is positive; eliminate the negative word *skeptical* in A and the neutral words *curious* and *detailed* in B and D, leaving *enthusiastic*, (C).

54. J
Category: Writing Strategy
Difficulty: High
Getting to the Answer: In context, this paragraph offers a specific example of the more general issues raised in paragraph 1.

55. C
Category: Wordiness
Difficulty: Medium
Getting to the Answer: Although the underlined segment is necessary, having *beginning* and *early stages* is redundant. Choice (C) is the most concise way to rephrase this.

56. J
Category: Sentence Sense
Difficulty: Medium
Getting to the Answer: As written, this is a run-on sentence, so eliminate F. To correct it, the new clause should be made subordinate by replacing the pronoun with a relative pronoun, so eliminate H. The correct form, because it follows a comma, is *which* rather than *that*, so eliminate G.

57. C
Category: Word Choice
Difficulty: Medium
Getting to the Answer: The passage has a formal, technical tone. It would, therefore, be inappropriate for the author to use the highly informal expressions "you know, is" or "is, like" eliminate A and B. The choice "however, is" is appropriate because this paragraph contrasts with the preceding one. Choice D would be appropriate if this paragraph drew a conclusion based on the prior paragraph, but it doesn't.

58. F
Category: Punctuation
Difficulty: High
Getting to the Answer: A colon is correct punctuation here because the material that follows it is an explanation of what precedes it.

59. D
Category: Organization
Difficulty: Medium
Getting to the Answer: Only sentence 2 and sentence 1 are choices for a first sentence. To put the sentences in logical order, first look for a good transition from paragraph 4, which discusses a problem. Sentence 1 explicitly refers to addressing the problem, so it's the better choice. Eliminate A and B. The second sentence should follow logically from sentence 1's description of the new color-changing pixel, and your choices are sentences 4 and 5. Sentence 4 in C refers to mirrors, which we haven't encountered before in the passage, rather than pixels, so eliminate this choice. That leaves us with (D), sentence 5, which refers to the pixels introduced in the first sentence.

60. F
Category: Organization
Difficulty: Medium
Getting to the Answer: To answer this question, you need an idea of the purpose of each

paragraph. Paragraph 1 introduces the "uniform of the future," paragraph 2 the Invisible Soldier program, paragraph 3 the program's early-stage solution, paragraph 4 a problem with that solution, and paragraph 5 a new advance that may solve that problem. The new sentences to be inserted do not discuss a problem with such a program. You can therefore eliminate G, H, and J. The material properly belongs in paragraph 2, (F), because it introduces camouflage generally.

PASSAGE V

61. B
Category: Sentence Sense
Difficulty: Low
Getting to the Answer: Choices A and C are too wordy, and D does not continue the verb tense established in the series.

62. F
Category: Punctuation
Difficulty: Medium
Getting to the Answer: The colon is used here to dramatically introduce California. The commas in G and H do not do this well, and the separate sentence in J does not work either.

63. D
Category: Verb Tenses
Difficulty: Low
Getting to the Answer: This paragraph is in the past tense, so the introductory sentence should be in the past tense as well.

64. G
Category: Punctuation
Difficulty: Medium
Getting to the Answer: This is a long nonessential clause that should be set off by a comma—eliminate F and H. Choice J is incorrect because it unnecessarily adds more words.

65. B
Category: Sentence Sense
Difficulty: Medium
Getting to the Answer: The word order is incorrect in A. Choice C creates a sentence fragment, and *did* in D is unnecessary.

66. F
Category: Wordiness
Difficulty: Medium
Getting to the Answer: The information is pertinent to the topic, and (F) is the clearest way to express it.

67. C
Category: Word Choice
Difficulty: Low
Getting to the Answer: The only choice that works here is (C), which uses the correct possessive form.

68. H
Category: Sentence Sense
Difficulty: Medium
Getting to the Answer: Choice F is a sentence fragment. Choices G and J are very awkward.

69. B
Category: Writing Strategy
Difficulty: Medium
Getting to the Answer: The last sentence of the previous paragraph talks about how workers began to quit their jobs to join the gold rush. The first sentence of this paragraph magnifies this point. Choice (B) is the only logical transition.

70. J
Category: Wordiness
Difficulty: Medium
Getting to the Answer: This information is not pertinent to the gold rush back in 1849.

71. B
Category: Wordiness
Difficulty: Low
Getting to the Answer: *Singularly* and *one* are redundant. Choice C is too wordy, and D is incorrect within the context of the sentence.

72. F
Category: Connections
Difficulty: Medium
Getting to the Answer: This sentence is a more specific detail that illustrates the preceding sentence. Choice (F) is the best transition between the two sentences.

73. B
Category: Word Choice
Difficulty: Medium
Getting to the Answer: Choice A makes it sound as though lives are changing the place rather than the other way around. Choice C does not make sense, and D is grammatically incorrect.

74. J
Category: Sentence Sense
Difficulty: Medium
Getting to the Answer: Choices F and H do not make sense because of the word *and*. Choice G is incorrect because the sentence is talking about people today, not the Forty-niners.

75. B
Category: Writing Strategy
Difficulty: High
Getting to the Answer: Though the Forty-niners are mentioned, the focus of the essay is on the history of the California gold rush. Therefore, the essay would not meet the requirements of the assignment.

MATHEMATICS TEST

1. A
Category: Proportions and Probability
Difficulty: Low
Getting to the Answer: To reduce a number by 20%, you could take 20% of the original number and subtract the result, or you could just take 80% of the original number:

$$\text{New price} = 80\% \text{ of original price}$$
$$= (0.80)(\$125)$$
$$= \$100$$

2. J
Category: Variable Manipulation
Difficulty: Low
Getting to the Answer: Plug in $x = -5$ and see what you get:

$$2x^2 - 6x + 5 = 2(-5)^2 - 6(-5) + 5$$
$$= 2 \times 25 - (-30) + 5$$
$$= 50 + 30 + 5$$
$$= 85$$

3. A
Category: Number Properties
Difficulty: Medium
Getting to the Answer: The prime factorization of 36 is $2 \times 2 \times 3 \times 3$. That factorization includes two distinct prime factors, 2 and 3.

4. G
Category: Plane Geometry
Difficulty: Medium
Getting to the Answer: The exterior angles of a triangle (or any polygon, for that matter) add up to $360°$:

$$x + 85 + 160 = 360$$
$$x = 115$$

5. B
Category: Number Properties
Difficulty: High
Getting to the Answer: Don't jump to hasty conclusions—don't just average the denominators. Do it right—add the fractions and divide by 2:

$$\text{Average of two numbers} = \frac{\text{Sum}}{2}$$

$$\frac{\frac{1}{20} + \frac{1}{30}}{2} = \frac{\frac{3}{60} + \frac{2}{60}}{2} = \frac{\frac{5}{60}}{2} = \frac{\frac{1}{12}}{2} = \frac{1}{12} \times \frac{1}{2} = \frac{1}{24}$$

6. H
Category: Variable Manipulation
Difficulty: Medium
Getting to the Answer: Everyone pays $1.50, and the rest of the toll is based on the number of miles traveled. Subtract $1.50 from Joy's toll to see how much is based on distance traveled: $25.00 − $1.50 = $23.50. Then divide that amount by 25 cents per mile:

$$\frac{\$23.50}{\$0.25 \text{ per mile}} = 94 \text{ miles}$$

7. C
Category: Operations
Difficulty: Medium
Getting to the Answer: Multiply the coefficients and add the exponents:

$$3x^2 \times 5x^3 = 3 \times 5 \times x^2 + x^3 = 15x^5$$

8. J
Category: Coordinate Geometry
Difficulty: High
Getting to the Answer: You could use the distance formula, but it's easier here to think about a right triangle. One leg is the difference between the x's, which is 3, and the other leg is the difference between the y's, which is 4, so you're looking at a 3-4-5 triangle. The hypotenuse, which is the distance from P to Q, is 5.

9. D
Category: Proportions and Probability
Difficulty: Medium
Getting to the Answer: Percent times whole equals part:

$$(\text{Percent}) \times 25 = 16$$
$$\text{Percent} = \frac{16}{25} = 0.64 = 64\%$$

10. F
Category: Proportions and Probability
Difficulty: Medium
Getting to the Answer: For $\frac{7}{x}$ to be greater than $\frac{1}{4}$, the denominator x has to be less than 4 times the numerator, or 28. And for $\frac{7}{x}$ to be less than $\frac{1}{3}$, the denominator x has to be greater than 3 times the numerator, or 21. Thus, x could be any of the integers 22 through 27, of which there are 6.

11. B
Category: Variable Manipulation
Difficulty: Medium
Getting to the Answer: To factor $6x^2 − 13x + 6$, you need a pair of binomials whose "first" terms will give you a product of $6x^2$ and whose "last" terms will give you a product of 6. Because the middle term of the result is negative, the two last terms must both be negative. You know that one of the factors is among the answer choices, so you can use them in your trial-and-error effort to factor. You know you're looking for a factor with a minus sign in it, so the answer's either (B) or D.

Try (B) first: Its first term is $3x$, so the other factor's first term would have to be $2x$ (to get that $6x^2$ in the product). Choice (B)'s last term is −2, so the other factor's last term would have to be −3. Check to see whether $(3x − 2)(2x − 3)$ works:

$$(3x − 2)(2x − 3) = (3x \times 2x) + [3x(−3)]$$
$$+ [(−2)(2x)] + [(−2)(−3)]$$
$$= 6x^2 − 9x − 4x + 6$$
$$= 6x^2 − 13x + 6$$

It works. There's no need to check D.

12. G

Category: Variable Manipulation

Difficulty: Medium

Getting to the Answer: The four fractions on the left side of the equation are all ready to be added, because they already have a common denominator: *a*.

$$\frac{1}{a} + \frac{2}{a} + \frac{3}{a} + \frac{4}{a} = 5$$

$$\frac{1+2+3+4}{a} = 5$$

$$\frac{10}{a} = 5$$

$$10 = 5a$$

$$a = 2$$

13. D

Category: Plane Geometry

Difficulty: Medium

Getting to the Answer: ∠CGE and ∠BGF are vertical angles, so∠BGF measures 105°. If you subtract ∠AGB from ∠BGF, you're left with ∠AGF, the angle you're looking for. So ∠AGF measures 105° − 40°, or 65°.

14. G

Category: Variable Manipulation

Difficulty: Medium

Getting to the Answer: You solve an inequality much the way you solve an equation: Do the same things to both sides until you've isolated what you're solving for. (Just remember to flip the sign if you ever multiply or divide both sides by a negative number.) Here, you want to isolate *x*:

$$-3 < 4x - 5$$

$$2 < 4x$$

$$\frac{2}{4} < x$$

$$x > \frac{1}{2}$$

15. D

Category: Plane Geometry

Difficulty: Medium

Getting to the Answer: Because *BD* bisects ∠ABC, the measure of ∠ABD is 50°. Now you know two of the three angles of ΔABD, so the third angle measures 180° − 60° − 50° = 70°.

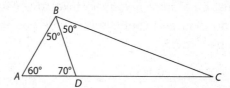

∠BDC, the angle you're looking for, is supplementary to the 70° angle, so ∠BDC measures 180° − 70° = 110°.

16. F

Category: Variable Manipulation

Difficulty: High

Getting to the Answer: To express *y* in terms of *x*, isolate *y*:

$$x + 2y - 3 = xy$$

$$2y - xy = -x + 3$$

$$y(2 - x) = 3 - x$$

$$y = \frac{3 - x}{2 - x}$$

17. E

Category: Proportions and Probability

Difficulty: Medium

Getting to the Answer: If you add the number of English-speakers and the number of Spanish-speakers, you get 28 + 37 = 65. But there are only 50 students, so 65 − 50 = 15 of them are being counted twice—because those 15 speak both languages.

18. K

Category: Proportions and Probability

Difficulty: Medium

Getting to the Answer: Set up a proportion:

$$\frac{288 \text{ miles}}{6 \text{ hours}} = \frac{x \text{ miles}}{8 \text{ hours}}$$

$$6x = 288 \times 8$$

$$6x = 2{,}304$$

$$x = 384$$

19. D
Category: Number Properties
Difficulty: Medium
Getting to the Answer: To convert a fraction to a decimal, you divide the denominator into the numerator. Clearly, you don't have time to take the division out to 100 places after the decimal point. There must be a pattern you can take advantage of. Start dividing and continue just until you see what the pattern is:

$$11\overline{)4.000000\ldots} = 0.363636\ldots$$

The 1st, 3rd, 5th, etc. digits are 3; and the 2nd, 4th, etc. digits are 6. In other words, every odd-numbered digit is a 3 and every even-numbered digit is a 6. The 100th digit is an even-numbered digit, so it's a 6.

20. G
Category: Variable Manipulations
Difficulty: Low
Getting to the Answer: Because it's x you're looking for, eliminate y. Fortunately, the equations are all ready for you—just add them and the $+4y$ cancels with the $-4y$:

$$3x + 4y = 31$$
$$3x - 4y = -1$$
$$6x = 30$$
$$x = 5$$

21. E
Category: Coordinate Geometry
Difficulty: Medium
Getting to the Answer: The coordinates of the midpoint are the averages of the coordinates of the endpoints. The average of the x's is $\frac{2+12}{2} = 7$, and the average of the y's is $\frac{3+(-15)}{2} = -6$, so the coordinates of the midpoint are $(7, -6)$.

22. H
Category: Trigonometry
Difficulty: Medium
Getting to the Answer: Cosine is "adjacent over hypotenuse." Here, the leg adjacent to θ is 4 and the hypotenuse is 5, so $\cos \theta = \frac{4}{5}$.

23. A
Category: Plane Geometry
Difficulty: High
Getting to the Answer: The center of Q is on P's circumference, and the radius of circle Q is twice the radius of circle P. You could use the circumference of circle P to find the radius of circle P, then double that radius to get the radius of circle Q, and finally use that radius to calculate the circumference of circle Q. It's much easier and faster, however, if you realize that "double the radius means double the circumference." If the circumference of circle P is 6, then the circumference of circle Q is twice that, or 12.

24. G
Category: Variable Manipulation
Difficulty: Medium
Getting to the Answer: This looks like a functions question, but in fact it's just a "plug in the number and see what you get" question:

$$f(x) = x^3 - x^2 - x$$
$$f(-3) = (-3)^3 - (-3)^2 - (-3)$$
$$= -27 - 9 + 3$$
$$= -33$$

25. C
Category: Plane Geometry
Difficulty: Medium
Getting to the Answer: Use the Triangle Inequality Theorem here. If the two unknown side lengths are integers, and the sum of the two lengths has to be greater than 4, then the least amount the two unknown sides could add up to would be 5, which would make the perimeter $4 + 5 = 9$.

26. J

Category: Variable Manipulation

Difficulty: Medium

Getting to the Answer: First factor out an x from each term, then factor what's left:

$$2x + 3x^2 + x^3 = x(2 + 3x + x^2)$$
$$= x(x^2 + 3x + 2)$$
$$= x(x + 1)(x + 2)$$

27. C

Category: Operations

Difficulty: Low

Getting to the Answer: Get rid of the parentheses in the denominator, and then cancel factors the numerator and denominator have in common:

$$\frac{x^2 y^3 z^4}{\left(xyz^2\right)^2} = \frac{x^2 y^3 z^4}{x^2 y^2 z^4} = \frac{x^2}{x^2} \cdot \frac{y^3}{y^2} \cdot \frac{z^4}{z^4} = y$$

28. H

Category: Number Properties

Difficulty: Medium

Getting to the Answer: Normally you would have a choice: either convert the fractions to decimals first and then add, or add the fractions first and then convert the sum to a decimal. In this case, however, both fractions would convert to endlessly repeating decimals, which would be unwieldy when adding. In this case, it makes sense to add first, then convert:

$$\frac{2}{3} + \frac{1}{12} = \frac{8}{12} + \frac{1}{12} = \frac{9}{12} = \frac{3}{4} = 0.75$$

29. D

Category: Variable Manipulation

Difficulty: High

Getting to the Answer: This looks like a physics question, but in fact it's just a "plug in the number and see what you get" question. Be sure you plug 95 in for C (not F):

$$C = \frac{5}{9}(F - 32)$$
$$95 = \frac{5}{9}(F - 32)$$
$$\frac{9}{5} \times 95 = F - 32$$
$$F - 32 = 171$$
$$F = 171 + 32 = 203$$

30. H

Category: Proportions and Probability

Difficulty: Medium

Getting to the Answer: Probability equals the number of favorable outcomes divided by the total number of possible outcomes. In this problem, a favorable outcome is choosing a green marble—that's 4. The "total number of possible outcomes" is the total number of marbles, or 20:

$$Probability = \frac{Favorable\ outcomes}{Total\ number\ of\ possible\ outcomes}$$
$$= \frac{4}{20}$$
$$= \frac{1}{5}$$

31. A

Category: Number Properties

Difficulty: Medium

Getting to the Answer: To find the average of three numbers—even if they're algebraic expressions—add them and divide by 3:

$$Average = \frac{Sum\ of\ terms}{Number\ of\ terms}$$
$$= \frac{(2x + 5) + (5x - 6) + (-4x + 2)}{3}$$
$$= \frac{3x + 1}{3}$$
$$= x + \frac{1}{3}$$

32. F

Category: Coordinate Geometry

Difficulty: High

Getting to the Answer: Parallel lines have the same slope. Use the first pair of points to figure out the slope:

$$Slope = \frac{y_2 - y_1}{x_2 - x_1} = \frac{16 - 1}{2 - 1} = 15$$

Then use the slope to figure out the missing coordinate in the second pair of points:

$$\text{Slope} = \frac{y_2 - y_1}{x_2 - x_1}$$

$$15 = \frac{(25 - (-5))}{a - (-10)}$$

$$15 = \frac{30}{a + 10}$$

$$15a + 150 = 30$$

$$15a = -120$$

$$a = -8$$

33. B

Category: Plane Geometry

Difficulty: Medium

Getting to the Answer: When parallel lines make a big triangle and a little triangle as they do here, the triangles are similar (because they have the same angle measurements). Side $\overline{PR}$ is three times the length of $\overline{QR}$, so each side of the big triangle is three times the length of the corresponding side of the smaller triangle, and therefore the ratio of the perimeters is also 3:1. So the perimeter of ΔPRT is 3 times 11, or 33.

34. K

Category: Plane Geometry

Difficulty: Medium

Getting to the Answer: It is a polygon because it's composed of straight line segments. It is a quadrilateral because it has four sides. It is not a rectangle because opposite sides are not equal. It is a trapezoid because it has one pair of parallel sides.

35. D

Category: Variable Manipulation

Difficulty: Medium

Getting to the Answer: Plug in $x = -3$ and solve for a:

$$2x^2 + (a - 4)x - 2a = 0$$

$$2(-3)^2 + (a - 4)(-3) - 2a = 0$$

$$18 - 3a + 12 - 2a = 0$$

$$30 - 5a = 0$$

$$-5a = -30$$

$$a = 6$$

36. K

Category: Proportions and Probability

Difficulty: Medium

Getting to the Answer: The total number of combinations of a first course, second course, and dessert is equal to the product of the three numbers:

$$\text{Total possibilities} = 4 \times 5 \times 3 = 60$$

37. B

Category: Number Properties

Difficulty: High

Getting to the Answer: An integer that's divisible by 6 has at least one 2 and one 3 in its prime factorization. An integer that's divisible by 9 has at least two 3s in its prime factorization. Therefore, an integer that's divisible by both 6 and 9 has at least one 2 and two 3s in its prime factorization. That means it's divisible by 2, 3, $2 \times 3 = 6$, $3 \times 3 = 9$, and $2 \times 3 \times 3 = 18$. It's not necessarily divisible by 12 or 36, each of which includes two 2s in its prime factorization. You could also do this one by Picking Numbers. Think of a common multiple of 6 and 9 and use it to eliminate some options. For example, $6 \times 9 = 54$ is an obvious common multiple—and it's not divisible by 12 or 36, but it is divisible by 18. The *least* common multiple of 6 and 9 is 18, which is also divisible by 18. In fact, every common multiple of 6 and 9 is also a multiple of 18.

38. F

Category: Variable Manipulation

Difficulty: Low

Getting to the Answer:

$$\frac{x^2 + x^2 + x^2}{x^2} = \frac{3x^2}{x^2} = 3$$

39. A

Category: Variable Manipulation

Difficulty: Medium

Getting to the Answer: Read carefully. This question's a lot easier than you might think. It's asking for the total number of coins, not the total value.

q quarters, *d* dimes, and *n* nickels add up to a total of *q* + *d* + *n* coins.

40. K
Category: Variable Manipulation
Difficulty: Medium
Getting to the Answer: You solve an inequality much the way you solve an equation: Do the same things to both sides until you've isolated what you're solving for. (Just remember to flip the sign if you ever multiply or divide both sides by a negative number.)

$$5x - 2(1 - x) \geq 4(x + 1)$$
$$5x - 2 + 2x \geq 4x + 4$$
$$5x + 2x - 4x \geq 4 + 2$$
$$3x \geq 6$$
$$x \geq 2$$

The "greater than or equal to" symbol is graphed as a solid circle.

41. B
Category: Coordinate Geometry
Difficulty: Low
Getting to the Answer: First find the slope of the line that contains the given points:

$$\text{Slope} = \frac{y_2 - y_1}{x_2 - x_1} = \frac{10 - 6}{6 - 5} = 4$$

Line *m* is perpendicular to the above line, so the slope of *m* is the negative reciprocal of 4, or $-\frac{1}{4}$.

42. H
Category: Trigonometry
Difficulty: Low
Getting to the Answer: Sine is "opposite over hypotenuse." Here, the leg opposite θ is 12 and the hypotenuse is 13, so:

$$\sin \theta = \frac{12}{13}$$

43. E
Category: Operations
Difficulty: Medium
Getting to the Answer: Express the left side of the equation so that both sides have the same base:

$$9^{2x - 1} = 3^{3x + 3}$$
$$(3^2)^{2x - 1} = 3^{3x + 3}$$
$$3^{4x - 2} = 3^{3x + 3}$$

Now that the bases are the same, just set the exponents equal:

$$4x - 2 = 3x + 3$$
$$4x - 3x = 3 + 2$$
$$x = 5$$

44. K
Category: Proportions and Probability
Difficulty: Medium
Getting to the Answer: Be careful with combined percent increase. You cannot just add the two percents, because they're generally percents of different wholes. In this instance, the 20% increase is based on the 1970 population, but the 30% increase is based on the larger 1980 population. If you just added 20% and 30% to get 50%, you fell into the testmaker's trap.

The best way to do a problem like this one is to pick a number for the original whole and just see what happens. As usual with percents, the best number to pick is 100. (That may be a small number for the population of a city, but verisimilitude is not important—all that matters is the math.)

If the 1970 population was 100, then a 20% increase would put the 1980 population at 120. Now, to figure the 30% increase, multiply 120 by 130%:

$$\text{New \#} = (\text{Original \#}) + (30\% \text{ of Original \#})$$
$$\text{New \#} = 130\% \text{ of Original \#}$$
$$x = 1.3(120)$$
$$= 156$$

The population went from 100 to 156, which is a 56% increase.

45. E
Category: Number Properties
Difficulty: Medium
Getting to the Answer: The best way to deal with changing averages is to go by way of the sums. Use the old average to figure out the total of the first four scores:

Sum of first 4 scores = 4 × 89 = 356

And use the new average to figure out the total he needs after the fifth score:

Sum of five scores = 5 × 90 = 450

To get his sum up from 356 to 450, Martin needs to score 450 − 356 = 94.

46. K
Category: Coordinate Geometry
Difficulty: High
Getting to the Answer: If you find the distance from the center to the given point on the circle, you'll have the radius. The difference between the x's is 8, and the difference between the y's is 6. If 8 and 6 are the lengths of the legs of a right triangle, then the hypotenuse is 10. The radius, then, is 10. Now you can plug the radius and the coordinates of the center point into the general form of the equation of a circle:

$$(x - h)^2 + (y - k)^2 = r^2$$
$$(x + 1)^2 + (y + 1)^2 = 10^2$$
$$(x + 1)^2 + (y + 1)^2 = 100$$

47. E
Category: Coordinate Geometry
Difficulty: Low
Getting to the Answer: In addition to picking coordinates from the line and plugging them into the answer choices, use the points where the line crosses the axes—(−1, 0) and (0, 2)—to find the slope:

$$\text{Slope} = \frac{y_2 - y_1}{x_2 - x_1} = \frac{2 - 0}{0 - (-1)} = 2$$

The y-intercept is 2. Now plug $m = 2$ and $b = 2$ into the slope-intercept equation form:

$$y = mx + b$$
$$y = 2x + 2$$

48. G
Category: Proportions and Probability
Difficulty: Medium

Getting to the Answer: Be careful. The question is not asking, "What is $\frac{1}{4}$ of 16?" It's asking, "What is $\frac{1}{4}$% of 16?" One-fourth of 1% is 0.25%, or 0.0025:

$$\frac{1}{4}\% \text{ of } 16 = 0.0025 \times 16 = 0.04$$

49. C
Category: Variable Manipulation
Difficulty: High
Getting to the Answer: Use FOIL to get rid of the parentheses, and then combine like terms:

$$(s + 4)(s - 4) + (2s + 2)(s - 2) = (s^2 - 16) + (2s^2 - 2s - 4)$$
$$= s^2 + 2s^2 - 2s - 16 - 4$$
$$= 3s^2 - 2s - 20$$

50. F
Category: Coordinate Geometry
Difficulty: Medium
Getting to the Answer: The easiest way to find the equation of a given parabola is to take a point or two from the graph and plug the coordinates into the answer choices, eliminating the choices that don't work. Start with a point with coordinates that are easy to work with. Here, you could start with (3, 0). Plug $x = 3$ and $y = 0$ into each answer choice, and you'll find that only (F) works.

51. C
Category: Trigonometry
Difficulty: Low

Getting to the Answer: Because $\sin a = \frac{4}{5}$, you could think of this as a 3-4-5 triangle:

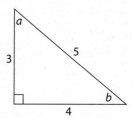

Cosine is "adjacent over hypotenuse." Here, the leg adjacent to b is 4, and the hypotenuse is 5, so $b = \dfrac{4}{5}$. (Notice that the sine of one acute angle in a right triangle is equal to the cosine of the other acute angle.)

52. F
Category: Variable Manipulation
Difficulty: Low
Getting to the Answer: Add the like terms in the numerator, and then divide by the denominator:

$$\frac{x^2 + x^2 + x^2}{x} = \frac{3x^2}{x} = 3x$$

If you weren't careful, you might have confused this with problem 38 and missed the change in the denominator.

53. B
Category: Variable Manipulation
Difficulty: Medium

Getting to the Answer: When you divide w by 4, you get $\dfrac{w}{4}$. When you subtract that result from r, you get $r - \dfrac{w}{4}$.

54. J
Category: Plane Geometry
Difficulty: Medium
Getting to the Answer: The formula for the volume of a cylinder is $V = \pi r^2 h$, where r is the radius of the circular base and h is the height. Here $r = 4$ and $h = 5$, so:

$$\begin{aligned}\text{Volume} &= \pi r^2 h \\ &= \pi (4)^2 (5) \\ &= \pi (16)(5) \\ &= 80\pi\end{aligned}$$

55. E
Category: Plane Geometry
Difficulty: Medium
Getting to the Answer: With a right triangle, you can use the two legs as the base and the height to figure out the area. Here, the leg lengths are expressed algebraically. Just plug the two expressions in for b and h in the triangle area formula:

$$\text{Area} = \frac{1}{2}(x - 1)(x + 1) = \frac{1}{2}(x^2 - 1) = \frac{x^2 - 1}{2}$$

56. G
Category: Proportions and Probability
Difficulty: Medium
Getting to the Answer: The difference between the populations in 1990 was $9,400 - 7,600 = 1,800$. Each year, as the larger population goes down by 100 and the smaller population goes up by 100, the difference decreases by 200. Thus, it will take $1,800 \div 200 = 9$ years to erase the difference.

57. B
Category: Number Properties
Difficulty: High
Getting to the Answer: The overall average is not simply the average of the two average ages. Because there are a lot more women than men, women carry more weight, and the overall average will be closer to 25 than 35. Pick particular numbers for the females and males, say 4 females and 1 male. The ages of the 4 females total 4 times 25, or 100, and the age of the 1 male totals 35. The average, then, is $(100 + 35)$ divided by 5, or 27.

58. J
Category: Trigonometry
Difficulty: High
Getting to the Answer: The height h of the tree is the leg opposite θ. The distance b from the base

of the tree is the leg adjacent to θ. "Opposite over adjacent" is tangent, but all the answer choices are in terms of the sine. Sine is "opposite over hypotenuse," so you're going to have to figure out the hypotenuse. Use the Pythagorean theorem:

$$(\text{hypotenuse})^2 = (\text{leg}_1)^2 + (\text{leg}_2)^2$$
$$(\text{hypotenuse})^2 = b^2 + h^2$$
$$\text{hypotenuse} = \sqrt{b^2 + h^2}$$

Now, to get the sine, put the opposite h over the hypotenuse $\sqrt{b^2 + h^2}$: $\sin\theta = \dfrac{h}{\sqrt{b^2 + h^2}}$

59. C
Category: Variable Manipulation
Difficulty: Medium
Getting to the Answer: This looks like a solid geometry question, but in fact it's just a "plug in the numbers" question:

$$S = \pi r \sqrt{r^2 + h^2} = \pi(3)\sqrt{3^2 + 4^2} = 3\pi\sqrt{9 + 16}$$
$$= 3\pi\sqrt{25} = 3\pi \times 5 = 15\pi$$

60. J
Category: Plane Geometry
Difficulty: Medium
Getting to the Answer: When a transversal crosses parallel lines, all the resulting acute angles are equal, and all the resulting obtuse angles are equal. (You can generally tell from looking which angles are equal.) In this problem's figure, $a = c = e = g$ and $b = d = f = h$. Only (J) is true: c and g are both obtuse. In all the other choices, you'll find an obtuse and an acute angle.

READING TEST

PASSAGE I

1. D
Category: Detail
Difficulty: Medium
Getting to the Answer: Lines 18–21 provide the answer: "I was brought up, from my earliest remembrance…by my godmother."

2. G
Category: Inference
Difficulty: Medium
Getting to the Answer: From the description of Dolly in the first two paragraphs, it is clear that Esther viewed her doll as her only friend. "I was such a shy little thing that I seldom dared to open my lips, and never dared to open my heart, to anybody else" (lines 6–9). This idea is repeated in lines 97–101: "I went up to my room, and crept to bed, and laid my doll's cheek against mine wet with tears, and holding that solitary friend upon my bosom, cried myself to sleep."

3. B
Category: Vocab-in-Context
Difficulty: Medium
Getting to the Answer: In this case, *stiff* is used to describe the tone of the letter that Esther's godmother wrote to decline the invitation to another student's birthday party. Choice (B), "rigidly formal," is the most appropriate definition in this context.

4. G
Category: Inference
Difficulty: High
Getting to the Answer: This is a Global question. Esther mentions that her birthday was never celebrated and the pivotal scene in the passage happens on her birthday. In lines 3–4, Esther tells her doll that she is not very clever, but that is not the focus of the passage. In lines 54–57, she mentions being invited to a friend's home for a party, so

H is not correct. In lines 79–82, you find out that Esther's mother did not die on her birthday, so J is not correct.

5. C
Category: Inference
Difficulty: Medium
Getting to the Answer: Although Esther's god-mother says that she has forgiven Esther's mother, her facial expression directly contradicts this. "I see her knitted brow and pointed finger...her face did not relent...." (lines 88–92).

6. G
Category: Detail
Difficulty: Low
Getting to the Answer: Esther is clearly lonely, as evidenced by her description of Dolly as her only friend and her explanation that there is a separation dividing her from the other girls at school. The birthday scene with her godmother also shows that Esther is quite confused about her own family past.

7. C
Category: Inference
Difficulty: Medium
Getting to the Answer: Her confrontation with her godmother gives Esther further reason to believe that no one loves her. The phrase before the cited line also points to (C) as the best answer: "I knew that I had brought no joy at any time to anybody's heart" (lines 102–103).

8. J
Category: Detail
Difficulty: Medium
Getting to the Answer: Choices F, G, and H are all mentioned in paragraph 5 (lines 44–59). At the end of the passage, Esther says, "I hope it is not self-indulgent to shed these tears as I think of it" (lines 111–112).

9. C
Category: Detail
Difficulty: Low
Getting to the Answer: Esther's evidence that her godmother is a "good, good woman" is explained in lines 22–27: "She went to church three times every Sunday, and to morning prayers on Wednesdays and Fridays, and to lectures whenever there were lectures, and never missed."

10. G
Category: Detail
Difficulty: High
Getting to the Answer: In the first paragraph, Esther says, "Now, Dolly, I am not clever..." (lines 3–4). In the second paragraph, Esther describes herself as "such a shy little thing" (lines 6–7).

PASSAGE II

11. B
Category: Vocab-in-Context
Difficulty: Low
Getting to the Answer: In the phrase "the Pantanal was a vast, soggy canvas, white with gleaming herds of Nelore cattle" (lines 73–75), *canvas* is used to mean "a background." None of the other choices makes sense.

12. J
Category: Detail
Difficulty: Medium
Getting to the Answer: The answer to this question can be found in lines 79–82: "As the jaguars grew scarce, their chief food staple, the capybaras—a meter-long rodent, the world's largest—overran farmers' fields..."

13. C
Category: Detail
Difficulty: Medium
Getting to the Answer: The answer to this question can be found in lines 15–20: "Exactly how dramatic

a comeback is difficult to say because jaguars—*Panthera onca*, the largest feline in the New World—are solitary, secretive, nocturnal predators. Each cat needs to prowl at least 35 square kilometers by itself."

14. G
Category: Inference
Difficulty: Medium
Getting to the Answer: The last sentence of the second paragraph provides the answer. "Hotels, campgrounds, and bed-and-breakfasts have sprung up to accommodate the half-million tourists a year…bent on sampling the Pantanal's wildlife, of which the great cats must be the most magnificent example" (lines 28–34). Tourists want to see the jaguars, and not having the jaguars might negatively affect the booming ecotourist business.

15. A
Category: Detail
Difficulty: Low
Getting to the Answer: The "green safari" example is mentioned as a way for "scientists to fit the cats with radio collars" (lines 103–105). The other three examples provided are listed in lines 109–113 as methods the scientists are teaching the ranchers.

16. G
Category: Generalization
Difficulty: Medium
Getting to the Answer: In lines 59–60, the author says, "Hard data on cattle losses due to jaguars in the Pantanal are nonexistent…." One reason for providing anecdotal information, then, is to tell the story of the hardships faced by the ranchers due to the jaguars. The author does not suggest that he empathizes with the ranchers more than the jaguars—in fact, he refers to the jaguars as "magnificent." The only examples that show rancher violence is Abel Monteiro shooting an attacking jaguar who had killed his two dogs (lines 37–43) and Ramos da Silva throwing burning sticks at a jaguar that was trying to invade his camp (43–47), both

acts of self-defense. The landscape of the Pantanal is not the focus of these two paragraphs, so J can be eliminated.

17. C
Category: Inference
Difficulty: Medium
Getting to the Answer: The passage explains that because of the decrease in the jaguar population, the capybara population increased. These rodents "spread trichomoniasis, a livestock disease that renders cows sterile" (lines 82–83). Lines 86–91 describe the effect of weather patterns and floods on the ranchers' land. "Weather patterns also shifted radically—due most likely to global warming—and drove annual floods to near-Biblical proportions. The waters are only now retreating from some inundated pasturelands."

18. G
Category: Detail
Difficulty: Medium
Getting to the Answer: The last sentence of the passage reads, "When the scholars go home and the greens log off, the *pantaneiros* will still be there—left on their own to deal with the jaguars as they see fit" (lines 117–120).

19. D
Category: Detail
Difficulty: Low
Getting to the Answer: Evidence is given throughout the passage that all three groups support protecting the jaguars. It is most concisely stated in lines 49–53: "a political catfight between the scientists, environmentalists, and ecotourists who want to protect the jaguars and the embattled ranchers…."

20. F
Category: Detail
Difficulty: Medium
Getting to the Answer: The answer to this question can be found in lines 59–61: "Hard data on cattle

losses due to jaguars in the Pantanal are nonexistent, but there are stories."

PASSAGE III

21. A
Category: Inference
Difficulty: Medium
Getting to the Answer: This question asks you why the aulos was considered "the instrument of the Dionysians." In the fifth paragraph, you find out that the Dionysians "represented the unbridled, sensual and passionate aspect of Greek culture" (lines 65–67). The passage also says that the aulos had a "far more exciting effect" (lines 71–72) than the lyre. The suggestion here is clearly that the aulos must have been able to express the unbridled passion and excitement of the Dionysians, making (A) the best answer. Choice B is out because the fact that the aulos was chosen as the official instrument of the Delphian and Pythian festivals doesn't explain why it was the instrument of the Dionysians. Choice C contradicts the passage. The kithara, not the aulos, represented the intellectual, idealistic side of Greek art. Finally, the author never says when the Dionysian cult originated, so D is also out.

22. J
Category: Detail
Difficulty: Medium
Getting to the Answer: All the author means by saying that the chelys can be "traced back to the age of fable" is that it is an ancient instrument. The chelys was an actual, not an imaginary, instrument, so H is incorrect. G is out because the kithara was used to accompany the epics, not the chelys.

23. D
Category: Generalization
Difficulty: Low
Getting to the Answer: Choice (D) is the only answer choice that adequately covers the entire passage. Choice A focuses only on the lyre. The connection between Greek music and drama, B, is

mentioned only in passing, as are the references to music in ancient Greek literature, C. The passage is really all about the "origin and development of various Greek instruments," (D).

24. H
Category: Detail
Difficulty: Medium
Getting to the Answer: The first thing the author says about the kithara is that it was used by "professional Homeric singers" (lines 15–16). The kithara, according to the author, probably came from Egypt, so F is incorrect. Choice G and J contradict information in the paragraph to the effect that the kithara was more powerful than the chelys and was played with both hands.

25. D
Category: Detail
Difficulty: Medium
Getting to the Answer: Skim through the third paragraph to find the changes that occurred to the lyre between the eighth and fifth centuries B.C. Musicians began to use a plectrum in the seventh century B.C., A; lyres featured an increasing number of strings, B, during this period; and musicians also began to use different scales and modes, C. That leaves (D). Nothing in the paragraph indicates that lyres were used to accompany dramatic productions.

26. J
Category: Inference
Difficulty: Medium
Getting to the Answer: The final paragraph says that "an early specimen" of the aulos was tuned to the chromatic tetrachord, "a fact that points to Oriental origin" (line 87). From this, you can infer that the chromatic tetrachord must have been used in ancient Oriental music, (J). Choice F is contradicted by the author's assertion that elegiac songs were composed in the mode of the chromatic tetrachord. There is no evidence to support either G or H.

27. C
Category: Detail
Difficulty: Low
Getting to the Answer: In the fourth sentence of the first paragraph (lines 8–10), the author indicates that the chelys is the most antique form of the lyre.

28. G
Category: Detail
Difficulty: Medium
Getting to the Answer: Sappho did two things that you know about from lines 44–47. She introduced a mode "in which Dorian and Lydian characteristics were blended," and she "initiated the use of the plectrum."

29. B
Category: Detail
Difficulty: High
Getting to the Answer: All of the details you need to answer this question are in the sixth paragraph (lines 68–78). The first sentence states that the aulos is more like our oboe than our flute, so III is false. This means C and D can be eliminated. The second sentence of the paragraph confirms that the aulos sounded more exciting than the lyre (II). Because (B) is the only remaining answer choice that includes II, you know it has to be the best answer.

30. F
Category: Generalization
Difficulty: Medium
Getting to the Answer: Greek instruments are discussed as a whole at the very beginning of the passage. The author says that our knowledge of Greek instruments comes from "representations on monuments, vases, statues, and friezes and from the testimony of Greek authors" (lines 4–6). These are all "secondary sources" of information about the instruments, so (F) is the best answer. Choice G is incorrect because quite a bit is known about the tuning of the instruments, as represented in the second paragraph. Choice H is contradicted by the

same sentence that supports (F). Finally, there is no evidence to suggest that more is known about one type of instrument than the other, J.

PASSAGE IV

31. B
Category: Detail
Difficulty: High
Getting to the Answer: The first paragraph in Passage A states, "In addition, saliva, tears, and mucous all contain the enzyme lysozyme, which can destroy bacterial cell walls (causing bacteria to rupture due to osmotic pressure) and some viral capsids" (lines 9–13).

32. G
Category: Detail
Difficulty: High
Getting to the Answer: As described in the passage, "macrophages are able to display to other more specific immune system cells the antigens (foreign proteins) they have just encountered. That, in turn, often results in a more intensive immune response from these more specific cells like B and T cells" (lines 45–50).

33. B
Category: Generalization
Difficulty: Medium
Getting to the Answer: The second paragraph says that macrophages engulf materials through a process called phagocytosis, and the third paragraph states that neutrophils are phagocytic-like macrophages.

34. J
Category: Vocab-in-Context
Difficulty: Medium
Getting to the Answer: A TH cell is a "helper" cell. Additionally, clues in the passage indicate that macrophages/APCs and B cells cooperate: the third paragraph indicates that T cells interact with APCs,

and the fourth paragraph indicates that helper T cells cue B cells to activate. Predict that TH cells "help" or intervene in the situation.

35. A
Category: Detail
Difficulty: High
Getting to the Answer: Paragraphs 5 and 6 discuss the activation of B and T cells. The passage states, "When a particular B or T cell gets activated, it begins to divide rapidly to produce identical clones. In the case of B cells, these clones will all produce antibodies of the same structure, capable of responding to the same invading antigens. B cell clones are known as plasma B cells and can produce thousands of antibody molecules per second as long as they live" (lines 116–123).

36. J
Category: Detail
Difficulty: Medium
Getting to the Answer: The end of the fourth paragraph states that helper T cells (TH) must recognize the proteins and then release chemicals to tell the B cell to replicate, which, according to paragraph 6, will then produce antibodies.

37. C
Category: Generalization
Difficulty: High
Getting to the Answer: The introductory information states, "The specific immune system is able to attack very specific disease-causing organisms by means of protein-to-protein interaction and is responsible for our ability to become immune to future infections from pathogens we have fought off already."

38. H
Category: Detail
Difficulty: Medium
Getting to the Answer: Passage A provides information about the nonspecific functions of the system, while Passage B provides additional

information about the system by addressing the specific functions.

39. A
Category: Inference
Difficulty: High
Getting to the Answer: Paragraph 4 in Passage B indicates that B cells can only be activated by TH cells that recognize pathogens the B cell has captured, but paragraph 3 indicates that T cells cannot recognize free antigens—they can only detect those displayed on cell surfaces. Additionally, paragraph 3 states that there are interactions between T cells and APCs, and paragraph 2 specifically states that TH cells will serve as mediators between the macrophages (certain APCs) and B cells. Passage A explains that macrophages are nonspecific functions that can display antigens on their cell walls for the specific system to see. It can thus be logically inferred that a macrophage in the nonspecific division must display information that a TH cell can see and pass to B cells before the B cells can be activated to then replicate and produce antibodies.

40. G
Category: Detail
Difficulty: Medium
Getting to the Answer: The first paragraph in Passage A states: "In addition, saliva, tears, and mucous all contain the enzyme lysozyme, which can destroy bacterial cell walls (causing bacteria to rupture due to osmotic pressure) and some viral capsids" (lines 9–13). The second paragraph of Passage B says, "Since virally infected cells display some viral proteins on their surfaces, TC cells can bind to those proteins and secrete enzymes that tear the cell membrane and kill the cell" (lines 85–88).

SCIENCE TEST

PASSAGE I

1. B
Category: Figure Interpretation
Difficulty: Medium
Getting to the Answer: Look at the *y*-axis of the graph between the region of pH 8 and pH 12, and then scan across at that level. The indicators that undergo color change in this pH range are thymol blue, phenolphthalein, and alizarin. These indicators correspond to (B).

2. H
Category: Figure Interpretation
Difficulty: Low
Getting to the Answer: Looking carefully at the graph, you can see that methyl orange changes from red to yellow between pH 3 and pH 5, and alizarin changes from yellow to red between pH 9 and pH 11. Thymol blue undergoes a yellow to blue color change, so it is not correct.

3. A
Category: Patterns
Difficulty: Medium
Getting to the Answer: In order to determine when the reaction is complete and the solution is basic, the chemist should select an indicator that turns color when the pH has risen into the region of basicity (above 7). When bromocresol green inches above the pH of 7, it turns blue, so (A) is correct.

4. J
Category: Scientific Reasoning
Difficulty: High
Getting to the Answer: This question requires you to form a broad conclusion about acid-base indicators. Choices F and G are incorrect because there are plenty of indicators that change colors above or below pH 7. Choice H is incorrect because different indicators change colors at different pH levels, and this fact also explains why (J) is correct.

5. A
Category: Figure Interpretation
Difficulty: Low
Getting to the Answer: Compare the two indicators on the graph, and you'll find that phenolphthalein undergoes a color change at a higher pH than bromothymol blue.

6. G
Category: Figure Interpretation
Difficulty: Low
Getting to the Answer: Locate black coffee in Table 1; it has a pH of 5. Then look in Figure 1 to determine which indicator responds to a pH of 5. Only Bromothymol Blue corresponds to this pH. Choice (G) is correct.

PASSAGE II

7. D
Category: Scientific Reasoning
Difficulty: Medium
Getting to the Answer: First, consider which of the listed options can be categorized as "atmospheric conditions." Because skin color is not an atmospheric condition, you can eliminate A and B. The other three options are atmospheric conditions. Choice (D) is correct.

8. F
Category: Figure Interpretation
Difficulty: Low
Getting to the Answer: The quickest way to answer the question is to eliminate the incorrect answer choices. A look at Table 1 rules out G because the total amount of oxygen absorbed is clearly affected by temperature. Choice H is incorrect because frog health is never an issue. The very mention of CO_2 makes J incorrect—Experiment 1 was only concerned with oxygen.

9. C
Category: Patterns
Difficulty: Medium
Getting to the Answer: There is no data for 17°C, so an estimate is necessary. The total (skin plus lungs) amount of carbon dioxide released per hour was about 100 mol/hr at 15°C and about 110 mol/hr at 20°C. The only choice that falls between these is (C).

10. H
Category: Scientific Reasoning
Difficulty: Medium
Getting to the Answer: To show that *Hyla faber* is an ectotherm, one must find evidence demonstrating that changes in temperature cause changes in gas exchange. Table 1 demonstrates that as temperature increases, *Hyla faber's* oxygen absorption increases, so (H) is correct. Choice F is not good evidence because data for only one temperature do not give an idea of how temperature changes affect gas exchange. Choice G is incorrect because the amount of carbon dioxide eliminated by the lungs is the same at 15°C, 20°C, and 25°C, making it look as though changes in temperature have little effect on gas exchange in the frog.

11. B
Category: Figure Interpretation
Difficulty: Low
Getting to the Answer: The amount of carbon dioxide eliminated by the skin increases over the range of temperatures; the increase levels off at the highest temperature. Carbon dioxide release by the lungs increases a bit over the lower temperatures and then levels off almost completely. The curve for skin release has to be much higher on the graph than the curve for lung release because the skin eliminated more carbon dioxide at each temperature than did the lungs. Choice (B) is the only graph that fits these patterns.

12. G
Category: Patterns
Difficulty: Medium
Getting to the Answer: When the answer choices all look similar, as in this problem, find the differences between them and rule out the ones that cannot be correct. You can eliminate H and J right away because the results show that as temperature increases, O_2 absorbed by the lungs increases. Choice F is not correct either—as temperature increases, CO_2 released by the skin increases, which is stated by (G).

13. B
Category: Figure Interpretation
Difficulty: Medium
Getting to the Answer: Here again, you want to be careful and refer to the answer choices as you review the tables to observe what happens as the temperature rises above 15°C. Each of the answer choices refers to the tree frog's ability to absorb oxygen through the skin, so start there. From Table 1, you can see that the skin's oxygen absorption rate goes down, so C and D are out. Now you need to refer to Table 2 to see what happens to the rate at which carbon dioxide is released from the lungs. It appears to remain about the same, so the correct answer is (B).

PASSAGE III

14. H
Category: Figure Interpretation
Difficulty: High
Getting to the Answer: This is a tricky question, so make sure you determine the opinions of both scientists. Scientist 1 states that deep-focus earthquakes are due to the release of water from crystalline structures, not magma. Because magma in the asthenosphere is not related to crystalline structures, it is unlikely to support Scientist 1's viewpoint. Scientist 2 states that deep-focus earthquakes are caused by slippage that occurs when rock in a descending plate undergoes a phase change. Liquid

magma in the asthenosphere fails to support Scientist 2's viewpoint. Because neither scientist is supported, (H) must be correct.

15. D
Category: Scientific Reasoning
Difficulty: Medium
Getting to the Answer: Scientist 1 states that "below 50 km, rock is under too much pressure to fracture normally." Scientist 2 gives the fact that "rock becomes ductile at the temperatures and pressures that exist at depths greater than 50 km" as the reason that "deep-focus earthquakes cannot result from normal fractures."

16. F
Category: Scientific Reasoning
Difficulty: High
Getting to the Answer: Scientist 1's theory is invalid unless water can be shown to exist in mantle rock at the level of deep-focus earthquakes. If researchers could subject mantle-like rock to those temperatures and pressures, and then extract water from it, (F), their experimental results would support the hypothesis of Scientist 1.

17. C
Category: Scientific Reasoning
Difficulty: Medium
Getting to the Answer: Both scientists believe that the Earth's crust (surface layer) is composed of mobile tectonic plates. In describing the plates as being "forced down into the mantle," Scientist 1 implies that they are normally in the crust, and Scientist 2 makes reference to "a descending tectonic plate." The introductory paragraph says that "most" earthquakes originate less than 20 km below Earth's surface, so A is incorrect. Neither scientist assumes that surface quakes are caused by trapped fluids, B; both state that such quakes are caused by normal fractures in Earth's crust. Neither scientist discusses how deep-focus earthquakes are detected, so D is not an assumption made by either scientist.

18. G
Category: Scientific Reasoning
Difficulty: Medium
Getting to the Answer: Scientist 2 believes that deep-focus quakes are the result of slippage caused by phase changes. Scientist 2 would, therefore, not expect deep quakes to occur below 680 km where, according to the last sentence of the passage, "no phase changes are predicted." Recording a quake with an origin below that depth would send Scientist 2 back to the drawing board, or at least in search of deeper phase changes.

19. D
Category: Scientific Reasoning
Difficulty: Low
Getting to the Answer: The final sentence of Scientist 1's paragraph mentions that when fluids were injected into the ground at the Rocky Mountain Arsenal, the unintended result was "a series of shallow-focus earthquakes." The opening words *in fact* signal that this final sentence is meant to illustrate the previous sentence, which refers to experiments in which trapped fluids caused rock to fail at lower than normal shear stresses. The implication is that the quakes at the arsenal occurred because the fluid wastes lowered the shear stress failure point of the rock, (D). Dehydration, A, is an important part of the hypothesis of Scientist 1 but is not specifically mentioned in the scientist's discussion of the Rocky Mountain Arsenal. The slab of calcium magnesium silicate, B, belongs in Scientist 2's paragraph. Choice C confuses the Rocky Mountain Arsenal incident with the deep-sea trenches that are mentioned in the previous two sentences.

20. H
Category: Scientific Reasoning
Difficulty: Medium
Getting to the Answer: Scientist 2 claims that the slippage involved in deep-focus quakes results from phase changes. To support this contention, she cites laboratory work that produced similar phase changes and slippage in a slab of calcium

magnesium silicate. But neither scientist says that mantle rock is composed of calcium magnesium silicate. If the slippery slab is to serve as evidence for Scientist 2's theory, it must at least be similar to mantle rock, so (H) is correct. Choice F might help refute Scientist 1's viewpoint, but it would not strengthen Scientist 2's theory. Choices G and J would tend to weaken Scientist 2's theory.

21. D
Category: Scientific Reasoning
Difficulty: Medium
Getting to the Answer: Phase changes are fundamental to the arguments of both scientists, and both agree that they occur deep beneath Earth's surface, so you can eliminate A and B. The release of water from minerals is part of the explanation of Scientist 1, so C is out as well. Only (D) agrees with the logic of Scientist 2.

PASSAGE IV

22. H
Category: Figure Interpretation
Difficulty: Medium
Getting to the Answer: The one variable that changes is the amount of moisture. Choice G cannot be correct because Experiment 2 says that the researcher used models representing equivalent mass as those in Experiment 1. There is no evidence for F or J.

23. B
Category: Scientific Reasoning
Difficulty: Medium
Getting to the Answer: The moisture in Experiment 1 is 86%, and the moisture in Experiment 2 is 12%. If the moisture were changed to 50%, the collision rating would fall between the lines of the two experiments on the graphs. At 400,000 kg, the collision rating would be between 4.5 and 5.5.

24. G
Category: Scientific Reasoning
Difficulty: High
Getting to the Answer: The collision ratings for Experiment 1, with a high percentage of moisture in the atmosphere, were mostly lower than those in Experiment 2. Therefore, an increase in moisture would decrease the impact of a collision. Eliminate H and J. However, for asteroids over 700,000 kg, the lines on the graph meet—the presence of moisture loses its effect. Choice (G) is correct.

25. C
Category: Figure Interpretation
Difficulty: Low
Getting to the Answer: Feel free to draw in your booklet on Test Day. To answer this question, draw a line from 4 on the x-axis straight up. Draw a line from 4 on the y-axis straight across. Those two lines meet on the line for Experiment 1. The moisture level for Experiment 1 was 86%, so (C) is correct.

26. H
Category: Figure Interpretation
Difficulty: Medium
Getting to the Answer: Again, it might help to draw on the graph to answer this question. Draw a vertical line up from 1 (100,000 kg) on the horizontal scale to see where it hits the curve representing Experiment 2. Then draw a horizontal line from this curve to the curve representing Experiment 1, and draw from that point down to the horizontal scale once again. You'll see that the size is closest to (H), 270,000 kg.

27. B
Category: Figure Interpretation
Difficulty: High
Getting to the Answer: To be minimally capable of regional destruction, an asteroid must have a collision rating of 4, so draw a horizontal line over from 4 on the vertical scale. If you do so, you'll see that size of an asteroid capable of such destruction goes from roughly 250,000 kg at a 12% moisture

level to about 400,000 kg at an 86% moisture level. Then 400,000 is roughly 70% larger than 250,000, so (B) is the correct answer.

28. J
Category: Patterns
Difficulty: Medium
Getting to the Answer: Use the graph to approximate where this collision would occur. A 1.5 on the Torino scale and a 350,000 kg asteroid would result in a point that is below and to the right of Experiment 1, so its moisture level would be above 86%. Choice (J) is the correct answer.

PASSAGE V

29. D
Category: Figure Interpretation
Difficulty: Medium
Getting to the Answer: Look at the graphs that clarify the relationship between conductivity and temperature for a conductor and a semiconductor. Semiconductors have a direct relationship: as temperature increases, so does conductivity. Look at the conductivity vs. temperature graph and find a temperature range in which both samples have positive slopes. Don't worry if you can't find a range—that means that both samples do not share a temperature range for semiconducting behavior, and therefore (D) is correct.

30. H
Category: Figure Interpretation
Difficulty: High
Getting to the Answer: Following HST-52 from right to left across the first figure (because the temperature is decreasing), conductivity increases and temperature decreases—just like the conductivity of a conductor—until 160 K, at which point HST-52's conductivity starts to decrease with decreasing temperature, like a semiconductor. With decreasing temperature, the sample undergoes a conductor to semiconductor transition, (H).

31. B
Category: Patterns
Difficulty: Low
Getting to the Answer: The plot for conductor-like behavior indicates that as the temperature increases, its conductivity decreases. Choices A and C describe the behavior of semiconductors, not conductors. Choice D is incorrect: If the conductivity of conductors were the same at all temperatures, the plot of conductivity versus temperature for conductors would be a horizontal line.

32. H
Category: Patterns
Difficulty: Medium
Getting to the Answer: A material that has a semiconductor to conductor transition at 10 K will show a brief increase and then, starting at 10 K, a steady decrease as the temperature increases. Choice (H) is the plot that shows this brief increase at low temperatures and then the decrease as the temperature rises.

33. D
Category: Scientific Reasoning
Difficulty: Medium
Getting to the Answer: The figure shows that HST-52 displays semiconductor behavior only up to about 150 K. Therefore, HST-52 will be usable as a semiconductor only at temperatures below about 150 K, (D). Choice A is incorrect because HST-52 is a semiconductor at certain temperatures, and B is incorrect because HST-52 is not a semiconductor at all temperatures. The brittleness of HST-52 is never discussed in the passage, so C should be eliminated from the outset.

34. J
Category: Patterns
Difficulty: High
Getting to the Answer: You are looking for the temperature at which the downward slope for Sample HST-52 is the steepest. This is somewhat difficult

to determine, but this much is clear: The slope does not begin to go down until the temperature rises above 160 K. Thus, the only answer that could make sense is (J), 180 K.

PASSAGE VII

35. C
Category: Figure Interpretation
Difficulty: Low
Getting to the Answer: The graph shows no difference in the percentage of body covered in dark fur for outdoor temperatures less than or equal to 2°C, making (C) correct. The phrase "According to the graph" should remind you to extract data directly from the graph. Based on the passage alone, you might incorrectly assume that because the temperature drops over that month the percentage of body covered in dark fur would increase, as in A. The graph shows, however, that this is only true for outdoor temperatures between 2°C and 7°C.

36. G
Category: Scientific Reasoning
Difficulty: High
Getting to the Answer: The key to this question is determining whether the cat in question is an outdoor or indoor cat. This cat goes outdoors a total of three hours per week, whereas an outdoor cat would spend at least six hours outdoors per week. Therefore, this cat is an indoor cat, and the percentage of dark fur on its body would remain just above 10%.

37. B
Category: Figure Interpretation
Difficulty: Medium
Getting to the Answer: You can draw a line from 45% dark fur across to the solid line representing outdoor cats. If you draw a line from that intersection straight down to the x-axis, you will hit 3°C.

38. G
Category: Patterns
Difficulty: High
Getting to the Answer: If the cat grew dark fur over 30% of its body, it must have been an outdoor cat as defined in the passage and, according to the graph, been exposed to temperature below 5°C (Statement I). To be an outdoor cat, a cat does not have to spend more time outdoors than indoors (Statement II), but it has to spend time outdoors for six consecutive days (Statement III).

39. C
Category: Patterns
Difficulty: Medium
Getting to the Answer: If a Siamese cat does not have dark fur over more than 10% of its body, then it must *either* be an indoor cat *or* live in an area where it is not regularly exposed to temperatures below 7°C.

40. H
Category: Scientific Reasoning
Difficulty: Medium
Getting to the Answer: Choice F is incorrect because the indoor cats will not help us, since they don't go outside. Choice G is not a good choice because the outdoor cats of the original experiment cannot be used as a control group: The time they spent outside was not monitored—you only know that they spent more than one hour outside a day. Choice J is incorrect because the data already gathered only show that outdoor cats turn darker in cold weather than indoor cats and do not provide any information about how varying the amount of time outdoors affects fur color. The correct answer is (H). A completely new experiment would have to be set up.

WRITING TEST

MODEL ESSAY

Below is an example of what a high-scoring essay might look like. Notice the author states her position clearly in the introductory paragraph and supports that position with evidence in the following paragraphs. This essay also uses transitions, some advanced vocabulary, and an effective "hook" to draw in the reader.

Teenagers have lots of opinions, many of which we share rather loudly. Taking into consideration the students' feelings about the courses they study in high school has both pros and cons. Some argue that schools should provide students a way to make their preferences known, others feel students are too young to make good decisions about what to study, and others argue that surveying students can help make the curriculum more relevant to them and provide another way to evaluate a teacher's effectiveness. I agree that students' interests should be surveyed as long as they are not, in and of themselves, the basis for creating a curriculum.

From the first perspective, it is argued that high schools should do what colleges do and survey students to see how they feel about their classroom lessons. Studies show that when high school students are engaged because they enjoy their studies and understand the relevance of what they are learning, they are more participatory in class and remember more of what they learn. However, one problem is that schools cannot let students create the lessons, since this would lead to chaos with so many students expressing different opinions. However, if it were made clear that not all suggestions would be used but that there would be some way to pare down the suggestions, implementing only those with most student support, it would be possible for the students' preferences to be included in a lesson. Schools could survey students, compile a list of five top suggestions, then have students vote on them. In this way at least some student suggestions, and hopefully the most popular ones, would be part of the curriculum and promote more interaction and learning in a classroom. Surely this is the goal of education, and therefore it should be encouraged.

On the other hand, there are those who think that only the teachers should be in charge of the curriculum because students are not qualified to make those changes. It's true that students don't have the education, knowledge, and maturity to design lessons, but the argument doesn't say that the curriculum would be totally in the hands of the students, but only that student preferences should be considered. Those who argue that students aren't capable of designing the curriculum have misunderstood the statement. Everybody can benefit from suggestions, including educators, so there is nothing wrong with finding out what students want and trying to incorporate at least some of it into the curriculum. Any good teacher does this already. For example, she tries to make her examples relevant to what the students are interested in, such as teaching math by using basketball or baseball examples. So the argument is already partially in force, and those who misread it by thinking that the entire curriculum would be made up by students are misinterpreting the argument and coming to a wrong conclusion.

Finally, some argue that allowing student surveys could make lessons more interesting and also be a way of evaluating a teacher's effectiveness. I personally think that this would be a better way to evaluate teachers than using test scores, which don't always reflect real learning. But surveys are completely subjective, and it would be very difficult to tell which responses really reflect student satisfaction and which are just written because the student needs to write something. So this option is better than cold test scores, but I also see problems in it and so can't support it fully.

If a school administration makes it really clear that, just because students are being asked to make lesson plan suggestions doesn't mean that all suggestions will be used and that students are not in charge of making the curriculum, then the first perspective—allowing students to give their opinion about what they would like to study—is a good one. This one will make at least some lesson plans more interesting and relevant, and that will lead to better learning.

You can evaluate your essay and the model essay based on the following criteria, which is covered in the Practice Makes Perfect section of this book:

- Does the author discuss all three perspectives provided in the prompt?

- Is the author's own perspective clearly stated?

- Does the body of the essay assess and analyze each perspective?

- Is the relevance of each paragraph clear?

- Does the author start a new paragraph for each new idea?

- Is each sentence in a paragraph relevant to the point made in that paragraph?

- Are transitions clear?

- Is the essay easy to read? Is it engaging?

- Are sentences varied?

- Is vocabulary used effectively? Is college-level vocabulary used?

ACT Practice Test Three
ANSWER SHEET

ENGLISH TEST

1. Ⓐ Ⓑ Ⓒ Ⓓ   11. Ⓐ Ⓑ Ⓒ Ⓓ   21. Ⓐ Ⓑ Ⓒ Ⓓ   31. Ⓐ Ⓑ Ⓒ Ⓓ   41. Ⓐ Ⓑ Ⓒ Ⓓ   51. Ⓐ Ⓑ Ⓒ Ⓓ   61. Ⓐ Ⓑ Ⓒ Ⓓ   71. Ⓐ Ⓑ Ⓒ Ⓓ
2. Ⓕ Ⓖ Ⓗ Ⓙ   12. Ⓕ Ⓖ Ⓗ Ⓙ   22. Ⓕ Ⓖ Ⓗ Ⓙ   32. Ⓕ Ⓖ Ⓗ Ⓙ   42. Ⓕ Ⓖ Ⓗ Ⓙ   52. Ⓕ Ⓖ Ⓗ Ⓙ   62. Ⓕ Ⓖ Ⓗ Ⓙ   72. Ⓕ Ⓖ Ⓗ Ⓙ
3. Ⓐ Ⓑ Ⓒ Ⓓ   13. Ⓐ Ⓑ Ⓒ Ⓓ   23. Ⓐ Ⓑ Ⓒ Ⓓ   33. Ⓐ Ⓑ Ⓒ Ⓓ   43. Ⓐ Ⓑ Ⓒ Ⓓ   53. Ⓐ Ⓑ Ⓒ Ⓓ   63. Ⓐ Ⓑ Ⓒ Ⓓ   73. Ⓐ Ⓑ Ⓒ Ⓓ
4. Ⓕ Ⓖ Ⓗ Ⓙ   14. Ⓕ Ⓖ Ⓗ Ⓙ   24. Ⓕ Ⓖ Ⓗ Ⓙ   34. Ⓕ Ⓖ Ⓗ Ⓙ   44. Ⓕ Ⓖ Ⓗ Ⓙ   54. Ⓕ Ⓖ Ⓗ Ⓙ   64. Ⓕ Ⓖ Ⓗ Ⓙ   74. Ⓕ Ⓖ Ⓗ Ⓙ
5. Ⓐ Ⓑ Ⓒ Ⓓ   15. Ⓐ Ⓑ Ⓒ Ⓓ   25. Ⓐ Ⓑ Ⓒ Ⓓ   35. Ⓐ Ⓑ Ⓒ Ⓓ   45. Ⓐ Ⓑ Ⓒ Ⓓ   55. Ⓐ Ⓑ Ⓒ Ⓓ   65. Ⓐ Ⓑ Ⓒ Ⓓ   75. Ⓐ Ⓑ Ⓒ Ⓓ
6. Ⓕ Ⓖ Ⓗ Ⓙ   16. Ⓕ Ⓖ Ⓗ Ⓙ   26. Ⓕ Ⓖ Ⓗ Ⓙ   36. Ⓕ Ⓖ Ⓗ Ⓙ   46. Ⓕ Ⓖ Ⓗ Ⓙ   56. Ⓕ Ⓖ Ⓗ Ⓙ   66. Ⓕ Ⓖ Ⓗ Ⓙ
7. Ⓐ Ⓑ Ⓒ Ⓓ   17. Ⓐ Ⓑ Ⓒ Ⓓ   27. Ⓐ Ⓑ Ⓒ Ⓓ   37. Ⓐ Ⓑ Ⓒ Ⓓ   47. Ⓐ Ⓑ Ⓒ Ⓓ   57. Ⓐ Ⓑ Ⓒ Ⓓ   67. Ⓐ Ⓑ Ⓒ Ⓓ
8. Ⓕ Ⓖ Ⓗ Ⓙ   18. Ⓕ Ⓖ Ⓗ Ⓙ   28. Ⓕ Ⓖ Ⓗ Ⓙ   38. Ⓕ Ⓖ Ⓗ Ⓙ   48. Ⓕ Ⓖ Ⓗ Ⓙ   58. Ⓕ Ⓖ Ⓗ Ⓙ   68. Ⓕ Ⓖ Ⓗ Ⓙ
9. Ⓐ Ⓑ Ⓒ Ⓓ   19. Ⓐ Ⓑ Ⓒ Ⓓ   29. Ⓐ Ⓑ Ⓒ Ⓓ   39. Ⓐ Ⓑ Ⓒ Ⓓ   49. Ⓐ Ⓑ Ⓒ Ⓓ   59. Ⓐ Ⓑ Ⓒ Ⓓ   69. Ⓐ Ⓑ Ⓒ Ⓓ
10. Ⓕ Ⓖ Ⓗ Ⓙ   20. Ⓕ Ⓖ Ⓗ Ⓙ   30. Ⓕ Ⓖ Ⓗ Ⓙ   40. Ⓕ Ⓖ Ⓗ Ⓙ   50. Ⓕ Ⓖ Ⓗ Ⓙ   60. Ⓕ Ⓖ Ⓗ Ⓙ   70. Ⓕ Ⓖ Ⓗ Ⓙ

MATHEMATICS TEST

1. Ⓐ Ⓑ Ⓒ Ⓓ Ⓔ   11. Ⓐ Ⓑ Ⓒ Ⓓ Ⓔ   21. Ⓐ Ⓑ Ⓒ Ⓓ Ⓔ   31. Ⓐ Ⓑ Ⓒ Ⓓ Ⓔ   41. Ⓐ Ⓑ Ⓒ Ⓓ Ⓔ   51. Ⓐ Ⓑ Ⓒ Ⓓ Ⓔ
2. Ⓕ Ⓖ Ⓗ Ⓙ Ⓚ   12. Ⓕ Ⓖ Ⓗ Ⓙ Ⓚ   22. Ⓕ Ⓖ Ⓗ Ⓙ Ⓚ   32. Ⓕ Ⓖ Ⓗ Ⓙ Ⓚ   42. Ⓕ Ⓖ Ⓗ Ⓙ Ⓚ   52. Ⓕ Ⓖ Ⓗ Ⓙ Ⓚ
3. Ⓐ Ⓑ Ⓒ Ⓓ Ⓔ   13. Ⓐ Ⓑ Ⓒ Ⓓ Ⓔ   23. Ⓐ Ⓑ Ⓒ Ⓓ Ⓔ   33. Ⓐ Ⓑ Ⓒ Ⓓ Ⓔ   43. Ⓐ Ⓑ Ⓒ Ⓓ Ⓔ   53. Ⓐ Ⓑ Ⓒ Ⓓ Ⓔ
4. Ⓕ Ⓖ Ⓗ Ⓙ Ⓚ   14. Ⓕ Ⓖ Ⓗ Ⓙ Ⓚ   24. Ⓕ Ⓖ Ⓗ Ⓙ Ⓚ   34. Ⓕ Ⓖ Ⓗ Ⓙ Ⓚ   44. Ⓕ Ⓖ Ⓗ Ⓙ Ⓚ   54. Ⓕ Ⓖ Ⓗ Ⓙ Ⓚ
5. Ⓐ Ⓑ Ⓒ Ⓓ Ⓔ   15. Ⓐ Ⓑ Ⓒ Ⓓ Ⓔ   25. Ⓐ Ⓑ Ⓒ Ⓓ Ⓔ   35. Ⓐ Ⓑ Ⓒ Ⓓ Ⓔ   45. Ⓐ Ⓑ Ⓒ Ⓓ Ⓔ   55. Ⓐ Ⓑ Ⓒ Ⓓ Ⓔ
6. Ⓕ Ⓖ Ⓗ Ⓙ Ⓚ   16. Ⓕ Ⓖ Ⓗ Ⓙ Ⓚ   26. Ⓕ Ⓖ Ⓗ Ⓙ Ⓚ   36. Ⓕ Ⓖ Ⓗ Ⓙ Ⓚ   46. Ⓕ Ⓖ Ⓗ Ⓙ Ⓚ   56. Ⓕ Ⓖ Ⓗ Ⓙ Ⓚ
7. Ⓐ Ⓑ Ⓒ Ⓓ Ⓔ   17. Ⓐ Ⓑ Ⓒ Ⓓ Ⓔ   27. Ⓐ Ⓑ Ⓒ Ⓓ Ⓔ   37. Ⓐ Ⓑ Ⓒ Ⓓ Ⓔ   47. Ⓐ Ⓑ Ⓒ Ⓓ Ⓔ   57. Ⓐ Ⓑ Ⓒ Ⓓ Ⓔ
8. Ⓕ Ⓖ Ⓗ Ⓙ Ⓚ   18. Ⓕ Ⓖ Ⓗ Ⓙ Ⓚ   28. Ⓕ Ⓖ Ⓗ Ⓙ Ⓚ   38. Ⓕ Ⓖ Ⓗ Ⓙ Ⓚ   48. Ⓕ Ⓖ Ⓗ Ⓙ Ⓚ   58. Ⓕ Ⓖ Ⓗ Ⓙ Ⓚ
9. Ⓐ Ⓑ Ⓒ Ⓓ Ⓔ   19. Ⓐ Ⓑ Ⓒ Ⓓ Ⓔ   29. Ⓐ Ⓑ Ⓒ Ⓓ Ⓔ   39. Ⓐ Ⓑ Ⓒ Ⓓ Ⓔ   49. Ⓐ Ⓑ Ⓒ Ⓓ Ⓔ   59. Ⓐ Ⓑ Ⓒ Ⓓ Ⓔ
10. Ⓕ Ⓖ Ⓗ Ⓙ Ⓚ   20. Ⓕ Ⓖ Ⓗ Ⓙ Ⓚ   30. Ⓕ Ⓖ Ⓗ Ⓙ Ⓚ   40. Ⓕ Ⓖ Ⓗ Ⓙ Ⓚ   50. Ⓕ Ⓖ Ⓗ Ⓙ Ⓚ   60. Ⓕ Ⓖ Ⓗ Ⓙ Ⓚ

READING TEST

1. Ⓐ Ⓑ Ⓒ Ⓓ   6. Ⓕ Ⓖ Ⓗ Ⓙ   11. Ⓐ Ⓑ Ⓒ Ⓓ   16. Ⓕ Ⓖ Ⓗ Ⓙ   21. Ⓐ Ⓑ Ⓒ Ⓓ   26. Ⓕ Ⓖ Ⓗ Ⓙ   31. Ⓐ Ⓑ Ⓒ Ⓓ   36. Ⓕ Ⓖ Ⓗ Ⓙ
2. Ⓕ Ⓖ Ⓗ Ⓙ   7. Ⓐ Ⓑ Ⓒ Ⓓ   12. Ⓕ Ⓖ Ⓗ Ⓙ   17. Ⓐ Ⓑ Ⓒ Ⓓ   22. Ⓕ Ⓖ Ⓗ Ⓙ   27. Ⓐ Ⓑ Ⓒ Ⓓ   32. Ⓕ Ⓖ Ⓗ Ⓙ   37. Ⓐ Ⓑ Ⓒ Ⓓ
3. Ⓐ Ⓑ Ⓒ Ⓓ   8. Ⓕ Ⓖ Ⓗ Ⓙ   13. Ⓐ Ⓑ Ⓒ Ⓓ   18. Ⓕ Ⓖ Ⓗ Ⓙ   23. Ⓐ Ⓑ Ⓒ Ⓓ   28. Ⓕ Ⓖ Ⓗ Ⓙ   33. Ⓐ Ⓑ Ⓒ Ⓓ   38. Ⓕ Ⓖ Ⓗ Ⓙ
4. Ⓕ Ⓖ Ⓗ Ⓙ   9. Ⓐ Ⓑ Ⓒ Ⓓ   14. Ⓕ Ⓖ Ⓗ Ⓙ   19. Ⓐ Ⓑ Ⓒ Ⓓ   24. Ⓕ Ⓖ Ⓗ Ⓙ   29. Ⓐ Ⓑ Ⓒ Ⓓ   34. Ⓕ Ⓖ Ⓗ Ⓙ   39. Ⓐ Ⓑ Ⓒ Ⓓ
5. Ⓐ Ⓑ Ⓒ Ⓓ   10. Ⓕ Ⓖ Ⓗ Ⓙ   15. Ⓐ Ⓑ Ⓒ Ⓓ   20. Ⓕ Ⓖ Ⓗ Ⓙ   25. Ⓐ Ⓑ Ⓒ Ⓓ   30. Ⓕ Ⓖ Ⓗ Ⓙ   35. Ⓐ Ⓑ Ⓒ Ⓓ   40. Ⓕ Ⓖ Ⓗ Ⓙ

SCIENCE TEST

1. Ⓐ Ⓑ Ⓒ Ⓓ   6. Ⓕ Ⓖ Ⓗ Ⓙ   11. Ⓐ Ⓑ Ⓒ Ⓓ   16. Ⓕ Ⓖ Ⓗ Ⓙ   21. Ⓐ Ⓑ Ⓒ Ⓓ   26. Ⓕ Ⓖ Ⓗ Ⓙ   31. Ⓐ Ⓑ Ⓒ Ⓓ   36. Ⓕ Ⓖ Ⓗ Ⓙ
2. Ⓕ Ⓖ Ⓗ Ⓙ   7. Ⓐ Ⓑ Ⓒ Ⓓ   12. Ⓕ Ⓖ Ⓗ Ⓙ   17. Ⓐ Ⓑ Ⓒ Ⓓ   22. Ⓕ Ⓖ Ⓗ Ⓙ   27. Ⓐ Ⓑ Ⓒ Ⓓ   32. Ⓕ Ⓖ Ⓗ Ⓙ   37. Ⓐ Ⓑ Ⓒ Ⓓ
3. Ⓐ Ⓑ Ⓒ Ⓓ   8. Ⓕ Ⓖ Ⓗ Ⓙ   13. Ⓐ Ⓑ Ⓒ Ⓓ   18. Ⓕ Ⓖ Ⓗ Ⓙ   23. Ⓐ Ⓑ Ⓒ Ⓓ   28. Ⓕ Ⓖ Ⓗ Ⓙ   33. Ⓐ Ⓑ Ⓒ Ⓓ   38. Ⓕ Ⓖ Ⓗ Ⓙ
4. Ⓕ Ⓖ Ⓗ Ⓙ   9. Ⓐ Ⓑ Ⓒ Ⓓ   14. Ⓕ Ⓖ Ⓗ Ⓙ   19. Ⓐ Ⓑ Ⓒ Ⓓ   24. Ⓕ Ⓖ Ⓗ Ⓙ   29. Ⓐ Ⓑ Ⓒ Ⓓ   34. Ⓕ Ⓖ Ⓗ Ⓙ   39. Ⓐ Ⓑ Ⓒ Ⓓ
5. Ⓐ Ⓑ Ⓒ Ⓓ   10. Ⓕ Ⓖ Ⓗ Ⓙ   15. Ⓐ Ⓑ Ⓒ Ⓓ   20. Ⓕ Ⓖ Ⓗ Ⓙ   25. Ⓐ Ⓑ Ⓒ Ⓓ   30. Ⓕ Ⓖ Ⓗ Ⓙ   35. Ⓐ Ⓑ Ⓒ Ⓓ   40. Ⓕ Ⓖ Ⓗ Ⓙ

ENGLISH TEST

45 Minutes—75 Questions

Directions: In the following five passages, certain words and phrases are underlined and numbered. In the right-hand column are alternatives for each underlined portion. Select the one that best conveys the idea, creates the most grammatically correct sentence, or is the most consistent with the style and tone of the passage. If you decide that the original version is best, select NO CHANGE. You may also find questions that ask about the entire passage or a section of the passage. These questions will correspond to small numbered boxes in the text. For these questions, decide which choice best accomplishes the purpose set out in the question stem. After you've selected the best choice, fill in the corresponding oval in your Answer Grid. For some questions, you'll need to read the context in order to answer correctly. Be sure to read until you have enough information to determine the correct answer choice.

PASSAGE I

A SWIMMING CHANGE

[1]

Until three years ago, I had never considered myself to be athletically talented. I have never been able to hit, catch, throw, or kick a ball with any degree of confidence or accuracy. For years, physical <u>education being</u> often the worst part of the school day for me. Units on tennis, touch football, volleyball, and basketball were torturous. I not only dreaded fumbling a pass,

<u>so</u> I also feared being hit in the face by a ball. However, at the beginning of my freshman year of high school, my attitude toward sports changed.

1. **A.** NO CHANGE
   B. education, was
   C. education was
   D. education,

2. **F.** NO CHANGE
   G. and
   H. but
   J. though

GO ON TO THE NEXT PAGE ▷

[2]

Somehow, my good friend Gretchen convinced me

to join <u>our schools</u> swim team.
     3

3.
  A. NO CHANGE
  B. our schools'
  C. our school's
  D. ours school

<u>Knowing that I enjoyed swimming, over the course of</u>
                4
<u>two summers, it was with Gretchen that I practically</u>
                4
<u>had lived at the pool.</u> My mother had
    4

4.
  F. NO CHANGE
  G. Because we had spent two summers practically living at the pool, it was Gretchen who knew that swimming was enjoyed by me.
  H. Having practically lived at the pool over two summers, the two of us, Gretchen knew it was swimming that I enjoyed.
  J. Gretchen knew I enjoyed swimming, as we had spent two summers practically living at the pool.

<u>insisted</u> that I take swimming lessons every summer
  5
since I was seven, so I was entirely comfortable in the

water. I was also eager to start my high school experience

with a new challenge and a new way to think of myself.

[3]

Of course, I had no idea what I was getting into

when Gretchen and I showed up for the first day of

practice. The team was made up of twenty young

<u>women, most of these swimmers</u> had been participat-
          6
ing in the community swim team for years. I couldn't do

a flip turn at the end of the lane without getting water

up my nose. In contrast, most of the other swimmers,

5. Of the four choices, which is the only one that does NOT indicate that the narrator's mother decided that the narrator must take swimming lessons?
  A. NO CHANGE
  B. suggested
  C. required
  D. demanded

6.
  F. NO CHANGE
  G. women, the majority of them
  H. women most of them
  J. women, most of whom

GO ON TO THE NEXT PAGE ⇒

who

<u>had been swimming competitively, since elementary</u>
                                7
<u>school,</u> were able to gracefully somersault and begin the
  7
next lap. By the end of the first hour of practice, I was

exhausted and waterlogged.

[4]

However, I had no intention of <u>giving up, which</u>
                                          8
<u>would mean quitting.</u> I came back the next day and the
      8
next day for practice. Things

<u>begun</u> to get serious in the second week, when we
  9
started the regular schedule of four early morning and

five afternoon practices. Our coach,

<u>whom</u> had led the team to several state championships,
  10
demanded dedication from everyone on the team. The

hard work

<u>eventually paid off. By</u> the end of the first month, I had
        11
discovered that I was good at the butterfly,

7. **A.** NO CHANGE
   B. had been swimming competitively since elementary school,
   C. had been swimming, competitively since elementary school,
   D. had been swimming competitively since elementary school

8. **F.** NO CHANGE
   G. giving up and resigning myself to failure.
   H. giving up and quitting what I had set out to do.
   J. giving up.

9. **A.** NO CHANGE
   B. had been begun
   C. had began
   D. began

10. **F.** NO CHANGE
    G. for whom
    H. who
    J. which

11. **A.** NO CHANGE
    B. eventually paid off, so, as a result
    C. paid off eventually, however, by
    D. paid off, eventually, by

GO ON TO THE NEXT PAGE

<u>a relatively new stroke that was first introduced in the</u>
                                                        12
<u>1930s.</u> I rarely won individual races, but I became a
12
solid member of our

<u>team's medley relay.</u>
          13

[5]

After that intimidating first season, I continued

swimming. I even <u>will have earned</u> a varsity letter last
                          14
year. Now I'm hoping to earn a spot in the state compe-

tition my senior year. [15]

12. Assuming each of the following creates a true statement, which provides the information most relevant to the narrator's experience on the swim team?

   F. NO CHANGE

   G. a difficult stroke that interested few other members of our team.

   H. which is faster than the backstroke but somewhat slower than the crawl.

   J. which is still sometimes called the dolphin because it incorporates a two-stroke dolphin kick.

13. **A.** NO CHANGE

   B. team's medley relay (it consists of four swimmers).

   C. team's medley relay, which the person swimming backstroke always begins.

   D. team.

14. **F.** NO CHANGE

   G. would have earned

   H. earned

   J. earn

15. If inserted here, which of the following would be the most appropriate sentence to conclude the essay?

   A. My coach continues to schedule demanding practices, but I have come to enjoy the early morning swims.

   B. For someone who thought she didn't have any athletic talent, I have come a long way.

   C. Gretchen is also still on the team, but she does not swim the medley relay.

   D. I've always enjoyed swimming, so I'm not all that surprised by my success as an athlete.

GO ON TO THE NEXT PAGE ⟹

PASSAGE II

EXPLORING DUBUQUE'S AQUARIUM

[1]

One lazy day last summer, my parents decided that my younger sister and I needed a break from our vacation from academics. They took us to the National Mississippi River Museum and Aquarium in Dubuque, Iowa. I was prepared to be bored by this family educational trip. However, from the moment I walked through the museum's doors, I was <u>captivated; by</u> all that there was
16
to learn about life in the Mississippi.

[2]

[1] A large tank stocked with fish and turtles <u>was there</u> to greet us as we walked into the main hall. [2]
17
There were also animals I had never before glimpsed, such as a fish called the long-nosed gar. [3] I was amazed by this fish in particular. [4] Its long, tubular shape and distinctive rod-shaped <u>nose that</u> made it
18
appear like something that lived in the dark depths of the ocean. [5] This first of five freshwater aquariums offered a close-up view of <u>familiar animals that I had seen</u>
19
<u>before,</u> such as ducks. [20]
19

16. F. NO CHANGE
    G. captivated, by
    H. captivated by,
    J. captivated by

17. A. NO CHANGE
    B. is there
    C. are there
    D. were there

18. F. NO CHANGE
    G. nose, which
    H. nose, and this
    J. nose

19. A. NO CHANGE
    B. animals that were familiar sights to me,
    C. familiar animals to which I was no stranger,
    D. familiar animals,

20. To make paragraph 2 coherent and logical, the best placement of sentence 5 is:
    F. where it is now.
    G. before sentence 1.
    H. after sentence 1.
    J. after sentence 2.

GO ON TO THE NEXT PAGE

[3]

In the next aquarium, I <u>see</u> a catfish bigger than I
                        21
had ever imagined this species could be. According to
the posted information, this specimen weighed more
than 100 pounds. With its long whiskers and slow, lazy
movements, this catfish looked like the grandfather of
all the other fish in the tank.

[4]

<u>I couldn't decide which I liked better, the catfish</u>
                                            22
<u>or the long-nosed gar.</u> The next floor-to-ceiling tank,
    22
which represented the ecosystem of the Mississippi
bayou, held an animal I had never seen: an alligator. At
first, I had a hard time spotting the creature—it blended
in almost completely with a half-submerged log. 23
Suddenly, though, it

21. **A.** NO CHANGE
    B. had been seeing
    C. saw
    D. spot

22. Which sentence most effectively connects this paragraph to the preceding paragraph?
    F. NO CHANGE
    G. Although the catfish was impressive, it was not the biggest animal on display in the museum.
    H. After seeing the catfish, I was interested in exhibits that were a bit more hands-on.
    J. Until my visit to the museum, I had never really considered what the Mississippi River was like south of my home.

23. At this point, the writer is considering removing the following phrase:

    it blended in almost completely with a half-submerged log.

    The primary effect of removing this phrase would be:

    A. a smoother transition between sentences.
    B. a greater contrast between images.
    C. a loss of descriptive information.
    D. an increased level of suspense.

slides into the water and aims itself right at the glass
24
separating me from its ferocious claws and skin-tearing

teeth. I had a

slightly moment of panic before I remembered that, try
25
as it might, this alligator would never successfully hunt

tourists like me. As

much of the onlookers squealed in delight as the alligator
26
moved through the tank, I noticed his companion. Far off

in a corner slept an enormous snapping turtle. I could im-

agine no better roommate for the alligator than this hook-

beaked turtle with rough ridges running along its shell.

[5]

Despite my initial expectations, I happily spent

the entire day soaking up information about creatures

that live in the Mississippi River. In one section of the

museum, I held a crayfish. 27 Later, I had the opportu-

nity to touch the cool, sleek skin of a stingray, which can

be found where the Mississippi empties into the Gulf of

Mexico.

24. **F.** NO CHANGE
    G. slides into the water to aim
    H. slid into the water and aiming
    J. slid into the water and aimed

25. **A.** NO CHANGE
    B. momentarily slight
    C. moment of slight
    D. momentarily of slight

26. **F.** NO CHANGE
    G. a large amount
    H. the many
    J. many

27. The writer would like to insert a sentence describing the appearance of the crayfish at this point. Which sentence would best accomplish the writer's goal?

    A. Also known as crawdads, crayfish are close relatives of the lobsters that live in freshwater.

    B. At an average length of three inches, the crayfish looks like a miniature lobster, complete with small but effective front pincers.

    C. Although they are found throughout the United States, crayfish populations are densest in Kentucky and Mississippi.

    D. At first, I was a bit nervous to touch the small creature, but then I relaxed and enjoyed the opportunity to look at it so closely.

GO ON TO THE NEXT PAGE ⟶

[6]

After seeing all, I could inside the museum, I wan-
                     28
dered outside, only to find even more exhibits.

Having just enough time, it was that I was able to see
                     29
the otters and watch a riverboat launching, but it was

closing time before I was able to see the most impressive

thing the museum had to offer. A football-field-sized

steamboat from the 1930s is open to

tourists. And operates as a "boat-and-breakfast" that
        30
hosts overnight guests. I'm hoping that my family will

plan another educational trip to Dubuque soon so I can

experience life on a steamboat.

28. **F.** NO CHANGE
    G. all I could inside the museum,
    H. all, I could inside the museum
    J. all I could inside the museum

29. **A.** NO CHANGE
    B. It was that I had just enough time, so I
        was able
    C. Having just enough time, it was possible
    D. I had just enough time

30. **F.** NO CHANGE
    G. tourists and that operates
    H. tourists, it operates
    J. tourists and operates

PASSAGE III

THE MYSTERY DINER

The paragraphs in this essay may or may not follow the most logical order. Each paragraph
is numbered, and question 45 will ask you to determine the best placement of paragraph 6.

[1]

Although secret identities and elaborate disguises are

typically associated with the world of spies and villains,

it has other uses. For six years, Ruth
31

31. **A.** NO CHANGE
    B. it does have
    C. they do have
    D. and they have

<u>Reichl the restaurant critic for the *New York Times,*</u> used
32
aliases and costumes as a regular part of her job.

[2]

Dining is big business in New York City, from the neighborhood noodle shops and diners to the upscale steak houses and four-star French restaurants.

33 Many of the more than one million people who read the *Times* each day

<u>look to</u> it for advice on where to eat. A positive review
34
from the *Times*

<u>could have brought</u> a restaurant unimagined suc-
35
cess and month-long waiting lists for reservations. A negative review, on the other hand, can undermine a

32. F. NO CHANGE
G. Reichl, the restaurant critic, for the *New York Times,*
H. Reichl, the restaurant critic for the *New York Times,*
J. Reichl the restaurant critic for the *New York Times*

33. Should the following sentence be inserted into the passage at this point?

> The legendary French restaurant Le Bernardin received a four-star rating from the *Times* shortly after opening in 1986, an honor it has maintained ever since.

A. Yes, because the added sentence emphasizes how important a positive review from the *Times* can be.
B. Yes, because the specific information helps the reader develop a clearer picture of the type of restaurant reviewed by the *Times*.
C. No, because it is unclear whether Reichl was responsible for reviewing this specific restaurant.
D. No, because the specific information about one restaurant leads the reader away from the main topic of the essay.

34. F. NO CHANGE
G. look with
H. look by
J. looking to

35. A. NO CHANGE
B. can bring
C. will have brought
D. will be bringing

GO ON TO THE NEXT PAGE

restaurant's popularity and seriously cut into its profits.

Obviously, restaurant owners and workers have a lot at
             36
stake when the restaurant critic for the *Times* walks in

the door. Waiters and chefs often pull out all of the stops

to impress the writer that the meal can make or break a
                     37
restaurant.

[3]

Reichl was acutely aware that she received special
                                           38
treatment once restaurant staff recognized her. She
38
would be graciously greeted and led to the best table

in the restaurant, offered dishes prepared specially by

the head chef, and given multiple courses of amazing

desserts. In other words, the dining experience of the

restaurant critic was nothing like that of the commonly
                                                 39
ordinary person walking in from the street.
39

[4]

To remedy this, Reichl decided a solution would be
                                           40
to become, for short periods of time, someone else.
40

36. F. NO CHANGE
    G. restaurant owners and workers;
    H. restaurant, owners and workers
    J. restaurant owners, and workers

37. A. NO CHANGE
    B. who's
    C. whose
    D. which

38. F. NO CHANGE
    G. special treatment was received by her
    H. she was the recipient of special treatment
    J. she was in the position of receiving special treatment

39. A. NO CHANGE
    B. common, representative, and average
    C. typical
    D. extravagant

40. F. NO CHANGE
    G. she created a solution to the problem by becoming,
    H. Reichl decided to become,
    J. Reichl found a way to fix the problem, which involved becoming,

GO ON TO THE NEXT PAGE ⟩

<u>Transforming herself into different personas, Reichl used</u>
41
<u>wigs, special makeup, and carefully selected clothing,</u>
41
such as an attractive blonde named Chloe, a redhead

named Brenda, and an older woman named Betty. [42]

41. A. NO CHANGE

 B. With wigs, special makeup, and carefully selected clothing, Reichl transformed herself into different personas,

 C. Transformed with wigs, special makeup, and carefully selected clothing, Reichl's different personas,

 D. Reichl used wigs, special makeup, and carefully selected clothing, that transformed herself into different personas,

42. Which of the following true statements would make the most effective and logical conclusion for paragraph 4?

 F. Reichl found that she could quickly disguise herself as Betty, but it took more time to become Chloe.

 G. Her true identity hidden, Reichl would then dine at a restaurant she was currently evaluating.

 H. After six years at the *Times,* Reichl moved on to become the editor of *Gourmet* magazine.

 J. The former restaurant critic for the *Times* did not always agree with Reichl's methods or her selection of restaurants to review.

[5]

 Sometimes, Reichl developed a different view about

the quality when she was not treated like a very impor-

tant person <u>of a restaurant</u>. Indeed, the difference be-
43
tween the treatment she received as herself and as one

43. For the sake of logic and coherence, the underlined portion should be placed:

 A. where it is now.

 B. after the word *developed.*

 C. after the word *view.*

 D. after the word *quality.*

GO ON TO THE NEXT PAGE

of her characters was occasionally so great that Reichl would revise her initial impression of a restaurant and write a more negative review. 44

[6]

By becoming an average customer, Reichl encouraged even the most expensive and popular restaurants to improve how they treated all of their customers. After all, waiters could never be certain when they were serving the powerful restaurant critic for the *New York Times*.

44. Would deleting the word *occasionally* from the previous sentence change the meaning of the sentence?

F. Yes, because without this word, the reader would not understand that Reichl had different experiences when she dined in disguise.

G. Yes, because without this word, the reader would think that Reichl always changed her impression of restaurants when she was not recognized and received different treatment as a result.

H. No, because this word repeats an idea that is already presented in the sentence.

J. No, because this word is used only to show emphasis, and it does not contribute to the meaning of the sentence.

Question 45 asks about the preceding passage as a whole.

45. To make the passage flow logically and smoothly, the best place for paragraph 6 is:

A. where it is now.

B. after paragraph 1.

C. after paragraph 3.

D. after paragraph 4.

GO ON TO THE NEXT PAGE

PASSAGE IV

THE BENEFITS OF A SQUARE-FOOT GARDEN

[1]

[1] I used to start every spring with great hopes for my backyard vegetable garden. [2] After the last freeze in late March or early April, I devoted an entire weekend to preparing the soil in the garden. [3] I thinned out the rows that had too many plants and spent hours tugging out each weed that threatened to rob my little plants of the nutrients they needed to thrive. [4] Once spring truly arrived, I marked out my rows and scattered the packets of seeds that I hoped, would develop into prize-winning vegetables. [5] In the first few weeks of the season, I was almost always in the garden. 47
46

46. **F.** NO CHANGE
    G. hoped, would,
    H. hoped would,
    J. hoped would

[2]

Despite my best intentions, my garden never lived up to the vision I had for it. After I had devoted several weekends to watering and weeding, the garden always started to become more of a

47. To make paragraph 1 more logical and coherent, sentence 3 should be placed:
    A. where it is now.
    B. before sentence 1.
    C. after sentence 1.
    D. after sentence 4.

burden less of a hobby. By July, the garden was usually
48
in disarray, and I didn't have the energy or time to save it.

48. **F.** NO CHANGE
    G. burden:
    H. burden and
    J. burden, but,

GO ON TO THE NEXT PAGE →

July and August are always the hottest parts of the year.
49

49. **A.** NO CHANGE
   B. The hottest months are July and August.
   C. (July, along with August, provides the hottest temperatures of the year.)
   D. OMIT the underlined portion.

[3]

This past year, <u>however,</u> my garden was finally the
50
success I had imagined it could be. Instead of planning the traditional garden of closely planted

50. Of the following choices, which would be the LEAST acceptable substitution for the underlined word?
   F. on the other hand
   G. indeed
   H. though
   J. in contrast

<u>rows that is modeled after large-scale farming,</u> I tried a
51
new technique. My new approach is called square-foot gardening.

51. **A.** NO CHANGE
   B. rows, which is modeled after large-scale farming,
   C. rows, which is based on the techniques for large-scale farming,
   D. rows,

[4]

<u>A square-foot garden is designed for efficiency.</u>
52

52. Which sentence most effectively links the topic of paragraph 3 to the topic of paragraph 4?
   F. NO CHANGE
   G. The technique of square-foot gardening was pioneered by Mel Bartholomew.
   H. One of the benefits of a square-foot garden is that it is less expensive to maintain than a traditional garden.
   J. My neighbor, who always has a beautiful garden, introduced me to the concept of square-foot gardening, and I have been grateful ever since.

GO ON TO THE NEXT PAGE ⟹

In a <u>traditionally</u> garden, you scatter a packet of seeds
                53
down a row. When the plants emerge,

<u>they spend</u> hours thinning each row by pulling out at
     54
least half of what was planted. In a square-foot garden,

you plant each seed individually, so there is never a need

for thinning

<u>in the garden</u>. You create the garden plan 1 square foot
        55
at a time, until you have a block of 16 squares. Sturdy

pieces of lumber

<u>which could make</u> effective borders for each square.
        56
Walking paths that are at least 2 feet wide separate each

16-square-foot garden. The design is clean and simple,

and it eliminates the problem of getting to the rows in

the middle of a large garden. In fact,

<u>you can do</u> all the weeding, watering, and harvesting
     57
from the walking paths.

[5]

In addition to being easier to weed and water, a

square-foot garden takes up much less space than a

regular garden. I was able to grow

<u>an increased number of more</u> vegetables in two square-
                58
foot gardens, which took up a total of 32 square feet,

than I ever had grown in my traditional garden, which

took up 84 square feet. Preparing the soil for the smaller

53. **A.** NO CHANGE
    B. conventionally
    C. traditional
    D. tradition

54. **F.** NO CHANGE
    G. he spends
    H. people spend
    J. you spend

55. **A.** NO CHANGE
    B. out the garden
    C. in that garden
    D. OMIT the underlined portion.

56. **F.** NO CHANGE
    G. that make
    H. make
    J. OMIT the underlined portion.

57. **A.** NO CHANGE
    B. you could have done
    C. one can do
    D. one is able to do

58. **F.** NO CHANGE
    G. a larger quantity of more
    H. an increased, bigger quantity
    J. more

GO ON TO THE NEXT PAGE ⟹

space only required a few hours instead of a whole weekend. There was so much less weeding to do that the task never felt overwhelming. One season of using the square garden techniques <u>were all</u> it took for me
⁵⁹
to convert to a completely new outlook on backyard gardening.

59. **A.** NO CHANGE
   B. were just what
   C. was all
   D. could be

> Question 60 asks about the preceding passage as a whole.

60. If the writer had intended to write an essay detailing how to plan, prepare, and care for a square-foot garden, would this essay meet the writer's goal?

   F. No, because the writer relies on generalities rather than specifics when describing her square garden.

   G. No, because the writer focuses on comparing two different types of gardens instead of explaining how to begin and care for one type of garden.

   H. Yes, because the writer states specific measurements for her square garden.

   J. Yes, because the writer maintains that square gardens are superior to traditional gardens.

GO ON TO THE NEXT PAGE

PASSAGE V

THE IMPORTANCE OF MAINTAINING YOUR CAR

[1]

Most new car owners glance briefly at the owner's manual before depositing it in the glove compartment of their recently purchased automobile. Owners may dig out their manuals when something goes <u>wrong, such as a flat tire or a flashing engine light</u> but few take the
61
time to learn the basics about maintaining their new purchase. This is truly unfortunate, as a few simple and routine steps

<u>improves the long-term performance of an automobile</u>
62
<u>and decreases</u> the possibility of a traffic accident.
62

[2]

One of the easiest and most overlooked maintenance steps is caring for a car's wiper blades. Most people don't

<u>notice a problem</u> until the blades fail to clear the wind-
63
shield during a rainstorm or heavy snowfall. When a driver's

<u>vision being</u> obscured, an accident is more likely to hap-
64
pen. Replacing the

61. A. NO CHANGE
  B. wrong; such as a flat tire or a flashing engine light
  C. wrong, such as a flat tire, or a flashing engine light
  D. wrong, such as a flat tire or a flashing engine light,

62. F. NO CHANGE
  G. improve the long-term performance of an automobile and decreases
  H. improve the long-term performance of an automobile and decrease
  J. improves the long-term performance of an automobile and decrease

63. A. NO CHANGE
  B. notice a problem that causes trouble
  C. recognize that their wiper blades are the source of a problem
  D. realize that their blades are failing and will become a problem

64. F. NO CHANGE
  G. vision, has been
  H. vision is
  J. vision,

GO ON TO THE NEXT PAGE →

set blades at a time each year greatly reduces this risk.
65
In addition, frequently refilling the windshield washer

fluid reservoir guarantees that there will always be

enough fluid to wash away grime that accumulates on

the windshield.

[3]

Much of car maintenance focuses on preventing

problems before they occur. For example, checking the

levels of coolant, oil, brake fluid, and transmission fluid

can avert serious malfunctions. In general, these fluids
66
should be checked monthly and refilled whenever the

need is indicated.

[4]

Cars are becoming more sophisticated every year,
67
but car owners without any expertise in mechanics can
67
still perform much of the basic upkeep of their vehicle.
67
You should change the oil in most cars every 3,000 to

7,000 miles. This task requires a willingness to get a bit

dirty,

so you don't have to be a mechanic to change a car's oil.
68
Before you get started, read the oil change

65. The underlined word would be most
logically placed:

A. where it is now.

B. before the word *time*.

C. before the word *year*.

D. before the word *risk*.

66. **F.** NO CHANGE

G. For generally,

H. With usual

J. By typically,

67. Which sentence is the most effective way to
begin paragraph 4?

A. NO CHANGE

B. Changing the oil and oil filter regularly
is another key to keeping your car's
engine performing at its best.

C. An entire industry now focuses on
providing regular car maintenance, such
as changing the oil and rotating the
tires.

D. Even if you haven't read your car
owner's manual, you probably know
that your car needs a tune-up every so
often.

68. **F.** NO CHANGE

G. but

H. for

J. because

GO ON TO THE NEXT PAGE ⟶

<u>section, in your owner's manual</u> and collect all of the
69
tools you will need. You

<u>won't need many tools, but you will definitely need a car</u>
70
<u>jack.</u> Never get under a car that is supported only by car
70

<u>jacks: you</u> do not want to risk being crushed by a car.
71
After you've secured the car, changing the oil is as

straightforward as sliding under the car with a drain

pan to catch the oil and a wrench to loosen the oil drain

plug. Then follow the instructions for changing the oil

filter, and fill the oil pan to the recommended level with

fresh oil. 72

[5]

These simple steps to maintaining the health of a

car can be done by just about anyone. However, success-

fully changing a car's oil does not turn a car owner into a

repair expert. More complicated tasks, such as adjusting

a carburetor or installing new brake pads, should be

69. **A.** NO CHANGE
    B. section, in your owner's manual,
    C. section in your owner's manual;
    D. section in your owner's manual,

70. In paragraph 4, the writer wants to provide an explanation of how to change the oil in an automobile. Which of the following would most logically fit the writer's intention for this paragraph?

    F. NO CHANGE
    G. need to get under the car to open the oil drain, so use car jacks to raise the car and sturdy car jack stands to support it.
    H. may find it helpful to watch someone else change the oil before you try to perform the job on your own.
    J. only need to follow a few basic steps in order to successfully change your car's oil.

71. **A.** NO CHANGE
    B. jacks, you
    C. jacks you
    D. jacks you,

72. Paragraph 4 of the essay uses the second person (*you*, *your*). Revising this paragraph to remove the second-person pronouns would have the primary effect of:

    F. disrupting the logical flow of the essay.
    G. making paragraph 4 more consistent with the voice used in the rest of the essay.
    H. underscoring the direct advice given to the reader.
    J. lightening the essay's formal tone.

GO ON TO THE NEXT PAGE

<u>performed by a qualified</u> auto mechanic.
            73

73. **A.** NO CHANGE
    B. professionally completed by a qualified
    C. performed by a certifiably qualified
    D. undertaken by qualifying

Questions 74–75 ask about the preceding passage as a whole.

---

74. After reading back through the essay, the writer decided that the following sentence contains important information:

    > The owner's manual provides instructions on how to test the levels of these different fluids used to lubricate and cool the engine.

    Logically, this sentence should be placed:

    F. after the last sentence of paragraph 2.
    G. before the first sentence of paragraph 3.
    H. after the last sentence of paragraph 3.
    J. after the last sentence of paragraph 4.

75. If the writer had intended to write an essay persuading readers to familiarize themselves with the basic safety features and maintenance needs of their cars, would this essay meet the writer's goal?

    A. Yes, because the essay repeatedly encourages readers to refer to the owner's manual for their car.
    B. Yes, because the essay lists many basic maintenance steps that owners can independently accomplish.
    C. No, because the essay encourages readers to go beyond learning about the features of their car and actually perform some of the basic upkeep.
    D. No, because the essay does not discuss a car's safety features in any detail.

MATHEMATICS TEST

60 Minutes—60 Questions

Directions: Solve each of the following problems, select the correct answer, and then fill in the corresponding space on your answer sheet.

Don't linger over problems that are too time-consuming. Do as many as you can, then come back to the others in the time you have remaining.

The use of a calculator is permitted on this test. Though you are allowed to use your calculator to solve any questions you choose, some of the questions may be most easily answered without the use of a calculator.

Note: Unless otherwise noted, all of the following should be assumed.

1. Illustrative figures are *not* necessarily drawn to scale.
2. All geometric figures lie in a plane.
3. The term *line* indicates a straight line.
4. The term *average* indicates arithmetic mean.

1. Tanya used $3\frac{3}{8}$ yards of fabric to make her dress, and she used $1\frac{1}{3}$ yards of fabric to make her jacket. What was the total amount, in yards, that Tanya used for the complete outfit of dress and jacket?

    A. $4\frac{1}{8}$

    B. $4\frac{1}{6}$

    C. $4\frac{4}{11}$

    D. $4\frac{1}{2}$

    E. $4\frac{17}{24}$

2. $5x^3y^5 \times 6y^2 \times 2xy$ is equivalent to:

    F. $13x^3y^7$.

    G. $13x^4y^8$.

    H. $60x^3y^7$.

    J. $60x^3y^{10}$.

    K. $60x^4y^8$.

3. Brandon puts 6% of his $36,000 yearly salary into savings, in 12 equal monthly installments. Jacqui deposits $200 every month into savings. At the end of one full year, what is the difference, in dollars, between the amount of money that Jacqui saved and the amount of money that Brandon saved?

    A. 20

    B. 24

    C. 240

    D. 1,960

    E. 2,800

4. Mikhail has received bowling scores of 190, 200, 145, and 180 so far in the state bowling tournament. What score must he receive on the fifth game to earn an average score of 180 for his five games?

    F. 179

    G. 180

    H. 185

    J. 200

    K. Mikhail cannot earn an average of 180.

GO ON TO THE NEXT PAGE

5. For steel to be considered stainless steel, it must have a minimum of 10.5% chromium in the metal alloy. If there are 262.5 pounds of chromium available, what is the maximum amount of stainless steel, in pounds, that can be manufactured?

    A.   27.56
    B.   252
    C.   262.5
    D.   2,500
    E.   25,000

6. A homeowner wants to put a wallpaper border on the top edge of all the walls of his kitchen. The kitchen measures 6.5 meters by 4 meters. What is the required length, in meters, of the border?

    F.   8
    G.   10.5
    H.   13
    J.   21
    K.   26

7. Which expression below is equivalent to $w(x - (y + z))$?

    A. $wx - wy - wz$
    B. $wx - wy + wz$
    C. $wx - y + z$
    D. $wx - y - z$
    E. $wxy + wxz$

8. If $6n - 4 = 3n + 24$, $n = ?$

    F.   28
    G. $\dfrac{28}{3}$
    H. $\dfrac{28}{9}$
    J. $\dfrac{20}{9}$
    K. $\dfrac{3}{28}$

9. What two numbers should be placed in the blanks below so that the difference between successive entries is the same?
    26, ___, ___, 53

    A. 36, 43
    B. 35, 44
    C. 34, 45
    D. 33, 46
    E. 30, 49

10. What is the real number value of $m^3 + \sqrt{12m}$ when $5m^2 = 45$?

    F.   5
    G.   27
    H.   33
    J.   38.09
    K. 739.39

11. The radius of a sphere is $3\dfrac{3}{5}$ meters. What is the volume of the sphere, to the nearest cubic meter? Use the formula $V = \dfrac{4}{3}\pi r^3$

    A.   42
    B.   45
    C.   157
    D.   195
    E.   3,429

GO ON TO THE NEXT PAGE ⇒

12. There are 10 peanuts, 6 cashews, and 8 almonds in a bag of mixed nuts. If a nut is chosen at random from the bag, what is the probability that the nut is NOT a peanut?

F. $\dfrac{5}{12}$

G. $\dfrac{7}{12}$

H. $\dfrac{5}{7}$

J. 10

K. 14

13. The number of people who shop at an electronics store during a given week is shown in the matrix below.

Adolescents	Adults	Senior Citizens
75	100	30

The ratio of people from each age group who will purchase a product to the number of people in that age group who shop at the store is shown in the following matrix:

Adolescents	0.20
Adults	0.35
Senior Citizens	0.10

Based on the matrices, how many people will make purchases?

A. 15

B. 41

C. 53

D. 133

E. 205

Use the following table to answer questions 14 and 15.

The table below shows the genres of radio music, broken down by the medium (AM, FM, or satellite) on which they are aired. In addition, the table shows the number of hours in which there is a live disc jockey.

Genre	Medium	# of Hours When There Is a Live Disc Jockey
Classical	AM	6
	FM	3
	Satellite	12
Country	AM	24
	FM	7
	Satellite	16
News	AM	24
	FM	24
	Satellite	24
Pop	AM	14
	Satellite	15
Rock	AM	12
	Satellite	24

14. What is the average number of hours, rounded to the nearest hour, that the country genre has a live disc jockey?

F. 3

G. 7

H. 14

J. 16

K. 24

GO ON TO THE NEXT PAGE

15. The time of day in which there is a live disc jockey does not matter, as long as there is a live disc jockey for the number of hours listed in the table. Assume that a disc jockey can switch from any genre and medium to another with the flip of a switch. Based on the table, what is the minimum number of disc jockeys needed to cover all genres and mediums, if each works an eight-hour shift?

   A.   5
   B.   13
   C.   25
   D.   26
   E.   205

16. In the following table, every row, column, and diagonal must have equivalent sums. Which term or value belongs in the lower left cell for this to be true?

m	$-4m$	$3m$
$2m$	0	$-2m$
	$4m$	$-m$

   F. $-4m$
   G. $-3m$
   H. -3
   J.   0
   K. m

17. The following standard coordinate plane is shown, with the four quadrants labeled. Point R, denoted by $R(x,y)$ is graphed on this plane, such that $x \neq 0$ and $y \neq 0$.

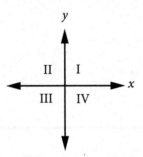

If the product xy is a positive number, then point R is located in:

   A.   quadrant I only.
   B.   quadrant II only.
   C.   quadrant III only.
   D.   quadrant I or IV only.
   E.   quadrant I or III only.

18. The cafeteria offers 7 different sandwiches, 3 different soups, and 4 different drink choices on the luncheon menu. How many distinct meals are available if a meal consists of 1 sandwich, 1 soup, and 1 drink?

   F.   7
   G.   14
   H.   21
   J.   84
   K.   Cannot be determined from the given information.

19. At the university, there are 5 females for every 3 males. If there are 6,000 male students, how many students are female?

   A.   10,000
   B.   12,000
   C.   16,000
   D.   18,000
   E.   30,000

GO ON TO THE NEXT PAGE ▷

20. What is the length, in inches, of the diagonal of a rectangle whose dimensions are 16 inches by 30 inches?

    F. 25
    G. 23
    H. 34
    J. 578
    K. 1,156

21. Which of the following expressions is NOT equivalent to $5n + 1$, if $n > 0$?

    A. $\dfrac{1}{5n + 1}$

    B. $5(n + 2) - 9$

    C. $\dfrac{1}{\dfrac{1}{5n + 1}}$

    D. $\dfrac{5n^2 + n}{n}$

    E. $\dfrac{25n^2 - 1}{5n - 1}$

22. Which of the following equations is equivalent to $3x + 2y = 16$?

    F. $y = -\dfrac{3}{2}x + 16$

    G. $y = -\dfrac{2}{3}x + 8$

    H. $y = \dfrac{3}{2}x + 8$

    J. $y = -\dfrac{3}{2}x + 8$

    K. $y = -\dfrac{2}{3}x + 8$

23. A solution to the equation $x^2 - 20x + 75 = 0$ is:

    A. –15.
    B. –5.
    C. 0.
    D. 3.
    E. 5.

24. Given the following right triangle, ΔLMN, what is the value of $\cos N$?

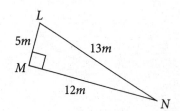

    F. $\dfrac{5}{13}$

    G. $\dfrac{5}{12}$

    H. $\dfrac{12}{13}$

    J. $\dfrac{13}{12}$

    K. $\dfrac{13}{5}$

GO ON TO THE NEXT PAGE ⟩

25. In the following circle, chord *AB* passes through the center of circle *O*. If radius *OC* is perpendicular to chord *AB* and has a length of 7 centimeters, what is the length of chord *BC*, to the nearest tenth of a centimeter?

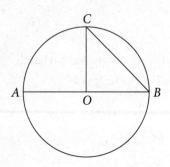

    A. 5.3

    B. 7.0

    C. 9.9

    D. 12.1

    E. 14.0

26. To convert a temperature in degrees Celsius to degrees Fahrenheit, the formula is $F = \frac{9}{5}C + 32$, where *C* is the temperature in degrees Celsius. What temperature, to the nearest degree Celsius, equals a temperature of 86 degrees Fahrenheit?

    F. 30

    G. 54

    H. 80

    J. 86

    K. 187

27. An Olympic-sized pool is 50 meters long, 25 meters wide, and holds 14,375 cubic meters of water. If the pool is the same depth in all parts, about how many meters deep is the water in the pool?

    A. Less than 9

    B. Between 9 and 10

    C. Between 10 and 11

    D. Between 11 and 12

    E. More than 12

28. In the following right triangle, *ΔDEF*, the measure of segment *DE* is 42 inches, and the tangent of angle *D* is $\frac{5}{8}$. What is the length of segment *EF*, to the nearest tenth of an inch?

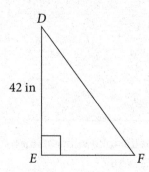

    F. 26.3

    G. 42.625

    H. 49.6

    J. 67.2

    K. 210.0

GO ON TO THE NEXT PAGE ⇒

29. The following bar graph shows the number of people at the spring prom, according to their grade level at the high school. According to the graph, what fraction of the people at the prom were sophomores?

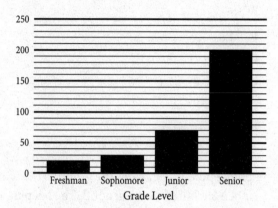

Number of Prom Attendees, by Grade Level

A. $\dfrac{1}{16}$

B. $\dfrac{3}{32}$

C. $\dfrac{3}{29}$

D. $\dfrac{3}{20}$

E. $\dfrac{3}{10}$

30. In the following segment, point X is the midpoint of segment WZ. If the measure of WY is 26 cm and the measure of WZ is 44 cm, what is the length, in centimeters, of segment XY ?

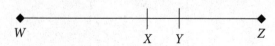

F. 4

G. 13

H. 18

J. 22

K. 70

31. What is the x-coordinate of the intersection point, in the (x,y) coordinate system, of the lines $2x + 3y = 8$ and $5x + y = 7$?

A. −1

B. $\dfrac{15}{7}$

C. 1

D. 2

E. 3

32. For all pairs of real numbers a and b, where $a = 2b − 8$, $b = ?$

F. $a + 4$

G. $2a − 8$

H. $2a + 8$

J. $\dfrac{a − 8}{2}$

K. $\dfrac{a + 8}{2}$

33. What is the area, in square millimeters, of parallelogram $RSUT$ shown?

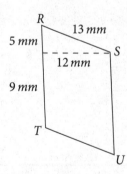

A. 30

B. 39

C. 54

D. 168

E. 182

GO ON TO THE NEXT PAGE

34. If $x = -(y + 3)$, then $(x + y)^3 = ?$

   F. −27

   G. −9

   H. 9

   J. 27

   K. Cannot be determined from the given information.

35. The following is a partial map of Centerville, showing 80 square miles: a total of 8 miles of Main Street and a total of 10 miles of Front Street. There is a fire station at the corner of Main and Front Streets, shown as point *F*. The town wants to build a new fire station exactly halfway between the hospital, at *H*, and the school, at *S*. What would be the driving directions to get from the current fire station to the new fire station, by way of Main and Elm streets? All streets and avenues shown intersect at right angles.

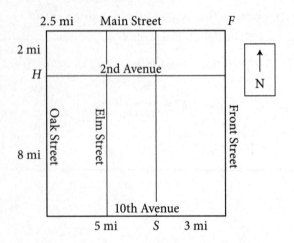

   A. 2.5 miles east, 4 miles north

   B. 2.5 miles west, 4 miles north

   C. 2.5 miles east, 6 miles south

   D. 5.5 miles west, 4 miles south

   E. 5.5 miles west, 6 miles south

36. There are two consecutive odd integers. The difference between four times the larger and twice the smaller is 36. If *x* represents the smaller integer, which of the following equations can be used to determine the smaller integer?

   F. $4x - 2x = 36$

   G. $4(x + 1) - 2x = 36$

   H. $4(x + 2) - 2x = 36$

   J. $(x + 3) - 2x = 36$

   K. $36 - 4x = 2x$

37. A 15-foot supporting wire is attached to a telephone pole 12 feet from the ground. The wire is then anchored to the ground. The telephone pole stands perpendicular to the ground. How far, in feet, is the anchor of the supporting wire from the base of the telephone pole?

   A. 3

   B. 6

   C. 9

   D. 12

   E. 15

38. In the following figure, the sides of the square are tangent to the inner circle. If the area of the circle is 100π square units, what is the unit length of a side of the square?

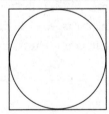

   F. 400

   G. 100

   H. 20

   J. 10

   K. π

GO ON TO THE NEXT PAGE

39. Rectangles *ABCD* and *EFGH* shown are similar. Using the given information, what is the length of side *EH*, to the nearest tenth of an inch?

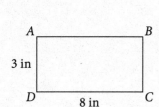
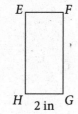

A. 0.8
B. 1.3
C. 5.3
D. 7.0
E. 8.0

40. In parallelogram *VWXY* shown, points *U, V, Y,* and *Z* form a straight line. Given the angle measures as shown in the figure, what is the measure of angle ∠*WYX* ?

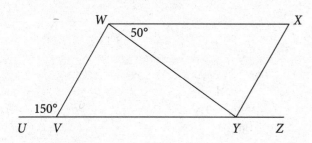

F. 25°
G. 30°
H. 50°
J. 100°
K. 150°

41. In the following figure, all interior angles are 90°, and all dimension lengths are given in centimeters. What is the perimeter of this figure, in centimeters?

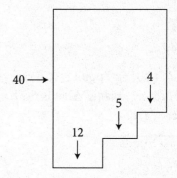

A. 40
B. 61
C. 82
D. 122
E. Cannot be determined from the given information.

42. In the mayoral election, $\frac{3}{4}$ of the eligible voters at one site cast a vote. Three-fifths of the votes at this site were for candidate Martinez. If there are 3,500 eligible voters at this site, how many of them voted for Martinez?

F. 417
G. 1,575
H. 2,100
J. 2,625
K. 4,725

43. Given that *a* and *b* are positive integers, and the greatest common factor of a^4b^2 and a^3b is 54, what is a possible value for *b* ?

A. 2
B. 3
C. 6
D. 9
E. 27

GO ON TO THE NEXT PAGE

44. If 40% of x is 70, then what is 160% of x ?

    F. 28

    G. 45

    H. 112

    J. 175

    K. 280

45. Point M (2,3) and point N (6,5) are points on the coordinate plane. What is the length of the segment MN ?

    A. $\sqrt{2}$ units

    B. $2\sqrt{3}$ units

    C. $2\sqrt{5}$ units

    D. 6 units

    E. 20 units

46. The ratio of the sides of two squares is 5:7. What is the ratio of the perimeters of these squares?

    F. 1:2

    G. 1:12

    H. 1:35

    J. 5:7

    K. 25:49

47. What is the equation of a circle in the coordinate plane with center (–2,3) and a radius of 9 units?

    A. $(x - 2)^2 + (y + 3)^2 = 9$

    B. $(x + 2)^2 + (y - 3)^2 = 9$

    C. $(x - 2)^2 + (y + 3)^2 = 81$

    D. $(x + 2)^2 + (y - 3)^2 = 3$

    E. $(x + 2)^2 + (y - 3)^2 = 81$

48. In the complex number system, $i^2 = -1$.

Given that $\dfrac{3}{5 - i}$ is a complex number, what is the result of $\dfrac{3}{5 - i} \times \dfrac{5 + i}{5 + i}$?

    F. $\dfrac{3}{5 + i}$

    G. $\dfrac{15 + 3i}{24}$

    H. $\dfrac{15 + 3i}{26}$

    J. $\dfrac{15 + i}{26}$

    K. $\dfrac{15 + i}{24}$

49. The following figures show regular polygons and the sum of the degrees of the angles in each polygon. Based on these figures, what is the number of degrees in an n-sided regular polygon?

    180°   360°   540°   720°

    A. $60n$

    B. $180n$

    C. $180(n - 2)$

    D. $20n^2$

    E. Cannot be determined from the information given.

GO ON TO THE NEXT PAGE

50. Fifty high school students were polled to see if they owned a cell phone and an MP3 player. A total of 35 of the students own a cell phone, and a total of 18 of the students own an MP3 player. What is the minimum number of students who own both a cell phone and an MP3 player?

    F.   0
    G.   3
    H. 17
    J. 32
    K. 53

51. What is the solution set of all real numbers n such that $-4n + 3 > -4n + 1$?

    A. All real numbers
    B. All positive numbers
    C. All negative numbers
    D. All numbers such that $n > -\dfrac{1}{2}$
    E. All numbers such that $n < -\dfrac{1}{2}$

52. If 3 people all shake hands with each other, there are a total of 3 handshakes. If 4 people all shake hands with each other, there are a total of 6 handshakes. How many total handshakes will there be if 5 people all shake hands with each other?

    F.   7
    G.   9
    H. 10
    J. 11
    K. 12

53. The following chart shows the percentages of a county's budget expenses by category. The remainder of the budget will be placed in the category Miscellaneous. If these data are to be put into a circle graph, what will be the degree measure of the Miscellaneous wedge, rounded to the nearest degree?

Budget Category	Percentage of Budget
Salaries	23
Road Repair	5
Employee Benefits	22
Building Mainte-nance/Utilities	18

    A.   32
    B.   58
    C.   68
    D. 115
    E. 245

54. If $\tan \theta = -\dfrac{4}{3}$, and $\dfrac{\pi}{2} < \theta < \pi$, then $\sin \theta = ?$

    F. $-\dfrac{4}{5}$
    G. $-\dfrac{3}{4}$
    H. $-\dfrac{3}{5}$
    J. $\dfrac{3}{5}$
    K. $\dfrac{4}{5}$

GO ON TO THE NEXT PAGE

55. Which of the following systems of inequalities is represented by the shaded region on the coordinate plane below?

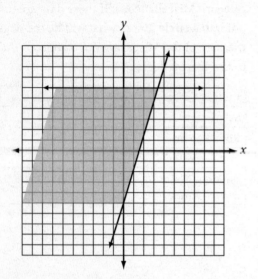

A. $y < 6$ and $y > 3x - 5$

B. $x < 6$ and $y > 3x - 5$

C. $y < 6$ and $y < 3x - 5$

D. $x < 6$ and $y < -3x - 5$

E. $y < 6$ and $y > \dfrac{1}{3}x - 5$

56. If $f(x) = 2(x + 7)$, then $f(x + c) = ?$

F. $2x + 2c + 7$

G. $2x + c + 7$

H. $2x + c + 14$

J. $2x + 2c + 14$

K. $2(x + 7) + c$

57. Which graph represents the solution set for the equation $y = \dfrac{2x^2 - 8}{x - 2}$?

A.

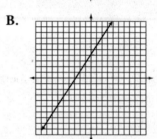

B.

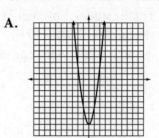

C.

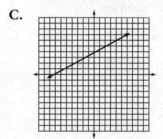

D.

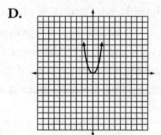

E.

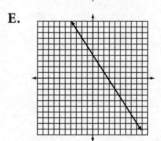

GO ON TO THE NEXT PAGE

58. What are the coordinates of Q', the reflection of the point $Q(r,s)$ over the y-axis?

   F. $(-r,s)$

   G. $(-r,-s)$

   H. $(s,-r)$

   J. $(r,-s)$

   K. $(-s,r)$

59. If $g = 4q + 3$ and $h = 2q - 8$, what is g in terms of h ?

   A. $g = \dfrac{h + 8}{2}$

   B. $g = \dfrac{4h + 11}{2}$

   C. $2h + 19$

   D. $2h + 11$

   E. $h = \dfrac{g - 3}{4}$

60. Find the $\cos(75°)$ knowing that $\cos(75°) = \cos(30° + 45°)$. Use the formula $\cos(\alpha + \beta) = \cos(\alpha)\cos(\beta) - \sin(\alpha)\sin(\beta)$ and the following table of values:

θ	$\sin \theta$	$\cos \theta$	$\tan \theta$
30°	$\dfrac{1}{2}$	$\dfrac{\sqrt{3}}{2}$	$\dfrac{\sqrt{3}}{3}$
45°	$\dfrac{\sqrt{2}}{2}$	$\dfrac{\sqrt{2}}{2}$	1
60°	$\dfrac{\sqrt{3}}{2}$	$\dfrac{1}{2}$	$\sqrt{3}$

   F. $\dfrac{\sqrt{3} - \sqrt{2}}{4}$

   G. $\dfrac{\sqrt{3} - \sqrt{2}}{2}$

   H. $\dfrac{\sqrt{6} - \sqrt{2}}{4}$

   J. $\dfrac{\sqrt{6} - \sqrt{2}}{2}$

   K. $\dfrac{3 - \sqrt{2}}{4}$

IF YOU FINISH BEFORE TIME IS CALLED, YOU MAY CHECK YOUR WORK ON THIS SECTION ONLY. DO NOT TURN TO ANY OTHER SECTION IN THE TEST.   **STOP**

READING TEST

35 Minutes—40 Questions

Directions: There are four passages in this test. Each passage is followed by several questions. After reading a passage, choose the best answer to each question and fill in the corresponding oval on your Answer Grid. You may refer to the passages as often as necessary.

PASSAGE I

PROSE FICTION

This excerpt from a short story describes a conversation between a woman and her husband, who is a twin.

Emily couldn't help but grin broadly after answering the phone. She frequently called us "two peas in a pod," but I'd always felt
Line like any time we were mentioned outside
(5) of my presence, he was "Bruce" and I was "Bruce's twin brother." Because of this, I wasn't surprised to hear my wife giggling uncontrollably and see her twirling the phone cord around her finger while talking
(10) to him. Despite the fact she was speaking to someone genetically identical to me, I couldn't help but wonder if she had ever responded so enthusiastically to one of my stories.
(15)   "Okay, I'll tell him. Talk to you soon." After Emily hung up, I watched her take a deep, almost wistful breath before walking over to me.
"Bruce seems well," I said, trying to
(20) sound casual. "He told me about the new job and everything. What did you guys talk about?"
"Not much." Emily replied. She walked behind my chair and patted my shoulder
(25) before sitting on the couch and opening her magazine. It didn't appear as if she were really reading. She seemed to stop and start, pausing and reflecting about something unrelated to the smiling celebrities featured
(30) in the article.
"It's funny to think that he knows some of these people," she said, pointing at her magazine.

I looked at the gleaming teeth and
(35) chiseled features of the actors, and then looked over at a picture of Bruce and me resting on the mantel. Looking closely at the photo always made my stomach turn; as with every picture of us, there was an
(40) unmistakable vitality in Bruce's face that wasn't present in mine. It were as if I were wearing a "Bruce" costume; I was trying to mimic one of his trademark smiles, but I always seemed to produce a different failed
(45) attempt.
"You all right?" Emily asked, noticing my expression.
I grabbed the picture from the mantel and brought it to her. She looked at it and
(50) looked up at me quizzically.
"Can you tell which one is me?" I asked.
She looked back at the picture and pushed her lip out as she looked from one face to the next. After about five seconds she
(55) pointed to my face, then turned and looked at me confidently.
"How could you tell?" I asked.
"Well, it wasn't very hard," she responded. "You are my husband, and I love
(60) the way you smile. Bruce looks exactly the same in every picture, it looks practiced, but for you it always seems like you're thinking about something, even concentrating, to make sure you smile right."
(65)   "Really?" I was surprised by how much thought she had put into this.
She took the picture and put it back on the mantel. I could still see the perfection in

GO ON TO THE NEXT PAGE →

Bruce's smile and hesitation in mine, but at
(70) least Emily found a way to compliment my
insecurities.

Emily went back to perusing her
magazine.

"At least you ended up with a Fairholm,"
(75) I said, "even if it wasn't the famous one."

"Oh, was I supposed to pursue the
famous one?" she shot back.

She closed her magazine and put it
down on the coffee table. There wasn't an
(80) argument coming, but I saw her disappointment.
The problem was not that she actually
would have married my brother before me;
it was the simple fact that I couldn't help but
believe that to be the case. I saw myself as
(85) second to him and always had. With embarrassing
relatives, people will always point
out that one can't choose his or her family,
but when you're a twin, it's not the association
that you fear—it's the comparison.

(90) "Do you want to be where he is?" she
inquired, with an empty tone.

"This is exactly where I want to be,"
I replied. "I just never know how to explain
to people that I'm an insurance adjuster,
(95) not a Hollywood agent. They always want
to know how it happened when we had the
same upbringing and education. They look
at me as if I did something wrong."

"Do you ever call him?" she asked.
(100) "I figure he's busy, and he calls enough,"
I said.

She cradled her chin in her hand and
looked at me in mild disbelief. "You realize
that by not calling and turning down his
(105) invitations to visit, you make him feel
rejected, right?"

"Come on, Emily. He's surrounded
by famous people—he doesn't need my
approval."

(110) "Maybe not," she sighed, "but his favorite
stories to tell me aren't about Hollywood—
they're about you two growing up."

"Well, he was popular then, too," I said,
shrugging.

(115) "He doesn't look at it that way," she
responded. "He would give up a lot to have
your approval, Dave. He wants to be your
brother, not a competitor."

"It's okay, Emily. I'll call him soon, but I
(120) think that he'll be okay either way."

1. Dave would probably agree with which of the
    following statements regarding his relation-
    ship with Bruce?

    A. They would be better off not talking at
       all.
    B. Their phone conversations are vital to
       their relationship.
    C. Their bond as twins is stronger due to
       Emily's effort.
    D. Their competition makes it harder for
       them to get along.

2. Emily is best described as:

    F. aloof and ineffectual.
    G. needling and meddlesome.
    H. caring and diplomatic.
    J. pained and inconsolable.

3. Which of the following statements does
    NOT describe a feeling Dave has toward his
    brother?

    A. He is jealous of the reaction his brother
       gets from Emily during their phone
       conversation.
    B. He believes he would be better suited
       for his brother's type of work.
    C. He is resentful of his brother's superior
       social skills.
    D. He is skeptical of his brother's desire for
       his approval.

GO ON TO THE NEXT PAGE ⟶

4. The primary focus of the first paragraph is:

    F. Emily's attempt to make her husband jealous.

    G. Emily's desire for the brothers to resolve their differences.

    H. Dave's hope to distance himself from his twin brother.

    J. Dave's feelings of inferiority to his twin brother.

5. Lines 99–120 ("Do you ever…either way") suggest that Dave does not contact Bruce because Dave:

    A. believes that Bruce has great need for him but does not want to admit to Emily that she is right.

    B. feels guilty about being distant toward Bruce and worries that he will have to explain himself.

    C. wants to prove to Emily that he is not impressed by Bruce's high-profile job.

    D. still harbors resentment over Bruce getting preferential treatment during their childhood.

6. According to the passage, when Dave looks at the photograph, he sees:

    F. his brother being cruel to him.

    G. two indistinguishable faces.

    H. a comparison unfavorable to him.

    J. his wife paying more attention to Bruce.

7. Which of the following best summarizes Dave's feelings when he asks Emily to pick him out in the picture?

    A. Dave is confident that Emily will prefer his image to Bruce's.

    B. Dave is insecure; he feels the picture compares him unfavorably to Bruce.

    C. Dave is worried, because he thinks Emily will want to talk more about Bruce after seeing a picture of him.

    D. Dave is angry because he did not want to talk about the picture in the first place.

8. It can be logically deduced from the passage that Dave and Bruce:

    F. tell Emily different-sounding stories about their shared childhood.

    G. are frequently at odds regarding their different professions.

    H. have often fought over Emily's attention.

    J. were much closer shortly before Bruce moved.

9. It can be inferred from the passage that both Emily and Dave conclude that when pictures are taken of the brothers:

    A. Bruce looks much better than Dave.

    B. Dave appears angry at Bruce.

    C. pictures of Bruce are more consistent than those of Dave.

    D. Dave's expression makes a greater impression on the viewer than Bruce's.

GO ON TO THE NEXT PAGE ⟹

10. According to the passage, the reason Emily tells Dave about the content of Bruce's stories is that Emily:

    F. wants to convince Dave that Bruce does not see himself as better than Dave.

    G. wishes to hear Dave's version of the stories.

    H. sees doing so as a way to make Dave more impressed with his brother.

    J. thinks that doing so will make Dave sympathetic to Bruce's loneliness.

PASSAGE II

SOCIAL SCIENCE

This passage discusses the relationship between the media and public opinion.

Large-scale media would likely be traced back to ancient tribes sharing information about the edibility of berries or the
Line aggressiveness of animals. Despite constant
(5) evolution, the information most sought after is that regarding personal safety, personal opportunity, and the triumphs and misdeeds of others—the larger the persona and more laudatory or despicable the act,
(10) the better. When a story is of continued national interest, however, the focus shifts even further from facts and more to theater. To step back and compose an objective plot of goings-on is a distant possibility, but
(15) establishing the hero or villain of the day is paramount. Ultimately, the public's desire to have cold, dry, and correct facts is virtually nonexistent.

Current newscasts exacerbate this by
(20) delivering an assault on the senses with meaningless graphics and theatrical music; meanwhile, the monotone newscaster reads, verbatim from a teleprompter, often using phrases identical to those on other
(25) networks. Additionally, the viewer has

probably already read the same story on the Internet earlier. When television was limited to three networks, rather than ubiquitous news-only channels, the newscaster
(30) was a national figure, and audience members would eagerly await information that was new to them and would expect a relatively thorough explanation of any complicated events. For example, to this day many
(35) people, in explaining the Watergate scandal to those too young to know of it, use Walter Cronkite's delineation as the basis for their understanding.

The objective, trustworthy anchorperson
(40) has also given way to vociferous demagogues promising truth but delivering oversimplified, bias-driven sound bites. The idea of allowing individuals to draw their own conclusions is notably absent; in fact, many
(45) personalities mock those with opinions differing from those presented. The availability of neutral online sources mitigates this slightly, but not to any large degree. While the actual article may be impartial,
(50) electronic periodicals will still sensationalize headlines in order to attract casual readers, and those very headlines sway many readers to certain opinions before the article is even read. For example, if a headline mentions
(55) an "enraged public," the reader is far more likely to both read and take umbrage at the information than he or she would if the article mentioned a subject that "irked locals."
(60) In truth, though, the public is as desirous for dry and objective facts as finicky children are for brussels sprouts. The personalities willing to shrug off accountability in favor of wild accusations and bombastic
(65) slogans captivate a large demographic, while one would be generous by saying that objective fact-based programs occupy even a niche market. This not only damages the general accuracy of so-called
(70) "news" but also further polarizes the public. People now have the option to receive their

GO ON TO THE NEXT PAGE ▷

news from hosts with a variety of political leanings, and one almost invariably chooses to watch the personality with opinions (75) closest to one's own. This is more harmful than convenient because it allows viewers to simply parrot information they are given, eliminating any thought or scrutiny. It is this intellectual laziness that aids in (80) distancing the general public from factual information: as a growing number become resigned to accept whatever their favorite host tells them, the more freedom networks have to pass sensationalist entertainment (85) off as news. It boils down to the unfortunate truth that most are far more likely to accept inaccurate information as fact than to question the legitimacy of something that seems to fit with opinions a particular (90) audience member holds.

Those who make the news also obfuscate objective facts. A legion of employees is dedicated solely to the purpose of making the decisions of political figures sound (95) flawless. Oftentimes, important decisions are made, yet throughout a lengthy press conference, not a single factual implication is discussed. The meeting becomes nothing more than an opportunity for political (100) employees to test their infallible-sounding slogans, while the media dissects the semantics rather than the facts. Semantics, however, are all the media is presented with.

Despite all these methods of prevarication, (105) people still are better informed than they were in the past. Public knowledge of events often occurs minutes after the fact, rather than days or weeks. The populace has a strong desire for news in general, (110) and amid all the unscrupulous presentation methods, facts do exist. However, the profitability of news has put a premium on presentation, not trustworthiness. Complicating matters further is the populace's impatience; (115) the standard consumer would rather be presented with a minute and potentially inaccurate statement—one that may or may

not be retracted the following day—than suffer through a lengthy treatise comprised (120) of all the known facts and nuances of a particular issue. The desire to know still exists, however; it just happens to be overshadowed by the public's desire for personal consensus and the media's desire to reel in (125) the public.

11. One of the primary points the author attempts to make regarding the current news media is that:

   A. the media passes off made-up stories as facts.

   B. the news anchors are not as opinionated as they were in decades past.

   C. the media focuses more on presentation than substance.

   D. the media goes directly against what news audiences truly desire to see.

12. The author makes what claim about impartial news stories?

   F. They no longer exist.

   G. They can be sensationalized in ways other than their content.

   H. They often have headlines that correctly reflect the emotional level of the story.

   J. They all have headlines that attempt to make the reader feel involved in the story.

13. The author brings up Walter Cronkite's coverage of Watergate in order to assert that:

   A. Walter Cronkite was a particularly adept newsperson.

   B. a previous standard for news rightly included clarification of complex issues.

   C. current newscasters are far more forgettable than those before them.

   D. the expanding number of television channels has made individual newscasters less famous.

GO ON TO THE NEXT PAGE ▷

14. By stating that "personal consensus" is of great importance to the public (lines 123–124), the author is probably suggesting that members of the public:

    F. do not want information that contradicts their own beliefs.

    G. work hard to find the source closest to truth, despite the difficulties present.

    H. wish to resolve any moral conflicts they may have with practices in news reporting.

    J. have difficulty finding news sources reflecting their personal views.

15. According to the passage, what type of news stories are sensationalized the most?

    A. Those with a fairly clear chain of events

    B. Those that stay in the public's consciousness for long periods of time

    C. Those that clearly support one political view

    D. Those with the most scandalous information

16. As it is used in line 14, the word *distant* most nearly means:

    F. separated.

    G. different.

    H. reserved.

    J. unlikely.

17. Based on the passage, which of the following headlines would the author be most likely to criticize?

    A. Earthquake Rocks Small Community, Arouses Questions Regarding Preparedness

    B. New Tax Protested by Idaho Farmers

    C. Parents Across Country Outraged at Offensive Song

    D. Governor Describes Proposed Legislation as "Monstrous"

18. The author asserts that individuals will often accept potentially inaccurate information because they:

    F. believe that most newscasters are honest.

    G. have no way to research correct facts.

    H. are forced to translate the guarded words of political employees.

    J. have political beliefs similar to those of specific media personalities.

19. In the fourth paragraph, the phrase "even a niche market" (line 68) expresses the author's feeling that:

    A. media companies are influenced greatly by public demand.

    B. cable television networks are unwilling to present objective facts.

    C. factual news media should look into better marketing practices.

    D. factual news would be profitable with greater exposure.

20. The author argues that in searching for a news source, audience members are most likely to choose the source that:

    F. features the most entertaining newscaster.

    G. validates the audience member's opinion.

    H. presents the shortest and simplest explanation for events.

    J. focuses on big stories rather than local ones.

GO ON TO THE NEXT PAGE

PASSAGE III

HUMANITIES

James Joyce was among the most influential writers of the early twentieth century and one of the leaders of a literary movement that became known as modernism. The following two passages are excerpted from essays written about Joyce during his lifetime.

PASSAGE A

Although the writer James Joyce has spent the majority of his adult life outside of Ireland, he has always thought
Line of himself as, and will be remembered
(5) as, a quintessentially Irish writer. His attachment to the nation, and especially his boyhood home of Dublin, is apparent in his works, which are invariably set in Ireland and often focus on the social
(10) and political issues of the Irish. One of his earliest works, a collection of short stories, is even entitled *Dubliners*, and his novel *Ulysses*, which is generally considered his greatest work, depicts 1904
(15) Dublin in almost staggering detail. Joyce was often quoted as saying that, were Dublin to be destroyed in some tremendous calamity, it could be re-created brick by brick from the depictions in
(20) *Ulysses*; in reading the novel, one finds it difficult to dispute the claim.

In addition to its focus on Dublin, *Ulysses* is somewhat narrowly focused in other ways as well. Its action takes place
(25) on a single day, and for the most part it is centered on a single protagonist. Its events are not the grand, sweeping historical landmarks found in other novels, such as Tolstoy's *War and Peace*, but
(30) rather the mundane events of everyday life; Joyce considered eating, running errands, and even making trips to the lavatory worthy of inclusion in his masterpiece. And yet, despite its tight focus,
(35) the novel is already considered one of

the most globally appealing of all time, a powerful representation of the complete human condition. Almost paradoxically, it is the level of detail in Joyce's micro-
(40) cosm of a single man on a single day in a single city that allows him to make statements and observations that apply to humanity as a whole. Perhaps human existence is not best contemplated on the
(45) great battlefields of history, which are experienced by only a few human beings for small portions of their lives. It might instead be better expressed in the minor struggles and idle musings of an ordi-
(50) nary Irishman who, by the very virtue of his ordinariness, is able to transcend the impediments of time and place in order to appeal to the entirety of the human dilemma.

PASSAGE B

(55) As one contemplates the state of literature in our modern era, it is hard to resist a longing for the great writers of eras gone by. At times, one must take great pains merely to remember that
(60) there were once authors such as Dante, Shakespeare, or Dickens: authors who were able to relate stories of great travels and struggles even as they compelled us to mull over the great philosophical
(65) questions of all time. They did not waste their time or ours with trivial affairs; their stories were unique and memorable, and they bore repeated readings and re-readings from generation to genera-
(70) tion. These writers never took perverse glee in conveying thoughts and actions that were better off forgotten. They took great care to depict accurately the best and worst aspects of human nature;
(75) they were well aware of the impact their works would have on culture and strove

GO ON TO THE NEXT PAGE ⇨

to ensure that they would enhance, rather than degrade, the public's intellect; they did not resort to tricks or devices in

(80) order to garner readership for their writings; and in all these regards, they are firmly distinguished from writers of the present day, the most notorious of which is the Irish novelist James Joyce.

(85)   The goal of art is to enlighten the consciousness of those who partake of it, to lift their minds and souls out of the trenches of ordinary activities and humanity's base instincts. It would seem

(90) that modern writers like Joyce have no interest in such enlightenment, instead preferring to revel in every detail of activities that should never have been committed to paper in the first place. In

(95) basing his novel *Ulysses* on Homer's *The Odyssey*, Joyce has sullied the very form of the epic genre. Whereas *The Odyssey* was a great tale of a noble hero's struggle against a seemingly insurmountable

(100) series of trials in order to restore order and honor to his household, Joyce's book is nearly the direct opposite. The protagonist is no hero, his actions are listless and forgettable, and his obsession with

(105) obscene and undignified behavior is virtually nauseating. It is a pity that Homer's epic hero has now been so distorted by his mere association with Joyce's antihero. And even more shame-

(110) ful is the waste of talent, for, subject matter aside, Joyce is no slouch as a wordsmith. Sadly, it is the literary world's loss that he was not born in a more dignified era where his talents could have been

(115) utilized in a more appropriate manner.

Questions 21–23 ask about Passage A.

21. Which of the following, if true, would most significantly weaken the main argument of Passage A?

   A. Historical events are often depicted inaccurately in fictional writing.

   B. Similar philosophical ideas often arise in cultures that have never had contact with each other.

   C. People from some cultures find the thoughts and motivations of people in other cultures impossible to comprehend.

   D. Thorough knowledge of the place where one grew up can lead to a stronger understanding of human nature.

22. Which of the following best conveys the meaning of "transcend...place" (lines 51–52)?

   F. Make a specific statement about a particular group of people.

   G. Write in such a way that precise information is obscured.

   H. Ignore setting in order to focus solely on character.

   J. Go beyond surface circumstance to reveal universal truth.

23. In lines 38–43 ("Almost paradoxically . . . as a whole"), the author of Passage A suggests that Joyce's widespread appeal is due to his:

   A. knowledge of geography.

   B. penchant for exciting prose.

   C. attention to ordinary details.

   D. use of exotic locales.

GO ON TO THE NEXT PAGE

Questions 24–26 ask about Passage B.

24. According to Passage B's first paragraph, the author is critical of James Joyce's writing on the grounds that Joyce:

   F. is not as dignified as the great authors of the past.

   G. lacks proper knowledge of his subject matter.

   H. copies too closely from the authors who preceded him.

   J. uses language that is unnecessarily elegant.

25. In the final sentence of Passage B (lines 112–115), the author suggests that Joyce:

   A. would sell many books whether his writing was obscene or not.

   B. never committed quite enough time to revising and improving his novels.

   C. would have been more successful if his prose style were stronger.

   D. might have produced greater literature in a more refined environment.

26. As used in line 89, the word *base* most nearly means:

   F. unrefined.

   G. foundational.

   H. nauseating.

   J. sophisticated.

Questions 27–30 ask about both passages.

27. It can be inferred that the author of Passage A would respond to Passage B's assertion that the goal of art is to enlighten by:

   A. providing evidence that Joyce's writing is more enlightened than older works.

   B. emphasizing the importance of appealing to readers throughout the world.

   C. agreeing that Joyce's attention to detail diminishes the value of his writing.

   D. refusing to acknowledge the significance of great philosophical questions.

28. Which of the following best captures the difference between the two authors' views of Joyce's writing?

   F. The author of Passage A despises its lack of importance, while the author of Passage B disparages its inaccuracy.

   G. The author of Passage A claims that it is insignificant, while the author of Passage B contends that it is obscene.

   H. The author of Passage A admires its universal appeal, while the author of Passage B deplores its lack of decorum.

   J. The author of Passage A laments its irrelevance, while the author of Passage B appreciates its craftsmanship.

29. Which of the following word pairs best reflects the perspective of each author on the word "detail" as used in Passage A (line 15) and Passage B (line 92)?

	Passage A	Passage B
A.	entertainment	dismay
B.	admiration	revulsion
C.	enthusiasm	shame
D.	support	glee

30. It can be inferred that the author of Passage B would most likely respond to Passage A's description of Joyce as "quintessentially Irish writer" (line 5) by:

   F. disagreeing that Joyce was of Irish descent.

   G. disagreeing that Joyce was an exemplary writer.

   H. agreeing that Joyce was a champion linguist.

   J. agreeing that Joyce was an unrelenting mystic.

GO ON TO THE NEXT PAGE ⟹

PASSAGE IV

NATURAL SCIENCE

This passage discusses the degree to which rattlesnakes pose a threat to humans.

In both recorded and oral history, rattlesnakes are categorized as malevolent beings.
Their lance-shaped heads and angular brow-lines
Line make them look the perfect villain, and their
(5) venom cements this classification. Publicized
reports of bite victims seem to prove their
nefarious nature.

Unlike mammalian predators such as
bears, rattlesnakes do not have the reputation
(10) of an animal deserving human respect.
One imagines the rattlesnake hiding in our
backyards, waiting to strike.

In recent long-term studies, however,
the social behavior of rattlesnakes has been
(15) found to be quite different than many would
expect. Herpetologists, scientists who study
snakes, had long suspected a more complex
and thoughtful existence for the reptiles,
and now have hard information to back up
(20) their theories. When examined, the sinister
opportunist lurking in the shadows better
resembles a mild-mannered domestic.
Unlike the nonvenomous king snake, rattlesnakes
are entirely noncannibalistic, and
(25) tend to spend their entire lives with a single
mate. The mating ritual in which two males
will extend almost half of their bodies off
the ground to wrestle is not lethal, and, once
bested, a rattlesnake peacefully retreats to
(30) find a new den of eligible mates. Female
rattlesnakes give birth to live young, and
rattlesnakes often share their dens, even
hibernating with tortoises without incident.

Sadly, it seems that only those with an
(35) existing fascination with snakes are aware of
this socially functional rattlesnake. Another
discovery that made little stir in the public
consciousness is an experiment in which
herpetologists tracked snakes with radio
(40) transmitters and saw their behavior when

humans entered their habitat. While a few
snakes did hold their ground and rattle,
most saw or sensed a disturbance (snakes
cannot hear) and immediately headed in
(45) the opposite direction. Many of the snakes
that were handled by herpetologists did not
coil or strike. This is not to say that a snake
will not bite a human if disturbed, but the
tendency is to retreat first and give warning
(50) second, before striking becomes a possibility.

Describing a more docile nature does
not imply that rattlesnakes would make
good pets for children, but considering the
aggressiveness often displayed by a South
(55) American pit viper, the fer-de-lance, one
familiar with both would have far less
trepidation about passing by a rattlesnake. For
one thing, rattlesnakes do coil and rattle,
giving humans an opportunity to move
(60) away, while fer-de-lances will often strike
at passersby without warning. Furthermore,
when it comes down to statistics,
American hospitals report an average of
7,000 snakebite patients a year; generally
(65) more than half are actually from nonvenomous
snakes thought by victims to be
venomous. On average, fewer than six people
die of snake envenomation annually, and
the vast majority of the serious bites are due
(70) to either handling the snake or stepping on
it; most people bitten by snakes they were
not engaging end up with very mild bites.
Compare this with an average of over one
million hospital visits for dog bites and
(75) twenty annual deaths at the jaws of man's
best friend. With such minuscule statistics
regarding snakebites, it is curious why they
are still viewed as unfathomably dangerous,
when bees, lightning—and yes, dogs—are
(80) responsible for far more human fatalities.
The fer-de-lance, however, is responsible for
thousands of deaths annually in Central and
South America.

GO ON TO THE NEXT PAGE ▷

If one is looking for proof that rattlesnakes
(85) do not intend to harm humans, one
should consider perhaps the most stunning
evidence regarding bite behavior. Over
half of the bites rattlesnakes administer to
humans are "dry," meaning the rattlesnake
(90) purposely does not release venom. While I
will not posit that this is due to rattlesnakes
possessing an awareness of the well-being of
their non-food-source bite victim, there is
a great deal of thought present. The snake
(95) acknowledges that venom is needed for
immobilizing and digesting prey (venom
is actually saliva), producing venom takes
time, and the human is not a food source.
Therefore, if the snake is not surprised or
(100) fearing death, the damage of a rattlesnake
bite will likely be far less severe than if the
snake used all its venom. This has been
known for some time, but, in many cases, it
is probably better for humans to believe that
(105) the snakes are more liberal with venom than
they are, simply because a frightened and
cornered rattlesnake is very dangerous.

Unfortunately, some people take the
traditional view of the rattlesnake and use
(110) it as an excuse to harm the animals. People
in various areas use the fearsome reputation
of rattlesnakes, along with the more docile
reality, for profit. Rattlesnake roundups are
held, where people collect snakes
(115) beforehand and join in a festival celebrating their
conquest. The events are billed as both
entertainment and as making surrounding
residential areas safer for children; however,
the vast majority of snakes are collected
(120) from uninhabited areas, and people are
frequently bitten at the festivals while
handling the snakes for the audience. Eventually,
the snakes are killed to make clothing
or trophies, and these events are estimated
(125) to be responsible for 100,000 rattlesnake
deaths annually, in comparison to fewer
than 6 human deaths from rattlesnakes.

Behavior like this provides a better
reason for crotalid mythology. With

(130) statistics categorically showing a low level of
danger from rattlesnakes to humans, and an
extremely high level vice versa, it would be
a wonder to see what human-related folklore
rattlesnakes would come up with if they
(135) were able to speak or write.

31. In relation to the entire passage, the phrase
"the sinister opportunist lurking in the shadows better resembles a mild-mannered domestic" (lines 20–22) most likely implies that:

   A. adult rattlesnakes are considerably less
   aggressive than juveniles.

   B. recent studies regarding rattlesnakes
   found few incidents of aggressive
   behavior.

   C. rattlesnakes are more similar to
   mammals than once thought.

   D. rattlesnakes are entirely predictable in
   behavior.

32. The passage implies that the rattlesnake's fearsome reputation can be beneficial because:

   F. it influences people to avoid or move
   away from rattlesnakes.

   G. it protects the lives of rattlesnakes.

   H. it inspires medical advancement in
   treating snakebites, despite a low
   mortality rate.

   J. adventurous people may seek rattlesnakes as pets.

33. What evidence does the passage give regarding the social ability of rattlesnakes?

   A. Rattlesnakes are aware of the uses of
   their venom.

   B. Wrestling between males establishes a
   social hierarchy.

   C. Rattlesnakes can share their habitat
   with other species.

   D. Rattlesnakes rarely eat other snakes.

GO ON TO THE NEXT PAGE ⇨

34. The statement "it would be a wonder to see what human-related folklore rattlesnakes would come up with if they were able to speak or write" (lines 132–135) means that:

    F. humans and rattlesnakes both present great risks to each other's safety.

    G. humans and rattlesnakes behave in many similar ways.

    H. humans are a much greater threat to rattlesnakes than rattlesnakes are to humans.

    J. humans have traditionally assigned human emotions to rattlesnakes in folklore.

35. According to the passage, what is the correlation between human behavior and serious rattlesnake bites?

    A. There is no statistical relationship.

    B. Humans who move with quick motions attract strikes.

    C. Humans who actively seek interaction with snakes are less likely to receive a "dry" bite.

    D. Rattlesnakes deliver a variable amount of venom based on how threatening humans act.

36. What is suggested by lines 51–53 when the author states that the new evidence "does not imply that rattlesnakes would make good pets for children"?

    F. Only professional herpetologists should keep rattlesnakes.

    G. Dogs can also be dangerous pets.

    H. Nonaggressive behavior does not make a venomous animal harmless.

    J. Rattlesnakes in the wild are more docile than those in captivity.

37. The passage states that the relative likelihood of a human being killed by a rattlesnake bite is:

    A. greater than that of a dog bite.

    B. less than that of a bee sting.

    C. equal to that of a lightning strike.

    D. comparable to that of the South American fer-de-lance.

38. Which of the following correctly categorizes a rattlesnake's strategy in venom usage?

    F. The larger the prey or predator, the more venom is used.

    G. Even when threatened, a rattlesnake reserves venom to use on prey.

    H. Rattlesnakes are aware that they will wound larger animals.

    J. Rattlesnakes would rather use venom solely for prey.

39. The author states that rattlesnake roundups use contradictory logic because:

    A. children are rarely bitten by rattlesnakes.

    B. the rattlesnakes that bite people at roundups would have been far less likely to bite someone in their natural habitat.

    C. organizers use erroneous statistics to make the rattlesnakes seem more dangerous and the events more impressive.

    D. many who go to the events are unaware of how many snakes are killed.

GO ON TO THE NEXT PAGE ⟶

40. As used in line 129, the term *crotalid* is most likely:

   F. an unfavorable characterization of humans.

   G. a scientific word meaning "rattlesnakes."

   H. a word describing a herpetologist who specializes in rattlesnakes.

   J. a general word for a group unfairly accused of wrongdoing.

SCIENCE TEST

35 Minutes—40 Questions

Directions: There are several passages in this test. Each passage is followed by several questions. After reading a passage, choose the best answer to each question and fill in the corresponding oval on your Answer Grid. You may refer to the passages as often as necessary. You are NOT permitted to use a calculator on this test.

PASSAGE I

Glaciers are large masses of ice that move slowly over Earth's surface due to the force of gravity and changes in elevation. Glacial *calving* occurs when one edge of a glacier borders a body of water. A calving glacier's *terminus* (the lower edge) periodically produces icebergs as they break away from the glacier and fall into the water.

STUDY 1

A computer was used to create a model of a typical calving glacier. It was hypothesized that a primary factor determining the calving rate is the glacier's velocity at its terminus. Figure 1 shows the calving rate, in meters per year, and length of the computer-generated glacier over a period of 2,000 years.

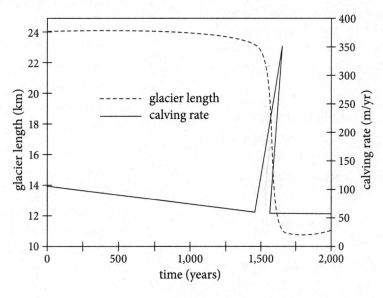

Figure 1

GO ON TO THE NEXT PAGE

STUDY 2

Four calving glaciers (A–D) were studied over a period of 10 years. The average velocity at the terminus of each glacier was recorded for years 1–5 and again for years 6–10. The calving rate of each glacier was estimated for the same time periods. The results are recorded in Table 1.

Table 1

Glacier	Years 1–5		Years 6–10	
	Average velocity (m/yr)	Calving rate (m/yr)	Average velocity (m/yr)	Calving rate (m/yr)
A	72	72	63	64
B	51	52	45	47
C	98	106	256	312
D	160	189	53	54

STUDY 3

Meteorologists reported unusually high average temperatures in the regions of Glacier C and Glacier D during the same 10-year period examined in Study 2. It was hypothesized that the high temperatures were responsible for the relatively rapid variations in velocity and calving rates evident for Glacier C and Glacier D in Table 1.

1. If the glacier model used in Study 1 is typical of all calving glaciers, the scientists would draw which of the following conclusions about the relationship between glacier length and calving rate?

   A. As calving rate decreases, glacier length always increases.

   B. As glacier length decreases, calving rate always decreases.

   C. A sharp increase in calving rate results in a sharp decrease in glacier length.

   D. A sharp increase in calving rate results in a sharp increase in glacier length.

2. The meteorologists in Study 3 hypothesized that the faster the calving rate, the faster the sea level at a calving glacier's terminus would rise. If this hypothesis is correct, which of the following glaciers resulted in the fastest rise in sea level during years 6–10?

   F. Glacier A

   G. Glacier B

   H. Glacier C

   J. Glacier D

3. Based on the results of Study 2, a calving glacier traveling at a velocity of 80 m/yr would most likely have a calving rate:

   A. between 72 m/yr and 106 m/yr.

   B. between 106 m/yr and 189 m/yr.

   C. between 189 m/yr and 312 m/yr.

   D. over 312 m/yr.

4. Which of the following statements best describes the behavior of the glaciers observed during Study 2?

   F. All of the glaciers observed traveled faster during the first five years than during the last five years.

   G. All of the glaciers observed traveled faster during the last five years than during the first five years.

   H. The calving rate is always less than the average velocity for all of the glaciers observed.

   J. The calving rate is always greater than or equal to the average velocity for all of the glaciers observed.

GO ON TO THE NEXT PAGE

5. Which of the following graphs best represents the relationship between the calving rate and the average velocity of the glaciers observed in Study 2 for years 6–10?

A.
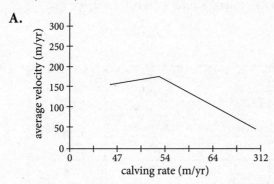

B.
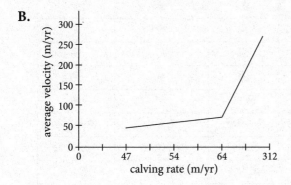

C.
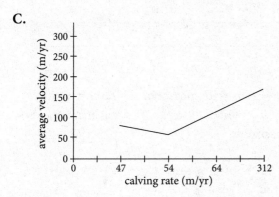

D.
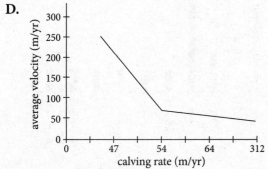

6. If the hypothesis made by the meteorologists in Study 3 is correct, the glacier modeled in Study 1 most likely experienced unusually high temperatures at approximately what time during the simulated 2,000-year study?

F. 500 years

G. 1,000 years

H. 1,500 years

J. 2,000 years

7. Based on Figure 1, what is the glacial length and calving rate, respectively, at 1,500 years?

A. 15 km and 125 m/yr

B. 23 km and 125 m/yr

C. 23 km and 350 m/yr

D. 125 km and 350 m/yr

GO ON TO THE NEXT PAGE

PASSAGE II

Allergic rhinitis refers to a person's nasal reaction to small airborne particles called *allergens*. Table 1 shows the specific allergen, its type, and the approximate number of reported cases of allergic symptoms for a population of 1,000 people living in northern Kentucky during a single year.

Table 1

Month	Allergen type — Specific allergen	Pollen — Trees	Grass	Weeds	Mold — Alternaria	Cladosporium	Aspergillus
January					❀	❀	❀
February					❀	❀	❀
March		❀❀			❀	❀	❀
April		❀❀❀❀❀			❀	❀	❀
May		❀❀❀	❀❀❀		❀	❀	❀
June			❀❀❀❀		❀	❀	❀
July			❀❀	❀	❀❀	❀	❀
August				❀❀❀	❀❀❀❀	❀❀❀	❀❀❀❀
September				❀❀	❀❀❀	❀❀❀❀	❀❀❀❀
October				❀❀	❀❀❀	❀❀	❀❀
November					❀❀	❀	❀
December					❀	❀	❀

Note: Each ❀ equals 100 reported cases of allergic rhinitis.

Weekly tree pollen and total mold spore concentrations were measured in grains per cubic meter (gr/m^3) for samples of air taken in southern Iowa for eight weeks. The pollen and mold spore counts are shown in Figures 1 and 2, respectively.

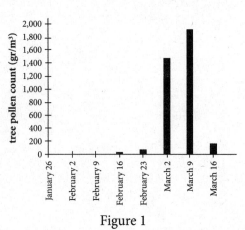

Figure 1

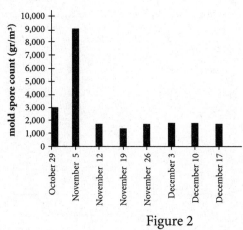

Figure 2

GO ON TO THE NEXT PAGE ⇨

8. If the 1,000 patients studied were given special air filters that greatly reduce allergic rhinitis symptoms, which of the following months would have the greatest decrease in the number of allergic rhinitis cases?

   F. March

   G. June

   H. September

   J. December

9. Based on Figure 1, the tree pollen count on March 2 was closest to:

   A.　　75 gr/m³.

   B.　　150 gr/m³.

   C. 1,500 gr/m³.

   D. 1,900 gr/m³.

10. According to Figure 2, the mold spore count in the weeks after November 5:

    F. increased.

    G. decreased.

    H. varied between 1,000 gr/m³ and 2,000 gr/m³.

    J. remained above 2,000 gr/m³.

11. Based on the data in Figure 1, the tree pollen count increased the most between which two dates?

    A. February 9 to February 16

    B. February 23 to March 2

    C. March 2 to March 9

    D. October 29 to November 5

12. According to Figure 1, which of the following conclusions about the tree pollen count is most valid?

    F. The tree pollen count was highest on March 9.

    G. The tree pollen count was highest on March 16.

    H. The tree pollen count was lowest on February 23.

    J. The tree pollen count was lowest on March 16.

13. Based on Table 1, most of the cases of allergic rhinitis in May in northern Kentucky were caused by which of the following allergens?

    A. Tree and grass pollen

    B. Grass and weed pollen

    C. Alternaria

    D. Aspergillus

GO ON TO THE NEXT PAGE

PASSAGE III

Simple harmonic motion (SHM) is motion that is *periodic*, or repetitive, and can be described by a frequency of oscillation. Students performed three experiments to study SHM.

EXPERIMENT 1

The students assembled the pendulum shown in Diagram 1. The mass at the end of the arm was raised to a small height, h, and released. The frequency of oscillation was measured in oscillations per second, or Hertz (Hz), and the process was repeated for several different arm lengths. The results are shown in Figure 1.

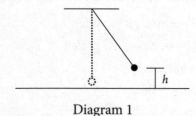

Diagram 1

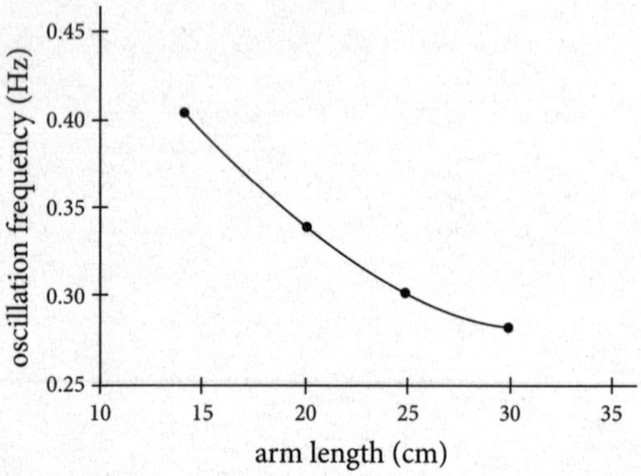

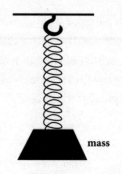

Diagram 2

Figure 1

EXPERIMENT 2

A spring was suspended vertically from a hook, and a mass was connected to the bottom of the spring, as shown in Diagram 2. The mass was pulled downward a short distance and released, and the frequency of the resulting oscillation was measured. The procedure was repeated with four different springs and four different masses, and the results are shown in Figure 2.

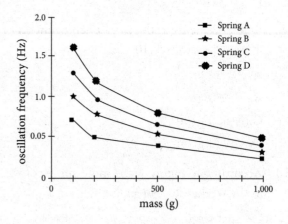

Figure 2

EXPERIMENT 3

Using the apparatus from Experiment 2, the mass-spring system was allowed to come to rest, and the *equilibrium length* of the spring was measured. The same four masses and four springs were used, and the results are shown in Figure 3.

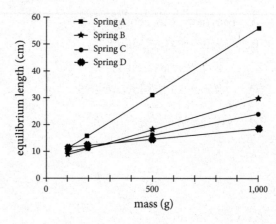

Figure 3

GO ON TO THE NEXT PAGE

14. In Experiment 3, for which of the following masses would Spring B, Spring C, and Spring D have closest to the same equilibrium lengths?

    F. 100 g
    G. 270 g
    H. 500 g
    J. 1,000 g

15. A student has hypothesized that as the length of the arm of a pendulum increases, the oscillation frequency of the pendulum during SHM will decrease. Do the results of Experiment 1 support her hypothesis?

    A. Yes; the oscillation frequency of the pendulum observed in Experiment 1 decreased as the arm length increased.
    B. Yes; although the longest pendulum arm resulted in the highest oscillation frequency, the frequency decreased with increasing arm length for the other three lengths tested.
    C. No; the oscillation frequency of the pendulum observed in Experiment 1 increased as the arm length increased.
    D. No; although the longest pendulum arm resulted in the lowest oscillation frequency, the frequency increased with increasing arm length for the other three lengths tested.

16. Based on the results of Experiment 2, if an engineer needs a spring that oscillates most slowly after being stretched and released, which of the following springs should be chosen?

    F. Spring A
    G. Spring B
    H. Spring C
    J. Spring D

17. Based on the results of Experiment 3, if a 700 g mass were suspended from Spring A, at what equilibrium length would the system come to rest?

    A. Less than 20 cm
    B. Between 20 cm and 30 cm
    C. Between 30 cm and 50 cm
    D. Greater than 50 cm

18. The students tested a fifth spring, Spring E, in the same manner as in Experiment 2. With a 100 g mass suspended from Spring E, the oscillation frequency was 1.4 Hz. Based on the results of Experiment 2, which of the following correctly lists the five springs by their oscillation frequency with a 100 g mass suspended from *fastest* to *slowest*?

    F. Spring E, Spring B, Spring C, Spring A, Spring D
    G. Spring D, Spring A, Spring C, Spring B, Spring E
    H. Spring A, Spring B, Spring C, Spring E, Spring D
    J. Spring D, Spring E, Spring C, Spring B, Spring A

GO ON TO THE NEXT PAGE

19. Experiment 1 was repeated using a larger pendulum mass. Which of the following figures best expresses the comparison between the results found using the larger pendulum mass and using the original mass?

A.

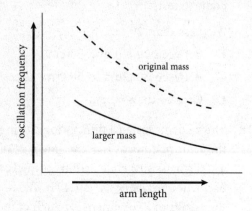

B.

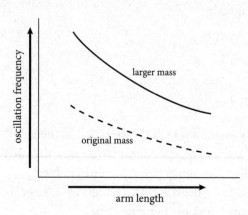

C.

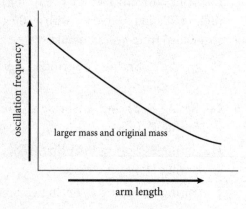

D.

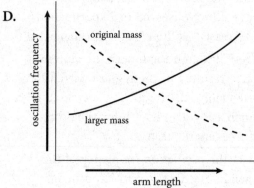

20. According to Figure 1, at what arm length will the oscillation frequency equal 0.35 Hz?

   F.   13 cm

   G.   16 cm

   H.   19 cm

   J.   21 cm

GO ON TO THE NEXT PAGE

PASSAGE IV

A person requires a certain percentage of oxygen in the blood for proper respiratory function. The amount of oxygen in the air varies enough with altitude that people normally accustomed to breathing near sea level may experience respiratory problems at significantly higher altitudes. Table 1 shows the average percentage of oxygen saturation in the blood, as well as the blood concentrations of three enzymes, GST, ECH, and CR, for three populations of high altitude (ha) dwellers and three populations of sea level (sl) dwellers. Enzyme concentrations are given in arbitrary units (a.u.). Figure 1 shows average oxygen partial pressure and average temperature at various altitudes.

Table 1

Population	Altitude range (m)	Oxygen saturation (%)	Enzyme concentration (a.u.)		
			GST	ECH	CR
ha 1	3,500–4,000	98.1	121.0	89.2	48.8
ha 2	3,300–3,700	99.0	108.3	93.5	45.6
ha 3	3,900–4,200	97.9	111.6	91.9	52.3
sl 1	0–300	98.5	86.7	57.1	44.9
sl 2	0–150	99.2	79.8	65.8	53.1
sl 3	0–200	98.7	82.5	61.4	47.0

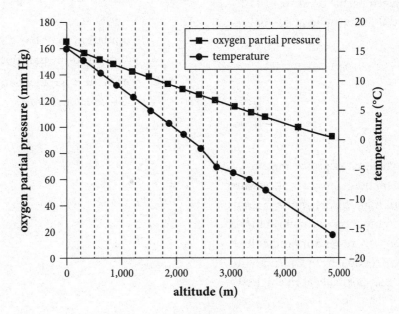

Figure 1

GO ON TO THE NEXT PAGE

21. Based on the data in Table 1, one would conclude that the blood of high altitude dwellers contains a higher concentration of:

    A. CR than ECH.
    B. CR than GST.
    C. ECH than GST.
    D. GST than CR.

22. Based on the information given, one would expect that, compared to the high-altitude dwellers, the sea-level dwellers:

    F. have blood with a lower percentage oxygen saturation.
    G. have blood with a lower GST concentration.
    H. can tolerate lower oxygen partial pressures.
    J. can tolerate lower temperatures.

23. According to Figure 1, an atmospheric sample found at an oxygen partial pressure of 110 mm Hg was most likely found at a temperature of about:

    A. 8.1°C.
    B. 0°C.
    C. –5.4°C.
    D. –12.5°C.

24. ECH is an enzyme that improves the efficiency of cellular energy production. Assume that people with higher ECH concentrations in the blood can function normally at higher altitudes without any respiratory difficulties. Based on Table 1, people from which population can function normally at the highest altitude?

    F. sl 1
    G. sl 2
    H. ha 2
    J. ha 3

25. Assume that a person's blood oxygen saturation percentage is determined only by the oxygen partial pressure at the location at which the person lives and the efficiency of the person's respiratory system at incorporating oxygen into the blood. Which of the following pieces of information supports the hypothesis that people from population ha 2 can incorporate oxygen into their blood more efficiently than can people from population sl 1?

    A. Population ha 2 lives where the oxygen partial pressure is lower than that of where population sl 1 lives, yet population ha 2 has a higher blood oxygen saturation percentage than does population ha 1.
    B. Population ha 2 lives where the oxygen partial pressure is higher than that of where population sl 1 lives, yet population ha 2 has a lower blood oxygen saturation percentage than does population ha 1.
    C. Population ha 2 has a higher CR concentration than does population sl 1.
    D. Population ha 2 has an unusually high GST concentration.

GO ON TO THE NEXT PAGE ▷

26. If a population of dwellers living at 1,500–1,800 m was studied, which of the following assumptions about the enzyme levels is most likely true?

   F. The levels of GST, ECH, and CR would be the same as the high-altitude populations.

   G. The levels of GST, ECH, and CR would be the same as the sea-level populations.

   H. The level of GST would be lower than the level of the sea-level population, and the levels of ECH and CR would be lower than the the level of the high-altitude populations.

   J. The levels of GST and ECH would be higher than the level of the sea-level population, and the level of CR would be the same as both populations.

PASSAGE V

Two students explain why lakes freeze from the surface downward. They also discuss the phenomenon of the melting of ice under the blades of an ice skater's skates.

STUDENT 1

Water freezes first at the surface of lakes because the freezing point of water decreases with increasing pressure. Under the surface, *hydrostatic pressure* causes the freezing point of water to be slightly lower than it is at the surface. Thus, as the air temperature drops, it reaches the freezing point of water at the surface before reaching that of the water beneath it. Only as the temperature becomes even colder will the layer of ice at the surface become thicker.

Pressure is defined as *force* divided by the *surface area* over which the force is exerted. An ice skater exerts the entire force of his or her body weight over the tiny surface area of two very thin blades. This

results in a very large pressure, which quickly melts a small amount of ice directly under the blades.

STUDENT 2

Water freezes first at the surface of lakes because the density of ice is less than that of liquid water. Unlike most liquids, the volume of a given mass of water expands upon freezing, and the density therefore decreases. As a result, the *buoyant force* of water acting upward is greater than the force of gravity exerted downward by any mass of ice, and all ice particles float to the surface upon freezing.

Ice melts under an ice skater's skates because of friction. The energy used to overcome the force of friction is converted to heat, which melts the ice under the skates. The greater the weight of the skater, the greater the force of friction, and the faster the ice melts.

27. According to Student 1, which of the following quantities is *greater* for water molecules beneath a lake's surface than for water molecules at the surface?

   A. Temperature

   B. Density

   C. Buoyant force

   D. Hydrostatic pressure

GO ON TO THE NEXT PAGE ⟶

28. When two ice skaters, wearing identical skates, skated across a frozen lake at the same speed, the ice under the blades of Skater B was found to melt faster than the ice under the blades of Skater A. What conclusion would each student draw about which skater is heavier?

   F. Both Student 1 and Student 2 would conclude that Skater A is heavier.

   G. Both Student 1 and Student 2 would conclude that Skater B is heavier.

   H. Student 1 would conclude that Skater A is heavier; Student 2 would conclude that Skater B is heavier.

   J. Student 1 would conclude that Skater B is heavier; Student 2 would conclude that Skater A is heavier.

29. Which student(s), if either, would predict that ice will melt under the blades of an ice skater who is NOT moving?

   A. Student 1 only

   B. Student 2 only

   C. Both Student 1 and Student 2

   D. Neither Student 1 nor Student 2

30. A beaker of ethanol is found to freeze from the bottom upward, instead of from the surface downward. Student 2 would most likely argue that the density of frozen ethanol is:

   F. greater than the density of water.

   G. less than the density of ice.

   H. greater than the density of liquid ethanol.

   J. less than the density of liquid ethanol.

31. A toy boat was placed on the surface of a small pool of water, and the boat was gradually filled with sand. After a certain amount of sand had been added, the boat began to sink. Based on Student 2's explanation, the boat began to sink because:

   A. hydrostatic pressure became greater than the buoyant force of the water on the boat.

   B. atmospheric pressure became greater than the buoyant force of the water on the boat.

   C. the force of gravity of the boat on the water became greater than the buoyant force of the water on the boat.

   D. the force of gravity of the boat on the water became less than the buoyant force of the water on the boat.

32. According to Student 2, if friction between the ice and the blades of an ice skater's skates is reduced, which of the following quantities simultaneously decreases at the point where the blades and the ice are in contact?

   F. Pressure exerted by the blades on the ice

   G. Heat produced

   H. Force of gravity of the blades on the ice

   J. Freezing point of water

33. Based on Student 2's explanation, the reason a hot air balloon is able to rise above the ground is that the balloon and the air inside it are:

   A. less dense than the air outside the balloon.

   B. more dense than the air outside the balloon.

   C. at a higher pressure than the air outside the balloon.

   D. less buoyant than the air outside the balloon.

GO ON TO THE NEXT PAGE ⟶

PASSAGE VI

In many communities, chemicals containing fluoride ions (F⁻) are added to the drinking water supply to help prevent tooth decay. Use of F⁻ is controversial because studies have linked F⁻ with bone disease. Students performed two experiments to measure F⁻ levels.

EXPERIMENT I

Five solutions, each containing a different amount of Na_2SiF_6 (sodium silicofluoride) in H_2O were prepared. Five identical *electrodynamic cells* were filled with equal volumes of each of the five solutions, and a sixth identical cell was filled with a *blank* solution (one containing no added Na_2SiF_6). The cells were activated to measure the electrical *conductivity* for each. The conductivities were then corrected by subtracting the conductivity of the blank solution from each value (see Table 1 and Figure 1).

Table 1

Concentration of F⁻ (mg/L*)	Measured conductivity (μS/cm**)	Corrected conductivity (μS/cm**)
0.0	15.96	0.00
0.1	16.13	0.17
0.5	16.80	0.084
1.0	17.63	1.67
2.0	19.30	3.34
4.0	22.64	6.68

*mg/L is milligrams per liter. **μS/cm is microsiemens per centimer.

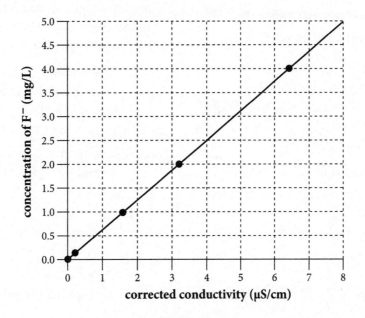

Figure 1

GO ON TO THE NEXT PAGE

EXPERIMENT 2

A water sample was taken directly from the drinking water supply of one community. An electrodynamic cell identical to those used in Experiment 1 was filled with water from this sample, and the cell was activated. The procedure was repeated for water samples from several communities, and the conductivities were measured (Table 2).

Table 2

Community	Measured conductivity (μS/cm)	Concentration of F⁻ (mg/L)
Newtown	22.31	3.8
Springfield	16.46	0.3
Lakewood	18.63	1.6
Reading	19.47	2.1

34. Students subtracted the measured conductivity of the blank solution from the sample solutions in order to:

    F. determine the amount of conductivity solely due to F- ions.

    G. calibrate the electrodynamic cells.

    H. correct for non-ionic impurities.

    J. test the solubility of F-.

35. Based on the results of Experiment 1, if the concentration of F⁻ in a solution is doubled, then the corrected conductivity of the solution will approximately:

    A. remain the same.

    B. halve.

    C. double.

    D. quadruple.

36. A sample was also taken from the drinking water supply of the community of Bluewater in Experiment 2, and its conductivity was measured to be 20.69 μS/cm. Which of the following correctly lists the drinking water supplies of Newtown, Lakewood, and Bluewater in increasing order of F⁻ concentration?

    F. Lakewood, Newtown, Bluewater

    G. Bluewater, Newtown, Lakewood

    H. Newtown, Bluewater, Lakewood

    J. Lakewood, Bluewater, Newtown

37. Based on the results of Experiment 1, if a solution with a concentration of 3.0 mg/L F⁻ had been tested, the corrected conductivity would have been closest to which of the following values?

    A. 1.3 μS/cm

    B. 3.3 μS/cm

    C. 5.0 μS/cm

    D. 6.5 μS/cm

38. If Experiments 1 and 2 were repeated to measure the concentration of chloride ions (Cl⁻) in drinking water, then which of the following changes in procedure would be necessary?

    F. The solutions in Experiment 1 should be prepared by adding different concentrations of NaCl (or another chemical containing Cl⁻) to H_2O.

    G. The conductivity of the blank solution should be added to the measured conductivities.

    H. The electrodynamic cells should be set to measure resistivity instead of conductivity.

    J. Both NaCl and Na_2SiF_6 should be added to all of the samples.

GO ON TO THE NEXT PAGE ⟩

39. Based on the results of Experiments 1 and 2, if the measured conductivities for the samples tested in Experiment 2 were compared with their corrected conductivities, the measured conductivities would be:

    A. lower for all of the samples tested.

    B. higher for all of the samples tested.

    C. lower for some of the samples tested, higher for others.

    D. the same for all of the samples tested.

40. The presence of other negative ions, such as Cl^-, results in an increase in the electrical conductivity of a solution. If all of the samples tested in Experiment 2 contained trace concentrations of Cl^-, how would the measurements have been affected? Compared to the actual F^- concentrations, the F^- concentrations apparently measured would be:

    F. higher.

    G. lower.

    H. the same.

    J. higher for some of the samples, lower for others.

IF YOU FINISH BEFORE TIME IS CALLED, YOU MAY CHECK YOUR WORK ON THIS SECTION ONLY. DO NOT TURN TO ANY OTHER SECTION IN THE TEST.   STOP

WRITING TEST

40 Minutes—1 Question

Directions: This is a test of your writing skills. You will have forty (40) minutes to write an essay in English. Before you begin planning and writing your essay, read the writing prompt carefully to understand exactly what you are being asked to do. Your essay will be evaluated on the evidence it provides of your ability to do the following:

- Express judgments by evaluating the three perspectives given in the prompt, taking a position on an issue, and explaining the relationship among all four ideas
- Develop a position by using logical reasoning and by supporting your ideas
- Maintain a focus on the topic throughout the essay
- Organize ideas in a logical way
- Use language clearly and effectively according to the conventions of standard written English

You may use a separate piece of paper to plan your essay. *You must write your essay in pencil on the lined pages provided after the prompt.* Your writing on those lined pages will be scored. You may not need all the lined pages, but to ensure you have enough room to finish, do NOT skip lines. You may write corrections or additions neatly between the lines of your essay, but do NOT write in the margins of the lined pages. *Illegible essays cannot be scored, so you must write (or print) clearly.*

DO NOT OPEN THIS BOOKLET UNTIL TOLD TO DO SO.

GO ON TO THE NEXT PAGE ⇒

EXPERIENTIAL EDUCATION

Experiential education is a philosophy that holds that students learn best through direct experience. Hands-on learning is said to promote deeper understanding because students are able to apply concepts and theories to physical situations. Rather than memorizing facts, students who are given the opportunity to create physical evidence of logical reasoning are better equipped to apply the same reasoning to new situations. Since all teachers aim to impart critical thinking in their classrooms, should they be expected to provide more hands-on learning opportunities? As educators aim to continuously improve the quality of the education they offer to students, consideration should be given to better incorporating hands-on learning.

Read and carefully consider these perspectives. Each suggests a particular approach regarding experiential education.

Perspective One	Perspective Two	Perspective Three
Some argue that to accept a theory without experiencing it is to learn nothing at all. Teachers need to provide opportunities for experiential involvement if they expect students to truly comprehend each lesson plan objective.	Experiential education is an integral part of readying students to pursue careers in the science, technology, engineering, and math fields, but not all disciplines. If students are expected to perform skill-based tasks in these fields after they graduate, they should be provided a strong foundation on which to build their careers. However, teachers should not be expected to supply experiential learning where it is not appropriate.	Schools cannot be expected to offer hands-on learning for students. Not only is it costly, but also it may not be effective for all learners. Students will be better served if schools invest money in other educational models and opportunities.

ESSAY TASK

Write a unified, coherent essay in which you evaluate multiple perspectives on experiential education. In your essay, be sure to:

- analyze and evaluate the perspectives given
- state and develop your own perspective on the issue
- explain the relationship between your perspective and those given

Your perspective may be in full agreement with any of the others, in partial agreement, or wholly different. Whatever the case, support your ideas with logical reasoning and detailed, persuasive examples.

GO ON TO THE NEXT PAGE

PLANNING YOUR ESSAY

You may wish to consider the following as you think critically about the task:

Strengths and weaknesses of the three given perspectives
- What insights do they offer, and what do they fail to consider?
- Why might they be persuasive to others, or why might they fail to persuade?

Your own knowledge, experience, and values
- What is your perspective on this issue, and what are its strengths and weaknesses?
- How will you support your perspective in your essay?

_____

_____

_____

_____

_____

_____

_____

_____

_____

_____

_____

_____

_____

_____

_____

_____

_____

GO ON TO THE NEXT PAGE

Practice Test Three
ANSWER KEY

ENGLISH TEST

1. C	11. A	21. C	31. C	41. B	51. D	61. D	71. A
2. H	12. G	22. G	32. H	42. G	52. F	62. H	72. G
3. C	13. A	23. C	33. D	43. D	53. C	63. A	73. A
4. J	14. H	24. J	34. F	44. G	54. J	64. H	74. H
5. B	15. B	25. C	35. B	45. A	55. D	65. B	75. D
6. J	16. J	26. J	36. F	46. J	56. II	66. F	
7. B	17. A	27. B	37. C	47. D	57. A	67. B	
8. J	18. J	28. G	38. F	48. H	58. J	68. G	
9. D	19. D	29. D	39. C	49. D	59. C	69. D	
10. H	20. H	30. J	40. H	50. G	60. G	70. G	

MATHEMATICS TEST

1. E	9. B	17. E	25. C	33. D	41. D	49. C	57. B
2. K	10. H	18. J	26. F	34. F	42. G	50. G	58. F
3. C	11. D	19. A	27. D	35. E	43. A	51. A	59. C
4. H	12. G	20. H	28. F	36. H	44. K	52. H	60. H
5. D	13. C	21. A	29. B	37. C	45. C	53. D	
6. J	14. J	22. J	30. F	38. H	46. J	54. K	
7. A	15. D	23. E	31. C	39. C	47. E	55. A	
8. G	16. G	24. H	32. K	40. J	48. H	56. J	

READING TEST

1. D	6. H	11. C	16. J	21. C	26. F	31. B	36. H
2. H	7. B	12. G	17. C	22. J	27. B	32. F	37. B
3. B	8. F	13. B	18. J	23. C	28. H	33. C	38. J
4. J	9. C	14. F	19. A	24. F	29. B	34. H	39. B
5. D	10. F	15. B	20. G	25. D	30. G	35. C	40. G

SCIENCE TEST

1. C	6. H	11. B	16. F	21. D	26. J	31. C	36. J
2. H	7. B	12. F	17. C	22. G	27. D	32. G	37. C
3. A	8. H	13. A	18. J	23. C	28. G	33. A	38. F
4. J	9. C	14. G	19. C	24. H	29. A	34. F	39. B
5. B	10. H	15. A	20. H	25. A	30. H	35. C	40. F

ANSWERS AND EXPLANATIONS

ENGLISH TEST

PASSAGE I

1. C
Category: Word Choice
Difficulty: Medium
Getting to the Answer: Choice (C) forms a complete sentence by using the simple past tense *was*. Choice A creates a sentence fragment; an *-ing* verb needs a helping verb, such as *was* or *is*, to be the main verb in a sentence. Choice B incorrectly uses a comma to separate the subject from the main verb. Choice D omits the verb entirely, creating a sentence fragment.

2. H
Category: Word Choice
Difficulty: Medium
Getting to the Answer: The phrase *not only* in the beginning of the sentence is your clue to the correct answer. Logically, the phrase *not only* is always followed by *but also*. The other choices neither complete the idiom correctly nor convey the necessary contrast between the ideas in the two clauses.

3. C
Category: Punctuation
Difficulty: High
Getting to the Answer: Add an apostrophe and an *s* to a singular noun to show possession. The narrator and Gretchen attend one school, so (C) is correct. Choice A omits the apostrophe needed to show that the *swim team* belongs to the *school*. Choice B incorrectly treats *school* as a plural, placing the apostrophe after the *s*. Choice D incorrectly uses *ours* and does not make *school* possessive.

4. J
Category: Wordiness
Difficulty: Medium
Getting to the Answer: The testmakers value simple and direct prose, so change passive constructions such as "it was with Gretchen that I" when you're given the opportunity. As is often the case on the English test of the ACT, the shortest choice—(J)—is correct. In addition to being verbose, F contains a sentence structure error: It is not clear who knows that the writer enjoyed swimming. Choices G and H are both also verbose.

5. B
Category: Writing Strategy
Difficulty: Low
Getting to the Answer: Slow down and carefully read a Nonstandard-Format question like this one. You just may see a question such as this that tests vocabulary. Choice (B) indicates that the narrator's mother recommended swimming lessons but did not decide that the narrator *must* take them. Choices A, C, and D all indicate that the mother's mind was made up.

6. J
Category: Sentence Sense
Difficulty: Medium
Getting to the Answer: If a sentence seems to have too many ideas, then it is probably a run-on. By itself, a comma cannot separate two clauses that could be independent sentences, as in F. Choice G replaces *swimmers* with a pronoun but does not correct the run-on. Similarly, H removes the comma but does not address the problem of two complete thoughts that are incorrectly joined. Choice (J) solves the problem by using *whom*, which turns the second half of the sentence into a dependent clause that describes the *women*.

7. B
Category: Punctuation
Difficulty: High
Getting to the Answer: This sentence contains a parenthetical phrase. If you omitted "who had been swimming competitively since elementary school," you would still have a complete sentence. Like all parenthetical phrases, this needs to be set off from the rest of the sentence. A comma is used at the beginning of the phrase, so a comma must also be used at the end of the phrase. This makes D incorrect. Choices A and C insert unnecessary commas within the parenthetical phrase.

8. J
Category: Wordiness
Difficulty: Low
Getting to the Answer: When in doubt, take it out. *Giving up,* by definition, means "quitting" or "failing." Choices F, G, and H create redundancies.

9. D
Category: Verb Tenses
Difficulty: Medium
Getting to the Answer: Trust your ear. *Begin* is an irregular verb; the simple past tense *began* can be used by itself, but the past participle *begun* cannot. Instead, *begun* always appears with *has,* *have,* or *had,* as in "I *have begun* to prepare for the ACT." Choice (D) correctly uses the simple past tense *began.* Choice B creates another verb usage error by inserting *been.* Choice C incorrectly uses *began* with *had.*

10. H
Category: Word Choice
Difficulty: High
Getting to the Answer: Don't panic if you see a question that tests the use of *who* and *whom.* The pronoun *who* serves as a subject, just like the pronouns *he* and *she* replace subjects. The pronoun *whom* serves as an object, just like the pronouns *him* and *her* replace objects. Here, *coach* is the subject

of the sentence, so *who,* (H), is correct. Never refer to a person as *which,* J.

11. A
Category: Wordiness
Difficulty: Medium
Getting to the Answer: Don't force a change where one isn't needed. The correct answer for some of the underlined portions will be NO CHANGE. The sentence "The hard work eventually paid off," is correct and concise as it is written. Choice B is verbose, and C and D create run-on sentences.

12. G
Category: Writing Strategy
Difficulty: Medium
Getting to the Answer: Start by asking yourself, "Does this information belong here?" The question asks for a sentence that is relevant to the narrator's experience on the swim team. Only (G) is connected to the narrator and the swim team; the sentence explains that the narrator was one of the only swimmers on the team to be interested in the butterfly. The history of the stroke, F; the relative speed of the stroke, H; and an alternative name for the stroke, J, are not as related to the narrator's personal experience.

13. A
Category: Writing Strategy
Difficulty: Medium
Getting to the Answer: The shortest answer is often, but not always, correct. Don't omit portions that add relevant information to the sentence. The sentence is about the narrator's swimming, so her participation in the medley relay is relevant. Choices B and C add descriptions of the medley relay that are not relevant to the topic.

14. H
Category: Verb Tenses
Difficulty: Medium
Getting to the Answer: The four choices offer different tenses of the same verb. The clue *last year* indicates that the narrator earned the varsity letter in the past. Choice (H), the simple past tense, is correct. Neither the future tense, F, nor the present tense, J, makes sense with the clue *last year.* Choice G would only make sense if something had prevented the narrator from earning the varsity letter.

15. B
Category: Writing Strategy
Difficulty: Low
Getting to the Answer: Keep the main point of the passage in mind. Before beginning high school, the narrator had never thought of herself as an athlete. Then she joined the swim team and became successful at the sport. Choice (B) is most relevant to the central ideas of the passage. Choices A and C focus too narrowly on details in the passage, while D contradicts the main point of the passage.

PASSAGE II

16. J
Category: Punctuation
Difficulty: Medium
Getting to the Answer: Don't assume that a comma or semicolon is needed just because a sentence is long. Read the sentence aloud to yourself, and you should be able to hear that a comma is not needed in the underlined portion. A semicolon, as in F, would only be correct if the second half of the sentence expressed a complete thought. Choices G and H both use an unnecessary comma.

17. A
Category: Word Choice
Difficulty: Low
Getting to the Answer: When a verb is underlined, check to see whether it agrees with its noun. Watch out for descriptive phrases that separate a verb from

its noun. Here, the verb *was* agrees with the singular noun *tank.* NO CHANGE is needed. Choice B uses the present tense, but the surrounding sentences use the past tense. Choices C and D incorrectly use a verb in the plural form.

18. J
Category: Sentence Sense
Difficulty: Medium
Getting to the Answer: When the word *that* or *which* is underlined, watch out for an incomplete sentence. As it is written, this is a sentence fragment; a complete verb is missing. Removing *that,* as in (J), turns *made* into the main verb of a complete and correct sentence. Choice G does not address the sentence fragment error, and H also fails to provide a clear and appropriate sentence.

19. D
Category: Wordiness
Difficulty: Medium
Getting to the Answer: If you are *familiar* with a type of animal, then you have almost certainly *seen it before.* Choice (D) creates a concise sentence that does not lose any of the original meaning. The other choices are redundant. Choice B repeats *sights* when *view* has already been used, and C uses the unnecessarily repetitive phrase "to which I was no stranger."

20. H
Category: Organization
Difficulty: High
Getting to the Answer: Scan the paragraph for connecting words and phrases that you can use as clues to determine the most logical order of sentences. In sentence 5, the word *first* suggests that the sentence should be placed close to the beginning of the paragraph. Sentence 2 says, "There were *also* animals I had never before glimpsed," which indicates that a preceding sentence discusses animals the writer had glimpsed. Sentence 5, which describes the writer's view of familiar animals, most logically belongs immediately after sentence 1.

21. C
Category: Verb Tenses
Difficulty: Low
Getting to the Answer: If an underlined verb agrees with its noun, then determine whether the verb's tense makes sense in the context of the passage. The surrounding verbs are in the past tense, so this sentence should use the simple past tense *saw*, (C). Choices A and D use the present tense, and B illogically uses the past progressive "had been seeing."

22. G
Category: Connections
Difficulty: High
Getting to the Answer: An effective first sentence for a paragraph will introduce the topic of the paragraph and connect that topic to ideas that have come before. Paragraph 3 focuses on the catfish, while paragraph 4 describes the large alligator and snapping turtle in the bayou tank. Choice (G) would provide an effective connection between these paragraphs, referring to the catfish and introducing the idea that there were even bigger animals on display. Neither F nor H leads into the topic of paragraph 4. Choice J doesn't provide a transition from the discussion of the catfish in paragraph 3.

23. C
Category: Writing Strategy
Difficulty: Medium
Getting to the Answer: The phrase in question provides a visual image; deleting the phrase would mean losing a description, (C). The removal of the phrase would not affect the transition between sentences, A. Contrary to B, the contrast between images would be decreased. The level of suspense may be somewhat decreased by the loss of the description, but it would not be increased, D.

24. J
Category: Verb Tenses
Difficulty: Medium
Getting to the Answer: The verbs *slides* and *aims* agree with the singular subject *it*, but they are in the wrong tense. The rest of the paragraph describes actions that took place in the past. For the sentence to make sense in context, these verbs should also be in the past tense, (J). Choices F and G use present-tense verbs. Choice H creates a logically incomplete sentence.

25. C
Category: Sentence Sense
Difficulty: Medium
Getting to the Answer: If something sounds awkward or unusual, there is probably an error. Most words that end in *-ly* are adverbs; they are used to modify verbs, adjectives, or other adverbs. Adverbs cannot be used to describe nouns, such as *moment*, A. Choice (C) correctly uses the adjective *slight* to modify *panic*. The sentences formed by B and D don't make sense.

26. J
Category: Idioms
Difficulty: Low
Getting to the Answer: The phrase "much of the onlookers" probably sounds strange to you. That's because *much* is used with noncountable things or concepts (as in "there isn't much time") or quantities (as in "there isn't much pizza left"). You could count the number of *onlookers*, so *many*, (J), is correct. Choices G and H also create idiomatic errors.

27. B
Category: Writing Strategy
Difficulty: Medium
Getting to the Answer: The question tells you that the writer's goal is to describe the appearance of the crayfish, so eliminate any sentences that do not have details about how crayfish look, C. Choice A suggests that crayfish look like lobsters, and D describes the crayfish as small. Neither of

these sentences offers the descriptive detail that is given in (B).

28. G
Category: Punctuation
Difficulty: Medium
Getting to the Answer: Trust your ear. You naturally pause when a comma or semicolon is needed in a sentence. A pause between *all* and *I* just doesn't sound right; that's because the full introductory phrase "After seeing all I could inside the museum" should not be interrupted. A comma should not separate a verb (*seeing*) from its object (*museum*). This eliminates F and H. A comma is needed between an introductory phrase and the complete thought that follows, making (G) correct and J incorrect.

29. D
Category: Wordiness
Difficulty: Medium
Getting to the Answer: Say it simply. The shortest answer here is correct: it turns the passive construction "it was that" in A and B into the active "I had." Choice C is unnecessarily wordy.

30. J
Category: Sentence Sense
Difficulty: High
Getting to the Answer: A sentence must have a subject and verb and express a complete thought. The sentence that begins "And operates" does not have a subject. Removing the period, (J), creates a grammatically correct sentence. Choice G is awkwardly worded. Choice H creates a run-on sentence; a coordinating conjunction such as *and* needs to be used along with a comma to link two complete thoughts.

PASSAGE III

31. C
Category: Pronouns
Difficulty: Medium
Getting to the Answer: When a pronoun is underlined, check to see that it agrees in number with the noun it replaces or refers to. In this sentence, the underlined pronoun refers back to the plural "secret identities and elaborate disguises." Choice (C) uses the correct plural pronoun *they*. Choices A and B create pronoun agreement errors by using the singular pronoun *it*. Choice D creates a sentence fragment.

32. H
Category: Punctuation
Difficulty: Medium
Getting to the Answer: Many English questions will focus on the correct use of commas. Commas should be used to separate an appositive or descriptive phrase from the main part of the sentence. The phrase "the restaurant critic for the *New York Times*" describes the noun *Ruth Reichl,* so the phrase should be set off with commas, (H). Choices F and J fail to use both necessary commas. On the other hand, G incorrectly inserts a third comma.

33. D
Category: Writing Strategy
Difficulty: High
Getting to the Answer: Only add sentences that are directly connected to the topic of a paragraph. Paragraph 2 discusses the importance of a *Times* review to restaurants in New York City. The suggested sentence provides a specific detail about one restaurant without explaining how the review from the *Times* affected business. Choice (D) best explains why the sentence should not be added.

34. F
Category: Idioms
Difficulty: Medium
Getting to the Answer: Trust your ear. You look *to* someone or something for advice. No change is needed. Choice G suggests that the paper is looking along *with* its readers, while H suggests that the readers are looking near the newspaper. Choice J uses an *-ing* verb without a helping verb, creating a sentence fragment.

35. B
Category: Verb Tenses
Difficulty: Low
Getting to the Answer: Verbs must make sense in the context of the passage. The next sentence says that a negative review "can undermine" a restaurant. Because the two sentences discuss possible results of a review, the underlined verb in this sentence should be in the same tense—"can bring," (B). Choice A illogically uses the conditional in the past tense, while C and D do not use the conditional at all.

36. F
Category: Punctuation
Difficulty: Medium
Getting to the Answer: The subject of the sentence is "restaurant owners and workers," and the verb is *have*. There isn't a descriptive phrase or clause separating the subject and verb, so no comma is needed. A semicolon should be used to connect two complete thoughts, G. Choice H incorrectly treats *restaurant* as the first item in a list; instead, *restaurant* identifies the type of *owners* and *workers*.

37. C
Category: Pronouns
Difficulty: Medium
Getting to the Answer: To whom does the meal belong? It belongs to the *writer,* so the possessive pronoun *whose* is correct. *Who's* is always a contraction for *who is* or *who has,* B. Choices A and D introduce sentence structure errors.

38. F
Category: Wordiness
Difficulty: Medium
Getting to the Answer: The shortest answer is often correct. The sentence is concise and direct as it is written. Each of the other choices adds unnecessary words to the underlined portion.

39. C
Category: Wordiness
Difficulty: Low
Getting to the Answer: On the ACT, there's no need to say the same thing twice. *Common, ordinary, representative,* and *average* all have very similar meanings; A and B use redundant language. Choice (C) makes the sentence concise by using only *typical.* Choice D uses a word that does not make sense in the context of the sentence.

40. H
Category: Wordiness
Difficulty: Medium
Getting to the Answer: If you have *decided* to do something to solve a problem, you have found a *solution*—there's no need to use both words. Choice (H) eliminates the redundancy and verbosity errors of the other choices.

41. B
Category: Sentence Sense
Difficulty: High
Getting to the Answer: As a rule, modifying words, phrases, and clauses should be as close as possible to the things or actions they describe. For instance, the list beginning "such as an attractive blonde named Chloe" describes the *different personas*. Therefore, *different personas* should come right before the list. This eliminates A. Choice (B) correctly uses an introductory phrase and makes *Reichl* the subject of the sentence. Choice C is a sentence fragment; a complete verb is missing. Choice D inserts an unnecessary comma between *clothing* and *that*, and the pronoun *herself* is incorrect in context.

42. G
Category: Writing Strategy
Difficulty: Medium
Getting to the Answer: The most logical and effective sentence will be connected to the main topic of the paragraph and make a transition to the following sentence. Paragraph 4 describes how Reichl turned herself into different characters, and paragraph 5 describes the result of reviewing a restaurant while in disguise. The best link between these ideas is (G). Choice F is a narrow detail that does not connect the two paragraphs, while H and J move completely away from the topic of Reichl's disguises.

43. D
Category: Organization
Difficulty: High
Getting to the Answer: Sometimes it helps to rephrase a question in your own words. For example, this question could be rewritten as "What does the phrase *of a restaurant* describe?" Reichl focuses on the quality of a restaurant, so the best placement is (D). The phrase does not describe *developed*, *view*, or *person*.

44. G
Category: Sentence Sense
Difficulty: High
Getting to the Answer: The word *occasionally* means "sometimes"; its placement in this sentence indicates that Reichl was sometimes treated very differently when she was in disguise, and sometimes she wasn't. Removing the word *occasionally* would indicate that Reichl always or typically had a different experience as one of her personas, (G).

45. A
Category: Organization
Difficulty: Medium
Getting to the Answer: Paragraph 6 describes the effect of Reichl's use of disguises when she reviewed restaurants. Logically, this information should follow

the explanation of why and how Ruth dined as different people, the topics of paragraphs 3 and 4. Paragraph 6 should remain where it is.

PASSAGE IV

46. J
Category: Punctuation
Difficulty: Medium
Getting to the Answer: Trust your ear. A comma indicates a short pause, which you won't hear when you read this part of the sentence aloud. No comma is needed, (J). A comma can be used to separate a descriptive phrase from the rest of the sentence, F and H, but neither "would develop into prize-winning vegetables" nor "develop into prize-winning vegetables" is a descriptive phrase. Choice G incorrectly treats the underlined portion of the sentence as part of a list.

47. D
Category: Organization
Difficulty: High
Getting to the Answer: The paragraph describes events in chronological order, from the last freeze of the year to the time that spring "truly arrived." Sentence 3 describes thinning out the plants and pulling weeds so the new plants would grow; it would only make sense to do this *after* the seeds have been planted and have started to grow. Sentence 4 is about planting seeds, so sentence 3 must come after sentence 4, (D).

48. H
Category: Connections
Difficulty: Medium
Getting to the Answer: When you read this sentence aloud, you should be able to hear a short pause between *burden* and *less*. This pause indicates that the conjunction *and* is needed to separate the two descriptions, (H). Choice G is incorrect because a colon is used to introduce a brief definition, explanation, or list. Choice J uses the inappropriate conjunction *but*, which doesn't make sense in context.

49. D
Category: Wordiness
Difficulty: Medium
Getting to the Answer: When "OMIT the underlined portion" is an option, consider whether the underlined portion is relevant to the topic of the sentence or paragraph. Paragraph 2 is about the writer's failure to maintain her garden, not about the weather in July and August. Choice (D) is correct.

50. G
Category: Connections
Difficulty: Low
Getting to the Answer: Always read the questions carefully! This one asks for the choice that would NOT work in the sentence. In other words, three of the answer choices would make sense in the sentence. The first sentence of paragraph 3 contrasts with paragraph 2, so the contrasting transitions in F, H, and J are all possible substitutions for the underlined word. *Indeed*, (G), is a word used to show emphasis, not contrast.

51. D
Category: Wordiness
Difficulty: Medium
Getting to the Answer: The shortest answer is often correct. Choices A, B, and C all refer to large-scale farming, which is only loosely related to the topic of gardening. Choice (D) keeps the sentence focused on the topic of paragraph 3.

52. F
Category: Connections
Difficulty: High
Getting to the Answer: Before you answer this question, read enough of paragraph 4 to identify its main idea. Paragraph 3 introduces the topic of square-foot gardening, and paragraph 4 describes several of its advantages. The best link between these ideas is the original sentence, (F). Paragraph 4 doesn't mention the history of square-foot gardening or the writer's neighbor, so G and J don't make sense. Choice H is a detail about square-foot

gardening, but it does not function as a topic sentence for the paragraph.

53. C
Category: Sentence Sense
Difficulty: Low
Getting to the Answer: If an underlined word ends in *-ly*, you can be pretty sure that it is an adverb. Remember that adverbs can be used to describe verbs, adjectives, and other adverbs but not nouns. The word *garden* is a noun, so A and B are incorrect. The adjective *traditional*, (C), is correct. The phrase *tradition garden*, D, does not make sense.

54. J
Category: Word Choice
Difficulty: Medium
Getting to the Answer: Who spends hours thinning each row? From this sentence, it's unclear: you have no idea who *they* are. Other sentences in paragraph 4 use the pronoun *you*, so it makes sense to use *you* here.

55. D
Category: Wordiness
Difficulty: Medium
Getting to the Answer: "OMIT the underlined portion" is an option, so check to see whether the information is irrelevant to the topic or repetitive. This sentence begins with the phrase "In a square-foot garden," so it is unnecessary to repeat "in the garden." Choice (D) is correct.

56. H
Category: Sentence Sense
Difficulty: Low
Getting to the Answer: "OMIT the underlined portion" isn't always the correct answer. As it is written, the sentence does not express a complete thought. To correct the error, remove *which could* so that *make* becomes the main verb of the sentence. Choices G and J create sentence fragments.

57. A
Category: Word Choice
Difficulty: Medium
Getting to the Answer: Don't look too hard for an error—many English test questions will require NO CHANGE. The present tense and the pronoun *you* are used throughout paragraph 4, so this sentence is correct as it is written.

58. J
Category: Wordiness
Difficulty: Low
Getting to the Answer: Remember that the ACT values economy. If you can express an underlined portion in fewer words without changing or losing the original meaning, then the shortest answer is probably correct. The only choice that does not use redundant language is (J).

59. C
Category: Word Choice
Difficulty: Medium
Getting to the Answer: The verb in this sentence is separated from its singular subject "one season" by the phrase "of using the square garden techniques." Choice (C) corrects the subject-verb agreement error of the original sentence. Incorrect choices use the plural form of the verb, A and B, or the future tense, D, which does not make sense in the context of the sentence.

60. G
Category: Writing Strategy
Difficulty: High
Getting to the Answer: This question asks about the passage as a whole, so take a moment to think about the main idea of the passage. Paragraphs 1 and 2 describe the writer's failed attempts at a traditional garden, while paragraphs 3, 4, and 5 focus on the writer's success with a square-foot garden. The essay is not instructive; instead, it compares two types of gardens, (G).

PASSAGE V

61. D
Category: Punctuation
Difficulty: Medium
Getting to the Answer: When a coordinating conjunction such as *but* or *and* combines two independent clauses (complete thoughts), a comma must come before it. In this sentence, a comma should be inserted after *light,* (D). Choice C incorrectly places a comma in a compound phrase and fails to add one before the coordinating conjunction. Choice B incorrectly uses a semicolon between an independent and a dependent clause. You'll likely see at least one semicolon question on the ACT, so remember that a semicolon is used to separate two complete thoughts or to separate items in a series or list when one or more of those items already contains commas.

62. H
Category: Word Choice
Difficulty: Medium
Getting to the Answer: The answer choices present different forms of the verbs *improves* and *decreases*, so you know the issue is subject-verb agreement. The two underlined verbs need to agree with the plural subject *steps*; only (H) puts both *improve* and *decrease* in the correct form.

63. A
Category: Wordiness
Difficulty: Low
Getting to the Answer: The simplest way to say something is often the most correct option. The original sentence is the most concise and correct version. Choice B is redundant, using both *problem* and *trouble*. Choices C and D are both unnecessarily wordy in comparison to (A), which expresses the same meaning.

64. H
Category: Sentence Sense
Difficulty: Medium
Getting to the Answer: An -*ing* verb needs a helping verb to function as the main verb in a clause or sentence. Changing *being* to *is*, as in (H), corrects the sentence structure error. Choice G inserts an incorrect comma between *vision* and *has been*, while J creates a new sentence structure error by omitting the verb *being*.

65. B
Category: Sentence Sense
Difficulty: Medium
Getting to the Answer: Something that is *set* is established or predetermined. For the sentence to make sense, *set* should describe *time*; the wiper blades should be replaced at an *established* time each year. Choice (B) is correct. It does not make sense for the *blades,* A, the *year,* C, or the *risk,* D, to be *set*, or established.

66. F
Category: Word Choice
Difficulty: Low
Getting to the Answer: Trust your ear. With some idiom questions, you have to rely on your ear to hear what sounds correct. *In general* is an introductory phrase used to mean "usually" or "typically." Choice (F) provides the correct idiom for this context. The other choices contain idioms that are not typical of spoken English and do not fit this context.

67. B
Category: Writing Strategy
Difficulty: Medium
Getting to the Answer: To pick the best first sentence for paragraph 4, you must be able to identify the main idea of the paragraph. If you scan a few sentences of paragraph 4 before you answer the question, you'll see that the topic of the paragraph is changing a car's oil and oil filter. Only (B) introduces this topic. Choice A is too general, while C and D refer to car maintenance procedures that are not discussed in paragraph 4.

68. G
Category: Connections
Difficulty: Medium
Getting to the Answer: The connecting word *so* is underlined, so consider the relationship between the two parts of the sentence. There is a slight contrast—the first part of the sentence explains what you *do* need, while the second part identifies what you *don't* need. The contrasting conjunction *but,* (G), makes the most sense in context. The other choices indicate a cause-and-effect relationship that is not present in the sentence.

69. D
Category: Punctuation
Difficulty: Medium
Getting to the Answer: Information that is key to the main idea of a sentence should not be set off by commas. Here, it's important to know that the section is "in your owner's manual," so commas are incorrect. Choice (D) is correct. Choice C incorrectly uses a semicolon; a complete thought is not expressed by "and collect all of the tools you need."

70. G
Category: Writing Strategy
Difficulty: High
Getting to the Answer: Carefully read the question so that you understand the writer's purpose. If the writer wants to explain how to change oil, then the sentence should explain at least one specific step in the process. Choice (G) provides the most detailed information about how to go about changing oil.

71. A
Category: Punctuation
Difficulty: Medium
Getting to the Answer: Use a semicolon to introduce or emphasize what follows. The warning "you do not want to risk being crushed by a car," is

certainly worthy of emphasis, so the sentence is correct as it is written. The other choices create run-ons, as the sentence expresses two complete thoughts; additionally, D incorrectly separates a subject noun from its verb with a comma.

72. G
Category: Writing Strategy
Difficulty: High
Getting to the Answer: Paragraph 4 uses the informal *you* and *your*, while the rest of the essay uses the more formal third person. Therefore, eliminating the second-person pronouns from paragraph 4 would make the paragraph match the tone and voice of the rest of the essay, (G). Choices H and J are opposite answers: eliminating *you* and *your* would make the advice less direct and would make the essay more formal.

73. A
Category: Wordiness
Difficulty: Low
Getting to the Answer: Watch out for redundant language! A "qualified mechanic" will do a *professional* job, just as a "qualified mechanic" is likely *certified*; B and C use repetitive language. Choice D introduces a sentence structure error. The best version of the underlined portion is (A).

74. H
Category: Writing Strategy
Difficulty: Medium
Getting to the Answer: Knowing the general topic of each paragraph will help you quickly answer a question like this one. The sentence refers to "these different fluids," so look for a part of the passage that discusses fluids. The second and third sentences of paragraph 3 refer to different fluids (*coolant, oil, brake fluid*, and *transmission fluid*), so the most logical placement for the sentence is at the end of paragraph 3, (H). Paragraph 2 and paragraph 4 each only refer to one fluid, so F and J are incorrect.

75. D
Category: Writing Strategy
Difficulty: Medium
Getting to the Answer: Use your Reading Comp skills to answer this question. Does the main idea of the passage fit with this purpose? Not really, as the passage focuses solely on basic maintenance that car owners can do themselves. The passage doesn't discuss the need to learn about a car's safety features. Choice (D) is correct.

MATHEMATICS TEST

1. E
Category: Operations
Difficulty: Medium
Getting to the Answer: To determine the total amount of fabric used, add the mixed numbers. To add mixed numbers, add the whole number parts, and then add the fractions. The whole number parts add to 4. To add the fractions, find the least common denominator of 8 and 3, which is 24. Convert each fraction to an equivalent fraction with a denominator of 24: $\frac{3 \times 3}{8 \times 3} = \frac{9}{24}$ and $\frac{1 \times 8}{3 \times 8} = \frac{8}{24}$.

Now, add the numerators, and keep the denominator: $\frac{9}{24} + \frac{8}{24} + \frac{17}{24}$. The total fabric used is $4\frac{17}{24}$. If you chose B, you found a common denominator, but you forgot to multiply the numerators by the same factor that you had multiplied the denominators by. A common error when adding fractions would result in C. This fraction was obtained by the incorrect procedure of adding the numerators, and then adding the denominators.

2. K
Category: Operations
Difficulty: Medium
Getting to the Answer: To simplify this expression, first multiply the numerical coefficients to get $5 \times 6 \times 2 = 60$. To multiply the variable

terms, keep the base of the variable and add the exponents. Remember that x denotes x^1. Multiply the x variable terms: $x^3 \times x = x^{3+1} = x^4$. Multiply the y variable terms: $y^5 \times y^2 \times y = y^{5+2+1} = y^8$. The resultant expression is $60x^4y^8$.

If your answer was J, you fell into the common trap of multiplying the exponents instead of using the correct method of adding the exponents. If your answer was either F or G, you added the numerical coefficients instead of multiplying. If your answer was H, you did not include the exponents of 1 for the single terms of x and y.

3. C
Category: Proportions and Probability
Difficulty: Medium
Getting to the Answer: First, find the amount each person saves yearly. Brandon saves 6% of his $36,000 salary, or $0.06 \times 36,000 = \$2,160$ each year. Jacqui saves $200 every month, or $12 \times 200 = \$2,400$ each year. The difference, in dollars, of their savings is therefore $2,400 - 2,160 = \$240$.

Choice A reflects the *monthly* difference in their savings. If you chose D, you incorrectly found the difference between Brandon's yearly savings and Jacqui's *monthly* savings. Choice E indicates Brandon's monthly *salary* minus Jacqui's monthly savings.

4. H
Category: Proportions and Probability
Difficulty: Medium
Getting to the Answer: An average is found by taking the total sum of the terms and dividing it by the total number of terms. Therefore, the sum = (average) × (number of terms). For Mikhail to have an average for the five games of 180, the sum = $180 \times 5 = 900$. The first four scores total $190 + 200 + 145 + 180 = 715$. Therefore, his score for the fifth game must be $900 - 715 = 185$.

Choice F is just the average of the first four scores. Choice G is the average of the first four scores added and averaged with 180.

5. D
Category: Proportions and Probability
Difficulty: Low
Getting to the Answer: The amount of chromium is a part of the whole alloy. Use the formula Part = Percent × Whole. There are 262.5 pounds of chromium available, which must reflect at least 10.5% of the whole. Let w represent the whole amount of alloy that can be manufactured, and write the algebraic equation: $262.5 = 10.5\%w$ or $262.5 = 0.105w$. Divide both sides of the equation by 0.105: $w = \dfrac{262.5}{0.105}$ pounds of steel.

Choice A represents 10.5% of 262.5. If you chose B, you simply subtracted 10.5 from 262.5, without regard to the percent or the whole amount. Choice C is simply the amount of chromium. If you chose E, you set up the problem correctly but incorrectly converted 10.5% to the decimal 0.0105.

6. J
Category: Plane Geometry
Difficulty: Low
Getting to the Answer: A wallpaper border is a strip that surrounds the perimeter of the kitchen. The perimeter of a rectangle = 2(length + width). The kitchen has a length of 6.5 meters and a width of 4 meters, so the amount of border needed is $2(6.5 + 4) = 2(10.5) = 21$ meters.

Choice G represents a common mistake made when calculating perimeter. This answer would result from just adding the two dimensions and not multiplying by 2. Choice K is the area, not the perimeter, of the kitchen.

7. A
Category: Operations
Difficulty: Medium
Getting to the Answer: To find an equivalent for the given expression, use the distributive property. First, evaluate the inner parentheses according to the order of operations, or PEMDAS. Distribute the negative sign to $(y + z)$ to get $w(x - y - z)$. Next,

distribute the variable *w* to all terms in parentheses to get *wx* – *wy* – *wz*.

Choice B fails to distribute the negative sign to the *z* term. Choices C and D only distribute the *w* to the first term. Choice E incorrectly distributes *wx* to the (*y* + *z*) term.

8. G

Category: Variable Manipulation
Difficulty: Medium
Getting to the Answer: This is an equation with a variable on both sides. To solve, work to get the *n* terms isolated on one side of the equation and the numerical terms on the other side. Subtract 3*n* from both sides to get 6*n* – 3*n* – 4 = 3*n* – 3*n* + 24. Combine like terms: 3*n* – 4 = 24. Now, add 4 to both sides: 3*n* – 4 + 4 = 24 + 4, or 3*n* = 28. Finally, divide both sides by 3: $n = \frac{28}{3}$. Choice F reflects a common trap: forgetting to divide by 3. If you chose H or J, you incorrectly added 6*n* and 3*n* and possibly subtracted 4 from 24 instead of adding 4. Dividing incorrectly at the last step would have led you to K.

9. B

Category: Patterns, Logic, and Data
Difficulty: Medium
Getting to the Answer: In this arithmetic sequence, you can think of the terms as 26, 26 + *s*, 26 + *s* + *s*, and 26 + *s* + *s* + *s*. In this example, *s* represents the difference between successive terms. The final term is 53, so set up an algebraic equation: 26 + *s* + *s* + *s* = 53. Solve this equation for *s*, by first combining like terms: 26 + 3*s* = 53. Subtract 26 from both sides to get 26 – 26 + 3*s* = 53 – 26, or 3*s* = 27. Divide both sides by 3 to find that *s*, the difference between terms, is 9. Therefore, the terms are 26, 26 + 9, 26 + 9 + 9, and 53 or 26, 35, 44, and 53.

Choice D results from taking 53 – 26, dividing by 4, adding this value to each term, and rounding. In all of the incorrect answer choices, there is a common difference between second-first and then fourth-third, but it is different from the difference between the third and the second terms.

10. H

Category: Variable Manipulation
Difficulty: High
Getting to the Answer: First, solve the equation $5m^2 = 45$ for *m*. Once a value is obtained for *m*, substitute this into the expression to evaluate and find the answer. To solve the equation, divide both sides of the equation by 5 to get $m^2 = 9$. Take the square root of each side to get *m* = 3, or *m* = –3.

Now, evaluate the expression. Because the expression contains the radical $\sqrt{12m}$, and the expression must be a real number, reject the value of *m* = –3. (When a radicand, the expression under the radical sign, is negative, the number does not have a value in the set of real numbers.) Substitute 3 for *m* in the expression:

$$(3)^3 + \sqrt{12(3)} = 27 + \sqrt{36} = 27 + 6 = 33$$

If you chose G, you just found the value of m^3. You might have selected J if you interpreted the 12*m* under the radical sign as the number 12^3 instead of 12 × 3. If you chose K, you probably failed to take the square root of 9 when solving the equation and used the value of 9 for *m*.

11. D

Category: Plane Geometry
Difficulty: Medium

Getting to the Answer: First, convert the mixed number radius to a decimal: $3\frac{3}{5} = 3.6$. Substitute 3.6 into the formula to get $V = \frac{4}{3} \times \pi \times (3.6)^3$. Use the π key on your calculator. If your calculator has fractional capability and follows the correct order of operations, type the entry in as listed above. Otherwise, first find 3.6 to the third power. Multiply the result by 4, then divide by 3. Finally, multiply by π. In either case, the result is approximately 195.43, or 195 to the nearest cubic meter.

If you chose A or B, you multiplied the radius by 3, instead of taking the radius to the third power. For C and A, you incorrectly converted $3\frac{3}{5}$ to 3.35, a common trap. If you arrived at E, you first multiplied $\frac{4}{3} \times \pi \times (3.6)$ and then raised this value to the third power.

12. G
Category: Proportions and Probability
Difficulty: Low
Getting to the Answer: Probability is a ratio that compares the number of favorable, or desired, outcomes to the total number of outcomes. Probability is always a number between 0 and 1. In this question, the favorable outcome is the number of nuts that are NOT peanuts, or $6 + 8 = 14$. The total number of outcomes is $10 + 6 + 8 = 24$. The probability that the nut is NOT a peanut is $\frac{14}{24} = \frac{7}{12}$, in lowest terms.

Choice F is the probability that the nut IS a peanut. Choice H is the ratio that compares peanuts to other nuts.

13. C
Category: Patterns, Logic, and Data
Difficulty: High
Getting to the Answer: The matrices outline the corresponding number of people who shop at the store to the ratio, written as a decimal, of the number of people who will make purchases, *with reference to their age group*. A ratio written as a decimal is essentially a percentage. So following the correspondence yields $75 \times 0.20 = 15$ adolescent purchases, $100 \times 0.35 = 35$ adult purchases, and $30 \times 0.10 = 3$ senior-citizen purchases. This is a total of $15 + 35 + 3 = 53$ people making purchases.

Choice A represents the adolescent purchases. If you chose B, you took the total number of people in the store, 205, and multiplied by the ratio for adolescents, 0.20. Choice D adds the total number of people, 205; multiplies by the sum of the ratios, 0.65; and then rounds. Choice E is the total number of people who shop at the store, not the total number of purchases.

14. J
Category: Patterns, Logic, and Data
Difficulty: Medium
Getting to the Answer: To find an average, calculate the sum of the data and then divide by the total number of data items. According to the table, the number of hours that the country genre has a live disc jockey is 24, 7, and 16. Find the sum: $24 + 7 + 16 = 47$. Divide: $47 \div 3 = 15.67$, which is 16 to the nearest hour.

Choice F is the number of *entries*, not hours, for the country genre.
Choice G is the average number of hours for the classical genre.
Choice K is the average number of hours for the news genre.

15. D
Category: Patterns, Logic, and Data
Difficulty: High
Getting to the Answer: When you add up all of the hours, you get 205. Divide 205 by 8 hours, which is the number of hours in each shift: $205 \div 8 = 25.625$. Round up to 26 because the question asks for the minimum number of disk jockeys needed to cover all genres and mediums if each works an eight-hour shift.

A common trap would be C because the answer would round down to 25 disc jockeys, but this would fall short of the requirement to cover all of the hours.

Choice E reflects the total number of hours needed. Choice A is the number of 24-hour segments that require a live disc jockey.

16. G
Category: Patterns, Logic, and Data
Difficulty: Medium
Getting to the Answer: To find the missing value, add the monomials in the first row: $m + -4m + 3m = 0$. This first row sums to zero. To be sure, check the rightmost column: $3m + -2m + -m = 0$. Every row, column, and diagonal must sum to 0. The first

column must therefore be $m + 2m + \square = 0$, or $3m + \square = 0$. Isolate the missing term on one side of the equation by subtracting $3m$ from both sides: $\square = -3m$.

If your choice was H, you ignored the m variable in the term. If your choice was F, J, or K, you may have just looked at the first column and the last row and found a value that would work with those, without considering the other rows, columns, and diagonals.

17. E
Category: Number Properties
Difficulty: Medium
Getting to the Answer: The algebraic expression xy means to multiply the point's x-value by its y-value. If the product is positive, then the x and y factors are either both positive or both negative, according to the rules for multiplying signed numbers. Positive x-coordinates are to the right of the origin. Positive y-coordinates are above the origin. In quadrant I, both coordinates are positive, and in quadrant III, both coordinates are negative. In quadrant II, the x-coordinate is negative (to the left of the origin), and the y-coordinate is positive (above the origin). In quadrant IV, the x-coordinate is positive (to the right of the origin), and the y-coordinate is negative (below the origin).

18. J
Category: Patterns, Logic, and Data
Difficulty: Medium
Getting to the Answer: The number of distinct lunches is determined by the fundamental counting principle. The counting principle directs you to multiply the different choices together to find the total number of combinations: $7 \times 3 \times 4 = 84$. If you consider just the sandwiches and soups alone, each sandwich can be paired with one of three soups, so there would be $7 \times 3 = 21$ different alternatives. These 21 alternatives would then become $21 \times 4 = 84$ different meals, because each of these 21 meals could be combined with four different drink choices.

A common trap answer is G, where the numbers are added together, instead of multiplied. Choice F is the number of sandwiches available, not the number of distinct meals. Choice H reflects the number of distinct choices of just sandwich and soup.

19. A
Category: Proportions and Probability
Difficulty: Low
Getting to the Answer: The question describes a comparison of the number of female to male students. This is a ratio—the ratio of female to male students is 5 to 3, or $\frac{5}{3}$. Let n represent the number of female students. Set up the proportion $\frac{5}{3} = \frac{n}{6,000}$ and cross multiply to get $3n = 5 \times 6,000$, or $3n = 30,000$. Divide both sides by 3 to get $n = 10,000$ females.

If you chose B, you may have used rounding and incorrectly considered the ratio to be twice as many females as males. Choice C represents the total number of students at the university. If you chose D or E, you may have stopped after multiplying 6,000 by 3 or by 5, respectively.

20. H
Category: Plane Geometry
Difficulty: Medium
Getting to the Answer: Draw a diagram of a rectangle:

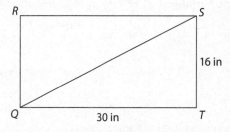

Because a rectangle has four right angles, you can treat the diagonal, QS, as the hypotenuse of a right triangle with legs of 16 and 30 inches. Use the Pythagorean theorem to solve for the length of the hypotenuse. If c represents the length of the hypotenuse and a and b represent the length of the legs, then $a^2 + b^2 = c^2$. Substitute into the formula:

$$c^2 = 16^2 + 30^2$$
$$c^2 = 256 + 900$$
$$c^2 = 1,156$$

Take the square root of both sides of the equation to find that $c = 34$ inches.

If you chose F, you used 30 inches for c (the hypotenuse) in the formula, and then solved for one of the legs. Choice G adds the two dimensions and divides by 2. If you chose J, you incorrectly divided by 2 instead of taking the square root; for K, you added the squares but did not take the square root of the sum.

21. A

Category: Variable Manipulation
Difficulty: Medium
Getting to the Answer: Choice (A) is not equivalent to $5n + 1$—it is the reciprocal. If you chose B, you may have incorrectly simplified by not multiplying 5×2. The expression simplifies as $5n + 10 - 9$, or $5n + 1$. Choice C is also equivalent to $5n + 1$—when you divide fractions, you multiply by the reciprocal of the denominator, and

$$\frac{1}{1} \div \frac{1}{5n+1} = \frac{1}{1} \times \frac{5n+1}{1} = 5n + 1.$$

If you chose either D or E, you may have thought that they could not be equivalent because they have a squared variable. But when D is factored and simplified, you can see it is equivalent: $\frac{n(5n+1)}{n} = 5n + 1$.

The same is true for E: $\frac{(5n+1)(5n-1)}{5n-1} = 5n + 1$.

22. J

Category: Variable Manipulation
Difficulty: Medium
Getting to the Answer: Each of the answer choices is in the form $y = ...$, so solve for y in terms of x. Isolate y on one side of the equation. First, subtract $3x$ from both sides: $3x - 3x + 2y = -3x + 16$. Combine

like terms to get $2y = -3x + 16$. Now, divide all terms on both sides by 2: $y = -\frac{3}{2}x + 8$.

In F, the numeric term 16 is not divided by 2. Choices G and K have the reciprocal of the coefficient of x. In H, $3x$ was added to both sides of the equation instead of subtracted, to get the incorrect term of $+\frac{3}{2}x$.

23. E

Category: Variable Manipulation
Difficulty: High
Getting to the Answer: To solve a quadratic equation, first factor the trinomial in the form $ax^2 + bx + c$. Because the c term is positive and the b term is negative, the factors will be $(x - \#)(x - \#)$. Look for factors of 75 that when added together will equal 20, the b coefficient. Some factor possibilities for 75 are 1 and 75, 3 and 25, and 5 and 15. Only the factors 5 and 15 will add to 20. The equation, after factoring, becomes $(x - 5)(x - 15) = 0$. The solutions are the values of x that result in either of the factors equaling 0: $x = 5$ or $x = 15$.

The common traps are A or B where you might have quickly looked at the factors and thought the answers were either −5 or −15. If you chose D, you may have thought the only factors of 75 were 3 and 25 and therefore chosen 3 as a solution. If you chose C, you may have ignored the term of 75 and found a solution of 0.

24. H

Category: Trigonometry
Difficulty: Medium
Getting to the Answer: The cosine (cos) ratio is the ratio of the side adjacent to angle N to the hypotenuse of the right triangle. The $\cos N = \frac{12}{13}$.

Choice F is the sine (sin) ratio of angle N. Choice G is the tangent (tan) ratio of angle N. Choice J is the secant (sec), or the reciprocal of the cos, to angle N. Choice K is the cosecant (csc), or the reciprocal of the sin, to angle N.

25. C
Category: Plane Geometry
Difficulty: Medium
Getting to the Answer: Because chord *AB* passes through the center, it is a diameter of the circle, and segment *OB* is a radius, equal to 7 cm. Because *OC* is perpendicular to *AB*, a right angle is formed. To find the length of chord *CB*, note that it is the hypotenuse of right triangle $\triangle COB$, with legs that each measure 7 cm. Because the legs have the same measure, this is a special right triangle, the 45°-45°-90° right triangle, and the sides are in the ratio of $n : n : n\sqrt{2}$. Chord *BC* is therefore $7\sqrt{2} \oplus 9.899$, or 9.9 to the nearest tenth of a centimeter. Alternately, you could have used the Pythagorean theorem, $a^2 + b^2 = c^2$, where $a = b = 7$:

$$7^2 + 7^2 = c^2$$
$$49 + 49 = c^2$$
$$c = \sqrt{98} \approx 9.9 \text{ cm}$$

If your answer was A, you used the Pythagorean theorem but evaluated 7^2 as 7×2, instead of 7×7. This is a common trap. Choice B is the length of the legs, not the hypotenuse. Choice D is $7\sqrt{3}$. Choice E is the length of the diameter of the circle.

26. F
Category: Variable Manipulation
Difficulty: Medium
Getting to the Answer: Substitute the value of 86 into the formula for *F*, the degrees in Fahrenheit, to get $86 = \frac{9}{5}C + 32$. Subtract 32 from both sides:

$$86 - 32 = \frac{9}{5}C + 32 - 32$$
$$54 = \frac{9}{5}C$$

Now, multiply both sides by the reciprocal of $\frac{9}{5}$ to isolate *C*:

$$\frac{5}{9} \times 54 = \frac{5}{9} \times \frac{9}{5} \times C$$
$$30 = C$$

If you chose G, you forgot to multiply by the reciprocal to get rid of the fraction on the right side of the equation. Choice H incorrectly multiplies 86 by $\frac{5}{9}$ first, then adds 32. Choice J is the degrees in Fahrenheit. Choice K would be the degrees in Fahrenheit of 86 degrees Celsius.

27. D
Category: Plane Geometry
Difficulty: Medium
Getting to the Answer: A swimming pool that is the same depth in all parts is a rectangular solid. The amount of water in the pool is the volume of the water. Use the formula $V = lwh$, and substitute in the volume, length, and width given in the problem. $14,375 = 50 \times 25 \times h$, or $14,375 = 1,250h$. Divide both sides of the equation by 1,250, to get $11.5 = h$. The depth is between 11 and 12 meters.

28. F
Category: Trigonometry
Difficulty: Medium
Getting to the Answer: The tangent is the ratio of the side opposite to the given angle over the side adjacent to the given angle. Segment *EF* is the side opposite to angle *D*, so call this side *m*. Segment *DE*, the adjacent side to angle *D*, equals 42 inches. Set up the equation:

$$\frac{5}{8} = \frac{m}{42}$$
$$(42)(5) = 8m$$
$$210 = 8m$$
$$m = 26.3$$

If you chose G, you added 42 and $\frac{5}{8}$. Choice H reflects the length of side *DF*, the hypotenuse of the right triangle. Choice J incorrectly uses 42 as the opposite side and side *EF* as the adjacent side.

29. B
Category: Proportions and Probability
Difficulty: Medium
Getting to the Answer: The fraction of the people who were sophomores would be the ratio of the number of sophomores to the total number of people at the prom. There were 30 sophomores and a total of $20 + 30 + 70 + 200 = 320$ people at the prom. The fraction is $\dfrac{30}{320} = \dfrac{3}{32}$.

Choice A is the fraction of the attendees who were freshmen. Choice C is the ratio of sophomores to those who are NOT sophomores. Choice D is the ratio of sophomores to seniors. Choice E is a common trap—it compares the number of sophomores to 100, instead of to the total number of students in attendance.

30. F
Category: Number Properties
Difficulty: Low
Getting to the Answer: This problem requires you to understand that the sum of the parts of a segment is equal to the whole segment. It is given that X is the midpoint of segment WZ. Because the length of $WZ = 44$ cm, the length of WX is one-half of this, or 22 cm. From the relative positions of the points in the segment, $WX + XY = WY$, or alternately, $WY - WX = XY$. It is given that $WY = 26$ and calculated that WX is 22. Therefore, $XY = 26 - 22$, or 4 centimeters.

If you chose K, you just added the two numbers given in the problem. Choice J is the length of one-half of segment WZ, or the length of WX. If your answer was H, you subtracted the two numbers given in the problem. Choice G is one-half of segment WY.

31. C
Category: Variable Manipulation
Difficulty: Medium
Getting to the Answer: Find the point of intersection of two lines by solving the system of equations.

Use the elimination method by lining up the equations by like terms:

$$5x + y = 7$$
$$2x + 3y = 8$$

The problem asks for the x-coordinate, so multiply one of the equations so that when they are combined, the y-values are eliminated. If you multiply all terms in the top equation by -3, when you combine them, the y-values will be eliminated:

$$-3(5x + y = 7) \qquad -15x - 3y = -21$$
$$2x + 3y = 8 \qquad\qquad 2x + 3y = 8$$

Combine like terms in the resulting equations: $(-15x + 2x) + (-3y + 3y) = -21 + 8$, or $-13x = -13$. Now, divide both sides of this simpler equation by -13 to get $x = 1$.

If you chose A, you probably divided the negative numbers incorrectly to get -1. Choice B may have resulted from only multiplying the y by -3 and not multiplying the terms of $5x$ and 7, and getting the result of $7x = 15$, or $x = \dfrac{15}{7}$. Choice D is the y-coordinate of the intersection of the two lines.

32. K
Category: Variable Manipulation
Difficulty: Medium
Getting to the Answer: To solve the equation for b, isolate b on one side of the equation. First, add 8 to both sides of the equation: $a + 8 = 2b - 8 + 8$, or $a + 8 = 2b$. Now, divide both sides by 2 to get $b = \dfrac{a + 8}{2}$.

If your answer was F, you forgot to divide a by 2. In G, you exchanged the variable a for the variable b, instead of solving for b. Choice H is similar to G, but the subtraction was changed to addition. In J, you may have subtracted 8 from both sides instead of adding 8.

33. D
Category: Plane Geometry
Difficulty: Low
Getting to the Answer: The area of a parallelogram is $A = bh$, where height h is the length of the perpendicular segment to one of the sides of the parallelogram. In the figure, segment RT, of length $9 + 5$, or 14 mm, is the base and the dotted segment, of length 12 mm, is the height. The area is $14 \times 12 = 168$ mm^2.

Choice A is the area of the little triangle at the top, not the parallelogram. If you chose B, you added the given numbers, without recognizing that the problem is asking for area. Choice C is the perimeter of the parallelogram. Choice E reflects a common error, where you multiplied the sides together instead of multiplying the base times the height.

34. F
Category: Variable Manipulation
Difficulty: Medium
Getting to the Answer: The problem asks you to evaluate $(x + y)^3$, so manipulate the given equation to isolate $x + y$ on one side of the equation. Once you have this value, cube it to find the answer to the problem. For the given equation $x = -(y + 3)$, first distribute the negative sign on the right-hand side to get $x = -y - 3$. Now add y to both sides of the equation: $x + y = -y + y - 3$. Combine like terms to arrive at $x + y = -3$. Now substitute -3 for $(x + y)$ in the expression to get $(-3)^3 = -3 \times -3 \times -3 = -27$.

Choice G is a common trap: evaluating $(-3)^3$ as $-3 \times 3 = -9$. Choices H and J result from not applying integer multiplication rules for negative numbers.

35. E
Category: Plane Geometry
Difficulty: High
Getting to the Answer: Because all streets and avenues shown intersect at right angles, the map is a rectangle in which opposite sides have the same measures. To find the location halfway between H and S, first think of the corner of Oak and 10th as

the origin, or (0, 0). Just as in coordinate geometry, the first ordered pair represents the east-west direction, and the second ordered pair represents the north-south direction. The distance from the origin at Oak Street to the school is 5 miles east. The distance from the origin at 10th Avenue to the hospital is 8 miles north. The new station will be halfway between these coordinates, or $\frac{5}{2} = 2.5$ miles east of the origin and $\frac{8}{2} = 4$ miles north of the origin.

To drive from F to the new fire station, you would have to drive $8 - 2.5 = 5.5$ miles west on Main Street, then $10 - 4 = 6$ miles south on Elm Street (the first 2 miles south to get to 2nd Avenue, and then 4 more miles south to be halfway between the hospital and the school). Choice A is the directions to the new fire station starting from the origin at Oak and 10th. Choice B is the directions to the new fire station starting from the school. Choice C is the directions from the corner of Main and Oak to the new station. If you answered D, you forgot to add in the 2 miles on Elm Street to get from Main to 2nd Avenue.

36. H
Category: Variable Manipulation
Difficulty: Medium
Getting to the Answer: Consecutive integers are integers that differ by 1, such as 3, 4, 5. Consecutive odd integers are odd integers that differ by 2, such as 7, 9, 11, 13. Because the answer choices use the variable x, let x represent the smaller of the consecutive odd integers, so $(x + 2)$ would be the larger of the integers. Four times the larger is represented by $4(x + 2)$ and twice the smaller by $2x$. The key word *difference* means to subtract the smaller from the larger, and the key word *is* means "equal." The equation is $4(x + 2) - 2x = 36$.

Choice F represents four times a number minus twice the same number. Choice G is incorrect because it represents two consecutive integers rather than two consecutive *odd* integers. Choice J is an equation for two integers that differ by 3, which means that the numbers are too far apart on the number line to be consecutive odd integers. Choice K is an equation for the difference between 36 and four times the smaller integer.

37. C

Category: Plane Geometry
Difficulty: Low
Getting to the Answer: The question states that the telephone pole is perpendicular to the ground and a wire is attached to the pole. This will result in a right triangle. It helps to draw a quick figure to represent the situation. The thicker side of the triangle represents the telephone pole, and the hypotenuse is the wire:

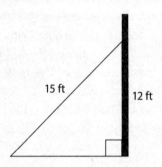

To find out how far the anchor of the supporting wire is from the base of the telephone pole, solve for the length of the missing leg. Use the Pythagorean theorem, which is $a^2 + b^2 = hypotenuse^2$. Let b represent the missing leg, and substitute in the given values to get $12^2 + b^2 = 15^2$, or $144 + b^2 = 225$. Subtract 144 from both sides: $b^2 = 81$. To solve for b, take the square root of both sides: $\sqrt{b^2} = \sqrt{81}$, so $b = 9$ or -9. A length cannot be negative, so the length is 9 ft.

Choice A subtracts $15 - 12$ to get 3. If you chose B, you may have thought that 15^2 meant 15×2 and calculated $30 - 24 = 6$. Choice D is the length up the pole, and E is the length of the wire.

38. H

Category: Plane Geometry
Difficulty: Medium
Getting to the Answer: The area of a circle is $A = \pi r^2$, where r is the radius of the circle. Use the equation $100\pi = \pi r^2$ and solve for r by dividing both sides by π: $100 = r^2$. If you take the square root of both sides, then $r = 10$ or -10. Reject the -10 value, because a radius length cannot be negative. The radius of the circle is 10, so the diameter of the circle, which is the same as the length of a side of the square, is $2 \times 10 = 20$ units.

Choice F is the area of the square. Choice G is r^2. Choosing J is a common error that mistakes the radius of the circle for the side of the square.

39. C

Category: Proportions and Probability
Difficulty: Medium
Getting to the Answer: When figures are similar, the side lengths are in proportion. Let x represent the missing side length, and set up the proportion of shorter side to longer side: $\dfrac{3}{8} = \dfrac{2}{x}$.
Cross multiply to get $3x = 16$. Divide both sides by 3 to get $x = 16 \div 3 \approx 5.3$, to the nearest tenth of an inch.

If you chose A or B, you set up the proportion incorrectly—make sure to match up the long sides and the short sides on the same side of the fraction. Choice D is the most common error made with similar figures, resulting if you assumed that because $3 - 1 = 2$, the missing side was $8 - 1 = 7$. Similar figures have sides that are in proportion, which is not an additive relationship.

40. J

Category: Plane Geometry
Difficulty: Medium
Getting to the Answer: The figure shown is a parallelogram. Extend the top side out to make a parallel line to line *UZ*. Line *WY* is a transversal to the parallel

lines, forming alternate interior angles, ∠*XWY* and ∠*WYV*, which have the same measures of 50°. Line *WV* is another transversal line to the parallel lines, forming alternate interior angles ∠*UVW* and ∠*VWX*. Because they have the same measure, ∠*VWX* = 150°. In addition, ∠*VWX* and ∠*VYX* have the same measure—they are opposite angles in a parallelogram. Now ∠*VYX* − ∠*WYV* = ∠*WYX*, or 150 − 50 = 100°.

If your answer was H, you incorrectly thought that ∠*WYX* had the same measure as ∠*XWY*. Choice K is the measure of ∠*VYX*, not ∠*WYX*.

41. D
Category: Plane Geometry
Difficulty: Medium
Getting to the Answer: The key to solving this problem is to simplify the drawing, knowing that you are looking for the perimeter. This figure, for perimeter purposes, can be thought of as a rectangle—just lower all the bottom pieces and move all left pieces to the right and you have a rectangle, with side lengths of 40 centimeters, and top/bottom lengths of 12 + 5 + 4 = 21 centimeters:

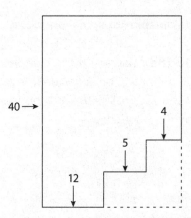

The perimeter is two times the length plus two times the width, or 2(40) + 2(21) = 80 + 42 = 122 centimeters.

Choice A is the measure of the length. Choice B is just the measure of two sides of the figure (just the numbers that are shown).

42. G
Category: Proportions and Probability
Difficulty: High
Getting to the Answer: Convert the fractions into decimal equivalents and remember that the key word *of* means to multiply. Because $\frac{3}{4}$ of the 3,500 eligible voters cast a vote, this is 0.75 × 3,500 = 2,625 votes that were cast at the site. Three-fifths of these votes were for Martinez, or 0.6 × 2,625 = 1,575 votes for Martinez.

If you answered F, you followed the correct procedure, but incorrectly converted the fractions. Choice H is $\frac{3}{5}$ of all the eligible voters. Choice J is $\frac{3}{4}$ of the eligible voters. Choice K is the sum of H and J.

43. A
Category: Number Properties
Difficulty: Medium
Getting to the Answer: To find the greatest common factor, find all factor pieces that the two expressions have in common. In this case, the factors in common are *a*, *a*, *a*, and *b*, or a^3b. It is given that the greatest common factor is 54, so think of a cubic number that is a factor of 54. The first cubic numbers are 1^3 (1), 2^3 (8), and 3^3 (27). Twenty-seven is a factor of 54: 27 × 2 = 54, so a possible value for *b* is 2.

Choice B is the value of the variable *a*. Choice C, 6, is a factor of 54, but that leaves the value of 9 for *a*, and 9 is not a perfect cube. The same reasoning would eliminate D. Choice E is the value of a^3.

44. K
Category: Proportions and Probability
Difficulty: Medium
Getting to the Answer: To tackle this problem, break it up into its parts. First, find the value of *x*, given that 40% of *x* is 70. The key word *of* means to multiply. Write this as the equation 0.40*x* = 70;

divide both sides by 0.40 to get $x = 175$. Now find 160% of x, or $1.60 \times 175 = 280$.

Choice F is 40% of 70. Choice G is 160% of 28, the incorrect value from F. Choice H is 160% of 70. A common trap is J, which is the value of the variable x.

45. C
Category: Coordinate Geometry
Difficulty: Medium
Getting to the Answer: To find the length of segment MN, use the distance formula: $d = \sqrt{(x_2 - x_1)^2 + (y_2 - y_1)^2}$. Substitute in the point values:

$$d = \sqrt{(6 - 2)^2 + (5 - 3)^2}$$
$$d = \sqrt{4^2 + 2^2}$$
$$d = \sqrt{20} = \sqrt{4} \times \sqrt{5} = 2\sqrt{5}$$

If you chose A, you may have used the distance formula incorrectly, using $(y_1 - x_1)$ and $(y_2 - x_2)$ instead of finding the difference between the x- and y-coordinates. Choice B multiplies by 2 instead of raising to the second power in the formula. Choice D is just the sum of the differences between the x- and y-coordinates. If your answer was E, you forgot to take the square root of 20, as indicated by the distance formula.

46. J
Category: Plane Geometry
Difficulty: Low
Getting to the Answer: If the sides are in the ratio of 5:7, the perimeter will be in this exact same ratio. When finding a perimeter, you add up the sides. Perimeter is measured in single units, just as is the side length. Therefore, the ratio will not change. If you are unsure about this fact, assign values and actually calculate the perimeters. Consider the smaller square to have sides $5s$ in length and the larger square to have sides $7s$ in length. The smaller square has a perimeter of $4 \times 5s = 20s$, and the larger $4 \times 7s = 28s$. The ratio $20s:28s$ is equivalent to 5:7, after dividing both terms of the ratio by $4s$.

If you chose F, you may have thought you needed to subtract $7 - 5 = 2$, to get the (incorrect) ratio 1:2. Likewise, G adds $7 + 5 = 12$. Choice H multiplies $7 \times 5 = 35$. Choice K confuses area and perimeter—the ratio of the *areas* is 25:49.

47. E
Category: Plane Geometry
Difficulty: Medium
Getting to the Answer: The equation of a circle, when you know the coordinates of the center (h,k) and the radius (r), is given by $(x - h)^2 + (y - k)^2 = r^2$. Substitute in the given values to get $(x - (-2))^2 + (y - 3)^2 = 9^2$. This simplifies to $(x + 2)^2 + (y - 3)^2 = 81$.

There are two common traps when finding the equation of a circle. One trap is to forget to square the radius, as in B. The other common trap is adding h and k to x and y, instead of subtracting, as in C. Choice A is both of these traps together. Choice D incorrectly takes the square root of the radius, instead of squaring the radius.

48. H
Category: Variable Manipulation
Difficulty: High
Getting to the Answer: In the complex number system, i^2 is defined to be equal to -1, as you are told in the question stem. Use the distributive property to multiply the fraction:

$$\frac{3}{5 - i} \times \frac{5 + i}{5 + i} = \frac{(3 \times 5) + 3i}{5^2 + 5i - 5i - i^2}$$
$$= \frac{15 + 3i}{25 - (-1)} = \frac{15 + 3i}{26}$$

If your answer was F, you may have cancelled incorrectly to simplify. Choice G reflects a common error when multiplying complex numbers: $25 - i^2$ was incorrectly interpreted as $25 - 1 = 24$. In J, the 3 in the numerator was not distributed to the i term. Choice K is the result of two errors—the common error described in G and the error in J.

49. C
Category: Plane Geometry
Difficulty: Low
Getting to the Answer: One way to solve this problem is to make a table. Each time the number of sides goes up by 1, the sum of the angles goes up by 180°. Make a third column in the table to discover a relationship.

Number of Sides	Sum of the Angles	
3	180°	180° × 1
4	360°	180° × 2
5	540°	180° × 3
6	720°	180° × 4

Notice that to find the sum of the angles, you can multiply 180 times 2 less than the number of sides of the polygon. This is (C).

If you chose A, you may have just considered the triangle and assumed that the relationship was 60n. If your answer was B, you may have noticed that the number of degrees rose by 180°, but this did not consider the sides of the polygons. Choice D is a relationship that works for the three-sided and six-sided polygons, but not the other two.

50. G
Category: Patterns, Logic, and Data
Difficulty: Medium
Getting to the Answer: The key to solving this problem is to first assume that there are no students who have both a cell phone and an MP3 player. If this were the case, then there would be 35 + 18 = 53 students polled. The problem states that 50 students were polled, so therefore at least 3 students have both electronic devices. This is the minimum number of students who own both.

If you chose F, you may have ignored the fact that 50 students were polled. Choice H is the difference between the number of cell phone owners and MP3 owners. Choice J is a possible number of students who own *only* a cell phone. Choice K is the sum of 35 and 18.

51. A
Category: Variable Manipulation
Difficulty: Medium
Getting to the Answer: To solve this inequality, attempt to get the variable on one side of the inequality by adding 4n to both sides: $-4n + 4n + 3 > -4n + 4n + 1$. Combine like terms to get 3 > 1. This inequality is always true for the set of real numbers.

If you chose answer B or C, you may have thought that the term $-4n$ would limit the set of solutions. If your answer was D or E, you may have mistakenly added $-4n$ to both sides and added 3 to both sides to get $-8n > 4$, and then solved for n.

52. H
Category: Patterns, Logic, and Data
Difficulty: High
Getting to the Answer: Make this question easier to visualize by naming the five people:

   A B C D E

Now you only need to identify the number of different combinations.

   AB, AC, AD, AE

   BC, BD, BE

   CD, CE

   DE

There are 10 distinct combinations, meaning 10 total handshakes.

If you chose F, you may have seen that 4 people have 2 more handshakes than other people and assumed this was the pattern for more people. If you chose G, you may have thought that the pattern in handshakes was multiples of 3. The key is to have a clear way to visualize the information given.

53. D
Category: Proportions and Probability
Difficulty: Medium
Getting to the Answer: First, determine the percentage in the category Miscellaneous. The total percentage must sum to 100%, so the percentage for Miscellaneous is 100 − 23 − 5 − 22 −18 = 32%. To find the number of degrees in a circle graph that corresponds with 32%, set up the ratio, where x represents the number of degrees for the Miscellaneous category. Recall that there are 360° in a circle: $\frac{32}{100} = \frac{x}{360}$. Cross multiply to get 32 × 360 = 100x, or 11,520 = 100x. Divide both sides by 100 to get $x = 115°$, rounded to the nearest degree.

Choice A is a common trap that represents the percentage, not the number of degrees in a circle graph. If your answer was B, you thought that there were 180° in a circle. Choice C is the percentage of categories that are *not* Miscellaneous, and E is the number of degrees that are *not* Miscellaneous.

54. K
Category: Trigonometry
Difficulty: High
Getting to the Answer: The information $\frac{\pi}{2} < \theta < \pi$ tells you that the angle is in quadrant II of the coordinate plane. In quadrant II, the sin values are positive. So the answer must be positive. Eliminate F, G, and H. You are given the value of tan θ, which is the ratio of the opposite side to the adjacent side of a right triangle. Sketch this triangle, using leg lengths of 4 and 3:

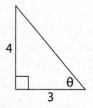

This is a special right triangle, the 3-4-5 Pythagorean triple, so the hypotenuse is 5 units in length. The sin of an angle is the ratio of the length of the opposite side to the length of the hypotenuse, or $\frac{4}{5}$.

If you chose F, you may have ignored the fact that the angle is in quadrant II and thought that the sin value would be negative. Choice G is the cotangent of the angle. Choices H and J are cosine values for the angle for quadrants II and I, respectively.

55. A
Category: Coordinate Geometry
Difficulty: Medium
Getting to the Answer: Look at the graphed boundary lines for the inequalities. Find the equation for these boundary lines and then determine whether the shading represents less than or greater than these boundary lines. The horizontal line has a slope of 0 and a y-intercept (where the line crosses the y-axis) of 6, so the equation of this boundary line is $y = 6$. It is shaded below this line, so the inequality is $y < 6$. The slanted line has a slope with a change in y-values of 3 and a change in x- values of 1, so the slope is $\frac{3}{1} = 3$. The y-intercept is −5. The line is increasing, so the slope is positive. The shading is greater than, or above, this boundary line, so the inequality is $y > 3x − 5$. If you chose B, you fell into a common trap of interpreting the horizontal boundary line equation to be $x < 6$. Choice C is another common error, representing the idea that the shading represents less than, or below, the slanted line. Choice D interprets the slope as −3. Negative slopes decrease, or slant downward, when going from left to right. Choice E represents a slope of $\frac{1}{3}$, not the correct slope of 3. A slope of $\frac{1}{3}$ would mean for every change of 1 in the y-values, the x-values would change by 3.

56. J

Category: Variable Manipulation

Difficulty: High

Getting to the Answer: The question asks you to evaluate the function $f(x)$, replacing x with $(x + c)$. Replace any instance of x in the function definition with $x + c$. This means that $2(x + 7)$ will be $2(x + c + 7)$. Use the distributive property and multiply each term in parentheses by 2 to get $2x + 2c + 2 \times 7$, or $2x + 2c + 14$.

In F, the 2 was not distributed to the constant term 7. Choice G only multiplies the 2 by the first term in the parentheses. In H and K, the c term was just added onto the end of the function definition, instead of replacing the x with $(x + c)$.

57. B

Category: Coordinate Geometry

Difficulty: Medium

Getting to the Answer: First, simplify the equation by simplifying the fraction on the right-hand side. Factor the numerator and then cancel the $(x - 2)$ factor from the numerator and denominator:

$$\frac{2x^2 - 8}{x - 2} = \frac{2(x^2 - 4)}{x - 2} = \frac{2(x + 2)(x - 2)}{x - 2} = 2(x + 2)$$

The simplified equation is $y = 2(x + 2)$, or $y = 2x + 4$. This equation is now in slope-intercept form, where the y-intercept is 4 and the slope is $\frac{2}{1}$. Choice (B) is the correct graph because the line has a slope of 2 and crosses the y-axis at 4.

If you ignored the denominator in the given equation, then you incorrectly chose A, the graph of the quadratic $y = 2x^2 - 8$.

Choice C is the graph of the equation $y = \frac{1}{2}x + 4$. If this was your choice, you may have misinterpreted the slope of a line. Choice D is the graph of a quadratic function, not the correct linear function. You cannot assume a function is a quadratic just because you see a variable that is squared; you must first try

to simplify the equation. Choice E is the graph of the linear function $y = -2x + 4$.

58. F

Category: Coordinate Geometry

Difficulty: Medium

Getting to the Answer: This problem tests your knowledge of line reflections in the coordinate plane.

When you reflect a point or a figure over the y-axis, the x-coordinate of each point is the opposite sign, and the y-coordinate stays the same. The reflection of the point Q (r,s) after a reflection over the y-axis is therefore Q' $(-r,s)$.

Choice G would be the result of a reflection over the y-axis, followed by a reflection over the x-axis. Choice H is incorrect—the x- and y-coordinates were switched. Choice J is a common trap that represents a reflection over the x-axis.

59. C

Category: Variable Manipulation

Difficulty: High

Getting to the Answer: The problem is asking what is the value of g in terms of h. The two given equations do not show a direct relationship between g and h, so you must solve for q in the second equation to get q in terms of h, and then substitute this value for q in the first equation. To solve for q in the second equation, isolate q by first adding 8 to both sides of the equation: $h + 8 = 2q - 8 + 8$, or $h + 8 = 2q$. Divide both sides by 2 to get $\frac{h + 8}{2} = q$.

Use this value of q in the first equation: $g = 4q + 3$ becomes $g = \frac{4(h + 8)}{2} + 3$.

Factor out a 2 from the numerator and the denominator of the first term to get $g = 2(h + 8) + 3$. Multiply the terms in parentheses by 2, so $g = 2h + 16 + 3$, or $g = 2h + 19$.

Choice A is the value of *q* in terms of *h* from the second equation. In B, the constant term 3 in the first equation was incorrectly added to the numerator of the transformed first equation, and the 4 was not distributed to both terms of *h* and 8. In D, the 2 was factored out correctly, but the remaining 2 was not distributed to the constant term of 8. Choice E is the value of *q*, not *h*, in terms of *g* from the first equation.

60. H

Category: Trigonometry

Difficulty: High

Getting to the Answer: In this problem, you are asked to use the formula $\cos(\alpha + \beta) = \cos(\alpha)\cos(\beta) - \sin(\alpha)\sin(\beta)$ and the table of values to find the value of $\cos(75°) = \cos(30° + 45°)$. Substitute 30° for α and 45° for β to get: $\cos(30°)\cos(45°) - \sin(30°)\sin(45°)$. Now use the table to replace each sin or cos with the corresponding values in the table:

$\frac{\sqrt{3}}{2} \times \frac{\sqrt{2}}{2} - \frac{1}{2} \times \frac{\sqrt{2}}{2}$. Using order of operations, multiply and then subtract the numerators and keep the denominator: $\frac{\sqrt{6}}{4} - \frac{\sqrt{2}}{4} = \frac{\sqrt{6} - \sqrt{2}}{4}$. Alternately, you could use your calculator to find the value of the $\cos(75°) \approx 0.2588$, and then test each answer choice to find the answer closest to this value. Choice (H) will be the only value to equal the $\cos(75°)$.

If you chose F or K, you probably used the wrong values in the table. In G, you used the wrong values in the table and also forgot to multiply the denominators, resulting in a denominator of 2 instead of 4. Choice J is a common trap—you correctly used the table but did not multiply the denominators to get a denominator of 4.

READING TEST

PASSAGE I

1. D

Category: Inference

Difficulty: Medium

Getting to the Answer: The question is asking about Dave's opinion specifically. Throughout the passage, Dave describes the problems with comparison between twins, and many of his comments to Emily are also focused on comparing himself to his twin. Choice (D) is correct because it mentions this competition and implies that it makes their relationship more difficult. Choice A is extreme, B implies that their relationship is stronger than it is, and C is not supported by the text because Emily doesn't seem to be able to convince Dave to make more of an effort.

2. H

Category: Detail

Difficulty: Low

Getting to the Answer: Emily has a good relationship with both brothers; she has an enjoyable conversation with Bruce and works to make Dave feel better. Also, she wants the brothers to be closer than they are. Because it reflects these details, (H) is the correct answer. Choice F is the opposite; Emily is very attentive, and G and J are both extreme and negative distortions of Emily's desire to help relations between the brothers.

3. B

Category: Detail

Difficulty: Medium

Getting to the Answer: This question is asking you to identify which answer choice is NOT represented in the passage, so the first step is to eliminate choices that ARE contained in the passage. In the first paragraph, Dave is envious of the reaction his wife has when talking to Bruce, eliminating A. The paragraph about Dave's reaction to the picture captures his negative feelings regarding the difference in their popularity, eliminating C. The final conversation shows Dave as doubtful of Bruce's need for his approval, eliminating D. This leaves (B), which is not found in the passage and is therefore the correct answer.

4. J
Category: Function
Difficulty: Medium
Getting to the Answer: The first paragraph starts with a description of Emily on the phone, but the focus quickly shifts to Dave's reaction. It then moves to Dave making some points about his brother's popularity and questioning whether his own wife has ever reacted so favorably to him. Choice (J) summarizes this well. Choices F and H are not found in the passage, and G occurs much later.

5. D
Category: Inference
Difficulty: High
Getting to the Answer: Emily attempts to make Dave believe that he is important to Bruce, but Dave still feels he is in Bruce's shadow. It is unclear whether or not Dave entirely believes Emily, but when she brings up Bruce's desire to talk about the brothers' childhood, Dave's response suggests that he does not want to talk about it because it again reminds him of how Bruce has always been the more popular of the two. This makes (D) the correct answer. Choice A is out of scope; the passage does not suggest that Dave does anything to spite Emily. Choice B is incorrect because Dave does not feel guilty; he sees Bruce's success as proof that it doesn't matter whether he calls Bruce or not. Choice C is out of scope; Dave's reasons for not calling Bruce have to do with his feelings toward his brother, not any feelings related to Emily.

6. H
Category: Detail
Difficulty: Medium
Getting to the Answer: In lines 39–45, Dave explicitly talks about how Bruce's image has positive aspects (vitality) that his image lacks. This is a perfect match for (H), which restates this generally. Choices F and J are not found in the passage, and G is contradicted by the fact that both Dave and Emily can tell the difference between the twins.

7. B
Category: Inference
Difficulty: Medium
Getting to the Answer: Dave is uncomfortable at this point, because Emily is clearly thinking about Bruce. The previous paragraph describes the picture as a source of insecurity for Dave, suggesting that he is nervous and seeking reassurance that Emily is with him for reasons other than his connection to Bruce. Only (B) describes these feelings. Choice A is the opposite of what Dave is feeling, and neither C nor D can be deduced from the information in the passage.

8. F
Category: Inference
Difficulty: Medium
Getting to the Answer: With an open-ended question like this, the answer choices must be individually tested. Choice (F) can be logically deduced, especially from the last exchange: Emily mentions that Bruce tells her stories about their childhood, and when Dave makes a comment about Bruce's popularity, Emily responds that "[Bruce] doesn't look at it that way" (line 115). This suggests that there is a difference between each brother's childhood stories. Choice G is too extreme and better describes the reaction other people have to the different professions of Bruce and Dave. Choice H is also too extreme: Dave feels competitive with Bruce, but that does not imply that they have fought. Choice J is not

supported by the text; their childhood is the only time when it is stated that they spent time together.

9. C
Category: Detail
Difficulty: High
Getting to the Answer: Dave and Emily have different opinions regarding the picture. Dave is displeased with his image, while Emily professes to like his smile. However, Dave describes Bruce's smile as "trademark" (line 43), and Emily says that Bruce looks "exactly the same" (lines 60–61) in every picture. This makes (C) correct. Choices A and D depict opinions that are strictly Dave's and Emily's, respectively, and B is not supported by the passage at all.

10. F
Category: Inference
Difficulty: Medium
Getting to the Answer: Emily follows her comment about Bruce's stories by dismissing Dave's comment about Bruce's popularity, saying that Bruce "doesn't look at it that way" (line 115). Her response is in reaction to Dave's frequent comments suggesting that Bruce has been more successful socially and Dave's implication that Bruce feels superior to Dave. This matches (F), which correctly restates this idea. Choice G is not supported by the passage; H is opposite because Emily wants Dave to focus less on his brother's successes; and J is extreme, because Bruce wants more attention from his brother but is not necessarily lonely.

PASSAGE II

11. C
Category: Generalization
Difficulty: Medium
Getting to the Answer: The author is critical of the media throughout the passage and focuses mostly on ways in which the current media is not concerned enough with factual accuracy. Choice (C) matches this nicely. Choice A is too extreme; the author talks about distorting facts, not making them

up. Choice B contradicts paragraph 3, which characterizes some news personalities as "demagogues" with biased views. Choice D contradicts paragraph 4; the public's desire for this type of news is one of the reasons for its existence.

12. G
Category: Inference
Difficulty: High
Getting to the Answer: In paragraph 3, the author mentions how impartial stories can sway the opinions of readers through headlines rather than content. Choices H and J both mention headlines, but H makes the opposite point, and J is far too specific, using the example as a basis for a point that the author does not explicitly make. Choice F is contradicted by the passage. Choice (G) is general, but correct: the headline is another method used to sensationalize the story, as illustrated by the example of the "enraged public" (line 55) versus the "irked locals" (lines 58–59).

13. B
Category: Function
Difficulty: Medium
Getting to the Answer: The sentence preceding the Walter Cronkite example states that audience members expected to have complicated events explained to them; the Cronkite example follows this logic. Choice (B) matches this perfectly. Choice A may be inferred, but it is not the point the author is making—the author's concern is the treatment of the news, not specific news personalities. This reasoning also eliminates C. Choice D is never mentioned in or suggested by the passage.

14. F
Category: Inference
Difficulty: Medium
Getting to the Answer: In order to research this statement, it is a good idea to look back at paragraph 4 because it discusses the public. "Personal consensus" applies to the author's point about people looking for news reported by someone with

a political opinion similar to their own. Choice (F) matches this. Choices G and J are both contradicted by information given in paragraph 4. Choice H is not supported by the passage and contradicts the author's main point.

15. B
Category: Detail
Difficulty: High
Getting to the Answer: In paragraph 1, the author states that in stories of "continued national interest" (lines 10–11), the focus shifts from facts to "theater" (line 12). Choice (B) is the best match. Choices A, C, and D are not explicitly mentioned as more or less likely to be sensationalized.

16. J
Category: Vocab-in-Context
Difficulty: Medium
Getting to the Answer: The sentence describes objective reporting as a "distant possibility." Questions like this are easier if you pick a word that means the same thing in context. In this case, you can predict *improbable* or something similar. This matches (J) perfectly. Choices F, G, and H do not address the likelihood of objective reporting.

17. C
Category: Writer's View
Difficulty: Medium
Getting to the Answer: The author is most likely to criticize a headline that sensationalizes or makes a value judgment, and the end of paragraph 3 gives an example. Choices A, B, and D are all basically factual and specific. Choice (C) is correct because it refers to a very broad group, like the example in paragraph 3 does, makes a value judgment by calling the song offensive, and uses emotional language.

18. J
Category: Detail
Difficulty: Low
Getting to the Answer: The fourth paragraph focuses on the flaws of the public and states that individuals who agree with certain politically biased hosts are unlikely to question the validity of the "facts" presented. This matches (J) perfectly. Choices F and G are not explicitly stated by the author. Choice H describes accuracy problems for the media, not the public.

19. A
Category: Detail
Difficulty: Medium
Getting to the Answer: The author makes the point that fact-based news only captures a small minority of the news audience. Also, the beginning of paragraph 4 states that the public is not interested in dry facts. Choice (A) can be inferred because the media companies are providing the type of programs that the public seems to want. Choice B is extreme—in fact, it could be inferred that if the greater public was interested in objective facts, the media (including cable) would provide programs of that sort. Choices C and D cannot be deduced from the passage; the author seems to believe that factual news will not draw a large audience no matter what.

20. G
Category: Inference
Difficulty: Low
Getting to the Answer: Because this question deals with the audience, paragraph 4 is a good place to look. The author states that audience members look for hosts who share their political opinions. Choice (G) is a general restatement of this idea, so it is correct. Choice F is not stated in the passage. Choice H distorts a detail from the last paragraph; audience members prefer short to lengthy, but there is no statement about audience members gravitating toward the shortest or simplest stories.

Choice J misuses the detail about headlines from paragraph 3.

PASSAGE III

21. C
Category: Generalization
Difficulty: Medium
Getting to the Answer: You should have already noted the main ideas of the passages, so all you need to do here is think about what statements could hinder the main idea of Passage A. The main idea of Passage A is that Joyce, despite, or even because of, the specific local detail in his work, has managed to create works of universal truth and appeal. Predict that the correct choice will somehow suggest a lack of ability to generate such widespread appeal. Choice A is a misused detail; though this author briefly mentions historical events in novels, the idea is not at all central to his point. Choice B is opposite; this might actually help the author's point, as it speaks to universal human ideals. Choice D is opposite; as is the case with B, this statement might actually help the author's point.

22. J
Category: Inference
Difficulty: Medium
Getting to the Answer: Use a paraphrase as your prediction, but keep in mind that the answer choices may be written in more general language. Here, the quoted phrase talks about escaping the boundaries of time and place to concentrate on greater truths that are independent of these factors. Expect to find a similar paraphrase among the answer choices. Choice F is opposite; the author is talking about revealing universal truths, not "specific" details. Choice G is out of scope; this author never claims that Joyce wrote in such a way as to "obscure information." Choice H is a distortion; although "ignoring setting" gets close to the right idea, focusing on "character" is not under discussion at this point.

23. C
Category: Inference
Difficulty: High
Getting to the Answer: When a question is phrased in this way, paraphrase the author's main point in the quoted lines to make a prediction. Remember that the answer choices may be phrased in more general language. Here, the author claims that Joyce's level of detail actually helps his work achieve greater appeal. Use such a paraphrase as the basis for your prediction. Choice A is a misused detail; though Dublin's "geography" is discussed earlier, it is not the main focus of discussion at this point in the passage. Choice B is opposite; the author of Passage A mostly describes Joyce's subject matter as mundane. Choice D is a distortion; though Dublin could perhaps be an "exotic locale" to some, this is not the point the author is making here.

24. F
Category: Detail
Difficulty: Medium
Getting to the Answer: One of the main criticisms in the first paragraph of Passage B is that Joyce's subject matter is more base and common than that of earlier authors. Use this idea as the foundation for your prediction. Choice G is out of scope; the author of Passage B never questions Joyce's factual knowledge. Choice H is opposite; if anything, Passage B argues that Joyce is too unlike his predecessors. Choice J is out of scope; the author of Passage B never makes claims about the elegance of Joyce's prose.

25. D
Category: Inference
Difficulty: Medium
Getting to the Answer: This is a fairly straightforward question; to make your prediction, just summarize the author's main point in the given sentence. In the final sentence, the author makes the claim that Joyce possessed the skill to have become a great writer, had he lived in an era more conducive to dignified writing. Use this as your

prediction. Choice A is out of scope; such a claim is never made in the passage and particularly not in the final sentence. Choice B is out of scope; this passage never mentions Joyce's need to "revise" his novels. Choice C is opposite; actually, the author suggests that Joyce's prose style was sufficiently strong and that all he needed was more refined subject matter.

26. F
Category: Vocab-in-Context
Difficulty: Medium
Getting to the Answer: Don't be fooled by familiar words; the challenge of questions like this is in the particular context, not the vocabulary itself. Here, the author uses "base" to describe crude details Joyce often includes, so you should predict something such as *indecent,* which matches (F), unrefined. Choice G is a distortion because it refers to the primary definition of the word. Choice H is a misused detail, referring to the phrase "virtually nauseating" later in the paragraph. Choice J is opposite; the author of Passage B is critical of Joyce's tendency to discuss unrefined activities.

27. B
Category: Inference
Difficulty: High
Getting to the Answer: Passage B criticizes Joyce for failing to provide enlightenment for readers, but Passage A has a favorable opinion of Joyce. The author of Passage A discusses how Joyce's works are globally appealing, which matches (B). Choice A is out of scope because Passage A does not discuss the level of enlightenment provided by older works. Choice C is opposite; the author of Passage A believes that Joyce's inclusion of details enhances his writing. Choice D is out of scope because Passage A does not address philosophical questions.

28. H
Category: Inference
Difficulty: Medium
Getting to the Answer: Although the question stem asks you to compare the passages, all you really have to do is summarize each author's opinion separately. Passage A is generally favorable towards Joyce, commending him for evoking many universal truths, while Passage B is mostly unfavorable, viewing him as undignified. Use this as the basis for your prediction. Choice F is opposite; the author of Passage A actually considers Joyce a great author, and "inaccuracy" is not really a criticism that Passage B employs. Choice G is opposite; similarly, this is incorrect because the author of Passage A promotes Joyce's "significance" as a writer. Choice J is a distortion; while Author B does mention Joyce's skill, Author A never laments any aspect of the writing nor deems it "irrelevant."

29. B
Category: Detail
Difficulty: Low
Getting to the Answer: Keep in mind the authors' general attitudes towards Joyce as you assess their tones at these particular points in the passages. In Passage A, the author is complementing the great degree of detail Joyce uses in describing Dublin, whereas the author of Passage B is expressing disgust at having to read the details of what he considers vulgar or insignificant acts. Use these tones as the basis for your predictions. Choice (B) is correct; this matches the perspectives of the authors. Choice A is a distortion; although both choices here get the general charge right, neither word is quite appropriate to the specific tone of each author. Choice C is a distortion; again, this choice gets the general positive/negative aspects of tone right, but the specifics aren't a good match with each author's attitude. Choice D is opposite; "glee" is contrary to the second author's tone.

30. G

Category: Inference

Difficulty: High

Getting to the Answer: The correct choice is likely to involve Passage B's main claim about Joyce's undignified writing. Choice (G) is correct; Passage B argues that Joyce's writing was not exemplary. Choice F is opposite; both authors agree that Joyce was of Irish descent. Choice H is out of scope; the author of Passage B is rarely complementary to Joyce, making this an unlikely choice. Choice J is out of scope; a "mystic" is someone concerned with religion or the occult, a choice inappropriate for either passage's discussion.

PASSAGE IV

31. B

Category: Inference

Difficulty: Medium

Getting to the Answer: The passage is most concerned with discrediting the myth that rattlesnakes are aggressive and very dangerous, and the selection refers to exactly that: the "sinister opportunist" is the myth, while the "mild-mannered domestic" is closer to fact. Choice (B) can be deduced from this. Choice A is incorrect, as juvenile snakes are not even mentioned. Choice C misuses the detail about rattlesnakes giving live birth, which is not treated as a recent discovery. Choice D is too extreme; the author describes rattlesnakes as fairly docile but not entirely predictable.

32. F

Category: Inference

Difficulty: Low

Getting to the Answer: At the end of paragraph 6, the author states that the reputation is good because a frightened and cornered rattlesnake is dangerous. Choice (F) fits this because if people did not avoid or move away from rattlesnakes, there would be more dangerous interaction between humans and snakes. Choices G and J are contradicted by the passage; in rattlesnake roundups, their reputation costs the snakes their lives, and the author, who is aware of their docile nature, would certainly never believe a rattlesnake should be a pet. Choice H misuses the detail about snakebite deaths.

33. C

Category: Detail

Difficulty: Medium

Getting to the Answer: The passage gives quite a few examples of the social behavior of rattlesnakes, so be prepared to find a restated fact among the answer choices. Choice (C) fits this nicely, because the second paragraph states that rattlesnakes have been known to hibernate with tortoises. Choice A is not a social behavior. Choice B goes beyond the text; the wrestling is used to claim a mate, but the losing snake will leave, rather than take a place within a hierarchy. Choice D also misuses a detail; rattlesnakes are described as "entirely noncannibalistic" (line 24), meaning they never eat other snakes.

34. H

Category: Inference

Difficulty: Medium

Getting to the Answer: The mythology referred to is that of the heartless, aggressive rattlesnake. This relates to rattlesnake roundups (line 113) to which the author clearly objects, so it would follow that the author sees this particular human behavior as heartless and aggressive. Choice (H) matches this perfectly, and the statistical comparison in paragraph 7 supports this. Choice F contradicts the author's belief that rattlesnakes are not as dangerous as commonly thought. Choices G and J do not relate to the point the author is making.

35. C

Category: Detail

Difficulty: Medium

Getting to the Answer: The sixth paragraph states that serious bites can usually be traced to people who either handle or step on snakes, in contrast to those who were not engaging the snakes. Choice (C) fits this nicely, specifically focusing on those handling snakes as an example of individuals purposefully seeking interaction. Choice A is incorrect because a relationship is mentioned. Choice B is not mentioned in the text. Choice D is a distortion because rattlesnakes deliver venom based on how threatened they feel, not necessarily based on how threatening humans act.

36. H
Category: Inference
Difficulty: High
Getting to the Answer: The selection's sentence starts with describing the docile behavior of rattlesnakes, as a follow-up to scientific findings in the previous paragraph. The implication is that snakes, while not as dangerous as often thought, can still be dangerous. Choice (H) matches this perfectly. Choice F is outside the scope of the passage; there is no mention of herpetologists keeping snakes. Choice G misuses a later detail; the author is not comparing the rattlesnake as a pet to dogs. Choice J states a comparison that is never made.

37. B
Category: Detail
Difficulty: Medium
Getting to the Answer: In paragraph 5, the author lists various statistics and states that dogs, bees, and lightning are all responsible for more annual deaths than rattlesnakes and that the fer-de-lance is responsible for substantially more. Choice (B) is the only answer that fits; every other choice is contradicted by the facts given.

38. J
Category: Detail
Difficulty: Medium
Getting to the Answer: In paragraph 6, the author explains that the rattlesnake knows that it needs its venom for food and goes on to state that the only situation in which a rattlesnake would release all of its venom is when it feels threatened. Choice (J) fits with this; the rattlesnake wishes to conserve its venom, specifically for prey. Choice F is incorrect because humans are large in comparison and

receive mostly "dry" bites. Choice G contradicts the statement about rattlesnakes potentially using all their venom if threatened. Choice H contradicts the statement that rattlesnakes are not aware of the well-being of nonfood sources.

39. B
Category: Inference
Difficulty: High
Getting to the Answer: The author examines two pieces of contradictory logic. The first is that the organizers use the reputation of the rattlesnake to promote interest but rely on the more docile nature of the snakes to manage the event. The second is the fact that most of the snakes are taken from areas without people and put into contact with people, thus creating a more dangerous situation. Choice (B) matches the second piece of information. Choice A is not stated as fact in the text. Choice C brings up erroneous statistics, but organizers use the rattlesnake's erroneous reputation. Choice D is not mentioned in the passage.

40. G
Category: Vocab-in-Context
Difficulty: Medium
Getting to the Answer: The answer lies in the last sentence, which speculates on the status of humans in rattlesnake folklore "if [rattlesnakes] were able to speak or write." This makes it clear that *crotalid* must have something to do with actual rattlesnakes. Choice (G) is the only choice that fits because the sentence is mocking the way that humans have characterized rattlesnakes within human mythology. Choices F, H, and J all are incorrect because they mention groups that are not specifically rattlesnakes.

SCIENCE TEST

PASSAGE I

1. C
Category: Patterns
Difficulty: High
Getting to the Answer: Be careful of extreme language, such as the use of *always* in A and B. While the general trend is that decreasing glacier length corresponds to decreasing calving rate, the opposite is true at the sharp peak in calving rate at around 1,500 years, which (C) correctly describes.

2. H
Category: Figure Interpretation
Difficulty: Low
Getting to the Answer: This question asks you to find the glacier with the largest calving rate for years 6–10 in Table 1. Make sure you are looking in the right place, which in this case is the far right column of Table 1.

3. A
Category: Patterns
Difficulty: Medium
Getting to the Answer: This question requires a little deeper understanding of the data presented in Table 1. For all four glaciers during both time periods, the calving rate is slightly greater than or equal to the average velocity. To predict the calving rate of a glacier with a velocity of 80 m/yr, you must look for glaciers traveling at similar velocities. The closest values come from glaciers A and C during years 1–5, which had velocities of 72 m/yr and 98 m/yr, respectively. The corresponding calving rates for these two glaciers are 72 m/yr and 106 m/yr. The correct answer should fall within this range, as described by (A).

4. J
Category: Figure Interpretation
Difficulty: Medium
Getting to the Answer: With open-ended questions like this one, a simple process of elimination is usually most efficient. Comparison of each choice with the data in Table 1 reveals that only (J) accurately reflects the "behavior of the glaciers."

5. B
Category: Figure Interpretation
Difficulty: Medium
Getting to the Answer: Don't be too concerned with the strange scale of the horizontal axis of each choice. The values on the axis correspond exactly to the calving rates for years 6–10 given in Table 1. Simply find the graph that correctly plots the four points given by the data in the last two columns of Table 1.

6. H
Category: Scientific Reasoning
Difficulty: Low
Getting to the Answer: The meteorologists in Study 3 hypothesized that high temperatures cause rapid variations in velocity and calving rate. Figure 1 shows a rapid change in calving rate at around 1,500 years. If the hypothesis is true, then the glacier modeled in Study 1 experienced a rapid change in temperature approximately 1,500 years ago, and (H) is correct.

7. B
Category: Figure Interpretation
Difficulty: Low
Getting to the Answer: The question is asking you to identify two data points—the glacier length and calving rate—in Figure 1. To get to the answer, find 1,500 years on the x-axis and draw a vertical line. Find where the vertical line intersects with glacier length curve and trace back to the y-axis on the left hand side to find that the glacier length is 23. You can eliminate A and D. Find the point where

the calving rate line intersects with the vertical line that was drawn, and trace over to the y-axis on the right hand side to find that the calving rate is approximately 125. Therefore, (B) is correct.

PASSAGE II

8. H
Category: Scientific Reasoning
Difficulty: Low
Getting to the Answer: The question states that the air filters greatly reduce rhinitis symptoms and asks which month would have the greatest decrease in the number of allergic rhinitis cases. To get to the answer, look at Table 1 and count the total number of cases associated with the four months in the answer choices. September has the greatest number of cases. Therefore, (H) is correct.

9. C
Category: Figure Interpretation
Difficulty: Low
Getting to the Answer: Sometimes, you will be asked to simply read information directly from a graph. If you are careful to refer to the right part of the right graph, you will find correct answers to these kinds of questions very quickly. The bar for March 2 on Figure 1 rises to approximately 1,500 gr/m^3, (C).

10. H
Category: Patterns
Difficulty: Medium
Getting to the Answer: You are asked to describe a trend in the data in Figure 1 beyond the high value given for November 5. After this value, the data maintain no discernible trend, but they do stay within a relatively small range of values, as is correctly described in (H).

11. B
Category: Figure Interpretation
Difficulty: Low
Getting to the Answer: Be careful to answer the correct question. "Increased the most" doesn't necessarily mean the count increased to its largest value, which is the trap set in C. Choice D is also a trap, set for those who refer to the wrong figure.

12. F
Category: Figure Interpretation
Difficulty: Medium
Getting to the Answer: This question asks about the tree pollen count shown in Figure 1. Process of elimination reveals that only (F) correctly reflects the data shown in the figure.

13. A
Category: Figure Interpretation
Difficulty: Low
Getting to the Answer: You are finally asked to refer to the rather complicated Table 1. Find the row for the month of May, and look for the corresponding column(s) containing the most reported cases of allergic rhinitis. In this case, that means the most ✿ symbols. Tree and grass pollen account for six of the nine total ✿ symbols in the May row and indeed constitute most of the cases.

PASSAGE III

14. G
Category: Figure Interpretation
Difficulty: Medium
Getting to the Answer: Notice that in Figure 3, the lines plotted for Springs B, C, and D intersect at approximately the same mass. The exact mass value is not completely clear from the figure, but it is definitely larger than F and smaller than H, which leaves (G) as the only possibility.

15. A
Category: Figure Interpretation
Difficulty: Medium
Getting to the Answer: According to Figure 1, oscillation frequency does indeed decrease with increasing arm length, so you can eliminate C and D. The second part of B is simply false, which leaves only (A).

16. F
Category: Scientific Reasoning
Difficulty: Medium
Getting to the Answer: This question requires a couple of steps of logic. First, you must realize what *slowly* means in terms of oscillation frequency. Recall from the passage that oscillation frequency is measured in "oscillations per second." The faster the spring oscillates, the more oscillations it will complete per second. Therefore, you are looking for the spring with the lowest value for oscillation frequency, which is Spring A.

17. C
Category: Figure Interpretation
Difficulty: Medium
Getting to the Answer: Refer to the line plotted for Spring A in Figure 3. On that line, a mass of 700 g corresponds to an equilibrium length of just less than 40 cm. Only (C) includes this estimate.

18. J
Category: Patterns
Difficulty: High
Getting to the Answer: According to Figure 2, an oscillation frequency of 1.4 Hz at a mass of 100 g would be represented by a data point that would fall in between the frequency values for Spring C and Spring D at that mass. Only H and (J) place Spring E correctly between Springs C and D, and (J) correctly lists the springs in order of *decreasing* oscillation frequency.

19. C
Category: Scientific Reasoning
Difficulty: High
Getting to the Answer: The effects of mass are not mentioned in Experiment 1. Only the pendulum arm length affects the oscillation frequency, so the plots for the original mass and the larger mass should be identical, as in (C).

20. H
Category: Figure Interpretation
Difficulty: Low
Getting to the Answer: Figure 1 shows the relationship between arm length and oscillation frequency. To find the corresponding arm length, draw a line from 0.35 on the *y*-axis to the curve. At the point of intersection, draw a line down to the *x*-axis. The line will be closer to 20 than 15, which is why the correct answer is 19 cm, (H).

PASSAGE IV

21. D
Category: Figure Interpretation
Difficulty: Low
Getting to the Answer: Make sure you refer to the correct part of Table 1 for the enzyme concentration values of populations ha 1, ha 2, and ha 3. The table shows that for all three high-altitude populations, GST levels are highest, CR levels are lowest, and ECH levels are intermediate. Only (D) does not violate this relationship.

22. G
Category: Figure Interpretation
Difficulty: Low
Getting to the Answer: The process of elimination works best here. Choice F is not universally true; the oxygen saturation percentages are pretty similar for high-altitude and sea-level dwellers. Neither Table 1 nor Figure 1 shows a comparison between high- or low-altitude populations and temperature or partial

oxygen pressure, so H and J cannot be correct. Only (G) is directly supported by the values in the table.

23. C
Category: Figure Interpretation
Difficulty: Medium
Getting to the Answer: The answer to this question comes directly from Figure 1, but you must be careful to not confuse the two data sets. You can draw a horizontal line from 110 mm Hg on the left vertical axis until it intersects with the oxygen partial pressure data (squares). That intersection happens at about 3,200 m. To find the temperature at this altitude, draw a horizontal line from the temperature plot (circles) at 3,200 m to the right axis. It intersects at between –5°C and –10°C, meaning the correct answer must be (C). Accidentally reversing the two data sets likely results in selecting trap answer A.

24. H
Category: Figure Interpretation
Difficulty: Medium
Getting to the Answer: You are asked to find the highest ECH concentration for any of the six populations, which occurs for population ha 2.

25. A
Category: Scientific Reasoning
Difficulty: High
Getting to the Answer: Only (A) and C agree with the information in Table 1. You can eliminate C, though, because nothing in the passage or data suggests that CR concentration has anything to do with efficiency at incorporating oxygen into the blood.

26. J
Category: Scientific Reasoning
Difficulty: High
Getting to the Answer: The question is asking you to identify the relationship between altitude and enzyme levels, and then predict the levels for an intermediate population. The population at 1,500-1,800 m (intermediate) is located between sea level and high altitude. When comparing GST between the sea-level and high-level populations, GST is higher for the high-altitude populations. It's safe to assume that the intermediate population would have a GST level higher than the sea level and lower than the high-altitude populations. Therefore, F, G, and H can be eliminated. Double-check EST and CR values to confirm that (J) is correct.

PASSAGE V

27. D
Category: Scientific Reasoning
Difficulty: Medium
Getting to the Answer: Recall that Student 1 credits pressure for the freezing phenomenon. Choices B and C reflect elements of the viewpoint of Student 2 and can therefore be eliminated. If A were true, the temperature and pressure effects would work against each other, so only (D) makes sense.

28. G
Category: Scientific Reasoning
Difficulty: Low
Getting to the Answer: According to Student 1, pressure causes the ice to melt, and pressure increases with increasing weight. Student 2 states that friction causes the ice to melt and that the force of friction increases with increasing weight. Therefore, the students would agree that ice would melt faster under the heavier skater, as in (G).

29. A
Category: Scientific Reasoning
Difficulty: Medium
Getting to the Answer: In the explanation of Student 2, ice melts when heat is generated as the skater overcomes the force of friction by *moving* across the ice. If the skater is not moving, then, no heat should be generated. Student 1, though, explains that ice melts due to pressure, which is

present whether or not the skater is moving, making (A) correct.

30. H
Category: Scientific Reasoning
Difficulty: Medium
Getting to the Answer: Student 2 explains that less dense materials float above more dense materials. Because the frozen ethanol remains below the liquid ethanol, (H) must be true.

31. C
Category: Scientific Reasoning
Difficulty: Low
Getting to the Answer: You can eliminate A and B due to the mention of pressure in both, which is a concept only Student 1 contemplates. Student 2 describes floating as the case in which the buoyant force exceeds the force of gravity, so the sinking boat is evidence of the opposite situation, as described in (C).

32. G
Category: Scientific Reasoning
Difficulty: Medium
Getting to the Answer: Eliminate F because only Student 1 considers pressure, and eliminate J because the only possible support for this explanation also comes from Student 1. Eliminate H because the force of gravity will only change as the mass of the skater changes. Student 2 states that heat is produced by overcoming friction, so less friction would mean less heat, as in (G).

33. A
Category: Scientific Reasoning
Difficulty: Medium
Getting to the Answer: Recall that the viewpoint of Student 2 focuses on a difference in *density*, and eliminate C. Choices B and D both actually mean the same thing, but the term *buoyant* is included in D to entice the unwary test taker. In either case, the balloon would remain on the ground. The less

dense balloon described in (A) would indeed rise above the ground.

PASSAGE VI

34. F
Category: Scientific Reasoning
Difficulty: Medium
Getting to the Answer: To get to the answer, focus on the relationship between measured and corrected conductivity in Table 1. The measured data demonstrates that there is conductivity in the sample solutions even when F- is not present. Subtracting the intrinsic conductivity allows the scientist to better see how much conductivity is due to just F-. Choice H is out of scope, because the passage does not mention the presence of impurities, and non-ionic molecules do not conduct electricity. Choice J is also incorrect because the question states that Na_2SiF_6 is already in solution. The data is normalized after it has been collected, so it would not be used to calibrate the electrodynamic cells.

35. C
Category: Patterns
Difficulty: Low
Getting to the Answer: Either Table 1 or Figure 1 can provide the answer here. Table 1 contains numerical examples of cases where the F⁻ concentration is indeed doubled (from 0.5 mg/L to 1 mg/L, for example) and gives the corresponding change in conductivity. Taking care to look in the *corrected* conductivity column, you can see that 2 times the concentration results in 2 times the corrected conductivity. Likewise, Figure 1 makes it clear that relationship between the two quantities is linear, which means that any multiplication of the concentration results in the same multiplication of the conductivity.

36. J
Category: Figure Interpretation
Difficulty: Medium
Getting to the Answer: Compare the new conductivity value to those given in Table 2, specifically those for Newtown and Lakewood, and recall

the direct relationship between conductivity and F⁻ concentration. Noticing that Bluewater's conductivity value lies between the values for Newtown and Lakewood allows you to eliminate F and G. Taking care to list the towns in order of *increasing* F⁻ leads you to (J).

37. C
Category: Patterns
Difficulty: Medium
Getting to the Answer: Refer to Table 1 to see where a value of 3.0 mg/L would fit in. This new concentration is between the 2.0 mg/L and 4.0 mg/L values given in the table, so the corrected conductivity should lie between 3.34 μS/cm and 6.68 μS/cm. Choices B and D are too close to the extremes of this range, but (C) is exactly in the middle as it should be. Alternatively, you could read the corrected conductivity for a concentration of 3.0 mg/L directly from Figure 1.

38. F
Category: Scientific Reasoning
Difficulty: Medium
Getting to the Answer: Questions that ask you to change the procedure of an experiment usually require you to review the original experiment before answering. In this case, the description of Experiment 1 tells you that F⁻ is added in the form of dissolved Na_2SiF_6. To study Cl⁻ concentrations, the students must use a chemical that contains Cl⁻ when preparing the solutions, as in (F).

39. B
Category: Scientific Reasoning
Difficulty: Low
Getting to the Answer: Experimental data are not required to answer this question. The last sentence of the description of Experiment 1 explains that the corrected conductivity is calculated by *subtracting* the measured conductivity of the blank solution. This always results in the corrected conductivity being less than the measured conductivity, as in (B).

40. F
Category: Scientific Reasoning
Difficulty: Medium
Getting to the Answer: You are told that Cl⁻ results in an increase in conductivity, and the data show that F⁻ results in an increase in conductivity. Therefore, in a solution containing both F⁻ and Cl⁻, it would be impossible to distinguish the contributions to conductivity from each ion given only conductivity measurements. Conductivity would be increased by the presence of Cl⁻, and the apparent values for F⁻ concentration would be falsely high, as in (F). If you miss this point, you could at least eliminate J because the question asks only about the case where *all* of the samples have Cl⁻ concentrations. The effect of the Cl⁻ should not be different for different solutions.

WRITING TEST

MODEL ESSAY

Below is an example of what a high-scoring essay might look like. Notice that the author states her position clearly in the introductory paragraph and supports that position with evidence in the following paragraphs. The essay also uses transitions, some advanced vocabulary, and an effective "hook" to draw in the reader.

Teachers often tell us that learning is fun, and the best way to convince us that learning is enjoyable is to give us activities that keep us engaged (and awake). The issue here is whether teachers should provide more hands-on learning experiences because doing so would help all students learn and remember better. On the other hand, others say that it's possible to learn without doing and that schools should use their money for other educational purposes rather than trying to make everything hands-on learning. I believe that the best learning comes from hands-on work.

I know from experience that I learn better when I can actually do something myself. When students do projects such as growing plants, they really learn about the science because they are part of making that science work. This is analogous to learning how to ride a bike. A child can read about it, watch videos on it and even watch someone actually ride a bike, but he doesn't learn how to do it until he gets on a bike and pedals away. Thus, it is important that the teacher provide opportunities for students to do as much hands-on learning as possible. However, those who think that students don't learn anything unless they actually do it are wrong. There are ideas that can't be experimented with. How can students re-create the Big Bang or evolution? But just because they can't actually do this doesn't mean students don't learn. There is a lot that can be learned from reading and learning from experts. However, if there is a choice between learning by doing and not having that opportunity, learning by doing is the better way to teach and learn.

On the other hand, other people think that experiential education is important only for students who will work in a career that requires that they do things themselves, such as engineering and technology. It is important that students who will enter careers that are skill based have the opportunity to practice this in school. School is supposed to teach what is needed for students later in life, and knowing how to do experiments or re-create what others have done should be part of this. But the people who argue for this say it is important only for students who will need it in their future careers. This means that some students, particularly those who don't know what career they want, will not get the benefit of hands-on experiences. That splits students into two groups: those who learn by doing and those who don't. All students learn well by doing, so it would not be fair to offer it only to some students. How can teachers know what is appropriate for students in their future careers if even the students don't yet know? This solution is not a good one because it assumes things that can't be supported.

Finally, it is shortsighted to argue that rather than create opportunities for hands-on learning, schools should spend their money on other things because learning by doing is expensive and may not be good for all students. There's always the problem that not all students learn in the same way so there's no one kind of learning that is best for everyone. But that doesn't mean teachers shouldn't provide hands-on opportunities. Actually, this is a good way to reach all students because it involves working with your hands, maybe some reading and talking too, and critical thinking, so it uses lots of ways of learning. It is foolish to have the opportunity to do something important and not do it just because some people may not benefit from it or it will cost money. Teachers should give students the opportunity to learn in a hands-on way as much as possible.

In the real world, when we need to learn something new, like how to cook or use a computer program, if it's possible to learn by doing while having someone help and direct us, that is the best way to learn and the way that schools should teach. Studies, and my own experience, show that everyone can benefit from hands-on education; that is the way we learn and remember best.

You can evaluate your essay and the model essay based on the following criteria, which is covered in the Practice Makes Perfect section of this book:

- Does the author discuss all three perspectives provided in the prompt?
- Is the author's own perspective clearly stated?
- Does the body of the essay assess and analyze each perspective?
- Is the relevance of each paragraph clear?
- Does the author start a new paragraph for each new idea?
- Is each sentence in a paragraph relevant to the point made in that paragraph?
- Are transitions clear?
- Is the essay easy to read? Is it engaging?
- Are sentences varied?
- Is vocabulary used effectively? Is college-level vocabulary used?

ACT Practice Test Four
ANSWER SHEET

ENGLISH TEST

1. Ⓐ Ⓑ Ⓒ Ⓓ 11. Ⓐ Ⓑ Ⓒ Ⓓ 21. Ⓐ Ⓑ Ⓒ Ⓓ 31. Ⓐ Ⓑ Ⓒ Ⓓ 41. Ⓐ Ⓑ Ⓒ Ⓓ 51. Ⓐ Ⓑ Ⓒ Ⓓ 61. Ⓐ Ⓑ Ⓒ Ⓓ 71. Ⓐ Ⓑ Ⓒ Ⓓ
2. Ⓕ Ⓖ Ⓗ Ⓙ 12. Ⓕ Ⓖ Ⓗ Ⓙ 22. Ⓕ Ⓖ Ⓗ Ⓙ 32. Ⓕ Ⓖ Ⓗ Ⓙ 42. Ⓕ Ⓖ Ⓗ Ⓙ 52. Ⓕ Ⓖ Ⓗ Ⓙ 62. Ⓕ Ⓖ Ⓗ Ⓙ 72. Ⓕ Ⓖ Ⓗ Ⓙ
3. Ⓐ Ⓑ Ⓒ Ⓓ 13. Ⓐ Ⓑ Ⓒ Ⓓ 23. Ⓐ Ⓑ Ⓒ Ⓓ 33. Ⓐ Ⓑ Ⓒ Ⓓ 43. Ⓐ Ⓑ Ⓒ Ⓓ 53. Ⓐ Ⓑ Ⓒ Ⓓ 63. Ⓐ Ⓑ Ⓒ Ⓓ 73. Ⓐ Ⓑ Ⓒ Ⓓ
4. Ⓕ Ⓖ Ⓗ Ⓙ 14. Ⓕ Ⓖ Ⓗ Ⓙ 24. Ⓕ Ⓖ Ⓗ Ⓙ 34. Ⓕ Ⓖ Ⓗ Ⓙ 44. Ⓕ Ⓖ Ⓗ Ⓙ 54. Ⓕ Ⓖ Ⓗ Ⓙ 64. Ⓕ Ⓖ Ⓗ Ⓙ 74. Ⓕ Ⓖ Ⓗ Ⓙ
5. Ⓐ Ⓑ Ⓒ Ⓓ 15. Ⓐ Ⓑ Ⓒ Ⓓ 25. Ⓐ Ⓑ Ⓒ Ⓓ 35. Ⓐ Ⓑ Ⓒ Ⓓ 45. Ⓐ Ⓑ Ⓒ Ⓓ 55. Ⓐ Ⓑ Ⓒ Ⓓ 65. Ⓐ Ⓑ Ⓒ Ⓓ 75. Ⓐ Ⓑ Ⓒ Ⓓ
6. Ⓕ Ⓖ Ⓗ Ⓙ 16. Ⓕ Ⓖ Ⓗ Ⓙ 26. Ⓕ Ⓖ Ⓗ Ⓙ 36. Ⓕ Ⓖ Ⓗ Ⓙ 46. Ⓕ Ⓖ Ⓗ Ⓙ 56. Ⓕ Ⓖ Ⓗ Ⓙ 66. Ⓕ Ⓖ Ⓗ Ⓙ
7. Ⓐ Ⓑ Ⓒ Ⓓ 17. Ⓐ Ⓑ Ⓒ Ⓓ 27. Ⓐ Ⓑ Ⓒ Ⓓ 37. Ⓐ Ⓑ Ⓒ Ⓓ 47. Ⓐ Ⓑ Ⓒ Ⓓ 57. Ⓐ Ⓑ Ⓒ Ⓓ 67. Ⓐ Ⓑ Ⓒ Ⓓ
8. Ⓕ Ⓖ Ⓗ Ⓙ 18. Ⓕ Ⓖ Ⓗ Ⓙ 28. Ⓕ Ⓖ Ⓗ Ⓙ 38. Ⓕ Ⓖ Ⓗ Ⓙ 48. Ⓕ Ⓖ Ⓗ Ⓙ 58. Ⓕ Ⓖ Ⓗ Ⓙ 68. Ⓕ Ⓖ Ⓗ Ⓙ
9. Ⓐ Ⓑ Ⓒ Ⓓ 19. Ⓐ Ⓑ Ⓒ Ⓓ 29. Ⓐ Ⓑ Ⓒ Ⓓ 39. Ⓐ Ⓑ Ⓒ Ⓓ 49. Ⓐ Ⓑ Ⓒ Ⓓ 59. Ⓐ Ⓑ Ⓒ Ⓓ 69. Ⓐ Ⓑ Ⓒ Ⓓ
10. Ⓕ Ⓖ Ⓗ Ⓙ 20. Ⓕ Ⓖ Ⓗ Ⓙ 30. Ⓕ Ⓖ Ⓗ Ⓙ 40. Ⓕ Ⓖ Ⓗ Ⓙ 50. Ⓕ Ⓖ Ⓗ Ⓙ 60. Ⓕ Ⓖ Ⓗ Ⓙ 70. Ⓕ Ⓖ Ⓗ Ⓙ

MATHEMATICS TEST

1. Ⓐ Ⓑ Ⓒ Ⓓ Ⓔ 11. Ⓐ Ⓑ Ⓒ Ⓓ Ⓔ 21. Ⓐ Ⓑ Ⓒ Ⓓ Ⓔ 31. Ⓐ Ⓑ Ⓒ Ⓓ Ⓔ 41. Ⓐ Ⓑ Ⓒ Ⓓ Ⓔ 51. Ⓐ Ⓑ Ⓒ Ⓓ Ⓔ
2. Ⓐ Ⓑ Ⓒ Ⓓ Ⓔ 12. Ⓕ Ⓖ Ⓗ Ⓙ Ⓚ 22. Ⓕ Ⓖ Ⓗ Ⓙ Ⓚ 32. Ⓕ Ⓖ Ⓗ Ⓙ Ⓚ 42. Ⓕ Ⓖ Ⓗ Ⓙ Ⓚ 52. Ⓕ Ⓖ Ⓗ Ⓙ Ⓚ
3. Ⓐ Ⓑ Ⓒ Ⓓ Ⓔ 13. Ⓐ Ⓑ Ⓒ Ⓓ Ⓔ 23. Ⓐ Ⓑ Ⓒ Ⓓ Ⓔ 33. Ⓐ Ⓑ Ⓒ Ⓓ Ⓔ 43. Ⓐ Ⓑ Ⓒ Ⓓ Ⓔ 53. Ⓐ Ⓑ Ⓒ Ⓓ Ⓔ
4. Ⓕ Ⓖ Ⓗ Ⓙ Ⓚ 14. Ⓕ Ⓖ Ⓗ Ⓙ Ⓚ 24. Ⓕ Ⓖ Ⓗ Ⓙ Ⓚ 34. Ⓕ Ⓖ Ⓗ Ⓙ Ⓚ 44. Ⓕ Ⓖ Ⓗ Ⓙ Ⓚ 54. Ⓕ Ⓖ Ⓗ Ⓙ Ⓚ
5. Ⓐ Ⓑ Ⓒ Ⓓ Ⓔ 15. Ⓐ Ⓑ Ⓒ Ⓓ Ⓔ 25. Ⓐ Ⓑ Ⓒ Ⓓ Ⓔ 35. Ⓐ Ⓑ Ⓒ Ⓓ Ⓔ 45. Ⓐ Ⓑ Ⓒ Ⓓ Ⓔ 55. Ⓐ Ⓑ Ⓒ Ⓓ Ⓔ
6. Ⓕ Ⓖ Ⓗ Ⓙ Ⓚ 16. Ⓕ Ⓖ Ⓗ Ⓙ Ⓚ 26. Ⓕ Ⓖ Ⓗ Ⓙ Ⓚ 36. Ⓕ Ⓖ Ⓗ Ⓙ Ⓚ 46. Ⓕ Ⓖ Ⓗ Ⓙ Ⓚ 56. Ⓕ Ⓖ Ⓗ Ⓙ Ⓚ
7. Ⓐ Ⓑ Ⓒ Ⓓ Ⓔ 17. Ⓐ Ⓑ Ⓒ Ⓓ Ⓔ 27. Ⓐ Ⓑ Ⓒ Ⓓ Ⓔ 37. Ⓐ Ⓑ Ⓒ Ⓓ Ⓔ 47. Ⓐ Ⓑ Ⓒ Ⓓ Ⓔ 57. Ⓐ Ⓑ Ⓒ Ⓓ Ⓔ
8. Ⓕ Ⓖ Ⓗ Ⓙ Ⓚ 18. Ⓕ Ⓖ Ⓗ Ⓙ Ⓚ 28. Ⓕ Ⓖ Ⓗ Ⓙ Ⓚ 38. Ⓕ Ⓖ Ⓗ Ⓙ Ⓚ 48. Ⓕ Ⓖ Ⓗ Ⓙ Ⓚ 58. Ⓕ Ⓖ Ⓗ Ⓙ Ⓚ
9. Ⓐ Ⓑ Ⓒ Ⓓ Ⓔ 19. Ⓐ Ⓑ Ⓒ Ⓓ Ⓔ 29. Ⓐ Ⓑ Ⓒ Ⓓ Ⓔ 39. Ⓐ Ⓑ Ⓒ Ⓓ Ⓔ 49. Ⓐ Ⓑ Ⓒ Ⓓ Ⓔ 59. Ⓐ Ⓑ Ⓒ Ⓓ Ⓔ
10. Ⓕ Ⓖ Ⓗ Ⓙ Ⓚ 20. Ⓕ Ⓖ Ⓗ Ⓙ Ⓚ 30. Ⓕ Ⓖ Ⓗ Ⓙ Ⓚ 40. Ⓕ Ⓖ Ⓗ Ⓙ Ⓚ 50. Ⓕ Ⓖ Ⓗ Ⓙ Ⓚ 60. Ⓕ Ⓖ Ⓗ Ⓙ Ⓚ

READING TEST

1. Ⓐ Ⓑ Ⓒ Ⓓ 6. Ⓕ Ⓖ Ⓗ Ⓙ 11. Ⓐ Ⓑ Ⓒ Ⓓ 16. Ⓕ Ⓖ Ⓗ Ⓙ 21. Ⓐ Ⓑ Ⓒ Ⓓ 26. Ⓕ Ⓖ Ⓗ Ⓙ 31. Ⓐ Ⓑ Ⓒ Ⓓ 36. Ⓕ Ⓖ Ⓗ Ⓙ
2. Ⓕ Ⓖ Ⓗ Ⓙ 7. Ⓐ Ⓑ Ⓒ Ⓓ 12. Ⓕ Ⓖ Ⓗ Ⓙ 17. Ⓐ Ⓑ Ⓒ Ⓓ 22. Ⓕ Ⓖ Ⓗ Ⓙ 27. Ⓐ Ⓑ Ⓒ Ⓓ 32. Ⓕ Ⓖ Ⓗ Ⓙ 37. Ⓐ Ⓑ Ⓒ Ⓓ
3. Ⓐ Ⓑ Ⓒ Ⓓ 8. Ⓕ Ⓖ Ⓗ Ⓙ 13. Ⓐ Ⓑ Ⓒ Ⓓ 18. Ⓕ Ⓖ Ⓗ Ⓙ 23. Ⓐ Ⓑ Ⓒ Ⓓ 28. Ⓕ Ⓖ Ⓗ Ⓙ 33. Ⓐ Ⓑ Ⓒ Ⓓ 38. Ⓕ Ⓖ Ⓗ Ⓙ
4. Ⓕ Ⓖ Ⓗ Ⓙ 9. Ⓐ Ⓑ Ⓒ Ⓓ 14. Ⓕ Ⓖ Ⓗ Ⓙ 19. Ⓐ Ⓑ Ⓒ Ⓓ 24. Ⓕ Ⓖ Ⓗ Ⓙ 29. Ⓐ Ⓑ Ⓒ Ⓓ 34. Ⓕ Ⓖ Ⓗ Ⓙ 39. Ⓐ Ⓑ Ⓒ Ⓓ
5. Ⓐ Ⓑ Ⓒ Ⓓ 10. Ⓕ Ⓖ Ⓗ Ⓙ 15. Ⓐ Ⓑ Ⓒ Ⓓ 20. Ⓕ Ⓖ Ⓗ Ⓙ 25. Ⓐ Ⓑ Ⓒ Ⓓ 30. Ⓕ Ⓖ Ⓗ Ⓙ 35. Ⓐ Ⓑ Ⓒ Ⓓ 40. Ⓕ Ⓖ Ⓗ Ⓙ

SCIENCE TEST

1. Ⓐ Ⓑ Ⓒ Ⓓ 6. Ⓕ Ⓖ Ⓗ Ⓙ 11. Ⓐ Ⓑ Ⓒ Ⓓ 16. Ⓕ Ⓖ Ⓗ Ⓙ 21. Ⓐ Ⓑ Ⓒ Ⓓ 26. Ⓕ Ⓖ Ⓗ Ⓙ 31. Ⓐ Ⓑ Ⓒ Ⓓ 36. Ⓕ Ⓖ Ⓗ Ⓙ
2. Ⓕ Ⓖ Ⓗ Ⓙ 7. Ⓐ Ⓑ Ⓒ Ⓓ 12. Ⓕ Ⓖ Ⓗ Ⓙ 17. Ⓐ Ⓑ Ⓒ Ⓓ 22. Ⓕ Ⓖ Ⓗ Ⓙ 27. Ⓐ Ⓑ Ⓒ Ⓓ 32. Ⓕ Ⓖ Ⓗ Ⓙ 37. Ⓐ Ⓑ Ⓒ Ⓓ
3. Ⓐ Ⓑ Ⓒ Ⓓ 8. Ⓕ Ⓖ Ⓗ Ⓙ 13. Ⓐ Ⓑ Ⓒ Ⓓ 18. Ⓕ Ⓖ Ⓗ Ⓙ 23. Ⓐ Ⓑ Ⓒ Ⓓ 28. Ⓕ Ⓖ Ⓗ Ⓙ 33. Ⓐ Ⓑ Ⓒ Ⓓ 38. Ⓕ Ⓖ Ⓗ Ⓙ
4. Ⓕ Ⓖ Ⓗ Ⓙ 9. Ⓐ Ⓑ Ⓒ Ⓓ 14. Ⓕ Ⓖ Ⓗ Ⓙ 19. Ⓐ Ⓑ Ⓒ Ⓓ 24. Ⓕ Ⓖ Ⓗ Ⓙ 29. Ⓐ Ⓑ Ⓒ Ⓓ 34. Ⓕ Ⓖ Ⓗ Ⓙ 39. Ⓐ Ⓑ Ⓒ Ⓓ
5. Ⓐ Ⓑ Ⓒ Ⓓ 10. Ⓕ Ⓖ Ⓗ Ⓙ 15. Ⓐ Ⓑ Ⓒ Ⓓ 20. Ⓕ Ⓖ Ⓗ Ⓙ 25. Ⓐ Ⓑ Ⓒ Ⓓ 30. Ⓕ Ⓖ Ⓗ Ⓙ 35. Ⓐ Ⓑ Ⓒ Ⓓ 40. Ⓕ Ⓖ Ⓗ Ⓙ

ENGLISH TEST

45 Minutes—75 Questions

Directions: In the following five passages, certain words and phrases are underlined and numbered. In the right-hand column are alternatives for each underlined portion. Select the one that best conveys the idea, creates the most grammatically correct sentence, or is the most consistent with the style and tone of the passage. If you decide that the original version is best, select NO CHANGE. You may also find questions that ask about the entire passage or a section of the passage. These questions will correspond to small numbered boxes in the text. For these questions, decide which choice best accomplishes the purpose set out in the question stem. After you've selected the best choice, fill in the corresponding oval in your Answer Grid. For some questions, you'll need to read the context in order to answer correctly. Be sure to read until you have enough information to determine the correct answer choice.

PASSAGE I

THE PARTHENON

[1]

If you are like most visitors to Athens, you will make your way to the Acropolis, the hill that once served as a fortified, strategic position over-looking the Aegean Sea—to see the Parthenon. This celebrated temple was dedicated in the fifth century B.C. to the goddess Athena. There is no more famous building in all of Greece; to

1. **A.** NO CHANGE
    B. Acropolis. The hill
    C. Acropolis—the hill
    D. Acropolis

GO ON TO THE NEXT PAGE ⟶

climb up its marble steps is <u>to have beheld</u> a human
                              2
creation that has attained the stature of a natural

phenomenon like the Grand Canyon. <u>You should also</u>
                                                 3
<u>make an attempt to sample Athenian cuisine while</u>
                         3
<u>you're there.</u>
       3

[2]

Generations of architects <u>have proclaimed</u> the Par-
                                   4
thenon to be the most brilliantly conceived structure in

the Western world. The genius of its construction

is <u>subtle for example</u> the temple's columns were made to
       5
bulge outward slightly in order to compensate for

the <u>fact, viewed from distance, that straight columns</u>
                              6
<u>appear concave.</u> Using this and other techniques, the
       6

architects strove to create an optical <u>illusion of; uprightness,</u>
                                                     7
solidity, and permanence.

2. **F.** NO CHANGE
    G. to behold
    H. beholding
    J. to be holding

3. **A.** NO CHANGE
    B. Also make an attempt to sample
              Athenian cuisine while you're there.
    C. While you're there, you should also
              make an attempt to sample Athenian
              cuisine.
    D. OMIT the underlined portion.

4. **F.** NO CHANGE
    G. has proclaimed
    H. proclaims
    J. are proclaiming

5. **A.** NO CHANGE
    B. subtle; for example
    C. subtle. For example
    D. subtle. For example,

6. **F.** NO CHANGE
    G. fact that straight columns, viewed from
              a distance, appear concave.
    H. view from a distance: straight columns
              appearing concave.
    J. fact, when viewed from far away, that
              straight columns appear concave.

7. **A.** NO CHANGE
    B. illusion of: uprightness
    C. illusion of, uprightness
    D. illusion of uprightness,

GO ON TO THE NEXT PAGE

[3]

Because of this, the overall impression you'll get
                    8
of the Parthenon will be far different from the one the

ancient Athenians had. Only by standing on the marble

steps of the Parthenon and allowing your imagination

to transport you back to the Golden Age of Athens. You
                                                      9
will be able to see the temple's main attraction, the leg-
9
endary statue of Athena Parthenos. It was 38 feet

high and made of ivory and over a ton of pure gold.

Removed from the temple in the fifth century C.E., all
                                              10
that remains is the slight rectangular depression on the

floor where it stood.

[4]

Many of the ornate carvings and sculptures that

adorned the walls of the Acropolis is no longer there,
                                    11
either. In the early nineteenth century, the British

diplomat Lord Elgins decision to "protect" the ones that
                          12
survived by removing them from the Parthenon and

carrying them back to Britain (he had the permission of

the Ottoman Turks, who controlled Greece at the time,

to do so).

[5]

After they gained independence from the Turks,

they began to demand the sculptures and carvings back
13
from the British, to no avail. Thus, if you want to gain

a complete picture of what the Parthenon once looked

like, you'll have to visit not only the Acropolis of Athens,

but the British Museum in London as well.

8. **F.** NO CHANGE
    G. Thus
    H. Rather
    J. Of course

9. **A.** NO CHANGE
    B. Athens; you will
    C. Athens will you
    D. Athens. You may

10. **F.** NO CHANGE
    G. Having been removed from the temple
            in the fifth century c.e.,
    H. Given its removal from the temple in
            the fifth century c.e.,
    J. The statue was removed from the
            temple in the fifth century c.e.;

11. **A.** NO CHANGE
    B. will be
    C. have been
    D. are

12. **F.** NO CHANGE
    G. Elgin's deciding that
    H. Elgin decided to
    J. Elgin's decision to

13. **A.** NO CHANGE
    B. the Turks
    C. the Greeks
    D. who

GO ON TO THE NEXT PAGE

Questions 14–15 ask about the preceding passage as a whole.

14. The writer wishes to insert the following material into the essay:

> Some of them were destroyed in 1687 when attacking Venetians bombarded the Acropolis, setting off explosives that had been stored in the Parthenon.

The new material best supports and therefore would most logically be placed in paragraph:

F. 1.

G. 2.

H. 3.

J. 4.

15. Suppose the editor of an architecture journal had requested that the writer focus primarily on the techniques the ancient Greek architects used in constructing the Parthenon. Does the essay fulfill this request?

A. Yes, because the essay makes it clear that the Parthenon was an amazing architectural achievement.

B. Yes, because the essay explains in the second paragraph the reason the temple's columns bulge outward slightly.

C. No, because the Parthenon's construction is only one of several topics covered in the essay.

D. No, because the author never explains what the architects who designed the Parthenon were trying to accomplish.

GO ON TO THE NEXT PAGE

PASSAGE II

THE LEGENDARY ROBIN HOOD

Although there is no conclusive evidence that a man named Robin Hood ever actually existed, the story of Robin Hood and his band of merry men has become one of the most popular traditional tales in English literature. Robin is the hero in a series of ballads dating from at least the fourteenth century. These ballads <u>are telling</u> of discontent among the lower classes in the
16
north of England during a turbulent era culminating in the Peasants' Revolt of 1381. A good deal of the rebellion against authority stemmed from restriction of hunting rights. These early ballads reveal the cruelty that was a part of medieval life. Robin Hood was a rebel, and many of the most striking episodes depict him and his companions robbing and killing representatives of authority and <u>they gave</u> the gains to the poor. Their
17

<u>most frequentest</u> enemy was the Sheriff of Nottingham,
18
a local agent of the central government. Other enemies included wealthy ecclesiastical landowners.

While Robin could be ruthless with those who abused their power, he was kind to the oppressed. He

16. **F.** NO CHANGE
    G. telling
    H. tell
    J. they are telling

17. **A.** NO CHANGE
    B. they were giving
    C. giving
    D. gave

18. **F.** NO CHANGE
    G. even more frequenter
    H. frequent
    J. frequently

GO ON TO THE NEXT PAGE

was a people's hero as King Arthur was a noble's.

(The Broadway musical *Camelot* and Walt Disney's *The*
                                    19
Sword in the Stone are based on the legend of King Arthur.)
                                    19
Some scholars have sought to prove that there was an

actual Robin Hood. However, references to the Robin

Hood legends by medieval writers make it clear that the

ballads were the only evidence for Robin's existence

available to <u>them.</u> A popular modern belief that Robin
              20
was of the time of Richard I probably stems from the

antiquary Richard <u>Stukely's fabrication</u> of a
                   21

"pedigree." 22

        In the eighteenth century, the nature of the legend

was distorted by the suggestion that Robin <u>was as a</u>
                                            23

19. **A.** NO CHANGE
    B. (The Broadway musical and the movie,
    respectively, *Camelot* and Walt Disney's
    The Sword in the Stone, are based on the
    legend of King Arthur.)
    C. (Movies and musicals, including
    The Sword in the Stone and *Camelot*,
    are derived from the legend of King
    Arthur.)
    D. OMIT the underlined portion.

20. **F.** NO CHANGE
    G. him.
    H. it.
    J. those writing ballads about him.

21. **A.** NO CHANGE
    B. Stukelys fabrication
    C. Stukelys fabrication,
    D. Stukely's, fabrication

22. Suppose that at this point in the passage,
    the writer wanted to add more information
    about Richard Stukely. Which of the
    following additions would be most relevant
    to the passage as a whole?

    F. A discussion of relevant books on
    England during the realm of Richard I
    G. A definition of the term *antiquary*
    H. An example of Stukely's interest in King
    Arthur
    J. A description of the influence Stukely's
    fabricated pedigree has had on later
    versions of the Robin Hood tale

23. **A.** NO CHANGE
    B. was like as if he was
    C. was a
    D. is as a

GO ON TO THE NEXT PAGE ⇨

fallen nobleman. Writers adopted this new element

as eagerly as puppies. Robin was also given a love
    24

24. **F.** NO CHANGE
    G. eagerly
    H. eagerly, like a puppy
    J. like a puppy's eagerness

interest; Maid Marian. Some critics say that these
    25
ballads lost much of their vitality and poetic value by

losing the social impulse that prompted their creation.

25. **A.** NO CHANGE
    B. interests—Maid
    C. interest: Maid,
    D. interest—Maid

Consequently, in the twentieth century, the legend
    26
of Robin Hood has inspired several movies and a

26. **F.** NO CHANGE
    G. (Do NOT begin new paragraph) In the twentieth century, on the one hand,
    H. (Begin new paragraph) In the twentieth century,
    J. (Begin new paragraph) In the twentieth century, therefore,

television series. Even a Broadway musical basing on the
                                        27
tale. So, whether or not a Robin Hood actually lived in

27. **A.** NO CHANGE
    B. has been based
    C. to base
    D. OMIT the underlined portion.

ancient Britain, and the legendary Robin has lived in the
        28
popular imagination for more than 600 years.

28. **F.** NO CHANGE
    G. Britain,
    H. Britain, therefore
    J. Britain;

GO ON TO THE NEXT PAGE

Questions 29–30 ask about the preceding passage as a whole.

29. Suppose this passage were written for an audience that was unfamiliar with the legend of Robin Hood. The writer could most effectively strengthen the passage by:

   A. citing examples of legendary rebels from Spanish and French literature.

   B. including further evidence of Robin Hood's actual existence.

   C. quoting a few lines from a Broadway musical about ancient Britain.

   D. including a brief summary of the Robin Hood legend.

30. This passage was probably written for readers who:

   F. are experts on how legends are handed down.

   G. are authorities on ancient British civilization and culture.

   H. are convinced that Robin Hood was an actual historical personage.

   J. have some familiarity with the Robin Hood legends.

GO ON TO THE NEXT PAGE

PASSAGE III

HOW MOTHER NATURE JUMP-STARTED MY CAREER

The following paragraphs may or may not be in the most logical order. Each paragraph is numbered in brackets, and question 45 will ask you to choose the most logical order of the paragraphs.

[1]

When Mt. St. Helens erupted, my training as a private pilot paid off. My editor asked me to write a feature story on the volcano. Only scientists and reporters were allowed within a <u>ten-mile radius</u> of the mountain.
                                   31
Eager to see Mt. St. Helens for himself, my brother Jeff volunteered to accompany me as an assistant on

the flight. He had never flown with me before, <u>and I</u>
                                              32
<u>looked forward at the opportunity to show off my skills.</u>
                    32

31. A. NO CHANGE
    B. radius, consisting of ten miles,
    C. measurement of a ten-mile radius
    D. radius, measuring ten miles,

32. F. NO CHANGE
    G. but looked forward to the opportunity of showing off my skills.
    H. and I looked forward to the opportunity to show off my skills.
    J. nevertheless I anticipated being able to show off my skills.

[2]

<u>If I could read a newspaper,</u> I entertained thoughts
              33
of becoming a photojournalist. I always envisioned

<u>myself</u> in some faraway exotic place performing
  34
dangerous deeds as a foreign correspondent. I was thrilled when I was hired for my first job as a cub reporter for the local newspaper in my rural hometown. However, some of the glamour began to fade after I

33. A. NO CHANGE
    B. Since I found it easy to read a newspaper,
    C. Although I could read a newspaper,
    D. Ever since I could read a newspaper,

34. F. NO CHANGE
    G. I
    H. me
    J. it

GO ON TO THE NEXT PAGE ⟹

covered the umpteenth garden party. Then one day,

Mother Nature <u>intervened,</u> giving me the opportunity to
35
cover an international event.

[3]

When we arrived at the airport, <u>filing my flight</u>
36
<u>plan; giving</u> my credentials as a reporter for the Gresh-
36
am *Outlook*. As we departed Troutdale airport, my

Cessna 152 ascended slowly on its way toward Mt. St.

Helens. As we neared the crater, I kept a <u>careful</u> watch
37
for other airplanes in the vicinity. A few other pilots

were also circling around the crater. I had to maintain a

high enough altitude to avoid both the smoke being

emitted <u>from: the crater</u> and the ashen residue already
38
in the atmosphere. Too much exposure to the volcanic

particles could put my plane out of service. This element

of danger served to increase not only my awareness, but

also my excitement.

[4]

Jeff and I were at first speechless <u>and mute</u> at the
39
awesome sight below us as we circled the crater. It was

as if the spectacular beauty of a Fourth of July celebra-

tion were contained in one natural phenomenon. Jeff

helped me, <u>steadying the plane and took notes,</u> while
40

35. A. NO CHANGE
   B. intervened:
   C. intervened;
   D. —intervened—

36. F. NO CHANGE
   G. I filed my flight plan and gave
   H. filing my flight plan, giving
   J. my flight plan was filed by me, and I gave

37. The best placement for the underlined portion would be:
   A. where it is now.
   B. after the word *other*.
   C. after the word *we*.
   D. before the word *crater*.

38. F. NO CHANGE
   G. (from: the crater)
   H. from, the crater,
   J. from the crater

39. A. NO CHANGE
   B. and also mute
   C. —and mute—
   D. OMIT the underlined portion.

40. F. NO CHANGE
   G. steadying the plane and taking notes,
   H. steadied the plane and taking notes,
   J. steadies the plane and takes notes

GO ON TO THE NEXT PAGE

I shot pictures and dictated story ideas to him. 41

41. The writer could most effectively strengthen the passage at this point by adding which of the following?

  A. A description of Mt. St. Helens

  B. The sentence, "Jeff, take this plane lower!" to add excitement

  C. The statement, "A volcano is a vent in the earth's crust through which lava is expelled," to inform the reader

  D. A discussion of other recent volcanic eruptions to provide a contrast

[5]

My story appeared as the front-page feature the following day. <u>However,</u> I have realized many of my
42
early dreams, working as a foreign correspondent in many different countries. And yet none of my experiences has surpassed that special pride and excitement I felt covering my first "international" story.

42. **F.** NO CHANGE

  G. Since that time,

  H. Furthermore,

  J. Nevertheless,

Questions 43–45 ask about the preceding passage as a whole.

---

43. Readers are likely to regard the passage as best described by which of the following terms?

  A. Optimistic

  B. Bitter

  C. Nostalgic

  D. Exhausted

44. Is the author's use of the pronoun *I* appropriate in the passage?

  F. No, because, as a rule, one avoids *I* in formal writing.

  G. No, because it weakens the passage's focus on volcanoes.

  H. Yes, because it gives immediacy to the story told in the passage.

  J. Yes, because *I* is, as a rule, appropriate in writing.

45. Choose the sequence of paragraph numbers that will make the passage's structure most logical.

  A. NO CHANGE

  B. 2, 1, 3, 4, 5

  C. 3, 4, 5, 1, 2

  D. 4, 5, 1, 2, 3

GO ON TO THE NEXT PAGE

PASSAGE IV

SIR ARTHUR CONAN DOYLE

[1]

Sherlock Holmes, the <u>ingenious and extremely clever</u> detective, with the deer-stalker hat, pipe, and
46
magnifying glass, is a universally recognizable character.
Everyone knows of Holmes's ability to solve even the
most bizarre mysteries through the application of cold
logic. <u>Therefore, everyone</u> is familiar with the phrase
47
"elementary, my dear Watson," Holmes's perennial
response to the requests of his baffled sidekick, Dr.
Watson, for an explanation of his amazing deductions.
<u>Strictly speaking, of course, Holmes's "deductions"</u>
48

[2]

<u>were not deductions at all, but inductive inferences.</u>
48
But how many people know anything about the
creator of Sherlock Holmes, Sir Arthur Conan Doyle?

Fans of Holmes might be surprised to discover that <u>he</u>
49

did not want <u>to be engraved forever in the memory of</u>
50
<u>the people</u> as the author of the Sherlock Holmes stories.
50

<u>In fact,</u> Conan Doyle sent Holmes to his death at the
51
end of the second book of short stories and

46. F. NO CHANGE
    G. ingenious
    H. ingenious, extremely clever
    J. cleverly ingenious

47. A. NO CHANGE
    B. Although everyone
    C. For this reason, everyone
    D. Everyone

48. F. NO CHANGE
    G. (Strictly speaking, of course, Holmes's "deductions" were not deductions at all, but inductive inferences.)
    H. Holmes's "deductions" were, strictly speaking, not deductions at all, but inductive inferences.
    J. OMIT the underlined portion.

49. A. NO CHANGE
    B. Conan Doyle
    C. they
    D. the detective

50. F. NO CHANGE
    G. to go down in the annals of history
    H. to be permanently thought of forever
    J. to be remembered

51. A. NO CHANGE
    B. Despite this,
    C. Regardless,
    D. Yet

GO ON TO THE NEXT PAGE

subsequently felt a great sense of relief. Having had

enough of his famous character by that time, <u>Sherlock
Holmes would never divert him again from more
serious writing, he promised himself.</u> It took eight years
and the offer of a princely sum of money before Conan

Doyle could be persuaded to revive the detective.

<u>Soap opera characters are sometimes brought back
to life after they've been pronounced dead, too.</u> [1]
Admirers of Holmes's coldly scientific approach to his

detective work may also be taken aback when they learn

that Conan Doyle <u>has been deeply immersed</u> in spiritualism. [2] Convinced by these experiences of the validity

of paranormal <u>phenomena, that he lectured</u> on spiritualism in towns and villages throughout Britain. [3] For

example, he and his family attempted to communicate

with the dead by automatic writing, <u>thought to be a
method of talking with those no longer among the living,</u>
and through a spiritual medium, an individual who

supposedly could contact those in the world beyond.

[4] Conan Doyle claimed to have grasped materialized

hands and watched heavy articles swimming through

52. F. NO CHANGE

G. the diversion of Sherlock Holmes, he promised himself, would never again keep him from more serious writing.

H. more serious writing consumed all his time from then on.

J. he promised himself that Sherlock Holmes would never again divert him from more serious writing.

53. A. NO CHANGE

B. (Soap opera characters are sometimes brought back to life after they've been pronounced dead, too.)

C. Sometimes you'll see soap opera charac-ters who were dead being brought back to life, just like Holmes.

D. OMIT the underlined portion.

54. F. NO CHANGE

G. is deeply immersed

H. was deeply immersed

J. has been immersed deeply

55. A. NO CHANGE

B. phenomena, he lectured

C. phenomena was he that he lectured

D. phenomena. He lectured

56. F. NO CHANGE

G. a means of getting in touch with those beyond the grave

H. thought to be a method of talking with the dead

J. OMIT the underlined portion.

GO ON TO THE NEXT PAGE

the air during sessions led by the medium. 57

[3]

Doyle seems never to have asked <u>himself: why they</u>
₅₈
would manifest themselves in such curious ways, or to

have reflected on the fact that many of these effects are

the standard trappings of cheating mediums. One has to

wonder, <u>what would Sherlock Holmes have to say?</u>
₅₉

57. For the sake of unity and coherence, sentence 2 should be placed:

A. where it is now.
B. before sentence 1.
C. after sentence 3.
D. after sentence 4.

58. F. NO CHANGE
    G. himself—why they
    H. himself why those in the other world
    J. himself why they

59. A. NO CHANGE
    B. what would Sherlock Holmes have said?
    C. what is Sherlock Holmes going to say?
    D. what had Sherlock Holmes said?

> Question 60 asks about the preceding passage as a whole.

60. Which of the following would be the most appropriate subtitle for the passage?

    F. The Truth about Spiritualists
    G. Rational or Superstitious?
    H. The Secret Life of Sherlock Holmes
    J. His Religious Beliefs

PASSAGE V

VISUAL LEARNING

Traditional educational theories stressed lecture-based methods in which students learned by listening to an instructor, but contemporary studies have noted that students learn best when they see, hear, and experience. Based on these studies, current educational theories emphasize auditory, visual, and experiential learning. Such theories <u>are not groundbreaking.</u> For example, medical education has stressed this model for decades. Young doctors in their residency training often repeat the mantra, "see it, do it, teach it." Interestingly, much of the development in the <u>area of</u> visual and experiential learning fields has come from the business world. Many businesses, from corporate management to consulting, utilize presentations. Traditionally, business presentations had included slides filled with dense text that merely repeated the presenter's words. Though these slides did provide a visual aspect, <u>the slides</u> were difficult to read, which detracted from their effectiveness.

[1] Over the past decade, <u>technological advances have created</u> additional presentation options, business leaders have teamed with public speaking experts to continue to refine the visual presentation style.

61. A. NO CHANGE
B. were not groundbreaking
C. had been groundbreaking
D. in groundbreaking

62. F. NO CHANGE
G. subject of
H. topic of
J. OMIT the underlined portion.

63. A. NO CHANGE
B. the slides'
C. the slide's
D. they

64. F. NO CHANGE
G. technological advances were creating
H. as technological advances have created
J. that technological advances have created

GO ON TO THE NEXT PAGE

[2] <u>A very important development revealed</u> that less
                                    65
cluttered visual aids work better than denser ones. [3]
This development led to the understanding that text

repeating a presenter's script did not <u>enhance or</u>
                                    66
<u>improve</u> student or audience learning. [4] Studies
   66
showed that visual aids should not simply present a

speaker's words, but instead <u>demonstrate or add to them</u>
                                    67
in some way. [5] These studies emphasized the efficacy
of visual representations of the presenter's dialogue in

the form of graphs, charts, art, or pictures. 68

65. **A.** NO CHANGE
    B. On the other hand, a very important development revealed
    C. A very important development similarly revealed
    D. In contrast, a very important development revealed

66. **F.** NO CHANGE
    G. lead to an improvement in
    H. better enhance or improve
    J. improve

67. **A.** NO CHANGE
    B. they can be demonstrated or added to
    C. demonstrating or adding to them
    D. demonstrate adding for them

68. After reviewing the essay, the writer is considering inserting the following true statement in this paragraph:

    > Audio aids, though infrequently used, can also help audiences focus on a presentation.

    Should this sentence be added to this paragraph, and if so, what is the most logical placement for it?

    F. Yes, after Sentence 2.
    G. Yes, after Sentence 4.
    H. Yes, after Sentence 5.
    J. No, the sentence should NOT be added.

GO ON TO THE NEXT PAGE ⟩

Several studies <u>in listeners have been published</u>
                                69
<u>in respected journals, that reveal that aesthetically</u>
                                69
<u>appealing presentations improve comprehension.</u>
                                69

69. A. NO CHANGE

    B. revealing that aesthetically appealing presentations improve comprehension in listeners have been published in respected journals.

    C. in listeners that reveal that aesthetically appealing presentations improve comprehension in respected journals have been published.

    D. have been published in respected journals by revealing in listeners that aesthetically appealing presentations improve comprehension.

<u>It has been determined by researchers that a learning aid</u>
                                70
<u>can be created from any pleasing image, even one that</u>
                                70
<u>is irrelevant.</u> Using this model, many presenters have
      70
begun projecting nature scenes or famous paintings to

70. F. NO CHANGE

    G. Researchers have determined that any pleasing image, even an irrelevant one, can serve as a learning aid.

    H. As researchers have determined, that any pleasing image, even an irrelevant one, can serve as a learning aid.

    J. A pleasing image, even an irrelevant one, researchers have determined it can serve as a learning aid.

accompany <u>presentations. Audience</u> members report
                        71
not being distracted by the irrelevant images. In fact,

most audience members find the pleasing images

helpful in creating a positive environment which, in

turn, helps <u>him or her</u> focus on the presentation.
                72

71. A. NO CHANGE

    B. presentations, audience

    C. presentations, and that audience

    D. presentations and that audience

72. F. NO CHANGE

    G. one

    H. you

    J. them

[1] <u>Even more recently, of late,</u> cognitive psycholo-
                73
gists have noted that students and audience members

73. A. NO CHANGE

    B. Not so long ago, in recent times,

    C. Lately, in addition,

    D. Recently,

GO ON TO THE NEXT PAGE ⟶

use multiple senses to take in information. [2] In fact,
74
many experts believe that a teacher's or presenter's body

language is the most important factor in student or

audience reaction. [3] Therefore, many education and

public speaking experts are interested in investigating
75
other factors in student and audience reaction. [4]
75
While these developments have not coalesced to form

one paradigm for public speaking and presenting, they

have underscored many of the new theories in the field

of communication. [5] These developments continue to

influence trends in the academic world.

74. Given that all of the following are true,
which choice would provide the most
effective and logical link between Sentences
1 and 2?

F. NO CHANGE

G. learn not only from images, but also
from body language.

H. pay more attention to visual images that
incorporate color or suggest movement.

J. recall more information when they are
asked by the presenter or speaker to
take notes or write questions.

75. At this point, the writer would like to show
how education and public speaking experts
have been influenced by the theory about
the importance of body language. Given that
all of the following are true, which choice
best achieves the writer's purpose?

A. NO CHANGE

B. now teach presenters to make
purposeful movements and focused
gestures.

C. have adjusted the focus of their public
speaking workshops for teachers and
business professionals.

D. question how the size of an audience
affects the power of a presenter's body
language.

IF YOU FINISH BEFORE TIME IS CALLED, YOU MAY CHECK YOUR WORK ON
THIS SECTION ONLY. DO NOT TURN TO ANY OTHER SECTION IN THE TEST. **STOP**

MATHEMATICS TEST

60 Minutes—60 Questions

Directions: Solve each of the following problems, select the correct answer, and then fill in the corresponding space on your answer sheet.

Don't linger over problems that are too time-consuming. Do as many as you can, then come back to the others in the time you have remaining.

The use of a calculator is permitted on this test. Though you are allowed to use your calculator to solve any questions you choose, some of the questions may be most easily answered without the use of a calculator.

Note: Unless otherwise noted, all of the following should be assumed.

1. Illustrative figures are *not* necessarily drawn to scale.
2. All geometric figures lie in a plane.
3. The term *line* indicates a straight line.
4. The term *average* indicates arithmetic mean.

1. What is the average of 230, 155, 320, 400, and 325?

   A. 205
   B. 286
   C. 300
   D. 430
   E. 490

2. Sarah has a wooden board that is 12 feet long. If she cuts three 28-inch pieces from the board, how much board will she have left?

   F. 14 inches
   G. 28 inches
   H. 36 inches
   J. 60 inches
   K. 72 inches

3. If $4x + 18 = 38$, then $x =$

   A. 3
   B. 4.5
   C. 5
   D. 12
   E. 20

4. John weighs 1.5 times as much as Ellen. If John weighs 165 lb, how much does Ellen weigh?

   F. 100 lb
   G. 110 lb
   H. 150 lb
   J. 165 lb
   K. 175 lb

5. What is the average of 237, 482, 375, and 210?

   A. 150
   B. 185
   C. 210
   D. 260
   E. 326

6. If $\sqrt[3]{x} = 4$, then $x =$

   F. 4
   G. 12
   H. 36
   J. 64
   K. 256

GO ON TO THE NEXT PAGE ⇨

7. If $x^2 + 14 = 63$, then $x =$

   A. 4.5
   B. 7
   C. 14
   D. 24.5
   E. 2.8

8. Which of the following is equivalent to $\sqrt{54}$?

   F. $2\sqrt{3}$
   G. $3\sqrt{6}$
   H. 15
   J. 9
   K. $9\sqrt{6}$

9. What whole number is closest to the solution of $\sqrt{90} \times \sqrt{32}$?

   A. 7
   B. 11
   C. 36
   D. 44
   E. 54

10. $5.2^3 + 6.8^2 =$

    F. 46.24
    G. 94.872
    H. 120.534
    J. 140.608
    K. 186.848

11. If x is a real number such that $x^3 = 512$, what is the value of x^2?

    A. 8
    B. 16
    C. 64
    D. 81
    E. 135

12. $3^3 \div 9 + (6^2 - 12) \div 4 =$

    F. 3
    G. 6.75
    H. 9
    J. 12
    K. 15

13. If bananas cost $0.24 and oranges cost $0.38, what is the total cost of x bananas and y oranges?

    A. $(x + y)(\$0.24 + \$0.38)$
    B. $\$0.24x + \$0.38y$
    C. $\$0.62(x + y)$
    D. $\dfrac{\$0.24}{x} + \dfrac{\$0.38}{y}$
    E. $\$0.38x + \$0.24y$

14. If $4x + 13 = 16$, what is the value of x?

    F. 0.25
    G. 0.50
    H. 0.55
    J. 0.70
    K. 0.75

15. What is 6% of 1,250?

    A. 75
    B. 208
    C. 300
    D. 500
    E. 750

GO ON TO THE NEXT PAGE

16. On her first three geometry tests, Sarah scored an 89, a 93, and an 84. If there are four tests total and Sarah needs at least a 90 average for the four, what is the lowest score she can receive on the final test?

    F. 86
    G. 90
    H. 92
    J. 94
    K. 96

17. What is the solution set of $3x - 11 \geq 22$?

    A. $x \geq -11$
    B. $x < -3$
    C. $x \geq 0$
    D. $x > 3$
    E. $x \geq 11$

18. The eighth grade girls' basketball team played a total of 13 games this season. If they scored a total of 364 points, what was their average score per game?

    F. 13
    G. 16
    H. 20
    J. 28
    K. 32

19. If $6x + 4 = 11x - 21$, what is the value of x?

    A. 2
    B. 3
    C. 4
    D. 5
    E. 6

20. The school band has a collection of 300 pieces of music. Of these, 10% are movie theme songs. Out of the rest of the pieces of music, 80 of the pieces are marches. How many of the band's pieces of music are neither marches nor movie theme songs?

    F. 190
    G. 198
    H. 210
    J. 220
    K. 270

21. A cooking class has 20 spaces available for each daily session. Data showed that 19 people attended the first session, 17 people attended the second session, and 15 people attended each of the remaining sessions. If the average number of attendees was exactly 16 per class session, how many total sessions of the cooking class were there?

    A. 3
    B. 4
    C. 6
    D. 11
    E. Cannot be determined from the given information

22. In the following figure, all of the small triangles are the same size. What percent of the entire figure is shaded?

    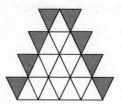

    F. 8
    G. 24
    H. $33\frac{1}{3}$
    J. 50
    K. $66\frac{2}{3}$

GO ON TO THE NEXT PAGE ⟩

23. A piece of letter-sized paper is $8\frac{2}{3}$ inches wide and 11 inches long. Suppose you want to cut strips of paper that are $\frac{5}{8}$ inch wide and 11 inches long. What is the maximum number of strips of paper you could make from 1 piece of letter-sized paper?

 A.   5
 B.   6
 C.   12
 D.   13
 E.   14

24. A scientist was studying a meadow and the birds that lived in the meadow. He kept a count of the birds that appeared in the meadow by tagging them so that the individual birds could be distinguished from one another. There are only three types of birds that live in the meadow: buntings, larks, and sparrows. He found that the ratio of buntings to total birds in the meadow was 35:176, while the ratio of larks to total birds was 5:11. If the scientist randomly chooses one individual bird that he had previously counted, which type of bird is he most likely to choose?

 F.   Bunting
 G.   Lark
 H.   Sparrow
 J.   All bird types are equally likely
 K.   Cannot be determined from the given information

25. For all x, $(x + 4)(x - 4) + (2x + 2)(x - 2) = ?$

 A. $x^2 - 2x - 20$
 B. $3x^2 - 12$
 C. $3x^2 - 2x - 20$
 D. $3x^2 + 2x - 20$
 E. $3x^2 + 2x + 20$

26. Which of these is equivalent to $(4x - 1)(x + 5)$?

 F. $4x^2 + 8x$
 G. $4x^2 - 10x - 5$
 H. $4x^2 - 15x + 5$
 J. $4x^2 + 19x - 5$
 K. $4x^2 + 19x + 5$

27. In the following triangle, if $\cos \angle BAC = 0.6$ and the hypotenuse of the triangle is 15, what is the length of side BC?

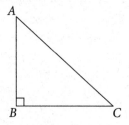

 A.   3
 B.   5
 C.   10
 D.   12
 E.   15

28. If a car drives 80 miles per hour for x hours and 60 miles per hour for y hours, what is the car's average speed, in miles, for the total distance traveled?

 F. $\dfrac{480}{xy}$

 G. $\dfrac{80}{x} + \dfrac{60}{y}$

 H. $\dfrac{80}{x} \times \dfrac{60}{y}$

 J. $\dfrac{80x + 60y}{x + y}$

 K. $\dfrac{x + y}{80x + 60y}$

GO ON TO THE NEXT PAGE

29. Four numbers are in a sequence with 8 as its first term and 36 as its last term. The first 3 numbers are in an arithmetic sequence with a common difference of –7. The last 3 numbers are in a geometric sequence. What is the common ratio of the last 3 terms of the sequence?

   A. –10
   B. –6
   C. 0
   D. 10
   E. 32

30. If $3^{3x+3} = 27^{\left(\frac{2}{3}x - \frac{1}{3}\right)}$, then $x = $?

   F. –4

   G. $-\dfrac{7}{4}$

   H. $-\dfrac{10}{7}$

   J. 2
   K. 4

31. A scientist had a container of liquid nitrogen that was at a temperature of –330°F. If the temperature of the room was 72°F, how much must the temperature of the liquid nitrogen change to become the room's temperature? (Note: "+" indicates a rise in temperature, and "–" indicates a drop in temperature.)

   A. –330°F
   B. –258°F
   C. +72°F
   D. +402°F
   E. +474°F

32. A playground is $(x + 7)$ units long and $(x + 3)$ units wide. If a square of side length x is sectioned off from the playground to make a sandpit, which of the following could be the remaining area of the playground?

   F. $x^2 + 10x + 21$
   G. $10x + 21$
   H. $2x + 10$
   J. 21
   K. $21x$

33. If u is an integer, then $(u - 3)^2 + 5$ must be:

   A. an even integer.
   B. an odd integer.
   C. a positive integer.
   D. a negative integer.
   E. Cannot be determined by the information given.

34. The point $(-3,-2)$ is the midpoint of the line segment in the standard (x,y) coordinate plane joining the point $(1,9)$ and (m, n). Which of the following is (m,n) ?

   F. $(-7,-13)$
   G. $(-1,7)$
   H. $(-2,5.5)$
   J. $(2,5.5)$
   K. $(5,20)$

35. If $f(x) = \dfrac{1}{3}x + 13$ and $g(x) = 3x^2 + 6x + 12$, what is the value of $f(g(x))$?

   A. $x^2 + 12x + 4$
   B. $\dfrac{x^2}{3} + 2x + 194$
   C. $x^2 + 2x + 17$
   D. $x^2 + 2x + 25$
   E. $x^2 + 2x + 54$

GO ON TO THE NEXT PAGE

36. What is the length of side *AC* in triangle *ABC* graphed on the following coordinate plane?

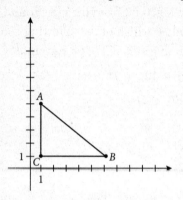

F. 3

G. 4

H. 5

J. 6

K. 7

37. If $f(x) = 16x^2 - 20x$, what is the value of $f(4)$?

A. −12

B. 36

C. 84

D. 144

E. 372

38. What is the equation of a line that is perpendicular to the line $y = \dfrac{2}{3}x + 5$ and contains the point $(4, -3)$?

F. $y = \dfrac{2}{3}x + 4$

G. $y = -\dfrac{2}{3}x + 3$

H. $y = -\dfrac{3}{2}x + 3$

J. $y = -\dfrac{3}{2}x - 9$

K. $y = -\dfrac{3}{2}x + 9$

39. What is the slope of the line through the points $(-10,0)$ and $(0,-6)$?

A. $-\dfrac{5}{3}$

B. $-\dfrac{3}{5}$

C. $\dfrac{3}{5}$

D. $\dfrac{5}{3}$

E. 0

40. The figure on the coordinate plane is a rectangle. What Coordinate pair corresponds to point *B*?

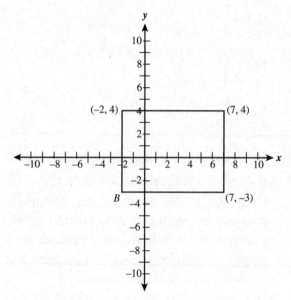

F. (−2,−3)

G. (−2,4)

H. (2,−3)

J. (−3,4)

K. (3,−2)

GO ON TO THE NEXT PAGE

41. What is the length of a line segment with endpoints (3,−6) and (−2,6)?

A. 1
B. 5
C. 10
D. 13
E. 15

42. What is the midpoint of the line segment in the following graph?

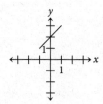

F. (0,1)
G. (0,2)
H. (1,2)
J. (1,1)
K. (1,3)

43. What is the volume of a sphere with a diameter of 6?

A. 3π
B. 9π
C. 27π
D. 36π
E. 288π

44. A rectangle has a side length of 8 and a perimeter of 24. What is the area of the rectangle?

F. 16
G. 24
H. 32
J. 64
K. 96

45. Isosceles triangle *ABC* has an area of 48. If $\overline{AB}$ = 12, what is the perimeter of *ABC*?

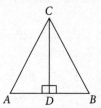

A. 32
B. 36
C. 48
D. 64
E. 76

46. The rectangular backyard of a house is 130 feet by 70 feet. If the backyard is completely fenced in, what is the length, in feet, of the fence?

F. 130
G. 200
H. 260
J. 400
K. 420

47. In the following figure, lines *m* and *l* are parallel and ∠*a* = 68°. What is the measure of ∠*f*?

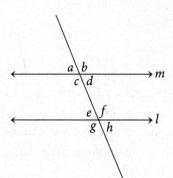

A. 22°
B. 68°
C. 80°
D. 112°
E. 292°

GO ON TO THE NEXT PAGE

48. Square *ABCD* is shown, with one side measuring 6 centimeters. What is the area of triangle *BCD*, in square centimeters?

F. 3

G. 6

H. 12

J. 18

K. 36

49. The hypotenuse of right triangle *RST* is 16. If the measure of ∠*R* = 30°, what is the length of *RS*?

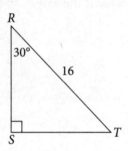

A. 4

B. 8

C. $8\sqrt{3}$

D. 12

E. 16

50. The radius of a circle is increased so that the radius of the resulting circle is double that of the original circle. How many times larger is the area of the resulting circle than that of the original circle?

F. 0.5

G. 1

H. 2

J. π

K. 4

51. What is the length of the diagonal of a square with sides of length 7?

A. 7

B. $7\sqrt{2}$

C. 14

D. 21

E. 28

52. What is the perimeter of a regular hexagon with a side of 11?

F. 33

G. 44

H. 66

J. 72

K. 78

53. A rectangle has a perimeter of 28, and its longer side is 2.5 times the length of its shorter side. What is the length of the diagonal of the rectangle, rounded to the nearest tenth?

A. 4.0

B. 10.0

C. 10.8

D. 12.4

E. 14.2

GO ON TO THE NEXT PAGE

54. In the following figure, $\overline{MN}$ and $\overline{PQ}$ are parallel. Point *A* lies on *MN*, and points *B* and *C* lie on $\overline{PQ}$. If *AB* = *AC* and ∠*MAB* = 55°, what is the measure of ∠*ACB*?

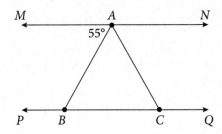

F.   35°

G.   55°

H.   65°

J.   80°

K.   125°

55. The following chord is 8 units long. If the chord is 3 units from the center of the circle, what is the area of the circle?

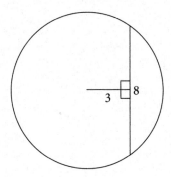

A.   9π

B.   16π

C.   18π

D.   25π

E.   28π

56. If isosceles triangle *QRS* has a base of length 16 and sides of length 17, what is the area of the triangle?

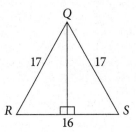

F.   50

G.   80

H.   110

J.   120

K.   180

57. In a high school senior class, the ratio of girls to boys is 5:3. If there are a total of 168 students in the senior class, how many girls are there?

A.   63

B.   100

C.   105

D.   147

E.   152

GO ON TO THE NEXT PAGE

58. What is the tangent of ∠*EFD* shown?

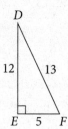

    F. $\dfrac{5}{13}$

    G. $\dfrac{5}{12}$

    H. $\dfrac{12}{13}$

    J. $\dfrac{13}{12}$

    K. $\dfrac{12}{5}$

59. In the following triangle, what is the value of sin ∠*QRS*?

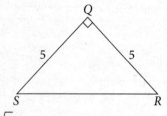

    A. $\dfrac{\sqrt{2}}{6}$

    B. $\dfrac{\sqrt{2}}{5}$

    C. $\dfrac{\sqrt{2}}{2}$

    D. $2\sqrt{2}$

    E. $5\sqrt{2}$

60. In the following right triangle, *JL* = 17 and *KL* = 8. What is the value of sin ∠*JLK*?

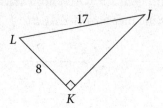

    F. $\dfrac{8}{15}$

    G. $\dfrac{8}{17}$

    H. $\dfrac{8}{20}$

    J. $\dfrac{3}{4}$

    K. $\dfrac{15}{17}$

IF YOU FINISH BEFORE TIME IS CALLED, YOU MAY CHECK YOUR WORK ON
THIS SECTION ONLY. DO NOT TURN TO ANY OTHER SECTION IN THE TEST.   **STOP**

READING TEST

35 Minutes—40 Questions

Directions: There are four passages in this test. Each passage is followed by several questions. After reading a passage, choose the best answer to each question and fill in the corresponding oval on your answer document. You may refer to the passages as often as necessary.

PASSAGE I

PROSE FICTION

This passage is an excerpt from the short story "Graduation," by John Krupp.

Rosemary sat at her kitchen table, working at a crossword puzzle. Crosswords were nice; they filled the time, and kept the mind
Line active. She needed just one word to complete
(5) this morning's puzzle; the clue was "a Swiss river," and the first of its three letters was "A." Unfortunately, Rosemary had no idea what the name of the river was, and could not look it up. Her atlas was on the
(10) desk, and the desk was in the guest room, currently being occupied by her grandson Victor. Looking up over the tops of her bifocals, Rosemary glanced at the kitchen clock: it was almost 10 A.M. *Land sakes!* Did
(15) the boy intend to sleep all day? She noticed that the arthritis in her wrist was throbbing, and put down her pen. At eighty-seven years of age, she was glad she could still write at all. She had decided long ago that
(20) growing old was like slowly turning to stone; you couldn't take anything for granted. She stood up slowly, painfully, and started walking to the guest room.

The trip, though only a distance of
(25) about twenty-five feet, seemed to take a long while. Late in her ninth decade now, Rosemary often experienced an expanded sense of time, with present and past tense intermingling in her mind. One minute she
(30) was padding in her slippers across the living room carpet, the next she was back on the farm where she'd grown up, a sturdy little

girl treading the path behind the barn just before dawn. In her mind's eye, she could
(35) still pick her way among the stones in the darkness, more than seventy years later… Rosemary arrived at the door to the guest room. It stood slightly ajar, and she peered through the opening. Victor lay sleeping
(40) on his side, his arms bent, his expression slightly pained. *Get up, lazy bones,* she wanted to say. Even in childhood, Rosemary had never slept past 4 A.M.; there were too many chores to do. How different
(45) things were for Victor's generation! Her youngest grandson behaved as if he had never done a chore in his life. Twenty-one years old, he had driven down to Florida to visit Rosemary in his shiny new car, a
(50) gift from his doting parents. Victor would finish college soon, and his future appeared bright—if he ever got out of bed, that is.

Something Victor had said last night over dinner had disturbed her. Now what
(55) was it? Oh yes; he had been talking about one of his college courses—a "gut," he had called it. When she had asked him to explain the term, Victor had said it was a course that you took simply because it was
(60) easy to pass. Rosemary, who had not even had a high school education, found the term repellent. If she had been allowed to continue her studies, she would never have taken a "gut"…The memory flooded back
(65) then, still painful as an open wound all these years later. It was the first day of high school. She had graduated from grammar

GO ON TO THE NEXT PAGE ⟶

school the previous year, but her father had forbidden her to go on to high school (70) that fall, saying that she was needed on the farm. After much tearful pleading, she had gotten him to promise that next year, she could start high school. She had endured a whole year of chores instead of books, with (75) animals and rough farmhands for company instead of people her own age. Now, at last, the glorious day was at hand. She had put on her best dress (she owned two), her heart racing in anticipation. But her father was (80) waiting for her as she came downstairs.

"Where do you think you're going?" he asked.

"To high school, Papa."

"No you're not. Take that thing off and (85) get back to work."

"But Papa, you promised!"

"*Do as I say*!" he thundered.

There was no arguing with Papa when he spoke that way. Tearfully, she had trudged (90) upstairs to change clothes. Rosemary still wondered what life would have been like if her father had not been waiting at the bottom of the stairs that day, or if somehow she had found the strength to defy him…

(95) Suddenly, Victor stirred, without waking, and mumbled something unintelligible. Jarred from her reverie, Rosemary stared at Victor. She wondered if he were having a nightmare.

1. According to the passage, Victor is Rosemary's:

   A. nephew.

   B. son.

   C. grandson.

   D. great-grandson.

2. It can be inferred from the passage that Rosemary is disturbed by Victor's:

   F. intention to drop out of college.

   G. disregard of her harsh upbringing.

   H. willingness to take courses that are easy to pass.

   J. inability to get out of bed in the morning.

3. The passage suggests that in the year after she finished grammar school, Rosemary most wanted:

   A. an escape from her father's company.

   B. the opportunity to go to college.

   C. the chance to study challenging subjects.

   D. the company of people her own age.

4. The passage suggests that Rosemary's attitude toward the physical afflictions of old age is generally one of:

   F. sadness.

   G. acceptance.

   H. resentment.

   J. optimism.

5. According to the passage, Rosemary does crossword puzzles in order to:

   A. keep her mind active.

   B. practice her handwriting.

   C. learn new geographical facts.

   D. make her more aware of time.

GO ON TO THE NEXT PAGE ⇨

6. The focus of the passage as a whole is on:

    F. Rosemary's concern at Victor's lack of motivation.

    G. the harsh treatment Victor received from his father.

    H. the contrast between Victor's and Rosemary's attitudes toward education.

    J. Rosemary's struggle to suppress painful memories.

7. It can be inferred from the passage that Victor's "shiny new car" (line 49) is mentioned in order to illustrate:

    A. the excessive generosity of Rosemary's parents.

    B. the contrast between Rosemary's generation and his.

    C. the strength of Victor's prospects for the future.

    D. the lack of physical hardship in Victor's life.

8. The third paragraph (lines 53–80) primarily portrays Rosemary in her youth as:

    F. resentful of her father's conduct.

    G. eager to continue her education.

    H. undecided about her future career.

    J. proud of her appearance.

9. Rosemary's recollection of growing up on the farm (lines 29–36) is mentioned as an example of her:

    A. nostalgia for her childhood experiences.

    B. determination to overcome her physical disabilities.

    C. ability to recall past and present events at the same time.

    D. disappointment at being denied an education.

10. The statement that Victor's "future appeared bright" (lines 51–52) most likely reflects the opinion of:

    F. Rosemary.

    G. Victor.

    H. Victor's parents.

    J. Rosemary's father.

PASSAGE II

SOCIAL SCIENCE

These two passages reflect two different views concerning the origins of modern liberal economic regulation in the United States. Passage A is from a 1980 newspaper article about the beginning of progressive reforms to the American economy. Passage B was written in the 1990s by a noted economic historian.

PASSAGE A

The Sherman Antitrust Act was introduced into Congress by Senator John Sherman of Ohio, and, after being first rewritten by pro-business Eastern senators, was passed into law
(5) in 1890. The Act made illegal "every contract, combination in the form of trust or otherwise, or conspiracy in the restraint of trade." Many have charged, at that time and since, that the decidedly vague wording introduced by the
(10) pro-business revisers resulted in the emasculation of the law's anti-monopoly message. Nevertheless, the Act was the first law to fight, even symbolically, against economic monopolies in the "open" market economy of the
(15) United States.

From the birth of the nation, many politicians and influential business leaders had felt that the most natural and ideal democratic economy was one in which the government
(20) played a very limited role in regulating commerce. It was argued that, by permitting businesses to pursue their own interests, the government was promoting the interests of

GO ON TO THE NEXT PAGE

the nation as a whole, or as GM chairman
(25) Charles E. Wilson reportedly quipped, "What's
good for General Motors is good for the
nation." Many of the leaders of trusts and
monopolies in the 1800s co-opted the then
cutting-edge terminology of Charles Darwin's
(30) theory of natural selection, arguing that in an
unrestrained economy, power and wealth
would naturally flow to the most capable
according to the principles of "Social Darwinism." Their monopolies were thus natural
(35) and efficient outcomes of economic development.

Towards the close of the 1800s, however,
an increasingly large and vocal number of lower-
and middle-class dissenters felt that the *laissez-
faire*[1] policies of the federal government allowed
(40) monopolistic trusts like Standard Oil to manipulate consumers by fixing prices, exploit workers
by cutting wages, and threaten democracy by
corrupting politicians. Most directly, the trusts
and monopolies completely destroyed the op-
(45) portunities for competitors in their industries
to do business effectively. The concerns of these
working-class dissenters thus created a ground-
swell of support for the Sherman Antitrust Act,
which attempted to outlaw these monopolies
(50) and trusts. Even more important than the direct
effects of the Act, however, was the sign of a new
era of reform against monopolistic economic
corruption, and the rise of deliberate economic
regulation in America. The federal government
(55) had finally realized that it had to take a more
active role in the economy in order to protect the
interests and rights of consumers, workers, and
small businesses while tempering the dominating
power of big business.

PASSAGE B

(60)   Some political historians contend that altera-
tions to the powers or role of the federal government are a violation of the democratic principles
and goals on which the United States was founded.
I hold that the evolution of democracy in America
(65) has been absolutely necessary and has led to
positive reform to correct injustices and suit the
needs of changing times. In no arena is this

more evident than in the field of economic policy,
especially during the presidency of Franklin D.
(70) Roosevelt.

Roosevelt was a liberal Democrat who looked
on his election in 1932 as a mandate from the
nation's voters to forge a bold path out of the
crippled economy, massive unemployment, and
(75) plummeting farm prices brought on by the Great
Depression[2]. Traditionally, it was believed that
in democratic nations the government should
balance its own budget and not attempt to manipulate the economy as a whole by expending
(80) money. According to traditional or conservative capitalist economists, busts and booms
in an open, unregulated economy were normal
and healthy, part of a natural cycle that self-
regulated excess or overproduction. There
(85) was thus no need for government intervention
during recessions. It seemed evident to
Roosevelt, however, that the Great Depression
would not "naturally" recede, and that he must,
in his own words, "reform democracy in order
(90) to save it." Roosevelt "pump-primed" the
economy using government funds for the
first time in American history by intentional
deficit spending. In the Agricultural Adjustment
Act, for example, Roosevelt controlled one
(95) of the causes and symptoms of the economic
recession, agricultural overproduction, by
using government funds to pay farmers to
produce fewer crops. Perhaps more than any
other, this act signaled the end of the *laissez-
(100) faire* economics era and ushered in the modern
era of liberal economic regulation.

Our nation's founders had planned for
a minimalist federal government that would
balance its own books and mind its own
(105) business, and, for some 150 years, this attitude
seemed intrinsic to the role of the federal
government. The deficit spending and deliberate manipulation of the national economy
by the Roosevelt administration marked a
(110) radical revision of the role of the federal
government, and it's likely that only the severe
crises of the Depression could have compelled
Americans to fully embrace the notion that

GO ON TO THE NEXT PAGE ⟶

government intervention in the economy was
(115) both beneficial and necessary. The success
of this approach in pulling the nation out of
a crippling depression was undeniable. Also
undeniable was the larger conclusion that the
national government must adapt in both
(120) scope and purpose to fit the needs of changing
times.

[1] from the French "to allow to do," an economic policy of non-intervention
[2] a prolonged and severe economic recession in America during the 1930s

---

Questions 11–13 ask about Passage A.

---

11. The revisions mentioned in line 3 illustrate the:

   A. support for Social Darwinism common in the nineteenth century.

   B. resistance from business proponents to antitrust reform.

   C. lengthy period of debate that preceded the passage of the Sherman Act.

   D. ineffective nature of Congressional legislation in the 1890s.

12. The phrase "Social Darwinism" (lines 33–34) is included in Passage A as:

   F. an illustration of the similarities between economic evolution and biological evolution.

   G. an argument to assert that only the strongest corporations could survive in a free market economy.

   H. a demonstration of the terms that monopolists utilized to justify their control of industries.

   J. an example of the influence of scientific theories on social and economic policy.

13. Based on information in the third paragraph of Passage A (lines 36–59), it seems most likely that the author of Passage A would agree with which of the following?

   A. All monopolistic trusts fixed prices and exploited workers.

   B. The overall effects of stifled competition were negative for many Americans.

   C. Outlawing monopolies was a necessary reform to save democracy.

   D. Standard Oil was prevented from freely competing by the Sherman Antitrust Act.

Questions 14–16 ask about Passage B.

---

14. The author cites the Agricultural Adjustment Act (lines 93–94) as:

   F. an important twentieth century antitrust act.

   G. an act that led to a resurgence of *laissez-faire* economic policy.

   H. a factor leading to the Great Depression.

   J. an example of aggressive government intervention in the economy.

15. In the last paragraph of Passage B (lines 102–121), the author primarily:

   A. argues that an alteration to the original plans for the American federal government was beneficial.

   B. shows that Roosevelt's economic reforms were unnecessary.

   C. cites an exception to his generalization that Roosevelt normally passed only beneficial legislation.

   D. explores weaknesses in the original design of the American federal government.

GO ON TO THE NEXT PAGE ▷

16. In the second paragraph of Passage B, the author includes the opinion of "conservative capitalist economists" (lines 80–81) as:

F. a demonstration of the conservative nature of the economic reforms introduced during the Roosevelt era.

G. evidence in support of the Agricultural Adjustment Act.

H. a view about the necessity of government economic regulation that the author will later refute.

J. an argument that only severe poverty can force radical changes in America.

Questions 17–20 ask about both passages.

---

17. Both passages cite which of the following as a necessary reform to the original design of the American democracy?

A. Lessening government control of the economy

B. Abandoning *laissez-faire* economic policy

C. Preventing unfair industry domination

D. Passing laws to limit agricultural overproduction

18. The author of Passage B would most likely respond to the description of monopolies as "natural and efficient outcomes of economic development" (lines 34–35) by:

F. arguing that theories of Social Darwinism were used as justification to promote the interests of the most wealthy.

G. noting that the most "natural" state of the economy is not necessarily the most preferable.

H. agreeing that government intervention in the economy is an abandonment of the ideals upon which the country was founded.

J. noting that the economic policies of Franklin Roosevelt were highly effective in battling such monopolies.

19. What aspect of government economic regulation is emphasized in Passage B, but not in Passage A?

A. Antitrust laws

B. Deficit spending

C. Congressional legislation

D. *Laissez-faire* policies

20. According to each passage, the term *laissez-faire* describes:

F. an economic policy that is beneficial to consumers and a period in history that has yet to conclude.

G. a natural, ideal democratic economy and a government's attempt to balance its own budget without creating interference.

H. a philosophy that Roosevelt championed and a presidential legacy that is in effect to this day.

J. an approach that allowed trusts to manipulate consumers and an era that the Agricultural Adjustment Act ended.

GO ON TO THE NEXT PAGE

PASSAGE III

HUMANITIES

This passage is an excerpt from A Short History of Western Civilization, *Volume 1, by John B. Harrison, Richard E. Sullivan, and Dennis Sherman, © 1990 by McGraw-Hill, Inc. Reprinted by permission of McGraw-Hill, Inc.*

Enlightenment ideas were put forth by a variety of intellectuals who in France came to be known as the *philosophes. Philosophes*
Line is French for philosophers, and in a sense
(5) these thinkers were rightly considered philosophers, for the questions they dealt with were philosophical: How do we discover truth? How should life be lived? What is the nature of God? But on the whole
(10) the term has a meaning different from the usual meaning of "philosopher." The philosophes were intellectuals, often not formally trained or associated with a university. They were usually more literary than scientific.
(15) They generally extended, applied, popularized, or propagandized ideas of others rather than originating those ideas themselves. The philosophes were more likely to write plays, satires, pamphlets or simply participate in
(20) verbal exchanges at select gatherings than to write formal philosophical books.

It was the philosophes who developed the philosophy of the Enlightenment and spread it to much of the educated elite
(25) in Western Europe (and the American colonies). Although the sources for their philosophy can be traced to the Scientific Revolution in general, the philosophes were most influenced by their understanding of
(30) Newton, Locke, and English institutions.

The philosophes saw Newton as the great synthesizer of the Scientific Revolution who rightly described the universe as ordered, mechanical, material, and only originally
(35) set in motion by God, who since then has remained relatively inactive. Newton's synthesis showed to the philosophes that reason and nature were compatible: Nature functioned logically and discernibly, and
(40) what was natural was also reasonable. Newton exemplified the value of reasoning based on concrete experience. The philosophes felt that his empirical methodology was the correct path to discovering truth.

(45) John Locke (1632–1704) agreed with Newton but went further. This English thinker would not exempt even the mind from the mechanical laws of the material universe. In his *Essay Concerning Human*
(50) *Understanding* (1691), Locke pictured the human brain at birth as a blank sheet of paper on which nothing would ever be written except sense perception and reason. What human beings become depends on
(55) their experiences—on the information received through the senses. Schools and social institutions could therefore play a great role in molding the individual from childhood to adulthood. Human beings were
(60) thus by nature far more malleable than had been assumed. This empirical psychology of Locke rejected the notion that human beings were born with innate ideas or that revelation was a reliable source of truth.

(65) Locke also enunciated liberal and reformist political ideas in his *Second Treatise of Civil Government* (1690), which influenced the philosophes. On the whole Locke's empiricism, psychology and politics were appealing
(70) to the philosophes.

England, not coincidentally the country of Newton and Locke, became the admired model for many of the philosophes. They tended to idealize it, but England did seem
(75) to allow greater individual freedom, tolerate religious differences, and evidence greater political reform than other countries, especially France. England seemed to have gone furthest in freeing itself from traditional
(80) institutions and accepting the new science of the seventeenth century. Moreover, England's approach seemed to work, for England was experiencing relative political

GO ON TO THE NEXT PAGE ⟹

stability and prosperity. The philosophes
(85) wanted to see in their own countries much
of what England already seemed to have.

Many philosophes reflected the influence
of Newton, Locke, and English institutions,
but perhaps the most representative in
(90) his views was Voltaire (1694–1778). Of all
leading figures of the Enlightenment, he was
the most influential. Voltaire, the son of a
Paris lawyer, became the idol of the French
intelligentsia while still in his early twenties.
(95) His versatile mind was sparkling; his wit
was mordant. An outspoken critic, he soon
ran afoul of both church and state authorities.
First he was imprisoned in the Bastille;
later he was exiled to England. There he
(100) encountered the ideas of Newton and Locke
and came to admire English parliamentary
government and tolerance. In *Letters on the
English* (1732), *Elements of the Philosophy
of Newton* (1738), and other writings, he
(105) popularized the ideas of Newton and Locke,
extolled the virtues of English society, and
indirectly criticized French society. Slipping
back into France, he was hidden for a time
and protected by a wealthy woman who
(110) became his mistress. Voltaire's facile mind
and pen were never idle. He wrote poetry,
drama, history, essays, letters, and scientific
treatises—ninety volumes in all. The special
targets of his cynical wit were the Catholic
(115) church and Christian institutions. Few
people in history have dominated their age
intellectually as did Voltaire.

21. The philosophes can best be described as:

   A. writers swept up by their mutual admiration of John Locke.

   B. professors who lectured in philosophy at French universities.

   C. intellectuals responsible for popularizing Enlightenment ideas.

   D. scientists who furthered the work of the Scientific Revolution.

22. Which of the following would most likely have been written by Voltaire?

   F. A treatise criticizing basic concepts of the Scientific Revolution

   G. A play satirizing religious institutions in France

   H. A collection of letters mocking the English Parliament

   J. A sentimental poem expounding the virtues of courtly love

23. According to the passage, Locke felt that schools and social institutions could "play a great role in molding the individual" (lines 57–58) primarily because:

   A. human beings were born with certain innate ideas.

   B. human nature becomes more malleable with age.

   C. society owes each individual the right to an education.

   D. the human mind is chiefly influenced by experience.

24. Based on the information in the passage, which of the following best describes Newton's view of the universe?

   I. The universe was initially set in motion by God.

   II. Human reason is insufficient to understand the laws of nature.

   III. The universe operates in a mechanical and orderly fashion.

   F. I only

   G. I and II only

   H. I and III only

   J. II and III only

GO ON TO THE NEXT PAGE ⇨

25. According to the passage, which of the following works questioned the idea that revelation was a reliable source of truth?

    A. *Letters on the English*
    B. *Second Treatise of Civil Government*
    C. *Elements of the Philosophy of Newton*
    D. *Essay Concerning Human Understanding*

26. The passage supports which of the following statements concerning the relationship between Newton and Locke?

    F. Locke's psychology contradicted Newton's belief in an orderly universe.
    G. Locke maintained that Newton's laws of the material universe also applied to the human mind.
    H. Newton eventually came to accept Locke's revolutionary ideas about the human mind.
    J. Newton's political ideas were the basis of Locke's liberal and reformist politics.

27. According to the passage, the philosophes believed that society should:

    I. allow individuals greater freedom.
    II. free itself from traditional institutions.
    III. tolerate religious differences.

    A. I only
    B. I and II only
    C. II and III only
    D. I, II, and III

28. It can be inferred from the passage that the author regards England's political stability and economic prosperity as:

    F. the reason why the philosophes did not idealize England's achievement.
    G. evidence that political reforms could bring about a better way of life.
    H. the result of Voltaire's activities after he was exiled to England.
    J. an indication that the Scientific Revolution had not yet started there.

29. The passage suggests that the French political and religious authorities during the time of Voltaire:

    A. allowed little in the way of free speech.
    B. overreacted to Voltaire's mild satires.
    C. regarded the philosophes with indifference.
    D. accepted the model of English parliamentary government.

30. How does the passage support the point that the philosophes were "more literary than scientific" (line 14)?

    F. It demonstrates how the philosophes' writings contributed to the political change.
    G. It compares the number of works that Voltaire authored to Newton's output.
    H. It traces the influences of English literary works on French scientists.
    J. It describes the kinds of literary activities the philosophes commonly engaged in.

GO ON TO THE NEXT PAGE ⇨

PASSAGE IV

NATURAL SCIENCE

This passage explores the theory that a large asteroid collided with the Earth 65 million years ago.

Sixty-five million years ago, something triggered mass extinctions so profound that they define the geological boundary between the Cretaceous and Tertiary periods (the K-T
(5) Boundary). Approximately 75 percent of all animal species, including every species of dinosaur, were killed off; those that survived lost the vast majority of their numbers. The Earth exists in a region of space teeming
(10) with asteroids and comets, which on collision have frequently caused enormous environmental devastation, including extinctions of animal species. Yet few traditional geologists or biologists considered the effect
(15) such impacts may have had on the geologic and biologic history of the Earth. Since gradual geologic processes like erosion or repeated volcanic eruptions can explain the topographical development of the Earth,
(20) they felt that there was no need to resort to extraterrestrial explanations.

An important theory proposed in 1980 by physicists Luis and Walter Alvarez challenged this view. The Alvarezes argued
(25) that an asteroid roughly six miles in diameter collided with the Earth in the K-T Boundary. Although the damage caused by the meteorite's impact would have been great, the dust cloud that subsequently
(30) would have enveloped the planet, completely blotting out the sun for up to a year—the result of soil displacement—would have done most of the harm, according to this theory. The plunge into darkness—and
(35) the resulting drastically reduced temperatures —would have interrupted plant growth, cutting off the food supply to herbivorous species, the loss of which in turn would have starved carnivores. Additional species
(40) would have perished as a result of prolonged

atmospheric poisoning, acid rain, forest fires, and tidal waves, all initiated by the asteroid's impact.

Some subsequent research not only
(45) tended to support the Alvarez theory, but suggested that similar impacts may have caused other sharp breaks in Earth's geologic and biologic history. Research in the composition of the Earth revealed a
(50) 160-fold enrichment of iridium all over the world in a thin layer of sediments formed at the K-T Boundary. The presence of this element, which is extremely uncommon in the Earth's crust but very common in
(55) asteroids and comets, suggested that a meteorite must have struck Earth at that time. Additional physical evidence of such a strike was found in rock samples, which contained shocked quartz crystals and
(60) microtektites (small glass spheres)—both byproducts of massive collisions.

Observation of the lunar surface provided further evidence of the likelihood of a massive strike. Since the moon
(65) and the Earth lie within the same swarm of asteroids and comets, their impact histories should be parallel. Although some lunar craters were of volcanic origin, over the last four billion years at least five impact craters
(70) ranging from 31 to 58 miles in diameter have marred the lunar surface. Therefore, over the same time span, Earth must have experienced some 400 collisions of similar magnitude. Although such an impact crater
(75) had not been found, Alvarez supporters didn't consider finding it necessary or likely. They reasoned that geologic processes over 65 million years, like erosion and volcanic eruptions, would have obscured the crater,
(80) which in any case probably formed on the ocean floor.

Traditional biologists and geologists resisted the Alvarez theory. They pointed to the absence of any impact crater; to the
(85) fact that iridium, while rare at the Earth's surface, was common at its core and could

GO ON TO THE NEXT PAGE ⇒

be transported to the surface by volcanic activity; and to the fact that the Alvarezes, though eminent physicists, were not biologists, (90) geologists, or paleontologists.

31. According to the Alvarez theory, the mass extinctions of animal species at the end of the Cretaceous period were caused by:

    A. animals being crushed by an enormous asteroid.

    B. processes like erosion and repeated volcanic eruptions.

    C. extreme global warming causing a global firestorm.

    D. environmental conditions following a meteorite impact.

32. Based on the information in the passage, the author probably believes that those who held the traditional views about the topographical development of the Earth were:

    F. proven incorrect by the Alvarezes.

    G. unrivaled at the present time.

    H. correct in challenging alternative views.

    J. unreceptive to new evidence.

33. As it is used in line 50, the word *enrichment* most nearly means:

    A. wealth.

    B. improvement.

    C. increase in amount.

    D. reward.

34. The views of scientists who opposed the Alvarez theory would have been strengthened if:

    F. major deposits of iridium were found in the lava flows of active Earth volcanoes.

    G. iridium were absent in sediments corresponding to several episodes of mass extinction.

    H. iridium were absent in fragments of several recently recovered meteorites.

    J. the Alvarezes were biologists as well as physicists.

35. The author's attitude toward the Alvarez theory is best characterized as:

    A. dismissive.

    B. neutral.

    C. skeptical.

    D. supportive.

36. According to the passage, which of the following is the correct order of events in the Alvarez theory explaining the mass extinction of species at the end of the Cretaceous period?

    F. Soil displacement, disappearance of the sun, decline of plant life, fall in temperature

    G. Soil displacement, disappearance of the sun, fall in temperature, decline of plant life

    H. Fall in temperature, decline of plant life, soil displacement, disappearance of the sun

    J. Disappearance of the sun, fall in temperature, decline of plant life, soil displacement

GO ON TO THE NEXT PAGE ⇨

37. It can be inferred from paragraph 2 that the author discusses the Alvarezes' description of environmental conditions at the end of the Cretaceous period in order to:

   A. demonstrate that an immense meteorite hit the Earth.
   B. explain why no trace of an impact crater has yet been found.
   C. show that the Earth is vulnerable to meteorite collisions.
   D. clarify how a meteorite may account for mass extinctions.

38. The author's statement (lines 9–10) that "Earth exists in a region of space teeming with asteroids and comets" is important to:

   F. the Alvarezes' claim that an asteroid's impact caused. atmospheric poisoning, acid rain, forest fires, and tidal waves.
   G. the Alvarezes' view that the resulting dust cloud, rather than the impact of the meteorite, did most of the harm.
   H. Alvarez supporters' argument based on the numbers of impact craters on the surface of the moon.
   J. traditionalists' view that to pographical development of the Earth can be explained by gradual geologic processes.

39. Supporters of the Alvarezes' theory believe finding the impact crater is not necessary because:

   I. the crater probably is on the ocean floor.
   II. iridium occurs at the Earth's core.
   III. processes like erosion and volcanic eruptions obscured the crater.

   A. I only
   B. I and II only
   C. I and III only
   D. II and III only

40. According to the passage, species died in mass extinctions as a result of all of the following EXCEPT:

   F. shocked quartz crystals and microtektites.
   G. reduced sunlight for up to a year.
   H. loss of food supplies.
   J. prolonged atmospheric poisoning.

SCIENCE TEST

35 Minutes—40 Questions

Directions: There are several passages in this test. Each passage is followed by several questions. After reading a passage, choose the best answer to each question and fill in the corresponding oval on your answer document. You may refer to the passages as often as necessary. You are NOT permitted to use a calculator on this test.

PASSAGE I

A *binary star system* consists of two stars that are gravitationally bound to each other. If two stars that orbit each other are viewed along a line of sight that is not perpendicular to the orbital plane, they will alternately appear to eclipse each other. The orbit of *eclipsing binary* System Q is shown in Figure 1.

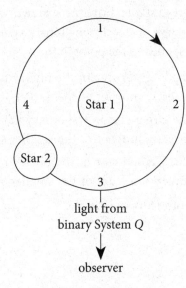

Figure 1

Notes: Diagram is not drawn to scale. Star 1 is brighter than Star 2.

Astronomers deduce that a given star is an eclipsing binary from its *light curve*—the plot of its surface brightness (observed from a fixed position) against time. The light curve of an eclipsing binary typically displays a deep primary minimum and a shallower secondary minimum. Figure 2 shows the light curve of System Q.

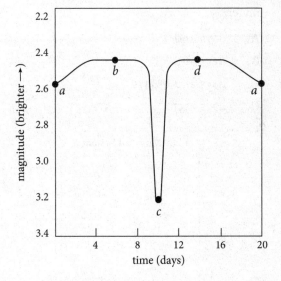

Figure 2

1. The point on the light curve labeled *c* corresponds to the position in Figure 1 labeled:

   A. 1.
   B. 2.
   C. 3.
   D. 4.

GO ON TO THE NEXT PAGE ▷

2. The period of revolution for eclipsing binary Q is about:

    F.   4 days.

    G. 10 days.

    H. 12 days.

    J.   20 days.

3. The stars in eclipsing binary Q alternately eclipse each other for periods of approximately:

    A. 2 days and 4 days.

    B. 2 days and 5 days.

    C. 2 days and 8 days.

    D. 5 days each.

Light Curve of System X

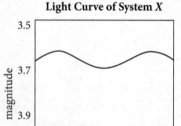

Light Curve of System Z

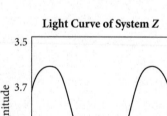

4. The light curves for two eclipsing binaries, Systems X and Z, are shown. Which of the following hypotheses would account for the deeper primary minimum of System Z?

    F.   There is a more extreme difference between the magnitudes of the two stars of System X than between those of the two stars of System Z.

    G. There is a more extreme difference between the magnitudes of the two stars of System Z than between those of the two stars of System X.

    H. System X has a longer period of revolution than does System Z.

    J.   System Z has a longer period of revolution than does System X.

5. The greatest total brightness shown on the light curve of an eclipsing binary system corresponds to the point in the orbit when:

    A. the brighter star in the binary pair is directly in front of the darker star.

    B. the larger star in the binary pair is directly in front of the smaller star.

    C. the brighter star in the binary pair is directly in front of the smaller star.

    D. both stars are visible.

GO ON TO THE NEXT PAGE

PASSAGE II

The utilization and replenishing of the Earth's carbon supply is a cyclic process involving all living matter. This cycle is shown here.

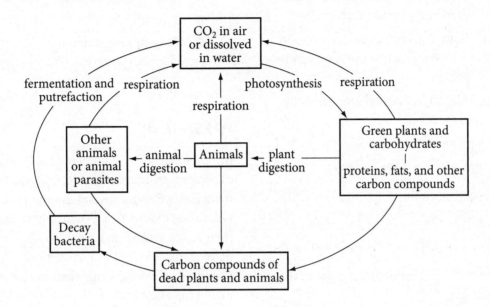

6. Carbon fixation involves the removal of CO_2 from the air and the incorporation of various compounds. According to the cycle shown, carbon fixation can form which compound(s)?

    I. Fat

    II. Starch

    III. Protein

    F. II

    G. II and III

    H. I and II

    J. I, II, and III

7. What effect would a sudden drop in the amount of the Earth's decay bacteria have on the amount of carbon dioxide in the atmosphere?

    A. The CO_2 level will drop to a life-threatening level since the bacteria is the sole source of CO_2.

    B. The CO_2 level will rise because the bacteria usually consume CO_2.

    C. The CO_2 level may decrease slightly, but there are other sources of CO_2.

    D. The CO_2 level will increase slightly due to an imbalance in the carbon cycle.

GO ON TO THE NEXT PAGE

8. Which of the following statements are consistent with the carbon cycle as presented in the diagram?

    I. A non-plant-eating animal does not participate in the carbon cycle.

    II. Both plant and animal respiration contribute CO_2 to the earth's atmosphere.

    III. All CO_2 is released into the air by respiration.

  F. I only

  G. II only

  H. I and II only

  J. II and III only

9. A direct source of CO_2 in the atmosphere is:

  A. the fermentation of green-plant carbohydrates.

  B. the photosynthesis of tropical plants.

  C. the digestion of plant matter by animals.

  D. the respiration of animal parasites.

10. Which of the following best describes the relationship between animal respiration and photosynthesis?

  F. Respiration and photosynthesis serve the same function in the carbon cycle.

  G. Animal respiration provides vital gases for green plants.

  H. Animal respiration prohibits photosynthesis.

  J. There is no relationship between respiration and photosynthesis.

11. The elimination of which of the following would cause the earth's carbon cycle to grind to a complete halt?

  A. Green plants

  B. Animals

  C. Animal predation

  D. Decay bacteria

PASSAGE III

Microbiologists have observed that certain species of bacteria are magnetotactic, i.e., sensitive to magnetic fields. Several species found in the bottom of swamps in the Northern Hemisphere tend to orient themselves toward magnetic north (the northern pole of the earth's magnetic field). Researchers conducted the following series of experiments on magnetotactic bacteria.

STUDY 1

A drop of water filled with magnetotactic bacteria was observed under high magnification. The direction of the first 500 bacterial migrations across the field of view was observed for each of five trials and the tally for each trial recorded in Table 1. Trial 1 was conducted under standard laboratory conditions. In Trial 2, the microscope was shielded from all external light and electric fields. In Trials 3 and 4, the microscope was rotated clockwise 90° and 180°, respectively. For Trial 5, the microscope was moved to another laboratory at the same latitude.

GO ON TO THE NEXT PAGE

Table 1

Trial #	Direction			
	North	**East**	**South**	**West**
1	474	7	13	6
2	481	3	11	5
3	479	4	12	5
4	465	9	19	7
5	484	3	11	6

STUDY 2

The north pole of a permanent magnet was positioned near the microscope slide. The magnet was at the 12:00 position for Trial 1 and was moved 90° clockwise for each of three successive trials. All other conditions were as in Trial 1 of Study 1. The results were tallied and recorded in Table 2.

Table 2

Trial #	Direction			
	12:00	**3:00**	**6:00**	**9:00**
1	472	6	15	9
2	8	483	3	6
3	17	4	474	5
4	5	19	9	467

12. The theory that light was not the primary stimulus affecting the direction of bacterial migration is:

   F. supported by a comparison of the results of Studies 1 and 2.

   G. supported by a comparison of the results of Trials 1 and 2 of Study 1.

   H. supported by a comparison of the results of Trials 3 and 4 of Study 1.

   J. not supported by any of the results noted in the passage.

13. If the south pole of the permanent magnet used in Study 2 had been placed near the microscope slide, what would the most likely result have been?

   A. The figures for each trial would have remained approximately the same, since the strength of the magnetic field would be unchanged.

   B. The bacteria would have become disoriented, with approximately equal numbers moving in each direction.

   C. The major direction of travel would have shifted by 180° because of the reversed direction of the magnetic field.

   D. The bacteria would still have tended to migrate toward Earth's magnetic north, but would have taken longer to orient themselves.

14. It has been suggested that magnetic sensitivity helps magnetotactic bacteria orient themselves downward. Such an orientation would be most advantageous from an evolutionary standpoint if:

   F. organisms that consume magnetotactic bacteria were mostly bottom-dwellers.

   G. the bacteria could only reproduce by migrating upwards to the water's surface.

   H. bacteria that stayed in the top layers of water tended to be dispersed by currents.

   J. the nutrients necessary for the bacteria's survival were more abundant in bottom sediments.

GO ON TO THE NEXT PAGE >

15. Researchers could gain the most useful new information about the relationship between magnetic field strength and bacterial migration by repeating Study 2 with:

   A. incremental position changes of less than 90°.

   B. a magnet that rotated slowly around the slide in a counterclockwise direction.

   C. more and less powerful magnets.

   D. larger and smaller samples of bacteria.

16. Which of the following statements is supported by the results of Study 1?

   F. The majority of magnetotactic bacteria migrate toward the Earth's magnetic north pole.

   G. The majority of magnetotactic bacteria migrate toward the north pole of the nearest magnet.

   H. The majority of magnetotactic bacteria migrate toward the 12:00 position.

   J. The effect of the Earth's magnetic field on magnetotactic bacteria is counteracted by electric fields.

17. What is the control in Study 1?

   A. Trial 1
   B. Trial 2
   C. Trial 3
   D. Trial 5

18. If each diagram below represents a microscopic field, which diagram best reflects the results of Trial 2 from Study 2?

   F.

   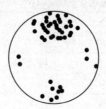

   G.

   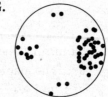

   H.

   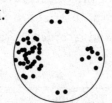

   J.

   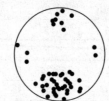

GO ON TO THE NEXT PAGE

PASSAGE IV

A process has been developed by which plastic bottles can be recycled into a clear, colorless material. This material, called *nu-PVC*, can be used to form park benches and other similar structures. A series of experiments was performed to determine the weathering abilities of *nu-PVC*.

EXPERIMENT 1

Fifteen boards of *nu-PVC*, each 150 × 25 × 8 cm in size, were sprayed with distilled water for 10 hours a day for 32 weeks. All 15 boards remained within 0.1 cm of their original dimensions. The surfaces of the boards displayed no signs of cracking, bubbling, or other degradation.

EXPERIMENT 2

Fifteen sheets of *nu-PVC*, each 2 m × 2 m × 5 cm, were hung in a chamber in which the humidity and temperature were held constant. The sheets were irradiated with ultraviolet light for 12 hours a day for 32 weeks. At the end of the experiment, the sheets' flexibility had decreased by an average of 17.5%. The surface of the sheets showed no signs of degradation, but they had all become milky white in color. Results from this experiment are shown in Figure 1.

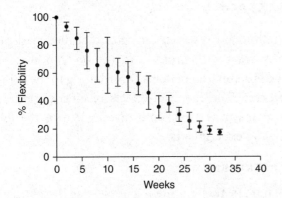

Figure 1

EXPERIMENT 3

Fifteen boards, as in Experiment 1, were each found to be capable of supporting an average of 963 pounds for 15 days without breaking or bending. These same boards were then kept for 32 weeks at temperatures ranging from 5°C to –15°C. At the end of the experiment, the boards were able to support an average of only 400 pounds without bending or breaking. This data is shown in Figure 2.

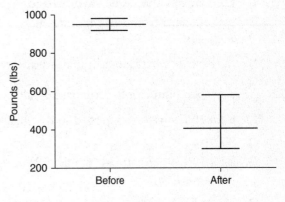

Figure 2

19. According to Figure 1, what would be the estimated percent flexibility if a sheet of *nu-PVC* was measured at 40 weeks?

    A. 3%

    B. 12%

    C. 20%

    D. 22.5%

20. Based on the results of Experiment 1, which of the following conclusions concerning the effect of rain on *nu-PVC* is valid?

    F. The material absorbs water over time, causing it to permanently swell.

    G. The material will be useful only in areas where there is no acid rain.

    H. The material's surface does not appear to require a protective coating to avoid water damage.

    J. The material loses flexibility after prolonged exposure to precipitation.

GO ON TO THE NEXT PAGE

21. Park benches in an often snow-covered region of Minnesota are to be replaced with new ones, made of *nu-PVC*. The experimental results indicate that:

   A. the benches will suffer little degradation due to weathering.

   B. the benches would have to be stored indoors during the winter to retain their initial strength.

   C. the benches should be varnished to prevent rain from seeping into the material.

   D. the benches will retain their initial flexibility.

22. A reasonable control for Experiment 1 would be:

   F. a *nu-PVC* board submerged in distilled water.

   G. a *nu-PVC* board stored in a dry warehouse.

   H. a wooden board subjected to the same conditions.

   J. a wooden board stored in a dry warehouse.

23. The purpose of the ultraviolet radiation used in Experiment 2 was to:

   A. simulate the effects of sunlight.

   B. avoid damage to the material's finish.

   C. turn the boards a uniform color.

   D. test the strength of the *nu-PVC*.

24. From the information given, it can be inferred that *nu-PVC*'s advantage over standard building materials, such as wood, is that it:

   F. is heavier and denser than other materials.

   G. can be developed in different colors and textures.

   H. is less subject to structural cracking and failure.

   J. is made from recycled plastic wastes.

25. Which of the following experiments would be the most likely to provide useful information concerning the weathering of *nu-PVC*?

   I. Repeating Experiment 1, increasing the length of the experiment from 32 weeks to 64 weeks

   II. Investigating the effects of sea water and salt-rich air on the material

   III. Repeating Experiment 3, decreasing the minimum temperature from $-15°C$ to $-40°C$

   A. II only

   B. III only

   C. I and II only

   D. I, II, and III

26. According to Figure 2, what is the approximate range of weight that the boards could hold after being kept in the cold?

   F. 100 lbs.

   G. 300 lbs.

   H. 563 lbs.

   J. 650 lbs.

PASSAGE V

Preliminary research indicates that dietary sugar may react with proteins in the body, damaging the proteins and perhaps contributing to the aging process. The chemical effects of glucose on lens proteins in the eye were investigated in the following experiments.

EXPERIMENT 1

A human tissue protein sample was dissolved in a glucose and water solution, resulting in a clear, yellow solution. After 30 minutes, the solution became opaque. Spectrographic analysis (Figure 1) revealed that an *Amadori* product had formed on the protein. It was determined that the *Amadori*

GO ON TO THE NEXT PAGE ⟶

products on one protein had combined with free amino groups on nearby proteins, forming brown pigmented cross-links between the two proteins. The cross-links are termed advanced glycosylation end products (AGE).

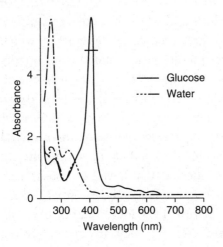

Figure 1

EXPERIMENT 2

Forty-six samples of human lens proteins taken from subjects ranging in age from 12–80 years were studied under an electron microscope. The lens proteins in the samples from older subjects occurred much more often in aggregates formed by cross-linked bonds than did the lens proteins in the samples from younger subjects. Fluorescent characteristics revealed the cross-links to be of two types: disulfide bonds and an indeterminate formation with brownish pigmentation.

EXPERIMENT 3

Two solutions containing lens proteins from cow lenses were prepared, one with glucose and one without. Only the glucose solution turned opaque. Analysis revealed that the lens proteins in the glucose solution had formed pigmented cross-links with the brownish color and fluorescence characteristics of those observed in Experiment 1.

27. According to Figure 1, what is the wavelength of the maximum absorbance of *Amadori* products?

   A. 250 nm
   B. 300 nm
   C. 350 nm
   D. 400 nm

28. It was assumed in the design of Experiment 3 that cow lens proteins:

   F. have a brownish pigment.
   G. react with sulfides.
   H. remain insoluble in water.
   J. react similarly to human lens proteins.

29. Based on the results in Experiment 1 only, it can be concluded that:

   A. proteins can form disulfide cross-links.
   B. glucose dissolved in water forms AGE.
   C. glucose can react with proteins to form cross-links.
   D. Amadori products are a result of glucose metabolism.

30. As people age, the lenses in their eyes sometimes turn brown and cloudy (known as senile cataracts). Based on this information and the results of Experiment 2, which of the following hypotheses is the most likely to be valid?

   F. As people age, the amount of sulfur contained in lens proteins increases.
   G. Senile cataracts are caused by cross-linked bonds between lens proteins.
   H. Lens proteins turn brown with age.
   J. Older lens proteins are more fluorescent than younger lens proteins.

GO ON TO THE NEXT PAGE ➡

31. Which of the following hypotheses about the brown pigmented cross-links observed in Experiment 2 is best supported by the results of the three experiments?

   A. Their brownish color is caused by disulfide bonds.

   B. They are a natural formation which can be found at birth.

   C. They are caused by glucose in the diet reacting with lens proteins.

   D. They form when proteins are dissolved in water.

32. Based on the experimental results, lens proteins from a 32-year-old man would most likely have:

   F. more cross-links than lens proteins from a 32-year-old woman.

   G. more cross-links than lens proteins from an 18-year-old cow.

   H. more cross-links than lens proteins from an 18-year-old man.

   J. fewer cross-links than lens proteins from an 80-year-old man.

33. People with uncontrolled diabetes have excess levels of blood glucose. Based on this information and the results of the experiments, a likely symptom of advanced diabetes would be:

   A. senile cataracts, due to an increase of free amino groups in the urine.

   B. senile cataracts, due to glucose interacting with disulfide cross-links on lens proteins.

   C. senile cataracts, due to AGE cross-links of lens proteins.

   D. kidney failure, due to high levels of free amino groups in the urine.

PASSAGE VI

Two scientists discuss their views about the Quark Model.

SCIENTIST 1

According to the Quark Model, each proton consists of three quarks: two up quarks, which carry a charge of +2/3 each, and one down quark, which carries a charge of –1/3. All mesons, one of which is the p+ particle, are composed of one quark and one antiquark, and all baryons, one of which is the proton, are composed of three quarks. The Quark Model explains the numerous different types of mesons that have been observed. It also successfully predicted the essential properties of the Y meson. Individual quarks have not been observed because they are absolutely confined within baryons and mesons. However, the results of deep inelastic scattering experiments indicate that the proton has a substructure. In these experiments, high-energy electron beams were fired into protons. While most of the electrons incident on the proton passed right through, a few bounced back. The number of electrons scattered through large angles indicated that there are three distinct lumps within the proton.

SCIENTIST 2

The Quark Model is seriously flawed. Conventional scattering experiments should be able to split the proton into its constituent quarks, if they existed. Once the quarks were free, it would be easy to distinguish quarks from other particles using something as simple as the Millikan oil drop experiment because they would be the only particles that carry fractional charge. Furthermore, the lightest quark would be stable because there is no lighter particle for it to decay into. Quarks would be so easy to produce, identify, and store that they would have been detected if they truly existed. In addition, the Quark Model violates the Pauli exclusion principle which originally was believed

GO ON TO THE NEXT PAGE

to hold for electrons but was found to hold for all particles of half-integer spin. The Pauli exclusion principle states that no two particles of half-integer spin can occupy the same state. The Δ^{++} baryon which supposedly has three up quarks violates the Pauli exclusion principle because two of those quarks would be in the same state. Therefore, the Quark Model must be replaced.

34. Which of the following would most clearly strengthen Scientist 1's hypothesis?

    F. Detection of the Δ^{++} baryon
    G. Detection of a particle with fractional charge
    H. Detection of mesons
    J. Detection of baryons

35. Which of the following are reasons why Scientist 2 claims quarks should have been detected, if they existed?

    I. They have a unique charge.
    II. They are confined within mesons and baryons.
    III. They are supposedly fundamental particles, and so could not decay into any other particle.

    A. I only
    B. II only
    C. I and III only
    D. I, II, and III

36. Which of the following could Scientist 1 use to counter Scientist 2's point about the Pauli exclusion principle?

    F. Evidence that quarks do not have half-integer spin
    G. Evidence that the Δ^{++} baryon exists
    H. Evidence that quarks have fractional charge
    J. Evidence that quarks have the same spin as electrons

37. If Scientist 1's hypothesis is correct, the Δ^{++} baryon should have a charge of:

    A. -1
    B. 0
    C. 1
    D. 2

38. Scientist 2 says the Quark Model is flawed because:

    F. the existence of individual baryons cannot be experimentally verified.
    G. the existence of individual quarks cannot be experimentally verified.
    H. particles cannot have fractional charge.
    J. it doesn't include electrons as elementary particles.

39. Scientist 1 says that some high-energy electrons that were aimed into the proton in the deep inelastic scattering experiments bounced back because they:

    A. hit quarks.
    B. hit other electrons.
    C. were repelled by the positive charge on the proton.
    D. hit baryons.

40. The fact that deep inelastic scattering experiments revealed a proton substructure of three lumps supports the Quark Model because:

    F. protons are mesons, and mesons supposedly consist of three quarks.
    G. protons are mesons, and mesons supposedly consist of a quark and an antiquark.
    H. protons are baryons, and baryons supposedly consist of three quarks.
    J. protons are baryons, and baryons supposedly consist of one quark and one antiquark.

IF YOU FINISH BEFORE TIME IS CALLED, YOU MAY CHECK YOUR WORK ON THIS SECTION ONLY. DO NOT TURN TO ANY OTHER SECTION IN THE TEST. **STOP**

WRITING TEST

40 Minutes—1 Question

Directions: This is a test of your writing skills. You will have forty (40) minutes to write an essay in English. Before you begin planning and writing your essay, read the writing prompt carefully to understand exactly what you are being asked to do. Your essay will be evaluated on the evidence it provides of your ability to do the following:

- Express judgments by evaluating the three perspectives given in the prompt, taking a position on an issue, and explaining the relationship among all four ideas
- Develop a position by using logical reasoning and by supporting your ideas
- Maintain a focus on the topic throughout the essay
- Organize ideas in a logical way
- Use language clearly and effectively according to the conventions of standard written English

You may use a separate piece of paper to plan your essay. *You must write your essay in pencil on the lined pages provided after the prompt.* Your writing on those lined pages will be scored. You may not need all the lined pages, but to ensure you have enough room to finish, do NOT skip lines. You may write corrections or additions neatly between the lines of your essay, but do NOT write in the margins of the lined pages. *Illegible essays cannot be scored, so you must write (or print) clearly.*

DO NOT OPEN THIS BOOKLET UNTIL TOLD TO DO SO.

GO ON TO THE NEXT PAGE ⇒

ATTENDANCE POLICIES

Students are required to be in attendance during the school day unless they are ill, have a doctor's appointment, or need to attend a funeral. Parents are allowed to take students out of school for other reasons, but prior approval is often required. Truancy, or unexcused absenteeism, is a problem that many schools have yet to solve. Since reducing truancy increases student success, should schools be doing more to prevent unexcused absences? Considering that students rely on educators to offer guidance and support, it is wise for schools to assist students in attending school as regularly as possible.

Read and carefully consider these perspectives. Each offers suggestions regarding attendance policies.

Perspective One	Perspective Two	Perspective Three
Schools should contact law enforcement officers to report students who skip school regularly. In addition to receiving detention for unexcused absences, students' truancy should be noted in criminal records. This additional consequence will help discourage students from missing school.	Truancy is a symptom rather than a core issue. Students who skip school regularly often do so because of transportation difficulties, social problems, violence concerns, or lack of interest. Addressing the core issues is the key to increasing student attendance, and schools should develop programs to help students overcome obstacles that prevent them from coming to school.	Schools should offer helpful alternative instruction for students who regularly miss school. Whether students are allowed to attend school on the weekends or are required to take classes online, schools should provide students every opportunity to complete their courses and graduate.

ESSAY TASK

Write a unified, coherent essay in which you evaluate multiple perspectives on experiential education. In your essay, be sure to:

- analyze and evaluate the perspectives given
- state and develop your own perspective on the issue
- explain the relationship between your perspective and those given

Your perspective may be in full agreement with any of the others, in partial agreement, or wholly different. Whatever the case, support your ideas with logical reasoning and detailed, persuasive examples.

GO ON TO THE NEXT PAGE ⇒

PLANNING YOUR ESSAY

You may wish to consider the following as you think critically about the task:

Strengths and weaknesses of the three given perspectives
- What insights do they offer, and what do they fail to consider?
- Why might they be persuasive to others, or why might they fail to persuade?

Your own knowledge, experience, and values
- What is your perspective on this issue, and what are its strengths and weaknesses?
- How will you support your perspective in your essay?

_____

_____

_____

_____

_____

_____

_____

_____

_____

_____

_____

_____

_____

_____

_____

_____

_____

_____

GO ON TO THE NEXT PAGE

_____

_____

_____

_____

_____

_____

_____

_____

_____

_____

_____

_____

_____

_____

_____

_____

_____

_____

_____

_____

_____

_____

_____

IF YOU FINISH BEFORE TIME IS CALLED, YOU MAY CHECK YOUR WORK ON THIS SECTION ONLY. DO NOT TURN TO ANY OTHER SECTION IN THE TEST.

STOP

Practice Test Four
ANSWER KEY

ENGLISH TEST

1. C	11. D	21. A	31. A	41. A	51. A	61. C	71. A
2. G	12. H	22. J	32. H	42. G	52. J	62. J	72. J
3. D	13. C	23. C	33. D	43. C	53. D	63. D	73. D
4. F	14. J	24. G	34. F	44. H	54. H	64. H	74. G
5. D	15. C	25. D	35. A	45. B	55. B	65. A	75. B
6. G	16. H	26. H	36. G	46. G	56. J	66. J	
7. D	17. C	27. B	37. A	47. D	57. D	67. A	
8. J	18. H	28. G	38. J	48. J	58. H	68. J	
9. C	19. D	29. D	39. D	49. B	59. B	69. B	
10. J	20. F	30. J	40. G	50. J	60. G	70. G	

MATHEMATICS TEST

1. B	9. E	17. E	25. C	33. C	41. D	49. C	57. C
2. J	10. K	18. J	26. J	34. F	42. G	50. K	58. K
3. C	11. C	19. D	27. D	35. C	43. D	51. B	59. C
4. G	12. H	20. F	28. J	36. G	44. H	52. H	60. K
5. E	13. B	21. C	29. B	37. C	45. A	53. C	
6. J	14. K	22. H	30. F	38. H	46. J	54. G	
7. B	15. A	23. D	31. D	39. B	47. D	55. D	
8. G	16. J	24. G	32. G	40. F	48. J	56. J	

READING TEST

1. C	6. H	11. B	16. H	21. C	26. G	31. D	36. G
2. H	7. B	12. H	17. B	22. G	27. D	32. H	37. D
3. D	8. G	13. B	18. G	23. D	28. G	33. C	38. H
4. G	9. C	14. J	19. B	24. H	29. A	34. F	39. C
5. A	10. F	15. A	20. J	25. D	30. J	35. D	40. F

SCIENCE TEST

1. C	6. J	11. A	16. F	21. B	26. G	31. C	36. F
2. J	7. C	12. G	17. A	22. G	27. D	32. J	37. D
3. C	8. G	13. C	18. G	23. A	28. J	33. C	38. G
4. G	9. D	14. J	19. B	24. J	29. C	34. G	39. A
5. D	10. G	15. C	20. H	25. A	30. G	35. C	40. H

ANSWERS AND EXPLANATIONS

ENGLISH TEST

PASSAGE I

1. C
Category: Punctuation
Difficulty: High
Getting to the Answer: At first glance, there may not seem to be anything wrong here. However, the dash after *Aegean Sea* alerts you that the writer has chosen to set off the parenthetical phrase describing *Acropolis* with dashes instead of commas. This means that you have to replace the comma after *Acropolis* with a dash, in order to have a matching pair. If there was a comma after *Aegean Sea,* this underlined part of the sentence would not need to be changed. Knowing that you need to "make it all match" will help you score points on ACT English.

2. G
Category: Sentence Sense
Difficulty: Medium
Getting to the Answer: This question tests your sense of parallelism. Your ear can often help you identify unparallel constructions. "To climb…is to have beheld" is unparallel. They should be in the same form: "to climb…is to behold."

3. D
Category: Writing Strategy
Difficulty: Low
Getting to the Answer: You have the option to OMIT in this question, which you should definitely take. Athenian cuisine has nothing to do with the subject of the paragraph or the passage, which is the Parthenon.

4. F
Category: Verb Tenses
Difficulty: Medium
Getting to the Answer: This verb is appropriately plural—the subject, *generations,* is plural—and in the present perfect tense. Choices G and H are singular verbs, while J is wrong because generations of architects can't all be proclaiming at the present time.

5. D
Category: Sentence Sense
Difficulty: High
Getting to the Answer: Run-on sentences are common on the English test. There are a couple of ways to deal with this run-on sentence. You could put a semicolon after *subtle* to separate the clauses, or you could put a period after *subtle* and make the clauses into separate sentences. Because the choices offer you both options, there must be something more. And there is: you need a comma after *For example* to set it off from the rest of the sentence. Choice (D) fixes both errors.

6. G
Category: Sentence Sense
Difficulty: Medium
Getting to the Answer: This part of the sentence sounds strange; it seems that *the fact* is what is being "viewed from a distance," not the *straight columns.* "Viewed from a distance" is a misplaced modifier that has to be moved to a position where it clearly modifies *columns.* Choice (G) accomplishes this.

7. D

Category: Punctuation

Difficulty: Medium

Getting to the Answer: Read the sentence out loud and you'll hear that it has punctuation problems. There is no need for a semicolon or any other kind of punctuation mark between *of* and *uprightness*. Don't place a comma before the first element of a series, C, and don't place a colon between a preposition and its objects, B.

8. J

Category: Connections

Difficulty: Medium

Getting to the Answer: The phrase "because of this" doesn't make sense here. The optical illusion the architects created is not the reason you'll get a different impression of the Parthenon from the one the ancient Athenians had; the reason is that the statue of Athena Parthenos isn't there anymore. The introductory phrase that makes sense won't suggest conclusion or contrast, it will emphasize the information in the sentence, making (J) correct.

9. C

Category: Sentence Sense

Difficulty: Medium

Getting to the Answer: "Only by standing…Golden Age of Athens" is a sentence fragment that has to be hooked up somehow to the sentence after it. You can't just use a semicolon to join the two, B, because then the first clause of the new sentence will still be only a fragment. You have to reverse the subject and verb of the second sentence to attach the fragment to it, as (C) does.

10. J

Category: Sentence Sense

Difficulty: High

Getting to the Answer: What was removed from the temple? The underlined part of the sentence is an introductory modifying phrase that you know describes the statue, but the word *statue* isn't

anywhere in the sentence. As a result, the sentence doesn't make sense at all; it's impossible that "all that remains" in the temple was removed in the fifth century c.e. Choice (J) makes the sentence make sense.

11. D

Category: Verb Tenses

Difficulty: Low

Getting to the Answer: Quite a few words come between the subject and the verb of this sentence. You shouldn't be fooled, though; *many* is the subject of the sentence, not *carvings, walls*, or *Acropolis*. Because *many* is plural, the verb of the sentence has to be plural as well. *Is* has to be changed to *are*, (D).

12. H

Category: Sentence Sense

Difficulty: High

Getting to the Answer: This sentence is really only a sentence fragment; it has a subject, *decision*, but no verb. Choice (H) rewords the underlined portion to make *Lord Elgin* the subject and *decided* the verb.

13. C

Category: Word Choice

Difficulty: Low

Getting to the Answer: *They* is an ambiguous pronoun because it's not immediately clear what group *they* refers to. You can figure out from the context that *they* is the Greeks; no other group could have won independence from the Turks and demanded the carvings back from the British. To make the first sentence clear, you have to replace *they* with the Greeks.

14. J

Category: Writing Strategy

Difficulty: Medium

Getting to the Answer: What could have been destroyed by explosions in the Parthenon? Carvings. The fact that some of the carvings were destroyed during a war is another good reason that many of them can no longer be found in the Parthenon, as paragraph 4 states. Therefore, the new material belongs in paragraph 4.

15. C
Category: Writing Strategy
Difficulty: Medium
Getting to the Answer: The answer to the question is clearly "no." The writer did not fulfill the request because only the second paragraph discusses techniques of construction at all; even then, only one technique, the bulging of the columns, is described in any detail. The author covers several topics in the essay in addition to construction techniques, including the statue of Athena Parthenos and the fate of the carvings.

PASSAGE II

16. H
Category: Verb Tenses
Difficulty: Low
Getting to the Answer: The previous sentence tells you that "Robin is the hero"; look for a verb form that matches the present tense *is*, because the sentence continues the discussion of the ballads. In (H), *tell* is in the right tense. Choice F switches to another tense, the present progressive, which makes it sound as if the ballads were literally speaking. Choice G lacks a main verb, creating a sentence fragment. Choice J has the same tense problem as F and compounds it by adding an extra, unnecessary subject, *they*.

17. C
Category: Sentence Sense
Difficulty: Medium
Getting to the Answer: You need a verb that is parallel to *robbing* and *killing*, so *giving*, (C), is the correct choice.

18. H
Category: Word Choice
Difficulty: Medium
Getting to the Answer: The adjective *frequent* is the correct choice to modify *enemy*. The underlined choice uses both the word *most* and the suffix *-est* to indicate the highest degree, or superlative form. Use one or the other, but not both. Likewise, G incorrectly uses *more* and the suffix *-er* together. Both of these express the comparative form—but again, you'd use one or the other, not both at once. In J, *frequently* is an adverb and so can't describe a noun.

19. D
Category: Writing Strategy
Difficulty: Medium
Getting to the Answer: When you see the OMIT option, ask yourself if the underlined portion is really necessary. The parentheses are a clue that the underlined part isn't really relevant. It goes off on a tangent about modern adaptations of the King Arthur legend, whereas Robin Hood is the focus of the passage. Choices B and C reword the irrelevant sentence.

20. F
Category: Word Choice
Difficulty: Medium
Getting to the Answer: This is correct as is. *Them* matches the plural noun it's standing in for: *writers*. Choice G, *him*, and H, *it*, are singular, so they don't. Choice J is wordy.

21. A
Category: Punctuation
Difficulty: Low
Getting to the Answer: This is correct because we need the possessive apostrophe. Choices B and C are wrong because they are the plural, not the possessive, form of Stukely, and there obviously aren't a lot of Stukelys running around. Choice D is wrong because if you read it out loud, you can tell that no pause—and so no comma—is called for.

22. J

Category: Writing Strategy

Difficulty: Medium

Getting to the Answer: Because this passage is aimed at discussing the historical development of the Robin Hood legend, (J) is most in keeping with the subject matter. Choice F goes way off track; you're asked to add more information on Stukely, not on English history. Choices G and H do relate their points to Stukely, but they pursue details. The main topic of the passage is Robin Hood, not antiquaries, G. (Remember, you want a choice that is most relevant to the passage as a whole.) As for H, King Arthur was mentioned earlier in the passage, but then only to make a point about Robin Hood. A discussion of Stukely's interest in King Arthur would stray from the topic of the passage.

23. C

Category: Sentence Sense

Difficulty: Low

Getting to the Answer: The shortest answer is the best choice. Choices A and D wrongly imply a comparison between Robin and a nobleman, when the claim was that Robin was a nobleman. B is incoherent.

24. G

Category: Writing Strategy

Difficulty: Medium

Getting to the Answer: The comparison with a puppy is silly in this context because it doesn't match the matter-of-fact tone of this passage; all choices except (G) can be eliminated. (The ACT will sometimes use a phrase that simply doesn't go with the passage's tone.)

25. D

Category: Punctuation

Difficulty: Medium

Getting to the Answer: The only choice that will tie in both parts of the sentence is (D). A dash in this context correctly makes an emphatic pause between *love interest* and its appositive, *Maid Marian*. All the rest of the choices have punctuation errors. Semicolons are used between independent clauses, and the part that would follow the semicolon in A isn't a clause. The plural form of the noun, *interests*, B, doesn't agree with the singular article. Choice C can be ruled out because there is no reason to pause in the middle of a name, and so the comma is incorrectly placed.

26. H

Category: Connections

Difficulty: High

Getting to the Answer: All the choices, with the exception of (H), have inappropriate connecting words. The passage moves to a discussion of a new time period, so you should begin a new paragraph, ruling out G. In addition, "on the one hand" should be followed by "on the other hand." *Consequently*, F, and *therefore*, J, wrongly imply that what follows is a result of something in the previous sentence.

27. B

Category: Verb Tenses

Difficulty: Medium

Getting to the Answer: The correct verb tense, and the only choice that doesn't create a sentence fragment, is (B). *Basing*, A, and *to base*, C, create sentence fragments. Of course, the omission of the verb would also result in a sentence fragment, so D is incorrect.

28. G

Category: Connections

Difficulty: Medium

Getting to the Answer: Choice (G) is the only choice that fits the rest of the sentence both logically and grammatically. *And* doesn't make sense as a connecting word in the original. Choice H also uses a connecting word that doesn't logically fit; *therefore* inaccurately suggests a cause-and-effect relationship. Choice J is wrong because a semicolon should be used between independent clauses, and the first clause can't stand alone.

29. D
Category: Writing Strategy
Difficulty: Medium
Getting to the Answer: You're told that the audience is unfamiliar with the story, so it would make sense to include a summary of the Robin Hood legend, (D), something the passage lacks. Choices A and C would do nothing for a reader curious about Robin Hood, because they go off on tangents about other issues. As the passage states that Robin Hood's existence is questionable (*legendary*), B doesn't fit in with the stance of the writer.

30. J
Category: Writing Strategy
Difficulty: Low
Getting to the Answer: Rarely are ACT English passages written for authorities or experts; they're usually written for the general public, as (J) correctly states in this question. If the passage were directed toward *experts*, F, or *authorities*, G, much of the basic information it presents would be unnecessary and not included. The passage states that the existence of Robin Hood is legendary, so the passage can't be aimed at readers craving confirmation that he "was an actual historical personage," so H is wrong.

PASSAGE III

31. A
Category: Wordiness
Difficulty: Low
Getting to the Answer: The shortest answer is correct. *Ten-mile* is correctly punctuated: the hyphen makes it an adjective modifying *radius*. The other answers are wordy and awkward.

32. H
Category: Word Choice
Difficulty: Medium
Getting to the Answer: You don't look forward *at* something. You look forward *to* something. Choice G wrongly implies that it is the brother who looks forward to the opportunity to show off the narrator's skills. Choice J wrongly implies a contrast between the two parts of the sentence. Actually, it is precisely because she hasn't flown with her brother that the writer anticipates showing off her skills to him.

33. D
Category: Connections
Difficulty: Medium
Getting to the Answer: *Ever since* means from the time the narrator first could read to the present time of the narrative. This span of time makes sense, since the writer is telling us how long she had planned on a journalism career. *If* in A signals a hypothetical situation, rather than a period of time. *Since* in B implies a cause-and-effect relationship that doesn't hold up. Why would her ability to easily read a newspaper be a reason for her career decision? *Although* in C signals a contrast, but there isn't one.

34. F
Category: Word Choice
Difficulty: Low
Getting to the Answer: It's true that you use *I* and *me*, in G and H, when you're writing about yourself. However, you can't say "I always envisioned I" or "I always envisioned me." Per the rules of grammar, you have to say "I always envisioned myself."

35. A
Category: Punctuation
Difficulty: Medium
Getting to the Answer: Choice (A) is correct because all you need to do is pause before the word *giving*, and this pause is signaled by the comma. You don't need a colon, as in B. Colons signal lists

or definitions. You don't need a semicolon in C either—a semicolon should be placed between clauses that could stand alone as sentences, but the second part of this sentence can't. Choice D creates a sentence with no verb.

36. G
Category: Sentence Sense
Difficulty: Medium
Getting to the Answer: This is an example of a misplaced modifier. Choices F and H make it sound as if it is the airport, and not the pilot, that is filing the flight plan. Choice J is awkward (it uses a passive construction) and wordy. Choice (G) is concise, and the verbs *filed* and *gave* are parallel.

37. A
Category: Sentence Sense
Difficulty: Low
Getting to the Answer: The adjective *careful* should be placed before *watch*, the noun it modifies. Choice B is wrong because the reference is not to "careful airplanes." *Neared* requires an adverb such as *carefully* before it, not an adjective. Choice D is wrong because it is the people, not the crater, that are *careful*.

38. J
Category: Punctuation
Difficulty: Medium
Getting to the Answer: The colon in the original interrupts the flow of the sentence. Colons often function like equal signs. ("Here's what we need for the picnic: salami, ham, cheese, and bread.") Colons signal lists or definitions, but nothing needs to be equated in this sentence.

39. D
Category: Wordiness
Difficulty: Low
Getting to the Answer: Because *speechless* and *mute* mean the same thing, it's redundant to use both of them.

40. G
Category: Verb Tenses
Difficulty: Medium
Getting to the Answer: *Steadying* and *took* should be in parallel form. This makes (G) correct. The verbs in J are parallel, but they're in the present tense, which doesn't fit with the past tense verbs *shot* and *dictated* in the nonunderlined part of the sentence.

41. A
Category: Writing Strategy
Difficulty: Medium
Getting to the Answer: Jeff and the narrator are circling the mountain, so "a description of Mt. St. Helens" would be appropriate. Choice B contradicts the information in the passage; we're told that the plane must stay high enough to avoid smoke and ash. In any case, the tone of B doesn't suit the calm tone of the rest of the passage. Choice C sounds as if it belongs in a science textbook rather than in a story. Choice D wanders too far from the direct observation of the Mt. St. Helens volcano, which is the paragraph's focus.

42. G
Category: Connections
Difficulty: Medium
Getting to the Answer: "Since that time" is an appropriate transition. It makes clear the time shift between the day at Mt. St. Helens and the present. The other choices contain inappropriate connecting words. *However* in F and *nevertheless* in J signal contrasts, but there isn't one in the passage. *Furthermore* suggests an elaboration of what came before, but there is no elaboration in the passage.

43. C
Category: Writing Strategy
Difficulty: Medium
Getting to the Answer: Because the author is favorably recalling a memorable past experience, *nostalgic* in (C) is the best choice. The passage is positive in tone. It's definitely not *bitter*, B, or *exhausted*,

D. *Optimistic* is close but wrong. *Optimistic* means "hopeful." The passage focuses on the excitement of the past, not on the good things that might happen.

44. H

Category: Writing Strategy
Difficulty: Medium
Getting to the Answer: The use of *I* is appropriate because this is a firsthand account. First-person narratives do tend to draw the reader in. Choice J is not true, because *I* is not appropriate in all types of writing. The passage is personal and chatty; it's not an example of "formal writing." The passage isn't focused on volcanoes in general, as G says, but on the Mt. St. Helens eruption, the narrator's first international story.

45. B

Category: Organization
Difficulty: High
Getting to the Answer: The passage reads best if the first and second paragraphs are switched. Choices A, C, and D confuse the time sequence of the narrative, which follows the narrator from her early dreams of becoming a photojournalist, to the memorable Mt. St. Helens story, to her present experience as a foreign correspondent.

PASSAGE IV

46. G

Category: Wordiness
Difficulty: Low
Getting to the Answer: The description of Sherlock Holmes as "ingenious and extremely clever" is redundant because ingenious and extremely clever mean the same thing. You need to use only one of the two to get the point across.

47. D

Category: Connections
Difficulty: High
Getting to the Answer: *Therefore* is supposed to be a signal that the sentence that follows is a logical conclusion based on information from the preceding sentence or sentences. The use of *therefore* doesn't make any sense here because you can't conclude that everyone knows the phrase "elementary, my dear Watson" just because everyone knows of Holmes's detective abilities. Choice C is wrong for the same reason—"for this reason" and *therefore* mean the same thing in this context. *Although*, B, indicates some sort of contrast; this would be wrong because there is no contrast within this sentence or between this sentence and the previous one. Really, there is no need for a structural signal here at all. Choice (D) is correct.

48. J

Category: Writing Strategy
Difficulty: Medium
Getting to the Answer: Note that this question has an OMIT option—a strong clue that the underlined portion is irrelevant to the paragraph. The theme of the first paragraph is "everyone knows who Sherlock Holmes is (or was)." The last sentence has absolutely nothing to do with this main idea, so it should be omitted. Putting parentheses around the sentence, as in G, will not make it more relevant, so that is not the way to solve the problem.

49. B

Category: Word Choice
Difficulty: Medium
Getting to the Answer: *He* is an ambiguous pronoun because it's unclear whether *he* refers to Conan Doyle or to Sherlock Holmes. You know after reading the entire sentence that *he* is Conan Doyle, so you have to replace *he* with *Conan Doyle* for the sake of clarity.

50. J

Category: Wordiness

Difficulty: Medium

Getting to the Answer: From a grammatical point of view, there is nothing wrong here; it's just unnecessarily wordy. The ACT prizes clarity and simplicity in style, which often means that the shortest answer is the best one. "To be remembered" is the most concise, and therefore the correct, answer.

51. A

Category: Connections

Difficulty: Medium

Getting to the Answer: *In fact* is the appropriate signal phrase here. *Despite this*, *regardless*, and *yet* would all indicate a contrast between this sentence and the previous one. There is no contrast, however; Conan Doyle did not want to be remembered as the author of Sherlock Holmes stories, so he killed the detective off (at least for a while).

52. J

Category: Sentence Sense

Difficulty: Medium

Getting to the Answer: A modifying phrase that begins a sentence refers to the noun or pronoun immediately following the phrase. According to that rule, the phrase "having had enough of his famous character by that time" modifies *Sherlock Holmes*, which doesn't make sense at all. The sentence has to be rearranged so that the introductory phrase describes Conan Doyle. Choice (J) is the choice that accomplishes this.

53. D

Category: Writing Strategy

Difficulty: Low

Getting to the Answer: Once again, take note of the OMIT choice. What do soap opera characters have to do with Arthur Conan Doyle and Sherlock Holmes? Nothing. This sentence disrupts the flow of the paragraph by being almost completely irrelevant, so it has to be omitted.

54. H

Category: Verb Tenses

Difficulty: Medium

Getting to the Answer: The verb is in the wrong tense. "Has been deeply immersed" is in the present perfect tense, which is used to describe an action that started in the past and continues to the present or that happened a number of times in the past and may happen again in the future. Conan Doyle's immersion in spiritualism is over and done with, so use the simple past: "was deeply immersed."

55. B

Category: Sentence Sense

Difficulty: Medium

Getting to the Answer: This is a sentence fragment because there is no subject and verb; all you have is an introductory phrase and a subordinate clause starting with *that*. By omitting *that*, you can turn the subordinate clause into a main clause, making "he lectured" the subject and verb, (B). Choice C would work if the sentence began with "so convinced." Choice D is wrong because the introductory phrase can't stand alone as a sentence.

56. J

Category: Wordiness

Difficulty: Low

Getting to the Answer: Because this sentence says that Conan Doyle and his family attempted to communicate with the dead by automatic writing, it's redundant to explain that automatic writing was thought to be a means of communicating with "those no longer among the living." Omit the underlined portion of the sentence.

57. D

Category: Organization

Difficulty: High

Getting to the Answer: The second sentence refers to "these experiences," so it should come directly after the sentence that describes the paranormal experiences Conan Doyle seemed to have had. The fourth sentence is the one that talks about materialized hands and heavy articles swimming through the air, so the second sentence should come after the fourth.

58. H

Category: Word Choice
Difficulty: Medium
Getting to the Answer: There are two problems with the underlined portion of the sentence: the colon does not belong there, and the pronoun *they* is ambiguous because it doesn't refer to anything in particular in the previous sentence. Choice (H) takes care of both of these problems by dropping the colon and by spelling out what the pronoun was supposed to refer to.

59. B

Category: Sentence Sense
Difficulty: Medium
Getting to the Answer: Here, you just have to pick the choice that makes sense. Sherlock Holmes is only a fictional character, so A, C, and D are wrong; Holmes could not possibly have said anything about Conan Doyle's spiritualism, nor will he ever. You can still wonder, however, what the esteemed detective would have said, if he were real. This is the idea behind the last sentence.

60. G

Category: Writing Strategy
Difficulty: High
Getting to the Answer: The passage contrasts the logical, deductive thinking used by Conan Doyle's fictional character, Sherlock Holmes, with Conan Doyle's own exploration of the paranormal. An appropriate subtitle must reflect this contrast. Choice (G) is the only choice that does.

PASSAGE V

61. A

Category: Verb Tenses
Difficulty: Medium
Getting to the Answer: Use context to determine correct verb tense usage. The first clause in the sentence uses the present tense "emphasize," so "are not groundbreaking" is correct in the second clause. NO CHANGE is needed. Choices B and C introduce inconsistent verb tenses. Choice D makes a sentence fragment.

62. J

Category: Wordiness
Difficulty: High
Getting to the Answer: "OMIT the underlined portion" is an answer choice, so you know that Wordiness is a potential issue. Check to see if the underlined selection repeats something that is stated elsewhere in the sentence. Reading the entire sentence tells you that "area of" is redundant; "fields," as it is used here, means essentially the same thing. OMIT is the correct choice. Choices G and H use similarly redundant language: "subject" and "topic," respectively.

63. D

Category: Wordiness
Difficulty: Medium
Getting to the Answer: If a clear, unambiguous antecedent is present, a pronoun will be correct. Because "the slides" is the only plural noun in this sentence, the pronoun "they" is the best choice here; (D) is correct. Choice A repeats "the slides" unnecessarily. Choices B and C incorrectly change the plural to the possessive.

64. H

Category: Sentence Sense
Difficulty: High
Getting to the Answer: There are several ways to join independent clauses, but only one choice will

do so without introducing additional errors. As written, the sentence is a run-on. Choice (H) correctly inserts "as" to make the first clause dependent. Choice G does not address the error. Choice J creates a grammatically incorrect sentence.

65. A
Category: Connections
Difficulty: Medium
Getting to the Answer: When two answer choices have transitions that convey the same meaning and create grammatically correct sentences, you can eliminate both choices, because they can't both be right. This sentence is correct as written. Choices B and D use transitions indicating a contrast, but the idea that people are working on improving visual presentation style does not contrast with the idea that "less cluttered" aids work better than "denser ones." Choice C uses the transition "similarly," but the second sentence is an example supporting the first.

66. J
Category: Wordiness
Difficulty: Low
Getting to the Answer: When the underlined selection consists of two words joined by "and" or "or," consider whether they mean essentially the same thing. If they do, the correct answer choice will eliminate one of them. "Enhance" and "improve," in this context, mean the same thing. Choice (J) omits the redundancy. Choice G is unnecessarily wordy. Choice H does not address the error.

67. A
Category: Sentence Sense
Difficulty: Medium
Getting to the Answer: Verbs in comparative structures, such as "not simply...but instead," require parallel structure, as do compounds joined by "and" or "or." This sentence uses correct parallel structure in both cases; NO CHANGE is needed here. Choices B and C violate the rules of parallel structure. Choice

D changes the meaning of the sentence by indicating that "adding" is the thing that is demonstrated.

68. J
Category: Writing Strategy
Difficulty: Medium
Getting to the Answer: In questions like this one, first answer the "yes" or "no" part of the question; you'll be able to eliminate at least one answer choice, and usually more. This paragraph focuses solely on how "visual presentation style" is being refined. The topic sentence of the paragraph doesn't discuss audio aids, nor does any other sentence in the paragraph. Therefore, the sentence should NOT be added; (J) is correct.

69. B
Category: Sentence Sense
Difficulty: High
Getting to the Answer: When you need to determine the correct order of words in a long sentence like this one, start by focusing on the correct placement of descriptive phrases and eliminate your way to the correct answer. "In respected journals" needs to follow the verb phrase "have been published." This eliminates C. "In listeners" belongs with "improve comprehension," which eliminates A and D. Choice (B) is correct here.

70. G
Category: Sentence Sense
Difficulty: Medium
Getting to the Answer: The passive voice will not always be wrong on the ACT, but passive constructions are generally wordier than active ones, so check for an active version of any underlined passives. "It has been determined by researchers" is a wordy and indirect way of saying "Researchers have determined"; (G) is the best choice here. Choice H is a sentence fragment with no independent clause. Choice J uses incorrect grammatical structure.

71. A

Category: Punctuation
Difficulty: Medium
Getting to the Answer: Don't expect to find an error in every underlined selection. About one-fourth of the English Test questions will require NO CHANGE. The end of one sentence and the beginning of the next are underlined, so determine if the sentences should be combined. None of the answer choices offers an option for correctly joining two independent clauses; NO CHANGE is needed. Choice B creates a run-on sentence. Choices C and D leave the meaning of the second clause incomplete.

72. J

Category: Word Choice
Difficulty: Medium
Getting to the Answer: When a pronoun is underlined, check that it agrees with its antecedent—the noun it replaces. The underlined pronoun refers back to the "audience members," so the third-person plural pronoun "them" is correct. Choices F and G use singular pronouns, which don't agree with the plural noun "audience members." Choice H uses the second person "you," but the writer is not directly addressing the reader.

73. D

Category: Wordiness
Difficulty: Medium
Getting to the Answer: Check underlined selections for words that mean essentially the same thing. "Recently" and "of late" mean essentially the same thing, so using them together is redundant. Only (D) eliminates all redundant language. B is also redundant; something that happened "in recent times" by definition happened "not so long ago." Choice C adds the transition "in addition," but the observations of psychologists are not a logical addition to the reactions of audience members discussed in the previous paragraph.

74. G

Category: Connections
Difficulty: High
Getting to the Answer: You need to pick the best Connection between sentences 1 and 2, so read sentence 2 before going to the answer choices. Sentence 2 discusses the importance of body language in presentations; the most effective link to this sentence will introduce this topic. Only (G) mentions body language. Choice F is much more general than (G), repeating ideas that have already been stated in the passage. Choice H focuses on visual images, which were discussed in the previous paragraph, not sentence 2 of this paragraph. Choice J is unnecessarily wordy, using the passive voice and redundant language.

75. B

Category: Writing Strategy
Difficulty: Medium
Getting to the Answer: Read the question stems carefully. Frequently, more than one answer choice will be both relevant and consistent, but only one will meet the specific criteria of the question. The writer wants to show how the theory about body language has "influenced" the education and public speaking experts who are the subject of the sentence. Choice (B) explains a specific way these experts have been influenced; they now focus on teaching presenters how to effectively use body language. Choices A and C are both too general; neither shows the specific influence of the body language theory. Choice D is out of scope; audience size isn't discussed in the passage.

MATHEMATICS TEST

1. B

Category: Proportions and Probability
Difficulty: Low
Getting to the Answer: Plug the terms into the average formula and solve:

$$\text{Average} = \frac{\text{Sum of terms}}{\text{Number of terms}}$$

$$= \frac{230 + 155 + 320 + 400 + 325}{5}$$

$$= \frac{1{,}430}{5}$$

$$= 286$$

That's (B).

2. J

Category: Operations
Difficulty: Medium
Getting to the Answer: Begin by converting Sarah's 12 feet of wood into inches. There are 12 inches in a foot, so Sarah has 12×12 inches = 144 inches. Cutting off three 28-inch pieces removes 3×28 = 84 inches, which leaves her with $144 - 84 = 60$ inches. That's (J).

3. C

Category: Variable Manipulation
Difficulty: Low
Getting to the Answer: To evaluate x, isolate it on one side of the equation, then solve.

$$4x + 18 = 38$$

$$4x = 20$$

$$x = 5$$

Choice (C) is correct.

4. G

Category: Proportions and Probability
Difficulty: Medium
Getting to the Answer: Because John weighs *more* than Ellen, begin by eliminating J and K, as doing so will reduce the chance of a miscalculation error. According to the problem, John's 165 lb represents 1.5 times Ellen's weight. Therefore, Ellen's

weight must be $\frac{165}{1.5}$ = 110 lb. Choice (G) is correct.

5. E

Category: Proportions and Probability
Difficulty: Low
Getting to the Answer: To find the average of four numbers, plug them into the average formula and solve:

$$\text{Average} = \frac{\text{Sum of terms}}{\text{Number of terms}}$$

$$= \frac{237 + 482 + 375 + 210}{4}$$

$$= \frac{1{,}304}{4}$$

$$= 326$$

Choice (E) is correct.

6. J

Category: Operations
Difficulty: Medium
Getting to the Answer: Cube both sides to solve for x.

$$\sqrt[3]{x} = 4$$

$$x = 64$$

7. B

Category: Variable Manipulation
Difficulty: Low
Getting to the Answer: Isolate the variable, then solve for x:

$$x^2 + 14 = 63$$

$$x^2 = 49$$

$$x = \pm 7$$

This is (B).

8. G

Category: Operations

Difficulty: Medium

Getting to the Answer: You *could* use your calculator to solve this problem, but there's a much easier way. Begin by eliminating H, as it is not a perfect square. J can also be eliminated for the same reason. To simplify the radical, factor out a perfect square from 54. The largest factor of 54 that's also a perfect square is 9, so $\sqrt{54} = \sqrt{9 \times 6} = 3\sqrt{6}$.

9. E

Category: Operations

Difficulty: Medium

Getting to the Answer: You *could* punch the expression into your calculator, but it may actually be quicker to estimate. $\sqrt{90} \approx \sqrt{81} = 9$ and $\sqrt{32} \approx \sqrt{36} = 6$, so $\sqrt{90} \times \sqrt{32} \approx 9 \times 6 = 54$. With the calculator, the actual value is 53.6656. That's closest to (E).

10. K

Category: Operations

Difficulty: Medium

Getting to the Answer: When the choices are spaced far apart, estimation is generally the quickest way to the correct answer. To estimate, round 5.2 to 5 and 6.8 to 7. Because $5^3 + 7^2 = 125 + 49 = 174$, the correct answer will be very close to 174. That would be (K).

11. C

Category: Operations

Difficulty: Medium

Getting to the Answer: $x^3 = 512$, so $x = \sqrt[3]{512} = 8$. Be careful not to stop too soon. The problem asks for x^2, not x. $8^2 = 64$, which is (C).

12. H

Category: Operations

Difficulty: Medium

Getting to the Answer: To solve this problem, you'll need to follow the order of operations (PEMDAS).

First, evaluate the parentheses: $3^3 \div 9 + (6^2 - 12) \div 4 = 3^3 \div 9 + (36 - 12) \div 4 = 3^3 \div 9 + 24 \div 4$.

Next, simplify the exponent: $3^3 \div 9 + 24 \div 4 = 27 \div 9 + 24 \div 4$.

Then, take care of any multiplication and/or division, from left to right: $27 \div 9 + 24 \div 4 = 3 + 6$.

Finally, take care of any addition and/or subtraction, from left to right: $3 + 6 = 9$.

So (H) is correct.

13. B

Category: Operations

Difficulty: Low

Getting to the Answer: Each banana costs \$.24, so the price of x bananas is \$.24x. Similarly, each orange costs \$.38, so the price of y oranges is \$.38y. Therefore, the total price of x bananas and y oranges is \$.24x + \$.38y. That's (B).

14. K

Category: Variable Manipulation

Difficulty: Low

Getting to the Answer: Isolate the variable, then solve for x:

$$4x + 13 = 16$$
$$4x = 3$$
$$x = \frac{3}{4}$$

Choice (K) is correct, when you convert $\frac{3}{4}$ to the decimal 0.75.

15. A

Category: Proportions and Probability

Difficulty: Low

Getting to the Answer: The quickest way to solve this problem is to estimate. While you may or may not know 6% of 1,250 off the top of your head, 10% of 1,250 is 125. Because 6% < 10%, the correct answer must be less than 125. Only (A) works.

To solve this the more traditional way, multiply 1,250 by the decimal form of 6%: $1,250 \times .06 = 75$.

16. J

Category: Proportions and Probability
Difficulty: High
Getting to the Answer: When an average problem involves variables, it often helps to think in terms of sum instead. For Sarah's exam scores to average at least a 90, they must sum to at least $90 \times 4 = 360$. She already has an 89, a 93, and an 84, so she needs at least $360 - (89 + 93 + 84) = 360 - 266 = 94$ points on her last test. Choice (J) is correct.

17. E

Category: Variable Manipulation
Difficulty: Medium
Getting to the Answer: Treat inequalities just as equations. The only exception is that if you multiply or divide by a negative number, you must flip the inequality sign. With inequalities, you are solving for a range of values.

$$3x - 11 \geq 22$$

$$3x \geq 33$$

$$x \geq 11$$

This matches (E).

18. J

Category: Proportions and Probability
Difficulty: Low

Getting to the Answer: The basketball team scored 364 points in 13 games, so they scored an average of $\frac{364}{13} = 28$ points per game. Choice (J) is correct.

19. D

Category: Variable Manipulation
Difficulty: Low
Getting to the Answer: Isolate the variable, then solve for x:

$$6x + 4 = 11x - 21$$

$$4 = 5x - 21$$

$$25 = 5x$$

$$5 = x$$

That's (D).

20. F

Category: Proportions and Probability
Difficulty: Medium
Getting to the Answer: Backsolving works well for word problems with numbers in the answer choices.

First, find the number of movie theme songs:

$$10\% \text{ of } 300 = 0.10 \degree\!\!- 300 = 30$$

Then subtract the number of movie theme songs and marches from the total number of pieces of music:

$$300 - (30 + 80) = 300 - 110 = 190$$

If you solve this answer by Backsolving, first remember that there are always 300 pieces of music; therefore, there will always be 30 movie theme songs and 80 marches. Start with H:

$$210 + 30 + 80 = 320 \neq 300.$$

Because the value is too big, eliminate H, J, and K, and then try G.

$$198 + 30 + 80 = 308 \neq 300.$$

Choice G is incorrect, so (F) must be the correct answer:

$$190 + 30 + 80 = 300$$

21. C

Category: Proportions and Probability
Difficulty: High
Getting to the Answer: Set up an expression that can be solved to find the total number of class sessions. Letting x = the total number of sessions:

$$16 = 19 + 17 + 15\frac{(x-2)}{x}$$

$$16x = 36 + 15x - 30$$

$$16x - 15x = 36 - 30$$

$$x = 6 \text{ sessions}$$

22. H

Category: Proportions and Probability
Difficulty: Medium
Getting to the Answer: To find the percent shaded, divide the number of shaded triangles by the total number of triangles. There are 24 small triangles in all, and 8 of them are shaded.

$$\frac{8}{24} = \frac{1}{3} = 33\frac{1}{3}\%$$

Choice (H) is correct.

23. D

Category: Proportions and Probability
Difficulty: Medium
Getting to the Answer: The piece of paper is $8\frac{1}{2}$ inches wide. To find the number of $\frac{5}{8}$ inch wide strips of paper you can cut, divide:

$$8\frac{1}{2} \div \frac{5}{8} = \frac{17}{2} \div \frac{5}{8} = \frac{17}{2} \times \frac{8}{5} = \frac{136}{10} = \frac{68}{5} = 13.6$$

Thus, you can make 13 strips of paper that are $\frac{5}{8}$ inch wide and 11 inches long, and you will have a small, thin strip of paper left over.

24. G

Category: Proportions and Probability
Difficulty: Medium
Getting to the Answer: The ratio of buntings to total birds and the ratio of larks to total birds are given as 35:176 and 5:11, respectively. Assume that the total number of birds that have been counted in the meadow is 176. This automatically means that 35 buntings have been counted. The problem also gives the information that 5 out of 11 of the birds are larks. Set up a proportion:

$$\frac{5}{8} = \frac{17}{2},$$ where x represents the number of larks on the field

$$x = 176 \times \frac{5}{11} = 80$$

Then find the number of sparrows, which is the number of birds remaining:

$$176 - 35 - 80 = 61$$

Because there is the greatest number of larks in the meadow (80 larks), there would be the greatest probability that a lark would be chosen at random (45% larks > 35% sparrows > 20% buntings).

25. C

Category: Variable Manipulation
Difficulty: Medium
Getting to the Answer: This problem seems long, but it actually isn't that complicated. The order of operations says that all of the multiplication should be taken care of first. Let's begin with the first two terms:

$$(x + 4)(x - 4)$$

(If you noticed the difference of squares here, that will save you some time. If not, use FOIL.)

First : $x \times x = x^2$ Outer : $x \times -4 = -4x$
Inner : $4 \times x = 4x$ Last : $4 \times -4 = -16$

Combine like terms:

$$x^2 + (-4x) + 4x + (-16) = x^2 - 16$$

Now for the other two terms:

$$(2x + 2)(x - 2)$$

First : $2x \times x = 2x^2$ Outer : $2x \times -2 = -4x$
Inner : $2 \times x = 2x$ Last : $2 \times -2 = -4$

Combine like terms:

$$2x^2 + (-4x) + 2x + (-4) = 2x^2 - 2x - 4$$

Finally, add the two polynomials:

$$(x^2 - 16) + (2x^2 - 2x - 4) = 3x^2 - 2x - 20$$

Choice (C) is correct.

26. J

Category: Variable Manipulation
Difficulty: Medium
Getting to the Answer: Use the acronym FOIL (First, Outside, Inside, Last) to multiply the binomials:

$$(4x - 1)(x + 5) =$$

$$4x^2 + 20x - x - 5 =$$

$$4x^2 + 19x - 5$$

27. D

Category: Trigonometry
Difficulty: High
Getting to the Answer: You are given the cosine of $\angle BAC$ and the hypotenuse of the triangle, so begin by using these to find the adjacent side:

$$\text{Cos } A = \frac{\text{Adjacent}}{\text{Hypotenuse}}$$

$$.6 = \frac{\text{Adjacent}}{15}$$

$$\text{Adjacent} = 9$$

So the adjacent side, $\overline{AB}$, is 9, and triangle ABC is a right triangle with a leg of 9 and a hypotenuse of 15. ABC must therefore be a 3-4-5 right triangle, and $\overline{BC}$ must be 12. Choice (D) is correct.

28. J

Category: Proportions and Probability
Difficulty: Low
Getting to the Answer: With variables in the question stem and the answer choices, this problem is perfect for Picking Numbers. Pick 2 for x and 3 for y. Now the problem reads: "If a car drives 80 miles per hour for two hours and 60 miles per hour for three hours, what is the car's average speed, in miles, for the total distance traveled?"

In this case, the car would have driven $80 \times 2 = 160$ miles and $60 \times 3 = 180$ miles, for a total of $160 + 180 = 340$ miles in five hours. The average speed is therefore $\frac{340}{5} = 68$ miles per hour. Plug 2 in for x and 3 in for y for each of the choices and see which comes out to 68:

F. $\frac{480}{2 \times 3} = \frac{480}{6} = 80.$ Eliminate.

G. $\frac{80}{2} = \frac{60}{3} = 40 + 20 = 60.$ Eliminate.

H. $\frac{80}{2} \times \frac{60}{3} = 40 \times 20 = 800.$ Eliminate.

J. $\frac{80(2) + 60(3)}{2 + 3} \times \frac{160 + 180}{5} = \frac{340}{5} = 68.$

Only (J) works, so it must be correct.

29. B

Category: Patterns, Logic, and Data
Difficulty: High
Getting to the Answer: Set up your sequence using blanks in place of the numbers you don't know. If the common difference is -7, then the second term must be $8 - 7 = 1$, and the third term must be $1 - 7 = -6$: 8, 1, -6, 36 To find the common ratio, find the rate of difference between the second and third

(or third and fourth) term: $1 \times - 6 = -6 - 6 \times - 6 = 36$ The common ratio is $- 6$.

$$8, \underline{\hspace{1cm}}, \underline{\hspace{1cm}}, 36$$

If the common difference is -7, then the second term must be $8 - 7 = 1$, and the third term must be $1 - 7 = - 6$:

$$8, 1, - 6, 36$$

To find the common ratio, find the rate of difference between the second and third (or third and fourth) term:

$$1 \times - 6 = -6$$

$$-6 \times - 6 = 36$$

The common ratio is $- 6$, (B).

30. F

Category: Operations
Difficulty: Medium
Getting to the Answer: When an exponent equation looks difficult on Test Day, try to rewrite the problem so that either the bases or the exponents themselves are the same. In this problem, the two bases seem different at first glance but, because 27 is actually 3^3, you can rewrite the equation as:

$$3^{3x+3} = 3^{3\left(\frac{2}{3}x-\frac{1}{3}\right)}$$

This simplifies to $3^{3}x^{+3} = 3^{2x-1}$. Now that the bases are equal, set the exponents equal to each other and solve for x:

$$3x + 3 = 2x - 1$$

$$x + 3 = -1$$

$$x = -4$$

Choice (F) is correct.

31. D

Category: Operations
Difficulty: Medium
Getting to the Answer: The temperature of the container of liquid nitrogen is lower than the temperature of the room, so it must rise to match the room's temperature. Eliminate A and B, which indicate that a drop in temperature is needed. To find the positive difference, subtract:

$$72°F - (-330°F) =$$

$$72°F + 330°F =$$

$$+402°F$$

32. G

Category: Variable Manipulation
Difficulty: Medium
Getting to the Answer: This is an area problem with a twist—we're cutting a piece out of the rectangle. To find the area of the remaining space, you will need to subtract the area of the sandpit from the area of the original playground. Recall that the area of a rectangle is length $\times$ width. The dimensions of the original playground are $x + 7$ and $x + 3$, so its area is $(x + 7)(x + 3) = x^2 + 10x + 21$. The sandpit is a square with side x, so its area is x^2. Remove the pit from our playground, and the remaining area is $x^2 + 10x + 21 - x^2 = 10x + 21$. Choice (G) is correct.

33. C

Category: Number Properties
Difficulty: Medium
Getting to the Answer: When a problem tests a number property, the easiest way to solve it is to Pick Numbers. Because u is an integer, pick some integers for u. If $u = 2$, then $(u - 3)^2 + 5 = (2 - 3)^2 + 5 = (-1)^2 + 5 = 1 + 5 = 6$. This eliminates B, D, and E. If $u = 3$, then $(u - 3)^2 + 5 = (3 - 3)^2 + 5 = 5$. This eliminates A, leaving (C) as the correct answer.

34. F

Category: Coordinate Geometry
Difficulty: High
Getting to the Answer: Use the midpoint formula to solve:

$$\left(\frac{x_1 + x_2}{2}, \frac{y_1 + y_2}{2}\right)$$

$$1 + \frac{m}{2} = -3 \quad 9 + \frac{n}{2} = -2$$

$$m = -3, n = -13$$
$$(m, n) = (-3, -13)$$

35. C

Category: Variable Manipulation
Difficulty: Medium
Getting to the Answer: With nested functions, work from the inside out. To solve this problem, substitute the entire function of $g(x)$ for x in the function $f(x)$, then solve:

$$f(g(x)) = \frac{1}{3}(3x^2 + 6x + 12) + 13$$
$$f(g(x)) = x^2 + 2x + 4 + 13$$
$$f(g(x)) = x^2 + 2x + 17$$

Choice (C) is correct.

36. G

Category: Coordinate Geometry
Difficulty: Low
Getting to the Answer: To find the length of a line segment on the coordinate plane, you would normally need to use the distance formula. This requires the coordinates of the segment's two endpoints. Because A (1,5) and C (1,1) have the same x-coordinate, a much faster way is to simply subtract the y-coordinate of C from the y-coordinate of A. The length of segment AC is $5 - 1 = 4$. Choice (G) is correct.

37. C

Category: Operations
Difficulty: High
Getting to the Answer: When given a function and a value of x, plug in the number value for x in the equation and simplify. Make sure to follow the order of operations.

$$f(x) = 16x^2 - 20x$$

$$f(3) = 16(3)^2 - 20(3)$$

$$f(3) = 16(9) - 60$$

$$f(3) = 144 - 60 = 84.$$

Choice (C) is the answer.

38. H

Category: Coordinate Geometry
Difficulty: Medium

Getting to the Answer: Perpendicular lines have negative reciprocal slopes. Because the line in the problem has a slope of $\frac{2}{3}$, the line you are looking for must have a slope of $-\frac{3}{2}$. The problem also says that this line contains the point (4,−3). Plugging all of this information into the equation of a line, $y = mx + b$, will allow us to find the final missing piece—the y-intercept:

$$y = mx + b$$
$$-3 = -\frac{3}{2}(4) + b$$
$$-3 = -6 + b$$
$$3 = b$$

With a slope of $-\frac{3}{2}$ and a y-intercept of 3, the line is $y = -\frac{3}{2}x + 3$. The correct answer is (H).

39. B

Category: Coordinate Geometry
Difficulty: Medium
Getting to the Answer: Use the slope formula to find the slope *m* of the line:

$$m = \frac{y_2 - y_1}{x_2 - x_1}$$
$$= \frac{-6 - 0}{0 - (-10)}$$
$$= \frac{-6}{10}$$
$$= -\frac{3}{5}$$

40. F

Category: Coordinate Geometry
Difficulty: Low
Getting to the Answer: Because the rectangle lies on a coordinate plane, Point B will have the same x-coordinate as the point directly above it (–2), and the same y-coordinate as the point to its right (–3). Therefore, the coordinates of point B are (–2,–3), so (F) is the correct answer.

41. D

Category: Coordinate Geometry
Difficulty: Medium
Getting to the Answer: To find the distance between two points, plug them into the distance formula and evaluate:

$$\text{Distance} = \sqrt{(x_2 - x_1)^2 + (y_2 - y_1)^2}$$
$$= \sqrt{(-2 - 3)^2 + (6 - (-6))^2}$$
$$= \sqrt{(-5)^2 + 12^2}$$
$$= \sqrt{25 + 144}$$
$$= \sqrt{169}$$
$$= 13$$

Choice (D) is correct.

42. G

Category: Coordinate Geometry
Difficulty: Low
Getting to the Answer: Plug given points [(–1,1) and (1,3)] into the midpoint formula and solve:

$$\text{Midpoint} = \left(\frac{x_1 + x_2}{2}, \frac{y_1 + y_2}{2} \right)$$
$$= \left(\frac{1 + (-1)}{2}, \frac{3 + 1}{2} \right)$$
$$= \left(\frac{0}{2}, \frac{4}{2} \right)$$
$$= (0, 2)$$

Choice (G) is correct.

43. D

Category: Plane Geometry
Difficulty: High
Getting to the Answer:

$$\text{Volume of a sphere} = \frac{4}{3}\pi r^3$$

Because you are told the diameter is 6, you know the radius of the sphere is 3. Watch out for this terminology on the ACT. If you knew the correct formula but use the diameter of the sphere instead of the radius, you would have selected E. If you don't recall the formula for the volume of a sphere, you should be able to eliminate some of the options and make an educated guess. Choice B is the area of a cross section of the sphere—too small—and A is even smaller, so you can eliminate both of these choices. Choice E seems pretty big (unless you fell for the trap), so you're down to C and (D). Hopefully you'll remember that the volume of a sphere is a little bigger than the radius cubed times π, C, and will select (D). But even if you guess between the two answers, you have a 50 percent chance of guessing correctly.

Choice (D) is correct.

44. H

Category: Plane Geometry

Difficulty: Medium

Getting to the Answer: The perimeter of a rectangle is twice its length plus twice its width, or Perimeter = $2l + 2w$. To find the area, you must first determine the value of w, so plug in the values for perimeter and length to solve:

$$\text{Perimeter} = 2l + 2w$$

$$24 = 2(8) + 2w$$

$$24 = 16 + 2w$$

$$8 = 2w$$

$$4 = w$$

So the width is 4. The area of the rectangle is length × width, or $8 × 4 = 32$. Choice (H) is correct.

45. A

Category: Plane Geometry

Difficulty: Medium

Getting to the Answer: With only one known side, you cannot find the area directly, as you will need to figure out more sides first. Given the area of triangle ABC and its base, the first step is to find height $\overline{CD}$:

$$\text{Area} = \frac{1}{2}bh$$

$$48 = \frac{1}{2}(12)h$$

$$48 = 6h$$

$$8 = h$$

So $\overline{CD} = 8$. Triangle ABC is an isosceles triangle, so $\overline{CD}$ also happens to be the perpendicular bisector of $\overline{AB}$, meaning $\overline{AD} = \overline{DB} = 6$. With legs of 6 and 8, each of the smaller right triangles must be 3-4-5 right triangles, making the hypotenuse of each—$\overline{AC}$ and $\overline{CB}$—10. (You can also use the Pythagorean theorem; if x equals the hypotenuse, then $6^2 + 8^2 = x^2$ which simplifies to $36 + 64 = 100 = x^2$. Therefore,

x equals 10.) Therefore, the perimeter of triangle ABC is $10 + 10 + 12 = 32$. Choice (A) is correct.

46. J

Category: Plane Geometry

Difficulty: Low

Getting to the Answer: It may sound a bit more complex, but this problem is only asking you for the perimeter of a rectangle with the given dimensions, so plug them into the perimeter formula and solve:

$$\text{Perimeter} = 2l + 2w$$

$$= 2(130) + 2(70)$$

$$= 260 + 140$$

$$= 400$$

Choice (J) is correct.

47. D

Category: Plane Geometry

Difficulty: Low

Getting to the Answer: When two parallel lines are cut by a transversal, half of the angles will be acute and half will be obtuse. Each acute angle will have the same measure as each other acute angle. The same is true of every obtuse angle. Furthermore, the acute angles will be supplementary to the obtuse angles. $\angle a$ is an acute angle measuring 68° while $\angle f$ is an obtuse angle, so $\angle a$ must be supplementary to $\angle f$. Therefore, $\angle f = 180° - 68° = 112°$.

Choice (D) is correct.

48. J

Category: Plane Geometry

Difficulty: Low

Getting to the Answer: Because $ABCD$ is a square, each side has the same length, which means the base and height of triangle BCD both equal 6 centimeters. Substitute these numbers in the formula for the area of a triangle:

$$\text{Area} = \frac{1}{2}bh$$

$$= \frac{1}{2}(6)6$$

$$= 18$$

The area of the triangle *BCD* is 18 cm².

49. C

Category: Plane Geometry

Difficulty: Medium

Getting to the Answer: You are told that triangle *RST* is a right triangle and that one of its angles is 30°, so *RST* must be a 30-60-90 right triangle, meaning its sides must be in the proportion $x : x\sqrt{3} : 2x$. Hypotenuse *RT* is 16, so *x* must be $\frac{16}{2} = 8$, and *RS* (the longer leg) must be $8\sqrt{3}$. (You can also use the Pythagorean theorem.) That matches (C).

50. K

Category: Plane Geometry

Difficulty: Medium

Getting to the Answer: Write the formula for the area of a circle, using r to represent the radius of the original circle in the problem. $A = \pi r^2$. This is the area of the original circle. Then write the formula for the area of the resulting circle, using 2r as the radius:

$$A = \pi(2r)^2 = \pi(4r^2) = 4\pi r^2$$

Now, divide the two areas (area of resulting circle/ area of original circle) to find out how many times larger the area of the resulting circle is compared to the area of the original circle.

$$\frac{\text{Area of resulting circle}}{\text{Area of original circle}} = \frac{4\pi r^2}{\pi r^2} = 4$$

51. B

Category: Plane Geometry

Difficulty: Low

Getting to the Answer: A square has four right angles and four equal sides. Its diagonal cuts the square into two identical isosceles right triangles. The square in this problem has a side length of 7, so the base and height of each isosceles right triangle is also 7. The sides of an isosceles right triangle are in the proportion $x : x : x\sqrt{2}$, so the length of the diagonal (the hypotenuse of both triangles) is $7\sqrt{2}$. (Again, you can also use the Pythagorean theorem.) Choice (B) is correct.

52. H

Category: Plane Geometry

Difficulty: Low

Getting to the Answer: A regular polygon is equilateral, so a regular hexagon is a hexagon with six equal sides. The regular hexagon in the problem has a side of 11, so its perimeter is $6 \times 11 = 66$.

Choice (H) is correct.

53. C

Category: Plane Geometry

Difficulty: Medium

Getting to the Answer: The perimeter of the rectangle is 28, and one of its sides is 2.5 times the length of the other, so call *x* the shorter side. Our rectangle now has sides of *x* and 2.5*x*. Draw a figure to help visualize this problem.

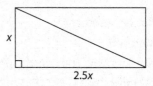

To find *x*, plug the information into the perimeter formula and solve:

$$\text{Perimeter} = 2l + 2w$$

$$28 = 2(x) + 2(2.5x)$$

$$28 = 2x + 5x$$

$$28 = 7x$$

$$4 = x$$

So $x = 4$, and the dimensions of the rectangle must be $4 \times 1 = 4$ and $2.5 \times 4 = 10$. These values are not parts of a special right triangle, so use the Pythagorean theorem to find the diagonal:

$$a^2 + b^2 = c^2$$
$$4^2 + 10^2 = c^2$$
$$16 + 100 = c^2$$
$$116 = c^2$$
$$\sqrt{116} = c$$

Because 116 isn't a perfect square but it lies between $10^2 = 100$ and $11^2 = 121$, $\sqrt{116}$ must be somewhere between 10 and 11 (it's approximately 10.77). The only choice that fits is (C).

54. G

Category: Plane Geometry

Difficulty: Medium

Getting to the Answer: This is a pair of parallel lines cut by a transversal, but this time, there's also a triangle thrown into the mix. Begin with AB. This is a transversal, so $\angle MAB$ and $\angle ABC$ are alternate interior angles and $\angle MAB = \angle ABC = 55°$. Because triangle ABC is isosceles with $AB = AC$, $\angle ACB$ is also 55°.

Choice (G) is correct.

55. D

Category: Plane Geometry

Difficulty: Medium

Getting to the Answer: The chord is perpendicular to the line segment from the center of the circle, so that line segment must be its perpendicular bisector. This allows us to add the following to the figure:

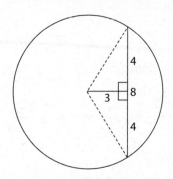

The two right triangles have legs 3 and 4, so they are both 3-4-5 right triangles with hypotenuse 5. This hypotenuse is also the radius of the circle, so plug that into the area formula to solve:

$$\text{Area} = \pi r^2$$
$$= \pi (5)^2$$
$$= 25\pi$$

The correct answer is (D).

56. J

Category: Plane Geometry

Difficulty: High

Getting to the Answer: Triangle QRS is an isosceles triangle, so its height is also the perpendicular bisector of RS. Each half of RS is $\frac{16}{2} = 8$ units long, so each of the smaller right triangles has a leg of 8 and a hypotenuse of 17. Using the Pythagorean theorem, a leg of 8 and hypotenuse of 17 means the other leg—the height—is 15.

$$\frac{1}{2} \times 16 \times 15 = \frac{1}{2} \times 240 = 120.$$

Choice (J) is correct.

57. C

Category: Proportions and Probability

Difficulty: Medium

Getting to the Answer: The ratio of girls to boys is 5:3, so the ratio of girls to the total number of seniors is 5:(3 + 5), or 5:8. Call x the number of girls in the senior class. Set up the proportion and solve for x:

$$\frac{5}{8} = \frac{x}{168}$$
$$8x = 840$$
$$x = 105$$

There are 105 girls in the senior class, which is (C).

58. K

Category: Trigonometry
Difficulty: Medium

Getting to the Answer: The tangent of an angle is defined by $\text{Tan } A = \dfrac{\text{Opposite}}{\text{Adjacent}}$. The side opposite $\angle EFD$ is 12 and the side adjacent to $\angle EFD$ is 5, so $\tan\angle EFD = \dfrac{12}{5}$. Choice (K) is correct.

59. C

Category: Trigonometry
Difficulty: Medium

Getting to the Answer: Because $QS = QR$, triangle QRS must be a 45-45-90 right triangle and the hypotenuse is $5\sqrt{2}$. Remember that $\sin\angle QRS = \dfrac{\text{opposite}}{\text{hypotenuse}}$. Therefore, $\sin\angle QRS = \dfrac{5}{5\sqrt{2}} = \dfrac{1}{\sqrt{2}} = \dfrac{\sqrt{2}}{2}$.

Choice (C) is correct.

60. K

Category: Trigonometry
Difficulty: Medium

Getting to the Answer: Using the Pythagorean theorem, a right triangle with leg 8 and hypotenuse 17 must have another leg of 15, so $JK = 15$. Because JK is opposite $\angle JLK$, $\sin\angle JLK = \dfrac{15}{17}$. Choice (K) is correct.

READING TEST

PASSAGE I

1. C

Category: Detail
Difficulty: Low

Getting to the Answer: Line 11 explicitly states that Victor is Rosemary's grandson. Choice (C) is correct.

2. H

Category: Inference
Difficulty: Medium

Getting to the Answer: Rosemary's unease with Victor's behavior is broadly in response to what she perceives as his laziness, but "laziness" isn't an answer choice. Choice J may be tempting, but Victor isn't unable to get out of bed, he's unwilling to. Paragraph 3 does specifically talk about something he had said that had "disturbed" her—his willingness to take an easy class, which matches (H). There is no evidence that Victor plans to drop out, so F is not correct, and her upbringing is never discussed with him, so G is incorrect.

3. D

Category: Inference
Difficulty: Medium

Getting to the Answer: The answer is strongly implied in the passage. Paragraph 3 notes that Rosemary wanted to go to high school after finishing grammar school. Her father would not permit her to go, so she had to spend time "with animals and rough farmhands for company instead of people her own age," (D). Choice B is flatly contradicted by paragraph 3, which indicates that Rosemary wanted to go to high school, not college. Choices A and C make inferences that are not supported by the passage.

4. G

Category: Inference

Difficulty: Medium

Getting to the Answer: Lines 19–20 say that Rosemary "had decided long ago that growing old was like slowly turning to stone." This sentiment suggests that she is resigned to the physical problems that accompany old age. *Acceptance*, (G), therefore, is correct. *Sadness*, F, and *resentment*, H, are too negative in tone, while *optimism*, J, is too positive. Rosemary, in short, isn't at all emotional about the aging process.

5. A

Category: Detail

Difficulty: Low

Getting to the Answer: Rosemary's interest in crossword puzzles is discussed in the opening sentences of paragraph 1. She does them for two reasons: to pass the time and to keep her mind active, (A). The other choices distort details in paragraphs 1 and 2. Choice B plays on Rosemary's happiness at still being able to write at 87, C plays on her need to consult an atlas to look up the Swiss river, and D plays on her experience of "an expanded sense of time" as she grows older.

6. H

Category: Generalization

Difficulty: Medium

Getting to the Answer: Most of the passage is about the different attitudes of Rosemary and Victor toward education, (H). The first two paragraphs serve as a lead-in to this topic, while the remainder of the passage concentrates on Rosemary's thoughts and memories about education. Rosemary mentions Victor's laziness, F, but this isn't the main focus of the passage. Education is the primary focus. There's no information at all to suggest that Victor's father has mistreated him, G. Indeed, just the opposite is implied: Victor's "doting parents," after all, have given him a new car. Finally, J doesn't mention education. Moreover, Rosemary doesn't try to suppress her memories.

7. B

Category: Inference

Difficulty: High

Getting to the Answer: A question that contains a line reference requires you to understand the context in which the reference appears. In the lines that precede the mention of Victor's "shiny new car," Rosemary considers his easy upbringing, how he looks as if he's never done a chore. In other words, Victor's car is a symbol of his generation, which has had a much easier time of it than Rosemary's. So (B) is correct. Rosemary's parents, A—her father anyway—can't be described as generous. Besides, her parents have nothing to do with Victor's car. Similarly, while Rosemary seems to feel that Victor's future prospects are bright, C, and that his life lacks hardship, D, neither has anything to do with his car.

8. G

Category: Detail

Difficulty: Medium

Getting to the Answer: Paragraph 3 says that Rosemary is disturbed by Victor's dismissive attitude toward his education. She doesn't like the idea that his only reason for taking a course is that he can pass it. In contrast to Victor's attitude, Rosemary, in her youth, was eager to continue her education, (G). Choices F and J refer to details from the wrong paragraphs, while H introduces an issue that the passage never tackles.

9. C

Category: Detail

Difficulty: Medium

Getting to the Answer: A few lines before Rosemary recalls what it was like growing up on the farm, the passage says that "Rosemary often experienced an expanded sense of time, with present and past tense intermingling in her mind," (C). Choice D, on the other hand, alludes to recollections from the wrong paragraphs. Choices A and B distort details in paragraph 2.

10. F
Category: Inference
Difficulty: Low
Getting to the Answer: The reference to Victor's bright future comes at the end of paragraph 2, which precedes Rosemary's opinion: "if he (Victor) ever got out of bed." It's clear from the text that it's Rosemary, (F), who thinks that he has a good future. The passage never says what Victor thought about his own future, G. Nor does it say what his parents thought about his future, H. And it's extremely unlikely that Victor and Rosemary's father, J, were even alive at the same time.

PASSAGE II

11. B
Category: Detail
Difficulty: High
Getting to the Answer: Use evidence in the passage and your own common sense to form a prediction before looking at the answer choices. The passage states that these revisions were written by "pro-business Eastern senators," and that these revisions worked to weaken the effectiveness of the Act. (B) is correct; the pro-business senators resisted the purpose of the bill. A is a misused detail; Social Darwinism is not discussed until the next paragraph, and the author makes no direct connection between it and the revisions. C is a distortion; there is evidence of "debate," because the bill got rewritten, but there is no evidence that the debate took a long time. D is extreme; the author is only discussing this bill, not the nature of all Congressional legislation at that time.

12. H
Category: Detail
Difficulty: High
Getting to the Answer: Remember to keep straight the opinion of the author and other opinions cited in the passage. The trust leaders used the theory of "Social Darwinism" to explain why it was natural for them to have monopolies. The author must have included this in order to explain how some people justified the existence of monopolies. Choice (H) is correct; this matches your prediction. F is a distortion; this is what the monopolists thought, not what the author thinks. G is out of scope; the author is not exploring what kind of corporations survived, except to the extent that monopolists artificially stifled competition. J is out of scope; the author is discussing a specific instance, not exploring the general "influence" of science on policy.

13. B
Category: Inference
Difficulty: Medium
Getting to the Answer: When a question stem refers you to a section of the passage but does not provide enough information to make a prediction, it is often helpful to take a quick scan through the passage before looking at the answer choices. The third paragraph states that *laissez-faire* policies created monopolies that had many negative effects. Many people objected to this, which eventually led to the Sherman Antitrust Act and other similar measures. (B) fits with the description of the many negative effects of the trusts. A is extreme; there is not enough evidence in the passage to use the word *all*. C is a misused detail; this idea comes from the second passage. The author of Passage A never states that it was necessary; maybe there were other ways to handle the situation. D is a distortion; the author would argue that all businesses, even big trusts like Standard Oil, could compete freely after the act.

14. J

Category: Detail
Difficulty: Medium
Getting to the Answer: Because the answer is in the passage, you should be able to move quickly through Detail questions, saving time for those you find more difficult. Read in the immediate vicinity of the given reference. The prior sentence states that Roosevelt used "government funds for the first time" in "intentional deficit spending." The sentence after the reference points out that this "ushered in the modern era of liberal economic regulation . . ." The Act is an example of active manipulation of the economy by the government, which matches (J). F is a misused detail; Passage A, not Passage B, refers to antitrust acts. G is opposite; the passage states that "this act signaled the end of the *laissez-faire* economics era . . ." H is opposite; the author says that the Agricultural Adjustment Act helped boost the nation out of the Great Depression.

15. A

Category: Generalization
Difficulty: High
Getting to the Answer: The first and last sentence of a paragraph will often help clue you into the author's purpose. Interestingly, the passage is not primarily about economics; the author simply uses economics as an example to make his larger point, that the role of the national government must change over time. In the last paragraph, the author reinforces this by saying that Roosevelt went against traditional attitudes about the role of government in the economy, and that he was very successful in doing so. In the last sentence, the author sums up by saying that "the national government must adapt in both scope and purpose to fit the needs of changing times." This matches (A). B is opposite; the author argues that reforms were quite necessary. C is out of scope; the author does not "cite" any exceptions. D is a distortion; the author is saying that the government must change because circumstances

change. This does not mean that there were "weaknesses in the original design" of the government.

16. H

Category: Detail
Difficulty: Medium
Getting to the Answer: opposite choices can be tricky if you do not take the time to read carefully. Many people, including the "conservative capitalist economists," felt that the economy would naturally rise and fall, and that the government should not interfere in that process. The author then goes on to state that Roosevelt felt the economy would not naturally recover and so he instituted policies and spent money to fix it. The author feels that Roosevelt was right to do so. (The author says that Roosevelt's success was "undeniable.") So, the author explains the viewpoint of the "conservative capitalist economists" in order to then argue that they were wrong, and that Roosevelt was right in working to change the economy. (H) fits nicely with the sentiments of the author. F is opposite; Roosevelt took the opposite view from the "conservative capitalist economists." G is opposite; the viewpoint of the "conservative capitalist economists" was in direct contradiction to policies like the Agricultural Adjustment Act. J is a misused detail; this does not come up until the final paragraph.

17. B

Category: Detail
Difficulty: Medium
Getting to the Answer: Watch out for choices that only apply to one of the Paired Passages. Both passages refer to economic reform. Passage A talks about preventing monopolies and trusts, and Passage B speaks in more general terms about spending money to pull the nation out of the Great Depression. Look for something that deals with government intervention in the economy. (B) is mentioned in both passages. A is opposite; both authors seem to agree that some degree of governmental control is necessary. C is a misused detail; this only

appears in Passage A. D is a misused detail; this only appears in Passage B.

18. G

Category: Inference
Difficulty: Medium
Getting to the Answer: When you are trying to infer how one author would react to an idea in another passage, look for a concept that the author specifically addresses. The author of Passage B argues that it is often a good idea for the government to intervene in the economy. Therefore he would probably not accept the argument that something should continue to exist simply because it is the most natural state of affairs. (G) is correct; this fits with Author B's view of *laissez-faire* economic policy. F is out of scope; we do not know how the author of Passage B feels about the theory of Social Darwinism. C is opposite; this viewpoint is what Author B is arguing against. D is a distortion; Author B never mentions monopolies.

19. B

Category: Detail
Difficulty: Low
Getting to the Answer: Use the passages to research your answer. It is tough to make a specific prediction here, so jump into the answer choices, and compare each one against the passages. (B) is correct; Passage B mentions Roosevelt's plan to "pump-prime" the depressed American economy through government deficit spending. A is opposite; this appears in Passage A but not Passage B. C is opposite; this is from Passage A, not Passage B. D is opposite; this appears in both passages.

20. J

Category: Detail
Difficulty: High
Getting to the Answer: In the third paragraph of Passage A, the author cites many negative consequences of *laissez-faire* policies, and the trusts and monopolies that arose from these policies. In the

third paragraph of Passage B, the author states that the Agricultural Adjustment Act "signaled the end of the *laissez-faire* economics era." These details match (J). F is opposite; Passage A describes how *laissez-faire* policies negatively affected consumers and Passage B states that the *laissez-faire* era ended by the end of the 19th century. G includes misused details that are mentioned in each passage but do not address the question. H is out of scope; Roosevelt's presidential legacy is not discussed.

PASSAGE III

21. C

Category: Detail
Difficulty: Medium
Getting to the Answer: This question asks for a description of the *philosophes*, so it's back to the first two paragraphs. Lines 15–17 say that they took the ideas of others and popularized them. The first sentence of paragraph 2 goes on to state that they "developed the philosophy of the Enlightenment and spread it to much of the educated elite in Western Europe (and the American colonies)." Thus, (C) is correct. Choices B and D are contradicted by information in the first paragraph, which states that the philosophes were generally neither professors nor scientists. Choice A, on the other hand, is too narrow in scope: true, the philosophes were influenced by Locke, but they were also influenced by Newton and English institutions.

22. G

Category: Inference
Difficulty: Low
Getting to the Answer: Your passage map of the passage should have sent you directly to the last paragraph, where Voltaire is discussed. This paragraph says that Voltaire criticized both French society and religious institutions, so you can infer that he might have attacked French religious institutions, (G). Choice H is contradicted by information in the paragraph, which states that Voltaire "came to admire" English government. It's unlikely that

he would have criticized the Scientific Revolution, F, because the philosophes were disciples of this revolution. Finally, the passage says nothing about Voltaire's views of "courtly love," J, so you can't infer what his position on this issue would have been.

23. D

Category: Detail

Difficulty: Medium

Getting to the Answer: The answer to a question that contains a line reference is found in the lines around that reference. Locke's idea that "schools and social institutions could…play a great role in molding the individual" comes up right after his belief that humans are shaped by their experiences, (D). Choice A is contradicted by lines 50–53, while B and C distort details in paragraph 4.

24. H

Category: Inference

Difficulty: High

Getting to the Answer: Your passage map should have pointed you to paragraph 3, where Newton is discussed. This paragraph says that Newton believed that "the universe [was]…originally set in motion by God," option I, and that "the universe operates in a mechanical and orderly fashion," option III. However, this paragraph doesn't say that Newton believed that "human reason is insufficient to understand the laws of nature," option II; if anything, it implies just the opposite. Choice (H), options I and III only, is correct.

25. D

Category: Detail

Difficulty: Medium

Getting to the Answer: Lines 61–64 reveal that it was Locke who questioned the notion that "revelation was a reliable source of truth." Thus, you're looking for a work written by him, so you can immediately eliminate A, *Letters on the English*, and C, *Elements of the Philosophy of Newton*, both of which were authored by Voltaire. The remaining

two works, *Second Treatise of Civil Government*, B, and *Essay Concerning Human Understanding*, (D), were both written by Locke; but *Second Treatise of Civil Government*, B, is a political, not a philosophical, work, so it can be eliminated as well. That leaves (D) as the correct answer.

26. G

Category: Inference

Difficulty: Medium

Getting to the Answer: The first sentence of paragraph 4 states that Locke "agreed with Newton but went further." Specifically, Locke also thought that the human mind was subject to "the mechanical laws of the material universe" (lines 48–49), (G). The other choices distort details in paragraphs 3 and 4.

27. D

Category: Generalization

Difficulty: Medium

Getting to the Answer: The philosophes—as paragraph 5 shows—were greatly influenced by an England that allowed more individual freedom, was more tolerant of religious differences, and was freer of traditional political institutions than other countries, particularly France. Indeed, the philosophes wanted other countries to adopt the English model. Thus (D), statements I, II, and III, is correct.

28. G

Category: Writer's View

Difficulty: High

Getting to the Answer: This question also asks about England, so refer back to paragraph 5. In the second-to-last sentence of the paragraph, the philosophes cite England's political stability and prosperity as evidence that England's system worked. The last sentence of the paragraph goes on to say that the philosophes "wanted to see in their own countries much of what England already seemed to have." Choice (G), therefore, is correct. Choice F, on the other hand, flatly contradicts the gist of paragraph 5. Finally, H and J distort details from the wrong part of the passage.

29. A

Category: Inference
Difficulty: Low
Getting to the Answer: The French political and religious authorities during the time of Voltaire are discussed in paragraph 6. Voltaire got in hot water with the authorities over his outspoken views, so it's safe to assume that they weren't advocates of free speech, (A). They first imprisoned and then exiled him, so they clearly didn't regard the philosophes with indifference, C. The passage doesn't say precisely what Voltaire was imprisoned and exiled for, so you can't infer that the authorities "overreacted to Voltaire's mild satires," B, which, in any case, weren't that mild. Finally, because Voltaire was an advocate of the English system of government, it's also safe to assume that the French hadn't accepted this model, making D wrong.

30. J

Category: Generalization
Difficulty: Medium
Getting to the Answer: The notion that the philosophes were "more literary than scientific" appears in the middle of paragraph 1. A few lines further down, the paragraph furnishes a list of the types of literary works produced by the philosophes, so (J) is correct. The passage never mentions any "political change," F. Nor does it compare the literary outputs of Newton and Voltaire, G. Finally, H is out because the philosophes were not scientists.

PASSAGE IV

31. D

Category: Detail
Difficulty: Low
Getting to the Answer: This question emphasizes the importance of reading all the choices before selecting one. The second paragraph tells us that

the Alvarezes believe conditions created by the impact of a meteorite led to mass extinctions. The impact of the asteroid, A, caused great damage, but it didn't do "most of the harm"—see the third sentence. Processes like B and C are the explanations of the traditional scientists.

32. H

Category: Writer's View
Difficulty: High
Getting to the Answer: This isn't easy, but (H) is the only possible choice. The author is an objective scientist or science journalist who wouldn't want opponents to give up their view until the new theory has been fully tested against all their criticisms. The traditionalists' arguments are given only briefly, and the author clearly believes the Alvarezes have added something valuable to the study of mass extinctions, but the traditional view has not proven wrong conclusively, F. And as the last paragraph indicates, traditionalists have produced their own theories to account for new evidence, such as iridium reaching the Earth's surface via volcanic activity, J. Choice G is clearly not true; the author believes the new theory challenged the old one.

33. C

Category: Vocab-in-Context
Difficulty: Medium
Getting to the Answer: As it is used in the sentence, *enrichment* means "increase in amount." It wouldn't make sense for the Earth to have wealth, A, improvement, B, or reward of iridium, D.

34. F

Category: Generalization
Difficulty: Low
Getting to the Answer: The arguments of Alvarez-theory opponents are given in the last paragraph: no crater, iridium comes from the Earth's core, and the Alvarezes are only physicists. If sufficient iridium deposits come from the Earth's core in lava flows, (F), Alvarez supporters can't rely on them as

evidence of impact. The Alvarezes didn't say extinctions never occurred without asteroid impact, G, or that all meteorites contain iridium, H. Choice J contradicts one of the opponents' arguments.

35. D

Category: Writer's View

Difficulty: Medium

Getting to the Answer: In the first sentence of paragraph 2, the author calls the Alvarez theory important. The bulk of the passage explains and supports this theory. The implication is that the author believes the Alvarezes were on the right track, so we want a positive answer. Choices A and C are negative, and B is neutral.

36. G

Category: Detail

Difficulty: High

Getting to the Answer: According to the information in the second paragraph, soil displacement was the immediate result of a meteorite's impact; it "blotted out" the sun, which reduced temperatures and caused plants to die.

37. D

Category: Inference

Difficulty: Medium

Getting to the Answer: Look back at the second paragraph; details there clarify how the impact led to extinctions—the crater didn't simply smash all species into extinction. Choice A uses the wrong verb. The lack of a known crater site, B, is mentioned at the end of paragraph 4, but that's not relevant to the discussion in paragraph 2. The conditions that result from meteorite collisions aren't evidence that the Earth is vulnerable to such collisions, C.

38. H

Category: Generalization

Difficulty: Medium

Getting to the Answer: The large number of asteroids implied by *teeming* in paragraph 1 explains why

Alvarez supporters believe frequent collisions must have occurred in Earth's history (paragraph 4). The fact that an impact would result in certain effects, F, or the idea that the dust cloud would do more harm than the impact itself, G, or the traditional view about gradual processes, J, are not related to the number of impacts that are likely.

39. C

Category: Detail

Difficulty: Medium

Getting to the Answer: The two sentences at the end of paragraph 4 offer the answer; only I and III explain this position. Iridium relates to a different argument entirely.

40. F

Category: Detail

Difficulty: Low

Getting to the Answer: As we've seen, the disastrous consequences of an asteroid's impact are covered in paragraph 2, where G, H, and J are mentioned. Choice (F) is evidence of impact from paragraph 3.

SCIENCE TEST

PASSAGE I

1. C

Category: Figure Interpretation

Difficulty: High

Getting to the Answer: Point *c* is the point on the light curve at which the eclipsing binary is the darkest. Take a look at Figure 1. From the point of view of the observer, System *Q* is going to be darkest when the light from the brighter star, Star 1, is being blocked by the light from the less bright Star 2. Star 2 interposes itself between Star 1 and the observer when Star 2 is in position 3, (C).

2. J

Category: Figure Interpretation

Difficulty: Medium

Getting to the Answer: According to the x-axis of the light curve, the complete cycle of changes in the system's surface brightness (from point *a* through points *b*, *c*, and *d* and back to point *a* again) lasts 20 days. This means that Star 2 requires 20 days to complete its orbit around Star 1 (it is this orbit, after all, that is causing the changes in the system's brightness). Choice (J) is the correct answer.

3. C

Category: Figure Interpretation

Difficulty: High

Getting to the Answer: The drops in brightness on the light curve (Figure 2) indicate when one star is eclipsing the other. The sharp drop known as the primary minimum—when the darker star eclipses the brighter star—lasts approximately two days. The secondary minimum—when the brighter star eclipses the darker star—goes from day 16 through day 20 to day 4, a total of eight days.

4. G

Category: Scientific Reasoning

Difficulty: Medium

Getting to the Answer: This question introduces two new light curve graphs. What gives System *Z* a deeper primary minimum than *X*? The reason *Q* had a deep primary minimum was that one star was brighter than the other; during the time that the brighter star's light was eclipsed by the darker star, the whole system became much darker. You can safely assume that this is the reason *Z* has a deep primary minimum as well. *X*'s lack of a deep primary minimum must mean, then, that neither of its stars is significantly brighter than the other. As you can see from *X*'s light curve, the drop in brightness of the system is about the same no matter which star is being eclipsed, so the two stars must be equally bright. Because the more extreme difference in the

magnitudes of System *Z*'s stars is the reason for *Z*'s deeper primary minimum, (G) is correct.

5. D

Category: Scientific Reasoning

Difficulty: Medium

Getting to the Answer: If either star in an eclipsing binary system is in front of the other, the brightness of the system will be reduced. The only time the system reaches maximum brightness is when both stars are completely visible—when the full brightness of one star is added to the full brightness of the other, (D).

PASSAGE II

6. J

Category: Scientific Reasoning

Difficulty: Medium

Getting to the Answer: The question requires you to identify what is formed when CO_2 leaves the air in the diagramed carbon cycle. The figure indicates that CO_2 leaves the air via photosynthesis and goes to green plants and carbohydrates. In the same box, proteins, fats, and other carbon compounds are also mentioned. Therefore, roman numeral II and III are correct. The only answer choice to have both II and III is (J). (J) is also correct because starch is an example of a carbohydrate. While this question is subtly testing background knowledge about carbohydrates, you are still able to get to the correct answer using the figure.

7. C

Category: Figure Interpretation

Difficulty: Medium

Getting to the Answer: Decay bacteria, according to the diagram, gets carbon from the carbon compounds of dead plants and animals and adds to the supply of carbon dioxide in air and water through fermentation and putrefaction. Because there is no other way to get carbon from dead plants and animals back to carbon dioxide, a drop in decay bacteria will reduce the amount of carbon available for forming carbon dioxide. The carbon dioxide level will not be greatly affected, though, because there are three other sources of carbon for carbon dioxide. Choice (C) is correct.

8. G

Category: Figure Interpretation
Difficulty: Medium
Getting to the Answer: Consider each of the statements one by one. Statement I is false because the diagram shows that the carbon in animals can move to "other animals" through the process of "animal digestion." An animal that only eats other animals is participating in the carbon cycle when it digests its prey. Statement II is clearly true; there are arrows labeled *respiration* going from the green plants, the animals, and the other animals stages back to the carbon dioxide stage. Statement III, however, is not true, because some carbon dioxide is released into the air by fermentation and putrefaction. Because only Statement II is true, (G) is correct.

9. D

Category: Figure Interpretation
Difficulty: High
Getting to the Answer: There are four direct sources of atmospheric carbon dioxide, according to the diagram: fermentation by decay bacteria and respiration by green plants, by animals, and by "other animals or animal parasites." Choice (D) correctly cites the respiration of animal parasites. If you were tempted by B, note the direction of the arrow for photosynthesis. Photosynthesis removes atmospheric carbon dioxide, using it as a source for carbon.

10. G

Category: Figure Interpretation
Difficulty: Medium
Getting to the Answer: The arrow signifying animal respiration and the arrow signifying photosynthesis are linked in the diagram by the "carbon dioxide in air or dissolved in water" box. Animal respiration is one of the sources of carbon for carbon dioxide, and the carbon dioxide in turn provides carbon for the process of photosynthesis. In this sense, "animal respiration provides vital gases for green plants," (G).

11. A

Category: Figure Interpretation
Difficulty: Medium
Getting to the Answer: Look closely at the diagram. The only way that carbon dioxide can enter the carbon cycle is through the process of photosynthesis in which it is taken up by green plants. Note that green plants also emit carbon dioxide back into the air via the process of respiration. Therefore, if green plants were eliminated, the carbon cycle would come to a complete stop, and (A) is correct.

PASSAGE III

12. G

Category: Scientific Reasoning
Difficulty: Medium
Getting to the Answer: In order to be able to tell whether light was the stimulus affecting the direction of bacterial migration, you have to compare two trials, one with the light on and one with the light off. If there is no difference in the direction of bacterial migration in the two trials, then light does not have an effect and is not the primary stimulus. The two trials you need to compare are Trial 1 and Trial 2 of Study 1, because Trial 1 was conducted under standard lab conditions (with the light on), and in Trial 2 the microscope was shielded from all external light. Because the results of the trials differed only minimally, they support the theory that light was not the primary stimulus. Choice (G) is correct.

13. C

Category: Scientific Reasoning
Difficulty: Medium
Getting to the Answer: The data shows that bacteria are sensitive to magnetic fields and tend to migrate in the direction of magnetic north. In Study 2, this meant that the bacteria moved toward the magnet because the magnet's north pole was near the slide. If the magnet's south pole were placed near the slide, the magnetic field would be reversed and the bacteria would migrate in exactly the opposite direction, away from the magnet. That makes (C) the correct answer.

14. J

Category: Scientific Reasoning
Difficulty: Medium
Getting to the Answer: You don't need experimental data to answer this question; you just have to figure out which answer choice provides the best reason a bacteria should be able to move downward. Choices F and G are out immediately because both are good reasons a bacteria should move upward, not downward. While it may have been somewhat advantageous for bacteria not to be dispersed by currents, H, it would have been much more important for them to move downward to find food, so (J) is the best answer.

15. C

Category: Scientific Reasoning
Difficulty: High
Getting to the Answer: Here, you have to determine which new study would yield new and useful information about the relationship between magnetic field strength and bacterial migrations. You should try to determine the experimental condition that the researchers should vary before you look at the answer choices. To gain new information about magnetic field strength and bacterial migrations, the researchers should vary the magnetic field strength and observe the effect on bacterial migrations. Choice (C) is correct because it suggests using

more and less powerful magnets, which would produce stronger and weaker magnetic fields than that of the magnet in Study 2.

16. F

Category: Figure Interpretation
Difficulty: Medium
Getting to the Answer: In each of the trials of Study 1, bacterial migrations were largely found to be in the direction of magnetic north. Shielding from light and electric fields, rotation of the microscope, and movement of the microscope to another lab all had no distinct effect on the direction of migration. It is fairly easy to conclude from Study 1 that "the majority of magnetotactic bacteria migrate toward the earth's magnetic north pole," (F).

17. A

Category: Scientific Reasoning
Difficulty: Low
Getting to the Answer: In any experiment, the control condition is the one used as a standard of comparison in judging the experimental effects of the other conditions. In Study 1, there would be no way to know what the effect of, say, rotating the microscope was on bacterial migration if you didn't know how the bacteria migrated before you rotated the microscope. The control condition is the trial that is run without any experimental manipulations: in this case, Trial 1, (A).

18. G

Category: Patterns
Difficulty: High
Getting to the Answer: To answer this question, refer to Table 2. Based on the data for Trial 2 in the table, 483 bacteria accumulated at the 3:00 direction on the microscope slide, whereas only a few accumulated at the other directions on the slide. Only (G) has a high density of dots at the 3:00 PM location and a low density of dots at the other locations.

PASSAGE IV

19. B

Category: Patterns
Difficulty: Low
Getting to the Answer: A data point does not exist for week 40 on Figure 1. In order to estimate the percent flexibility of the *nu-PVC*, extend the line of the graph and make sure that it is consistent with the downward trend. Use 40 on the *x*-axis to trace back to the *y*-axis, which reveals that the closest value is indeed 12%. The answer cannot be H or J because they are greater than 17.5%, the last data point that is at 32 weeks. The downward trend of the graph tapers off at the end, between weeks 24 and 32. If the extended line did not follow the trend and was too steep, A would be incorrectly selected.

20. H

Category: Figure Interpretation
Difficulty: Medium
Getting to the Answer: According to the results of Experiment 1, *nu-PVC* does not suffer any kind of damage when exposed to water for a long period of time. It seems safe to say, then, that *nu-PVC* would not need a protective coating to avoid water damage, (H).

21. B

Category: Scientific Reasoning
Difficulty: Medium
Getting to the Answer: The results that are relevant here are those from Experiment 3, in which *nu-PVC*'s ability to withstand cold temperatures was tested. The *nu-PVC* boards did not fare well during this experiment; they lost more than half of their capacity to support weight without bending or breaking. In a cold environment, the benches could not be kept outside during the winter without sustaining damage. Choice (B) is correct.

22. G

Category: Scientific Reasoning
Difficulty: Medium
Getting to the Answer: Remember that a control is an experimental condition in which nothing special is done to the thing being tested. The control serves as a standard of comparison for the experimental effects found in other conditions. In Experiment 1, the *nu-PVC* boards were sprayed with distilled water for a long period of time to see what effect the water would have. In order to assess the water's effects accurately, though, you have to compare the results of Experiment 1 to the results of a condition in which *nu-PVC* boards are not exposed to water, (G).

23. A

Category: Scientific Reasoning
Difficulty: Medium
Getting to the Answer: Although at first this question seems to require outside knowledge, it can be answered by the process of elimination using the information in the introduction. The introduction of the passage states that the series of experiments was performed to test the weathering abilities of *nu-PVC*. The only weather phenomenon in the answer choices is sunlight, (A).

24. J

Category: Scientific Reasoning
Difficulty: High
Getting to the Answer: You know nothing in particular about standard building materials from the passage—you don't know how well they stand up to rain or ultraviolet radiation or how well they support weight after exposure to cold weather. This means you cannot compare *nu-PVC* to other materials at all, which rules out F and H. Choice G is out because there is no information in the passage about the "different colors and textures" of *nu-PVC*. That leaves (J). Choice (J) is correct because it is an advantage of *nu-PVC* (perhaps the only one) that it is made of recycled plastic wastes. *Nu-PVC* helps to solve the garbage problem at the same time that it

fills the need for building materials; wood and other standard building materials don't do that.

25. A

Category: Scientific Reasoning

Difficulty: High

Getting to the Answer: The conditions of the original experiments were clearly chosen so that *nu-PVC* would be subjected to extremes of water, radiation, and cold. There is little point in making the conditions even more extreme when a park bench would never have to survive such weather. It is unlikely, for example, that a park bench will be exposed to 32 weeks of continuous rain, much less 64 weeks, or that a bench will have to endure eight months of −40°C temperature. Thus, Statements I and III are not going to provide useful information. Statement II, on the other hand, is an important experiment, because sea water and salt-rich air may well have a corrosive effect on *nu-PVC* whereas distilled water did not. Choice (A) is correct.

26. G

Category: Figure Interpretation

Difficulty: Medium

Getting to the Answer: The data for each treatment in Figure 2 is represented with three lines: One that reflects the greatest value, one that reflects the mean, and one that reflects the lowest value. In order to answer the question, direct your attention to the After data in the graph. Draw a line from the top line of the data to the *y*-axis, which is approximately 600 lbs. Repeat with the bottom line of the data to find that it is approximately 300 lbs. The distance between the two is 300 lbs, which matches (G). Choice F is a trap because it is the range for the Before data.

27. D

Category: Figure Interpretation

Difficulty: Medium

Getting to the Answer: The passage states that *Amadori* products form when the protein samples are incubated with glucose but not with water. On Figure 1, locate the peak that represents the glucose treated protein (the solid line). Draw a line from the top of the glucose peak, which is the maximum absorbance of the sample, to the *x*-axis to find that the wavelength is closest to 400 nm. Choice A is a trap because it is the wavelength for the maximum absorbance of the sample that had been incubated in water.

28. J

Category: Scientific Reasoning

Difficulty: Medium

Getting to the Answer: The researcher who designed the experiments was interested in the effect of dietary glucose on lens proteins in the human eye, not the cow eye. There would be no reason to use cow lens proteins in Experiment 3 if cow lens proteins were expected to react any differently from human lens proteins, especially when human lens proteins were readily available for use—they were used, after all, for Experiment 1. Therefore, you know that the researcher assumed that cow lens proteins would react the same as human lens proteins, (J).

29. C

Category: Scientific Reasoning

Difficulty: Medium

Getting to the Answer: Make sure that you stick to the results of Experiment 1 only when you answer this question. All you know from Experiment 1 is that when a human tissue protein was dissolved in a glucose and water solution, the proteins formed Amadori products that combined with other proteins to make brown cross-links. You can conclude from this that the glucose reacted with the proteins to form cross-links, (C). Based on Experiment 1, though, you know nothing about disulfide cross links, A, or glucose metabolism, D. Choice B contradicts the results of Experiment 1 because it is protein, not glucose, that forms AGE.

30. G

Category: Scientific Reasoning
Difficulty: Medium
Getting to the Answer: Take another look at the results of Experiment 2. It was found that in the samples from older subjects, the lens proteins often formed cross-linked bonds, some of which were brown. The senile cataracts in the lenses of older people are also brown. The conclusion suggested by the identical colors of the cataracts and the cross-linked bonds is that the senile cataracts are made up of, or caused by, cross-linked bonds, (G).

31. C

Category: Scientific Reasoning
Difficulty: Medium
Getting to the Answer: You don't know from the results of Experiment 2 how the brown pigmented cross-links developed among the lens proteins of older humans. Experiments 1 and 3 indicate, however, that glucose reacts with lens proteins in such a way that brown pigmented cross-links form among the proteins. And remember the main purpose of the experiments: The researcher is investigating the effects of glucose on lens proteins in order to see whether dietary sugar (glucose) damages proteins. The hypothesis that dietary sugar reacted with lens proteins to cause the brown pigmented cross-links found in older subjects would seem to be supported by the results of the three experiments, (C).

32. J

Category: Scientific Reasoning
Difficulty: Medium
Getting to the Answer: The relevant results are those from Experiment 2: the lens proteins of

younger subjects were found to have formed cross-linked aggregates much less frequently than the lens proteins of older subjects did. So you would expect that the lens proteins of a 32-year-old man would have fewer cross-links than the lens proteins of an 80-year-old man, (J). Choice H appears true, but the lens proteins appear "much more often" in older samples. The age difference is greater from 32 years to 80 than 18 years to 32; (J) is, thus, the most likely, and correct, answer.

33. C

Category: Scientific Reasoning
Difficulty: High
Getting to the Answer: String together the hypotheses that were the correct answers from questions 30 and 31, and you have the following overall hypothesis: dietary glucose causes brown pigmented (AGE) cross-links to form among lens proteins, and these brown cross-links in turn cause the formation of brown senile cataracts. According to this hypothesis, the excess glucose in an uncontrolled diabetic's blood should cause the formation of AGE cross-links among lens proteins and subsequently the development of senile cataracts, (C).

PASSAGE VI

34. G

Category: Scientific Reasoning
Difficulty: High
Getting to the Answer: Scientist 1 is a proponent of the Quark Model, which says that baryons (including the proton) and mesons are made up of quarks, which have fractional charge. Quarks have never been observed, however. You find out from Scientist 2 that quarks should be easy to distinguish from other particles because they would be the only ones with fractional charge. If a particle with fractional charge was detected, then, it would most likely be a quark, and this would strengthen Scientist 1's hypothesis that the Quark Model is correct. Mesons, baryons, and the Δ^{++} baryon have all been

detected, but mere detection of them does not tell us anything about their substructure, so it cannot be used to support the Quark Model.

35. C

Category: Scientific Reasoning
Difficulty: Medium
Getting to the Answer: Scientist 2 says that it should be easy to split the proton into quarks, that the quarks should be easy to distinguish because of their unique charge (Statement I), and that they should be stable because they can't decay into lighter particles (Statement III). Statement II is wrong because it is Scientist 1's explanation of why quarks cannot be detected. Therefore, (C) is correct.

36. F

Category: Scientific Reasoning
Difficulty: Low
Getting to the Answer: Scientist 2 says that the Quark Model is wrong because it violates the Pauli exclusion principle, which states that no two particles of half-integer spin can occupy the same state. He says that in the Δ^{++} baryon, for example, the presence of two up quarks in the same state would violate the principle, so the model must be incorrect. If Scientist 1 were able to show, however, that quarks do not have half-integer spin, (F), she could argue that the Pauli exclusion principle does not apply to quarks and thus counter Scientist 2's objections. Evidence that the Δ^{++} baryon exists, G, or that quarks have fractional charge, H, isn't going to help Scientist 1 because neither has anything to do with the Pauli exclusion principle. Evidence that quarks have the same spin as electrons, J, would only support Scientist 2's position.

37. D

Category: Scientific Reasoning
Difficulty: Medium
Getting to the Answer: According to Scientist 2, the Δ^{++} baryon has three up quarks. Each up quark has a charge of $+2/3$ each, so the three quarks together have a total charge of 2, (D).

38. G

Category: Scientific Reasoning
Difficulty: High
Getting to the Answer: Scientist 2 thinks that the Quark Model is flawed for two reasons: 1) quarks have not been detected experimentally, and they would have been if they existed, and 2) the Quark Model violates the Pauli exclusion principle. The first reason is paraphrased in (G), the correct answer. Choice F is incorrect because the existence of individual baryons, including protons, has been verified experimentally. Scientist 2 never says that he thinks particles cannot have fractional charge, nor does he complain that the Quark Model doesn't include electrons as elementary particles, so H and J are incorrect as well.

39. A

Category: Scientific Reasoning
Difficulty: Medium
Getting to the Answer: The deep inelastic scattering experiments, according to Scientist 1, showed that the proton has a substructure. The three distinct lumps that were found to bounce high-energy electrons back and scatter them through large angles were the three quarks that make up the proton (at least in Scientist 1's view), so (A) is correct.

40. H

Category: Scientific Reasoning
Difficulty: High
Getting to the Answer: This question is a follow-up to the last one. If the three lumps were indeed quarks, then this supports the Quark Model because in the Quark Model, the proton consists of three quarks. "Protons supposedly consist of three quarks" is not one of the choices, though, so you have to look for a paraphrase of this idea. Protons are baryons and not mesons, so F and G are out. Baryons, like protons, are all supposed to consist of three quarks, so this rules out J and makes (H) the correct answer.

WRITING TEST

MODEL ESSAY

Below is an example of what a high-scoring essay might look like. Notice the author states her position clearly in the introductory paragraph and supports that position with evidence in the following paragraphs. This essay also uses transitions, some advanced vocabulary, and an effective "hook" to draw in the reader.

"Be cool; stay in school," is the type of saying that may sound silly to most people. Even though that phrase isn't really sophisticated, it does provide very wise advice. Attending school is incredibly important, and some people argue that unexcused absences should be reported to the police. Other people want focus on treating the underlying causes of truancy rather than doling out harsh punishments. Still others think that schools should provide alternative instruction options for students who have trouble getting to school on a regular basis. All three options have the same goal, which is to help students most at risk for missing school, and I think that schools should incorporate the best parts of all three approaches into their truancy-reduction policies.

The idea of having a police record because I skipped school is extremely scary and would certainly prevent me from missing school. If students know that their school will report them to the police after a specific number of unexcused absences, they will be more likely to find a way to get to school. Teenagers don't always do the right thing because it's a good idea but rather because not doing the right thing will get them in a lot of trouble. For example, many high school students turn in their assignments on time because they don't want teachers to deduct points for late submissions. The fear of consequence can promote good behavior in both homework habits and school attendance.

While avoiding a harsh consequence is a good reason to get to school, it's sometimes not compelling enough for students who are struggling with issues that make attending school very difficult. The best way to increase attendance for these students is to address the underlying problem. If students have transportation trouble, schools should help coordinate carpools and bus schedules. School counselors should be available to help students who have social issues or violence concerns. As for lack of interest, schools can offer before and after-school activities such as intramural sports and social clubs to give students a reason to stay throughout the day.

Even with the best efforts, some students will still struggle with attendance. For those students, schools should offer as many opportunities for them to complete their coursework as possible. It is in society's best interest to facilitate education, especially for at-risk youth. Now that technology allows students to learn from nearly anywhere, schools should offer students the option to study remotely. Students will benefit from a high school diploma, of course, and they will be able to say that their teachers did everything they could to give them the best chance at a good life.

Attending school isn't just about learning facts. The school environment gives students the opportunity to learn how to use social skills, collaborate with peers, and communicate effectively. The only way for students to work on these skills is to actually attend school. Every measure should be taken to reduce truancy, including the threat of a criminal record, the mitigation of underlying causes, and the option to pursue alternative instruction. That way, students don't have to just take our "be cool; stay in school" word for it - they'll show up because, really, with all those measures in place, how could they not?

You can evaluate your essay and the model essay based on the following criteria, which is covered in the Practice Makes Perfect section of this book:

- Does the author all three perspectives provided in the prompt?

- Is the author's own perspective clearly stated?

- Does the body of the essay assess and analyze each perspective?

- Is the relevance of each paragraph clear?

- Does the author start a new paragraph for each new idea?

- Is each sentence in a paragraph relevant to the point made in that paragraph?

- Are transitions clear?

- Is the essay easy to read? Is it engaging?

- Are sentences varied?

- Is vocabulary used effectively? Is college-level vocabulary used?

ACT Practice Test Five
ANSWER SHEET

ENGLISH TEST

1. Ⓐ Ⓑ Ⓒ Ⓓ 11. Ⓐ Ⓑ Ⓒ Ⓓ 21. Ⓐ Ⓑ Ⓒ Ⓓ 31. Ⓐ Ⓑ Ⓒ Ⓓ 41. Ⓐ Ⓑ Ⓒ Ⓓ 51. Ⓐ Ⓑ Ⓒ Ⓓ 61. Ⓐ Ⓑ Ⓒ Ⓓ 71. Ⓐ Ⓑ Ⓒ Ⓓ
2. Ⓕ Ⓖ Ⓗ Ⓙ 12. Ⓕ Ⓖ Ⓗ Ⓙ 22. Ⓕ Ⓖ Ⓗ Ⓙ 32. Ⓕ Ⓖ Ⓗ Ⓙ 42. Ⓕ Ⓖ Ⓗ Ⓙ 52. Ⓕ Ⓖ Ⓗ Ⓙ 62. Ⓕ Ⓖ Ⓗ Ⓙ 72. Ⓕ Ⓖ Ⓗ Ⓙ
3. Ⓐ Ⓑ Ⓒ Ⓓ 13. Ⓐ Ⓑ Ⓒ Ⓓ 23. Ⓐ Ⓑ Ⓒ Ⓓ 33. Ⓐ Ⓑ Ⓒ Ⓓ 43. Ⓐ Ⓑ Ⓒ Ⓓ 53. Ⓐ Ⓑ Ⓒ Ⓓ 63. Ⓐ Ⓑ Ⓒ Ⓓ 73. Ⓐ Ⓑ Ⓒ Ⓓ
4. Ⓕ Ⓖ Ⓗ Ⓙ 14. Ⓕ Ⓖ Ⓗ Ⓙ 24. Ⓕ Ⓖ Ⓗ Ⓙ 34. Ⓕ Ⓖ Ⓗ Ⓙ 44. Ⓕ Ⓖ Ⓗ Ⓙ 54. Ⓕ Ⓖ Ⓗ Ⓙ 64. Ⓕ Ⓖ Ⓗ Ⓙ 74. Ⓕ Ⓖ Ⓗ Ⓙ
5. Ⓐ Ⓑ Ⓒ Ⓓ 15. Ⓐ Ⓑ Ⓒ Ⓓ 25. Ⓐ Ⓑ Ⓒ Ⓓ 35. Ⓐ Ⓑ Ⓒ Ⓓ 45. Ⓐ Ⓑ Ⓒ Ⓓ 55. Ⓐ Ⓑ Ⓒ Ⓓ 65. Ⓐ Ⓑ Ⓒ Ⓓ 75. Ⓐ Ⓑ Ⓒ Ⓓ
6. Ⓕ Ⓖ Ⓗ Ⓙ 16. Ⓕ Ⓖ Ⓗ Ⓙ 26. Ⓕ Ⓖ Ⓗ Ⓙ 36. Ⓕ Ⓖ Ⓗ Ⓙ 46. Ⓕ Ⓖ Ⓗ Ⓙ 56. Ⓕ Ⓖ Ⓗ Ⓙ 66. Ⓕ Ⓖ Ⓗ Ⓙ
7. Ⓐ Ⓑ Ⓒ Ⓓ 17. Ⓐ Ⓑ Ⓒ Ⓓ 27. Ⓐ Ⓑ Ⓒ Ⓓ 37. Ⓐ Ⓑ Ⓒ Ⓓ 47. Ⓐ Ⓑ Ⓒ Ⓓ 57. Ⓐ Ⓑ Ⓒ Ⓓ 67. Ⓐ Ⓑ Ⓒ Ⓓ
8. Ⓕ Ⓖ Ⓗ Ⓙ 18. Ⓕ Ⓖ Ⓗ Ⓙ 28. Ⓕ Ⓖ Ⓗ Ⓙ 38. Ⓕ Ⓖ Ⓗ Ⓙ 48. Ⓕ Ⓖ Ⓗ Ⓙ 58. Ⓕ Ⓖ Ⓗ Ⓙ 68. Ⓕ Ⓖ Ⓗ Ⓙ
9. Ⓐ Ⓑ Ⓒ Ⓓ 19. Ⓐ Ⓑ Ⓒ Ⓓ 29. Ⓐ Ⓑ Ⓒ Ⓓ 39. Ⓐ Ⓑ Ⓒ Ⓓ 49. Ⓐ Ⓑ Ⓒ Ⓓ 59. Ⓐ Ⓑ Ⓒ Ⓓ 69. Ⓐ Ⓑ Ⓒ Ⓓ
10. Ⓕ Ⓖ Ⓗ Ⓙ 20. Ⓕ Ⓖ Ⓗ Ⓙ 30. Ⓕ Ⓖ Ⓗ Ⓙ 40. Ⓕ Ⓖ Ⓗ Ⓙ 50. Ⓕ Ⓖ Ⓗ Ⓙ 60. Ⓕ Ⓖ Ⓗ Ⓙ 70. Ⓕ Ⓖ Ⓗ Ⓙ

MATHEMATICS TEST

1. Ⓐ Ⓑ Ⓒ Ⓓ Ⓔ 11. Ⓐ Ⓑ Ⓒ Ⓓ Ⓔ 21. Ⓐ Ⓑ Ⓒ Ⓓ Ⓔ 31. Ⓐ Ⓑ Ⓒ Ⓓ Ⓔ 41. Ⓐ Ⓑ Ⓒ Ⓓ Ⓔ 51. Ⓐ Ⓑ Ⓒ Ⓓ Ⓔ
2. Ⓕ Ⓖ Ⓗ Ⓙ Ⓚ 12. Ⓕ Ⓖ Ⓗ Ⓙ Ⓚ 22. Ⓕ Ⓖ Ⓗ Ⓙ Ⓚ 32. Ⓕ Ⓖ Ⓗ Ⓙ Ⓚ 42. Ⓕ Ⓖ Ⓗ Ⓙ Ⓚ 52. Ⓕ Ⓖ Ⓗ Ⓙ Ⓚ
3. Ⓐ Ⓑ Ⓒ Ⓓ Ⓔ 13. Ⓐ Ⓑ Ⓒ Ⓓ Ⓔ 23. Ⓐ Ⓑ Ⓒ Ⓓ Ⓔ 33. Ⓐ Ⓑ Ⓒ Ⓓ Ⓔ 43. Ⓐ Ⓑ Ⓒ Ⓓ Ⓔ 53. Ⓐ Ⓑ Ⓒ Ⓓ Ⓔ
4. Ⓕ Ⓖ Ⓗ Ⓙ Ⓚ 14. Ⓕ Ⓖ Ⓗ Ⓙ Ⓚ 24. Ⓕ Ⓖ Ⓗ Ⓙ Ⓚ 34. Ⓕ Ⓖ Ⓗ Ⓙ Ⓚ 44. Ⓕ Ⓖ Ⓗ Ⓙ Ⓚ 54. Ⓕ Ⓖ Ⓗ Ⓙ Ⓚ
5. Ⓐ Ⓑ Ⓒ Ⓓ Ⓔ 15. Ⓐ Ⓑ Ⓒ Ⓓ Ⓔ 25. Ⓐ Ⓑ Ⓒ Ⓓ Ⓔ 35. Ⓐ Ⓑ Ⓒ Ⓓ Ⓔ 45. Ⓐ Ⓑ Ⓒ Ⓓ Ⓔ 55. Ⓐ Ⓑ Ⓒ Ⓓ Ⓔ
6. Ⓕ Ⓖ Ⓗ Ⓙ Ⓚ 16. Ⓕ Ⓖ Ⓗ Ⓙ Ⓚ 26. Ⓕ Ⓖ Ⓗ Ⓙ Ⓚ 36. Ⓕ Ⓖ Ⓗ Ⓙ Ⓚ 46. Ⓕ Ⓖ Ⓗ Ⓙ Ⓚ 56. Ⓕ Ⓖ Ⓗ Ⓙ Ⓚ
7. Ⓐ Ⓑ Ⓒ Ⓓ Ⓔ 17. Ⓐ Ⓑ Ⓒ Ⓓ Ⓔ 27. Ⓐ Ⓑ Ⓒ Ⓓ Ⓔ 37. Ⓐ Ⓑ Ⓒ Ⓓ Ⓔ 47. Ⓐ Ⓑ Ⓒ Ⓓ Ⓔ 57. Ⓐ Ⓑ Ⓒ Ⓓ Ⓔ
8. Ⓕ Ⓖ Ⓗ Ⓙ Ⓚ 18. Ⓕ Ⓖ Ⓗ Ⓙ Ⓚ 28. Ⓕ Ⓖ Ⓗ Ⓙ Ⓚ 38. Ⓕ Ⓖ Ⓗ Ⓙ Ⓚ 48. Ⓕ Ⓖ Ⓗ Ⓙ Ⓚ 58. Ⓕ Ⓖ Ⓗ Ⓙ Ⓚ
9. Ⓐ Ⓑ Ⓒ Ⓓ Ⓔ 19. Ⓐ Ⓑ Ⓒ Ⓓ Ⓔ 29. Ⓐ Ⓑ Ⓒ Ⓓ Ⓔ 39. Ⓐ Ⓑ Ⓒ Ⓓ Ⓔ 49. Ⓐ Ⓑ Ⓒ Ⓓ Ⓔ 59. Ⓐ Ⓑ Ⓒ Ⓓ Ⓔ
10. Ⓕ Ⓖ Ⓗ Ⓙ Ⓚ 20. Ⓕ Ⓖ Ⓗ Ⓙ Ⓚ 30. Ⓕ Ⓖ Ⓗ Ⓙ Ⓚ 40. Ⓕ Ⓖ Ⓗ Ⓙ Ⓚ 50. Ⓕ Ⓖ Ⓗ Ⓙ Ⓚ 60. Ⓕ Ⓖ Ⓗ Ⓙ Ⓚ

READING TEST

1. Ⓐ Ⓑ Ⓒ Ⓓ 6. Ⓕ Ⓖ Ⓗ Ⓙ 11. Ⓐ Ⓑ Ⓒ Ⓓ 16. Ⓕ Ⓖ Ⓗ Ⓙ 21. Ⓐ Ⓑ Ⓒ Ⓓ 26. Ⓕ Ⓖ Ⓗ Ⓙ 31. Ⓐ Ⓑ Ⓒ Ⓓ 36. Ⓕ Ⓖ Ⓗ Ⓙ
2. Ⓕ Ⓖ Ⓗ Ⓙ 7. Ⓐ Ⓑ Ⓒ Ⓓ 12. Ⓕ Ⓖ Ⓗ Ⓙ 17. Ⓐ Ⓑ Ⓒ Ⓓ 22. Ⓕ Ⓖ Ⓗ Ⓙ 27. Ⓐ Ⓑ Ⓒ Ⓓ 32. Ⓕ Ⓖ Ⓗ Ⓙ 37. Ⓐ Ⓑ Ⓒ Ⓓ
3. Ⓐ Ⓑ Ⓒ Ⓓ 8. Ⓕ Ⓖ Ⓗ Ⓙ 13. Ⓐ Ⓑ Ⓒ Ⓓ 18. Ⓕ Ⓖ Ⓗ Ⓙ 23. Ⓐ Ⓑ Ⓒ Ⓓ 28. Ⓕ Ⓖ Ⓗ Ⓙ 33. Ⓐ Ⓑ Ⓒ Ⓓ 38. Ⓕ Ⓖ Ⓗ Ⓙ
4. Ⓕ Ⓖ Ⓗ Ⓙ 9. Ⓐ Ⓑ Ⓒ Ⓓ 14. Ⓕ Ⓖ Ⓗ Ⓙ 19. Ⓐ Ⓑ Ⓒ Ⓓ 24. Ⓕ Ⓖ Ⓗ Ⓙ 29. Ⓐ Ⓑ Ⓒ Ⓓ 34. Ⓕ Ⓖ Ⓗ Ⓙ 39. Ⓐ Ⓑ Ⓒ Ⓓ
5. Ⓐ Ⓑ Ⓒ Ⓓ 10. Ⓕ Ⓖ Ⓗ Ⓙ 15. Ⓐ Ⓑ Ⓒ Ⓓ 20. Ⓕ Ⓖ Ⓗ Ⓙ 25. Ⓐ Ⓑ Ⓒ Ⓓ 30. Ⓕ Ⓖ Ⓗ Ⓙ 35. Ⓐ Ⓑ Ⓒ Ⓓ 40. Ⓕ Ⓖ Ⓗ Ⓙ

SCIENCE TEST

1. Ⓐ Ⓑ Ⓒ Ⓓ 6. Ⓕ Ⓖ Ⓗ Ⓙ 11. Ⓐ Ⓑ Ⓒ Ⓓ 16. Ⓕ Ⓖ Ⓗ Ⓙ 21. Ⓐ Ⓑ Ⓒ Ⓓ 26. Ⓕ Ⓖ Ⓗ Ⓙ 31. Ⓐ Ⓑ Ⓒ Ⓓ 36. Ⓕ Ⓖ Ⓗ Ⓙ
2. Ⓕ Ⓖ Ⓗ Ⓙ 7. Ⓐ Ⓑ Ⓒ Ⓓ 12. Ⓕ Ⓖ Ⓗ Ⓙ 17. Ⓐ Ⓑ Ⓒ Ⓓ 22. Ⓕ Ⓖ Ⓗ Ⓙ 27. Ⓐ Ⓑ Ⓒ Ⓓ 32. Ⓕ Ⓖ Ⓗ Ⓙ 37. Ⓐ Ⓑ Ⓒ Ⓓ
3. Ⓐ Ⓑ Ⓒ Ⓓ 8. Ⓕ Ⓖ Ⓗ Ⓙ 13. Ⓐ Ⓑ Ⓒ Ⓓ 18. Ⓕ Ⓖ Ⓗ Ⓙ 23. Ⓐ Ⓑ Ⓒ Ⓓ 28. Ⓕ Ⓖ Ⓗ Ⓙ 33. Ⓐ Ⓑ Ⓒ Ⓓ 38. Ⓕ Ⓖ Ⓗ Ⓙ
4. Ⓕ Ⓖ Ⓗ Ⓙ 9. Ⓐ Ⓑ Ⓒ Ⓓ 14. Ⓕ Ⓖ Ⓗ Ⓙ 19. Ⓐ Ⓑ Ⓒ Ⓓ 24. Ⓕ Ⓖ Ⓗ Ⓙ 29. Ⓐ Ⓑ Ⓒ Ⓓ 34. Ⓕ Ⓖ Ⓗ Ⓙ 39. Ⓐ Ⓑ Ⓒ Ⓓ
5. Ⓐ Ⓑ Ⓒ Ⓓ 10. Ⓕ Ⓖ Ⓗ Ⓙ 15. Ⓐ Ⓑ Ⓒ Ⓓ 20. Ⓕ Ⓖ Ⓗ Ⓙ 25. Ⓐ Ⓑ Ⓒ Ⓓ 30. Ⓕ Ⓖ Ⓗ Ⓙ 35. Ⓐ Ⓑ Ⓒ Ⓓ 40. Ⓕ Ⓖ Ⓗ Ⓙ

ENGLISH TEST

45 Minutes—75 Questions

Directions: In the following five passages, certain words and phrases are underlined and numbered. In the right-hand column are alternatives for each underlined portion. Select the one that best conveys the idea, creates the most grammatically correct sentence, or is most consistent with the style and tone of the passage. If you decide that the original version is best, select NO CHANGE. You may also find questions that ask about the entire passage or a section of the passage. These questions will correspond to small, numbered boxes in the test. For these questions, decide which choice best accomplishes the purpose set out in the question stem. After you've selected the best choice, fill in the corresponding oval on your Answer Grid. For some questions, you'll need to read the context in order to answer correctly. Be sure to read until you have enough information to determine the correct answer choice.

PASSAGE I

AMERICAN JAZZ

<u>One of the earliest</u> music forms to originate in the United
1
States was Jazz. Known as truly Mid-American because of

<u>it's</u> having origins in several locations in middle
2
America, this music developed almost simultaneously

in New Orleans, Saint Louis, Kansas City, and Chicago.

    At the start of the twentieth century, musicians all

along the Mississippi River familiar with West African

1. **A.** NO CHANGE
    B. One of the most earliest
    C. The most early
    D. The earliest

2. **F.** NO CHANGE
    G. its
    H. its's
    J. its,

GO ON TO THE NEXT PAGE ⇒

folk music [3] blended it with European classical music from the early nineteenth century. This combination was adopted by artists in the region who began to use minor

chords and <u>syncopation, in their own music,</u> ragtime
                        4
and blues. At the same time, brass bands and gospel choirs adopted Jazz music, and it became a true blend

of cultures. Eventually, a unique music <u>style developed;</u>
                                          5
<u>based on</u> a blend of the many different cultures in
  5

America at the time. <u>It was American Jazz and</u> became
                              6
the first indigenous American style to affect music in the rest of the world.

[1] One of the true greats of American Jazz was Cabell "Cab" Calloway III. [2] He was born in New York in 1907, but his family moved to Chicago during

3. At this point, the writer is considering adding the following phrase:

—rich with syncopation—

Given that it is true, would this be a relevant addition to make here?

A. Yes, because it can help the reader have a better understanding of the music being discussed.

B. Yes, because it helps explain to the reader why this music became popular.

C. No, because it fails to explain the connection between this music and the button accordion.

D. No, because it is inconsistent with the style of this essay to mention specific musical forms.

4. F. NO CHANGE
   G. syncopation in their own music,
   H. syncopation, in their own music
   J. syncopation in their own music

5. A. NO CHANGE
   B. style developed based on
   C. style developed based on,
   D. style, developed based on

6. F. NO CHANGE
   G. This style, known as American Jazz,
   H. Being known as American Jazz, it
   J. It being American Jazz first

GO ON TO THE NEXT PAGE

his teen years. [3] Growing up, Cab <u>made his living</u>
                                              7
working as a

7. Which of the following alternatives to the underlined portion would NOT be acceptable?

    A. earned his living by

    B. made his living from

    C. made his living on

    D. earned his living

shoe shiner and <u>he was</u> a waiter. [4] During these years,
                      8
he also spent time at the racetrack, where he walked
horses to keep

8.   **F.** NO CHANGE

    G. as well

    H. being

    J. OMIT the underlined portion

them in good shape. 9 [5] After graduating from high

9. The writer is considering deleting the following clause from the preceding sentence (placing a period after the word *racetrack*):

    where he walked horses to keep them in good shape.

Should the writer make this deletion?

    A. Yes, because the information is unrelated to the topic addressed in this paragraph.

    B. Yes, because the information diminishes the musical accomplishments and successes of Cab Calloway.

    C. No, because the information explains the reference to the racetrack, which might otherwise puzzle readers.

    D. No, because the information shows how far Cab Calloway came in his life.

school in Chicago, <u>where</u> Cab got his first performance
                        10
job in a revue called "Plantation Days." [6] His strong

10. **F.** NO CHANGE

    G. it was there that

    H. was where

    J. OMIT the underlined portion

GO ON TO THE NEXT PAGE ▷

and impressive voice soon gained him <u>popularity in the</u>
                                                            11
<u>top Jazz circles</u> of the
      11

United States. [12]

11. A. NO CHANGE
     B. popularity: in the top Jazz circles
     C. popularity, in the top Jazz circles,
     D. popularity in the top Jazz circles,

12. Upon reviewing this paragraph and finding that some information has been left out, the writer composes the following sentence incorporating that information:

   He became widely known as "The man in the zoot suit with the reet pleats."

   This sentence would most logically be placed after sentence:

     F. 3.
     G. 4.
     H. 5.
     J. 6.

Many others have followed Cab's lead <u>and have</u>
                                                  13
<u>moved from the east coast to middle America</u>. Like
      13
other folk music forms, American Jazz has a rich

history and unique

13. Given that all the choices are true, which one would most effectively tie together the two main subjects of this essay?

     A. NO CHANGE
     B. and have added to the rich tradition of American Jazz.
     C. such as George Duke and Earl Klugh.
     D. and have signed large recording contracts.

sound that <u>means it'll stick around for a while</u>.
                                    14

14. F. NO CHANGE
     G. causes it to be an enduring institution with a timeless appeal.
     H. makes many people enjoy it.
     J. ensures its continued vitality.

Question 15 asks about the essay as a whole.

15. Suppose the writer's goal was to write a brief essay focusing on the history and development of American Jazz music. Would this essay successfully fulfill this goal?

 A. Yes, because the essay describes the origins of American Jazz music and one of its important figures.

 B. Yes, because the essay mentions the contributions American Jazz music has made to other folk music traditions.

 C. No, because the essay refers to other musical forms besides American Jazz music.

 D. No, because the essay focuses on only one American Jazz musician, Cab Calloway.

PASSAGE II

MY GRANDFATHER'S INTERNET

My grandfather is possibly the least technologically

capable writer in the <u>world. He refused</u> to use anything
16

but his pen and paper to write until last year. (He <u>said,</u>
17
he didn't need any keys or mouse pads between his

words and himself.) Consequently, when he

<u>has went</u> to buy a computer—
18

16. F. NO CHANGE
 G. world he refused
 H. world refusing,
 J. world, and has been refusing

17. A. NO CHANGE
 B. said
 C. said, that
 D. said, that,

18. F. NO CHANGE
 G. had went
 H. went
 J. goes

GO ON TO THE NEXT PAGE

because of the knowledge that his editor refused to read
               19
another hand-written novel—he resisted connecting it

to the Internet for several months. He said he had no

need to find information on a World Wide Web. [20]

    Grandpa's editor, however, was clever and, knowing

exactly how my grandfather could use it, described how

the Internet would improve his life.

However, Grandpa could get instant
        21

feedback, and praise from the publishing company, read
            22
online reviews, and do research for his characters much

faster. Finally, Grandpa connected to the Internet, and

he hasn't logged off yet.

    Grandpa is fascinated by all the things he can do

on the World Wide Web. He has found that chat rooms

are wonderful places to have long conversations with

people interesting enough to be characters in his books.

For example, he says, by clicking the "close" button he
    23

19. **A.** NO CHANGE
    B. due to the fact that
    C. because
    D. so

20. Given that all are true, which of the following additions to the preceding sentence (after *World Wide Web*) would be most relevant?
    F. that was on his computer.
    G. when he had a set of encyclopedias right there in his office.
    H. with other people on it.
    J. where he might get a computer virus.

21. **A.** NO CHANGE
    B. Additionally, Grandpa
    C. Conversely, Grandpa
    D. Grandpa

22. **F.** NO CHANGE
    G. feedback and, praise
    H. feedback and praise
    J. feedback and praise,

23. **A.** NO CHANGE
    B. To illustrate,
    C. On the one hand,
    D. On the other hand,

GO ON TO THE NEXT PAGE ⇒

can just ignore <u>them</u> who aren't interesting. Grandpa's
24
favorite website is Google.com. Google.com is a search

engine that searches millions of sites for whatever word

he types in, which is very <u>convenient when</u> he needs to
25
know how the native people of Africa developed the

game Mancala. <u>For him, Grandpa says that, in merely</u>
26
<u>a few seconds, to be able to find anything he wants is a</u>
26
<u>source of pure joy.</u>
26

[1] As for his writings, Grandpa uses the Internet

not only for research but also for making them more

creative and checking his word choice. [2] Explaining

his new vocabulary to his editor, <u>Grandpa points</u> to his
27
new computer and admits that an Internet connection

was a good idea after all. [3] I am sure Grandpa hasn't

24. F. NO CHANGE
G. the people
H. it
J. their talking

25. A. NO CHANGE
B. convenient, when
C. convenient. When
D. convenient; when

26. F. NO CHANGE
G. For him, Grandpa says that to be able to find anything he wants, is a source of pure joy for him, in merely a few seconds.
H. Grandpa says a source of pure joy for him is that he is able to find anything he wants, in merely a few seconds.
J. Grandpa says that being able to find anything he wants in merely a few seconds is source of pure joy for him.

27. A. NO CHANGE
B. pointing
C. having pointed
D. Grandpa has pointed

GO ON TO THE NEXT PAGE

explored the entire Internet yet, <u>but I am sure he will</u>
                                  28
<u>continue to find new and better ways of using it.</u> 29
                   28

28. **F.** NO CHANGE

    G. and he probably won't explore the rest of it either.

    H. and so his editor will have to teach him to find things faster.

    J. and his editor knows just that.

29. Upon reviewing Paragraph 5 and realizing that some information has been left out, the writer composes the following sentence:

> He uses the dictionary and thesaurus websites religiously.

The most logical placement for this sentence would be:

    A. before sentence 1.

    B. after sentence 1.

    C. after sentence 2.

    D. after sentence 3.

Question 30 asks about the essay as a whole.

---

30. The writer is considering deleting the first sentence of Paragraph 1. If the writer removed this sentence, the essay would primarily lose:

    F. information about aspects of technology that his grandfather does not use.

    G. humor that sets the mood for the piece.

    H. important details about the Internet that his grandfather might enjoy.

    J. a justification for his grandfather's reluctance to use the Internet.

GO ON TO THE NEXT PAGE

PASSAGE III

CHICKASAW WANDERING

<u>In</u> the twilight of a cool autumn evening, I walked with
31
a gathering of people to the center of a field in

Oklahoma. Although I didn't know <u>more of the people</u>
32

<u>who</u> walked with me,
32

<u>a few of them I did know quite well.</u> We were
33
Chickasaw Indians, and some of us had waited for years

to make this journey <u>across</u> the Chickasaw territory to
34
the ornately

31. **A.** NO CHANGE
    B. On
    C. With
    D. From

32. **F.** NO CHANGE
    G. more of the people whom
    H. most of the people who
    J. most of the people whom

33. The writer wants to balance the statement made in the earlier part of this sentence with a related detail that suggests the unity of the people. Given that all of the following choices are true, which one best accomplishes this goal?

    A. NO CHANGE
    B. we each had our own reasons for being there.
    C. I hoped I would get to know some of them.
    D. I felt a kinship with them.

34. Which of the following alternatives to the underlined portion would NOT be acceptable?

    F. among
    G. over
    H. on
    J. through

GO ON TO THE NEXT PAGE

decorated capital of Tishomingo. 35

35. The writer is considering revising the preceding sentence by deleting the phrase "to the ornately decorated capital of Tishomingo" (placing a period after the word *territory*). If the writer did this, the paragraph would primarily lose:

A. information comparing the narrator's own journey to similar ones made by members of other tribes.

B. details describing the destination of the people the narrator is traveling with.

C. details that establish the time and place of the events of the essay.

D. interesting but irrelevant information about the Chickasaw.

For my whole life I had been shown <u>other Chickasaw's pictures</u>— many of them the ancestors

36

36. F. NO CHANGE

G. pictures in which other Chickasaw were present

H. pictures of other Chickasaw

J. other Chickasaw whose pictures had been taken

of the <u>people, who walked along with me,</u> to the Festival

37

37. A. NO CHANGE

B. people who, walked along with me

C. people, who walked along, with me

D. people who walked along with me

that evening. <u>My father and grandmother helped preserve tribal history by collecting books and newspaper clippings.</u> Books about the history and

38

traditions of our tribe were stacked on the bookshelves,

and framed portraits of members of our tribe decorated

the walls of these rooms. When I was growing up,

I would often find my father or grandmother in

one of the rooms, my father reading a book and my

grandmother listening to ancient tribal music

38. F. NO CHANGE

G. Some of those pictures had been reprinted in books my father and grandmother collected.

H. My grandmother and father proudly displayed these pictures in their homes.

J. Like other Chickasaw, my father and grandmother had each set aside a room in their own home to the tribe.

GO ON TO THE NEXT PAGE ⇨

That room held everything I knew about being
39

a Chickasaw, and unlike many Chickasaw, my family
40
had moved away from Oklahoma all the way to Seattle.

Once a year, the tribe held a Festival and Annual

Meeting that was always well attended. Before they
41
moved to Seattle, my grandmother and father had

always attended this event. However, the tribe owned

no land in Seattle on which a ceremonial house

could be built and Chickasaw ceremonies conducted.
42
Since I had never been to Oklahoma, I had never been

to a Chickasaw event or walked in our territory. Still, I
43
had never even known any other Chickasaw children.

Finally, my father, grandmother, and I all took a trip

to participate in the Festival. As we walked together

through the open plain, hundreds of crickets chirping
44
softly from the grass. The insects accompanied our

march like the spirits of our ancestors singing to us on
45
our way home.

39. **A.** NO CHANGE
    B. Her rooms
    C. Those rooms
    D. This room

40. **F.** NO CHANGE
    G. Chickasaw unlike
    H. Chickasaw, unlike
    J. Chickasaw. Unlike

41. Given that all of the choices are true, which one provides information most relevant to the main focus of this paragraph?
    A. NO CHANGE
    B. notable for its exquisite dancing.
    C. in south central Oklahoma.
    D. that lasted several days.

42. **F.** NO CHANGE
    G. Chickasaw ceremonies were conducted there.
    H. there were Chickasaw ceremonies conducted there.
    J. the conducting of Chickasaw ceremonies.

43. **A.** NO CHANGE
    B. Meanwhile
    C. In fact,
    D. On the other hand,

44. **F.** NO CHANGE
    G. crickets, which chirped
    H. crickets that chirped
    J. crickets chirped

45. **A.** NO CHANGE
    B. just as
    C. as like
    D. such as

GO ON TO THE NEXT PAGE ⇨

PASSAGE IV

TOPPING THE WASHINGTON MONUMENT

During the midday hours of December 6, <u>1884, engineers</u>
46

and workers braced themselves for the <u>days</u> dangerous
47
mission. Winds that rushed past the workers at speeds

of nearly sixty miles per hour <u>threatened</u> to postpone
48

<u>and delay</u> the capstone ceremony marking the
49
placement of the capstone atop the Washington

Monument. 50

46. F. NO CHANGE
G. 1884, and engineers
H. 1884. Engineers
J. 1884; engineers

47. A. NO CHANGE
B. days'
C. day's
D. days's

48. F. NO CHANGE
G. had been threatened
H. will have threatened
J. threatens

49. A. NO CHANGE
B. to a later time
C. by delaying
D. OMIT the underlined portion

50. The writer is considering deleting the following from the preceding sentence:

marking the placement of the capstone atop the Washington Monument.

If the writer were to delete this phrase, the essay would primarily lose:

F. a minor detail in the essay's opening paragraph.
G. an explanation of the term *capstone ceremony*.
H. the writer's opinion about the significance of the capstone ceremony
J. an indication of the capstone ceremony's significance to the American people.

GO ON TO THE NEXT PAGE

Eighty-five years of fundraising and planning had brought about this moment. In 1799, <u>attorney and</u>
51
<u>Congressman</u> John Marshall proposed a monument to
51
honor the young nation's Revolutionary War hero and

first president. 52 Architect Robert

<u>Mills, who planned</u> the monument that would
53
memorialize Washington.

<u>Meanwhile, the</u> monument would be in the form of
54
a 500-foot obelisk made of marble and topped with a

100-pound capstone of aluminum.

In 1861, construction on the monument was halted because supplies and men were needed to fight the Civil War. During the war, the monument stood only 176 feet tall, and the ground around it served as grazing land for livestock used to feed the Union army. Fifteen years

51. **A.** NO CHANGE
B. attorney, and Congressman
C. attorney and Congressman,
D. attorney, and Congressman,

52. If the writer were to delete the preceding sentence, the paragraph would primarily lose:
F. an explanation of Washington's heroic acts of war.
G. details about what John Marshall thought the monument he envisioned should look like.
H. background information about why Washington was being honored with a monument.
J. biographical information about John Marshall.

53. **A.** NO CHANGE
B. Mills, planner of
C. Mills planned
D. Mills creating

54. **F.** NO CHANGE
G. Therefore, the
H. However, the
J. The

GO ON TO THE NEXT PAGE

passed before work <u>resumed</u> on the monument. The
55
workers had the entire monument's history in their

55. **A.** NO CHANGE
    B. started
    C. began
    D. restarted again

minds during <u>they're attempt to place its</u> capstone.
56

56. **F.** NO CHANGE
    G. they're attempt to place it's
    H. their attempt to place its
    J. their attempt to place it's

<u>The crowd cheered as, attached to the top of the</u>
57
<u>monument, the capstone was hoisted up.</u> More than
57

57. **A.** NO CHANGE
    B. As the crowd cheered, the capstone was hoisted up and attached to the top of the monument.
    C. As the crowd cheered, attached to the top of the monument, the capstone was hoisted up.
    D. The capstone was hoisted up as the crowd cheered and attached to the top of the monument.

eight <u>decades and more than eighty years</u> of planning
58

58. **F.** NO CHANGE
    G. decades amounting to more than eighty years
    H. decades–over eighty years–
    J. decades

and building had <u>come to a conclusion,</u> and the
59
Washington Monument was finally complete.

59. Which of the following alternatives would be LEAST acceptable in terms of the context of this sentence?
    A. reached completion,
    B. come to a halt,
    C. come to an end,
    D. ended,

GO ON TO THE NEXT PAGE

Question 60 asks about the essay as a whole.

60. Suppose the writer had intended to write a brief essay that describes the entire process of designing and building the Washington Monument. Would this essay successfully fulfill the writer's goal?

  F. Yes, because it offers such details as the materials used to make the capstone and shaft of the monument.

  G. Yes, because it explains in detail each step in the design and construction of the monument.

  H. No, because it focuses primarily on one point in the development of the monument rather than on the entire process.

  J. No, because it is primarily a historical essay about the early stages in the development of the monument.

PASSAGE V

WHY LIONS ROAR

Research by biologists and environmental scientists has found several reasons that lions roar. Lions, which live in groups called prides, are very social creatures that communicate with one another in many ways. Roaring,
61

the sound most often associated with lions, perform
62
several key functions within the pride.

61. A. NO CHANGE
  B. Roaring
  C. Roaring:
  D. Roaring is

62. F. NO CHANGE
  G. perform,
  H. performs,
  J. performs

GO ON TO THE NEXT PAGE

<u>One of these defense</u> involves protecting the
            63
pride's land. When prides take large pieces of land and

claim them as their own, they will roar to keep away

intruders,

<u>those are usually</u> other lions. This "No Trespassing"
        64

warning serves to keep the peace <u>because</u> it helps
                                    65
prevent competing prides from fighting over food or for

mates.

<u>Lions also roar</u> to stay in contact with one another
         66
when members of a pride are separated by long

distances. Like all large cats, lions have <u>intense</u> hearing,
                                              67
which makes it possible for them to hear other members

of their pride from great distances. <u>Frequently, everyday</u>
                                          68

63. **A.** NO CHANGE
    B. One of these, defense,
    C. One of these being defense,
    D. One of these is defense and it

64. **F.** NO CHANGE
    G. most often these are
    H. and are typically
    J. usually

65. Which of the following alternatives to the underlined portion would be the LEAST acceptable?
    A. although
    B. in that
    C. since
    D. as

66. **F.** NO CHANGE
    G. It's also the case that roaring is employed
    H. In addition, roaring is a way
    J. Roaring is also used

67. **A.** NO CHANGE
    B. cunning
    C. acute
    D. vivid

68. **F.** NO CHANGE
    G. Quite regularly, everyday
    H. Many times, everyday
    J. Everyday

GO ON TO THE NEXT PAGE ▷

activities like hunting <u>call upon animals' sharp instincts;</u>
69
in order to reunite, the pride members roar to find one

another.

     <u>Finally,</u> lions use roars to attract potential mates.
70
During mating season, males will try to attract females

from the pride by roaring, displaying their manes,

<u>they rub</u> against females and fighting one another. Often
71
a male that does not belong to a pride will try to enter

the pride and mate with females inside the pride. When

this occurs, the <u>alpha or, dominant, male</u> instructs all
72
the other males in the pride to roar toward the outsider.

<u>The outsider is scared during his preparation for the</u>
73
<u>fight partly by the roaring.</u> The combined roaring of the
73

69. Given that all of the choices are true, which is the best replacement for the underlined selection to provide a logical reason for the action described in the second clause of the sentence?

  A. NO CHANGE

  B. disperse a pride over large areas of land

  C. require the pride to travel some distance

  D. involve the entire pride.

70. **F.** NO CHANGE

  G. Nevertheless,

  H. Second,

  J. Thus,

71. **A.** NO CHANGE

  B. rubbing

  C. rubbed

  D. rub

72. **F.** NO CHANGE

  G. alpha, or dominant, male

  H. alpha or dominant male,

  J. alpha or, dominant male

73. **A.** NO CHANGE

  B. The purpose of the roaring is to help scare the outsider during his preparation for the fight.

  C. Fear in the outsider is raised, during preparation for the fight, by the roaring.

  D. The roaring helps scare the outsider during his preparation for the fight.

GO ON TO THE NEXT PAGE ⇒

males <u>make</u> the pride sound much larger than it actually is.
74
    Future research on lions will help us understand

more about the reasons they roar. What is already

<u>clear, is that</u> often the lion's roar is meant to be
75
heard. Whether communicating with one another or

threatening intruders, lions roar to get attention.

74. **F.** NO CHANGE
    G. have the effect of making
    H. are intended to make
    J. makes

75. **A.** NO CHANGE
    B. clear is that,
    C. clear is, that
    D. clear is that

MATHEMATICS TEST

60 Minutes—60 Questions

Directions: Solve each of the following problems, select the correct answer, and then fill in the corresponding space on your answer sheet.

Don't linger over problems that are too time-consuming. Do as many as you can, then come back to the others in the time you have remaining.

The use of a calculator is permitted on this test. Though you are allowed to use your calculator to solve any questions you choose, some of the questions may be most easily answered without the use of a calculator.

Note: Unless otherwise noted, all of the following should be assumed.

1. Illustrative figures are *not* necessarily drawn to scale.
2. All geometric figures lie in a plane.
3. The term *line* indicates a straight line.
4. The term *average* indicates arithmetic mean.

1. In a class, 10 students are receiving honors credit. This number is exactly 20% of the total number of students in the class. How many students are in the class?

    A. 12
    B. 15
    C. 18
    D. 20
    E. 50

2. In the figure below, points *A*, *B*, and *C* are on a straight line. What is the measure of angle *DBE* ?

    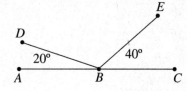

    F. 60°
    G. 80°
    H. 100°
    J. 120°
    K. 140°

3. What is the fifth term of the arithmetic sequence 7, 4, 1, … ?

    A. –5
    B. –2
    C. 1
    D. 4
    E. 14

4. What value of *c* solves the following proportion?

    $$\frac{20}{8} = \frac{c}{10}$$

    F. 4
    G. 16
    H. 18
    J. 22
    K. 25

GO ON TO THE NEXT PAGE

5. If G, H, and K are distinct points on the same line, and $\overline{GK} \cong \overline{HK}$, then which of the following must be true?

　A. G is the midpoint of $\overline{HK}$

　B. H is the midpoint of $\overline{GK}$

　C. K is the midpoint of $\overline{GH}$

　D. G is the midpoint of $\overline{KH}$

　E. K is the midpoint of $\overline{KG}$

6. Four pieces of yarn, each 1.2 meters long, are cut from the end of a ball of yarn that is 50 meters long. How many meters of yarn are left ?

　F. 45.2

　G. 45.8

　H. 46.8

　J. 47.2

　K. 47.8

7. If $x = -2$, then $14 - 3(x + 3) = ?$

　A. -1

　B. 11

　C. 14

　D. 17

　E. 29

8. $-|-6| - (-6) = ?$

　F. -36

　G. -12

　H. 0

　J. 12

　K. 36

9. A car dealership expects an increase of 15% in its current annual sales of 3,200 cars. What will its new annual sales be?

　A. 3,215

　B. 3,248

　C. 3,680

　D. 4,700

　E. 4,800

10. If $x^4 = 90$ (and x is a real number), then x lies between which two consecutive integers?

　F. 2 and 3

　G. 3 and 4

　H. 4 and 5

　J. 5 and 6

　K. 6 and 7

11. If $47 - x = 188$, then $x = ?$

　A. -235

　B. -141

　C. 4

　D. 141

　E. 235

12. To complete a certain task, Group A requires 8 more hours than Group B, and Group B requires twice as long as Group C. If h is the number of hours required by Group C, how long does the task take Group A, in terms of h ?

　F. $10h$

　G. $16h$

　H. $10 + h$

　J. $2(8 + h)$

　K. $8 + 2h$

GO ON TO THE NEXT PAGE

13. In the standard (x,y) coordinate plane, three corners of a rectangle are $(2,-2)$, $(-5,-2)$, and $(2,-5)$. Where is the rectangle's fourth corner?

    A. $(2,5)$

    B. $(-2,5)$

    C. $(-2,2)$

    D. $(-2,-5)$

    E. $(-5,-5)$

14. Which of the following is a simplified form of $5a - 5b + 3a$?

    F. $5(a - b + 3)$

    G. $(a - b)(5 + 3a)$

    H. $a(8 - 5b)$

    J. $8a - 5b$

    K. $2a - 5b$

15. In the parallelogram below, what is the measure of angle FEG ?

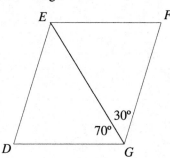

    A. $30°$

    B. $40°$

    C. $50°$

    D. $60°$

    E. $70°$

16. What is the slope of any line parallel to the line $4x + 3y = 9$?

    F. -4

    G. $-\dfrac{4}{3}$

    H. $\dfrac{4}{9}$

    J. 4

    K. 9

17. If $x > 0$ and $3x^2 - 7x - 20 = 0$, then $x = $?

    A. $\dfrac{5}{3}$

    B. 3

    C. 4

    D. 7

    E. 20

18. The lengths of the sides of a triangle are 2, 5, and 8 centimeters. How many centimeters long is the shortest side of a similar triangle that has a perimeter of 30 centimeters?

    F. 4

    G. 7

    H. 10

    J. 15

    K. 16

19. A shirt that normally sells for $24.60 is on sale for 15% off. How much does it cost during the sale, to the nearest dollar?

    A. $ 4

    B. $10

    C. $20

    D. $21

    E. $29

GO ON TO THE NEXT PAGE

20. Which of the following is a factored form of $3xy^4 + 3x^4y$?

   F. $3x^4y^4(y + x)$

   G. $3xy(y^3 + x^3)$

   H. $6xy(y^3 + x^3)$

   J. $3x^4y^4$

   K. $6x^5y^5$

21. If $x - 2y = 0$ and $3x + y = 7$, what is the value of x ?

   A. −1

   B. 0

   C. 1

   D. 2

   E. 3

22. There are three feet in a yard. If 2.5 yards of fabric cost $4.50, what is the cost per foot?

   F. $ 0.60

   G. $ 0.90

   H. $ 1.50

   J. $ 1.80

   K. $11.25

23. The figure below shows a square overlapping with a rectangle. One vertex of the rectangle is at the center of the square. What is the area of the shaded region, in square inches?

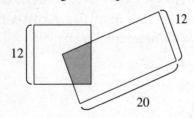

   A. 9

   B. 18

   C. 36

   D. 72

   E. 144

24. A salesperson earns $7h + 0.04s$ dollars, where h is the number of hours worked, and s is the total amount of her sales. What does she earn for working 15 hours with $120.50 in sales?

   F. $109.82

   G. $153.20

   H. $226.10

   J. $231.50

   K. $848.32

25. A floor has the dimensions shown below. How many square feet of tiles are needed to cover the entire floor?
(Note: All angles are right angles)

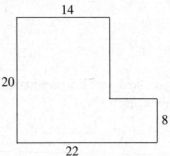

   A. 64

   B. 96

   C. 160

   D. 344

   E. 484

26. Which of the following is the graph of the solution set of $x - 2 < -4$?

GO ON TO THE NEXT PAGE

27. Which of the following is less than $\frac{3}{5}$?

    A. $\frac{4}{6}$

    B. $\frac{8}{13}$

    C. $\frac{6}{10}$

    D. $\frac{7}{11}$

    E. $\frac{4}{7}$

28. What is the area, in square feet, of a right triangle with sides of length 7 feet, 24 feet, and 25 feet?

    F.   56

    G.   84

    H. $87\frac{1}{2}$

    J.   168

    K.   300

29. When the graduating class is arranged in rows of 6 people each, the last row is one person short. When it is arranged in rows of 7, the last row is still one person short. When arranged in rows of 8, the last row is *still* one person short. What is the least possible number of people in the graduating class?

    A.   23

    B.   41

    C.   71

    D.   167

    E.   335

30. A triangle has sides of length 3.5 inches and 6 inches. Which of the following CANNOT be the length of the third side, in inches?

    F.   2

    G.   3

    H.   4

    J.   5

    K.   6

31. For all $b > 0$, $\frac{4}{5} + \frac{1}{b} = ?$

    A. $\frac{4}{5b}$

    B. $\frac{5}{5b}$

    C. $\frac{4b+5}{5b}$

    D. $\frac{5}{5+b}$

    E. $\frac{4b+5}{5+b}$

32. In the right triangle below, how long is side $\overline{EF}$?

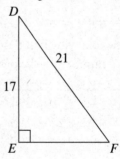

    F. $\sqrt{21^2 - 17^2}$

    G. $\sqrt{21^2 + 17^2}$

    H. $21^2 - 17^2$

    J. $21^2 + 17^2$

    K. $21 - 17$

GO ON TO THE NEXT PAGE ▷

33. If the length of a square is increased by 2 inches and the width is increased by 3 inches, a rectangle is formed. If each side of the original square is b feet long, what is the area of the new rectangle, in square inches?

A. $2b + 5$

B. $4b + 10$

C. $b^2 + 6$

D. $b^2 + 5b + 5$

E. $b^2 + 5b + 6$

34. If $\sin \beta = \dfrac{8}{17}$ and $\cos \beta = \dfrac{15}{17}$, then $\tan \beta = $?

F. $\dfrac{7}{17}$

G. $\dfrac{8}{15}$

H. $\dfrac{23}{17}$

J. $\dfrac{15}{8}$

K. $\dfrac{120}{17}$

35. Which of the following best describes the graph on the number line below?

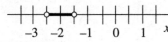

A. $-|x| = -2$

B. $-|x| < 0.5$

C. $-3 < x < -1$

D. $-1.5 < x < -2.5$

E. $-1.5 > x > -2.5$

36. A basketball team made 1-point, 2-point, and 3-point baskets. 20% of their baskets were worth 1 point, 70% of their baskets were worth 2 points, and 10% of their baskets were worth 3 points. To the nearest tenth, what was the average point value of their baskets?

F. 1.4

G. 1.7

H. 1.8

J. 1.9

K. 2.0

37. In the triangle below, if $\overline{CD}$ is 3 centimeters long, how many centimeters long is $\overline{CE}$?

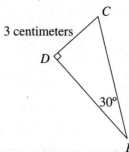

A. 3

B. $3\sqrt{2}$

C. $3\sqrt{3}$

D. 6

E. 9

38. What is the largest possible product for two odd integers whose sum is 42 ?

F. 117

G. 185

H. 259

J. 377

K. 441

GO ON TO THE NEXT PAGE

39. In the figure below, lines *l* and *m* are parallel, lines *n* and *p* are parallel, and the measures of two angles are as shown. What is the value of *x* ?

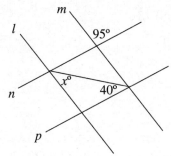

A. 40

B. 45

C. 50

D. 70

E. 85

40. In the (*x*,*y*) coordinate plane, what is the *y*-intercept of the line $12x - 3y = 12$?

F. –4

G. –3

H. 0

J. 4

K. 12

41. Among the points graphed on the number line below, which is closest to *e* ? (Note: $e \approx 2.718281828$)

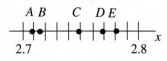

A. *A*

B. *B*

C. *C*

D. *D*

E. *E*

42. For what value of *a* would the following system of equations have no solution?

$$-x + 6y = 7$$
$$-5x + 10ay = 32$$

F. $\dfrac{5}{3}$

G. 3

H. 6

J. 30

K. 60

43. The expression $(360 - x)°$ is the degree measure of a nonzero obtuse angle if and only if:

A. $0 < x < 90$

B. $0 < x < 180$

C. $180 < x < 270$

D. $180 < x < 360$

E. $270 < x < 360$

44. If $p - q = -4$ and $p + q = -3$, then $p^2 - q^2 = $?

F. 25

G. 12

H. 7

J. –7

K. –12

45. The sides of a triangle are 6, 8, and 10 meters long. What is the angle between the two shortest sides?

A. 30°

B. 45°

C. 60°

D. 90°

E. 135°

GO ON TO THE NEXT PAGE

46. In the standard (x,y) coordinate plane, if the x-coordinate of each point on a line is 9 more than three times the y-coordinate, the slope of the line is:

F. −9

G. −3

H. $\dfrac{1}{3}$

J. 3

K. 9

47. A tree is growing at the edge of a cliff, as shown below. From the tree, the angle between the base of the cliff and the base of the house near it is 62°. If the distance between the base of the cliff and the base of the house is 500 feet, how many feet tall is the cliff?

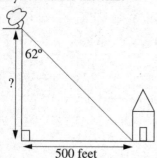

500 feet

A. 500cos 62°

B. 500tan 62°

C. $\dfrac{500}{\sin 62°}$

D. $\dfrac{500}{\cos 62°}$

E. $\dfrac{500}{\tan 62°}$

48. Two numbers have a greatest common factor of 9 and a least common multiple of 54. Which of the following could be the pair of numbers?

F. 9 and 18

G. 9 and 27

H. 18 and 27

J. 18 and 54

K. 27 and 54

49. Five functions, each denoted $b(x)$ and each involving a real number constant $k > 1$, are listed below. If $a(x) = 5^x$, which of these 5 functions yields the greatest value of $a(b(x))$, for all $x > 2$?

A. $b(x) = \dfrac{k}{x}$

B. $b(x) = \dfrac{x}{k}$

C. $b(x) = kx$

D. $b(x) = x^k$

E. $b(x) = \sqrt[k]{x}$

50. Line segments $\overline{WX}$, $\overline{XY}$, and $\overline{YZ}$ which represent the 3 dimensions of the rectangular box shown below, have lengths of 12 centimeters, 5 centimeters, and 13 centimeters, respectively. What is the cosine of $\angle ZWY$?

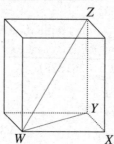

F. $\dfrac{13\sqrt{2}}{12}$

G. 1

H. $\dfrac{12}{13}$

J. $\dfrac{\sqrt{2}}{2}$

K. $\dfrac{5}{13}$

GO ON TO THE NEXT PAGE

51. A certain circle has an area of 4π square centimeters. How many centimeters long is its radius?

   A. $\dfrac{1}{4}$

   B. 2

   C. 4

   D. 2π

   E. 4π

52. The equation of line l below is $y = mx + b$. Which of the following could be an equation for line q ?

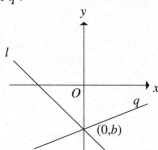

   F. $y = \dfrac{1}{2}mx$

   G. $y = \dfrac{1}{2}mx - b$

   H. $y = \dfrac{1}{2}mx + b$

   J. $y = -\dfrac{1}{2}mx - b$

   K. $y = -\dfrac{1}{2}mx + b$

53. The equation $x^2 - 6x + k = 0$ has exactly one solution for x. What is the value of k ?

   A. 0

   B. 3

   C. 6

   D. 9

   E. 12

54. In the standard (x,y) coordinate plane, what is the slope of the line through the origin and $\left(\dfrac{1}{3}, \dfrac{3}{4}\right)$?

   F. $\dfrac{1}{4}$

   G. $\dfrac{1}{3}$

   H. $\dfrac{5}{12}$

   J. $\dfrac{3}{4}$

   K. $\dfrac{9}{4}$

55. If R, S, and T are real numbers and $RST = 2$, which of the following *must* be true?

   A. $RT = \dfrac{2}{S}$

   B. R, S, and T are all positive

   C. Either $R = 2$, $S = 2$ or $T = 2$

   D. Either $R = 0$, $S = 0$ or $T = 0$

   E. Either $R > 2$, $S > 2$ or $T > 2$

56. A square has sides of length $(w + 5)$ units. Which of the following is the remaining area of the square, in square units, if a rectangle with sides of length $(w + 2)$ and $(w - 3)$ is removed from the interior of the square?

   F. 31

   G. $9w + 19$

   H. $11w + 31$

   J. $w^2 + 10w + 25$

   K. $2w^2 + 9w + 19$

GO ON TO THE NEXT PAGE

57. What is the smallest positive value for θ where $\sin 2\theta$ reaches its minimum value?

A. $\dfrac{\pi}{4}$

B. $\dfrac{\pi}{2}$

C. $\dfrac{3\pi}{4}$

D. π

E. $\dfrac{3\pi}{2}$

58. In the standard (x,y) coordinate plane, if the distance between the points $(r,6)$ and $(10,r)$ is 4 coordinate units, which of the following could be the value of r ?

F. 3

G. 4

H. 7

J. 8

K. 10

59. Calleigh puts 5 nickels into an empty hat. She wants to add enough pennies so that the probability of drawing a nickel at random from the hat is $\dfrac{1}{6}$. How many pennies should she put in?

A. 1

B. 5

C. 10

D. 25

E. 30

60. How many different integer values of x satisfy the inequality $\dfrac{1}{5} < \dfrac{3}{x} < \dfrac{1}{3}$?

F. 1

G. 2

H. 3

J. 4

K. 5

READING TEST

35 Minutes—40 Questions

Directions: There are four passages in this test. Each passage is followed by several questions. After reading a passage, choose the best answer to each question and fill in the corresponding oval on your Answer Grid. You may refer to the passages as often as necessary.

PASSAGE I

PROSE FICTION

This passage is adapted from Nathaniel Hawthorne's short story "Rappaccini's Daughter."

Giovanni still found no better occupation than to look down into the garden beneath his window. From its appearance, he judged it one
Line of those botanic gardens that were of earlier date
(5) in Padua than elsewhere in Italy or in the world. Or, not improbably, it might once have been the pleasure-place of an opulent family; for there was the ruin of a marble fountain in the center, sculptured with rare art, but so woefully shattered
(10) that it was impossible to trace the original design from the chaos of remaining fragments. The water, however, continued to gush and sparkle into the sunbeams as cheerfully as ever. A little gurgling sound ascended to the young man's window,
(15) and made him feel as if the fountain were an immortal spirit that sung its song unceasingly and without heeding the vicissitudes around it, while one century embodied it in marble and another scattered the perishable embellishments
(20) on the soil. All about the pool into which the water subsided grew various plants that seemed to require a plentiful supply of moisture for the nourishment of gigantic leaves, and, in some instances, flowers gorgeously magnificent. There
(25) was one shrub in particular, set in a marble vase in the midst of the pool, that bore a profusion of purple blossoms, each of which had the luster and richness of a gem; and the whole together made a show so resplendent that it seemed enough to
(30) illuminate the garden, even had there been no sunshine. Every portion of the soil was peopled with plants and herbs, which, if less beautiful, still

bore tokens of assiduous care, as if all had their individual virtues, known to the scientific mind
(35) that fostered them. Some were placed in urns, rich with old carving, and others in common garden pots; some crept serpent-like along the ground or climbed on high, using whatever means of ascent was offered them. One plant had wreathed itself
(40) round a statue of Vertumnus, which was thus quite veiled and shrouded in a drapery of hanging foliage, so happily arranged that it might have served a sculptor for a study.

While Giovanni stood at the window he heard
(45) a rustling behind a screen of leaves, and became aware that a person was at work in the garden. His figure soon emerged into view, and showed itself to be that of no common laborer, but a tall, emaciated, sallow, and sickly-looking man, dressed
(50) in a scholar's garb of black. He was beyond the middle term of life, with gray hair, a thin, gray beard, and a face singularly marked with intellect and cultivation, but which could never, even in his more youthful days, have expressed much warmth
(55) of heart.

Nothing could exceed the intentness with which this scientific gardener examined every shrub that grew in his path: it seemed as if he were looking into their inmost nature, making
(60) observations in regard to their creative essence, and discovering why one leaf grew in this shape and another in that, and why such and such flowers differed among themselves in hue and perfume. Nevertheless, in spite of this deep intelligence
(65) on his part, there was no approach to intimacy between himself and these vegetable existences. On the contrary, he avoided their actual touch or

GO ON TO THE NEXT PAGE ▷

the direct inhaling of their odors with a caution
that impressed Giovanni most disagreeably; for the
(70) man's demeanor was that of one walking among
malignant influences, such as savage beasts, or
deadly snakes, or evil spirits, which, should he
allow them one moment of license, would wreak
upon him some terrible fatality. It was strangely
(75) frightful to the young man's imagination to see this
air of insecurity in a person cultivating a garden,
that most simple and innocent of human toils,
and which had been alike the joy and labor of the
unfallen parents of the race. Was this garden, then,
(80) the Eden of the present world? And this man, with
such a perception of harm in what his own hands
caused to grow—was he the Adam?

    The distrustful gardener, while plucking away
the dead leaves or pruning the too luxuriant
(85) growth of the shrubs, defended his hands with
a pair of thick gloves. Nor were these his only
armor. When, in his walk through the garden,
he came to the magnificent plant that hung its
purple gems beside the marble fountain, he placed
(90) a kind of mask over his mouth and nostrils, as if
all this beauty did but conceal a deadlier malice;
but, finding his task still too dangerous, he drew
back, removed the mask, and called loudly, but in
the infirm voice of a person affected with inward
(95) disease.

1. Of the plants mentioned in the passage, which
   of the following did Giovanni find to be the
   most exceptional?

   A. The plant wreathed around the statue
   B. The plant that crept along the ground
   C. The plant with the gigantic leaves
   D. The plant with the purple blossoms

2. In order to ensure that he is safe from the
   plants, the gardener:

       I. handles them only indirectly.
       II. avoids looking directly at them.
       III. avoids breathing their odors.

   F. I and II only
   G. I and III only
   H. II and III only
   J. I, II, and III

3. It can reasonably be inferred from the passage
   that the gardener, as compared with Giovanni,
   is a:

   A. more religious man.
   B. less cautious man.
   C. more cautious man.
   D. less religious man.

4. Which of the following actions performed by
   the gardener disturbs Giovanni?

       I. Indicating disregard or disapproval
          of the plants
       II. Avoiding directly inhaling the odors
          of the plants
       III. Looking at the inmost nature of the
          plants

   F. I only
   G. II only
   H. III only
   J. I and II only

GO ON TO THE NEXT PAGE ⇨

5. As described in the third paragraph (lines 56–82), the gardener's actions suggest that he is a man who:

   A. is very alert.

   B. knows all there is to know about plants.

   C. loves nature.

   D. resembles Adam.

6. The narrator suggests that the plant with "a profusion of purple blossoms" (lines 26–27) could:

   F. sprout gems.

   G. produce light.

   H. overrun the garden.

   J. grow very quickly.

7. The narrator takes the point of view of:

   A. a gardener.

   B. Giovanni.

   C. a scientist.

   D. an unknown third party.

8. When Giovanni questions whether the garden is "the Eden of the present world" and whether the gardener is Adam (lines 79–82), he is expressing his belief that the gardener:

   F. goes about his work with great care.

   G. has every reason to be distressed by the plants.

   H. should treat the plants with reverence.

   J. should not appear so afraid of the plants.

9. According to the passage, Giovanni characterizes the area beneath his window as a:

   A. botanic garden.

   B. center for rare art.

   C. place for people with plants.

   D. pleasure-place for the community.

10. In the third paragraph (lines 56–82), the author suggests that the gardener's relationship with the plants was partly characterized by:

   F. the gardener's impatience with the plants.

   G. the gardener's interest in understanding the plants.

   H. the gardener's desire to harm the plants.

   J. the gardener's anger toward the plants.

PASSAGE II

SOCIAL SCIENCE

This passage is adapted from "Look First to Failure" by Henry Petroski, which appeared in the October 2004 issue of Harvard Business Review. *It discusses a paradox in the field of engineering.*

Engineering is all about improvement, and so it is a science of comparatives. "New, improved" products are ubiquitous, advertised as making teeth whiter, wash fluffier, and meals faster. Larger
Line
(5) engineered systems are also promoted for their comparative edge: the taller building with more affordable office space, the longer bridge with a lighter-weight roadway, the slimmer laptop with greater battery life. If everything is a new, improved
(10) version of older technology, why do so many products fail, proposals languish, and systems crash?

To reengineer anything—be it a straight pin, a procurement system, or a Las Vegas resort—we first must understand failure. Successes give us
(15) confidence that we are doing something right, but they do not necessarily tell us what or why. Failures, on the other hand, provide incontrovertible proof that we have done something wrong. That is invaluable information.

(20) Reengineering anything is fraught with risk. Take paper clips. Hundreds of styles were introduced in the past century, each claiming to be an improvement over the classic Gem. Yet none displaced it. The Gem maintains its privileged
(25) position because, though far from perfect, it strikes

GO ON TO THE NEXT PAGE ➡

an agreeable balance between form and function.
Each challenger may improve on one aspect of
the Gem but at the expense of another. Thus, a
clip that is easier to attach to a pile of papers is
(30) also more likely to fall off. Designers often focus
so thoroughly on the advantages that they fail to
appreciate (or else ignore) the disadvantages of
their new design.

Imagine how much more complex is the
(35) challenge of reengineering a jumbo jet. The
overall external form is more or less dictated by
aerodynamics. That form, in turn, constrains the
configuration of the interior space, which must
accommodate articulated human passengers as
(40) well as boxy luggage and freight. As much as
shipping clerks might like fuselages with square
corners, they must live with whale bellies. It is no
wonder that Boeing invited stakeholders, including
willing frequent flyers, to participate in designing
(45) its Dreamliner—so the users would buy into the
inevitable compromises. The resulting jetliner will
succeed or fail depending on how convincingly
those compromises are rationalized.

Logically speaking, basing a reengineering
(50) project—whether of a product or a business
process—on successful models should give
designers an advantage: They can pick and choose
the best features of effective existing designs.
Unfortunately, what makes things work is often
(55) hard to express and harder to extract from the
design as a whole. Things work because they work
in a particular configuration, at a particular scale,
and in a particular culture. Trying to reverse-
engineer and cannibalize a successful system
(60) sacrifices the synergy of success. Thus John
Roebling, master of the suspension bridge form,
looked for inspiration not to successful examples
of the state of the art but to historical failures.
From those he distilled the features and forces
(65) that are the enemies of bridges and designed his
own to avoid those features and resist those forces.
Such failure-based thinking gave us the Brooklyn
Bridge, with its signature diagonal cables, which
Roebling included to steady the structure in winds
(70) he knew from past example could be its undoing.

But when some bridge builders in the 1930s
followed effective models, including Roebling's,
they ended up with the Tacoma Narrows Bridge,
the third-longest suspension bridge in the world
(75) and the largest ever to collapse in the wind. In the
process of "improving" on Roebling's design, the
very cables that he included to obviate failure were
left out in the interests of economy and aesthetics.

When a complex system succeeds, that success
(80) masks its proximity to failure. Imagine that the
Titanic had not struck the iceberg on her maiden
voyage. The example of that "unsinkable" ship
would have emboldened success-based shipbuilders to model larger and larger ocean liners after her.
(85) Eventually the Titanic or one of those derivative
vessels would probably have encountered an iceberg
with obvious consequences. Thus, the failure of the
Titanic contributed much more to the design of safe
ocean liners than would have her success. That is
(90) the paradox of engineering—and of reengineering.

11. All of the following are mentioned as con-
straints on the design of a jumbo jet EXCEPT:

A. the shape of the human body.
B. fuel consumption.
C. aerodynamics.
D. freight handling.

12. When the author says Boeing wants stakeholders to "buy into" the Dreamliner's inevitable compromises (line 45), he means the
company hopes that:

F. passengers will be willing to invest in
the company to support Dreamliner
development.
G. engineers will be able to satisfy all the
needs of passengers, freight handlers,
and pilots.
H. users will be willing to pay extra to
have their specific needs met.
J. users will understand and accept that
the jet will not meet all their needs
perfectly.

GO ON TO THE NEXT PAGE

13. The author believes the sinking of the Titanic contributed more to the safety of ocean travel than its success would have because:

   A. engineers realized they could not be so careless.

   B. later ships carried more lifeboats.

   C. shipbuilders were able to learn from mistakes in the Titanic's design before they built more ships with the same weakness.

   D. passengers were more likely to take out insurance before a voyage.

14. The purpose of the passage is to convey the idea that:

   F. failed systems often have more to teach us than do successful ones.

   G. sophisticated engineering projects are more difficult than they seem.

   H. the best way to design a system is to reverse-engineer successful models.

   J. today's engineering is so technically advanced that there is little to learn from the past.

15. Based on the passage, which of the following contributed to the failure of the Tacoma Narrows Bridge?

   A. The engineers copied the design for the Brooklyn Bridge too closely.

   B. The wind at Tacoma Narrows was stronger than in Brooklyn.

   C. The engineers ignored the aesthetic aspect of the design.

   D. The final design omitted diagonal cables.

16. The author inserts the final paragraph (lines 79–90) in order to:

   F. emphasize that the designers of the Titanic should have studied earlier ships more thoroughly.

   G. make the point that all ocean liners will eventually encounter icebergs and sink.

   H. illustrate how the failure of a complex design may contribute more to long-term technical development than its success would have.

   J. point out that the designs of ocean liners and bridges both involve significant risks.

17. The main purpose of the Gem paper clip example is to show that:

   A. paper clips are indispensable to modern business.

   B. attempting to redesign a paper clip is a waste of time.

   C. engineers should study the effectiveness of the paper clip before beginning a design project.

   D. redesigning a successful product risks damaging its effectiveness.

18. According to the passage, the Gem paper clip continues to be the most popular because:

   F. it features an excellent compromise between ease of attachment and security.

   G. it was invented long before alternative designs.

   H. people are familiar with the name and don't want to risk trying new products.

   J. it is unlikely to fall off in use.

GO ON TO THE NEXT PAGE

19. In the context of this passage, "failure-based thinking" (line 67) refers to:

   A. a counterproductive habit that engineers adopt that inhibits their creativity.

   B. the process of taking inspiration from analyzing the causes of past failures.

   C. an example of how cannibalizing a successful system can create synergy.

   D. an approach to design that was discredited with the collapse of the Tacoma Narrows Bridge.

20. When the author says engineering is a "science of comparatives" (line 2), he means that:

   F. engineers are always compared to other scientists.

   G. engineered products are only better if they are bigger or faster than other products.

   H. engineers' designs are generally evaluated based on whether they offer improvements over previous designs of the same product.

   J. engineering tools are used to compare the discoveries of scientists.

PASSAGE III

HUMANITIES

The following passages are excerpted from two books that discuss fairy tales. Passage A was written by a specialist in psychology and children's literature and was published in 1965. Passage B was written by a folklore methodologist and was published in 1986.

PASSAGE A

Most of the stories that our society tells have only enjoyed a comparatively short period of popularity in comparison with the sweep of

Line human history, flaming into popular consciousness
(5) in books, television, or film for a period reaching anywhere from a few months to a few centuries. Fads come and go as fickle as the weather, and today's hit may be tomorrow's forgotten relic. But one particular kind of story that our society tells, the
(10) fairy tale, has a kind of popularity that is uniquely persistent. Literally since time immemorial, fairy tales have been told and retold, refined and adapted across generations of human history. Folk tales that spoke to people in some deeper way, and thus
(15) proved popular, endured and were passed down through the ages. Tales that had only temporal and fleeting appeal are long since lost. Since, as we know, it is a truism that time sifts out the literary wheat and discards the chaff, fairy tales can be said
(20) to have undergone the longest process of selection and editing of any stories in human history.

Consider, for example, the story of Snow White. Here is reflected the tale of the eternal struggle for supremacy between the generations. The evil
(25) mother queen grows jealous of the competition of the young Snow White for supremacy in the realm of youth and beauty, so she contrives to do away with her rival. The innocent Snow White survives by a twist of whim and circumstance, and then
(30) retreats into the forest—the traditional symbol of the site of psychological change—where she hides among the Seven Dwarves. Small supernatural spirits or homunculi, often depicted in folk tales as tiny elves, spirit men, trolls, or fairies, represent
(35) unconscious forces, and thus Snow White must care for and nurture the Seven Dwarves while she undergoes her psychological transformation. The dwarves' mining activities can be said to symbolize this process of mental delving into the depths in
(40) hopes of uncovering the precious materials of the developing psyche.

Yet Snow White's road to her new identity is not without incident. The breaching of the secure space by the disguised queen mother and Snow White's
(45) giving in to the temptation of the apple—representative of the same youth and beauty that the queen seeks to deprive her of—causes her to fall into the slumberous mock death. Only the prince can deliver Snow White and metaphorically resurrect

GO ON TO THE NEXT PAGE ⇨

(50) her with a kiss, itself a motif that suggests her entry into the identity of a mature person ready to leave the dwarves and forest of the unconscious behind and take on adult responsibilities.

(55) The popularity of this tale, and others like it, across time and in widely scattered societies confirms its power in tapping into unconscious forces and common motifs that all humans share. All humans in all ages experience generational rivalry and the impact that it has on patterns of
(60) growth and maturity. The specific symbols used to represent these dynamics are less important than their universality; indeed the very adaptability of the symbolism is what allows tales to remain popular over time. By dramatizing these psycho-
(65) logical progressions, the fairy tale helps its audience to process the ill-understood unconscious psychological forces that are a part of human life. Can it be any wonder that such powerful avenues to the cosmic unconscious can be shown to have
(70) remained popular across the eons?

PASSAGE B

The contention that folklore represents a cosmic tale that encapsulates cross-cultural human universalities in narrative form is naïve in the extreme. The notion that folk tales somehow embody
(75) a symbolically encoded map of human consciousness suffers from a fundamental flaw: It assumes that each tale has a more-or-less consistent form. In fact, the forms of most folk tales that we have today recorded in collections and in the popular
(80) media represent nothing more than isolated snapshots of narratives that have countless forms, many of which are so different as to drastically change the interpretations that some critics want to say are universal.

(85) Consider, for example, the story of Little Red Riding Hood. Some psychological interpretations might conjecture, for example, that this is a tale about obedience and parental authority. Straying from the path in the forest, in this context, might
(90) represent rebelling against that authority, and the wolf then symbolizes the dangerous unconscious forces from which parents seek to protect Little Red. The red color of the riding hood might be

seen as representing the subdued emotions of anger
(95) and hostility. Being consumed by the wolf signifies a period of isolation and transformation. Finally, the rescuing huntsman at the end of the story then symbolizes the return of parental authority to deliver the innocent child from being metaphorically
(100) consumed by ill-understood emotional states.

It is an apparently consistent analogy, and one that is difficult to dispute, until one investigates the circumstances of the composition and recording of the version of Little Red Riding Hood that we have
(105) today. Earlier editions of the story simply don't have many of the components that critics would like to present as so-called "universal symbols." For example, in the vast majority of the older and simpler versions of this tale, the story ends after the wolf
(110) eats the girl. So there can be no theme of parental rescue because, in all but a few of the examples of this tale, there is no rescue and no kind huntsman. In some versions the girl even saves herself, completely contradicting the assumption that it is a
(115) story about rescue. Story elements such as the path, the hunter, and the happy ending, which are seen as essential symbolic components of our interpretation above, were introduced to this ancient tale by the Brothers Grimm in the 19th century. Even the
(120) introduction of the "symbolic" red garment dates only from the seventeenth century, when it was put into the story by Charles Perrault.

In fact, every fairy tale known to the study of folklore has so many different versions that there
(125) are encyclopedic reference books to catalog the variations and the differences between them. A creature that is an elf in one country and era might be a troll in another. A magic object represented as a hat in one version of a tale might be a cloak in ten
(130) other tellings. If folk tales actually represent universal human truths in symbolic form, the symbols in them would have to reflect universal consistency across time. Any attempt to pinpoint a consistent symbolic meaning or underlying scheme in such a
(135) field of moving, blending, and ever-changing targets is doomed to fail before it even begins. Instead, we should embrace all such variations on a theme, searching for insights into the cultural conditions that prompt such divergence.

GO ON TO THE NEXT PAGE

Questions 21–23 ask about Passage A.

21. The "motifs" mentioned in line 57 support the author's primary argument that motifs:

   A. represent experiences that all humans have undergone.

   B. reflect the views of critics.

   C. signify the transition from childhood to adult identity.

   D. embody unconscious forces that must be cared for and nurtured.

22. The word "avenues" in line 68 conveys the author's belief that fairy tales offer:

   F. boulevards into the human subconscious.

   G. beginnings of life-changing adventures.

   H. approaches for understanding common experiences.

   J. homecomings for people's true feelings toward others.

23. In discussing "fairy tales" in lines 7–21, the author of Passage A suggests that:

   A. which stories endure and which are forgotten has nothing to do with the quality of the story.

   B. stories written by a single author and not endlessly retold and edited may well not have the lasting appeal of fairy tales.

   C. many folk tales that spoke deeply to their audiences have been lost and forgotten over the ages.

   D. folk tales undergo the same degree of selection and editing as other kinds of literature.

Questions 24–26 ask about Passage B.

24. The final sentence of Passage B provides information about:

   F. the author's opinion that only fairy tales written in modern times can be accurately interpreted.

   G. folklore methodologists that seek out oral versions of folk tales themselves instead of getting them from books.

   H. the earliest recorded versions of folk tales, which are more accurate and authoritative than later versions.

   J. the variations among versions of fairy tales, which can tell us something about the cultures in which these versions developed.

25. The author of Passage B specifically disagrees with critics who extract simple symbolic interpretations from fairy tales because of their:

   A. disregard for the rigorous principles of modern psychology.

   B. willingness to assume that minor details of a specific version of a folk tale are universal.

   C. failure to make proper use of reference materials pertaining to folklore methodology.

   D. naïve view of the complexity of human nature.

GO ON TO THE NEXT PAGE

26. The statement that "there can be no theme of parental rescue . . . huntsman" in Passage B (lines 115–118) suggests that fairy tales:

    F. cannot be said to have a single authoritative form.

    G. are generally not interested in historical accuracy.

    H. should make a greater effort to capture universal human themes.

    J. are usually not concerned with themes of rescue.

    Questions 27–30 ask about both passages.

    ---

27. The authors of both passages state that fairy tales are:

    A. intuitively meaningful.

    B. critically misunderstood.

    C. historically changeable.

    D. symbolically rich.

28. Which of the following best describes the primary disagreement that the author of Passage B would most likely raise against the statement in Passage A (lines 32–37) that "Small supernatural spirits . . . transformation"?

    F. The specific details in different versions of this folk tale show too much variation to make any consistent interpretations based on this particular version.

    G. The popularity of this tale is no indication of its value in expressing a psychological truth.

    H. This version of the tale is not necessarily the most accurate, because it is recent and may have deviated too much from the true version over time.

    J. Small supernatural spirits could represent many things other than unconscious forces.

29. The author of Passage A would probably respond to the statement in lines 78–84 of Passage B with the argument that:

    A. many modern folk tales originated relatively recently and haven't been subjected to centuries of editing.

    B. the changes in the symbolism of more-recent revisions of folk tales are less important psychologically than the broad themes.

    C. there is no evidence that the symbolism of folk tales is related to psychological forces.

    D. Snow White is a poor example to use as evidence because it has changed so much over time.

30. With which of the following statements about fairy tales would the authors of both passages most likely agree?

    F. The popularity of fairy tales is due to their deeper meanings.

    G. Fairy tales speak to all humans in the language of universal psychological symbols.

    H. Fairy tales have resulted from a compositional process very different from that of modern literature written by a single author.

    J. The study of folklore is undergoing extensive changes because of new information about different versions of particular tales.

GO ON TO THE NEXT PAGE

PASSAGE IV

NATURAL SCIENCE

This passage is adapted from a Wikipedia.com entry on particle accelerators. It describes two different devices used to accelerate subatomic particles.

In linear accelerators, particles are accelerated in a straight line, with the target at the end of the line. Low energy accelerators such as cathode ray
Line tubes and X-ray generators use a single pair of
(5) electrodes with a DC voltage of a few thousand volts between them. In an X-ray generator, the target is one of the electrodes.

Higher energy accelerators use a linear array of plates to which an alternating high energy field is
(10) applied. As the particles approach a plate, they are accelerated toward it by an opposite polarity charge applied to the plate. As they pass through a hole in the plate, the polarity is switched so that the plate now repels the particles, which are now accelerated
(15) by it toward the next plate. Normally, a stream bunches particles that are accelerated, so a carefully controlled AC voltage is applied to each plate to repeat this for each bunch continuously.

As the particles approach the speed of light,
(20) the switching rate of the electric fields becomes so high as to operate at microwave frequencies, and so microwave cavities are used in higher energy machines instead of simple plates. High energy linear accelerators are often called linacs.

(25) Linear accelerators are very widely used. Every cathode ray tube contains one, and they are also used to provide an initial low-energy kick to particles before they are injected into circular accelerators. They can also produce proton beams,
(30) which can produce "proton-heavy" medical or research isotopes, as opposed to the "neutron-heavy" ones made in reactors.

In circular accelerators, the accelerated particles move in a circle until they reach sufficient levels
(35) of energy. The particle track is bent into a circle using dipole magnets. The advantage of circular accelerators over linacs is that components can be reused to accelerate the particles further, as the particle passes a given point many times. However,

(40) they suffer a disadvantage in that the particles emit synchrotron radiation.

When any charged particle is accelerated, it emits electromagnetic radiation. As a particle travelling in a circle is always accelerating
(45) towards the center of the circle, it continuously radiates. This has to be compensated for by some of the energy used to power the accelerating electric fields, which makes circular accelerators less efficient than linear ones. Some circular
(50) accelerators have been deliberately built to generate this radiation (called synchrotron light) as X-rays—for example, the Diamond Light Source being built at the Rutherford Appleton Laboratory in England. High energy X-rays are useful for X-ray
(55) spectroscopy of proteins, for example.

Synchrotron radiation is more powerfully emitted by lighter particles, so these accelerators are invariably electron accelerators. Consequently, particle physicists are increasingly using heavier
(60) particles, such as protons, in their accelerators to achieve higher levels of energy. The downside is that these particles are composites of quarks and gluons, which makes analyzing the results of their interactions much more complicated.

(65) The earliest circular accelerators were cyclotrons, invented in 1929 by Ernest O. Lawrence. Cyclotrons have a single pair of hollow "D"-shaped plates to accelerate the particles and a single dipole magnet to curve the track of the
(70) particles. The particles are injected in the center of the circular machine and spiral outwards toward the circumference.

Cyclotrons reach an energy limit because of relativistic effects at high energies, whereby
(75) particles gain mass rather than speed. As the Special Theory of Relativity means that nothing can travel faster than the speed of light in a vacuum, the particles in an accelerator normally travel very close to the speed of light. In high energy
(80) accelerators, there is a diminishing return in speed as the particle approaches the speed of light. The effect of the energy injected using the electric

GO ON TO THE NEXT PAGE ⇒

fields is therefore to increase their mass markedly, rather than their speed. Doubling the energy might
(85) increase the speed a fraction of a percent closer to that of light, but the main effect is to increase the relativistic mass of the particle.

Cyclotrons no longer accelerate electrons when they have reached an energy for about 10 million
(90) electron volts. There are ways of compensating for this to some extent—namely, the synchrocyclotron and the isochronous cyclotron. They are nevertheless useful for lower energy applications.

To push the energies even higher—into
(95) billions of electron volts—it is necessary to use a synchrotron. This is an accelerator in which the particles are contained in a doughnut-shaped tube, called a storage ring. The tube has many magnets distributed around it to focus the particles and
(100) curve their track around the tube, and microwave cavities similarly distributed to accelerate them. The size of Lawrence's first cyclotron was a mere four inches in diameter. Fermilab now has a ring with a beam path of four miles.

31. The main idea of the passage is that:

   A. linear accelerators are more efficient than circular accelerators.

   B. particles in accelerators cannot travel at the speed of light.

   C. linear and circular accelerators have important, but different, uses.

   D. the cyclotron is a useful type of circular accelerator.

32. The passage states that magnets affect particles by:

   F. influencing the direction particles travel.

   G. creating curved particles.

   H. increasing the acceleration of particles.

   J. causing an increase in the particles' energy levels.

33. The passage states that which of the following causes an increase in particle mass?

   A. A particle reaching the speed of light

   B. Acceleration of a particle in a vacuum

   C. Using heavier particles

   D. Injecting energy using electric fields

34. As it is used in line 62, the word *quarks* most nearly refers to:

   F. objects made up of electrons.

   G. objects made up of radiation.

   H. components of protons.

   J. components of gluons.

35. According to the passage, which of the following CANNOT be a result of using a circular accelerator?

   A. Particles that emit electromagnetic radiation

   B. Reuse of components to accelerate particles

   C. Particles that emit synchrotron radiation

   D. An initial low kick of energy in particles

36. Which of the following statements would the author most likely agree with?

   F. Linear accelerators are of limited use.

   G. Using particles such as protons in such experiments is not possible, since they are composites of quarks and gluons.

   H. Circular accelerators have improved little since Lawrence's first cyclotron.

   J. Depending on the desired result, both linear and circular accelerators are valuable tools.

GO ON TO THE NEXT PAGE ⟹

37. According to the passage, what is one effect of particles passing through the hole in the plate of higher energy accelerators?

    A. The mass of the particles increases.

    B. The charge of the particles changes.

    C. The particles lose energy.

    D. The particles are repelled and accelerated toward the next plate.

38. The passage suggests that the greatest difference between a cyclotron and a synchrotron is that:

    F. cyclotrons are not useful.

    G. synchrotrons accelerate particles in a circle.

    H. synchrotrons can overcome limitations that cyclotrons cannot.

    J. synchrotrons are capable of causing particles to curve more closely to the edge of the tube.

39. How does the information about the size of Lawrence's first cyclotron and the size of Fermilab's ring function in the passage?

    A. It suggests that, over time, there has been progress in improving the size and capabilities of particle accelerators.

    B. It proves that cyclotrons are important for particle acceleration because they were invented by Lawrence.

    C. It indicates that the inventors at Fermilab were more capable than Lawrence was.

    D. It emphasizes the difference between cyclotrons and synchrotrons.

40. What is the main idea of the ninth paragraph (lines 73–87)?

    F. Cyclotrons can accelerate particles to nearly the speed of light.

    G. As the speed of particles in an accelerator approaches the speed of light, they gain more mass than speed.

    H. The speed of particles diminishes when particles get close to the speed of light.

    J. Energy limits are reached in cyclotrons because the mass of the particles becomes too high.

SCIENCE TEST

35 Minutes—40 Questions

Directions: There are several passages in this test. Each passage is followed by several questions. After reading a passage, choose the best answer to each question and fill in the corresponding oval on your Answer Grid. You may refer to the passages as often as necessary. You are NOT permitted to use a calculator on this test.

PASSAGE I

A panel of engineers designed and built a pressurized structure to be used for shelter by geologists during extended research missions near the South Pole. The design consisted of 4 rooms, each with its own separate heating and air pressure control systems. During testing, the engineers found the daily average air temperature, in degrees Celsius (°C), and daily average air pressure, in millimeters of mercury (mm Hg), in each room. The data for the first 5 days of their study are given in Table 1 and Table 2.

Table 1

Day	Daily average air temperature (°C)			
	Room 1	Room 2	Room 3	Room 4
1	19.64	19.08	18.67	18.03
2	20.15	19.20	18.46	18.11
3	20.81	19.19	18.62	18.32
4	21.06	19.51	19.08	18.91
5	21.14	19.48	18.60	18.58

Table 2

Day	Daily average air pressure (mm Hg)			
	Room 1	Room 2	Room 3	Room 4
1	748.2	759.6	760.0	745.2
2	752.6	762.0	758.7	750.3
3	753.3	760.2	756.5	760.4
4	760.1	750.8	755.4	756.8
5	758.7	757.9	754.0	759.5

1. The lowest daily average air pressure recorded during the first 5 days of the study was:

   A. 762.0 mm Hg.

   B. 745.2 mm Hg.

   C. 21.14 mm Hg.

   D. 18.03 mm Hg.

2. According to Table 2, daily average air pressures were recorded to the nearest:

   F. 0.01 mm Hg.

   G. 0.1 mm Hg.

   H. 1.0 mm Hg.

   J. 10 mm Hg.

GO ON TO THE NEXT PAGE

3. Which of the following graphs best represents a plot of the daily average air temperature versus the daily average air pressure for Room 4?

A.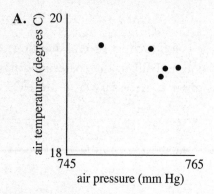

B.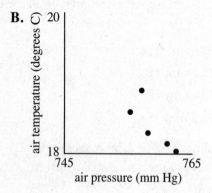

C.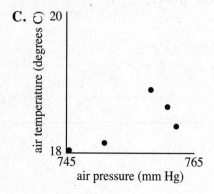

D.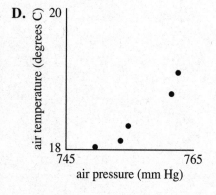

4. Which of the following most accurately describes the changes in the daily average air pressure in Room 3 during days 1–5?

F. The daily average air pressure increased from days 1 to 4 and decreased from days 4 to 5.

G. The daily average air pressure decreased from days 1 to 2, increased from days 2 to 4, and decreased again from days 4 to 5.

H. The daily average air pressure increased only.

J. The daily average air pressure decreased only.

5. Suppose the *heat absorption modulus* of a room is defined as the quantity of heat absorbed by the contents of the room divided by the quantity of heat provided to the entire room. Based on the data, would one be justified in concluding that the heat absorption modulus of Room 1 was higher than the heat absorption modulus of any of the other rooms?

A. Yes, because the quantity of heat provided to Room 1 was greater than the quantity of heat provided to any of the other rooms.

B. Yes, because the quantity of heat not absorbed by the contents of Room 1 was greater than the quantity of heat not absorbed by the contents of any of the other rooms.

C. No, because the quantity of heat absorbed by the contents of Room 1 was less than the quantity of heat absorbed by the contents of any of the other room.

D. No, because the information provided is insufficient to determine heat absorption modulus.

GO ON TO THE NEXT PAGE

6. If the geologists were to use equipment that malfunctions in warm environments, which room would be most likely to cause the equipment to malfunction?

F. Room 1

G. Room 2

H. Room 3

J. Room 4

PASSAGE II

Humans can experience toxic symptoms when concentrations of mercury (Hg) in the blood exceed 200 parts per billion (ppb). Frequent consumption of foods high in Hg content contributes to high Hg levels in the blood. On average, higher Hg concentrations are observed in people whose diets consist of more extreme amounts of certain types of seafood. A research group proposed that sea creatures that live in colder waters acquire greater amounts of Hg than those that reside in warmer waters. The researchers performed the following experiments to examine this hypothesis.

EXPERIMENT 1

Samples of several species of consumable sea life caught in the cold waters of the northern Atlantic Ocean were chemically prepared and analyzed using a cold vapor atomic fluorescence spectrometer (CVAFS), a device that indicates the relative concentrations of various elements and compounds found within a biological sample. Comparisons of the spectra taken from the seafood samples with those taken from samples of known Hg levels were made to determine the exact concentrations in ppb. Identical volumes of tissue from eight different specimens for each of four different species were tested, and the results

are shown in Table 1, including the average concentrations found for each species.

Table 1

Specimen	Hg concentration in cold-water species (ppb):			
	Cod	Crab	Swordfish	Shark
1	160	138	871	859
2	123	143	905	820
3	139	152	902	839
4	116	177	881	851
5	130	133	875	818
6	134	148	880	836
7	151	147	910	847
8	109	168	894	825
Average	133	151	890	837

EXPERIMENT 2

Four species caught in the warmer waters of the Gulf of Mexico were examined using the procedure from Experiment 1. The results are shown in Table 2.

Table 2

Specimen	Hg concentration in warm-water species (ppb):			
	Catfish	Crab	Swordfish	Shark
1	98	113	851	812
2	110	122	856	795
3	102	143	845	821
4	105	128	861	803
5	94	115	849	798
6	112	136	852	809
7	100	129	863	815
8	117	116	837	776
Average	105	125	852	804

GO ON TO THE NEXT PAGE ⟹

7. According to Table 1 and Table 2, which species shows the greatest difference in average mercury concentration between cold and warm climates?

   A. Crab

   B. Swordfish

   C. Shark

   D. The greatest difference in the average mercury concentration cannot be determined from the information provided.

8. Given that shark and swordfish are both large predatory animals, and catfish and crab are smaller non-predatory animals, do the results of Experiment 2 support the hypothesis that the tissue of larger predatory fish exhibits higher levels of Hg than does the tissue of smaller species?

   F. Yes; the lowest concentration of Hg was found in swordfish.

   G. Yes; both swordfish and shark had Hg concentrations that were higher than those found in either catfish or crab.

   H. No; the lowest concentration of Hg was in catfish.

   J. No; both catfish and crab had concentrations of Hg that were higher than those found in either swordfish or shark.

9. A researcher, when using the CVAFS, was concerned that lead (Pb) in the tissue samples might be interfering with the detection of Hg. Which of the following procedures would best help the researcher explore this trouble?

   A. Flooding the sample with a large concentration of Pb before using the CVAFS

   B. Using the CVAFS to examine a non-biological sample

   C. Collecting tissue from additional species

   D. Testing a sample with known concentrations of Hg and Pb

10. Based on the results of the experiments and the data in the table below, sharks caught in which of the following locations would most likely possess the largest concentrations of Hg in February?

Location	Average water temperature (°F) for February
Northern Atlantic Ocean	33
Gulf of Mexico	70
Northern Pacific Ocean	46
Tampa Bay	72

   F. Northern Atlantic Ocean

   G. Northern Pacific Ocean

   H. Gulf of Mexico

   J. Tampa Bay

11. Which of the following factors was intentionally varied in Experiment 2?

   A. The volume of tissue tested

   B. The method by which the marine organisms were caught

   C. The species of marine organism tested

   D. The method of sample analysis

GO ON TO THE NEXT PAGE ⟩

12. Which of the following specimens would most likely have the highest concentration of Hg?

F. A crab caught in cold water

G. A swordfish caught in cold water

H. A catfish caught in warm water

J. A swordfish caught in warm water

13. How might the results of the experiments be affected if the chemical preparation described in Experiment 1 introduced Hg-free contaminants into the sample, resulting in a larger volume of tested material? The measured concentrations of Hg would be:

A. the same as the actual concentrations for both cold-water and warm-water specimens.

B. higher than the actual concentrations for both cold-water and warm-water specimens.

C. lower than the actual concentrations for cold-water specimens, but higher than the actual concentrations for warm-water specimens.

D. lower than the actual concentrations for both cold-water and warm-water specimens.

PASSAGE III

A student performed three exercises with a battery and four different light bulbs.

EXERCISE 1

The student connected the battery to a fixed outlet designed to accept any of the four bulbs. She then placed four identical light sensors at different distances from the outlet. Each sensor was designed so that a green indicator illuminated upon the sensor's detection of incident light, while a red indicator remained illuminated when no light was detected. The student darkened the room and recorded the state of each sensor while each bulb was lit. The results are shown in Table 1.

Table 1

Sensor distance (cm)	Sensor indicator color			
	Bulb 1	Bulb 2	Bulb 3	Bulb 4
50	green	green	green	green
100	red	green	green	green
150	red	red	green	green
200	red	red	red	green

EXERCISE 2

The battery produced an *electromotive force* of 12 Volts. The student was given a device called an ammeter, which is used to measure the *current* passing through an electric circuit. She completed the circuit by connecting the battery, the ammeter, and each of the four light bulbs, one at a time. She measured the associated current in Amperes (A) for each bulb and calculated the *impedance* ($\dot{Z}$) in Ohms (Ω) for each from the following formula:

$$Z = \text{electromotive force} \div \text{current}.$$

The results are shown in Table 2.

GO ON TO THE NEXT PAGE ⟹

Table 2

Light bulb	Current (A)	Z (Ω)
1	0.2	60
2	0.3	40
3	0.4	30
4	0.6	20

EXERCISE 3

The *power rating* (P) of each light bulb was printed near its base. P gives the time rate of energy consumption of the bulb and is related to the *brightness* (B) of light at a given distance from the bulb. B is calculated in Watts per meter squared (W/m^2) from the following formula:

$$B = \frac{P}{4r\pi^2}$$

where r is the distance in meters (m) from the bulb, and P is measured in Watts (W).

The student calculated B for each bulb at a distance of 1 m. The results are shown in Table 3.

Table 3

Light bulb	P (W)	B (W/m2)
1	2.4	0.19
2	3.6	0.29
3	4.8	0.38
4	7.2	0.57

14. If the student had tested a fifth light bulb during Exercise 2 and measured the current passing through it to be 1.2 A, the Z associated with this bulb would have been:

    F.   1 Ω.

    G. 10 Ω.

    H. 14.4 Ω.

    J. 100 Ω.

15. Based on the results of Exercise 2, a circuit including the combination of which of the following batteries and light bulbs would result in the highest current in the circuit? (Assume Z is a constant for a given light bulb.)

    A. A 10 V battery and Bulb 1

    B. An 8 V battery and Bulb 2

    C. A 6 V battery and Bulb 3

    D. A 5 V battery and Bulb 4

16. With Bulb 3 in place in the circuit in Exercise 1, how many of the sensors were unable to detect any incident light?

    F. 1

    G. 2

    H. 3

    J. 4

17. Which of the following equations correctly calculates B (in W/m^2) at a distance of 2 m from Bulb 2?

    A. $B = \dfrac{2}{4\pi(3.6)^2}$

    B. $B = \dfrac{2}{4\pi(2.4)^2}$

    C. $B = \dfrac{3.6}{4\pi(2)^2}$

    D. $B = \dfrac{2.4}{4\pi(2)^2}$

18. Another student used the approach given in Exercise 3 to calculate B at a distance of 1 m from a fifth light bulb. He determined that, for this fifth bulb, B = 0.95 W/m^2. Accordingly, P for this bulb was most likely closest to which of the following values?

    F.   0.1 W

    G.   6 W

    H. 12 W

    J.   18 W

GO ON TO THE NEXT PAGE ⟩

19. Exercise 1 and Exercise 2 differed in that in Exercise 1:

　　A. 4 light sensors were used.

　　B. 4 different light bulbs were used.

　　C. the electromotive force of the battery was varied.

　　D. the current was highest for Bulb 1.

20. According to Table 3, which light bulb with a brightness greater than 0.30 (W/m²) has the lowest power consumption?

　　F. Light bulb 1

　　G. Light bulb 2

　　H. Light bulb 3

　　J. Light bulb 4

PASSAGE IV

The electrons in a solid occupy *energy states* determined by the type and spatial distribution of the atoms in the solid. The probability that a given energy state will be occupied by an electron is given by the *Fermi-Dirac distribution function*, which depends on the material and the temperature of the solid. Fermi-Dirac distribution functions for the same solid at 3 different temperatures are shown in the figure below.

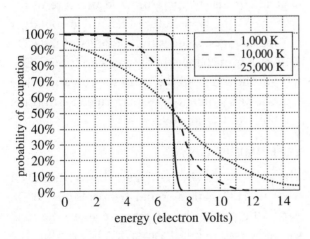

Figure 1

(Note: 1 electron Volt (eV) = 1.66×10^{-19} Joules (J); eV and J are both units of energy. At energies above 15 eV, the probability of occupation at each temperature continues to decrease.)

21. The information in the given figure supports which of the following statements about energy states?

　　A. Cooler materials have a larger range of energy states than hotter materials.

　　B. Materials have the same range of energy states regardless of temperature.

　　C. Cooler materials are more capable of occupying higher energy states than hotter materials.

　　D. Hotter materials are more capable of occupying higher energy states than cooler materials.

22. The steepness of the slope of each distribution function at the point where its value equals 50% is inversely proportional to the average *kinetic energy* of the atoms in the solid. Which of the following correctly ranks the 3 functions, from *least* to *greatest*, according to the average kinetic energy of the atoms in the solid?

　　F. 25,000 K; 10,000 K; 1,000 K

　　G. 25,000 K; 1,000 K; 10,000 K

　　H. 10,000 K; 1,000 K; 25,000 K

　　J. 1,000 K; 10,000 K; 25,000 K

23. Based on the figure, at a temperature of 1,000 K, the probability of a state at an energy of 20 eV being occupied by an electron will most likely be:

　　A. less than 5%.

　　B. between 5% and 50%.

　　C. between 50% and 90%.

　　D. greater than 90%.

GO ON TO THE NEXT PAGE ⇨

24. Based on the figure, which of the following sets of Fermi-Dirac distribution functions best represents an unknown solid at temperatures of 2,000 K, 20,000 K, and 50,000 K?

F.

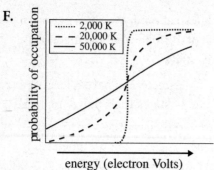

G.

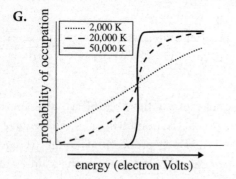

H.

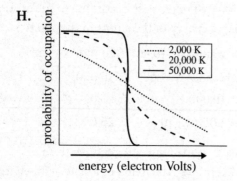

J.

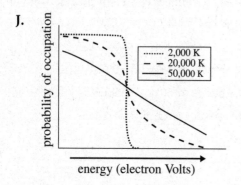

25. Based on the figure, the probability of a 5 eV energy state being occupied by an electron will equal 80% when the temperature of the solid is closest to:

A. 500 K.

B. 5,000 K.

C. 20,000 K.

D. 30,000 K.

26. The *de Broglie wavelength* of an electron energy state decreases as the energy of the state increases. Based on this information, over all energies in the figure, as the de Broglie wavelength of an electron energy state decreases, the probability of that state being occupied by an electron:

F. increases only.

G. decreases only.

H. increases, then decreases.

J. decreases, then increases.

PASSAGE V

A soda beverage is typically a solution of water, various liquid colorings and flavorings, and CO_2 gas. *Solubility* is defined as the ability of a substance to dissolve, and the solubility of CO_2 in a soda depends on the temperature and pressure of the system. As the temperature of a sealed container of soda changes, so does the solubility of the CO_2. This results in changes in the concentration of CO_2 in both the soda and the air in the container. The following experiments were performed to study the solubility of CO_2 in sodas.

EXPERIMENT 1

The apparatus shown in Figure 1 was assembled with an H_2O bath at room temperature (25°C). After 10 minutes, the air pressure above the soda was measured in kilo-Pascals (kPa) by reading the

GO ON TO THE NEXT PAGE ▷

value directly from the pressure gauge. Additional trials were performed at different temperatures and with other sodas in the container. The results are shown in Table 1.

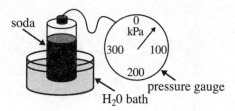

Figure 1

Table 1

Soda	Pressure (kPa) at:		
	0°C	25°C	50°C
A	230	237	256
B	214	234	253
C	249	272	294
D	223	243	282
E	209	228	247

EXPERIMENT 2

An apparatus similar to those used by companies that produce soda was constructed so that measured amounts of compressed CO_2 gas could be injected into each soda until the solution reached its maximum concentration of CO_2. The apparatus consisted of an air-sealed flask containing only soda and no air. Starting with sodas from which all of the CO_2 had been carefully removed, CO_2 was injected and the maximum CO_2 concentration for each soda was recorded. From the maximum concentrations, the solubility of CO_2 in each soda was calculated for three different temperatures at equal pressures. Solubility was recorded in centi-Molars per atmosphere (cM/atm), and the results are shown in Table 2.

Table 2

Soda	CO_2 solubility (cM/atm) at:		
	0°C	25°C	50°C
A	3.59	3.51	3.45
B	3.58	3.50	3.37
C	3.67	3.57	3.48
D	3.62	3.53	3.41
E	3.54	3.46	3.29

27. Which of the following bar graphs best expresses the pressures of the container contents from Experiment 1 at 25°C?

A.

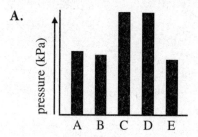

B.

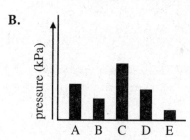

C.

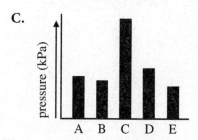

D.

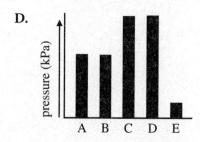

GO ON TO THE NEXT PAGE

28. Which of the following figures best depicts the change in position of the needle on the pressure gauge while attached to the container holding Soda C in Experiment 1?

needle position at 0°C | needle position at 50°C

F.

0 kPa
300   100
200

0 kPa
300   100
200

G.

0 kPa
300   100
200

0 kPa
300   100
200

H.

0 kPa
300   100
200

0 kPa
300   100
200

J.

0 kPa
300   100
200

0 kPa
300   100
200

29. A student hypothesized that, at a given pressure and temperature, the higher the sugar content of a soda, the higher the solubility of CO_2 in that soda. Do the results of Experiment 2 and all of the information in the table below support this hypothesis?

Soda	Sugar content (grams per 12 ounces)
A	23
B	32
C	38
D	40
E	34

A. Yes; Soda A has the lowest sugar content and the lowest CO_2 solubility.

B. Yes; Soda D has a higher sugar content and CO_2 solubility than Soda C.

C. No; the higher a soda's sugar content, the lower the soda's CO_2 solubility.

D. No; there is no clear relationship in these data between sugar content and CO_2 solubility.

30. According to the results of Experiment 2, as the temperature of the soda increases, the CO_2 solubility of the soda:

F. increases only.

G. decreases only.

H. increases, then decreases.

J. decreases, then increases.

GO ON TO THE NEXT PAGE ⟶

31. Which of the following figures best illustrates the apparatus used in Experiment 2?

   A.

   B.
   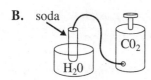

   C.

   D.
   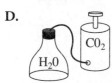

32. Which of the following statements best explains why, in Experiment 1, the experimenter waited 10 minutes before recording the pressure of the air above the soda? The experimenter waited to allow:

   F. all of the CO_2 to be removed from the container.

   G. time for the soda in the container to evaporate.

   H. the contents of the container to adjust to the temperature of the H_2O bath.

   J. time for the pressure gauge to stabilize.

33. Table 2 shows that the soda's CO_2 solubility:

   A. increases as temperature increases.

   B. decreases as temperature increases.

   C. sometimes increases and sometimes decreases as temperature increases.

   D. is not affected by changes in temperature.

PASSAGE VI

Straight-chain conformational isomers are carbon compounds that differ only by rotation about one or more single carbon bonds. Essentially, these isomers represent the same compound in a slightly different position. One example of such an isomer is butane (C_4H_{10}), in which two methyl (CH_3) groups are each bonded to the main carbon chain. The straight-chain conformational isomers of butane are classified into 4 categories.

1. In the *anti* conformation, the bonds connecting the methyl groups to the main carbon chain are rotated 180° with respect to each other.

2. In the *gauche* conformation, the bonds connecting the methyl groups to the main carbon chain are rotated 60° with respect to each other.

3. In the *eclipsed* conformation, the bonds connecting the methyl groups to the main carbon chain are rotated 120° with respect to each other.

4. In the *totally eclipsed* conformation, the bonds connecting the methyl groups to the main carbon chain are parallel to each other.

The anti conformation is the lowest energy and most stable state of the butane molecule, since it allows for the methyl groups to maintain maximum separation from each other. The methyl groups are much closer to each other in the gauche conformation, but this still represents a relative minimum or *meta-stable* state, due to the relative orientations of the other hydrogen atoms in the molecule. Molecules in the anti or gauche conformations tend to maintain their shape. The eclipsed conformation represents a relative maximum energy state, while the totally eclipsed conformation is the highest energy state of all of butane's straight-chain conformational isomers.

Two organic chemistry students discuss straight-chain conformational isomers.

GO ON TO THE NEXT PAGE ▷

STUDENT 1

The *active shape* (the chemically functional shape) of a butane molecule is always identical to the molecule's lowest-energy shape. Any other shape would be unstable. Because the lowest-energy shape of a straight-chain conformational isomer of butane is the anti conformation, its active shape is always the anti conformation.

STUDENT 2

The active shape of a butane molecule is dependent upon the energy state of the shape. However, a butane molecule's shape may also depend on temperature and its initial isomeric state. Specifically, in order to convert from the gauche conformation to the anti conformation, the molecule must pass through either the eclipsed or totally eclipsed conformation. If the molecule is not given enough energy to reach either of these states, its active shape will be the gauche conformation.

34. According to the passage, molecules in conformation states with relatively low energy tend to:

    F. convert to the totally eclipsed conformation.

    G. convert to the eclipsed conformation.

    H. maintain their shape.

    J. chemically react.

35. The information in the passage indicates that when a compound changes from one straight-chain conformational isomer to another, it still retains its original:

    A. energy state.

    B. shape.

    C. number of single carbon bonds.

    D. temperature.

36. Student 2's views differ from Student 1's views in that only Student 2 believes that a butane molecule's active shape is partially determined by its:

    F. initial isomeric state.

    G. energy state.

    H. hydrogen bonding angles.

    J. proximity of methyl groups.

37. A student rolls a ball along the curved path shown below. Given that points closer to the ground represent states of lower energy, the ball coming to rest at the position shown corresponds to a butane molecule settling into which conformational isomer state?

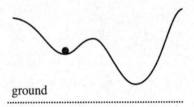

ground

    A. Anti

    B. Gauche

    C. Eclipsed

    D. Totally eclipsed

38. Suppose butane molecules are cooled so that each molecule is allowed to reach its active shape. Which of the following statements is most consistent with the information presented in the passage?

    F. If Student 1 is correct, all of the molecules will be in the anti conformation.

    G. If Student 1 is correct, all of the molecules will have shapes different from their lowest-energy shapes.

    H. If Student 2 is correct, all of the molecules will be in the anti conformation.

    J. If Student 2 is correct, all of the molecules will have shapes different than their lowest-energy shapes.

GO ON TO THE NEXT PAGE

39. Which of the following diagrams showing the relationship between a given butane molecule's shape and its relative energy is consistent with Student 2's assertions about the energy of butane molecules, but is NOT consistent with Student 1's assertions about the energy of butane molecules?

A.

B.

C.

D.

Key
- ☐ eclipsed conformation
- ▨ active shape
- ■ most stable shape

40. Student 2 says that a butane molecule may settle into a moderately high-energy conformation. Which of the following findings, if true, could be used to *counter* this argument?

F. Once a molecule has settled into a given conformation, all of its single carbon bonds are stable.

G. Enough energy is available in the environment to overcome local energy barriers, driving the molecule into its lowest-energy conformation.

H. During molecule formation, the hydrogen bonds are formed before the carbon bonds.

J. Molecules that change their isomeric conformation tend to lose their chemical functions.

IF YOU FINISH BEFORE TIME IS CALLED, YOU MAY CHECK YOUR WORK ON THIS SECTION ONLY. DO NOT TURN TO ANY OTHER SECTION IN THE TEST. **STOP**

WRITING TEST

40 Minutes

Directions: This is a test of your writing skills. You will have forty (40) minutes to write an essay in English. Before you begin planning and writing your essay, read the writing prompt carefully to understand exactly what you are being asked to do. Your essay will be evaluated on the evidence it provides of your ability to do the following:

- Express judgments by evaluating the three perspectives given in the prompt, taking a position on an issue, and explaining the relationship among all four ideas
- Develop a position by using logical reasoning and by supporting your ideas
- Maintain a focus on the topic throughout the essay
- Organize ideas in a logical way
- Use language clearly and effectively according to the conventions of standard written English

You may use the unlined pages in this test booklet to plan your essay. These pages will not be scored. *You must write your essay in pencil on the lined pages in the answer folder.* Your writing on those lined pages will be scored. You may not need all the lined pages, but to ensure you have enough room to finish, do NOT skip lines. You may write corrections or additions neatly between the lines of your essay, but do NOT write in the margins of the lined pages. *Illegible essays cannot be scored, so you must write (or print) clearly.*

If you finish before time is called you may review your work. Lay your pencil down immediately when time is called.

DO NOT OPEN THIS BOOKLET UNTIL TOLD TO DO SO.

GO ON TO THE NEXT PAGE

COLLEGIATE FIELDS OF STUDY

Students pursuing higher education with the intent to commit to a particular field of study often determine that a different concentration is a better fit and subsequently make a change. Many students base their initial field of study on their interests, strengths, and experiences in high school. Some students complete the program they originally selected, but many others find that college unearths new passions and prospects. Additionally, collegiate study often exposes students to job markets, which help students evaluate the availability of jobs in their desired field; this is often a driving factor in changing their concentration since students seek financial security upon graduation. Should high schools incorporate career-oriented programs to help students make better decisions regarding their majors? Making better-informed choices before entering college will help students wisely allocate their time and money during their college careers, and will prevent graduates from entering a career field without background knowledge regarding job availability.

Read and carefully consider these perspectives. Each discusses the importance of providing high school students with the necessary knowledge to choose appropriate fields of study in college.

Perspective One	Perspective Two	Perspective Three
High schools should hold career-oriented seminars at least once a semester during the regular school day to help students make more directed decisions when choosing collegiate fields of study. These seminars will help students explore career options, post-graduate position availability, and job requirements. Armed with this knowledge, students can make better-informed choices that will help them to avoid spending unnecessary time and money in both college and job markets.	High schools should retain their current primary focus, but should offer optional after-school career-focused seminars conducted by professionals so students can learn about options before attending college. Students who take advantage of this resource will be able to make better decisions, and these seminars will allow teachers to continue to focus on the core curriculum and assist students academically.	High schools should partner with colleges and professionals to embed career-oriented options into current courses. The job market information will be relevant to the class in which it is presented. Although students will only receive career-based information centered on the courses in which they are enrolled, this approach guarantees that each student is offered course-specific advice.

GO ON TO THE NEXT PAGE

ESSAY TASK

Write a unified, coherent essay in which you evaluate multiple perspectives regarding academic programs that assist students in choosing appropriate fields of study. In your essay, be sure to:

- analyze and evaluate the perspectives given
- state and develop your own perspective on the issue
- explain the relationship between your perspective and those given

Your perspective may be in full agreement with any of the others, in partial agreement, or wholly different. Whatever the case, support your ideas with logical reasoning and detailed, persuasive examples.

PLANNING YOUR ESSAY

You may wish to consider the following as you think critically about the task:

Strengths and weaknesses of the three given perspectives

- What insights do they offer, and what do they fail to consider?
- Why might they be persuasive to others, or why might they fail to persuade?

Your own knowledge, experience, and values

- What is your perspective on this issue, and what are its strengths and weaknesses?
- How will you support your perspective in your essay?

_____

_____

_____

_____

_____

_____

_____

_____

_____

_____

GO ON TO THE NEXT PAGE ⇨

GO ON TO THE NEXT PAGE

Practice Test Five
ANSWER KEY

ENGLISH TEST

1. A	11. A	21. D	31. A	41. C	51. A	61. A	71. B
2. G	12. J	22. H	32. H	42. F	52. H	62. J	72. G
3. A	13. B	23. D	33. D	43. C	53. C	63. B	73. D
4. G	14. J	24. G	34. F	44. J	54. J	64. J	74. J
5. B	15. A	25. A	35. B	45. A	55. A	65. A	75. D
6. G	16. F	26. J	36. H	46. F	56. H	66. F	
7. C	17. B	27. A	37. D	47. C	57. B	67. C	
8. J	18. H	28. F	38. J	48. F	58. J	68. J	
9. C	19. C	29. B	39. C	49. D	59. B	69. B	
10. J	20. G	30. J	40. J	50. G	60. H	70. F	

MATHEMATICS TEST

1. E	9. C	17. C	25. D	33. E	41. B	49. D	57. C
2. J	10. G	18. F	26. G	34. G	42. G	50. J	58. K
3. A	11. B	19. D	27. E	35. E	43. C	51. B	59. D
4. K	12. K	20. G	28. G	36. J	44. G	52. K	60. K
5. C	13. E	21. D	29. D	37. D	45. D	53. D	
6. F	14. J	22. F	30. F	38. K	46. H	54. K	
7. B	15. E	23. C	31. C	39. B	47. E	55. A	
8. H	16. G	24. F	32. F	40. F	48. H	56. H	

READING TEST

1. D	6. G	11. B	16. H	21. A	26. F	31. C	36. J
2. G	7. D	12. J	17. D	22. H	27. C	32. F	37. D
3. C	8. J	13. C	18. F	23. D	28. F	33. D	38. H
4. J	9. A	14. F	19. B	24. J	29. B	34. H	39. A
5. A	10. G	15. D	20. H	25. B	30. H	35. D	40. G

SCIENCE TEST

1. B	6. F	11. C	16. F	21. D	26. G	31. A	36. F
2. G	7. B	12. G	17. C	22. J	27. C	32. H	37. B
3. C	8. G	13. D	18. H	23. A	28. G	33. B	38. F
4. J	9. D	14. G	19. A	24. J	29. D	34. H	39. D
5. D	10. F	15. D	20. H	25. C	30. G	35. C	40. G

ANSWERS AND EXPLANATIONS

ENGLISH TEST

PASSAGE I

1. A
Category: Word Choice
Difficulty: Low
Getting to the Answer: The superlative adjective form will use –est or most—not both. This sentence needs (A), NO CHANGE. "Earliest" is the correct superlative adjective to refer to all "music forms." Choice B uses "most" with "earliest," which is grammatically incorrect. Choice C uses "most early," which is also incorrect; "most" is only used with words that do not have an –est superlative form. Choice D uses the right adjective, but creates a subject–verb agreement error; "The earliest…forms" does not agree with the singular verb form "was."

2. G
Category: Punctuation
Difficulty: High
Getting to the Answer: "It's" is a contraction of *it is* or *it has*. If neither of these makes sense when substituted for the contraction, the contraction is incorrect. It doesn't make sense to say "because of it is (or has) having," so we know F is incorrect. Choice (G) substitutes the correct singular possessive adjective, "*its*," meaning that the "origins" belong to American Jazz. Choices H and J use spellings that are never correct.

3. A
Category: Writing Strategy
Difficulty: High
Getting to the Answer: Just determining whether or not the suggested information is relevant gives you a 50–50 chance of getting the question right. First, determine if the new information is relevant or not. Here, it is, since the paragraph discusses the way that different musical forms came together to form American Jazz; eliminate C and D. Choice B is

out of scope for the paragraph, which concerns the development, not the popularity, of American Jazz. Choice (A) is correct.

4. G
Category: Punctuation
Difficulty: Medium
Getting to the Answer: If a phrase is set off by a comma or commas, the sentence must make sense without it. The phrase "ragtime and blues" should be set of from the rest of the sentence with a comma because it is not essential to the meaning of the sentence; (G) is correct. Removing the phrase set off by commas in F does not result in a logical sentence. Choice H incorrectly separates a prepositional phrase from the rest of the sentence. Choice J eliminates the commas, making the sentence difficult to understand.

5. B
Category: Punctuation
Difficulty: Medium
Getting to the Answer: If a semicolon is used to combine clauses, the clauses must be independent. This sentence incorrectly places a semicolon between an independent and a dependent clause. Choice (B) eliminates the incorrect semicolon. Choice C incorrectly inserts a comma between a preposition and its object. Choice D separates a subject from its verb with a comma, which is also incorrect.

6. G
Category: Word Choice
Difficulty: Medium
Getting to the Answer: When an underlined selection includes a pronoun, make sure its antecedent is clear and unambiguous. There are several singular nouns in the sentence previous to this one ("style," "blend," "America," "the time") that could be antecedents for the pronoun "It." Choice (G) replaces the pronoun with the appropriate noun. Choices H and J do not address the ambiguity issue.

7. C
Category: Word Choice
Difficulty: Medium
Getting to the Answer: When an English Test question has a stem, read it carefully. This one asks you to determine the unacceptable choice, which means three of the choices will be correct in context. Although "made his living on" is a properly constructed idiom, it is inappropriate in this context, since it refers to the location where the living was made, rather than the occupation itself. Choice (C) is the correct choice here. Choices A, B, and D are all acceptable in the sentence.

8. J
Category: Connections
Difficulty: Medium
Getting to the Answer: When OMIT is an option, check to see if the underlined selection is necessary to the meaning of the sentence. "He was" isn't necessary here; "working as a shoe shiner and a waiter" properly provides a compound object for the preposition, so (J) is correct. Choice G uses incorrect grammatical structure and H leaves the meaning of the second clause incomplete.

9. C
Category: Writing Strategy
Difficulty: High
Getting to the Answer: When facing a question about deleting information, read the sentence without the suggested deletion. The information that Cab Calloway "spent time at the racetrack" doesn't make sense coming directly after a sentence that discusses the jobs he held, unless we also know that Calloway worked at the track. Choice (C) is correct; without this explanation, readers might be confused. Choice A is incorrect; the information does relate to the topic at hand. Choice B is also wrong; the information has nothing to do with Calloway's accomplishments or successes. Other information in the sentence tells us how far Cab Calloway came in his life; it's not necessary to keep this clause for the reason that D suggests.

10. J
Category: Sentence Sense
Difficulty: Medium
Getting to the Answer: Although OMIT will not always be the correct answer when it's offered, always consider the possibility that the selection is either redundant or used incorrectly. As written, this sentence is a fragment, with no independent clause. Eliminating "where," as (J) suggests, corrects this error. Choice G is unnecessarily wordy. Choice H does not address the fragment error.

11. A
Category: Punctuation
Difficulty: Medium
Getting to the Answer: The ACT tests only a few very specific punctuation rules; make sure your answer choice follows these rules. Choice (A) is correct; no punctuation is needed here. Choice B inserts a colon which, on the ACT, will only be correct when used to introduce a brief explanation, definition, or list. Choice C treats the phrase "in the top Jazz circles" as nonessential information, but the sentence does not make sense when read without it. Choice D inserts an unneeded comma before a prepositional phrase.

12. J
Category: Organization
Difficulty: Medium
Getting to the Answer: Because NO CHANGE is not an answer choice, the sentence must be relevant; you'll need to determine its most logical placement. "Widely known" is a good context clue. It doesn't make sense that he was well-known when he was a shoe-shiner and waiter, when he was walking racehorses, and when he first began performing, so you can eliminate F, G, and H. Choice (J) places the sentence logically.

13. B
Category: Writing Strategy
Difficulty: Low
Getting to the Answer: Your Reading skills will be helpful in answering questions like this one. The two

topics of this essay are Cab Calloway and American Jazz. Choice (B) is the only choice that mentions both of these topics and relates them to one another. Choices A, C, and D all fail to mention American Jazz, the second main subject of the passage.

14. J
Category: Writing Strategy
Difficulty: Medium
Getting to the Answer: In addition to following the rules of grammar, style, and usage, the correct answer choice must also be consistent with the tone of the passage. The phrase "it'll stick around for a while" is too informal and slangy for the rest of this passage. Choice (J) matches the tone of the essay and provides a logical conclusion. Choice G is unnecessarily wordy. Choice H doesn't provide a logical conclusion to the passage; it concerns Jazz's popularity rather than its endurance.

15. A
Category: Writing Strategy
Difficulty: Medium
Getting to the Answer: Once you determine whether or not the passage satisfies the conditions in the question stem, you can immediately eliminate two of the four choices. First, you'll need to determine whether or not this essay focuses on "the history and development of American Jazz music." Since it does, you can eliminate both "no" choices, C and D. Now focus on the reasoning. Choice B misstates the information in the passage, which tells us that Jazz developed from folk music, not the other way around. Choice (A) is the correct choice here.

PASSAGE II

16. F
Category: Sentence Sense
Difficulty: Medium
Getting to the Answer: Approximately 25% of ACT English Test questions will require NO CHANGE. This sentence contains no error; (F) is correct. Choice G creates a run-on sentence. Choice H would be acceptable if the comma were placed after "world," but is incorrect punctuated this way. Choice J intro-

duces a verb tense that is inappropriate in context.

17. B
Category: Punctuation
Difficulty: Medium
Getting to the Answer: When commas are the issue, remember your tested rules. This sentence does not meet any of the tested conditions for proper comma usage; (B) is correct. Choice A separates the verb from its object. Choices C and D do not address the error; "said that" would be acceptable without the commas but, as written, these choices are incorrect.

18. H
Category: Verb Tenses
Difficulty: Medium
Getting to the Answer: Unless context tells you that more than one time frame is referred to, verb tenses should remain consistent. This sentence discusses something that happened in the past; (H) is correct. Choices F and G incorrectly use "went" with "has" and "had," respectively; the correct past participle for the verb to go is "gone." Choice J uses the present tense, which is incorrect in context.

19. C
Category: Wordiness
Difficulty: Low
Getting to the Answer: Many ACT Style questions will have four answer choices that are grammatically correct; your goal is to find the best one. "Because" is all that is needed here; (C) is the best choice. Choices A and B are unnecessarily wordy. Choice D creates an illogical relationship between the clauses; the editor's refusal to read hand-written manuscripts was the cause, not the result, of the grandfather's decision to buy a computer.

20. G
Category: Writing Strategy
Difficulty: High
Getting to the Answer: An added sentence or clause must be relevant to the topic of the passage and consistent with its tone. The theme of this passage up to this point is the grandfather's preference for

the old-fashioned way of doing things. Choice (G) provides a low-tech alternative to the Internet: "a set of encyclopedias." Choices F and H are redundant; we already know the World Wide Web is on the computer and that other people use it. Choice J is out of scope; nothing in the passage indicates that the writer's grandfather is concerned about computer viruses.

21. D
Category: Connections
Difficulty: Medium
Getting to the Answer: Make sure Connections words are both logical and necessary. This sentence needs nothing to link it to the sentence that precedes it. Choice (D) eliminates the unnecessary words. Choice A incorrectly uses "however" to link the two sentences. This would indicate that the second sentence contradicts the first, which it does not. Choice B uses "additionally," which means the second sentence is building upon the first sentence. This is not the case here either. "Conversely," in C, indicates a contradiction to what came before, which is inappropriate here.

22. H
Category: Punctuation
Difficulty: Medium
Getting to the Answer: Use commas only between items in a series of three or more items; a compound does not require a comma. This sentence treats the compound "feedback and praise" as two separate items in this series of clauses. The conjunction "and," however, is not correct between the first two items in a longer series. Choice (H) eliminates the incorrect comma. Choice G places a comma after the conjunction "and," which is not correct in a series. Choice J treats "from the publishing company" as an item in the series, which does not make sense in a list of uses for a computer.

23. D
Category: Connections
Difficulty: Medium
Getting to the Answer: Make sure Connections words properly relate the words or clauses they con-

nect. The second sentence here provides a different point than the first; Grandpa is saying that he can talk to interesting people for a long time or he can ignore uninteresting people. Choice (D) uses the appropriate connection. Choices A and B indicate that the second sentence will provide a specific example of the first, but this is not the case. Choice C suggests that the writer will introduce a contrasting perspective after discussing Grandpa's use of the "close" button, but she does not do so.

24. G
Category: Word Choice
Difficulty: Low
Getting to the Answer: When the underlined word is a pronoun, make sure its antecedent is clear and that it is in the proper case. Since you wouldn't say "them people," F is incorrect; *those* would be the proper pronoun here. However, since *those* is not among the answer choices, you'll need to find a logical replacement for the pronoun. Choice (G) correctly indicates who isn't interesting. Choice H incorrectly uses "it" to refer to people. Choice J creates a sentence that is grammatically incorrect.

25. A
Category: Punctuation
Difficulty: Medium
Getting to the Answer: If you read the sentence and don't find a problem with it, don't be afraid to choose NO CHANGE. It will be the correct choice about 25% of the time. This sentence contains no error; (A) is correct here. Choice B treats the phrase "which is very convenient" as nonessential information, but the sentence does not make sense without it. The second sentence created by C is a fragment. Choice D misuses the semicolon splice, which is only correct when combining two independent clauses.

26. J
Category: Sentence Sense
Difficulty: High
Getting to the Answer: When an entire sentence is underlined, choose the clearest revision. As written, this sentence is wordy and convoluted. While not much briefer, (J) is easier to understand; "in

merely a few seconds" is placed directly after the phrase it modifies, "being able to find anything he wants," and "for him" follows the phrase it modifies, "a source of pure joy." Choices F, G, and H are all less concise and more awkward than (J); additionally, Choice G incorrectly places a comma between the sentence's subject and predicate verb.

27. A
Category: Verb Tenses
Difficulty: Medium
Getting to the Answer: Unless context makes it clear that more than one time frame is being referenced, verb tenses should remain consistent. This sentence needs (A), NO CHANGE; the present tense is correct in context. Choices B and C create sentence fragments. Choice D introduces a verb tense that is inappropriate in context.

28. F
Category: Sentence Sense
Difficulty: Low
Getting to the Answer: Don't just read for errors in grammar and usage; read for logic as well. Here, (F) is the only choice that is both consistent with the passage and uses the proper contrast transition "but." Nothing in the passage indicates that Grandpa won't continue to explore the Internet, as G suggests, or that his editor believes this to be the case, as in J. Choice H doesn't follow logically from the first clause of the sentence.

29. B
Category: Organization
Difficulty: Medium
Getting to the Answer: When asked to add information, read the new sentence into the passage at the suggested points to determine its best placement. This sentence adds information about how Grandpa uses the websites he accesses, so placing it before sentence 1, as A suggests, is illogical. Choices C and D both place the new information too far from the discussion of Grandpa's use of the Internet. Choice (B) is the most logical place for this new sentence.

30. J
Category: Writing Strategy
Difficulty: Medium
Getting to the Answer: Whenever you are asked to consider deleting something, think about why the author included that information—what purpose does it serve? The first sentence of this passage tells us that Grandpa does not know how to use technology. This explains why Grandpa did not want to use the Internet; (J) is correct. Choice F misstates a detail from the passage; the sentence in question tells us only that Grandpa does not like to use technology, not the specific technologies he avoids. The first sentence is not particularly humorous, which eliminates G. Choice H can be eliminated as well, since no justification for Grandpa's technophobia is provided.

PASSAGE III

31. A
Category: Word Choice
Difficulty: Low
Getting to the Answer: Most Idioms question will hinge on preposition usage. This sentence needs (A), NO CHANGE; "In the twilight" is the appropriate idiom in this context. Choice B is idiomatically incorrect usage. Choices C and D would require more information to be correct; neither "With the twilight" nor "From the twilight" is an acceptable idiom by itself.

32. H
Category: Word Choice
Difficulty: High
Getting to the Answer: Some constructions might be grammatically correct but inappropriate in context. Although "more of the people who" is a grammatically correct construction, it is used incorrectly here, so F is incorrect. It was "most of the people" the writer did not know; (H) makes the correction without introducing a new error. Choice G does not address the error; additionally, it uses the objective pronoun form "whom" where "who" is correct. Choice J corrects the incorrect use of "more", but adds a new error by changing "who" to "whom."

33. D

Category: Writing Strategy
Difficulty: Medium
Getting to the Answer: Read question stems carefully and use Keywords to determine the correct answer choice. The Keyword in this question stem is "unity." Choice (D) mentions "kinship," which suggests a family-like relationship between the writer and the other walkers. Choice A indicates that the writer knew some of the people, but you can know people without feeling unity with them. Choice B's mention of each walker having his or her own reasons for being there suggests the opposite of unity. Being interested in knowing people, as C suggests, does not convey unity.

34. F

Category: Word Choice
Difficulty: Low
Getting to the Answer: Read question stems carefully to determine what the question is asking. Here, you are looking for the one unacceptable answer, which means that three of the choices will be appropriate in context. You can "journey over," "journey on," and "journey through" a territory; you cannot "journey among" it. Choices G, H, and J would be acceptable and (F) would not be acceptable, so (F) is the correct choice here.

35. B

Category: Writing Strategy
Difficulty: Medium
Getting to the Answer: Questions like this one require you to use the "purpose of a detail" skills from your Reading lessons. When a question stem asks you to determine what a paragraph would lose with information deleted, it's asking the purpose of that information. Here, what's being deleted is the information about the writer's destination; (B) is the correct choice. The phrase in question does not compare "the narrator's…journey" to any others or "establish the time and place of the events of the essay" as A and C suggest, nor is it "about the Chickasaw," as D suggests.

36. H

Category: Sentence Sense
Difficulty: High
Getting to the Answer: When all of the answer choices are wordier than the original selection, ask yourself if there is a grammatical or logical need for a longer phrase. As written, the sentence does not make clear whether the writer is talking about pictures *of* other Chickasaw or pictures *belonging to* other Chickasaw, so F is incorrect. Choice (H) makes this clear. Choice G is unnecessarily wordy. Choice J changes the meaning of the phrase, indicating that it was "Chickasaw," and not "pictures," that the writer had been shown.

37. D

Category: Punctuation
Difficulty: Medium
Getting to the Answer: Only very specific comma uses are tested on the ACT. If commas are used in any other way, they will be incorrect. The underlined selection does not meet any of the tested requirements for comma usage; (D) is correct. Choice A treats the phrase "who walked along with me" as nonessential information, but the sentence does not make sense without it. Choice B inserts a comma within a phrase modifying "people." Choice C treats another necessary phrase, "who walked along," as nonessential.

38. J

Category: Connections
Difficulty: High
Getting to the Answer: Each sentence in the passage must lead logically into the next. Look at the sentence preceding the selection and the one that follows. You need to find a choice that transitions from the idea of the pictures the writer had been shown and somewhere that "Books...were stacked on the bookshelves." (J) does this best. Choices F, G, and H all explain where the pictures came from but do not lead logically into the sentence that follows.

39. C
Category: Word Choice
Difficulty: Low
Getting to the Answer: Remember to read for logic as well as grammar and usage. We know there are two rooms: the father's and the grandmother's; (C) correctly conveys this. Choices A and D refer to a single room, but the writer has been talking about two rooms. Choice B seems to indicate that both rooms belong to the writer's grandmother, but this contradicts the passage.

40. J
Category: Connections
Difficulty: Medium
Getting to the Answer: Connection words, such as conjunctions, must logically join the ideas they are used to combine. The two clauses here do not relate to one another in a way that makes it logical for them to be joined into a single sentence; one clause concerns the rooms displaying pictures of Chickasaw and the other the writer's family's move to Seattle, so a change is needed and F is wrong. Choice (J) makes each clause a separate sentence. Choices G and H create run-on sentences.

41. C
Category: Writing Strategy
Difficulty: High
Getting to the Answer: When NO CHANGE is offered as an option, you'll need to determine the logic and relevance of any potential new material. The information in the underlined sentence, while related to the topic being discussed, does not logically lead from the idea that the writer and his family had moved to Seattle to the reason they were then unable to attend the Annual Meetings. This means you can eliminate A. By pointing out the location of these meetings, (C) connects the two ideas: the meetings were too far away from the family's new home. Choice B is out of scope—dancing at the Festivals is never mentioned in the passage—and still fails to logically connect the ideas. Choice D also fails to provide a logical reason for the writer's family not attending the meetings.

42. F
Category: Wordiness
Difficulty: Medium
Getting to the Answer: Be wary of answer choices that are significantly longer than the original selection. Barring errors of grammar or logic, these will be incorrect. There is no need to make this sentence any longer; (F) is correct. Choices G, H, and J are all wordier than the original and violate the parallel structure required for the compound "built and... conducted."

43. C
Category: Connections
Difficulty: Low
Getting to the Answer: Connections words and phrases must logically combine the ideas they connect. This sentence builds on the preceding one by giving more evidence to make the point of the first sentence. Choice (C) correctly reflects this relationship. Choices A and D use inappropriate contrast connections. Choice B indicates two events occurring simultaneously, which is illogical in context.

44. J
Category: Sentence Sense
Difficulty: Medium
Getting to the Answer: A sentence can have multiple verbs and still be a fragment. Remember, the –ing verb form by itself can never be the predicate (main) verb in a sentence. As written, this sentence is a fragment; neither clause is independent. Choice (J) gives the sentence a correct predicate verb, "chirped." Choices G and H do not address the error.

45. A
Category: Word Choice
Difficulty: Medium
Getting to the Answer: Some idiomatic phrases are only correct as part of a longer construction. Choice (A) is correct here; "like" can stand alone as a comparison in this context. Choice B does not properly complete the idiomatic construction "just as...so." Choice C uses the grammatically incorrect "as like." Choice D uses an idiom that means "for example," which is inappropriate in context.

PASSAGE IV

46. F
Category: Punctuation
Difficulty: Medium
Getting to the Answer: An introductory clause should be set off with a comma. This sentence is punctuated appropriately; (F) is correct. Choice G incorrectly places a comma and a coordinating conjunction between an independent clause and a prepositional phrase. The first sentence created by H is a fragment. Choice J improperly places a semicolon between an independent clause and a prepositional phrase.

47. C
Category: Punctuation
Difficulty: Medium
Getting to the Answer: When apostrophe use is the issue, use context to determine whether a plural or a possessive is required; eliminate answer choices that use the apostrophe in ways that are never correct. As written, this sentence uses the plural "days," which doesn't make sense in context, so you can eliminate A. Although there are circumstances in which a noun ending in *s* will be made possessive by adding 's, the rules for this usage are quite complicated and are not tested on the ACT; eliminate D. Since the sentence is discussing one specific day (December 6, 1884), the plural possessive in B can also be eliminated. "Day's," the singular possessive, is what is called for here; (C) is correct.

48. F
Category: Verb Tenses
Difficulty: Low
Getting to the Answer: Use context to determine the appropriate tense of underlined verbs. There is no contextual reason to change verb tenses in this sentence; since "rushed" is in the past tense, (F) "threatened" is correct. Choice G changes the meaning of the sentence, making the wind the object of the threat, rather than its cause. Choice H uses a tense that indicates actions that will happen in the future, but these actions have already occurred. Choice J uses the singular verb form "threatens" with the plural noun "winds."

49. D
Category: Wordiness
Difficulty: Low
Getting to the Answer: Whenever OMIT is presented as an option, check the underlined selection for relevance and redundancy. Here, "postpone" and "delay" mean essentially the same thing, so eliminate A; (D), OMIT, is the correct choice here. Choice B still contains redundant wording; "to a later time" is understood in "postpone." Choice C is also redundant; there is no other way to "postpone" something than "by delaying" it.

50. G
Category: Writing Strategy
Difficulty: Medium
Getting to the Answer: Remember your "purpose of a detail" skills from ACT Reading; that's what question stems like this one are asking for. Here, the phrase marked for deletion is the definition of "capstone ceremony"; (G) correctly explains what the essay would lose if the clause were deleted. Since the term "capstone ceremony" is not something most people are familiar with, this "detail" is not "minor," as F suggests. Nothing in the phrase reflects the writer's opinion or the ceremony's significance to the American people, which eliminates H and J.

51. A
Category: Punctuation
Difficulty: Medium
Getting to the Answer: Remember your tested comma rules; if a comma is used in any other way in the underlined selection, it will be incorrect. None of the conditions for comma usage are met by this sentence, so (A) is correct. Choices B and D insert commas between the two parts of a compound; this is never correct comma usage. Choice C treats "attorney and Congressman" as nonessential information, but leaving it out makes it unclear who John Marshall was.

52. H
Category: Writing Strategy
Difficulty: High
Getting to the Answer: When a question stem suggests deleting a sentence, first determine the

sentence's purpose in the passage. The sentence in question says that the monument was proposed to honor a war hero and president; (H)'s "background information about why Washington was being honored" is the purpose of this detail in the passage. Choice F is out of scope; the sentence merely tells us that Washington was a Revolutionary War hero, not what he did to become one. Choice G is also out of scope; nowhere in the passage is this discussed. Choice J is out of scope as well; the passage contains no biographical information about John Marshall.

53. C
Category: Sentence Sense
Difficulty: Medium
Getting to the Answer: A sentence may be a fragment even if it contains multiple nouns and verb forms. As written, this sentence consists of a single dependent clause, so eliminate A. Only (C) creates a complete sentence by adding an appropriate predicate verb, "planned." Choices B and D do not address the fragment error.

54. J
Category: Connections
Difficulty: Low
Getting to the Answer: When evaluating Connections words, consider the possibility that no Connection is needed. This sentence needs nothing to link it to the sentence that precedes it; (J) is the best choice here. Choice F indicates that the actions in the two sentences occurred concurrently, which is illogical. Choice G indicates that the second sentence is the result of the first, which also doesn't make sense in context. Choice H links the two sentences with a contrast Connection, which is inappropriate here as well.

55. A
Category: Word Choice
Difficulty: Medium
Getting to the Answer: If two answer choices mean the same thing and work in grammatically similar ways, you can eliminate them both, since only one answer choice can be correct. Since work was done on the monument, stopped, and then started again,

"resumed," (A), is the most appropriate. Choices B and C do not convey the idea that this work was a continuation of work that was done in the past. Choice D is redundant; "again" is indicated by the prefix *re–* in "restarted."

56. H
Category: Word Choice
Difficulty: Medium
Getting to the Answer: Replacing contractions with the full phrase can help you determine correct usage. "They're" is a contraction of they are, so first determine if the contraction is appropriate here. Since "during they are attempt" doesn't make sense, you can quickly eliminate F and G. Now turn to the difference between the remaining choices: the possessive "its" versus the contraction "it's." Try replacing the contraction with it is or it has; neither makes sense, so you can eliminate J as well. Choice (H) is correct here.

57. B
Category: Sentence Sense
Difficulty: Medium
Getting to the Answer: In most cases, a descriptive phrase will modify the first noun that follows it. As written, this sentence refers to the capstone as "attached to the top of the monument." However, this doesn't make sense, since the sentence concerns placing the capstone there, so eliminate A. Choice (B) creates the most logical sentence: The crowd cheers while the capstone is hoisted up, then the capstone is attached. Choices C and D make it sound as if the crowd, not the capstone, was "attached to the top of the monument."

58. J
Category: Wordiness
Difficulty: Low
Getting to the Answer: Look for words and phrases that mean the same thing; using them together will not be correct on the ACT. "Eight decades" and "eighty years" are the same amount of time. Choice (J) eliminates the redundancy. Choices F, G, and H all include redundant information.

59. B
Category: Writing Strategy
Difficulty: High
Getting to the Answer: Read question stems carefully. This one asks for the LEAST acceptable alternative, which means that three choices will work in context. "Conclusion," "completion," "end," and "halt" all have similar meanings but, in this context, "come to a halt" implies that the project was not completed. Since context tells us the project was completed, Choice (B) is the least acceptable choice. Choices A, C, and D would all be acceptable in context.

60. H
Category: Writing Strategy
Difficulty: Medium
Getting to the Answer: Question stems like this one appear frequently on the ACT. Answer the "yes" or "no" part of the question first, then tackle the reasoning behind your choice. The question stem asks if this essay would satisfy an assignment to write about "the entire process of designing and building the Washington Monument." Since the passage focuses primarily on the capstone ceremony, you can immediately eliminate the "yes" choices, F and G. Choice J's reasoning is that the essay focuses on "the early stages" of the monument's construction, but the opposite is true. Choice (H) is correct here.

PASSAGE V

61. A
Category: Punctuation
Difficulty: Medium
Getting to the Answer: Keep tested punctuation rules in mind; uses other than these will be incorrect on the ACT. This sentence is punctuated correctly; the phrase separated out by the commas is not essential to the meaning of the sentence. Choice (A) is correct. By eliminating the first comma, B incorrectly leaves the subject and verb of the sentence separated by a comma. Choice C misuses the colon which, on the ACT, will only be correct when used to introduce or emphasize a brief explanation, description, or list.

Choice D creates a sentence that is grammatically incorrect.

62. J
Category: Word Choice
Difficulty: Medium
Getting to the Answer: The test maker frequently places a plural object near a verb with a singular subject. Always determine the proper subject of an underlined noun; it will generally not be the noun closest to it in the sentence. The singular "Roaring," not the plural "lions," is the subject of the verb "perform," so eliminate F. Choice (J) puts the verb in the proper singular form without introducing any additional errors. Choice G does not address the error and also incorrectly places a comma between the verb and its object. Choice H corrects the agreement error, but also inserts the incorrect comma.

63. B
Category: Punctuation
Difficulty: High
Getting to the Answer: Always read for logic as well as usage and style. As written, this sentence uses the plural "these" to modify the singular "defense." This is incorrect, so eliminate A. By putting commas around "defense," (B) makes "One of these" refer to "functions," and identifies "defense" as a function of roaring. Choice C creates a sentence that is grammatically incorrect. Choice D is unnecessarily wordy.

64. J
Category: Sentence Sense
Difficulty: Medium
Getting to the Answer: There are several ways to correct a run-on sentence, but only one answer choice will do so without introducing any new errors. This sentence is a run-on; the underlined selection begins a new independent clause, which means F is incorrect. Choice (J) corrects the error by making the final clause dependent. Choice G does not address the error. Choice H eliminates the run-on error, but it is unnecessarily wordy.

65. A

Category: Connections

Difficulty: Low

Getting to the Answer: Read question stems carefully. You can determine the least acceptable Connections word simply by finding the one that is inconsistent with the other three. Because NO CHANGE is not given as an option, you're looking for the connection that cannot be substituted for "because." "In that," "since," and "as" can all mean "because"; therefore, B, C, and D are all considered acceptable. "Although" indicates contrast, not cause-and-effect, and is therefore considered unacceptable, so (A) is correct.

66. F

Category: Wordiness

Difficulty: Low

Getting to the Answer: Be suspicious of answer choices that are significantly longer than the original selection. They won't always be incorrect, but make sure the longer phrase is necessary for logic or grammatical correctness. There is no reason for a longer sentence; (F) is correct. Choices G, H, and J are all unnecessarily wordy.

67. C

Category: Word Choice

Difficulty: High

Getting to the Answer: Some Word Choice questions will require you to use skills you've learned in your Reading sessions. "Intense" means *extreme* or *forceful*, "cunning" means *clever*, "acute" means *extremely sharp or intense*, and "vivid" means *having the clarity and freshness of immediate experience*. Of these, the one most logical to modify "hearing" in this context is (C), "acute."

68. J

Category: Wordiness

Difficulty: Medium

Getting to the Answer: Use context clues to determine when words are used redundantly. Something that is described as "everyday" can be assumed to be done "frequently"; (J) eliminates the redundancy.

Choices F, G, and H all use words or phrases that are redundant with "everyday."

69. B

Category: Writing Strategy

Difficulty: High

Getting to the Answer: Remember the first rule in the Kaplan Method: Read until you have enough information to answer the question. The second clause here tells us the pride members have to "reunite," so the logical answer choice will concern their being separated. Choice (B) is the choice most consistent with the question stem. Neither A nor D involve the pride becoming separated. Although C mentions the pride traveling, it does not indicate that they become separated when they do so.

70. F

Category: Connections

Difficulty: Medium

Getting to the Answer: Connections words and phrases must logically transition between the ideas they combine. Each paragraph in this essay describes a way in which roaring helps lions survive. This paragraph discusses the final use lions have for their roars; "Finally" is the best Connection here, so (F) is correct. Choice G uses "nevertheless," which indicates a contrast that is not present here. Choice H uses "second," but this is the essay's third point. Choice J signifies a conclusion, which is inappropriate in this context.

71. B

Category: Sentence Sense

Difficulty: Low

Getting to the Answer: Run-on sentences can be corrected in a number of ways, but only one answer choice will do so without introducing additional errors. As written, this sentence is a run-on, so you can eliminate A right away. Choices (B), C, and D all make the second clause dependent, but only (B) follows the rules of parallel structure required in the series "roaring...displaying...and fighting."

72. G

Category: Punctuation

Difficulty: High

Getting to the Answer: Commas are never correct when used to separate a subject and verb. As written, the sentence treats the word "dominant" as nonessential information, so F is incorrect; however, the sentence does not make sense without it. Choice (G) correctly sets off the phrase "or dominant" from the rest of the sentence; the sentence is still both logical and grammatically correct with this information removed. Choice H incorrectly places a comma between a subject and its predicate verb. Choice J places a comma after a non-coordinating conjunction, which is also incorrect.

73. D

Category: Sentence Sense

Difficulty: Medium

Getting to the Answer: In most cases, the passive voice will make a sentence unnecessarily wordy and may cause modifier errors as well. This sentence is written in the passive voice, making it unclear what the phrase "by the roaring" is intended to modify, so A is incorrect. Choice (D) creates the clearest sentence. The passive voice in B and C makes them unnecessarily wordy.

74. J

Category: Word Choice

Difficulty: Medium

Getting to the Answer: Don't mistake the object of a preposition for the subject of a verb. Here, the plural "males" is the object of the preposition "of"; the subject of the verb here in the singular "roaring." Choice F is incorrect; G, H, and (J) all correct the agreement error, but G and H are unnecessarily wordy.

75. D

Category: Punctuation

Difficulty: Medium

Getting to the Answer: Remember your tested comma rules. If a sentence doesn't satisfy one or more of those requirements, commas will be incorrect. This sentence does not meet any of the tested requirements for comma usage; (D) is correct. Choice A puts a comma between the sentence's subject and its predicate verb. Choice B incorrectly places a comma between "that" and the clause it introduces. The comma in C separates the verb "is" from its object.

MATHEMATICS TEST

1. E

Category: Proportions and Probability

Difficulty: Low

Getting to the Answer: This is a great question for Backsolving, because you know 20% of the answer should turn out to be 10. Alternatively, you could use your knowledge that $\text{Percent} = \dfrac{\text{part}}{\text{whole}} \cdot 100\%$ to set up an equation. Let x be the number of students in the class. Then 20% of x is 10:

$0.2x = 10$

$\quad x = 50$, (E)

2. J

Category: Plane Geometry

Difficulty: Low

Getting to the Answer: Questions like this are simply testing whether you remember how many degrees are in a line. Remember that the arc between two points on a line is a half circle, or 180°.

$20° + 40° + x° = 180°$

$\qquad x° = 120°$, (J)

3. A

Category: Patterns, Logic, & Data

Difficulty: Low

Getting to the Answer: Even if you forget what "arithmetic" means, you should still be able to recognize the pattern. Each term is 3 less than the previous term.

Fourth term = $1 - 3 = -2$

Fifth term = $(-2) - 3 = -5$, (A)

Be sure not to stop too soon—the fourth term is a tempting, but wrong, answer choice.

4. K

Category: Proportions and Probability

Difficulty: Low

Getting to the Answer: Whenever you see a proportion (two fractions set equal to each other), you can cross-multiply to solve.

$$\frac{20}{8} = \frac{c}{10}$$

$$20(10) = 8c$$

$$c = 25, (K)$$

5. C

Category: Coordinate Geometry

Difficulty: Low

Getting to the Answer: On problems like this without a diagram, drawing one is an excellent idea. $\overline{GK} \cong \overline{HK}$ means that the line segments $\overline{GK}$ and $\overline{HK}$ are congruent, or equal in length. For these two segments to have equal lengths, the points must be arranged like this:

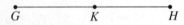

K is the midpoint of $\overline{GH}$, so (C) is correct.

6. F

Category: Operations

Difficulty: Low

Getting to the Answer: On early problems, you can sometimes let your calculator do most of the work for you. Yarn cut off = 4(1.2) = 4.8 yards. Yarn remaining = 50 – 4.8 = 45.2 yards, (F).

7. B

Category: Variable Manipulation

Difficulty: Low

Getting to the Answer: Be careful with positives and negatives, and remember to follow the order of operations. You can count on some of the wrong answer choices resulting from careless mistakes.

$$14 - 3[(-2) + 3]$$

$$= 14 - 3(1)$$

$$= 11, (B)$$

8. H

Category: Operations

Difficulty: Low

Getting to the Answer: Use the order of operations. In PEMDAS, absolute value counts as parentheses, so you must evaluate it first.

$$-|-6| - (-6)$$

$$= -(6) - (-6)$$

$$= -6 + 6$$

$$= 0, (H)$$

9. C

Category: Proportions and Probability

Difficulty: Low

Getting to the Answer: Remembering how to convert between percents, fractions, and decimals will be a key skill on the ACT.

15% of 3,200 = 0.15(3,200) = 480

3,200 + 480 = 3,680, (C)

10. G

Category: Operations

Difficulty: Low

Getting to the Answer: You can use your calculator to quickly find the fourth root of 90, or you can compare the fourth power of the integers in the answer choices.

$$2^4 = 16$$

$$3^4 = 81$$

$$4^4 = 256$$

If $x^4 = 90$, then x must be between 3 and 4, because 90 is between 3^4 and 4^4, so (G) is correct.

11. B

Category: Variable Manipulation

Difficulty: Low

Getting to the Answer: You can use your calculator for the arithmetic here. It will take only a few seconds and will help you avoid mistakes.

$$47 - x = 188$$

$$47 = 188 + x$$

$$-141 = x, (B)$$

12. K
Category: Variable Manipulation
Difficulty: Low
Getting to the Answer: Don't jump at the first answer that seems right; on the other hand, don't think that the most complicated answer has to be right, either!
Time for Group C = h
Time for Group B = $2h$
Time for Group A = $8 + 2h$, (K)

13. E
Category: Coordinate Geometry
Difficulty: Low
Getting to the Answer: Draw a quick sketch. Notice that the answers are fairly different, so you just need a general idea in order to get the correct answer.

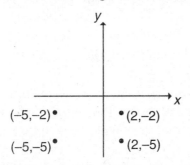

As you can see in the diagram above, the fourth coordinate must be (E), (–5,–5).

14. J
Category: Variable Manipulation
Difficulty: Low
Getting to the Answer: Before you try anything too fancy, check for like terms. Combine the like variables $5a$ and $3a$ to find that $5a - 5b + 3a = 8a - 5b$, (J).

15. E
Category: Plane Geometry
Difficulty: Medium
Getting to the Answer: Even if you forget all the properties of a parallelogram, you can figure out problems like this by using the fact that opposite sides are parallel. Redraw the diagram, and it's clear that *FEG* and *EGD* are alternate interior angles.

Therefore, the measure of *FEG* is also 70°, so (E) is correct.

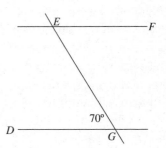

16. G
Category: Coordinate Geometry
Difficulty: Medium
Getting to the Answer: The easiest way to find the slope of a line is to write the equation in slope-intercept form, $y = mx + b$.
$$4x + 3y = 9$$
$$3y = -4x + 9$$
$$y = -\frac{4}{3}x + 3$$
The slope, m, is the coefficient of x, or $-\frac{4}{3}$, which matches (G).

17. C
Category: Variable Manipulation
Difficulty: Medium
Getting to the Answer: When you need to factor a quadratic equation, make sure one side is equal to zero before you begin. Then you know that one factor or the other must be equal to zero. Because 3 is a prime number, the two binomial factors must look like $(3x \pm \_\_)(x \pm \_\_)$. One of the last two numbers must be positive and the other negative, because they multiply to a negative number (–20). At this point you can use trial and error with the factors of –20 to find $(3x + 5)(x - 4) = 0$. If the product is equal to zero, then one of the factors must be equal to zero, so $3x + 5 = 0$ or $x - 4 = 0$. The left equation gives you a negative value for x, which contradicts the question stem, while the right equation gives you $x = 4$, which matches (C).

18. F

Category: Plane Geometry

Difficulty: Medium

Getting to the Answer: In similar shapes, each side is scaled up or down by the same factor, and the perimeter is scaled up or down by that same factor. The perimeter of the original triangle is $2 + 5 + 8 = 15$. Because the similar triangle has a perimeter twice as long, each side must also be twice as long. The smallest side is $2(2) = 4$, (F).

19. D

Category: Proportions and Probability

Difficulty: Low

Getting to the Answer: You can often save a step in percentage problems if you figure out what percentage is left. If the shirt is 15% off, then the sale price is $100\% - 15\% = 85\%$ of the original price. $\$24.60(0.85) = \$20.91 \approx \$21$, (D).

20. G

Category: Variable Manipulation

Difficulty: Medium

Getting to the Answer: One way to tackle problems like this is to multiply out the factored answers to see if they match the expression in the problem. Each term has a 3, an x, and a y, so you can take out a greatest common factor of $3xy$. What's left from each factor when you divide this out? The first term has no more coefficient or x, and it has 3 ys left, so the term turns into y^3. Similarly, the second term becomes x^3. The factored form is (G), $3xy(y^3 + x^3)$, which you can check by distributing.

21. D

Category: Variable Manipulation

Difficulty: Medium

Getting to the Answer: If the question asks you for x, that means you don't care about y—get rid of it! You can eliminate y using one of two methods.

Substitution:

$$3x + y = 7$$
$$y = 7 - 3x$$
$$x - 2y = x - 2(7 - 3x) = 0$$
$$x - 14 + 6x = 0$$
$$7x = 14$$
$$x = 2, \text{(D)}$$

Combination:

Multiply the second equation by 2: $2(3x + y) = 2(7)$

$$6x + 2y = 14$$

Add to the first equation:

$$
\begin{aligned}
6x + 2y &= 14 \\
+ x - 2y &= 0 \\
\hline
7x &= 14 \\
x &= 2
\end{aligned}
$$

22. F

Category: Operations

Difficulty: Low

Getting to the Answer: Writing out the units on conversion problems will help you avoid mistakes. First find the cost per yard: $\dfrac{4.50 \text{ dollars}}{2.5 \text{ yards}} = 1.80 \dfrac{\text{dollars}}{\text{yards}}$.

Then find the cost per foot (notice that yards cancel):

$1.80 \dfrac{\text{dollars}}{\text{yards}} \cdot \dfrac{1 \text{ yard}}{3 \text{ feet}} = 0.60 \dfrac{\text{dollars}}{\text{foot}}$, (F)

23. C

Category: Plane Geometry

Difficulty: High

Getting to the Answer: Sometimes the answer choices give you a hint about how to solve the problem. Here, they are simple enough that you know you don't have to do any fancy calculations. In fact, they're different enough that you might even be able to eyeball the answer. Draw in lines that go from the center of the square to the edge at right angles.

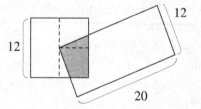

The gray triangle is the same size as the white triangle. (The portion of the upper 90° angle formed by the gray triangle is the same as the portion of the rectangle's 90° angle formed by the gray triangle. Therefore, the portion of the lower 90° angle formed by the white triangle is also the same.) If you move the gray triangle to where the white triangle is, the shaded area is exactly $\dfrac{1}{4}$ of the square.

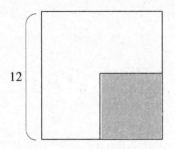

Because the area of the square is 12 · 12 = 144, the area of the shaded region is $\frac{1}{4}$ (144) = 36, (C).

24. F
Category: Operations
Difficulty: Low
Getting to the Answer: Questions like this may seem complicated at first, but all you need to do is plug the given numbers into the formula.

$h = 15$ and $s = 120.50$
$7h + 0.04s$
$= 7(15) + 0.04(120.50)$
$= 105 + 4.82$
$= 109.82$, (F)

25. D
Category: Plane Geometry
Difficulty: Low
Getting to the Answer: Whenever you're faced with an odd shape, try to divide it into two or more shapes that are familiar. This shape can be divided into two rectangles. The width of the smaller one is the difference between the width of the entire shape and the width of the larger rectangle, or 22 – 14 = 8. The area of any rectangle is length times width.

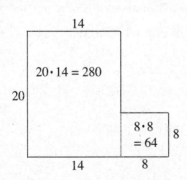

The total area of this shape is 280 + 64 = 344, (D).

26. G
Category: Variable Manipulation
Difficulty: Low
Getting to the Answer: Don't forget that inequalities work exactly the same as equalities, except that the direction of the sign changes when you multiply or divide by a negative number. $x - 2 < -4$ Add 2 to both sides: $x < -2$ Everything less than –2 is everything to the left of –2, exactly what (G) shows.

27. E
Category: Operations
Difficulty: Low
Getting to the Answer: On the ACT Mathematics test, you have an average of one minute per question. If a problem can be solved quickly using your calculator, take advantage of it. For example, you can use your calculator to compare fractions by finding the decimal equivalents.

$\frac{3}{5} = 0.6$

A: $\frac{4}{6} = 0.\overline{66}$

B: $\frac{8}{13} = 061538...$

C: $\frac{6}{10} = 0.6$

D: $\frac{7}{11} = 0.\overline{63}$

(E): $\frac{4}{7} = 0.57142...$

Only (E) is smaller than 0.6.

28. G
Category: Plane Geometry
Difficulty: Medium
Getting to the Answer: In a right triangle, the hypotenuse is always the longest side, and the other two sides are the legs.
The legs are 7 and 24. Area $= \frac{1}{2}bh$

$= \left(\frac{1}{2}\right)(7)(24)$

$= 84$, (G)

29. D

Category: Number Properties

Difficulty: Medium

Getting to the Answer: You need to figure out how to turn this word problem into math. If the last row is one person short of 6, how does the number of students relate to multiples of 6? This is just another way of saying that the number of students is one less than a multiple of 6, one less than a multiple of 7, and one less than a multiple of 8. The least common multiple of 6, 7, and 8 is 168. One less is 167, (D). You can find the least common multiple by finding the prime factors of each number:

$6 = 2 \cdot 3$

$7 = 7$

$8 = 2 \cdot 2 \cdot 2$

To have all these factors in one number, you need one 3, one 7, and three 2s, or $3 \cdot 7 \cdot 2 \cdot 2 \cdot 2 = 168$. E produces the right arrangement, but it is not the smallest possible number. Choice A is 2 *more* then a multiple of 7, which means the last row will have 2 people (or be 5 people short). Choice B is 1 *more* than a multiple of 8, which means the last row will be 7 people short. Choice C is 1 *more* than a multiple of 7, which means the last row will be 6 people short.

30. F

Category: Plane Geometry

Difficulty: Low

Getting to the Answer: There will usually be one question that tests your knowledge of the Triangle Inequality Theorem. If you're not sure how to proceed, try drawing a sketch. The Triangle Inequality Theorem states that any side of a triangle is less than the sum of and more than the difference between the other two, so the third side must be at least $6 - 3.5 = 2.5$ inches. Choice (F) is too small.

31. C

Category: Variable Manipulation

Difficulty: Medium

Getting to the Answer: Fractions are always added in the same way, whether they include variables or not. You must write both fractions in terms of a common denominator, then add the numerators.

$$\frac{4}{5} = \frac{4b}{5b}$$

$$\frac{1}{b} = \frac{5}{5b}$$

$$\frac{4b}{5b} + \frac{5}{5b} = \frac{4b+5}{5b}, \text{(C)}$$

32. F

Category: Plane Geometry

Difficulty: Medium

Getting to the Answer: In the Pythagorean Theorem, $a^2 + b^2 = c^2$, c represents the hypotenuse (the longest side).

$$a^2 + b^2 = c^2$$

$$17^2 + b^2 = 21^2$$

$$b^2 = 21^2 - 17^2$$

$$b = \sqrt{21^2 - 17^2}, \text{(F)}$$

33. E

Category: Variable Manipulation

Difficulty: Medium

Getting to the Answer: When you multiply binomials, don't forget to use FOIL. If you only multiply the first terms together and the last terms together, you're missing two terms.

The new length is $b + 2$, and the new width is $b + 3$.

$$\text{Area} = l \cdot w$$

$$= (b + 2)(b + 3)$$

$$= b^2 + 3b + 2b + 6$$

$$= b^2 + 5b + 6, \text{(E)}$$

34. G

Category: Trigonometry

Difficulty: Low

Getting to the Answer: If you have sine and cosine, find tangent using the formula $\tan x = \dfrac{\sin x}{\cos x}$.

$$\tan x = \frac{\sin x}{\cos x} = \frac{\frac{8}{17}}{\frac{15}{17}} = \frac{8}{17} \cdot \frac{17}{15} = \frac{8}{15}, \text{(G)}$$

35. E
Category: Variable Manipulation
Difficulty: Medium
Getting to the Answer: If you're not sure which answer is correct, try plugging in points from the number line. The shaded region includes all the values between –1.5 and –2.5. Because –1.5 is larger than –2.5, the inequality should be $-1.5 > x > -2.5$. Plugging in $x = -2 \cdot 2.5$ eliminates A, B, and D. Choice C includes numbers that aren't in the shaded region, such as –2.9, so (E) is correct.

36. J
Category: Operations
Difficulty: Medium
Getting to the Answer: To make the question a little easier to follow, Pick Numbers for the total number of baskets. Imagine that they made a total of 100 baskets. If the team made 100 baskets, then they made 20 1-point baskets, 70 2-point baskets, and 10 3-point baskets. The average point value of all the baskets is the total number of points divided by the total number of baskets:

$$\frac{20(1) + 70(2) + 10(3)}{100}$$
$$= \frac{20 + 140 + 30}{100}$$
$$= \frac{190}{100}$$
$$= 1.9, (J)$$

37. D
Category: Plane Geometry
Difficulty: Medium
Getting to the Answer: If you can use 45-45-90 triangles or 30-60-90 triangles instead of trigonometry, do it. (Similarly, look for the Pythagorean Triplets before you use the Pythagorean Theorem.) The sides in a 30-60-90 triangle are in the ratio $x : x\sqrt{3} : 2x$. You have been given the side opposite the 30 degree angle, which is x. You want the side opposite the 90 degree angle, which is $2x$. Because $x = 3$, $CE = 2x = 6$, (D).

38. K
Category: Number Properties
Difficulty: Medium
Getting to the Answer: On this type of problem, you want the numbers to be either as close together or as far apart as possible. Try a few possibilities; you should see a pattern.
$3 \cdot 39 = 117$
$5 \cdot 37 = 185$
$7 \cdot 35 = 245$
The products are increasing, so it looks like you want the two numbers to be as close together as possible. Because half of 42 is 21, try $21 \cdot 21 = 441$. Because (K) is the largest possible answer choice, you can be sure it's correct.

39. B
Category: Plane Geometry
Difficulty: Medium
Getting to the Answer: Parallel lines provide lots of information—look for congruent and supplementary angles.

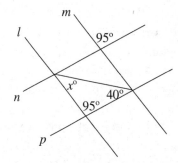

Because both sets of lines are parallel, the missing angle in the triangle corresponds to the angle marked 95°. The three interior angles of the triangle sum to 180°.
$40° + 95° + x° = 180°$
$x° = 45°$, (B)

40. F
Category: Coordinate Geometry
Difficulty: Medium
Getting to the Answer: Don't jump right in to using your graphing calculator; often some simple algebra is the best route to the correct answer. The easiest way to find the y-intercept (the value of y

when the graph crosses the *y*-axis) is to plug in $x = 0$:

$$12(0) - 3y = 12$$
$$-3y = 12$$
$$y = -4, \text{(F)}$$

41. B

Category: Operations

Difficulty: Medium

Getting to the Answer: If the labels are missing on a number line, you can find the length of each interval by finding the difference in the endpoints (how much the total interval is) and dividing by the number of subintervals. The unmarked interval goes from 2.7 to 2.8, so it must be 0.1 units long. It's divided into 10 equally spaced subintervals, each of which must be $\frac{0.1}{10} = 0.01$ units long.

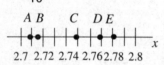

$$A \ B \qquad C \quad D \ E$$
$$2.7 \ 2.72 \ 2.74 \ 2.76 \ 2.78 \ 2.8$$

E is approximately 2.718, so you want a point between 2.71 and 2.72. Choice (B) is the closest.

42. G

Category: Coordinate Geometry

Difficulty: High

Getting to the Answer: If a system has no solution, there are no values of *x* and *y* that make both equations true. If a system has infinitely many solutions, then every set of *x* and *y* that works in one equation will also work in the other. These two linear equations will have no solutions (points of intersection) if they are parallel. Write both equations in slope-intercept form, then set the slopes equal and solve for *a*.

$$-x + 6y = 7$$
$$6y = x + 7$$
$$y = \frac{1}{6}x + \frac{7}{6}$$

$$-5x + 10ay = 32$$
$$10ay = 5x + 32$$
$$y = \frac{5}{10a}x + \frac{32}{10a}$$

$$\frac{1}{6} = \frac{5}{10a}$$
$$10a = 30$$
$$a = 3, \text{(G)}$$

43. C

Category: Plane Geometry

Difficulty: Medium

Getting to the Answer: "If and only if" means the answer always gives you an obtuse angle, and it gives you all obtuse angles. An angle is obtuse if its measure is between 90° and 180°, non-inclusive. That's everything wider than a right angle and smaller than a straight line. Try plugging in the end values of each range. A: $0 < x < 90 : 360 - 0 = 360$, $360 - 90 = 270$. This answer gives angles from 270° to 360°. B: $0 < x < 180 : 360 - 0 = 360$, $360 - 180 = 180$. This answer gives angles from 180° to 360°. (C): $180 < x < 270 : 360 - 180 = 180$, $360 - 270 = 90$. This answer gives angles from 90° to 180°—exactly what you're looking for. D: $180 < x < 360 : 360 - 180 = 180$, $360 - 360 = 0$. This answer gives angles from 0° to 180°. E: $270 < x < 360 : 360 - 270 = 90$, $360 - 360 = 0$. This answer gives angles from 0° to 90°. Only (C) gives the entire set of obtuse angles and nothing more.

44. G

Category: Variable Manipulation

Difficulty: Medium

Getting to the Answer: Always be on the lookout for the three classic quadratics—they'll save you a lot of time.

$$p^2 - q^2 = (p + q)(p - q)$$
$$= (-3)(-4)$$
$$= 12, \text{(G)}$$

45. D

Category: Plane Geometry

Difficulty: Low

Getting to the Answer: Remember, time is short on the ACT. Do they really expect you to apply something like the law of cosines here? If you recognized the Pythagorean Triplet (3:4:5) scaled up by 2, then you realized that this is a right triangle. The right angle is always between the two shortest sides (and opposite the longest side, the hypotenuse), so the angle is 90 degrees, (D).

46. H
Category: Coordinate Geometry
Difficulty: Medium
Getting to the Answer: Be sure to read the question carefully. This one gives you an equation where x is in terms of y, not y in terms of x. First, translate the description into an equation: $x = 9 + 3y$. Then put it into slope-intercept form:

$$x = 9 + 3y$$

$$\frac{1}{3}x - 3 = y$$

The slope is the coefficient of x, which is $\frac{1}{3}$, (H).

47. E
Category: Trigonometry
Difficulty: High
Getting to the Answer: Use SOHCAHTOA. When you're presented with a trigonometry problem, your first step should be to identify the sides you're given and the side you're trying to find. Then figure out which trig function gives you a relationship between the side you know and the side you want to know. The distance between the cliff and the house is opposite the given angle. The height of the cliff is adjacent. The trig function that gives a relationship between the opposite and the adjacent sides is tangent.

$$\tan 62^\circ = \frac{500}{\text{height}}$$

$$\text{height} \cdot \tan 62^\circ = 500$$

$$\text{height} = \frac{500}{\tan 62^\circ}, \text{(E)}$$

48. H
Category: Number Properties
Difficulty: Medium
Getting to the Answer: Prime factorizations can help you find the greatest common factor and least common multiple.

$9 = 3 \cdot 3$
$18 = 2 \cdot 3 \cdot 3$
$27 = 3 \cdot 3 \cdot 3$
$54 = 2 \cdot 3 \cdot 3 \cdot 3$

	GCF	LCM
9 and 18	$3 \cdot 3 = 9$	$2 \cdot 3 \cdot 3 = 18$
9 and 27	$3 \cdot 3 = 9$	$3 \cdot 3 \cdot 3 = 27$
18 and 27	$3 \cdot 3 = 9$	$2 \cdot 3 \cdot 3 \cdot 3 = 54$
18 and 54	$2 \cdot 3 \cdot 3 = 18$	$2 \cdot 3 \cdot 3 \cdot 3 = 54$
27 and 54	$3 \cdot 3 \cdot 3 = 27$	$2 \cdot 3 \cdot 3 \cdot 3 = 54$

Only (H) fits the description. All the other pairs have either a lower common multiple or a greater common factor.

49. D
Category: Patterns, Logic, & Data
Difficulty: High
Getting to the Answer: You can make abstract questions like this one easier to handle by Picking Numbers. Be sure the numbers you pick obey any restrictions in the question stem. Try $k = 2$ and $x = 4$. (These numbers will make the radical in E easy to calculate.)

A $b(4) = \dfrac{2}{4} = \dfrac{1}{2}$

B $b(4) = \dfrac{4}{2} = 2$

C $b(4) = 2(4) = 8$

D $b(4) = 4^2 = 16$

E $b(4) = \sqrt[2]{4} = 2$

The largest $b(x)$ is (D). When this is plugged into $a(b(x)) = 5^{b(x)}$, the largest value of $b(x)$ will produce the largest value of $a(b(x))$. For the values of k and x allowed in this question, (D) is always the largest, so it is correct. Another way to approach this problem is to use a graphing calculator. Pick a value for k, then graph each answer choice on your calculator at the same time to see which one has the largest value when x is greater than 2.

50. J
Category: Trigonometry
Difficulty: High
Getting to the Answer: If you're not sure where to get started, try working backwards. What are you looking for? The cosine of $\angle ZWY$. What do you need to find that? The lengths of the hypotenuse and the adjacent leg, WZ and WY. How can you find those

lengths? By using the given side lengths and your knowledge of right triangles. Now that you've figured out how to get from what you have to what you need, you can go ahead and get there. *WXY* is a right triangle. You know that *WX* is 12 and *XY* is 5, so *WY* must be 13. If you didn't spot the 5:12:13 triplet, you could have used the Pythagorean Theorem.) *WYZ* is also a right triangle. You know that *WY* and *YZ* are both 13, so *WZ* must be $13\sqrt{2}$. (Again, you could have used the Pythagorean Theorem if you didn't spot the 45–45–90 triangle.) The cosine of an angle is the adjacent leg over the hypotenuse, so the cosine of $\angle ZWY$ is *WY* over *WZ*, or $\dfrac{13}{13\sqrt{2}} = \dfrac{1}{\sqrt{2}} = \dfrac{\sqrt{2}}{2}$.

51. B
Category: Plane Geometry
Difficulty: Low
Getting to the Answer: On circle questions, it's important to distinguish between radius and diameter.

$$\text{Area} = \pi r^2 = 4\pi$$
$$r^2 = 4$$
$$r = 2, \text{ (B)}$$

52. K
Category: Coordinate Geometry
Difficulty: Medium
Getting to the Answer: Lines with positive slope rise to the right, and lines with negative slope rise to the left. The lines have the same *y*-intercept, so line *q* must also have "+ *b*" at the end of its equation. You may have been fooled by the fact that *b* is negative, but imagine that the *y*-intercept was at –2: The equation would be $y = mx + (-2)$. This eliminates F, G, and J. Line *l* has a negative slope, so $m < 0$, and line *q* has a positive slope. Because $\dfrac{1}{2}m < 0$, this cannot be the slope of line *q*, so its equation must be $y = -\dfrac{1}{2}mx + b$, (K).

53. D
Category: Variable Manipulation
Difficulty: Medium
Getting to the Answer: When you solve a quadratic equation by factoring, each factor will give you a solution. If the equation has only one solution, that

means the factors are the same. To get a middle term of –6*x*, you must have factors of $(x - 3)(x - 3)$. Multiply it out to get $(x - 3)(x - 3) = x^2 - 3x - 3x + 9 = x^2 - 6x + 9$. This means that $k = 9$, (D).

54. K
Category: Coordinate Geometry
Difficulty: Low
Getting to the Answer: Most coordinate geometry questions rely on the slope. Make sure you remember that slope is $\dfrac{\text{rise}}{\text{run}}$.

$$\frac{y_2 - y_1}{x_2 - x_1} = \frac{\dfrac{3}{4} - 0}{\dfrac{1}{3} - 0}$$
$$= \frac{\dfrac{3}{4}}{\dfrac{1}{3}}$$
$$= \frac{3}{4} \cdot \frac{3}{1}$$
$$= \frac{9}{4}, \text{ (K)}$$

55. A
Category: Number Properties
Difficulty: Medium
Getting to the Answer: Don't accidentally add your own assumptions. For example, the question never says that the variables are integers. (A) is true. It follows immediately from dividing both sides by *S*. Choices B, C, and E are disproved by $R = -3$, $S = -2$, and $T = \dfrac{1}{3}$. Choice D can never be true, because then the product would be 0.

56. H
Category: Plane Geometry
Difficulty: High
Getting to the Answer: Although this is a geometry question, the part that's most likely to trip you up is the variable manipulation. Work carefully, and remember that you can Pick Numbers if you run into trouble with *w*. The area of the square is $(w + 5)^2 = w^2 + 10w + 25$. The area of the rectangle is $(w + 2)(w - 3) = w^2 - w - 6$. The area of the square after the

rectangle is removed is $w^2 + 10w + 25 - (w^2 - w - 6) = 11w + 31$, (H). If you had any trouble with the math, Picking Numbers can simplify things. Let $w = 5$. Then the square has sides of length 10 and an area of 100. The rectangle's sides are length 7 and length 2, so its area is 14. The area of the square after the rectangle is removed is $100 - 14 = 86$. Plug $w = 5$ into each answer choice to find that only (H) equals 86.

57. C

Category: Trigonometry
Difficulty: Medium
Getting to the Answer: First figure out where sine reaches a minimum, then worry about where the 2θ comes in. The sine function first reaches its minimum of -1 at $\dfrac{3\pi}{2}$, so:

$$2\theta = \frac{3\pi}{2}$$

$$\theta = \frac{3\pi}{4}, \text{(C)}$$

58. K

Category: Coordinate Geometry
Difficulty: High
Getting to the Answer: Backsolving is a great option here if you're not sure how to set this problem up algebraically or if you're not confident about your variable manipulation skills. Plug the given coordinates into the distance formula ($\sqrt{(x_1 - x_2)^2 + (y_1 - y_2)^2}$), set the distance equal to 4, and solve for r:

$$\sqrt{(r-10)^2 + (6-r)^2} = 4$$
$$(r-10)^2 + (6-r)^2 = 16$$
$$(r^2 - 20r + 100) + (36 - 12r + r^2) = 16$$
$$2r^2 - 32r + 136 = 16$$
$$2r^2 - 32r + 120 = 0$$
$$r^2 - 16r + 60 = 0$$
$$(r-10)(r-6) = 0$$
$$r = 10 \text{ or } r = 6$$

Only 10 is an answer choice, so (K) is correct. To Backsolve, you still need to know the distance formula to figure out whether F, G, H, and J are correct, but notice that (K) gives the points (10,6) and (10,10).

Because the x-coordinate is the same, you can see that the distance between the points is $10 - 6 = 4$ without using the formula.

59. D

Category: Proportions and Probability
Difficulty: Medium
Getting to the Answer: This is a great candidate for Backsolving. For each answer, add that number to 5 to find the total. Is the probability of getting a nickel $\dfrac{1}{6}$? You know that $\dfrac{1}{6}$ of the total should be 5 nickels. Let x be the total:

$$\frac{1}{6}x = 5$$
$$x = 30$$

If the total is 30, the number of pennies is $30 - 5 = 25$, (D).

60. K

Category: Variable Manipulation
Difficulty: High
Getting to the Answer: Each question is worth the same amount, so don't spend too much time on any one. Problems that ask how many different values of something there are tend to be particularly lengthy, so it's a good idea to save them for the end of the test. One way to solve this is to make all of the numerators 3:

$$\frac{3}{15} < \frac{3}{x} < \frac{3}{9}$$

This inequality is true for all values of x between 9 and 15. That's 10, 11, 12, 13, and 14: five integer values of x, making (K) correct. You can also solve this algebraically. The fastest way is to first take the reciprocals, which will reverse the inequalities (Because $\dfrac{1}{3} < \dfrac{1}{2}$ but $3 > 2$):

$$5 > \frac{x}{3} > 3$$

Multiply everything by 3 to find $15 > x > 9$. Again, the five integer values of x are 10, 11, 12, 13, and 14. There are five different integer values of x, so (K) is correct.

READING TEST

PASSAGE I

1. D
Category: Detail
Difficulty: Medium
Getting to the Answer: Good notes will help lead you quickly to the section of the passage you need to research. In lines 25–30, Giovanni notices "one shrub in particular" that seems to "illuminate the garden." The plant he is speaking about is the one with "a profusion of purple blossoms." In the next sentence, he considers other plants that are "less beautiful" than the one with purple blossoms. This should lead you to (D). Choice A is a misused detail; the plant that is wreathed around the statue (lines 39–43) is shown in a positive light, but these lines do not indicate that Giovanni finds the plant to be exceptional. Choice B is a misused detail; in lines 37–39, there is information about plants that "crept serpent-like along the ground," yet no specific plant is mentioned, nor are any viewed as being special. Choice C is a misused detail; in line 23, "gigantic leaves" are mentioned, but not a specific plant's leaves.

2. G
Category: Detail
Difficulty: Medium
Getting to the Answer: If you are able to determine that a certain statement is correct (or incorrect), you can include (or eliminate) all answer choices that include that statement. Normally, you would start with the statement that appears most frequently, but all statements here appear an equal number of times. Your notes should indicate that the narrator discusses the gardener's interaction with the plants principally in paragraphs 3 and 4. Skim those paragraphs for the information in the three statements. In lines 67–68, you see that the gardener avoids the "actual touch or the direct inhaling of [the plants'] odors." Based on this, you know that Statements I and III are valid; eliminate all choices that don't include both of them (F and H). Paragraph 4 offers

alternate confirmation of these two statements. A quick skim of the paragraphs offers no support for Statement II; eliminate J. Choice (G) is correct; the passage supports both statements. Choice F is a distortion; this lacks Statement III. Choice H is a distortion; this lacks Statement I. Choice J is out of scope; the passage doesn't support the second statement.

3. C
Category: Generalization
Difficulty: Medium
Getting to the Answer: Generalization questions can be challenging because the answers will not be directly stated in the passage. Remember, though, that the answers will be supported by information within the passage, usually in more than one spot. Your notes should help you to see that the gardener is shown as being very cautious when he gardens. For instance, in lines 85–86, it is stated that the gardener wears gloves to protect himself. He also wears other "armor," the mask that he puts over his mouth and nostrils, in lines 89–90. In lines 67–74, Giovanni is disturbed by the fact that the gardener takes so much caution with the plants, indicating that Giovanni himself would not take these types of precautions. A good prediction is *cautious man*. Choice (C) matches this. Choice A is a distortion; Giovanni alludes to Adam and the Garden of Eden, but this does not indicate that the gardener is more religious. Choice B is opposite; the narrator depicts the gardener as being very cautious, behavior that disturbs Giovanni. Choice D is a distortion; Giovanni alludes to Adam and the Garden of Eden, but this does not indicate that the gardener is less religious.

4. J
Category: Detail
Difficulty: Medium
Getting to the Answer: In Roman numeral questions, start with the statements that appear more frequently. Statements I and II appear more frequently than the third one does, so start there. In line 69, the gardener "impressed Giovanni most disagreeably" by avoiding the inhalation of the plants'

odors; Statement II is valid then. Eliminate F and H. (Note that this means you don't have to investigate Statement III.) In the following lines, Giovanni becomes upset that "the man's demeanor was that of one walking among malignant influences," which supports Statement I. Choice (J) is the correct choice. Choice F is a distortion; this does not include Statement II. Choice G is a distortion; this does not include Statement I. Choice H is a misused detail; the narrator describes the gardener as doing this, but not that it disturbs Giovanni.

5. A

Category: Generalization
Difficulty: Medium
Getting to the Answer: Some questions will ask you to read between the lines. Although this can sometimes be difficult, remember that the answer will always be supported by information in the passage. The gardener, in lines 67–68, avoids directly touching the plants or "inhaling… their odors." He is also described as a "scientific gardener," who seems to be "looking into" the nature of the plants. You can infer that he is observant and seems to understand the essence of the plants. Predict that he is *focused* or *attentive*. Choice (A) matches this prediction. Choice B is extreme; lines 56–63 indicate that the gardener knows a lot about plants. The narrator suggests, however, that he discovers this information as he works, not that he already knows all there is to know about plants. Choice C is opposite; the fact that he refuses to touch or smell the plants goes against the idea that he loves nature. Choice D is a misused detail; Giovanni mentions Adam in lines 80–82, but there is no indication that the gardener actually resembles him.

6. G

Category: Inference
Difficulty: Medium
Getting to the Answer: Don't "over-infer." The correct choice will be closely related to something stated in the passage. In lines 30–31, the plant is described as seemingly able to "illuminate the garden, even had there been no sunshine." From this, you

can infer that the plant seemed capable of producing light, which matches (G). Choice F is a distortion; in lines 27–28 the narrator states that each blossom "had the luster and richness of a gem." To say that the plant could sprout gems stretches the metaphor too far. Choice H is a distortion; the narrator suggests that the plant could shed light on the garden, not overrun it like a weed. Choice J is out of scope; nowhere in the passage is there any indication that the plant grows very quickly.

7. D

Category: Writer's View
Difficulty: Low
Getting to the Answer: Take the time to predict an answer before looking at the answer choices; this will help you avoid being tempted by incorrect answer choices. The passage is not told directly from Giovanni's point of view; the reader understands what Giovanni is thinking, yet this information comes from an unidentified narrator. Look for this among the choices; (D) matches. Choice A is a misused detail; the narrator refers to the gardener in the third person. Choice B is a misused detail; the narrator refers to Giovanni in the third person. Choice C is a misused detail; the gardener is described as being scientific, yet that does not indicate that the narrator is a scientist.

8. J

Category: Function
Difficulty: Medium
Getting to the Answer: Read the referenced lines carefully to determine the author's intent. These statements are made after the narrator describes Giovanni as being disturbed by the insecurities the gardener shows while cultivating the garden. The narrator mentions Eden and Adam to show how far the gardener's behavior is from these ideals—he should display more positive feelings for the plants he tends. Choice (J) matches this prediction. Choice F is a misused detail; Giovanni seems to recognize this in the gardener earlier in the paragraph, but this has no relation to the references to Adam and Eden. Choice G is opposite; Giovanni finds the gardener's

behavior inexplicable. Choice H is a distortion; while these are Biblical references, Giovanni never implies that the gardener should show the plants respect, religious or otherwise.

9. A
Category: Detail
Difficulty: Low
Getting to the Answer: When you don't receive line references, good notes will help you know where to research. Your notes should indicate that every paragraph but the first focuses on Giovanni's observation of the gardener, so look to the first paragraph. Scan the choices first, then look for the match. Choice (A) is correct; in lines 3–4, Giovanni refers to the garden as "one of those botanic gardens," different from most in the world. Choice B is a distortion; rare art is mentioned in line 9, but this refers specifically to the marble fountain, not to the garden as a whole. Choice C is a distortion; this answer is a misreading of lines 31–32, where the narrator states that "the soil was peopled with plants and herbs." He is not referring to actual people. Choice D is a distortion; in lines 6–7, the narrator states that the garden "might once have been the pleasure-place of an opulent family." He never states that it was such a locale for "the community."

10. G
Category: Generalization
Difficulty: High
Getting to the Answer: When given line references in the question stem, go back to those lines in the text and, if necessary, read the sentences before and after those lines. The paragraph begins by describing the gardener as examining the plants intently and "looking into [the plants'] inmost nature," "discovering why one leaf grew in this shape and another in that" (lines 61–62). He seems interested in understanding what the plants are made up of. The remainder of the paragraph discusses his apparent fear of the plants. Look for one of these ideas in the correct choice. Choice (G) matches the first part of the paragraph. Choice F is opposite; the paragraph indicates that he is quite patient, intently seeking to understand the plants' inmost qualities. Choice H is a distortion; the gardener seems to fear the plants may harm him, but he does not seem to want to harm the plants. Choice J is out of scope; there is no indication that the gardener is angry with the plants.

PASSAGE II

11. B
Category: Detail
Difficulty: Low
Getting to the Answer: You are looking for three things that ARE mentioned and one that IS NOT. Don't get the two confused. First check your notes to see that the author mentions jumbo jet design in paragraph 4. Research the passage and cross off each choice that is referenced in the paragraph. Choice (B) is not referenced in this paragraph. Choice A is opposite; the author mentions this in line 39. Choice C is opposite; the author mentions this in line 37. Choice D is opposite; the author mentions this in line 40.

12. J
Category: Vocab-in-Context
Difficulty: Medium
Getting to the Answer: The test maker frequently gives you uncommon usages of common words. You need to read carefully to understand the intended meaning of the phrase. The Boeing example starts by pointing out that the plane's design will be limited in ways that will make it impossible to satisfy everyone. You can assume that the company wants to come close enough to satisfying all the plane's users that those users will be happy with the final design. Choice (J) matches the thrust of the text. Choice F is out of scope; the author doesn't discuss such investments. Choice G is extreme; the passage tells you that there will be compromises. Choice H is out of scope; the cost to users is not mentioned.

13. C
Category: Detail
Difficulty: Medium
Getting to the Answer: You need to find the details

used as evidence for this belief. Therefore, your answer will come straight from the passage. Your passage notes should send you to the last paragraph. The author asks you to "imagine" that the Titanic hadn't sunk on her first trip. In the author's opinion, there would have been many ships designed just like the Titanic and potentially many more disasters. Look for an answer choice that reflects this idea. Choice (C) is correct. Choice A is out of scope; there is no evidence that ship designers were careless before the Titanic sank. Choice B is out of scope; the number of lifeboats is not mentioned. Choice D is out of scope; the passage never discusses insurance.

14. F
Category: Generalization
Difficulty: Medium
Getting to the Answer: The answer should come from your overall understanding of the passage, not from specific details. Your active reading told you that this passage is about the importance of learning from failure. The passage title—"Look First to Failure"—is an excellent clue. Therefore, look for an answer choice that mentions the positive aspects of studying failures. Choice (F) matches this prediction. Choice G is out of scope; the author does not address whether or not projects "seem" difficult. Choice H is opposite; in lines 58–60, the author tells you that reverse engineering "sacrifices the synergy of success." Choice J is opposite; the author says that studying past failures is an excellent way to learn.

15. D
Category: Detail
Difficulty: Medium
Getting to the Answer: Use your notes to find the correct paragraph and predict the answer before looking at the choices; you will reach your answer more quickly and be less likely to fall into traps set by the test maker. Based on your notes, you should go directly to paragraph 6. It tells you that the engineers for the Tacoma Narrows Bridge tried to improve on Roebling's design for the Brooklyn Bridge and left out "the very cables that he included to obviate failure." The prior paragraph identifies those cables. Choice

(D) is correct. Choice A is opposite; deviations from the design of the Brooklyn Bridge were the cause of the failure of the Tacoma Narrows Bridge. Choice B is out of scope; the author doesn't discuss any difference in the wind strength between the two bridges. Choice C is opposite; the engineers' concern for "economy and aesthetics" were what caused them to leave out the critical cables.

16. H
Category: Function
Difficulty: High
Getting to the Answer: Use your notes to help you understand the writer's purpose in selecting this specific example. Because this is the final paragraph, it is likely that its meaning will be closely related to the overall purpose of the passage. Lines 80–84 state that Titanic's failure contributed more to ocean liner safety than its success would have. Note that the correct choice may not be stated so specifically; (H) is correct. Choice F is a distortion; the author's point is about design in general, not just the Titanic. Choice G is a distortion; the article is not about the fate of ocean liners. Choice J is out of scope; this is true, but it's not the function of the paragraph.

17. D
Category: Function
Difficulty: Medium
Getting to the Answer: Focus on how an example fits into the overall point the author is making. Use your notes to locate the paper clip example—paragraph 3. The author points out that challengers to the Gem may be able to improve on one aspect of its design but not another. This reiterates the topic sentence, "Reengineering anything is fraught with risk." The example is probably meant to emphasize this point. Choice (D) is correct. Choice A is out of scope; the paragraph is not about the importance of paper clips. Choice B is extreme; the example points out the risks of reengineering in general. Choice C is a distortion; the author does not suggest any redesign of the paper clip.

18. F
Category: Detail
Difficulty: Low
Getting to the Answer: Use your notes to research paragraph 3. To avoid traps, predict your answer before reading the choices. The paragraph tells you that the Gem clip is easy to use and doesn't fall off. Challengers have improved on one aspect of the Gem clip but have sacrificed the other. Choice (F) addresses the compromise predicted. Choice G is out of scope; function, not timing, determines success. Choice H is out of scope; brand awareness and familiarity are not mentioned. Choice J is a distortion; this mentions only one of the benefits the author lists.

19. B
Category: Detail
Difficulty: Medium
Getting to the Answer: When dealing with unfamiliar or passage-specific terms, read around the reference carefully. "Failure-based thinking" in this reference is related to Roebling's *successful* design of the Brooklyn Bridge. A careful reading shows you that Roebling was able to succeed because he understood where others had failed. You need to look for a positive use of "failure" in your answer choice. Choice (B) matches this prediction. Choice A is out of scope; the author doesn't discuss such a habit. Choice C is a distortion; this choice can be tempting because it uses several key words from the paragraph, but the passage says cannibalizing can *sacrifice* synergy, not *create* it. Choice D is opposite; the Tacoma Bridge collapse supports the author's theory because the designers of that bridge failed to use "failure-based thinking."

20. H
Category: Vocab-in-Context
Difficulty: Medium
Getting to the Answer: To answer this question, you need to understand the author's use of the term *in context*. First, read the entire sentence and, if necessary, the sentences before and after. "So" in the middle of the sentence tells you that the first and second halves of the sentence are closely linked.

From this, you conclude that "comparatives" relates to improvements. Choice (H) is correct. You need to look for an answer choice that tells you that engineering is measured by its ability to make improvements. Choice F is out of scope; the comparison is between products, not individuals. Choice G is a distortion; "bigger" and "faster" are only two possible measures of improvement. Choice J is out of scope; the author doesn't deal with such comparisons.

PASSAGE III

21. A
Category: Generalization
Difficulty: Medium
Getting to the Answer: When a line reference occurs in the first line of a paragraph, you'll often need to read the following sentence to answer the question fully. Research the passage to find that the "motifs" mentioned are a shared reality with the common human experience, so predict something such as, *all humans go through such experiences*. This prediction matches (A). Choice B is out of scope; the author doesn't mention "critics." Choice C is a distortion; this comes up in the prior paragraph, but it doesn't fit with the author's intention here. Choice D is out of scope; the paragraph doesn't address this.

22. H
Category: Writer's View
Difficulty: Low
Getting to the Answer: Read the sentence referenced in the question stem to make a prediction. The passage says that these avenues are used to get at "the cosmic unconscious," so predict that the author believes fairy tales are one method to help people process human experiences. Choice (H) matches this prediction. Choice F reflects the standard meaning of the word, which doesn't fit here. Choices G and J don't make sense in context.

23. D
Category: Inference
Difficulty: Low
Getting to the Answer: Correct answers to Inference questions will only be a step removed from

what is stated in the passage. The lines indicated in the passage, along with those preceding them, discuss how popular fairy tales survive, while unpopular ones die out ("time . . . discards the chaff"). Look for an answer close to that. Choice (D) matches the passage's emphasis on "editing" and "appeal." A Choice A is out of scope; "quality" is not discussed at this point. Choice B is a distortion; fairy tales "can be said to have" undergone an editing process, but not to "the same degree" as other forms of writing. Choice C is opposite; such tales would have "endured."

24. J
Category: Detail
Difficulty: Medium
Getting to the Answer: Don't range too far from the text given and the ideas in that text when drawing your conclusion. The final sentence of Passage B says that we should acknowledge the many variations among versions of fairy tales and search "for insights into the cultural conditions which prompt such divergence." In other words, we should question what these variations tell us about the specific cultures in which they appear. This matches (J) nicely. Choice F is a distortion; the author of Passage B indicates that there is no "accurate" interpretation of such tales. Choice G is out of scope; the passage doesn't explore the difference between written and "oral versions" of the stories. Choice H is a distortion; the author of Passage B does not suggest that any version of a tale is more valid or authoritative than any other.

25. B
Category: Detail
Difficulty: Medium
Getting to the Answer: Remember not to confuse something said by one author with something said by the other author. You know that the author of Passage B disagrees with the kinds of symbolic interpretations made in Passage A, and this question asks specifically why. Predict something about the way that they fail to take multiple versions of tales into account. Choice (B) matches this prediction.

Choice A is opposite; if anything, Author B thinks that Author A pays too much attention to "psychology." Choice C is out of scope; the problem that Author B sees goes beyond simple failure to use reference materials. Choice D is a misused detail; it's not the "naïve view of . . . human nature," but rather the naïve view of folklore methodology.

26. F
Category: Inference
Difficulty: High
Getting to the Answer: Beware of answer choices that pull from details in the passage but have nothing to do with the inference at hand. The indicated section of the passage makes the argument that an interpretation based on details about the huntsman can't be valid when most versions of the folk tale don't have a huntsman in them. Predict something along the lines of fairy tales having too many variations to interpret. Choice (F) is the best match for this prediction. Choice H is a distortion; this original idea comes from Passage A. Choice G is out of scope; the passage doesn't raise the question of historical accuracy. Choice J is a distortion; "themes of rescue" are not what the author is striving for here.

27. C
Category: Detail
Difficulty: Low
Getting to the Answer: Some questions don't lend themselves easily to prediction; work your way through the answer choices if you need to. This question calls for a detail that the passages have in common, but it doesn't give you any real hints as to where to look. Eliminate wrong answers, paying special attention to those that come from one passage only. Choice (C) is the correct choice. Both authors admit that fairy tales have changed over time. Choice A is a distortion; only Passage A states this. Choice B is a distortion; this idea appears only in Passage B. Choice D is a distortion; this appears only in Passage A. The author of Passage B would not agree that symbolic interpretation of folk tales is valid.

28. F
Category: Generalization
Difficulty: Medium
Getting to the Answer: Return to the main point made by Author B. The correct answer should be consistent with this overall idea. The main argument made by Author B is that it isn't possible to interpret the symbolism of specific tales as reflecting general psychological truth, so eliminate any answer choice that contradicts that idea. Only (F) captures the central argument of Author B against this type of interpretation. Choice G is out of scope; Author B does not address the "popularity" of such tales. Choice H is a distortion; Author B does not believe that there is such a thing as a definitive version of a tale. Choice J is a distortion; this choice doesn't reflect the overall opinion of Author B that interpretations can't be made at all.

29. B
Category: Inference
Difficulty: High
Getting to the Answer: In questions asking what one author might say to the other, be careful not to confuse the respective viewpoints of the authors. Author A mentions that these motifs are common to all humans in "widely-scattered" societies across time, so he'd probably argue that the specifics of a given version are less important than these universal psychological trends. This prediction matches (B). Choice A is out of scope; Author A makes no mention of recent versions of folk tales or advances in methodology. Choice C is opposite; Author A believes in the relevance of "psychological forces." Choice D is opposite; Author A chooses Snow White as the principal example of his argument.

30. H
Category: Inference
Difficulty: Low
Getting to the Answer: For broadly stated questions, work through the choices, eliminating clearly incorrect answers, and then return to the passages to support your choice. Because a prediction for this question might be difficult, check and eliminate answer choices that don't match both passages. Because both authors would concur that folk tales are developed and passed down through generations (certainly a unique "compositional process"), they would agree with (H). Choice F is a distortion; only Author A emphasizes this. Choice G is a distortion; the contention that folk tales have "universal" truth comes from Passage A only. Choice J is out of scope; neither passage says anything about "new information about . . . particular tales."

PASSAGE IV

31. C
Category: Generalization
Difficulty: Low
Getting to the Answer: Be sure to predict an answer before looking at the answer choices; predicting will help you avoid trap answers. Your notes should help you to predict an answer for this on every passage. Throughout this passage, the author discusses how linear and circular accelerators work and how they differ in their uses. Choice (C) matches this prediction well. Choice A is a misused detail; although this does appear, it is not the main idea of the entire passage. Choice B is a misused detail; this appears in the passage, but it is not the main idea. Choice D is a misused detail; based on the passage, cyclotrons do seem to be a useful type of circular accelerator, but this is not the main idea of the entire passage.

32. F
Category: Detail
Difficulty: Medium
Getting to the Answer: Think of Detail questions as matching questions. The answer choice will always match a detail stated directly in the passage. In lines 98–100, the author writes, "The tube has many magnets distributed around it to focus the particles and curve their track around the tube." The magnets, by focusing the particles and their curve, influence the direction in which the particles travel; use this as your prediction. Choice (F) matches this prediction well. Choice G is a distortion; this misconstrues the statement that the magnets curve the particles'

track "around the tube" (line 100). The particles' track is curving, not the particles themselves. Choice H is a distortion; the microwave cavities accelerate the particles (lines 100–101), not the magnets. Choice J is out of scope; there is no indication that the magnets impact the energy levels of the particles.

33. D
Category: Detail
Difficulty: Medium
Getting to the Answer: On Detail questions, avoid incorrect choices that contain details from the passage not relevant to the question being asked. According to lines 81–83, "The effect of the energy injected using the electric fields is therefore to increase their mass." Choice (D) is correct. Choice A is a distortion; the passage states that particles do not reach the speed of light. Choice B is a distortion; this misconstrues the reference to a vacuum in line 77. Choice C is out of scope; there is no indication in the passage that using heavier particles will cause particle mass to increase.

34. H
Category: Vocab-in-Context
Difficulty: Medium
Getting to the Answer: The entire sentence that contains the vocabulary word to decipher its meaning; then look at the choices. In lines 58–61, the author states that heavier particles, such as protons, are being used in accelerators. In the following sentence, you see that "these particles are composites of quarks and gluons." It follows that quarks help make up protons. Choice (H) matches this prediction. Choice F is a misused detail; electron accelerators are mentioned in lines 56–58, but there is no indication that electrons are what make up a quark. Choice G is out of scope; there is no mention of radiation in this paragraph, nor is there any indication that a quark is made up of radiation. Choice J is a distortion; gluons and quarks seem to be roughly equivalent. Neither is a component of the other.

35. D
Category: Detail
Difficulty: Medium
Getting to the Answer: Some questions will ask you what CANNOT be possible. Make sure you take the time to read the question carefully, so that you don't select what is possible. In lines 27–29, the passage states that linear accelerators "are also used to provide an initial low-energy kick to particles before they are injected into circular accelerators." These lines show that linear accelerators provide this kick, not the circular accelerator, as (D) suggests. Choice A is opposite; in lines 42–43, the author states that "When any charged particle is accelerated, it emits electromagnetic radiation," which means that the circular accelerator can cause this. Choice B is opposite; in lines 37–38, the author states that parts of circular accelerators "can be reused to accelerate the particles further." Choice C is opposite; in lines 39–41, the author states that circular accelerators suffer a disadvantage in that the particles emit synchrotron radiation.

36. J
Category: Generalization
Difficulty: Medium
Getting to the Answer: Some questions will ask you to read between the lines. Although this can sometimes be difficult, remember that the answer will always be supported by information in the passage. The passage discusses how linear and circular accelerators work. Some information is also given on how they differ, how they can be used, and some different types of accelerators. Based on this information, it would seem that they have different uses, yet both linear and circular accelerators are valuable in their own ways; (J) is correct. Choice F is extreme; the author states, for example, that linear accelerators can be used to "provide an initial low energy kick." Choice G is extreme; the author states in lines 58–61 that physicists are using particles like protons in accelerators. Choice H is a distortion; besides the first circular accelerator invented by Lawrence in 1929, the passage mentions other types of circular

accelerators, such as the synchrotron, which is able to push energies into the billions of electron volts versus the 10 million electron volts that a cyclotron can push energies to.

37. D
Category: Detail
Difficulty: Medium
Getting to the Answer: To get more points on Test Day, predict answers; this will keep you from being tempted to pick incorrect choices that distort or misuse information from the passage. Your notes can help direct you to the second paragraph. Lines 12–15 include the information needed to answer this question. Once the particles have passed through the hole in the plate, the plate repels the particles, which are accelerated towards the next plate. Choice (D) matches this. Choice A is out of scope; the author does not state this. Choice B is out of scope; the author does not state this. Choice C is out of scope; the author does not state this.

38. H
Category: Inference
Difficulty: High
Getting to the Answer: Remember that even though the answers for Inference questions will not be directly stated in the passage, they will be supported by information in the passage. Use your notes to find where the author discusses these items. The author writes that synchrotrons can push energy levels higher than cyclotrons can. Look for this distinction among the choices. Choice (H) is correct. Choice F is extreme; as stated in lines 92–93, cyclotrons are still useful for lower energy applications. Choice G is a distortion; circular accelerators accelerate particles in a circle, and cyclotrons and synchrotrons are both types of circular accelerators. Choice J is out of scope; the author never indicates that synchrotrons cause particles to move closer to the edge of the tube.

39. A
Category: Function
Difficulty: Medium
Getting to the Answer: When you come across Function questions, remember that context is cru-

cial to understanding the purpose of a particular passage element. After discussing the "storage ring," the author recalls the earliest cyclotron, from 1929, and shows the size difference between it and a modern counterpart. You can predict that the author means to *show the progress made in the technology*. Choice (A) matches this prediction. Choice B is a misused detail; the passage indicates that cyclotrons are important, but not because Lawrence invented them. Choice C is a distortion; simply due to the passage in time and the natural pace of progress, this is likely true. This is not, however, the author's purpose in making this statement. Choice D is a distortion; this is not the purpose of this reference.

40. G
Category: Generalization
Difficulty: Medium
Getting to the Answer: Go back and read the lines mentioned in the question. Taking the time to research the passage will help ensure that the answer you choose is supported by the passage, which means more points on Test Day. Throughout this paragraph, the main focus is on how particles in high energy accelerators approach the speed of light, and that when they do so, the main effect is an increase in the relativistic mass of the particle. Choice (G) matches this. Choice F is a misused detail; the author references this in line 79, but it is not the main idea of the paragraph. Choice H is a distortion; this choice is a misinterpretation of the information in lines 79–81. Choice J is a distortion; energy limits are not reached because the mass increases. The mass increases in particles as they come closer to traveling at the speed of light.

SCIENCE TEST

PASSAGE I

1. B
Category: Figure Interpretation
Difficulty: Low
Getting to the Answer: This question represents a

case where it's faster to go to the answer choices first. Searching for the lowest value of the 20 in Table 2 is time consuming. Instead, start with the lowest value among the answer choices. Choice D, like C, is far lower than the values in Table 2—in fact, both are values from Table 1. Choice (B) is the lowest value in Table 2. It was recorded in Room 4 on Day 1. Choice A is the highest value in Table 2.

2. G
Category: Figure Interpretation
Difficulty: Low
Getting to the Answer: Don't answer low-difficulty questions like this one from memory. It's worth taking an extra ten seconds to look back at the table to be sure you get the right answer. All of the values in Table 2 are recorded to the nearest 0.1 mm Hg. Choice (G) is correct. Choice F is a trap for those who mistakenly refer to Table 1, in which values are recorded to the nearest 0.01°C.

3. C
Category: Patterns
Difficulty: Medium
Getting to the Answer: Pick one data point at a time and check it against the answer choices. Eliminate any that don't contain that data point. Start by checking the answer choices for the point from Day 1 (745.2 mm Hg, 18.03°C). Eliminate A, B, and D, as they don't contain this point. Only (C) correctly represents this data point, so this must be the correct answer.

4. J
Category: Patterns
Difficulty: Low
Getting to the Answer: For questions that ask you to describe a data trend in words, be sure to make a prediction before checking the answer choices. Circle the Room 3 column in Table 2, so your eye doesn't accidentally wander. Reading down the column, you can see that the average daily air pressure decreases every day. Choice (J) matches this perfectly. Choice F describes the pressure changes for Room 1. Choice G describes the temperature changes (Table 1) for Room 3. Choice H is the opposite of the correct answer.

5. D
Category: Scientific Reasoning
Difficulty: Medium
Getting to the Answer: Pay close attention to the definitions of new terms introduced in the question stem. Make sure to account for all referenced quantities. Choice (D) is correct because you are given only the temperatures of each room. You know nothing about the exact quantities of heat provided to the room or the amount absorbed by the room's contents. Choices A, B, and C all suggest knowledge of these quantities.

6. F
Category: Figure Interpretation
Difficulty: Low
Getting to the Answer: In Table 1, the room with the highest daily average air temperate is Room 1, so (F) is correct.

PASSAGE II

7. B
Category: Figure Interpretation
Difficulty: High
Getting to the Answer: The last rows of Tables 1 and 2 provide the average Hg concentration for each species of sea creature. To find the difference, subtract the cold-water value (Table 1) from the warm-water value (Table 2). Swordfish, with a difference of 38 Hg concentration (ppb), is the sea creature with the greatest difference, (B).

8. G
Category: Scientific Reasoning
Difficulty: Low
Getting to the Answer: Before looking at the choices, determine for yourself what factors would support the given hypothesis or cause it to be rejected. In this case, the hypothesis would be supported only if the results showed higher Hg concentrations in swordfish and shark than in catfish and crab. The results do indeed show higher Hg concentrations for swordfish and shark, so the hypothesis is confirmed as in (G). The "Yes" part of F is correct, but the reason given contradicts the data in Table 2, so it is incorrect.

Choice H is also incorrect; the lowest Hg concentration was indeed in catfish, but this does not cause the hypothesisto be rejected. Choice J contradicts the data in Table 2.

9. D
Category: Scientific Reasoning
Difficulty: High
Getting to the Answer: Refer to the passage to understand the process in question on Scientific Method questions. In this case, refer to the description of CVAFS. The passage mentions that CVAFS "indicates the relative concentrations of various elements and compounds." A properly working CVAFS, then, should be able to correctly measure the relative concentrations of Hg and Pb. Using a sample of known concentrations of Hg and Pb, as in (D), would support or reject the accuracy of the CVAFS in detecting the presence of Pb. Nothing in the passage supports either A or C. Choice B is similarly unrelated to the passage.

10. F
Category: Patterns
Difficulty: Medium
Getting to the Answer: Try to find a correlation between any new information given in the question stem and the information in the passage. Because new data on water temperature is introduced, try to find a correlation between water temperature and Hg concentration. Compare the average Hg concentrations in Tables 1 and 2 to see that, for all three common species (crab, swordfish, and shark), the cold-water specimens have higher Hg concentrations than do the warm-water specimens. Choice (F) is correct, because the Northern Atlantic Ocean is the coldest location.

11. C
Category: Scientific Reasoning
Difficulty: Low
Getting to the Answer: The factors intentionally varied are the ones researchers purposefully changed in the course of the experiment. Look back at Table 2. It shows that researchers intentionally tested four different kinds of fish, which matches (C). Choice A is incorrect, because the volume of tissue was never discussed. Choice B is incorrect because all four species in Experiment 2 were extracted from water of the same temperature. Choice D is incorrect, because CVAFS is the only method of analysis mentioned.

12. G
Category: Patterns
Difficulty: Medium
Getting to the Answer: Use Tables 1 and 2 to locate the Hg concentrations for each of the answer choices. A swordfish caught in cold water would have the highest Hg concentration. Choice (G) is correct.

13. D
Category: Scientific Reasoning
Difficulty: Medium
Getting to the Answer: Think about the experimental method used, and try to predict an answer before looking at the choices. Increasing the volume of tested material while maintaining the same volume of Hg in the sample would lead to a smaller fraction of Hg content, regardless of water temperature. Choice (D) is perfect. Choice C is incorrect, because nothing in the passage indicates that the contamination would affect warm- and cold-water fish differently.

PASSAGE III

14. G
Category: Patterns
Difficulty: Medium
Getting to the Answer: When a question introduces new data, try to relate it to patterns in the data given. Occasionally, some basic math may be required. The equation in Exercise 2 tells you how to calculate the answer. Z = electromotive force ÷ current = (12 V) ÷ (1.2 A) = 10 Ω, (G). Even if you missed the equation, you can note from Table 2 that Z decreases as current increases and at least eliminate J. Also, if you noticed that Z and current are inversely proportional (either by looking at the equation or

Table 2), you could see that *double* the current of Bulb 4 results in *half* the Z of Bulb 4.

15. D
Category: Patterns
Difficulty: High
Getting to the Answer: Challenging Pattern Analysis questions may require you to do some basic math. Here, noticing the pattern of decreasing Z with increasing current is not enough. You must actually apply the given equation. Because Z = electromotive force ÷ current, current = electromotive force ÷ Z. You have to apply this equation to each answer choice and calculate which gives the highest current. You must use the Z values for each light bulb from Table 2.

For A, current = (10 V) ÷ (60 Ω) = $\frac{1}{6}$ A.

For B, current = (8 V) ÷ (40 Ω) = $\frac{1}{5}$ A.

For C, current = (6 V) ÷ (30 Ω) = $\frac{1}{5}$ A.

For (D), current = (5 V) ÷ (20 Ω) = $\frac{1}{4}$ A. (D), then, gives the largest current.

16. F
Category: Figure Interpretation
Difficulty: Medium
Getting to the Answer: Sometimes, a question may require you to combine a detail from the passage with data in a figure. Read the question carefully for clues regarding which part of the passage and which table you'll need. According to Table 1, Bulb 3 produced one red indicator light and three green indicator lights. The text above Table 1 explains that green indicators illuminate when light is detected and red indicators illuminate when no light is detected. For Bulb 3, then, only one sensor did not detect any light, (F). Beware of the trap in H for those who confuse the meaning of red and green indicators.

17. C
Category: Figure Interpretation
Difficulty: Medium
Getting to the Answer: This question certainly looks more intimidating than it is. Work methodically and you'll get the answer in no time. First, find the equation for B in the passage. It's listed in *Exercise* 3 as B = $\frac{P}{4\pi r^2}$. The text explains that P is the power rating in Watts and r is the distance in meters from the bulb. You're given r in the question stem (2 meters), but you'll need to find P. P is listed in Table 3 as 3.6 watts for Bulb 2. Plugging in P = 3.6 and r = 2 gives you (C). Choice A is the result if you accidentally swap the values of P and r. Choices B and D are the results if you mistakenly use the P for Bulb 1.

18. H
Category: Scientific Reasoning
Difficulty: High
Getting to the Answer: Because you are not permitted to use your calculator during the Science Test, there must be a way to estimate seemingly involved calculations. Look for ways to make the math easier than it appears. Because B = $\frac{P}{4\pi r^2}$, P = $4\pi r^2 B$. You're given in the question stem that the bulb is 1 m away, so you can plug r = 1 into the equation. You're also given that B = 0.95 W/m². Plugging r and B into the equation for P gives: P = $4\pi(1 \text{ m})^2(0.95 \text{ W/m}^2)$. Because π is slightly larger than 3, and 0.95 is slightly smaller than 1, P ≈ 4(3) (1 m²)(1 W/m²) = 12 W, (H). Even without calculating, you can eliminate F and G by comparing B for the fifth bulb with all of the B values from Table 3. 0.95 is just less than double the B value for Bulb 4, which had a P value of 7.2 Watts. Because B increases with P, you know your answer must be greater than 7.2.

19. A
Category: Scientific Reasoning
Difficulty: Low
Getting to the Answer: Look first at the tables for the similarities and differences between the

two exercises. It's often easier to read information from those than from the text. No light sensors were used in Exercise 2, so (A) is correct. Choice B is incorrect because 4 different light bulbs were used in both exercises. Choice C is incorrect because a 12 V battery was used for both exercises. Choice D is incorrect because Table 2 shows that the current was lowest for Bulb 1.

20. H
Category: Figure Interpretation
Difficulty: Medium
Getting to the Answer: According to Table 3, light bulb 1 and light bulb 2 are not bright enough to consider. Light bulb 3's P is greater than 0.30 (W/m^2) and has a lower power rating than light bulb 4. Thus, (H) is the best answer given the criteria.

PASSAGE IV

21. D
Category: Patterns
Difficulty: High
Getting to the Answer: The figure shows how energy relates to the probability of occupation. The passage states that the figure shows the same solid at 3 different temperatures. The hottest solid (25,000 K) is able to reach beyond 14 electron Volts, which is greater than both of the other temperature solids. Therefore (D) is the correct choice.

22. J
Category: Scientific Reasoning
Difficulty: High
Getting to the Answer: Don't be intimidated by presentation of unfamiliar science. All three curves happen to intersect at 50%, so look at their slopes at this point of intersection. "Inversely proportional" means that the average kinetic energy is lower for steeper slopes. The 1,000 K curve has the steepest slope and therefore the lowest average kinetic energy. The 10,000 K curve has the next steepest slope and therefore the next lowest kinetic energy, and the 25,000 K curve has the least steep slope and the highest kinetic energy. Choice (J) is correct.

23. A
Category: Patterns
Difficulty: Low
Getting to the Answer: Locate the correct data set and extrapolate beyond the given data by using your pencil to continue the curve. The 1,000 K curve appears to reach 0% at energies above approximately 8 eV. The note under the graph says that the curves all continue to decrease beyond 15 eV, so the value of the 1,000 K curve should still be 0% at an energy of 20 eV. Only (A) agrees with this.

24. J
Category: Patterns
Difficulty: Medium
Getting to the Answer: The correct answer will depict the same trends as the figure in the passage. Identify those trends before you check the answer choices. There are two trends in the figure that accompanies Passage IV: probability of occupation decreases as energy increases, and the curves get shallower as temperature increases. Look for both of these patterns to be represented in the correct answer. You can immediately eliminate F and G, because the curves in these choices increase in value with an increase in energy, behavior opposite to that of the curves in the figure. Choice (J) is perfect because these curves decrease with increasing energy and because the lowest temperature (2,000 K) curve has the steepest slope, just as the figure shows.

25. C
Category: Figure Interpretation
Difficulty: High
Getting to the Answer: Sometimes a question will ask you to predict the placement of data points that are in between those actually shown on a graph. The answer choices for these questions will be spaced far enough apart so that a rough estimate will be enough. Locate the point corresponding to an 80% probability of occupation of a 5 eV energy state. It lies between the 10,000 K and 25,000 K curves. The temperature of the solid, then, must be between 10,000 K and 25,000 K. Choice (C) must be correct, because it is the only choice in this range.

26. G
Category: Patterns
Difficulty: High
Getting to the Answer: Questions that introduce technical terms can be very confusing. Remember, though, that you don't need to understand what they mean, just how they fit into the question. It doesn't matter whether you've ever heard of the de Broglie wavelength before (or whether you can pronounce it!). Everything you need to know is in the question stem. As the de Broglie wavelength decreases, the energy increases. What happens to probability as energy increases? The figure clearly shows that the values on all three curves decrease with increasing energy. Choice (G), then, is the correct answer. You can eliminate H and J because the figure doesn't show any curve changing from an increase to a decrease, or vice versa, so these can't be correct.

PASSAGE V

27. C
Category: Patterns
Difficulty: Medium
Getting to the Answer: On questions that ask you to generate a graph from a data set, identify a few points and check for the answer choice in which they all appear. The bars on the graph need to represent the values in the 25°C column of Table 1. Soda C gives the largest value, and Soda D gives the second largest value. Eliminate A and D because neither shows this trend. Choice (C) shows Sodas A, B, and E all very close to each other, and B shows Soda A higher than Sodas B and E. Checking back with Table 1, you'll see that the pressures in Sodas A, B, and E are fairly equally spaced at 25°C, so (C) is correct.

28. G
Category: Patterns
Difficulty: Low
Getting to the Answer: Make sure you understand the meaning of new and unusual diagrams. Start by looking back at Table 1 and jotting down the pressures of Soda C at 0°C (249 kPa) and 50°C (294 kPa). Choice (G) shows the gauge at 249 kPa at 0°C and 294 kPa at 50°C, so this is the correct answer.

Choice F shows the opposite relationship between 0°C and 50°C. Beware of H, which shows the values for Soda B.

29. D
Category: Scientific Reasoning
Difficulty: Medium
Getting to the Answer: Pick a few data points that stand out and look for correlations between the two relevant sets of data (in this case, sugar content and solubility). Soda D has the highest sugar content (40 grams per 12 ounces), but, according to Table 2, it has lower solubility than Soda C. This means higher sugar content doesn't always give higher solubility. The theory is not true, so eliminate A and B. Choice C is incorrect because, while Soda D has the highest sugar content, it doesn't have the lowest solubility (Soda E does). Only (D), then, is true.

30. G
Category: Patterns
Difficulty: Low
Getting to the Answer: Read across each row to identify the trend in the data. If you read across each row in Table 2, you'll see that the solubility values for each soda decrease with increasing temperature, with no exceptions. Choice (G), then, is the correct answer.

31. A
Category: Scientific Reasoning
Difficulty: Medium
Getting to the Answer: Refer to the passage for a description of the experiment in question, paying close attention to detail. Experiment 2 says, "The apparatus consisted of an air-sealed flask containing only soda and no air," and "CO_2 was injected." So you're looking for an apparatus built to allow CO_2 to be injected into a sealed container of soda. Only (A) shows this setup. Choice B is incorrect because it shows the soda immersed in an H_2O bath, which was only the case in Experiment 1. Choice C is incorrect because it shows an apparatus that injects H_2O into soda. Choice D is incorrect because it shows an apparatus that injects CO_2 into H_2O.

32. H

Category: Scientific Reasoning

Difficulty: Medium

Getting to the Answer: Sometimes a question requires you to infer things not directly stated in the passage. Draw only conclusions that MUST follow from the passage. The passage states that the H_2O bath is at room temperature, but soda temperatures are what matter. You can predict that 10 minutes allows the soda to reach the same temperature as the H_2O. Choice (H) correctly explains how the H_2O and soda reach the same temperature. Choices F and G are incorrect because CO_2 and soda evaporation aren't mentioned in Experiment 1. In J the chronology is backwards—you need the pressure gauge to stabilize during the reading of the pressure, not beforehand.

33. B

Category: Figure Interpretation

Difficulty: Low

Getting to the Answer: Table 2 shows that for Soda A, as temperature increases from 0 to 50 degrees Celsius, the value for CO_2 solubility decreases. Eliminate F and J. By checking the other 4 sodas, you can see the same pattern. Choice (B) describes this trend.

PASSAGE VI

34. H

Category: Scientific Reasoning

Difficulty: Medium

Getting to the Answer: Reread where the passage discusses "low energy," paying close attention to the details. The passage states, "The anti conformation is the lowest energy and most stable state of the butane molecule," and "Molecules in the anti or gauche conformations tend to maintain their shape." Choice (H), then is a perfect match. Choices F and G are the opposite of what you're looking for—the low energy molecules *don't* change their shape. Choice J is incorrect because the passage never mentions chemical reactions.

35. C

Category: Scientific Reasoning

Difficulty: Medium

Getting to the Answer: Refer to the passage, paying close attention to detail. Eliminate choices that contradict the passage or ones that don't logically follow from statements made in the passage. The passage states that "*Straight-chain conformational isomers* are carbon compounds that differ only by rotation about one or more single carbon bonds," and "isomers represent the same compound in a slightly different position." The number of carbon bonds, then, must not vary between different isomers of the same compound. Choice (C) matches perfectly. Choices A and B contradict the statements in the passage. Choice D is not mentioned in the passage.

36. F

Category: Scientific Reasoning

Difficulty: Medium

Getting to the Answer: When the question stem says "only Student 2 believes," you know you're looking for an answer choice with which Student 1 would disagree. Student 1 believes that a molecule's active shape is *always* identical to its lowest-energy shape. Student 2 believes that "The active shape of a butane molecule is dependent upon the energy state of the shape," but also that there are two other factors, namely temperature and initial isomeric state, that affect active shape. Temperature does not appear in the choices, so (F) is the only possibility.

37. B

Category: Scientific Reasoning

Difficulty: High

Getting to the Answer: Don't be intimidated by questions that ask you to apply the logic of the passage to a totally different situation. Try to find structural similarities between the passage and the new situation. The question stem tells you that the two dips in the path represent states of lower energy. The lowest dip is closer to the ground and represents the lowest energy state, and the smaller, higher dip is a higher energy state. The ball is in the dip that is higher off the ground, so check the passage to find the name of the second-lowest energy state. According to the information at the beginning of the passage, the anti conformation is the lowest energy state, and the gauche conformation is the next lowest ("The methyl groups are much closer to each other in the gauche conformation, but this still represents a relative minimum or *meta-stable* state"). Choice (B), then, is the correct answer.

38. F

Category: Scientific Reasoning
Difficulty: Medium
Getting to the Answer: Make sure you understand the fundamentals of both arguments presented in the passage before you tackle this question. Student 1 believes that a molecule's active shape and its lowest-energy shape are the same thing. Therefore, Student 1 believes that all molecules in their active shape are in the anti conformation. This matches (F). Student 2 believes that some of the molecules will settle into the gauche conformation, so you can eliminate H. Choice G is incorrect and the opposite of what Student 1 believes. Choice J is incorrect because Student 2 only believes that some of the molecules will have shapes different from that of their lowest-energy shapes.

39. D

Category: Scientific Reasoning
Difficulty: High
Getting to the Answer: Look for agreements between the graphs and the viewpoint of each student. Student 2 believes that the energy of a molecule's active shape may be slightly higher than that of its most stable shape, while Student 1 believes that a molecule's most stable shape and its active shape are always the same. Choice (D), then, depicts a situation in which the active shape has a higher energy than the most stable shape, so it is the correct answer. Choice C is incorrect because Student 1 believes that the active shape and most stable shape are always the same, and you're looking for a choice Student 1 would disagree with. Both students agree that the energy of the eclipsed conformation is higher than that of either the active or most stable shape, so you could immediately eliminate A and B.

40. G

Category: Scientific Reasoning
Difficulty: High
Getting to the Answer: Be sure to understand an argument thoroughly before attempting to counter it. Student 2 says that a butane molecule may settle into a moderately high-energy conformation. This, he says, is because "in order to convert from the gauche conformation to the anti conformation, the molecule must pass through either the eclipsed or totally eclipsed conformation. If the molecule is not given enough energy to reach either of these states, its active shape will be the gauche conformation." According to Student 2, then, without being given enough energy, the butane molecule can't always settle from the gauche (second-lowest energy) to the anti (lowest energy) state. If (G) was true, and the molecule could get enough energy from the environment to get into the lowest state, then this would counter his argument. Choices H and J are incorrect because hydrogen bonds, carbon bonds, and chemical functions aren't related to Student 2's argument. Choice F is not clearly relevant, and, if anything, supports the argument of Scientist 2.

WRITING TEST

LEVEL 6 ESSAY

It is the rare high school student who knows exactly what his career will be and pursues it singlemindedly. High school is a time to master a solid educational base and explore future opportunities, therefore high schools need to expose students to career opportunities. The question is how this is best done. Some argue that required attendance at career-oriented seminars will allow students to explore careers and job requirements. Others emend this to optional after-school career-focused seminars, while still others feel that schools, colleges and professionals should partner to embed career-oriented options into existing courses. Because exploring options is so important to deciding on a career, I agree that students should be required to attend career seminars at least once a semester, and that they should be given by college representatives and career professionals.

The second option, that of providing optional seminars after-school, would be helpful to students already interested in exploring options, but unfortunately many students don't think that far ahead. Some do not have a family background that encourages college or professional careers, and those students would likely not attend seminars that they feel is of no interest to them. This does not serve the purpose of exposing all students to career options. Although after-school seminars do not interrupt the core curriculum, some students are not able to stay after school and would miss the seminars. In any case, a seminar of an hour or two per semester would not interfere with core instruction. There is no need to make students stay after school, or to exclude the very students who need college and career information the most. This option does not consider any but the already-interested student, the exact opposite of what is intended.

Those who go much further and would have career-oriented options embedded into current courses miss the fact that not all students take the same courses, so those who do not take courses with career-options embedded in them will not be exposed to these opportunities. Also, if the options are taught in a class relevant to it, who would choose which classes and options to incorporate? Some might be ok but others might not interest anyone. Furthermore, this option would take up class time and teachers may not be able to teach everything they need to. The argument says that all students would be given course-specific advice, but to guarantee that every student gets that advice means that there will have to be a lot of options offered in every class, from art to history, and a lot of classes interrupted. This approach takes up school time. The same professionals and college representatives can give seminars and not have to develop whole programs that would go into high school classes. This may be overkill. We don't need to have entire embedded programs to be exposed to career possibilities.

The first perspective of required seminars is the best one. The seminars would only take up a few hours each semester, so would not interrupt classes, and could be held during assembly times. In my school weekly assemblies are required and have various programs. Career-oriented seminars could be one of those programs once a semester. When this is required, all students will be exposed to career options and have some background knowledge before they go to college. I don't agree that not going to college already knowing what you want to do is a waste of time and money, since you learn a great deal before you decide on a career. But I do agree that if you have some information about a lot of different careers, you have a good basis to keep exploring, and that basis should be provided in high school to give students a jump start on their thinking about careers.

GRADER'S COMMENTS

This essay stays squarely focused on the prompt, explores the implications of all three perspectives, and presents the author's opinion in both the opening and closing paragraphs. Specific examples are provided, including school assemblies, reference to art and history classes, students who will and will not take advantage of seminars, and those who cannot attend after-school seminars.

The writer displays good use of the conventions of writing, including high-level vocabulary with phrases such as "core curriculum" and "solid educational base." Though the writer also uses lower-level words ("overkill," "ok"), they do not reduce the impact of the writing. There is a clear introduction covering all perspectives and introducing the writer's point of view, and though there is no concluding paragraph, the last sentence of the final paragraph serves the purpose. Grammar and punctuation are correct, with only one misused word ("emend"). Transition words and phrases are well-placed ("Some," "Others," "Furthermore") and though not every paragraph opens with a transition, each paragraph is clearly separate and discusses one of the three options.

The author's position is well-reasoned and supported, and critical thinking is clearly displayed. Though her point of view could be developed somewhat further, it is evident that this writer has understood the argument and different points of view, considered the pros and cons of each, and taken a solid stand of her own.

LEVEL 4 ESSAY

I think it's really important to tell students about jobs and careers and high school is a good place to do this but we already spend enough time in school without having to go to lectures after school. Seminars should be scheduled during the school day when we are already there. Also, we have so much work to do in all of our classes that there shouldn't be more added even though it might be helpful. Also, I like airplane mechanics and I'll bet there wouldn't be anything about that in any of my current classes.

My school has assemblys that are mostly a waste of time since nobody pays attention. Now, if they did something interesting like having people talk about what they do, we'd be more likely to actually listen, especially if the people talking to us had really impressive jobs. I doubt we'd listen to a lab technician, but someone who builds airplanes would have a lot of good info to share.

Asking students to stay after school to learn about careers is a great way to have really terrible attendance at the seminars. Plus, it's really unfair to students who have after-school activities. There is no way that the star of the football team is going to miss practice just to attend an assembly.

My friends and I are always thinking about what we should do after high school, and I know my mom and dad are super worried about it, so learning about jobs in school would really help. Maybe someone who comes to talk to us will tell us about a job I didn't even know existed. I once met a flebologist, which was really neat because I had no idea what that even meant. When he told me that he studies vains, I was really interested. Who knew that you could spend your whole career helping people with disorders in their vains? I don't think I want to be a flebologist, but I might miss out on knowing what that is if my school only talks about medical careers in bio or chem class. Since I am taking physics, maybe an engineer would come to talk to my class, but I know for sure that I don't want to be an engineer. Plus physics is hard enough without trying to fit in extra time to talk about careers, we barely get through everything we need to discuss in one class period as it is.

In-school assemblies are the best way to get information about careers to students since we'll actually pay attention, we won't have to stay after school, and we won't take up important class time.

GRADER'S COMMENTS

The writer stays on topic throughout the essay, but doesn't explore each perspective with the same depth of analysis. While the writer adequately expresses her views, she needs to offer a full discussion of each perspective rather than concentrating on her own opinion.

The writing style is adequate, but the essay includes grammatical errors that should be avoided, such as run-on sentences ("I think it's really important to tell students about jobs and careers and high school is a good place to do this but we already spend enough time in school without having to go to lectures after school") and comma splices ("Plus physics is hard enough without trying to fit in extra time to talk about careers, we barely get through everything we need to discuss in one class period as it is"). The writer has a few spelling mistakes, writing "assemblys" for "assemblies," "vains" for "veins," and "flebologist" for "phlebologist." Though the writer has organized the essay into five paragraphs, there are no transitions at the beginning of each paragraph, and the last paragraph includes only one sentence.

Word choice could be improved by avoiding simpler words and phrases ("I'll bet", "super worried, and "for sure"). In addition, the writer should write "biology" instead of "bio" and "chemistry" instead of "chem." In all, the writer needs to offer a more comprehensive analysis of the issue and express her ideas with more complex vocabulary and sentence structure.

LEVEL 2 ESSAY

I dont need anyone to tell me what to do when I get out of school I already know I will work in my uncles garage and hes going to teach me everything I need to no about it. I only go to school because I have to and noone can tell me that I need to learn more than I need.

Maybe other kids want to go to colege and they dont know what they will work at so they can listen to poeple tell them what to do but not me. I like cars and my uncle says I good at them so thats what I will do. Besides people talk a lot but that dosnt mean there right so maybe you wont find out what you want even if you listen to them.

GRADER'S COMMENTS

The essay is off-topic, misses the point of the prompt and task, is very poorly written and shows little, if any, logical reasoning. The author has a definite point of view but it is not relevant to any of the perspectives, thus does not fulfill the requirements of the essay. He has not considered any point of view other than his own and a fleeting, derogatory reference to other students and those who may present job information. His only support is that he already knows what he will do and needs no other information about careers.

Conventions of English are flaunted in every category. There are numerous misspellings, including "no" for "know," "noone" for "no one," "poeple" for "people," and "colege" for "college." Contractions lack apostrophes, sentences are confusing ("noone can tell me that I need to learn more than I need"), necessary words are missing ("uncle says I good at them"), and the first sentence is a run-on one.

Though there are two paragraphs, there is no introduction or conclusion, and neither paragraph attempts to reference any perspective. The author seems to have taken this task as an opportunity to vent his own annoyance at school and those students who are not sure of their career paths, but does so without logical reasons, support, or clarity.

You can evaluate your essay and the model essay based on the following criteria, which is covered in the Practice Makes Perfect section of this book:

- Does the author discuss all three perspectives provided in the prompt?

- Is the author's own perspective clearly stated?

- Does the body of the essay assess and analyze each perspective?

- Is the relevance of each paragraph clear?

- Does the author start a new paragraph for each new idea?

- Is each sentence in a paragraph relevant to the point made in that paragraph?

- Are transitions clear?

- Is the essay easy to read? Is it engaging?

- Are sentences varied?

- Is vocabulary used effectively? Is college-level vocabulary used?

ACT Practice Test Six
ANSWER SHEET

ENGLISH TEST

1. Ⓐ Ⓑ Ⓒ Ⓓ	11. Ⓐ Ⓑ Ⓒ Ⓓ	21. Ⓐ Ⓑ Ⓒ Ⓓ	31. Ⓐ Ⓑ Ⓒ Ⓓ	41. Ⓐ Ⓑ Ⓒ Ⓓ	51. Ⓐ Ⓑ Ⓒ Ⓓ	61. Ⓐ Ⓑ Ⓒ Ⓓ	71. Ⓐ Ⓑ Ⓒ Ⓓ
2. Ⓕ Ⓖ Ⓗ Ⓙ	12. Ⓕ Ⓖ Ⓗ Ⓙ	22. Ⓕ Ⓖ Ⓗ Ⓙ	32. Ⓕ Ⓖ Ⓗ Ⓙ	42. Ⓕ Ⓖ Ⓗ Ⓙ	52. Ⓕ Ⓖ Ⓗ Ⓙ	62. Ⓕ Ⓖ Ⓗ Ⓙ	72. Ⓕ Ⓖ Ⓗ Ⓙ
3. Ⓐ Ⓑ Ⓒ Ⓓ	13. Ⓐ Ⓑ Ⓒ Ⓓ	23. Ⓐ Ⓑ Ⓒ Ⓓ	33. Ⓐ Ⓑ Ⓒ Ⓓ	43. Ⓐ Ⓑ Ⓒ Ⓓ	53. Ⓐ Ⓑ Ⓒ Ⓓ	63. Ⓐ Ⓑ Ⓒ Ⓓ	73. Ⓐ Ⓑ Ⓒ Ⓓ
4. Ⓕ Ⓖ Ⓗ Ⓙ	14. Ⓕ Ⓖ Ⓗ Ⓙ	24. Ⓕ Ⓖ Ⓗ Ⓙ	34. Ⓕ Ⓖ Ⓗ Ⓙ	44. Ⓕ Ⓖ Ⓗ Ⓙ	54. Ⓕ Ⓖ Ⓗ Ⓙ	64. Ⓕ Ⓖ Ⓗ Ⓙ	74. Ⓕ Ⓖ Ⓗ Ⓙ
5. Ⓐ Ⓑ Ⓒ Ⓓ	15. Ⓐ Ⓑ Ⓒ Ⓓ	25. Ⓐ Ⓑ Ⓒ Ⓓ	35. Ⓐ Ⓑ Ⓒ Ⓓ	45. Ⓐ Ⓑ Ⓒ Ⓓ	55. Ⓐ Ⓑ Ⓒ Ⓓ	65. Ⓐ Ⓑ Ⓒ Ⓓ	75. Ⓐ Ⓑ Ⓒ Ⓓ
6. Ⓕ Ⓖ Ⓗ Ⓙ	16. Ⓕ Ⓖ Ⓗ Ⓙ	26. Ⓕ Ⓖ Ⓗ Ⓙ	36. Ⓕ Ⓖ Ⓗ Ⓙ	46. Ⓕ Ⓖ Ⓗ Ⓙ	56. Ⓕ Ⓖ Ⓗ Ⓙ	66. Ⓕ Ⓖ Ⓗ Ⓙ	
7. Ⓐ Ⓑ Ⓒ Ⓓ	17. Ⓐ Ⓑ Ⓒ Ⓓ	27. Ⓐ Ⓑ Ⓒ Ⓓ	37. Ⓐ Ⓑ Ⓒ Ⓓ	47. Ⓐ Ⓑ Ⓒ Ⓓ	57. Ⓐ Ⓑ Ⓒ Ⓓ	67. Ⓐ Ⓑ Ⓒ Ⓓ	
8. Ⓕ Ⓖ Ⓗ Ⓙ	18. Ⓕ Ⓖ Ⓗ Ⓙ	28. Ⓕ Ⓖ Ⓗ Ⓙ	38. Ⓕ Ⓖ Ⓗ Ⓙ	48. Ⓕ Ⓖ Ⓗ Ⓙ	58. Ⓕ Ⓖ Ⓗ Ⓙ	68. Ⓕ Ⓖ Ⓗ Ⓙ	
9. Ⓐ Ⓑ Ⓒ Ⓓ	19. Ⓐ Ⓑ Ⓒ Ⓓ	29. Ⓐ Ⓑ Ⓒ Ⓓ	39. Ⓐ Ⓑ Ⓒ Ⓓ	49. Ⓐ Ⓑ Ⓒ Ⓓ	59. Ⓐ Ⓑ Ⓒ Ⓓ	69. Ⓐ Ⓑ Ⓒ Ⓓ	
10. Ⓕ Ⓖ Ⓗ Ⓙ	20. Ⓕ Ⓖ Ⓗ Ⓙ	30. Ⓕ Ⓖ Ⓗ Ⓙ	40. Ⓕ Ⓖ Ⓗ Ⓙ	50. Ⓕ Ⓖ Ⓗ Ⓙ	60. Ⓕ Ⓖ Ⓗ Ⓙ	70. Ⓕ Ⓖ Ⓗ Ⓙ	

MATHEMATICS TEST

1. Ⓐ Ⓑ Ⓒ Ⓓ Ⓔ	11. Ⓐ Ⓑ Ⓒ Ⓓ Ⓔ	21. Ⓐ Ⓑ Ⓒ Ⓓ Ⓔ	31. Ⓐ Ⓑ Ⓒ Ⓓ Ⓔ	41. Ⓐ Ⓑ Ⓒ Ⓓ Ⓔ	51. Ⓐ Ⓑ Ⓒ Ⓓ Ⓔ
2. Ⓕ Ⓖ Ⓗ Ⓙ Ⓚ	12. Ⓕ Ⓖ Ⓗ Ⓙ Ⓚ	22. Ⓕ Ⓖ Ⓗ Ⓙ Ⓚ	32. Ⓕ Ⓖ Ⓗ Ⓙ Ⓚ	42. Ⓕ Ⓖ Ⓗ Ⓙ Ⓚ	52. Ⓕ Ⓖ Ⓗ Ⓙ Ⓚ
3. Ⓐ Ⓑ Ⓒ Ⓓ Ⓔ	13. Ⓐ Ⓑ Ⓒ Ⓓ Ⓔ	23. Ⓐ Ⓑ Ⓒ Ⓓ Ⓔ	33. Ⓐ Ⓑ Ⓒ Ⓓ Ⓔ	43. Ⓐ Ⓑ Ⓒ Ⓓ Ⓔ	53. Ⓐ Ⓑ Ⓒ Ⓓ Ⓔ
4. Ⓕ Ⓖ Ⓗ Ⓙ Ⓚ	14. Ⓕ Ⓖ Ⓗ Ⓙ Ⓚ	24. Ⓕ Ⓖ Ⓗ Ⓙ Ⓚ	34. Ⓕ Ⓖ Ⓗ Ⓙ Ⓚ	44. Ⓕ Ⓖ Ⓗ Ⓙ Ⓚ	54. Ⓕ Ⓖ Ⓗ Ⓙ Ⓚ
5. Ⓐ Ⓑ Ⓒ Ⓓ Ⓔ	15. Ⓐ Ⓑ Ⓒ Ⓓ Ⓔ	25. Ⓐ Ⓑ Ⓒ Ⓓ Ⓔ	35. Ⓐ Ⓑ Ⓒ Ⓓ Ⓔ	45. Ⓐ Ⓑ Ⓒ Ⓓ Ⓔ	55. Ⓐ Ⓑ Ⓒ Ⓓ Ⓔ
6. Ⓕ Ⓖ Ⓗ Ⓙ Ⓚ	16. Ⓕ Ⓖ Ⓗ Ⓙ Ⓚ	26. Ⓕ Ⓖ Ⓗ Ⓙ Ⓚ	36. Ⓕ Ⓖ Ⓗ Ⓙ Ⓚ	46. Ⓕ Ⓖ Ⓗ Ⓙ Ⓚ	56. Ⓕ Ⓖ Ⓗ Ⓙ Ⓚ
7. Ⓐ Ⓑ Ⓒ Ⓓ Ⓔ	17. Ⓐ Ⓑ Ⓒ Ⓓ Ⓔ	27. Ⓐ Ⓑ Ⓒ Ⓓ Ⓔ	37. Ⓐ Ⓑ Ⓒ Ⓓ Ⓔ	47. Ⓐ Ⓑ Ⓒ Ⓓ Ⓔ	57. Ⓐ Ⓑ Ⓒ Ⓓ Ⓔ
8. Ⓕ Ⓖ Ⓗ Ⓙ Ⓚ	18. Ⓕ Ⓖ Ⓗ Ⓙ Ⓚ	28. Ⓕ Ⓖ Ⓗ Ⓙ Ⓚ	38. Ⓕ Ⓖ Ⓗ Ⓙ Ⓚ	48. Ⓕ Ⓖ Ⓗ Ⓙ Ⓚ	58. Ⓕ Ⓖ Ⓗ Ⓙ Ⓚ
9. Ⓐ Ⓑ Ⓒ Ⓓ Ⓔ	19. Ⓐ Ⓑ Ⓒ Ⓓ Ⓔ	29. Ⓐ Ⓑ Ⓒ Ⓓ Ⓔ	39. Ⓐ Ⓑ Ⓒ Ⓓ Ⓔ	49. Ⓐ Ⓑ Ⓒ Ⓓ Ⓔ	59. Ⓐ Ⓑ Ⓒ Ⓓ Ⓔ
10. Ⓕ Ⓖ Ⓗ Ⓙ Ⓚ	20. Ⓕ Ⓖ Ⓗ Ⓙ Ⓚ	30. Ⓕ Ⓖ Ⓗ Ⓙ Ⓚ	40. Ⓕ Ⓖ Ⓗ Ⓙ Ⓚ	50. Ⓕ Ⓖ Ⓗ Ⓙ Ⓚ	60. Ⓕ Ⓖ Ⓗ Ⓙ Ⓚ

READING TEST

1. Ⓐ Ⓑ Ⓒ Ⓓ	6. Ⓕ Ⓖ Ⓗ Ⓙ	11. Ⓐ Ⓑ Ⓒ Ⓓ	16. Ⓕ Ⓖ Ⓗ Ⓙ	21. Ⓐ Ⓑ Ⓒ Ⓓ	26. Ⓕ Ⓖ Ⓗ Ⓙ	31. Ⓐ Ⓑ Ⓒ Ⓓ	36. Ⓕ Ⓖ Ⓗ Ⓙ
2. Ⓕ Ⓖ Ⓗ Ⓙ	7. Ⓐ Ⓑ Ⓒ Ⓓ	12. Ⓕ Ⓖ Ⓗ Ⓙ	17. Ⓐ Ⓑ Ⓒ Ⓓ	22. Ⓕ Ⓖ Ⓗ Ⓙ	27. Ⓐ Ⓑ Ⓒ Ⓓ	32. Ⓕ Ⓖ Ⓗ Ⓙ	37. Ⓐ Ⓑ Ⓒ Ⓓ
3. Ⓐ Ⓑ Ⓒ Ⓓ	8. Ⓕ Ⓖ Ⓗ Ⓙ	13. Ⓐ Ⓑ Ⓒ Ⓓ	18. Ⓕ Ⓖ Ⓗ Ⓙ	23. Ⓐ Ⓑ Ⓒ Ⓓ	28. Ⓕ Ⓖ Ⓗ Ⓙ	33. Ⓐ Ⓑ Ⓒ Ⓓ	38. Ⓕ Ⓖ Ⓗ Ⓙ
4. Ⓕ Ⓖ Ⓗ Ⓙ	9. Ⓐ Ⓑ Ⓒ Ⓓ	14. Ⓕ Ⓖ Ⓗ Ⓙ	19. Ⓐ Ⓑ Ⓒ Ⓓ	24. Ⓕ Ⓖ Ⓗ Ⓙ	29. Ⓐ Ⓑ Ⓒ Ⓓ	34. Ⓕ Ⓖ Ⓗ Ⓙ	39. Ⓐ Ⓑ Ⓒ Ⓓ
5. Ⓐ Ⓑ Ⓒ Ⓓ	10. Ⓕ Ⓖ Ⓗ Ⓙ	15. Ⓐ Ⓑ Ⓒ Ⓓ	20. Ⓕ Ⓖ Ⓗ Ⓙ	25. Ⓐ Ⓑ Ⓒ Ⓓ	30. Ⓕ Ⓖ Ⓗ Ⓙ	35. Ⓐ Ⓑ Ⓒ Ⓓ	40. Ⓕ Ⓖ Ⓗ Ⓙ

SCIENCE TEST

1. Ⓐ Ⓑ Ⓒ Ⓓ	6. Ⓕ Ⓖ Ⓗ Ⓙ	11. Ⓐ Ⓑ Ⓒ Ⓓ	16. Ⓕ Ⓖ Ⓗ Ⓙ	21. Ⓐ Ⓑ Ⓒ Ⓓ	26. Ⓕ Ⓖ Ⓗ Ⓙ	31. Ⓐ Ⓑ Ⓒ Ⓓ	36. Ⓕ Ⓖ Ⓗ Ⓙ
2. Ⓕ Ⓖ Ⓗ Ⓙ	7. Ⓐ Ⓑ Ⓒ Ⓓ	12. Ⓕ Ⓖ Ⓗ Ⓙ	17. Ⓐ Ⓑ Ⓒ Ⓓ	22. Ⓕ Ⓖ Ⓗ Ⓙ	27. Ⓐ Ⓑ Ⓒ Ⓓ	32. Ⓕ Ⓖ Ⓗ Ⓙ	37. Ⓐ Ⓑ Ⓒ Ⓓ
3. Ⓐ Ⓑ Ⓒ Ⓓ	8. Ⓕ Ⓖ Ⓗ Ⓙ	13. Ⓐ Ⓑ Ⓒ Ⓓ	18. Ⓕ Ⓖ Ⓗ Ⓙ	23. Ⓐ Ⓑ Ⓒ Ⓓ	28. Ⓕ Ⓖ Ⓗ Ⓙ	33. Ⓐ Ⓑ Ⓒ Ⓓ	38. Ⓕ Ⓖ Ⓗ Ⓙ
4. Ⓕ Ⓖ Ⓗ Ⓙ	9. Ⓐ Ⓑ Ⓒ Ⓓ	14. Ⓕ Ⓖ Ⓗ Ⓙ	19. Ⓐ Ⓑ Ⓒ Ⓓ	24. Ⓕ Ⓖ Ⓗ Ⓙ	29. Ⓐ Ⓑ Ⓒ Ⓓ	34. Ⓕ Ⓖ Ⓗ Ⓙ	39. Ⓐ Ⓑ Ⓒ Ⓓ
5. Ⓐ Ⓑ Ⓒ Ⓓ	10. Ⓕ Ⓖ Ⓗ Ⓙ	15. Ⓐ Ⓑ Ⓒ Ⓓ	20. Ⓕ Ⓖ Ⓗ Ⓙ	25. Ⓐ Ⓑ Ⓒ Ⓓ	30. Ⓕ Ⓖ Ⓗ Ⓙ	35. Ⓐ Ⓑ Ⓒ Ⓓ	40. Ⓕ Ⓖ Ⓗ Ⓙ

ENGLISH TEST

45 Minutes—75 Questions

Directions: In the following five passages, certain words and phrases are underlined and numbered. In the right-hand column are alternatives for each underlined portion. Select the one that best conveys the idea, creates the most grammatically correct sentence, or is most consistent with the style and tone of the passage. If you decide that the original version is best, select NO CHANGE. You may also find questions that ask about the entire passage or a section of the passage. These questions will correspond to small, numbered boxes in the test. For these questions, decide which choice best accomplishes the purpose set out in the question stem. After you've selected the best choice, fill in the corresponding oval on your Answer Grid. For some questions, you'll need to read the context in order to answer correctly. Be sure to read until you have enough information to determine the correct answer choice.

PASSAGE I

MY OLD FASHIONED FATHER

My father, though he is only in his early 50s, is stuck in his old-fashioned <u>ways. He has a</u> general mistrust of any
1
innovation or technology that he can't immediately grasp and

1. **A.** NO CHANGE
   B. ways he has a
   C. ways having a
   D. ways, and still has a

he always <u>tells us, that</u> if something isn't broken, then you
2
shouldn't fix it.

2. **F.** NO CHANGE
   G. tells us, that,
   H. tells us that,
   J. tells us that

He <u>has run</u> a small grocery store in town, and if you
3
were to look at a snapshot of his back office taken when he opened

3. **A.** NO CHANGE
   B. was running
   C. runs
   D. ran

the store in 1975, you would <u>see that not much has</u>
4
<u>changed since</u>. He is the most disorganized person I
4
know and still

4. **F.** NO CHANGE
   G. not be likely to see very much that has changed since.
   H. be able to see right away that not very much has changed since.
   J. not change very much.

GO ON TO THE NEXT PAGE ▷

uses a pencil and paper to keep track of his <u>inventory.</u>
₅
His small office is about to burst with all the various

documents,

notes, and receipts he has accumulated over the <u>years,</u>
₆
<u>his filing cabinets</u> have long since been filled up. The
₆
centerpiece of all the clutter is his ancient typewriter,

which isn't even electric. In the past few years, Father's

search for replacement typewriter ribbons has become

an increasingly difficult task, because they are no longer

being produced. He is perpetually tracking down the

few remaining places that still have these antiquated

ribbons in their dusty inventories. When people ask

him why he doesn't get upgrade his equipment, he tells

them, "Electric typewriters won't work in a blackout. All

I need is a candle and some paper, and I'm fine." Little

does Father <u>know, however, is that</u> the "upgrade" people
₇
are speaking of is not to an electric typewriter but to a

computer.

[1] Hoping to bring Father out of the dark ages, <u>my</u>
₈
<u>sister, and I</u> bought him a brand new computer for his
₈
fiftieth birthday. [2] We offered to help him to transfer all

of his records onto it and to teach him how to use it.

5. Assuming that all are true, which of the following replacements for "inventory" would be most appropriate in context?

   A. inventory of canned and dry goods.

   B. inventory, refusing to consider a more current method.

   C. inventory, which he writes down by hand.

   D. inventory of goods on the shelves and in the storeroom.

6. F. NO CHANGE

   G. years; his filing cabinets

   H. years, and besides that, his filing cabinets

   J. years and since his filing cabinets

7. A. NO CHANGE

   B. know, besides, that

   C. know, however, that

   D. know, beyond that,

8. F. NO CHANGE

   G. me and my sister

   H. my sister and I

   J. my sister and I,

GO ON TO THE NEXT PAGE ▷

[3] <u>Eagerly,</u> we told him about all the new spreadsheet
$\qquad$9

programs that would help simplify his recordkeeping

and organize his

<u>accounts; and</u> emphasized the advantage of not having
$\quad$10

to completely retype any document when he found a

typo. [4] Rather than offering us a look of joy for the

life-changing gift we had presented him, however, he

again brought up the blackout scenario. [5] To Father,

this is a concrete argument, <u>never mind the fact that</u> our
$\qquad\qquad$11

town hasn't had a blackout in five

years, and that one only lasted an hour or two. ☐12

    My father's state-of-the-art computer now serves

as a very expensive bulletin board for the hundreds of

adhesive notes

he uses to keep himself organized. <u>Sooner than later,</u> we
$\qquad\qquad$13

fully expect it will completely disappear under the

mounting

---

9. **A.** NO CHANGE
    B. On the other hand,
    C. In addition
    D. Rather,

10. **F.** NO CHANGE
    G. accounts and
    H. accounts and,
    J. accounts, we

11. **A.** NO CHANGE
    B. although,
    C. although
    D. despite the fact that

12. The author wants to include the following statement in this paragraph:

    We expected it to save him a lot of time and effort.

    The most logical placement for this sentence would be:

    F. before Sentence 1
    G. after Sentence 1
    H. after Sentence 4
    J. after Sentence 5

13. **A.** NO CHANGE
    B. Sooner rather than later,
    C. Sooner or later,
    D. As soon as later,

GO ON TO THE NEXT PAGE ⇨

files and papers in the back office. <u>In the depths of that</u>
                                              14
<u>disorganized office, the computer will join the cell</u>
                                    14
<u>phone my mom gave him a few years ago.</u> Interestingly
                           14
enough, every once in a while, that completely forgotten

cell phone will ring

from under the heavy clutter of the past. ⑮

14. **F.** NO CHANGE

    G. Deep in the disorganization of that office's, the computer will join the cell phone my mom gave him a few years back.

    H. In the disorganized depths of the office, the computer will soon be joined by the cell phone my mom gave him a few years ago.

    J. The computer will join the cell phone my mom gave him a few years back in the disorganized depths of that office.

15. Which of the following would provide the most appropriate conclusion for the passage?

    A. It's hard to say what else might be lost in there.

    B. We tell my father it's a reminder that he can't hide from the future forever.

    C. We have no idea who might be calling.

    D. Maybe one day I will try to find it and answer it.

PASSAGE II

BREAKING BASEBALL'S COLOR BARRIER

A quick perusal of any modern major league base-

ball team will reveal a roster of players of multiple eth-

nicities <u>from the farthest</u> reaches of the globe. Second
                16
only to soccer, baseball has evolved into a global sport

and a symbol for equality among races.

<u>It's</u> diversity today presents a stark contrast to
17
the state of the sport just sixty years ago. As late as the

1940s, there existed an unwritten rule in baseball that

16. **F.** NO CHANGE

    G. from the most far

    H. from the most farthest

    J. from farther

17. **A.** NO CHANGE

    B. Its'

    C. Its

    D. Its own

GO ON TO THE NEXT PAGE ⟹

prevented all but white players <u>to participate</u> in the
18
major leagues. This rule was known as the "color

barrier" or "color line." The color line in baseball

actually predated the birth of the major leagues. Prior

to the official formation of any league of professional

baseball teams, there existed an organization of ama-

teur baseball clubs known as the National Association

of Baseball Players, <u>which was the precursor to today's</u>
19
<u>National League.</u> On December 11, 1868, the governing
19
body of this association had unanimously adopted a rule

that effectively

barred any team that <u>had, any "colored persons"</u> on its
20
roster. However, when baseball started to organize into

leagues of

professional teams in the early <u>1880s; the</u> National
21
Association of Baseball Players' decree no longer had any

weight, especially in the newly formed American

18. F. NO CHANGE
G. to be able to participate
H. from participating
J. to participation

19. Is the underlined portion relevant here?
A. Yes, because it helps familiarize the reader with the range of baseball associations that once existed.
B. Yes, because it helps clarify the development the author traces.
C. No, because the names of the organizations are not important.
D. No, because it is inconsistent with the style of the essay to provide specific historical data.

20. F. NO CHANGE
G. had any, "colored persons"
H. had any "colored persons"
J. had any "colored persons,"

21. A. NO CHANGE
B. 1880s, the
C. 1880s. The
D. 1880s, and the

GO ON TO THE NEXT PAGE ⟩

Association. <u>For a brief period in those early years, a few</u>
                                                        22
<u>African Americans played side by side with white players</u>
                                                        22
<u>on major league diamonds.</u>
            22

[1] Most baseball historians believe that the first

African American to play in the major leagues was

Moses "Fleet"

Walker. [2] <u>Walker was a catcher</u> for the Toledo Blue
                            23
Stockings of the American Association between 1884

and 1889. [3] During that time, a few other

African Americans, <u>including</u> Walker's brother Weldy,
                          24

<u>would be joining him</u> on the Blue Stockings.
          25
[4] Unfortunately, this respite from segregation did not

last for very long; as Jim Crow laws took their hold on

the nation, many of the most popular white ballplayers

started to refuse to take the field with their

African-American teammates. [5] By the 1890s, the

22. The writer is considering deleting the underlined portion. Should the writer make this deletion?

F. Yes, because the information is not relevant to the topic of the paragraph.

G. Yes, because the information contradicts the first sentence of the paragraph.

H. No, because the information shows that white players did not object to integration.

J. No, because the statement provides a smooth transition to the specific information about early African-American players in the next paragraph.

23. A. NO CHANGE
    B. Walker, being a catcher
    C. Walker, a catcher
    D. Walker who was a catcher

24. F. NO CHANGE
    G. which included
    H. who would include
    J. including among them

25. A. NO CHANGE
    B. joined him
    C. were to join him
    D. will join him

GO ON TO THE NEXT PAGE

color barrier had fully returned to baseball, where it would endure for more than half a century. 26

Jackie Robinson would become the first African American to cross the color line <u>at the time when</u> he
27
debuted for the Brooklyn Dodgers in 1947. For Robinson's landmark

achievements on and off the diamond, he will <u>forever be</u>
28
<u>recognized as</u> a hero of the civil rights movement and a
28
sports icon. The path that he blazed through the prejudices of American society during the 1940s and 1950s opened the door for the multi-racial and multi-national face of modern baseball, and fans of the sport worldwide <u>will be in his debt for all time to come.</u>
29

26. Upon reviewing this paragraph, the author discovers that he has neglected to include the following information:

    A handful of African Americans played for other teams as well.

    This sentence would be most logically placed after:

    F. Sentence 1.

    G. Sentence 2.

    H. Sentence 3.

    J. Sentence 4.

27. A. NO CHANGE

    B. when

    C. while

    D. when the time came that

28. F. NO CHANGE

    G. one day be recognized

    H. forever recognize

    J. be admired by a lot of people for being

29. A. NO CHANGE

    B. will be forever in his debt.

    C. will owe him a lot.

    D. being in his debt forever.

GO ON TO THE NEXT PAGE

Question 30 asks about the essay as a whole.

30. Suppose the writer had been assigned to develop a brief essay on the history of baseball. Would this essay successfully fulfill that goal?

   F. Yes, because it covers events in baseball over a period of more than a century.

   G. Yes, because it mentions key figures in baseball history.

   H. No, because people played baseball before 1868.

   J. No, because the focus of this essay is on one particular aspect of baseball history.

PASSAGE III

THE BEAR MOUNTAIN BRIDGE

When the gleaming Bear Mountain Bridge officially opened to traffic on Thanksgiving Day in 1924, it was known as the Harriman Bridge, after
31
Edward H. Harriman, wealthy philanthropist and

patriarch of the family most influential in the bridges
32
construction. Before the Harriman Bridge was constructed, there were no bridges spanning the Hudson River south of Albany. By the early 1920s, the ferry services used to transport people back and forth across the river had become woefully inadequate. In February of 1922, in an effort to alleviate some of the burden on the ferries and create a permanent link across the Hudson, the New York State Legislature

31. A. NO CHANGE
    B. 1924; it
    C. 1924. It
    D. 1924 and it

32. F. NO CHANGE
    G. bridges'
    H. bridge's
    J. bridges's

had authorized a group of private investors, led by
33
Mary Harriman, to build a bridge. The group, known

as the Bear Mountain Hudson Bridge Company

(BMHBC), was allotted thirty years to build, construct,
34
and maintain the structure, at which time the span
34
would be handed over to New York State.

    The BMHBC invested almost $4,500,000 into the

suspension bridge and hired the world-renowned

design team of Howard Baird and George Hodge as
35

architects. 36 Baird and Hodge enlisted the help of

John A. Roebling and Sons,

33. **A.** NO CHANGE
    B. authorized
    C. was authorized
    D. would authorize

34. **F.** NO CHANGE
    G. build and construct and maintain
    H. construct and maintain
    J. construct, and maintain

35. **A.** NO CHANGE
    B. of Howard Baird, and George Hodge
    C. of Howard Baird and, George Hodge
    D. of, Howard Baird and George Hodge

36. The author wants to remove the following from the preceding sentence:

    invested almost $4,500,00 into the suspension bridge

If this language were deleted, the essay would primarily lose:

    F. a piece of information critical to the point of the essay.
    G. a necessary transition between the second and third paragraphs.
    H. a detail contributing to the reader's understanding of the magnitude of the project.
    J. an explanation of how the group raised money to invest in the bridge.

GO ON TO THE NEXT PAGE ▷

<u>who were</u> instrumental in the steel work of the Brooklyn
                37
Bridge and would later work on the Golden Gate and

George Washington Bridges.

    Amazingly, the bridge took only twenty months

and eleven days to complete, and not one life was lost.

[38] It was a technological marvel and would stand as

a model for the suspension bridges of the future. At

the time of the Harriman Bridge's completion, it was,

at 2,257 feet, the longest single-span steel suspension

bridge in the world.

<u>Therefore, the</u> two main cables used in the suspension
                39
were 18 inches in diameter, and each contained 7,752

individual steel wires wrapped in 37 thick strands. If

completely unraveled, the single wires in both cables

would be 7,377 miles <u>longer</u>. The bridge links Bear
                                            40
Mountain on the western bank of the Hudson to

Anthony's Nose on the eastern side, and it lies so

precisely on an east-west plane that one can check a

compass by it. It carries Routes 6 and 202 across the

Hudson, <u>as well as being</u> the point of river crossing for
                        41
the Appalachian Trail.

37. A. NO CHANGE
   B. who was
   C. a company
   D. a company that had been

38. If the writer were to delete the preceding sentence, the essay would lose primarily:

   F. information about how long the project had been expected to take.

   G. a warning about the dangers of large-scale construction projects.

   H. crucial information about the duration of the project.

   J. a necessary transition between paragraphs 3 and 4.

39. A. NO CHANGE
   B. Nonetheless, the
   C. At the same time, the
   D. The

40. F. NO CHANGE
   G. long.
   H. in total length.
   J. lengthy.

41. A. NO CHANGE
   B. and is as well
   C. and is
   D. besides being

GO ON TO THE NEXT PAGE ⇨

In an attempt to recoup some of its investment after the bridge opened, the BMHBC charged an exorbitant
42
toll of eighty cents per crossing. Even with the high toll, however, it operated at a loss for thirteen of its first sixteen years. Finally it was acquired, more than ten years—a full decade—earlier than planned, by the New
43
York State Bridge Authority. The bridge was renamed the Bear Mountain Bridge. Today, the Bear Mountain

Bridge sees more than six million vehicles cross its
44
concrete decks each year.

42. **F.** NO CHANGE
    G. opened the BMHBC charged
    H. opened: the BMHBC charged
    J. opened; the BMHBC charged

43. **A.** NO CHANGE
    B. years and a full decade
    C. years, a full decade,
    D. years

44. **F.** NO CHANGE
    G. over
    H. even more than
    J. a higher amount than

Question 45 asks about the essay as a whole.

---

45. Suppose the author had been assigned to write a brief history of bridge building in the United States. Would this essay successfully fulfill that requirement?

    A. Yes, because it provides information on the entire process from the initial funding through the opening of the bridge.

    B. Yes, because Bear Mountain Bridge is historically significant.

    C. No, because it focuses on only one bridge.

    D. No, because the essay is primarily concerned with the financial aspects of building and maintaining the bridge.

GO ON TO THE NEXT PAGE ➤

PASSAGE IV

THE DREAM OF THE AMERICAN WEST

As the sun <u>was slowly rising</u> over the Atlantic
          46
Ocean and painted New York harbor a spectacular fiery

orange, I started my old Toyota's engine. At this early

hour, there was still some semblance of the night's

tranquility left on the city sidewalks, but I knew that,

as the minutes ticked by, <u>the streets would flood</u>
                                 47

<u>with humanity.</u>
 47

I smiled <u>with</u> the thought that soon all the wonderful
        48
chaos of New York City would be disappearing behind

me as I <u>embarked on my trip to the other side of</u> the
                  49
country.

<u>As the morning sun climbed into the sky,</u>
              50

46. **F.** NO CHANGE
    G. rising slowly
    H. rose slowly
    J. continued to rise

47. The author wants to contrast the statement about the quiet of the night streets with a related detail about the daytime activity. Assuming that all of the choices are true, which of the following best accomplishes that goal?

    A. NO CHANGE
    B. some people might appear.
    C. everything would be different.
    D. the tranquility would be unbroken.

48. **F.** NO CHANGE
    G. along with
    H. at
    J. all because of

49. **A.** NO CHANGE
    B. embarked on this journey across
    C. traveled to the other side of
    D. traveled across

50. Which of the following alternatives to the underlined portion would NOT be acceptable?

    F. At sunrise,
    G. Watching the morning sun climb into the sky,
    H. The morning sun climbed into the sky,
    J. As the sun rose,

GO ON TO THE NEXT PAGE ▷

I shuddered with excitement <u>to think that my final stop</u>
₅₁
<u>would be in California, where the sun itself ends its</u>
₅₁
<u>journey across America.</u> Like the sun, however, I still
₅₁
had quite a journey before me.

I had been planning this road trip across the United States for as long as I could remember. In my life, I had been fortunate enough to see some of the most beautiful countries in the world. However, it had always bothered me that although I'd stood in the shadow of the <u>Eiffel Tower, marveled in the desert heat at the</u>
₅₂
<u>Pyramids of Giza,</u> I'd never seen any of the wonders of
₅₂
my own country, except those found in my hometown of New York City. All of that was about to change.

<u>As I left the city, the tall buildings began to give way</u>
₅₃
<u>to smaller ones, then to transform into the quaint rows</u>
₅₃
<u>of houses that clustered the crowded suburbs.</u> Trees and
₅₃
grass, then the yellow-green of cornfields and the golden wash of wheat

51. The writer is considering revising this sentence by deleting the underlined portion. If she did so, the paragraph would primarily lose:

   A. information about the reasons for the writer's trip.

   B. information about the writer's destination.

   C. a description of the writer's planned route.

   D. a comparison between the sunrise in New York and the sunset in California.

52. F. NO CHANGE

   G. Eiffel Tower and had marveled in the desert heat at the Pyramids of Giza,

   H. Eiffel Tower and marveled in the desert heat at the Pyramids of Giza

   J. Eiffel Tower, and had marveled, in the desert heat, at the Pyramids of Giza

53. Given that all are true, which of the following provides the most effective transition between the third paragraph and the description of the Midwest in the fourth paragraph?

   A. NO CHANGE

   B. In fact, there were changes on the horizon almost immediately.

   C. My excitement hadn't diminished.

   D. I realized that people who lived in other areas might feel the same way about visiting New York.

GO ON TO THE NEXT PAGE ⇒

were rapidly <u>replacing the familiar mazes of cement and</u>
                                          54
<u>steel.</u> My world no longer stretched vertically toward
54

54. Assuming that all are true, which of the following provides information most relevant to the main focus of the paragraph?
   F. NO CHANGE
   G. appearing before me.
   H. racing past my window.
   J. becoming monotonous.

<u>the sky, it now spread</u> horizontally towards eternity.
            55

55. A. NO CHANGE
   B. the sky but it now spread
   C. the sky; it now spread
   D. the sky spreading

<u>For two days</u> I pushed through the wind-whipped farm-
       56
lands of Mid-America, hypnotized by the beauty of the

undulating yet unbroken lines. At night, the breeze from

my car would stir the wheat fields to dance beneath the

moon, and the silos hid in the shadows, quietly impos-

ing their simple serenity upon everything.

56. F. NO CHANGE
   G. For two days,
   H. During two days,
   J. During two days

   Then, as the <u>night's shadows</u> gave way to light, there
                          57

57. A. NO CHANGE
   B. nights shadows
   C. shadows from the night
   D. night shadow

seemed to be a great force rising to meet the <u>sun as it</u>
                                                    58
<u>made its reappearance.</u>
        58

58. F. NO CHANGE
   G. sun as it reappeared
   H. reappearing sun
   J. sun as it was also rising

<u>Still,</u> I had no idea what I was looking at. Then, there
 59
was no

59. A. NO CHANGE
   B. Even so,
   C. At first,
   D. Eventually,

GO ON TO THE NEXT PAGE

<u>mistaking it.</u> The unbroken lines of Mid-America had
 60
given way to the jagged and majestic heights of the

Rockies and the gateway to the American west.

PASSAGE V

TRAVELING AT THE SPEED OF SOUND

The term "supersonic" refers to anything that travels faster than the speed of sound. When the last of the

supersonic Concorde passenger planes made its

final trip across the Atlantic in <u>November of 2003, an</u>
                                              61
<u>interesting</u> chapter in history was finally closed. The
 61
fleet of supersonic Concorde SSTs, or "Supersonic

Transports," which were jointly operated by Air France

and British Airways, had been making the interconti-

nental trip across the Atlantic for almost thirty years.

These amazing machines cruised at <u>Mach 2 which is</u>
                                          62
more than twice the speed of sound. They flew

<u>to a height</u> almost twice that of standard passenger
  63
airplanes. The Concorde routinely made the trip from

New York to London in less than three hours and was

much more expensive than normal transatlantic flights.

Though the majority of the passengers who traveled on

the Concorde were celebrities or the extremely wealthy,

it also attracted ordinary people who simply wanted to

know how it felt to travel faster than the speed of sound.

60. F. NO CHANGE
 G. mistake to be made.
 H. chance to mistake it.
 J. having made a mistake.

61. A. NO CHANGE
 B. November, of 2003 an interesting
 C. November of 2003 an interesting
 D. November of 2003; an interesting

62. F. NO CHANGE
 G. Mach 2, which
 H. Mach 2,
 J. a speed of Mach 2, which is

63. A. NO CHANGE
 B. at an altitude
 C. toward an altitude
 D. very high

GO ON TO THE NEXT PAGE

<u>Some of these,</u> would save money for years just to gain
    64
that knowledge.

      What is the speed of sound? Many people are

surprised to learn that there is no fixed answer to this

question. The speed <u>that</u> sound travels through a given
            65
medium depends on a

number of factors. <u>So that we may better begin to</u>
                  66
<u>understand</u> the speed of sound, we must first under-
 66
stand what a "sound" really is.

      The standard dictionary definition of sound is "a

vibration or disturbance transmitted, like waves through

water, through a material medium such as a gas." Our

ears are able to pick up those sound waves and <u>convert</u>
                                  67
them into what we hear. This means that the speed at

which sound travels through gas

<u>directly depends on what gas it is traveling through,</u>
                    68
<u>and the temperature and pressure of the gas.</u> When
                  68
discussing aircraft breaking the speed of sound, that gas

medium, of course, is

air. As air temperature and pressure decrease <u>with alti-</u>
                                      69
<u>tude,</u> so does the speed of sound. An airplane flying at
 69
the speed of sound at sea level is traveling roughly at

64. **F.** NO CHANGE
     G. Among these were those who
     H. Some
     J. Some,

65. **A.** NO CHANGE
     B. to which
     C. at which
     D. where

66. **F.** NO CHANGE
     G. In order that we may understand
     H. To understand
     J. For understanding

67. Which of the following alternatives to the underlined portion would be the LEAST acceptable?
     A. change
     B. translate
     C. alter
     D. transform

68. **F.** NO CHANGE
     G. depends directly on the type, temperature, and pressure of the gas it is traveling through.
     H. directly depends on what gas it is, and also on the temperature and pressure of that gas.
     J. depends directly on the type, temperature, and pressure of the gas.

69. **A.** NO CHANGE
     B. with height
     C. with a drop in altitude
     D. at higher altitudes

GO ON TO THE NEXT PAGE ⟹

761 mph; <u>however</u> when that same plane climbs to
            70
20,000 feet, the speed of sound is only about 707 mph.

This is why the Concorde's cruising attitude was so

much higher than

that of a regular passenger aircraft; <u>planes can reach</u>
                                              71
<u>supersonic speeds more easily at higher altitudes.</u>
                        71

In the years since the Concorde <u>has been</u> decom-
                                    72
missioned, only fighter pilots and astronauts have

been able to experience the sensation of breaking

"the sound barrier." <u>But that is all about to change very</u>
                                          73
<u>soon.</u> Newer and faster supersonic passenger planes are
  73
being developed that will be technologically superior

to the Concorde and much cheaper to operate.

<u>That means we can expect that in the very near future,</u>
                        74
supersonic passenger travel will be available

not only to the rich and famous, <u>but also be for</u> the
                                          75
masses, so they, too, can experience life at faster than

the speed of sound.

70. **F.** NO CHANGE
    G. however,
    H. and so,
    J. even so

71. Given that all are true, which of the following
    provides the most logical conclusion for this
    sentence?
    A. NO CHANGE
    B. they're much faster.
    C. they use much more fuel than regular
    aircraft.
    D. they're rarely visible because they fly
    above the cloud cover.

72. **F.** NO CHANGE
    G. came to be
    H. was
    J. had been

73. **A.** NO CHANGE
    B. Soon, however, that is about to change.
    C. Soon, however, that will change.
    D. That is about to change soon.

74. **F.** NO CHANGE
    G. So then, in the near future
    H. Soon,
    J. We can expect, then, that in the near
    future

75. **A.** NO CHANGE
    B. but also be available to
    C. but also to
    D. but for

MATHEMATICS TEST

60 Minutes—60 Questions

Directions: Solve each of the following problems, select the correct answer, and then fill in the corresponding oval on your Answer Grid.

Don't linger over problems that are too time-consuming. Do as many as you can, then come back to the others in the time permitted.

You may use a calculator on this test. Some questions, however, may be easier to answer without the use of a calculator.

Note: Unless the question says otherwise, assume all of the following:

1. Illustrative figures are *not* necessarily drawn to scale.

2. All geometric figures lie in a plane.

3. The term *line* indicates a straight line.

4. The term *average* indicates arithmetic mean.

1. A *rod* is a unit of length equivalent to 5.5 yards. If a field is 127 yards long, then how many rods long is the field, to the nearest tenth?

    A. 231.9
    B. 69.9
    C. 43.3
    D. 23.1
    E. 4.3

2. Because of increased rents in the area, a pizzeria needs to raise the cost of its $20.00 extra large pizza by 22%. What will the new cost be?

    F. $20.22
    G. $22.20
    H. $24.00
    J. $24.40
    K. $42.00

3. Increases in membership for 5 different organizations are indicated in the table below.

Organization	A	B	C	D	E
Increase in Membership	120	210	0	210	180

What is the average increase in membership for the 5 organizations?

    A. 127.5
    B. 144
    C. 170
    D. 180
    E. 240

4. Train A travels 50 miles per hour for 3 hours; Train B travels 70 miles per hour for $2\frac{1}{2}$ hours. What is the *difference* between the number of miles traveled by Train A and the number of miles traveled by Train B?

    F. 0
    G. 25
    H. 150
    J. 175
    K. 325

GO ON TO THE NEXT PAGE

5. Which of the following is a value of b for which $(b-3)(b+4)=0$?

    A. 3

    B. 4

    C. 7

    D. 10

    E. 12

6. In the parallelogram $RSTU$ shown below, $\overline{ST}$ is 8 feet long. If the parallelogram's perimeter is 42 feet, how many feet long is $\overline{UT}$?

    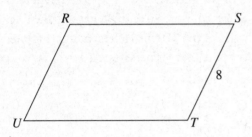

    F. 34

    G. 26

    H. 21

    J. 13

    K. $15\frac{1}{4}$

7. If the measure of each interior angle of a regular polygon is 60°, how many sides does the polygon have?

    A. 3

    B. 4

    C. 6

    D. 10

    E. 12

8. For all nonzero a, b, and c values, $\dfrac{12a^5bc^7}{-3ab^5c^2} = ?$

    F. $\dfrac{-4c^5}{a^4b^4}$

    G. $\dfrac{-4a^4c^5}{b^4}$

    H. $\dfrac{-4ac}{b}$

    J. $-4a^6b^6c^9$

    K. $-4a^4b^4c^5$

9. In the figure below, P and Q lie on the sides of $\triangle WXY$, and $\overline{PQ}$ is parallel to $\overline{WY}$. What is the measure of $\angle QPX$?

    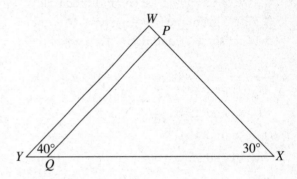

    A. 110°

    B. 120°

    C. 130°

    D. 140°

    E. 150°

10. $|-4| \bullet |2| = ?$

    F. -8

    G. -6

    H. -2

    J. 6

    K. 8

GO ON TO THE NEXT PAGE

11. A company conducted a taste test of its new soft drink. Of the 1250 participants, 800 liked the soft drink, 150 didn't like it, and the rest were undecided. What percent of the participants were undecided about the new soft drink?

   A.   24%

   B.   46%

   C.   64%

   D.   76%

   E. 300%

12. Two whole numbers have a greatest common factor of 15 and a least common multiple of 225. Which of the following pairs of numbers will satisfy this condition?

   F.   9 and 25

   G. 15 and 27

   H. 25 and 45

   J.   30 and 45

   K. 45 and 75

13. If $x = 2$ and $y = -3$, then $x^5y + xy^5 = ?$

   A.   −60

   B. −192

   C. −390

   D. −582

   E. −972

14. How many units long is one side of a square with perimeter $16 - 24h$ units?

   F. $16 - 24h$

   G. $16 - 6h$

   H. $8h$

   J. $4 - 24h$

   K. $4 - 6h$

15. If $(x - k)^2 = x^2 - 26x + k^2$ for all real numbers x, then $k = ?$

   A.   13

   B.   26

   C.   52

   D. 104

   E. 208

16. Helena bought her daughter a game system and two game cartridges for her birthday, all on sale. The game system, regularly $180, was 10% off, and the game cartridges, regularly $40 each, were 20% off. What was the total price of the 3 items Helena bought? (Note: Assume there is no sales tax.)

   F. $186

   G. $194

   H. $221

   J. $226

   K. $250

17. Which of the following expressions gives the slope of the line connecting the points (5,9) and (−3,−12)?

   A. $\dfrac{9 + (-12)}{-5 - (-3)}$

   B. $\dfrac{9 + (-12)}{-3 + 5}$

   C. $\dfrac{9 - (-12)}{5 - (-3)}$

   D. $\dfrac{9 - (-12)}{-3 - 5}$

   E. $\dfrac{9 - (-12)}{-5 + 3}$

GO ON TO THE NEXT PAGE ⟹

18. In the standard (x,y) coordinate plane, how many times does the graph of $y = (x + 1)(x + 2)(x - 3)(x + 4)(x + 5)$ intersect the x-axis?

 F. 15
 G. 9
 H. 5
 J. 4
 K. 1

19. Which of the following is an equivalent, simplified version of $\dfrac{4 + 8x}{12x}$?

 A. $\dfrac{2x + 1}{3x}$

 B. $\dfrac{1 + 8x}{3x}$

 C. 1

 D. $\dfrac{7}{3}$

 E. $\dfrac{8}{3}$

20. Four friends about to share an airport shuttle for $21.50 for each ticket discover that they can purchase a book of 5 tickets for $95.00. How much would each of the 4 save if they can get a fifth person to join them and they divide the cost of the book of 5 tickets equally among all 5 people?

 F. $ 2.25
 G. $ 2.50
 H. $ 3.13
 J. $ 9.00
 K. $12.50

21. What is the sum of the polynomials $-2x^2y^2 + x^2y$ and $3x^2y^2 + 2xy^2$?

 A. $-6x^4y^4 + 2x^3y^3$
 B. $-2x^2y^2 + x^2y + 2xy^2$
 C. $x^2y^2 + x^2y + 2xy^2$
 D. $x^2y^2 + x^2y$
 E. $x^2y^2 + 3x^2y$

22. A 12 foot flagpole casts a 7 foot shadow when the angle of elevation of the sun is θ (see figure below). What is $\tan(\theta)$?

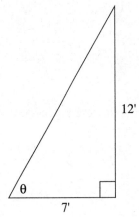

 F. $\dfrac{7}{12}$
 G. 1
 H. $\dfrac{12}{7}$
 J. 19
 K. 84

23. Yousuf was x years old 15 years ago. How old will he be 7 years from now?

 A. $x + 7$
 B. $(x - 15) + 7$
 C. $(x + 15) - 7$
 D. $(x - 15) - 7$
 E. $(x + 15) + 7$

GO ON TO THE NEXT PAGE

24. Which of the following is a factor of $x^2 - 4x - 12$?

F. $(x + 1)$

G. $(x - 2)$

H. $(x + 2)$

J. $(x - 3)$

K. $(x - 4)$

25. What is the length, in inches, of the hypotenuse of a right triangle with legs measuring 8 inches and 15 inches?

A. 7

B. 17

C. 23

D. $\sqrt{23}$

E. $\sqrt{161}$

26. Which of the following expressions is a simplified form of $(-2x^5)^3$?

F. $-6x^8$

G. $8x^8$

H. $-2x^{15}$

J. $-6x^{15}$

K. $-8x^{15}$

27. The *relative atomic mass* of an element is the ratio of the mass of the element to the mass of an equal amount of carbon. If 1 cubic centimeter of carbon has a mass of 12 grams, what is the relative atomic mass of an element that has a mass of 30 grams per cubic centimeter?

A. 1

B. 1.2

C. 2.5

D. 3

E. 30

28. If $2x + 3 = -5$, what is the value of $x^2 - 7x$?

F. -44

G. -12

H. -4

J. 12

K. 44

29. Which of the following is a graph of the solution set for $2(5 + x) < 2$?

A.

B.

C.

D.

E.

30. Which of the following equations has m varying directly as the cube of b and inversely as the square of c?

F. $\dfrac{m^3}{c^2} = b$

G. $\dfrac{b^3}{c^2} = m$

H. $\dfrac{c^3}{b^2} = m$

J. $\dfrac{\sqrt[3]{b}}{\sqrt{c}} = m$

K. $\dfrac{b^3}{m^2} = c$

GO ON TO THE NEXT PAGE

31. Points $V(-2,-7)$ and $W(4,5)$ determine line segment $\overline{VW}$ in the standard (x,y) coordinate plane. If the midpoint of $\overline{VW}$ is $(1,p)$, what is the value of p?

    A. -2
    B. -1
    C. 1
    D. 2
    E. 6

32. If the graphs of $y = 3x$ and $y = mx + 6$ are parallel in the standard (x,y) coordinate plane, then $m = $?

    F. -6
    G. $\dfrac{1}{3}$
    H. 2
    J. 3
    K. 6

33. When 3 times x is increased by 5, the result is less than 11. Which of the following is a graph of the real numbers x for which the previous statement is true?

    A.
    B.
    C.
    D.
    E.

34. It costs 54 cents to buy x pencils and 92 cents to buy y erasers. Which of the following is an expression for the cost, in cents, of 7 pencils and 3 erasers?

    F. $\dfrac{54}{7+x} + \dfrac{92}{3+y}$

    G. $3\left(\dfrac{54}{x}\right) + 7\left(\dfrac{92}{y}\right)$

    H. $7\left(\dfrac{x}{54}\right) + 3\left(\dfrac{y}{92}\right)$

    J. $7\left(\dfrac{54}{x}\right) + 3\left(\dfrac{92}{y}\right)$

    K. $7\left(\dfrac{92}{x}\right) + 3\left(\dfrac{54}{x}\right)$

35. When graphed in the standard (x,y) coordinate plane, 3 points from among $(-9,-7)$, $(-5,-3)$, $(-2,-1)$, $(1,-1)$ and $(10,-8)$ lie on the same side of the line $y - x = 0$. Which of the three points are they?

    A. $(-9,-7)$, $(-2,-1)$, $(-5,-3)$
    B. $(-9,-7)$, $(-2,-1)$, $(1,-1)$
    C. $(-9,-7)$, $(-5,-3)$, $(10,-8)$
    D. $(-9,-7)$, $(1,-1)$, $(10,-8)$
    E. $(-5,-3)$, $(1,-1)$, $(10,-8)$

GO ON TO THE NEXT PAGE

36. What is the sine of angle E in right triangle DEF below?

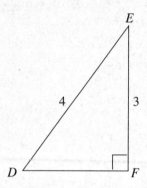

F. $\dfrac{\sqrt{7}}{3}$

G. $\dfrac{3}{4}$

H. $\dfrac{\sqrt{7}}{4}$

J. $\dfrac{3}{\sqrt{7}}$

K. $\dfrac{4}{\sqrt{7}}$

37. The graph of the solution set for the system of linear equations below is a single line in the (x,y) coordinate plane.

$$12x - 20y = 108$$
$$3x + ky = 27$$

What is the value of k?

A. -5

B. -3

C. $-\dfrac{1}{4}$

D. $\dfrac{3}{5}$

E. 4

38. A common rule of thumb is that each additional inch of height (H) will add 10 pounds to a person's weight (W). Doctors recommend finding your Body Mass Index (BMI) as a measure of health. BMI is computed as follows (H is in inches, and W is in pounds):

$$BMI = \frac{703W}{H^2}$$

If a 68 inch tall person typically weighs 150 pounds, which of the following is closest to the expected BMI of a 72 inch tall person?

F. 1

G. 2

H. 20

J. 26

K. 42

39. Dave's math tutor reminded him not to calculate $\left(\dfrac{x}{y}\right)^2$ as $\dfrac{x^2}{y}$. Dave thinks there are some numbers for which that calculation works. Eventually, he was able to show that $\left(\dfrac{x}{y}\right)^2$ equals $\dfrac{x^2}{y}$ if and only if:

(Note: Assume that $y \neq 0$.)

A. $x = 0$

B. $x = 1$

C. $y = 1$

D. $x = 0$ and $y = 1$

E. $x = 0$ or $y = 1$

GO ON TO THE NEXT PAGE

40. In the figure below, $\overline{BD}$ is a perpendicular bisector of $\overline{AC}$ in equilateral triangle $\triangle ABC$. If $\overline{BD}$ is $4\sqrt{3}$ units long, how many units long is $\overline{BC}$?

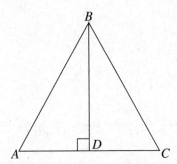

F. $2\sqrt{3}$

G. 4

H. 8

J. $8\sqrt{3}$

K. 16

41. What is the perimeter, in meters (m), of the figure below?

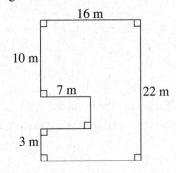

A. 58

B. 83

C. 90

D. 208

E. 352

42. Isosceles trapezoid $ABCD$ is inscribed in a circle with center O, as shown below. Which of the following is the most direct explanation of why $\triangle AOD$ is isosceles?

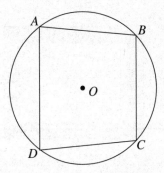

F. If two angles in a triangle are congruent, the sides opposite them are congruent.

G. Two sides are radii of the circle.

H. Side-angle-side congruence

J. Angle-side-angle congruence

K. Angle-angle-angle similarity

43. A circle with radius 4 meters is cut out of a circle with radius 12 meters, as shown in the figure below. Which of the following gives the area of the shaded figure, in square meters?

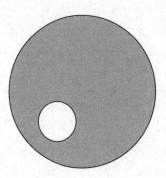

A. $\pi(12 - 2)^2$

B. $\pi 12^2 - 2^2$

C. $\pi 12^2 - 4^2$

D. $\pi(12 - 4^2)$

E. $\pi(12^2 - 4^2)$

GO ON TO THE NEXT PAGE

44. A walkway, 31 by $32\frac{1}{2}$ feet, surrounds a pool that is $27\frac{1}{2}$ by 29 feet, as shown below.

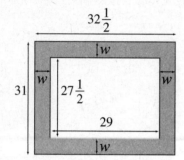

What is the width, w, of the walkway?

F. $1\frac{1}{4}$

G. 1

H. $1\frac{1}{2}$

J. $1\frac{3}{4}$

K. $3\frac{1}{2}$

45. The area of a rectangular floor is 323 square feet. The width of the floor is 21 feet less than twice the length. How many feet long is the floor?

A. 8.5

B. 11

C. 13.5

D. 17

E. 19

46. For the area of a circle to double, the new radius must be the old radius multiplied by:

F. $\frac{1}{2}$

G. $\sqrt{2}$

H. 2

J. π

K. 4

47. If $\log_x 64 = 3$, then $x = ?$

A. 4

B. 8

C. $\frac{64}{3}$

D. $\frac{64}{\log 3}$

E. 64^3

48. If $A = \begin{bmatrix} 3 & -6 \\ 0 & 9 \end{bmatrix}$ and $B = \begin{bmatrix} -3 & 6 \\ 0 & -9 \end{bmatrix}$, then $A - B = ?$

F. $\begin{bmatrix} 0 & 0 \\ 0 & 0 \end{bmatrix}$

G. $\begin{bmatrix} 1 & 0 \\ 0 & 1 \end{bmatrix}$

H. $\begin{bmatrix} 0 & -12 \\ 0 & 18 \end{bmatrix}$

J. $\begin{bmatrix} -6 & 0 \\ 0 & 0 \end{bmatrix}$

K. $\begin{bmatrix} 6 & -12 \\ 0 & 18 \end{bmatrix}$

49. If a and b are real numbers, and $a > 0$ and $b < a$, then which of the following inequalities must be true?

A. $b \leq 0$

B. $b \geq 0$

C. $b^2 \geq 0$

D. $b^2 \geq a^2$

E. $b^2 \leq a^2$

GO ON TO THE NEXT PAGE

50. The ratio of the lengths of the sides of a right triangle is $2:\sqrt{5}:3$. What is the cosine of the smallest angle in the triangle?

F. $\dfrac{2}{3}$

G. $\dfrac{\sqrt{5}}{3}$

H. $\dfrac{2\sqrt{5}}{5}$

J. $\dfrac{9}{10}$

K. 2

51. What is the amplitude of the graph of the equation $y + 3 = 4\sin(5\theta)$?

(Note: the amplitude is $\dfrac{1}{2}$ the difference between the maximum and the minimum values of y.)

A. 3

B. 4

C. 5

D. 7

E. 10

52. Each of the following determines a unique plane in 3-dimensional Euclidian space EXCEPT:

F. 1 line and 1 point NOT on the line.

G. 3 distinct points NOT on the same line.

H. 2 lines that intersect in exactly 1 point.

J. 2 distinct parallel lines.

K. 2 lines that are NOT parallel and do NOT intersect.

53. The measure of the vertex angle of an isosceles triangle is $(x - 10)°$. The base angles each measure $(3x + 18)°$. What is the measure in degrees of one of the base angles?

A. 12

B. 22

C. $37\dfrac{1}{2}$

D. $43\dfrac{1}{2}$

E. 84

54. To make a set of potholders of various sizes to give as a gift, Margot needs the following amounts of fabric for each set:

Pieces of Fabric	Length (inches)
6	8
5	12
2	18

If the fabric costs $1.95 per yard, which of the following would be the approximate cost of fabric for 5 sets of potholders?

(Note: 1 yard = 36 inches)

F. $ 8

G. $ 24

H. $ 39

J. $ 58

K. $117

GO ON TO THE NEXT PAGE

55. The formula for the surface area (S) of a rectangular solid with square bases (shown below) is $S = 4wh + 2w^2$, where w is the side length of the bases and h is the height of the solid. Doubling each of the dimensions (w and h) will increase the surface area to how many times its original size?

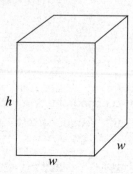

A. 2
B. 4
C. 6
D. 8
E. 24

56. The average of a set of four integers is 14. When a fifth number is included in the set, the average of the set increases to 16. What is the fifth number?

F. 16
G. 18
H. 21
J. 24
K. 26

57. Which of the following is the equation of the largest circle that can be inscribed in the ellipse with equation $\dfrac{(x-4)^2}{16} + \dfrac{y^2}{4} = 1$?

A. $(x - 4)^2 + y^2 = 64$
B. $(x - 4)^2 + y^2 = 16$
C. $(x - 4)^2 + y^2 = 4$
D. $x^2 + y^2 = 16$
E. $x^2 + y^2 = 4$

58. One of the graphs below is that of $y = x^3 + C$, where C is a constant. Which one?

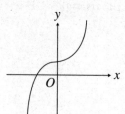

F.

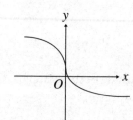

G.

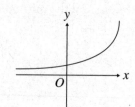

H.

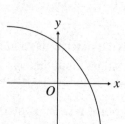

J.

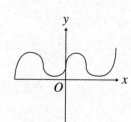

K.

GO ON TO THE NEXT PAGE

59. How many points do the graphs of all three equations below have in common?

$$x = y + 8$$
$$-x = y - 8$$
$$6x = 2y + 4$$

A. 0
B. 1
C. 2
D. 3
E. Infinitely many

60. In 4 fair coin tosses, what is the probability of obtaining exactly 3 heads?

(Note: In a fair coin toss, the 2 outcomes, heads and tails, are equally likely.)

F. $\dfrac{1}{16}$

G. $\dfrac{1}{8}$

H. $\dfrac{3}{16}$

J. $\dfrac{1}{4}$

K. $\dfrac{1}{2}$

READING TEST

35 Minutes—40 Questions

Directions: There are four passages in this test. Each passage is followed by several questions. After reading a passage, choose the best answer to each question and fill in the corresponding oval on your Answer Grid. You may refer to the passages as often as necessary.

PASSAGE I

PROSE FICTION

This passage is adapted from The Age of Innocence, *by Edith Wharton (1920).*

It was generally agreed in New York that the Countess Olenska had "lost her looks."

She had appeared there first, in Newland
Line Archer's boyhood, as a brilliantly pretty little girl of
(5) nine or ten, of whom people said that she "ought to be painted." Her parents had been continental wanderers, and after a roaming babyhood she had lost them both, and been taken in charge by her aunt, Medora Manson, also a wanderer, who was herself
(10) returning to New York to "settle down."

Poor Medora, repeatedly widowed, was always coming home to settle down (each time in a less expensive house), and bringing with her a new husband or an adopted child, but after a few
(15) months she invariably parted from her husband or quarrelled with her ward, and, having got rid of her house at a loss, set out again on her wanderings. As her mother had been a Rushworth, and her last unhappy marriage had linked her to one of
(20) the crazy Chiverses, New York looked indulgently on her eccentricities, but when she returned with her little orphaned niece, whose parents had been popular in spite of their regrettable taste for travel, people thought it a pity that the pretty child should
(25) be in such hands.

Everyone was disposed to be kind to little Ellen Mingott, though her dusky red cheeks and tight curls gave her an air of gaiety that seemed unsuitable in a child who should still have been in
(30) black for her parents. It was one of the misguided Medora's many peculiarities to flout the unalterable rules that regulated American mourning, and when

she stepped from the steamer her family was scandalized to see that the crepe veil she wore for her
(35) own brother was seven inches shorter than those of her sisters-in-law, while little Ellen wore a crimson dress and amber beads.

But New York had so long resigned itself to Medora that only a few old ladies shook their heads
(40) over Ellen's gaudy clothes, while her other relations fell under the charm of her high spirits. She was a fearless and familiar little thing, who asked disconcerting questions, made precocious comments, and possessed outlandish arts, such as dancing a
(45) Spanish shawl dance and singing Neapolitan love-songs to a guitar. Under the direction of her aunt, the little girl received an expensive but incoherent education, which included "drawing from the model," a thing never dreamed of before, and play-
(50) ing the piano in quintets with professional musicians.

Of course no good could come of this, and when, a few years later, poor Chivers finally died, his widow again pulled up stakes and departed with Ellen, who had grown into a tall bony girl
(55) with conspicuous eyes. For some time no more was heard of them; then news came of Ellen's marriage to an immensely rich Polish nobleman of legendary fame. She disappeared, and when a few years later Medora again came back to New York, subdued,
(60) impoverished, mourning a third husband, and in quest of a still smaller house, people wondered that her rich niece had not been able to do something for her. Then came the news that Ellen's own marriage had ended in disaster, and that she was herself
(65) returning home to seek rest and oblivion among her kinsfolk.

GO ON TO THE NEXT PAGE ⟶

These things passed through Newland Archer's mind a week later as he watched the Countess Olenska enter the van der Luyden drawing room (70) on the evening of the momentous dinner. In the middle of the room she paused, looking about her with a grave mouth and smiling eyes, and in that instant, Newland Archer rejected the general verdict on her looks. It was true that her early radiance (75) was gone. The red cheeks had paled; she was thin, worn, a little older-looking than her age, which must have been nearly thirty. But there was about her the mysterious authority of beauty, a sureness in the carriage of the head, the movement of the (80) eyes, which, without being in the least theatrical, struck him as highly trained and full of a conscious power. At the same time she was simpler in manner than most of the ladies present, and many people (as he heard afterward) were disappointed that her (85) appearance was not more "stylish"—for stylishness was what New York most valued. It was, perhaps, Archer reflected, because her early vivacity had disappeared; because she was so quiet—quiet in her movements, her voice, and the tones of her (90) voice. New York had expected something a good deal more resonant in a young woman with such a history.

1. The author describes which of the following practices as undesirable to New York society?

    A. Playing the piano
    B. Performing Spanish shawl dances
    C. Traveling
    D. Adopting children

2. As a result of her "peculiarities" (line 31), Medora offends her family by:

    F. allowing Ellen to marry a Polish nobleman.
    G. wearing a veil that is too short for mourning.
    H. returning to New York with no money.
    J. refusing to dress stylishly when meeting Newland Archer.

3. It is most reasonable to infer that, after the death of Medora's third husband, Ellen did not help her aunt primarily because:

    A. Ellen was no longer wealthy, since her own marriage had failed.
    B. Medora had become embittered because she hadn't heard from Ellen for so long.
    C. Ellen resented the incoherent education she received from her aunt.
    D. receiving help from her niece would interfere with Medora's desire to be eccentric.

4. Based on the characterization of Newland Archer in the last paragraph, he can best be described as:

    F. reflective and nonjudgmental.
    G. likable but withdrawn.
    H. disinterested but fair.
    J. stylish and gregarious.

5. The third paragraph (lines 11–25) suggests that Medora's lifestyle was primarily viewed by others as:

    A. acceptably different from societal norms.
    B. a terrible example to set for her niece.
    C. unfortunate and pitiful.
    D. disturbingly inconsistent.

6. Which of the following conclusions about the relationship between Medora and Ellen is best supported by the passage?

    F. Ellen is grateful that her aunt unselfishly adopted her.
    G. Medora is jealous of her niece's marriage to a wealthy husband.
    H. Both women share a distaste for New York society.
    J. Ellen has adopted some of her aunt's unconventional traits.

GO ON TO THE NEXT PAGE ⟹

7. What does the narrator suggest is a central characteristic of Medora Manson?

   A. Arrogance

   B. Immodesty

   C. Non-conformity

   D. Orthodoxy

8. Which of the following characters learns to do something otherwise unheard of by New York society?

   F. Ellen Mingott

   G. Newland Archer

   H. Medora Manson

   J. Count Olenska

9. Newland Archer would most likely agree with which of the following characterizations of Ellen?

   A. She is confident and poised.

   B. She is lonely and unhappy.

   C. She is intelligent and outspoken.

   D. She is highly-educated and intimidating.

10. One can reasonably infer from the passage that on the occasion of the dinner, Newland and Ellen:

    F. had not seen each other for some time.

    G. were interested in becoming romantically involved.

    H. were both disappointed with New York society.

    J. had just met, but were immediately attracted to each other.

PASSAGE II

SOCIAL SCIENCE

The following passage is excerpted from a magazine article discussing scientific research on traditional methods of predicting the timing and character of the Indian monsoon.

Can traditional rules of thumb provide accurate weather forecasts? Researchers in Junagadh, India, are trying to find out. Most farmers in the region
Line grow one crop of peanuts or castor per year. In a
(5) wet year, peanuts give the best returns, but if the rains are poor, the more drought-tolerant castor is a better bet. In April and May, before the monsoon comes, farmers decide what to plant, buy the seed, prepare the soil and hope for the best. An accurate
(10) forecast would be extremely helpful.

Little wonder, then, that observant farmers have devised traditional ways to predict the monsoon's timing and character. One such rule of thumb involves the blooming of the *Cassia fistula*
(15) tree, which is common on roadsides in southern Gujarat. According to an old saying which has been documented as far back as the 8th century, the monsoon begins 45 days after *C. fistula's* flowering peak. Since 1996, Purshottambhai Kanani, an
(20) agronomist at Gujarat Agricultural University, has been collecting data to test this rule. He records the flowering dates of trees all over the university's campus and plots a distribution to work out when the flowering peak occurs. While not perfect,
(25) *C. fistula* has so far done an admirable job of predicting whether the monsoon will come early or late.

Similarly, with help from local farmers, Dr Kanani has been investigating a local belief
(30) regarding the direction of the wind on the day of Holi, a Hindu festival in spring. The wind direction at certain times on Holi is supposed to indicate the strength of the monsoon that year. Wind from the north or west suggests a good monsoon, whereas
(35) wind from the east indicates drought. Each year before Holi, Dr Kanani sends out postcards to more than 400 farmers in Junagadh and neighbouring districts. The farmers note the wind direction at the

GO ON TO THE NEXT PAGE ⟶

specified times, and then send the postcards back.

(40)   In years of average and above-average monsoons (1994, 1997, 1998, and 2001), the wind on Holi tended to come from the north and west. In the drier years of 1995 and 1996 the majority of farmers reported wind from the east (Dr Kanani

(45) did not conduct the study in 1999 and 2000). As with the *C. fistula* results, the predictions are not especially precise, but the trend is right.

Dr Kanani first became interested in traditional methods in 1990, when an old saying attributed to

(50) a tenth-century sage named Bhadli—that a storm on a particular day meant the monsoon would come 72 days later—proved strikingly correct. This prompted Dr Kanani to collect other rules from old texts in Gujarati and Sanskrit.

(55)   Not all of his colleagues approve. Damaru Sahu, a meteorologist at Gujarat Agricultural University and a researcher for India's director-general of meteorology, says that traditional methods are "OK as a hobby." But, he goes on, they cannot be relied

(60) upon, and "may not be applicable to this modern age." Yet Dr Sahu concedes that meteorological science has failed to provide a useful alternative to traditional methods. For the past 13 years, he notes, the director-general for meteorology has predicted

(65) "normal monsoon" for the country. Every year, the average rainfall over the whole country is calculated, and this prediction is proved correct. But it is no use at all to farmers who want to know what will happen in their region.

(70)   Dr Kanani hopes that his research will put traditional methods on a proper scientific footing. He and his colleagues have even set up a sort of peer-review forum for traditional meteorology. Each spring, he hosts a conference for 100 local

(75) traditional forecasters, each of whom presents a monsoon prediction with supporting evidence—the behaviour of a species of bird, strong flowering in a certain plant, or the prevailing wind direction that season. Dr Kanani records these predictions and

(80) publishes them in the local press.

He has also started a non-governmental organisation, the Varsha Vigyan Mandal, or Rain Science Association, which has more than 400 members. Its vice-president, Dhansukh Shah, is a scientist at

(85) the National Directorate of Meteorology in Pune. By involving such mainstream meteorologists as Dr Shah in his work, Dr Kanani hopes to bring his unusual research to the attention of national institutions. They could provide the funding for

(90) larger studies that could generate results sufficiently robust to be published in peer-reviewed science journals.

11. According to the passage, all of the following traditional methods of weather prediction have been scientifically tested EXCEPT:

   A. wind direction during the Hindi festival of Holi.

   B. the behavior of certain bird species.

   C. the flowering *Cassia fistula* trees.

   D. a tenth century prediction connecting storm activity to later monsoons.

12. When the author uses the phrase "useful alternative" (line 62), she means that:

   F. modern meteorology rarely provides an accurate forecast.

   G. equipment needed for accurate forecasting is too expensive for many in India.

   H. modern meteorology doesn't give as specific predictions as traditional methods do.

   J. today's science cannot explain why traditional methods work so well.

GO ON TO THE NEXT PAGE

13. The main purpose of the last three paragraphs (lines 55–92) is to:

 A. project the role of traditional weather prediction methods in the scientific community into the future.

 B. suggest that both traditional and scientific methods can co-exist because they serve very different functions.

 C. remind us that traditional methods have been around too long to be easily eclipsed by modern science.

 D. introduce us to a general respect for ancient knowledge in the sciences.

14. The author's attitude toward traditional methods of weather forecasting may reasonably be described as:

 F. curious as to their development.

 G. cautious hopefulness that they are useful.

 H. skeptical regarding their real scientific value.

 J. regretful of the "fad" of interest in these methods.

15. Based on information in the passage, which of the discussed methods gives the most advanced prediction of monsoon arrival?

 A. The behavior of the birds

 B. The flowering of the fistula tree

 C. The wind direction on Holi

 D. Bhadli's prediction based on storms

16. The function of the second paragraph in relation to the passage as a whole is most likely to provide:

 F. a reason that farmers need techniques to predict monsoons earlier.

 G. examples of the inexact nature of predictions made from traditional methods.

 H. an explanation of the ancient saying that the rest of the passage will examine.

 J. an introduction to the modern research of traditional methods.

17. According to the passage, the purpose of Dr. Kanani's springtime conferences is to:

 A. record the traditional methods of weather prediction before they disappear.

 B. help gain acceptance for traditional methods in the academic community.

 C. publish the methods in the local press.

 D. facilitate the exchange of ideas between farmers from far-flung regions of India.

18. According to the passage, the reason farmers use traditional methods to predict the weather is that:

 F. traditional methods are more accessible to rural populations.

 G. "normal" monsoons can still be very different from each other.

 H. they need to anticipate the local conditions for the coming growing season.

 J. traditional methods get the basic trends right.

GO ON TO THE NEXT PAGE

19. The author uses the term "admirable job" (line 25) to indicate that:

    A. the flowering of the fistula tree provides remarkably predictive data on the coming monsoon.

    B. precision isn't everything.

    C. predictions based on the peak of *C. fistula's* flowering do provide some reliable answers.

    D. sometimes rules of thumb are better than complex formulas.

20. According to Damaru Sahu, traditional weather prediction:

    F. can be curiously accurate.

    G. has a defined place in meteorology.

    H. is useful in some ways despite its lack of scientific foundation.

    J. appeals to an instinct different than the rational brain.

PASSAGE III

HUMANITIES

One of the most enjoyable ways to analyze culture is through music. By analyzing musical styles and lyrics, one can explore quintessential characteristics of particular cultures.

PASSAGE A

Country music has its roots in the southern portions of the United States, specifically in the remote and undeveloped backcountry of the central and
Line southern areas of the Appalachian mountain range.
(5) Recognized as a distinct cultural region since the late nineteenth century, the area became home to European settlements in the eighteenth century, primarily led by Ulster Scots from Ireland. Early inhabitants have been characterized as fiercely independent, to the
(10) point of rudeness and inhospitality. It was in this area

that the region's truly indigenous music, now known as country music, was born.

Rooted in spirituals as well as folk music, cowboy songs, and traditional Celtic melodies,
(15) country music originated in the 1920s. The motifs are generally ballads and dance tunes, simple in form and accompanied mostly by guitar, banjo, and violin. Though today there are many genres of country music, all have their roots in this mélange
(20) of sources.

The term "country" has replaced the original pejorative term, "hillbilly." Hillbillies referred to Appalachian inhabitants who were considered poor, uneducated, isolated, and wary; the name
(25) change reflects a more accepting characterization of these mountain dwellers.

Hank Williams put country music on the map nationally, and is credited with the movement of country music from the South to more national
(30) prominence. Other early innovators include the Carter family, Ernest Tubb, Woody Guthrie, Loretta Lynn, and Bill Monroe, father of bluegrass music. More recently, Faith Hill, Reba McEntire, and Shania Twain have carried on the tradition.
(35) What might be considered the "home base" of country music is in Nashville, Tennessee, and the legendary music hall, the Grand Ole Opry. Founded in 1925 by George D. Hay, it had its genesis in the pioneer radio station WSM's program
(40) *Barn Dance*. Country singers are considered to have reached the pinnacle of the profession if they are asked to become members of the Opry. While noted country music performers and acts take the stage at the Opry numerous times, Elvis Presley
(45) performed there only once, in 1954. His act was so poorly received that it was suggested he return to his job as a truck driver.

The offshoots and relatives of country music highlight the complexity of this genre. In a move
(50) away from its mountain origins, and turning a focus to the West, honky-tonk music became popular in the early twentieth century. Its name is a reference to its roots in honky-tonk bars, where the music was played. Additionally, Western Swing
(55) emerged as one of the first genres to blend country

GO ON TO THE NEXT PAGE ➡

and jazz musical styles, which required a great deal of skill and creativity. Some of the most talented and sophisticated musicians performing in any genre were musicians who played in bluegrass (60) string bands, another relative of country music.

Country music has always been an expression of American identity. Its sound, lyrics, and performers are purely American, and though the music now has an international audience, it remains (65) American in its heart and soul.

PASSAGE B

A style of music closely related to country is the similarly indigenous music known as bluegrass, which originated in the Appalachian highland regions extending westwards to the Ozark (70) Mountains in southern Missouri and northern Arkansas. Derived from the music brought over by European settlers of the region, bluegrass is a mixture of Scots, Welsh, Irish, and English melodic forms, infused, over time, with African-American (75) influences. Indeed, many bluegrass songs, such as "Barbara Allen" and "House Carpenter" preserve their European roots, maintaining the traditional musical style and narratives almost intact. Story-telling ballads, often laments, are common themes. (80) Given the predominance of coal mining in the Appalachian region, it is not surprising that ballads relating to mining tragedies are also common.

Unlike country music, in which musicians commonly play the same melodies together, (85) bluegrass highlights one player at a time, with the others providing accompaniment. This tradition of each musician taking turns with solos, and often improvising, can also be seen in jazz ensembles. Traditional bluegrass music is typically played on (90) instruments such as banjo, guitar, mandolin, bass, harmonica, and Dobro (resonator guitar.) Even household objects, including washboards and spoons, have, from time to time, been drafted for use as instruments. Vocals also differ from country (95) music in that, rather than featuring a single voice, bluegrass incorporates baritone and tenor harmonies.

Initially included under the catch-all phrase "folk music," and later referred to as "hillbilly," (100) bluegrass did not come into his own category until the late 1950s, and appeared first in the comprehensive guide, *Music Index*, in 1965. Presumably it was named after Bill Monroe's Blue Grass band, the seminal bluegrass band. A rapid, almost frenetic (105) pace, characterizes bluegrass tempos. Even today, decades after their most active performing era, *The Foggy Mountain Boys* members Lester Flatt, a bluegrass guitarist and mandolinist, and Earl Scruggs known for his three-finger banjo picking (110) style, are widely considered the foremost artists on their instruments.

Partially because of its pace and complexity, bluegrass has often been recorded for movie soundtracks. "Dueling Banjos," played in the movie (115) *Deliverance*, exemplifies the skill required by the feverish tempo of the genre. The soundtrack for *O Brother Where Art Thou?* incorporates bluegrass, and its musical cousins folk, country, gospel, and blues. Bluegrass festivals are held throughout the (120) country and as far away as the Czech Republic. Interactive, often inviting audience participation, they feature performers such as Dolly Parton and Alison Krauss.

Central to bluegrass music are the themes of (125) the working class—miners, railroad workers, farmers. The phrase "high, lonesome sound" was coined to represent the bluegrass undertones of intensity and cheerlessness, symbolizing the hard-scrabble life of the American worker. As with so much of a (130) nation's traditional music, and for better or worse, bluegrass music reflects America.

Questions 21–23 ask about Passage A.

21. According to the passage, country music originated from all of the following EXCEPT:

A. Celtic melodies.

B. spirituals.

C. jazz.

D. cowboy songs.

GO ON TO THE NEXT PAGE

22. Which of the following would be the most logical place to hear the best of country music?

    F. Honky-tonk bars
    G. Ireland
    H. The Appalachian backcountry
    J. The Grand Ole Opry

23. It can be inferred that the author considers that from its many roots, country music became:

    A. the most influential of all music genres.
    B. a reflection of Appalachian mountain people.
    C. best performed at the Grand Ole Opry.
    D. representative of the American character.

Questions 24–26 ask about Passage B.

---

24. The themes of the working class are best characterized by:

    F. songs performed by the Bill Monroe band.
    G. country music.
    H. a genre influenced by Scottish music.
    J. ballads with high, lonesome sounds.

25. According to the passage, the instruments played in bluegrass music are:

    A. both typical and unusual.
    B. derived from African-American influences.
    C. made famous by the piece "Dueling Banjos."
    D. restricted to those used in the Ozarks.

26. In addition to highlighting one player at a time, bluegrass music differs from country music because it often:

    F. features harmonies sung by bass and tenor voices.
    G. features a single voice.
    H. is characterized by musicians commonly playing the same melodies together.
    J. is played on instruments such as the banjo and guitar.

Questions 27–30 ask about both passages.

---

27. As it is used in the introductory information, "quintessential" means:

    A. old-fashioned.
    B. representative.
    C. charming.
    D. unconventional.

28. It can be inferred that both authors would agree that:

    F. country and bluegrass music are popular genres.
    G. both genres are showcased at the Grand Ole Opry.
    H. music genres can evolve.
    J. country and bluegrass music are gaining in acceptance.

GO ON TO THE NEXT PAGE

29. Passage A states that there were "talented and sophisticated" (line 57-58) musicians playing bluegrass music. Which sentence in Passage B suggests this claim?

   A. "Central to bluegrass music are the themes of the working class—miners, railroad workers, farmers."

   B. "Partially because of its pace and complexity, bluegrass has often been recorded for movie soundtracks."

   C. "Lester Flatt, a bluegrass guitarist and mandolinist, and Earl Scruggs known for his three-finger banjo picking style, are widely considered the foremost artists on their instruments."

   D. "A style of music closely related to country is the similarly indigenous music known as bluegrass . . ."

30. It can be inferred that laments and high, lonesome sounds both reflect:

   F. the influence of Irish music.

   G. American themes.

   H. songs sung by Shania Twain.

   J. hillbilly music.

PASSAGE IV

NATURAL SCIENCE

The following passage appeared in Science *magazine as "Pluto: The Planet That Never Was" by Govert Schilling. (© Science, Inc., 1999)*

Nearly 70 years ago, Pluto became the ninth member of the sun's family of planets, but now it's on the verge of being cast out of that exclusive clan.
Line The International Astronomical Union (IAU) is
(5) collecting votes on how to reclassify the icy body: as the first (and largest) of the so-called trans-Neptunian objects, or as the 10,000th entry in the growing list of minor bodies orbiting the sun.

In either case, Pluto may officially lose its
(10) planetary status, leaving the solar system with only eight planets.

Children's books and planetariums may not acknowledge the loss. And Brian Marsden of the Harvard-Smithsonian Center for Astrophysics
(15) in Cambridge, Massachusetts, who launched the discussion six years ago, says no one is trying to demote Pluto. "If anything, we're going to add to Pluto's status," he says, "by giving it the honor of a very special designation."

(20) Cold comfort for Pluto, maybe, but its reclassification will at least end a long identity crisis, which began soon after its 1930 discovery at Lowell Observatory in Flagstaff, Arizona, by Clyde Tombaugh, who died in 1997. Pluto turned out to be
(25) much smaller than all the other planets (according to recent estimates, its diameter is only 2200 kilometers), and its orbit is strangely elongated. It didn't belong with either the Earth-like rocky planets or the gas giants.

(30) A clue to its true nature came in 1992, when David Jewitt of the University of Hawaii, Honolulu, and Jane Luu, then at the University of California, Berkeley, discovered a small, icy object beyond the orbit of Neptune. Provisionally cataloged as 1992
(35) QB1, this ice dwarf measures a mere 200 kilometers in diameter. Since then many more trans-Neptunian objects (TNOs) have been detected, some of which move in very Pluto-like orbits around the sun. These "supercomets" populate the Kuiper Belt,
(40) named after Dutch-American astronomer Gerard Kuiper, who predicted its existence in the early 1950s. "Pluto fits the picture [of the solar system] much better if it's viewed as a TNO," says Luu, who is now at Leiden University in the Netherlands.

(45) At present, more than 70 TNOs are known, and apparently, Pluto is just the largest member of this new family, which explains why it was found more than 60 years before number two. If astronomers had known about the other TNOs back in the
(50) 1930s, Pluto would never have attained the status of a planet, Luu says: "Pluto was lucky."

A couple of months ago, the kinship between Pluto and the TNOs led Richard Binzel of the Massachusetts Institute of Technology to propose

GO ON TO THE NEXT PAGE ⟶

(55) that Pluto be made the first entry in a new catalog of TNOs for which precise orbits have been
determined. It would then enter the textbooks as
something like TN-1 (or TN-0, as some astronomers have suggested).

(60)   Marsden agrees that Pluto is a TNO, but he
doesn't like the idea of establishing a new catalog of
solar system objects, arguing that astronomers already
have a perfectly serviceable list of numbered minor
bodies (mostly asteroids). "The question is: Do we

(65) want to recognize [trans-Neptunian objects] with a
different designation?" he asks. He points out that the
Centaurs—TNOs that have been nudged well inside
Neptune's orbit—have been classified as asteroids and
says he sees "no reason for introducing a new designa-

(70) tion system for objects of which we have representations in the current [catalog of minor bodies]."

Instead of making Pluto the founding member of a new catalog, Marsden wants to add it to
the existing list. "The current number is 9826," he

(75) says. "With the current detection rate, we should
arrive at number 10,000 somewhere in January
or February." He notes that asteroids 1000, 2000,
3000, and so on have all been honored by the IAU
with special names, including Leonardo and Isaac

(80) Newton. "What better way to honor Pluto than to
give it this very special number?"

But the prospect of lumping Pluto with the
solar system's riffraff outrages supporters of a new
TNO category. "It's the most idiotic thing" she's ever

(85) heard, says Luu. "Pluto is certainly not an asteroid,"
she says.

To try to settle the issue, Mike A'Hearn of the
University of Maryland, College Park, is collecting
e-mail votes from 500 or so members of IAU divi-

(90) sions on the solar system, comets and asteroids,
and other relevant topics. "I wanted to arrive at a
consensus before Christmas [1998]," he says, "but it
may take a while, since the community as a whole
doesn't seem to have a consensus." Neither proposal

(95) has attracted a majority. Although many people
opposed Marsden's proposal, a comparable number
were unhappy with Binzel's idea, A'Hearn says,
because Pluto would still be an anomaly,
being much larger than the other trans-Neptunian

(100) objects. A'Hearn says that if no consensus can be

reached, Pluto will probably not end up in any
catalog at all, making it the ultimate outcast of the
solar system.

However the debate settles out, Pluto's career as
(105) a planet seems to be ending, and even astronomers
are wistful at the prospect. "No one likes to lose a
planet," says Luu. A'Hearn agrees. "It will probably
always be called the ninth planet" by the general
public, he says.

31. According to the passage, regarding the view
that Pluto should be categorized as an asteroid,
Jane Luu expressed which of the following?

A. Shock

B. Excitement

C. Confusion

D. Forceful opposition

32. It can be inferred that Pluto's original designation as a planet would have never happened if
scientists had:

F. understood its size from the beginning.

G. seen the icy core of Pluto sooner.

H. been able to detect the many smaller
TNOs when Pluto was discovered.

J. understood the popular misconceptions
about Pluto's planet-hood that would
follow.

33. According to the passage, Pluto has historically been regarded as:

A. closer in relation to rocky planets such
as Earth.

B. unlikely to keep its title as a planet.

C. an outlier among planetary bodies.

D. destined for an honorable place in
astronomy history.

GO ON TO THE NEXT PAGE

34. According to the passage, large objects similar to the makeup and orbit of Pluto found nearer to the sun than Neptune are called:

    F. Centaurs.
    G. IAUs.
    H. TNOs.
    J. ice-dwarves.

35. According to lines 64–71, the central issue in the debate over Pluto is:

    A. whether Pluto is more similar to rocky planets or the gas giants.
    B. the distance of Pluto from the sun.
    C. whether or not the issues raised by Pluto's differences from the other TNOs are substantial enough to create a new classification for it.
    D. scientists' conception of Pluto versus the view of the general public.

36. As used in line 63, the term *serviceable* most nearly means:

    F. able to be fixed.
    G. adequate.
    H. beneficial.
    J. durable.

37. One slightly less scientific concern expressed by most of the scientists in the passage is:

    A. the role of the IAU in making classification decisions.
    B. respect for the views of the public.
    C. who gets the credit for Pluto's reclassification.
    D. the preservation of Pluto's fame and importance.

38. According to the passage, what is the major reason for lack of consensus regarding the status of Pluto?

    F. The general population resists the scientific community's belief that Pluto is not a planet.
    G. Pluto seems very different than the other members of any classification.
    H. Pluto's strange orbit makes it asteroid-like, but its surface more closely resembles a planet.
    J. There have been numerous discoveries of other Pluto-like objects nearer to the sun than to Neptune.

39. Details in the passage suggest that Pluto is much different from other planets in:

    A. its distance from the sun and the shape of its orbit.
    B. its size and the shape of its orbit.
    C. the year of its discovery and its size.
    D. its shape and surface composition.

40. Pluto's size accounts for:

    F. its classification as a TNO.
    G. its dissimilarity to asteroids.
    H. its early discovery relative to other TNOs.
    J. its bizarre orbit.

SCIENCE TEST

35 Minutes—40 Questions

Directions: There are several passages in this test. Each passage is followed by several questions. After reading a passage, choose the best answer to each question and fill in the corresponding oval on your Answer Grid. You may refer to the passages as often as necessary. You are NOT permitted to use a calculator on this test.

PASSAGE I

Soil, by volume, consists on the average of 45% minerals, 25% water, 25% air, and 5% organic matter (including both living and nonliving organisms). Time and topography shape the composition of soil and cause it to develop into layers known as *horizons*. The soil horizons are collectively known as the *soil profile*. The composition of soil varies in each horizon, as do the most common minerals (see Figure 1). Figure 1 also shows the depth of each horizon and the overall density of the soil.

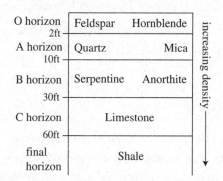

Figure 1

Table 1 lists the percents (%) of zinc and calcium in the minerals that compose soil.

Table 1

Mineral	Zinc content (%)	Calcium content (%)
Feldspar	35–40	0–10
Hornblende	30–35	10–20
Quartz	25–30	20–30
Mica	20–25	30–40
Serpentine	15–20	40–50
Anorthite	10–15	50–60
Limestone	5–10	60–70
Shale	0–5	70–80

Table 2 shows the percent of minerals that compose granite and sandstone, 2 rock types that are commonly found in soil.

Table 2

Mineral	Percent of mineral in:	
	Sandstone	Granite
Feldspar	30	54
Hornblende	2	0
Quartz	50	33
Mica	10	10
Serpentine	0	0
Anorthite	0	0
Limestone	5	0
Shale	0	0
Augite	3	3

GO ON TO THE NEXT PAGE

1. An analysis of an unknown mineral found in soil revealed its zinc content to be 32% and its calcium content to be 12%. Based on the data in Table 1, geologists would most likely classify this mineral as:

   A. hornblende.
   B. anorthite.
   C. serpentine.
   D. mica.

2. Geologists digging down to the A horizon would most likely find which of the following minerals?

   F. Limestone
   G. Shale
   H. Serpentine
   J. Mica

3. Based on the data presented in Figure 1 and Table 1, which of the following statements best describes the relationship between the zinc content of a mineral and the depth below surface level at which it is dominant? As zinc content increases:

   A. depth increases.
   B. depth decreases.
   C. depth first increases, then decreases.
   D. depth first decreases, then increases.

4. If geologists were to drill through to the C horizon, which minerals would they most likely encounter?

   F. Quartz, mica, and limestone
   G. Feldspar, shale, and serpentine
   H. Feldspar, quartz, and anorthite
   J. Hornblende, limestone, and serpentine

5. If augite is most likely found at a depth between that of the other minerals found in granite, then augite would most likely be found at a depth of:

   A. 10 feet or less.
   B. 30 feet or less.
   C. 60 feet or less.
   D. greater than 60 feet.

6. How is the percentage of zinc content related to the percentage of calcium content in the minerals that make up soil?

   F. The percentage of zinc content increases as the percentage of calcium content increases.
   G. The percentage of zinc content increases as the percentage of calcium content decreases.
   H. Both the percentage of zinc content and the percentage of calcium content remain constant.
   J. There is no relationship between the percentage of zinc content and the percentage of calcium content.

PASSAGE II

Conductivity is the ability of a material to transmit electricity. All materials have electrical properties that divide them into three broad categories: conductors, insulators and semiconductors.

A conductor is a substance that allows an electric charge to travel from one object to another. An insulator is a substance that prevents an electric charge from traveling between objects. Substances with levels of conductivity between that of a conductor and that of an insulator are called semiconductors. A voltammeter is an instrument used to measure voltage (see Figure 1).

GO ON TO THE NEXT PAGE

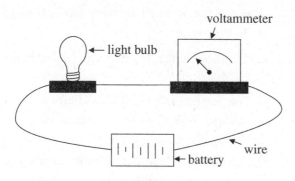

Figure 1

Three studies were executed to determine the validity of the hypothesis that a wire's conductivity increases when either the diameter or the temperature of the wire decreases.

STUDY 1

Wires were made from 5 different materials. Each strand of wire had a diameter of exactly 4 millimeters (mm). The strand of wire connecting the battery, light bulb and voltammeter was 0.5 meters (m) long and was kept at a temperature of 50°C. Table 1 displays the voltage, in millivolts (mV), recorded by the voltammeter.

Table 1

Material	Voltammeter (mV)
Silicon carbide (SiC)	4.6
Copper (Cu)	9.4
Rubber	0.0
Zinc Telluride (ZnTe)	5.2
Steel	3.5

STUDY 2

The conditions in Study 1 were repeated, except the diameter of the wires was decreased to 2 mm. The length between the battery and the light bulb and the light bulb and the voltammeter was held constant at 0.5 m and the wires were kept at 50°C. Table 2 displays the findings.

Table 2

Material	Voltammeter (mV)
Silicon carbide (SiC)	6.5
Copper (Cu)	11.3
Rubber	0.0
Zinc Telluride (ZnTe)	7.1
Steel	8.6

STUDY 3

Study 2 was repeated at 30°C. Table 3 displays the findings.

Table 3

Material	Voltammeter (mV)
Silicon carbide (SiC)	7.3
Copper (Cu)	12.1
Rubber	0.0
Zinc Telluride (ZnTe)	8.9
Steel	6.6

7. Which of the following ranges represents the voltage of all five wires with diameters of 2 mm at 30°C?

   A. 6.5 mV to 11.3 mV

   B. 0.0 mV to 9.4 mV

   C. 0.0 mV to 11.3 mV

   D. 0.0 mV to 12.1 mV

8. The scientist hypothesized that decreasing the diameter of a wire increases its conductivity. The results from the studies for each of the following materials prove the scientist's hypothesis to be true, EXCEPT the results for:

   F. silicon carbide.

   G. rubber.

   H. copper.

   J. steel.

GO ON TO THE NEXT PAGE

9. According to the results of all 3 experiments, a wire made from ZnTe would have the highest conductivity with which of the following dimensions?

   A. 1 mm diameter, 0.5 m length at 20°C

   B. 4 mm diameter, 0.5 m length at 20°C

   C. 4 mm diameter, 0.5 m length at 40°C

   D. 10 mm diameter, 0.5 m length at 40°C

10. What would the voltammeter read if a scientist used two wires, one copper and one rubber, both with diameters of 2 mm, lengths of 0.5 m, and at 30°C, to conduct electricity to the light bulb?

    F. 0.0 millivolts

    G. 9.4 millivolts

    H. 12.1 millivolts

    J. 14.7 millivolts

11. How would the conductivity of the materials be affected if Study 3 was repeated and the temperature of the wires was increased to 100°C?

    A. The conductivity would decrease with the exception of rubber.

    B. The conductivity would remain unchanged.

    C. The conductivity would increase only.

    D. The conductivity would increase with the exception of rubber.

12. Why was the conductivity of rubber examined in all three studies?

    F. To show that rubber conducts electricity well.

    G. To determine whether the diameter and temperature of rubber affect its insulating abilities.

    H. To show that the use of rubber with any other material will increase that material's conductivity.

    J. To determine if the length of a rubber wire affects its insulating abilities.

13. Which of the following effects would be most appropriate for the scientists to test next to learn more about conductivity?

    A. The changes in wire conductivity when diameter and temperature are modified

    B. The effect of wire color on conductivity

    C. The effect of wire temperature on conductivity

    D. The effect of different wire lengths on conductivity

PASSAGE III

Engineers designing a roadway needed to test the composition of the soil that would form the roadbed. In order to determine whether their two sampling systems (System A and System B) give sufficiently accurate soil composition measurements, they first conducted a study to compare the two systems.

Soil samples were taken with varying levels of *humidity* (concentration of water). The concentrations of the compounds that form the majority of soil were measured. The results for the sampling systems were compared with data on file with the US Geological Survey (USGS), which compiles extremely

GO ON TO THE NEXT PAGE

accurate data. The engineers' and USGS' results are presented in the table below.

Table 1

Concentration (mg/L) of:	Level of Humidity				
	10%	25%	45%	65%	80%
Nitrogen (N)					
USGS	105.2	236	598	781	904
System A	111.6	342	716	953	1,283
System B	196.4	408	857	1,296	1,682
Potassium Oxide (K_2O)					
USGS	9.4	9.1	8.9	8.7	8.2
System A	9.4	9.0	8.7	8.5	8.0
System B	9.5	9.2	9.0	8.8	8.3
Calcium (Ca)					
USGS	39.8	24.7	11.4	5.0	44.8
System A	42.5	31.4	10.4	8.0	42.9
System B	37.1	23.2	11.6	11.1	45.1
Phosphorus Oxide (P_2O_5)					
USGS	69.0	71.2	74.8	78.9	122.3
System A	67.9	69.9	72.2	76.7	123.1
System B	74.0	75.6	78.7	82.1	126.3
Zinc (Zn)					
USGS	0.41	0.52	0.64	0.74	0.70
System A	0.67	0.80	0.88	0.97	0.93
System B	0.38	0.48	0.62	0.77	0.73

Note: Each system concentration measurement is the average of 5 measurements.

14. The hypothesis that increasing humidity increases the concentration (mg/L) of a compound is supported by all of the following EXCEPT:

   F. nitrogen.

   G. potassium oxide.

   H. phosphorous oxide.

   J. zinc.

15. At a humidity level of 25%, it could be concluded that System B least accurately measures the concentration of which of the following compounds, relative to the data on file with the USGS?

   A. Nitrogen

   B. Calcium

   C. K_2O

   D. P_2O_5

16. The engineers hypothesized that the concentration of potassium oxide (K_2O) decreases as the level of humidity increases. This hypothesis is supported by:

   F. the data from the USGS only.

   G. the System A measurements only.

   H. the data from the USGS and the System B measurements only.

   J. the data from the USGS, the System A measurements, and the System B measurements.

17. Do the results in the table support the conclusion that System B is more accurate than System A for measuring the concentration of zinc?

   A. No, because the zinc measurements from System A are consistently higher than the zinc measurements from System B.

   B. No, because the zinc measurements from System A are closer to the data provided by the USGS than the zinc measurements from System B.

   C. Yes, because the zinc measurements from System B are consistently lower than the zinc measurements from System A.

   D. Yes, because the zinc measurements from System B are closer to the data provided by the USGS than the zinc measurements from System A.

GO ON TO THE NEXT PAGE ⟩

18. The relationship between humidity level and calcium concentration, as measured by System B, is best represented by which of the following graphs?

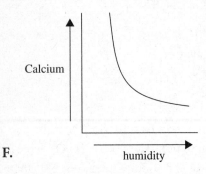

F.

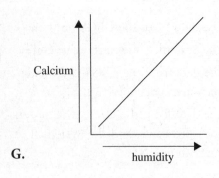

G.

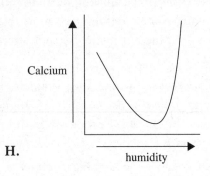

H.

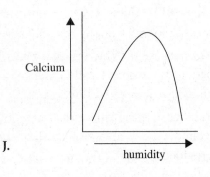

J.

19. After conducting their comparisons, the engineers used System B to test a soil sample at the future road site. They measured the concentrations, in mg/L, of selected compounds in the sample and found that they were: potassium oxide (K_2O) = 9.1, calcium = 17.3, and zinc = 0.57. According to the data in the table, the engineers should predict that the level of humidity is approximately:

A. 16%.

B. 37%.

C. 49%.

D. 57%.

PASSAGE IV

An increasing number of individuals over 50 develop type II diabetes, which occurs when the body does not produce enough insulin or when the cells ignore the insulin and as a result, the body's blood sugar level rises dangerously. Although type II diabetes occurs in people of all ages and races, it is more common in adults. Several hypotheses have been proposed to explain the cause of type II diabetes.

DIETARY HYPOTHESIS

Most Americans consume too much sugar. Sugar from food is absorbed into the bloodstream and insulin is required for the body to be able to use that sugar. In a study of individuals 18–25 years old who consumed more than the recommended amount of sugar daily, and were thus considered at risk for developing type II diabetes, it was shown that the majority had significantly elevated levels of sugar in their blood but normal levels of insulin. When these individuals received small injections of insulin once a day, their blood sugar levels decreased to more normal levels. If abundant levels of sugar are supplied by the diet, sugar dissolving insulin injections should be given to avoid type II diabetes.

GO ON TO THE NEXT PAGE ⟩

GENETIC HYPOTHESIS

Genes, which primarily come from parents and grandparents, contribute to many medical problems that individuals will experience through life. Type II diabetes mainly depends on one's genes, but also on one's lifestyle. Diabetes occurs when the pancreas produces little or no insulin or when the insulin it produces does not work properly. As individuals grow older, the processes of their body do not run as efficiently as they did when the individuals were younger. Therefore, the same behaviors may be more detrimental to a person when he or she is older than when he or she was younger, especially for those over the age of 50. This is the main reason that type II diabetes is more common in adults.

Scientists compared the genetics and lifestyles of 4 groups of individuals over 50. The results are shown in the table below.

Table 1

Group	Attributes	% with type II diabetes
A	One parent with type II	55%
B	Healthy lifestyle, no parents with type II	20%
C	One parent with type II and healthy lifestyle	40%
D	Two parents with type II	70%

EXERCISE HYPOTHESIS

A lack of exercise results in high body fat content, and a high body fat content does not allow the body to work efficiently. Conversely, regular weight-bearing exercise can boost the body's efficiency. One study showed that 10 weeks of weight training lowered blood sugar in adults over 50. A second study on another group of adults over 50 showed that walking 2 miles a day for 12 weeks also lowered blood sugar levels.

20. Dietary Hypothesis would be strengthened if it were proven that high blood sugar levels are indicative of:

F. a low efficiency of insulin.

G. a low-sugar diet.

H. high levels of insulin produced by the body.

J. sugar being stored elsewhere in the body.

21. The Genetic Hypothesis best explains why type II diabetes is more common in which of the following groups?

A. Individuals under the age of 25 as opposed to individuals over the age of 25

B. Individuals over the age of 25 as opposed to individuals under the age of 25

C. Individuals over the age of 50 as opposed to individuals under the age of 50

D. Individuals under the age of 50 as opposed to individuals over the age of 50

22. According to the Genetic Hypothesis, adults who have had their pancreas removed should exhibit:

F. increased blood insulin levels.

G. decreased blood sugar levels.

H. increased blood sugar levels.

J. decreased body fat content.

23. Supporters of the Dietary Hypothesis might criticize the experimental results in the Exercise Hypothesis for which of the following reasons?

A. Not enough sugar was included in the diets of the test subjects in both groups.

B. The sugar intake of the individuals in the two groups was not monitored.

C. The genetics of each individual in both groups should have been determined.

D. Type II diabetes is more common in children than adults.

GO ON TO THE NEXT PAGE →

24. Assume that individuals with elevated blood sugar levels have a greater chance of developing type II diabetes. How would supporters of the Genetic Hypothesis explain the experimental results presented in the Dietary Hypothesis?

    F. The test subjects probably had high levels of sugar in their diets.

    G. The test subjects did not perform any weight-bearing exercise.

    H. The test subjects probably had no occurrence of type II diabetes in their genetic backgrounds.

    J. The test subjects were given too little insulin.

25. How might proponents of the Dietary Hypothesis explain the results of Group D in the Genetics Hypothesis experiment?

    A. Insulin supplements should not have been taken by this group.

    B. These individuals and both parents had an unhealthy diet that was high in sugar.

    C. More genetic background should be researched for all the groups.

    D. Not enough insulin was given to this group to affect the onset of type II diabetes.

26. The experiments cited in the Genetics Hypothesis and in the Exercise Hypothesis are similar in that each test subject:

    F. has at least one parent with type II diabetes.

    G. was given a shot of insulin.

    H. had their pancreas previously removed.

    J. was an adult over 50 years old.

PASSAGE V

Human blood is composed of approximately 45% *formed elements*, including blood cells, and 50% plasma. The formed elements of blood are further broken down into red blood cells, white blood cells, and platelets. The mass of a particular blood sample is determined by the ratio of formed elements to plasma, as the formed elements weigh approximately 1.10 grams per milliliter (g/mL), and plasma approximately 1.02 g/mL. This ratio varies according to an individual's diet, health, and genetic makeup.

The following experiments were performed by a phlebotomist to determine the composition and mass of blood samples from three different individuals, each of whom was required to fast overnight before the samples were taken.

EXPERIMENT 1

A 10 mL blood sample was taken from each of the three patients. The densities of the blood samples were measured using the *oscillator technique*, which determines fluid densities by measuring sound velocity transmission.

EXPERIMENT 2

Each 10 mL blood sample was spun for 20 minutes in a centrifuge to force the heavier formed elements to separate from the plasma. The plasma was then siphoned off and its mass recorded.

EXPERIMENT 3

The formed elements left over from Experiment 2 were analyzed using the procedure from Experiment 2, except this time they were spun at a slower speed for 45 minutes so that the red blood cells, white blood cells, and platelets could separate out. The mass of each element was then recorded. The results of the three experiments are shown below:

GO ON TO THE NEXT PAGE

Table 1

Patient	Plasma (g)	Red blood cells (g)	White blood cells (g)	Platelets (g)	Total density (g/mL)
A	4.54	2.75	1.09	1.32	1.056
B	4.54	2.70	1.08	1.35	1.054
C	4.64	2.65	1.08	1.34	1.050

27. The results of the experiments indicate that the blood sample with the lowest density is sample with the most:

A. plasma.

B. red blood cells.

C. white blood cells.

D. platelets.

28. Why did the phlebotomist likely require each patient to fast overnight before taking blood samples?

F. It is more difficult to withdraw blood from patients who have not fasted.

G. Fasting causes large, temporary changes in the composition of blood.

H. Fasting ensures that blood samples are not affected by temporary changes caused by consuming different foods.

J. Blood from patients who have not fasted will not separate when spun in a centrifuge.

29. Which of the following best explains why the amount of plasma, red blood cells, white blood cells, and platelets do not add up to 10.5 g?

A. Some of the red blood cells might have remained in the plasma, yielding low red blood cell measurements.

B. Some of the platelets might not have separated from the white blood cells, yielding high white blood cell counts.

C. The centrifuge might have failed to fully separate the plasma from the formed elements.

D. There are likely components other than plasma, red and white blood cells, and platelets in blood.

30. From the data presented in the experiment, it is possible to determine that, as total density increases, the mass of red blood cells:

F. increases only.

G. increases, then decreases.

H. decreases only.

J. decreases, then increases.

31. A 10 mL blood sample from a fourth individual contains 5 mL of plasma and 4 mL of formed elements. Approximately what is the mass of this blood sample?

A. 6.5 g

B. 9.5 g

C. 11.5 g

D. 15.5 g

GO ON TO THE NEXT PAGE

32. The phlebotomist varied which of the following techniques from Experiment 2 to Experiment 3?

    F. The volume of blood taken from each patient

    G. The mass of blood taken from each patient

    H. The instrument used to separate the elements of the blood samples

    J. The amount of time the samples were left in the centrifuge

33. The patient with the greatest mass of red blood cells is:

    A. Patient 1.

    B. Patient 2.

    C. Patient 3.

    D. not possible to determine from the information given.

GO ON TO THE NEXT PAGE

PASSAGE VI

A student performed experiments to determine the relationship between the electrical conductivity of a metal rod and its length, mass density (mass per unit length of metal), and temperature.

EXPERIMENT 1

The student used several lengths of iron rods. The student weighed the rods and calculated their mass densities. The rods were then heated to the specified temperature by being held over a flame. To test the conductivity, pairs of rods were placed at opposite sides of a container containing an *electrolyte solution* (a solution containing positive ions with a positive electrical charge and negative ions with a negative electrical charge) and then connected to a battery. The movement of the ions in the solution was detected and displayed on the screen of an oscilloscope, where the conductivity could be measured. The results are presented in Table 1.

Table 1

Trial	Length (cm)	Mass density (g/cm)	Temperature (°C)	Conductivity (μΩ/cm)
1	16	100	20	240
2	16	100	80	120
3	16	400	20	60
4	16	400	80	30
5	8	100	20	120
6	8	100	80	60
7	8	400	20	30

EXPERIMENT 2

The student repeated the procedure in Experiment 1, this time using rods made from silver and tungsten. The results are presented in Table 2.

Table 2

Trial	Material	Length (cm)	Mass density (g/cm)	Temperature (°C)	Conductivity (μΩ/cm)
8	Silver	16	400	20	30
9	Silver	16	100	80	120
10	Silver	16	225	20	60
11	Silver	16	225	5	120
12	Tungsten	16	100	20	60
13	Tungsten	16	225	80	240

GO ON TO THE NEXT PAGE

34. Which of the following would most likely be the conductivity of a silver rod with a length 16 cm, a mass density of 225 g/cm, and a temperature of 15°C?

    F. 60 $\mu\Omega$/cm

    G. 80 $\mu\Omega$/cm

    H. 100 $\mu\Omega$/cm

    J. 130 $\mu\Omega$/cm

35. Between Trials 8 and 10, the student directly manipulated which of the following variables?

    A. The temperature of the metal rods

    B. The conductivity of the metal rods

    C. The material from which the metal rods were composed

    D. The mass density of the metal rods

36. Instead of immersing the rods in an electrolyte solution, the student could have measured conductivity by:

    F. shortening the rods to 8 cm.

    G. connecting the rods with a low-resistance wire.

    H. increasing the mass density of the rods to 200 *g*/cm.

    J. insulating the rods with rubber.

37. If the rods used in Trial 11 were heated to a temperature of 60°C, the conductivity would most likely be:

    A. less than 60 $\mu\Omega$/cm

    B. 80 $\mu\Omega$/cm

    C. 120 $\mu\Omega$/cm

    D. greater than 120 $\mu\Omega$/cm

38. Based on the results of both experiments, which of the following statements regarding the relationship between observed conductivity and the other physical variables is false?

    F. Increasing temperature increases observed conductivity.

    G. Increasing mass density decreases observed conductivity.

    H. Increasing length increases conductivity.

    J. The observed conductivity depends on the material.

39. A student is given several metal rods of identical length but unknown mass density. The rod with the lowest mass density could be found by:

    A. placing all the rods under identical temperature conditions and selecting the rod with the lowest conductivity.

    B. placing all the rods under identical temperature conditions and selecting the rod with the highest conductivity.

    C. varying the voltage until all the rods have the same conductivity and selecting the rod with the lowest temperature.

    D. selecting the rod capable of sustaining the highest temperature without melting.

40. An ordinary table lamp requires a conductivity level of less than 30 $\mu\Omega$/cm. An electrician wants to use an iron rod with the mass density 400 *g*/cm at a temperature of 80°C in order to conduct electricity to the lamp. Approximately what length should the rod be for the electrician to connect the table lamp to the source of the electricity?

    F. 48 cm

    G. 24 cm

    H. 16 cm

    J. Less than 16 cm

WRITING TEST

40 Minutes

Directions: This is a test of your writing skills. You will have forty (40) minutes to write an essay in English. Before you begin planning and writing your essay, read the writing prompt carefully to understand exactly what you are being asked to do. Your essay will be evaluated on the evidence it provides of your ability to do the following:

- Express judgments by evaluating the three perspectives given in the prompt, taking a position on an issue, and explaining the relationship among all four ideas
- Develop a position by using logical reasoning and by supporting your ideas
- Maintain a focus on the topic throughout the essay
- Organize ideas in a logical way
- Use language clearly and effectively according to the conventions of standard written English

You may use the unlined pages in this test booklet to plan your essay. These pages will not be scored. *You must write your essay in pencil on the lined pages in the answer folder.* Your writing on those lined pages will be scored. You may not need all the lined pages, but to ensure you have enough room to finish, do NOT skip lines. You may write corrections or additions neatly between the lines of your essay, but do NOT write in the margins of the lined pages. *Illegible essays cannot be scored, so you must write (or print) clearly.*

If you finish before time is called you may review your work. Lay your pencil down immediately when time is called.

DO NOT OPEN THIS BOOKLET UNTIL TOLD TO DO SO.

GO ON TO THE NEXT PAGE

SCIENTIFIC RESEARCH

A great deal of pure research, undertaken without specific goals but generally to further man's understanding of himself and his world, is subsidized at least partly, if not fully, by the nation's government to help drive progress and promote outcomes that improve overall quality of life for citizens. Though pure research often involves considerable time, energy, and money without any assurances of positive outcomes, it can result in economic, medical, and technological benefits. However, it can also result in negative, harmful, and perhaps irreversible outcomes, in which case taxpayer dollars can be wasted and society put at risk. Should governments fund research when the outcome is unclear? Given that taxpayers prefer that their dollars be spent efficiently and effectively, it may be unwise to allocate significant funding to endeavors that may not benefit society as a whole.

Read and carefully consider these perspectives. Each discusses government funding of scientific research.

Perspective One	Perspective Two	Perspective Three
Governments should fund as much pure research as they can afford when the intent is to benefit the mass population. Without the government's money, many research projects would have to cease unless alternative funding is secured. Even research without clear, positive consequences should be pursued because the outcome may prove beneficial, and the research can always be paused or stopped entirely if negative repercussions begin to emerge.	Governments should be very cautious and limit efforts to fund research programs with unclear consequences. Rather, these programs should demonstrate their worth and intended results in order to seek government money. Governments should evaluate the merit and benefit of each program and on a case-by-case basis, fund only those projects that are designed to create, and will likely achieve, clear and acceptable outcomes.	Governments should partner with private contributors to fund research. Private contributors include companies doing research and development as well as nonprofit foundations. These partnerships will distance the government from taking responsibility for any unintended or undesired consequences and relieve the burden on the taxpayer for efforts that do not prove beneficial. Additionally, this approach incentivizes research teams to provide results-based research that can generate private funding, thus increasing the chance that the research will prove useful to multiple entities, including the government.

GO ON TO THE NEXT PAGE

ESSAY TASK

Write a unified, coherent essay in which you evaluate multiple perspectives regarding government funding of scientific research. In your essay, be sure to:

- analyze and evaluate the perspectives given
- state and develop your own perspective on the issue
- explain the relationship between your perspective and those given

Your perspective may be in full agreement with any of the others, in partial agreement, or wholly different. Whatever the case, support your ideas with logical reasoning and detailed, persuasive examples.

PLANNING YOUR ESSAY

You may wish to consider the following as you think critically about the task:

Strengths and weaknesses of the three given perspectives

- What insights do they offer, and what do they fail to consider?
- Why might they be persuasive to others, or why might they fail to persuade?

Your own knowledge, experience, and values

- What is your perspective on this issue, and what are its strengths and weaknesses?
- How will you support your perspective in your essay?

_____

_____

_____

_____

_____

_____

_____

_____

_____

_____

_____

_____

GO ON TO THE NEXT PAGE ▶

Practice Test Six
ANSWER KEY

ENGLISH TEST

1. A	11. C	21. B	31. A	41. C	51. B	61. A	71. A
2. J	12. G	22. J	32. H	42. F	52. G	62. H	72. H
3. C	13. C	23. A	33. B	43. D	53. A	63. B	73. C
4. F	14. F	24. F	34. H	44. F	54. F	64. H	74. H
5. B	15. B	25. B	35. A	45. C	55. C	65. C	75. C
6. G	16. F	26. H	36. H	46. H	56. G	66. H	
7. C	17. C	27. B	37. D	47. A	57. A	67. C	
8. H	18. H	28. F	38. J	48. H	58. H	68. J	
9. A	19. B	29. B	39. D	49. D	59. C	69. D	
10. G	20. H	30. J	40. G	50. H	60. F	70. G	

MATHEMATICS TEST

1. D	9. A	17. C	25. B	33. D	41. C	49. C	57. C
2. J	10. K	18. H	26. K	34. J	42. G	50. G	58. F
3. B	11. A	19. A	27. C	35. A	43. E	51. B	59. A
4. G	12. K	20. G	28. K	36. H	44. J	52. K	60. J
5. A	13. D	21. C	29. D	37. A	45. E	53. E	
6. J	14. K	22. H	30. G	38. J	46. G	54. H	
7. A	15. A	23. E	31. B	39. E	47. A	55. B	
8. G	16. J	24. H	32. J	40. H	48. K	56. J	

READING TEST

1. C	6. J	11. B	16. J	21. C	26. F	31. D	36. G
2. G	7. C	12. H	17. B	22. J	27. B	32. H	37. D
3. A	8. F	13. A	18. H	23. D	28. H	33. C	38. G
4. F	9. A	14. G	19. C	24. J	29. C	34. F	39. B
5. A	10. F	15. D	20. H	25. A	30. G	35. C	40. H

SCIENCE TEST

1. A	6. G	11. A	16. J	21. C	26. J	31. B	36. G
2. J	7. D	12. G	17. D	22. H	27. A	32. J	37. A
3. B	8. G	13. D	18. H	23. B	28. H	33. A	38. F
4. H	9. A	14. G	19. B	24. H	29. D	34. G	39. B
5. A	10. H	15. A	20. F	25. B	30. F	35. D	40. J

ANSWERS AND EXPLANATIONS

ENGLISH TEST

PASSAGE I

1. A
Category: Sentence Sense
Difficulty: Low
Getting to the Answer: When a period appears in the underlined portion, check to see if each "sentence" is complete. Here, each sentence is complete and correct; therefore (A), NO CHANGE, is correct. Choice B creates a run-on sentence. Choices C and D create sentences that are awkward and overly wordy.

2. J
Category: Punctuation
Difficulty: Medium
Getting to the Answer: The ACT tests very specific punctuation rules. If punctuation is used in a way not covered by these rules, it will be incorrect. No commas are required in the underlined selection; (J) is correct. Choices F, G, and H all contain unnecessary commas.

3. C
Category: Verb Tenses
Difficulty: Medium
Getting to the Answer: When a verb is underlined, make sure it places the action properly in relation to the other events in the passage. This passage is written primarily in the present tense; "runs," (C), is the best answer here. Choices A and B use verb tenses that do not make sense in context. The past tense verb in D is inconsistent with the rest of the passage.

4. F
Category: Wordiness
Difficulty: Medium
Getting to the Answer: Very rarely will a correct answer choice be significantly longer than the original selection. The underlined selection is grammatically and logically correct, so check the answer choices for a more concise version. You can eliminate G and H, both of which are wordier than the original. Choice J may be tempting because it's shorter than the underlined selection, but it changes the meaning of the sentence; the back office, not the reader, is what hasn't changed. Choice (F) is correct.

5. B
Category: Writing Strategy
Difficulty: Medium
Getting to the Answer: When an English Test question contains a question stem, read it carefully. More than one choice is likely to be both relevant and correct, but only one will satisfy the conditions of the stem. This paragraph deals with the author's father's refusal to give up his old-fashioned ways. Choice (B) is the most consistent choice. Choices A and D describe the items being inventoried, which is irrelevant to the point of the paragraph. Choice C is redundant; since we already know he uses paper and pencil to keep his inventory, it's understood that he's writing it by hand.

6. G
Category: Sentence Sense
Difficulty: Medium
Getting to the Answer: Commas cannot be used to combine independent clauses. Here, the comma connects two independent clauses. Choice (G) correctly replaces the comma with a semicolon. Choice H corrects the run-on error but is unnecessarily wordy. Choice J leaves the meaning of the second clause incomplete.

7. C
Category: Sentence Sense
Difficulty: High
Getting to the Answer: Beware of answer choices that make changes to parts of the selection that

contain no error; these choices will rarely be correct. As written, this sentence uses incorrect grammatical structure; the verb "is" is incorrect here, so you should eliminate A. Choice (C) eliminates it without introducing additional errors. Choices B and D correct the sentence's grammatical error, but neither uses the necessary contrast Connection to relate this sentence to the one before it.

8. H
Category: Punctuation
Difficulty: Low
Getting to the Answer: Commas are used in a series of three or more; they are incorrect in compounds. "My sister and I" is a compound; no comma is needed, so F is correct. Choice (H) corrects the error without adding any new ones. Choice G uses the incorrect pronoun case; since you wouldn't say "me bought him a brand new computer," "me" is incorrect in the compound as well. Choice J incorrectly separates the sentence's subject and its predicate verb with a comma.

9. A
Category: Connections
Difficulty: High
Getting to the Answer: When a Connections word or phrase is underlined, make sure it properly relates the ideas it connects. The underlined word is the Connection between the offer to help transfer records and the information about other ways the computer could be helpful. The second sentence is a continuation of the first, so you can eliminate B and D, both of which suggest a contrast. Choosing between (A) and C is a little more difficult, but remember that new errors may be introduced in answer choices. "In addition" in C would be acceptable if it were followed by a comma, but as written, it's incorrect.

10. G
Category: Punctuation
Difficulty: Medium
Getting to the Answer: Semicolons can only com-

bine independent clauses. Here, the second clause is not independent, so the semicolon is incorrect; eliminate F. Choice (G) eliminates the semicolon. Choice H incorrectly places a comma after the conjunction. Choice J creates a run-on sentence.

11. C
Category: Wordiness
Difficulty: Medium
Getting to the Answer: If you don't spot a grammar or usage error, check for errors of style. This sentence is grammatically correct, but "although" in (C) is a much more concise way of saying "never mind the fact that." Choice B corrects the wordiness error but places an incorrect comma after "although." Choice D is still unnecessarily wordy.

12. G
Category: Writing Strategy
Difficulty: Medium
Getting to the Answer: When asked to add new information, read it into the passage at the points suggested to choose its most logical placement. There are three pronouns in this new sentence; clarity requires that it be placed somewhere that these pronouns have logical antecedents. Placing it after Sentence 1, as (G) suggests, gives each pronoun a clear antecedent: "we" is the author and his sister, "him" is their father, and "it" is the computer. Choice F puts the siblings' hopes about how a computer could help their father before the information that they bought him one. Choice H's placement makes the antecedent for "it" Father's "blackout scenario," which doesn't make sense in context. Placing the new sentence where Choice J suggests gives the pronoun the antecedent "blackout," which is also illogical.

13. C
Category: Word Choice
Difficulty: Medium
Getting to the Answer: Idioms questions often offer more than one idiomatically correct answer choice; use context to determine which is appropriate. "Sooner than later" is idiomatically incorrect, so you

should eliminate A; these are comparison words, but nothing is compared here. Both B and (C) offer proper idioms, but (C) is the one that's appropriate here. Choice D is also incorrect idiomatic usage.

14. F
Category: Sentence Sense
Difficulty: Medium
Getting to the Answer: Remember to read for logic as well as for grammar and usage. The best version of this sentence is the way it is written; (F) is correct. Choice G redundantly uses the possessive "office's" where possession has already been indicated by "of." Choice H misstates the information in the passage; the writer's father received the cell phone before the computer. In J, "the disorganized depths of that office" is where the writer's father received his cell phone, not where the cell phone ended up.

15. B
Category: Writing Strategy
Difficulty: Low
Getting to the Answer: When asked to add information, consider both subject matter and tone. This essay is about the author's father's resistance to technology. Choice (B) concludes the essay by referencing something stated at the beginning: that the writer's father tries to "hide" from the future. Choices A, C, and D, while relevant to the paragraph, do not provide strong conclusions to a passage about the father's aversion to technology.

PASSAGE II

16. F
Category: Word Choice
Difficulty: Medium
Getting to the Answer: *More* or *–er* adjectives are used to compare two items; for more than two, use *most* or *–est*. This sentence is correct as written, (F); "farthest" is appropriate when comparing all areas of the globe. Choice G uses "most far," but "most" is only correct with adjectives that don't have *–est* forms. Choice H combines "most" with the *–est* suf-

fix, which is never correct. Choice J uses "farther," which indicates a comparison that is not present here.

17. C
Category: Punctuation
Difficulty: Medium
Getting to the Answer: "It's" has an apostrophe only when it's used as a contraction; possessive pronouns do not have apostrophes. To check for the correctness of "It's," substitute *It is* or *It has* for the contraction. Since "It is diversity today presents a stark contrast" does not make sense, the contraction is incorrect; eliminate A. Choice (C) is the appropriate possessive here. Choice B uses a spelling that is never correct. Choice D adds the word "own" unnecessarily.

18. H
Category: Word Choice
Difficulty: Medium
Getting to the Answer: Most ACT Idioms questions will hinge on preposition usage. "Prevented… to participate" is idiomatically incorrect, so you can eliminate F; the proper idiom in this context is "prevented from participating," (H). Choices G and J are both idiomatically incorrect.

19. B
Category: Writing Strategy
Difficulty: Medium
Getting to the Answer: When you're asked whether a piece of text is relevant, first determine the topic of the paragraph. This paragraph is about the evolution of the "color line" in baseball. Therefore, information that talks about the development of the industry and the shift in authority is relevant to the paragraph; (B) is correct. Choice A is incorrect because, although the text does talk about previous associations, knowing that range doesn't further the purpose of the paragraph. Choices C and D can be eliminated, since they indicate that the information is irrelevant.

20. H
Category: Punctuation
Difficulty: Medium
Getting to the Answer: A verb should not be separated from its object by a comma. As written, this sentence places an incorrect comma between the verb "had" and its object; eliminate F. Choice (H) eliminates the comma without introducing any additional errors. Choices G and J both add incorrect commas.

21. B
Category: Punctuation
Difficulty: Medium
Getting to the Answer: A semicolon can only be used to combine clauses if both of them are independent. The first clause of this sentence is not independent, so the semicolon is incorrect; a comma correctly joins it to the independent clause that follows. Choices A, C, and D all treat the first clause as independent. Choice (B) is correct.

22. J
Category: Writing Strategy
Difficulty: Medium
Getting to the Answer: Determining whether or not the underlined text should be deleted will help you quickly eliminate two answer choices. If you eliminate the underlined selection, the passage skips abruptly from the decree losing its force to a discussion of specific African-American players. The underlined text introduces those players generally, as a result of the decree losing its impact, and therefore provides a necessary transition, as indicated in (J). Choice F and G can be eliminated, since they advocate deleting the selection. The reasoning in H is not supported by the passage.

23. A
Category: Sentence Sense
Difficulty: Medium
Getting to the Answer: Expect about 25% of your English Test questions to have no error. This sentence is correct as written, (A). Choices B, C, and D all create sentence fragments.

24. F
Category: Word Choice
Difficulty: Medium
Getting to the Answer: Beware of answer choices that are longer than the original; barring errors of grammar or logic, they will not be correct. The phrase "including his brother Weldy" is properly used here to modify "a few other African Americans"; (F), NO CHANGE is needed. Choices G, H, and J all make the sentence wordier unnecessarily.

25. B
Category: Verb Tenses
Difficulty: Medium
Getting to the Answer: Use context to determine appropriate verb tense usage. The previous sentence says that Walker "was" a catcher; the introductory phrase in this sentence refers us to the same time period. Only (B) uses a consistent tense. Choices A, C, and D all refer to future actions.

26. H
Category: Writing Strategy
Difficulty: Medium
Getting to the Answer: Since NO CHANGE is not presented as an option, you'll need to find the most logical placement for the new sentence. "Other teams" must contrast with teams already mentioned, and the only place that happens is in Sentences 2 and 3. Sentence 2 talks about one player for the Blue Stockings and Sentence 3 mentions some additional players for the same team. Sentence 4 turns to the time when segregation returned, so the information about African Americans playing for other teams must come before that, between Sentences 3 and 4, (H).

27. B
Category: Wordiness
Difficulty: Low
Getting to the Answer: When you don't spot an error in grammar or usage, check for errors of style. "At the time when" is a longer way of saying "when"; (B) is correct here. Choice C uses "while," which indi-

cates a continuing period of time, but this sentence refers to a specific moment when Jackie Robinson crossed the color line. Choice D is even wordier than the original.

28. F
Category: Word Choice
Difficulty: Medium
Getting to the Answer: Make sure answer choices that are more concise than the original selection do not alter the meaning of the sentence. The best version of this sentence is the way it is written, (F). Choice G changes the meaning of the sentence, implying that Robinson has yet to be recognized as a hero. Choice H also changes the sentence's meaning, indicating that Robinson is doing the recognizing rather than being recognized. Choice J is unnecessarily wordy.

29. B
Category: Wordiness
Difficulty: Medium
Getting to the Answer: When looking for a more concise version of the underlined selection, keep style, tone, and point of view in mind as well. As written, this sentence is unnecessarily wordy, so A is incorrect; (B) is more concise without introducing any errors. Choice C is too casual for the tone of this passage. Choice D leaves the meaning of the second clause incomplete.

30. J
Category: Writing Strategy
Difficulty: Medium
Getting to the Answer: This question format appears frequently on the ACT; what it's asking for is the passage's main idea. This essay is about the color barrier in baseball; it would not fulfill an assignment to write about the history of baseball, so you can eliminate F and G. The fact that baseball was played before 1868, H, is not the reason this essay does not fulfill an assignment on baseball's history. Choice (J) correctly states the reasoning: the essay focuses only on one aspect of the game.

PASSAGE III

31. A
Category: Punctuation
Difficulty: Medium
Getting to the Answer: An introductory phrase should be separated from the rest of the sentence by a comma. The introductory phrase is set off by a comma; the sentence is correct as written, (A). Choices B and C incorrectly treat the introductory phrase as an independent clause. Choice D incorrectly connects a dependent and an independent clause with the conjunction "and."

32. H
Category: Punctuation
Difficulty: Low
Getting to the Answer: Possessive nouns use apostrophes; plural nouns do not. Here, the noun is possessive; the writer is discussing the construction of a bridge, so F is incorrect. Choice (H) places the necessary apostrophe correctly. Choice G uses the plural possessive, but only one bridge is referred to. (Don't be fooled by the fact that it's been known by two different names.) Choice J uses 's to make a plural noun possessive. While there are cases where this is correct, it is not here. (Plural possessives are not generally tested on the ACT, although they may appear in wrong answer choices.)

33. B
Category: Verb Tenses
Difficulty: Medium
Getting to the Answer: Make sure verb tenses make sense within the chronology of the passage. The past perfect is used in this sentence, but this tense is only correct when used to describe one past action completed before another. That is not the case here, so A is incorrect; (B) correctly replaces the verb with its past tense form. Choice C changes the meaning of the sentence (the legislature did the authorizing; it wasn't authorized by someone else) and creates a sentence that is grammatically incorrect. Choice D uses a conditional verb phrase, which is inappropriate in context.

34. H
Category: Wordiness
Difficulty: Low
Getting to the Answer: When the underlined selection contains a compound, check to see if the words mean the same thing. If so, the correct answer choice will eliminate one of them. "Build" and "construct" mean the same thing, so you can eliminate F and G right away. The only difference between (H) and J is a comma, which is incorrect in a compound; eliminate J.

35. A
Category: Punctuation
Difficulty: Medium
Getting to the Answer: Where the only difference among the answer choices is comma placement, remember your tested rules. This sentence needs NO CHANGE, (A). Choice B incorrectly places a comma between items in a compound. Choice C places a comma after the conjunction in a compound, which is also incorrect. Choice D incorrectly inserts a comma between a preposition and its object.

36. H
Category: Writing Strategy
Difficulty: Medium
Getting to the Answer: Read the sentence without the material in question to determine how its meaning changes. Looking at the paragraph as a whole, you can see that the author mentions the amount of money invested, the prominence of the architects, and the accomplishments of the firm the architects brought in to help. Removing one of these details detracts from that description; (H) is the best choice here. Choice F can be eliminated because this is not the only detail that supports the larger point; in and of itself, it's not critical. Removing this one phrase wouldn't impact the transition, as G suggests. Choice J is a trap. The segment in question does concern finances, but the text only mentions the amount of money invested, not how it was raised.

37. D
Category: Word Choice
Difficulty: High
Getting to the Answer: On the ACT, "who" will only be correct when used to refer to people. Despite the fact that it's named after a person, "John A. Roebling and Sons" is the name of a company, so "who" isn't appropriate. That eliminates A and B. Choice C might be tempting because it's shorter than (D), but when C is read into the sentence, it creates a grammatical problem: "a company...and would later" requires another verb. Choice (D) is correct.

38. J
Category: Writing Strategy
Difficulty: Medium
Getting to the Answer: Consider context when you're asked about the role a piece of text plays. A question that asks what would be lost if text were deleted is really just asking for the Function of that text. If you read the paragraphs before and after the sentence in question, you'll see that what is missing is a clear transition; (J) is correct. Choice F distorts the meaning of the sentence, which discusses how long the project actually took, not how long it was expected to take. Choice G is out of scope; danger is only mentioned in this one sentence and then only in terms of how few lives were lost constructing the bridge. Choice H overstates the significance of the detail regarding construction time.

39. D
Category: Connections
Difficulty: Medium
Getting to the Answer: When Connections words are underlined, focus on the relationship between the sentences or clauses they combine. The preceding sentence talks about the length of the bridge, and the sentence in which the underlined segment appears goes on to describe the cables in more detail. Since the second isn't a result of the first, you can eliminate A. Choice B inaccurately suggests an inconsistent or contradictory relationship between

the sentences. Choice C is illogical; these are facts about the bridge, not events occurring simultaneously. The best choice here is no transition at all, as in (D).

40. G
Category: Word Choice
Difficulty: Low
Getting to the Answer: Word Choice wrong answers may have the wrong word in context. They may also be wordy or passive. "Longer" means a comparison: one thing is longer *than* something else. Since this sentence doesn't offer a comparison, "longer" can't be correct. Eliminate F. Choices (G) and H are both grammatically correct in context, but H is unnecessarily wordy. "Lengthy," in J, is not correct when used to describe a specific length.

41. C
Category: Wordiness
Difficulty: Medium
Getting to the Answer: If all of the answer choices create grammatically correct sentences, check for errors of style. "As well as being" is just a wordier way of saying "and is"; (C) is the best choice here. Choices B and D are still unnecessarily wordy.

42. F
Category: Punctuation
Difficulty: Medium
Getting to the Answer: Introductory phrases and clauses should be set off from the rest of the sentence by a comma. The comma here is used correctly; (F), NO CHANGE is needed Choice G eliminates the comma, making the sentence difficult to understand. Both the colon in H and the semicolon in J would only work if the first clause were independent, which it is not.

43. D
Category: Wordiness
Difficulty: Low
Getting to the Answer: Look for words that restate information, either explicitly or implicitly. "Ten

years" and "a decade" are the same thing, so A is incorrect; (D) removes the redundancy. Choices B and C do not address the error.

44. F
Category: Word Choice
Difficulty: Medium
Getting to the Answer: Use "over" for physical location and "more than" for numbers or amounts. This sentence is correct as written, (F). Choice G replaces "more than" with "over," which, despite its common usage, is actually a preposition and indicates location, not amount. Choice H is unnecessarily wordy. Choice J is also wordy and uses "amount," which is incorrect for a countable noun like "vehicles."

45. C
Category: Writing Strategy
Difficulty: Medium
Getting to the Answer: As you read ACT English passages, develop a sense of topic or "big idea," just like you do in Reading; this question format is very common on the ACT. This passage is about one specific bridge, so it would not satisfy the requirement set out in the question stem. You can therefore eliminate A and B right away. Now turn to the reasoning. Choice D misstates the topic of the passage; (C) is correct.

PASSAGE IV

46. H
Category: Verb Tenses
Difficulty: Medium
Getting to the Answer: Verbs in a compound should be in the same tense. The compound verb in this clause is "was…rising…and painted." Since the second verb is in the past tense, the first should be as well, so F is incorrect; (H) is correct. Choice G uses the gerund verb form without the necessary helping verb. Choice J is unnecessarily wordy.

47. A
Category: Writing Strategy
Difficulty: Medium
Getting to the Answer: Read English Test question stems carefully. Often, all of the choices will be relevant and grammatically correct, but only one will fulfill the requirements of the stem. This question stem asks for a detail that shows a contrast between the quiet night streets and the daytime activity. The original text does this best. The verb in B does not convey the difference in the streets at these two times as well as "flood" in (A). Choice C is too general. Choice D does not provide the necessary contrast.

48. H
Category: Word Choice
Difficulty: Medium
Getting to the Answer: There are no "rules" to learn that will help you answer idioms questions; use your Kaplan resources to familiarize yourself with commonly tested ones. Although all four answer choices form idioms that would be correct in some contexts, one smiles *at* someone or something; (H) is correct.

49. D
Category: Wordiness
Difficulty: Medium
Getting to the Answer: When you don't spot an error in grammar or usage, look for errors in style. The underlined selection is a wordy way of saying "traveled across," (D). Choices B and C are unnecessarily wordy.

50. H
Category: Sentence Sense
Difficulty: Low
Getting to the Answer: Read question stems carefully. This one asks which answer choice would NOT be acceptable, which means that three of the choices will be correct in context. Choices F, G, and J are appropriate introductory clauses, but (H) is an independent clause, which makes the sentence a run-on.

51. B
Category: Writing Strategy
Difficulty: Medium
Getting to the Answer: Use your Reading skills for questions like this one that ask for the function of a detail. The underlined portion tells us that the writer's journey will end in California. Choice (B) is correct. The underlined selection does not mention the reasons for the writer's trip, describe her route, or make any comparisons, so A, C, and D are incorrect.

52. G
Category: Punctuation
Difficulty: Medium
Getting to the Answer: Use commas in a list or series only if there are three or more items. Since the writer only mentions two places she has been, the first comma here is incorrect; eliminate F. Choice (G) corrects this without introducing any additional errors. Choice H eliminates the incorrect comma but removes the one at the end of the selection, which is needed to separate the introductory clause from the rest of the sentence. Choice J does not address the error.

53. A
Category: Connections
Difficulty: Medium
Getting to the Answer: To identify the most effective Connection, you'll need to read both paragraphs. Paragraph 3 is about how the author has traveled to foreign countries but, within the United States, only knows New York City. Paragraph 4 describes her drive through the Midwest. The text as written takes the reader from New York City (tall buildings) to the less populated areas, leading to the description of the cornfields. Choice (A), NO CHANGE, is the best choice here. Choice B misstates the passage; the cornfields didn't appear "almost immediately," but gradually. Choice C and D do not provide appropriate transitions between the paragraphs.

54. F
Category: Writing Strategy
Difficulty: Medium
Getting to the Answer: When you're asked to identify the "most relevant" choice, use context clues. The paragraph is about the change the author experiences as she drives from New York across the country. That contrast is clear in the passage as written; (F) is the best choice here. Choices G and H do not relate to the paragraph's topic. Choice J is opposite; the writer describes many different settings, which is the opposite of "monotonous."

55. C
Category: Sentence Sense
Difficulty: Medium
Getting to the Answer: There are a number of ways to correct a run-on sentence, but only one answer choice will do so without introducing any additional errors. Each of the clauses in this sentence is independent; (C) corrects the run-on by replacing the comma with a semicolon. Choice B omits the comma necessary with the coordinating conjunction "but." Choice D loses the contrast between the clauses that is present in the original.

56. G
Category: Punctuation
Difficulty: Medium
Getting to the Answer: Introductory phrases and clauses should be set off from the rest of the sentence with a comma. The underlined portion here is an introductory phrase, which should be followed by a comma, so F is incorrect; (G) makes the correction. Choice H corrects the error but changes "For" to "During," which is incorrect for a fixed period of time such as the one referred to here. Choice J does not address the error and also changes "For" to "During."

57. A
Category: Punctuation
Difficulty: Medium
Getting to the Answer: Only two apostrophe uses are tested on the ACT: possessive nouns and contractions. The noun here is possessive; the apostrophe is used correctly, (A). Choice B uses the plural "nights" instead of the possessive. Choice C is unnecessarily wordy and uses the idiomatically incorrect "shadows from the night." Choice D changes the meaning of the sentence.

58. H
Category: Wordiness
Difficulty: Medium
Getting to the Answer: If you don't spot a grammar or usage error, check for errors in style. As written, this sentence is unnecessarily wordy, so F is wrong; (H) provides the best revision. Choices G and J are still unnecessarily wordy.

59. C
Category: Connections
Difficulty: Medium
Getting to the Answer: When a Connections word or clause is underlined, determine the relationship between the ideas being connected. Look at the relationship between the sentences in this paragraph. The ideas are presented chronologically—that is, in the order in which they happened. Choice (C), "At first," is the best transition into this series of events. Choice A and B imply contradiction or qualification, which is incorrect in context. Choice D implies that a lot went on prior to the writer's not having any idea what she was looking at, but this is presented as the first in a series of events.

60. F
Category: Word Choice
Difficulty: High
Getting to the Answer: The correct answer will rarely be longer than the original selection. This question requires NO CHANGE, (F). The pronoun's antecedent appears in the previous sentence ("what I was looking at") and the —*ing* verb form is used correctly. Choices G, H, and J are wordy; additionally, G introduces the passive voice unnecessarily.

PASSAGE V

61. A
Category: Punctuation
Difficulty: Low
Getting to the Answer: Commas are used to combine an independent and a dependent clause. This sentence is correct as written, (A), with the comma properly placed after the introductory clause. Choice B places the comma incorrectly; "of 2003" is part of the introductory clause. Choice C omits the necessary comma. Choice D incorrectly uses a semicolon between a dependent and an independent clause.

62. H
Category: Wordiness
Difficulty: Medium
Getting to the Answer: Always read the shortest answer into the sentence to determine how much information can be omitted without changing the meaning of the sentence. Choice (H) eliminates everything but "Mach 2." If you read it back into the sentence, you see that the rest of the phrase isn't necessary. Choice (H) also adds the necessary comma that was omitted in F. Choice G adds the comma, but omits the verb, making the sentence grammatically incorrect. Choice J is unnecessarily wordy; we know from context that Mach 2 is a speed.

63. B
Category: Word Choice
Difficulty: Medium
Getting to the Answer: Word Choice questions require you to look at context; frequently words will have similar meanings but be used differently. "Height" means "the distance from the top to the bottom of something"; "altitude" means "height above sea level." Since "altitude" is correct in this context, you can eliminate A. Choices (B) and C both use "altitude," but "at an altitude" is the correct idiom here; (B) is correct. Choice D creates a grammatically incorrect sentence.

64. H
Category: Wordiness/Punctuation
Difficulty: Medium
Getting to the Answer: When an underlined segment contains more than one error, make sure your answer choice addresses all of them. The underlined segment contains a punctuation error. The subject and predicate of a sentence should not be separated by a single comma, so you can eliminate F and J. Of the remaining two choices, G is unnecessarily wordy. Choice (H) is correct.

65. C
Category: Word Choice
Difficulty: High
Getting to the Answer: Words like "that," which are commonly misused in everyday speech, can make a question more challenging. Sound doesn't travel a speed, it travels *at* a speed; eliminate A. Only (C) makes the correction. Sound doesn't travel *to* a speed, as in B; D, "where" will only be correct on the ACT when used to indicate location or direction.

66. H
Category: Wordiness
Difficulty: Medium
Getting to the Answer: Phrases like "In order to" are often superfluous. Check to see if the answer choices include a more concise version. Choice (H) is concise, without changing the meaning of the sentence. Choice G is still unnecessarily wordy. "For understanding" in J is a proper idiom, but it is not correct in this context.

67. C
Category: Word Choice
Difficulty: Medium
Getting to the Answer: Read English Test question stems carefully. This one asks for the LEAST acceptable alternative, which means that three of the choices will be correct in the sentence. All of the answer choices mean "change," so read each of them into the sentence. "Change them into," "translate them into," and "transform them into" are all ap-

propriate usage, but "alter them into" is not. Choice (C) is the correct choice here.

68. J
Category: Wordiness
Difficulty: High
Getting to the Answer: Look for constructions that repeat words unnecessarily; these will be incorrect on the ACT. The sentence tells us that the speed at which sound travels through gas depends on three things: what kind of gas it is, the temperature, and the pressure; "it is traveling through" is redundant, so F is incorrect. Choice (J) is the most concise answer, and it does not lose any of the meaning of the underlined selection. Choices G and H do not address the error.

69. D
Category: Word Choice
Difficulty: High
Getting to the Answer: Don't choose the shortest answer if it fails to make the writer's meaning clear. "Air temperature and pressure decrease with altitude" isn't clear; "air temperature" and "pressure" themselves do not have altitude, and we're not told "the altitude of what?" so A is incorrect. Choice (D) makes the writer's meaning clear; when altitudes are higher, the decrease in temperature and pressure occur. Choice B does not address the error and even compounds it by replacing "altitude" with "height." Choice C contradicts the facts in the passage; higher, not lower, altitudes have this effect.

70. G
Category: Punctuation
Difficulty: Medium
Getting to the Answer: Beware of answer choices that make unnecessary changes to the sentence. The information provided in the two clauses contrasts, so "however" is correct, but it requires a comma to separate it from the rest of the clause. Eliminate F. Choice (G) is correct. Choice H creates an inappropriate cause-and-effect relationship between the clauses. Choice J does not address the punctuation error.

71. A
Category: Writing Strategy
Difficulty: Medium
Getting to the Answer: When you're asked to choose the most logical conclusion, first determine the sentence's function within the paragraph. The first half of this sentence previews a reason that the Concorde cruises at a higher altitude than regular planes, and it ties that reason back to the contrast between the speed of sound at two different altitudes. You need, then, a conclusion to the sentence that both explains why the planes would fly higher and does so in light of the information about altitude in the preceding sentence. The best choice here is (A); the original version of the sentence is the most logical. Choice B doesn't provide a reason; it simply repeats information that has already been stated. Choice C is out of scope; fuel consumption isn't mentioned in the passage. Choice D is a result of the plane's higher altitude, not its cause.

72. H
Category: Verb Tenses
Difficulty: High
Getting to the Answer: The use of "since" creates a specific marking point in the past and requires a verb that does the same. You need a simple past verb with "since; (H) is correct. Choice F uses a tense that indicates an action that is ongoing, but the decommissioning of the Concorde has been completed. Choice G is unnecessarily wordy. The past perfect in J is only correct when used to indicate one past action competed prior to another stated past action, which is not the case here.

73. C
Category: Sentence Sense/Wordiness
Difficulty: Medium
Getting to the Answer: Sentences beginning with coordinating (FANBOYS) conjunctions will not be correct on the ACT. This sentence incorrectly begins with "But", so you should eliminate A; additionally, "about to" and "very soon" are redundant. Only (C) makes the necessary changes. Choices B and D do not address the redundancy error.

74. H
Category: Wordiness
Difficulty: Medium
Getting to the Answer: Try the shortest answer first; it will frequently be correct. Choice (H) replaces the long introductory clause with a single word without losing any of the sentence's meaning. Choices G and J are still unnecessarily wordy.

75. C
Category: Sentence Sense
Difficulty: Medium
Getting to the Answer: Here, the items combined by "not only…but also" are "to the rich and famous" and "be for the masses." Choice (C) corrects the error. Choices B and D do not address the error; additionally, D fails to correctly complete the idiom.

MATHEMATICS TEST

1. D
Category: Proportions and Probability
Difficulty: Low
Getting to the Answer: When you're converting units, writing out the units will help you determine if you've made a mistake.

$127 \text{ yards} \cdot \dfrac{1 \text{ rod}}{5.5 \text{ yards}} \approx 23.1 \text{ rods, (D)}$

2. J
Category: Proportions and Probability
Difficulty: Low
Getting to the Answer: Instead of finding the increase and adding it to the original cost, you can do the computation in one step by adding 100% to the percent increase. When the cost of the pizza is raised by 22%, the new cost will be 122% of the original cost.

$\$20 \cdot 1.22 = \$24.40$, (J)

3. B
Category: Proportions and Probability
Difficulty: Low
Getting to the Answer: Phrases like "average increase" may sound a little complicated, but there's nothing difficult going on here. The chart shows increases, so you just need to find the average to get the "average increase." Remember, the average of a set of terms is the sum of the terms divided by the number of terms.

$\text{average} = \dfrac{120 + 210 + 0 + 210 + 180}{5} = \dfrac{720}{5} = 144,$

which is (B).

4. G
Category: Proportions and Probability
Difficulty: Low
Getting to the Answer: The formula rate · time = distance will take you far on the ACT. Some people find it easier to remember as rate $= \dfrac{\text{distance}}{\text{time}}$. It's the same equation no matter how you rearrange it. Train A travels 50 · 3 = 150 miles. Train B travels 70 · 2.5 = 175 miles. The difference is 175 − 150 = 25 miles, or (G).

If you got this one wrong, you probably didn't answer the right question; the distance each train traveled is a trap, waiting to catch you if you stop too soon.

5. A
Category: Variable Manipulation
Difficulty: Low
Getting to the Answer: When a factored product equals 0, one of the factors must be 0.
$b - 3 = 0$ or $b + 4 = 0$
$b = 3$ or $b = -4$
Only one of these, 3, appears in the answers, as (A). Although B might be tempting if you looked too quickly, 4 is not the same as −4.

6. J
Category: Plane Geometry
Difficulty: Medium
Getting to the Answer: Many of the wrong answers

are designed to catch you making a careless mistake. Just because you got one of the 5 answers doesn't mean you did the problem correctly, so work carefully! In a parallelogram, opposite sides have the same length, so $RU = ST = 8$ and $RS = UT$. The perimeter is the sum of the sides, so $RS + ST + UT + RU = 42$. Substitute in the known sides and solve for the length of UT:

$$RS + 8 + UT + 8 = 42$$
$$2UT + 16 = 42$$
$$2UT = 26$$
$$UT = 13, \text{(J)}$$

7. A

Category: Plane Geometry
Difficulty: Medium
Getting to the Answer: In a "regular polygon," all of the angles have the same measure. This is one you could eyeball. What figure with equal angles has 60° angles? If you said an equilateral triangle, you're absolutely right. If you're not sure off the top of your head, consider each possible answer choice. Choice (A): This is a triangle, and the interior angles of a triangle add up to 180 degrees. Therefore, if all three angles are the same, they each measure $\frac{180}{3} = 60$ degrees—just right. Choice B: A regular four-sided polygon is a square, so all four angles are 90 degrees. Even if you didn't notice that at first, you should know that the sum of the interior angles of a quadrilateral is 360 degrees, so each angle in a regular quadrilateral must be $\frac{360}{4} = 90$ degrees. This is clearly too large. Choice C: A six-sided figure's interior angles add up to 720 degrees. For a regular hexagon, each angle would be $\frac{720}{6} = 120$ degrees. Notice the pattern here: As the number of sides goes up, so does the measure of each angle. It's clear that to get a small angle like 60°, you need a small number of sides, so there is no need to check D or E.

8. G

Category: Variable Manipulation
Difficulty: Low
Getting to the Answer: If you forget the rules of exponents, try writing out an example and canceling. For example, $\frac{a^2}{a^3} = \frac{a \cdot a}{a \cdot a \cdot a} = \frac{1}{a}$. When you're dividing, you subtract the exponents of powers with the same base.

$$\frac{12a^5bc^7}{-3ab^5c^2} = \frac{12}{-3} \cdot \frac{a^5}{a} \cdot \frac{b}{b^5} \cdot \frac{c^7}{c^2} = -4 \cdot a^4 \cdot \frac{1}{b^4} \cdot c^5$$
$$= \frac{-4a^4c^5}{b^4}, \text{ which is (G).}$$

9. A

Category: Plane Geometry
Difficulty: Medium
Getting to the Answer: Whenever you see parallel lines, look for corresponding angles and alternate interior angles. They're most obvious when you're just given two parallel lines and a transversal, so questions that include parallel lines as parts of shapes like triangles or parallelograms can be a little sneaky. Because is $\overline{PQ}$ parallel to $\overline{WY}$, by corresponding angles, $\angle YWX$ has the same measure as $\angle QPX$ and $\angle WYX$ has the same measure as $\angle POX$:

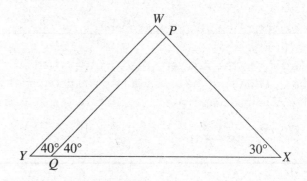

Using the fact that the angles of $\triangle PXQ$ sum to 180 degrees:
$$40° + 30° + \angle QPX = 180°$$
$$\angle QPX = 110°, \text{ which is (A).}$$

10. K

Category: Operations
Difficulty: Low
Getting to the Answer: Absolute value is a special type of parentheses, so PEMDAS says to take the absolute values before multiplying. $|-4| \cdot |2| = 4 \cdot 2 = 8$, (K).

11. A

Category: Proportions and Probability

Difficulty: Low

Getting to the Answer: The math in this question isn't too challenging—just basic percents. The question is really testing whether you pay attention to detail and work carefully. 1250 − 800 − 150 = 300 participants were undecided. $\frac{300}{1250} = 0.24 = 24\%$, (A)

12. K

Category: Number Properties

Difficulty: Medium

Getting to the Answer: The greatest common factor is the largest factor that the two numbers share. The least common multiple is the smallest number that is a multiple of both numbers. Many questions about factors and multiples are made easier by considering the prime factorization of the numbers involved. Choice F: 15 is not a factor of 9 or 25, so these numbers can't have a greatest common factor of 15. Choice G: 15 is not a factor of 27, so these numbers can't have a greatest common factor of 15. Choice H: 15 is not a factor of 25, so these numbers can't have a greatest common factor of 15. Choice J: 30 = 15 · 2 and 45 = 15 · 3, so 15 is the greatest common factor here. The least common multiple of 30 and 45 is 90, which you can find by looking at the prime factorizations: 30 = 3 · 2 · 5 and 45 = 5 · 3 · 3, so the least common multiple must be 2 · 3 · 3 · 5 = 90. Choice (K): 45 = 15 · 3 and 75 = 15 · 5, so 15 is the greatest common factor here. The least common multiple is 225: 45 = 5 · 3 · 3 and 75 = 5 · 5 · 3, so the least common multiple is 5 · 5 · 3 · 3 = 225.

13. D

Category: Operations

Difficulty: Medium

Getting to the Answer: Remember that if you raise a negative number to an odd power, the result is negative. (If the power is even, the result is positive.) Any question that involves negative numbers will require extra attention. It's very easy to lose track of negative signs.

$x^5y + xy^5 = (2)^5(-3) + (2)(-3)^5 = (32)(-3) + (2)(-243) = -96 - 486 = -582$, which is (D).

14. K

Category: Plane Geometry

Difficulty: Medium

Getting to the Answer: The first step is to recall the definition of perimeter—the distance around the sides of a figure. For a square, the perimeter is four times the length of a side. $\frac{1}{4}(16 - 24h) = 4 - 6h$, which is (K). If you got this one wrong, you probably only took $\frac{1}{4}$ of one of the terms, not of the entire expression for the perimeter. For example, J is $\frac{1}{4}(16) - 24h = 4 - 24h$.

15. A

Category: Variable Manipulation

Difficulty: Medium

Getting to the Answer: Memorizing the three classic quadratics will save you valuable time on questions like this. Remember, $(x - y)^2 = x^2 - 2xy + y^2$. Multiply out the quadratic, or better yet, write down the formula from memory. $(x - k)^2 = x^2 - 2kx + k^2 = x^2 - 26x + k^2$. Because the coefficient of x must be the same on both sides of the equation, $-2k = -26$. $k = 13$, which is (A).

16. J

Category: Proportions and Probability

Difficulty: Low

Getting to the Answer: Remember that 20% off means the sale price was 100% − 20% = 80% of the original price. The game system cost 0.9($180) = $162. Each game cartridge cost 0.8($40) = $32. The total was $162 + 2($32) = $226, (J). Be sure you have all the parts to avoid trap answers. Choice G, for instance, is the price of the system and *one* cartridge, so work carefully!

17. C
Category: Coordinate Geometry
Difficulty: Medium
Getting to the Answer: The slope of a line is $\frac{y_2 - y_1}{x_2 - x_1}$. Either point could be used first, but you must be sure that the first x- and y-coordinate come from the same point. If $(5,9) = (x_1,y_1)$ and $(-3,-12) = (x_2,y_2)$, then slope $= \frac{y_2 - y_1}{x_2 - x_1} = \frac{-12 - 9}{-3 - 5}$. Because this doesn't look like any of the answers, try the other ordering: If $(-3,-12) = (x_1,y_1)$ and $(5,9) = (x_2,y_2)$, then slope $= \frac{y_2 - y_1}{x_2 - x_1} = \frac{9 - (-12)}{5 - (-3)}$, which is (C).

18. H
Category: Coordinate Geometry
Difficulty: Medium
Getting to the Answer: You don't have to find the solutions, just the number of solutions. As long as you know the technique you would use to solve it, you can eyeball the answer in seconds. An equation crosses the x-axis when $y = 0$, so set the equation equal to 0: $(x + 1)(x + 2)(x - 3)(x + 4)(x + 5) = 0$ There are 5 factors, any of which could be 0 (for example, if $x + 1 = 0$, then $x = -1$), so there will be 5 roots, which is (H). Specifically, they are -1, -2, 3, -4, and -5, but you don't need to know that to answer the question. If you have a graphing calculator, you might be tempted to use it to graph this equation and see how many times the graph intersects the x-axis. Like solving for all the roots, this is more trouble than it's worth. The time taken up by typing the equation would be better used to think about the problem and realize that it actually asks for something very simple.

19. A
Category: Variable Manipulation
Difficulty: Medium
Getting to the Answer: To reduce, you must factor out the same number from the top and the bottom, then divide. You *cannot* only reduce the 4, neglecting the $8x$ (or vice versa).
$\frac{4 + 8x}{12x} = \frac{4(1 + 2x)}{4(3x)} = \frac{1 + 2x}{3x} = \frac{2x + 1}{3x}$, which is (A).

20. G
Category: Operations
Difficulty: Low
Getting to the Answer: Always read the problem carefully before you jump into your calculations. If 5 people buy 5 tickets for $95, each pays $\frac{\$95}{5} = \$19$. Because the individual rate is $21.50, this is a savings of $21.50 - $19 = $2.50 per person, which is (G). If you got this one wrong, you might have found the total savings for all five people, K, or split the savings just among the original four people, H.

21. C
Category: Variable Manipulation
Difficulty: Low
Getting to the Answer: Small mistakes will add up quickly—keep yourself focused! The key to this one is that x^2y and $2xy^2$ are <u>not</u> like terms. Like terms must have the same exponent on each variable. Combine the two first terms to get: $-2x^2y^2 + x^2y + 3x^2y^2 + 2xy^2 = x^2y^2 + x^2y + 2xy^2$, which is (C).

22. H
Category: Trigonometry
Difficulty: Low
Getting to the Answer: On sine and cosine questions, you can eliminate any answer that's not between -1 and 1, but remember that tangent can get very large or small. Use SOHCAHTOA to help you remember which trig function uses which sides of the triangle.
$\tan(\theta) = \frac{\text{opposite}}{\text{adjacent}} = \frac{12}{7}$, which is (H).

23. E
Category: Variable Manipulation
Difficulty: Low
Getting to the Answer: If you're not sure which operation is appropriate, try Picking Numbers. If Yousuf was 10 years old fifteen years ago, then he's 25 today. In another 7 years, he will be 32. Plug $x = 10$ into each answer choice to see which one equals 32:

A: 10 + 7 = 17 No.
B: (10 – 15) + 7 = 2 No.
C: (10 + 15) – 7 = 18 No.
D: (10 – 15) – 7 = –12 No.
(E): (10 + 15) + 7 = 32 Yes!
The key to solving this problem algebraically is to realize that if Yousef was x years old 15 years ago, he is now $(x + 15)$ years old, not $(x - 15)$ years old. Seven years from now, he'll be another 7 years older, or $(x + 15) + 7$, (E).

24. H
Category: Variable Manipulation
Difficulty: Medium
Getting to the Answer: It's a good idea to check your factoring by multiplying it back out. You want two numbers that multiply to –12 and sum to –4; those numbers are –6 and + 2: $x^2 - 4x - 12 = (x - 6)(x + 2)$. The latter factor is (H).

25. B
Category: Plane Geometry
Difficulty: Low
Getting to the Answer: When using the Pythagorean Theorem, $a^2 + b^2 = c^2$, remember that a and b are the legs and c is the hypotenuse. Wrong answer choices may come from plugging numbers into the wrong part of the formula.

$$8^2 + 15^2 = c^2$$
$$64 + 225 = c^2$$
$$289 = c^2$$
$$c = \sqrt{289} = 17, \text{(B)}$$

26. K
Category: Variable Manipulation
Difficulty: Medium
Getting to the Answer: As with every question involving negative numbers, be careful with the negative signs. Also pay attention to the location of the parentheses. Here you need to cube both the –2 and the x^5 because both are inside the parentheses.

$$(-2x^5)^3 = (-2)^3(x^5)^3 = -8x^{15}, \text{(K)}$$

27. C
Category: Proportions and Probability
Difficulty: High
Getting to the Answer: Don't worry when you see an unfamiliar term, like "relative atomic mass." On questions with terms the test makers don't expect you to be familiar with (including ones they just made up), they'll tell you everything that you need to know. 1 cubic centimeter of carbon masses 12 grams. 1 cubic centimeter of the unknown element is 30 grams. Because these are equal amounts (1 cubic centimeter of each), the relative atomic mass is simply the ratio of the mass of the unknown element to the mass of the carbon, which is $\frac{30}{12} = 2.5$, (C).

28. K
Category: Variable Manipulation
Difficulty: Medium
Getting to the Answer: Don't stop until you're sure you've answered the exact question asked. It's tempting to bubble in the value of x and move on, but that's not what this question is asking for.

$$2x + 3 = -5$$
$$2x = -8$$
$$x = -4$$
$$x^2 - 7x = (-4)^2 - 7(-4) = 16 + 28 = 44, \text{(K)}$$

Be wary of sign errors; it's easy to subtract 28 instead of adding.

29. D
Category: Coordinate Geometry
Difficulty: Medium
Getting to the Answer: Inequalities work exactly like equalities, except that the direction of the sign changes if you multiply or divide by a negative.

$$2(5 + x) < 2$$
$$5 + x < 1$$
$$x < -4$$

The numbers less than –4 are to the left, which means the correct graph is (D).

30. G

Category: Variable Manipulation

Difficulty: Medium

Getting to the Answer: When two things vary directly, one rises as the other rises and falls as the other falls. If x and y vary directly, they can be represented by the equation $y = kx$, where k is a constant. When two things vary inversely, one rises as the other falls and falls as the other rises. If x and y vary inversely, they can be represented by $y = \frac{k}{x}$. The question describes how m relates to the other variables, so the equation will be $m =$ something. Variables that it varies directly with will be in the numerator, and variables that it varies inversely with will be in the denominator. Therefore, $\frac{b^3}{c^2} = m$, which is (G). As the cube of b increases, so does m. As the square of c rises, m will fall.

31. B

Category: Coordinate Geometry

Difficulty: Low

Getting to the Answer: Occasionally you'll be given information in the problem that you don't need. Here, the x-coordinates are irrelevant because the variable is the midpoint of the y-coordinates. The midpoint formula states that the x- and y-coordinates of the midpoint are the averages of the x- and y-coordinates of the endpoints.

$$\frac{-7+5}{2} = p$$

$-1 = p$, so (B) is correct.

32. J

Category: Coordinate Geometry

Difficulty: Medium

Getting to the Answer: Understanding the slope-intercept equation of a line, $y = mx + b$, is essential on the ACT. In the equation $y = mx + b$, the slope is the coefficient of x. In the first equation, the slope is 3. In the second equation, the slope is m. To be parallel, the two equations must have the same slope, so $m = 3$, which is (J).

33. D

Category: Coordinate Geometry

Difficulty: Medium

Getting to the Answer: Problems like this that require two skills (translating English to algebra and graphing on a number line) can be skipped until you've done the more basic problems. "3 times x is increased by 5" translates to $3x + 5$, which is "less than 11":

$$3x + 5 < 11$$
$$3x < 6$$
$$x < 2$$

This is graphed with an open circle at 2 (because x cannot equal 2) and shaded to the left, where x is less than 2. Your graph should look like (D).

34. J

Category: Variable Manipulation

Difficulty: Medium

Getting to the Answer: If you decide to Pick Numbers, make sure they're easy to work with. For example, $x = 6$ would be a good number of pencils because 54 is divisible by 6. If $x = 6$, then each pencil costs $\frac{54}{6} = 9$ cents. If $y = 4$, then each eraser costs $\frac{92}{4} = 23$ cents. The cost of 7 pencils and 3 erasers is $9(7) + 23(3) = 63 + 69 = 132$ cents. Then plug $x = 6$ and $y = 4$ into each answer choice to see which also equals 132 cents. Alternatively, you could think through the algebra to avoid having to calculate all those complicated answer choices. If x pencils cost 54 cents, then each one costs $\left(\frac{54}{x}\right)$ cents. Similarly, each eraser will cost $\left(\frac{92}{y}\right)$ cents. To find the cost of 7 pencils, multiply 7 by the cost per pencil: $7\left(\frac{54}{x}\right)$. Similarly, the cost of 3 erasers is $3\left(\frac{92}{y}\right)$. Add these together to get (J).

35. A
Category: Coordinate Geometry
Difficulty: Medium
Getting to the Answer: You don't always need to make an exact plot. Make a rough sketch, and then, if you have to, you can go back and make it better. Rearrange $y - x = 0$ to get $y = x$. This is a line with slope 1 that goes through the origin. You could plot this line and the points, then find the three on the same side of the line. Another way to think about the line is that it's all the points where the x and y coordinates are equal. Above the line y will be greater than x (which is true of the first three points listed in the problem), and below the line x will be greater than y (which is true of the last two points). So the answer is the first 3 points, which is (A).

36. H
Category: Trigonometry
Difficulty: Medium
Getting to the Answer: Just because two of the sides are 3 and 4 doesn't mean it's a 3-4-5 triangle—remember that 3 and 4 are the legs, and 5 is the hypotenuse! The third side is $\sqrt{4^2 - 3^2} = \sqrt{7}$, so $\sin E = \dfrac{\text{opposite}}{\text{hypotenuse}} = \dfrac{\sqrt{7}}{4}$, which is (H).

37. A
Category: Coordinate Geometry
Difficulty: Medium
Getting to the Answer: If the solution set is a single line, then both equations describe the same line. When two equations are the same line, one is an exact multiple of the other. Look for a multiple. Because $3 \cdot 4 = 12$ and $27 \cdot 4 = 108$, you can get the first equation by multiplying the second by 4:

$4(3x + ky) = 4(27)$
$12x + 4ky = 108$
Therefore:
$4k = -20$
$k = -5$, (A)

38. J
Category: Variable Manipulation
Difficulty: High
Getting to the Answer: Sometimes on the ACT you will need to put together several pieces of information in the right way to get the answer. Because each extra inch adds approximately 10 pounds, a 72 inch person should weigh about 40 pounds more than a 68 inch person, for a total of 190 pounds. Now use the formula:

$BMI = \dfrac{703W}{H^2} = \dfrac{703(190)}{72^2} \approx 26$, which is (J).

39. E
Category: Variable Manipulation
Difficulty: High
Getting to the Answer: Sometimes questions will look harder than they actually are because they're written to intimidate you. Set the expressions equal to each other and see what you can deduce:

$$\left(\frac{x}{y}\right)^2 = \frac{x^2}{y}$$

$$\frac{x^2}{y^2} = \frac{x^2}{y}$$

$$x^2 y = x^2 y^2$$

At this point, you can divide by x^2y if x^2y is not equal to zero, leaving $1 = y$. If $x^2y = 0$, then either x or y equals 0. Because the question tells you to assume y does not equal 0, $x = 0$. There are two possible ways that $\left(\dfrac{x}{y}\right)^2$ can equal $\dfrac{x^2}{y}$: if $x = 0$ or if $y = 1$. If the algebra is confusing, Pick Numbers. Let $x = 0$ and $y = 2$. Then $\left(\dfrac{x}{y}\right)$ is $\left(\dfrac{0}{2}\right) = 0^2 = 0$ and $\left(\dfrac{x}{y}\right)$ is $\left(\dfrac{0}{2}\right)^2 = 0$.

These are equal. You can eliminate B, C, and D. To test whether A or (E) is true, try $x = 2$, $y = 1$:

$$\left(\frac{x}{y}\right)^2 = \left(\frac{2}{1}\right)^2 = 2^2 = 4$$

$$\frac{x^2}{y} = \frac{2^2}{1} = \frac{4}{1} = 4$$

These are equal, so (E) is correct.

40. H

Category: Plane Geometry
Difficulty: Medium
Getting to the Answer: Always be on the lookout for special triangles. What kind of triangles are formed when a perpendicular bisector is added to an equilateral triangle?

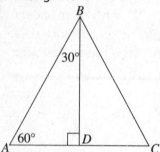

Because $\triangle ABC$ is equilateral, each of its angles is 60 degrees. Angle BDA is 90 degrees, because $\overline{BD}$ is perpendicular to $\overline{AC}$. Then each half of ABC is a 30-60-90 triangle, with side ratios of $x:x\sqrt{3}:2x$. The side opposite the 60-degree angle is $x\sqrt{3} = 4\sqrt{3}$ units long, so $x = 4$. The hypotenuse, $\overline{BC}$, is $2x = 8$ units long, which is (H).

41. C

Category: Plane Geometry
Difficulty: Medium
Getting to the Answer: To find the perimeter of a complicated figure like this one, it can be easy to leave out some sides. Try marking each side as you add it so that you don't accidentally forget any or add any twice. First find the missing lengths:

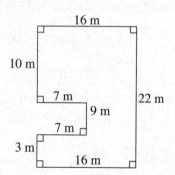

The small horizontal side must be the same length as the small horizontal side above it, because all the angles are right angles. The interior vertical

side must be $22 - (10 + 3) = 9$ meters long, because the total vertical distance on each side of the figure must be the same. Now add the length of each side to find the perimeter: $16 + 22 + 16 + 10 + 7 + 9 + 7 + 3 = 90$, or (C).

42. G

Category: Plane Geometry
Difficulty: High
Getting to the Answer: The advantage of a multiple choice test is that you don't have to come up with the answer yourself; you just have to pick it out. However, remember that if you can predict your own answer and then compare, you're less likely to fall into a trap. Sides $\overline{AO}$ and $\overline{DO}$ will be radii of the circle, which means they are congruent. Choice (G) is the most direct explanation. All the other choices depend on this deduction to be proven true.

43. E

Category: Plane Geometry
Difficulty: Medium
Getting to the Answer: If your answer doesn't look quite like any of the answer choices, rearrange it so that it does. Don't just pick an answer that looks similar; make sure it actually means the same thing. Parentheses make a big difference, so you should carefully consider where they should be! The outer circle has area $\pi r^2 = \pi(12^2)$. The inner circle has area $\pi r^2 = \pi(4^2)$. The shaded area is $\pi(12^2) - \pi(4^2) = \pi(12^2 - 4^2)$, which is (E).

44. J

Category: Plane Geometry
Difficulty: High
Getting to the Answer: Be sure to examine the diagram carefully. Each dimension is $2w$ longer in the outer rectangle; there's w more above and w more below, and w more to the left and w more to the right. It will be very tempting to solve for $2w$ and stop, instead of finding the value the question asks for. You can use either dimension to find w. Using the length:

$$32\frac{1}{2} = 29 + 2w$$

$$3\frac{1}{2} = 2w$$

$$1\frac{3}{4} = w, \text{ so (J) is correct.}$$

Using the width:

$$27\frac{1}{2} + 2w = 31$$

$$2w = 3\frac{1}{2}$$

$$w = 1\frac{3}{4}, \text{ (J)}$$

45. E

Category: Variable Manipulation

Difficulty: Medium

Getting to the Answer: If you're trying to factor a quadratic and you're not getting anywhere, use one of the Kaplan strategies. Here, there are numbers in the answer choices, so Backsolving will work well. If you Backsolve, be sure you plug the answer choices into the right part of the problem. Here, they represent possible lengths. Start with C: If the length of the floor is 13.5 feet, then the width is 2(13.5) – 21 = 27 – 21 = 6 feet. This would produce an area of 13.5(6) = 81 square feet—not big enough. Try D:

length = 17 feet

width = 2(17) – 21 = 34 – 21 = 13 feet

area = 17(13) = 221 square feet

This still isn't big enough, so (E) must be correct:

length = 19 feet

width = 2(19) – 21 = 38 – 21 = 17 feet

area = 19(17) = 323 square feet

Perfect!

You could also solve algebraically:

An equation for the width (W) in terms of the length (L) is $W = 2L - 21$.

$$\text{area} = L \cdot W = 323$$

$$L(2L - 21) = 323$$

$$2L^2 - 21L = 323$$

$$2L^2 - 21L - 323 = 0$$

$$(2L + 17)(L - 19) = 0$$

$$2L + 17 = 0 \text{ or } L - 19 = 0$$

$$2L = -17 \text{ or } L = 19$$

$$L = \frac{-17}{2} \text{ or } L = 19$$

Length must be positive, so the length is 19, (E).

46. G

Category: Plane Geometry

Difficulty: Medium

Getting to the Answer: Picking Numbers can make a theoretical problem much more concrete. Say the original radius was 1. Then the area of the circle would be $\pi r^2 = \pi(1^2) = \pi$. Twice this area would be 2π. Find the radius of a circle with area 2π:

$$\pi r^2 = 2\pi$$

$$r^2 = 2$$

$$r = \sqrt{2}$$

The new radius is $\sqrt{2}$ times the old radius, so (G) is correct.

47. A

Category: Operations

Difficulty: Medium

Getting to the Answer: On some questions you won't be able to depend on your calculator. You simply have to know the formula or rule. Rewrite this equation using an exponent: $x^3 = 64$. If you're not sure what to the third power will give you 64, you can always Backsolve. You'll find that $4^3 = 64$, which means (A) is correct.

48. K

Category: Patterns, Logic & Data

Difficulty: Medium

Getting to the Answer: Some things in math actually work like you expect them to. To subtract two matrices, just subtract the elements that are in the same position. After you've subtracted one position, eliminate the answer choices that don't have the correct number in that position. You may be able to get away with only subtracting one or two positions before you eliminate all the wrong answer choices.

$$\begin{bmatrix} 3 & -6 \\ 0 & 9 \end{bmatrix} - \begin{bmatrix} -3 & 6 \\ 0 & -9 \end{bmatrix} = \begin{bmatrix} (3)-(-3) & (-6)-(6) \\ (0)-(0) & (9)-(-9) \end{bmatrix} = \begin{bmatrix} 6 & -12 \\ 0 & 18 \end{bmatrix},$$

so (K) is correct.

49. C

Category: Number Properties

Difficulty: Medium

Getting to the Answer: When you're Picking Numbers for a question with few limits, don't forget to try both positives and negatives, integers and fractions. Try $a = 1$ and $b = -2$. This immediately eliminates B. Then $a^2 = 1$ and $b^2 = 4$, which eliminates E. Now try $a = 2$ and $b = 1$. This eliminates A. Then $a^2 = 4$ and $b^2 = 1$, which eliminates D. Choice (C) must be correct, because the square of a number cannot be negative. No matter what b is, b^2 must be greater than or equal to zero.

50. G
Category: Trigonometry
Difficulty: Medium
Getting to the Answer: On trigonometry problems, it usually helps to draw the triangle. Use SOHCAH-TOA to remember which trig function uses which sides of the triangle.

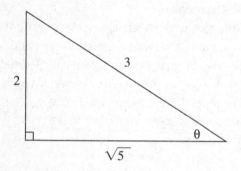

The smallest angle is the one opposite the shortest side. Here, it's marked θ. Based on the diagram, $\cos \theta = \dfrac{\text{adjacent}}{\text{hypotenuse}} = \dfrac{\sqrt{5}}{3}$, which is (G).

51. B
Category: Trigonometry
Difficulty: High
Getting to the Answer: A graphing calculator can be a good backup, but understanding the math will always be faster. You could plug this equation into your graphing calculator, find the highest and lowest values, find their difference, and divide by 2. Alternatively, you could use algebra. Rewrite the equation as $y = 4\sin(5\theta) - 3$. The −3 at the end moves the entire graph down by 3; it doesn't affect the difference between the largest and smallest values. The 5 inside the sin affects how often the function repeats itself in the same space on the x-axis. It's the 4 in front that multi-

plies the y values and makes the extreme values of the function higher and lower. Sine usually goes from −1 to 1, so if you multiply all the values by 4, it will go from −4 to 4. The difference is 8, and half of the difference is 4. So the amplitude is 4, (B).

52. K
Category: Plane Geometry
Difficulty: Medium
Getting to the Answer: A line is like a pencil that goes forever in both directions, and a plane is like a piece of paper that goes forever in all directions. If you model each situation using pencils and paper, you'll see that you can only make one plane with the paper in every case but (K). To make (K), hold two pencils parallel, one above the other. Now rotate one. You cannot put a piece of paper flat against both of these lines, so they do not define a plane.

53. E
Category: Plane Geometry
Difficulty: Medium
Getting to the Answer: The wording of this problem is a giveaway. One of the angles is a "vertex angle" and the other two are "base angles." This will allow you to solve the problem even if you forgot what an isosceles triangle is! The angles sum to 180 degrees, so:

$$(x - 10) + (3x + 18) + (3x + 18) = 180$$
$$7x + 26 = 180$$
$$7x = 154$$
$$x = 22$$

Base angle $= 3x + 18 = 3(22) + 18 = 84$, (E). Notice that A and B are the answers to other questions; they are, respectively, the measure of the vertex angle and the value of x. Be sure to solve for the right thing.

54. H
Category: Proportions and Probability
Difficulty: Medium
Getting to the Answer: If you don't take the time to read carefully, you'll lose a lot of points on careless

mistakes. You might want to leave a question you know will take a long time until after you've gotten points from easier questions. One set of potholders requires: $(6 \cdot 8) + (5 \cdot 12) + (2 \cdot 18) = 48 + 60 + 36 = 144$ inches of fabric. This is 144 inches $\cdot \dfrac{1 \text{ yard}}{36 \text{ inches}}$ = 4 yards. Each yard costs $1.95, so one set of potholders costs 4($1.95) = $7.80. Margot is making five sets of potholders, so the total cost is 5($7.80) = $39, which is (H).

55. B
Category: Plane Geometry
Difficulty: High
Getting to the Answer: Picking Numbers is a great way to deal with abstract questions like this one. Say the original dimensions were $w = 2$, $h = 3$. The surface area would be $S = 4(2)(3) + 2(2)^2 = 24 + 8 = 32$. If you double each dimension, you'll have $w = 4$, $h = 6$, $S = 4(4)(6) + 2(4)^2 = 96 + 32 = 128$. The surface area has gone up by a factor of 4, (B), because $32 \cdot 4 = 128$.

56. J
Category: Proportions and Probability
Difficulty: Medium
Getting to the Answer: The average of a set of terms is the sum of the terms divided by the number of terms. Even if you're not sure what to do on an averages problem, plugging the given information into this formula can help you figure out where to go.

For the first 4 numbers: $\dfrac{\text{sum}}{4} = 14$

$$\text{sum} = 56$$

When you include the fifth number, x, the new sum will be $56 + x$. The new average is:

$$\frac{56 + x}{5} = 16$$
$$56 + x = 80$$
$$x = 24$$

The fifth number is 24, which is (J). Don't forget to divide by 5 in the second equation, because there are now five numbers.

57. C
Category: Coordinate Geometry
Difficulty: High
Getting to the Answer: If you can tell at a glance that a problem is going to take several minutes, save it until you've done all the easier problems. In the equation of an ellipse, $\dfrac{(x - h)^2}{a^2} + \dfrac{(y - k)^2}{b^2} = 1$, the center is at (h, k), the length of the horizontal axis is $2a$, and the length of the vertical axis is $2b$. This particular ellipse is:

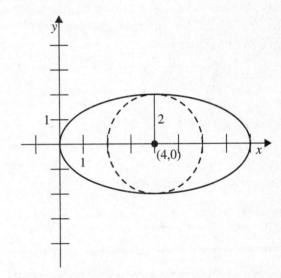

The largest circle possible is dotted on the diagram. Notice that it has the same center as the ellipse, and has radius 2 (the shortest dimension of the ellipse). In the equation of a circle, $(x - h)^2 + (y - k)^2 = r^2$, (h, k) is the center and r is the radius. Plug this information into the formula to find this circle's equation: $(x - 4)^2 + y^2 = 4$, which is (C).

58. F
Category: Coordinate Geometry
Difficulty: Medium
Getting to the Answer: The highest power in the equation determines the general shape. The graph of $y = x^3$ will always have the general shape of the graph in F. Adding a constant C will move it up by C units (if C is positive—if C is negative the graph will move down). If you're not familiar with the shape

of the graph $y = x^3$, you could either plug it into a graphing calculator or plot a few points. Don't worry too much about specific values. As soon as you realize that when x is negative, y will also be negative, you can eliminate all the graphs except (F).

59. A

Category: Coordinate Geometry
Difficulty: High
Getting to the Answer: Equations share points when the same values of x and y work for all the equations involved. Start with the first two equations. Rewrite the second so that both equations have the same term on one side, then set them equal to each other:

$$-x = y - 8$$
$$x = -y + 8$$
$$x = y + 8$$
$$-y + 8 = y + 8$$
$$-y = y$$

This is only true when y equals 0. Plug $y = 0$ into either equation and solve for x:

$$x = y + 8$$
$$x = 0 + 8$$
$$x = 8$$

The point (8,0) is shared between the first two equations. Does it work in the third?

$$6x = 2y + 4$$
$$6(8) = 2(0) + 4$$
$$48 = 4$$

That's not true, so this point is not shared between all three equations. There are no points that work in every equation, so (A) is correct.

60. J

Category: Proportions and Probability
Difficulty: High
Getting to the Answer: ACT probability questions are simple enough that you can write out all the possible outcomes if you need to. Remember that probability is the number of desired outcomes over the number of possible outcomes. The easiest way to think about this problem is to look at

it backwards. If there are three heads, how many tails are there? In 4 coin tosses, if there are 3 heads there must be exactly one tail. That tail could be the first, second, third, or fourth coin, so there are four ways to get one tail and three heads. There are two possible positions for each coin, so the total number of possible arrangements of heads and tails is $2 \cdot 2 \cdot 2 \cdot 2 = 16$. Therefore, the probability that, in 4 tosses, there will be exactly 3 heads is $\frac{4}{16} = \frac{1}{4}$. (J) is correct. If you're in doubt, write it out! All the possible arrangements of 4 coins are:

HHHH	**THHH**	HTTH	THTT
HHHT	HHTT	THTH	TTHT
HHTH	HTHT	TTHH	TTTH
HTHH	THHT	HTTT	TTTT

The ones with three heads are in bold type. There are 4 arrangements with exactly three heads, and 16 total possible arrangements. Again, the probability of getting exactly three heads is $\frac{4}{16} = \frac{1}{4}$, so (J) is correct.

READING TEST

PASSAGE I

1. C

Category: Detail
Difficulty: Low
Getting to the Answer: Remember that the correct answer to Detail questions will be directly stated in the passage. Your notes should guide you as you locate specific references to the details in question. Line 23 mentions Ellen's parents' "regrettable taste for travel," and lines 22–23 make it clear that New York society agrees with this characterization. Predict something like *travel*. Choice (C) matches this prediction. Choice A is a misused detail; Medora does teach her niece to play the piano, but nothing in the passage suggests that this was undesirable. Choice B is a misused detail; Spanish shawl dances are described as "outlandish," but this description is

never directly attributed to New York Society. Choice D is a misused detail; while Medora often adopted children, this is never described as undesirable.

2. G
Category: Detail
Difficulty: Low
Getting to the Answer: Each of the answer choices may be a detail from the passage, but only one will be the correct response to the question. Predicting an answer will help keep you from being distracted by the irrelevant details. The only time in the passage in which Medora's family is clearly upset is when they are "scandalized" that she wears a veil that is shorter than those of her sisters-in-law (lines 33–37); this makes an excellent prediction. Choice (G) is an exact match. Choice F is a distortion; the author tells you neither that Medora allowed Ellen to marry, nor that her family raised any objections. Choice H is a misused detail; although Medora does return to New York impoverished (line 60), the passage does not indicate that her family is upset by this. Choice J is a distortion; this refers to Countess Olenska, not Medora.

3. A
Category: Inference
Difficulty: Medium
Getting to the Answer: To answer Inference questions, you will have to go beyond what is directly stated in the passage. However, the correct answer choice will be supported by evidence from the passage, so make sure that you make a prediction that has solid textual support. You can predict, based on lines 55–66, that Ellen was unable to help her aunt because her own marriage to the immensely rich Polish nobleman "had ended in disaster." Choice (A) matches this prediction. Choice B is a distortion; although the passage does state that no one had heard from Ellen in some time, there is nothing to suggest that Medora had strong feelings about this. Choice C is a distortion; while the author tells you that Ellen had an incoherent education, nothing in the passage suggests that she resented this. Choice

D is a distortion; though the passage makes it clear that Medora was eccentric, this is in no way related to receiving help from her niece.

4. F
Category: Generalization
Difficulty: Medium
Getting to the Answer: Generalization questions require you to synthesize information, sometimes from the entire passage. Predicting an answer is particularly important for questions like this. Make sure you can support your prediction with information in the passage. Lines 67–68 suggest that Newland has spent time thinking about Ellen, and lines 74–92 all describe Newland's observations of Ellen. Newland is not disappointed that Ellen is not as "stylish" as others expected (lines 84–86). You can predict that Newland is *thoughtful* and, unlike many of the other characters in the passage, *non-judgmental*. Choice (F) matches this prediction. Choice G is out of scope; It might seem reasonable to conclude that Newland is likeable, but the passage does not provide any evidence to directly support this. Also, there is nothing to suggest that he is withdrawn. Choice H is 0pposite; Newland's observations about Ellen in the last paragraph clearly indicate that he is interested in her. Choice J is a distortion; Newland's observation that Ellen is not as stylish as New York society might expect says nothing about his own stylishness. Also, the author never implies that Newland behaves in the same way as New York society, so there is no reason to believe that he is gregarious.

5. A
Category: Inference
Difficulty: Medium
Getting to the Answer: The answer to questions like this can be found in the passage, but you may have to put a few pieces of information together to get to the correct answer. Lines 20–21 state that "New York looked indulgently on her eccentricities." Predict that *Medora's eccentric nature was largely accepted.* Choice (A) matches your prediction. Choice B is extreme; although lines 24–25 state that

others thought it was a pity that Ellen should be in Medora's care, to call Medora's lifestyle a "terrible example" goes too far. Choice C is a distortion; although Medora's life is described as unfortunate, the passage does not suggest that this is the way in which others viewed her life. Choice D is a distortion; it may be reasonable to describe Medora's life as inconsistent, but nothing suggests that others viewed her life that way.

6. J
Category: Generalization
Difficulty: Medium
Getting to the Answer: Answering Generalization questions like this might require you to pull together information from throughout the entire passage. It is clear from lines 38–50 and lines 82–86 that Ellen, like Medora, is unconventional and eccentric. Predict that *Ellen has taken on some of her Aunt's uniqueness and eccentricity*. Choice (J) matches this prediction. Choice F is out of scope; nothing in the passage suggests that Medora is necessarily grateful or that her aunt was unselfish in adopting her. Choice G is out of scope; nothing suggests that Medora is jealous of Ellen's marriage. Choice H is a distortion; while the passage makes it clear that New York society is suspicious of both Ellen and Medora, you don't necessarily know that they, in turn, dislike New York society.

7. C
Category: Generalization
Difficulty: Medium
Getting to the Answer: Make sure you have good evidence for your prediction, and the right answer choice will be easy to find. Line 21 mentions Medora's "eccentricities," line 31 mentions her "peculiarities," and line 44 mentions the "outlandish arts" that Medora teaches Ellen. From these descriptions, you can predict that Medora is *unconventional* or *eccentric*. Choice (C) matches this prediction. Choice A is out of scope; although Medora does not adhere to conventions, as indicated by lines 31–32, there is nothing to suggest that this is attributable to arro-

gance. Choice B is a distortion; the description of the short veil that Medora wore to her brother's funeral in lines 34–36 might suggest immodesty, but the author makes clear that this is evidence of Medora's willingness to flout social conventions. Choice D is opposite; you're told in lines 31–32 that one of her peculiarities is to "flout the unalterable rules that regulated American mourning."

8. F
Category: Detail
Difficulty: Low
Getting to the Answer: Detail questions like this one are straightforward, but it can sometimes be difficult to find exactly where in the passage the relevant information comes from. Make sure that you are answering the specific question being asked, so that other details don't distract you. Medora teaches Ellen "drawing from the model" (lines 48–49), which is described as "a thing never dreamed of before," so predict *Ellen* or *Countess Olenska*. Choice (F) matches your prediction. Choice G is out of scope; Newland is not described as having learned anything at all, let alone something controversial. Choice H is a distortion; Medora teaches Ellen, but the passage does not mention Medora learning anything herself. Choice J is a distortion; Count Olenska is only mentioned indirectly as the rich nobleman who Medora marries. The passage makes it clear that Ellen is *Countess* Olenska; don't be fooled by this initially tempting, but incorrect, choice.

9. A
Category: Inference
Difficulty: Medium
Getting to the Answer: You won't be able to predict an answer to Inference questions like this. Instead, examine each of the answer choices and find the one that is best supported by the passage. Although some details might seem to support several answer choices, only one will have strong support in the text. Most of the passage describes Ellen in her childhood, so focus on the last paragraph, which describes Ellen as Newland encounters her. Lines 78–82

describe her sureness, and her "conscious power." Later, in lines 88–90, she is also described as quiet. Choice (A) matches these characterizations. Choice B is a distortion; while the passage does state that Ellen's marriage had ended (lines 63–64), it's never inferred that Ellen is necessarily unhappy about it. Choice C is opposite; you might infer that Ellen is intelligent, but she is quiet, which contradicts describing her as *outspoken*. Choice D is extreme; Ellen is described as confident; *intimidating* goes too far.

10. F

Category: Inference
Difficulty: High
Getting to the Answer: Remember that Inference questions will have details in the wrong answer choices that are meant to throw you off. Making a good prediction before reviewing the choices will guard against this. The beginning of the passage (line 4) makes it clear that Newland knew Ellen when he was young. Lines 55–59 state that no one had heard from Ellen for some time, and after a few years, she came back to New York, as Medora had done before her. Predict that at the dinner, Newland and Ellen *had not seen one another for an extended period of time*. Choice (F) matches your prediction. Choice G is extreme; although Newland is clearly paying attention to Ellen in the last paragraph, there is nothing to suggest that either of them is interested in a romantic relationship. Choice H is extreme; while Ellen's lack of "stylishness" (lines 85–86) might suggest that she is not interested in New York society's conventions, it goes too far to say that she is disappointed. Choice J is opposite; the passage clearly portrays Ellen and Newland's encounter as a reacquaintance.

PASSAGE II

11. B

Category: Detail
Difficulty: Medium
Getting to the Answer: More difficult Detail questions can be approached using elimination and

careful reading. Remember the EXCEPT. For "except" questions, review the answer choices methodically, eliminating those which fail to meet the conditions of the question stem. The passage deals in some depth with both the flowering of the fistula tree, C, and the wind during Holi, A, so you can eliminate those first. Paragraph 5 states that Dr. Kanani became interested in traditional methods when a tenth century rule of thumb "proved strikingly correct," which suggests that D has been tested. In contrast, the bird behavior is merely listed as an example of a rule of thumb uncovered in one of Kanani's conferences, making (B) the correct answer.

12. H

Category: Inference
Difficulty: Medium
Getting to the Answer: Read through the part of the passage that uses the word or phrase in question, using context to inform your prediction. Look at the sentence directly following the phrase. It compares the usefulness of modern predictions to the information provided by traditional methods. The farmers need more specific evidence than the averages over time and geography provided by meteorology. Predict that *Meteorology is not always useful for the farmers' purposes.* Choice (H) matches this prediction. Choice F is a distortion; the author here does not make a statement regarding the accuracy of meteorology, and, in fact, suggests that meteorologists have been right in the past. What's important is that the information they predict is of little use to farmers. Choice G is out of scope; the passage never makes a statement regarding the expense of equipment. Choice J is a distortion; the phrase quoted intends to *compare* modern and traditional meteorology, not to apply the modern to the traditional.

13. A

Category: Generalization
Difficulty: High
Getting to the Answer: Generalization questions that ask about multiple paragraphs often require you to interpret how the main ideas of each para-

graph are related. Paraphrase the main idea of each paragraph, then note the way in which these ideas progress. The sixth paragraph deals with scientific skepticism for traditional methods. The seventh details efforts by those studying traditional methods to gain recognition in the mainstream. The last introduces you to new groups and projects to achieve the goals of the seventh. In general, you can see that *achieving acceptance of traditional methods by a skeptical scientific community* is the general story told by these paragraphs and a good prediction for the correct answer choice. Choice (A) clearly fits this view. Choice B is a misused detail; while the sixth paragraph mentions the differences in the methods, the next two still deal with the controversy over accepting traditional approaches. Choice C is opposite; the paragraphs tell the story of an uphill battle for advocates of traditional methods. Choice D is a out of scope; these paragraphs never leave the main topic of weather.

14. G
Category: Inference
Difficulty: Medium
Getting to the Answer: Inference questions encompassing the whole text will draw on evidence from the entire passage. A good prediction depends on your ability to synthesize the major ideas from throughout the passage. The passage mentions several traditional methods and their amazing accuracy. Even the scientific skepticism described in the passage admits a place for traditional methodology. The passage validates traditional methods, so predict that the author finds these methods to be *valuable*. Choice (G) matches this prediction. Choice F is out of scope; while the author briefly discusses the origins of each method, she never asks any questions. Choice H is a distortion; the skepticism gets relatively little treatment and is followed by a detailed discussion of the progress toward making a real science of traditional methods. Choice J is opposite; the author never casts interest in traditional methods as a "fad," and, as noted before, mentions the success of traditional methods more than once.

15. D
Category: Detail
Difficulty: Low
Getting to the Answer: Look to your notes to find specific locations for tested details. According to paragraph 5, Bhadli's storm method offers a 72-day warning. None of the other cited methods provide the same sort of accuracy over such a specific and extended time period, so look for Bhadli's method among the choices. Choice (D) matches this prediction. Choice A is a distortion; while the author suggests that bird behavior can serve as a predictor, this is never viewed as a particularly precise method. Choice B is a distortion; the flowering of the *fistula* tree does provide a specific and accurate prediction, but it gives only 45 days advance warning. Choice C is a distortion; while the passage describes a loose correlation between the character of the monsoon and the wind direction on Holi, this method doesn't predict when the monsoon will arrive.

16. J
Category: Function
Difficulty: Low
Getting to the Answer: Beware of answer choices that present details that are narrower than the main point of the paragraph or sum up surrounding paragraphs instead of the target of the question. Focus on the overall topic of the paragraph and how it helps build the story or argument in the passage. The passage in general describes the accuracy of traditional methods of weather prediction. The paragraph introduces you to Dr. Kanani and his interest in applying scientific rigor to these methods. Predict that the correct answer will describe this paragraph as an introduction to a central character and a description of his particular interests. Choice (J) matches this prediction. Choice F is a misused detail; this sums up the first paragraph. Choice G is a misused detail; this accounts only for the last sentence of the cited paragraph. Choice H is a distortion; while the ancient saying is examined in passage, this choice casts this examination as the central issue.

17. B
Category: Detail
Difficulty: Low
Getting to the Answer: For Detail questions, rely on your notes to direct your research to the relevant part of the passage. Lines 70–73 read: "Dr Kanani hopes that his research will put traditional methods on a proper scientific footing. He and his colleagues have even set up a sort of peer-review forum." Predict that the conference's goal is this *establishment of traditional methods as worthy subjects of scientific inquiry*. Choice (B) matches this prediction. Choice A is out of scope; the passage never discusses the disappearance of traditional methods. Choice C is a misused detail; while Dr. Kanani does, in fact, publish the methods in the local press, this is not the objective of the conference. Choice D is out of scope; the passage never mentions the exchange of ideas between geographically distant farmers.

18. H
Category: Inference
Difficulty: Medium
Getting to the Answer: Beware of general answer choices. Attack the question stem, get a good understanding of what it's really asking, and make a solid prediction. The question asks you for the reason farmers predict the weather using traditional methods. What do they hope to accomplish? When the question is rephrased, the answer seems more obvious; predict that the correct choice will show that *they want to know what to plant*, so they need to know what's coming. Choice (H) matches this prediction. Choice F is out of scope; the passage never mentions the accessibility of the methods. Choice G is a distortion; while "'normal' monsoons" are discussed in paragraph 6, this in reference to modern meteorology, not traditional methods of forcasting. Choice J is a distortion; while traditional methods do get the basics right, the question asks why the farmers are trying to get the basics right in the first place.

19. C
Category: Function
Difficulty: Medium
Getting to the Answer: Context clues can be important in Function questions in which simple replacement is difficult. Eliminate answers that are inconsistent with the central concerns of the passage. Reread the specific reference and the surrounding text, which talks about the flowering of *C. fistula* as a monsoon predictor that isn't "perfect," but still of value and interest. Predict that the correct choice will account for both an *appreciation of this traditional method* and *an awareness of its limitations*. Choice (C) matches this prediction. Choice A is extreme; while the author feels that the predictive data are useful and noteworthy, calling them *remarkable* goes too far. Choice B is out of scope; the author never attempts to generalize on the relative value of precision. Choice D is out of scope; again, the author neither casts traditional methods as rules of thumb and scientific methods as complex formulas nor attempts to elevate one over the other.

20. H
Category: Detail
Difficulty: Low
Getting to the Answer: Consult your notes to direct your research to the relevant text. Sahu says in lines 58–61 that traditional prediction may be "OK as a hobby," but "may not be applicable to this modern age," but then concedes that modern era forecasts are not always helpful to farmers in the way traditional methods claim to be. That *some utility exists despite scientific skepticism* serves as a good prediction and an accurate paraphrase of his attitude. Choice (H) summarizes Sahu's attitude and matches this prediction. Choice F is out of scope; Sahu does not comment directly on the accuracy of the methods. Choice G is opposite; Sahu rejects traditional methods from the scientific view. Choice J is out of scope; Sahu never mentions the "appeal" of the methods, only their trustworthiness as predictors.

PASSAGE III

21. C
Category: Detail
Difficulty: Medium
Getting to the Answer: It is very difficult to predict the answer to this type of question because the answer choices themselves give the clues. Go directly to the choices and research each one in the passage. Paragraph 2 includes information about the origins of country music. Choice (C) is correct because country music is not rooted in jazz. Rather, jazz was combined with country music to create Western Swing. Paragraph 6 states, "Additionally, Western Swing emerged as one of the first genres to blend country and jazz musical styles, which required a great deal of skill and creativity." Choice A is opposite; paragraph 2 describes the many sources of country music with the phrase, "Rooted in spirituals as well as folk music, cowboy songs, and traditional Celtic melodies, country music originated in the 1920s." Choice B is opposite; spirituals influenced the development of country music. Choice D is opposite; country music is rooted in cowboy songs.

22. J
Category: Detail
Difficulty: Medium
Getting to the Answer: The answer to a Detail question is stated in the passage. However, because all answer choices are in the passage, be careful to assess each one in terms of the actual question asked. A look at your notes, or a quick scan of the passage, should provide enough information to make a prediction about where to find the best country music. Match that prediction to the correct answer. Choice (J) is correct; in paragraph 5, the author writes "Country singers are considered to have reached the pinnacle of the profession if they are asked to become members of the Opry." To hear the best music, it makes sense to go to the place where those at the pinnacle, or top of their field, perform. Choice F is a misused detail; one would hear honky-tonk music, a derivative of country, but not country music itself, in these bars. Choice G is a misused detail; Ireland is the original home of the Ulster Scots, many of whom settled in Appalachia. Choice H is a misused detail; though country music had its origins in the mixture of music created in Appalachia, the author does not state that it is the place to hear the best music.

23. D
Category: Inference
Difficulty: Medium
Getting to the Answer: An inference is a conclusion not directly stated in the passage, but one that must be true given the information that is stated. In the last paragraph, the author concludes his discussion of country music by putting it in the context of American identity. Look for an answer that is very close to this statement. Choice (D) is correct; in the last paragraph, the author clearly states, "Country music has always been an expression of American identity." The word "character" is another word that can mean the same thing as "identity," both describing qualities representative of a person or, in this case, a country. Choice A is a distortion; the word "most" makes this answer an extreme one, taking it far beyond the author's intended meaning. Furthermore, the author writes nothing about which genre is most influential. Choice B is a misused detail; though country music rose from the mountain people of Appalachia, the author calls this music reflective of the American identity, not specific to one area of the nation. Choice C is out of scope; the Grand Ole Opry is the hub of country music, but not necessarily the place where it is best performed. Indeed, the example of Presley's failure shows that some performances are quite bad.

24. J
Category: Inference
Difficulty: Low
Getting to the Answer: Though the answer is not directly stated in the passage, look for an answer that can be assumed based on what is stated. Locate where mining disasters are referred to, consider what kind of event this is, then which of the possible answers it would exemplify. Choice (J) is correct; ballads are mentioned in paragraph 1, where they

are given as an example of the stories told in laments. That connects well with the meaning of high, lonesome sound, which is described as "the bluegrass undertones of intensity and cheerlessness, symbolizing the hard-scrabble life of the American worker." Choice F is out of scope; mining disasters are not relevant to the Blue Grass Band, and furthermore, there are no examples of the songs performed by the band. Choice G is out of scope; country music is the topic of Passage A, not Passage B. Choice H is a misused detail; though Scottish music is referred to as one of the sources of bluegrass, it is the actual genre of bluegrass, which is characterized by the phrase, "high, lonesome sound."

25. A

Category: Detail
Difficulty: Medium
Getting to the Answer: Locate the paragraph in which bluegrass instruments are described, and match those descriptions with the correct answer choice. Your notes point to only one paragraph in which musical instruments are mentioned. Scan the answer choices, then re-read the information in that paragraph to determine which answer choice characterizes the information given. Choice (A) is correct; musical instruments are described in the second paragraph, and include typical ones such as "banjo, guitar, mandolin, bass, harmonica, and Dobro (resonator guitar.)" But the paragraph goes on to include far less typical ones, such as "household objects, including washboards and spoons," which are not usually considered musical instruments, but are sometimes included in a bluegrass band. Choice B is a misused detail; African-American influences are provided as one more source of the bluegrass genre but do not refer to instrumentation. Choice C is a misused detail; this is an example of a bluegrass piece, which was used in a movie soundtrack. Choice D is out of scope; the reference to the Ozark mountains concerns the origin of bluegrass and has nothing to do with a description of musical instruments.

26. F

Category: Detail
Difficulty: High
Getting to the Answer: The answer to a Detail question is stated in the passage. Locate the paragraph in which the differences between country and bluegrass music are discussed. Paragraph 2 includes the information you need to answer the question. Be sure to keep straight which details describe each genre of music. Choice (F) is correct; paragraph 2 details two characteristics of bluegrass music; first, that "bluegrass highlights one player at a time, with the others providing accompaniment," and second, that "bluegrass incorporates baritone and tenor harmonies." Choice G is opposite; country music features a single voice. Choice H is opposite; country musicians commonly play the same melodies together. Choice J is opposite; both country music and bluegrass music feature banjo and guitar.

27. B

Category: Vocab-in-context
Difficulty: Medium
Getting to the Answer: Vocab-in-Context questions require that you understand the context of a cited word or phrase. Locate the reference and focus your research on the text immediately preceding and immediately following the word or phrase in question. The introductory paragraph states, "One of the most enjoyable ways to analyze culture is through music." Look for an answer choice that indicates that music can provide specific insight about a culture as a whole. Choice (B) matches this prediction. Choice A is a distortion; quintessential does not mean old-fashioned. Choice C is a distortion; quintessential does not mean charming. Choice D is opposite; quintessential means conventional, or typical.

28. H

Category: Inference
Difficulty: Medium
Getting to the Answer: When looking for something on which both authors would agree, first

determine what each one actually states in the passage, then consider what must be true based on those statements. The evolution, or gradual change, in music, as with anything else, must start from somewhere, so look to the parts of each passage that detail the genesis of the music genres, then consider the progression from there. Choice (H) is correct; both authors detail the various music sources that became either country or bluegrass. In the first passage, the author mentions "folk music, cowboy songs, and traditional Celtic melodies," and in the second passage, the author refers to "Scots, Welsh, Irish, and English melodic forms, infused, over time, with African-American influences." Both authors affirm that the two music genres are "indigenous." Thus, it must be true that both country and bluegrass music have evolved from their various roots to become American music, supporting agreement on the fact that music can evolve. Choice F is out of scope; there is no reference to how popular these genres are. Though this might be assumed in Passage B, where the author notes that bluegrass festivals are held even in the Czech Republic, this is not matched by any similar information in Passage A. Choice G is a misused detail; the Grand Ole Opry showcases country music only, not bluegrass. Choice J is out of scope; neither passage indicates that the music is gaining in acceptance.

29. C
Category: Inference
Difficulty: Medium
Getting to the Answer: When asked to use a quote to find support in one paragraph for information in another, be sure to read the quote in the context of the paragraph. First find the paragraph in which the quote from Passage A appears, then match the quote to one in Passage B. Choice (C) is correct; Flatt and Scruggs are mentioned in Passage B, paragraph 3, in which they are characterized as "the foremost artists on their instruments." The best artists are certainly "talented and sophisticated." Choice A is a misused detail; this quote refers to bluegrass themes, whereas the question asks for one that supports talented and

sophisticated musicians. Choice B is out of scope; music soundtracks are not support for the artistry of the musicians. Choice D is out of scope; the relation between bluegrass and country music refers to the kinship of the genres, not the musicians.

30. G
Category: Inference
Difficulty: Medium
Getting to the Answer: There are several points at which bluegrass and country music intersect. Focus on the one specifically asked for in the question. Locate the paragraphs that mention laments and high, lonesome sound, and consider what the author means by including these two themes. Choice (G) is correct; the reference to "laments" is in the first paragraph of Passage A, where it serves as an example of country music themes. The reference to "high, lonesome sound" is in the last paragraph of the second passage, and is an example of "the hard-scrabble life of the American worker." Passage A ends with the phrase "it remains American in its heart and soul," while Passage B states "for better or worse, bluegrass music reflects America." Thus, both kinds of music reflect American subject matter. Choice F is out of scope; Irish music is one of the sources of both bluegrass and country genres, which are included in the sources of the music, not the themes. Choice H is a misused detail; Shania Twain is an example of a country singer, and is mentioned in Passage A only. Choice J is a misused detail; though both types of music were originally called "hillbilly," this is the name for the genres, not the themes.

PASSAGE IV

31. D
Category: Inference
Difficulty: Medium
Getting to the Answer: After reading the question stem, you'll be aware of what to look for. Predict before looking at the answer choices and trust your judgment. Luu strongly disagrees with the view that Pluto should be labeled an asteroid (lines 82–86). She goes so far as to use the term "idiotic" in reference

to others in her profession, so predict something like *indignation*. Choice (D) matches this prediction. Choice A is a distortion; while "shock" may be an initially tempting choice, it's clear that Luu's surprise stems from her disagreement with the opinion, not her lack of preparation to hear it. Choice B is opposite; excitement suggests some degree of positive response, which Luu clearly does not display. Choice C is opposite; Luu quite clearly expresses her feelings on the classification controversy.

32. H
Category: Inference
Difficulty: Medium
Getting to the Answer: If you get stuck, eliminating answers that have no support in the passage will greatly reduce the number of choices. The passage states that, if astronomers had known about the other TNOs, Pluto would not have been named a planet (lines 48–51). The size of Pluto is indicated as the reason it was discovered before the others. You can infer that a better system of detection would have discovered other TNOs, eliminating Pluto's status as a planet. Account for this in your prediction. Choice (H) matches your prediction. Choice F is opposite; Pluto's size separates it from other TNOs. Choice G is out of scope; the article never mentions Pluto's icy core. Choice J is a distortion; the controversy that would later surround Pluto's initial classification as a planet was never drawn into the discussion of the original classification.

33. C
Category: Generalization
Difficulty: Low
Getting to the Answer: Since you've been summarizing the main idea of each paragraph as you've moved through the passage, you're well equipped to predict an answer to Generalization questions. Think about overarching, recurrent themes. The majority of statements in the passage, including the title, should point you to the conclusion that Pluto was difficult to classify from the beginning. Your prediction should focus on this difficulty. Choice

(C) matches this prediction. Choice A is opposite; the passage only mentions such a comparison once, and describes Pluto as out of place among rocky planets such as earth. Choice B is a misused detail; while Pluto does appear likely to lose its planetary status within the scientific community, this has not historically been the case. Choice D is a misused detail; it is the current controversy, rather than the traditional view, that will ultimately give Pluto special status in the history of astronomy.

34. F
Category: Detail
Difficulty: Low
Getting to the Answer: Your notes on the passage should show the location of key details and terminology, so you can quickly find them as you research the question stem. Neptune is mentioned only a few times and all but once merely appeared as part of the longer name of TNOs, trans-Neptunian objects. This single reference is in connection with a description of Centaurs, one of the answer choices. Sure enough, an examination of the description reveals that *Centaurs*, a great prediction, are asteroids similar to Pluto "nudged" inside Neptune's orbit. Choice (F) matches this prediction. Choice G is a misused detail; the passage states that IAU stands for International Astronomical Union. Choice H is a misused detail; TNO stands for TRANS-Neptunian objects, things beyond Neptune. Choice J is a misused detail; the term "ice dwarf" is used in connection with the discovery of a TNO.

35. C
Category: Inference
Difficulty: Low
Getting to the Answer: Inference questions such as this ask that you interpret the referenced lines, drawing on your reading of the passage as a whole. The quote making up the majority of the referenced lines comes from a scientist who, in the passage, takes a position against creating a new classification. Your prediction should reflect the issue of *whether the existing categories are suitable*. Choice

(C) matches this prediction. Choice A is a misused detail; this is certainly discussed in the passage, but this doesn't pertain to the cited lines or the speaker in question. Choice B is a misused detail; distance from the sun and from Neptune is significant to certain classification schemes, but this is not the central issue in Pluto's specific case. Choice D is a misused detail; that the scientific community and general public have differing opinions is irrelevant to the cited lines.

36. G
Category: Vocab-in-Context
Difficulty: High
Getting to the Answer: Vocab-in-Context questions require that you understand the context of a cited word or phrase. Locate the reference and focus your research on the text immediately preceding and immediately following the word or phrase in question. Investigating the word in question contextualizes it within the argument of a scientist who "doesn't like the idea of establishing a new catalog of solar system objects" (lines 61–62) and argues that "astronomers already have a perfectly serviceable list of numbered minor bodies" (lines 62–64). Predict something like *sufficient* to replace the word in question. Choice (G) matches this prediction. Choice F invokes the most common meaning of the word, which doesn't make sense in context and is usually a trap answer. Choices H and J don't work in context, since describing a particular classification system as "beneficial" or "durable" is awkward.

37. D
Category: Generalization
Difficulty: Low
Getting to the Answer: Remember that Generalization questions will attempt to make tempting answer choices out of issues discussed in the passage only briefly. A recurring theme throughout the passage is giving Pluto a "very special designation" (line 19) or "honor" (line 80), which differs from the predominantly scientific concerns over Pluto's classification discussed elsewhere. Predict an answer that touches on this

idea of honoring or distinguishing Pluto in some way. Choice (D) matches this prediction. Choice A is out of scope; the role of the IAU is never discussed by the cited experts. Choice B is a misused detail; the author does relay some information about the ways in which public opinion is unlikely to change, but this is not a significant concern for scientists dealing with deeper issues. Choice C is out of scope; none of the cited scientists seem particularly concerned with being credited for solving the problem.

38. G
Category: Inference
Difficulty: Medium
Getting to the Answer: Use your reading of the passage as a whole to guide your predictions when tackling Inference questions; the answer is in your ability to synthesize ideas that recur throughout. The passage ends the debate about Pluto's classification with a discussion of one scientist's attempt to find consensus. In this part of the passage, the major ideas are listed. Binzel's idea is rejected because Pluto "would still be an anomaly." Luu forcefully asserts that "Pluto is certainly not an asteroid." Both criticisms are based on the idea that neither category adequately describes Pluto, so predict that the correct answer will focus the inadequacy of any categorization scheme. Choice (G) matches this prediction. Choice F is a misused detail; the public's recognition of Pluto's controversial status or a potential change in category is not a significant issue to scientists. Choice H is a distortion; Pluto's orbit plays little role in the discussion of its classification, and its surface is never mentioned. Choice J is a misused detail; the existence of Pluto-like objects nearer to the sun than Neptune functions as a criticism of only one theory.

39. B
Category: Detail
Difficulty: Medium
Getting to the Answer: Detail questions will sometimes require a broad approach to information from a variety of locations in the text. Your notes will help you to sort out the specifics. Lines 24–27 discuss

Pluto's size in relation to other planets and line 27 describes its orbit as anomalous. A good prediction will account for both. Choice (B) matches this prediction. Choice A is a misused detail; distance from the sun versus distance from Neptune is significant only in certain classification systems for non-planets. Choice C is out of scope; the year of Pluto's discovery in relation to those of other planets is never discussed. Choice D is out of scope; neither Pluto's shape nor surface composition are ever substantially compared to those of other planets.

40. H
Category: Detail
Difficulty: High
Getting to the Answer: Tougher Detail questions will require an investigation of several sections of text. Count on your notes to direct you, even when the search is fairly extensive. Lines 24–27 tell you that Pluto is smaller than other planets, which is why scientists need to reclassify it, yet its large size compared to asteroids and TNOs (lines 99–100) is what keeps many scientists confused about its proper category. Lines 45–48 cite Pluto's size as the exact reason that it was found 60 years before the next body like it. Your prediction should account for this classification difficulty as well as Pluto's early discovery. Choice (H) matches this prediction. Choice F is a distortion; categorizing of Pluto as a TNO is only a proposed solution to the classification problem and takes into consideration issues other than size. Choice G is opposite; it is Pluto's relatively small size that potentially allows it the same classification as an asteroid. Choice J is a misused detail; the passage never relates Pluto's size to the nature of the planet's orbit.

SCIENCE TEST

PASSAGE I

1. A
Category: Figure Interpretation
Difficulty: Low
Getting to the Answer: The key to quickly answering many Figure Interpretation questions will be finding the data you need. When you examined the figures during Step 2 of the Kaplan Method for ACT Science, you should have noted that Table 1 lists the percents of calcium and zinc in a group of minerals. Look there for the answer. The question stem tells you that you're looking for a mineral composed of 32% zinc and 12% calcium. According to Table 1, hornblende is composed of 30 to 35 percent zinc and 10 to 20 percent calcium, so (A) is correct.

2. J
Category: Figure Interpretation
Difficulty: Low
Getting to the Answer: The key to answering this question is identifying the relevant figure. Where have you seen information about soil horizons? The answer is in Figure 1, which shows the two most common minerals in each horizon. A geologist digging down to the A horizon would encounter mostly quartz and mica. Quartz isn't listed as an answer choice, but mica is. Choice (J) is correct. Choice F is incorrect because limestone isn't commonly found until the C horizon. Choice G is incorrect because shale isn't common until the final horizon. Choice H is incorrect because serpentine is commonly found in the B horizon.

3. B
Category: Patterns
Difficulty: Medium
Getting to the Answer: Be careful that you don't accidentally reverse the relationship in this otherwise straightforward question. First, look at Table 1. The minerals are arranged from highest zinc content to lowest zinc content. Next, use Figure 1 to check the depth at which each mineral is most commonly found. You can see that the minerals are arranged in Table 1 so that the shallowest are at the top of the column and the deepest are at the bottom. Be careful to note that the question stem gives the beginning of the relationship ("As zinc content increases:"). Zinc content increases if you read the table from the bottom up, which corresponds to the deepest

minerals first. As zinc content *increases*, then, depth *decreases*, (B) .

4. H
Category: Figure Interpretation
Difficulty: Low
Getting to the Answer: You can answer this question either by looking through the answer choices for the minerals you would find or by crossing off choices that contain minerals you wouldn't find. The only minerals geologists wouldn't commonly find at a depth of 60 feet or lower (through the C horizon) are limestone and shale. You can eliminate F, G, and J because these contain one of these minerals. Choice (H), then, is correct.

5. A
Category: Patterns
Difficulty: Medium
Getting to the Answer: The question stem doesn't name a figure or table for you to look at, so you'll have to ask yourself where best to find the answer. The mineral content of granite is the subject of Table 2, so start there. Table 2 shows that granite is composed of feldspar, quartz, mica, and augite. If augite is found at a depth between the other minerals in granite, then it's found at a depth between that of feldspar, quartz, and mica. Now use Figure 1 to find the depths at which those three minerals are most commonly found. Feldspar is found in the O horizon, at a depth of 2 feet or less. Quartz and mica are found in the A horizon, at a depth of 10 feet or less. So you should expect to find augite at a depth of between 2 and 10 feet. Only (A) captures this range.

6. G
Category: Patterns
Difficulty: Low
Getting to the Answer: When asked to identify relationships, make sure you identify the correct table or figure to analyze. Zinc content percentage and calcium content percentage are found in Table 1. Zinc decreases as calcium increases. Choice (G) matches this nicely.

PASSAGE II

7. D
Category: Patterns
Difficulty: Medium
Getting to the Answer: Each of the tables includes rubber, which has a voltage of 0.0. Eliminate choice A. Use the information given in the question stem to determine the correct table to use. Study 2 and Study 3 both use 2 mm wire. Study 3 was conducted at 30°C, so use Table 3 to find the range. The highest value is 12.1 mV, so the range is 0.0 mV to 12.1 mV. Choice (D) matches this range.

8. G
Category: Figure Interpretation
Difficulty: Low
Getting to the Answer: Questions like this one require you to look at the results in the table; there is no need to even refer to the written paragraphs about the experiment. Trace the activity of each material in Tables 1 and 2. Silicon carbide conducts more voltage in Table 2, with a diameter of 2 mm, than in Table 1, with a diameter of 4 mm, so F proves the hypothesis and is incorrect. Copper's conductivity does the same thing, so H likewise supports the hypothesis. Steel's conductivity increases as its diameter decreases, so J again supports the hypothesis. Only rubber fails to support the hypothesis. It conducts 0 mV in Table 1 and Table 2, so decreasing the diameter does not increase the conductivity. Choice (G), therefore, fails to prove the hypothesis and is the correct answer.

9. A
Category: Patterns
Difficulty: Medium
Getting to the Answer: Look at one variable at a time when you're asked to determine the relationship between multiple variables. Start by looking at what happens to conductivity when the diameter of a Zinc Telluride (ZnTe) wire increases. Tables 1 and 2 show that when diameter increases, the amount of voltage conducted decreases. You can cross off B and D because they represent increased diameters at a

constant temperature. Now check how temperature affects conductivity. Tables 2 and 3 show that when the temperature of a Zinc Telluride (ZnTe) wire increases, its conductivity decreases. Therefore, you're looking for the sample with the smallest diameter and lowest temperature. Choice (A) is correct.

10. H
Category: Figure Interpretation
Difficulty: Medium
Getting to the Answer: This question might seem confusing at first, but approach it one step at a time. You'll only need to refer to one table to determine the combined conductivity. Use Table 3 to find the voltage because the conditions in the question (2 mm diameter, 0.5 m long, and 30°C) match those in Study 3. Copper is listed in Table 3 as conducting 12.1 mV and rubber is listed as conducting 0.0 mV. No voltage will travel through the rubber wire, then, and only the voltage through the copper wire will be measured. The correct answer is 12.1 millivolts, (H).

11. A
Category: Patterns
Difficulty: Medium
Getting to the Answer: Start by determining which studies tested the effect of temperature on conductivity. Studies 2 and 3 held every variable constant except for temperature, so look there for the patterns in the data. Tables 2 and 3 show the amount of voltage conducted when temperature is decreased from 50°C to 30°C and the other variables are kept constant. You can see that when temperature is decreased, the conductivity of all the materials increases *except* rubber, which remains at 0.0 millivolts. If conductivity increases when temperature decreases, you can expect that conductivity will decrease when temperature increases. Choice (A) is correct. Choices B, C, and D all contradict the results shown in the tables.

12. G
Category: Scientific Reasoning
Difficulty: High
Getting to the Answer: Scientific Reasoning ques-

tions can usually be cracked either by focusing on the variables that were intentionally manipulated or by checking the opening paragraphs for information. You can see by looking at the tables that rubber conducts 0.0 millivolts of electricity throughout all three studies. Therefore, rubber is unable to conduct electricity. The second paragraph of the passage defines a material that is unable to conduct electricity as an insulator. Therefore, rubber must have been tested to see how temperature and diameter affect its insulating abilities. Choice (G) is correct. Choices F and H are incorrect because they contradict the results of the studies. Choice J could be immediately eliminated, as changes in wire length were never tested.

13. D
Category: Scientific Reasoning
Difficulty: Medium
Getting to the Answer: For this type of question, either look for an answer that further probes a variable that was shown to have some effect on the outcome of the experiment but leaves more to be learned, or look for a choice that examines another logical variable. This question can best be answered by the process of elimination. You can eliminate A because the experiments in this passage already tested the effects of diameter and temperature. You can eliminate B because you're given no reason to suspect that color could have any effect on conductivity. You can eliminate C because, as in A, temperature was already tested in the studies. Choice (D) is the best answer. The studies showed that increasing the diameter of a wire affected its conductivity, so you can expect that changing the length would likewise provide additional information about conductivity.

PASSAGE III

14. G
Category: Patterns
Difficulty: Medium
Getting to the Answer: First look at nitrogen in Table 1. For all three systems, as the level of hu-

midity (%) increases, the concentration of nitrogen also increases. Analyzing the other three elements confirms the same pattern for each of them except potassium oxide. As the level of humidity (%) increases, potassium oxide concentrations decrease in all three systems. This matches (G).

15. A
Category: Figure Interpretation
Difficulty: Low
Getting to the Answer: Don't complicate this type of question; the answer is right there in Table 1. The question is asking you to find the compound for which System B gives a concentration that is the farthest from the USGS concentration results. Make sure you're looking in the column that represents 25% humidity, and jot down the difference between System B's concentration results and the USGS's concentrations, so that you don't get confused. Choice (A) is correct. System B gives a nitrogen concentration of 408 mg/L at 25% humidity, and the USGS, 236 mg/L. That's a difference of more than 100 mg/L. Choice B is incorrect. System B gives a calcium concentration just 1.5 mg/L lower than the USGS. Choice C is incorrect. System B gives a K_2O concentration just 0.1 mg/L higher than the USGS. Choice D is likewise incorrect. System B gives a P_2O_5 concentration only 4.4 mg/L higher than the USGS.

16. J
Category: Patterns
Difficulty: Low
Getting to the Answer: When you're asked to identify how one variable changes with respect to another, check whether the variables always increase together, always decrease together, stay the same, or have no relationship at all. Look at the row for potassium oxide (K_2O) and determine if it continually decreases as humidity increases in the USGS data, System A, and System B measurements. From the table, you can see that potassium oxide concentration continually decreases from 9.4 to 8.2 as humidity increases from 10% to 80% in the USGS data, continually decreases from 9.4 to 8.0 in

System A, and continually decreases from 9.5 to 8.3 in System B. Therefore, (J) is the correct answer.

17. D
Category: Patterns
Difficulty: Medium
Getting to the Answer: For yes and no questions, decide if the answer to the question is "yes" or "no" before reading each answer choice thoroughly. This way, you can eliminate two answer choices right away. The question asks you to determine which system gives measurements that are closer to the data from the USGS, not which system is higher than the other. Looking at the rows for zinc, you can see that the measurements from System B are closer to the data from the USGS than are the measurements from System A. Therefore, you know the answer to the question is yes, and you can eliminate A and B. Don't be tricked by C. System B does give lower measurements than System A, but that alone doesn't mean it is more accurate. The measurements from System B are closer to the data from the USGS than are the measurements from System A, so the answer is (D).

18. H
Category: Patterns
Difficulty: Medium
Getting to the Answer: For questions that ask you to choose the best graph, identify the patterns in the data *before* you look at the answer choices. Look at the row in the table that represents calcium and System B. You can see that the numbers gradually decrease from 10% humidity to 65% humidity, then increase quickly from 65% to 85% humidity. The only graph that represents this curve is (H).

19. B
Category: Patterns
Difficulty: High
Getting to the Answer: When new data falls between two columns in the table, don't be afraid to use your pencil to draw in the new values. Using the table, determine which levels of humidity each

of the new concentrations falls between for System B. A potassium oxide level of 9.1 falls between 25% and 45% humidity, a calcium level of 17.3 falls between 25% and 45% humidity, and a zinc level of 0.57 likewise falls between 25% and 45% humidity. Therefore, the level of humidity for this sample must be between 25% and 45%. Only (B) falls within this range.

PASSAGE IV

20. F
Category: Scientific Reasoning
Difficulty: Low
Getting to the Answer: Following the Kaplan Method for Conflicting Viewpoints passages, you should answer this question first, because it deals with the first hypothesis only. Start this question by making sure you understand what the Dietary Hypothesis says about blood sugar levels. The hypothesis says that individuals with high blood sugar levels and low insulin levels were able to lower their blood sugar levels by receiving insulin. To strengthen the hypothesis, look for a choice that supports the idea that high blood sugar is caused by or otherwise related to low insulin. Choice (F) does just that. Choice G is incorrect because it would weaken the Dietary Hypothesis, which states that high blood sugars are caused by a high-sugar diet. Choice H is incorrect. If it were proven that high blood sugars indicate high levels of insulin produced by the body, giving *more* insulin wouldn't lower blood sugar. Choice J is incorrect because the hypothesis doesn't address where sugar is stored.

21. C
Category: Scientific Reasoning
Difficulty: Low
Getting to the Answer: Review the Genetic Hypothesis to see what it says about age and type II diabetes. The last sentence of the first paragraph states, "Therefore, the same behaviors may be more detrimental to a person when he or she is older than when he or she was younger, especially for those over the age of 50. This is the main reason that type

II diabetes is more common in adults." Choice (C), then, is the correct answer.

22. H
Category: Scientific Reasoning
Difficulty: Medium
Getting to the Answer: As always, use key words from the question stem to point you to the part of the passage that contains the answer. In this case, those are "Genetic Hypothesis" and "pancreas." What does the Genetic Hypothesis say about the pancreas? The passage states that "Diabetes occurs when the pancreas produces little or no insulin at all or when the insulin it produces does not work properly." If diabetes is caused when the pancreas doesn't produce enough insulin, then removing the pancreas should lead to diabetes. None of the answer choices state this explicitly, but (H) gives the major symptom of diabetes as stated in the introductory paragraph. Choices F and G are incorrect because they state the opposite of what you should expect. You can eliminate J because you're given no reason to suspect a link between the pancreas and body fat content.

23. B
Category: Scientific Reasoning
Difficulty: Medium
Getting to the Answer: Be sure you understand the crux of both hypotheses before you answer this question. The Dietary Hypothesis states, in effect, that eating too much sugar causes high blood sugar levels and that giving insulin can lower blood sugar. The Exercise Hypothesis states that adults who exercise regularly lower their blood sugar levels. You should expect, then, that supporters of the Dietary Hypothesis would want to know how much sugar was included in the diets of the exercisers over the course of the study. This matches (B). Choice A is incorrect because supporters of the Dietary Hypothesis wouldn't know how much sugar was in the diets of the exercisers. Therefore, they couldn't criticize the experiment for not including enough sugar. You can eliminate C because it discusses a detail from

the Genetic Hypothesis and is therefore not a criticism supporters of the Dietary Hypothesis would likely levy. Choice D is incorrect according to the passage and, therefore, couldn't be a valid criticism.

24. H

Category: Scientific Reasoning
Difficulty: Medium
Getting to the Answer: Look for an answer choice that allows both the experimental results presented in the Dietary Hypothesis and those in the Genetic Hypothesis to be true. Supporters of the Genetic Hypothesis would look for an element of genetics in the results presented by the Dietary Hypothesis. If it were true that the test subjects had no diabetes in their genetic background, then the results from the Dietary Hypothesis experiment wouldn't violate the Genetic Hypothesis. Choice (H), then, is the correct answer. Choice F is incorrect because supporters of the Genetic Hypothesis aren't concerned with dietary sugar levels. Choice G is incorrect because it is a detail from the Exercise Hypothesis. Choice J is incorrect because supporters of the Genetic Hypothesis wouldn't be concerned with how much insulin the subjects were given; that's related to the Dietary Hypothesis.

25. B

Category: Scientific Reasoning
Difficulty: High
Getting to the Answer: Just as in the previous question, look for an answer choice that accounts for the results in the Genetics Hypothesis experiment but doesn't violate the Dietary Hypothesis. If you're unsure about the position of the Dietary Hypothesis, you'll have to review it before answering this question. Essentially, it states that eating too much sugar causes high blood sugar levels and adding insulin lowers blood sugar levels. Group D in the Genetics Hypothesis experiment showed that 70% of individuals who had two parents with type II diabetes also had type II diabetes. You can expect that supporters of the Dietary Hypothesis will look for a dietary reason for this link. Choice (B) is the correct answer because

it blames the *diet* of the parents rather than genetics. Choices A and D are irrelevant because none of the groups took insulin supplements. Choice C is incorrect because Dietary Hypothesis supporters wouldn't look for a genetic explanation for the results.

26. J

Category: Scientific Reasoning
Difficulty: Low
Getting to the Answer: Move straight to the answer choices and eliminate those that aren't common to both experiments; it'll be quicker than trying to find the answer in the passage and then looking for a match in the choices. You're looking for what the subjects of both studies have in common, so eliminate those answer choices that apply to one or neither of the studies. Choice F is incorrect because parents were only discussed in the Genetics Hypothesis study. Choice G refers only to the Dietary Hypothesis, so it is likewise incorrect. Choice H is incorrect because neither study mentions whether test subjects had their pancreases removed. Choice (J) is correct because both studies focused on adults over 50.

PASSAGE V

27. A

Category: Figure Interpretation
Difficulty: Low
Getting to the Answer: Don't read too much into easy questions. Here, you're simply asked to find which element is highest in the blood sample with the lowest density. Start by looking at Table 1. The lowest-density blood sample is 1.050 *g*/mL, that of Patient C. Looking at each column, you can see that Patient C has more platelets than Patient A but fewer than Patient B, fewer white blood cells than Patient A, the fewest red blood cells, but the most plasma. Choice (A), then, is correct.

28. H

Category: Scientific Reasoning
Difficulty: Medium
Getting to the Answer: Look for an answer choice that relates blood composition or density, the purpose of the experiment. You know that the phlebotomist is studying the blood composition of three different patients. His method, then, should include taking steps to make sure the samples weren't affected by temporary changes in composition. If what a patient eats can affect his blood composition, then it would make sense to require the patients to fast, (H). Choice F is incorrect because you're given no reason to suspect that taking blood is easier if a patient has fasted. Choice G is incorrect because if fasting could greatly change the composition of blood, then the phlebotomist would likely have made sure the patients ate before having blood withdrawn. The passage also states that diet can affect the composition of blood, so it would make sense that the phlebotomist tried to control this factor by requiring the patients to fast. Choice J is incorrect because you're given no indication in the passage that anything can affect the ability of blood to separate.

29. D

Category: Scientific Reasoning
Difficulty: High
Getting to the Answer: Even for the most difficult questions, you know the answer *must* be true based on what's in the passage. You can always start by eliminating answer choices that aren't supported by the passage. If the resulting masses of the blood samples are less than their starting masses, you can assume that either some of the mass was lost during one or more of the experiments, or that there are more components to blood than plasma, red and white blood cells, and platelets. Choices A and C are incorrect because even if some of the formed elements remained in the plasma, they would have been weighed with the plasma, and their mass would still be included. Choice B is incorrect for the same reason. If platelets and white blood cells were

mixed, the total amounts still wouldn't be affected. Additionally, the mass of the four elements was always lower than 10.5 *g*, so it's unlikely that any one element was overestimated. Choice (D) is correct. You're told in the opening paragraph that "Human blood is composed of approximately 45% *formed elements*, including blood cells, and 50% plasma." That leaves 5% of blood unaccounted for in the experiments.

30. F

Category: Patterns
Difficulty: Low
Getting to the Answer: Don't rush through the easier questions. Make sure you take the time to get them right and grab points. Go back to Table 1 and look at the columns for total density and red blood cell mass. (Circle each column if you tend to get distracted by the other information.) Reading the table from the bottom up, you can see that, as total density increases, the mass of the red blood cells also increases, (F).

31. B

Category: Patterns
Difficulty: Medium
Getting to the Answer: You can't use your calculator on the Science Test, but rest assured that any calculations required will be very simple. The beginning of the passage states that "formed elements weigh approximately 1.10 grams per milliliter (*g*/mL) and plasma approximately 1.02 *g*/mL." Here, you have 5 mL of plasma, so the total mass of plasma is (5 mL) (1.02 *g*/mL) = 5.1 g. You also have 4 mL of formed elements, so the total mass of formed elements is (4 mL)(1.10 *g*/mL) = 4.4 g. The total mass is then 5.1 *g* + 4.4 *g* = 9.5 *g*, (B).

32. J

Category: Scientific Reasoning
Difficulty: Low
Getting to the Answer: If you followed the Kaplan Method for ACT Science and circled the methods as you read the passage, this question offers some quick,

easy points. The paragraph describing each experiment states that the phlebotomist placed the blood samples in a centrifuge for 20 minutes in Experiment 2 and at a slower speed for 45 minutes in Experiment 3. Only (J) captures any element of this difference. Choice F is incorrect because you're told at the beginning of the passage that 10 mL of blood were taken from each patient. Choice G is incorrect because, while the mass of the blood samples did vary from patient to patient, the masses weren't intentionally varied by the phlebotomist from Experiment 2 to Experiment 3. Choice H is incorrect because a centrifuge was used in both Experiment 2 and 3.

33. A
Category: Figure Interpretation
Difficulty: Medium
Getting to the Answer: Using Table 1, find the column labeled "Red blood cells (g)" and compare the data. Patient A has the greatest mass of red blood cells with 2.75 grams. Choice (A) matches this observation.

PASSAGE VI

34. G
Category: Patterns
Difficulty: Medium
Getting to the Answer: First, locate the correct table required to answer this question. Table 2 contains silver rods, so that is the best place to start. Looking at silver with a mass density of 225 yields two results. One result includes a temperature of 5°C and a conductivity of 120 μΩ/cm. The other result shows a temperature of 20°C and a conductivity of 60 μΩ/cm. This indicates that for every 5°C that the temperature is increased, the conductivity decreases by 20 μΩ/cm. Choice (G) matches this trend.

35. D
Category: Scientific Reasoning
Difficulty: Medium
Getting to the Answer: Remember, the answer is in the passage! Find where Trials 8 and 10 appear, and

check to see which variable is different. The only differences in the two rows for Trial 8 and 10 are the mass density and the conductivity. Choice (D) is correct, because the student can manipulate the mass density, but conductivity is a measured property of the material that can't be *directly* manipulated by the student. Choice A is incorrect because the temperature of the rods in both trials was 20°C. Choice C is incorrect because both rods were made of silver.

36. G
Category: Scientific Reasoning
Difficulty: Low
Getting to the Answer: When you're asked to find another method, make sure the new method accomplishes the goals of the original. This question is just asking you to determine another way to measure electric current. You don't have to know anything about circuitry to recognize that only (G) even deals with the issue of measuring voltage. Choices F and H are incorrect because shortening the rods or increasing their mass density won't help the student measure conductivity. Choice J is incorrect because insulating the rods will only make it more difficult to measure conductivity.

37. A
Category: Patterns
Difficulty: Medium
Getting to the Answer: To find the patterns in the data here, make sure you identify two trials where only temperature was varied. Look at the rows for Trials 10 and 11. Length and mass density are identical in those two trials, but temperature and conductivity are different. You can see that when length and mass density are kept constant, conductivity decreases as temperature increases. Trial 11 shows that the conductivity falls from 120 to 60 μΩ/cm when the temperature rises from 5 to 20°C, so you can expect that at an even higher temperature, the conductivity will be even less than 60 μΩ/cm. The only answer choice less than 60 μΩ/cm is (A).

38. F

Category: Patterns

Difficulty: Medium

Getting to the Answer: Determine the relationship between each variable and the conductivity one at a time. Don't forget, you are looking for the statement that is *false*. Trials 10 and 11 show that when temperature increases, conductivity decreases. Choice (F) says the opposite of this, so it is false and the answer you're looking for. Trials 1 and 3 show that increasing mass density decreases conductivity, so G is true. Trials 1 and 5 show that increasing length increases conductivity, so H is true. Trials 3 and 8 show that when all other variables are held constant, different materials have different conductivities. Choice J is true.

39. B

Category: Scientific Reasoning

Difficulty: Medium

Getting to the Answer: In order to successfully manipulate just one variable, the rest of the variables must be kept constant. In the last question, you determined that as mass density increases conductivity decreases. If you didn't remember this, you could check Trials 1 and 3. Therefore, the rod with the lowest mass density could be found by heating the rods to the same temperature and finding the rod with the highest conductivity, (B). Choice A is the opposite of what you're looking for. Choice C is incorrect because you're given no information regarding how voltage affects conductivity. Choice D is incorrect because the passage never relates mass density to melting point.

40. J

Category: Patterns

Difficulty: High

Getting to the Answer: This question involves several steps. Don't rush just because you're anxious to finish the test! Use Table 1 to answer this question, since it deals with an iron rod rather than a rod made of silver or tungsten. Trial 4 is the row with a mass density of 400 *g*/cm and a temperature of 80°C. The length of the rod in Trial 4 is 16 cm and the conductivity is 30 $\mu\Omega$/cm. There isn't a trial conducted with all of the same properties and a different length, so you will have to identify the pattern between length and conductivity by looking at two other rows. Use Trials 1 and 5. These rows have the same mass density and temperature but different lengths. These trials show that as length increases, conductivity increases. Therefore, the longer the rod, the more electricity it can conduct. Trial 4 has a conductivity of 30 $\mu\Omega$/cm, but you need conductivity less than that. To decrease the conductivity, then, you'll need a length shorter than the 16 cm used in Trial 4. Choice (J), then, is the correct answer.

WRITING TEST

LEVEL 6 ESSAY

I fully agree that pure scientific research is vital to increase our understanding of ourselves and our world, and that this research, even without specific goals, can result in important benefits to society. Louis Pasteur did not set out to discover penicilin, but in doing so accidentally, saved millions of people from death. Putting a man on the moon didn't help people on Earth but it certainly taught us a lot about our universe. This kind of research must continue and the cost should be shared by the government, drug companies and non-profit groups. Those who argue that the government should fund only that research that is specific to a goal do not understand that general research can be very beneficial, and goal-directed research, though necessary, can fail just as much as general research can. Positive results cannot be assured even with a specific goal. Others who argue that the government alone, without private partners, should fund pure research are on the right track, but put too much control in government hands.

If only the government funds pure research, it will have to spend a great deal of money on it. The government has other responsibilities and is accountable to taxpayers for how it spends their money, and many taxpayers would think this is a waste of money. As the perspective says, without government money research would stop unless other sources of money were found. This is a dangerous situation, because if there is no other money, important research would end. Thus to make pure research completely reliant on government funding would make that research likely to stop if the government can't put as much money as possible in it. What would happen if the government suddenly had to pay for more anti-terrorist protection? It would have to take money away from research, the research would stop, and possibly important outcomes would never be found. Furthermore, any research, whether funded by the government alone or along with other groups, can be stopped if it becomes dangerous.

On the other hand, people who say the government should fund only research which has demonstrated its worth and intended results don't understand the function of pure research. It is not possible for researchers to say they are going to find a cure for cancer, then be sure they can find it. Researchers have to be able to say they are searching for something as yet unknown with the hope that it will be beneficial. And what is a clear and acceptable outcome? If cancer researchers find a cure for diabetes, but not cancer, is that acceptable if it is not the stated intention? A lot of science is luck and perserverance, but that doesn't mean it can't be very important. According to this perspective, if a researcher wanted government money to go to the rain forest and explore plants, the government wouldn't fund it because there is no clear objective. But that's exactly how quinine was found, and the general exploration was certainly worth funding. However, the government has to be careful to use its money for all the programs it funds, and for unexpected threats to the people, so it should not have to spend as much as possible on any research, but partner with others who will also benefit.

Finally, when the government partners with drug companies, funding is assured and not in the hands of one entity only. Drug companies are always searching for something new. They send scientists out to the field to come back with anything interesting, which is then researched and, if promising, developed into a new drug. As I already wrote, penicilin was discovered by accident. So was the relation between blood sugar and diabetes, leading to the insulin that my cousin takes because he has diabetes; without insulin, he would die. If a drug company develops an important drug, it can make millions of dollars from it, leading to funding more pure research. Non-profit organizations also have a stake in pure research, since another accidental discovery could prove to be beneficial to the group. If the government doesn't need to spend too much money helping with this research, it is not at risk for being fully blamed if the research doesn't work out because not much taxpayer money has been spent for it. A partnership would insure continued funding and the funders, as well as all citizens, would benefit from discoveries.

In reference to the prompt, it is unlikely that pure research, no matter who funds it, will result in disaster. Researchers are very careful to prevent this, and even if it did happen, it would not be a result of who is funding the research but of lab accidents. Pure research is very important but very expensive, and doesn't always bring about positive results. It is necessary to fund it but not necessary that the government alone fund it. Drug companies and others that make money from positive results of pure research should also have a part in funding it.

GRADER'S COMMENTS:

This essay is clearly focused on the prompt, logically assesses the implications of all three perspectives, and puts forth the author's point of view in both the first and fourth paragraphs. There is a clear and strong introduction and a summary conclusion, both of which enlarge the specifics of the prompt to the larger issues involved. The third and fourth paragraphs are introduced with transition words, and the others, though lacking specific transitions, are obviously independent and focus on one perspective only. Support is explicit and relevant, with references to the invention of penicillin (by Fleming, not Pasteur, though this incorrect fact is not important to the essay score), space exploration, insulin and diabetes, research in the rain forest, and pharmaceutical companies' goals and earnings.

The grammar and punctuation are mostly correct, though there are some spelling errors ("penicilin," "perserverance"). Despite the confusion of "insure" for "ensure," the writing is mostly high-level with the use of a rhetorical question, and words such as "perseverance," "accountable" and "reliant." Several sentences are varied and complex with an appropriate use of a semi-colon in the fourth paragraph.

The writer shows good understanding of the persuasive nature of the prompt, the differences between the three perspectives, and the pros and cons of each. Her own perspective is clear and well-written, with unified, coherent and logical organization. Overall, the writer displays a clear, focused, well-supported assessment of the prompt, the perspectives, and her own point of view.

LEVEL 4 ESSAY

It's hard to predict what new scientific discoveries may happen in the next few years, let alone the next few decades. Scientific research is really important, but people disagree about who should pay for it. Some people think that the government should give money to scientists unless the outcome isn't good. Other people think that the government should only give money to research that will be helpful. Others think that the government and private companies should work together to give scientists the money they need, which is the best way to do it.

My little brother has asthma and he takes a lot of medication every day. I'm not sure who paid for the research that helped make his meds, but I'm guessing that they didn't get it right the very first time they tried it. If the government was giving money to scientists making inhalers and the inhalers didn't work right, the government may stop funding the project. But then what? There are still kids who need inhalers that actually work. If there is a private company that is helping to pay for everything, the scientists can keep working until they get it right.

Some people think that scientists should have to show the government that their projects will be helpful in order to get money. That isn't going to work for a whole bunch of scientists who haven't had any major breakthroughs yet. Louis Pasture wouldn't have gotten money from his government to make penicillin since it was a total accident. The government and companies should pick an amount of money they want to spend each year on scientific research and give it to a variety of research groups. Then, if any of the groups make a major discovery, they can get more money on top of the amount they already get.

The government can't do everything on its own and companies shouldn't have to work by themselves either. If they team up, lots of research can get done. Asthma is now manageable, but there are plenty of other illnesses that are very deadly. Everybody is hoping for a cure for cancer one day, and scientists need money to figure it out.

I know the government might be scared to keep giving money to research that doesn't turn out right the first time, but scientists need money to work through all the kinks. Maybe big businesses with lots of money can help. Either way, scientists need us to believe in them and the best way to do that is to give them money.

GRADER'S COMMENTS:

The writer provides an adequate discussion of all three perspectives but fails to consider any implications that are outside of her own view. She doesn't fully consider counterarguments, but she does provided relevant support for her opinion.

The writing style is adequate, with few spelling and grammar errors. Word choice could be improved by avoiding simpler words and phrases ("kids", "whole bunch", and "total accident"). In addition, the writer should write out the word "medications" instead of using the abbreviation "meds."

Though the writer has organized the essay into five paragraphs, she doesn't use transition words at the beginning of each paragraph. The writer needs to provide a broader analysis of the issue beyond her own perspective and express her ideas with more complex vocabulary and sentence structure.

LEVEL 2 ESSAY

I did a school sience project and I did it with too other kids so we were sort of partners and that worked out good because everyone did something difrent and we got a B so we did a good job. So I think when you have partners its good so the govement needs partners to do a good job for lots of people. Also if everyone puts money in theirs a lot of money and that can pay for a lot of things that people and the govemnet need.

I like sience in school and maybe I can get a job about sience and maybe the govement can pay for it because topic for this paper says the government should pay for sience. Thats a good idea and I can have partners so maybe we can find out some good sience that can help a lot of people. So I think the govement and partners can get a lot of money for sience and that could be really good like finding a way to stop cancer.

But sometime you fight with partners so its also good to work alone.

GRADER'S COMMENTS:

This essay is completely off topic, indicating lack of understanding of the prompt and task, and poor reasoning and writing skills. The author has focused solely on the reference to partners (introduced in the third perspective), and misinterpreted this to mean working with others on a science project. He has not understood the prompt's discussion of how to pay for pure research, and provides his own opinion on a different topic (partners) with personal support that is irrelevant to the given perspectives.

There are numerous spelling errors, several run-on sentences, poorly-worded phrases, poor organization without a clear introduction or conclusion, and misuse of paragraph structure.

The writer's focus on one word in the prompt, and his misunderstanding of the persuasive function of the prompt and perspectives, has led to an essay which disregards the task, has no developed ideas, and is so poorly written as to make parts of it almost incomprehensible.

You can evaluate your essay and the model essay based on the following criteria, which is covered in the Practice Makes Perfect section of this book:

- Does the author discuss all three perspectives provided in the prompt?

- Is the author's own perspective clearly stated?

- Does the body of the essay assess and analyze each perspective?

- Is the relevance of each paragraph clear?

- Does the author start a new paragraph for each new idea?

- Is each sentence in a paragraph relevant to the point made in that paragraph?

- Are transitions clear?

- Is the essay easy to read? Is it engaging?

- Are sentences varied?

- Is vocabulary used effectively? Is college-level vocabulary used?

ACT Practice Test Seven
ANSWER SHEET

ENGLISH TEST

1. Ⓐ Ⓑ Ⓒ Ⓓ   11. Ⓐ Ⓑ Ⓒ Ⓓ   21. Ⓐ Ⓑ Ⓒ Ⓓ   31. Ⓐ Ⓑ Ⓒ Ⓓ   41. Ⓐ Ⓑ Ⓒ Ⓓ   51. Ⓐ Ⓑ Ⓒ Ⓓ   61. Ⓐ Ⓑ Ⓒ Ⓓ   71. Ⓐ Ⓑ Ⓒ Ⓓ
2. Ⓕ Ⓖ Ⓗ Ⓙ   12. Ⓕ Ⓖ Ⓗ Ⓙ   22. Ⓕ Ⓖ Ⓗ Ⓙ   32. Ⓕ Ⓖ Ⓗ Ⓙ   42. Ⓕ Ⓖ Ⓗ Ⓙ   52. Ⓕ Ⓖ Ⓗ Ⓙ   62. Ⓕ Ⓖ Ⓗ Ⓙ   72. Ⓕ Ⓖ Ⓗ Ⓙ
3. Ⓐ Ⓑ Ⓒ Ⓓ   13. Ⓐ Ⓑ Ⓒ Ⓓ   23. Ⓐ Ⓑ Ⓒ Ⓓ   33. Ⓐ Ⓑ Ⓒ Ⓓ   43. Ⓐ Ⓑ Ⓒ Ⓓ   53. Ⓐ Ⓑ Ⓒ Ⓓ   63. Ⓐ Ⓑ Ⓒ Ⓓ   73. Ⓐ Ⓑ Ⓒ Ⓓ
4. Ⓕ Ⓖ Ⓗ Ⓙ   14. Ⓕ Ⓖ Ⓗ Ⓙ   24. Ⓕ Ⓖ Ⓗ Ⓙ   34. Ⓕ Ⓖ Ⓗ Ⓙ   44. Ⓕ Ⓖ Ⓗ Ⓙ   54. Ⓕ Ⓖ Ⓗ Ⓙ   64. Ⓕ Ⓖ Ⓗ Ⓙ   74. Ⓕ Ⓖ Ⓗ Ⓙ
5. Ⓐ Ⓑ Ⓒ Ⓓ   15. Ⓐ Ⓑ Ⓒ Ⓓ   25. Ⓐ Ⓑ Ⓒ Ⓓ   35. Ⓐ Ⓑ Ⓒ Ⓓ   45. Ⓐ Ⓑ Ⓒ Ⓓ   55. Ⓐ Ⓑ Ⓒ Ⓓ   65. Ⓐ Ⓑ Ⓒ Ⓓ   75. Ⓐ Ⓑ Ⓒ Ⓓ
6. Ⓕ Ⓖ Ⓗ Ⓙ   16. Ⓕ Ⓖ Ⓗ Ⓙ   26. Ⓕ Ⓖ Ⓗ Ⓙ   36. Ⓕ Ⓖ Ⓗ Ⓙ   46. Ⓕ Ⓖ Ⓗ Ⓙ   56. Ⓕ Ⓖ Ⓗ Ⓙ   66. Ⓕ Ⓖ Ⓗ Ⓙ
7. Ⓐ Ⓑ Ⓒ Ⓓ   17. Ⓐ Ⓑ Ⓒ Ⓓ   27. Ⓐ Ⓑ Ⓒ Ⓓ   37. Ⓐ Ⓑ Ⓒ Ⓓ   47. Ⓐ Ⓑ Ⓒ Ⓓ   57. Ⓐ Ⓑ Ⓒ Ⓓ   67. Ⓐ Ⓑ Ⓒ Ⓓ
8. Ⓕ Ⓖ Ⓗ Ⓙ   18. Ⓕ Ⓖ Ⓗ Ⓙ   28. Ⓕ Ⓖ Ⓗ Ⓙ   38. Ⓕ Ⓖ Ⓗ Ⓙ   48. Ⓕ Ⓖ Ⓗ Ⓙ   58. Ⓕ Ⓖ Ⓗ Ⓙ   68. Ⓕ Ⓖ Ⓗ Ⓙ
9. Ⓐ Ⓑ Ⓒ Ⓓ   19. Ⓐ Ⓑ Ⓒ Ⓓ   29. Ⓐ Ⓑ Ⓒ Ⓓ   39. Ⓐ Ⓑ Ⓒ Ⓓ   49. Ⓐ Ⓑ Ⓒ Ⓓ   59. Ⓐ Ⓑ Ⓒ Ⓓ   69. Ⓐ Ⓑ Ⓒ Ⓓ
10. Ⓕ Ⓖ Ⓗ Ⓙ   20. Ⓕ Ⓖ Ⓗ Ⓙ   30. Ⓕ Ⓖ Ⓗ Ⓙ   40. Ⓕ Ⓖ Ⓗ Ⓙ   50. Ⓕ Ⓖ Ⓗ Ⓙ   60. Ⓕ Ⓖ Ⓗ Ⓙ   70. Ⓕ Ⓖ Ⓗ Ⓙ

MATHEMATICS TEST

1. Ⓐ Ⓑ Ⓒ Ⓓ Ⓔ   11. Ⓐ Ⓑ Ⓒ Ⓓ Ⓔ   21. Ⓐ Ⓑ Ⓒ Ⓓ Ⓔ   31. Ⓐ Ⓑ Ⓒ Ⓓ Ⓔ   41. Ⓐ Ⓑ Ⓒ Ⓓ Ⓔ   51. Ⓐ Ⓑ Ⓒ Ⓓ Ⓔ
2. Ⓕ Ⓖ Ⓗ Ⓙ Ⓚ   12. Ⓕ Ⓖ Ⓗ Ⓙ Ⓚ   22. Ⓕ Ⓖ Ⓗ Ⓙ Ⓚ   32. Ⓕ Ⓖ Ⓗ Ⓙ Ⓚ   42. Ⓕ Ⓖ Ⓗ Ⓙ Ⓚ   52. Ⓕ Ⓖ Ⓗ Ⓙ Ⓚ
3. Ⓐ Ⓑ Ⓒ Ⓓ Ⓔ   13. Ⓐ Ⓑ Ⓒ Ⓓ Ⓔ   23. Ⓐ Ⓑ Ⓒ Ⓓ Ⓔ   33. Ⓐ Ⓑ Ⓒ Ⓓ Ⓔ   43. Ⓐ Ⓑ Ⓒ Ⓓ Ⓔ   53. Ⓐ Ⓑ Ⓒ Ⓓ Ⓔ
4. Ⓕ Ⓖ Ⓗ Ⓙ Ⓚ   14. Ⓕ Ⓖ Ⓗ Ⓙ Ⓚ   24. Ⓕ Ⓖ Ⓗ Ⓙ Ⓚ   34. Ⓕ Ⓖ Ⓗ Ⓙ Ⓚ   44. Ⓕ Ⓖ Ⓗ Ⓙ Ⓚ   54. Ⓕ Ⓖ Ⓗ Ⓙ Ⓚ
5. Ⓐ Ⓑ Ⓒ Ⓓ Ⓔ   15. Ⓐ Ⓑ Ⓒ Ⓓ Ⓔ   25. Ⓐ Ⓑ Ⓒ Ⓓ Ⓔ   35. Ⓐ Ⓑ Ⓒ Ⓓ Ⓔ   45. Ⓐ Ⓑ Ⓒ Ⓓ Ⓔ   55. Ⓐ Ⓑ Ⓒ Ⓓ Ⓔ
6. Ⓕ Ⓖ Ⓗ Ⓙ Ⓚ   16. Ⓕ Ⓖ Ⓗ Ⓙ Ⓚ   26. Ⓕ Ⓖ Ⓗ Ⓙ Ⓚ   36. Ⓕ Ⓖ Ⓗ Ⓙ Ⓚ   46. Ⓕ Ⓖ Ⓗ Ⓙ Ⓚ   56. Ⓕ Ⓖ Ⓗ Ⓙ Ⓚ
7. Ⓐ Ⓑ Ⓒ Ⓓ Ⓔ   17. Ⓐ Ⓑ Ⓒ Ⓓ Ⓔ   27. Ⓐ Ⓑ Ⓒ Ⓓ Ⓔ   37. Ⓐ Ⓑ Ⓒ Ⓓ Ⓔ   47. Ⓐ Ⓑ Ⓒ Ⓓ Ⓔ   57. Ⓐ Ⓑ Ⓒ Ⓓ Ⓔ
8. Ⓕ Ⓖ Ⓗ Ⓙ Ⓚ   18. Ⓕ Ⓖ Ⓗ Ⓙ Ⓚ   28. Ⓕ Ⓖ Ⓗ Ⓙ Ⓚ   38. Ⓕ Ⓖ Ⓗ Ⓙ Ⓚ   48. Ⓕ Ⓖ Ⓗ Ⓙ Ⓚ   58. Ⓕ Ⓖ Ⓗ Ⓙ Ⓚ
9. Ⓐ Ⓑ Ⓒ Ⓓ Ⓔ   19. Ⓐ Ⓑ Ⓒ Ⓓ Ⓔ   29. Ⓐ Ⓑ Ⓒ Ⓓ Ⓔ   39. Ⓐ Ⓑ Ⓒ Ⓓ Ⓔ   49. Ⓐ Ⓑ Ⓒ Ⓓ Ⓔ   59. Ⓐ Ⓑ Ⓒ Ⓓ Ⓔ
10. Ⓕ Ⓖ Ⓗ Ⓙ Ⓚ   20. Ⓕ Ⓖ Ⓗ Ⓙ Ⓚ   30. Ⓕ Ⓖ Ⓗ Ⓙ Ⓚ   40. Ⓕ Ⓖ Ⓗ Ⓙ Ⓚ   50. Ⓕ Ⓖ Ⓗ Ⓙ Ⓚ   60. Ⓕ Ⓖ Ⓗ Ⓙ Ⓚ

READING TEST

1. Ⓐ Ⓑ Ⓒ Ⓓ   6. Ⓕ Ⓖ Ⓗ Ⓙ   11. Ⓐ Ⓑ Ⓒ Ⓓ   16. Ⓕ Ⓖ Ⓗ Ⓙ   21. Ⓐ Ⓑ Ⓒ Ⓓ   26. Ⓕ Ⓖ Ⓗ Ⓙ   31. Ⓐ Ⓑ Ⓒ Ⓓ   36. Ⓕ Ⓖ Ⓗ Ⓙ
2. Ⓕ Ⓖ Ⓗ Ⓙ   7. Ⓐ Ⓑ Ⓒ Ⓓ   12. Ⓕ Ⓖ Ⓗ Ⓙ   17. Ⓐ Ⓑ Ⓒ Ⓓ   22. Ⓕ Ⓖ Ⓗ Ⓙ   27. Ⓐ Ⓑ Ⓒ Ⓓ   32. Ⓕ Ⓖ Ⓗ Ⓙ   37. Ⓐ Ⓑ Ⓒ Ⓓ
3. Ⓐ Ⓑ Ⓒ Ⓓ   8. Ⓕ Ⓖ Ⓗ Ⓙ   13. Ⓐ Ⓑ Ⓒ Ⓓ   18. Ⓕ Ⓖ Ⓗ Ⓙ   23. Ⓐ Ⓑ Ⓒ Ⓓ   28. Ⓕ Ⓖ Ⓗ Ⓙ   33. Ⓐ Ⓑ Ⓒ Ⓓ   38. Ⓕ Ⓖ Ⓗ Ⓙ
4. Ⓕ Ⓖ Ⓗ Ⓙ   9. Ⓐ Ⓑ Ⓒ Ⓓ   14. Ⓕ Ⓖ Ⓗ Ⓙ   19. Ⓐ Ⓑ Ⓒ Ⓓ   24. Ⓕ Ⓖ Ⓗ Ⓙ   29. Ⓐ Ⓑ Ⓒ Ⓓ   34. Ⓕ Ⓖ Ⓗ Ⓙ   39. Ⓐ Ⓑ Ⓒ Ⓓ
5. Ⓐ Ⓑ Ⓒ Ⓓ   10. Ⓕ Ⓖ Ⓗ Ⓙ   15. Ⓐ Ⓑ Ⓒ Ⓓ   20. Ⓕ Ⓖ Ⓗ Ⓙ   25. Ⓐ Ⓑ Ⓒ Ⓓ   30. Ⓕ Ⓖ Ⓗ Ⓙ   35. Ⓐ Ⓑ Ⓒ Ⓓ   40. Ⓕ Ⓖ Ⓗ Ⓙ

SCIENCE TEST

1. Ⓐ Ⓑ Ⓒ Ⓓ   6. Ⓕ Ⓖ Ⓗ Ⓙ   11. Ⓐ Ⓑ Ⓒ Ⓓ   16. Ⓕ Ⓖ Ⓗ Ⓙ   21. Ⓐ Ⓑ Ⓒ Ⓓ   26. Ⓕ Ⓖ Ⓗ Ⓙ   31. Ⓐ Ⓑ Ⓒ Ⓓ   36. Ⓕ Ⓖ Ⓗ Ⓙ
2. Ⓕ Ⓖ Ⓗ Ⓙ   7. Ⓐ Ⓑ Ⓒ Ⓓ   12. Ⓕ Ⓖ Ⓗ Ⓙ   17. Ⓐ Ⓑ Ⓒ Ⓓ   22. Ⓕ Ⓖ Ⓗ Ⓙ   27. Ⓐ Ⓑ Ⓒ Ⓓ   32. Ⓕ Ⓖ Ⓗ Ⓙ   37. Ⓐ Ⓑ Ⓒ Ⓓ
3. Ⓐ Ⓑ Ⓒ Ⓓ   8. Ⓕ Ⓖ Ⓗ Ⓙ   13. Ⓐ Ⓑ Ⓒ Ⓓ   18. Ⓕ Ⓖ Ⓗ Ⓙ   23. Ⓐ Ⓑ Ⓒ Ⓓ   28. Ⓕ Ⓖ Ⓗ Ⓙ   33. Ⓐ Ⓑ Ⓒ Ⓓ   38. Ⓕ Ⓖ Ⓗ Ⓙ
4. Ⓕ Ⓖ Ⓗ Ⓙ   9. Ⓐ Ⓑ Ⓒ Ⓓ   14. Ⓕ Ⓖ Ⓗ Ⓙ   19. Ⓐ Ⓑ Ⓒ Ⓓ   24. Ⓕ Ⓖ Ⓗ Ⓙ   29. Ⓐ Ⓑ Ⓒ Ⓓ   34. Ⓕ Ⓖ Ⓗ Ⓙ   39. Ⓐ Ⓑ Ⓒ Ⓓ
5. Ⓐ Ⓑ Ⓒ Ⓓ   10. Ⓕ Ⓖ Ⓗ Ⓙ   15. Ⓐ Ⓑ Ⓒ Ⓓ   20. Ⓕ Ⓖ Ⓗ Ⓙ   25. Ⓐ Ⓑ Ⓒ Ⓓ   30. Ⓕ Ⓖ Ⓗ Ⓙ   35. Ⓐ Ⓑ Ⓒ Ⓓ   40. Ⓕ Ⓖ Ⓗ Ⓙ

ENGLISH TEST

45 Minutes—75 Questions

Directions: In the following five passages, certain words and phrases are underlined and numbered. In the right-hand column are alternatives for each underlined portion. Select the one that best conveys the idea, creates the most grammatically correct sentence, or is most consistent with the style and tone of the passage. If you decide that the original version is best, select NO CHANGE. You may also find questions that ask about the entire passage or a section of the passage. These questions will correspond to small, numbered boxes in the text. For these questions, decide which choice best accomplishes the purpose set out in the question stem. After you've selected the best choice, fill in the corresponding oval on your Answer Grid. For some questions, you'll need to read the context in order to answer correctly. Be sure to read until you have enough information to determine the correct answer choice.

PASSAGE I

MY COUSIN NICOLA

My father and his two younger brothers emigrated

from Italy to New York in the early 1970s. Only their

older sister Lucia, <u>which</u> was already married, remained
                      1
behind in their small home

1. **A.** NO CHANGE
    B. whom
    C. who
    D. she who

<u>town, this village</u> lies in the shadow of Mount Vesuvius.
        2
Growing up in America, my cousins and I were as close

2. **F.** NO CHANGE
    G. town, it can be seen where it
    H. town it
    J. town that

as brothers and sisters, but we hardly <u>known</u> our family
                                        3
across the Atlantic. When I was a young child, my par-

ents and I went to Italy to visit Aunt Lucia and her family

3. **A.** NO CHANGE
    B. knew
    C. had knew
    D. been known

for a week. I first met my cousin <u>Nicola however,</u> I
                                   4
remember that we were not only about the same age,

4. **F.** NO CHANGE
    G. Nicola, so then
    H. Nicola because
    J. Nicola then.

GO ON TO THE NEXT PAGE ⟹

<u>and</u> we also got along well. But because
5

 <u>I being</u> so young, I remember little else. I hadn't seen
    6
him again up until this last summer.

   Nicola decided that he wanted to join the Italian

Air Force after finishing high school. Before beginning

his service, though, he wanted to travel for a bit. <u>He had</u>
                                                      7
<u>never been to America, even though so many of his rela-</u>
                      7
<u>tives live here, but he had been to England already.</u> When
                      7
the rest of the cousins heard the news, they were

<u>ecstatic</u>. Most of them had never met Nicola or, like me,
8

<u>hadn't seen him, since we were kids;</u> they were eager to
                      9
get to know him.

   Two weeks later, we picked Nicola up at JFK

Airport. Right away, I was surprised by his height. I am

the tallest of all the cousins in America, and Nicola was

easily a couple of inches taller than me. In addition to

---

5. **A.** NO CHANGE
     B. so
     C. but
     D. then

6. **F.** NO CHANGE
     G. I, who was
     H. I was
     J. I,

7. Assuming that each choice is true, which one
     provides the most relevant information about
     Nicola's travel plans?

     A. NO CHANGE
     B. He had never been to America, so he
          called my father and asked if he could
          come spend the summer with us in
          New York.
     C. He had never been to America, which is
          most easily reached from Italy by plane.
     D. Because it was expensive for his whole
          family to travel overseas, Nicola had
          never been to America before.

8. Three of these choices indicate that the cous-
     ins looked forward to meeting Nicola. Which
     choice does NOT do so?

     F. NO CHANGE
     G. excited
     H. apprehensive
     J. thrilled

9. **A.** NO CHANGE
     B. hadn't seen him since we were kids
     C. hadn't seen him since we were kids;
     D. hadn't seen, him since we were kids,

GO ON TO THE NEXT PAGE ⇨

our height, he and I had another similarity in common:
₁₀
we were both musicians. The moment I saw the acoustic

guitar slung over his shoulder, I knew he and I would

get along just fine. None of my American cousins plays

an instrument, and I always thought that I was the only

musician in the family (even though some relatives have
₁₁
lovely singing voices). I was happy to find out I was
₁₁
wrong.

Throughout that summer, Nicola and I shared the

gift of music. We would sing and play our guitars long

into the night, only stopping when my mother came

downstairs and forced us to quit. We liked many of the

same bands, and we taught each other to play our fa-

vorite songs. Taught to him as a child before she passed
₁₂
away in Italy, I was taught by him the Italian folk songs
₁₂
of our grandmother more importantly. It was through
₁₂
those songs that I truly connected to the beauty of our

ancestry. On the night before Nicola returned to Italy,

my father would have thrown a big party for all of the
₁₃
relatives.

10. F. NO CHANGE
    G. another similar trait in common:
    H. another similarity that we shared:
    J. another similarity:

11. A. NO CHANGE
    B. in the family, which has at least 20 members that I know of.
    C. in the family.
    D. OMIT the underlined portion (ending the sentence with a period).

12. F. NO CHANGE
    G. Teaching him as a child before she passed away, our grandmother in Italy more importantly taught to me many of the Italian folk songs.
    H. Teaching him as a child, more importantly, by our grandmother in Italy, I was taught by him many Italian folk songs.
    J. More importantly, however, he taught me many of the Italian folk songs our grandmother in Italy had taught him as a child before she passed away.

13. A. NO CHANGE
    B. will have thrown
    C. threw
    D. throws

GO ON TO THE NEXT PAGE ⟶

Nicola and I played the folk songs of <u>our grand-</u>
                                              14
<u>mothers</u> country for the American side of our family.
    14
When we were done, my Uncle Vittorio had a tear in his

eye. Since coming to America so long ago, he had never

been able to return to Italy. [15]

14. F. NO CHANGE
     G. our grandmother's
     H. our grandmothers'
     J. are grandmother's

15. Which of the following sentences, if included
     here, would best conclude the essay as well as
     maintain the tone established in this paragraph?

     A. In the music and our singing, Nicola
         and I brought the beautiful country
         back to Uncle Vittorio.
     B. Uncle Vittorio is the youngest member
         of his generation of the family, so he
         probably misses Italy the least.
     C. I had a good time singing in front of an
         audience.
     D. Nicola is better at playing the guitar
         than singing.

PASSAGE II

THE HANDSOME BEAN

On the ground floor of the apartment <u>building</u>
                                             16
<u>where, I live,</u> the Handsome Bean coffee shop is
    16
almost always bustling with customers. During the

warm months, the shop sets up outdoor tables on the

sidewalk, and the chatter of conversation mixed with

the aroma of coffee often floats in through my window

to wake me in the mornings. Next to the Handsome

Bean is a used bookstore, and the two shops share many

of the same <u>customers who are interested in purchasing</u>
                                                          17
<u>items.</u> People come to find a book and stay to enjoy a
    17
cup of coffee. Across the street from the building is the

neighborhood Little League field. The Handsome Bean

16. F. NO CHANGE
     G. building where I live,
     H. building, where I live
     J. building where I live

17. A. NO CHANGE
     B. people who express interest in acquiring
         items by shopping.
     C. customers who shop for items to
         purchase or consume.
     D. customers.

GO ON TO THE NEXT PAGE ⟶

often <u>sponsors</u> a local team. During the games, the
18

coffee shop offers a discount to parents whose children

are competing across the street. [19] It is a pleasure to

have as a neighbor a business that <u>children. And adults</u>
20
enjoy so much.

18. **F.** NO CHANGE
    G. had sponsored
    H. was a sponsor of
    J. supported

19. At this point, the writer wants to add a sentence that provides additional detail about the customers who come to the Handsome Bean. Which of the following sentences would best achieve the writer's purpose?

    A. In addition to this discount, the shop offers all patrons a punch card to receive a tenth coffee for free.

    B. The shop also sells ice cream, so it often gets very crowded with children and parents after the Little League games are over.

    C. The Handsome Bean also provides uniforms for an elementary school soccer team.

    D. The Little League field doesn't have a concession stand, so the coffee shop doesn't have much competition for the parents' business.

20. **F.** NO CHANGE
    G. children and adults
    H. children and that adults
    J. children. Adults

GO ON TO THE NEXT PAGE

<u>Over the past few years, I have become friends with</u>
                                        21
<u>Mary, the owner of the shop.</u> The store's main counter is
      21
a century-old antique that Mary bought and restored

to its <u>originally conditional,</u> and the photos that adorn
                              22
the back wall

<u>depicts</u> our town during the 1920s and 1930s. My
  23
favorite detail of the shop, however, is the original tin

ceiling. One afternoon, while staring at the intricate pat-

terns etched into the tin tiles, I noticed a name camou-

flaged within the ornate design: Harvey. I pointed it out

to Mary, and she said the original owner of the building

was named Harvey Wallaby. Her guess was that he had

probably written it there more than 70 years ago. 24

That night after the coffee shop had closed, Mary and I

etched our names into the ceiling right next to Harvey's,

hoping that our names would similarly be discovered in

the far-off future.

21. Which choice most effectively leads the reader
    into the topic of this paragraph?

    A. NO CHANGE

    B. Mary, the shop's owner, has a great
       appreciation for history.

    C. The Handsome Bean has only been open
       for a couple of years, but the owner,
       Mary, has taken great care to make it
       look like it has been there for decades.

    D. Before Mary, the shop's owner, opened
       the Handsome Bean, the space had been
       unoccupied for six months.

22. F. NO CHANGE

    G. original conditional,

    H. original condition,

    J. conditionally original,

23. A. NO CHANGE

    B. depict

    C. has depicted

    D. shows

24. The writer is considering deleting the sentence
    below from the passage:

    > Her guess was that he had probably
    > written it there more than 70 years ago.

    If the writer were to delete this sentence, the
    essay would primarily lose:

    F. an additional detail about the building
       that houses the coffee shop.

    G. an explanation of the action taken by
       Mary and the writer.

    H. an emphasis on the original owner's
       influence.

    J. a description of the shop's interior.

GO ON TO THE NEXT PAGE

On Friday nights, the Handsome Bean has live entertainment, usually in the form of, a band or a poetry reading. For a small town coffee shop, the HandsomeBean
25

attracts a good amount of talented musicians and poets.
26

It being that I am amazed by the performances, they transpire within its cozy walls.
27

[1] The clientele of the coffee shop is as varied as the selection of flavored brews. [2] In the mornings, the Handsome Bean is abuzz with the 9-to-5 crowd stopping in for some java before heading off to work. [3] During the days, the tables are home to local artists lost in their thoughts and cappuccinos. [4] The evening finds the Handsome Bean filled with bleary-eyed college students loading up on caffeine so they can cram all night for their upcoming exams or finishing their research papers with
28
looming due dates. [5] Then there's me, sitting in the corner, maybe talking to Mary or reading the paper, smiling at the thought that the best cup of coffee in town is found right beneath my bedroom window. [6] In the afternoons, a group of high school students who stops
29

25. A. NO CHANGE
B. form; of a
C. form, of a
D. form of a

26. F. NO CHANGE
G. better amount
H. better number
J. good number

27. A. NO CHANGE
B. Amazing the performances, it is that I know they
C. I am amazed by the performances that
D. Amazing the performances, they

28. F. NO CHANGE
G. finish
H. finishes
J. finalizing

29. A. NO CHANGE
B. students that
C. students, and they
D. students

GO ON TO THE NEXT PAGE

by to have an ice cream cone or an egg cream. 30

30. For the sake of logic and coherence, Sentence 6 should be placed:

    F. where it is now.

    G. before Sentence 2.

    H. before Sentence 4.

    J. before Sentence 5.

PASSAGE III

MR. MIDSHIPMAN MARRYAT

The paragraphs below may or may not be in the most logical order. A number in brackets appears above each paragraph. At the end of the passage, Question 45 will ask you to determine the most logical place for Paragraph 1.

[1]

    Born to an upper-class English family in 1792, Marryat had a thirst for <u>naval adventure</u> and exploration
31
very early in his childhood. As a young boy at private school, he tried to run away to sea a number of times.

<u>Finally, his exasperated parents</u> at last granted him his
32

wish in 1806; <u>they were</u> enlisted in the British Navy as a
33
midshipman. Marryat had the luck to be assigned to sail upon the frigate *HMS Imperieuse* under the command of

Lord Cochrane. Cochrane, <u>that's</u> naval exploits are
34

31. **A.** NO CHANGE

    B. naval, adventure,

    C. naval, adventure

    D. naval adventure;

32. **F.** NO CHANGE

    G. His exasperated parents

    H. In the end, his exasperated parents

    J. Ultimately, the result was that his exasperated parents

33. **A.** NO CHANGE

    B. they

    C. he

    D. and he

34. **F.** NO CHANGE

    G. who's

    H. whose

    J. who the

GO ON TO THE NEXT PAGE ⟩

legendary, would later serve as the inspiration for

a number of Marryat's fictional characters. [36]
    35

35. The writer is considering deleting the phrase "a number of." If the writer decided to delete the phrase, would the meaning of the sentence change?

   A. Yes, because without this phrase, the reader would think that all of Marryat's fictional characters were based on Cochrane.

   B. Yes, because without this phrase, the reader would not understand that Marryat used Cochrane as a model for more than one fictional character.

   C. No, because this phrase is an example of wordiness that should be eliminated from the sentence.

   D. No; although the phrase adds a detail about Marryat's character, this detail is not essential to the meaning of the sentence.

36. At this point, the writer is considering adding the sentence below:

   > The well-known writer Patrick O'Brian also modeled his Captain Jack Aubrey after Cochrane.

   Should the writer make this addition?

   F. Yes, because if readers know that other writers were inspired by Cochrane, they will better understand that Cochrane was an impressive person.

   G. Yes, because the added detail provides information about a writer who used a style similar to Marryat's.

   H. No, because the essay doesn't reveal the relationship between O'Brian and Marryat.

   J. No, because the detail distracts from the main focus of the essay.

GO ON TO THE NEXT PAGE

[2]

Unlike most of the other <u>prominently famous</u> authors who have spun tales of brave British naval officers fighting for king and country on the high seas, Frederick Marryat actually served as a captain in the British Royal Navy. While others could only use their imagination and accounts to describe what life must have been like for a young man rising through the ranks from lowly midshipman to all-powerful captain <u>from historical records,</u> Marryat needed only to dip into the vast library of adventure stored in his memory.

[3]

Marryat's three years aboard the *Imperieuse* were filled with experiences that would later serve him well in his writing career. The *Imperieuse* saw much action off the coast of Spain, where Marryat took part in capturing a Spanish castle and numerous vessels in the Mediterranean. Marryat willingly accepted any chance to distinguish himself in the eyes of his revered <u>captain and literary inspiration, Cochrane.</u> In fact, Marryat once jumped into the turbulent sea to save the life of another midshipman

who <u>had fallen</u> overboard. Not only did Marryat have the privilege of knowing first-hand a character as illustrious as Cochrane, but his own bold experiences as a midshipman would also be the basis for his most famous novel, *Mr. Midshipman Easy.*

37. **A.** NO CHANGE
    B. prominent famous
    C. prominent
    D. prominent and famous

38. The best placement for the underlined portion is:
    F. where it is now.
    G. after the word "accounts."
    H. after the word "others."
    J. after the word "adventure."

39. **A.** NO CHANGE
    B. captain, and literary inspiration Cochrane.
    C. captain and literary inspiration Cochrane.
    D. captain and, literary inspiration, Cochrane.

40. **F.** NO CHANGE
    G. would have fallen
    H. had been falling
    J. falls

GO ON TO THE NEXT PAGE

[4]

As Marryat quickly climbed through the ranks of the

Royal Navy, <u>many feats were accomplished by him.</u> These
              41
included single-handedly saving his ship during a hor-

rific storm and fighting in a number of sea battles against

the United States Navy during the War of 1812. ☐42

[5]

<u>Marryat earned his greatest acclaim for his novels</u>
                        43
<u>and short stories during this time,</u> which were published
                  43
in England while he was at sea. He retired from the navy

shortly after being awarded the rank of post captain

in 1825 to concentrate <u>for writing</u> full-time. Marryat's
                          44
thrilling stories of sea adventure still live today because,

as the old cliché goes, the best stories are the ones that

are true.

41. **A.** NO CHANGE
    B. his accomplishment of many feats occurred.
    C. his many feats were accomplished.
    D. he accomplished many feats.

42. Which of the following true statements would most effectively conclude this paragraph?
    F. The British eventually lost the War of 1812.
    G. He also earned a medal from the Royal Humane Society for inventing a special lifeboat.
    H. The British Navy was considered the world's most powerful navy until the time of World War II.
    J. Marryat considered it a privilege to serve his country.

43. **A.** NO CHANGE
    B. During this time, Marryat earned his greatest acclaim for his novels and short stories,
    C. His greatest acclaim was earned by him, for his novels and short stories during this time,
    D. During this time for his novels and short stories, earned him his greatest acclaim,

44. **F.** NO CHANGE
    G. at writing
    H. on writing
    J. in writing of

GO ON TO THE NEXT PAGE ➡

Question 45 asks about the preceding passage as a whole.

45. The most logical placement of Paragraph 1 is:
   A. where it is now.
   B. after Paragraph 2.
   C. after Paragraph 3.
   D. after Paragraph 4.

PASSAGE IV

THE TOUGHEST TASK IN SPORTS

[1]

I've often heard others make the comment that the hardest single act in all of sports is to hit a major league fastball. I'm not going to deny that hitting a ball traveling at upwards of 95 miles per hour is a daunting task, but I can think of something even tougher than taking a major league at-bat: stopping a crank shot in men's lacrosse. <u>Football quarterbacks facing oncoming defensive linemen are also in a difficult position.</u>
                                 46

[2]

[1] Lacrosse <u>that is</u> often referred to as "the fastest
                 47
sport on two feet," and with good reason. [2] The game is

46. F. NO CHANGE
   G. Also in a challenging position are football quarterbacks facing oncoming defensive linemen.
   H. (Football quarterbacks also face a daunting task when they are rushed by defensive linemen.)
   J. OMIT the underlined portion.

47. A. NO CHANGE
   B. which has been
   C. is
   D. OMIT the underlined portion.

GO ON TO THE NEXT PAGE

often <u>brutally</u>, and the best players normally possess
48

a bit of <u>toughness</u>, a bit of finesse. [3] As in hockey or
49
soccer, the only thing that stands between the ball and

the goal is the goalkeeper. [4] Using sticks known as

"crosses" to pass a hard rubber ball back and forth

through the air, players on two teams sprint around a

field; <u>they then attempted</u> to set up a shot on the
50
opposing team's goal. [5] Using just his body and his

crosse, the keeper must protect the six-foot by six-foot

goal from being penetrated by a ball that is less than

eight inches in circumference. 51

[3]

    This brings me to the heart of my argument. A

regulation lacrosse ball is almost an inch narrower than

a regulation baseball, with an unstitched, smooth rubber

surface. The fastest baseball pitch on record was clocked

at 100.9 mph, though only a handful of major league

pitchers can approach even the upper nineties in speed.

In men's lacrosse, because the crosse acts as a lever, the

fastest "crank shots" on <u>goal, can</u> reach 110 mph. Even at
52
the high school level, crank shots of more than 90 mph

<u>made by high school players</u> are not uncommon. Unlike
53
a baseball pitcher throwing his fastball from a fixed posi-

tion on the mound, a lacrosse player may shoot from

---

48. F. NO CHANGE
    G. brutal
    H. brute
    J. brutality

49. A. NO CHANGE
    B. toughness;
    C. toughness
    D. toughness, and,

50. F. NO CHANGE
    G. they must attempt
    H. one then attempts
    J. one must attempt

51. The most logical placement of Sentence 3 in
    Paragraph 2 is:
    A. where it is now.
    B. after Sentence 1.
    C. after Sentence 4.
    D. OMITTED, because the paragraph does
        not discuss hockey or soccer.

52. F. NO CHANGE
    G. goal, can,
    H. goal can
    J. goal can,

53. A. NO CHANGE
    B. made by these high school players
    C. shot by high school players
    D. OMIT the underlined portion.

GO ON TO THE NEXT PAGE

anywhere on the field, which is typically grass. This means
                        54
that a lacrosse goalie may be asked to stop a crank shot

from a distance of only six feet away! To make the goalie's
        55
job even more difficult, a lacrosse player may shoot from

over his shoulder, from his side, or drop his stick down

and wind up from the ground. On top of that, the best
                                  56
players often employ a variety of fakes, and most have

the ability to shoot left-handed or right-handed, de-

pending upon their angle to the goal.

                        [4]

        Like hitting a major league fastball, stopping a crank
                        57
shot in lacrosse is tough. Both of these endeavors,
        57

however, require the same set of skills. One must possess
        58

54.
F. NO CHANGE
G. field, which is covered with natural turf.
H. field that is covered with grass.
J. field.

55.
A. NO CHANGE
B. merely a length of six feet
C. just a mere six feet
D. only six feet

56. Of the following possible replacements for the underlined portion, which would be LEAST acceptable?
F. In addition,
G. On the other hand,
H. Furthermore,
J. What's more,

57. Which choice is the most effective and logical transition from the topic of Paragraph 3 to the topic of Paragraph 4?
A. NO CHANGE
B. The combination of these unknown variables makes stopping a crank shot in lacrosse tougher than hitting a major league fastball.
C. Though baseball is less challenging than lacrosse, both sports require tremendous skill and dedication from athletes.
D. There is little question that stopping a crank shot in lacrosse is among the toughest tasks an athlete can face.

58.
F. NO CHANGE
G. requires
H. required
J. would have required

GO ON TO THE NEXT PAGE ⇨

superlative athleticism, great hand-eye coordination, and

catlike quickness. Above all, <u>you must be</u> fearless.
59

59. A. NO CHANGE

    B. one must be

    C. they must be

    D. he must have been

Question 60 asks about the preceding passage as a whole.

60. Suppose that the writer had wanted to write an essay comparing the strategies used by baseball pitchers and lacrosse goalies. Would this essay fulfill the writer's goal?

    F. Yes, because the writer compares both sports throughout the essay.

    G. Yes, because the writer details the challenges that lacrosse goalies face.

    H. No, because the writer does not provide any specific details about baseball pitchers.

    J. No, because the writer focuses on comparing the difficulty of hitting a ball pitched by a major league pitcher to the difficulty of blocking a crank shot in men's lacrosse.

GO ON TO THE NEXT PAGE

GO ON TO THE NEXT PAGE

PASSAGE V

THOMAS EDISON, TINFOIL CYLINDERS, AND MP3 PLAYERS

[1]

Thomas Edison first recorded sounds on tinfoil cylinders in the 1870s, and since then, <u>formats for recording music have come and gone</u> at a breakneck
61
pace. Innovation in recording music has been constant, and the popularity and lifespan of the newest format have always been transitory at best. Those first tinfoil cylinders, which were hailed as a miracle in their day, quickly progressed to wax cylinders, then hard plastic cylinders and, within a decade, were completely replaced by the next "miracle," the gramophone disc record.

[2]

The vinyl phonograph record, which sounded, soon <u>better</u> supplanted the gramophone in the 1940s. This
62
new-fangled format dominated the music landscape for the next 30 years, but like its predecessors, it would

eventually fall into obsolescence. The vinyl <u>record being</u>
63
no longer mass marketed to the public. For that matter, neither is its successor, the 8-track cartridge of the 1970s.

61. **A.** NO CHANGE
    B. formats for recording music have come and gone,
    C. formats for recording music, have come and gone
    D. formats, for recording music have come and gone

62. The most logical placement for the underlined word would be:
    F. where it is now.
    G. before the word "vinyl."
    H. after the word "sounded."
    J. before the word "gramophone."

63. **A.** NO CHANGE
    B. record, having been
    C. record is
    D. record,

GO ON TO THE NEXT PAGE

[3]

It may seem curious to a 40-year-old man today that the average high-school student is well acquainted with the older vinyl record format, <u>so</u> has never even
64
heard of an 8-track cartridge. DJs and those who mix

popular music still <u>uses and appreciates</u> the vinyl
65

record format cherished by them.
66

They have kept records from <u>potentially vanishing into</u>
67
<u>oblivion,</u> along with the 8-track and the more recent
67
recording format, the cassette tape.

[4]

That same 40-year-old man witnessed the rise and fall of the cassette tape, so he may not be surprised that many in today's recording industry view the compact disc as similarly spiraling towards its own doom. For the first <u>time, though</u> it is not the sound quality of the
68
recording that is ushering in the change. Now the

driving force is something <u>different</u> the quality of the
69
player itself.

64. F. NO CHANGE
    G. yet
    H. thus
    J. or

65. A. NO CHANGE
    B. use and appreciates
    C. uses and appreciate
    D. use and appreciate

66. F. NO CHANGE
    G. record format that they cherish.
    H. format for records they play on turntables.
    J. record format.

67. A. NO CHANGE
    B. disappearing into oblivion
    C. a disappearance into being oblivious
    D. disappearance toward the oblivion

68. F. NO CHANGE
    G. time; though
    H. time, though,
    J. time though,

69. A. NO CHANGE
    B. different;
    C. different:
    D. different,

GO ON TO THE NEXT PAGE

[5]

<u>Lack of portability was one of the drawbacks of the</u>
70
<u>vinyl record and even of the compact disc.</u> In contrast,
70
recently introduced small personal music players, such as

the iPod, can have up to an impressive 60 gigabytes worth

of storage space. For those who are music lovers, this has

completely changed the experience of listening

to their favorite songs. <u>Contrasting by</u> the few hours'
71
worth of songs stored on a single CD, a 60-gigabyte MP3

player can store a month's worth of uninterrupted music

on a machine about the size of an old cassette tape.

<u>It's no wonder that MP3 players are among the most</u>
72
<u>popular technology purchases for people of all ages.</u>
72

[6]

Has the apex in the climb towards better and better

ways to play recorded music been reached? For those

who believe it has, history teaches that they are wrong;

such a proclamation will surely prove to be shortsighted

when the next "miracle" in music arrives.

70. Which sentence makes the most effective
beginning for Paragraph 5?

   F. NO CHANGE

   G. A standard audio compact disc can
store only about 700 megabytes worth
of digital data, which equates to only a
few hours worth of songs.

   H. Most music listeners want a format with
a great sound that also provides ample
storage space for all of their favorite songs.

   J. Recording devices have become smaller
and smaller over the years, from the
unwieldy gramophone to the pocket-
sized cassette player.

71. A. NO CHANGE

   B. Compared to

   C. While

   D. In contrast of

72. In this paragraph, the writer wants to help
readers understand the storage capacity and
size of the new personal music players. Which
true statement would best help the writer
accomplish this goal?

   F. NO CHANGE

   G. It is not unreasonable to expect that
technological improvements will soon
allow personal music players to have an
even more compact size and store twice
as many songs.

   H. Experts in the music industry predict
that personal music players will quickly
replace compact disc players, just
as compact disc players so recently
replaced vinyl record players.

   J. Entire music libraries once confined to
the living room wall can now fit into a
music lover's pocket, and be taken and
listened to anywhere.

GO ON TO THE NEXT PAGE ⇒

Questions 73–75 ask about the preceding passage as a whole.

73. Paragraphs 5 and 6 of this essay are written in the third person, using the pronouns *those*, *their*, and *they*. If the writer revised these paragraph using the second-person pronouns *you* and *your*, the essay would primarily:

   A. gain a sense of urgency by suggesting actions to be taken by the reader.

   B. gain a more personal tone by speaking directly to the reader.

   C. lose the formal and removed tone that matches the content and purpose of the essay.

   D. lose a sense of the author's knowledge on the subject by personalizing the essay.

74. After reading the essay, the writer realized that some information had been left out. The writer then composed the sentence below to convey that information:

   > Though the gramophone record's disc shape proved to have longevity, the gramophone record itself did not.

   The most effective and logical placement of this sentence would be before the first sentence of Paragraph:

   F. 2.

   G. 3.

   H. 4.

   J. 5.

75. Suppose the writer had set out to write an essay explaining the process of recording sounds in a variety of formats. Does this essay meet that purpose?

   A. Yes, because the essay describes the different recording formats used since the 1870s.

   B. Yes, because the writer provides specifics about how each new recording format has improved upon earlier formats.

   C. No, because the essay discusses a limited number of recording formats.

   D. No, because the essay does not discuss the mechanics of how sounds are recorded and played back in different formats.

MATHEMATICS TEST

60 Minutes—60 Questions

Directions: Solve each of the following problems, select the correct answer, and then fill in the corresponding space on your answer sheet.

Don't linger over problems that are too time-consuming. Do as many as you can, then come back to the others in the time you have remaining.

The use of a calculator is permitted on this test. Though you are allowed to use your calculator to solve any questions you choose, some of the questions may be most easily answered without the use of a calculator.

Note: Unless otherwise noted, all of the following should be assumed.

1. Illustrative figures are *not* necessarily drawn to scale.

2. All geometric figures lie in a plane.

3. The term *line* indicates a straight line.

4. The term *average* indicates arithmetic mean.

1. Khristina walked $1\frac{2}{3}$ miles on Sunday and $2\frac{3}{4}$ on Monday. What was the total distance, in miles, that she walked over those two days?

   A. $3\frac{1}{2}$

   B. $3\frac{5}{7}$

   C. $3\frac{11}{12}$

   D. $4\frac{1}{4}$

   E. $4\frac{5}{12}$

2. $2y^3 \cdot 3xy^2 \cdot 6xy^2$ is equivalent to which of the following?

   F. $11x^2y^7$

   G. $11x^2y^{12}$

   H. $36x^2y^7$

   J. $36xy^{12}$

   K. $36x^2y^{12}$

3. Ms. Ruppin is a machinist who works 245 days a year and earns a salary of $51,940. She recently took an unpaid day off from work to attend a bridge tournament. The company pays temporary replacements $140 a day. How much less did the company have to pay in salary by paying the replacement instead of Ms. Ruppin that day?

   A. $ 72

   B. $113

   C. $140

   D. $196

   E. $212

4. On his first four 100-point tests this quarter, a student has earned the following scores: 52, 70, 76, 79. What score must the student earn on the fifth, final 100-point test in order to earn an average test grade of 75 for all five tests?

   F. 69

   G. 70

   H. 71

   J. 98

   K. The student cannot earn an average of 75.

GO ON TO THE NEXT PAGE

5. Relative humidity is found by dividing the grams of water vapor per cubic meter of air by the maximum possible grams of water vapor per cubic meter of air, then converting to a percentage. If on a given day the air has 6.7 grams of water vapor per cubic meter, and the maximum possible at that temperature is 19.2 grams of water vapor per cubic meter, what is the relative humidity, to the nearest percent?

   A. 19%
   B. 30%
   C. 35%
   D. 67%
   E. 87%

6. A fence completely surrounds a pool that is 30 feet by 10 feet. What is the approximate length, in feet, of the fence?

   F. 20 feet
   G. 40 feet
   H. 60 feet
   J. 80 feet
   K. 160 feet

7. The expression $w[x - (y + z)]$ is equivalent to:

   A. $wx - wy - wz.$
   B. $wx - wy + wz.$
   C. $wx - wy - z.$
   D. $wx - y + z.$
   E. $wx - y - z.$

8. If $2x - 5 = 7x + 3$, then $x = ?$

   F. $-\dfrac{8}{5}$
   G. $-\dfrac{5}{8}$
   H. $-\dfrac{2}{5}$
   J. $\dfrac{2}{5}$
   K. $\dfrac{8}{9}$

9. What two numbers should be placed in the blanks below so that each pair of consecutive numbers has the same difference?

   13, ____, ____, 49

   A. 22, 31
   B. 23, 39
   C. 24, 38
   D. 25, 37
   E. 26, 39

10. If x is a real number such that $x^3 = 729$, then $\sqrt{x} + x^2 = ?$

    F. 9
    G. 21
    H. 53
    J. 84
    K. 90

11. The formula for the volume of a sphere with radius r is $V = \dfrac{4}{3}\pi r^3$. If the radius of a spherical ball is $1\dfrac{1}{3}$ inches, what is its volume to the nearest cubic inch?

    A. 6
    B. 7
    C. 10
    D. 17
    E. 66

12. If a ball is randomly chosen from a bag with exactly 10 purple balls, 10 yellow balls, and 8 green balls, what is the probability that the ball chosen will NOT be green?

    F. $\dfrac{2}{7}$
    G. $\dfrac{2}{5}$
    H. $\dfrac{1}{2}$
    J. $\dfrac{9}{14}$
    K. $\dfrac{5}{7}$

GO ON TO THE NEXT PAGE

13. The number of employees at a company in each division can be shown by the following matrix.

	Public		
Marketing	Relations	Development	Recruitment
[30	20	60	10]

The head of recruitment estimates the proportion of current employees who will leave within the next year with the following matrix.

$$\begin{matrix} \text{Marketing} \\ \text{Public Relations} \\ \text{Development} \\ \text{Recruitment} \end{matrix} \begin{bmatrix} 0.3 \\ 0.5 \\ 0.2 \\ 0.4 \end{bmatrix}$$

Given these matrices, what is the head of recruitment's estimate of the number of current employees in these departments who will leave within the next year?

A. 27
B. 35
C. 42
D. 49
E. 53

Use the following information to answer questions 14–15.

The following chart shows the current enrollment in all the English classes offered at King High School.

Course title	Section	Period	Number of students
English I	1	5	29
	2	1	27
	3	2	22
English II	1	3	26
	2	6	25
	3	4	24
British Literature	1	6	23
African-American Literature	1	2	26
	2	5	25

14. What is the average number of students per section in English I?

F. 22
G. 25
H. 26
J. 27
K. 29

15. The school has 2 computer labs with 30 computers each. There are 3 computers in one lab that are broken, and 5 in the other lab that are broken, all of which are not available to be used by students. For which of the following class periods, if any, are there NOT enough computers available for each English student to use a computer without having to share?

A. Period 2 only
B. Period 5 only
C. Period 6 only
D. Periods 5 and 6 only
E. None

GO ON TO THE NEXT PAGE

16. What expression must be in the center cell of the table below so that the sums of each row, each column, and each diagonal are equivalent?

$-3x$	$4x$	$-7x$
$-6x$	?	$2x$
$3x$	$-8x$	$-x$

F. $-6x$

G. $-4x$

H. $-2x$

J. $2x$

K. $4x$

17. Point Z is to be graphed in a quadrant, not on an axis, in the standard (x,y) coordinate plane, as shown below.

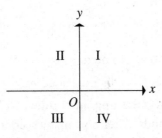

If the x-coordinate and the y-coordinate of point Z have the same sign, then point Z must be located in which of the following?

A. Quadrant I only

B. Quadrant III only

C. Quadrant I or II only

D. Quadrant I or III only

E. Quadrant III or IV only

18. Leila has 5 necklaces, 8 pairs of earrings, and 3 hair clips. How many distinct sets of accessories, each consisting of a necklace, a pair of earrings, and a hair clip, can Leila choose?

F. 16

G. 55

H. 64

J. 120

K. 360

19. At a factory, 90,000 tons of grain are required to make 150,000 tons of bread. How many tons of grain are required to produce 6,000 tons of bread?

A. 3,600

B. 10,000

C. 25,000

D. 36,000

E. 60,000

20. If a rectangle measures 42 meters by 56 meters, what is the length, in meters, of the diagonal of the rectangle?

F. 48

G. 49

H. 70

J. 98

K. 196

21. For all positive integers a, b, and c, which of the following is false?

A. $\dfrac{a \cdot b}{c \cdot b} = \dfrac{a}{c}$

B. $\dfrac{a \cdot a}{b \cdot b} = \dfrac{a^2}{b^2}$

C. $\dfrac{a \cdot b}{b \cdot a} = 1$

D. $\dfrac{a + b}{b} = \dfrac{a}{b} + 1$

E. $\dfrac{a + b}{c + b} = \dfrac{a}{c} + 1$

GO ON TO THE NEXT PAGE

22. What is the slope-intercept form of $-3x - y + 7 = 0$?

   F. $y = 3x - 7$

   G. $y = 3x + 7$

   H. $y = -7x + 3$

   J. $y = -3x - 7$

   K. $y = -3x + 7$

23. Which of the following is a solution to the equation $x^2 - 16x = 0$?

   A. 32

   B. 16

   C.   8

   D.   4

   E. −4

24. For right triangle $\triangle ABC$ below, what is tan C ?

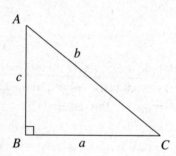

   F. $\dfrac{c}{a}$

   G. $\dfrac{c}{b}$

   H. $\dfrac{a}{c}$

   J. $\dfrac{a}{b}$

   K. $\dfrac{b}{a}$

25. A chord 30 centimeters long is 8 centimeters from the center of a circle, as shown below. What is the radius of the circle, to the nearest tenth of a centimeter?

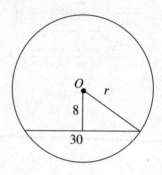

   A. 38.0

   B. 34.0

   C. 31.2

   D. 22.8

   E. 17.0

26. The velocity, in meters per second, of an object is given by the equation $V = \dfrac{5}{3}t + 0.05$, where t is the amount of time that has passed, in seconds. After how many seconds will the object be traveling at 0.575 meters per second?

   F. 0.28

   G. 0.315

   H. 0.365

   J. 0.525

   K. 0.57

GO ON TO THE NEXT PAGE

27. The city has decided to store an estimated 15,000 cubic yards of sand for later distribution to the city's beaches. If this sand were spread evenly over the entire soccer field shown below, about how many yards deep would the sand be?

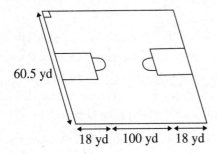

60.5 yd

18 yd   100 yd   18 yd

  A. Less than 1

  B. Between 1 and 2

  C. Between 2 and 3

  D. Between 3 and 4

  E. More than 4

28. The hypotenuse of the right triangle $\triangle ABC$ shown below is 18 feet long. The cosine of $\angle A$ is $\frac{4}{5}$. About how many feet long is $\overline{AC}$?

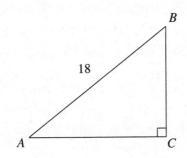

18

  F. 15.2

  G. 14.4

  H. 13.9

  J. 12.6

  K. 10.8

29. The graph below shows the number of beds in each of several hotels, rounded to the nearest 50 beds. According to the graph, what fraction of the beds in these four hotels is at the Bedtime Hotel?

	Key = 100 beds

Hotel	Number of Beds
Comf-E	
Just Like Home	
Budget	
Bedtime	

  A. $\frac{1}{4}$

  B. $\frac{1}{3}$

  C. $\frac{2}{5}$

  D. $\frac{5}{11}$

  E. $\frac{1}{2}$

30. Points B and C lie on $\overline{AD}$ as shown below. The length of $\overline{AD}$ is 38 units, $\overline{AC}$ is 26 units long, and $\overline{BD}$ is 20 units long. If it can be determined, how many units long is $\overline{BC}$?

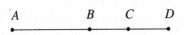

  A   B   C   D

  F. 6

  G. 8

  H. 12

  J. 18

  K. Cannot be determined from the given information

GO ON TO THE NEXT PAGE

31. What is the *x*-coordinate of the point in the standard (*x*,*y*) coordinate plane at which the two lines $y = 4x + 10$ and $y = 5x + 7$ intersect?

A. 2

B. 3

C. 7

D. 10

E. 22

32. For all pairs of real numbers *V* and *W* where $V = 5W + 4$, $W = ?$

F. $\dfrac{V}{5} - 4$

G. $\dfrac{V}{5} + 4$

H. $\dfrac{V - 4}{5}$

J. $\dfrac{V + 4}{5}$

K. $5V - 4$

33. Parallelogram *FGHJ*, with dimensions in centimeters, is shown in the figure below. What is the area of the parallelogram, in square centimeters?

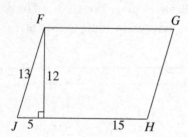

A. 45

B. 130

C. 240

D. 260

E. 480

34. If $s = 4 + t$, then $(t - s)^3 = ?$

F. −64

G. −12

H. −1

J. 12

K. 64

35. A zoo has the shape and dimensions in yards given below. The viewing point for the giraffes is halfway between points *B* and *F*. Which of the following is the location of the viewing point from the entrance at point *A* ?

(Note: The zoo's borders run east/west or north/south.)

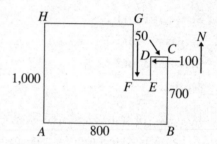

A. 400 yards east and 350 yards north

B. 400 yards east and 500 yards north

C. 600 yards east and 350 yards north

D. 750 yards east and 300 yards north

E. 750 yards east and 350 yards north

36. The larger of two numbers is six less than triple the smaller one. The sum of four times the larger and twice the smaller is 77. If *x* represents the smaller number, which of the following equations determines the correct value for *x* ?

F. $2(3x - 6) + 4x = 77$

G. $2(3x + 6) + 4x = 77$

H. $(12x - 6) + 2x = 77$

J. $4(3x - 6) + 2x = 77$

K. $4(3x + 6) + 2x = 77$

GO ON TO THE NEXT PAGE

37. A painter leans a 35 foot ladder against a house. The side of the house is perpendicular to the level ground, and the base of the ladder is 15 feet away from the base of the house. To the nearest foot, how far up the house will the ladder reach?

    A. 15
    B. 20
    C. 32
    D. 38
    E. 50

38. A circle of radius 6 inches is inscribed in a square, as shown below. What is the area of the square, in square inches?

    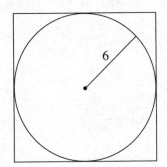

    F. 36
    G. 42
    H. 72
    J. 36π
    K. 144

39. The sides of a triangle are in the ratio of exactly 15:17:20. A second triangle, similar to the first, has a longest side of length 12. To the nearest tenth of a unit, what is the length of the shortest side of the second triangle?

    A. 15.9
    B. 10.2
    C. 9.0
    D. 7.0
    E. Cannot be determined from the given information

40. In the figure below, WXZY is a trapezoid, point X lies on $\overline{WT}$, and the angles are as marked. What is the measure of ∠ZXT ?

    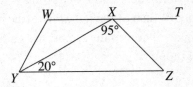

    F. 20°
    G. 30°
    H. 40°
    J. 55°
    K. 65°

41. In the figure below, all angles are right angles, and all lengths are in feet. What is the perimeter, in feet, of the figure?

    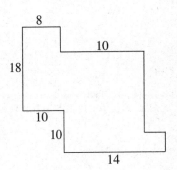

    A. 70
    B. 76
    C. 84
    D. 92
    E. 104

GO ON TO THE NEXT PAGE

42. Of 896 seniors at a certain college, approximately $\frac{1}{3}$ are continuing their studies after graduation, and approximately $\frac{2}{5}$ of those continuing their studies are going to law school. Which of the following is the best estimate of how many seniors are going to law school?

    F. 120
    G. 180
    H. 240
    J. 300
    K. 360

43. If $a = -2$, $b = 4$, and $c = 7$, what is the value of the expression below?

    $$(a + b)(c - a)$$

    A. −30
    B. −10
    C. 10
    D. 18
    E. 30

44. If 135% of a number is 405, what is 80% of the number?

    F. 205
    G. 240
    H. 270
    J. 300
    K. 324

45. What is the distance in the standard (x,y) coordinate plane between the points $(2,0)$ and $(0,7)$?

    A. 5
    B. 9
    C. 25
    D. 81
    E. $\sqrt{53}$

46. The ratio of the radii of two circles is 9:16. What is the ratio of their circumferences?

    F. 3:4
    G. 9:16
    H. 81:256
    J. $9:18\pi$
    K. $16:32\pi$

47. A circle in the standard (x,y) coordinate plane is tangent to the x-axis at 4 and tangent to the y-axis at 4. Which of the following is an equation of the circle?

    A. $x^2 + y^2 = 4$
    B. $x^2 + y^2 = 16$
    C. $(x - 4)^2 + (y - 4)^2 = 4$
    D. $(x - 4)^2 + (y - 4)^2 = 16$
    E. $(x + 4)^2 + (y + 4)^2 = 16$

48. In complex numbers, where $i^2 = -1, \dfrac{(i+1)(i+1)}{(i-1)(i-1)} = ?$

    F. $\dfrac{i+1}{i-1}$
    G. $\dfrac{i}{2}$
    H. $\dfrac{2}{i}$
    J. $2i$
    K. -1

49. One Saturday, an art-museum ticket office sold 120 adult tickets for $10 each and x student tickets for $5 each. Which expression represents the total ticket sales for Saturday, in dollars?

    A. $5(120 + x)$
    B. $10(120) + 5x$
    C. $10x + 5(120)$
    D. $10(120 + x)$
    E. $10(120 + 5x)$

GO ON TO THE NEXT PAGE

50. In a dance school with 35 students, a poll shows that 12 are studying tap dance and 19 are studying ballet. What is the minimum number of students in the school who are studying both tap dance and ballet?

F.   0
G.   7
H.   9
J.   12
K.   31

51. Which of the following is the solution set for all real numbers x such that $x - 2 < x - 5$?

A.   The empty set
B.   The set containing all real numbers
C.   The set containing all negative real numbers
D.   The set containing all nonnegative real numbers
E.   The set containing only zero

52. Hexagons have 9 diagonals, as illustrated below.

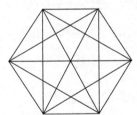

How many diagonals does the octagon below have?

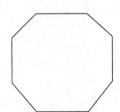

F.   8
G.   11
H.   16
J.   20
K.   40

53. Diane wants to draw a circle graph showing the favorite teachers at her school. When she polled her classmates, 25% said Mr. Green, 15% said Ms. Brown, 35% said Mrs. White, 5% said Mr. Black, and the remaining classmates said teachers other than Mr. Green, Ms. Brown, Mrs. White, or Mr. Black. The teachers other than Mr. Green, Ms. Brown, Mrs. White, or Mr. Black will be grouped together in an Other sector. What will be the degree measure of the Other sector?

A.   144°
B.   72°
C.   36°
D.   20°
E.   15°

54. If $\cos \theta = -\dfrac{12}{13}$ and $\dfrac{\pi}{2} < \theta < \pi$, then $\tan \theta = $?

F. $-\dfrac{12}{5}$

G. $-\dfrac{12}{13}$

H. $-\dfrac{5}{12}$

J. $\dfrac{5}{13}$

K. $\dfrac{5}{12}$

GO ON TO THE NEXT PAGE

55. Which of the following systems of inequalities is represented by the shaded region of the graph below?

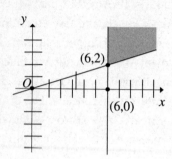

A. $y \geq \frac{1}{3}x$ and $x \geq 6$

B. $y \geq \frac{1}{3}x$ or $x \geq 6$

C. $y \leq \frac{1}{3}x$ and $x \geq 6$

D. $y \leq \frac{1}{3}x$ or $x \geq 6$

E. $y \leq \frac{1}{3}x$ and $x \leq 6$

56. If $f(x) = 1 - x^2$, then $f(x + h) = ?$

F. $1 - x^2 + h$

G. $1 - x^2 - h$

H. $-x^2 - 2xh - h^2$

J. $1 - x^2 - 2xh - h^2$

K. $1 - x^2 + 2xh + h^2$

57. Which of the following is the graph, in the standard (x,y) coordinate plane, of
$$y = \frac{3x^2 + 2x}{x} ?$$

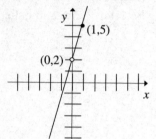

A.

B.

C.

D.

E.

GO ON TO THE NEXT PAGE

58. A triangle, $\triangle ABC$, is reflected across the y-axis to create the image $\triangle A'B'C'$ in the standard (x,y) coordinate plane; for example, A reflects to A'. The coordinates of point A are (v,w). What are the coordinates of point A' ?

F. $(v,-w)$

G. $(-v,w)$

H. $(-v,-w)$

J. (w,v)

K. Cannot be determined from the given information

59. If $a = 6c + 7$ and $b = 3 - 2c$, which of the following expresses a in terms of b ?

A. $a = \dfrac{16 - b}{3}$

B. $a = \dfrac{17 - b}{2}$

C. $a = 16 - 3b$

D. $a = 25 - 12b$

E. $a = 6b + 7$

60. In a contest, the weight of a first-place watermelon is 15 pounds less than 3 times the weight of the second-place watermelon. If w is the weight of the second-place watermelon, which of the following expresses the weight, in pounds, of the first-place watermeon?

F. $w - 5$

G. $w + 15$

H. $w - 15$

J. $3w + 15$

K. $3w - 15$

READING TEST

35 Minutes—40 Questions

Directions: There are four passages in this test. Each passage is followed by several questions. After reading a passage, choose the best answer to each question and fill in the corresponding oval on your Answer Grid. You may refer to the passages as often as necessary.

PASSAGE I

PROSE FICTION

This passage is an adapted excerpt from Tess of the d'Urbervilles, *by Thomas Hardy. In this excerpt, Tess is working as a milkmaid at a dairy, where she has met and finds herself attracted to a gentleman by the name of Angel Clare.*

They came downstairs yawning next morning; but skimming and milking were proceeded with as usual, and they went indoors to breakfast. Dairy-
Line man Crick was discovered stamping about the
(5) house. He had received a letter, in which a customer had complained that the butter had a twang.

"And begad, so 't have!" said the dairyman, who held in his left hand a wooden slice on which a lump of butter was stuck. "Yes—taste for yourself!"

(10) Several of them gathered round him; and Mr. Clare tasted, Tess tasted, also the other indoor milkmaids, one or two of the milking-men, and last of all Mrs. Crick, who came out from the waiting breakfast-table. There certainly was a twang.

(15) The dairyman, who had thrown himself into abstraction to better realize the taste, and so divine the particular species of noxious weed to which it appertained, suddenly exclaimed, "'Tis garlic! and I thought there wasn't a blade left in that meadow!"

(20) Then all the old hands remembered that a certain dry meadow, into which a few of the cows had been admitted of late, had, in years gone by, spoiled the butter in the same way. The dairyman had not recognized the taste at that time, and thought the
(25) butter bewitched.

"We must overhaul that meadow," he resumed; "this mustn't continue!"

All having armed themselves with old pointed knives, they went out together. As the inimical plant
(30) could only be present in very microscopic dimensions to have escaped ordinary observation, to find it seemed rather a hopeless attempt in the stretch of rich grass before them. However, they formed themselves into line, all assisting, owing to the
(35) importance of the search; the dairyman at the upper end with Mr. Clare, who had volunteered to help; then Tess, Marian, Izz Huett, and Retty; then Bill Lewell, Jonathan, and the married dairywomen—Beck Knibbs, with her woolly black hair and rolling
(40) eyes; and flaxen Frances, consumptive from the winter damps of the water-meads—who lived in their respective cottages.

With eyes fixed upon the ground, they crept slowly across a strip of the field, returning a lit-
(45) tle further down in such a manner that, when they should have finished, not a single inch of the pasture would escape falling under the eye of some one of them. It was a most tedious business, not more than half a dozen shoots of garlic being
(50) discoverable in the whole field; yet such was the herb's pungency that probably one bite of it by one cow had been sufficient to season the whole dairy's produce for the day.

Differing one from another in natures and
(55) moods so greatly as they did, they yet formed, bending, a curiously uniform row—automatic, noiseless. As they crept along, stooping low to discern the plant, a soft yellow gleam was reflected from the buttercups into their shaded faces, giving
(60) them an elfish, moonlit aspect, though the sun was pouring upon their backs in all the strength of noon.

GO ON TO THE NEXT PAGE ⇨

Angel Clare, who communistically stuck to his rule of taking part with the rest in everything,
(65) glanced up now and then. It was not, of course, by accident that he walked next to Tess.

"Well, how are you?" he murmured.

"Very well, thank you, sir," she replied demurely. After a moment, she said, "Don't
(70) they look pretty?"

"Who?"

"Izzy Huett and Retty."

Tess had moodily decided that either of these maidens would make a good farmer's wife, and that
(75) she ought to recommend them, and obscure her own wretched charms.

"Pretty? Well, yes—they are pretty girls. I have often thought so."

"Though, poor dears, prettiness won't last
(80) long!"

"Oh no, unfortunately."

"They are excellent dairywomen."

"Yes—though not better than you."

"They skim better than I."
(85) "Do they?"

Clare remained observing them—not without their observing him.

"She is coloring up," continued Tess heroically.

"Who?"
(90) "Retty Priddle."

"Oh! Why is that?"

"Because you are looking at her."

Self-sacrificing as her mood might be, Tess could not well go further and cry, "Marry one of
(95) them, if you really do want a dairywoman and not a lady; and don't think of marrying me!" She followed Dairyman Crick, and had the mournful satisfaction of seeing that Clare remained behind.

From this day she forced herself to take pains to
(100) avoid him—never allowing herself, as formerly, to remain long in his company, even if their juxtaposition were purely accidental. She gave the other three every chance.

1. At the time of the events of the story, Tess is:

   A. reflecting on the qualities required of a good farmer's wife.

   B. struggling with conflicting feelings for Clare.

   C. frustrated by the tedium of daily life.

   D. excited about securing a romantic interest for one of her friends.

2. It can reasonably be inferred that the characters view the search for garlic shoots as a task that is:

   F. impossibly monotonous and made more complicated by the number of people participating.

   G. relatively simple but made more complicated by the number of people participating.

   H. quite dull but something that demands everyone's participation.

   J. engaging but something that results in the loss of the dairy's production for the day.

3. It can reasonably be inferred from the passage that garlic presented such a nuisance to the dairy primarily because of which of its following traits?

   A. Its status as an unsightly weed

   B. Its pungency

   C. Its microscopic size

   D. Its limited presence in the field

4. The passage states that Tess claims Izzy Huett and Retty Priddle are superior to her in all of the following aspects EXCEPT their:

   F. ladylike nature.

   G. skills as dairywomen.

   H. prettiness.

   J. skimming ability.

GO ON TO THE NEXT PAGE

5. It can reasonably be inferred that Tess views her statements and behavior in her conversation with Clare with a mixture of:

A. sorrow and regret.

B. confusion and discomfort.

C. pride and shame.

D. resolution and sadness.

6. The passage states that Dairyman Crick became aware of the "twang" in the butter as a result of:

F. the tasting of the butter by the members of the dairy.

G. discovering the small garlic plants in the meadow that had caused a similar twang years ago.

H. a letter directly expressing a customer's complaint.

J. an angry customer's breakfast-time visit to Crick's house.

7. The distinction the author makes between the characters' everyday actions and the characters' actions in the search is that the search:

A. renders their individual differences less important than their pulling together in the common task.

B. lets the characters take on an other-worldly aspect that contrasts sharply with their everyday personalities.

C. makes them more willing to overlook the status differences among the group.

D. causes them to lose their individual identities.

8. Which of the following statements best describes the way the ninth paragraph (lines 54–62) functions in the passage as a whole?

F. It sets the stage for a transition from discussion of the "twang" to the conversation between Tess and Clare.

G. It contrasts the initial disorder of the dairy to the structure and order that emerges after the search.

H. It emphasizes how the search process transforms the members of the group.

J. It moves the narrative from a discussion of everyday events to an idealization of the surrounding landscape.

9. The statement "She gave the other three every chance" (lines 102–103) functions in the passage to support Tess' view that:

A. the other milkmaids are not capable of attracting Clare's attention by themselves.

B. chance plays an important role in matchmaking.

C. Clare would never marry Tess, despite her charms.

D. the other milkmaids are more suitable companions for Clare than she is.

10. The author considers "Marry one of them... don't think of marrying me!" (lines 94–96) to be a statement that:

F. exposes the high level of competition Tess feels with the other girls.

G. goes beyond the limits of Tess's commitment to self-sacrifice.

H. reveals feelings Tess has for Clare that she has put fully behind her.

J. demonstrates the strength of Tess' wish to have Clare leave her alone.

GO ON TO THE NEXT PAGE ⟩

PASSAGE II

SOCIAL STUDIES

The following two passages were written in the early 1990s and present two viewpoints about the ways that the public responds to the results of scientific research.

PASSAGE A

The way that people in present-day industrial societies think about science in the modern world actually tends to cultivate the very unscientific
Line perception that science supplies us with unques-
(5) tionable facts. If there is one unquestionable fact about science, it is that science is inherently uncertain. Research consists not so much of a search for truth as a search for some degree of certainty in an uncertain world. Every research study,
(10) every experiment, and every survey incorporates an extensive statistical analysis that is meant to be taken as qualifying the probability that the results are consistent and reproducible. Yet policy makers, public relations interests, and so-called experts in
(15) the popular media continue to treat the results of every latest study as if they were surefire truths.

History is filled with examples of the fallibility of scientific certainties. From the medieval monks who believed the sun orbited around Earth and the
(20) world was only 4,000 years old, to the early twentieth-century scientists who thought that X-rays were a hoax and that exploding a nuclear bomb would set off a chain reaction that would destroy all matter in the universe, it has been demonstrated repeatedly
(25) that science deals primarily with possibilities and is subject to the same prejudices as other kinds of opinions and beliefs. Yet statistics are complicated, and in our need to feel that we live in a universe of predictable certainties, it is tempting to place our
(30) faith in the oversimplified generalities of headlines and sound bites rather than the rigorous application of probabilities. Ironically, even though the intent of science is to expand the realm of human knowledge, an unfounded prejudice stemming from a
(35) desire for scientific constancy can actually discourage inquiry.

Science serves an important practical function; predictability and reproducibility are vital to making sure that our bridges remain standing, our
(40) nuclear power plants run smoothly, and our cars start in the morning so we can drive to work. When these practicalities become everyday occurrences, they tend to encourage a complacent faith in the reliability and consistency of science. Yet faced
(45) with so many simple conveniences, it is important to remember that we depend on the advance of science for our very survival. With progress expanding into those gray areas at the boundaries of scientific exploration, caution and prudence are
(50) just as important as open-mindedness and imagination. As technological advances engage increasingly complex moral questions within fields such as pharmaceutical developments, indefinite extension of life, and the potential for inconceivably potent
(55) weapons, an understanding of the limitations of science becomes just as important as an understanding of its strengths.

PASSAGE B

While it is important that scientific knowledge be taken into consideration in significant matters
(60) of public interest, such consideration must be tempered with critical rigor. In the early days during the ascendance of science as a practical discipline, the public was inclined to view every new advance and discovery with a healthy skepticism. In the late
(65) 19th century, when Italian astronomer Giovanni Schiaparelli first detected seas and continents on the planet Mars, many people balked at the idea of Earth-like topography on the Red Planet. Just a few decades later, when fellow Italian astronomer
(70) Vincenzo Cerulli provided evidence that the seas and continents Schiaparelli observed were merely optical illusions, public disbelief proved to be entirely appropriate.

Since then, the historic tendency of the public
(75) to question scientific findings has unfortunately been lost. Yet in present-day industrial societies, and especially where public policy is at issue, response to scientific research needs more than ever to pursue an informed, critical viewpoint. Who

GO ON TO THE NEXT PAGE ⟶

(80) performs a research study, what kind of study it is, what kinds of review and scrutiny it comes under, and what interests support it are every bit as important as a study's conclusions.

Studies of mass media and public policy reveal (85) that, all too often, scientific findings presented to the public as objective and conclusive are actually funded at two or three degrees of removal by corporate or political interests with a specific agenda related to the outcome of those findings. For (90) example, some critics question the issue of whether a study of the effectiveness of a new drug is more likely to produce favorable results when the study is funded by the pharmaceutical company that owns the drug patent. In cases where such findings (95) conflict with the interests of the funding parties, analysts sometimes wonder if information was repressed, altered, or given a favorable public relations slant in order to de-emphasize dangerous side effects. Some critics of company-funded studies (100) argue that the level of misrepresentation included in such studies borders on immoral.

Part of the problem grows from the public's willingness to place blind faith in the authority of science without an awareness of the interests that (105) lie behind the research. Public officials then, in turn, may sometimes be too willing to bend in the face of public or private political pressure rather than pursuing the best interests of the constituency. Issues such as genetics, reproductive health, (110) and preventative care are particularly fraught with political angst. Where the safety of individuals is at stake, a precautionary principle of allowing for unpredictable, unforeseen negative effects of technological advances should be pursued. It is the (115) duty of active citizens in a free society to educate themselves about the real-world application of risk-assessment and statistical analysis, and to resist passive acceptance of the reassurances of self-styled scientific authorities. The most favorable approach (120) to policy decisions based on realistic assessments finds a middle ground between the alarmism of political "Chicken Littles" and the recklessness of profit-seeking risk takers.

Questions 11–13 ask about Passage A.

11. The viewpoint of the author of Passage A toward the results of modern scientific studies can most closely be described as one of:

 A. anger.
 B. enthusiasm.
 C. acceptance.
 D. skepticism.

12. The word "probabilities" in line 32 is used to express the author's belief that:

 F. scientific theories will eventually be proven true.
 G. current scientific findings will be regarded as outdated by future scientists.
 H. viewing scientific results as possibly wrong is a wise approach.
 J. refusing to question science is unavoidable because people prefer certainty.

13. In lines 46–47, the author of Passage A points out that "we depend on . . . very survival" in order to:

 A. strengthen the authority of the central thesis.
 B. emphasize an important argument.
 C. introduce a new line of reasoning.
 D. provide reassurance to the reader.

GO ON TO THE NEXT PAGE

Questions 14–16 ask about Passage B.

14. The main idea of Passage B is that:

    F. the human desire for stability can lead people to resist scientific inquiry.

    G. scientific findings are always repressed or altered to de-emphasize contradicting results.

    H. citizens should regard scientific advancements with reasonable skepticism.

    J. it is in the best interest of society to embrace new scientific developments without restraint.

15. The author of Passage B uses the first paragraph to explain:

    A. a new scientific hypothesis.

    B. a historical contrast.

    C. a public policy generality.

    D. the underlying cause of an issue.

16. With which of the following statements would the author of Passage B most likely agree?

    F. People should not unquestioningly accept the results of scientific studies.

    G. More government control and regulation are needed to ensure that science serves the best interests of the public.

    H. Society should place less emphasis on modern conveniences and more on understanding the limitations of science.

    J. The results that scientists derive from research are less reliable now than in former times.

Questions 17–20 ask about both passages.

17. What does the author of Passage A believe is the biggest obstacle to reaching the solution described by the author of Passage B in lines 114–119 ("It is the duty...authorities")?

    A. Policymakers are too willing to bend to public pressure when it comes to regulating scientific research.

    B. The interests that fund research are the same interests that stand to profit by favorable results, making impartiality impossible.

    C. Statistics are too abstract when compared with the concrete evidence of technological conveniences.

    D. Unanswered ethical questions are increasingly coming under scrutiny at the forefront of our most advanced scientific research.

18. Both passages refer to which of the following in their introductory paragraphs?

    F. Present-day industrial societies

    G. Early twentieth-century scientists

    H. Critics of company-funded studies

    J. Significant matters of public interest

19. According to Passage B, which of the following is an example of the "fallibility of scientific certainties" (lines 17–18) mentioned in Passage A?

    A. Medieval monks who believed the sun orbited around Earth

    B. People who balked at the idea of Earth-like topography on Mars

    C. Issues such as genetics, reproductive health, and preventative care

    D. Early twentieth-century scientists who thought that X-rays were a hoax

GO ON TO THE NEXT PAGE ⟹

20. The authors of both passages mention the term "pharmaceutical" in order to:

    F. highlight a particular scientific field in which moral questions may arise.

    G. point out an example of the recklessness of profit-seeking risk takers.

    H. identify unfounded prejudice stemming from a desire for scientific constancy.

    J. cite the usefulness of the current approach regarding drug testing and analysis.

PASSAGE III

HUMANITIES

This passage is adapted from an article found on Wikipedia.com.

Born in Edinburgh in 1771, the young Walter Scott survived a childhood bout of polio that would leave him lame in his right leg for the rest of his
Line life. After studying law at Edinburgh University,
(5) he followed in his father's footsteps and became a lawyer in his native Scotland. Beginning at age 25, he started dabbling in writing, first translating works from German, then moving on to poetry. In between these two phases of his literary career, he
(10) published a three-volume set of collected Scottish ballads, *The Minstrelsy of the Scottish Border*. This was the first sign of his interest in Scotland and history in his writings.

After Scott had founded a printing press, his
(15) poetry, beginning with *The Lay of the Last Minstrel* in 1805, brought him great fame. He published a number of other poems over the next ten years, including in 1810 the popular *Lady of the Lake*, portions of which (translated into German) were
(20) set to music by Franz Schubert. Another work from this time period, *Marmion*, produced some of his most quoted (and most often misattributed) lines, such as

    Oh! what a tangled web we weave
(25)   *When first we practise to deceive!*

When Scott's press became embroiled in financial difficulties, Scott set out, in 1814, to write a successful (and profitable) work. The result was *Waverley*, a novel that did not name its author. It
(30) was a tale of the last Jacobite rebellion in the United Kingdom, the "Forty-Five," and the novel met with considerable success. There followed a large number of novels in the next five years, each in the same general vein. Mindful of his reputation as a poet,
(35) he maintained the anonymity he had begun with *Waverley*, always publishing the novels under a name such as "Author of Waverley" or attributed as "Tales of..." with no author. Even when it was clear that there would be no harm in coming out into
(40) the open, he maintained the façade, apparently out of a sense of fun. During this time, the nickname "The Wizard of the North" was popularly applied to the mysterious best-selling writer. His identity as the author of the novels was widely rumored, and
(45) in 1815 Scott was given the honour of dining with George, Prince Regent, who wanted to meet "the author of Waverley."

In 1820, Scott broke away from writing about Scotland with *Ivanhoe*, a historical romance set in
(50) twelfth-century England. It too was a runaway success and, as he did with his first novel, he unleashed a slew of books along the same lines. As his fame grew during this phase of his career, he was granted the title of Baronet, becoming Sir Walter Scott. At
(55) this time he organized the visit of King George IV to Scotland, and when the King visited Edinburgh in 1822, the spectacular pageantry Scott had concocted to portray the King as a rather tubby reincarnation of Bonnie Prince Charlie made
(60) tartans and kilts fashionable and turned them into symbols of national identity.

Beginning in 1825, Scott fell into dire financial straits again, and his company nearly collapsed. That he was the author of his novels became gen-
(65) eral knowledge at this time as well. Rather than declare bankruptcy he placed his home, Abbotsford House, and income into a trust belonging to his creditors, and proceeded to write his way out of debt. He kept up his prodigious output of fiction
(70) (as well as producing a biography of Napoleon Bonaparte) through 1831. By then his health was

GO ON TO THE NEXT PAGE ⟶

failing, and he died at Abbotsford in 1832. Though not in the clear by then, his novels continued to sell, and he made good his debts from beyond the
(75) grave. He was buried in Dryburgh Abbey; nearby, fittingly, a large statue can be found of William Wallace—one of Scotland's great historical figures.

Scott was responsible for two major trends that carry on to this day. First, he popularized the
(80) historical novel; an enormous number of imitators (and imitators of imitators) would appear in the nineteenth century. It is a measure of Scott's influence that Edinburgh's central railway station, opened in 1854, is called Waverley Station. Second,
(85) his Scottish novels rehabilitated Highland culture after years in the shadows following the Jacobite rebellions.

Scott was also responsible, through a series of pseudonymous letters published in the *Edinburgh*
(90) *Weekly News* in *1826*, for retaining the right of Scottish banks to issue their own banknotes, which is reflected to this day by his continued appearance on the front of all notes issued by the Bank of Scotland.

21. The main idea of the passage is that:

A. historical novels can be very successful in rehabilitating a country's culture.

B. Sir Walter Scott's writings achieved both financial success and cultural impact.

C. Scott became known more for his financial failures than for his literary talents.

D. the success of Scott's novels was largely due to the anonymity of the author.

22. According to the passage, Walter Scott turned to writing novels because:

F. his childhood bout with polio made it difficult for him to continue working as a lawyer.

G. his printing press business was being sued over copyright violations.

H. his three-volume set of Scottish ballads did not sell well.

J. his printing press business was losing money.

23. According to the author, Scott published *Waverly* anonymously because:

A. he didn't want to damage his reputation as a lawyer.

B. he had fun watching people try to determine who the author was.

C. his novels sold faster without an author's name on them.

D. he was afraid writing fiction would take away from his reputation as a poet.

24. The author would most likely describe Scott's effect on how Scotland was viewed as:

F. damaging, since Scott degraded Scottish culture by popularizing tartans and kilts.

G. unimportant, since Scott's novels were no more than popular fiction.

H. ground-breaking, since Scott was the first to write serious analyses of Scottish history.

J. positive, since Scott made Scottish culture acceptable again after years of neglect.

GO ON TO THE NEXT PAGE

25. Based on the passage, it is reasonable to assume that Scott's reputation after his death:

    A. remained favorable.

    B. waned because there were no more of his novels being published.

    C. declined because he died without paying all of his debts.

    D. was debased because of all his imitators.

26. The author describes how Scott influenced Scotland's right to continue issuing its own banknotes in order to:

    F. show a way in which Scott helped overcome his own financial difficulties.

    G. establish the level of Scott's influence with the Prince Regent.

    H. emphasize Scott's continued impact on his native country.

    J. point out a way for the reader to find out what Scott looked like.

27. The author most likely uses "fittingly" (line 76) when describing the presence of a statue of William Wallace near Scott's grave in Dryburgh Abbey because:

    A. Scott's first major novel was about the achievements of William Wallace.

    B. Scott wrote novels about Scottish history and Wallace is a famous historical figure from Scotland.

    C. Scott was a very religious man and deserved to be buried in an abbey.

    D. Wallace was an avid fan of Scott's poetry.

28. The passage suggests that the author's attitude toward Sir Walter Scott is:

    F. restrained and skeptical.

    G. derisive and contemptuous.

    H. interested and appreciative.

    J. passionate and envious.

29. Based on the fifth paragraph (lines 62–77), it is reasonable to infer that Sir Walter Scott's attitude toward his debts was:

    A. irresponsible, since he left them to be taken care of after his death.

    B. resentful, for he believed that they were caused by his partners.

    C. impatient, because he became annoyed that his creditors hounded him so.

    D. accepting, since he acknowledged his responsibility and tried to pay them back.

30. The author's use of "dabbling" in line 7 suggests that:

    F. Scott sought to establish himself in a field in which he had little experience.

    G. the financial losses eventually suffered by Scott's printing press began with this activity.

    H. Scott's inexperience led to the poor quality of his literary work.

    J. Scott's initial work led to his interest in Scottish history.

PASSAGE IV

NATURAL SCIENCE

The following is adapted from Wikipedia articles titled "Lemur" and "Ring-tailed Lemur."

Lemurs are part of a suborder of primates known as prosimians, and make up the infraorder Lemuriformes. This type of primate was the evolutionary predecessor of monkeys and apes (simians). The term "lemur" is derived from the Latin word *lemures*, which means "spirits of the night." This likely refers to many lemurs' nocturnal behavior and their large, reflective eyes. It is generically used for the members of the four lemuriform families, but it is also the genus of one of the lemu-

Line (5)

(10)

GO ON TO THE NEXT PAGE

riform species. The two flying lemur species are not lemurs, nor are they even primates.

(15) Lemurs are found naturally only on the island of Madagascar and some smaller surrounding islands, including the Comoros (where it is likely they were introduced by humans). While they were displaced in the rest of the world by monkeys, apes, and other primates, the lemurs were safe from competition on Madagascar and differentiated into a number of (20) species. These range in size from the tiny 30-gram pygmy mouse lemur to the 10-kilogram indri. The larger species have all become extinct since humans settled on Madagascar, and since the early twentieth century the largest lemurs reach about seven (25) kilograms. Typically, the smaller lemurs are active at night (nocturnal), while the larger ones are active during the day (diurnal).

All lemurs are endangered species, due mainly to habitat destruction (deforestation) and hunting. (30) Although conservation efforts are underway, options are limited because of the lemurs' limited range and because Madagascar is desperately poor. Currently, there are approximately 32 living lemur species.

The ring-tailed lemur is a relatively large pros- (35) imian, belonging to the family Lemuridae. Ring-tailed lemurs are the only species within the genus *Lemur* and are found only on the island of Mada-gascar. Although threatened by habitat destruction and therefore listed as vulnerable by the IUCN (40) Red List, ring-tailed lemurs are the most populous lemurs in zoos worldwide; they reproduce readily in captivity.

Mostly grey with white underparts, ring-tailed lemurs have slender frames; their narrow faces are (45) white with black lozenge-shaped patches around the eyes and black vulpine muzzles. The lemurs' trademark, their long, bushy tails, are ringed in black and white. Like all lemurs, ring-tailed lemurs have hind limbs longer than their forelimbs; their (50) palms and soles are padded with soft, leathery skin and their fingers are slender and dextrous. On the second toe of their hind limbs, ring-tailed lemurs have claws specialized for grooming purposes.

The very young animals have blue eyes while (55) the eyes of all adults are a striking yellow. Adults may reach a body length of 46 centimeters (18 inches) and a weight of 5.5 kilograms (12 pounds). Their tails are longer than their bodies, at up to 56 centimeters (22 inches) in length.

(60) Found in the southwest of Madagascar and ranging farther into highland areas than any other lemur, ring-tailed lemurs inhabit deciduous forests with grass floors or forests along riverbanks (gallery forests); some may also inhabit dry, open (65) brush where few trees grow. Ring-tailed lemurs are thought to require primary forest (that is, forests that have remained undisturbed by human activity) in order to survive; such forests are now being cleared at a troubling rate.

(70) While primarily frugivores (fruit-eating), ring-tailed lemurs will also eat leaves, seeds, and the odd insect. Ring-tailed lemurs are diurnal and primarily arboreal animals, forming troops of up to 25 individuals. Social hierarchies are determined (75) by sex, with a distinct hierarchy for each gender; females tend to dominate the troop, while males will alternate between troops. Lemurs claim a siz-able territory, which does not overlap with those of other troops; up to 5.6 kilometers (3.5 miles) of this (80) territory may be covered in a single day's foraging.

Both vocal and olfactory signals are important to ring-tailed lemurs' communication: 15 distinct vocalizations are used. A fatty substance is exuded from the lemurs' glands, which the lemurs run (85) their tails through; this scent is used by both sexes to mark territory and to challenge would-be rivals amongst males. The males vigorously wave their tails high in the air in an attempt to overpower the scent of others.

(90) The breeding season runs from April to June, with the female fertile period lasting for only a day. Gestation lasts for about 146 days, resulting in a litter of either one or two. The young lemurs begin to eat solid food after two months and are fully (95) weaned after five months.

GO ON TO THE NEXT PAGE ⟶

31. According to the passage, lemurs survived on the island of Madagascar because:

    A. their large, reflective eyes allowed them to move around at night when predators were asleep.

    B. their ability to mark their territory by scent gave them adequate territory for foraging.

    C. monkeys, apes and other primates were not a threat to them on Madagascar.

    D. their strong social hierarchy allowed them to band together for safety.

32. According to the passage, the social organization of the ring-tailed lemur:

    F. places females at the top of the hierarchy.

    G. functions to ensure adequate food supplies.

    H. has followed the same structure since antiquity.

    J. is notable for its equality of the sexes.

33. The main purpose of the passage is to:

    A. propose a means of preventing the extinction of lemurs.

    B. compare different species of lemurs.

    C. provide information regarding the ring-tailed lemur.

    D. argue that the lemur should not have been introduced into the Comoros Islands.

34. According to the passage, why are ring-tails the most populous species of lemurs in zoos?

    F. They inhabit deciduous forests, which make the lemurs' capture relatively easy.

    G. They have no difficulty giving birth in a zoo environment.

    H. Their attractive appearance makes them popular with patrons.

    J. Their eating preferences are easily accommodated.

35. The passage suggests that the rate at which primary forests are being cleared is "troubling" (line 69) because:

    A. it is causing significant soil erosion in the lemurs' primary habitat.

    B. valuable hardwoods are being destroyed.

    C. lemurs' predators inhabit the cleared area.

    D. lemurs need to live in primary forests to survive.

36. All of the following are given as ways in which ring-tailed lemurs use olfactory signals EXCEPT:

    F. to put male challengers on notice.

    G. to mask the scent of other lemurs.

    H. to signify group identification.

    J. to mark their territory.

37. According to the passage, which of the following describes a characteristic of the infraorder Lemuriformes?

    A. They are nocturnal.

    B. They evolved before monkeys and apes did.

    C. They include two species of flying lemurs.

    D. They are found only on Madagascar.

38. Which of the following can reasonably be inferred from information in the second paragraph (lines 13–27)?

    F. The pygmy mouse lemur is diurnal.

    G. The larger species of lemur were hunted for their fur.

    H. The indri lemur is extinct.

    J. Lemurs are descended from monkeys.

GO ON TO THE NEXT PAGE

39. The primary purpose of the seventh paragraph (lines 60–69) is to:

   A. distinguish between nocturnal and diurnal lemurs.

   B. explain the demise of primary forests.

   C. describe the lemur's habitat.

   D. argue that lemurs inhabit only forested areas.

40. Which of the following questions is NOT answered by the passage?

   F. Will conservationists be able to prevent the extinction of lemurs?

   G. Why did lemurs survive on Madagascar?

   H. How many offspring can a female lemur produce per year?

   J. What makes up the lemur's diet?

SCIENCE TEST

35 Minutes—40 Questions

Directions: There are several passages in this test. Each passage is followed by several questions. After reading a passage, choose the best answer to each question and fill in the corresponding oval on your Answer Grid. You may refer to the passages as often as necessary. You are NOT permitted to use a calculator on this test.

PASSAGE I

Blood samples of equal volumes were collected from five students on one day immediately after waking in the morning and one hour after a breakfast of pancakes and syrup with orange juice. The samples were then analyzed. Tables 1 and 2 show the color, mass, and sugar concentration of the blood samples taken before and after breakfast, respectively. *Sugar concentration* was calculated in milligrams per deciliter (mg/dL) as follows:

$$\text{sugar concentration (mg/dL)} = \frac{\text{mass of sugars (mg)}}{\text{volume of blood (dL)}}$$

The normal range for blood sugar concentration is 90 mg/dL–120 mg/dL.

Table 1

Before-breakfast blood samples			
Student	Color*	Mass(g)	Sugar concentration (mg/dL)
A	9	1.067	116
B	4	1.049	93
C	3	1.051	94
D	6	1.058	108
E	7	1.064	112

*Note: Color values were assigned according to the following scale: 0 = pale red; 10 = dark red

Table 2

After-breakfast blood samples			
Student	Color*	Mass(g)	Sugar concentration (mg/dL)
A	8	1.069	119
B	5	1.051	96
C	4	1.055	102
D	6	1.060	110
E	7	1.066	115

*Note: Color values were assigned according to the following scale: 0 = pale red; 10 = dark red

1. Based on the information presented, which of the following blood samples most likely had the highest water content per milliliter?

   A. The before breakfast blood sample from Student A

   B. The before breakfast blood sample from Student B

   C. The after breakfast blood sample from Student C

   D. The after breakfast blood sample from Student D

GO ON TO THE NEXT PAGE

2. Do the data in Tables 1 and 2 support the conclusion that as the mass of a given volume of blood decreases, blood color darkens?

   F. Yes, because blood samples with the lowest masses had lower color values.

   G. Yes, because blood samples with the lowest masses had higher color values.

   H. No, because blood samples with the lowest masses had lower color values.

   J. No, because blood samples with the lowest masses had higher color values.

3. Based on the results provided, as the sugar concentration of a given volume of blood increases, the mass of that volume of blood:

   A. increases, then decreases.

   B. decreases, then increases.

   C. increases only.

   D. decreases only.

4. One of the five students had a common cold on the day the blood samples were collected. Given that the sugar concentration of blood tends to increase during periods of illness, the student with a cold was most likely:

   F. Student A.

   G. Student B.

   H. Student C.

   J. Student D.

5. A volume of 0.5 mL from which of the following blood samples would weigh the most?

   A. The before breakfast blood sample from Student B

   B. The before breakfast blood sample from Student D

   C. The after breakfast blood sample from Student C

   D. The after breakfast blood sample from Student E

6. What is the positive difference in mass, in milligrams, between the before and after samples from Student C?

   F. 0.0004

   G. 0.004

   H. 0.04

   J. 4

PASSAGE II

The following experiments were performed to study the effects of adding various amounts of a *solute* (a substance that is dissolved in a solution) on the boiling points and freezing points of two different *solvents* (substances that dissolve other substances). The two solvents, isopropyl alcohol (IPA) and acetone, boil at 108°C and 56°C, respectively, and freeze at –88°C and –95°C, respectively, at standard atmospheric pressure.

EXPERIMENT 1

A student dissolved 0.05 moles of potassium chloride (KCl) in 200 g of IPA. Each mole of KCl produces 2 moles of solute particles (1 mole of potassium ions and 1 mole of chloride ions in solution). After the KCl dissolved, the boiling point of the solution was determined. This procedure was repeated dissolving different amounts of KCl in IPA and acetone. The results are shown in Table 1.

Table 1

Solution	Solvent	Amount of KCl added (moles)	Boiling point (°C)
1	IPA	0.05	109.5
2	IPA	0.1	111.2
3	IPA	0.2	114.4
4	IPA	0.4	119.7
5	acetone	0.05	56.4
6	acetone	0.1	56.8
7	acetone	0.2	57.9
8	acetone	0.4	59.2

Note: Boiling points were measured at standard atmospheric pressure.

GO ON TO THE NEXT PAGE

EXPERIMENT 2

A student dissolved 0.05 moles of KCl in 200 g of IPA. After the KCl dissolved, the freezing point of the solution was determined. The procedure was repeated using various amounts of KCl. The results are shown in Table 2.

Table 2

Solution	Amount of KCl added (moles)	Freezing point (°C)
9	0.05	−88.5
10	0.1	−89.0
11	0.2	−90.0
12	0.4	−92.0

Note: Freezing points were measured at standard atmospheric pressure.

7. A solution containing 200 g of IPA and an unknown amount of KCl freezes at −93.0°C. Based on the results of Experiment 2, the number of moles of KCl dissolved in the solution is closest to:

   A. 0.4.

   B. 0.5.

   C. 0.6.

   D. 0.7.

8. Which of the following factors was NOT directly controlled by the student in Experiment 2?

   F. The substance added to the IPA

   G. The amount of IPA used

   H. The amount of solute added to the IPA

   J. The freezing points of the IPA solutions

9. From the results of Experiment 2, which of the following statements most accurately reflects the effect of the number of solute particles dissolved in IPA on the freezing point of a solution?

   A. The number of solute particles produced does not affect the freezing point.

   B. The more solute particles that are present, the higher the freezing point is.

   C. The more solute particles that are present, the lower the freezing point is.

   D. No hypothesis can be made because only one solute was tested.

10. According to the results of Experiments 1 and 2, which of the following conclusions can be made about the changes in the boiling point and freezing point of IPA solutions when 0.4 moles of KCl are added to 200 g of IPA? The boiling point is:

   F. raised more than the freezing point is lowered.

   G. raised less than the freezing point is raised.

   H. lowered more than the freezing point is lowered.

   J. lowered less than the freezing point is raised.

11. Based on the results of Experiment 1, as the number of potassium particles and chloride particles in 200 g of IPA increases, the boiling point of the solution:

   A. increased only.

   B. decreased only.

   C. increased, then decreased.

   D. remained the same.

GO ON TO THE NEXT PAGE ⟶

12. $MgCl_2$ produces 3 moles of solute particles per mole when dissolved. Experiment 1 was repeated using a solution containing 200 g of IPA and 0.2 moles $MgCl_2$. Assuming that $MgCl_2$ has the same effect on the boiling point of IPA as does KCl per particle produced when dissolved, the boiling point of the solution would most likely be:

    F. between 109.5°C and 111.2°C.

    G. between 111.2°C and 114.4°C.

    H. between 114.4°C and 119.7°C.

    J. above 119.7°C.

13. Based on the relationship between moles and boiling point in Table 1 and the trend with the freezing point of IPA in Table 2, which value is the best approximation of the freezing point for acetone when 0.1 moles of KCl are added?

    A. −88.5

    B. −89

    C. −95

    D. −95.5

PASSAGE III

The study of carbon isotopes present in an archeological sample can help us closely approximate the age of the sample. The ratio of the isotopes ^{14}C and ^{12}C in a sample of formerly living tissue such as skeletal remains is compared to the $^{14}C/^{12}C$ ratio in a sample of air from Earth's *biosphere*. The biosphere is the layer of the atmosphere closest to Earth's surface, where living organisms constantly exchange levels of carbon isotopes with the environment. The comparison of a sample's ratio to that of the biosphere is called the *C-14 index* ($\delta^{14}C$). The $\delta^{14}C$ is calculated using the following formula:

$$\delta^{14}C = \frac{(^{14}C/^{12}C)_{biosphere} - (^{14}C/^{12}C)_{sample}}{(^{14}C/^{12}C)_{biosphere}} \times 100$$

Scientists conducted 3 studies to examine the $\delta^{14}C$ of human remains excavated from tombs in Mexico and Africa and learn about the ancient civilizations that once existed there.

STUDY 1

Human remains from 10 different tombs throughout Mexico were examined and the average $\delta^{14}C$ was calculated for each tomb. Figure 1 shows a comparison between the calculated values of $\delta^{14}C$ and the ages of the remains as determined by other methods.

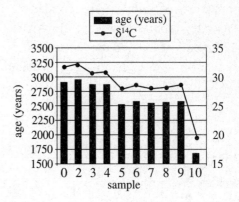

Figure 1

STUDY 2

The remains from one of the largest tombs from Mexico in Study 1 were organized according to the depth beneath the surface from which they were excavated. Since layers of soil and rock were deposited at a known rate at this location, each depth corresponded to a different sample age. In total, 20 m of earth represented the last 4,000 years of soil and rock accumulation. The calculated values of $\delta^{14}C$ for samples taken from different depths are shown in Figure 2.

GO ON TO THE NEXT PAGE ⟩

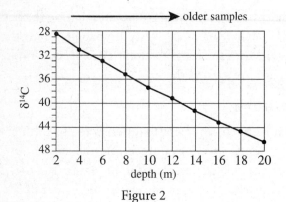

Figure 2

STUDY 3

The procedures of Study 2 were repeated for samples excavated from a large tomb in Africa. The past 4,000 years of soil and rock accumulation was represented by 40 m of depth. The calculated values of $\delta^{14}C$ for the samples are shown in Figure 3.

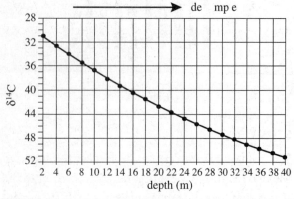

Figure 3

14. According to Study 1, average $\delta^{14}C$ values for the samples from Mexico were closest for which of the following pairs of tombs?

   F. Tomb 2 and Tomb 3
   G. Tomb 4 and Tomb 5
   H. Tomb 5 and Tomb 10
   J. Tomb 6 and Tomb 9

15. According to Study 1, which of the following best describes the relationship between the average $\delta^{14}C$ and the ages of the samples from Mexico? As the ages of the samples increased, the average $\delta^{14}C$ of the samples:

   A. increased only.
   B. decreased only.
   C. increased, then decreased.
   D. decreased, then increased.

16. Which of the following statements best describes why Mexico and Africa were chosen as locations for these studies? These locations had to have:

   F. sample ages greater than 2,000 years for all tomb sites.
   G. tombs over which a significant amount of soil and rock was deposited over the last 4,000 years.
   H. several sites at which little soil and rock was deposited over the last 4,000 years.
   J. large areas of undeveloped land.

17. According to Study 2, a sample excavated from a depth of 25 m under the surface in Mexico most likely had a $\delta^{14}C$ value that was:

   A. less than 30.
   B. between 30 and 40.
   C. between 40 and 50.
   D. greater than 50.

GO ON TO THE NEXT PAGE

18. According to Studies 2 and 3, 4,000 years of soil and rock accumulation was represented by 20 m of earth in Mexico and 40 m of earth in Africa. Which of the following statements best explains why the relationships between time and depth were different? The average rate of soil and rock accumulation over that time period in Africa:

   F. was less than the rate in Mexico.

   G. was the same as the rate in Mexico.

   H. was greater than the rate in Mexico.

   J. could not be determined in comparison with the rate in Mexico.

19. According to the information provided, a sample that has a calculated $\delta^{14}C$ of zero must have a $^{14}C/^{12}C$ ratio that compares in which of the following ways to the $^{14}C/^{12}C$ ratio of the biosphere? The sample's $^{14}C/^{12}C$ ratio is:

   A. 1/4 of the $^{14}C/^{12}C$ ratio of the biosphere.

   B. 1/2 of the $^{14}C/^{12}C$ ratio of the biosphere.

   C. the same as the $^{14}C/^{12}C$ ratio of the biosphere.

   D. twice as large as the $^{14}C/^{12}C$ ratio of the biosphere.

20. What is the approximate age, in years, of a sample from the Mexican tomb that was unearthed 5 meters beneath the surface?

   F. 2,750

   G. 2,850

   H. 3,050

   J. The age can not be determined due to the decomposition of the soil.

PASSAGE IV

Scientists discuss two possible events that may have caused the extinction of dinosaurs approximately 65 million years ago.

SCIENTIST 1

The extinction of the dinosaurs was caused by a meteorite of about 10 km in diameter that struck Earth at a location along what is now the northwestern coast of the Yucatan Peninsula in Mexico. The initial impact incinerated everything on Earth's surface within a radius of approximately 500 km from the point of impact. The resulting shock wave set massive fires and generated tidal waves that caused destruction across much larger distances.

Also, trillions of tons of debris were thrown into the air, blocking light from the sun and causing a significant decrease in global temperatures. The worldwide fires and the large amounts of CO_2 they released later resulted in an equally significant increase in temperatures and chemical reactions leading to downpours of acid rain.

SCIENTIST 2

The extinction of the dinosaurs was caused by an extended period of widespread volcanic activity. Volcanic eruptions around the world introduced large amounts of soot into the atmosphere, causing dramatic climatic changes. Combined with the excess CO_2 released by fires ignited by lava flows, the soot and the change in climate resulted in the production of acid rain. The atmosphere and the sources of food and water became too toxic for the dinosaurs.

The volcanoes also expelled huge amounts of sulfates (SO_4) into the atmosphere, and the mixing of sulfates with water vapor caused more acid rain. Also, SO_4 in the atmosphere led to a breakdown of the ozone layer, allowing high levels of ultraviolet radiation to reach the surface.

GO ON TO THE NEXT PAGE

21. Which of the following statements best explains why Scientist 1 mentioned acid rain?

    A. Acid rain is beneficial to many living things.

    B. Acid rain is harmful to many living things.

    C. Acid rain helps create CO_2 in the atmosphere.

    D. Acid rain results in fires.

22. Sulfates in the atmosphere help to reflect solar radiation back into space, resulting in a reduction of Earth's surface temperature. Based on the information provided, this fact would most likely weaken the viewpoint(s) of:

    F. Scientist 1.

    G. Scientist 2.

    H. both Scientist 1 and Scientist 2.

    J. neither Scientist 1 nor Scientist 2.

23. Scientist 2 would most likely agree that the ozone layer present in today's atmosphere is maintained, at least in part, by:

    A. frequent meteor showers.

    B. periodically active volcanoes.

    C. the high level of CO_2 in the atmosphere.

    D. the low level of SO_4 in the atmosphere.

24. Both scientists would most likely agree that worldwide climate changes occurred partially as a result of:

    F. the impact of a meteorite.

    G. acid rain.

    H. the presence of high levels of CO_2 in the atmosphere.

    J. the presence of high levels of SO_4 in the atmosphere.

25. According to the information provided, radioactive dating of fragments of the meteorite described by Scientist 1 would show the fragments to be about how many million years old?

    A. 2

    B. 10

    C. 50

    D. 65

26. Sulfates are produced in large amounts by a variety of industrial processes. Scientist 2 would most likely predict that in an area of many SO_4-producing industries, if the industries were to alter their processes such that sulfates were no longer produced, the climatic effect in that area would be an increase in the:

    F. average pH of rainfall.

    G. amount of rainfall.

    H. average temperature.

    J. amount of ultraviolet radiation reaching Earth's surface.

27. *Inorganic sulfates* are rocks containing sulfates like barium sulfate ($BaSO_4$) that are formed when minerals combine with sulfates in a high-temperature environment. If scientists found large amounts of inorganic sulfates that had formed about 65 million years ago, this discovery would most likely support the viewpoint(s) of:

    A. Scientist 1.

    B. Scientist 2.

    C. both Scientist 1 and Scientist 2.

    D. neither Scientist 1 nor Scientist 2.

GO ON TO THE NEXT PAGE

PASSAGE V

Under certain conditions, mixtures of hydrogen and chlorine will form hydrochloric acid (HCl). In their chemistry class, students performed the following experiments to study how HCl forms.

EXPERIMENT 1

A clear, thick-walled gas syringe was filled with 20 mL of hydrogen gas (H_2) and 20 mL of chlorine gas (Cl_2), as shown in Figure 1.

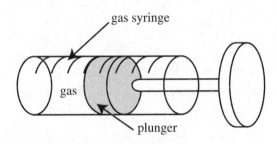

gas syringe

gas

plunger

Figure 1

The syringe plunger was then locked into place, and the syringe was covered in a black cloth. After a few minutes, the cloth was removed and an ultraviolet light bulb was flashed to briefly illuminate the gas from close range. A reaction occurred, forming droplets of HCl. The plunger was then released, and the final volume of gas was recorded after the system was allowed to adjust to room temperature. The composition of the remaining gas, if any, was analyzed. The procedure was repeated with different gas volumes, and the results were recorded in Table 1.

Table 1

	Volume (mL)			
Trial	Initial H_2	Initial Cl_2	Final H_2	Final Cl_2
1	20	20	0	0
2	20	30	0	10
3	20	40	0	20
4	10	40	0	30
5	40	40	0	0
6	30	20	10	0

Since equal numbers of different gas molecules are known to occupy equal volumes at the same pressure and temperature, the students proposed the following equation:

$$H_2 + Cl_2 \rightarrow 2\ HCl$$

EXPERIMENT 2

As shown in Figure 2, streams of silicon tetrachloride ($SiCl_4$) and hydrogen (H_2) gases were allowed to mix in a high-temperature furnace, producing HCl vapor and solid Si. The vapor was released into a cooler chamber, where it condensed to form liquid HCl.

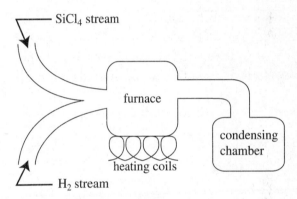

$SiCl_4$ stream

furnace

condensing chamber

heating coils

H_2 stream

Figure 2

The changes in mass of the contents of the furnace and condensing chamber were used to calculate the mass of $SiCl_4$ reacted and the mass of HCl formed. It was determined that 4 molecules of HCl were produced for every 1 molecule of $SiCl_4$ reacted:

$$SiCl_4 + 2\ H_2 \rightarrow Si + 4\ HCl$$

28. When sodium hydroxide (NaOH) and HCl are combined, both compounds decompose, and sodium chloride (NaCl) and H_2O are formed. Which of the following correctly represents this reaction?

  F. $NaCl + H_2O \rightarrow NaOH + HCl$

  G. $NaCl + 2\ H_2O \rightarrow NaOH + HCl$

  H. $NaOH + HCl \rightarrow NaCl + H_2O$

  J. $NaOH + HCl \rightarrow NaCl + 2\ H_2O$

GO ON TO THE NEXT PAGE

29. In Trial 5 of Experiment 1, immediately after the reaction began but before the syringe plunger was released, one would predict that, compared to the pressure in the syringe before the flash, the pressure in the syringe after the flash was:

   A. lower, because the total amount of gas increased.

   B. lower, because the total amount of gas decreased.

   C. higher, because the total amount of gas increased.

   D. higher, because the total amount of gas decreased.

30. If 10 mL of H_2 and 20 mL of Cl_2 were reacted using the procedure from Experiment 1, the final volume of Cl_2 would most likely be:

   F. 0 mL.

   G. 5 mL.

   H. 10 mL.

   J. 20 mL.

31. In Experiment 1, which of the following assumptions about the chemical reactions were made before the final measurements were taken?

   A. Each reaction had run to completion.

   B. Excess Cl_2 must be present for HCl to form.

   C. HCl vapor is not absorbed by solid Si.

   D. $SiCl_4$ and H_2 will only react when heated.

32. When oxygen gas (O_2) is reacted with H_2 under certain conditions, the following reaction occurs:

$$2\ H_2 + O_2 \rightarrow 2\ H_2O$$

   Based on the results of Experiment 1, if 10 mL of O_2 were completely reacted with 25 mL of H_2 at the same pressure and temperature, what volume of H_2 would remain unreacted?

   F. 0 mL

   G. 5 mL

   H. 10 mL

   J. 15 mL

33. Which of the following events would NOT cause an error in interpreting the results of Experiment 2?

   A. Other reactions occurring between $SiCl_4$ and H_2 that produced different products

   B. HCl condensing before it reached the condensing chamber

   C. Using $SiCl_4$ contaminated with nonreactive impurities

   D. Using H_2 contaminated with reactive impurities

34. In which trial is Cl_2 a limiting reagent?

   F. Trial 1

   G. Trial 4

   H. Trial 5

   J. Trial 6

GO ON TO THE NEXT PAGE

PASSAGE VI

A wooden box was held in place on a plastic track a distance, d_0, from one end of the track, which was inclined at an angle, θ, above the floor, as shown in Figure 1.

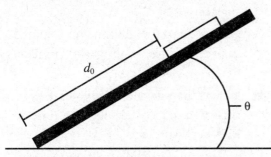

Figure 1

When the box was released it slid down the plane, as shown in Figure 2.

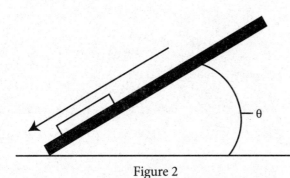

Figure 2

The *slide time* was the time required for the leading face of the box to reach the end of the track. The slide time is graphed in Figure 3 for a fixed θ and various d_0 on the surfaces of Neptune, Earth, and Mercury. The slide time is graphed in Figure 4 for $d_0 = 60$ cm and various θ on the same three surfaces. The acceleration due to gravity on these surfaces is shown in Table 1.

Table 1

Planet	Acceleration due to gravity on surface of planet (m/sec²)
Neptune	13.3
Earth	9.8
Mercury	3.6

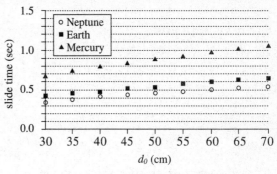

Figure 3

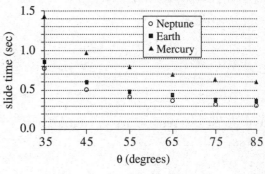

Figure 4

35. Which pair of values for θ produce slide times that are equal for Earth and Mercury, respectively?

   A. 45° and 85°

   B. 35° and 65°

   C. 45° and 55°

   D. 35° and 55°

36. Based on Figure 3, if d_0 were 25 cm, the slide time on Mercury would be closest to:

   F. 0.3 sec.

   G. 0.4 sec.

   H. 0.6 sec.

   J. 1.1 sec.

GO ON TO THE NEXT PAGE

37. According to Figure 4, the box with $d_0 = 60$ cm will have a slide time on Mercury of 1.2 sec if θ is approximately:

    A. 27°.

    B. 30°.

    C. 38°.

    D. 51°.

38. After the box traveled a distance, x, down the track, the distance from the leading face of the box to the end of the track equaled:

    F. $d_0 - x$.

    G. $d_0 + x$.

    H. d_0.

    J. x.

39. Suppose the box represented in Figure 4 has a 0.8 sec slide time on Mercury's surface. For the same box released from the same d_0 to have a 0.8 sec slide time on Earth's surface, θ on Earth's surface would have to be approximately:

    A. 23° greater than on Mercury's surface.

    B. 23° less than on Mercury's surface.

    C. 17° greater than on Mercury's surface.

    D. 17° less than on Mercury's surface.

40. The acceleration due to gravity on the surface of the planet Jupiter is approximately 24.9 m/sec^2. Based on Figure 3, a box's slide time, calculated for Jupiter's surface and a given θ, would be:

    F. less than its slide time on Neptune's surface.

    G. greater than its slide time on Neptune's surface, and less than its slide time on Earth's surface.

    H. greater than its slide time on Earth's surface, and less than its slide time on Mercury's surface.

    J. greater than its slide time on Mercury's surface.

WRITING TEST

40 Minutes

Directions: This is a test of your writing skills. You will have forty (40) minutes to write an essay in English. Before you begin planning and writing your essay, read the writing prompt carefully to understand exactly what you are being asked to do. Your essay will be evaluated on the evidence it provides of your ability to do the following:

- Express judgments by evaluating the three perspectives given in the prompt, taking a position on an issue, and explaining the relationship among all four ideas
- Develop a position by using logical reasoning and by supporting your ideas
- Maintain a focus on the topic throughout the essay
- Organize ideas in a logical way
- Use language clearly and effectively according to the conventions of standard written English

You may use the unlined pages in this test booklet to plan your essay. These pages will not be scored. *You must write your essay in pencil on the lined pages in the answer folder.* Your writing on those lined pages will be scored. You may not need all the lined pages, but to ensure you have enough room to finish, do NOT skip lines. You may write corrections or additions neatly between the lines of your essay, but do NOT write in the margins of the lined pages. *Illegible essays cannot be scored, so you must write (or print) clearly.*

If you finish before time is called you may review your work. Lay your pencil down immediately when time is called.

DO NOT OPEN THIS BOOKLET UNTIL TOLD TO DO SO.

GO ON TO THE NEXT PAGE

STUDENT LOANS

Despite the rising cost of higher education, financial experts agree that a college diploma is worth the investment. As students enroll in college to increase their life-time earning potential, broaden their opportunities, and pursue careers, many worry about the challenge of paying off student loans once they graduate. Student loan repayment includes both the original amount borrowed as well as interest accrued over time, which often takes students years to repay. Should colleges and financial institutions be expected to develop programs and policies to address student concern regarding loans? Given the fact that affording college is a primary factor in deciding whether or not to pursue higher education, it is prudent for institutions to develop practices to better assist students in financing their degrees.

Read and carefully consider these perspectives. Each suggests a particular way of thinking about student loans.

Perspective One	Perspective Two	Perspective Three
Student loans should not be subject to interest rates if a student is able to pay off the loan within a reasonable amount of time. Financial lenders, including the United States government, should not be making a profit on loans that students need to complete their degrees. Should a student request additional time to repay the loan beyond the agreed-upon repayment schedule, interest or a penalty fee can then be applied to the remaining balance.	Higher education is a commodity and is subject to supply and demand principles inherent in a capitalist market. Colleges, financial institutions, and the United States government should not make special accommodations for college students. All loans should be held to the same standard and should not differ according to a borrower's intended use.	The amount of money students can borrow should be proportional to the annual salary they are projected to earn once they graduate. Students should not be allowed to borrow more money than they can pay back in a reasonable amount of time. Reducing or eliminating interest rates does not address the more concerning issue of disproportionate debt and future earning potential.

ESSAY TASK

Write a unified, coherent essay in which you evaluate multiple perspectives regarding student loans. In your essay, be sure to:

- analyze and evaluate the perspectives given
- state and develop your own perspective on the issue
- explain the relationship between your perspective and those given

Your perspective may be in full agreement with any of the others, in partial agreement, or wholly different. Whatever the case, support your ideas with logical reasoning and detailed, persuasive examples.

GO ON TO THE NEXT PAGE ⇨

PLANNING YOUR ESSAY

You may wish to consider the following as you think critically about the task:

Strengths and weaknesses of the three given perspectives
- What insights do they offer, and what do they fail to consider?
- Why might they be persuasive to others, or why might they fail to persuade?

Your own knowledge, experience, and values
- What is your perspective on this issue, and what are its strengths and weaknesses?
- How will you support your perspective in your essay?

_____

_____

_____

_____

_____

_____

_____

_____

_____

_____

_____

_____

_____

_____

_____

_____

GO ON TO THE NEXT PAGE

_____

_____

_____

_____

_____

_____

_____

_____

_____

_____

_____

_____

_____

_____

_____

_____

_____

_____

_____

_____

_____

_____

Practice Test Seven
ANSWER KEY

ENGLISH TEST

1. C	11. C	21. C	31. A	41. D	51. C	61. A	71. B
2. J	12. J	22. H	32. G	42. G	52. H	62. H	72. J
3. B	13. C	23. B	33. C	43. B	53. D	63. C	73. B
4. J	14. G	24. F	34. H	44. H	54. J	64. G	74. F
5. C	15. A	25. D	35. A	45. B	55. D	65. D	75. D
6. H	16. G	26. J	36. J	46. J	56. G	66. J	
7. B	17. D	27. C	37. C	47. C	57. B	67. B	
8. H	18. F	28. G	38. G	48. G	58. F	68. H	
9. C	19. B	29. D	39. A	49. A	59. B	69. C	
10. J	20. G	30. H	40. F	50. G	60. J	70. G	

MATHEMATICS TEST

1. E	9. D	17. D	25. E	33. C	41. E	49. B	57. A
2. H	10. J	18. J	26. G	34. F	42. F	50. F	58. G
3. A	11. C	19. A	27. B	35. D	43. D	51. A	59. C
4. J	12. K	20. H	28. G	36. J	44. G	52. J	60. K
5. C	13. B	21. E	29. A	37. C	45. E	53. B	
6. J	14. H	22. K	30. G	38. K	46. G	54. H	
7. A	15. B	23. B	31. B	39. C	47. D	55. A	
8. F	16. H	24. F	32. H	40. K	48. K	56. J	

READING TEST

1. B	6. H	11. D	16. F	21. B	26. H	31. C	36. H
2. H	7. A	12. H	17. C	22. J	27. B	32. F	37. B
3. B	8. F	13. B	18. F	23. D	28. H	33. C	38. H
4. F	9. D	14. H	19. B	24. J	29. D	34. G	39. C
5. D	10. G	15. B	20. F	25. A	30. F	35. D	40. F

SCIENCE TEST

1. B	6. J	11. A	16. G	21. B	26. F	31. A	36. H
2. H	7. B	12. H	17. D	22. G	27. B	32. G	37. C
3. C	8. J	13. D	18. H	23. D	28. H	33. C	38. F
4. F	9. C	14. J	19. D	24. H	29. B	34. J	39. D
5. D	10. F	15. A	20. G	25. D	30. H	35. A	40. F

ANSWERS AND EXPLANATIONS

ENGLISH TEST

PASSAGE I

1. C
Category: Word Choice
Difficulty: Medium
Getting to the Answer: Use "who" or "whom" to refer to a person. The underlined word begins a description of Lucia; the correct pronoun is "who," because Lucia is a person. Choice (C) is correct. "Which," in A, is incorrect when used to refer to a person. Choice B uses the objective case "whom"; you wouldn't say "*her* was already married," so "*whom* was already married" is incorrect. "She who," in D, makes the sentence unnecessarily wordy and awkward.

2. J
Category: Sentence Sense
Difficulty: Medium
Getting to the Answer: Independent clauses should either be joined by a semicolon or connected with a coordinating conjunction; otherwise, one of the clauses must be made subordinate. As written, the sentence is a run-on. None of the answer choices offers a semicolon or a comma and a coordinating conjunction, but (J) makes the second clause dependent by using "that." Choices G and H do not address the run-on error.

3. B
Category: Verb Tenses
Difficulty: Medium
Getting to the Answer: Use context to determine appropriate verb tenses. This sentence uses the simple past tense "were" and doesn't indicate any time shift, so the simple past tense "knew" makes the most sense. Choice (B) is correct. Choice A uses the past participle "known" without the necessary helping verb "had." Choice C incorrectly uses "had knew"; the past participle of "know" is "known." Choice D uses "been

known" without the necessary helping verb "had"; it also creates a sentence that is grammatically incorrect.

4. J
Category: Connections
Difficulty: Medium
Getting to the Answer: Remember to read for logic, as well as grammar and usage. This sentence inappropriately uses the contrast word "however"; "then," a Connection indicating time, is the best choice here. Choices G and H use cause-and-effect Connections, which are inappropriate in context.

5. C
Category: Word Choice
Difficulty: Medium
Getting to the Answer: When an idiomatic construction begins with "not only," it must conclude with "but also." Only (C) correctly completes the idiom. "And" A, "so," B, and "then," D, all fail to correctly complete the idiom.

6. H
Category: Verb Tenses
Difficulty: Medium
Getting to the Answer: The –*ing* form can serve several functions; when used as a verb, it requires a helping verb to be correct. "I being" here is grammatically incorrect; (H) substitutes the correct verb form "was." Choice G creates a grammatically incorrect sentence, and J omits the verb.

7. B
Category: Writing Strategy
Difficulty: Medium
Getting to the Answer: With Writing Strategy questions like this one, you need to identify the choice that matches the purpose stated in the question stem. The question asks you to select the sentence that gives the most relevant information

about Nicola's travel plans. Only (B) tells you about Nicola's plans; he intends to spend the summer with his family in New York. Choice A mentions Nicola's trip to England, which is out of scope for the passage. Choice C provides general information about the easiest way to travel from Italy to America, but it doesn't tell you anything about Nicola's specific plans to visit America. Choice D also focuses on the past, explaining why Nicola had not previously come to America; this doesn't match the question stem's call for information about Nicola's travel plans.

8. H
Category: Writing Strategy
Difficulty: Medium
Getting to the Answer: Always read question stems carefully; it's easy to miss an important word like NOT or EXCEPT. The question asks for the word that does NOT show that the cousins looked forward to meeting Nicola. The only negatively charged word here is "apprehensive," which suggests that the cousins feared Nicola's arrival. Choice (H) is correct. Choices F, G, and J all use positively charged words that indicate the cousins were looking forward to Nicola's visit.

9. C
Category: Punctuation
Difficulty: Medium
Getting to the Answer: A phrase set off between commas must be nonessential: that is, the sentence must still make sense without it. As written, this sentence treats the phrase "hadn't seen him" as nonessential, but "like me, since they were kids" does not make sense. Choice (C) eliminates the incorrect comma without introducing any additional errors. Choices B and D create run-on sentences; additionally, D incorrectly inserts a comma between a verb and its object.

10. J
Category: Wordiness
Difficulty: Low
Getting to the Answer: Eliminate answer choices that contain redundant language. It is redundant to use "similarity" and "in common" together; (J) eliminates the redundancy. Choices G and H both contain redundant language.

11. C
Category: Wordiness
Difficulty: Medium
Getting to the Answer: The shortest answer isn't always correct. The sentence must make sense, both logically and grammatically. Choices A and B include information irrelevant to the topic of the writer meeting Nicola. Choice D omits a phrase necessary for the sentence to make sense. That leaves (C), which eliminates the irrelevant information without losing the logic of the sentence.

12. J
Category: Sentence Sense
Difficulty: Medium
Getting to the Answer: As a general rule, descriptive phrases modify the nouns that immediately follow them. As written, this sentence tells us that "I" was "Taught to him before she passed away in Italy." Choice (J) is the most concise and logical version of this sentence. Choice G incorrectly indicates that the grandmother, not Nicola, taught the songs to the writer. Choice H gives the introductory phrase no logical noun to modify, making its grammatical structure incorrect.

13. C
Category: Verb Tenses
Difficulty: Low
Getting to the Answer: A verb is underlined, so start by checking to see if the tense is correct. The simple past tense is used in this paragraph: "shared" and "connected." The correct tense here is the simple past "threw," as in (C). Choice A uses the conditional tense "would have thrown," but the sentence

describes something the writer's father actually did, not something hypothetical. Choice B uses the future perfect tense, but the sentence describes something that happened in the past, not an upcoming event. Choice D uses the present tense, but the action happened in the past.

14. G
Category: Punctuation
Difficulty: Low
Getting to the Answer: "Possessive versus plural" questions can often be answered quickly: does the sentence refer to more than one grandmother or something belonging to a grandmother? This sentence is discussing the country that "belongs" to the grandmother, so an apostrophe is needed to make "grandmother" possessive. Only (G) does this without introducing an additional error. Choice F is missing the necessary apostrophe; "grandmothers" is plural, not possessive. Choice H uses the plural possessive "grandmothers'" but only one grandmother is discussed in the paragraph. Choice J corrects the punctuation error but substitutes the homophone "are" for the plural possessive pronoun "our."

15. A
Category: Writing Strategy
Difficulty: Medium
Getting to the Answer: The question stem asks for the best conclusion to the essay, so keep the main idea of the essay in mind. Narrow details or new topics will be incorrect here. The essay focuses on the connection between the New York and Italian members of the writer's family, particularly the relationship that developed between the writer and Nicola. Choice (A) maintains the tone and topic of the final paragraph by describing Uncle Vittorio's reaction to the music performed by the two cousins; it also reflects the essay's topic of family in New York and Italy. Choice B addresses Uncle Vittorio's age, which is not relevant to this essay. Choice C changes the focus from the writer and his family to the writer's feelings about performing music. Choice D abruptly changes the topic of the paragraph, moving from a description of Uncle Vittorio's emotional reaction to the music to a comparison of the writer and Nicola.

PASSAGE II

16. G
Category: Punctuation
Difficulty: Medium
Getting to the Answer: When the only difference in the answer choices is the use of commas, focus on sentence structure. Are there items in a list that need to be separated by commas? A nonessential phrase that needs to be set off from the rest of the sentence with a pair of commas? An introductory phrase or clause that needs to be separated from the rest of the sentence? This sentence treats the phrase "I live" as nonessential, but removing it creates a sentence fragment. Choice (G) properly places a comma between the introductory phrase describing the location of the Handsome Bean coffee shop and the sentence's independent clause. Choice H creates an introductory clause with no noun to modify, which is grammatically incorrect. Choice J fails to set off the introductory phrase from the body of the sentence, making the sentence difficult to understand.

17. D
Category: Wordiness
Difficulty: Low
Getting to the Answer: Be aware of words or phrases that mean essentially the same thing; using them together will be incorrect on the ACT. "Customers" are by definition "people who are interested in purchasing items," so these descriptions are redundant. Choice (D) eliminates the redundancy. Choices A, B, and C all contain redundant language.

18. F
Category: Verb Tenses
Difficulty: Low
Getting to the Answer: Use context to determine the answers to Verb Tenses questions. The verbs in this paragraph are in the present tense: "come," "stay," "is," and "offers." The present tense "spon-

sors" is correct, so NO CHANGE is needed, (F). Choice G uses the past perfect "had sponsored," incorrectly suggesting that the coffee shop sponsored the Little League team before another past event. Choices H and J use the past tense, which is inconsistent with the rest of the paragraph.

19. B
Category: Writing Strategy
Difficulty: Medium
Getting to the Answer: Read question stems carefully. Often, all four answer choices to Writing Strategy questions will be relevant to the passage, but only one will fulfill the specific requirements of the question. The question asks for additional detail about the customers who come to the coffee shop. Only (B) focuses on customers—the parents and children who come for ice cream after the Little League games. Choice A focuses on an additional discount provided by the coffee shop, not on the customers of the shop. Choice C provides a detail about another sport supported by the coffee shop; this doesn't match the purpose stated in the question stem. Choice D provides more information about the Little League field, not about the coffee shop's customers.

20. G
Category: Sentence Sense
Difficulty: Medium
Getting to the Answer: When the end of one sentence and the beginning of the next are underlined, consider whether one or both are sentence fragments. As written, both of these sentences are fragments, since neither expresses a complete thought. Choice (G) correctly combines the two fragments into a single sentence. Choice H is unnecessarily wordy. Choice J does not address the error.

21. C
Category: Writing Strategy
Difficulty: Medium
Getting to the Answer: Remember the first step in the Kaplan Method: Read until you have enough information to answer the question. Here, you need to select the sentence that best introduces the topic of the paragraph, so you'll need to read the paragraph. The paragraph describes the antique décor of the coffee shop—its "century-old" counter, the photos from the 1920s and 1930s, and the "original tin ceiling." Choice (C) effectively leads into this description by explaining that the owner wants the shop to "look like it has been there for decades." Choice A focuses on the friendship between the writer and Mary; this doesn't connect with the details of the antique counter, old photos, and original tin ceiling. Choice B is too general; (C) provides a more specific reason for the decorating decisions Mary has made. Choice D explains that the space was vacant before the Handsome Bean opened, but this doesn't introduce the description of the décor.

22. H
Category: Word Choice
Difficulty: Low
Getting to the Answer: The object of a preposition must be a noun, pronoun, or gerund (–ing verb form functioning as a noun). For this sentence to make sense, the noun "condition" is required as the object of "to." Since nouns can only be modified by adjectives, (H) is correct. Choices F and G use the adjective "conditional" as the object of the preposition, which is grammatically incorrect. Although "original" can function as a noun, it could not then be modified by an adverb, so J is incorrect.

23. B
Category: Word Choice
Difficulty: Medium
Getting to the Answer: The ACT will often separate a tested verb from its subject with an intervening phrase or clause. Make sure that you've correctly identified the subject with which an underlined

verb must agree. As in many sentences on the ACT, a description separates the subject and verb here; the subject of the verb "depicts" is the plural "photos." The plural form "depict" is needed; (B) is correct. Choices C and D do not address the error; additionally, C introduces an unwarranted verb tense change.

24. F
Category: Writing Strategy
Difficulty: Medium
Getting to the Answer: To answer this type of question, focus on the function of the sentence. What purpose does it serve in the paragraph? The sentence provides the reader with the information that the building is at least 70 years old. Therefore, if the sentence were deleted, you would lose information about the age of the building. Choice (F) is correct. Choice G refers to Mary and the writer etching their names in the ceiling, but the time at which the original owner etched his name in the ceiling has little to do with why Mary and the writer did the same thing. Choice H relates the sentence to the influence of the original owner; however, the time at which Harvey etched his name has little to do with his influence on Mary, the writer, or anyone else. Choice J treats the sentence as a description of the interior of the coffee shop, but no description of the ceiling is given in this sentence.

25. D
Category: Punctuation
Difficulty: Medium
Getting to the Answer: A comma should not be inserted between a preposition and its object. This sentence requires no comma; (D) is correct. Choice B uses a semicolon, which is only correct when used to connect two independent clauses. Choice C treats "usually in the form" as a nonessential phrase. However, deleting this phrase does not leave a logical sentence; some additional form of punctuation would be needed to make it correct.

26. J
Category: Word Choice
Difficulty: Medium
Getting to the Answer: Use "number" for items that are countable and "amount" for quantities that are not. The talented musicians and poets are countable, so "number" should be used instead of "amount." Since the number of talented performers isn't compared to anything, "good" is the correct adjective. The answer is (J). Choices F and G use "amount" where "number" would be correct; additionally, Choice G uses the comparative adjective "better," but nothing is compared here. Choice H also uses "better," which is only correct in a comparison.

27. C
Category: Wordiness
Difficulty: Medium
Getting to the Answer: Be aware of phrases like "It being that" here; they add no real meaning to the sentence and provide no clear antecedent for the pronoun. "It being that" is unnecessary here, but eliminating it creates a run-on sentence. Choice (C) eliminates the unnecessary language and makes the second clause subordinate. Choices B and D both use incorrect grammatical structure.

28. G
Category: Sentence Sense
Difficulty: Medium
Getting to the Answer: Elements in a compound must be parallel in structure. The conjunction "or" creates a compound: students load up on caffeine "so they can cram all night…or finishing their research papers." Choice (G) makes the two verbs, *cram* and *finish*, parallel. Choices H and J do not address the parallelism error.

29. D
Category: Sentence Sense
Difficulty: Medium
Getting to the Answer: A sentence may have multiple nouns and verbs and still be a fragment. A complete sentence requires a subject and a verb

in an independent clause that expresses a complete thought. The subject here is "a group of high school students," but the clause "who stops by to have an ice cream cone or an egg cream" describes the students without providing a predicate verb. Choice (D) eliminates the pronoun, making "stops" the predicate verb. Choice B does not address the error and incorrectly uses "that" to refer to people. Choice C creates an error in subject–verb agreement; the plural pronoun "they" does not agree with the verb "stops."

30. H
Category: Organization
Difficulty: Medium
Getting to the Answer: When you need to add or move information, read the new information into the passage at the suggested points to determine its logical placement. The paragraph describes different customers at the coffee shop throughout a typical day, starting in the morning and ending in the evening. This sentence talks about customers who come to the coffee shop in the afternoon, so it should be placed between sentence 3, which talks about daytime customers, and sentence 4, which describes customers in the evening. Choice (H) is correct. Choices F and J both place the information about customers in the afternoon after information about customers in the evening. Choice G places the information about afternoon customers before the information about morning customers.

PASSAGE III

31. A
Category: Punctuation
Difficulty: Medium
Getting to the Answer: Remember your tested comma rules. If a sentence doesn't satisfy a tested condition, the comma will be incorrect. NO CHANGE is needed here. Choice B treats "naval," "adventure," and "exploration" as three items in a list, but "naval" is an adjective, not a noun. Choice C places a comma between the adjective "naval" and "adventure," the

noun it describes. Choice D adds a semicolon, but the second clause is not independent.

32. G
Category: Wordiness
Difficulty: Low
Getting to the Answer: Follow the Kaplan Method and read until you have enough information to identify the issue. A problem that isn't apparent in the underlined portion may be clear when you consider the whole sentence. The sentence is grammatically correct, but it uses redundant language: "Finally" and "at last" mean the same thing. Choice (G) is correct. Choice H changes "Finally" to "In the end," but this doesn't correct the redundancy problem. Choice J makes the redundancy problem worse by using both "Ultimately" and "the result."

33. C
Category: Word Choice
Difficulty: Medium
Getting to the Answer: Every pronoun must have a clear and logical antecedent. Marryat, not his parents, enlisted in the British Navy, so the pronoun here should be "he," not "they." Both (C) and D correct the pronoun, but D introduces a new error; a comma, not a semicolon, is used with a coordinating conjunction ("and"). Choice B does not address the error.

34. H
Category: Word Choice
Difficulty: Low
Getting to the Answer: Remember the difference between "who's" and "whose." "Who's" always stands for "who is" or "who has," while "whose" shows possession. The "naval exploits" were Cochrane's, so the pronoun "whose" is correct here. Choice F uses "that's," which is a contraction for "that is"; "that is naval exploits are legendary" doesn't make sense in context. Choice G uses "who's," a contraction for "who is or "who has"; "who is (or has) naval exploits are legendary" doesn't make sense. Choice J creates a grammatically incorrect sentence.

35. A
Category: Writing Strategy
Difficulty: Medium
Getting to the Answer: Use your elimination skills here. Once you've answered the question "yes" or "no," you can immediately eliminate two choices and focus your attention on the remaining two. The question asks you if the phrase "a number of" adds meaning to the sentence, so take a look at the sentence without the phrase. Omitting the phrase leaves you with Cochrane "as the inspiration for Marryat's fictional characters." A reader could easily assume that this means that Cochrane was the inspiration for all of Marryat's characters, which definitely changes the meaning of the sentence. Choice (A) provides the correct answer. Choice B is incorrect because "characters" is plural, which indicates that Cochrane was a model for more than one character. Choices C and D incorrectly state that omitting the phrase would not change the meaning of the sentence.

36. J
Category: Writing Strategy
Difficulty: Medium
Getting to the Answer: When you're asked about adding a new phrase or sentence, consider both relevance and tone. The focus of this essay is Marryat and how his adventures at sea influenced his writing. The description of Cochrane as an inspiration for Marryat is directly related to the essay's focus, but the information that Cochrane inspired another writer is irrelevant. The sentence should not be added because it is not connected to the main idea of the essay, so (J) is correct. Choices F and G would both incorrectly add the sentence to the essay. Choice H is incorrect because even adding an explanation of the relationship between O'Brian and Marryat would not make this detail relevant to the topic of the essay.

37. C
Category: Wordiness
Difficulty: Medium
Getting to the Answer: Watch out for words that

mean essentially the same thing. Someone who is "famous" is, by definition, "prominent," so describing someone as "prominently famous" is redundant. Only (C) eliminates all redundant language. Choices B and D still contain redundant language.

38. G
Category: Sentence Sense
Difficulty: Medium
Getting to the Answer: The question asks you to correctly place the prepositional phrase in the sentence, so start by determining what came "from historical records." The sentence explains that Marryat had vast experiences at sea, while other writers had only "their imaginations and accounts." It makes sense that these accounts came "from historical records," so the placement in (G) is correct. Choice F indicates that the captain himself, not stories about him, came "from historical records." Choice H indicates that the other writers came "from historical records," which doesn't make sense. Choice J indicates that Marryat's memories of adventures came "from historical records"; this contradicts the information in the passage.

39. A
Category: Punctuation
Difficulty: Medium
Getting to the Answer: Not every underlined portion will contain an error; about 25% of English Test questions will require NO CHANGE. In this sentence, "captain and literary inspiration" describes Cochrane; (A) correctly sets "Cochrane" off from the rest of the sentence. Choices B and D incorrectly place commas within a compound; commas are used to set off items in a series of three or more. Choice C omits the comma necessary to set off "Cochrane" from the rest of the sentence.

40. F
Category: Verb Tenses
Difficulty: Medium
Getting to the Answer: Verb tenses must make sense in the context of the sentence, so consider

whether one action logically occurs before another. This sentence tells you about two past events—a midshipman falling overboard and Marryat jumping into the sea to save him. The first event was the midshipman falling, so the past perfect "had fallen" in (F) is correct. Choice G uses the conditional "would have fallen," but Marryat didn't prevent the midshipman from falling into the sea; he jumped in after the midshipman. Choice H illogically suggests that the midshipman was still in the process of falling overboard when Marryat jumped in to save him. Choice J incorrectly uses the present tense; all of the actions in this sentence took place in the past.

41. D
Category: Wordiness
Difficulty: Low
Getting to the Answer: The passive voice is not always incorrect, but it is generally wordier than the active. If a passive construction can be easily made active, the correct answer choice will do so. Marryat is the one who accomplished the feats, so an active sentence will focus on him, rather than his actions. Choice (D) makes "he" the subject and uses the active verb "accomplished." Choices A and C make "feats," not Marryat, the subject, requiring passive and unnecessarily wordy constructions. Choice B is also unnecessarily wordy.

42. G
Category: Writing Strategy
Difficulty: Medium
Getting to the Answer: The correct sentence will be related to the topic of this paragraph and reflect the passage's overall tone and style. This paragraph discusses the "feats" Marryat accomplished while in the Navy. Choice (G) adds a new feat—inventing a lifeboat—to the list. This choice is most closely related to the ideas presented in the paragraph. Choice F continues on the topic of the War of 1812, but is not the best choice to conclude the paragraph, which concerns Marryat's feats. Choice H concerns the British Navy, which is

a detail in the passage, not the paragraph's topic. Choice J is a general statement that is not necessarily related to Marryat's accomplishments in the Navy.

43. B
Category: Sentence Sense
Difficulty: Medium
Getting to the Answer: Modifying words and phrases should be as close as possible to the person, thing, or action they describe. Marryat's "novels and short stories" were published in England while he was at sea; (B) makes this clear. In A, "during this time" seems to be what was published in England, which is illogical. Choice C is awkwardly worded and "by him" is redundant with "His greatest acclaim." The sentence created by D is grammatically incorrect.

44. H
Category: Word Choice
Difficulty: Medium
Getting to the Answer: Most ACT Idioms questions will hinge on preposition choice. The correct idiom here is "concentrate on writing," as in (H). Choice F uses "concentrate for"; you might concentrate for a period of time, but you don't concentrate *for* writing. Choice G uses "concentrate at"; you might concentrate at a place, such as school, but you don't concentrate *at* writing. Choice J uses two idioms that are inappropriate in context. You might major in writing at college, but you don't *concentrate* in writing; additionally, "writing of full-time" suggests that Marryat was writing about the topic of full-time.

45. B
Category: Organization
Difficulty: Medium
Getting to the Answer: The first paragraph in a passage typically introduces the passage's topic. Only Paragraph 2 uses Marryat's full name: "Frederick Marryat." This paragraph also introduces the topic: Marryat wrote about the adventures he had at sea. This makes Paragraph 2 a better opening paragraph than Paragraph 1; (B) is correct. Choice C interrupts the chronology by placing information about Marryat's

enlistment in the navy after details about his first few years in the navy. Choice D similarly disrupts the chronological order by placing information about Marryat's enlistment in the Navy after all of the details about his experiences in the navy.

PASSAGE IV

46. J
Category: Wordiness
Difficulty: Low
Getting to the Answer: When OMIT is an option, read the underlined selection for relevance. The first paragraph compares the challenge of hitting a major league fastball to that of stopping a crank shot in lacrosse. The rest of the passage focuses on lacrosse, returning to the comparison to baseball in the third and fourth paragraphs. The description of quarterbacks is out of scope, so it should be omitted, (J). Choices G and H also concern the challenge faced by quarterbacks.

47. C
Category: Sentence Sense
Difficulty: Medium
Getting to the Answer: The words "that" and "which" often begin dependent clauses; when one of these words is included in an underlined portion, make sure it doesn't create a sentence fragment. As written, this sentence has no predicate verb. "Lacrosse" is the subject, but "is often referred to" is the verb for the clause that begins with "that" and describes "Lacrosse." Removing "that" makes "is often referred to" the main verb; (C) is correct. Choices B and D do not correct the fragment error.

48. G
Category: Word Choice
Difficulty: Medium
Getting to the Answer: An adverb can modify a verb, adjective, or another adverb; it cannot be used to modify a noun. Here, the adverb "brutally" is used to modify the noun "game." The adjective form "brutal" in (G) is correct. Although "brute", H, can

be used as an adjective, it is incorrect in this context. Choice J uses "brutality," which is a noun, where the adjective form is needed.

49. A
Category: Punctuation
Difficulty: Medium
Getting to the Answer: When the only difference in the answer choices is punctuation, remember your tested rules. A comma is correctly used here to separate the two qualities players possess. NO CHANGE is needed, (A). Choice B uses a semicolon, which would only be correct if an independent clause followed it. Choice C omits the comma, making the meaning of the sentence unclear. Choice D inserts a comma after "and"; commas are incorrect after the conjunctions in compounds.

50. G
Category: Verb Tenses
Difficulty: High
Getting to the Answer: A pronoun and a verb are underlined, so you have several things to check. Make sure that the pronoun has a clear antecedent and is used consistently. Then make sure that the verb agrees with its subject and is in the correct tense. The pronoun "they" correctly refers to the "players," but this paragraph is written in the present tense ("is," "possess," "stands," "sprint"). The present tense "attempt" in (G) is correct. Choice F incorrectly uses the past tense. Choices H and J both incorrectly use the pronoun "one," which does not agree with its plural antecedent "players."

51. C
Category: Organization
Difficulty: Medium
Getting to the Answer: Use context clues to help you answer Organization questions. Sentence 5 describes the job of "the keeper" in lacrosse. Because sentence 3 introduces the role of the goalkeeper, sentence 3 should be placed right before sentence 5. Choice (C) creates the most logical order of sentences in this paragraph. Choices A and B both put a specific detail

about lacrosse before a general description of how the game is played; this paragraph moves from the general to the specific, not the other way around. Choice D incorrectly omits the sentence; because it identifies the role of the goalkeeper in lacrosse, the sentence is relevant to this paragraph.

52. H
Category: Punctuation
Difficulty: High
Getting to the Answer: If you're not sure how to approach a tough Punctuation question, try boiling the sentence down to its basics. Identify the subject and verb in each clause. Remember that a single comma should not separate a subject from its verb. Eliminate the introductory phrase and dependent clause from this sentence, and you're left with "the fastest 'crank shots' on goal, can reach 110 mph." The subject is "crank shots," and the verb is "can reach." There should be no comma separating them, so (H) is correct. Choice F treats "the fastest 'crank shots' on goal" as a nonessential phrase, but the sentence does not make sense without it. Choice G inserts two commas, treating "can" as nonessential. However, "can" is a necessary part of the verb phrase "can reach." Choice J places the comma between the two verbs in the verb phrase, which will never be correct.

53. D
Category: Wordiness
Difficulty: Medium
Getting to the Answer: Always consider redundancy when OMIT is an answer choice. "By high school players" is redundant in a sentence that begins "Even at the high school level." Choice (D) removes the redundant language. Choices B and C both contain redundancies.

54. J
Category: Wordiness
Difficulty: Low
Getting to the Answer: When one answer choice is significantly shorter than the others, consider Wordiness. For this question, ask yourself whether

a description of the field is relevant to the sentence. The sentence compares the single position from which a baseball pitcher throws to the multiple positions from which a lacrosse player can shoot. A description of the field is not related to the main point of this sentence or the following one, so the description should be deleted. Choice (J) is correct. Choices F, G, and H all describe the field, adding irrelevant information to the sentence.

55. D
Category: Wordiness
Difficulty: Medium
Getting to the Answer: Look for the most concise and direct way to express a sentence's meaning. By definition, "six feet" is both a "distance" and a "length"; including either of these words is redundant. Choice (D) is the only choice without redundancy. Choices A and B unnecessarily describe "six feet" as "a distance" and "a length," respectively. Choice C uses both "just" and "mere"; these words have essentially the same meaning and their use together is redundant.

56. G
Category: Connections
Difficulty: Low
Getting to the Answer: Think about what relationships these transitions depict. The preceding sentence gives an explanation of why a lacrosse goalie has a difficult task. This sentence adds to that explanation, telling you that players can make fake moves to trick the goalie. Choices F, H, and J all use transitions that indicate one idea is being added to another. Only (G) indicates a different relationship; "On the other hand" suggests a contrast between the ideas in the two sentences.

57. B
Category: Connections
Difficulty: Medium
Getting to the Answer: When asked to connect paragraphs, be sure you read through them, considering both subject matter and tone. The

Keyword "however" in the second sentence of paragraph 4 tells you that there must be some sort of contrast between the first and second sentences. The second sentence also refers to "Both of these endeavors," so the sentence in question should discuss both hitting a major league pitch and blocking a crank shot. Only (B) meets both of these requirements. Choices A and C do not provide the contrast indicated by "however"; additionally, the slang phrase "is tough" in A is inconsistent with the tone of the rest of the passage. Choice D does not mention hitting a major league pitch, making "Both of these endeavors" in the second sentence illogical.

58. F
Category: Word Choice
Difficulty: Medium
Getting to the Answer: Get in the habit of "matching" verbs with their subject nouns. Since the subject of the underlined verb is the plural "Both," this sentence needs NO CHANGE, (F). Choice G is singular and does not agree with the plural subject "both." Choice H changes the verb to the past tense, but the passage is in the present tense. Choice J uses the conditional "would have required," but there is nothing conditional or hypothetical about the writer's opinion.

59. B
Category: Word Choice
Difficulty: Medium
Getting to the Answer: A pronoun is underlined, so the issue may be pronoun–antecedent agreement, ambiguity, or a pronoun shift. Check context clues. The preceding sentence uses the third-person pronoun "One." Because the underlined sentence adds a thought to the preceding sentence, the pronouns should be consistent. This makes (B) correct. Choice A uses the second-person pronoun "you." Choice C shifts to the third-person plural "they." Choice D shifts from "One" to "he"; it also illogically changes the verb tense.

60. J
Category: Writing Strategy
Difficulty: Medium
Getting to the Answer: This type of question requires you to determine the main idea of the passage. Your Reading skills will come in handy here. In the first paragraph, the writer argues that "stopping a crank shot in men's lacrosse" is "even tougher than taking a major league at-bat." All of the following details support this position. Choice (J) correctly identifies the main idea of the passage. Choices F and G are both automatically out, because the passage does not go into any depth about the strategies employed by baseball pitchers. Choice H is incorrect because the passage provides details in paragraph 3 about the speeds achieved by baseball pitchers.

PASSAGE V

61. A
Category: Punctuation
Difficulty: Medium
Getting to the Answer: If you're not sure whether a phrase or clause should be set off from the sentence by commas, try reading the sentence without it. If the sentence no longer makes sense, then the commas are incorrect. The sentence is correct as written, (F). Choice B incorrectly separates the prepositional phrase "at a breakneck pace" from the verb it describes. Choices C and D both incorrectly insert a comma between the subject "formats" and the verb phrase "have come and gone."

62. H
Category: Sentence Sense
Difficulty: High
Getting to the Answer: More than one placement may create a grammatically correct sentence, so make sure that the sentence is also logical. What word in this sentence does "better" most logically describe? The main idea of the sentence is that the vinyl record replaced the gramophone, so something about the vinyl record must have been better than the gramophone. It makes the most sense to describe vinyl record as "sounding better," as in (H).

Choice F places "better" before "supplanted," which means "replaced", but the sentence isn't comparing the way the vinyl record replaced the gramophone to the way another technology replaced the gramophone. Choice G puts "better" before "vinyl," but "vinyl" isn't being compared to anything in the sentence that results. Choice J creates an illogical sentence, indicating that the gramophone was the better recording format even though it was replaced by the vinyl record.

63. C
Category: Sentence Sense
Difficulty: Medium
Getting to the Answer: The –*ing* verb form cannot be the predicate (main) verb in a sentence. As written, this sentence is a fragment. Choice (C) corrects this by providing a predicate verb without introducing any additional errors. Choices B and D do not address the error.

64. G
Category: Connections
Difficulty: High
Getting to the Answer: With Connections questions, focus on the relationship between ideas. The two ideas here are contrasted—the "average high school student" knows about one type of recording but not the other. Choice (G) has the only contrasting Connections word. Choices F and H incorrectly indicate a cause-and-effect relationship; it doesn't make sense that familiarity with the vinyl record would lead to unfamiliarity with the 8-track. Choice J uses "or," which doesn't make sense in context. It wouldn't seem "curious" that younger people had never heard of either of these recording techniques; what's "curious" is that they are familiar with the older one, but not the more recent.

65. D
Category: Word Choice
Difficulty: Medium
Getting to the Answer: A compound subject joined with "and" requires a plural verb form. The

subject here is "DJs and those", so the two verbs need to be in the plural form. Choice (D) is correct. Choices B and C change one verb but not the other.

66. J
Category: Wordiness
Difficulty: Medium
Getting to the Answer: Redundant information may be contained within the underlined selection, or the underlined information may be redundant because of information elsewhere in the sentence or paragraph. Since we already know that DJs and music-mixers "appreciate" vinyl recordings, it is redundant to also say that they "cherish" them; (J) is correct. Choice G does not address the error. Choice H repeats the information that vinyl records are played on turntables.

67. B
Category: Wordiness
Difficulty: Medium
Getting to the Answer: When you don't spot an error in grammar or usage, check for errors in style. The simplest way to express what the DJs have done is given in (B): "They have kept records from disappearing into oblivion." Choices A and C are unnecessarily wordy. Choice D uses the idiomatically incorrect "disappearance toward."

68. H
Category: Punctuation
Difficulty: Medium
Getting to the Answer: "Aside" words like "though," "for example," and "however" should be set off with commas, since the sentence would still make sense without them. Choice (H) places the commas correctly. Choices F and J only use one of the necessary commas to separate "though" from the rest of the sentence. Choice G uses a semicolon, which is only correct when used to combine independent clauses.

69. C

Category: Punctuation
Difficulty: High
Getting to the Answer: Colons are used to introduce or emphasize a brief definition, explanation, or list. The information after the underlined selection serves as an explanation of the "something different" to which the writer refers. Choice (C) correctly places a colon before this information. Choice A uses no punctuation, which makes the sentence hard to understand. Choice B incorrectly uses a semicolon between an independent and a dependent clause. Choice D uses a comma, which doesn't set off the explanation as well as the colon does.

70. G

Category: Writing Strategy
Difficulty: Medium
Getting to the Answer: Use context and Keywords to determine the correct answers to Writing Strategy questions. The second sentence in the paragraph begins "In contrast" and explains that personal music players have an impressive amount of storage space. The correct answer choice, then, will have something to do with the limited amount of storage space provided by other recording formats. Choice (G) does this, explaining that "A… compact disc can store only…a few hours worth of songs." Choice F focuses on portability, not storage, making the transition "In contrast" illogical. Choice H describes what music listeners want, but this does not contrast with the storage capacity of personal music players discussed in the second sentence. Choice J focuses on the size of music players, not their storage capacity.

71. B

Category: Word Choice
Difficulty: Medium
Getting to the Answer: Read idioms for both proper construction and logic in context. "Contrasting by" is idiomatically incorrect; the best choice here is (B), "Compared to." Choice C uses incorrect grammatical structure. Choice D is idiomatically incorrect.

72. J

Category: Writing Strategy
Difficulty: Medium
Getting to the Answer: Read all question stems carefully. The correct answer choice will maintain the passage's tone and satisfy the stated purpose. The question stem asks for a choice that will "help readers understand the [MP3 player's] storage capacity and size," so you can immediately eliminate Choices F and H, which address the player's popularity, not its storage capacity. Both G and (J) discuss the MP3 player's storage capacity, but J's information is more specific and better satisfies the requirement of the question stem.

73. B

Category: Writing Strategy
Difficulty: High
Getting to the Answer: Read the paragraphs in question with the suggested changes. How do they affect the essay? If the writer uses the pronouns "you" and "your," he is directly addressing the reader. The effect is a more personal tone, (B). Choice A mentions suggested actions, which are not present in paragraphs 5 and 6. The tone of the essay is not "formal and removed," as C indicates. Choice D focuses on the writer's knowledge, but changing the pronouns would not affect the facts presented by the writer.

74. F

Category: Organization
Difficulty: Medium
Getting to the Answer: The first sentence of a paragraph typically introduces the topic of the paragraph, so look for the paragraph that contains details related to this sentence. Paragraph 2 explains how the gramophone record was replaced by the vinyl phonograph record. The new sentence introduces the idea that the gramophone record's popularity did not last, so the beginning of paragraph 2 is the most logical placement. Choice (F) is correct. The gramophone is not mentioned in paragraph 3, 4, or 5.

75. D
Category: Writing Strategy
Difficulty: Medium
Getting to the Answer: This is a question about the main idea of the essay. By determining this, you can quickly eliminate two answer choices. The main idea of the essay is that recording formats have changed and improved rapidly over the past 135 years and are likely to continue changing rapidly. This main idea does not include any technical explanation of how sounds are recorded, so you can immediately eliminate A and B. Choice C can also be ruled out since, far from discussing "a limited number of recording formats," this essay mentions nearly all of them; (D) is correct.

MATHEMATICS TEST

1. E
Category: Operations
Difficulty: Low
Getting to the Answer: To add or subtract fractions, you must first write them over the same denominator.

$$1\frac{2}{3} + 2\frac{3}{4} = \frac{5}{3} + \frac{11}{4} = \frac{20}{12} + \frac{33}{12} = \frac{53}{12} = 4\frac{5}{12}$$

Or, alternatively, plug the numbers into your calculator: 1.6667 + 2.75 = 4.4167. When you enter (E) into your calculator, you get the same result.

2. H
Category: Variable Manipulation
Difficulty: Low
Getting to the Answer: The signs between these terms say to *multiply*—keep that in mind as you apply the rules for exponents. Be careful not to leave any parts out or multiply by any part more than once. First, multiply the number parts together: $2 \cdot 3 \cdot 6 = 36$, which immediately eliminates F and G. Then, x times x is x^2, which eliminates J. Now multiply the ys: $y^3 \cdot y^2 \cdot y^2 = y^{3+2+2} = y^7$, so (H) is correct. Remember that you're counting the number of ys that are being multiplied, so add the exponents.

3. A
Category: Operations
Difficulty: Low
Getting to the Answer: Make sure you solve for what the problem is asking. Wrong answer choices will often be other parts of the question or steps along the way. Ms. Ruppin earns $\frac{\$51,940}{245} = \$212$ per day. The company will save $212 - $140 = $72 by paying the replacement instead, which is (A). Note that E is Ms. Ruppin's pay and C is the replacement's pay. Don't fall for the traditional traps.

4. J
Category: Proportions and Probability
Difficulty: Medium
Getting to the Answer: Questions about averages always start the same way: write the equation using the given information. The average is always equal to the sum of the terms divided by the number of terms. Let x be the fifth test score. Then the situation in this question is:

$$\frac{52 + 70 + 76 + 79 + x}{5} = 75$$
$$\frac{277 + x}{5} = 75$$
$$277 + x = 375$$
$$x = 98, \text{ (J) is correct.}$$

5. C
Category: Proportions and Probability
Difficulty: Medium
Getting to the Answer: If reading isn't your strength, skip problems like this until the end of the test. Divide the amount of water vapor per cubic meter, 6.7 grams, by the maximum, 19.2 grams:

$$\frac{6.7}{19.2} \oplus 0.34896 = 34.896\% \approx 35\%, \text{ (C).}$$

6. J
Category: Plane Geometry
Difficulty: Low
Getting to the Answer: Try to translate what you're asked for into concepts that you know. This question asks for the distance around the pool, also known as

the perimeter. To find the perimeter of a rectangle, add up all the sides: $2(30) + 2(10) = 80$ feet, which is (J).

7. A
Category: Variable Manipulation
Difficulty: Medium
Getting to the Answer: When there is a minus before a parentheses, it gets distributed to *everything* inside the parentheses.

$$w\left[x - (y + z)\right] = w\left[x - y - z\right] = wx - wy - wz, \text{ or (A).}$$

You can also Pick Numbers for w, x, y, and z if you're not comfortable with the algebra involved.

8. F
Category: Variable Manipulation
Difficulty: Medium
Getting to the Answer: Watching your positives and negatives is key! Subtracting when you mean to add (or vice versa) will lead you straight to a wrong answer choice.

$$2x - 5 = 7x + 3$$
$$-5 = 5x + 3$$
$$-8 = 5x$$
$$-\frac{8}{5} = x, \text{ (F)}$$

9. D
Category: Patterns, Logic, & Data
Difficulty: Medium
Getting to the Answer: Sometimes Backsolving will be much easier than trying to work out the algebra. You're not going to be able to tell whether you need a larger or smaller number here, so start with A and work your way down until you have the answer. Choice A: $22 - 13 = 9$ and $49 - 31 = 18$. The difference between the first pair and the last pair is not the same. Eliminate. Choice B: $23 - 13 = 10$ and $49 - 39 = 10$. So far so good, but what about going from the second to the third number? $39 - 23 = 16$, which is not the same as the difference between the other pairs. Eliminate. Choice C: $24 - 13 = 11$ and $49 - 38 = 11$. However, $38 - 24 = 14$. Eliminate. Choice D: $25 - 13 = 12$, $49 - 37 = 12$, and $37 - 25 =$

12. With a difference of 12, the sequence 13, 25, 37, 49 works. Choice (D) is correct. If you want to do the algebra, imagine that you're adding the same thing three times in order to get from 13 to 49 (since you always add the same thing to get the next number). This means that:

$$13 + 3x = 49$$
$$3x = 36$$
$$x = 12$$

The difference is 12, which means the next two numbers are $13 + 12 = 25$ and $25 + 12 = 37$. You can check that $37 + 12 = 49$. Choice (D) is correct.

10. J
Category: Variable Manipulation
Difficulty: Medium
Getting to the Answer: Keeping the values for $\sqrt{x}$, x, and x^2 straight is important. It's easy to quit a step too soon and confuse x with $\sqrt{x}$.

$$x = \sqrt[3]{729} = 729^{\frac{1}{3}} = 9$$
$$\sqrt{x} + x^2 = \sqrt{9} + 9^2 = 3 + 81 = 84, \text{ which is (J).}$$

11. C
Category: Plane Geometry
Difficulty: Medium
Getting to the Answer: It's usually easier to work with fractions if they're written as improper fractions instead of as mixed fractions.

$$r = 1\frac{1}{3} = \frac{4}{3}$$
$$V = \frac{4}{3}\pi \left(\frac{4}{3}\right)^3 \approx 9.93, \text{ which is closest to (C).}$$

12. K
Category: Proportions and Probability
Difficulty: Medium
Getting to the Answer: Pay close attention to words like "not" and "except"—these will make all the difference in a problem. Probability can always be calculated using the fraction $\frac{\text{desired outcomes}}{\text{possible outcomes}}$. The total number of balls is $10 + 10 + 8 = 28$. The number of non-green balls is $10 + 10 = 20$. The probability of choosing a ball that isn't green is $\frac{20}{28} = \frac{5}{7}$, which is (K).

13. B
Category: Patterns, Logic, & Data
Difficulty: Medium
Getting to the Answer: Even if you're not sure how to perform operations on matrices, you can probably reason out the answer. The number of people who will leave Marketing is 0.3(30) = 9. You can compute the number for each department, then add them all together. This will give you the same result as multiplying the matrices.

$$[30\ 20\ 60\ 10]\begin{bmatrix} 0.3 \\ 0.5 \\ 0.2 \\ 0.4 \end{bmatrix} = 30(0.3) + 20(0.5) + 60(0.2) +$$

10(0.4) = 9 + 10 + 12 + 4 = 35, or (B).

Note that even though the information is expressed in matrices, you do not need to know how to multiply matrices to solve the problem.

14. H
Category: Patterns, Logic, & Data
Difficulty: Low
Getting to the Answer: This first question simply tests whether you understand the table. Averages are always calculated by dividing the sum of the terms by the number of terms. You need to know this for Test Day. Using the three sections of English I (rows 1, 2, and 3): $\frac{29 + 27 + 22}{3} = \frac{78}{3} = 26$, which is (H).

15. B
Category: Patterns, Logic, & Data
Difficulty: Medium
Getting to the Answer: Instead of getting overwhelmed by all the data and combinations, try to think of a systematic way to check if each period has enough computers. One good method would be to find the total number of students for each period.

Period	1	2	3	4	5	6
# Students	27	48	26	24	54	48

The number of computers available is 30 + 30 – 3 – 5 = 52. This means there aren't enough for period 5, which is (B).

16. H
Category: Patterns, Logic, & Data
Difficulty: Medium
Getting to the Answer: You don't need to calculate every row, column, and diagonal—since they should all be equal, you just need to look at one row or column that doesn't contain the middle square and one row, column, or diagonal that does contain the middle square. The first column sums to –3x – 6x + 3x = –6x. The second column should have the same sum. Call the missing square q:

$$4x + q - 8x = -6x$$
$$q - 4x = -6x$$
$$q = -2x, \text{ which is (H)}.$$

17. D
Category: Coordinate Geometry
Difficulty: Low
Getting to the Answer: Certain things, such as where in the coordinate plane x and y are positive or negative, are essential knowledge on the ACT. The x-coordinate of an ordered pair is positive to the right of the y-axis and negative to the left. The y-coordinate is positive above the x-axis and negative below. Both coordinates have the same sign in quadrant I and quadrant III, which is (D).

18. J
Category: Patterns, Logic, & Data
Difficulty: Low
Getting to the Answer: Once you know the rule, all problems like this are straightforward. Simply multiply the number of possibilities for each type: 5 • 8 • 3 = 120, or (J).

19. A
Category: Proportions and Probability
Difficulty: Medium
Getting to the Answer: Blindly doing calculations is not a good way to approach a question like this—many wrong answers involve doing the wrong calculations with the given numbers. Make a plan before you start manipulating numbers. Set up a proportion using the ratio of grain to bread. Be sure to keep track of the zeroes.

$$\frac{90,000}{150,000} = \frac{x}{6,000}$$
$$\frac{9}{15} = \frac{x}{6,000}$$
$$54,000 = 15x$$
$$3,600 = x, \text{ (A)}$$

20. H
Category: Plane Geometry
Difficulty: Low
Getting to the Answer: Draw a picture to help you see which concept is being tested.

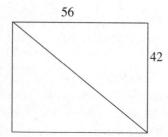

The diagram reveals that this problem is really about the Pythagorean Theorem. The diagonal of the rectangle forms two right triangles. Each triangle is actually a multiple of the 3:4:5 triangle, but that's a little hard to see with such a large multiple. The diagonal, which is the hypotenuse of each right triangle, is $\sqrt{56^2 + 42^2} = \sqrt{4,900} = 70$, or (H).

21. E
Category: Variable Manipulation
Difficulty: Medium
Getting to the Answer: If you're not comfortable simplifying the expressions on the left to see if they match the expressions on the right, you can Pick Numbers for *a*, *b*, and *c*. A is true. All you need to do is cancel out the factor *b* from the expression on the left to get the expression on the right. Choice B is true. It's just using the rules of exponents. Choice C is true. Both the numerator and the denominator are *ab*, and anything divided by itself equals 1 (except for zero, but that's not relevant here). Choice D is true $\frac{a+b}{b} = \frac{a}{b} + \frac{b}{b} = \frac{a}{b} + 1$. Choice (E) is false because you cannot divide the first terms and the second terms separately. When you divide, you can only

divide out factors (things that are multiplied in both the numerator and denominator), not terms (things that are added or subtracted in the numerator and denominator).

22. K
Category: Coordinate Geometry
Difficulty: Low
Getting to the Answer: Even if you forgot what slope-intercept form looks like, the answers tell you to solve for *y*. Add *y* to both sides to arrive at the equation $-3x + 7 = y$, which is (K).

23. B
Category: Variable Manipulation
Difficulty: Medium
Getting to the Answer: Before you factor a quadratic equation, make sure one side is equal to zero. Here, that's already been done.
$$x^2 - 16x = 0$$
$$x(x - 16) = 0$$
$$x = 0 \text{ or } x - 16 = 0$$
$$x = 0 \text{ or } x = 16$$
The latter answer is (B).

24. F
Category: Trigonometry
Difficulty: Low
Getting to the Answer: On Trigonometry questions, be sure you know which angle you're dealing with before you determine which sides are opposite or adjacent. Remember the method for finding the three basic trigonometric functions—SOHCAHTOA tells you that tangent is calculated by dividing the opposite side length by the adjacent side length. Relative to angle *C*, the opposite side is *c* and the adjacent side is *a*, so $\tan C = \frac{c}{a}$, which is (F).

25. E
Category: Plane Geometry
Difficulty: Medium
Getting to the Answer: Even if a question talks about rounding, the correct answer may require no rounding whatsoever. The distance from a point to

a line is measured perpendicularly, so you can be sure that the triangle is a right triangle. Because this distance is perpendicular and measured from the radius, it bisects the chord, which means the base of the triangle is 15. Use the Pythagorean Theorem to find the length of the hypotenuse, r.

$$8^2 + 15^2 = r^2$$
$$r = \sqrt{8^2 + 15^2} = \sqrt{289} = 17, \text{ which is (E).}$$

26. G
Category: Variable Manipulation
Difficulty: Medium
Getting to the Answer: Don't confuse your variables—here you're given V and you need to solve for t.

$$0.575 = \frac{5}{3}t + 0.05$$
$$0.525 = \frac{5}{3}t$$
$$t = \left(\frac{3}{5}\right)0.525 = 0.315, \text{ which is (G).}$$

27. B
Category: Plane Geometry
Difficulty: Medium
Getting to the Answer: If a problem seems confusing, try rewording it in simpler terms. The sand over the soccer field will make a rectangular prism, and you're looking for the height if the volume is 15,000 cubic yards. The volume of a rectangular prism is length times width times height. The length of this soccer field is $100 + 18 + 18 = 136$ yards, the width is 60.5 yards, and the height is unknown. Put this information into an equation with the volume of sand:

$$60.5 \cdot 136 \cdot h = 15,000$$
$$8,228h = 15,000$$
$$h \approx 1.82, \text{ which is between 1 and 2 yards.}$$

28. G
Category: Trigonometry
Difficulty: Low
Getting to the Answer: Most of the trigonometry on the ACT simply tests whether you know the definitions of sine, cosine, and tangent. Remember the method for finding the three basic trigonometric functions. SOHCAHTOA tells you that cosine is calculated by dividing the adjacent side by the hypotenuse. Let x be the length of $\overline{AC}$.

$$\cos A = \frac{adjacent}{hypotenuse}$$
$$\frac{4}{5} = \frac{x}{18}$$
$$5x = 72$$
$$x = 14.4, \text{ which is (G).}$$

29. A
Category: Patterns, Logic, & Data
Difficulty: Medium
Getting to the Answer: Don't automatically start calculating the actual numbers of beds—the graph is already sufficient to answer this question. Bedtime has 2.5 pictures of beds (each representing 100 actual beds). There's a total of $1.5 + 2 + 4 + 2.5 = 10$ pictures of beds. So the fraction of the total beds that are at Bedtime is $\frac{2.5}{10} = \frac{25}{100} = \frac{1}{4}$, which is (A).

30. G
Category: Plane Geometry
Difficulty: Medium
Getting to the Answer: Sometimes drawing a good diagram (or strategically using the given one) will be key to solving a problem.

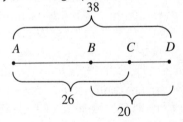

Since $26 + 20 = 46$, the overlapping part, BC, must be $46 - 38 = 8$, which is (G). If you didn't see that right away, you can always calculate from one piece to another. If $AC = 26$ and $AD = 38$, CD must be 12. If $CD = 12$ and $BD = 20$, BC must be 8, (G).

31. B
Category: Coordinate Geometry
Difficulty: Medium
Getting to the Answer: The intersection of two

lines is simply the one (x, y) point that makes both equations true. You can solve this like any system of equations.

$4x + 10 = y = 5x + 7$
$4x + 10 = 5x + 7$
$10 = x + 7$
$3 = x$, which is (B).

If you had accidentally solved for the y-coordinate, you would have gotten E. Look out for traps like this in Coordinate Geometry problems.

32. H
Category: Variable Manipulation
Difficulty: Medium
Getting to the Answer: When you're solving for a variable, remember to get rid of anything added or subtracted to it before multiplying or dividing.

$V = 5W + 4$
$V - 4 = 5W$
$W = \dfrac{V - 4}{5}$, or (H).

33. C
Category: Plane Geometry
Difficulty: Medium
Getting to the Answer: The area of a parallelogram is base times height. Remember, though, that the height has to be perpendicular to the base. It's not the same as the length of a side of the parallelogram. The base of this parallelogram measures 5 + 15 = 20 centimeters. The height is the perpendicular line, which is 12 centimeters long. So the area is 12(20) = 240 square centimeters, which is (C). If you forget the formula for the area of a parallelogram, you can always break the shape into rectangles and triangles and solve from there.

34. F
Category: Variable Manipulation
Difficulty: Medium
Getting to the Answer: A negative number raised to an odd power will always be negative, while a negative number raised to an even power will always be positive. This is an important concept on the ACT.

$s = 4 + t$
$0 = 4 + t - s$
$-4 = t - s$
$(t - s)^3 = (-4)^3 = -64$, (F)

Remember that $(-4)^3$ is not the same as $3(-4)$, which is how you might have gotten wrong answer choice G.

35. D
Category: Coordinate Geometry
Difficulty: Medium
Getting to the Answer: Feel free to draw all over your test booklet—that's what it's there for. This question tests coordinates and midpoint (although you may not realize this at first glance). Set up a coordinate system to compare points B and F. Because you're trying to find the distance relative to A, make A (0,0). Then B is at (800,0). Use the labeled distances to find the x-value of F, which is 700 ($AB - DC - FE$), and the y-value, which is 600 ($CB - DE$). This means F is at (700,600). The lookout point is at the midpoint of B and F, so you can use the midpoint formula:

$$\left(\frac{800 + 700}{2}, \frac{0 + 600}{2}\right) = (750, 300)$$

Using these coordinates, the lookout is 750 yards to the right (east) of point A and 300 yards up (north), which is (D).

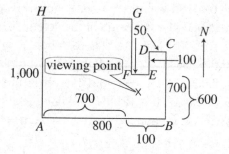

36. J
Category: Variable Manipulation
Difficulty: Medium
Getting to the Answer: When you're translating from English to math, it's easiest to first translate literally (word by word) and then simplify the expression.

Smaller number = x

Larger number = $3x - 6$

Four times the larger = $4(3x - 6)$

Sum of four times the larger and twice the smaller = $4(3x - 6) + 2x$

This sum is supposed to be 77, so $4(3x - 6) + 2x = 77$, which is (J). Remember that "6 less than x" means $x - 6$, not $6 - x$.

37. C

Category: Plane Geometry

Difficulty: Medium

Getting to the Answer: Draw a picture, carefully labeling the sides with the given lengths so that you can see which lengths are the legs and which is the hypotenuse.

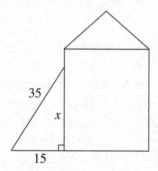

Using the Pythagorean Theorem, $15^2 + x^2 = 35^2$

$$225 + x^2 = 1,225$$
$$x^2 = 1,000$$

$x = \sqrt{1,000} \approx 32$, which is (C).

If you got D, you probably thought 35 was a leg of the triangle instead of the hypotenuse.

38. K

Category: Plane Geometry

Difficulty: Medium

Getting to the Answer: When one figure is inscribed in or circumscribed around another, think about how they relate. The key to every composite figure is moving information from one part of the figure (here, the circle) to another (the square).

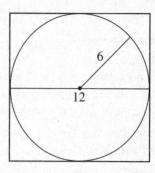

The length of each side of the square is the same as the diameter of the circle, which is $2(6) = 12$. So the area of the square is $12^2 = 144$, which is (K). Note that J is the area of the circle—answering the wrong question is a trap you should avoid on Test Day.

39. C

Category: Plane Geometry

Difficulty: Medium

Getting to the Answer: Similar triangles have equal angles and proportional sides. Be sure to keep track of which side is proportional to which—the longest side of one triangle goes with the longest side of the other triangle and so on. Set up a proportion comparing the longest sides of both triangles and the shortest sides of both triangles:

$$\frac{12}{20} = \frac{x}{15}$$
$$20x = 180$$
$$x = 9, \text{ which is (C).}$$

40. K

Category: Plane Geometry

Difficulty: Medium

Getting to the Answer: Sometimes it is easier to spot corresponding or alternate interior angles if you redraw the diagram with just the two parallel lines and the transversal. The angles of triangle YXZ sum to 180 degrees, so

$$\angle YZX + 20° + 95° = 180°$$
$$\angle YZX = 65°$$

The bases of the trapezoid, $\overline{WX}$ and $\overline{YZ}$, are parallel, making $\angle YZX$ and $\angle TXZ$ alternate interior angles, so $\angle TXZ = 65°$, which is (K).

41. E
Category: Plane Geometry
Difficulty: High
Getting to the Answer: You don't always need to add up all the sides—because all angles are right angles, just find the total vertical distance and the total horizontal distance. On the left side, the distance up is 10 + 18 = 28, so this must be the sum of the vertical sides on the right as well. The total distance going in the up/down direction is 2(28) = 56. Similarly, from the bottom, the total left/right distance is 10 + 14 = 24, so the total distance going left and then right is 2(24) = 48. The total perimeter is 56 + 48 = 104, or (E).

42. F
Category: Proportions and Probability
Difficulty: Medium
Getting to the Answer: When given two ratios, make sure you check whether the second one is a fraction of the first group or a fraction of the total population. Number of students continuing their studies $= \frac{1}{3}(896) \approx 299$. Of that 299, the number of students going to law school is $\frac{2}{5}(299) \approx 120$, which is (F).

43. D
Category: Operations
Difficulty: Medium
Getting to the Answer: Knowing what each letter in the mnemonic "PEMDAS" represents will make simple Operations questions a breeze on Test Day. Substitute the values for a, b, and c, and evaluate the expression following the order of operations: $(a + b)(c - a) = (-2 + 4)[7 - (-2)] = (2)(9) = 18$, so (D) is correct.

44. G
Category: Proportions and Probability
Difficulty: Medium
Getting to the Answer: When it comes to percents, remember that "of" means multiply and "is" means equals.

135% of x is 405
$1.35x = 405$
  $x = 300$
80% of 300 = 0.8(300) = 240, which is (G).

45. E
Category: Coordinate Geometry
Difficulty: Medium
Getting to the Answer: Thinking of the distance formula as a form of the Pythagorean Theorem can help you remember it. Here, the line segment between (2,0) and (0,7) is the hypotenuse of a triangle which has a third vertex at (0,0).

$$d = \sqrt{(y_2 - y_1)^2 + (x_2 - x_1)^2} = \sqrt{(7-0)^2 + (0-2)^2}$$
$$= \sqrt{7^2 + (-2)^2} = \sqrt{49 + 4} = \sqrt{53}, \text{ (E)}$$

46. G
Category: Plane Geometry
Difficulty: Medium
Getting to the Answer: Just because a problem happens to involve perfect squares doesn't mean that you need to square them or take the square root! One way for the ratio to be 9:16 is for the first radius to be 9 and the second to be 16. Then the circumference of the first is $2\pi r = 18\pi$ and the circumference of the second is 32π. The ratio of the circumferences is $\frac{18\pi}{32\pi} = \frac{18}{32} = \frac{9}{16}$ or 9:16, which is (G). No matter what the radii actually are, as long as they are in this ratio their circumferences will be in the same ratio. The circles could have radii of 18 and 32, 90 and 160, or any other radii in a ratio of 9:16.

47. D
Category: Coordinate Geometry
Difficulty: Medium
Getting to the Answer: Concepts like "tangent" are less scary if you work on becoming more comfortable with math vocabulary. Math in a Nutshell in your ACT Lesson Book is a good place to review the concepts you'll need to know.

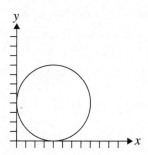

As you can see in the diagram, the center of the circle is at (4,4), and the radius is 4. In the equation of a circle, $(x - h)^2 + (y - k)^2 = r^2$, the center is at (h,k), and the radius is r. Plug in the information you know to get $(x - 4)^2 + (y - 4)^2 = 4^2$, which is (D). If you're stuck, try plugging in a few points. Using either (4,0) or (0,4) eliminates all answers except B and (D), and (4,8) eliminates B.

48. K
Category: Variable Manipulation
Difficulty: High
Getting to the Answer: You don't have to know anything about complex numbers ahead of time. All the information you need is in the question stem. Treat i as a variable, and replace i^2 with -1 whenever it appears.

$$\frac{(i + 1)(i + 1)}{(i - 1)(i - 1)} = \frac{i^2 + 2i + 1}{i^2 - 2i + 1} = \frac{-1 + 2i + 1}{-1 - 2i + 1} = \frac{2i}{-2i} = -1, \text{ (K)}$$

49. B
Category: Variable Manipulation
Difficulty: Medium
Getting to the Answer: Work step-by-step when translating English to math. The total adult ticket sales is $10(120), and the total student ticket sales is $5($x$). The total ticket sales for adult and student tickets in dollars is 10(120) + 5x, or (B).

50. F
Category: Patterns, Logic, & Data
Difficulty: High
Getting to the Answer: A small fraction of the questions are designed to be tricky. On a late question, if it seems like the test maker is leaving something

out, don't doubt yourself. The maximum number of students who are studying tap, ballet, or both is 12 + 19 = 31. This leaves 4 people unaccounted for. So the minimum number possible who do both is 0, which is (F). For example, the school could have 12 tap-only students, 19 ballet-only students, and 4 hip-hop-only students.

51. A
Category: Variable Manipulation
Difficulty: Medium
Getting to the Answer: Don't get too caught up in the language—figure out what the solution is, then think about which answer choice means that. Subtract x from both sides: $-2 < -5$. When is -2 less than -5? Never. What set has nothing in it? The empty set, (A).

52. J
Category: Plane Geometry
Difficulty: Medium
Getting to the Answer: Unless you happen to know the formula for the number of diagonals in a polygon, this one will take you a while. Problems you know will take more than a minute to complete should be saved for the end of the test. Be very careful not to count any diagonals twice. A good way to be sure you don't is to sketch in all the diagonals from one vertex at once, then move to the next vertex and add those diagonals, and so on.

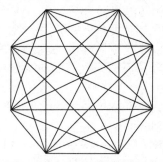

The formula for the number of diagonals in a polygon with n sides is $\frac{n(n - 3)}{2}$. For an octagon, the number of diagonals is $\frac{8(8 - 3)}{2} = \frac{40}{2} = 20$, which is (J).

53. B
Category: Proportions and Probability
Difficulty: Medium
Getting to the Answer: Once you're strong on the basics, combining two concepts on seemingly complex questions like this one will be a breeze! The percent who chose one of the 4 named teachers is 25% + 15% + 35% + 5% = 80%. This means that 20% of the answers were grouped under "Other." A circle has 360 degrees, so the measure of this sector will be 20% of 360, or 0.2(360) = 72 degrees, which is (B).

54. H
Category: Trigonometry
Difficulty: Medium
Getting to the Answer: Most Trigonometry questions will be easier if you draw the triangle. Even though a real triangle couldn't have a side of negative length, drawing a triangle is still a good way to think about trigonometry.

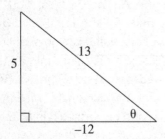

$\cos \theta = \dfrac{\text{adjacent}}{\text{hypotenuse}} = \dfrac{-12}{13}$. Using the 5:12:13 Pythagorean Triplet, the opposite side must be 5. Then $\tan \theta = \dfrac{\text{opposite}}{\text{adjacent}} = \dfrac{5}{-12}$, which is (H).

55. A
Category: Coordinate Geometry
Difficulty: Medium
Getting to the Answer: A great way to test inequalities is to plug in a point. All the points in the shaded region should work, and all the points in the unshaded region should not work. Because only values of x greater than 6 are shaded, $x \geq 6$ should be one of the inequalities, eliminating E. Because the area above the slanted line is shaded, the other inequality should read $y \geq \frac{1}{3}x$. Only the region where both

inequalities are true is shaded, so the answer is (A). Notice that you didn't even have to find the slope of the slanted line, since it's the same in all the answers. All you needed to decipher was that you wanted the region above it.

56. J
Category: Patterns, Logic, & Data
Difficulty: High
Getting to the Answer: Don't let function notation scare you. All you need to do is a little substitution. To find $f(x + h)$ from $f(x)$, plug in $x + h$ wherever you see x. $f(x + h) = 1 - (x + h)^2 = 1 - (x^2 + 2xh + h^2) = 1 - x^2 - 2xh - h^2$, which is (J).

57. A
Category: Coordinate Geometry
Difficulty: Medium
Getting to the Answer: Always look for ways to simplify algebra in the question stem.

$$y = \frac{3x^2 + 2x}{x} = \frac{x(3x + 2)}{x} = 3x + 2$$

Even though the equation looks complicated at first, it's really just a line! The graph is a line with y-intercept 2 and slope 3. Only (A) fits this description. The missing point at $x = 0$ disappears because x cannot equal 0 in the original equation (that would be dividing by 0, which is undefined).

58. G
Category: Coordinate Geometry
Difficulty: Medium
Getting to the Answer: Drawing a triangle and flipping it over the y-axis will help you visualize this situation and others like it.

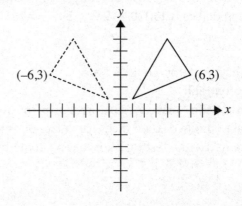

Based on the diagram, the *y*-coordinate stays the same, and the *x*-coordinate goes from positive to negative. This means that (v,w) will become $(-v,w)$, which is (G).

59. C

Category: Variable Manipulation
Difficulty: High
Getting to the Answer: To get *a* in terms of *b*, you'll first need to get *c* in terms of *b*, because *c* is the variable the two equations have in common.

$$b = 3 - 2c$$
$$b + 2c = 3$$
$$2c = 3 - b$$
$$c = \frac{3-b}{2}$$
$$a = 6\left(\frac{3-b}{2}\right) + 7$$
$$a = 3(3-b) + 7$$
$$a = 9 - 3b + 7$$
$$a = 16 - 3b, \text{ (C)}$$

60. K

Category: Variable Manipulation
Difficulty: Low
Getting to the Answer: Carefully translate potentially intimidating word problems. "Fifteen pounds less than" tells you to subtract 15 from some quantity. That quantity is three times the weight of the second-place watermelon, or $3w$, so $3w - 15$ is the correct expression. Choice (K) is correct. Picking Numbers can also help if you have difficulty translating. Pick $w = 10$. Three times this quantity is 30 and 15 less than 30 is 15. Plug $w = 10$ into the answer choices, eliminating any answer choice that does not equal 15:

F. $10 - 5 = 5$
G. $10 + 15 = 25$
H. $10 - 15 = -5$
J. $3(10) + 15 = 45$
K. $3(10) - 15 = 15$

The only answer choice that works is (K).

READING TEST

PASSAGE I

1. B
Category: Generalization
Difficulty: Medium
Getting to the Answer: Although it does not ask for the "purpose" of the passage, this question is asking you to look at the big picture. The question stem doesn't leave much room for a prediction. Note, however, that the focus only turns to Tess in the second half of the passage. Based on your notes, you should at least keep in mind that she seems to like Clare, but also feels that she must encourage him to date other women. Choice (B) matches the author's primary characterization of Tess. Choice A is out of scope; the passage does not describe what Tess thinks is required of a "good farmer's wife." Choice C is a distortion; the search for garlic seems "tedious," but the author never characterizes Tess in this way. Choice D is opposite; lines 93–98 make clear that Tess feels sad about having to steer Clare toward the other women.

2. H
Category: Inference
Difficulty: Medium
Getting to the Answer: Remember that the answer to an Inference question will not stray far from something said in the passage. The passage indicates that the search required all possible assistance because of its importance. The process also sounds very laborious. Look for a choice that incorporates these ideas. Choice (H) matches your prediction. Choice F is opposite; the difficulty of the search required the participation of many people. Choice G is opposite; the passage makes clear that the search was far from "simple." Choice J is a distortion; the passage does not say that the search resulted in lowered production, but states that garlic consumption by a cow can affect a day's dairy produce.

3. B
Category: Inference
Difficulty: High
Getting to the Answer: Some questions may be phrased in a complex way; make sure you know what is being asked before making your prediction. The complaint arose because of the taste the garlic lent the milk. Look for the trait that would affect the milk's taste. Choice (B) says that the root's pungency is such that "one bite of it by one cow" (lines 51–52) could taint a whole day's produce. Choice A is out of scope; the passage doesn't focus on the appearance or classification of a shoot of garlic. Choice C is a misused detail; the "microscopic dimensions" (lines 30–31) of the offending shoot make it hard to find, but this is not the primary reason it presents a nuisance. Choice D is a misused detail; while there are not that many shoots in the field, there were nonetheless enough to cause a problem.

4. F
Category: Detail
Difficulty: Medium
Getting to the Answer: In EXCEPT questions, even the correct answer may appear in the passage, just in the wrong place. Your notes should lead you back to lines 69–92, where Tess considers the other two girls' supposed advantages. She later thinks to herself that Clare should choose Izzy or Retty if he wants "a dairywoman and not a lady" (lines 95–96) which matches (F). Choice G is opposite; Tess states that Izzy and Retty are "excellent dairywomen" while recommending them to Clare. Choice H is opposite; Tess begins her conversation with Clare by drawing his attention to how "pretty" Izzy and Retty are. Choice J is opposite; Tess explicitly states that Izzy and Retty "skim better" than she does.

5. D
Category: Generalization
Difficulty: High
Getting to the Answer: Some questions deal with a character's attitude. Examine the author's choice of language regarding the subject and look at the character's own language and actions to help uncover how she feels. The key reference comes in lines 93–98, where the author describes Tess's "mournful satisfaction" at steering Clare to the other girls. Look for a choice that incorporates these conflicting emotions. Choice (D) works. Tess is certainly sad about rejecting Clare's attention, and she seems resolved—she took "pains to avoid him." Choice A is a distortion; though her conversation makes her feel "mournful," Tess also took "satisfaction" from the results. This suggests that she did not regret them. Choice B is a distortion; "discomfort" makes some sense, but Tess does not exhibit any confusion in recommending Izzy and Retty to Clare. Choice C is out of scope; neither of these emotions is supported by the passage.

6. H
Category: Detail
Difficulty: Low
Getting to the Answer: Sometimes the answer to a question is right in the passage. Reference your notes and the passage directly instead of relying on memory. The end of the first paragraph tells us that Crick had "received a letter, in which a customer had complained that the butter had a twang." Use this as your prediction. The passage confirms (H). Choice F is a misused detail; this tasting served to confirm the presence of the twang, not to cause awareness of it. Choice G is a distortion; the garlic plants are responsible for the twang, but Crick knew first of the twang and later of its cause. Choice J is out of scope; the customer wrote a letter but did not appear at Crick's house.

7. A
Category: Inference
Difficulty: Medium
Getting to the Answer: Many Inference questions may seem like Detail questions in that the inferences will be very close to the passage. The author writes in lines 54–55, "Differing…in natures and moods," the characters "yet formed…a curiously uniform row." This means that their usual differences were

obscured in the effort to work as a team, which matches (A). Choice B is a distortion; in line 60, the characters are described as having an "elfish, moon-lit aspect," but this is due to the buttercups and not directly to their participation in a search. Choice C is out of scope; status differences are not discussed. Choice D is extreme; the author does indicate that individual differences are put aside for this task, but the passage doesn't support the more permanent idea suggested by this choice.

8. F
Category: Function
Difficulty: High
Getting to the Answer: Parts of a passage can have widely varying functions. Pay attention to changes in attitude and tone as well as to those in content. The paragraph moves the focus of the narrative from the nuisance of the garlic to some of the individuals involved in the search. The next paragraph leads into the more personal concerns of Tess's and Clare's relationship, which matches (F). Choice G is a distortion; the passage doesn't suggest that the dairy is disordered before the twang is reported. Choice H is a misused detail; this choice summarizes the paragraph but does not explain what it does for the passage as a whole. Choice J is a distortion; the paragraph does describe the surroundings of the search, but this doesn't describe the paragraph's function in the passage.

9. D
Category: Function
Difficulty: Medium
Getting to the Answer: This question appears to be asking about a detail, but it is really asking you to understand a character's viewpoint. Think more broadly about the context of the passage before predicting an answer. Tess gives Clare several reasons why he should be interested in the other girls, and then takes "pains to avoid him." Tess is trying to encourage Clare to seek the company of the other milkmaids because she believes each of them to be a more suitable wife for him than she would be.

Choice A is out of scope; the passage never suggests that Tess believes the other milkmaids are unable on their own to get Clare's attention. Choice (D) is also supported by lines 73–76. Choice B is a distortion; "chance" in the citation refers to an opportunity, not luck, as used in this choice. Choice C is extreme; nothing in the passage supports such a strong statement. The author appears to suggest that Clare is more interested in Tess than in the others.

10. G
Category: Writer's View
Difficulty: High
Getting to the Answer: The context of the cited material is usually essential to understanding it. Go back to the passage before predicting an answer. The information before the cited statement tells you that Tess was willing to sacrifice her own interests, but not so committed as to say something as strong as this. Her conflicting feelings about the situation prohibit her from making this statement. Choice F is a distortion; Tess does not wish to compete with the other girls. Choice (G) matches the thrust of the text. Choice H is opposite; the author suggests that she is still wrestling with these feelings. Choice J is a distortion; Tess only partly wants Clare to leave her alone. She was unable to make the cited statement because she partly does not wish this.

PASSAGE II

11. D
Category: Generalization
Difficulty: Medium
Getting to the Answer: Generalization questions require you to find an answer choice that correctly interprets the entire passage. Consult your passage notes to predict an answer for this Generalization question. Work through the choices, looking for something consistent with the author's purpose and tone. Choice (D) is correct; in paragraph 1, the author describes science as "inherently uncertain," which matches well with skepticism. Choice A is ex-

treme; while the author is reluctant to embrace the results of modern scientific studies wholeheartedly, the author isn't angry. Choice B is a distortion; the author has a positive view of science, but the author stresses the importance of questioning the scientific results. Choice C is opposite; the author recommends questioning the results of modern scientific studies rather than accepting them as fact.

12. H
Category: Writer's View
Difficulty: Low
Getting to the Answer: Because the question cites a specific part of the passage, reread the relevant text to make a prediction. In line 32, the author uses the word "probabilities" to refer to the scientific discipline that studies the comparative chances of events taking place, which matches (H). Choice F is opposite; the author believes that science is uncertain, so theories will not necessarily be proven true. Choice G is out of scope; the author does not include information about how future scientists will impact current data. Choice J is a distortion; the author does state that "an unfounded prejudice stemming from a desire for scientific constancy can actually discourage inquiry," but that is not related to the idea that science is an implementation of probabilities.

13. B
Category: Function
Difficulty: Medium
Getting to the Answer: Beware of answer choices that twist the meaning of details from the passage. This Function question asks about the role that a detail plays in the argument. In the middle of the third paragraph of Passage A, the author argues that it is important not to be complacent about scientific advances, and the quoted detail is used to support this point. Choice (B) fits well with the intended function of the phrase. Choice A is out of scope; nothing in the paragraph refers to some kind of authority. Choice C is out of scope; the example continues a line of reasoning that has already been developed. Choice D is opposite; the author's purpose is to warn, not to reassure.

14. H
Category: Generalization
Difficulty: Medium
Getting to the Answer: Focus on your notes to help in predicting and solving Generalization questions. Your notes should confirm that the author of Passage B recommends questioning science in paragraph 1, and in paragraph 4 the author urges citizens to resist passive acceptance. Choice (H) matches well. Choice F is out of scope; this information comes from Passage A. Choice G is extreme; while the author says that "analysts sometimes wonder if information was repressed, altered, or given a favorable public relations slant in order to de-emphasize dangerous side effects," the author doesn't argue that *all* scientific findings are repressed or altered. Choice J is opposite; the passage refutes this idea because the author does not want citizens to simply accept scientific information presented to them.

15. B
Category: Function
Difficulty: Medium
Getting to the Answer: Use your passage notes to help predict an answer for a Function question that refers to an entire paragraph. The first paragraph of Passage B outlines the way that skepticism toward science has changed over time. Choice (B) matches the function of paragraph 1. Choice A is out of scope; no new hypothesis is introduced in this paragraph. Choice C is a misused detail; paragraph 2 introduces the issue of public policy, but this question asks specifically about paragraph 1. Choice D is a misused detail; underlying causes are discussed in the third paragraph, not the first.

16. F
Category: Inference
Difficulty: High
Getting to the Answer: Remember not to make too big a logical leap; the correct inference will not stray far from the text. The author believes that people are too ready to believe the results of scientific studies. Choice (F) fits well with the text and represents

a logical, supportable inference. Choice G is out of scope; neither author supports the idea of government control and regulation. Choice H is a misused detail; this idea applies to Passage A. Choice J is out of scope; the belief that the reliability of science has decreased isn't discussed in the passage.

17. C
Category: Writer's View
Difficulty: High
Getting to the Answer: Keeping track of each author's primary viewpoints or beliefs can help you to more quickly evaluate and eliminate answer choices. Passage B describes a solution in which people understand enough about science to assess its reliability for themselves, but Passage A claims that people don't do this because they desire a world of certainties. The contrast between striving for more knowledge and clinging to easy beliefs is captured in (C). Choice A is a distortion; the actions and attitudes of policymakers don't prevent people from becoming better educated. Choice B is a misused detail; Passage B discusses the difficulties of obtaining impartial results, but this is not relevant to the question. Choice D is out of scope; the author of Passage A discusses ethical questions, but this is not related to the solution specified in Passage B.

18. F
Category: Detail
Difficulty: Low
Getting to the Answer: Remember that the answers to Detail questions are always stated directly. By turning first to the passages, you can accurately predict the correct answer and not be misled by misused details. Passage A includes the phrase "present-day industrial societies" in the first sentence, and Passage B mentions "present-day industrial societies" in the third sentence. Choice (F) matches your research. Choice G is a misused detail; this phrase is from paragraph 2 in Passage A. Choice H is a misused detail; this is included in paragraph 3 in Passage B. Choice J is a misused detail; this is mentioned in the first paragraph of Passage B only.

19. B
Category: Detail
Difficulty: Medium
Getting to the Answer: Prediction is key in Detail questions. Wrong answer choices will often reference other details erroneously. In paragraph 2, the passage directly states "In the late 19th century, when Italian astronomer Giovanni Schiaparelli first detected seas and continents on the planet Mars, many people balked at the idea of Earth-like topography on the Red Planet." Use this as a prediction. Choice (B) matches the prediction. Choice A is a misused detail; this example is mentioned in Passage A, not Passage B. Choice C is a distortion; the author of Passage B discusses this in paragraph 4, but these are not examples of the fallibility of scientific certainties. Choice D is a misused detail; this example is mentioned in Passage A, not Passage B.

20. F
Category: Function
Difficulty: Low
Getting to the Answer: When a question stem includes a specific line reference, you usually need to read a little before and a little after those particular lines in order to understand the full context of the quoted portion. The word cited in the question stem comes from the third paragraphs of Passage A and Passage B. Passage A says, "technological advances engage increasingly complex moral questions within fields such as pharmaceutical developments" and Passage B states that, "Some critics of company-funded studies argue that the level of misrepresentation included in such studies borders on immoral." Choice (F) matches with the references to moral questions in both passages. Choice G is a misused detail; this is mentioned in Passage B only, in the last paragraph. Choice H is a misused detail; this is mentioned in Passage A only, in the third paragraph. Choice J is a misused detail; drug testing and analysis is discussed in paragraph 3 of Passage A but not in paragraph 3 of Passage B.

PASSAGE III

21. B
Category: Generalization
Difficulty: Medium
Getting to the Answer: This question focuses on the big picture. You should be predicting the purpose and main idea of every passage you read so you can deal with questions like this quickly. Your notes should tell you that the author is writing more about Scott's achievements than about his weaknesses. You can predict that the answer will be favorable overall. Choice A is out of scope; this choice lacks a sufficient focus on Scott. Choice (B) matches your prediction. Scott's success is stressed throughout and the last two paragraphs point out Scott's impact in several areas. Choice C is a distortion; although you read that Scott had financial difficulties, the financial aspect is much less important than is the success of his writing. Choice D is a distortion; the passage offers no support for this claim.

22. J
Category: Detail
Difficulty: Medium
Getting to the Answer: On Detail questions, first find the appropriate section in the passage. Read the question carefully; sometimes a single word can make a major difference in selecting the correct answer. Note that the question asks about why Scott started writing *novels*, not poetry, so look to paragraph 3, where the author first talks about Scott's novels. The first line tells you that financial difficulties led Scott to write a novel, which met with great success. Look for a choice that matches this idea. Choice F is out of scope; the author doesn't list this outcome as a result of Scott's polio. Choice G is out of scope; nothing in the passage mentions "copyright violations." Choice H is out of scope; the author doesn't reference whether the ballads sold well or not. Choice (J) fits the prediction.

23. D
Category: Detail
Difficulty: Low
Getting to the Answer: If your notes don't help, titles, whether italicized or capitalized, are easier to spot when skimming. In the third paragraph, you see that the author references *Waverly* to mention that Scott left his name off it because he was "mindful of his reputation as a poet." Use this as your prediction. Choice A is a distortion; your research tells you that it was his reputation as a poet, not as a lawyer, that concerned Scott. Choice B is a misused detail; the author tells you that Scott found writing anonymously "fun" only after he believed that it would not damage his reputation as a poet. Choice C is out of scope; although the fact that Scott was "widely rumored" to be the author indicates that there was public interest in the novels' author, there is nothing to suggest that interest spurred sales. Choice (D) matches the prediction.

24. J
Category: Writer's View
Difficulty: Medium
Getting to the Answer: Use the passage to help you understand the author's view of this concept. First find where he refers to Scott and Scottish history, and then focus on the tone of that discussion. Consider the author's overall attitude toward Scott, which is positive. In paragraph 4, the author mentions Scott's popularization of the tartan and kilt, and writes that he turned them into symbols of national identity. Also, in paragraph 6, you see in lines 85–86 that Scott's novels "rehabilitated Highland culture after years in the shadows." Choice F is opposite; the author's tone is more admiring than this. Choice G is opposite; to say that Scott "rehabilitated Highland culture" sounds important. Choice H is a distortion; Scott wrote novels, not "serious analyses of Scottish history." Choice (J) matches the research above.

25. A
Category: Generalization
Difficulty: Medium
Getting to the Answer: When in doubt, keep in mind the overall tone that the author takes in the passage. This question asks about Scott's reputation *after his death*. Since the overall structure of the passage is chronological, it is likely that the answer will come toward the end. The last three paragraphs give evidence of Scott's continued popularity: you read that his novels continued to sell after his death, eventually covering his debts; that Edinburgh's central railroad station was named after his first successful novel; and that his picture is on Scottish currency today. You can predict that his reputation *has only grown* or *is still positive*. Choice (A) matches the prediction, and a quick check of the other choices shows that this is the only one with a positive description. Choice B is opposite; the passage clearly states that Scott's novels continued to sell well after his death. Choice C is a distortion; his debts were unpaid, but this did not affect Scott's reputation. Choice D is a distortion; the passage does mention such imitators (lines 80–81), but the author doesn't suggest that they damaged Scott's reputation.

26. H
Category: Function
Difficulty: Medium
Getting to the Answer: To determine what the author was trying to accomplish here, read around the applicable reference for context. First you must find the reference to Scottish currency. This appears in the last paragraph, but it helps to put it in the context of what comes before: a discussion of Scott's continuing impact. Based on that, you can predict that Scott's influence on the issuance of bank notes is a continuation of the list of achievements. Choice F is a distortion; the author mentions Scott's financial difficulties earlier, but never relates them to the currency issue. Choice G is a misused detail; the author refers to the Prince Regent earlier in the passage but does not tie him into the currency discussion. Choice

(H) varies a bit from the prediction, but matches with the idea of a legacy for Scott. Choice J is out of scope; one could do this, but the author never suggests such an idea.

27. B
Category: Function
Difficulty: Low
Getting to the Answer: To understand the function of a word in context, reading the entire sentence it appears in should be enough. Ask yourself why the placement of this statue would be fitting—the author has not referred to Wallace before this point. The author has, however, previously stressed Scott's affinity for his native land, Scotland, for which Wallace is a great historical figure. Look for a connection with Scotland among the choices. Choice A is out of scope; nothing in the passage suggests that Scott ever wrote a novel about Wallace. Choice (B) fits your prediction. Choice C is out of scope; this fails to address the choice of Wallace. Choice D is out of scope; the passage doesn't support this.

28. H
Category: Writer's View
Difficulty: Low
Getting to the Answer: You will need to answer this question from your overall impression of the passage rather than any specific paragraph. First you need to decide whether the author's attitude is positive or negative. Look to the close of the passage; you know that the author believes Scott was responsible for two major trends. The focus on Scott's achievements indicates that the author admires Scott's work. Choice F is a distortion; nothing indicates that the author is skeptical toward Scott's achievements. Choice G is opposite; both of these adjectives are too negative. Choice (H) matches your prediction. Choice J is out of scope; the passage gives no such indication of jealousy.

29. D
Category: Generalization
Difficulty: Low
Getting to the Answer: Paragraph references focus your research. Use your notes and reference the passage as needed. The author writes that Sir Walter refused to declare bankruptcy, insisting on putting his home and income into a trust that would eventually pay back his creditors completely. Predict that he was committed to paying his debts back. Choice A is opposite; the passage clearly contradicts this. Choice B is out of scope; the author never discusses the cause of Scott's debts. Choice C is out of scope; the author doesn't mention such annoyance on Scott's part. Choice (D) matches the prediction.

30. F
Category: Writer's View
Difficulty: Low
Getting to the Answer: Read the complete sentence for context. You may need to read the ones before and after as well. The prior sentence states that Scott was working as a lawyer, after which you read the first mention of Scott's writings. The subsequent sentences make clear that the emphasis has shifted to Scott's literary career. So the sentence including "dabbling" deals with Scott's first forays into writing. Look for a choice that captures that idea. Choice (F) matches the thrust of the prediction. Choice G is a misused detail; Scott's printing press is not mentioned until paragraph 3, and the author draws no connection between his "dabbling" and his financial troubles. Choice H is a distortion; he was certainly inexperienced, but there is no evidence that his work was inferior. Choice J is a distortion; "dabbling" refers to Scott's writing, not to his interest in history.

PASSAGE IV

31. C
Category: Detail
Difficulty: Low
Getting to the Answer: Wrong answers on Detail questions often include material relevant to other sections of the passage. Be sure you research the passage carefully to interpret the context correctly. You are looking for a factor that is responsible for the lemurs' survival. Your notes should help you find your way to paragraph 2, where the author first discusses Madagascar. The author says the lemurs "were safe from competition" on the island. That should factor into the correct choice. Choice A is a misused detail; the author does mention that lemurs have large reflective eyes, but doesn't relate this to survival. Choice B is a misused detail; scent marking is related to their social organization, not their survival. Choice (C) paraphrases the relevant sentence in paragraph 2. Choice D is a misused detail; the author mentions "hierarchy" later, but not as an explanation for the lemurs' survival.

32. F
Category: Detail
Difficulty: Medium
Getting to the Answer: Taking good notes and marking the passage will help you on Detail questions that lack line references. From your notes, you should see that social organization is discussed in paragraph 8. The writer states that there are separate hierarchies for each gender and that "females tend to dominate the troop." Look for this among the choices. Choice (F) matches your prediction. Choice G is a distortion; the author does reference "foraging," but not in the context of social organization. Choice H is out of scope; the author doesn't offer support for such a sweeping statement. Choice J is opposite; the author writes that females tend to dominate the troop.

33. C
Category: Generalization
Difficulty: Medium
Getting to the Answer: You should be predicting this on every passage you read. Answering a question like this should then take very little time. Based on your notes, you can predict that the author is describing aspects of the ring-tailed lemur, and not making any particular argument. Look for

this among the choices. Choice A is a misused detail; paragraph three references conservation efforts, but this is not the author's purpose in writing. Choice B is a misused detail; the author mentions other species only in passing. Choice (C) matches the prediction nicely. Choice D is out of scope; the author never mentions whether or not lemurs should have been introduced into the Comoros.

34. G
Category: Detail
Difficulty: Medium
Getting to the Answer: The answers to Detail questions are stated directly in the passage—can you find the answer with research. This point is fairly obscure, and may not be reflected in your notes. If you have to, skim for "zoo," which appears in paragraph 4. The author states that ring-tailed lemurs are the most populous lemurs in zoos, and follows that by writing that "they reproduce readily in captivity." Use that as your prediction. Choice F is out of scope; the author doesn't make such a contention. Choice (G) is a good paraphrase of the text referenced above. Choice H is out of scope; the author does not make this point. Choice J is a distortion; the author addresses "foraging," but not in connection with zoos.

35. D
Category: Inference
Difficulty: Medium
Getting to the Answer: When given a line reference, move quickly and read at least that entire sentence to discern context. The author indicates that lemurs need to live in primary forest to survive. The clearing will likely endanger the lemurs' continued survival. Look for a match to this idea. Choice A is out of scope; the author does not refer to this. Choice B is out of scope; the author does not refer to this. Choice C is out of scope; the author doesn't reference such predators here. Choice (D) matches the research above.

36. H
Category: Detail
Difficulty: Low
Getting to the Answer: This is an EXCEPT question. That means you need to find three choices that are mentioned in the text and one that is not mentioned. Don't confuse the two. Your notes can help you to locate "olfactory signals"; they appear in paragraph 9. Work through the paragraph, crossing off the three choices that do appear. Choice F is opposite; this appears in line 86–87. Choice G is opposite; this appears in line 88–89. The author does not reference (H), which makes it the correct answer. Choice J is opposite; this appears in line 86.

37. B
Category: Detail
Difficulty: Medium
Getting to the Answer: Detail questions are answered directly in the passage. Referencing it before making a prediction will help you avoid misused details. Note that the question concerns all Lemuriformes, not only ring-tailed lemurs. This leads you to the first paragraph, which discusses lemurs in general. You may be unsure exactly which characteristic to predict, so compare this paragraph to the choices. Choice A is a distortion; many lemurs are nocturnal, but not all lemurs are. Choice (B) makes sense. Paragraph 1 states that lemurs represent the "evolutionary predecessor" of monkeys and apes, a paraphrase of what you see here. Choice C is opposite; at the end of paragraph 1, the author clearly states that these species are not actually lemurs (*Lemuriformes*). Choice D is opposite; the first sentence in paragraph 2 states that lemurs are found on Madagascar "and some smaller surrounding islands."

38. H
Category: Inference
Difficulty: Medium
Getting to the Answer: You need to "read between the lines" to find the correct answer. But don't make too great a logical leap. Check your notes for the

second paragraph, and read it again if necessary. The question is very open-ended, so work through the choices and compare them to the information in the paragraph. Choice F is opposite; the author states that the pygmy mouse lemur is the smallest species and that smaller species are typically nocturnal, not diurnal. Choice G is out of scope; the author does not discuss why certain species of lemur have become extinct. Choice (H) works. The author writes that the indri was the largest lemur. The next sentence states that "the larger species" are all extinct. Therefore, you can infer that the indri is extinct. Choice J is opposite; in paragraph one, you learn that lemurs are described as evolutionary *predecessors* of monkeys, meaning monkeys are descended from them.

39. C
Category: Generalization
Difficulty: Medium
Getting to the Answer: This question is asking for the purpose of a single paragraph. Your first step should be to check your notes on that paragraph. This paragraph discusses the habitat of ring-tailed lemurs. Look for a choice that incorporates this. Choice A is a misused detail; nocturnal and diurnal lemurs are discussed in paragraph 2. Choice B is a misused detail; you do read that primary forests are being cleared, but that is a small part of this paragraph. Choice (C) matches the prediction. Choice D is a distortion; the passage states that some inhabit dry open brush.

40. F
Category: Detail
Difficulty: Medium
Getting to the Answer: Because this question asks which question is not answered, it functions as an EXCEPT question. Find the issue that is not addressed in the passage. The answers to these questions could fall anywhere in the passage. Your notes, though, should help you find the information you need. The author touches on (F) in paragraph 3, saying that "options are limited." This implies that the question of

survival has not been fully answered. If you're unsure at this point, work through the others to see that they are answered. Choice G is opposite; this is answered in the second sentence of paragraph 2. Lemurs survived because they did not have to compete with monkeys and apes. Choice H is opposite; looking at the last paragraph, you see that the female is fertile for only one day a year, and that gestation lasts 146 days. So the female can have only one litter, and the author states that a litter consists of one or two babies. Choice J is opposite; this is answered in paragraph 8. The author states lemurs eat fruit, "leaves, seeds, and the odd insect."

SCIENCE TEST

PASSAGE I

1. B
Category: Figure Interpretation
Difficulty: High
Getting to the Answer: When a question asks about a quantity that is not given in the figures, think about how that quantity relates to those that *are* given. The highest water content per millimeter means the highest water concentration, which means the lowest concentration of other substances. The blood sample with the highest water content per millimeter is then most likely the sample with the lowest sugar concentration, as in (B).

2. H
Category: Patterns
Difficulty: Medium
Getting to the Answer: Focus on the relevant data. You're only looking at the mass and color columns for both tables. Compare blood color to mass in both tables. The higher blood masses generally have a darker color. So, the conclusion in the question stem is wrong. Eliminate F and G as they state that the conclusion is correct. Choice (H) correctly states that as blood mass decreases, blood color lightens.

Choice J is incorrect because the data shows that lower masses have lighter blood color.

3. C
Category: Patterns
Difficulty: Low
Getting to the Answer: Usually, relationships on the ACT will either be direct (one goes up as the other goes up), or inverse (one goes up as the other goes down). Look for these types of relationships first. The data in Tables 1 and 2 show that sugar concentration goes up as mass goes up. Choice (C) is perfect. Choice D is the exact opposite of what you're looking for.

4. F
Category: Scientific Reasoning
Difficulty: Low
Getting to the Answer: Pay close attention to any new concepts introduced in the question, but don't let them confuse you. Everything you need to know will be in either the question stem or the passage. The passage doesn't tell you anything about illness, but the question stem provides the link you need. It states that blood sugar concentration tends to increase during illness. So, the student with the cold is most likely the student with the highest blood sugar concentration. The highest sugar concentration values occur for the samples taken from Student A in both Tables 1 and 2, so (F) is correct.

5. D
Category: Figure Interpretation
Difficulty: Medium
Getting to the Answer: Sometimes a question will ask you to compare the choices with each other, rather than develop a new conclusion. Be meticulous in your comparison. Since the volumes of the samples in both tables are the same, the heaviest sample is the one with the largest mass. Although Student A had the sample with the overall highest mass, Student A is not represented in the choices. The sample with the highest mass represented in the choices is given by (D).

6. J
Category: Figure Interpretation
Difficulty: Low
Getting to the Answer: To find the positive difference in mass, locate the mass of the before and after samples for Student C in Tables 1 and 2. The after sample is 1.055 and the before sample is 1.051, so the positive difference is 0.004. Choice G, however, is a trap. The question is asking for the value in milligrams, but the data in the tables in grams. There 1,000 milligrams per gram. To convert units, multiply 0.004 grams by 1,000 to get 4 milligrams, (J).

PASSAGE II

7. B
Category: Patterns
Difficulty: Medium
Getting to the Answer: Patterns in the data may not always be obvious. Look carefully at each set of data and proceed step by step. The pattern here is that for every 0.1 moles of KCl added, the freezing point rises 1.0°C. Because 0.4 moles yields a freezing point of –92.0°C, 0.5 moles, (B), will yield a freezing point of –93.0°C. Choice A is incorrect, and could be easily eliminated, because you can see from Table 2 that a freezing point of –92.0°C corresponds to 0.4 moles of KCl, (B).

8. J
Category: Scientific Reasoning
Difficulty: Low
Getting to the Answer: Sometimes a question asks you for specific details. Refer back to the passage and figures to eliminate wrong answer choices. Choices F, G, and H, were all factors directly manipulated by the student: the substance added to the IPA was KCl, which was controlled by the student; 200 g of IPA was used by the student, so that was controlled by the student; and the amount of solute (KCl) added was varied by the student between 0.05 and 0.4 moles. Only (J) describes properties controlled by nature alone.

9. C

Category: Patterns
Difficulty: Medium
Getting to the Answer: Be careful when data include negatives—it's easy to mistakenly think of moving from $-80°C$ to $-90°C$ as an increase, not a decrease. Start by looking at Table 2. As more KCl was added, the freezing point dropped from $-88.5°C$ to $-92°C$. So, according to Experiment 2, more solute particles mean a lower freezing point, (C). Choice A is incorrect because the freezing point does indeed change as the number of solute particles changes. Choice B is incorrect and the opposite of what you're looking for. Choice D is incorrect because the question stem asks you to draw a conclusion based on the results of Experiment 2 alone, so it doesn't matter that only one solute was tested.

10. F

Category: Figure Interpretation
Difficulty: High
Getting to the Answer: Some questions may ask you to compare the data from two experiments. Make sure you understand each experiment separately before making the comparison. According to Table 1, when 0.4 moles of KCl are added to 200g of IPA, the boiling point is raised $119.7°C - 108°C = 11.7°C$. According to Table 2, when 0.4 moles of KCl are added to 200 g of IPA, the freezing point is lowered $-88°C - (-92.0°C) = 4.0°C$. Choice (F) expresses this perfectly.

11. A

Category: Patterns
Difficulty: Low
Getting to the Answer: "Based on the results of Experiment 1" tells you to look only at Experiment 1 and Table 1 when answering this question. With each increase in the amount of KCl (potassium chloride) added, the boiling point of the solution increased. Choice (A) is perfect. Choice B is incorrect and the opposite of what you're looking for.

12. H

Category: Scientific Reasoning
Difficulty: High
Getting to the Answer: Read this question carefully. Challenging questions often require you to pick up on subtle points. The big clue in the question stem is the statement "Assuming that $MgCl_2$ has the same effect on the boiling point of IPA as does KCl per particle produced when dissolved." To answer this challenging question, you must think in terms of the individual solute particles, K and Cl for KCl, and Mg, Cl, and Cl for $MgCl_2$. Adding 0.2 moles of $MgCl_2$ results in 3×0.2 moles = 0.6 moles of solute particles (0.2 moles of Mg and 0.4 moles of Cl). According to Table 1, 0.4 moles of *solute particles* (0.2 moles of K plus 0.2 moles of Cl) result in a boiling point of $114.4°C$, while 0.8 moles of solute particles (0.4 moles of K plus 0.4 moles of Cl) result in a boiling point of $119.7°C$. Since $0.4 < 0.6 < 0.8$, the boiling point resulting from the addition of 0.2 moles of $MgCl_2$ should be (H). Note that all three incorrect choices involve boiling points taken directly from Table 1.

13. D

Category: Patterns
Difficulty: Medium
Getting to the Answer: Table 1 shows that adding KCl increases the boiling point of both acetone and IPA. Table 2 shows that the freezing point of IPA is depressed by the addition of KCl. Therefore, it is reasonable to conclude that the freezing point of acetone would be depressed as well. Since -95 is the freezing point of acetone, given in the introductory paragraph, the correct value for this answer would be even lower. Therefore, -95.5, (D), is the best answer for this question. Both -88.5 and -89 are incorrect because they are values for IPA.

PASSAGE III

14. J

Category: Figure Interpretation
Difficulty: Low
Getting to the Answer: Before you evaluate the an-

swer choices, go back to Figure 1 and make sure you understand where to find the tombs and the $\delta^{14}C$ values. For $\delta^{14}C$ values, look at the line graph portion of Figure 1. The tombs are numbered 1–10 and each is represented on the x-axis. The correct answer is the pair of samples for which the $\delta^{14}C$ values are the closest. Go through the answer choices one by one and compare the $\delta^{14}C$ values for the tombs in each choice. The plotted points for the pair in (J) appear to be at the same height, while the pairs in the other choices have unequal heights.

15. A
Category: Patterns
Difficulty: Medium
Getting to the Answer: Start this question by finding which axis plots the age of the samples. Then, find where the $\delta^{14}C$ value is expressed. Both age and $\delta^{14}C$ value are plotted on the y-axis of Figure 1. The height of the bars represents the age of the samples, and the line with the plotted points represents the $\delta^{14}C$ value. If you compare the height of the plotted points to the height of the bars for the same samples, you'll see that they are directly proportional. In other words, high $\delta^{14}C$ values correspond to greater ages, and lower $\delta^{14}C$ values correspond to lower ages. Choice (A), then, is correct.

16. G
Category: Scientific Reasoning
Difficulty: Medium
Getting to the Answer: Go straight to the answer choices when the question is vague. A is directly contradicted by Sample 10 in Study 1, so cross this choice off. Choice (G) seems good. Studies 2 and 3 relied upon 20 m and 40 m of soil and rock accumulation over the past 4,000 years, so it's reasonable to assume that this factor was important in the selection of these sites. Choice H doesn't make sense—there was a great deal of soil and rock. Choice J requires knowledge out of scope for this passage—nowhere is land development mentioned. This leaves only (G), which is correct.

17. D
Category: Patterns
Difficulty: Medium
Getting to the Answer: Follow trends in the given data to extrapolate data outside of the boundaries of the figures. The curve in Figure 2 clearly decreases with increasing depth. A depth of 25 m is greater than any depth shown, so the $\delta^{14}C$ value must be less than any of those shown, as in (D).

18. H
Category: Scientific Reasoning
Difficulty: Medium
Getting to the Answer: Sometimes a question requires an intuitive leap from the given information. Just as with a Reading passage, infer only what MUST follow from the given information. Over the same time period, twice as much soil and rock accumulated at the African sites than at the Mexican sites. Therefore, the rate of accumulation must have been faster in Africa than in Mexico, as in (H).

19. D
Category: Scientific Reasoning
Difficulty: High
Getting to the Answer: Don't be afraid of complicated-looking equations. Search for the simple concepts hiding beneath the intimidating presentation. Start this question by looking back at the equation that describes how $\delta^{14}C$ is calculated. The equation given in the first paragraph of the passage shows that $\delta^{14}C$ is equal to the $^{14}C/^{12}C$ ratio of the biosphere minus the $^{14}C/^{12}C$ ratio of the sample divided by the $^{14}C/^{12}C$ ratio of the biosphere. $\delta^{14}C$ can only equal 0 if the numerator of the equation equals 0. This is only true when the $^{14}C/^{12}C$ ratio of the biosphere equals the $^{14}C/^{12}C$ ratio of the sample. Choice (D) is correct.

20. G
Category: Figure Interpretation
Difficulty: Medium
Getting to the Answer: The question asks for the age of a sample based on its depth. Figure 2 has the

carbon index vs. depth for a Mexican tomb. A depth of 5 meters corresponds to $32\delta^{14}$C. δ^{14} is on the right-hand y-axis of Figure 1, which correlates with age. The δ^{14}C line has two data points near 32, directly over samples 3 and 4. The ages of samples 3 and 4 are greater than 2,750 and less than 3,000. Therefore, the answer is 2,850, (G).

PASSAGE IV

21. B
Category: Scientific Reasoning
Difficulty: Low
Getting to the Answer: Make sure you understand Scientist 1's viewpoint before you answer the questions that relate to it. Scientist 1's second paragraph contains examples of events that were detrimental to the dinosaurs, so you can predict that he mentioned acid rain because it was also harmful to the dinosaurs. A is is the opposite of what you've predicted, so eliminate that. C contradicts the information in the passage—CO_2 helped cause the acid rain, not vice versa. D contradicts the passage, which states that fires helped cause the acid rain. Only (B) matches your prediction.

22. G
Category: Scientific Reasoning
Difficulty: Medium
Getting to the Answer: Begin this question by reviewing where sulfates appear in the passage. Only Scientist 2 mentioned sulfates, so you can immediately eliminate F and H, because they mention Scientist 1. Scientist 2 states that sulfates caused acid rain and led to the breakdown of the ozone layer, which allowed more ultraviolet radiation to reach Earth's surface. If it were shown that sulfates reflect radiation back into space, this would counteract the mechanism described by Scientist 2, so (G) is correct.

23. D
Category: Scientific Reasoning
Difficulty: Medium
Getting to the Answer: The correct answer MUST

follow from the passage. Begin this question by reviewing what Scientist 2 says about the ozone layer. The only thing Scientist 2 says about the ozone layer is that the introduction of SO_4 into the atmosphere depleted it. Scientist 2 would then likely agree that lower sulfate levels mean a healthier ozone layer, as in (D).

24. H
Category: Scientific Reasoning
Difficulty: Low
Getting to the Answer: Make sure you understand each scientist's viewpoint before you move to the answer choices. F is incorrect because while Scientist 1 believes the climate change was caused by the impact of a meteorite, Scientist 2 believes it was caused by volcanic eruptions. Choice G is tempting. Both scientists mentioned acid rain, but neither called it a cause of climate change. Both listed it as a result of other changes. Eliminate this choice. Choice (H) looks good. Both scientists mention excess CO_2 as a cause of climate change. Keep this choice. J can't be correct, because only Scientist 2 mentions SO_4. Choice (H), then, is correct.

25. D
Category: Scientific Reasoning
Difficulty: Medium
Getting to the Answer: Sometimes key information is located in the introduction of the passage, before the viewpoints are presented. The very first sentence of the passage makes the only reference to the time of the dinosaurs' extinction. It states that the extinction of the dinosaurs occurred approximately 65 million years ago. The meteor described by Scientist 1 would have to have landed at the same time, so (D) is correct.

26. F
Category: Scientific Reasoning
Difficulty: High
Getting to the Answer: You must understand how sulfates fit into Scientist 2's viewpoint to an-

swer this question. According to Scientist 2, sulfates caused acid rain and helped break down the atmosphere, allowing more ultraviolet radiation to reach Earth's surface. (F) is possible. Even if you're not sure whether an increase in pH means less acid, you know from the passage that sulfates affect the acidity of rain, so you should keep this choice. Choice G is incorrect. Scientist 2 discussed the affect of sulfates on the acidity of rain, but not on the amount of rainfall. Choice H is incorrect. Scientist 2 doesn't relate sulfates to temperature. Choice J is also incorrect and the opposite of what you're looking for. Scientist 2 says that increasing sulfates increases the amount of ultraviolet radiation reaching Earth. So, decreasing the amount of sulfates would decrease the amount of ultraviolet radiation reaching Earth's surface. Choice (F) is correct.

27. B
Category: Scientific Reasoning
Difficulty: Medium
Getting to the Answer: Keep track of which details belong to which scientist. Eliminate A and C, because only Scientist 2 mentions sulfates. Scientist 2 stated that a large amount of sulfates was released at the time of the dinosaurs' extinction, so finding rocks high in sulfates that date from the time of the extinction would support Scientist 2's viewpoint. Choice (B) is correct.

PASSAGE V

28. H
Category: Scientific Reasoning
Difficulty: High
Getting to the Answer: Questions like this one would be easier with some chemistry knowledge, so you might want to save it for last if you don't like chemistry. Remember, though, there's still a way to the answer without outside knowledge. Two chemical equations appear in the passage. Both have the starting chemicals on the left and the resulting chemicals on the right. So, you can eliminate F and

G, because you want NaOH and HCl on the left side. The only difference between (H) and J is that J has 2 H_2Os on the right side, and (H) has just one. According to the equations in the passage, the total number of each element is the same on each side of the equation; there are two Hs and two Cls on the left side of the first equation, and two of each on the right. The same relationship holds in the second equation. So, you can determine that J is incorrect because it gives 4 Hs and 2 Os on the right side, and 2 Hs and 1 O on the left. Choice (H), then, is correct.

29. B
Category: Scientific Reasoning
Difficulty: High
Getting to the Answer: If you look at the answer choices first on this question, you'll see that you're really asked to explain whether there is more gas at this point in the experiment compared to the starting point, or less. Table 1 shows that the syringe was filled with 40 mL of H_2 and 40 mL of Cl_2 at the beginning of Trial 5. The light was flashed, and HCl was formed. Table 1 also shows that no H_2 or Cl_2 was left over after the reaction. So, you know that all of the gas was used up to make a liquid. You're also told at the end of the description of Experiment 1 that "equal numbers of different gas molecules are known to occupy equal volumes at the same pressure and temperature." So, decreasing the amount of gas over the course of the reaction, also decreases the pressure in the syringe. Choice (B) matches this perfectly.

30. H
Category: Patterns
Difficulty: Medium
Getting to the Answer: Ask yourself, "What are the patterns in the information?" Look at the reactions in Table 1 that use more Cl_2 than H_2—Trials 2, 3, and 4. In each of these trials, the amount of Cl_2 left over was equal to the amount of starting Cl_2 minus the amount of starting H_2. So, you can predict that 20 mL of Cl_2 reacting with 10 mL of H_2 will leave 10 mL of Cl_2 left over. This matches (H).

31. A
Category: Scientific Reasoning
Difficulty: Medium
Getting to the Answer: It's difficult to predict the researchers' assumptions, so work backwards from the answer choices on questions like this. Start by eliminating the answer choices that contain information not included in Experiment 1. C and D refer to Si, which appears only in Experiment 2, so you can eliminate those choices. B contradicts Trials 1, 5, and 6 of Experiment 1—each of these were successful without having Cl_2 left over. Only (A), then, must be true.

32. G
Category: Patterns
Difficulty: Medium
Getting to the Answer: Apply the patterns shown in the passage to new situations. Experiment 1 states that 1 H_2 and 1 Cl_2 combine to form 2 HCl; that is, 1 mL of H_2 requires 1 mL of Cl_2 to form 2 mL of HCl. The equation in the question stem states that 2 H_2 and 1 O_2 combine to form 2 H_2O; 2 mL of H_2 and 1 mL of O_2 form 2 mL of H_2O. So, to follow the patterns in the data, you can predict that 10 mL of O_2 will react with 20 mL of H_2 and leave 5 mL of H_2 unreacted. Choice (G) is correct.

33. C
Category: Scientific Reasoning
Difficulty: High
Getting to the Answer: You'll need the scientific method to answer this question. What were the results of Experiment 2? Experiment 2 combined $SiCl_4$ and H_2 to form liquid HCl. By measuring the changes in mass, students were able to tell how many $SiCl_4$ and H_2 molecules were needed to form one molecule of HCl. Go through the answer choices one by one and ask if each could cause an error in these results. Choice A could certainly cause an error. If unaccounted for reactions that produce different products took place, the $SiCl_4$, H_2, and $SiCl_4$ measurements would be wrong. Choice B could cause an error, since only the HCl that condensed in the conden-

sation chamber was measured. If some was missed, the equation students produced would be wrong. Choice (C) is correct. Nonreactive impurities would have no effect on the measured masses. Choice D is incorrect for the same reason (C) is correct. Reactive impurities would change the measured masses.

34. J
Category: Figure Interpretation
Difficulty: Low
Getting to the Answer: A limiting reagent is completely used up in a chemical reaction, which causes the reaction to stop before other reagents can be used up. Cl_2 is completely used up in Trials 1, 5, and 6. Because Trial 6 has leftover H_2, Cl_2 is a limiting reagent for that trial, making (J) the correct answer.

PASSAGE VI

35. A
Category: Figure Interpretation
Difficulty: Low
Getting to the Answer: Figure 4 compares slide time to θ. Find the slide time line on which points for both Earth and Mercury lie (the horizontal line that has both a square and a triangle marker). The slide time is 0.6 seconds, which represents a θ of 45° on Earth and a θ of 85° on Mercury, (A). Choice D is a trap because it gives the values of θ for which Neptune and Mercury (not Earth and Mercury) have the same slide time.

36. H
Category: Patterns
Difficulty: Medium
Getting to the Answer: Follow the shape of the given curve to extrapolate beyond the boundaries of the figures. Mercury is represented by the set of triangles. Follow the triangles to the far left of the graph and estimate where the next one would appear for $d_0 = 25$ cm. The slide time is just under 0.7 seconds for $d_0 = 30$ cm, and just over 0.7 seconds for $d_0 = 35$ cm. So you're looking for a slide time of a little less than 0.7 seconds. Choice (H), 0.6 seconds, makes the best

approximation. You could have immediately eliminated J because it is higher than 0.7 seconds. Choices
F and G are both too low, and do not fall in line with
the shape of the curve.

37. C
Category: Figure Interpretation
Difficulty: Medium
Getting to the Answer: Draw on the figures for questions like this. Draw a horizontal line from 1.2 seconds
on the *y*-axis until it intersects the curve that represents Mercury (the one with triangles). Then, draw a
line straight down from that point to the *x*-axis. The
line hits the *x*-axis somewhere between $\theta = 35°$ and
$\theta = 45°$. Only (C) falls within this range.

38. F
Category: Scientific Reasoning
Difficulty: Medium
Getting to the Answer: Don't be intimidated by the
equations in the answer choices. Any math on the
Science Test will be very straightforward. Figure 1
shows the box on the track. The distance between
the end of the track and the beginning of the box
is labeled d_0. If the box slides a distance *x* down the
track, you know that it must be closer to the edge of
the track than it started, so eliminate G and H. As the
box slides further down the track, *x* increases, and
the distance remaining must decrease. This is only
the case in (F).

39. D
Category: Figure Interpretation
Difficulty: High
Getting to the Answer: This question sounds
tough, but breaks down into a few simple steps if
you approach it methodically. According to Figure 4,
the slide time on Mercury's surface was 0.8 sec when
θ was approximately 55°. Interpolating between the
given points, the slide time on Earth's surface would
be 0.8 sec for a θ of approximately 38°. Because 38°
is 17° less than 55°, (D) is correct.

40. F
Category: Patterns
Difficulty: Medium
Getting to the Answer: Apply trends from the figures to make deductions about similar experiments.
According to Figure 3, slide times are shorter on the
surface of planets with larger accelerations due to
gravity. The acceleration due to gravity on Jupiter is
larger than that on any of the given planets, so the
slide times on Jupiter should be less than those on
any planet, as in (F).

WRITING TEST

LEVEL 6 ESSAY

The argument is about how student college loans should be structured, particularly whether interest should be charged and if there should be a cap on the loan amount concomitant with what the student will earn in his later career. There are several ways to look at each option, but the first perspective is the best, since it is fair and workable.

Firstly, as the issue states, student loans can take years to repay, even when the former students earn good salaries and repay the loan month by month. This is simply because the cost of a college education is so high. For all but the wealthiest of students, paying for college without a loan is prohibitive. My cousin spent years paying off her student loans and, in the long run, defaulted and had to declare bankruptcy. Surely this is not the intention of either the government or colleges. Loans are not special entitlements; they are fundamental to allow students of all economic backgrounds to attend college. As such, the government should not be making money from student loans. Interest rates make the loan amount even higher and more difficult to pay off, and can result in loan default. Charging only the principal needed to pay for college insures that students can not only pay the yearly tuition, but are also more likely to be able to settle the entire loan. If some students need more time, this would be a special circumstance, and it is then fair to add some further amount of payment as recognition that the original agreement was not fulfilled. This is the fairest solution and one that provides the greatest opportunity for students to go to college and pay off their loans.

The second option defines a college education as a commodity, which is something that can be bought and sold. Although it can be argued that a college education can be bought, it is not like oil or wheat. It is not used for the moment but for the future and it cannot be compared to loans for things such as cars or refrigerators. As we have all learned, college is an investment in the future. When considered on a supply and demand basis, it is even more important, since studies show that jobs requiring a college degree are in more and more demand. A capitalist market requires the ability to be competitive and creative; this is exactly what a college education provides. Educated students are far more important than almost anything else a loan can support, and any accommodations, including making college loans less expensive than other loans, is for the benefit of society and the future, and should be promoted, not prohibited.

Finally, the third point of view is simply ridiculous. There is absolutely no way to determine how much money a person will earn in the future. We can make considered guesses—lawyers will earn more than waiters—but there is no guarantee that the lawyer will not be fired and the waiter will not become a restaurant owner. Basing the loan amount on future earnings can also mean that the graduate has no opportunity to change his career from a high-earning one, such as a lawyer, to one that may truly be his heart's desire, such as being an artist. Furthermore, even if one were to train to be a lawyer, it is possible that he will not find a job that pays him the same amount of money the loan projected him to earn. At one time, investment counselors were earning a lot of money, and therefore would have been able to borrow a lot, but these days most investment counselors are doing other jobs, have no job, or may even be in jail. College graduates are just starting their careers; how well they do, what they earn, and whether they stay in their original jobs are unknown and cannot be used to determine a loan amount since it cannot be used to determine their future debt.

There is nothing more important than an educated and far-sighted generation of college graduates. They are the ones who will run the government, captain business, teach children. To deprive them of their college opportunity by making it too hard for them to either get or repay adequate loans is to deprive this country of those who will steer its future.

GRADER'S COMMENTS:

This essay exhibits strong and consistent writing skills. The introduction summarizes the arguments to come and heralds the author's point of view. Each following paragraph then discusses one perspective and its implications, using specific and appropriate examples. The conclusion reiterates the writer's opinion and moves it from specific to general, connecting it to a wider concept.

The organization is excellent, with good transitions ("Firstly," "The second option," "Finally") and word choice is on a college-level vocabulary with the use of words such as "concomitant," "entitlements," and "prohibited." There are no grammar mistakes or punctuation errors, and only one spelling error ("insures" for "ensures"). Sentence structure is somewhat varied, particularly with use of dashes in paragraph four. The inclusion of the cousin's loan experience provides a solid example, as do references to the need for an educated future generation. This is a strong essay and indicates good thinking, evaluating, and communication skills.

LEVEL 4 ESSAY

Almost all my friends in my high school are planning on going to college, but most of us won't be able to pay for it without loans. I know from the home loan my parents have that it's hard to pay loans back every month, so the less money you have to pay every month, the better it will be. That means that the best way to structure college loans is to not have to pay anything extra, like interest, so I can pay back my school loans as fast as possible. If I have to pay more, it will take me longer and be harder, and I may not be able to do it at all. The government makes plenty of money off taxes, and banks make plenty of money from credit cards, so why do they have to make more money from student loans?

People who think the loans should have extra money added to the total probably don't have kids in college and don't know how expansive it is and hard to pay back. They think that kids should have to pay the same kind of loans that my brother pays for his car, but cars and colleges are two different things, so why shouldn't the loans be different?

If people want to base my school loans on my future job, I think they are going to run into a lot of problems. I don't know what I want to be when I get out of college so I can't figure out what salary I'll earn. I guess by the time I'm a junior in college I'll know what I want to be so maybe the loans for the last two years can be figured out with my salary, but that won't work for the freshman and sophomore loans. And what if you can't find a job right after school or you decide to change your career? There are too many ways this approach could wind up being really complicated for it to be a good idea.

Since financial institutions only get their money back if people actually pay their monthly install-ments, you'd think they would do what they can to make it easy. Students are borrowing money for something that actually benefits society as a whole. We're not asking for college to be free (although that would be great!). All we want is a fair chance at paying the money we owe back. If the government and the banks want to get their money back they definitely should make the loans cheaper by not charging interest.

GRADER'S COMMENTS:

The writer of this essay remains focused on the issue throughout and develops a clear opinion in the first paragraph. Even though the support is couched primarily in terms of the author's own expectations, it does show some recognition of the complexity of the issue by providing some response to counter-arguments to the author's position. The rhe-torical questions at the ends of the first and second paragraphs are nice writing devices, but are not followed through.

The development of ideas is adequate, with a clear discussion of each perspective. In the second paragraph, rather than discussing the implications of the perspective, the writer primarily makes assumptions about the people who propose it. The thinking is underde-veloped, though the example of the car loan is solid. The first part of the third paragraph lacks a cogent argument. However, the author thinks more broadly about the issue when discussing the job market and career changes.

Though each perspective is clearly set apart in its own paragraph, there are few transition words to help it flow better. Word choice is correct but simple, with words such as "kids" and "cheaper," and "I guess," and sentence structure is awkward. There are a few spelling errors ("its" for "it's" and "expansive" for "expensive,") but overall, the grammar and spelling are correct.

The last paragraph reiterates the writer's viewpoint but is not developed in any way in order to extend the essay's ideas. The writer needs to think more deeply about the issue, develop her point of view with stronger arguments and more complex writing, and extend her ideas to a wider viewpoint.

LEVEL 2 ESSAY

Getting a goverment loan for college is really hard because you have to fill out a long and really hard application and even then if you get the loan you have to make sure you can pay it back on time. That means you have to make a lot of money so you can pay your loan and also have money to live. I think a better way to get money for college is to get a scholarship because you don't have to pay that back. I hope I will get a football scholarship because I'm good at that. Im the quarterback on the varsity team and I score a lot of points in football games and we're one of the top three teams in the high school division. If I get a football scholaship I can go to college and still play football and I won't have to pay any money for a loan. It doesnt matter if loans have extra money to pay back like interest because all that money is hard to pay back no matter how much it is. So a scholarship is better and that's what I want so I can go to college.

GRADER'S COMMENTS:

The author has written off-topic and completely missed the point of this issue; thus he has neglected to consider it from any perspective but his own. Though scholarships are available for college tuition, they are irrelevant to the task, thus the writer has neither understood the tasks nor fulfilled them in any way. He does not take a position on any perspective, nor support any one of them in a relevant way.

Sentence structure and word choice are simplistic, and there are multiple spelling and punctuation errors ("goverment" for "government," "scholaship" for "scholarship"). There is a noticeable lack of commas within sentences and missing apostrophes in the words "I'm" and "doesn't." The writing is redundant, especially the phrase "really hard," which appears twice in the first sentence.

The entire essay is contained in one paragraph with no transition words and no discernable introduction or conclusion. This essay does not show college-level thinking, writing, or attention to the task.

You can evaluate your essay and the model essay based on the following criteria, which is covered in the Practice Makes Perfect section of this book:

- Does the author discuss all three perspectives provided in the prompt?

- Is the author's own perspective clearly stated?

- Does the body of the essay assess and analyze each perspective?

- Is the relevance of each paragraph clear?

- Does the author start a new paragraph for each new idea?

- Is each sentence in a paragraph relevant to the point made in that paragraph?

- Are transitions clear?

- Is the essay easy to read? Is it engaging?

- Are sentences varied?

- Is vocabulary used effectively? Is college-level vocabulary used?

ACT Practice Test Eight
ANSWER SHEET

ENGLISH TEST

1. Ⓐ Ⓑ Ⓒ Ⓓ   11. Ⓐ Ⓑ Ⓒ Ⓓ   21. Ⓐ Ⓑ Ⓒ Ⓓ   31. Ⓐ Ⓑ Ⓒ Ⓓ   41. Ⓐ Ⓑ Ⓒ Ⓓ   51. Ⓐ Ⓑ Ⓒ Ⓓ   61. Ⓐ Ⓑ Ⓒ Ⓓ   71. Ⓐ Ⓑ Ⓒ Ⓓ
2. Ⓕ Ⓖ Ⓗ Ⓙ   12. Ⓕ Ⓖ Ⓗ Ⓙ   22. Ⓕ Ⓖ Ⓗ Ⓙ   32. Ⓕ Ⓖ Ⓗ Ⓙ   42. Ⓕ Ⓖ Ⓗ Ⓙ   52. Ⓕ Ⓖ Ⓗ Ⓙ   62. Ⓕ Ⓖ Ⓗ Ⓙ   72. Ⓕ Ⓖ Ⓗ Ⓙ
3. Ⓐ Ⓑ Ⓒ Ⓓ   13. Ⓐ Ⓑ Ⓒ Ⓓ   23. Ⓐ Ⓑ Ⓒ Ⓓ   33. Ⓐ Ⓑ Ⓒ Ⓓ   43. Ⓐ Ⓑ Ⓒ Ⓓ   53. Ⓐ Ⓑ Ⓒ Ⓓ   63. Ⓐ Ⓑ Ⓒ Ⓓ   73. Ⓐ Ⓑ Ⓒ Ⓓ
4. Ⓕ Ⓖ Ⓗ Ⓙ   14. Ⓕ Ⓖ Ⓗ Ⓙ   24. Ⓕ Ⓖ Ⓗ Ⓙ   34. Ⓕ Ⓖ Ⓗ Ⓙ   44. Ⓕ Ⓖ Ⓗ Ⓙ   54. Ⓕ Ⓖ Ⓗ Ⓙ   64. Ⓕ Ⓖ Ⓗ Ⓙ   74. Ⓕ Ⓖ Ⓗ Ⓙ
5. Ⓐ Ⓑ Ⓒ Ⓓ   15. Ⓐ Ⓑ Ⓒ Ⓓ   25. Ⓐ Ⓑ Ⓒ Ⓓ   35. Ⓐ Ⓑ Ⓒ Ⓓ   45. Ⓐ Ⓑ Ⓒ Ⓓ   55. Ⓐ Ⓑ Ⓒ Ⓓ   65. Ⓐ Ⓑ Ⓒ Ⓓ   75. Ⓐ Ⓑ Ⓒ Ⓓ
6. Ⓕ Ⓖ Ⓗ Ⓙ   16. Ⓕ Ⓖ Ⓗ Ⓙ   26. Ⓕ Ⓖ Ⓗ Ⓙ   36. Ⓕ Ⓖ Ⓗ Ⓙ   46. Ⓕ Ⓖ Ⓗ Ⓙ   56. Ⓕ Ⓖ Ⓗ Ⓙ   66. Ⓕ Ⓖ Ⓗ Ⓙ
7. Ⓐ Ⓑ Ⓒ Ⓓ   17. Ⓐ Ⓑ Ⓒ Ⓓ   27. Ⓐ Ⓑ Ⓒ Ⓓ   37. Ⓐ Ⓑ Ⓒ Ⓓ   47. Ⓐ Ⓑ Ⓒ Ⓓ   57. Ⓐ Ⓑ Ⓒ Ⓓ   67. Ⓐ Ⓑ Ⓒ Ⓓ
8. Ⓕ Ⓖ Ⓗ Ⓙ   18. Ⓕ Ⓖ Ⓗ Ⓙ   28. Ⓕ Ⓖ Ⓗ Ⓙ   38. Ⓕ Ⓖ Ⓗ Ⓙ   48. Ⓕ Ⓖ Ⓗ Ⓙ   58. Ⓕ Ⓖ Ⓗ Ⓙ   68. Ⓕ Ⓖ Ⓗ Ⓙ
9. Ⓐ Ⓑ Ⓒ Ⓓ   19. Ⓐ Ⓑ Ⓒ Ⓓ   29. Ⓐ Ⓑ Ⓒ Ⓓ   39. Ⓐ Ⓑ Ⓒ Ⓓ   49. Ⓐ Ⓑ Ⓒ Ⓓ   59. Ⓐ Ⓑ Ⓒ Ⓓ   69. Ⓐ Ⓑ Ⓒ Ⓓ
10. Ⓕ Ⓖ Ⓗ Ⓙ   20. Ⓕ Ⓖ Ⓗ Ⓙ   30. Ⓕ Ⓖ Ⓗ Ⓙ   40. Ⓕ Ⓖ Ⓗ Ⓙ   50. Ⓕ Ⓖ Ⓗ Ⓙ   60. Ⓕ Ⓖ Ⓗ Ⓙ   70. Ⓕ Ⓖ Ⓗ Ⓙ

MATHEMATICS TEST

1. Ⓐ Ⓑ Ⓒ Ⓓ Ⓔ   11. Ⓐ Ⓑ Ⓒ Ⓓ Ⓔ   21. Ⓐ Ⓑ Ⓒ Ⓓ Ⓔ   31. Ⓐ Ⓑ Ⓒ Ⓓ Ⓔ   41. Ⓐ Ⓑ Ⓒ Ⓓ Ⓔ   51. Ⓐ Ⓑ Ⓒ Ⓓ Ⓔ
2. Ⓕ Ⓖ Ⓗ Ⓙ Ⓚ   12. Ⓕ Ⓖ Ⓗ Ⓙ Ⓚ   22. Ⓕ Ⓖ Ⓗ Ⓙ Ⓚ   32. Ⓕ Ⓖ Ⓗ Ⓙ Ⓚ   42. Ⓕ Ⓖ Ⓗ Ⓙ Ⓚ   52. Ⓕ Ⓖ Ⓗ Ⓙ Ⓚ
3. Ⓐ Ⓑ Ⓒ Ⓓ Ⓔ   13. Ⓐ Ⓑ Ⓒ Ⓓ Ⓔ   23. Ⓐ Ⓑ Ⓒ Ⓓ Ⓔ   33. Ⓐ Ⓑ Ⓒ Ⓓ Ⓔ   43. Ⓐ Ⓑ Ⓒ Ⓓ Ⓔ   53. Ⓐ Ⓑ Ⓒ Ⓓ Ⓔ
4. Ⓕ Ⓖ Ⓗ Ⓙ Ⓚ   14. Ⓕ Ⓖ Ⓗ Ⓙ Ⓚ   24. Ⓕ Ⓖ Ⓗ Ⓙ Ⓚ   34. Ⓕ Ⓖ Ⓗ Ⓙ Ⓚ   44. Ⓕ Ⓖ Ⓗ Ⓙ Ⓚ   54. Ⓕ Ⓖ Ⓗ Ⓙ Ⓚ
5. Ⓐ Ⓑ Ⓒ Ⓓ Ⓔ   15. Ⓐ Ⓑ Ⓒ Ⓓ Ⓔ   25. Ⓐ Ⓑ Ⓒ Ⓓ Ⓔ   35. Ⓐ Ⓑ Ⓒ Ⓓ Ⓔ   45. Ⓐ Ⓑ Ⓒ Ⓓ Ⓔ   55. Ⓐ Ⓑ Ⓒ Ⓓ Ⓔ
6. Ⓕ Ⓖ Ⓗ Ⓙ Ⓚ   16. Ⓕ Ⓖ Ⓗ Ⓙ Ⓚ   26. Ⓕ Ⓖ Ⓗ Ⓙ Ⓚ   36. Ⓕ Ⓖ Ⓗ Ⓙ Ⓚ   46. Ⓕ Ⓖ Ⓗ Ⓙ Ⓚ   56. Ⓕ Ⓖ Ⓗ Ⓙ Ⓚ
7. Ⓐ Ⓑ Ⓒ Ⓓ Ⓔ   17. Ⓐ Ⓑ Ⓒ Ⓓ Ⓔ   27. Ⓐ Ⓑ Ⓒ Ⓓ Ⓔ   37. Ⓐ Ⓑ Ⓒ Ⓓ Ⓔ   47. Ⓐ Ⓑ Ⓒ Ⓓ Ⓔ   57. Ⓐ Ⓑ Ⓒ Ⓓ Ⓔ
8. Ⓕ Ⓖ Ⓗ Ⓙ Ⓚ   18. Ⓕ Ⓖ Ⓗ Ⓙ Ⓚ   28. Ⓕ Ⓖ Ⓗ Ⓙ Ⓚ   38. Ⓕ Ⓖ Ⓗ Ⓙ Ⓚ   48. Ⓕ Ⓖ Ⓗ Ⓙ Ⓚ   58. Ⓕ Ⓖ Ⓗ Ⓙ Ⓚ
9. Ⓐ Ⓑ Ⓒ Ⓓ Ⓔ   19. Ⓐ Ⓑ Ⓒ Ⓓ Ⓔ   29. Ⓐ Ⓑ Ⓒ Ⓓ Ⓔ   39. Ⓐ Ⓑ Ⓒ Ⓓ Ⓔ   49. Ⓐ Ⓑ Ⓒ Ⓓ Ⓔ   59. Ⓐ Ⓑ Ⓒ Ⓓ Ⓔ
10. Ⓕ Ⓖ Ⓗ Ⓙ Ⓚ   20. Ⓕ Ⓖ Ⓗ Ⓙ Ⓚ   30. Ⓕ Ⓖ Ⓗ Ⓙ Ⓚ   40. Ⓕ Ⓖ Ⓗ Ⓙ Ⓚ   50. Ⓕ Ⓖ Ⓗ Ⓙ Ⓚ   60. Ⓕ Ⓖ Ⓗ Ⓙ Ⓚ

READING TEST

1. Ⓐ Ⓑ Ⓒ Ⓓ   6. Ⓕ Ⓖ Ⓗ Ⓙ   11. Ⓐ Ⓑ Ⓒ Ⓓ   16. Ⓕ Ⓖ Ⓗ Ⓙ   21. Ⓐ Ⓑ Ⓒ Ⓓ   26. Ⓕ Ⓖ Ⓗ Ⓙ   31. Ⓐ Ⓑ Ⓒ Ⓓ   36. Ⓕ Ⓖ Ⓗ Ⓙ
2. Ⓕ Ⓖ Ⓗ Ⓙ   7. Ⓐ Ⓑ Ⓒ Ⓓ   12. Ⓕ Ⓖ Ⓗ Ⓙ   17. Ⓐ Ⓑ Ⓒ Ⓓ   22. Ⓕ Ⓖ Ⓗ Ⓙ   27. Ⓐ Ⓑ Ⓒ Ⓓ   32. Ⓕ Ⓖ Ⓗ Ⓙ   37. Ⓐ Ⓑ Ⓒ Ⓓ
3. Ⓐ Ⓑ Ⓒ Ⓓ   8. Ⓕ Ⓖ Ⓗ Ⓙ   13. Ⓐ Ⓑ Ⓒ Ⓓ   18. Ⓕ Ⓖ Ⓗ Ⓙ   23. Ⓐ Ⓑ Ⓒ Ⓓ   28. Ⓕ Ⓖ Ⓗ Ⓙ   33. Ⓐ Ⓑ Ⓒ Ⓓ   38. Ⓕ Ⓖ Ⓗ Ⓙ
4. Ⓕ Ⓖ Ⓗ Ⓙ   9. Ⓐ Ⓑ Ⓒ Ⓓ   14. Ⓕ Ⓖ Ⓗ Ⓙ   19. Ⓐ Ⓑ Ⓒ Ⓓ   24. Ⓕ Ⓖ Ⓗ Ⓙ   29. Ⓐ Ⓑ Ⓒ Ⓓ   34. Ⓕ Ⓖ Ⓗ Ⓙ   39. Ⓐ Ⓑ Ⓒ Ⓓ
5. Ⓐ Ⓑ Ⓒ Ⓓ   10. Ⓕ Ⓖ Ⓗ Ⓙ   15. Ⓐ Ⓑ Ⓒ Ⓓ   20. Ⓕ Ⓖ Ⓗ Ⓙ   25. Ⓐ Ⓑ Ⓒ Ⓓ   30. Ⓕ Ⓖ Ⓗ Ⓙ   35. Ⓐ Ⓑ Ⓒ Ⓓ   40. Ⓕ Ⓖ Ⓗ Ⓙ

SCIENCE TEST

1. Ⓐ Ⓑ Ⓒ Ⓓ   6. Ⓕ Ⓖ Ⓗ Ⓙ   11. Ⓐ Ⓑ Ⓒ Ⓓ   16. Ⓕ Ⓖ Ⓗ Ⓙ   21. Ⓐ Ⓑ Ⓒ Ⓓ   26. Ⓕ Ⓖ Ⓗ Ⓙ   31. Ⓐ Ⓑ Ⓒ Ⓓ   36. Ⓕ Ⓖ Ⓗ Ⓙ
2. Ⓕ Ⓖ Ⓗ Ⓙ   7. Ⓐ Ⓑ Ⓒ Ⓓ   12. Ⓕ Ⓖ Ⓗ Ⓙ   17. Ⓐ Ⓑ Ⓒ Ⓓ   22. Ⓕ Ⓖ Ⓗ Ⓙ   27. Ⓐ Ⓑ Ⓒ Ⓓ   32. Ⓕ Ⓖ Ⓗ Ⓙ   37. Ⓐ Ⓑ Ⓒ Ⓓ
3. Ⓐ Ⓑ Ⓒ Ⓓ   8. Ⓕ Ⓖ Ⓗ Ⓙ   13. Ⓐ Ⓑ Ⓒ Ⓓ   18. Ⓕ Ⓖ Ⓗ Ⓙ   23. Ⓐ Ⓑ Ⓒ Ⓓ   28. Ⓕ Ⓖ Ⓗ Ⓙ   33. Ⓐ Ⓑ Ⓒ Ⓓ   38. Ⓕ Ⓖ Ⓗ Ⓙ
4. Ⓕ Ⓖ Ⓗ Ⓙ   9. Ⓐ Ⓑ Ⓒ Ⓓ   14. Ⓕ Ⓖ Ⓗ Ⓙ   19. Ⓐ Ⓑ Ⓒ Ⓓ   24. Ⓕ Ⓖ Ⓗ Ⓙ   29. Ⓐ Ⓑ Ⓒ Ⓓ   34. Ⓕ Ⓖ Ⓗ Ⓙ   39. Ⓐ Ⓑ Ⓒ Ⓓ
5. Ⓐ Ⓑ Ⓒ Ⓓ   10. Ⓕ Ⓖ Ⓗ Ⓙ   15. Ⓐ Ⓑ Ⓒ Ⓓ   20. Ⓕ Ⓖ Ⓗ Ⓙ   25. Ⓐ Ⓑ Ⓒ Ⓓ   30. Ⓕ Ⓖ Ⓗ Ⓙ   35. Ⓐ Ⓑ Ⓒ Ⓓ   40. Ⓕ Ⓖ Ⓗ Ⓙ

ENGLISH TEST

45 Minutes—75 Questions

Directions: In the following five passages, certain words and phrases are underlined and numbered. In the right-hand column are alternatives for each underlined portion. Select the one that best conveys the idea, creates the most grammatically correct sentence, or is most consistent with the style and tone of the passage. If you decide that the original version is best, select NO CHANGE. You may also find questions that ask about the entire passage or a section of the passage. These questions will correspond to small, numbered boxes in the text. For these questions, decide which choice best accomplishes the purpose set out in the question stem. After you've selected the best choice, fill in the corresponding oval on your Answer Grid. For some questions, you'll need to read the context in order to answer correctly. Be sure to read until you have enough information to determine the correct answer choice.

PASSAGE I

A SCREENWRITING CAREER

[1]

Wanting to have success as a Hollywood screenwriter, if
                                                        1
you do, you should be aware of the difficulties that come
  1
along

with this career and its development. Very <u>less</u> budding
                                                2
screenwriters attain success by selling, let alone producing, their screenplays. Furthermore, even successful
screenwriters report living stressful and dissatisfied,
though wealthy, lives.

[2]

The first difficulty encountered by budding screenwriters is the lack of a formal career path. A recent college graduate cannot approach the career center at his

1. **A.** NO CHANGE
    B. If you want to succeed as a Hollywood screenwriter,
    C. Whether or not wanting to succeed as a Hollywood screenwriter,
    D. Having decided if you want to or not succeed as a Hollywood screenwriter,

2. **F.** NO CHANGE
    G. little less
    H. many few
    J. few

GO ON TO THE NEXT PAGE ⟶

or her school or <u>find time for extracurricular activities.</u>
3
While several successful screenwriters have written

guides that outline possibilities for success, their

<u>proposed suggestions only highlight and draw attention</u>
4
<u>to the</u> disparity of their experiences.
4

[3]

Unlike its value in other professional pursuits,

<u>a college education are</u> not necessarily a career boost for
5
a budding screenwriter. In fact, a college education can

have the reverse effect on a screenwriter. The academic

study of literature or film may help a budding screen-

writer to produce higher quality work, but such an edu-

cation delays its recipient from competing in the film

industry. <u>This also tends to hold true for actors.</u> While
6
a college graduate spends his or her late teens and early

twenties studying, the budding screenwriters

who do not attend college <u>begins honing</u> their craft and
7
competing for work several years earlier. In a career

3. Assuming that all are true, which choice is the most logical and appropriate in context?

A. NO CHANGE

B. read the classified ads in order to find screenwriting opportunities.

C. understand the difficulties of his or her chosen career.

D. stumble into an opportunity to work in the field.

4. F. NO CHANGE

G. proposed suggestions only draw attention to the noteworthy

H. proposed plans merely highlight the emphasized

J. suggestions only highlight the

5. A. NO CHANGE

B. a college education, is

C. a college education is

D. it is, a college education

6. F. NO CHANGE

G. Actors also find this to be true for themselves.

H. This has similar repercussions for actors.

J. OMIT the underlined portion.

7. A. NO CHANGE

B. begins to hone

C. begin honing

D. has begun honing

GO ON TO THE NEXT PAGE ⟹

path that usually requires years to develop, <u>you can see</u>
₈
<u>that education is relevant.</u>
₈

[4]

Moreover, <u>the debt of a college education</u>
₉
<u>acquired at a prestigious school</u> may lead many young
₉
screenwriters to surrender early to the allure of steady, if

not glamorous, work and pay. Those without college

educations often cannot escape to "fallback" <u>careers; this</u>
₁₀
lack of options bolsters their drive to succeed. Further-

more, those without college educations are less averse to

the low-wage <u>jobs, aspiring screenwriters</u> are forced to
₁₁
take in order to pay living expenses while saving blocks

of time to hone their craft.

[5]

The very few screenwriters who succeed often

find <u>that's the realities of their</u> day-to-day lives are far
₁₂
different from their glamorous preconceptions and the

media's idealistic portrayals. While they can earn very

high salaries, successful Hollywood screenwriters often

feel more stressed and powerless than they did when

they struggled. A <u>Hollywood screenwriters reputation</u>
₁₃
always hinges on the success of his or her last screen-

play. This volatile situation produces a high level of

8. Which choice provides the clearest and most logical transition to Paragraph 4?
   F. NO CHANGE
   G. late entry can create a substantial disadvantage.
   H. the months in school add up quickly.
   J. one can recognize that delayed entry may be disadvantageous.

9. A. NO CHANGE
   B. though universities offer work-study programs to help students pay for school, many graduate with debt; this burden
   C. the burden of student loans
   D. student loans which

10. F. NO CHANGE
    G. careers; this,
    H. careers so, this
    J. careers this

11. A. NO CHANGE
    B. jobs, these aspiring screenwriters
    C. jobs these aspiring screenwriters
    D. jobs that aspiring screenwriters

12. F. NO CHANGE
    G. that the realities of there
    H. there the realities of their
    J. that the realities of their

13. A. NO CHANGE
    B. Hollywood screenwriter's reputation
    C. screenwriters Hollywood reputation
    D. reputation of a Hollywood screenwriter's

GO ON TO THE NEXT PAGE ⇨

stress and pressure to <u>continually produce more and</u>
                                                    14
<u>better</u> work. Furthermore, the Hollywood hierarchy
14
places studio executives, producers, directors, and star

actors above screenwriters in both pay and importance.

Thus, even the most successful screenwriters must yield

creative power to individuals who often have very little

knowledge of the craft of screenwriting.

[6]

Regardless of the hardships of initially succeed-

ing and then thriving in the screenwriting profession,

young people move to Los Angeles every year to pursue

this career. <u>If they succeed, they will find that studio</u>
                                           15
<u>executives have more decision-making power than they</u>
                                                           15
<u>do.</u> If you are one of these people, please research and

learn as much as possible about the vicissitudes as well as

the potential triumphs of this profession.

PASSAGE II

THE SWALLOWS OF SAN JUAN CAPISTRANO

[1]

The oldest building still in use in California is the

Mission at San Juan Capistrano, the seventh in the chain

of California missions built by Spanish priests in the late

eighteenth and early nineteenth centuries. The mission has

gained fame as the <u>well-known summer residence</u> of
                                          16

14. F. NO CHANGE
   G. churn out improving and increasing
   H. be more productive and improved
   J. raising the stakes of

15. A. NO CHANGE
   B. Those who become successful find that studio executives have the power to make decisions.
   C. The power to make most decisions rests with studio executives, not successful screenwriters.
   D. OMIT the underlined portion.

16. F. NO CHANGE
   G. seasonal residence for the summer
   H. summer residence
   J. residential summer home

birds.
17

[2]

[1] For centuries, these cliff swallows have migrated to and from California every year in a cloud-like formation. [2] The swallows leave the town of San Juan Capistrano, halfway between San Diego and Los Angeles, around October 23. [3] They then journey 7,000 miles to spend the winter in Argentina. [4] Every spring, the birds faithfully return from Argentina to nest and for bearing their young in the valley near the
18
mission. [5] On March 19, mission bells ring, a fiesta is held, and

a parade snaking through the streets as throngs of locals
19
and tourists celebrate the birds' return.

[3]

According to legend, the swallows were seeking refuge from an innkeeper who had destroyed their muddy nests when they discovered the mission. Biolo-
20
gists have a different explanation for how the birds

might of developed their fondness for the mission. After
21
observing the swallows' behavior and noting that the birds build their nests out of mud, biologists have

postulated that the swallows real chose the mission due
22
to its proximity to two rivers. These rivers provide the

17. Which choice creates the most specific and logical transition to the following paragraph?
   A. NO CHANGE
   B. migrating animals.
   C. the swallows of San Juan Capistrano.
   D. Argentinean species.

18. F. NO CHANGE
    G. with bearing
    H. bearing
    J. bear

19. A. NO CHANGE
    B. snaked
    C. snakes
    D. is snaking

20. F. NO CHANGE
    G. nests when discovering
    H. nests, when
    J. nests, when finding

21. A. NO CHANGE
    B. might have
    C. may of
    D. may

22. F. NO CHANGE
    G. really chosened
    H. really chose
    J. real choosing

GO ON TO THE NEXT PAGE

swallows with ample mud for building their funnel-like

nests <u>of which</u>
      23

they return year after year. ⬚24

[4]

[1] One aspect of the legend, however, rings

true. [2] The swallows, sensing that they will be pro-

tected within the mission walls, return to the compound

every spring. [3] In fact, beyond the church walls, the

entire city has sought toprotect the swallows. ⬚25

[5]

[1] Although the <u>community clearly</u> sees the
                  26

importance of providing a home for the swallows, some

problems have arisen in recent years. [2] Due to the

23. **A.** NO CHANGE
    B. to which
    C. by which
    D. which

24. Of the following true statements, which is the best choice to insert here in order to further support the biologists' explanation that the swallows chose the mission because of its proximity to two rivers?

    F. The swallows will repair a damaged nest instead of building an entirely new nest.
    G. The rivers also supply insects upon which the swallows feed.
    H. Both rivers are also home to a wide variety of fish.
    J. The location of the mission near the rivers also provides other advantages for the swallows.

25. Which of the following true sentences, if added here, would make the most logical transition from Paragraph 4 to Paragraph 5?

    A. The crowds that welcome the swallows back each spring reveal the delight that people take in the swallows.
    B. The birds have benefited from the community's interest in them.
    C. San Juan Capistrano municipal ordinances declare the city a bird sanctuary and outlaw the destruction or damaging of swallow nests.
    D. However, these protections do not extend to other migrating species.

26. **F.** NO CHANGE
    G. community, clearly
    H. community clearly,
    J. community clear

GO ON TO THE NEXT PAGE ⇨

city's growth and development, the number of insects has declined, causing many of the swallows to locate farther from the mission in the town center and closer to the open areas where their food source thrives. [3] Large groups of swallows have found other nesting sites in the <u>area, usually in the hills</u> due to
27
disruptions from recent restorations of the historic

buildings at the mission. [4] <u>Fortunately, city and mis-</u>
28
<u>sion officials have started,</u> to respond to these prob-
28
lems.

[5] For example, <u>to attempt at enticing</u> the birds back
29
home, mission workers have strewn insects about the mission's grounds.

27. **A.** NO CHANGE
     B. area; usually in the hills,
     C. area—usually in the hills—
     D. area, having been usual in the hills,

28. **F.** NO CHANGE
     G. Fortunately city and mission officials have started,
     H. Fortunately, city and mission officials have started
     J. Fortunately, city and mission officials, have started

29. **A.** NO CHANGE
     B. in an attempt to entice
     C. in an attempt's enticement
     D. in an attempt of enticing

Question 30 asks about the preceding passage as a whole.

30. The writer is considering adding the following sentence to further explain how residents of San Juan Capistrano feel about the swallows:

     Many residents and visitors miss the huge clouds of swallows descending upon the mission as in the past decades.

     The most logical place to insert this sentence would be directly after:

     F. Sentence 5 in Paragraph 2.
     G. Sentence 3 in Paragraph 4.
     H. Sentence 1 in Paragraph 5.
     J. Sentence 3 in Paragraph 5.

GO ON TO THE NEXT PAGE ⟶

PASSAGE III

ROOT FOR THE HOME TEAM?

If you are young and love football, it is advantageous to live near a large sporting-goods store that carries a wide variety of paraphernalia from different teams. My daughter and I visit our local store at least once a year to buy another new football jersey for yet another team. Although my daughter is a fan of our <u>city</u> professional
31
team, she frequently changes her jersey to match that of her favorite player.

A free agent is a professional football player who is no longer under contract with a team, which means he can choose the team <u>which</u> he wants to play.
32

In the NFL today, players can become free agents <u>easy,</u>
33
so they often switch teams several times during their careers. Things were much different when I was growing up. My favorite player was on the same team for his entire <u>career I had</u> one jersey. My daughter has bought
34
over eight team jerseys in the past six years! At seventy-five dollars a shirt, this is not a sustainable trend.

There are many disadvantages to <u>free agency.</u>
35
<u>When my</u> daughter and I went to pre-season training
35
practice to get a preview of this year's home team, we constantly consulted the team roster to figure out the new line-up, because there were so many new players. At one point, a number of fans even started to cheer for

31. **A.** NO CHANGE
    B. city's
    C. cities
    D. cities'

32. **F.** NO CHANGE
    G. at which
    H. for which
    J. OMIT the underlined portion.

33. **A.** NO CHANGE
    B. easily
    C. easiest
    D. easier

34. **F.** NO CHANGE
    G. career, so I had
    H. career, because I had
    J. career, and then I had

35. **A.** NO CHANGE
    B. free agency: for when my
    C. free agency, when my
    D. free agency when my

GO ON TO THE NEXT PAGE ⟶

a player who, was no longer with the team, because they
                    36
did not realize someone new was wearing his number.

A second disadvantage of free agency is lack of camara-
            37
derie and cohesion.

Football is the ultimate team sport, in which

players must depend upon each other to win. A team
                      38
trains strategizes and plays together for months. The
        39
players learn each other's strengths and weaknesses.

Eleven players are on the field at one time, and their goal
                                          40
is to stop the other team from progressing down the

field. If any one of those eleven players leaves the team,

it disrupt the dynamics and cohesion that the entire
   41
team has worked together to build.

A third disadvantage is the loss of team dynas-
         42
ties. When I was a teenager, my home team made the

playoffs for three years in a row. Since free agency was

introduced, our team has not made it back to the playoffs

for ten years. When we did return 10 years later, my
                                  43
daughter fell in love with the team and our star quarter-

back.

36. **F.** NO CHANGE
  G. player who was no longer with the team,
  H. player, who was no longer, with the team
  J. player who was no longer, with the team

37. **A.** NO CHANGE
  B. (Begin new paragraph) A second disad-
       vantage of
  C. (Begin new paragraph) Secondly
  D. (Do NOT begin new paragraph) A final
       disadvantage of

38. **F.** NO CHANGE
  G. to win on each other
  H. upon winning with each other
  J. OMIT the underlined portion.

39. **A.** NO CHANGE
  B. trains, strategizes, and plays,
  C. trains strategizes, and plays
  D. trains, strategizes, and plays

40. **F.** NO CHANGE
  G. at one time, because their goal
  H. at one time, yet their goal
  J. at one time, or their goal

41. **A.** NO CHANGE
  B. disrupted
  C. disrupts
  D. disrupting

42. **F.** NO CHANGE
  G. A loss is the third disadvantage
  H. A disadvantage is the third loss
  J. The third loss is a disadvantage

43. **A.** NO CHANGE
  B. to the Super Bowl
  C. 10 years' later
  D. OMIT the underlined portion.

GO ON TO THE NEXT PAGE

That player moved to another team; <u>because</u> our home
44
team has not had a winning season since he left, his new

team has won the

Superbowl for the last two years. 45

PASSAGE IV

THE RIGHT TO WRITE

[1]

Going to see a play is a cultural tradition that

has been passed on for thousands of years. Although

theater is a form of art and entertainment, it is also a

highly competitive business, especially for playwrights.

Many plays are written, but <u>it is only</u> a select few are
46
produced and seen by the public, and often with strings

attached. Playwright José Rivera is an example of a

contemporary playwright <u>that</u> has fought for the right
47
to have his work produced and seen in the way he

intended it.

[2]

Rivera was born in San Juan, Puerto Rico, in

1955, but his family moved to New York when he was

four years old. <u>Yet</u> many of Rivera's relatives had already
48
moved to the Bronx, a bustling neighborhood in

New York, Rivera's father wanted to live in a place that

felt more like a small town. So they moved to a quarter

acre of land in Long Island, New York, which at the time

had dirt roads and woods.

44. **F.** NO CHANGE
   G. however
   H. therefore
   J. while

45. Which of the following sentences, if added, would best conclude the essay?
   A. Football is a great sport that will never decrease in popularity.
   B. Free agency has a variety of benefits, but the negatives outweigh the positives.
   C. Free agency allows players to change teams frequently, which has made it increasingly difficult to root for a home team that never stays the same.
   D. One thing will never change, and that is the home team.

46. **F.** NO CHANGE
   G. there are only
   H. only
   J. there only is

47. **A.** NO CHANGE
   B. who
   C. which
   D. whom

48. **F.** NO CHANGE
   G. Meanwhile,
   H. However,
   J. Although

GO ON TO THE NEXT PAGE

[3]

[49] From an early age, Rivera knew that he
wanted to be a writer. As a kid, he wrote comic strips, a

novel about baseball, <u>and essays in response to photo-</u>
                                          50
<u>graphs, from</u> *Life* magazine. When he was in middle
     50
school, he saw a play

that inspired him <u>when he saw the play that he wanted</u>
                                     51

to become a playwright. He <u>writes</u> several plays during
                                         52
high school and in college.

[4]

<u>Rivera, after graduating, returned to New York,</u>
                            53
<u>from college</u> determined to continue writing. He
   53
worked at a bookstore

and became <u>then</u> a copy editor at a publishing company.
                  54
Eventually, Rivera found an artistic home in a

playwriting group called the Theater Matrix; the group

49. The most logical placement of Paragraph 3 is

   A. where it is now.

   B. after Paragraph 1.

   C. after Paragraph 4.

   D. after Paragraph 5.

50. **F.** NO CHANGE

   G. and essays in response to photographs from

   H. and essays in response to photographs from:

   J. and essays in response to photographs; from

51. **A.** NO CHANGE

   B. that when he saw the play he wanted

   C. that he wanted when he saw that play

   D. OMIT the underlined portion.

52. **F.** NO CHANGE

   G. is writing

   H. has written

   J. wrote

53. **A.** NO CHANGE

   B. Rivera returned from college after graduating, to New York,

   C. After graduating from college, Rivera returned to New York,

   D. Rivera, from graduating, returned to New York,

54. **F.** NO CHANGE

   G. (Place before *became*)

   H. (Place before *publishing*)

   J. (Place after *company*)

GO ON TO THE NEXT PAGE ⟩

met on Monday nights to share their work. One of the

plays he wrote and produced, *The House of Roman*
                                              55
Iglesia, received a good review by *The New York Times.*
                55
This was an important step

in Rivera's career receiving a good review from a major
                  56
publication led to more work. The famous television

producer Norman Lear read the review and immedi-

ately offered Rivera a job writing for Embassy Television

in California.

[5]

In order to make a living, Rivera accepted the job. He

learned a lot from the process of writing for television

shows, but there were sacrifices he had to make. He

missed writing plays and living in New York. [57] Rivera

also discovered that in the entertainment business, he

was often labeled and identified by his ethnicity. Rivera

was proud of his cultural heritage but wanted to be

acknowledged for his talent.

[5]

After many years of hard work and perseverance,

Rivera has received the recognition he deserves through

countless productions of his plays and the numer-

ous awards he has won for playwriting. Despite the

---

55. A. NO CHANGE

B. produced *The House of Roman Iglesia,* received

C. produced, *The House of Roman Iglesia* received

D. produced *The House of Roman Iglesia* received

56. F. NO CHANGE

G. career, receiving

H. career; receiving

J. career receiving.

57. If the writer wanted to reinforce the main point made in Paragraph 5, which sentence would she add here?

A. He also missed the reward of owning his work, because his writing became the property of the television shows.

B. California is a beautiful state with a variety of places to visit, from beaches to major cities.

C. He had the opportunity to write for television shows such as *Family Matters* and *Eerie, Indiana.*

D. While in California, he became a founding member of a theater company in the city of Los Angeles.

GO ON TO THE NEXT PAGE ⟩

challenges of show business, José Rivera <u>has became</u>
                                              58
an important playwright whose work has an impact on

audiences worldwide.

58. **F.** NO CHANGE

  G. is became

  H. has become

  J. have become

Questions 59 and 60 ask about the preceding passage as a whole.

59. Does this essay successfully describe the challenges faced by playwrights in the entertainment business?

  A. The essay is not successful; it is a biography of the playwright José Rivera.

  B. The essay is not successful; it portrays playwriting as a fun and rewarding career.

  C. The essay is successful; it describes playwriting as an impossible dream for only the very lucky.

  D. The essay is successful; it demonstrates the challenges through the life and work of José Rivera.

60. The writer is considering adding the following sentence:

  The contrast between small-town and city life became an influence on Rivera's work.

  The best placement for this detail is in:

  F. Paragraph 1.

  G. Paragraph 2.

  H. Paragraph 5.

  J. Paragraph 6.

GO ON TO THE NEXT PAGE

PASSAGE V

SIGNATURE OF THE TIME

[1] The home of Tyler Gregory looks like an abandoned bureaucratic archive. [2] Almost all of the available space <u>being crammed with old books</u> or
61
covered with folios and documents. [3] Dr. Gregory, a psychologist, first began collecting old documents as a hobby.

[4] What was initially a <u>hobby quickly became a life's</u>
62
passion and devotion. [5] Predictably, several papers in Dr. Gregory's collection, which includes a faded

but detailed inn receipt, <u>is</u> signed by John Hancock.
63
[6] Proudly displayed, the John Hancock documents

<u>had represented</u> Dr. Gregory's work: graphology. [7]
64
Unlike other rare and vintage document enthusiasts, Dr. Gregory collects only documents that bear famous signatures. [65]

61. **A.** NO CHANGE
    B. was crammed with old books or is
    C. is crammed with old books or
    D. crammed with old books or

62. **F.** NO CHANGE
    G. hobby, quickly became a life's
    H. hobby quickly became a life's,
    J. hobby: quickly became a life's

63. **A.** NO CHANGE
    B. are
    C. was
    D. OMIT the underlined portion.

64. **F.** NO CHANGE
    G. represent
    H. represented
    J. would have represented

65. To maintain the logic and coherence of this paragraph, Sentence 7 should be placed:

    A. where it is now.
    B. after Sentence 1.
    C. after Sentence 3.
    D. after Sentence 4.

GO ON TO THE NEXT PAGE ⇨

Graphology, <u>a growing field,</u> is used to authenticate
                    66
documents in court trials and other legal proceedings,

but it has other, less familiar uses as well. Psychologists

can use graphology to analyze a patient's psyche. Many

patients

cannot explain their problems, <u>but psychologists have</u>
                                              67
<u>techniques to help patients learn to express themselves.</u>
                      67
Psychologists and graphologists have noted that hand-

writing

is a subconscious expression of inner thoughts. Many

of the issues involuntarily revealed <u>of</u> a subject's
                                       68
handwriting remain unknown to the subject herself.

Unlike the patients of most psychologists who use

graphology, however, Dr. Gregory's subjects are dead.

Dr. Gregory once practiced clinical <u>psychology in the</u>
                                            69
<u>past,</u> but his interest in graphology is a more historical

one. He studies the handwriting of

66. Which of the following true choices provides information that is most relevant and meaningful to the essay in its entirety?

   F. NO CHANGE
   G. or handwriting analysis,
   H. which has been practiced for decades,
   J. as a professional endeavor,

67. After reviewing the essay, the writer wants to insert a statement at this point that would lead into the next sentence. Given that all of the choices are true, which one best accomplishes the writer's purpose?

   A. NO CHANGE
   B. and this is one reason they seek help from professionals.
   C. but their handwriting often can.
   D. so analyzing the psyche can be challenging.

68. F. NO CHANGE
    G. from
    H. by
    J. as

69. A. NO CHANGE
    B. psychology for a time,
    C. psychology at an earlier period in his life,
    D. psychology,

GO ON TO THE NEXT PAGE

historical <u>figures, hoping to</u> better understand their
                        70
personalities. Dr. Gregory's interest in historical

personalities stems from an interdisciplinary desire

to apply psychological theories to the explanation of

historical events. Historians and political scientists have

long sought to apply psychology and its theories to

their work, but they have not always met with success.

While such theories as organizational psychology and

cognitive dissonance have illuminated some historical

decisions, they have done so neither definitively nor

broadly. 71

70. Of the following alternatives to the under-
    lined portion, which choice would NOT be
    acceptable?

    F. figures in order to
    G. figures since hoping to
    H. figures with the hope that he will
    J. figures. He hopes to

71. If added here, which of the following
    sentences would be the best choice to
    conclude this paragraph and create an
    effective transition to the next one?

    A. This lack of widespread success has
       discouraged many in the field, but not
       Dr. Gregory.

    B. The scarcity of information regarding
       the personalities of historical figures has
       been the biggest obstacle.

    C. However, these theories are likely to
       gain ground as more historians and
       political scientists study their subjects
       through a psychological lens.

    D. These theories have most frequently
       been applied to events from the 18th
       and 19th centuries.

GO ON TO THE NEXT PAGE

Unlike current in-depth information from multiple media sources, scarcely any record exists of the private personalities and lives of history's greatest figures. The records that do exist paint skewed <u>pictures, for they</u> come almost entirely from friends, enemies, or the historical figures themselves. Thus, Dr. Gregory uses graphology to study and understand the personalities and inner lives of important men and women who lived so long ago.

Dr. Gregory, along with most graphologists, believes that a person's signature reveals more about that person's personality than normal handwriting. The signature legally and traditionally conveys the mark of an individual. This supports Dr. Gregory's <u>belief that</u> the shape of a signature also serves as a psychological

stamp. According to Dr. Gregory, a person <u>has been</u> both consciously and unconsciously imprinting key aspects of his personality while he forms a signature. Those aspects have led Dr. Gregory to infer many personal details about historical figures. Such details are now being used by historians in their analysis of historical decisions.

72. Of the following alternatives to the underlined portion, which choice would NOT be acceptable?

    F. pictures; they

    G. pictures. They

    H. pictures, as they

    J. pictures they

73. **A.** NO CHANGE

    B. belief, that

    C. belief that,

    D. belief: that

74. **F.** NO CHANGE

    G. had been

    H. will be

    J. is

GO ON TO THE NEXT PAGE ▷

Question 75 asks about the preceding passage as a whole.

75. Suppose the writer had intended to write a short essay about an example of one area of study influencing another area of study. Would this essay achieve the writer's goal?

   A. Yes, because the essay explains how personality traits determined through analyzing a historical individual's handwriting can be used to form a psychological study of such figures and their roles in historical events.

   B. Yes, because the essay compares the research process of graphologists to the research process of historians.

   C. No, because the essay focuses on Dr. Gregory, who turned his hobby into an intellectual pursuit.

   D. No, because the essay does not discuss the findings of historians who have applied psychological theories to historical figures and events.

MATHEMATICS TEST

60 Minutes—60 Questions

Directions: Solve each of the following problems, select the correct answer, and then fill in the corresponding oval on your Answer Grid.

Don't linger over problems that are too time-consuming. Do as many as you can, then come back to the others in the time permitted.

You may use a calculator on this test. Some questions, however, may be easier to answer without the use of a calculator.

Note: Unless the question says otherwise, assume all of the following:

1. Illustrative figures are *not* necessarily drawn to scale.

2. All geometric figures lie in a plane.

3. The term *line* indicates a straight line.

4. The term *average* indicates arithmetic mean.

1. If $2x - 6 = 18$, then $x = $?

   A. 1.5
   B. 3.0
   C. 6.0
   D. 12.0
   E. 24.0

2. Consider the following two logical statements relating to triangle *RST*.

   If the length of side $\overline{RS}$ is 5, then the length of side $\overline{ST}$ is 8.

   The length of side $\overline{ST}$ is not 8.

   If both of these statements are true, then it follows that the length of:

   F. $\overline{RS}$ is NOT 5.
   G. $\overline{RS}$ is 5.
   H. $\overline{RS}$ is 8.
   J. $\overline{ST}$ is 5.
   K. $\overline{ST}$ is NOT 5.

3. In a raffle, Mark must draw a ticket at random from a bag. The probability that he will draw a winning ticket is 0.3. What is the probability that he will draw a losing ticket?

   A. 0.0
   B. 0.1
   C. 0.7
   D. 1.0
   E. 1.3

4. On the last geometry test, Anna's score was 94. Two of her friends each scored 89. What is the average score of these three students?

   F. $94 + \dfrac{89}{2}$

   G. $\dfrac{94}{3} + \dfrac{89}{2}$

   H. $\dfrac{94 + 89}{2}$

   J. $\dfrac{94 + 89}{3}$

   K. $\dfrac{94 + 2(89)}{3}$

GO ON TO THE NEXT PAGE ▷

5. On Monday Tom received a bag of candy for his birthday and ate half of it. On Tuesday he ate half of the remaining candy, and on Wednesday he ate half of what remained from Tuesday. If 6 pieces of candy then remained, how many pieces of candy did he receive originally?

    A. 18
    B. 24
    C. 36
    D. 48
    E. 96

6. If $R = 4x$ and $S = 3y - x$, then what is the value of $R + S$?

    F. $3x + 3y$
    G. $3x - 3y$
    H. $4x + 3y$
    J. $4x - 3y$
    K. $5x + 3y$

7. In the figure below, l_1 is parallel to l_2, l_3 is parallel to l_4, and the lines intersect as shown. What is the measure of angle y?

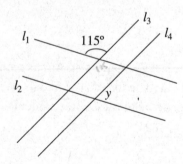

    A. 60°
    B. 65°
    C. 70°
    D. 75°
    E. Cannot be determined from the given information

8. If $x = -3$, then $-x^2 - 7x + 5 = ?$

    F. –25
    G. –7
    H. 14
    J. 17
    K. 35

9. The average of five numbers is 85. If each of the numbers is increased by 4, what is the average of the five new numbers?

    A. 80
    B. 81
    C. 85
    D. 87
    E. 89

10. The expression $3x + 9y$ is equivalent to which of the following?

    F. $3(x + y)$
    G. $12(x + y)$
    H. $3(x + 3y)$
    J. $3xy$
    K. $12xy$

11. For each month on your phone bill you pay $20 plus a fixed amount for every minute of long distance calls. In May you used 80 long distance minutes and your bill was $28. In June you used 20 more long distance minutes than in May. What was the charge on your phone bill in June?

    A. $20.00
    B. $28.20
    C. $29.00
    D. $30.00
    E. $32.50

GO ON TO THE NEXT PAGE ⟩

12. If $\dfrac{6}{x} \geq \dfrac{3}{4}$, what is the largest possible value for x?

    F. $\dfrac{1}{2}$

    G. 2

    H. 4

    J. 7

    K. 8

13. The hands of a clock are both pointing to 12 at noon. By 8 PM, what is the number of degrees the *hour* hand has moved?

    A. 80°

    B. 96°

    C. 120°

    D. 160°

    E. 240°

14. In the standard (x,y) coordinate plane below, $\triangle LMN$ and $\triangle NOP$ are right isosceles triangles with equal areas. Points M, N, O, and P are located on the axes as shown. Which of the following could be the coordinates of point L?

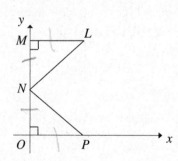

    F. (0,6)

    G. (6,0)

    H. (6,12)

    J. (12,0)

    K. (12,6)

15. Which of the following equations has both $x = 5$ and $x = -7$ as solutions?

    A. $(x - 5)(x + 7) = 0$

    B. $(x - 5)(-x + 7) = 0$

    C. $(x + 5)(x + 7) = 0$

    D. $(x + 5)(x - 7) = 0$

    E. $x - 5 = x + 7$

16. The grocery store opens each day with $(r + s)$ dollars in each cash register. If the store has t cash registers, which of the following is an expression for the total amount of money, in dollars, in the grocery store?

    F. $(t \cdot r) + s$

    G. $(t \cdot r) + (t \cdot s)$

    H. $(t \cdot s) + r$

    J. $(t \cdot r \cdot s)$

    K. $t + r + s$

17. If 30% of x equals 60, then $x = ?$

    A. 2

    B. 18

    C. 200

    D. 1,800

    E. 2,000

18. A school is selling t-shirts as a fund raiser. For the first 100 t-shirts that are sold, the school will earn 7 dollars per shirt. For each additional shirt that is sold, the school will earn 10 dollars. How much will the school earn if 350 t-shirts are sold?

    F. $ 245

    G. $ 250

    H. $2,450

    J. $3,200

    K. $4,200

GO ON TO THE NEXT PAGE

19. You want to buy a salad for lunch. The price on the menu is $3.99, and the cashier is going to add a sales tax of 7% of the $3.99 (rounded to the nearest cent) to the price of the salad. You are going to pay with a five-dollar bill. How much change should the cashier return to you?

   A.   7¢

   B.   27¢

   C.   28¢

   D.   73¢

   E.   93¢

20. For which nonnegative value of x is the expression $\dfrac{1}{x^2 - 4}$ undefined?

   F.   0

   G.   2

   H.   4

   J.   8

   K.   16

21. What is the correct ordering of π, $3\frac{1}{4}$, and 3.5, from greatest to least?

   A. $\pi > 3\frac{1}{4} > 3.5\pi$

   B. $\pi > 3.5 > 3\frac{1}{4}$

   C. $3.5 > 3\frac{1}{4} > \pi$

   D. $3.5 > \pi > 3\frac{1}{4}$

   E. $3\frac{1}{4} > 3.5 > \pi$

22. Ashley has wrapped a box that measures 20 inches (in) wide, 15 in long, and 4 in tall, as shown below. She wants to tie a single piece of string around the box. If Ashley needs 4 additional inches of string to tie a bow, what is the minimum length, in inches, of string she will need to wrap around the box in both directions, as shown below?

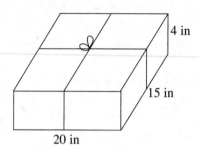

   F.   39

   G.   43

   H.   47

   J.   82

   K.   90

23. To make the color you want to paint your house, you have to mix 5 parts white paint with 3 parts blue paint. How many quarts of blue paint will you need to make 24 quarts of this color?

   A.   3

   B.   5

   C.   8

   D.   9

   E.   15

24. Which of the following gives all of the solutions of $x^2 + x = 30$?

   F.   −6 and 5

   G.   −5 and 6

   H.   −2 and 15

   J.   2 and 15

   K.   15 only

GO ON TO THE NEXT PAGE

25. If $(a - b)^2 = 36$ and $ab = 24$, then $a^2 + b^2 = ?$

  A. −12

  B. 12

  C. 60

  D. 84

  E. 96

26. If, for all x, $(x^{3b-1})^2 = x^{16}$, then $b = ?$

  F. 1

  G. $\dfrac{5}{3}$

  H. $\dfrac{5}{4}$

  J. 3

  K. $\dfrac{16}{3}$

27. Given the complex number i such that $i^2 = -1$, what is the value of $i^2 - i^4$?

  A. −2

  B. −1

  C. 0

  D. 1

  E. 2

28. $\overline{AB}$ is a line segment in the standard (x,y) coordinate plane with endpoints A and B. If point A has the coordinates $(5,-4)$ and the midpoint of $\overline{AB}$ has coordinates $(-2,4)$ what are the coordinates of point B?

  F. (−9,12)

  G. (−3,−16)

  H. (3,−16)

  J. (3,−1)

  K. (9,12)

29. A circle in the standard (x,y) coordinate plane has the equation $(x + 2)^2 + (y - 2)^2 = 5$. What is the radius of the circle?

  A. −2

  B. $\sqrt{2}$

  C. 2

  D. $\sqrt{5}$

  E. 5

30. The right triangle pictured below has side lengths a, b, and c. What is the value of $\sin \beta$?

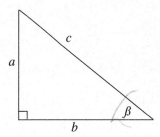

  F. $\dfrac{a}{b}$

  G. $\dfrac{a}{c}$

  H. $\dfrac{b}{a}$

  J. $\dfrac{b}{c}$

  K. $\dfrac{c}{a}$

31. For all nonzero x and y, $\dfrac{(16x^2 y^2)(6x^2 y^4)}{-8x^2 y^3} = ?$

  A. $-12y^3$

  B. $-12x^2 y^2$

  C. $-12x^2 y^3$

  D. $\dfrac{x^2 y^2}{12}$

  E. $\dfrac{12}{y}$

GO ON TO THE NEXT PAGE

32. Three parallel lines are intersected by transversals, as shown below. The points of intersection are labeled. $\overline{QR}$ measures 3 inches, $\overline{RS}$ measures 5 inches, and $\overline{UV}$ measures 7 inches. What is the length of $\overline{TU}$, in inches?

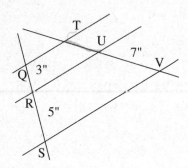

F. 3
G. 4
H. 5
J. $\dfrac{21}{5}$
K. $\dfrac{16}{5}$

33. In the figure below, the circle centered at O has radii $\overline{OA}$ and $\overline{OB}$. $\triangle AOB$ is a right isosceles triangle. If the area of $\triangle AOB$ is 18 square units, what is the area of the circle, in units?

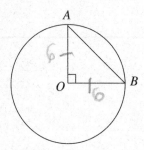

A. 12π
B. 18π
C. 36π
D. 72π
E. 81π

34. Which of the following represents the same set as the figure shown below?

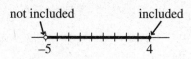

E. $x \le -5$ or $x > 4$
G. $x > -5$ or $x \le 4$
H. $x \ge -5$ or $x < 4$
J. $x > -5$ and $x \le 4$
K. $x \ge -5$ and $x < 4$

35. Jen has built a straight slide from her tree house to her sand box. The top of the slide, directly above the base of the tree house, is 9 feet from the ground. The slide touches the ground 12 feet from the base of the tree house. What is the length of the slide, in feet?

A. $3\sqrt{7}$
B. $6\sqrt{3}$
C. 15
D. 25
E. 108

36. If a and b are real numbers, and $\sqrt{3\left(\dfrac{a^2}{b}\right)} = 2$, then what must be true of b?

F. b must be positive
G. b must be negative
H. b must equal $\dfrac{2}{3}$
J. b must equal 3
K. b may have any value

GO ON TO THE NEXT PAGE ▷

37. The numbers 84 and 96 are both divisible by n, a real positive integer. Neither 18 nor 16 is divisible by n. What is the sum of the digits of n?

    A. 1
    B. 3
    C. 4
    D. 5
    E. 6

38. In the standard (x,y) coordinate plane, line R is parallel to the x-axis. What is the slope of R?

    F. –1
    G. 0
    H. 1
    J. Undefined
    K. Cannot be determined from the given information

39. Which of the following lines has the same slope as $y = 2x - 1$?

    A. $-y = 2x - 1$
    B. $y = 3x - 1$
    C. $y = 4x + 2$
    D. $4y = 2x + 6$
    E. $5y = 10x + 2$

40. The two triangles in the figure below share a common side. What is $\sin(x + y)$?

    (Note: For all x and y, $\sin(x + y) = \sin x \cos y + \sin y \cos x$.)

    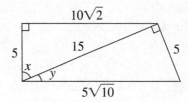

    F. $\dfrac{1}{5\sqrt{10}}$

    G. $\dfrac{12\sqrt{5} + \sqrt{10}}{30}$

    H. $\dfrac{6\sqrt{5} + 3\sqrt{10}}{20}$

    J. $\dfrac{2\sqrt{2} + \sqrt{10}}{3}$

    K. $5\sqrt{10}$

41. Julie can type 3 pages in x minutes. How many minutes will it take her to type 11 pages?

    A. $33x$

    B. $\dfrac{3}{11x}$

    C. $\dfrac{11}{3x}$

    D. $\dfrac{3x}{11}$

    E. $\dfrac{11x}{3}$

GO ON TO THE NEXT PAGE

42. Which of the following will result in an odd integer for any integer a?

    F. a^2

    G. $3a^2$

    H. $4a^2$

    J. $3a^2 + 1$

    K. $4a^2 + 1$

43. In $\triangle RST$, $\angle R$ is a right angle and $\angle S$ measures 60°. If $\overline{ST}$ is 8 inches long, what is the area of $\triangle RST$ in square inches?

    A. 8

    B. $8\sqrt{3}$

    C. 16

    D. 32

    E. $32\sqrt{3}$

44. Right triangle ABC, below, has lengths as marked. If $\overline{DE}$ is the perpendicular bisector of $\overline{AC}$, what is the ratio of the length of $\overline{AB}$ to the length of $\overline{DE}$?

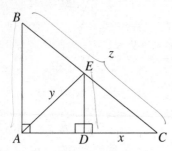

    F. $\dfrac{1}{2}$

    G. $\dfrac{x}{y}$

    H. $\dfrac{y}{x}$

    J. $\dfrac{y}{z}$

    K. $\dfrac{z}{y}$

45. The figure below is composed of a square and a semicircle. The radius of the semicircle is r and the side of the square is $2r$. Suppose r is doubled. How many times the area of the original figure is the area of the new figure?

    A. 2

    B. 3

    C. 4

    D. 8

    E. 10

46. For what value of x would the following system of equations have an infinite number of solutions?

$$4a - b = 4$$
$$16a - 4b = 8x$$

    F. 2

    G. 4

    H. 6

    J. 16

    K. 24

GO ON TO THE NEXT PAGE ▷

47. Sally and Samir left their camp at the same time. Sally walked at a constant rate of 3 miles per hour. She walked 20 minutes north, then 40 minutes east. Samir walked at a constant rate of 2 miles per hour. He walked 20 minutes south, then 40 minutes east. Which of the following is an expression for the number of miles apart Samir and Sally were one hour after they left camp?

A. $1(3 - 2)$

B. $\sqrt{\left(1 - \frac{2}{3}\right)^2 + \left(2 - \frac{4}{3}\right)^2}$

C. $\sqrt{\left(1 + \frac{2}{3}\right)^2 + \left(2 - \frac{4}{3}\right)^2}$

D. $\sqrt{\left(1 + \frac{2}{3}\right)^2 + \left(2 + \frac{4}{3}\right)^2}$

E. $\sqrt{\left(1 - \frac{2}{3}\right)^2 \left(2 - \frac{4}{3}\right)^2}$

48. A golf ball is at a point on the ground that is 20 feet from the base of a flag pole, as shown below. The angle of elevation from this point to the top of the vertical flag pole is 35°. What is the height, in feet, of the flag pole?

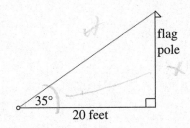

F. 20cos 35°

G. 20cot 35°

H. 20sec 35°

J. 20sin 35°

K. 20tan 35°

49. The shaded portion of the figure below represents a parallelogram. Side lengths are indicated in inches. What is the area of the parallelogram, in square inches?

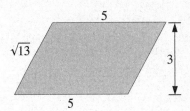

A. 5

B. 15

C. $\sqrt{13}$

D. $\sqrt{26}$

E. $2\sqrt{13}$

50. Three points, A, B, and C, lie on the same line. The length of $\overline{AB}$ is 8 units, and the length of $\overline{BC}$ is 2 units. Which of the following gives all of the possible lengths for $\overline{AC}$?

F. 6 only

G. 10 only

H. 6 and 10 only

J. Any number less than 6 or greater than 10

K. Any number greater than 6 and less than 10

GO ON TO THE NEXT PAGE

51. Given the vertices of $\triangle ABC$ in the standard (x,y) coordinate plane below, what is the area of $\triangle ABC$ in square units?

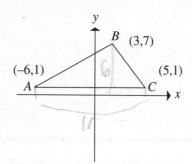

A. 22.0

B. 32.0

C. 33.0

D. 40.0

E. 66.0

52. If $-3x^2y^3 > 0$, which of the following CANNOT be true?

F. $x = y$

G. $x < 0$

H. $x > 0$

J. $y < 0$

K. $y > 0$

53. If the first term in a geometric sequence is x, and the second term is nx, what is the 30th term in the sequence?

A. $n^{29}x$

B. $n^{30}x$

C. $n^{31}x$

D. $(nx)^{29}$

E. $(nx)^{30}$

54. A system of two linear equations in two variables has NO solution. One of the equations is graphed in the (x,y) coordinate plane as shown below. Which of the following could be the equation of the other line?

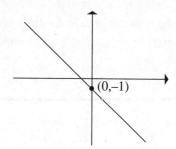

F. $y = x + 1$

G. $y = -x - 1$

H. $y = x + 2$

J. $y = -x + 2$

K. $y = 1$

55. If $0° \leq n \leq 90°$ and $\cos n = \dfrac{15}{17}$, then $\tan n = ?$

A. $\dfrac{8}{17}$

B. $\dfrac{8}{15}$

C. $\dfrac{17}{15}$

D. $\dfrac{15}{8}$

E. $\dfrac{17}{8}$

GO ON TO THE NEXT PAGE

56. For every cent decrease in the price of milk, a grocery sells 10 more gallons of milk per day. Right now, the store is selling 65 gallons of milk per day at $2.25 per gallon. Which of the following expressions represents the number of gallons that will be sold per day if the cost is reduced by c cents?

    F. $65(2.25 - c)$

    G. $2.25(10c + 65)$

    H. $(2.25 - c)(10c + 65)$

    J. $2.25 - c$

    K. $65 + 10c$

57. A group of 100 students are being divided into 10 teams for a relay race. Each student will draw and keep a token from a bag of tokens numbered 00 through 99. Students who draw tokens numbered with the same tens digit will be on the same team. (Students with numbers between 00 and 09, for example, will be on the same team.) Ann is the first student to draw, and she draws 56. If Elizabeth is the second student to draw, what is the probability that she will be on Ann's team?

    A. $\dfrac{1}{8}$

    B. $\dfrac{1}{9}$

    C. $\dfrac{1}{10}$

    D. $\dfrac{1}{11}$

    E. $\dfrac{1}{99}$

58. The figure below shows a cross-section of Dave's room, which is 10 feet long and 8 feet wide. The walls are perfectly vertical, and the floor is horizontal. The ceiling is horizontal for 6 feet, then slopes down as shown. The ceiling is 7 feet from the floor at one end of the room and 4 feet from the floor at the other end. As a prank, Dave's friends are planning to fill his room with packing peanuts. How many cubic feet of packing peanuts will they need to fill Dave's entire room from floor to ceiling (assuming there is nothing in the room)?

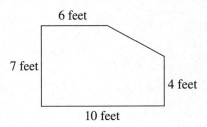

    F.   64

    G. 336

    H. 368

    J.   512

    K. 560

GO ON TO THE NEXT PAGE

59. In the figure below, line l has the equation $y = x$. Line m is perpendicular to l and intercepts the x-axis at (3,0). Which of the following is an equation for m?

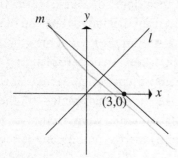

A. $y = x + 3\sqrt{2}$

B. $y = x + 3$

C. $y = -x + 3$

D. $y = -x + 3\sqrt{2}$

E. $y = -3x + 3$

60. What is the smallest possible value for the product of two real numbers that differ by 8?

F. -64

G. -16

H. -8

J. 0

K. 16

READING TEST

35 Minutes—40 Questions

Directions: There are four passages in this test. Each passage is followed by several questions. After reading a passage, choose the best answer to each question and fill in the corresponding oval on your Answer Grid. You may refer to the passages as often as necessary.

PASSAGE I

PROSE FICTION

This passage is adapted from Howard's End, *by E.M. Forster (1910). Two sisters, Helen and Margaret, are attending an orchestra performance with friends and family.*

It will be generally admitted that Beethoven's *Fifth Symphony* is the most sublime noise that has ever penetrated into the ear of man. All sorts and
Line conditions are satisfied by it. Whether you are like
(5) Mrs. Munt, and tap surreptitiously when the tunes come—of course, not so as to disturb the others— or like Helen, who can see heroes and shipwrecks in the music's flood; or like Margaret, who can only see the music; or like Tibby, who is profoundly
(10) versed in counterpoint, and holds the full score of the symphony open on his knee; or like Fraulein Mosebach's young man, who can remember nothing but Fraulein Mosebach: in any case, the passion of your life becomes more vivid, and you
(15) are bound to admit that such a noise is cheap at two shillings. It is cheap, even if you hear it in the Queen's Hall, dreariest music-room in London, though not as dreary as the Free Trade Hall, Manchester; and even if you sit on the extreme left
(20) of that hall, so that the brass bumps at you before the rest of the orchestra arrives, it is still cheap.

"Whom is Margaret talking to?" said Mrs. Munt, at the conclusion of the first movement. She was again in London on a visit to Wickham Place.
(25) Helen looked down the long line of their party, and said that she did not know.

"Would it be some young man or other whom she takes an interest in?"

"I expect so," Helen replied. Music enwrapped
(30) her, and she could not be bothered by the

distinction that divides young men whom one takes an interest in from young men whom one knows.

"You girls are so wonderful in always having—
(35) Oh dear! One mustn't talk."

For the Andante had begun—very beautiful, but bearing a family likeness to all the other beautiful andantes that Beethoven had written, and, to Helen's mind, rather disconnecting the heroes
(40) and shipwrecks of the first movement from the heroes and goblins of the third. She heard the tune through once, and then her attention wandered, and she gazed at the audience, or the organ, or the architecture. Then Beethoven started decorating
(45) his tune, so she heard him through once more, and then she smiled at her Cousin Frieda. But Frieda, listening to classical music, could not respond. Herr Liesecke, too, looked as if wild horses could not make him inattentive; there were lines across his
(50) forehead, his lips were parted, his glasses at right angles to his nose, and he had laid a thick, white hand on either knee. And next to her was Aunt Juley, so British, and wanting to tap. How interesting that row of people was! What diverse influences
(55) had gone into the making of them! Here Beethoven, after humming and hawing with great sweetness, said "Heigho," and the Andante came to an end. Applause ensued, and a round of praise volleying from the audience. Margaret started talking to her
(60) new young man; Helen said to her aunt: "Now comes the wonderful movement: first of all the goblins, and then a trio of elephants dancing"; and Tibby implored the company generally to look out for the transitional passage on the drum.

GO ON TO THE NEXT PAGE ⟹

(65) "On the what, dear?"

"On the drum, Aunt Juley."

"No—look out for the part where you think you are done with the goblins and they come back," breathed Helen, as the music started with a goblin (70) walking quietly over the universe, from end to end. Others followed him. They were not aggressive creatures; that was what made them so terrible to Helen. They merely observed in passing that there was no such thing as splendor or heroism in the (75) world. Helen could not contradict them, for once, she had felt the same, and had seen the reliable walls of youth collapse. Panic and emptiness! Panic and emptiness! The goblins were right. Her brother raised his finger; it was the transitional passage on (80) the drum.

Helen pushed her way out during the applause. She desired to be alone. The music had summed up to her all that had happened or could happen in her life.

(85) She read it as a tangible statement, which could never be superseded. The notes meant this and that to her, and they could have no other meaning, and life could have no other meaning. She pushed right out of the building and walked slowly down the (90) outside staircase, breathing the autumnal air, and then she strolled home.

1. Helen would most likely agree with which of the following statements about her relationship with Margaret?

   A. Helen disapproves of Margaret's actions.

   B. Helen's feelings toward Margaret are affected by Helen's jealousy of the attention Margaret receives from suitors.

   C. Helen is not interested in Margaret's actions, at least as long as the music is playing.

   D. They are drawn together principally by their mutual love of music.

2. Helen can most accurately be characterized as:

   F. creative and effervescent.

   G. analytical yet optimistic.

   H. imaginative and introspective.

   J. curt and insensitive.

3. Which of the following statements does NOT describe one of Helen's reactions to the goblins?

   A. She feels that their presence is a denial of the good in the world.

   B. She is frightened by the goblins' aggressive nature.

   C. She cannot deny the viewpoint that the goblins seem to represent.

   D. She believes that the goblins will return after they appear to have left.

4. The main point of the first paragraph is that:

   F. the characters in the story react to the performance in different ways.

   G. Beethoven's *Fifth Symphony* is an outstanding musical accomplishment.

   H. musicians are not being paid in proportion to their talents.

   J. the poor quality of the auditorium keeps Helen's party from enjoying the concert.

5. The main point of the last paragraph is that Helen believes that:

   A. peace can only be found through acceptance of her fate.

   B. life is a meaningless endeavor that must be endured alone.

   C. the music has foretold her future.

   D. the music has told her unchangeable truths about life.

GO ON TO THE NEXT PAGE

6. According to the passage, when Tibby listens to the symphony he is:

  F. most interested in the technical aspects of the music.

  G. caught up in imagery that the music conveys to him.

  H. distracted from the performance as a whole because of his focus on the drum.

  J. depressed by his dreary surroundings.

7. Which of the following statements most accurately expresses Helen's feelings as she leaves after the symphony?

  A. Helen feels alienated by the indifference of her companions.

  B. Helen is meditative, pondering the music's immutable meaning.

  C. Helen is upset with Tibby's constant focus on the technical aspects of the music.

  D. Helen is relieved to have escaped the crowding and discomfort of the performance hall.

8. It can most reasonably be inferred from the passage that the reason Aunt Juley refrains from tapping along with the music is because:

  F. Aunt Juley is concentrating instead on the drum.

  G. Aunt Juley does not want to distract Helen.

  H. British custom only permits snapping one's fingers along with the music.

  J. Aunt Juley feels it would not be appropriate.

9. Based on the passage, it can be inferred that each of the following characters is deeply interested in the music being played EXCEPT:

  A. Herr Liesecke.

  B. Margaret.

  C. Fraulein Mosebach's young man.

  D. Tibby.

10. According to the passage, the reason why Helen's attention returns to the Andante after it had wandered is because she:

  F. hears changes in the tune.

  G. is directed to do so by Tibby.

  H. no longer wishes to speak with Mrs. Munt.

  J. believes the Andante is nearing its end.

PASSAGE II

SOCIAL SCIENCE

The following passage is adapted from the article "What Causes Overweight and Obesity" released by the National Heart, Lung and Blood Institute.

The past 10 years have seen a dramatic rise in "diseases of affluence" in the United States. Americans suffer from type II diabetes, obesity, and cardiovascular disease in epidemic proportions.
Line
(5) Indeed, American culture is often perceived to be entrenched in fast-food, excessive consumption, and minimal physical exertion. Supermarkets and restaurants in the United States serve a panoply of processed foods loaded with sugar, preservatives,
(10) trans-fats and cholesterol. Children develop poor eating habits—from sugar-laden cereals to school lunches drenched in saturated fat—that, unfortunately, last into adulthood. While changes in diet are partly responsible for American obesity, the
(15) primary cause of obesity is the sedentary lifestyle that 40 percent of Americans currently lead.

GO ON TO THE NEXT PAGE ⟩

For most of human history, people worked as farmers, hunters, laborers, and tradesmen—all physically demanding occupations. Blacksmiths
(20) hammered metal, servants washed dirty linen, and farmers lifted hay bails by hand. At the time, the only sources of work energy were animals or man power. However, these lifestyles afforded people vast stretches of idle time—winter
(25) months, religious holidays, and festivals—to rest and recover. Furthermore, routine and leisure activities also required more physical exertion. For all but the wealthy, everyday life was similar to a balanced gym routine. Despite high mortality
(30) from infectious diseases and malnutrition (and debilitating physical injuries suffered in far more hazardous working environments than today's workplace), physical fitness was standard.

Urbanization and industrialization during the
(35) 19th and 20th centuries drastically changed people's life-styles. Agricultural advances have led to increasingly larger farms manned by fewer workers. Machines are used for most aspects of farming, from sowing seeds to harvesting. Manufacturing,
(40) meanwhile, transformed into a system of mass production facilitated by machines—a process that does not require the range or degree of physical exertion from workers as was necessitated by pre-industrial fabrication. People began to move less
(45) and sit more. During the 20th century, increasingly elaborate systems of government and finance brought about the most sedentary workplace of all: the office building. Suddenly massive complexes peopled by legions of clerks, salespeople, analysts,
(50) and secretaries manning telephones, computers, and typewriters began to fill the American city. Urbanization condensed all aspects of living into a few square blocks. The conveniences of the modern urban environment are also conducive to inactivity.
(55) Transportation has also exacerbated the problem by offering city dwellers numerous options for travel, none of which require any real physical exertion. Therefore, the average 9-to-5 worker can go to work, run errands, and seek entertainment with
(60) little more effort than what is required to walk to and from a car or a mass transit station.

Leisure has likewise contributed to the obesity epidemic. Watching television and playing video games have supplanted sports, leisurely strolls,
(65) and horse-riding as popular pastimes. Pre-studies have revealed a positive correlation between hours of television viewing and levels of obesity. In fact, video games are found to play an especially significant role in childhood obesity.

(70) Despite the proliferation of gimmick diets and fancy gadgets, losing weight is actually a simple matter of burning more calories than one consumes. Active living initiatives are working hard to bring more movement into the average
(75) American's life. Urban planners are designing cities that include more sidewalks, crosswalks, parks, and bicycle trails. Education programs and advertising campaigns seek to reform the deleterious habits of adults and create more active lifestyles in children.
(80) Parents and nutritionists are working together to banish some of the more egregious offenders— fries, pizza, and soda—from public school cafeterias.

In the 21st century, the stakes for combating
(85) obesity in the United States are increasingly high. As an overweight baby boom generation enters its twilight, insurance providers and health care professionals are encountering alarming rates of diabetes and heart disease. American life
(90) expectancy has begun to drop from all-time highs during the late 1990s. Even more concerning is the earlier onset of obesity in younger generations. Given that the World Health Organization has estimated 60 percent of the global population get
(95) insufficient exercise, finding a way to get people back in shape is perhaps the greatest health care issue that the world currently faces.

GO ON TO THE NEXT PAGE

11. The main purpose of the first paragraph in relation to the passage as a whole is to:

A. emphasize the role of overeating in America's health problems.

B. undermine the theory that Americans don't get enough exercise.

C. discuss the factors at play in America's obesity pandemic.

D. criticize the lifestyles of pre-industrial Americans.

12. According to the passage, all of the following are aspects of pre-industrial culture responsible for promoting physical fitness EXCEPT:

F. the hazardous conditions of the 19th century workplace.

G. the variation of physical activity required by most occupations.

H. the absence of alternative energy source for performing tasks.

J. the vigor of pastime activities.

13. The author most likely included lines 17–33 to:

A. provide examples of typical pre-industrial occupations that have been rendered obsolete.

B. cite occupations that necessitated human energy for successful completion.

C. recommend jobs that modern Americans should pursue to counter obesity.

D. explain why consuming foods rich in calories was more acceptable in past eras.

14. The third paragraph details the effects of industrialization on the workplace by:

F. citing the hazards of the modern workplace.

G. lamenting the working conditions in office buildings.

H. praising the efficiency of modern farming and manufacturing.

J. indicating specific ways in which modern workers do less physical work.

15. The author's attitude toward the 9-to-5 worker mentioned in lines 58–61 can best be described as:

A. dismayed.

B. envious.

C. judgmental.

D. objective.

16. The passage suggests which of the following about television?

F. There is an inverse relationship between television viewing and obesity.

G. Watching television directly causes obesity in viewers.

H. People who watch more television are more likely to be obese.

J. The obese enjoy television more than fit viewers.

17. According to the passage, losing weight:

A. is essential to avoiding health problems in later life.

B. can be achieved only through excessive levels of physical exertion.

C. is possible when caloric intake exceeds energy burned through activity.

D. requires a deficit between consumption and metabolism.

GO ON TO THE NEXT PAGE

18. The author most likely mentions diets and exercise machines to:

    F. contrast public opinion with the simplicity of losing weight.

    G. give examples of effective weight loss techniques.

    H. critique nontraditional methods of combating obesity.

    J. emphasize the ease of using modern exercise machines.

19. Based on the passage, health-conscious families and experts' attitudes toward public school lunches can best be described as:

    A. ambivalent.

    B. inimical.

    C. apathetic.

    D. enthralled.

20. The author most likely mentions *life expectancy* in lines 89–90 in order to:

    F. emphasize the longevity of Americans during the 1990s.

    G. indicate that obesity has innocuous effects on older Americans.

    H. illustrate long-term effects of obesity in the U.S. population.

    J. contrast American health with the health of people in other countries.

PASSAGE III

HUMANITIES

This passage is excerpted from "Mr. Bennett and Mrs. Woolf," by Irving Howe. Reprinted by permission of The New Republic, © *1990, The New Republic, LLC.*

Literary polemics come and go, sparking a season of anger and gossip, and then turning to dust. A handful survive their moment:

Line Dr. Johnson's demolition of Soames Jenyn, Hazlitt's
(5) attack on Coleridge. But few literary polemics can have been so damaging, or so lasting in consequences, as Virginia Woolf's 1924 essay "Mr. Bennett and Mrs. Brown," about the once widely read English novelists Arnold Bennett,
(10) H. G. Wells, and John Galsworthy. For several literary generations now, Woolf's essay has been taken as the definitive word finishing off an old-fashioned school of fiction and thereby clearing the way for literary modernism. Writing with her glistening
(15) charm, and casting herself as the voice of the new (always a shrewd strategy in literary debate), Woolf quickly seized the high ground in her battle with Bennett. Against her needling thrusts, the old fellow never had a chance.

(20) The debate has been nicely laid out by Samuel Hynes in *Edwardian Occasions*, and I owe to him some of the following details. It all began in 1917, with Woolf's review of a collection of Bennett's literary pieces, a rather favorable review marred
(25) by the stylish snobbism that was becoming a trademark of the Bloomsbury circle. Bennett, wrote Woolf, had a materialistic view of the world—"he had been worrying himself to achieve infantile realisms." A catchy phrase, though exactly what
(30) "infantile realisms" meant Woolf did not trouble to say. During the next few years she kept returning to the attack, as if to prepare for "Mr. Bennett and Mrs. Brown." More than personal sensibilities or rivalries of status was involved here, though
(35) both were quite visible; Woolf was intent upon discrediting, if not simply dismissing, a group of literary predecessors who enjoyed a large readership.

GO ON TO THE NEXT PAGE →

In 1923 Bennett reviewed Woolf's novel *Jacob's Room*, praising its "originality" and "exquisite" prose
(40) but concluding that "the characters do not vitally survive in the mind." For Bennett, this was a fatal flaw. And for his readers, too—though not for the advanced literary public that by now was learning to suspect this kind of talk about "characters
(45) surviving" as a lazy apology for the shapeless and perhaps even mindless Victorian novel.

A year later Woolf published her famous essay, brilliantly sketching an imaginary old lady named Mrs. Brown whom she supplied with anecdotes
(50) and reflections as tokens of inner being. These released the sort of insights, suggested Woolf, that would not occur to someone like Bennett, a writer obsessed with dull particulars of setting (weather, town, clothing, furniture, and so on). Were Bennett
(55) to write about a Mrs. Brown, he would describe her house in conscientious detail but never penetrate her essential life, for—what a keen polemicist!— "he is trying to hypnotize us into the belief that, because he has made a house, there must be a
(60) person living there." (Herself sensitive to the need for a room with a view, Woolf seemed indifferent to what a house might mean for people who had risen somewhat in the world. For a writer like Bennett, however, imagining a house was part of the way to
(65) locate "a person living there.") And in a quiet put-down of Bennett's novel *Hilda Lessways* (not one of his best), Woolf gave a turn of the knife: "One line of insight would have done more than all those lines of description."

(70) From the suave but deadly attack of "Mr. Bennett and Mrs. Brown" Bennett's literary reputation never quite recovered. He remained popular with the general public, but among literary readers, the sort that became the public for the emerging modernists,
(75) the standard view has long been that he was a middling, plodding sort of Edwardian writer whose work has been pushed aside by the revolutionary achievements of Lawrence, Joyce, and to a smaller extent Woolf herself.

(80) When Bennett died in 1930, Woolf noted in her diary that "he had some real understanding power, as well as a gigantic absorbing power [and] direct contact with life"—all attributes, you might suppose, handy for a novelist but for her
(85) evidently not sufficient. In saying this, remarks Hynes, "Woolf gave Bennett, perhaps, the 'reality gift' that [she] doubted in herself, the gift that she despised and envied." Yes; in much of her fiction Woolf resembles Stevens's man with the blue guitar
(90) who "cannot bring a world quite round/Although I patch it as I can." Still, none of this kept Woolf from steadily sniping at Bennett's "shopkeeping view of literature." Bennett was a provincial from the Five Towns; Bennett was commercially successful;
(95) Bennett was an elder to be pulled down, as elders must always be pulled down even if they are also admired a little.

21. Which of the following statements best characterizes the author's view of Virginia Woolf?

   A. Woolf criticized others only in areas where she felt strong, leaving her own weaknesses out of the discussion.

   B. Woolf only disparaged Bennett and his school of authors because she envied the strides they had made.

   C. Woolf almost single-handedly changed the prevailing opinion about a particular writer and laid the path for a new school of literature.

   D. Woolf's views toward the venerated authors of the day were abusive, and her reputation has rightly suffered as a result of those attacks.

GO ON TO THE NEXT PAGE

22. In lines 58–60, the phrase "he is trying to hyp-notize us into the belief that, because he has made a house, there must be a person living there" is an example of which of the following general ideas in the passage?

    F. Woolf's dismissal of the social and economic differences between herself and Bennett, and the effect of that difference on their priorities in writing

    G. Woolf's view that Bennett fails to address the elements necessary to portray fully developed characters

    H. Woolf's recognition of Bennett's obsession with material goods

    J. The author's belief that Woolf revolu-tionized the view of literary polemics

23. In the first paragraph, the author compares Woolf's polemic against Bennett to other literary attacks. This comparison supports the author's view that:

    A. Bennett's dull style of writing would soon have fallen out of fashion anyway.

    B. many such attacks are remembered as turning points for the arts.

    C. Woolf fought with other authors often.

    D. Woolf's criticisms of Bennett were espe-cially important and memorable.

24. According to the passage, Bennett's literary output was marked by:

    F. description of the scene rather than insight into the characters.

    G. the use of colorful characters who frequently reveal their deepest emotions.

    H. fewer essays than Woolf wrote.

    J. exhaustive description of minute details.

25. It can be reasonably inferred from the passage that the author means to:

    A. demonstrate an effective strategy for writing a literary polemic.

    B. suggest a new interpretation of a well-known literary polemic.

    C. analyze one literary polemic and its effect on the literature of its era.

    D. assess the significance of a literary polemic in the context of similar works.

26. Based on the passage, it is most reasonable to infer that Woolf's phrase *infantile realisms* (line 30) means:

    F. a focus on things rather than on people.

    G. the values of the Bloomsbury Circle.

    H. the type of writing that doesn't survive in the reader's mind.

    J. the superficial details of Mrs. Brown's house.

27. In the final sentence of the passage, the author suggests that Woolf believed that "elders must always be pulled down." This same sentiment is most closely exemplified by which of the following examples from the passage?

    A. The author's view of Woolf's novel *Jacob's Room*

    B. The author's view of *Edwardian Occasions* by Samuel Hynes

    C. The author's comparison of Woolf to "Stevens's man with the blue guitar"

    D. The author's reference to Bennett's *Hilda Lessways* as "not one of his best"

GO ON TO THE NEXT PAGE

28. Bennett's general opinion of Woolf's novel *Jacob's Room* was that it was:

   F. inferior to other novels published at that time.

   G. a keen example of a new style of literature.

   H. a success, despite one or two minor failings.

   J. generally original and inspired, but with significant problems.

29. It is Woolf's opinion that the thoughts and feelings of characters are more important than the details of a scene because:

   A. scenic descriptions were part of a literary style that she disliked.

   B. scenic details cannot convey a sense of the character within.

   C. good authors know to include at least one line of insight into a character.

   D. scenic details create characters that are easily forgettable.

30. Without the last paragraph, the passage as a whole would not include an example of:

   F. Woolf criticizing Bennett.

   G. Woolf praising Bennett.

   H. Bennett praising Woolf.

   J. the author of the passage criticizing Woolf.

PASSAGE IV

NATURAL SCIENCE

Fossil fuels are energy-rich substances formed from the remains of organisms. Both coal and petroleum help power commercial energy throughout the world.

PASSAGE A

Coal is a solid fossil fuel formed from the remains of land plants that flourished 300 to 400 million years ago. It is composed primarily of
Line carbon but also contains small amounts of sulfur.
(5) When the sulfur is released into the atmosphere as a result of burning, it can form SO_2, a corrosive gas that can damage plants and animals. When it combines with H_2O in the atmosphere, it can form sulfuric acid, one of the main components of acid
(10) rain, which has been demonstrated to be an environmental hazard. Burning coal has also been shown to contain trace amounts of mercury and radioactive materials, similarly dangerous substances. The type of coal that is burned directly affects the amount of
(15) sulfur that is released into the atmosphere.

The formation of coal goes through discrete stages as, over millions of years, heat and pressure act on decomposing plants. Coal begins as peat, partially decayed plant matter, which is still found
(20) today in swamps and bogs, and can be burned, but produces little heat. As the decayed plant material is compressed over time, lignite is formed. Lignite is a sedimentary rock with low sulfur content and, like peat, also produces a small amount of heat
(25) when burned. With further compaction, lignite loses moisture, methane, and carbon dioxide, and becomes bituminous coal, the form of coal most widely used. Bituminous coal is also a sedimentary rock, but it has a high sulfur content.
(30) Anthracite, or hard coal, is a metamorphic rock formed when heat and pressure are added to bituminous coal. Anthracite coal is most desirable because it burns very hot and also contains a much smaller amount of sulfur, meaning that it burns
(35) cleaner.

However, the supplies of anthracite on Earth are limited. In the United States, most anthracite

GO ON TO THE NEXT PAGE

is extracted from the valleys of northeastern Pennsylvania, which is known as the Coal Region.
(40) The major American reserve of bituminous coal is in West Virginia, while the largest coal producer in the world is The People's Republic of China. The United States and China are also foremost among the world's coal consumers. There are many other
(45) coal-producing areas throughout the world, though in some cases, the coal is essentially tapped out, or other, cleaner sources of coal are preferred.

Coal is extracted from mines. For subsurface mines, machines dig shafts and tunnels underground
(50) to allow the miners to remove the material. Buildup of poisonous gases, explosions, and collapses are all dangers that underground miners must face. The Sago Mine disaster of January 2006 in West Virginia—where only 1 of 13 trapped miners
(55) survived an explosion—shows how extracting these underground deposits of solid material is still a very dangerous process. Strip mining, or surface mining, is cheaper and less hazardous than underground mining. However, it often leaves the land scarred and
(60) unsuitable for other uses.

PASSAGE B

Petroleum, or crude oil, is a thick liquid that contains organic compounds of hydrogen and carbon, called hydrocarbons. The term "crude oil" refers to both the unprocessed petroleum and the
(65) products refined from it, such as gasoline, heating oil, and asphalt. Petroleum contains many types of hydrocarbons in liquid, solid and gaseous forms, as well as sulfur, oxygen, and nitrogen.

When organic material such as zooplankton
(70) and algae settled on the bottom of oceans millions of years ago, the material mixed with mud and was covered in sediment more quickly than it could decay. Thousands of years later, the sediments that contained the organic material were subjected to
(75) intense amounts of heat and pressure, changing it into a waxy material called kerogen. From this substance, liquid hydrocarbons can be produced to create oil shale. When more heat was added to the kerogen, it liquefied into the substance we know
(80) as oil. Since hydrocarbons are usually lighter than rock or water, they migrate upward through the

permeable rock layers until they reach impermeable rocks. The areas where oil remains in the porous rocks are called reservoirs.
(85) Oil is traditionally pumped out of the layer of reserves found under the surface of Earth. In order to penetrate the earth, an oil well is created using an oil rig, which turns a drill bit. After the hole is drilled, a casing—a metal pipe with a slightly
(90) smaller diameter than the hole—is inserted and bonded to its surroundings, usually with cement. This strengthens the sides of the hole, or wellbore, and keeps dangerous pressure zones isolated. This process is repeated with smaller bits and thinner
(95) casings, going deeper into the surface to reach the reservoir. Drilling fluid is pushed through the casings to break up the rock in front of the bit and to clean away debris and lower the temperature of the bit, which grows very hot. Once the reservoir is
(100) reached, the top of the wellbore is usually equipped with a set of valves encased in a pyramidal iron cage called a Christmas Tree.

The natural pressure within the reservoir is usually high enough to push the oil or gas up to the
(105) surface. But sometimes, additional measures, called secondary recovery, are required. This is especially true in depleted fields. Installing thinner tubing is one solution, as are surface pump jacks—the structures that look like horses repeatedly dipping their heads.
(110) It is impossible to remove all of the oil in a single reservoir. In fact, a 30 percent to 40 percent yield is typical. However, technology has provided a few ways to increase drilling yield, including forcing water or steam into the rock to "push" out more of the oil.
(115) Even with this technique, only about 50 percent of the deposit will be extracted.

There are also more unconventional sources of oil, including oil shale and tar sands. The hydrocarbons obtained from these sources require
(120) extensive processing to be useable, reducing their value. The extraction process also has a particularly large environmental footprint.

GO ON TO THE NEXT PAGE →

Questions 31–33 ask about Passage A.

31. The author would be most likely to support:

   A. the use of oil over that of coal.

   B. the continued use of fossil fuels.

   C. the use of lignite for fuel.

   D. secondary recovery.

32. The passage suggests that which of the following has the smallest amount of moisture, methane, and carbon dioxide?

   F. Lignite

   G. Peat

   H. Bituminous coal

   J. Kerogen

33. It can be inferred that the author believes that:

   A. acid rain is a direct contrast to carbon in coal.

   B. acid rain provides proof that burning coal is dangerous.

   C. acid rain is a direct result of decaying plant matter.

   D. the amount of acid rain produced can be reduced by burning anthracite coal instead of bituminous coal.

Questions 34–36 ask about Passage B.

34. As used in the passage, the phrase "environmental footprint" (line 122) most likely means:

   F. indentations in the surface of the earth.

   G. the positive environmental results of extracting oil.

   H. the effect that a person or activity has on the environment.

   J. irreversible damage to the earth.

35. According to the passage, the second step in extracting the oil is:

   A. drilling a hole.

   B. pushing in draining fluid.

   C. topping with valves.

   D. inserting a pipe.

36. What is most likely true about an oil field in which a pump jack is installed?

   F. Oil is being extracted in the safest way.

   G. The oil reserves in the field are greatly diminished.

   H. About 50 percent of the available oil is recovered.

   J. The wellbore is strengthened.

Questions 37–40 ask about both passages.

37. Both passages include details regarding all of the following EXCEPT:

   A. the transformation of organic material into usable energy sources.

   B. the lengthy nature of converting organic material into fossil fuel.

   C. the limited supply of fossil fuels.

   D. evidence to support the claim that solar power is a safer energy source than oil or coal.

38. The formation of both coal and oil requires all of the following EXCEPT:

   F. proper extraction techniques

   G. pressure.

   H. heat.

   J. organic material.

GO ON TO THE NEXT PAGE ⇨

39. Fossil fuel is formed in a multi-step process, as stated in Passage A where the author writes that "The formation of coal goes through discrete stages. . ." Which sentence in Passage B confirms a similar step process for the formation of oil?

   A. The areas where oil remains in the porous rocks are called reservoirs.

   B. The natural pressure within the reservoir is usually high enough to push the oil or gas up to the surface.

   C. When more heat was added to the kerogen, it liquefied into the subtance we know as oil.

   D. Petroleum contains many different types of hydrocarbons in liquid, solid, and gaseous forms, as well as sulfur, oxygen, and nitrogen.

40. The final sentence in each passage conveys which of the following?

   F. The land cannot recover after fossil fuels have been extracted.

   G. The process of extracting coal and oil present environmental repercussions.

   H. New technology can reduce the amount of sulfur released into the air.

   J. Lead is as equally hazardous to people as are coal and oil.

SCIENCE TEST

35 Minutes—40 Questions

Directions: There are several passages in this test. Each passage is followed by several questions. After reading a passage, choose the best answer to each question and fill in the corresponding oval on your Answer Grid. You may refer to the passages as often as necessary. You are NOT permitted to use a calculator on this test.

PASSAGE I

The growth of flowering plants and trees can depend on a number of factors, including the type of plant and the latitude where it is grown. Table 1 below contains typical adult heights for several different varieties of a particular flowering plant.

The rate of flowering for many plants and trees, such as the pecan tree, depends on the age of the organism. Growth occurs in several distinct phases, which reflect changes in the development of the organism over time. See Figure 1.

Table 1

Variety	Soil type	Latitude (degrees)	Height (meters)
Lagerstroemia Apalachee	Soil alone	28	5.2
Lagerstroemia indica Catawba	Soil and organic compost	28	2.7
Lagerstroemia Chickasaw	Soil alone	28	0.9
Lagerstroemia Choctaw	Soil and mulch	28	7.3
Lagerstroemia indica Conestoga	Soil alone	28	2.4
Lagerstroemia fauriei Kiowa	Soil and organic compost	28	8.3
Lagerstroemia Miami	Soil alone	28	6.4
Lagerstroemia Natchez	Soil and mulch	33	5.8
Lagerstroemia Natchez	Soil and natural fertilizer	28	8.6
Lagerstroemia Natchez	Soil and artificial fertilizer	28	7.6
Lagerstroemia indica Potomac	Soil alone	28	4.6
Lagerstroemia Tuscarora	Soil alone	25	4.9

GO ON TO THE NEXT PAGE

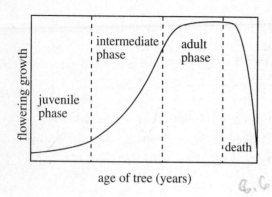

age of tree (years)

Figure 1

1. Based on the information presented in Table 1, if a young *Lagerstroemia Natchez* was planted at a latitude of 28 degrees, one would predict its adult height to most likely be:

   A. less than 6.0 meters.

   B. between 6.0 and 6.5 meters.

   C. between 6.5 and 7.5 meters.

   D. between 7.5 and 9.0 meters.

2. Flowering growth increases most rapidly during which of the following phases?

   F. Juvenile phase

   G. Intermediate phase

   H. Adult phase

   J. Death

3. Based on the information contained within Table 1, which of the following varieties grown in soil alone reached the greatest adult height?

   A. *Lagerstroemia indica Conestoga*

   B. *Lagerstroemia Miami*

   C. *Lagerstroemia indica Potomac*

   D. *Lagerstroemia Tuscarora*

4. Seedlings of the plant varieties shown in Table 1 were planted in a patch of soil enriched with organic compost at a latitude of 28 degrees. Which of the following varieties would probably come closest to an adult height of 3 meters?

   F. *Lagerstroemia indica Catawba*

   G. *Lagerstroemia Chickasaw*

   H. *Lagerstroemia fauriei Kiowa*

   J. *Lagerstroemia Natchez*

5. Which of the following hypotheses about flowering trees is supported by the information displayed in Figure 1?

   A. Flowering growth increases at a constant rate throughout the life cycle of the tree.

   B. The flowering growth of juvenile trees begins to increase sharply immediately after they are planted.

   C. The flowering growth of juvenile trees begins to decrease immediately after they are planted.

   D. Young trees experience little flowering growth until they reach a certain point in their developmental cycle.

6. If a *Lagerstroemia indica Potomac* shrub that is five meters tall and is located at 28 degrees latitude were observed for one year to determine its flowering rate, what trend would be observed?

   F. The shrub would not produce flowers during that time.

   G. The growth rate would increase slowly.

   H. The growth rate would increase quickly.

   J. The growth rate would remain the same.

GO ON TO THE NEXT PAGE ⟶

PASSAGE II

An isotope is a species of an element characterized by the number of neutrons it contains. Some isotopes are stable, while others are radioactive. Radioactive isotopes emit particles in radioactive decay. The process of bombardment involves shooting beams of particles at a sample material, often provoking radioactive decay. Scientists performed a series of experiments with 2 different isotopes in order to study 2 different types of radiation. One radiation, called alpha radiation, consists in the release of alpha particles (composed of 2 protons and 2 neutrons). Another radiation, called beta negative radiation, consists in the release of beta negative particles (composed of 1 electron).

EXPERIMENT 1

A sample of Isotope 1 was placed in a chamber and was bombarded with 1 of 4 particles (Particles A–D). The sample was then placed in a cloud chamber, allowing scientists to view the paths traced by any particles emitting from the sample (see Figure 1).

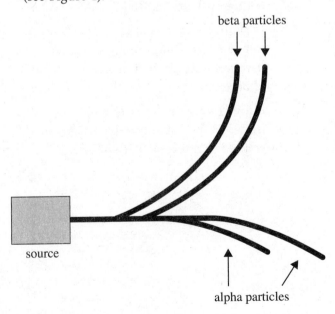

Figure 1

This procedure was repeated for Isotope 2. The particles emitted from the isotopes after bombardment were recorded in Table 1:

Table 1

Bombarding particle	Isotope 1		Isotope 2	
	alpha	beta	alpha	beta
A	−	−	+	−
B	+	−	−	+
C	+	+	+	+
D	−	+	−	−
None	−	−	+	−

EXPERIMENT 2

When a radioactive isotope emits particles, its properties change and it can transform into a different radioactive isotope. This decay process, called a decay chain, will continue until a relatively stable isotope is reached. In order to study decay chains, the resulting isotopes (Isotopes 1b and 2b) from Experiment 1 were monitored for their next decay process. The results were recorded in Table 2:

Table 2

Associated particle (from Experiment 1)	Isotope 1b		Isotope 2b	
	alpha	beta	alpha	beta
A	−	−	+	−
B	+	−	−	−
C	−	−	+	+
D	+	−	−	−
None	−	−	+	+

GO ON TO THE NEXT PAGE

7. What is the difference in the number of protons emitted by Isotope 1 before being bombarded with Particle D and after being bombarded with Particle D?

   A. 0
   B. 1
   C. 2
   D. 4

8. In Experiment 1, which of the bombarding particles caused alpha decay in Isotope 1?

   F. Particle B only
   G. Particle D only
   H. Particle B and Particle C only
   J. Particle A and Particle D only

9. Suppose that, after Experiment 2, scientists bombarded Isotopes 1b and 2b again with beams of Particle A. Which of the following could be the decay patterns from the resulting isotopes?

Isotope 1b		Isotope 2b	
alpha	beta	alpha	beta

   A.   +   –   +   +
   B.   –   –   –   +
   C.   +   +   –   –
   D.   –   +   +   –

10. Suppose that a scientist randomly selects one of the particle beams from Experiment 1 and bombards both initial isotopes with it. Following this bombardment, Isotope 1 emits only beta particles and Isotope 2 appears relatively stable. Based on the results of Experiment 1, it is most likely that the beam used for this bombardment consists of:

    F. Particle A.
    G. Particle B.
    H. Particle C.
    J. Particle D.

11. What is the evidence from Experiments 1 and 2 that suggests that bombardment by Particle C will trigger a relatively short decay chain in Isotope 1?

    A. No particles were emitted at all from Isotope 1 following bombardment by Particle C.
    B. Alpha particles were emitted from Isotope 1, but only beta particles were emitted in a second stage of decay.
    C. Initially both alpha and beta particles were emitted from Isotope 1, but no particles were emitted in a second stage of decay.
    D. Initially no particles were emitted from Isotope 1, but beta particles were emitted in a second stage of decay.

GO ON TO THE NEXT PAGE ⇨

12. Which of the following figures best represents the results from the bombardment of Isotope 2 with Particle B in Experiment 1?

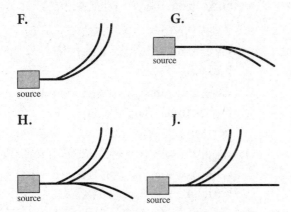

F.   G.

H.   J.

13. Is the conclusion that Isotope 2 will become relatively stable upon bombardment by Particle A supported by the results of Experiments 1 and 2?

   A. Yes, because alpha particles were emitted in both experiments.

   B. Yes, because beta particles were emitted in Experiment 1 and no particles were emitted in Experiment 2.

   C. No, because no particles were emitted in either experiment.

   D. No, because alpha particles were emitted in both experiments.

PASSAGE III

Ultraviolet (UV) light, a component of natural sunlight, can be damaging to human skin at high doses. UV light occurs in several ranges, including less damaging UV-A light and more damaging UV-B and UV-C light. Scientists designed two experiments to investigate the various factors affecting levels of UV light in a certain region of the United States.

EXPERIMENT 1

Scientists studied how levels of UV-A light vary seasonally and with elevation. They measured UV-A energy over a 10-minute span of time for several days to determine an average daily UV-A value for each site. Three sites were studied at three different elevations, and measurements from each site were obtained once in the winter and once in the summer. UV-A levels for an average 10-minute period beginning 30 minutes after the sun appeared directly overhead were calculated in millijoules per square centimeter (mJ/cm^2). The results are shown in Table 1.

Table 1

Season	Elevation (meters above sea level)	Average UV-A level (mJ/cm^2)
Winter	0	1,270
	1,000	1,400
	2,000	1,530
Summer	0	1,580
	1,000	1,740
	2,000	1,900

EXPERIMENT 2

Next, the levels of UV-A and UV-B were measured at 0, 1, and 2 hours past the time of day at which the sun was directly overhead during the winter at the site with an elevation of 2,000 meters above sea level. The level of UV-A decreased from 1,620 mJ/cm^2 at 0 hours to 1,430 mJ/cm^2 at 2 hours. The level of UV-B decreased from 48 mJ/cm^2 at 0 hours to 42 mJ/cm^2 at 2 hours.

GO ON TO THE NEXT PAGE

EXPERIMENT 3

UV-B light is another component of sunlight that occurs at a lower rate than UV-A but with higher energy. Levels of UV-B light, in millijoules per square centimeter (mJ/cm^2), were measured at various times of day during the summer at the site with an elevation of 2,000 meters above sea level. The results are shown in Table 2.

Table 2

Hours after sun is directly overhead	Average UV-B level (mJ/cm^2)
0	68
1	63
2	57
3	49
4	41

14. Which of the following variables was changed in Experiment 3?

  F. Background levels of UV-A light
  G. Background levels of UV-B light
  H. Time of day
  J. Season of the year

15. According to the results of these experiments, one way to reduce exposure to UV-A light would be to:

  A. spend time in environments with higher levels of UV-B light.
  B. live in an area with shorter summers and longer winters.
  C. live in an area with longer summers and shorter winters.
  D. make sure that all windows are designed to filter out UV-B light.

16. Based on the results of these experiments, if one compared UV-B levels when the sun is directly overhead to those when the sun is low on the horizon, the UV-B levels:

  F. when the sun is overhead would be lower than when the sun is low on the horizon.
  G. when the sun is overhead would be higher than when the sun is low on the horizon.
  H. when the sun is overhead would be the same as when the sun is low on the horizon.
  J. would be measurable only when the sun is overhead.

17. UV-C light is a third type of UV light that was not directly studied in the experiments above. However, if it behaves like the other types of UV light in the experiments, one would expect that UV-C levels:

  A. would decrease from year to year.
  B. would increase from year to year.
  C. are higher when the sun is directly overhead.
  D. are lower when the sun is directly overhead.

18. Based on the experimental results, as the number of hours after the sun is directly overhead increases:

  F. UV-A and UV-B levels both increase.
  G. UV-A levels increase and UV-B levels decrease.
  H. UV-A levels increase and UV-B levels stay the same.
  J. UV-A and UV-B levels both decrease.

GO ON TO THE NEXT PAGE

19. A community near the region studied has an elevation of 3,000 meters above sea level. At a time 30 minutes after the sun is directly overhead, one would predict that UV-A levels during the summer are:

   A. less than 1,580 mJ/cm².

   B. between 1,580 and 1,740 mJ/cm².

   C. between 1,740 and 1,900 mJ/cm².

   D. above 1,900 mJ/cm².

20. Which of the following would best represent the average UV-B level at an altitude of 2,000 meters in winter, one hour after the sun is directly overhead?

   F. 45 mJ/cm²

   G. 48 mJ/cm²

   H. 57 mJ/cm²

   J. 63 mJ/cm²

PASSAGE IV

The following experiments were performed to study the motion of gyroscopes, objects on a surface that spin quickly around an axis of rotation. These experiments focus on the gyroscopes' rate of *precession*, or the rate at which they revolve around the point where the axis of rotation touches a surface (see Figure 1).

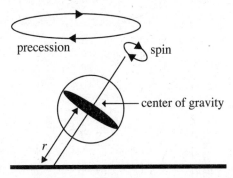

Figure 1

EXPERIMENT 1

A scientist tested several different gyroscopes that differed only in the distance from the gyroscope's center of gravity to the surface (r). A mechanical device was used to spin each gyroscope at the exact same rate of spin on the same surface, and the rate of precession was measured for each gyroscope in revolutions per minute (rpm). These rates are given in Table 1.

Table 1

r (centimeters)	Precession rate (rpm)
4	9
6	14
8	19
10	24
12	28

EXPERIMENT 2

Then, the scientist used a gyroscope of fixed size and varied the settings on the mechanical device spinning the gyroscope. The precession rate was measured several times for different spin rates, also measured in revolutions per minute (rpm). The results of this experiment are given in Table 2.

Table 2

Spin rate (rpm)	Precession rate (rpm)
250	41
400	25.5
600	17
750	14
1,200	8.5

GO ON TO THE NEXT PAGE ⟩

EXPERIMENT 3

A scientist placed a gyroscope similar to that used in the first two experiments on board a satellite orbiting Earth. It was found that for a gyroscope of fixed size and spin rate, its precession rate on the satellite was about one-eighth of its precession rate on the surface of Earth. For example, a precession rate of approximately 24 rpm would become approximately 3 rpm on the satellite.

21. If, during Experiment 1, the scientists had tested a sixth gyroscope with a center of gravity that was 9 cm from the surface, its precession rate would most likely have been:

   A. 4 rpm.
   B. 9 rpm.
   C. 21.5 rpm.
   D. 23.5 rpm.

22. According to the results of Experiment 1, one can conclude that the gyroscope's precession rate increases as the gyroscope's center of gravity:

   F. decreases in distance from the surface.
   G. increases in distance from the surface.
   H. remains the same distance from the surface.
   J. changes in mass.

23. Of the following graphs, which best represents how changes in precession rate are related to changes in spin rate, as shown in Experiment 2?

A.

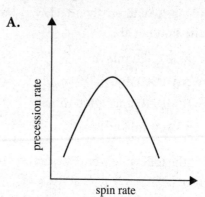

B.

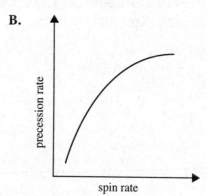

C.

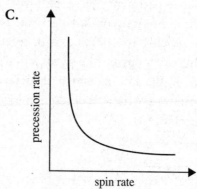

D.

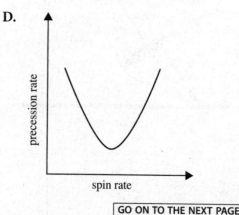

GO ON TO THE NEXT PAGE

24. The hypothesis of the scientist in Experiment 3 was that precession rate is related to gravity, which decreases as one's distance from Earth increases. To confirm this hypothesis, the scientist should repeat this experiment on:

F. several different satellites at varying distances from Earth.

G. another satellite at the exact same distance from Earth as the first satellite.

H. a satellite orbiting in the opposite direction.

J. Earth's surface while varying the gyroscope's spin rate.

25. If an *r* of 6 cm was used throughout Experiment 2, what was the most likely spin rate used in Experiment 1?

A. 400 rpm

B. 600 rpm

C. 750 rpm

D. 1,200 rpm

26. If the effects tested in Experiment 1 had not been known during the design of Experiment 2, how might this have affected Experiment 2?

F. The scientist might have used gyroscopes with different masses.

G. The scientist might not have always used the same size gyroscope.

H. The scientist might have tested the gyroscope on a different surface.

J. The scientist might have used a different-shaped gyroscope.

27. Which is the best way to investigate the effect of gyroscope mass on precession rate while keeping the spin rate constant?

A. Use gyroscopes made by different companies.

B. Use gyroscopes that are the same size and shape, but that are made from different types of metal.

C. Use several different gyroscopes that are each measured on both Earth and on a satellite.

D. Use gyroscopes that are all the same mass but that have different sizes.

PASSAGE V

Precipitation is a general term for a form of water, such as rain, snow, sleet, or hail, that falls from the sky to the surface of Earth. There are two theories that attempt to explain how the tiny water droplets in clouds combine to form precipitation.

COLLISION AND COALESCENCE THEORY

As shown in Stage I of Figure I, a cloud is initially composed of numerous droplets of liquid water of varying sizes, but all microscopic. As these droplets move about within the cloud, they can collide with one another. These collisions can either result in the droplets bouncing apart again or sticking together (*coalescence*) to form a larger droplet (see Stage II). The process continues until large drops are formed which are too heavy to remain suspended in the cloud any longer. Some of these drops will then split apart into smaller drops that continue the collision and coalescence process, while others will fall to the ground in the form of precipitation (see Stage III).

GO ON TO THE NEXT PAGE

ICE CRYSTAL THEORY

In this theory, the tiny droplets in clouds rise to a point in Earth's atmosphere where the temperature is lower than the freezing point of water. Initially, the cloud is composed of many supercooled water droplets, still in liquid form (see Stage I of Figure II). Some of these droplets then condense around tiny impurities in the air to form miniature ice crystals (see Stage II). Water vapor in the air can then freeze onto the surface of the crystals, causing some of the droplets to evaporate in order to maintain a constant level of water vapor (see Stage III). The ice crystals quickly become too heavy to remain suspended in the air and fall to the ground, often melting again in the warmer temperatures near the ground to form rain (see Stage IV). The net effect is that the formation of ice crystals takes moisture out of the air, allowing the crystals to grow larger at the expense of the droplets.

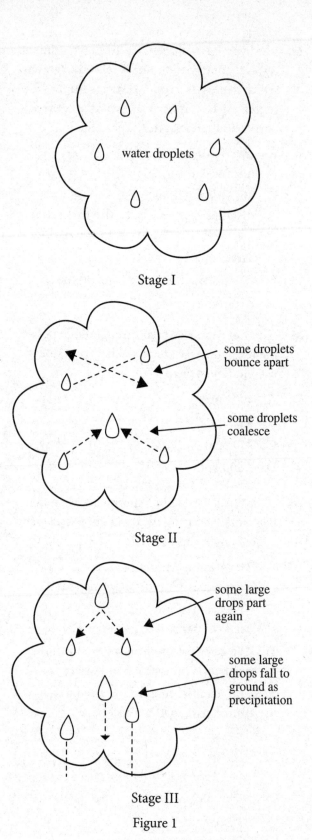

Figure 1

GO ON TO THE NEXT PAGE ⇨

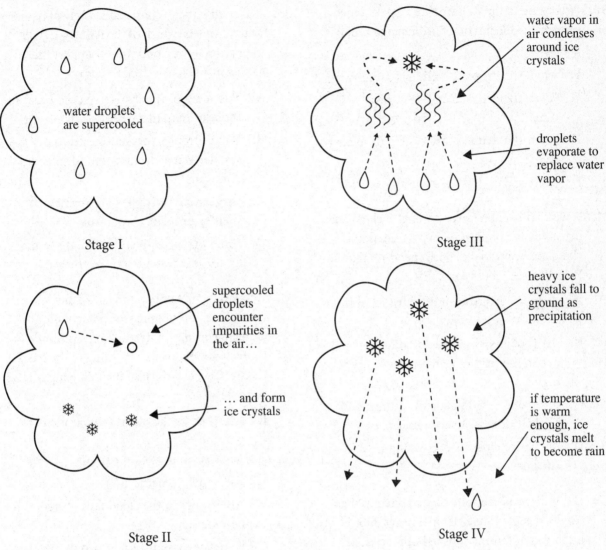

water vapor in air condenses around ice crystals

droplets evaporate to replace water vapor

Stage I

Stage III

water droplets are supercooled

supercooled droplets encounter impurities in the air…

… and form ice crystals

heavy ice crystals fall to ground as precipitation

if temperature is warm enough, ice crystals melt to become rain

Stage II

Stage IV

Figure 2

28. In which of the following situations would supporters of both theories agree that precipitation should NOT occur?

F. A cloud with water droplets colliding and coalescing to produce larger droplets

G. A cloud with water droplets forming crystals around impurities in the air

H. A cloud with an insufficient number of water droplets

J. A cloud containing elements too heavy to remain suspended in the air

29. The Collision and Coalescence and Ice Crystal Theories differ on which of the following points?

A. Exterior shape of cloud formation

B. State of matter of precipitation before falling from the cloud

C. Amount of precipitation that reaches the ground

D. Climate required for precipitation to occur

GO ON TO THE NEXT PAGE

30. According to the Collision and Coalescence Theory, the likelihood of producing rainfall is greater:

    F. when the droplets collide at a high rate.

    G. when the droplets collide at a variable rate.

    H. when the temperature causes droplets to freeze.

    J. shortly after the last rainfall occurred.

31. A weather balloon travels through a cloud and detects a high proportion of particles in the cloud too heavy to remain suspended in the air. Both theories would agree that:

    A. there are insufficient impurities in the air to form ice crystals.

    B. the probability of precipitation occurring in the near future is very high.

    C. the water-based particles in the cloud are colliding at a very rapid rate.

    D. the entire cloud is decreasing in altitude.

32. City A has a higher rate of precipitation than City B, despite similar temperatures, humidity, and cloud formations in both locations. The Ice Crystal Theory would suggest that the higher rate of precipitation in City A most likely results from which of the following?

    F. The greater frequency of thunder and lightning storms in City A

    G. Large atmospheric density differences between City A and City B

    H. A greater number of impurities released into the air by factories in City A

    J. The lower rate of air pollution in City A

33. If a cloud initially consisted entirely of liquid water droplets, which of the following statements about the cloud would support the Collision and Coalescence Theory?

    A. The mass of the droplets is too great for them to remain suspended in the air.

    B. Water droplets crystallize around smaller water droplets found in the atmosphere.

    C. Larger water droplets are formed by smaller droplets combining.

    D. Some of the droplets evaporate to make up for lost water vapor in the air.

34. Depending on temperature and other conditions, it is possible for precipitation to change forms on its way to the ground. If precipitation forms according to the Ice Crystal Theory, which of the following is NOT possible?

    F. After ice in the cloud falls, it melts to become rain.

    G. After ice in the cloud falls, it partially melts to become sleet.

    H. After water in the cloud falls, it freezes to become snow.

    J. Some ice crystals formed around impurities in the air first melt and then evaporate before they fall from the cloud.

PASSAGE VI

Elements as shown in the periodic table have a number of different properties which depend on the structure of the element's atoms. For example, these properties might depend on the atom's number of *electrons* (negatively charged particles), which move in patterns called *shells* (see Figure 1).

GO ON TO THE NEXT PAGE

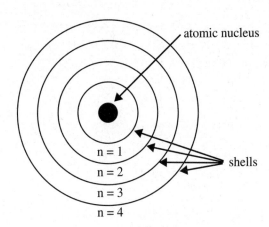

atomic nucleus

n = 1
n = 2
n = 3
n = 4

shells

Figure 1
Note: Drawing is NOT to scale.

Table 1 lists properties for several chemical elements. The table includes the number of shells in the atom (n), the number of electrons in the atom's outer shell (e), the atomic radius (r), the energy (I) required to remove one electron from the atom's outer shell (in electron volts, eV), and a measure of attraction (c) to electrons in a chemical bond (in Pauling units).

Table 1

Element	n	e	r (× 10⁻¹¹ m)	I (eV)	c
C	2	4	9.1	11.2	2.5
N	2	5	7.5	14.5	3.0
O	2	6	6.5	13.6	3.5
F	2	7	5.7	17.4	4.0
Si	3	4	14.6	8.2	1.8
P	3	5	12.6	10.5	2.1
S	3	6	10.9	10.4	2.5
Cl	3	7	9.7	13.0	3.0
Ge	4	4	15.2	7.9	1.8
As	4	5	13.3	9.8	2.0
Se	4	6	12.2	9.8	2.4
Br	4	7	11.2	11.8	2.8

35. For any value of n, Table 1 indicates that as e increases, r:

    A. increases only.
    B. first increases, then decreases.
    C. decreases only.
    D. remains unchanged.

36. According to Table 1, for an element with n = 2 and e = 3, the most likely value of r would be:

    F. 11.7 × 10⁻¹¹ m.
    G. 8.8 × 10⁻¹¹ m.
    H. 7.4 × 10⁻¹¹ m.
    J. 6.2 × 10⁻¹¹ m.

37. According to the information in the passage, it is possible to decrease an atom's negative charge by:

    A. decreasing the radius of the atom.
    B. forming a chemical bond with the atom.
    C. applying energy to the atom.
    D. changing the number of shells in the atom.

38. The hypothesis that for a given value of n, c increases as the number of electrons in the atom's outer shell increases, is supported by the data in Table 1 when:

    F. n = 2 only.
    G. n = 2 or 3 only.
    H. n = 4 only.
    J. n = 2, 3, or 4.

39. The most energy will be required to remove an electron from shell:

    A. n = 3 in Si
    B. n = 3 in Cl
    C. n = 2 in C
    D. n = 2 in F

GO ON TO THE NEXT PAGE

40. Which of the following pairs of elements does not have the same value in Pauling units?

   F. Se and As
   G. N and Cl
   H. Ge and Si
   J. C and S

WRITING TEST

40 Minutes

Directions: This is a test of your writing skills. You will have forty (40) minutes to write an essay in English. Before you begin planning and writing your essay, read the writing prompt carefully to understand exactly what you are being asked to do. Your essay will be evaluated on the evidence it provides of your ability to do the following:

- Express judgments by evaluating the three perspectives given in the prompt, taking a position on an issue, and explaining the relationship among all four ideas
- Develop a position by using logical reasoning and by supporting your ideas
- Maintain a focus on the topic throughout the essay
- Organize ideas in a logical way
- Use language clearly and effectively according to the conventions of standard written English

You may use the unlined pages in this test booklet to plan your essay. These pages will not be scored. *You must write your essay in pencil on the lined pages in the answer folder.* Your writing on those lined pages will be scored. You may not need all the lined pages, but to ensure you have enough room to finish, do NOT skip lines. You may write corrections or additions neatly between the lines of your essay, but do NOT write in the margins of the lined pages. *Illegible essays cannot be scored, so you must write (or print) clearly.*

If you finish before time is called you may review your work. Lay your pencil down immediately when time is called.

GO ON TO THE NEXT PAGE

ACT PRACTICE TEST EIGHT

ACCESS TO TECHNOLOGY

To help ready students to become productive members of the workforce, schools concentrate on providing a strong foundation on which students can build their careers. Since job applicants who are proficient in word processing applications, email programs, and storage tools are more likely to be hired than applicants who do not have technology experience, it is to the benefit of students that schools offer technology instruction in high school. Given the importance of technology in today's society, should schools be responsible for providing ongoing access to computers for every student? Since many students will need to use computers in various capacities throughout their lifetimes, how well a school provides access to technology directly affects its student body.

Read and carefully consider these perspectives. Each discusses the importance of student access to technology.

Perspective One	Perspective Two	Perspective Three
Schools should be encouraged to incorporate technology objectives into homework assignments and class projects, but schools do not have an obligation to provide unlimited access to computers. Teachers can provide time during the school day for students to use on-site computer labs, which will allow students the tools they need to complete assignments that require computer technology.	Schools should be required to provide personal computers for students to use at least throughout their high school careers, if not during middle and elementary school as well. Unlimited access to a personal computer for every student will foster continual development of technological abilities, which is a highly valued skill set.	Schools and computer companies should work together to provide significant student discounts so that the majority of parents who have school-age children can afford to purchase at least one personal computer. Students who do not have their own computers can use their schools' computer labs or go to their local libraries to complete homework assignments that require computer technology.

ESSAY TASK

Write a unified, coherent essay in which you evaluate multiple perspectives regarding access to technology. In your essay, be sure to:

- analyze and evaluate the perspectives given

- state and develop your own perspective on the issue

- explain the relationship between your perspective and those given

Your perspective may be in full agreement with any of the others, in partial agreement, or wholly different. Whatever the case, support your ideas with logical reasoning and detailed, persuasive examples.

GO ON TO THE NEXT PAGE

PLANNING YOUR ESSAY

You may wish to consider the following as you think critically about the task:

Strengths and weaknesses of the three given perspectives

- What insights do they offer, and what do they fail to consider?

- Why might they be persuasive to others, or why might they fail to persuade?

Your own knowledge, experience, and values

- What is your perspective on this issue, and what are its strengths and weaknesses?

- How will you support your perspective in your essay?

_____

_____

_____

_____

_____

_____

_____

_____

_____

_____

_____

_____

_____

_____

_____

_____

_____

GO ON TO THE NEXT PAGE

Practice Test Eight
ANSWER KEY

ENGLISH TEST

1. B	11. D	21. B	31. B	41. C	51. D	61. C	71. B
2. J	12. J	22. H	32. H	42. F	52. J	62. F	72. J
3. B	13. B	23. B	33. B	43. D	53. C	63. B	73. A
4. J	14. F	24. G	34. G	44. J	54. G	64. G	74. J
5. C	15. D	25. C	35. A	45. C	55. A	65. D	75. A
6. J	16. H	26. F	36. G	46. H	56. H	66. G	
7. C	17. C	27. C	37. B	47. B	57. A	67. C	
8. G	18. J	28. H	38. F	48. J	58. H	68. H	
9. C	19. C	29. B	39. D	49. A	59. D	69. D	
10. F	20. F	30. J	40. F	50. G	60. G	70. G	

MATHEMATICS TEST

1. D	9. E	17. C	25. D	33. C	41. E	49. B	57. D
2. F	10. H	18. J	26. J	34. J	42. K	50. H	58. J
3. C	11. D	19. D	27. A	35. C	43. B	51. C	59. C
4. K	12. K	20. G	28. F	36. F	44. K	52. K	60. G
5. D	13. E	21. C	29. D	37. B	45. C	53. A	
6. F	14. H	22. K	30. G	38. G	46. F	54. J	
7. B	15. A	23. D	31. C	39. E	47. C	55. B	
8. J	16. G	24. F	32. J	40. G	48. K	56. K	

READING TEST

1. C	6. F	11. C	16. H	21. C	26. F	31. B	36. G
2. H	7. B	12. F	17. D	22. G	27. C	32. H	37. D
3. B	8. J	13. B	18. F	23. D	28. J	33. D	38. F
4. F	9. C	14. J	19. B	24. F	29. B	34. H	39. C
5. D	10. F	15. C	20. H	25. C	30. G	35. D	40. G

SCIENCE TEST

1. D	6. J	11. C	16. G	21. C	26. G	31. B	36. F
2. G	7. C	12. F	17. C	22. G	27. B	32. H	37. C
3. B	8. H	13. D	18. J	23. C	28. H	33. C	38. J
4. F	9. B	14. H	19. D	24. F	29. B	34. H	39. D
5. D	10. J	15. B	20. F	25. C	30. F	35. C	40. F

ANSWERS AND EXPLANATIONS

ENGLISH TEST

PASSAGE I

1. B
Category: Wordiness
Difficulty: Medium
Getting to the Answer: Look for the answer choice that expresses the sentence's Idea in the clearest, most concise way. The clearest version here is (B): "If you want to succeed as a Hollywood screenwriter." This is grammatically correct and sets up the if–then relationship between the clauses. Choice A is awkward and unnecessarily wordy. Choices C and D create sentences that are grammatically incorrect.

2. J
Category: Word Choice
Difficulty: Low
Getting to the Answer: Use "few" for items that can be counted and "less" for quantities that cannot. Because screenwriters can be counted, "few" in (J) is correct. Choices F and G both incorrectly use "less." Choice H uses the idiomatically incorrect "Very many few."

3. B
Category: Writing Strategy
Difficulty: Medium
Getting to the Answer: Don't forget to read for logic as well as for grammar and usage. The preceding sentence explains that screenwriters don't have "a formal career path." The first part of the sentence in question gives an example of what a formal career path might involve—going to a school career center for help. The correct answer will provide another example along these lines. Someone with a formal career path could find job opportunities in the classified ads, but a screenwriter cannot. Choice (B) is correct. Choice A refers to "extracurricular activities," which is out of scope for a sentence concern-

ing a career path. There's no reason to believe that a college graduate can't understand how difficult it is to become a screenwriter, as C suggests. Choice D is an example of something involved in an *informal* career path, not a formal one.

4. J
Category: Wordiness
Difficulty: Low
Getting to the Answer: Using words that mean essentially the same thing together is redundant. A suggestion is, by definition, "proposed," so using the two words together is redundant; you can eliminate F, G and H. Choice H also uses both "highlight" and "emphasized," but when you highlight something, you emphasize it. Choice (J) is the only choice that does not contain redundant language.

5. C
Category: Word Choice
Difficulty: Low
Getting to the Answer: Beware of answer choices that make changes to parts of a sentence that contain no error; these choices will almost never be correct. The subject of the sentence is "a college education," so the verb needs to be the singular "is." Choices B, C, and D all correct the subject–verb error, but Choice B incorrectly separates the subject from the verb with a comma and D creates a sentence that is grammatically incorrect. Choice (C) is correct.

6. J
Category: Wordiness
Difficulty: Low
Getting to the Answer: When "OMIT the underlined portion" is an option, read the underlined selection for relevance. The topic of this paragraph, and the entire essay, is the career of screenwriting. No matter how it is worded, a sentence about an acting career is out of scope. This sentence should be omitted, (J).

7. C

Category: Word Choice

Difficulty: Low

Getting to the Answer: The ACT often separates a subject from its verb with an intervening phrase or clause containing another noun. Although the singular noun "college" is closer to the verb "begins" in this sentence, its subject is the plural "screenwriters." The verb needs to be in the plural form, which eliminates all answer choices but (C). Choice B does not address the error. "Has begun" in D is also singular.

8. G

Category: Connections

Difficulty: Medium

Getting to the Answer: This is a Connections question, so the correct answer will create a bridge between the last sentence of paragraph 3 and the topic of paragraph 4. Paragraph 3 suggests that a college education may not be the best path for aspiring screenwriters. As indicated by the transition "Moreover," paragraph 4 adds to this idea. The best transition between the two paragraphs, then, will relate to the possible disadvantages of college for screenwriters. Choice (G) does this without introducing any errors. Choice F contradicts both paragraphs, which suggest that college may not be relevant for screenwriters. Choice H is much more general than (G), making it a less effective transition. Choice J is unnecessarily wordy.

9. C

Category: Wordiness

Difficulty: Medium

Getting to the Answer: Be wary of answer choices that are significantly longer than the underlined selection; they will rarely be correct. As written, the underlined portion is unnecessarily wordy and the phrase "at a prestigious school" is misleading, since it is not just some colleges that the writer deems irrelevant for screenwriters. Choice (C) corrects this error by focusing only on the student loans. Choice B is much wordier than the original and includes ir-

relevant information about "work study programs." Choice D creates a sentence fragment.

10. F

Category: Punctuation

Difficulty: Medium

Getting to the Answer: To check if a semicolon is correctly used, try replacing it with a period and making the second clause a separate sentence. If two complete sentences are formed, then the semicolon is correct. A semicolon is correctly used here to join two independent clauses. NO CHANGE is needed, (F). Choice G incorrectly inserts a comma between "this" and the noun it modifies. Choice H incorrectly places a comma after "so"; a comma should be placed before a coordinating conjunction. Choice J creates a run-on sentence.

11. D

Category: Punctuation

Difficulty: Medium

Getting to the Answer: If you're unsure about punctuation, read the sentence without the descriptive words and phrases to focus on its structure. Stripped of some of the descriptive phrases, this sentence becomes easier to deal with: "Those without college educations are less averse to the jobs, aspiring screenwriters are forced to take." There is no reason for a comma here. Choice (D) correctly uses "that" to indicate that the phrase "aspiring screenwriters are forced to take" is meant to modify "jobs." Choice B creates a run-on sentence. Choice C incorrectly specifies "these" aspiring screenwriters alone are forced to take low-wage jobs.

12. J

Category: Word Choice

Difficulty: Low

Getting to the Answer: Many words can function as more than one part of speech; use context to help you eliminate choices that use these words incorrectly. The word "that's" in the underlined selection is a contraction of the pronoun "that" and the verb "is," but context tells us that this sentence requires "that" to be used as a conjunction. Choice (J) uses "that" correctly and does not introduce any new errors. Choice G replaces the correct possessive pronoun "their" with its homophone "there"; familiarize yourself with the correct uses of "their," "there," and "they're" before Test Day. Choice H creates a grammatically incorrect sentence.

13. B
Category: Punctuation
Difficulty: Low
Getting to the Answer: To check for correct usage of the possessive, use context to determine if something that is discussed belongs to someone. Here, the "reputation" belongs to the "Hollywood screenwriter," so an apostrophe is needed to show possession. Choice (B) corrects the error. Choice A uses the plural "screenwriters" instead of the possessive "screenwriter's." Choice C does not address the error. Choice D indicates possession with the word "of"; because possession has already been shown, the 's in "screenwriter's" isn't necessary.

14. F
Category: Word Choice
Difficulty: Medium
Getting to the Answer: About one in four English Test questions will require NO CHANGE. This sentence is correct as written, (F). Choice G illogically states the screenwriter's work must be "increasing." Choice H suggests that screenwriters face pressure to "be . . . work," which does not make sense. Choice J is idiomatically incorrect; "to raise," not "to raising," is the correct infinitive.

15. D
Category: Wordiness
Difficulty: Medium
Getting to the Answer: Always consider relevance when "OMIT the underlined portion" is an option. A sentence may be related to the topic of the passage but irrelevant in the context in which it is used. Paragraph 5 discusses the power of studio executives, so the underlined portion, if it were to be included, would logically go there. The flow of the passage is improved when you OMIT the underlined sentence, (D).

PASSAGE II

16. H
Category: Wordiness
Difficulty: Medium
Getting to the Answer: The underlined selection may repeat something said elsewhere in the sentence, so take the whole sentence into consideration before choosing an answer. This sentence already indicates that the mission "gained fame," so it is unnecessary to repeat that it is "well known." Eliminate F. Choice G unnecessarily uses the adjective "seasonal" along with "summer"; summer is a season, so you can eliminate G. Choice J describes the "home" as "residential," but a home is, by definition, residential. Choice (H) is the only choice that eliminates all redundant language.

17. C
Category: Connections
Difficulty: Medium
Getting to the Answer: When a question stem asks you to provide a transition between paragraphs, read both paragraphs through before trying to select an answer. This question stem asks for "the most specific and logical transition." The most specific language is used in (C): "the swallows of San Juan Capistrano." These are the "cliff swallows" referred to in the first sentence of paragraph 2. Choices A, B, and D all offer more general terms; naming the swallows is more specific than referring to them as "birds," "migrating animals," or an "Argentinean species."

18. J
Category: Sentence Sense
Difficulty: Medium
Getting to the Answer: Items in a compound must be parallel in form. The two verbs joined by "and" in the original sentence are "nest" and "bearing." Only (J) provides the needed parallel verb. Choices F, G, and H all use the *-ing* form, violating the rules of parallel structure.

19. C
Category: Sentence Sense
Difficulty: Medium
Getting to the Answer: Items in a series or list require parallel structure. There are three verbs in this series. The first two verbs, "ring" and "is," are in the simple present tense, so the underlined verb should be also. Choice (C) is correct. Choices A, B, and D all violate the rules of parallel structure.

20. F
Category: Sentence Sense
Difficulty: Medium
Getting to the Answer: NO CHANGE will be the answer to about 25% of English Test questions. This sentence is correct as written, so (F) is the answer. The past tense verb "discovered" used after the past progressive "were seeking" indicates that the birds found the mission while in the process of looking for "refuge." Choices G and J omit the pronoun "they," suggesting that it was the innkeeper, not the birds, who found the mission. Choice H creates a grammatically incorrect sentence.

21. B
Category: Word Choice
Difficulty: Low
Getting to the Answer: The preposition "of" cannot be part of a verb phrase. The preposition "of" in the original version should actually be the verb "have." Choice (B) corrects this error. Choices A and C both use the preposition "of" instead of the verb "have." Choice D omits the verb "have," leaving the grammatically incorrect "may developed."

22. H
Category: Word Choice
Difficulty: Low
Getting to the Answer: Before Test Day, know the past participles of irregular verbs such as "to choose." This will help you quickly eliminate some wrong answer choices. An adverb, not an adjective, is needed to modify the verb "chose." Choice (H) corrects the error. "Chosened," in G, is not a word. Choice J creates a grammatically incorrect sentence.

23. B
Category: Word Choice
Difficulty: Low
Getting to the Answer: Many word choice questions will present you with four grammatically correct idioms; use context to determine which is correct. "Of which," A, "to which," B, and "by which," C, are all proper idioms, but the only one that makes sense in context is (B): the swallows "return *to*" their nests. Choice D omits the preposition, incorrectly suggesting that the birds return the nests to some person or place.

24. G
Category: Writing Strategy
Difficulty: Medium
Getting to the Answer: When an English Test question has a question stem, read it carefully. Frequently, all of the answer choices will be both consistent and relevant, but only one will fulfill the requirements of the stem. Only one sentence gives a specific reason for the swallows choosing the mission based on its location near two rivers. Choice (G) explains that the rivers provide a food supply for the swallows, which is a logical reason for the swallows to live nearby. Choice F provides information about swallow nest-building, not about swallows choosing the mission based on its location near the rivers. Choice H provides a detail about the rivers, but it is unclear how this detail relates to the swallows. Choice J is a generalization; it doesn't tell you anything specific about the "other advantages" provided by the rivers.

25. C
Category: Connections
Difficulty: Medium
Getting to the Answer: Remember to read until you have enough information. When asked to transition between paragraphs, read them both. The end of paragraph 4 talks about protecting the swallows; the beginning of paragraph 5 sets up a contrast with the introductory phrase "Although the community clearly sees the importance of providing a home for

the swallows." The best Connection should relate to both of these ideas. Choice (C) does so, describing specific steps the community has taken to protect the swallows' nests. Choice A focuses on how people enjoy the swallows, not on how the community tries to provide a home for them. Choice B doesn't mention anything specific about "providing a home for the swallows," as referred to in paragraph 5. "Other migrating species" in D are out of scope for this passage.

26. F
Category: Punctuation
Difficulty: Medium
Getting to the Answer: Remember your tested comma rules; no other uses will be correct on the ACT. The sentence is correct as written; NO CHANGE is needed, (F). Choices G and H both incorrectly insert a comma between the noun "community" and its verb "sees." Choice J uses an adjective ("clear"), instead of an adverb, to modify the verb "sees."

27. C
Category: Punctuation
Difficulty: Medium
Getting to the Answer: Dashes may be used to offset supplementary material within a sentence. Here, "usually in the hills" is descriptive information about "the area." Such descriptive phrases can be offset from the main sentence with commas or dashes; (C) correctly uses dashes to offset and emphasize the phrase. Choice A omits one of the commas necessary to correctly offset the phrase. Choice B uses a semicolon, but the second clause is not independent. Choice D is awkward and unnecessarily wordy.

28. H
Category: Punctuation
Difficulty: Medium
Getting to the Answer: If you're unsure whether a phrase or clause should be offset with commas, try reading the sentence without it. If the absence of the phrase or clause makes the sentence incomplete or illogical, then the commas are incorrect. Only one

comma is needed here to set off the introductory word "Fortunately." Choice (H) provides the correct punctuation. Choice F treats "city and mission officials have started" as nonessential information, but removing this clause does not leave a complete sentence. Choice G incorrectly treats "Fortunately city and mission officials have started" as in introductory clause. Choice J treats "city and mission officials" as nonessential information, but this is the subject of the sentence.

29. B
Category: Word Choice
Difficulty: Medium
Getting to the Answer: Some Idioms will be properly constructed but incorrect in context. The phrase "in an attempt" requires the infinitive verb form; (B) is correct. Choice A uses "to attempt at," which is idiomatically incorrect. Choices C and D change the infinitive "to attempt" to the noun "an attempt"; this creates an illogical sentence in C and an idiomatically incorrect one in D.

30. J
Category: Organization
Difficulty: Medium
Getting to the Answer: Since NO CHANGE is not offered as an option, you'll need to find the most logical place to insert the new sentence. Paragraph 5 discusses the problems that "have arisen in recent years," so this sentence about a problem with the swallows belongs in paragraph 5; eliminate F and G. Sentences 2 and 3 in paragraph 5 explain the specific problems that are leading to a decline in the swallow migration. It is reasonable that one result of the changes discussed in sentences 2 and 3 would be the lack of "huge clouds of swallows descending upon the mission as in the past decades." The best placement for the new sentence is after sentence 3 in paragraph 5; (J) is correct.

PASSAGE III

31. B
Category: Punctuation
Difficulty: Low
Getting to the Answer: The possessive form of most singular nouns is formed by adding "'s." Context tells us that the singular possessive, not the plural, form is needed here. Choice (B) retains the singular form and places the apostrophe correctly. Choice C creates the plural of the noun and does not show possession. Choice D creates the plural possessive of the noun, but the context is referring to one city.

32. H
Category: Sentence Sense
Difficulty: Medium
Getting to the Answer: Be sure to read ACT passages for logic as well as grammatical correctness. The word "which" modifies "team," and a preposition is necessary. Choice (H) is the correct answer, because it adds the preposition "for." Choice G introduces an incorrect preposition. Omitting the selection, as J suggests, creates an incomplete sentence.

33. B
Category: Wordiness
Difficulty: Medium
Getting to the Answer: Adjectives are used to modify nouns and pronouns; all other parts of speech are modified by adverbs. Here, the adjective "easy" is incorrectly used to modify the verb "become." Choice (B) replaces the adjective with its adverb form, "easily." Choices C and D change the adjective to an adverb, but each case is either comparative or superlative.

34. G
Category: Sentence Sense
Difficulty: Medium
Getting to the Answer: A complete sentence must have a subject and predicate verb that express a complete thought. In this case, there are two subjects and predicates which create a run-on sentence and an incomplete thought. Choice (G) properly uses the conjunction "so" to join two independent clauses expressing connected thoughts. Choice H creates a grammatically correct sentence, but the thought loses its clarity when the second phrase indicates a cause-and-effect relationship. Choice J uses a comma but creates the same error as F by maintaining a run-on sentence.

35. A
Category: Punctuation
Difficulty: Low
Getting to the Answer: Make sure punctuation correctly reflects the intention of a sentence as well as its grammar. The sentences in question are correctly separated by a period because they express two separate, complete thoughts. This matches (A). Choice B is incorrect because, while the colon draws the reader's attention to a specific point directly related to what precedes it, the words "for when" makes the sentence structure awkward. The first sentence says there are "many" disadvantages to free agency, but the information in the second sentence expresses only one disadvantage. Choice C is also incorrect because the comma separates two independent clauses. Choice D is incorrect because it creates a run-on.

36. G
Category: Punctuation
Difficulty: Medium
Getting to the Answer: When a word or phrase is offset from the rest of the sentence with commas, the sentence must make sense without that phrase. The sentence is grammatically incorrect as written. A comma incorrectly separates "who" from the remainder of the phrase. Choice (G) corrects this by placing a comma only at the end of the complete phrase. Choices H and J maintain the incorrect use of a comma, which breaks up the thought.

37. B
Category: Organization
Difficulty: High
Getting to the Answer: Use context clues to help determine the answer to Organization questions. The paragraph starts with "There are many disadvantages," and the final paragraph starts with "A third disadvantage." Choice (B) connects these thoughts with "A second disadvantage" and sequentially supports the strength of the argument as a whole. Choice C incorrectly uses an adverb to introduce the fourth paragraph and is missing a comma to separate the introductory phrase. Choice D makes the final sentence of the paragraph a conclusion, rather than another item in a series.

38. F
Category: Wordiness
Difficulty: Low
Getting to the Answer: When OMIT is an option, first determine if the underlined information is necessary to the meaning of the sentence. The underlined information is necessary to the sentence, which means J can be eliminated. In the correct answer, (F), "upon" correctly precedes the direct object "each other." Choice G uses incorrect prepositions, "to" and "on," and separates the direct object from "depend." Choice H is illogical; the players depend on each other, not on winning.

39. D
Category: Punctuation
Difficulty: Low
Getting to the Answer: A list must be set off with serial commas. Choice (D) is the correct answer because it correctly places the commas between each item. Choice A is incorrect because it is a run-on sentence. Choice B is incorrect because it uses a comma to separate the adverb "together" from the verb it modifies, "plays." Choice C is incorrect because the comma that separates the first item from the second is missing.

40. F
Category: Connections
Difficulty: Low
Getting to the Answer: When determining whether two thoughts are correctly combined, check for proper punctuation and the use of a conjunction. This sentence correctly uses a comma and conjunction to join two independent clauses. The sentence is correct as written, so (F) is the correct answer. Choices G, H, and J use incorrect conjunctions.

41. C
Category: Verb Tenses
Difficulty: Medium
Getting to the Answer: Unless context clearly indicates a change in time periods, verb tenses with a sentence, paragraph, or passage should remain consistent. The context of the paragraph is present tense; (C) is the correct answer. Choices B and D both introduce inconsistent verb tenses.

42. F
Category: Sentence Sense
Difficulty: Medium
Getting to the Answer: Make sure modifying phrases are placed so as to modify logical things. Choice (F) is the correct answer because it concludes the sequence of three major disadvantages to free agency and correctly modifies "the loss of team dynasties." Choice G is incorrect because "loss" modifies "team dynasties." Choices H and J are incorrect because the adverb "third" modifies "disadvantage," not "loss."

43. D
Category: Wordiness
Difficulty: Medium
Getting to the Answer: Read the sentence without the underlined information to see if it still makes sense, and eliminate answer choices that contain redundant language. In the context of the paragraph, the sentence still makes sense without the underlined information. Choice (D) is the correct answer. Choice B contains redundant language. Adding an

apostrophe to "years" in C is grammatically incorrect and the phrase is redundant.

44. J
Category: Connections
Difficulty: High
Getting to the Answer: Remember to read for logic, as well as grammar and usage. Choice (J) is the only choice that logically connects ideas in this sentence by setting up the contrast between the simultaneous failure of the home team and the success of the player's new team. Choice F is incorrect because it creates a causal relationship between the home team failing and the player's new team winning (as a result of the home team's failure). The author is trying to convey that the player's new team is winning because of the player. Choices G and H do not logically connect the ideas in this sentence.

45. C
Category: Writing Strategy
Difficulty: Medium
Getting to the Answer: Read question stems carefully. Often, the wrong answer choices will be consistent with the passage but fail to answer the question posed. The question stem is looking for the choice that best reflects the main idea of the essay. This paragraph concerns the author's dislike of what free agency has done to his experience of football; Choice (C) makes this point best. Choice A is a general opinion that does not relate to the specific argument in the essay. Choice B is incorrect because the author does not describe any benefits of free agency. Choice D is incorrect because it takes the opposite point of view from the main point of persuasion in the essay.

PASSAGE IV

46. H
Category: Wordiness
Difficulty: Medium
Getting to the Answer: Be aware of phrases like "it is only," because they add no real meaning to the

sentence and provide no clear antecedent for the pronoun. "It is only" is unnecessary here. Choice (H) eliminates the unnecessary language and makes the second clause subordinate. Choices G and J both use incorrect grammatical structure.

47. B
Category: Word Choice
Difficulty: Medium
Getting to the Answer: Use "who" or "whom" to refer to a person. The underlined word refers to José Rivera; the correct pronoun is "who," because José Rivera is a person. Choice (B) is correct. "Which," in C, is incorrect when used to refer to a person. Choice D uses the objective case "whom"; you wouldn't say "him has fought for the right," so "whom has fought for the right" is incorrect.

48. J
Category: Connections
Difficulty: Medium
Getting to the Answer: Remember to read for logic, as well as grammar and usage. This sentence inappropriately uses the coordinating conjunction "yet." "Although," a subordinating conjunction that introduces subordinate clauses, is the best choice here. Choice (J) is correct. Choice G is inappropriate for the context. Choice H is a coordinating conjunction that connects clauses.

49. A
Category: Organization
Difficulty: Low
Getting to the Answer: When you need to consider moving information, first read it to determine the main idea. Then consider the context of this information in the essay as a whole to determine its logical placement. The paragraph describes the early years in Rivera's schooling when he discovered he wanted to be a writer. In the essay as a whole, this information is in the right sequence; the paragraph before describes his childhood and the paragraph after describes his employment as an adult. Choice (A) is the correct answer. Choices B, C, and D would place the information out of sequence.

50. G
Category: Punctuation
Difficulty: Low
Getting to the Answer: A comma should not be inserted between a preposition and its object. The concluding conjunction "and" completed the list of the different things Rivera wrote. The direct object, "photographs," and the indirect object, "*Life* magazine," are part of one thought. Choice (G) is the correct answer. Choice H uses a colon, which is only correct when used to introduce a list or following an independent clause. Choice J uses a semicolon, which is only correct when used to connect two independent clauses.

51. D
Category: Wordiness
Difficulty: Low
Getting to the Answer: When OMIT is an option, read the underlined selection for relevance. Eliminate answer choices that contain redundant language. It is redundant to use "he saw a play" and "when he saw the play" together; (D) eliminates the redundancy. Choices A, B, and C all contain redundant language.

52. J
Category: Verb Tenses
Difficulty: Low
Getting to the Answer: When a verb is underlined, start by checking to see if the tense is correct. The simple present tense, "writes," is used in this sentence to describe an event that happened in the past. The correct tense here is the simple past tense, "wrote," as in (J). Choice G uses the present continuous tense, and H uses the present perfect tense, but the sentence describes something that happened in the past.

53. C
Category: Sentence Sense
Difficulty: High
Getting to the Answer: Remember to read for logic, as well as grammar and usage. In the underlined portion, the subject and predicate are split

by misplaced prepositional phrases. The subject is "Rivera," and the predicate is "returned to New York determined to continue writing." The prepositional phrase, "After graduating from college," modifies the action. Choice (C) is the correct answer. Choices B and D both use incorrect grammatical structure.

54. G
Category: Organization
Difficulty: Low
Getting to the Answer: When you need to consider moving information, read it into the passage at the suggested points to determine its logical placement. "Then" modifies "became," so (G) is the correct answer. Choices H and J are illogical.

55. A
Category: Punctuation
Difficulty: Medium
Getting to the Answer: A phrase offset between commas must be nonessential. The sentence must still make sense without it. If you read the sentence without the information in commas, "*The House of Ramon Iglesia*," it still makes sense. Choice (A) is the correct answer. Choices C and D are incorrect because an appositive must be offset by commas.

56. H
Category: Punctuation
Difficulty: Medium
Getting to the Answer: When the only difference in the answer choices is punctuation, remember your tested rules. A semicolon is used to join independent clauses closely related in meaning. Choice (H) is the correct answer. Choice G is incorrect because a comma does not join two independent clauses without a conjunction. Choice J is incorrect because the period is placed in the middle of the predicate.

57. A
Category: Writing Strategy
Difficulty: Medium
Getting to the Answer: Read question stems and the paragraph that is being questioned carefully.

Often, all four answer choices to Writing Strategy questions will be relevant to the passage, but only one will fulfill the specific requirements of the question. The question asks for a detail that supports Paragraph 5, which is about the sacrifices Rivera had to make to be a writer. Choice (A) is the only answer choice that supports this idea. Choices B and C are incorrect because they are off topic and do not support the main idea. Choice D is incorrect because it describes the writing he did for television as an opportunity, which is a positive charge.

58. H
Category: Verb Tenses
Difficulty: Medium
Getting to the Answer: When a verb is underlined, start by checking to see if the tense is correct. The correct tense here is the past continuous tense, "has become," as in (H). Choice G uses "is," which is incorrect. Choice J uses the past continuous tense, but José Rivera is singular, not plural as "have" would imply.

59. D
Category: Writing Strategy
Difficulty: Medium
Getting to the Answer: By determining the main idea of the passage, you can quickly eliminate two answer choices. The main idea of the essay is that being a playwright is challenging, but there are people like José Rivera who have succeeded despite the odds. Choice (D) is the correct answer. Choice A is incorrect because the essay is persuasive, not biographical. Choices B and C are incorrect because they convey the opposite of what the passage is arguing.

60. G
Category: Organization
Difficulty: Medium
Getting to the Answer: The first sentence of a paragraph typically introduces the topic of the paragraph, so look for the paragraph that contains details related to the sentence in question. Paragraph 2

describes Rivera's upbringing and contrasts the "bustling neighborhood of the Bronx" with the "dirt roads and woods" of Long Island. Choice (G) is the correct answer. Choices F, H, and J can be eliminated because the detail does not support the main idea of any of these paragraphs.

PASSAGE V

61. C
Category: Sentence Sense
Difficulty: Medium
Getting to the Answer: Remember that an –*ing* verb form by itself cannot serve as the predicate (main) verb in a sentence. As written, this sentence is a fragment. Choice (C) corrects this error by replacing "being" with "is" and does not introduce any additional errors. Choice B uses verb tenses inconsistently. Choice D does not address the error.

62. F
Category: Punctuation
Difficulty: Medium
Getting to the Answer: Remember the tested punctuation rules. If punctuation isn't needed for one of those reasons, it will be incorrect on the ACT. This sentence is correct as written, (F); no additional punctuation is needed in the underlined portion. Choice G incorrectly places a comma between the subject "What was initially a hobby" and the verb phrase "quickly became." Choice H incorrectly places a comma between a possessive noun (which functions grammatically as an adjective) and the noun it modifies. Choice J uses a colon, but what follows is not a brief definition, explanation, or list of what comes before.

63. B
Category: Word Choice
Difficulty: Medium
Getting to the Answer: Don't fall for the common testmaker trick of putting a singular noun near a verb with a plural subject. Always determine the correct subject of an underlined verb. The subject of

the verb "is" is not the singular "receipt" that immediately precedes it, but the plural "papers" ("several papers…is signed by John Hancock"). The underlined verb must be in the plural form; (B) is correct. Choices A and C both use singular verb forms, which do not agree with the plural subject. Choice D eliminates the verb, creating a sentence fragment.

64. G
Category: Verb Tenses
Difficulty: Medium
Getting to the Answer: The past perfect verb tense is only correct when describing an action that was completed prior to another stated past action. Checking context, you can see that the verbs used to describe Dr. Gregory's collection of signatures are all in the present tense: "includes" and "are" (your correction to the underlined "is" in question 63). The verb here should also be in the present tense; (G) is correct. Choice F uses the past perfect, but there is no stated past action here to justify this tense. Choice H uses the past tense, which is inconsistent with the rest of the description of the collection. Choice J uses the conditional, but there is nothing hypothetical about the meaning of the Hancock documents.

65. D
Category: Organization
Difficulty: Medium
Getting to the Answer: When you need to determine the best placement for a sentence, look for Keywords that show how the sentence relates to other ideas in the paragraph. Sentence 7 identifies the type of documents that Dr. Gregory collects, and sentences 5 and 6 specifically describe some of those documents. The Keyword "Predictably" in sentence 5 tells you that sentence 7 should come right before sentence 5; it is only predictable for Dr. Gregory to have Hancock documents if it has already been stated that Dr. Gregory collects famous signatures. Choice (D) is correct. Choice A disrupts the logical general-to-specific order set up in the paragraph; it also interrupts the transition

between sentence 6, which gives the name of Dr. Gregory's field, and the beginning of paragraph 2, which provides an explanation of that field. Choice B interrupts the description of Dr. Gregory's home. Choice C interrupts the explanation of how Dr. Gregory's interest in collecting documents developed.

66. G
Category: Writing Strategy
Difficulty: Medium
Getting to the Answer: Since NO CHANGE is offered as an answer choice, you must first decide whether a change is warranted. If so, you must then decide what the change should be. Graphology is discussed throughout the essay, so a definition of the term would be relevant and helpful to readers. Choice (G) provides this definition. The other choices do not provide information related to the topic discussed in the rest of the essay—the analysis of the handwriting of historical figures.

67. C
Category: Connections
Difficulty: Medium
Getting to the Answer: Remember the first step of the Kaplan Method: Read until you have enough information to identify the issue. To determine the best Connection to the following sentence, you must first read that sentence. The sentence following the underlined portion explains how psychologists and graphologists use handwriting. Only (C) mentions handwriting, identifying it as a tool to diagnose patients' problems. This is the most logical lead-in to the next sentence. Choice A changes the focus from handwriting to the general topic of how patients learn to express themselves. Choice B similarly moves the topic to an explanation of why patients seek help; this doesn't lead in to the next sentence's explanation of how psychologists use handwriting. Choice D is too general; it doesn't lead in to the specific information of why handwriting analysis can be helpful.

68. H
Category: Word Choice
Difficulty: Medium
Getting to the Answer: There are no specific rules for idiom construction, so use the meaning of each preposition to help you determine the correct answer choice. The correct preposition to follow "revealed" in this context is "by," (H). Choices F and G create idiomatic errors; something is not "revealed of" or "revealed from" something else. Choice J creates an illogical sentence, making "a subject's handwriting," and not "the issues," the thing that is revealed.

69. D
Category: Wordiness
Difficulty: Medium
Getting to the Answer: If a sentence is grammatically correct, check for errors in style. The sentence already tells you that "Dr. Gregory *once* practiced clinical psychology," so there is no need to repeat the information that this occurred "in the past." Choice (D) eliminates this redundant language. Choices B and C both contain redundant language.

70. G
Category: Sentence Sense
Difficulty: High
Getting to the Answer: Read question stems carefully. This one asks which revision is NOT acceptable, which means three choices can be logically and grammatically substituted for the underlined selection. Choice G) leaves the meaning of the second clause incomplete; "since hoping to better understand their personalities" requires additional information to make sense. Choice F replaces "hoping" with "in order to," correctly setting up a cause-and-effect relationship in the sentence. Choice H is considerably longer than the original selection, but it is both grammatically and logically correct in context. Choice J creates two separate sentences, both of which are complete and grammatically correct.

71. B
Category: Connections
Difficulty: High
Getting to the Answer: An effective Connection between paragraphs functions as a bridge between them; the best choice will be relevant to the ideas in both paragraphs. This paragraph explains that some historians and political scientists have tried to apply psychology to the study of historical events; however, this attempt has not been completely successful. The next paragraph describes the few types of personal historical documents that are available for study. Choice (B) provides the best bridge between these ideas, explaining that the lack of success in applying psychology to historical events comes from a lack of "information regarding the personalities of historical figures." Choice A brings the focus back to Dr. Gregory, but he is not mentioned again until the last sentence of the next paragraph. Choice C focuses on the future of the theories, which doesn't connect to the next paragraph's description of the available historical documents from individuals' private lives. Choice D provides information about the theories, but the theories are not the focus of the next paragraph.

72. J
Category: Punctuation
Difficulty: Medium
Getting to the Answer: You need to find the choice that is NOT acceptable; in other words, the correct answer will create an error in the sentence. It is not acceptable to connect two independent clauses, such as the ones in this sentence, without the proper punctuation and/or coordinating conjunction. Choice (J) creates a run-on sentence. Choice F correctly uses a semicolon to connect two independent clauses. Choice G forms two complete sentences. Choice H keeps the second clause dependent, replacing "for" with "as."

73. A
Category: Punctuation
Difficulty: Medium
Getting to the Answer: Don't expect to find a grammatical or stylistic error in every underlined selection. About 25% of your English Test questions will require NO CHANGE. No punctuation is needed here; the sentence is correct as written, (A). Choice B incorrectly inserts a comma before "that," which is used here as a conjunction. Choice C incorrectly uses a comma after "that"; commas are not correct after conjunctions. Choice D uses a colon, which would be appropriate only if it also eliminated "that," but it does not.

74. J
Category: Verb Tenses
Difficulty: High
Getting to the Answer: Use context to make sure verb tenses properly sequence the actions discussed in a sentence. As indicated by the word "while," the two actions in this sentence take place at the same time. The second verb, "forms," is in the present tense, so the underlined verb should also be in the present tense. Choice (J) is correct. Choices F and G both put the action of "imprinting key aspects of his personality" in the past; this would only make sense if the rest of the sentence were also in the past tense. Choice H indicates that the action of "imprinting key aspects of his personality" takes place in the future, not "while" he "forms a signature."

75. A
Category: Writing Strategy
Difficulty: High
Getting to the Answer: To make sure you understand the question, take a moment to put it in your own words. Here, you might rephrase the questions as "Does the essay talk about how one area of study can influence another?" The essay explains how Dr. Gregory, a psychologist, has used graphology to identify personality traits in historical figures; the essay concludes by explaining that these "details are now being used by historians in their analysis of historical decisions." This satisfies the condition of the question stem, so you can eliminate both "no" answers, C and D. Now move on to the reasoning. Choice (A) is an accurate paraphrase of the main idea of the essay. Choice B is incorrect because the essay does not compare different research processes.

MATHEMATICS TEST

1. D
Category: Variable Manipulation
Difficulty: Low
Getting to the Answer: In straightforward algebra problems like this one, you are asked to find the value of a variable. Collect all the terms with the variable on one side, and all the terms without the variable on the other.

$$2x - 6 = 18$$
$$2x = 24$$
$$x = 12, \text{ (D)}$$

2. F
Category: Patterns, Logic, & Data
Difficulty: Medium
Getting to the Answer: This is a logic problem, not a geometry problem. You don't need to do any calculations, just to find the answer choice that follows the logic of the two statements. Logic problems can be easier to understand if you replace statements about numbers with statements about real-life situations. Like this: If John gets out of bed before noon, he takes a shower. John did not take a shower. It follows logically that John did not get out of bed before noon, because if he did, he would have showered. In this problem, it follows logically that the length of $\overline{RS}$ is not 5, (F), because if it had been 5, the length of $\overline{ST}$ would have been 8.

3. C
Category: Proportions and Probability
Difficulty: Low
Getting to the Answer: Don't get thrown off when you see probability expressed as a decimal rather than as a ratio or as a fraction. You could think of

0.3 as a 30% chance of something happening, or a probability of $\frac{3}{10}$. Because you know that every ticket either will win or will not win, the probability that Mark will draw a winning ticket and the probability that he will draw a losing ticket will add up to 1. The probability that he will draw a losing ticket is 1.0 − 0.3 = 0.7, (C). If it is easier for you to think in terms of percents, look at the problem this way: If Mark has a 30% chance of drawing a winning ticket, the other 70% of the time he will draw a losing ticket. That's $\frac{70}{100}$, or 0.7, which is (C).

4. K
Category: Proportions and Probability
Difficulty: Medium
Getting to the Answer: This problem challenges you to translate a word problem into an algebraic expression. You already know that to find an average, you find the sum of the terms and divide this sum by the total number of terms. Your task is to find the answer choice that expresses this operation accurately. The sum of the three test scores is 94 + 89 + 89, or 94 + 2(89). To find the average score, you divide the sum by the total number of scores, 3, so $\frac{94 + 2(89)}{3}$ is the correct expression for the average of the scores. Choice (K) is correct.

5. D
Category: Patterns, Logic, & Data
Difficulty: Low
Getting to the Answer: If you get confused trying to solve this problem using algebra, you can always Backsolve. The correct answer choice, divided in half three times, will equal 6. Try translating the problem into algebra. You are looking for the amount of candy that Tom started with, which you can call x. Tom reduced that number by half 3 times, and ended up with 6 pieces.

$$\left(\frac{1}{2}\right)\left(\frac{1}{2}\right)\left(\frac{1}{2}\right)x = 6$$

$$\frac{1}{8}x = 6$$

$$x = 48, \text{(D)}$$

6. F
Category: Variable Manipulation
Difficulty: Low
Getting to the Answer: This problem asks you to combine two algebraic expressions. Pay attention to the signs as you combine like terms and you won't have any trouble. $R + S$ is equivalent to $4x + 3y − x$. Combining the x terms will give you the answer, $3x + 3y$, which matches (F).

7. B
Category: Plane Geometry
Difficulty: Medium
Getting to the Answer: If you are familiar with the properties of parallel lines that are intersected by transversals, this problem will be quick and easy for you. Make sure you are familiar with these properties before Test Day! In a figure like this one, formed by intersecting parallel lines, you only need the measure of one angle to quickly find the measure of every other angle. The angle adjacent to the angle that measures 115° must be supplementary to 115°, so its measure is 180° − 115° = 65°. This angle corresponds to angle y, so angle y must also measure 65°, (B).

8. J
Category: Operations
Difficulty: Medium
Getting to the Answer: Some algebra problems, like this one, will require you to substitute a given value for the variable. Be careful to get the signs right when substituting a negative value! Replace x with −3 and apply the rules of PEMDAS:

$$-x^2 − 7x + 5 = -(-3)^2 − 7(-3) + 5 = -9 + 21 + 5 = 17, \text{(J)}$$

9. E
Category: Proportions and Probability
Difficulty: Medium
Getting to the Answer: If you increase or decrease each of a set of numbers by the same amount, the average of those numbers will also increase or decrease by the same amount. This problem is not so

difficult if you imagine using specific numbers. If the average of 5 numbers is 85, each of the five numbers could be 85, right? Now, if you increase each of those numbers by 4, the average will be $\frac{5(89)}{5}$, or 89. Choice (E) is correct.

10. H
Category: Variable Manipulation
Difficulty: Low
Getting to the Answer: This problem involves factoring. If you are not comfortable with factoring, be sure to practice problems like this before Test Day. To simplify this expression, you can factor out a 3. This will give you the new, equivalent expression, $3(x + 3y)$, which matches (H). When in doubt, you can Pick Numbers for the variables and find the equivalent expression.

11. D
Category: Proportions and Probability
Difficulty: Medium
Getting to the Answer: Word problems like this one give you all of the information you need, but in a roundabout way. Stay on your toes and remember to ask yourself what you are really looking for. For instance, don't forget that the June bill will be $20 plus the cost of *100* long distance minutes, not 20. First, determine the price per minute based on what you were charged in May. Subtract the $20 fee from your total of $28, and you will find that you paid $8 for 80 minutes of long distance. That means that 1 minute costs 10 cents. In June you talked 20 minutes more than in May.
$80 + 20 = 100$
100 minutes · 10 cents per minute = $10
Add this per-minute fee to your monthly $20, and the bill is $30, (D).

12. K
Category: Variable Manipulation
Difficulty: Medium
Getting to the Answer: Problems that ask you to find the greatest or least possible value are often great opportunities to use Backsolving. When asked

to find the greatest possible value, start by plugging in the greatest answer choice. Here, the greatest answer choice is 8, so plug in 8 for x: $\frac{6}{8} = \frac{3}{4}$, so 8 is a possible value for x. Because 8 is the largest answer choice, there is no need to evaluate the other answers. Choice (K) is correct.

13. E
Category: Plane Geometry
Difficulty: Medium
Getting to the Answer: Always be on the lookout for basic geometric figures. If you remember that a clock is just a circle, and you are familiar with the properties of circles, you will have all of the tools you need to solve this problem. You already know that a whole circle is 360°. You also know that a clock is divided into 12 hours. Use this information to calculate how many degrees the hour hand will move in 1 hour. $\frac{360°}{12} = 30°$, so the hour hand will move 30° in one hour. In the 8 hours between noon and 8 PM, the hour hand will move $8 \cdot 30° = 240°$, (E).

14. H
Category: Coordinate Geometry
Difficulty: Medium
Getting to the Answer: Pay attention to all of the clues you are given about triangles in figure problems like this. You can often use them to find similar or congruent triangles. You can eliminate F, G, and J immediately, since each of those points would be on the x- or y-axis. To decide which of the remaining two choices is correct, examine the clues in the question stem. Because both triangles are right isosceles triangles, you know that they are similar triangles. Because the two triangles also have equal areas, you can conclude that they have equal side lengths. Now, can you see how the lengths of the sides of the two triangles are related to the coordinates of L? The length of $\overline{LM}$ will be half the length of $\overline{MO}$. Therefore, the x-coordinate of L will be half the y-coordinate. Choice (H) is the only answer that fits this proportion.

15. A

Category: Variable Manipulation

Difficulty: Low

Getting to the Answer: Be sure to be familiar with the properties of zero before Test Day! Remember that when two terms are multiplied to equal zero, at least one of those terms must equal zero. You could substitute the two values for x into each answer choice to find which equation has both 5 and –7 as solutions, but all that work is not necessary. When you have an equation in which the product of two binomials is zero, one of the binomials will have to equal zero. So, if $(x - 5)(x + 7) = 0$, then $x - 5 = 0$ or $x + 7 = 0$. The solutions to this equation, then, would be $x = 5$ and $x = -7$. Choice (A) is correct.

16. G

Category: Variable Manipulation

Difficulty: Low

Getting to the Answer: You might have predicted that the correct expression would be $t(r + s)$. Don't panic when that expression doesn't appear among the answer choices; just look for an expression that is equivalent. If this is too confusing, try Picking Numbers. To find the total number of dollars in all of the cash registers, you would multiply the number of registers times the number of dollars in each one, or $t(r + s)$. If you distribute the t in this expression, you will get $(t \cdot r) + (t \cdot s)$, so this is an equivalent expression. To solve this problem by Picking Numbers, choose a small, easily workable number to replace each variable. If $t = 3$, $r = 4$, and $s = 5$, then there will be 3 cash registers with $(4 + 5)$ dollars in each, which gives you $3(\$9) = \$27$ in the store. Plug the same values into the answer choices, and you will find that Choice (G) gives the same result.

17. C

Category: Proportions and Probability

Difficulty: Low

Getting to the Answer: Focus on what you are looking for in percent problems like this. Don't make the mistake of calculating 30 percent of 60. Percentages can be much more workable if you convert

them to decimals. If 30 percent of x is 60, solve for x using the equation $0.3x = 60$.

$$x = \frac{60}{0.3} = 200, \text{ (C)}$$

18. J

Category: Operations

Difficulty: Low

Getting to the Answer: When you are calculating a total price, you usually multiply the number of units sold times the price per unit. The challenge in this word problem is that 100 of the units (t-shirts) were sold at a different price. Calculate the price for the first 100, and add that to the total price of the remaining shirts. The total number of t-shirts sold was 350. The school earned 7 dollars for each of the first 100 shirts, and 10 dollars for each of the remaining shirts. Translate this problem into algebra, with p representing the total price:

$$7(100) + 10(350 - 100) = p$$
$$700 + 10(250) = p$$
$$700 + 2{,}500 = p$$
$$3{,}200 = p$$

Choice (J) is correct.

19. D

Category: Proportions and Probability

Difficulty: Medium

Getting to the Answer: Getting comfortable converting percentages to decimals will save you some time. To increase a number by 7 percent, you don't need to calculate 7 percent and add it to the original number. Instead, multiply the original number by 1.07. First calculate the total charge for the salad with sales tax. Add 7 percent to $3.99:

$$(1.07)(\$3.99) = \$4.2693$$

The price, rounded to the nearest cent, is $4.27. Subtract the price from $5.00 to find that the amount of change is 73¢, (D).

20. G

Category: Variable Multiplication

Difficulty: Medium

Getting to the Answer: Reviewing the properties

of fractions before Test Day will give you an edge on questions like this one. If you remember what causes a fraction to be "undefined," you can solve this problem quickly using algebra. An undefined fraction is a fraction with zero as the denominator. So, you're looking for the value of x that will give the denominator ($x^2 - 4$) a value of 0. Find it by setting up an equation:

$$x^2 - 4 = 0$$
$$(x - 2)(x + 2) = 0$$
$$x = 2 \text{ or } x = -2$$

Because the question asks for a nonnegative value of x, the answer is 2, (G). You can also Backsolve by plugging in each answer choice for x, and see which one results in a denominator of zero.

21. C
Category: Number Properties
Difficulty: Low
Getting to the Answer: Comparing values is always easier when all of the values are expressed in the same form. The numbers in this question would be much easier to compare if they were all decimals, so convert them. You might remember that π has a value of approximately 3.14. The mixed number $3\frac{1}{4}$ is equivalent to 3.25. These numbers are much easier to compare, but don't forget to order them from *greatest* to *least*.

$3.5 > 3.25 > 3.14$, so
$3.5 > 3\frac{1}{4} > \pi$, (C)

22. K
Category: Plane Geometry
Difficulty: Medium
Getting to the Answer: Stop and take a minute to visualize when you are faced with a 3-dimensional figure. Remember that you can't see 3 of the sides of this box. Don't make the mistake of adding up only the lengths that are visible in the figure. If you imagine that this figure is a 3-dimensional box, you can see that the string will have to cross the width (20 in) twice, the length (15 in) twice, and the height (4 in)

four times. Don't forget to add 4 inches to the total, so that Ashley can tie a bow. Converting this from a word problem into algebra, you have:

$$x = 2(20) + 2(15) + 4(4) + 4$$
$$x = 40 + 30 + 16 + 4$$
$$x = 90, \text{(K)}$$

23. D
Category: Proportions and Probability
Difficulty: Medium
Getting to the Answer: Be careful not to confuse a part:part ratio with a part:whole ratio. The correct ratio between white and blue paint needed to produce the desired color is 5 parts white to 3 parts blue, which gives a total of 8 parts. To find the correct amount of blue paint in 24 quarts of the mixed color, use the ratio of blue paint to the total: 3:8 or $\frac{3}{8}$. Therefore, for 24 quarts of paint, you need $24 \cdot \frac{3}{8} = 9$ quarts of blue paint, (D).

24. F
Category: Variable Manipulation
Difficulty: Medium
Getting to the Answer: The answer choices in this problem give you a clue that the problem involves a quadratic that can be factored. You could also substitute each of the answer choices for x to see which one is true. Backsolving or algebra may be faster for you—use whichever will get you to the answer more quickly.

$$x^2 + x = 30$$
$$x^2 + x - 30 = 0$$
$$(x + 6)(x - 5) = 0$$
$$x + 6 = 0 \text{ or } x - 5 = 0$$
$$x = -6 \text{ or } x = 5, \text{(F)}$$

25. D
Category: Variable Manipulation
Difficulty: High
Getting to the Answer: When you get stuck on a problem involving variables, look for ways to write the expressions that will produce like terms to

work with. Keep an eye out for the classic quadratic equations.

Start with the first expression:

$$(a - b)^2 = 36$$

This can also be written as:

$$(a - b)(a - b) = 36$$

Use the FOIL method (or recognize the classic quadratic):

$$a^2 - 2ab + b^2 = 36$$

Now you have something you can work with! Substitute in the value of ab that was given in the question:

$$a^2 - 2(24) + b^2 = 36$$
$$a^2 - 48 + b^2 = 36$$
$$a^2 + b^2 = 84, \text{(D)}$$

26. J

Category: Variable Manipulation

Difficulty: High

Getting to the Answer: Be sure to get familiar with the rules regarding exponents! When an exponent is raised to another exponent, multiply the exponents. Because the variable you want to solve for is part of an exponent, try to make the bases the same so that you can compare the exponents.

$$(x^{3b - 1})^2 = x^{16}$$

Simplify the left side by multiplying the exponents:

$$x^{6b - 2} = x^{16}$$

Now that the bases are the same, set up an equation comparing the exponents:

$$6b - 2 = 16$$
$$6b = 18$$
$$b = 3, \text{(J)}$$

27. A

Category: Variable Manipulation

Difficulty: Medium

Getting to the Answer: You don't have to know about imaginary numbers to solve a problem like this. Because you are given that $i^2 = -1$, plug in -1 for i^2. Remember that $i^4 = (i^2)^2$.

$$i^2 - i^4 = i^2 - (i^2)^2 = (-1) - (-1)^2 = -1 - 1 = -2, \text{(A)}$$

28. F

Category: Coordinate Geometry

Difficulty: Medium

Getting to the Answer: Don't forget what you are really looking for in this problem. You will use the midpoint formula, but be sure to solve for an endpoint (B) rather than the midpoint. Remember that the x-coordinate of the midpoint of a line segment is the average of the x-coordinates of the endpoints. The y-coordinate of the midpoint is the average of the y-coordinates of the endpoints. Use the midpoint formula:

$$\left(\frac{x_1 + x_2}{2}, \frac{y_1 + y_2}{2}\right)$$

First, calculate the x-coordinate of B by solving for x_2:

$$\frac{5 + x_2}{2} = -2$$
$$5 + x_2 = -4$$
$$x_2 = -9$$

The x-coordinate of B is -9. You could continue by finding the y-coordinate in the same way, but that is not necessary because only (F) has the correct x-coordinate.

29. D

Category: Coordinate Geometry

Difficulty: Medium

Getting to the Answer: This problem is much simpler than it first appears. You just need to know the formula for the equation of a circle. The formula for the equation of a circle is $(x - h)^2 + (y - k)^2 = r^2$, where the center of the circle is (h,k) and r is the radius of the circle. Therefore, in this problem:

$$r^2 = 5$$
$$r = \sqrt{5}, \text{(D)}$$

30. G

Category: Trigonometry

Difficulty: Medium

Getting to the Answer: Some trig problems will simply require you to remember the definitions of sin, cos, and tan. Use SOHCAHTOA to help you remember.

$$\sin = \frac{\text{opposite}}{\text{hypotenuse}}$$

According to the figure, the hypotenuse is c, and the side opposite β is a. Therefore, $\sin \beta = \frac{a}{c}$, (G).

31. C
Category: Variable Manipulation
Difficulty: Medium
Getting to the Answer: When multiplying terms with the same base, exponents are *added*, not multiplied. When dividing terms with the same base, exponents are subtracted. You can simplify the numerator, then divide:

$$\frac{\left(16x^2y^2\right)\left(6x^2y^4\right)}{-8x^2y^3} = \frac{96x^4y^6}{-8x^2y^3} = -12x^2y^3$$

Or you can cancel out as much as possible, then simplify:

$$\frac{\left(16x^2y^2\right)\left(6x^2y^4\right)}{-8x^2y^3} = \frac{\left(2y^2\right)\left(6x^2y\right)}{-1} = -12x^2y^3, \text{(C)}$$

32. J
Category: Plane Geometry
Difficulty: Low
Getting to the Answer: Whenever 3 or more parallel lines are intersected by 2 transversals, the transversals are divided proportionally by the parallel lines. The ratio of the length of $\overline{TU}$ to the length of $\overline{UV}$ will be equal to the ratio of the length of $\overline{QR}$ to the length of $\overline{RS}$. Therefore, you can set up the following proportion:

$$\frac{x}{7} = \frac{3}{5}$$
$$5x = 21$$
$$x = \frac{21}{5}, \text{(J)}$$

33. C
Category: Plane Geometry
Difficulty: High
Getting to the Answer: To solve this problem, you will have to remember the area formulas for both triangles and circles. To find the area of a circle, use the equation πr^2. You don't know the value of r yet,

but you might have noticed that the sides of $\triangle AOB$ are also radii of the circle. Use the area formula for triangles ($\frac{1}{2}$ base $\cdot$ height = area) to find the base and height. In this case, the base and height are both equal and are both radii of the circle.

$$\frac{1}{2}r^2 = 18$$
$$r^2 = 36$$

The area of a circle is πr^2, so the area of this circle is 36π, (C). Even if you were completely stuck, you could narrow down your options and make a strategic guess. The area of the circle must be more than 4 times the area of the triangle, so you can eliminate A and B, which are less than 4 times the area of the triangle.

34. J
Category: Coordinate Geometry
Difficulty: Medium
Getting to the Answer: The symbol $\leq$ means less than *or equal to*, and $\geq$ means greater than *or equal to*. You will use one of these symbols when you want to include a number in a set. The bold part of the number line represents the numbers that should be included in the set, including 4 and excluding –5. Therefore, $x > -5$ and $x \leq 4$, which matches (J).

35. C
Category: Plane Geometry
Difficulty: Medium
Getting to the Answer: Always be on the lookout for special triangles! This problem involves a 3-4-5 right triangle. If you draw a diagram for this problem, you will find that you are working with a right triangle.

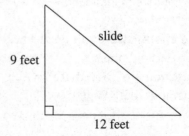

The length of the slide is the hypotenuse of a triangle with side lengths 9 and 12. If you didn't notice that this is a 3-4-5 triangle, you could solve for the hypotenuse using the Pythagorean Theorem:

$$9^2 + 12^2 = c^2$$
$$81 + 144 = c^2$$
$$225 = c^2$$
$$15 = c, \text{(C)}$$

36. F
Category: Number Properties
Difficulty: Medium
Getting to the Answer: Think of a few possible values for a and b and use these values to evaluate the answer choices. First, simplify the expression:

$$\sqrt{3\left(\frac{a^2}{b}\right)} = 2$$

$$\left(\sqrt{3\left(\frac{a^2}{b}\right)}\right)^2 = 2^2$$

$$3\left(\frac{a^2}{b}\right) = 4$$

$$\frac{a^2}{b} = \frac{4}{3}$$

If $\frac{a^2}{b} = \frac{4}{3}$, then one set of possible values is $a = 2$ and $b = 3$. This eliminates G and H. Another set of possible values is $a = 4$ and $b = 12$. This eliminates J. Now, since $\frac{a^2}{b}$ results in $\frac{4}{3}$, which is positive, and because a^2 will always be positive, you know that b CANNOT be a negative number, because a positive number divided by a negative number would result in a negative number. Therefore, you can eliminate K. The answer is (F).

37. B
Category: Number Properties
Difficulty: Medium
Getting to the Answer: Because the difference between 84 and 96 is 12, no number greater than 12

can be a common factor. First, think of all of the integers that divide both 84 and 96. 1, 2, 3, 4, 6, and 12 are all common factors of 84 and 96. 1, 2, 3, 4, and 6 are all factors of either 18 or 16, though, so they can be eliminated. The only integer left is 12. The digits of 12 (1 and 2) add up to 3, (B).

38. G
Category: Coordinate Geometry
Difficulty: Low
Getting to the Answer: If you are tempted to say you don't have enough information to answer this question, look again. Knowing that line R is parallel to the x-axis is an important clue. The x-axis is the horizontal axis. Any line that is parallel to the x-axis is also horizontal, and the slope of a horizontal line is always 0. Remember, slope is change in y over change in x. If the line is horizontal, there is no change in y. This means (G) is correct.

39. E
Category: Coordinate Geometry
Difficulty: Medium
Getting to the Answer: The quickest way to compare the slopes among equations is to put the equations in slope-intercept form: $y = mx + b$. In slope-intercept form, the slope is represented by m. Therefore, the slope of the line in the question, $y = 2x - 1$, is 2. Which of the answer choices has a slope of 2? A and D may appear to at first, but be careful—they are not in slope-intercept form. In slope-intercept form, A is $y = -2x + 1$ and D is $\frac{1}{2}x + \frac{3}{2}$. Neither has a slope of 2. B and C are already in slope-intercept form, with slopes that do not equal 2. Take a look at (E):

$$5y = 10x + 2$$
$$y = 2x + \frac{2}{5}$$

The slope of this line is 2.

40. G

Category: Trigonometry

Difficulty: High

Getting to the Answer: Use SOHCAHTOA to find the sine and cosine of each angle. The presence of the complicated formula in the note warns you that this question will take a while, so it's a good one to leave for the end of the test. The question stem tells you how to calculate $\sin(x + y)$, so your job is to find $\sin x$, $\cos x$, $\sin y$, and $\cos y$ and plug those values into the given equation.

Since $\sin = \dfrac{\text{opposite}}{\text{hypotenuse}}$, $\sin x = \dfrac{10\sqrt{2}}{15}$ and $\sin y = \dfrac{5}{5\sqrt{10}}$.

Since $\cos = \dfrac{\text{adjacent}}{\text{hypotenuse}}$, $\cos x = \dfrac{5}{15}$ and $\cos y = \dfrac{15}{5\sqrt{10}}$.

Plug those values into $\sin(x + y) = \sin x \cos y + \sin y \cos x$ to get:

$$\frac{10\sqrt{2}}{15} \cdot \frac{15}{5\sqrt{10}} + \frac{5}{5\sqrt{10}} \cdot \frac{5}{15} = \frac{150\sqrt{2}}{75\sqrt{10}} + \frac{25}{75\sqrt{10}}$$

$$= \frac{150\sqrt{2} + 25}{75\sqrt{10}} = \frac{6\sqrt{2} + 1}{3\sqrt{10}} = \frac{\sqrt{10}\left(6\sqrt{2} + 1\right)}{\sqrt{10}\left(3\sqrt{10}\right)}$$

$$= \frac{6\sqrt{20} + \sqrt{10}}{3 \cdot 10} = \frac{12\sqrt{5} + \sqrt{10}}{30}, \text{ (G)}$$

41. E

Category: Proportions and Probability

Difficulty: Medium

Getting to the Answer: When the answer choices include variables, Picking Numbers may make the problem look less complicated. Choose a small, easily workable number to replace the variable. Suppose $x = 3$. If it takes Julie 3 minutes to type 3 pages, her rate is 1 page per minute. So, it will take her 11 minutes to type 11 pages. Now plug 3 into each of the answer choices, and you will find that (E) gives you the same answer, 11 minutes. Want to solve the problem with algebra? Let m equal the number of minutes it takes for Julie to type 11 pages. If she types 3 pages in x minutes, you can use the proportion:

$$\frac{m}{11} = \frac{x}{3}$$

$$m = \frac{11x}{3}, \text{ (E)}$$

42. K

Category: Number Properties

Difficulty: Low

Getting to the Answer: If you are unsure, you can check your answer by Picking Numbers for a. Any time you multiply an integer by an even integer, the resulting product is even. $4a^2$ is an even integer for any integer a. What happens when you add 1 to an even integer? The sum will always be odd, so $4a^2 + 1$ will result in an odd integer given any integer a. Choice (K) is correct.

43. B

Category: Plane Geometry

Difficulty: Medium

Getting to the Answer: Did you recognize that $\triangle RST$ is a 30–60–90 triangle? You should always be on the lookout for special triangles. Drawing a quick diagram of $\triangle RST$ may help you to organize the information in this problem. Since $\angle R$ is a right angle, you know that the side opposite $\angle R$, $\overline{ST}$, will be the hypotenuse.

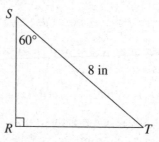

Remember that a 30–60–90 triangle has sides in the ratio $x{:}x\sqrt{3}{:}2x$. This allows you to calculate the other two sides of $\triangle RST$. Since $2x = 8$, $x = 4$. $\overline{RT}$ is 4 inches long and $\overline{SR}$ is $4\sqrt{3}$ inches long. These two sides are the base and height of $\triangle RST$, so you can plug their lengths into the area formula for triangles:

$$\text{area} = \frac{1}{2}bh$$

$$\text{area} = \frac{1}{2}(4)\left(4\sqrt{3}\right)$$

$$\text{area} = 8\sqrt{3}, \text{ (B)}$$

44. K
Category: Plane Geometry
Difficulty: High
Getting to the Answer: Whenever there doesn't seem to be enough information to solve a geometry problem, look for special or similar triangles. You know that $\triangle ABC$ is similar to $\triangle DEC$ since both are right triangles that share $\angle DCE$. $\triangle DEC$ is the same as $\triangle DEA$, since the two triangles share height $\overline{DE}$ are both right triangles, and have bases of the same length (since $\overline{DE}$ bisects $\overline{AC}$, $\overline{AD}$ and $\overline{DC}$ are the same length). Therefore, $CE = y$. The ratio between corresponding sides of similar triangles is the same, so $\frac{AB}{DE} = \frac{BC}{CE} = \frac{z}{y}$, (K).

45. C
Category: Plane Geometry
Difficulty: Medium
Getting to the Answer: If you get confused about the variable, try Picking Numbers. The area of the original figure is the area of the square plus the area of the semicircle. The square has sides of length $2r$, so its area is $(2r)^2 = 4r^2$. The area of the semicircle is $\frac{1}{2}\pi r^2$, so the area of the original figure is $4r^2 + \frac{1}{2}\pi r^2$. If r is doubled, the new figure will be composed of a square with sides of length $4r$ and a semicircle with radius $2r$. The new figure's area will be $(4r)^2 + \frac{1}{2}\pi(2r)^2 = 16r^2 + \frac{1}{2}\pi 4r^2 = 16r^2 + 2\pi r^2$. This is $\frac{16r^2 + 2\pi r^2}{4r^2 + \frac{1}{2}\pi r^2} = \frac{2r^2(8+\pi)}{\frac{1}{2}r^2(8+\pi)} = \frac{2}{\frac{1}{2}} = 4$ times the area of the original figure. To make the problem more concrete, you could Pick Numbers. If $r = 1$, then the area of the original figure is $2^2 + \frac{1}{2}\pi(1^2) = 4 + \frac{1}{2}\pi$. When r is doubled, it becomes 2, and the area of the new figure is $4^2 + \frac{1}{2}\pi(2^2) = 16 + 2\pi$. This is $\frac{16 + 2\pi}{4 + \frac{1}{2}\pi} = 4$ times the area of the original figure. Choice (C) is correct.

46. F
Category: Coordinate Geometry
Difficulty: Medium
Getting to the Answer: A system of equations has an infinite number of solutions when both equations say the same thing. So, you just have to find the value of x that will make the second equation equivalent to the first one. Compare the two equations. The left side of the second equation is 4 times the left side of the first equation. If the term on the right side of the second equation is also 4 times the term on the right side of the first equation, the two equations will be equivalent.

$$4(4a - b) = 4(4)$$
$$16a - 4b = 16$$
$$16 = 8x$$
$$2 = x, \text{(F)}$$

47. C
Category: Plane Geometry
Difficulty: High
Getting to the Answer: This question combines rates with plane geometry. The first step is to figure out where Samir and Sally have gone. Only then can you come up with an expression that describes the distance between them. Sally walked north for 20 minutes, or $\frac{1}{3}$ of an hour. Since she was walking at a rate of 3 miles per hour, she went $\frac{1}{3}(3) = 1$ mile north. She walked east for 40 minutes, or $\frac{2}{3}$ of an hour, so she went $\frac{2}{3}(3) = 2$ miles east. Samir walked south at a rate of 2 miles per hour for $\frac{1}{3}$ of an hour, so he went $\frac{1}{3}(2) = \frac{2}{3}$ miles south. Then he went $\frac{2}{3}(2) = \frac{4}{3}$ miles east. A sketch will help you see where they are:

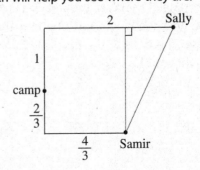

The distance between them is the hypotenuse of a right triangle. The height of the triangle is the north–south distance between them, and the base of the triangle is the east–west distance. The north–south distance is $1 + \frac{2}{3}$, and the east–west distance is $2 - \frac{4}{3}$. Don't bother to simplify these, because the answer choices don't either. Instead, plug them into the Pythagorean Theorem, which can be written as $c = \sqrt{a^2 + b^2}$, to find that the hypotenuse of this triangle must be $\sqrt{\left(1+\frac{2}{3}\right)^2 + \left(2-\frac{4}{3}\right)^2}$, (C).

48. K
Category: Trigonometry
Difficulty: Medium
Getting to the Answer: Think about how this problem can be translated from a word problem into a trig problem. Notice that the flag pole forms a 90° angle with the ground. In this problem you are looking for the height of the flag pole, so call that length x. The flag pole (x) is also the side opposite of the angle of elevation, and you know that the adjacent side is 20 ft. Which trig function uses the opposite and adjacent sides? Use SOHCAHTOA to find that:

$$\tan = \frac{\text{opposite}}{\text{adjacent}}$$
$$\tan 35° = \frac{x}{20}$$
$$x = 20\tan 35°, \text{ (K)}$$

49. B
Category: Plane Geometry
Difficulty: Medium
Getting to the Answer: The area of a parallelogram is base times height, just like the area of a rectangle. Remember that the height must be perpendicular to the base. The base of the parallelogram in this figure is 5 inches. The height is 3.

area = base · height
area = 5 · 3
area = 15, (B)

50. H
Category: Coordinate Geometry
Difficulty: Low
Getting to the Answer: It may be helpful to draw a number line and plot the possible positions for point C. B is 8 units away from A, and C is 2 units away from B, so there are only 2 possible positions for C—2 units before B or 2 units after B. Therefore, C must be either 6 units or 10 units away from A, which matches (H).

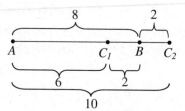

51. C
Category: Coordinate Geometry
Difficulty: Medium
Getting to the Answer: You don't need to use the distance formula to solve this problem. Look for a quick way to find the base and height of the triangle. The area of a triangle is $\frac{1}{2}$(base)(height). Because the base of this triangle, $\overline{AC}$, is a horizontal line segment (both vertices have the same y-coordinate), you can determine its length by finding the difference between the x-coordinates of A and C.

$5 - (-6) = 11$

The height will be the shortest distance from the base to B, so you can calculate the height by finding the difference between the y-coordinates of B and any point on the base.

$7 - 1 = 6$

Now use the area formula for triangles:

$$\text{area} = \frac{1}{2}(\text{base})(\text{height})$$
$$\text{area} = \frac{1}{2}(11)(6)$$
$$\text{area} = 33, \text{ (C)}$$

52. K

Category: Number Properties

Difficulty: Medium

Getting to the Answer: Stop and think about what it means to say that a number is greater than 0. That's just another way of saying that the number is positive. Your task is to find which of the answer choices will always yield a positive result for $-3x^2y^3$. Since one of the factors (-3) is negative, exactly one of the other 2 factors must also be negative. x^2 will never be negative, because any real number squared will always be positive or zero. That means that y^3 must be negative, and when y^3 is negative, y must also be negative. Therefore, y cannot be greater than 0. Choice (K) is correct.

53. A

Category: Patterns, Logic, & Data

Difficulty: High

Getting to the Answer: In a geometric sequence, you calculate each successive term by multiplying the previous term by the same value. If the first number in a geometric sequence is x, and the second number is nx, the third number will be $(n)(n)x$, or n^2x, and the fourth number will be $(n)(n)(n)x$, or n^3x, and so on. As you can see, the exponent of n will always be *one less* than the number of successions in the sequence. The 30th term in the sequence, then, will be $n^{30-1}x$, or $n^{29}x$, (A).

54. J

Category: Coordinate Geometry

Difficulty: Medium

Getting to the Answer: When a system of linear equations has NO solution, you are dealing with parallel lines. How can you tell if any of the equations form a line parallel to the one in the figure? Parallel lines have the same slope, and the two lines cannot have the same y-intercept, because they would be the same line. The given equations are all in the same form: $y = mx + b$, where m is the slope. You don't know the exact slope of the line in the graph, but you can see that it has a negative slope, because it goes down as it goes to the right. Therefore, you

can eliminate F, H, and K, because they do not have negative slopes. Next, you can eliminate G, because it has the same y-intercept as the line in the figure. That leaves you with the correct answer, (J).

55. B

Category: Trigonometry

Difficulty: Medium

Getting to the Answer: Don't worry when a trig problem doesn't include a diagram. You have all of the information you need, and you can always draw your own triangle if you are confused. Imagine a triangle with angle n. If $\cos n = \dfrac{15}{17}$, then you can assume that the adjacent side is 15 and the hypotenuse is 17, because $\cos = \dfrac{\text{adjacent}}{\text{hypotenuse}}$.

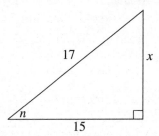

$\tan = \dfrac{\text{opposite}}{\text{adjacent}}$, so all you need now is the length of the side opposite angle n.

Use the Pythagorean Theorem:

$$15^2 + x^2 = 17^2$$
$$225 + x^2 = 289$$
$$x^2 = 64$$
$$x = 8$$

So, $\tan n = \dfrac{8}{15}$, (B).

56. K

Category: Patterns, Logic, & Data

Difficulty: Medium

Getting to the Answer: Some word problems include unnecessary information. Do you really need to know the current price of milk? Imagine the price of milk drops by 3 cents. How many gallons of milk would you expect the grocery store to sell? You know there will be 10 extra gallons sold for every cent decrease, so 3(10) more than the current 65 gallons will be sold. This is represented by the expression $65 + 10c$, (K).

57. D
Category: Proportions and Probability
Difficulty: Medium
Getting to the Answer: Probability is the ratio between the total *favorable* outcomes and the total *possible* outcomes. For Elizabeth to be on Ann's team, she has to draw one of the remaining tokens that has the number 5 in the tens digit. 56 is no longer available, so that leaves 50 through 55, plus 57, 58, and 59. That makes 9 tokens that would put Elizabeth on Ann's team, or 9 possibilities for a favorable outcome. Now how many tokens are there for Elizabeth to draw from? There were 100 to start with, but Ann took one, so there are 99. That leaves a probability of $\frac{9}{99}$, which reduces to $\frac{1}{11}$, (D).

58. J
Category: Plane Geometry
Difficulty: High
Getting to the Answer: It's very tempting to find the area of the cross-section shown and stop, but that's not what this question asks for. Keeping track of the units can help you spot this type of error. The volume of Dave's room is the area of this cross-section times the width of the room. The cross-section looks like a rectangle with a right triangle taken out of it, and that's the easiest way to find its area:

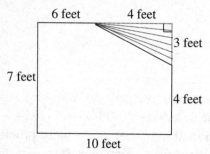

The area of the entire rectangle is $7 \cdot 10 = 70$ square feet, and the area of the triangle is $\frac{1}{2}(3 \cdot 4) = 6$ square feet, so the area of the cross-section is $70 - 6 = 64$ square feet. The question stem says that Dave's

room is 8 feet wide, so its volume is $64 \cdot 8 = 512$ cubic feet, (J).

59. C
Category: Coordinate Geometry
Difficulty: High
Getting to the Answer: When lines in the coordinate plane are perpendicular, the slopes of the two lines are negative reciprocals. Because *m* is perpendicular to *l*, and *l* has a slope of 1, the slope of *m* must be −1. That eliminates A, B, and E. To distinguish between C and D, you'll need to find the *y*-intercept of line *m*. Because the slope is −1, the line goes down one unit for every unit it goes to the right. You can also think of it as going up one unit for every unit it goes to the left. Start at (3,0) and count units until you reach the *y*-axis: (3,0), (2,1), (1,2), (0,3). The *y*-intercept of line *m* is 3, so (C) is correct.

60. G
Category: Number Properties
Difficulty: Medium
Getting to the Answer: Try a few different values for the two numbers. Let the answer choices be clues as to which numbers you experiment with. To get the smallest possible product, you want to have a negative product. That means that one of the factors will have to be negative, and the other will have to be positive. Don't forget that the factors differ by 8. So, use numbers that are close to zero. You'll find that 4 and −4 give you the smallest possible product, −16. Choice (G) is correct.

READING TEST

PASSAGE I

1. C
Category: Inference
Difficulty: Medium
Getting to the Answer: When the passage offers you little information about the subject of the question, make a conservative inference based only on

what the text supports. Helen and Margaret interact very little in the passage, though you do see in lines 25–35 that Helen appears uninterested in Margaret's conversation with the young man. Helen is too engrossed in the symphony being played. Don't make too big a leap here; they don't seem that close, but this is just a single incident in the course of a novel. Choice (C) is correct as it captures the sense of this section nicely. Choice A is extreme; Helen "could not be bothered" by Margaret's conversation. She does not express disapproval. Choice B is out of scope; the passage does not suggest that Helen is jealous of Margaret. Choice D is out of scope; the passage doesn't allow you to draw much of a conclusion about what draws them together.

2. H
Category: Generalization
Difficulty: High
Getting to the Answer: When answer choices consist of pairs of words, both words in a choice have to be correct for that choice to be correct. Consult your notes to come up with a prediction for Helen's personality. She certainly gives the music great consideration, to the exclusion of communing with those in her party. Predict something like *given to deep thought* or *tending to keep to herself*. Both of the adjectives in (H) match the prediction and the gist of the text. Choice F is a distortion; her analysis of the music definitely shows creativity, but she does not display an animated personality. Choice G is a distortion; Helen does analyze the music, but the results of her analysis are more pessimistic: "there was no such thing as splendor or heroism in the world . . . Panic and emptiness!" (lines 73–78) Choice J is extreme; Helen doesn't speak much to those around her, but these adjectives are too strong to be supported by the text.

3. B
Category: Detail
Difficulty: Low
Getting to the Answer: With "NOT" questions, find the section that the question draws from, then cross off the three answer choices mentioned there. Your notes should help you see that Helen considers the goblins in depth in lines 67–78. Compare the choices to the description here and work your way to the one NOT mentioned. In lines 65–66, Helen says, "They were not aggressive creatures; that was what made them so terrible to Helen." This line directly contradicts (B), which is the correct choice. Choice A is opposite; in lines 73–74, Helen feels that the goblins communicate the sense that "there was no such thing as splendor or heroism in the world." Choice C is opposite; in lines 75–78, Helen admits she "could not contradict them . . . The goblins were right" in their pessimistic worldview. Choice D is opposite; in lines 67–68, Helen warns her aunt to "look out for the part where you think you are done with the goblins and they come back."

4. F
Category: Generalization
Difficulty: Medium
Getting to the Answer: When answering questions asking for the main point, don't be distracted by details that a choice inflates in significance. The first paragraph introduces the characters and tells you in its first two sentences that "all sorts" of people are "satisfied" by the "sublime noise" of this symphony. The remainder of the paragraph provides a broad overview of the characters and their varied responses to the music; use this as your prediction. Choice (F) perfectly captures the predicted response. Choice G is a misused detail; Beethoven's *Fifth Symphony* is described as a "sublime noise," but this is not the main point of the paragraph. Choice H is a distortion; the fact that "such a noise is cheap" means that it is a bargain for the audience, not that the performers are underpaid. Choice J is a distortion; the author comments on the deficiency of the hall, but the group appears to enjoy the music regardless.

5. D
Category: Generalization
Difficulty: High
Getting to the Answer: When a question asks

you to focus on a specific section of the passage, you may need to read before or after that section. Be careful, however, not to incorporate ideas from those other sections. Use your notes to predict what Helen believes. The author writes that the "statement" made by the music "could never be superseded" and that the notes and life "could have no other meaning." She seems to accept this "statement" as indisputable fact. Choice (D) correctly matches this prediction. Choice A is out of scope; the "statement" has more to do with life in general than with Helen's fate or sense of peace. Choice B is a distortion; Helen "desired to be alone" in the previous paragraph, but this does not imply that "life . . . must be endured alone." Choice C is a distortion; the previous paragraph does suggest that the music has told her everything that "could happen in her life," but this is not a specific prediction of her future, nor is it the main point of this paragraph.

6. F
Category: Detail
Difficulty: Low
Getting to the Answer: Remember that "according to the passage" indicates a Detail question; the answer will be a paraphrase of something directly stated in the passage. Your notes can remind you where the author discusses Tibby (paragraphs 1, 7, and 10). He listens to the symphony with "the full score . . . open on his knee" and draws the company's attention to "the transitional passage on the drum." Predict that he is *fascinated by details within the performance.* Choice (F) correctly matches the thrust of this prediction and of the text. Choice G is a misused detail; this more correctly defines Helen. Choice H is a distortion; Tibby's attention to the drum exemplifies his focus on the more technical aspects of the music. Choice J is a distortion; the author refers to the hall as dreary, but nothing indicates that this affects Tibby in this way.

7. B
Category: Inference
Difficulty: Medium
Getting to the Answer: Good notes and a good

sense of the passage help when you don't receive a line or paragraph reference. The symphony performance takes up most of the passage, so research the last few paragraphs. The symphony leaves Helen with a hopeless feeling, but also feelings of certainty and acceptance of that outcome—a sense of resolution. Look for a match to this idea among the choices. Choice (B) correctly captures Helen's sentiments as she leaves. Choice A is out of scope; the passage paints Helen as unconcerned with her companions, who also seem anything but indifferent. Choice C is a out of scope; the passage does not describe Helen's reaction to Tibby. Choice D is a distortion; though Helen "pushed her way out" of the hall, nothing indicates that conditions in the hall affected her decision to leave.

8. J
Category: Inference
Difficulty: Medium
Getting to the Answer: With Prose Fiction passages, be careful to keep straight which character does or thinks what. This passage contains a number of different characters. Use your notes to find where the author mentions Aunt Juley—principally in line 53. He describes her as "so British, and wanting to tap." You also might have found the reference to Mrs. Munt in lines 5–6: she would tap along with the music, but surreptitiously. You can infer that tapping must be frowned upon, and Aunt Juley is aware of that. Choice (J) is the most reasonable inference based on the text. Choice F is a misused detail; Tibby draws Aunt Juley's attention to the drum, but this comes after her decision not to tap. Choice G is a distortion; the passage does not suggest that Aunt Juley was considering how her tapping might affect Helen. Choice H is out of scope; "snapping one's fingers" is not mentioned in the passage

9. C
Category: Generalization
Difficulty: Medium
Getting to the Answer: Some inferences will seem so "small" that they appear more like details. Big "leaps of logic" will lead you astray. The passage

contains many characters. Count on your recollection of the passage and your notes to whittle down the choices, then research further as needed. In lines 12–13, you read that, though the music enthralls nearly everyone else, he "can remember nothing but Fraulein Mosebach." He must be infatuated with her, and not the music. Choice (C) logically follows from this portion of the passage. Choice A is opposite; the author writes, "wild horses could not make him inattentive" (lines 48–49). Choice B is opposite; though Margaret seems interested in the young man she is speaking with, when the performance is going on, she "can only see the music" (lines 8–9). Choice D is opposite; the author describes Tibby's interest in the music in multiple spots in the passage.

10. F
Category: Detail
Difficulty: Low
Getting to the Answer: If your notes don't help, skim the passage, especially when looking for italicized or capitalized text. The author deals with the *Andante* in paragraph 7. Helen listened to the *Andante* "once more" after "Beethoven started decorating his tune." Predict that she was drawn by a change in the music. Choice (F) matches the prediction nicely. Choice G is a misused detail; Tibby does gesture her way, but this occurs later in the passage. Choice H is a distortion; the two women had already stopped speaking once the *Andante* began. Choice J is out of scope; the author doesn't indicate that Helen believed this.

PASSAGE II

11. C
Category: Generalization
Difficulty: Low
Getting to the Answer: Questions that ask you to take into account the whole passage require you to look back at your notes to make a prediction. The first paragraph typically introduces the main idea of the passage. The paragraph introduces the topic of American obesity and contributing factors. Choice (C) fits this prediction well. Choice A is extreme;

overeating is one of many causes of obesity. Choice B is opposite; the passage doesn't undermine this idea but supports it emphatically. Choice D is extreme; the purpose of the paragraph is to focus on Americans' obesity problems, not to criticize the people themselves.

12. F
Category: Detail
Difficulty: Low
Getting to the Answer: Whenever a question uses the phrase "EXCEPT," eliminating obviously wrong answer choices first can make finding the correct choice easier. The author lists several aspects of pre-industrial life that contributed to overall physical fitness. The author never suggests that (F), hazardous conditions of the 19th-century workplace, is conducive to being fit. Choice G is incorrect because author mentions variation in activity in paragraph 2. Choice H is incorrect because the second paragraph cites animal and manpower as the primary sources of pre-industrial work energy. Choice J is incorrect because paragraph 4 discusses the physicality of pre-industrial pastimes.

13. B
Category: Writer's View
Difficulty: Medium
Getting to the Answer: When answer choices begin with verbs, eliminate choices that don't match the author's purpose. Put yourself in the author's shoes and ask yourself, "Why would I include that information?" The author mentions these occupations to support the main idea of the second paragraph—jobs in pre-industrial society required more physical activity. Choice (B) matches the prediction well. Choice A is out of scope; the passage does not mention jobs that are obsolete. Choice C is extreme; while the passage focuses on obesity, the author does not recommend specific occupations for people. Choice D is a misused detail; caloric intake and nutrition are mentioned in the first paragraph, not the second.

14. J
Category: Inference
Difficulty: Medium
Getting to the Answer: It is sometimes helpful to consider information from the author's viewpoint to determine what it implies. The author describes how the modern workplace promotes obesity by showing ways in which modern work requires less energy from people. Choice (J) is correct. Choice F is opposite; the passage describes pre-industrial work as hazardous. Choice G is extreme; the word "lament" is too strong for the context of the passage. Choice H is extreme; the passage does not praise modern working conditions.

15. C
Category: Generalization
Difficulty: Medium
Getting to the Answer: Determining the tone of a statement requires reading not just the tested detail, but a few lines before and after. The tone of the entire passage is critical of American exercise habits. The 9-to-5 worker is given as a stereotypical example of a person whose lifestyle doesn't require exertion. Choice (C) matches the tone of the passage well. Choice A is extreme; "dismayed" suggests extreme distress, which does not match the passage. Choice B is out of scope; nothing in the passage suggests that the author is jealous of American workers. Choice D is opposite; the passage is critical of sedentary lifestyle, not objective.

16. H
Category: Inference
Difficulty: Medium
Getting to the Answer: Correct answers to Inference questions tend to be more general and avoid absolute language. The passage suggests a correlation between television viewing and obesity. In other words, a relationship exists between watching television and obesity, but one doesn't necessarily cause the other. Choice (H) is the best fit. Choice F is opposite; the passage suggests a direct, not inverse, relationship. Choice G is extreme; correlation should not be confused with causation. Choice J is out of scope; the passage doesn't discuss enjoyment of television.

17. D
Category: Detail
Difficulty: High
Getting to the Answer: Wrong answers on Detail questions often employ language from the passage. Look for the idea that matches your prediction, not the exact wording. Lines 72–73 state that losing weight requires burning more calories than one consumes. Choice (D) expresses the same basic concept. Choice A is out of scope; while the passage suggests that weight loss is beneficial, the author never directly states this information. Choice B is extreme; the passage does not state that excessive levels of exercise are required for weight loss. Choice C is opposite; the passage states that one must burn more calories than are consumed, not consume more calories than are burned.

18. F
Category: Writer's View
Difficulty: High
Getting to the Answer: Writer's View questions require you to figure out why the author does what he does. Consider how the information relates to the paragraph topic and passage as a whole. The paragraph topic relates measures that people could take to combat obesity. The author mentions gimmick diets and exercise machines as a means of explaining how losing weight is simpler than people realize. Choice (F) matches your prediction. Choice G is a opposite; the passage does not suggest that these methods are effective. Choice H is a distortion; the author's purpose is not to criticize these methods, but rather to focus on the simplicity of losing weight. Choice J is a distortion; the passage focuses more on the ease, or rather simplicity, of losing weight, not of using exercise machines.

19. B
Category: Inference
Difficulty: High
Getting to the Answer: Questions that ask about tone often require you to choose between subtle shades of emotion. A little vocabulary study can help make such differences clear. The author states that parents and nutritionists have banished certain foods from public schools, indicating hostility to such foods. Choice (B) fits this prediction. Choice A is incorrect because the passage doesn't mention any uncertainty in feelings. Choice C is incorrect because the passage clearly indicates that parents and nutritionists care and, thus, are not apathetic. Choice D is incorrect because "enthralled," or "fascinated," is not at all mentioned in the passage.

20. H
Category: Writer's View
Difficulty: Medium
Getting to the Answer: Remember that a Writer's View answer will always be consistent with the main idea of the passage. The last paragraph discusses the increasing need to deal with the obesity problem. Choice (H) supports this. Choice F is a misused detail; while Americans during the 1990s lived longer, this choice has nothing to do with the paragraph topic. Choice G is opposite; the passage does not characterize the effects of obesity as innocuous, or harmless. Choice J is out of scope; American health is not directly compared to the health of people in other countries.

PASSAGE III

21. C
Category: Writer's View
Difficulty: High
Getting to the Answer: Questions that encompass the whole passage will often offer choices that distort or misuse details from the passage. Your notes should give you a good read on "big-picture" question like this. The author seems to feel that Woolf treated Bennett harshly, detracting from her own reputation, at least in his eyes. The passage makes clear that Bennett's career was never the same, and that Woolf's essay paved the way for literary modernism. Choice (C) matches that idea. Choice A is a distortion; the author of the passage compares the authors' strengths and weaknesses, but you receive no indication as to what Woolf considered her own advantages or disadvantages compared to Bennett et al. Choice B is a distortion; the passage lists only the slightest of praise on Woolf's part for Bennett and his peers. Choice D is out of scope; the author references no such repercussions for Woolf.

22. G
Category: Generalization
Difficulty: Medium
Getting to the Answer: Read around the quote for context, and put it into your own words. Then decide how it fits in with similar statements in the passage. The difference between describing "a house" and the person inside represents a key theme in the passage. Woolf uses it to charge Bennett with putting too great a focus on characters' surroundings and not enough on the characters' inner emotions. Choice (G) correctly incorporates this idea. Choice F is out of scope; the author does not focus on this issue. Choice H is a distortion; this draws from an earlier review Woolf wrote of some of Bennett's work, and is unrelated to the point she makes in the quoted phrase. Choice J is out of scope; the author doesn't suggest such a belief.

23. D
Category: Writer's View
Difficulty: Medium
Getting to the Answer: Ask yourself what the writer is attempting to accomplish—why he says what he does. In the paragraph, the author claims that only "a handful" of such disputes "survive their moment," after which he lists two presumably famous ones. But he follows that by saying that few others "can have been so damaging, or so lasting in consequences." Predict that the author feels that this polemic *may have been the most important one yet.*

Choice (D) matches this prediction. Choice A is a distortion; the author doesn't indicate this. Choice B is extreme; even among the others in the "handful," none is characterized by the author as being so pivotal. Choice C is a distortion; the author doesn't use the comparison to make this point.

24. F
Category: Detail
Difficulty: Medium
Getting to the Answer: Use your notes to help find the paragraph where the author discusses this. Discussion of Bennett's work appears in several paragraphs, but the most in-depth treatment comes in paragraph 4: for example, "a writer obsessed with dull particulars of setting" (lines 52–53), and "he would describe her house in conscientious detail but never penetrate her essential life." Choice (F) correctly matches these ideas. Choice G is opposite; this contradicts the information found in paragraph 4. Choice H is out of scope; you know of the one essay Woolf wrote attacking Bennett, but not any more than that on this subject. Choice J is extreme; the passage indicates that Bennett did focus on certain details, but it doesn't indicate that he did so to the degree suggested here.

25. C
Category: Generalization
Difficulty: Medium
Getting to the Answer: Some questions will be so generally worded that making a prediction won't be feasible. Start working through the choices, and you should see which part of the passage to research. All of the choices reference the term "polemic." The author deals with this term most directly in the first paragraph. Compare the choices against that paragraph, only researching further as required. The passage deals primarily with Woolf's polemic and its effect on twentieth century literature, which matches (C). Choice A is out of scope; the author would likely agree that Woolf provides a great example of a successful polemic, but he never offers advice about formulating such a work. Choice B is a

distortion; the author doesn't offer a "new interpretation." He discusses and expands on the generally understood view of the dispute. Choice D is out of scope; the author mentions other polemics only as introduction to discussing Woolf's essay. He doesn't rank or compare multiple polemics.

26. F
Category: Vocab-in-Context
Difficulty: Medium
Getting to the Answer: Always try to make a prediction based on context before moving to the choices. When you go to the reference, you'll remember that even the author seems unsure of what Woolf means in using this phrase. Directly before this, however, you read that Woolf wrote that Bennett "had a materialistic view of the world." Look for a choice that incorporates this idea. Choice (F) is correct. Choice G is a distortion; this group is mentioned before the comment on Bennett, but there is no indication that he and the group are related in any way. Choice H is a distortion; this quotes a criticism that Bennett made about Woolf. Choice J is a misused detail; this may be an example of the concept, but is too specific to represent the entire meaning of the phrase.

27. C
Category: Writer's View
Difficulty: High
Getting to the Answer: Take the citation given and put it in your own words. Then review each specific example to see if it matches the general idea of your paraphrase. The quotation refers to Woolf's criticism of a writer whom most observers of that era considered well established and successful. Work through the choices looking for a match to this general idea. The analogy suggests that Woolf tried to achieve something but couldn't. The "Yes" that begins that sentence (lines 88–91) indicates a continuation of the idea in the previous sentence—a criticism of Woolf, who supposedly envied the "reality gift" displayed by Bennett. Choice (C) matches well. Choice A is a distortion; the author doesn't express an opinion of *Jacob's Room*. He only cites Bennett's opinion of it.

Choice B is out of scope; the author refers to this book as an authority for his own essay, but expresses no "view" on it. Choice D is a distortion; this parenthetical comment by the author is not strong enough to "pull down" Bennett's reputation.

28. J
Category: Detail
Difficulty: Medium
Getting to the Answer: A good set of notes will help you to move quickly, even when you don't receive a line reference. Your notes should show you that the author addresses *Jacob's Room* in paragraph 3. Bennett praised the novel's "originality" and writing style but concluded that "the characters do not vitally survive in the mind." Bennett found this to be a serious deficiency. Only (J) matches the thrust of the citation. Choice F is out of scope; Bennett never compares the work to other novels. Choice G is out of scope; the author does not cite Bennett referring to this. Choice H is opposite; Bennett feels the novel does well in small ways but fails where it counts.

29. B
Category: Inference
Difficulty: Medium
Getting to the Answer: Find the relevant spot in the text, and predict an inference that is close to something said in the text. You find Woolf's opinion on "details of scene" in paragraph 4. As the author paraphrases, Woolf charged that Bennett would describe Mrs. Brown's "house in conscientious detail but never penetrate her essential life." Predict that *such details can't capture a character's inner feelings.* Choice (B) accurately matches this prediction. Choice A is a distortion; Woolf criticizes much of the work of these writers, but such feelings are not her reason for devaluing details of scene. Choice C is a distortion; this draws from Woolf's quote on one of Bennett's works. Choice D is a distortion; she might feel this way, but this pulls more from a comment made by Bennett.

30. G
Category: Generalization
Difficulty: Medium
Getting to the Answer: Questions like this can be hard to predict. Work through the choices, comparing them to the paragraph. This paragraph offers a summation of the passage, including some final analysis of the impact of Bennett, Woolf, and Woolf's essay. Only this paragraph shows Woolf giving credit to Bennett, beginning with "he had some real understanding power" in line 74. Choice (G) is correct. Choice F is a distortion; the author cites Woolf's "sniping," but removing this paragraph would still leave a number of examples of Woolf criticizing Bennett. Choice H is a misused detail; no examples of Bennett praising Woolf appear in the paragraph. His faint praise for one of Woolf's works (paragraph 3) seems to have precipitated her essay on him. Choice J is a distortion; the author does criticize her here, but he also does so, for example, in lines 61–63 ("Woolf seemed indifferent . . . ").

PASSAGE IV

31. B
Category: Generalization
Difficulty: Medium
Getting to the Answer: To determine what the author would likely support, consider what the author already supports as evidenced by the topics of the passages. Unless an author specifically states that he or she disagrees with some idea in the passage, it can be fairly assumed that he or she is comfortable with what is written. Since the author writes about the use of one or another type of fossil fuel, it's likely he or she would support further use of them. Choice (B) is correct; since coal is a fossil fuel, and the author does not comment that this kind of fuel shouldn't be used, it's likely the author would agree on the continued use of fossil fuels. Choice A is out of scope; oil is not discussed in Passage A. Choice C is a misused detail; the author states, "Lignite is a sedimentary rock with low sulfur content and, like peat, also produces a small amount of heat when

burned," so it is not a desirable source of fuel. Choice D is out of scope; recovery refers to an additional step taken to extract oil from depleted fields, and is relevant only to Passage B.

32. H
Category: Inference
Difficulty: High
Getting to the Answer: The best way to answer a question like this is to research each answer separately, using your notes or scanning the passage for the words. Look for an answer that the author specifically indicates has low levels of moisture, methane, and carbon dioxide. Since the author states, "With further compaction, lignite loses moisture, methane, and carbon dioxide, and becomes bituminous coal," it must be true that the bituminous coal has less moisture, methane, and carbon dioxide than lignite. Since peat is found in swamps and bogs, it would have more moisture than both lignite and bituminous coal. Choice (H) is the best choice. Choice F is a misused detail; lignite is a sedimentary rock that has more moisture, methane, and carbon dioxide than bituminous coal. Choice G is a misused detail; peat is found in swamps and bogs, so it would have more moisture than both lignite and bituminous coal. Choice J is out of scope; kerogen is waxy material found in shale that can be heated to produce oil (Passage B), not coal.

33. D
Category: Inference
Difficulty: Medium
Getting to the Answer: It's hard to predict the answer to a question like this, since many things could be inferred. Rather than make a prediction, use the answers to research the passage. Your notes, or a quick scan of the passages, show that the reference to acid rain is in paragraph one in Passage A, and falls within the context of the author's discussion of SO_2, which he says "is a corrosive gas that can damage plants and animals." When combined with water, SO_2 produces acid rain, which serves as an example of another danger of SO_2. Combine that

information with, "Anthracite coal is most desirable because it burns very hot and also contains a much smaller amount of sulfur, meaning that it burns cleaner," and you will be able to infer that burning anthracite coal rather than bituminous coal would reduce the amount of sulfur released, which would in turn reduce the amount of acid rain. Choice (D) correctly matches our research of the passage. Choice A is a misused detail; there is no comparison; just the statement that coal contains both carbon and sulfur. Choice B is a distortion; it is true that burning coal releases sulfur, but the author is just making a point about the dangers of coal, not proving it. Be careful of extreme words like "prove;" they often take the author's meaning beyond what the author intended. Choice C is a misused detail; it is coal, not acid rain, which is a result of plant matter, which decays over time.

34. H
Category: Vocab-in-Context
Difficulty: Medium
Getting to the Answer: Questions like this require you to consider the meaning of the phrase in the context not only of the sentence in which it appears, but also in terms of the surrounding sentences. The phrase relates to the "extraction process" of oil shale and tar sands. In the last paragraph, the author writes, "The hydrocarbons obtained from these sources require extensive processing to be usable, reducing their value. The extraction process also has a particularly large environmental footprint," which sounds negative. An environmental footprint refers to how much a person or action affects the health of the environment. In this case, it's a big, and seemingly negative effect, which matches (H). Choice F is a distortion; in this case, "footprint" does not refer to the imprint of a foot, but to the effect on the environment of the extraction of oil. Choice G is opposite; the phrase "extensive processing" seems like a negative one, as it is associated with a reduction in value. Choice J is out of scope; the author does not state that all effects on the environment, even negative ones, are irreversible.

35. D
Category: Detail
Difficulty: Medium
Getting to the Answer: Use your notes to research where to find the details about how oil is pumped from under the Earth's surface. All the information about the process of extracting oil is in paragraph three. Look for keywords that signal the steps in the process, such as "after" and "the process is repeated." Paragraph three outlines the steps in erecting a well: "An oil well is created using an oil rig, which turns a drill bit. After the hole is drilled, a casing—a metal pipe with a slightly smaller diameter than the hole—is inserted and bonded to its surroundings, usually with cement." In these three steps, drilling the hole is the second one; thus, (D) is the correct answer. Choice A is a misused detail; drilling a hole is the first step in the process. Choice B is a misused detail; draining fluid is pushed in after casings are in place, one of the last steps in extraction. Choice C is a misused detail; topping the wellbore is the very last part of the procedure.

36. G
Category: Inference
Difficulty: High
Getting to the Answer: It's hard to predict the answer to a question like this, since many things could be inferred. Rather than make a prediction, use the answers to research the passage. Pump jacks are mentioned in paragraph four, where it states that they are used in one particular circumstance. Determine what that circumstance is, then match it with the correct answer. When writing about pump jacks in paragraph four, the author states, "But sometimes, additional measures, called secondary recovery, are required. This is especially true in depleted fields . . . " Depleted fields are those in which the oil reserves are greatly diminished, meaning very low. Choice (G) correctly matches the circumstances described in paragraph four. Choice F is out of scope; the passage does not provide any information about the safety of using pump jacks. Choice H is opposite; paragraph five states that

even with new technology, only about 50% of the oil can be recovered. Choice J is a misused detail; the wellbore (paragraph 3) is the drilling hole, strengthened by metal pipes, not pump jacks.

37. D
Category: Detail
Difficulty: Low
Getting to the Answer: Read the question carefully. Though not worded in the most straightforward way, it's really just saying that, given the information in the passage, it can be inferred that both authors would agree on three of the four answers; the one on which the authors would not agree is the correct one. The key here is that the passages must include information relevant to the question. If there is no information given, there is no basis from which to draw an inference. Look for an answer that is not referred to in any part of either passage. Neither author says anything about solar power, so we don't have evidence regarding the safety of solar power; therefore, (D) is correct. Choice A is opposite; here's a point of agreement. Both authors write about organic material being used as energy sources. Choice B is opposite; in passage A, the author writes: "Coal is a solid fossil fuel formed from the remains of land plants that flourished 300 to 400 million years ago" and in passage B the author notes that "When organic material such as zooplankton and algae settled on the bottom of ocean[s] millions of years ago." Both statements clearly mean that both oil and coal are created from organic material, and the process takes a very long time. Choice C is opposite; in passage A, the author refers to limited supplies of anthracite (paragraph three), while the reference to "depleted fields" in passage B (paragraph four) indicates that, at least in some oil fields, the supply has dwindled.

38. F
Category: Detail
Difficulty: Low
Getting to the Answer: Use your notes to research where to find the details about how coal and oil are formed. The information you need regarding the

formation of coal and oil is located in the second paragraphs of each passage. According to the passages, extraction does not affect the formation of coal and oil since extraction occurs millions of years after the formation of fossil fuels; therefore, (F) is correct. Choice G is opposite; passage A states, "The formation of coal goes through discrete stages as, over millions of years, heat and pressure act on decomposing plants." Passage B states, "Thousands of years later, the sediments that contained the organic material were subjected to intense amounts of heat and pressure, changing it into a waxy material called kerogen." Choice H is opposite; heat is mentioned in the second paragraphs of both Passages A and B. Choice J is opposite; there appears to be an extra space here. Organic material is mentioned in the second paragraphs of both Passages A and B.

39. C
Category: Detail
Difficulty: Medium
Getting to the Answer: The formation of oil is described in the third paragraph, a likely place to research when looking for support for a multistep process. Though the information in paragraph three is not given in a step-by-step process with key words such as "first," and "then," look for a phrase that indicates a process which evolves over time, with different steps at different points. The phrase "'when more heat is added" means that the addition of heat is a step taken after a previous one. Even though the passage says that this takes a long time, it's still a step-by-step procedure, which results in oil as we know it. Choice (C) matches this description. Choice A is out of scope; this answer is about the terminology for an oil field, not the process of oil formation. Choice B is out of scope; how oil is pushed to the surface is irrelevant to how it is formed. Choice D is out of scope; the components of oil are also irrelevant.

40. G
Category: Function
Difficulty: Medium
Getting to the Answer: When answering Function questions, consider the author's purpose in doing something. Read both final sentences, focusing on each author's tone. Both authors include negative descriptions of the consequences of extracting fossil fuels. In passage A, the author states, "However, it often leaves the land scarred and unsuitable for other uses." Passage B states "The extraction process also has a particularly large environmental footprint." Given the information that sulfur is dangerous, it is likely that the authors would agree that extracting coal and oil results in negative consequences. Choice (G) matches these descriptions. Choice F is a distortion; both passages mention negative impacts of extracting fossil fuels, but only Passage A conveys the idea that the land may not recover. The "environmental footprint" mentioned in Passage B does not guarantee irreparable harm to the land. Choice H is out of scope; new technology is mentioned only in passage B, where it is referenced as a way to increase oil recovery. Since it is not discussed at the end of both Passages A and B it cannot be the correct answer. Choice J is out of scope; since neither author writes about lead, you can eliminate this answer choice.

SCIENCE TEST

PASSAGE I

1. D
Category: Figure Interpretation
Difficulty: Low
Getting to the Answer: Pay attention to all of the conditions in the question stem—finding the answer to this question depends on locating the right line in the table. There are two rows in the table that refer to *Lagerstroemia Natchez* grown at a latitude of 28 degrees. (Make sure to ignore the row containing *Lagerstroemia Natchez* grown at

a latitude of 33 degrees!) Reading across the two rows, you can see that the plants have heights of 8.6 and 7.6 meters. Only (D) encompasses this range.

2. G
Category: Figure Interpretation
Difficulty: Low
Getting to the Answer: Grab low difficulty points like these by making sure you're looking at the right figure. Flowering growth is on the y-axis of Figure 1, so start by looking at that figure. The slope of the line indicates the rate of flowering growth, so you should look for the segment that has the steepest positive slope. According to the figure, flowering growth increases only slightly in the Juvenile and Adult phases, and it decreases during the Death phase. The only phase containing a large increase in flowering growth, indicated by a steep upward slope, is the Intermediate phase, (G).

3. B
Category: Figure Interpretation
Difficulty: Low
Getting to the Answer: Don't rely on memory alone here—copy a few numbers or circle rows on the table so you don't get your data mixed up. This question merely requires you to read the table accurately. The four species mentioned in the answer choices grew to heights of 2.4, 6.4, 4.6, and 4.9 meters, respectively. Of these four numbers, 6.4 is clearly the greatest, so (B) is correct.

4. F
Category: Figure Interpretation
Difficulty: Medium
Getting to the Answer: Don't overthink problems that require only a little bit of interpretation; the data in the table will probably take you closer to the answer than you think. Take a look at the table and summarize what you know about each plant variety. *Lagerstroemia indica Catawba* reached a height of 2.7 meters in soil and compost, and *Lagerstroemia fauriei Kiowa* was 8.3 meters tall in soil and compost. *Lagerstroemia Chickasaw* and *Lagerstroemia Natchez*

were not grown in compost, so eliminate G and J. *Lagerstroemia indica Catawba* comes closest to a height of 3 meters, so (F) is the correct answer.

5. D
Category: Patterns
Difficulty: Medium
Getting to the Answer: This sort of question should not involve overly complex reasoning—you're simply looking for the answer choice that describes, in words, the data in the figure. Simply compare the statement in each choice to the information in the figure—only one choice should agree closely with the data. Choice A cannot be correct, since the rate of increase for flowering growth changes in each phase. Choices B and C don't match the data either—the graph during the Juvenile phase is mostly flat with just a small increase towards the end. Choice (D) is correct. Figure 1 depicts little increase in flowering growth until the onset of the Intermediate phase.

6. J
Category: Patterns
Difficulty: Medium
Getting to the Answer: The introductory paragraph states that Table 1 includes the typical adult height, and a typical adult *Lagerstroemia indica Potomac* is 4.6 m tall. The question asks about a *Lagerstroemia indica Potomac* shrub that is five meters tall, which would be classified as an adult based on Table 1. To find the flowering growth rate, look at the adult phase in Figure 1. The flowering growth rate does not increase or decrease during the adult phase, meaning that the general trend is the same during that period of time, (J).

PASSAGE II

7. C
Category: Patterns
Difficulty: Medium
Getting to the Answer: The introductory paragraph defines alpha radiation as the release of two

protons and two neutrons. Based on Table 1, Isotope 1 does not undergo alpha decay after its first bombardment with Particle D. However, Table 2 indicates that Isotope 1b undergoes one alpha decay after being bombarded with Particle D. Between both experiments, one alpha decay is observed, so two protons were emitted, (C).

8. H
Category: Figure Interpretation
Difficulty: Low
Getting to the Answer: Make sure to read the correct portion of a corresponding table. According to Table 1, alpha decay occurs in Isotope 1 after being bombarded by both Particles B and C. Choice (H) is correct. Choice F is only half right. Particle C also caused alpha decay. Choice G suggests Particle D, which caused only beta decay. Choice J suggests Particles A and D, neither of which caused alpha decay.

9. B
Category: Patterns
Difficulty: Medium
Getting to the Answer: Pay close attention to what a trend implies about the concepts involved. Tables 1 and 2 reveal that Isotope 1, when bombarded by Particle A, undergoes no decay. Therefore, if it were to continue to be bombarded by Particle A, there would still be no decay. The only answer choice which shows no decay for Isotope 1 is (B). Choice A shows alpha decay for Isotope 1b. Choice C shows both alpha and beta decay for Isotope 1b. Choice D shows beta decay for Isotope 1b.

10. J
Category: Figure Interpretation
Difficulty: Medium
Getting to the Answer: Sometimes you will need to read a figure in a counterintuitive direction. The particle that caused beta decay in Isotope 1 and no decay in Isotope 2 was Particle D. Choice (J) is correct. Choice F suggests Particle A, which caused no decay in Isotope 1. Choice G suggests Particle

B, which caused alpha decay in Isotope 1. Choice H suggests Particle C, which caused both alpha and beta decay in Isotope 1.

11. C
Category: Scientific Reasoning
Difficulty: Medium
Getting to the Answer: Think about what is implied by the data in a figure. A decay chain will have reached an end once a stable isotope is reached. In the second stage of decay, the Isotope 1b sample showed no decay. Choice (C) is correct. Choice A suggests that Isotope 1 exhibited no initial decay, which is not supported by Table 1. Choice B references the data regarding Particle D. Choice D reverses the data regarding Particle D.

12. F
Category: Figure Interpretation
Difficulty: Medium
Getting to the Answer: When you are asked to create a new figure, pay close attention to the original. The bombardment of Isotope 2 with Particle B results in beta decay only, as shown in Table 1. Beta decay is marked by a strong curve upward, as noted in Figure 1. Choice (F) shows such a figure. Choice G shows only alpha decay. Choice H shows both alpha and beta decay. Choice J shows alpha, beta, and a third type of decay (presumably gamma).

13. D
Category: Scientific Reasoning
Difficulty: Medium
Getting to the Answer: Consider the implications of the data when asked to go beyond a given experiment. A stable isotope will show no decay. Both alpha and beta decay are seen in both experiments, so (D) is correct. Choice A suggests that the isotope will become stable, which is not the case. Choice B also suggests that the isotope will become stable. Choice C is half right, but suggests that the reason is because no decay is seen. This would imply stability.

PASSAGE III

14. H
Category: Scientific Reasoning
Difficulty: Low
Getting to the Answer: In passages with multiple experiments, it's even more important to circle the methods during Step 1 of the Kaplan Method for ACT Science so that you don't get mixed up from one experiment to the next. The table and description for Experiment 3 both indicate that the experiment studied how levels of UV-B light varied by the time of day they were measured. Choice (H) is the only choice that correctly indicates the changing variable; the other choices refer to quantities that are not manipulated in Experiment 3.

15. B
Category: Patterns
Difficulty: Medium
Getting to the Answer: Focus on the variables that affect only UV-A light—don't get distracted by any others. You first need to figure out which factors lead to higher and lower levels of UV-A light to answer this question. From Experiment 1, you can see that UV-A levels are higher in summer and at higher elevations, and from Experiment 2, you can see that time of day also makes a difference. Experiment 3 does not deal with UV-A light. Choices A and D both deal with UV-B light. Since the relationship between UV-A and UV-B light is never discussed, you can't assume that reducing one will reduce the other. Eliminate these. B is consistent with the passage. Shorter summers and longer winters should result in fewer days of high UV-A levels. Keep this one. Choice C is the opposite of B and would likely increase exposure to UV-A light. Choice (B), then, is correct.

16. G
Category: Patterns
Difficulty: Medium
Getting to the Answer: If a question asks how one variable affects another, there is bound to be an experiment that addresses that relationship—you just have to find it. Essentially, this question is asking how UV-B levels are different when the sun is overhead, in the middle of the day, and when it is low on the horizon, later in the day. Experiments 2 and 3 both discuss the relationship between time of day and UV-B levels, though it is probably easier to see this relationship in Experiment 3. According to the table, UV-B levels decrease every hour after the sun is directly overhead, so you should predict that UV-B levels will be lower when the sun is low on the horizon, which corresponds to (G).

17. C
Category: Patterns
Difficulty: Medium
Getting to the Answer: Questions that introduce a new variable that behaves just like the other variables in the experiment are really just complicated ways of asking you to identify the patterns in the data. This question is too open-ended to make a prediction, so go directly to the answer choices. The issue of how UV levels change from year to year is never mentioned in the passage, so rule out A and B. That leaves C and D, which ask about UV levels when the sun is directly overhead. Experiments 2 and 3 indicate that both UV-A and UV-B levels are higher when the sun is overhead, so if UV-C behaves similarly, as stated in the question stem, (C) must be correct.

18. J
Category: Patterns
Difficulty: Medium
Getting to the Answer: If one question repeats concepts or relationships used in previous questions, you're in luck—you have a chance to get some quick, easy points and double-check your earlier work at the same time. This question also asks about the relationship between UV levels and time of day, but in a slightly different manner—don't let the altered phrasing throw you off. You've previously found that both UV-A and UV-B are higher when the sun is overhead and lower at later times of day, so that means both levels *decrease* as the number of hours after the sun is overhead *increases*. Choice

(J) is the only choice that captures this relationship accurately.

19. D
Category: Patterns
Difficulty: Medium
Getting to the Answer: If you're not sure which table to examine, you might get some help from the answer choices—check and see if the numbers in them are unique to one particular table or experiment. This question looks complicated, but the mention of UV-A levels, the summer, and measuring 30 minutes after the sun is overhead all point to the design of Experiment 1, particularly the information in the second half of Table 1. Since the elevation mentioned in the question stem is higher than all of those in the table, and because UV-A levels increase with greater elevation, predict that the levels of UV-A in this community will be higher than all of the values in the "Summer" section of Table 1. Only (D) matches this prediction.

20. F
Category: Patterns
Difficulty: Low
Getting to the Answer: Experiment 2 investigated the change in UV-B rays over time at an altitude of 2,000 meters and was conducted in the winter. The UV-B measurement when the sun is directly overhead is 48 mJ/cm^2 and, after two hours, it is 42 mJ/cm^2. The only answer choice that has a value between 42 mJ/cm^2 and 48 mJ/cm^2 is (F). Choice J is a trap because it represents the value of UV-B after one hour in the summer.

PASSAGE IV

21. C
Category: Patterns
Difficulty: Medium
Getting to the Answer: The question is asking for the precession rate of a gyroscope that has an r of 9 cm. Using the information provided in Table 1, you can see that a gyroscope with an r of 8 cm has a

precession rate of 19 rpm, and a gyroscope with an r of 10 cm has a precession rate of 24 rpm. A gyroscope with an r of 9 cm is exactly halfway between 8 cm and 10 cm, so its precession rate is likely to be exactly halfway between 19 rpm and 24 rpm, which is 21.5 rpm. Choice (C) is correct.

22. G
Category: Patterns
Difficulty: Low
Getting to the Answer: When presented with multiple tables, always make sure you're reading the right one—you don't want to miss a straightforward question because you read the wrong table. As you look down the information presented in Table 1, the number in the "Precession rate" column increases. So does the corresponding value of r, representing the distance from the surface to the gyroscope's center of gravity. Thus you can conclude that precession rate increases as r increases, which matches (G). Choices F and H contrast this data. You should immediately have eliminated J because mass is not addressed in Experiment 1.

23. C
Category: Patterns
Difficulty: Medium
Getting to the Answer: You don't have to figure out the exact shape of the graph—just enough to distinguish it from the incorrect answer choices. Experiment 2 shows a steady decrease in precession rate as spin rate increases, with no sign of this trend reversing indicated in the table. This best corresponds to (C), which also shows the precession rate (y-axis) decreasing as the spin rate (x-axis) increases. Choice A shows an initial increase in precession rate before it decreases, which is not supported by the data in the table. Choice B shows the opposite trend—precession rate increasing as spin rate increases. Choice D shows an initial decrease in precession rate, but the subsequent increase is not supported by the table.

24. F
Category: Scientific Reasoning
Difficulty: Medium
Getting to the Answer: In any scientific method question, make sure you have a firm understanding of the hypothesis before going any further. To test a hypothesis about precession rate and gravity, the scientist would have to measure the precession rate at several different gravities. The question tells you that gravity decreases as distance from the Earth increases. One way to test this hypothesis would be to measure gyroscopes at different distances from Earth, which matches (F). Choice G would not provide any new data about gravity, as the conditions are the same as in Experiment 3. Choice H is incorrect because nothing in the passage or question stem indicates that orbit direction has anything to do with gravity. Choice J would tell you something about changing precession rates with spin rate (as in Experiment 2), but it has little to do with gravity.

25. C
Category: Patterns
Difficulty: High
Getting to the Answer: Save difficult questions like this one for last, but don't guess without even trying to find your way to the answer. Start this question by looking back at Tables 1 and 2. Table 1 relates r and precession rate, and Table 2 relates spin rate and precession rate. You're told in the question stem that r in Experiment 2 is 6 cm. Because r only appears in Table 1, examine Table 1 to find that the precession rate for an r of 6 cm is 14 rpm. Now you know r and the precession rate. However, the question is asking you to find the spin rate in Experiment 1. To find that, look at Table 2 (you can move back and forth because, according to the question, r equals 6 in Experiment 2). The spin rate for a gyroscope with an r of 6 and a precession rate of 14 rpm is 750 rpm. So, you can assume that 750 rpm was the spin rate used throughout Experiment 1, which matches (C).

26. G
Category: Scientific Reasoning
Difficulty: High
Getting to the Answer: When you have multiple experiments to keep track of, make sure you always know exactly what effect or variable was tested in each one. The main effect tested in Experiment 1 was the effect of the gyroscope's size on its precession rate, specifically the distance from the spinning surface to the gyroscope's center of mass. If it had not been known that size affects precession rate, the scientist might not have been as careful to use the same size gyroscope throughout Experiment 2, which matches (G). Choice F is unlikely, as gyroscope mass was not addressed in either experiment. Choice H can't be correct. Although surface type could influence precession, that was not the factor tested in Experiment 1. Choice J was a factor not explicitly tested in Experiment 1.

27. B
Category: Scientific Reasoning
Difficulty: High
Getting to the Answer: Always remember—any good experiment should involve manipulating the variable being tested while keeping all other quantities constant. To investigate the effects of gyroscope mass, one needs a way to vary mass without changing any other properties of the gyroscope. One way to do this is by using different materials, as suggested in (B). Choice A is too vague to be correct. Although gyroscopes from different companies could potentially have different masses, they might also have different shapes or sizes. Mass is the only variable you want to manipulate in this investigation. Choice C doesn't address mass, so it's not a good answer. There is no need to test different gravities when the main variable in question can be manipulated right on Earth. Choice D is the reverse of what you want—it tests the effects of gyroscope size, which is already investigated in Experiment 1.

PASSAGE V

28. H
Category: Scientific Reasoning
Difficulty: Low
Getting to the Answer: In questions like this, the correct answer will be one that conflicts with both theories, rather than simply being irrelevant to one theory or another. The two theories differ widely, but they both broadly involve water droplets in clouds coming together in some way until they fall to the ground. Examine the answer choices one by one to find a situation that violates *both* viewpoints. Since both theories rely on water droplets to produce precipitation, (H) is the correct choice. Choice F agrees with the first theory, so this can't be a situation with which supporters of both viewpoints would disagree. Choice G agrees with the second theory, so this is incorrect. Choice J agrees with both theories, so it's also incorrect.

29. B
Category: Scientific Reasoning
Difficulty: Medium
Getting to the Answer: In questions like this one, you can easily rule out answer choices that are irrelevant to one theory or both. The two theories differ with regard to the mechanism of how precipitation forms in clouds, but the net result—precipitation—appears to be the same. The first theory has liquid drops forming in the cloud while the second refers to ice crystals. Choice (B) matches this description. Choice A cannot be correct. The shape of the cloud formation is not mentioned in either theory, so they cannot differ on this point. Choice C cannot be correct. Neither theory makes predictions about the amount of precipitation, so they cannot differ on this point. Choice D cannot be correct either. Neither theory makes any mention of climate, so they cannot differ on this point.

30. F
Category: Scientific Reasoning
Difficulty: Medium
Getting to the Answer: When you see two answer choices that are exact opposites of each other, it's often a good bet that one of them will be correct. This theory essentially relies on droplets colliding and sticking together until the drops are large enough to form precipitation. Anything that increases the likelihood of these events occurring, then, should increase the likelihood of rainfall. Choice F looks like a good choice, as a high rate of collisions would mean more collisions, which in turn would mean more coalescence and more raindrops. Keep this one. Choice G is too vague to be correct. A variable rate could mean fewer collisions, and therefore less coalescence and fewer raindrops, reducing the likelihood of producing rain. Choice H is incorrect, as the theory does not rely on temperature. Choice J is irrelevant, as nothing in the theory mentions time since the last rainfall. Choice (F) is the correct answer.

31. B
Category: Scientific Reasoning
Difficulty: Medium
Getting to the Answer: Even if they are not emphasized, pay close attention to words in the question stem that indicate both theories, one theory, or neither theory. Both theories state that heavy particles end up falling to the ground as precipitation. So, a likely conclusion of both would be that the heavy particles found by the weather balloon will be turning into precipitation soon. Choice (B) is the best match for this prediction. Choice A is incorrect because the idea of impurities in the air is relevant only to the second theory. Choice C is incorrect because the idea of particles colliding is only relevant to the first theory. Choice D is incorrect because the idea of clouds changing altitude is not addressed in either theory.

32. H
Category: Scientific Reasoning
Difficulty: Medium
Getting to the Answer: Remember, you should answer this question after reading the Ice Crystal Theory, but before you answer questions addressing both theories. The major point of the Ice Crystal Theory is that impurities in the air lead to precipitation, so look for an answer choice that addresses impurities. Only (H) mentions impurities, and it is the correct answer. Choice F cannot be correct, as thunder and lightning are not mentioned in the Ice Crystal Theory. Choice G cannot be correct, as the Ice Crystal Theory never mentions atmospheric density. Choice J is the opposite of the correct answer; fewer impurities would mean less precipitation according to the Ice Crystal Theory.

33. C
Category: Scientific Reasoning
Difficulty: Medium
Getting to the Answer: You should answer this question before you read the Ice Crystal Theory. The main point of the Collision and Coalescence Theory is that precipitation is formed when small droplets collide in clouds, resulting in bigger droplets that are too heavy to remain suspended in the cloud. You can predict that the correct choice will have to do with the collision and coalescence of water droplets. Choice A does not support the idea that smaller droplets collide and combine to form bigger droplets, which is the crux of the Collision and Coalescence Theory. Choice B can't be right, as the theory never mentions crystallization. Choice C corresponds fairly well to Step II of the Collision and Coalescence Theory. Choice D, like B, is not mentioned in the theory. (Both answer choices are drawn from the Ice Crystal Theory, and might be tempting if you had answered this question after reading that theory.) Choice (C) is the correct choice.

34. H
Category: Scientific Reasoning
Difficulty: Medium
Getting to the Answer: Don't try to answer questions based on your own world knowledge—stick to figuring out whether choices agree or disagree with the theory presented. The theory states that precipitation forms in a cloud as ice crystals and often melts as it falls to produce rain. However, as this is the Ice Crystal Theory, any possibility that does not begin with precipitation in the clouds in ice form will not contradict the theory. Choice F is incorrect, as the passage says it is possible. Choice G is not directly stated to be possible, but it does not contradict anything in the theory. Choice (H) begins with water in the clouds rather than ice, making it incompatible with the Ice Crystal Theory. This looks good. Choice J, like G, is not directly mentioned, but is not ruled out by the theory. Choice (H) is therefore the correct answer.

PASSAGE VI

35. C
Category: Patterns
Difficulty: Medium
Getting to the Answer: Detecting patterns is more difficult when three variables are involved. To simplify this question, work methodically through one variable at a time. The question asks you to identify the trend between e and r for any value of n. If you look back at the table, you'll see that n can be either 2, 3, or 4. Start by looking at the n = 2 data. As the values of e increase from 4 to 7, the values of r decrease steadily from 9.1 to 5.7. Next, look at the n = 3 data—the same holds true, as it does for the n = 4 data. Choice (C), then, is the correct answer.

36. F
Category: Patterns
Difficulty: Medium
Getting to the Answer: Use the trends in the data to make a prediction for the correct answer. You saw in question 31 that for a given value of n, higher values

of e give lower values of r, and vice versa. For n = 2, the lowest value of e given is 4, with a corresponding r = 9.1. If the trend continues as expected, you can predict a lower e will have an r value that is higher than 9.1. The only answer choice given that is larger than 9.1 is (F).

37. C

Category: Scientific Reasoning

Difficulty: High

Getting to the Answer: Don't try thinking back to chemistry class—as the question states, all the information you need is right in the passage. Start this question by asking yourself how you might decrease an atom's negative charge—that is, how you might make it *less* negative. Check to see where negative charge is mentioned in the passage. The opening paragraph states that electrons are an atom's negatively charged particles. You can expect, then, that removing electrons will decrease an atom's negative charge. Removing electrons isn't one of the answer choices, so you'll have to think further about which answer choice might result in the removal of an electron, thus decreasing the atom's charge. Choice A is incorrect. According to Table 1, decreasing the radius (r) corresponds to an increased number of electrons in the outer shell (e), which would only increase the atom's negative charge. Eliminate this. B is incorrect, as nothing in the passage suggests a link between chemical bonds and electron loss. Choice (C) looks good. After Figure 1, the passage says that I is the energy required to remove an electron, so you can infer that the application of energy causes the electron to be removed. Keep this. Choice D is incorrect. The passage doesn't tell you how the number of shells and the total number of electrons in an atom are related. Choice (C) is the correct answer.

38. J

Category: Patterns

Difficulty: Medium

Getting to the Answer: If the question stem and answer choices group the data in particular ways, examine the table in the same groupings. This question asks you to examine the trend between the number of electrons in an atom's outer shell (e) and c according to each value of n. Just like with question 31, look at e and c for each value of n separately. For n = 2, c increases as e increases. Cross off H, as this doesn't contain n = 2. For n = 3, c again increases as e increases. Cross off F, because it doesn't contain n = 3. For n = 4, again, c increases as e increases. The correct answer must be (J).

39. D

Category: Figure Interpretation

Difficulty: Medium

Getting to the Answer: If a question does not use the same symbols as the table to refer to variables, make sure to go back and check what each symbol represents. Since the question asks about removing electrons from shells, look for the row in the table with the greatest value of I (which, according to the passage, is "the energy required to remove one electron from the atom's outer shell.") Each element mentioned only has one entry in the table, so its value of I should be easy to find. The I values for Si, Cl, C, and F are 8.2, 13.0, 11.2, and 17.4, respectively. Of these, 17.4, the value for F, is greatest, so the answer is (D).

40. F

Category: Figure Interpretation

Difficulty: Medium

Getting to the Answer: Pauling units are the unit of measurement for the attraction of electrons in a chemical bond, which is represented by the variable c. N and Cl, C and S, and Si and G pairs each share a c value. The elements As and SE have the same value for electron volts, but they do not have the same c value, so (F) is correct.

WRITING TEST

LEVEL 6 ESSAY

The question posed is if schools should provide computers to all students so that they can become proficient in using computers, since in today's world, computers are important for jobs and general communication. Since there is no going back to a pre-computer time, and the odds are the computer use will continue to grow, it will be necessary for everyone to know how to use a computer. The question is how schools will contribute to this and the best answer is to provide opportunities for all students to have access to computers.

On one hand, there are people who posit that schools should give homework that requires students to use computers, and that schools should then ensure that all students have access to a computer in a computer lab. This means the school doesn't have to give computer to all students, but all students will have the ability to work on a computer at some time in a computer lab. This seems as if it would work but in reality, there are many problems. School computer labs are open during school hours and an hour or two before and after school. But that may not be enough time for all students who need to use computers to take their turns in a lab. Also, many students have after-school jobs, or sports team practice, or family obligations, and may not be able to take advantage of time in the computer lab. If teachers give students class projects, that work may require that several students work on computers at the same time and in the same place, and possibly for hours at a time. This becomes unworkable. In general, I can't support this option not because it's not a good one, but because it is not one that can be well implemented.

Other people argue that schools should give computers to all high school students throughout their years in school, and perhaps all middle school and elementary students as well. If every student has a computer, there is no doubt that they will be very proficient at using it, and that will be good for their careers in a world of technology. However, I live in Los Angeles and I know from experience that there are problems with giving students their own computers. The school board did that in Los Angeles and it has run into trouble with students using the computers for all sorts of non-academic work. Also, given the size of the Los Angeles school district, and other very large school districts, giving every student a computer, even if it's only for high school students, will cost a great deal of money, and some school districts may not be able to support it. If that's the case, we create two groups: the haves and have-nots. This is inequitable and not something the schools should support.

Finally, the perspective is to have schools and business work together to lower the cost of computers so most parents who need computers for their children can buy them at a large discount. This will allow most students to have computers, and reduce the number of students who still need to use the school computer center, so there should be enough time for everyone to get on a computer. Not only that, but students who have their own computers can not only do their school work, but can also email their friends and even play video games. Indeed, some studies have shown that playing games can increase critical thinking, which is what teachers work to do. Computers have multiple benefits that all students should be able to take advantage of.

The third option is the best one because it provides either personal or school computers for all students, and is not a financial burden for parents. It is vital today that all students be computer literate, and this will become even more vital in the future. School is the proper place to prepare students for their working or college careers, and it is incumbent on them to provide all the tools needed for this. Thus, when business and schools work together to make computers affordable, all students will have the tools they need for school and career success.

Since computers will certainly become more and more important for people in the future, and teachers are giving students more computer school work, it makes sense for students in all grades to be able to learn on a computer and become computer literate. Thus, giving all students access to computers, either their own affordable ones or school computers for those who still cannot afford a personal computer, is the best solution.

GRADER'S COMMENTS

This essay is well developed and shows a clear focus on the issue, with sophisticated language and thought. Paragraph one restates and frames the issue, indicating that the author had understood and will focus on it, and immediately states the author's opinion.

Paragraphs two, three, and four show in-depth understanding of all points of view, and give well thought out consideration to both sides. Transitions are incorporated well ("on the one hand," "other people feel," "finally") and provide good organization, making the essay flow well. In each case the writer has developed pertinent examples (Los Angeles' computer experience) and notes his point of view and implications for all perspectives. Paragraph four firmly restates the author's opinion, while the last paragraph moves his personal point of view to more general ideas, while maintaining focus on the issue, thus providing a logical conclusion.

Word choice, grammar, spelling, and sentence construction are sophisticated and correct. Vocabulary is well-chosen and appropriate, using words such as "posit, " argue," and "inequitable." Sentences are complex with use of commas, but could be more varied by using semicolons or colons.

Overall this essay shows clear, in-depth thinking and good communication skills, as well as the ability to focus on the issue and all its perspectives.

LEVEL 4 ESSAY

Everybody should have a computer because computers are important to all kids for their schoolwork, among other things. Some people think that teachers should give lots of computer homework so kids can get used to using computers. They think that if teachers let students use school computers during the day in the computer lab, that will be enough time for everyone to have a turn on the computer and do their work. Others suggest giving all high school students personal computers, which is a lot more drastic than the third idea to provide kids with big discounts so they can actually buy their own laptops. Discounts are the best idea because it's the easiest way to get most of students in the nation to use computers daily.

It does make sense for teachers to give students work that requires computers because students could use their study hall time or lunch to work on computers. Good students will probably jump at the chance to work on computers, and that will raise their grades even more. Even the students who are not so great at school would also have a chance to use the computers to and that might help them. But really, the best way to make sure all kids have computer time is for business and schools to work together to make sure everyone can afford a computer, and if some people can't, make sure they can use a library or school computer.

Some people argue that schools give computers to high school students and maybe also to middle and elementary school kids. If the schools do that, kids don't have to buy their own computers and that will save a lot of money for the kids and their parents. And if young kids have computers, by the time their in high school they will really know how to use them and can have careers that require computer use. Also, if everyone has their own computers, they can do their homework on them and also play games and email their friends, so it would also be a lot of fun. But this would cost a lot of money and some schools probably can't afford that.

Other people think that if computers are cheap because schools and businesses work together to make them that way, then everyone will have a computer and that would make kids really happy. Everyone wants a computer but some people cant afford them, so this is a way to make them cheaper so parents can buy them. If parents still can't buy them, kids can go to the library or computer lab and there should be lots of room for them there because most kids will have their own computers so don't need to use the library or lab. I think computers are great and everyone should have one, either because everyone can afford one or because people can use library and school computers.

GRADER'S COMMENTS

This essay stays on task throughout its entirety and shows an adequate understanding of the perspectives. All perspectives are addressed, though the implications aren't fully explored. Though the writer expresses a point of view, the vague support provided centers primarily around the fact that computers could be helpful in school and students like computers. The writer takes a position in the first paragraph but the support given for this position isn't fully discussed and, in general, ideas are underdeveloped.

Transitions are included, but they are simple; paragraph three opens with "Some people argue," and paragraph four begins with "Other people think." Throughout the essay, the language is simple, employing words such as "kids", "cheap," and "other things" rather than explicit examples.

Sentence structure is adequate, but could be more complex and show more variety. There are several grammatical errors with noun/antecedent mistakes ("everyone" and "their" in paragraphs one and three), and spelling mistakes ("to" for "too" in paragraph one, "their" for "they're" in paragraph two, "cant" for "can't" in paragraph three).

The introduction and conclusion are adequately developed and organized. The introduction addresses all three perspectives and provides the author's opinion. The conclusion includes a discussion of the author's opinion but does not offer enough specific, relevant support. In general, the essay stays on topic but the writer shows a narrow depth of understanding. The writer needs to offer a more comprehensive analysis of the issue, develop her perspective with specific, relevant support, and express her ideas with complex vocabulary and sentence structure.

LEVEL 2 ESSAY

I love to play on my computer and I think all kids should be able to play on computers to. You can use them for homework and for fun and if you have to share them with your little brother you can learn about sharing. Schools should give computers to all kids because that's how kids learn to use computers, that's important because a lot of work is done on computers. Computers cost a lot of money so its better that schools give them away because a lot of kids can't afford to buy their own. When you don't have a computer you miss out on a lot of fun. Also can't do your homework if you need a computer for it. Then you'll really do bad in school but teachers want you to do good, so they'll be sad. Everyone will be happy if all kids have computers, and kids will learn a lot to. Also, parents can learn to use them so they'll get better jobs. People who don't want schools to give out computers are wrong because then a lot of kids won't get computers and the won't be able to do there homework or play or have any fun on it.

GRADER'S COMMENTS

This essay, though on the topic of computers, displays no attention to the task almost no understanding of the perspectives. Ideas about the perspectives and their implications are not explored. The first perspective is mentioned briefly but without real consideration, and no other perspective is addressed. Though there is an author viewpoint about computers, it is not supported with appropriate or in-depth reasons, and centers primarily around the writer's enjoyment of computers. Critical thinking is lacking and there is no development of ideas. The primary writer opinion (computers are fun and can be helpful) is simply restated without movement between general to specific ideas.

Introduction and conclusion are lacking. The entire passage is one paragraph long with several errors of grammar, punctuation, and spelling. The third sentence is a run-on, grammar is poor ("you'll really do bad in school but teachers want you to do good,"), and there are several misspellings ("to" for "too," "there" for "their," "its" for "it's). The writer displays a lack of coherent and correct writing skills, and only a very basic understanding of the issue with little focus on it.

You can evaluate your essay and the model essay based on the following criteria, which is covered in the Practice Makes Perfect section of this book:

- Does the author discuss all three perspectives provided in the prompt?

- Is the author's own perspective clearly stated?

- Does the body of the essay assess and analyze each perspective?

- Is the relevance of each paragraph clear?

- Does the author start a new paragraph for each new idea?

- Is each sentence in a paragraph relevant to the point made in that paragraph?

- Are transitions clear?

- Is the essay easy to read? Is it engaging?

- Are sentences varied?

- Is vocabulary used effectively? Is college-level vocabulary used?